THIRD EDITION

ON BAKING

A TEXTBOOK OF BAKING AND PASTRY FUNDAMENTALS

Approach and Philosophy of ON BAKING

On Baking, Third Edition, follows the model established in our previous editions, which has prepared thousands of students for successful careers in the baking and pastry arts by building a strong foundation based upon sound fundamental techniques. *On Baking* focuses on teaching the hows and whys of baking. *On Baking* starts with general procedures, highlighting fundamental principles and skills, and then presents specific applications and sample recipes. Core baking and pastry principles are explained as the background for learning proper techniques. Once mastered, these techniques can be used in the preparation of a wide array of baked goods, pastries and confections. The baking and pastry arts are shown in a cultural and historical context as well so that students understand how different techniques and flavor profiles developed.

Chapters focus on four areas essential to a well-rounded baking and pastry professional:

❶ Professionalism Background chapters introduce students to the field with material on culinary and baking history, food safety, tools and ingredients.

❷ Breads Four chapters focus on breadmaking, from basic quickbreads to yeast breads and advanced artisan specialties such as sourdough breads and laminated doughs.

❸ Desserts and Pastries Fundamental baking techniques used in the preparation of cookies, pies, cakes, custards and frozen desserts are explained and then demonstrated with a wide range of recipes. Healthy baking concludes this section.

❹ Advanced Pastry Work Chapters on tortes and modern entremets, petits fours, plated desserts, chocolate and sugar work demonstrate advanced concepts and techniques.

NEW TO THIS EDITION

▶ **Fresh new design,** including more than 350 new photographs, line drawings and illustrations provide clear representations of core preparations that are the foundation of any good baking textbook.

▶ Content updates reflect **current trends in the world of baking and pastry,** such as the interest in artisan baking, sensory science, flavor pairing and professionalism.

▶ **Expanded coverage of flavors** and **advanced pastry techniques** is offered in new sidebars and recipes; expanded troubleshooting material is covered in photographs and tables.

▶ **Greatly enhanced support package** includes MyCulinary Lab™ 2.0, instructor's manual featuring performance-based learning activities, improved test bank and lecture-based PowerPoint™ slides.

▶ **Expanded Recipe Testing Program** Hundred of recipes featured in this third edition of *On Baking* were tested by chef-instructors at leading culinary schools across the country. This unparalleled program ensures accuracy, clarity and instructional value. We invite qualified chef-instructors to test recipes for upcoming projects. If you would like more information regarding the program, or would like to sign up to be part of the Pearson Test Kitchen, please visit www.pearsontestkitchen.com.

GUIDED TOUR

Easy to navigate, *On Baking* is divided into bite-sized subsections to optimize your learning experience. We invite you to explore this new edition with the following Guided Tour through the features presented.

HALLMARK FEATURES

◀ Learning Objectives

Each chapter begins with clearly stated objectives that guide you to focus on what can be achieved by completing the chapter.

After studying this chapter, you will be able to:

- understand the various mixing methods used in the bakeshop
- understand how heat affects batters and doughs, the basis of most bakeshop items
- identify and understand the basic baking and cooking methods employed in the bakeshop
- understand the science of taste and basic flavor principles

▶ Chapter Introduction

Introductory paragraphs summarize the main themes in each chapter and help reinforce topics.

BREAD MAKING IS AN ART THAT DATES BACK TO ANCIENT TIMES. Over the centuries, bakers have learned to manipulate the basic ingredients—flour, water, salt and leavening—to produce a vast variety of breads. Thin-crusted baguettes, tender Parker House rolls, crisp flatbreads and chewy bagels derive from careful selection and handling of the same key ingredients. A renewed interest in the traditional craft of baking has seen many new artisan bread bakeries open in recent years. Customers are demanding, and more restaurants are serving, exciting bread assortments to their guests at every meal. Although few baked goods intimidate novice bakers as much as yeast breads, few baked goods are actually as forgiving to prepare. By mastering a few basic procedures and techniques, restaurants and bakeshops can offer their customers delicious, fresh yeast products.

Yeast breads can be divided into two major categories: lean doughs and rich doughs. Lean doughs, such as those used for crusty French and Italian artisan breads, contain little or no sugar or fat. Traditional sourdough and rye breads are lean doughs that require special handling to bring out their unique flavor. Rich doughs, such as brioche and challah, contain significantly more sugar and fat than lean doughs. Rich dough bakes into softer products with a tender crust and interior crumb and is discussed in Chapter 8, Enriched Yeast Breads. A specific type of rich, flaky dough is made by incorporating layers of fat and flour and is covered in Chapter 9, Laminated Doughs.

This chapter covers in detail the basic production techniques for making lean and sourdough bread products. The principles discussed in this chapter apply to working with all types of yeast-raised products, including artisan-style breads also discussed here. Rereading the discussion of the function of ingredients found in Chapter 4, Bakeshop Ingredients, is recommended before beginning this chapter.

▶ Margin Definitions

Important terms are defined in margin notes to help you quickly master new terminology.

flavor an identifiable or distinctive quality of a food, drink or other substance perceived with the combined senses of taste, touch and smell

mouthfeel the sensation created in the mouth by a combination of a food's taste, smell, texture and temperature

aroma the sensations, as interpreted by the brain, of what we detect when a substance comes in contact with sense receptors in the nose

taste the sensations, as interpreted by the brain, of what we detect when food, drink or other substances come in contact with our taste buds

SAFETY ALERT
Milk Storage

Canned milks, aseptically packaged milks and dry milk powders are shelf-stable products needing no refrigeration. After the can or box is opened or the powder is reconstituted with water, however, these become potentially hazardous foods and must be handled just as carefully as fresh milk. Do not store an open can of milk in its original container, and keep all milk products refrigerated at or below 40°F (4°C).

◀ Safety Alerts

Brief notes remind you of safety concerns and encourage you to incorporate food safety and sanitation into your regular kitchen activities.

① A vol-au-vent cutter looks like a double cookie cutter with one cutter about 1 inch (2.5 centimeters) smaller than the other. To cut the pastry, simply position the cutter and press down.

② To shape with rings, use two rings, one approximately 1 inch (2.5 centimeters) smaller than the other. The larger ring is used to cut two rounds. One will be the base and is set aside. Use the smaller ring to cut out an interior circle from the second round, leaving a border ring of dough.

◄ Procedures

Step-by-step color photographs of various stages in the preparation of ingredients and dishes help you visualize unfamiliar techniques and encourage you to organize kitchen activities.

► Product Identification

Hundreds of original color photographs help you identify ingredients. Descriptions let you explore a huge variety of items such as fruits, sugars, nuts or chocolates.

Pomegranates

MISE EN PLACE

► Allow the butter, eggs and buttermilk to come to room temperature.

► Zest the lemon and orange.

► Grease pans.

► Preheat oven to 400°F (200°C).

◄ Mise en Place

French for "put in place," this margin feature accompanying in-chapter recipes lists what needs to be done *before* starting to prepare the recipe, such as preheating the oven, chopping nuts or melting butter.

► Line Drawings

Detailed line drawings illustrate tools and equipment commonly used in a bakeshop.

Bench Brush

▼ Formulas

Recipes, more appropriately called *formulas* in professional bakeshops, demonstrate techniques and provide delicious laboratory experiments for all skill levels.

Pastry Wheel

 BRAN MUFFINS WITH RAISINS

Yield: 36 Muffins, 3½ oz. (105 g) each **Method:** Muffin

Buttermilk	1 qt.	960 ml	152%
Wheat bran	10 oz.	300 g	47%
Salt	0.75 oz.	22 g	3.5%
All-purpose flour	1 lb. 5 oz.	630 g	100%
Baking powder	0.6 oz. (4 tsp.)	18 g	3%
Baking soda	0.6 oz. (4 tsp.)	18 g	3%
Cinnamon, ground	0.4 oz. (2 Tbsp.)	12 g	2%
Eggs	6.5 oz. (4 eggs)	195 g	31%
Vegetable oil	12 fl. oz.	360 ml	57%
Brown sugar	1 lb. 8 oz.	720 g	114%
Raisins, conditioned	1 lb.	480 g	75%
Streusel Topping (page 145; optional)	as needed	as needed	
Total batter weight:	7 lb. 11 oz.	3697 g	587%

Rasp-Style Grater

▼ Icons

 Our adaptation of the MyPlate icon identifies healthy formulas.

The scale icon identifies formulas for which larger quantity measurements are provided in Appendix III.

Balloon and Rigid Whisks

Formulas are illustrated with both step-by-step photographs showing procedural techniques, as well as photographs of finished products or plated desserts.

❼ The finished dessert.

Measurements

All formulas include ingredient quantities in both U.S. and metric measurements. U.S. and metric measurements for all temperatures, pan sizes and other quantities are provided throughout the text.

Baker's Percentage

A way of expressing the ratio of ingredients unique to professional baking, baker's percentages are used primarily with breads, cakes and dough products and are provided with those formulas.

Variations

Variations show how to modify a formula to create different flavor profiles and new dishes.

Nutritional Analysis

All formulas include a nutritional analysis prepared by a registered dietitian.

TRADITIONAL SHORTBREAD

Yield: 7 Dozen Cookies, approximately ½ oz. (15 g) each

Method: Icebox cookies

Unsalted butter, softened	1 lb.	480 g	84%
Powdered sugar	8 oz.	240 g	42%
Vanilla extract	0.5 fl. oz.	15 ml	3%
Salt	0.2 oz. (1 tsp.)	5 g	1%
Pastry or all-purpose flour	1 lb. 3 oz.	570 g	100%
Egg wash	as needed	as needed	
Total dough weight:	2 lb. 11 oz.	1310 g	230%

❶ Blend the butter and powdered sugar in a mixing bowl without creaming. Stir in the vanilla and salt, mixing thoroughly. Add the flour and mix until just combined.

❷ Divide the dough into four equal portions. Roll each piece of dough into 8-inch (20-centimeter) disks. Wrap in plastic. Freeze until hard, approximately 30 minutes.

❸ Remove from the freezer and unwrap, then lightly brush each disk with egg wash. Cut each disk into eight wedges. Dock the wedges with a fork.

❹ Bake at 375°F (190°C) until pale golden brown, approximately 15 to 20 minutes.

VARIATIONS:

Bergamot Shortbread—Add 12 drops of oil of bergamot with the vanilla in Step 1. Divide the dough into four equal portions. Roll each piece into a 10-inch- (25-centimeter-) long cylinder. Freeze until hard, approximately 30 minutes. Brush each cyclinder with egg wash. Roll each cyclinder in granulated sugar. Cut the cylinders into ½-inch- (1.2-centimeter-) thick slices, then place the slices cut side down on paper-lined sheet pans. Dock the cookies with a fork and bake.

Pecan Shortbread—Add 7 ounces (210 grams/37%) of finely chopped pecans to the dough in Step 1.

Approximate values per cookie: **Calories** 70, **Total fat** 4.5 g, **Saturated fat** 3 g, **Cholesterol** 10 mg, **Sodium** 30 mg, **Total carbohydrates** 8 g, **Protein** 1 g

Bergamot Shortbread

Pecan Shortbread

▶ Color Illustrations of Torte Assembly

Full-color illustrations accompany torte formulas to show the internal assembly of these finished desserts.

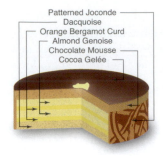

Patterned Joconde
Dacquoise
Orange Bergamot Curd
Almond Genoise
Chocolate Mousse
Cocoa Gelée

▼ New! Flavor Sidebars

These features show how flavoring ingredients may be used to change the character of a dessert preparation.

VARIETAL HONEY

More than three hundred types of varietal honey are available in the United States. Each nectar source contributes a distinct color and flavor to the honey. Use this to advantage when selecting honey to use in ice cream, mousses and custards. From the rich buttery flavor of avocado honey to the delicate floral taste of tupelo honey, alternating honeys will change the flavor profile of a dish. Do taste these honeys before using them. The pronounced taste of buckwheat or heather blossom honey may be better suited to baked goods or chocolate desserts. Edible honeycomb makes an attractive garnish, as do granules of dried honey.

▼ Troubleshooting Charts

Troubleshooting charts enhance the learning experience by clarifying "how" and "why," and by helping you diagnose and correct problems.

TABLE 10.2	TROUBLESHOOTING CHART FOR COOKIES	
PROBLEM	**CAUSE**	**SOLUTION**
Cookies too dense or hard	Too little liquid in the dough	Adjust formula or measure carefully; add more eggs
	Too little fat in the dough	Adjust formula or measure fat carefully
	Too much flour in the dough	Adjust formula or measure flour carefully
	Dough overmixed	Cream properly; avoid overmixing after adding dry ingredients
	Cookies overbaked	Remove cookies from oven promptly
Cookies tough	Improper flour used	Use lower-protein flour
	Too much flour in the dough	Adjust formula or measure flour carefully
	Too little fat in the dough	Adjust formula or measure fat carefully
	Too little sugar in the dough	Adjust formula or measure sugar carefully
	Dough overmixed	Avoid overmixing after adding dry ingredients
	Dough reworked during rolling	Roll dough carefully; do not re-roll scrap dough
Cookies too crumbly	Dough lacks gluten development	Mix longer; use higher-protein flour
	Too much chemical leavening, fat or sugar used in the dough	Adjust formula or measure carefully
	Too few eggs in the dough	Adjust formula
	Dough too thin	Roll or cut dough thicker
Cookies flatten and spread too much	Wrong type of flour used	Use higher-protein flour
	Too little flour in the dough	Adjust formula or measure flour carefully
	Too much chemical leavening, fat or liquid in the dough	Adjust formula or measure ingredients carefully
	Too much grease on baking sheets	Grease equipment carefully
	Dough too warm before baking	Chill dough thoroughly before using
	Oven too cool	Adjust oven

▼ Tables

Tables and charts offer visual support and organization of material to enhance your understanding.

TABLE 10.1	COOKIE TEXTURES					
DESIRED TEXTURE	**FAT**	**SUGAR**	**LIQUID**	**FLOUR**	**SIZE OR SHAPE**	**BAKING**
Crispness	High	High; use granulated sugar	Low	Strong	Thin dough	Well done; cool on baking sheet
Softness	Low	Low; use hygroscopic sugars	High	Weak	Thick dough	Use parchment-lined pan; underbake
Chewiness	High	High; use hygroscopic sugars	High	Strong	Not relevant; chilled dough	Underbake; cool on rack
Spread	High	High; use coarse granulated sugar	High; especially from eggs	Weak	Not relevant; room-temperature dough	Use greased pan; low temperature

▼ Sidebars

Sidebars present additional information on food history, food in culture and the background of professional food service. These sidebars help you understand baking and pastry arts in a wider social context.

THE RISE OF YEAST BREADS

How and when the first yeast-leavened breads came into being, no one knows. Perhaps some wild yeasts—the world is full of them—drifted into a dough as it awaited baking. Perhaps some ancient baker substituted fermented ale or beer for water one day. In any case, the resulting bread was different, lighter and more appetizing.

Based on models, images and writings found in excavated tombs, historians are fairly certain that the ancient Egyptians saved a bit of fermented dough from one day's baking to add to the next day's. This use of sourdough starter continues today, enjoying widespread popularity.

Other cultures developed their own leavening methods. The Greeks and Romans prepared a wheat porridge with wine, which caused their doughs to ferment. The Gauls and Iberians added the foamy head from ale to their doughs. Both methods resulted in lighter breads that retained their fresh textures longer. Since ancient times, bread baking has been one of the first household tasks readily turned over to professionals. The first cooks to work outside homes during the Greek and Roman empires were bakers. The bakery trade flourished during the Middle Ages, with a wide variety of breads being produced. Yeast-leavened breads remained the exception, not the

norm, until well into the 17th century, however. The first real collection of bread recipes is found in Nicolas Bonnefon's *Les Délices de la campagne*, published in 1654. Bonnefon's instructions, meant for those dissatisfied with commercial products of the time, included the use of beer yeast. By the end of the 17th century, published works included recipes for breads leavened with sourdough starter and the yeasts used in breweries.

Louis Pasteur finally identified yeast as a living organism in 1857. Soon after, a process for distilling or manufacturing baker's yeast was developed. By 1868, commercial baking yeast was available in stores.

▼ Questions for Discussion

Questions for Discussion appear at the end of each chapter to encourage you to integrate theory and technique into a broader understanding of the material. Web-based activities, as indicated by the WWW icon, encourage you to conduct research and seek answers from outside your primary classroom material.

QUESTIONS FOR DISCUSSION

1. Explain the differences among active dry yeast, instant dry yeast and compressed yeast. Describe the correct procedures for working with these yeasts.

2. Explain the differences between a sponge and a sourdough starter. How is each of these items used?

3. Describe the straight dough mixing method and give two examples of products made with this procedure.

4. List the 10 production stages for yeast breads. Which of these production stages would also apply to quick bread production? Explain your answer.

5. Locate a professional organization for bread bakers. What services are available to its members? WWW

6. Locate two recipes each for typical French, German and Italian yeast breads and determine whether they are made with the straight dough, sponge or other pre-fermentation method. WWW

Terms to Know

leavening	kneading
active dry yeast	windowpane test
instant dry yeast	pickup stage
starter	punching down
dough	rounding
temperature	proofing
straight dough	scoring
method	refresh
sponge method	lactic acid
sourdough	acetic acid
method	poolisch
old dough	biga

◄ New! Terms to Know

A list of important terms used in each chapter is provided to help enhance your vocabulary and reinforce professionalism.

Comprehensive Teaching

FOR THE INSTRUCTOR

PowerPoint Presentations, Instructor's Manual and MyTest

Available on Pearson's online catalog and at www.pearsonhighered.com, adopters may access PowerPoint presentations featuring lecture outlines for the entire textbook, and an Instructor's Manual with answers to each chapter's Questions for Discussion, problem-based learning exercises and examination questions. MyTest contains text-based questions in a format that enables instructors to select questions and create their own examinations.

To access supplementary materials online, instructors need to request an instructor access code. Go to www.pearsonhighered.com/irc, where you can register for an instructor access code. Within 48 hours after registering, you will receive a confirming e-mail, including an instructor access code. Once you have received your code, go to the site and log on for full instructions on downloading the materials you wish to use.

and Learning Package

FOR THE STUDENT

We believe in learning—all kinds of learning for all kinds of people, delivered in a personal style. MyCulinaryLab™ 2.0 supports the many ways in which students learn. By engaging the learner through media–rich competency and skills-based Learning Modules that are mapped to learning objectives and industry recognized accreditation standards, MyCulinaryLab™ 2.0 helps students master the content online on their own time and at their own pace.

Available standalone, or integrated within MyCulinaryLab™ 2.0, the Pearson Kitchen Manager is a robust web-based recipe management application created by a team of culinary professionals, educators and interactive experts. Pearson Kitchen Manager is a valuable resource for chef instructors and students alike. Featuring trusted recipes tested in the kitchens of top culinary schools, Pearson Kitchen Manager bridges the gap between learning to cook and learning how to manage a successful foodservice organization.

MyCulinaryLab®

PEARSON KITCHENMANAGER

Student Study Guide

An indispensable resource, the **Study Guide** (ISBN-10: 0-13-237305-X) assists the student in learning terminology and theory. It includes review questions with answers to help the student comprehend the techniques and processes illustrated in the textbook. The Student Study Guide may be purchased through local bookstores or at **www.pearsonhighered.com**.

THIRD EDITION

ON BAKING

A TEXTBOOK OF BAKING AND PASTRY FUNDAMENTALS

SARAH R. LABENSKY, CCP

and PRISCILLA MARTEL

with EDDY VAN DAMME
Houston Community College

Photographs by Richard Embery and Eddy Van Damme
Drawings by Stacey Winters Quattrone and William E. Ingram

Boston Columbus Indianapolis New York San Francisco Upper Saddle River
Amsterdam Cape Town Dubai London Madrid Milan Munich Paris Montreal Toronto
Delhi Mexico City São Paulo Sydney Hong Kong Seoul Singapore Taipei Tokyo

Editorial Director: Vernon Anthony
Senior Acquisitions Editor: William Lawrensen
Editorial Assistant: Lara Dimmick
Director of Marketing: David Gesell
Senior Marketing Manager: Thomas Hayward
Assistant Marketing Manager: Alicia Wozniak
Senior Marketing Assistant: Les Roberts
Associate Managing Editor: Alexandrina Benedicto Wolf
Project Manager: Kris Roach
Senior Operations Supervisor: Pat Tonneman
Operations Specialist: Deidra Skahill

Senior Art Director: John Christiana
Text and Cover Designer: John Christiana
Cover Photo: © Photolibrary/Corbis
Media Director: Karen Bretz
Full-Service Project Management: Linda Zuk, WordCraft LLC
Composition: S4Carlisle Publishing Services
Printer/Binder: Courier Kendallville
Cover Printer: Lehigh-Phoenix Color/Hagerstown
Text Font: 10 point Garamond Light

Credits and acknowledgments borrowed from other sources and reproduced, with permission, in this textbook appear on page 827.

Library of Congress Cataloging-in-Publication Data
Labensky, Sarah R.
   On baking: a textbook of baking and pastry fundamentals / Sarah R Labensky and
Priscilla Martel with Eddy Van Damme; photographs by Richard Embery and Eddy Van Damme;
drawings by Stacey Winters Quattrone and William E. Ingram. — 3rd ed.
      p. cm.
   ISBN 0-13-237456-0 (978-0-13-237456-9)
   1. Baking. 2. Pastry. I. Martel, Priscilla. II. Van Damme, Eddy. III. Title.
TX763.B3233 2013
641.8'15--dc23
                                                              2011044530

V011
10 9 8 7 6 5 4

ISBN 10:   0-13-237456-0
ISBN 13:   978-0-13-237456-9

CONTENTS

CONTENTS

CONTENTS

PREFACE

On Baking: A Textbook of Baking and Pastry Fundamentals builds on the successful approach developed in *On Cooking: A Textbook of Culinary Fundamentals*. This is a carefully designed text intended to teach both the principles and practices of baking and the pastry arts. The baking information presented in *On Cooking* is suitable for culinary students seeking a general knowledge of baking. *On Baking* takes the same clear, organized approach and expands the material into far greater depth, covering techniques and formulas required for core and advanced baking and pastry programs.

This book aims to teach professional culinary students core baking principles and the skills necessary to produce a wide array of baked goods and confections. Our goal is not merely to offer a collection of recipes, although there are over 750 recipes for a wide variety of baked goods and confections. We include these formulas to illustrate the techniques presented in the teaching sections of each chapter. Throughout the text, we discuss both the "how" and "why" of baking. Extensive step-by-step photographs help you visualize the techniques used to form bread dough, shape cookies or temper chocolate while recipes illustrate the baking principles and procedures. Throughout the book we provide extensive illustrated sections identifying bakeshop ingredients and equipment. We believe that a thorough understanding of the function of ingredients will serve you well throughout your baking career.

Winner of the 2004 **Gourmand World Cookbook Award** as the **"Best Book for Food Professionals in the World,"** *On Baking* has been uniformly praised for its organization, clarity, ease of use and use of quality photography to illustrate professional techniques. This third edition seeks to further enhance the content included in prior editions.

THE STORY BEHIND THIS NEW EDITION

Baking programs vary in terms of content and depth. After speaking with instructors and hearing from reviewers, we wanted to incorporate material at a wide range of skill levels and interests.

Our commitment to offering a range of formulas for various skill levels led us to institute an in-classroom testing program for many of the recipes in both the second and third editions. The testing enabled chef instructors to share useful feedback about how they approach a particular topic.

Much of the feedback we received since *On Baking* was first published indicated that students and instructors appreciate a book with clear, thorough explanations of fundamental techniques used in professional bakeries. Users also look for an assortment of formulas for making classic pastries and items served at modern bakery cafes, as well as dishes that reflect a wider ethnic influence. We have expanded this coverage and sought to add more formulas that speak to these trends. All of the formulas featured in *On Baking*, Third Edition, as well as many formulas found in previous editions, are available online through the Pearson Kitchen Manager application, which is accessible at www .pearsonhighered.com/pkm or integrated within MyCulinaryLab™ 2.0 at www.myculinarylab.com. By creating an online database of formulas, we are able to expand the content covered and support the book with photographs and illustrations while maintaining an acceptable size and cost.

A NOTE ON RECIPES AND FORMULAS

The featured recipes are designed to reinforce and demonstrate techniques that are presented within the text. Many of these formulas intentionally produce low yields, which are more appropriate for students beginning to learn about baking and for small schools and teaching kitchens. Selected larger volume formulas appear in Appendix III and are noted with the scale icon shown at left . We provide volume measurements only when the quantity of an ingredient is difficult to weigh without specialized equipment: less than ½ ounce of salt, leavening or spices, for example. We list all ingredients in both **U.S. and metric measurements.** In most instances we round off the metric equivalents to even, easily measured amounts.

Consider the U.S. and metric ingredient lists as separate recipes or formulas; do not measure some ingredients according to the metric amounts and other ingredients according to the U.S. amounts or the proportions will not be accurate and the intended result will not be achieved.

Baker's percentages are included with many formulas, especially those for breads. Widely used in the professional bakeshop, baker's percentages are very useful for increasing or decreasing yields as needed. We provide **yields** in either total batch weight or total yield and offer suggested portion sizes where appropriate.

We present detailed procedures for standard techniques, then generally do not repeat them in each recipe (for example, "apply egg wash" or "divide the dough"). A **mise en place** feature is included with recipes that appear in the front section of recipe chapters. Ingredients that require preparation before beginning to prepare the recipe are listed in the margin. You should consult this brief checklist after you read the recipe but before you begin to bake. No matter how detailed the written recipe, however, we must assume that you possess certain knowledge, skills and judgment.

Variations appear at the end of selected recipes. These variations enable you to see how a set of techniques or procedures can be used to prepare different dishes with only minor modifications. Variations also provide the advanced baker or pastry chef the opportunity to customize recipes for different applications. **Headnotes** that describe the cultural or historical background of a bread or pastry or the unique techniques used in its preparation appear with many of the recipes. This short text should enhance your understanding of a baking style or technique.

A registered dietitian analyzed each recipe using nutritional analysis software that incorporates data from the U.S. Department of Agriculture, research laboratories and food manufacturers. The **nutrient information** provided here should be used only as a reference, however. A margin of error of approximately 20 percent can be expected because of natural variations in ingredients. Preparation techniques and serving sizes may also significantly alter the values of many nutrients. In the nutritional analysis for a recipe that offers a choice of ingredients, the first-mentioned ingredient is the one used unless stated otherwise. Ingredients listed as "as needed" are omitted from the analysis. Corn oil and whole milk are used throughout for "vegetable oil" and "milk," respectively. In cases of a range of ingredient quantities or numbers of servings, the average was used.

Throughout this book the MyPlate symbol, shown at left marks various recipes. This symbol identifies dishes that are particularly low in calories, fat, saturated fat or sodium; if appropriate, they may also be a good source of vitamins, protein, fiber or calcium.

Bakeshop products are often challenging to produce from start to finish in a single two- to three-hour class session. Formulas that can be produced in a limited amount of time are printed in blue in the master recipe list on pages xxiii through xxx. If a dough, pastry or frozen dessert base needs to chill overnight before using, it will not be highlighted even if the preparation can be made quickly. Should components such as tart dough or puff pastry be available, additional formulas in this book may be prepared in a two- to three-hour class time. As in restaurant and bakery settings, however, many breads and pastries will need to be made in stages. For example, puff pastry can be produced one day, then refrigerated for baking and assembly during a subsequent day. This reinforces the component approach to pastry preparation, in which fillings, doughs, toppings, icings and such can be prepared in advance and assembled in various ways to complete desserts and pastries. Similarly, starters for yeast breads, doughs for Danish pastries and many dessert sauces can be prepared days in advance of final use.

Baking is both an art and a science. It is best learned through hands-on experience combined with study of the principles that underlie each technique. You should rely on the knowledge and skills of your instructor for guidance. Although some skills and an understanding of theory can be acquired through reading and study, no book can substitute for repeated, hands-on preparation and observations. We hope you enjoy *On Baking*!

ACKNOWLEDGMENTS

This book would not have been possible without the assistance and support of many people. Special thanks go to photographer Richard Embery for his talent, professionalism and commitment to quality; to Eddy Van Damme for his artistry with both recipes and photographs; and to Sharon Salomon, MS, RD, for help with preparation of Chapter 16, Healthful and Special-Needs Baking.

PREFACE

The nutritional analysis was prepared by Mindy Herman, MS, RD, whose thoroughness and prompt replies were greatly appreciated. Thanks also go to Stacey Winters Quattrone, Bill Ingram and Anna Moreno for their artistry. We thank Suzanne Fass for her expertise in creating the indexes for this edition. We are grateful to the many chefs, restaurateurs, writers and culinary professionals who provided recipes and essays for this book. We extend our special thanks to the baking and pastry professionals who took time out of their busy schedules to contribute to this edition. Among them: Dan Fox, Gale Gand, Will Goldfarb, En-Ming Hsu, Emily Luchetti and Craig Nielsen.

Sarah offers her sincere thanks and appreciation to her co-authors for adding their expertise, insight and artistry to this edition. She is especially grateful to Priscilla Martel for her friendship as well as her many contributions to this project, including her ability to synthesize mountains of information and express a clear vision for the book.

Eddy would like to thank his parents for gently guiding him into the amazing field of baking, Patricia for being the best sister anyone could ask for and Kyle for being the greatest. He would like to commend Dr. William Harmon, President, Dean Linda Koffel and Suzette Brimmer for their support, dedication and vision of excellence for the academic and culinary and pastry programs at Houston Community College, and Dr. Mary Spangler, Chancellor, and other members of the College for their relentless commitment to making the College superb. He thanks Chef Younes Kay for being the very best colleague, Anna Moreno for her beautiful illustrative work and Samiha Hashem and Eva Hsu for their tremendous help in the pastry lab. He also would like to thank Hyuna Lee, Quynh Luu Ha and the Imperial Sugar Company for their generous support.

Priscilla would like to recognize the personal and professional support of Victor Frumolt, Jacques Pépin, Carole Pierce, J. Patrick Truhn, Sylvia Barnes, and James Trimble with this project. She would also like to thank Dennis Hibdon, Technical Service, Bunge Corporation; Beth Hillson, President, American Celiac Disease Alliance; Stuart A. Hirsch; Warren Patterson, General Mills; Bill Weekley, CMB, General Mills; and William "Bill" Yosses, White House Executive Pastry Chef, for their professional help with this project. And special thanks to Charlie van Over for always keeping the wood oven stoked.

The authors wish to thank the following companies for their generous contributions to the production of this book: Belshaw Brothers Inc., South Seattle, WA; Cambro Manufacturing Company, Huntington Beach, CA; Chicago Metallic Bakeware Company, Chicago, IL; Demarle USA, Cranbury, NJ; FBM Baking Machines, Cranbury, NJ; Gemini Baking Equipment Co., Philadelphia, PA; Houston Community College, Houston, TX; JB Prince, New York, NY; Nor-Lake Manufacturing, Hudson, WI; Sveba Dahlen AB, Fristad, Sweden; Taylor, Rockton, IL, and the Edlund Co., Burlington, VT.

Finally we wish to thank everyone involved in this project at Pearson Education, including Vernon Anthony, Editorial Director for Career Publishing; William Lawrensen, Senior Acquisitions Editor, Hospitality Management & Culinary Arts; John Christiana, Manager of Design Development; Alex Wolf, Associate Managing Editor; Kris Roach, Project Manager; Janet Portisch, AV Project Manager; Joe Conti, Color Supervisor; Ronald Walko, Imaging Specialist; David Gesell, Director of Marketing; Leigh Ann Sims, Marketing Manager; and Alicia Dysert, Marketing Coordinator. We offer special thanks to Linda Zuk, our tireless Project Manager at WordCraft LLC. Not only do we appreciate her eagle eye; working with her is always a pleasure.

We also remain indebted to Robin Baliszewski, Acquisitions Editor of the first edition of *On Cooking* and current Director for People at Pearson, for her support and friendship.

We would like to extend our thanks to the following chefs and instructors who took the time to review the accuracy and relevance of the content, as well as those who participated in our recipe testing program. Their feedback has contributed greatly to the production of our text's accuracy, level of difficulty, and appropriateness.

Maurietta Amos
Gwinett Technical College

Sheila Beckley
Front Range Community College

Leslie Bartosch, CEC, FMP
Alvin Community College

Carol Bennett
Central Arizona College

Beatrice C. Beasley
Santa Rosa Jr. College

Frank Benowitz
Mercer County Community College

Jeffery Alan Bricker
Ivy Tech Community College -
Indianapolis

Scott Bright
The Chef's Academy

Tracey Brigman
University of Georgia

Melinda Casady
Pioneer Pacific College

Jonathan M. Deutsch
Kingsborough Community College
(CUNY)

Katherine Donaho-Wessman
Le Cordon Bleu College of Culinary
Arts – Las Vegas

Jodi Lee Duryea
University of North Texas

William Easter
Des Moines Area Community College

Sari Edelstein
Simmons College

Stephen C. Fernald
Lake Tahoe Community College

Carolyn Fludd
Atlanta Technical College

Kristen Grissom
Daytona State College

Brandon Harpster
Southeast Community College

Eunice Alicia Harris
County College of Morris

James Haynes
Central Arizona College - Coolidge

Michael Herbert
Northern Virginia Community College

Deborah A. Hutcheon
Bob Jones University

Dorothy Johnston
Erie Community College (SUNY)

Debbie C. Kern
Delgado Community College

Cynthia Kruth
Naugatuk Valley Community College

Julie K. Lee
Western Kentucky University

Laura Marone
Jefferson College, St. Louis Community
College

Fiona McKenzie
Sand Hills Community College

Prema Monteiro
J. F. Drake State Technical College

Mark Moritz
Bob Jones University

Adrienne O'Brien
Luna Community College

Jayne Pearson
Manchester Community College

Donna Pease
Technical College of the Low Country

Anthony J. Pisacano
Ogeechee Technical College

Lou Rice
Northwest Arkansas Community College

Bryan Richard
Ogeechee Technical College

Alan Scheidhauer
Culinary Institute of the Carolinas at
Greenville Technical College

Janet L. Shaffer
Lake Washington Institute of Technology

Casey Shiller
St. Louis Community College

Jim Switzenberg
Harrisburg Area Community College

Daniel Taylor
The International Culinary Schools at the
Art Institutes – Raleigh-Durham

Paul Vida
Ivy Tech Community College

Chris Villa
Wallace State Community College -
Hanceville

Katrina Warner
Tarrant County College

Robert Weir
Allan Hancock College

RECIPES

Recipes printed in red are available online. Recipes printed in blue can be prepared in a 2- to 3-hour class period.

CHAPTER EIGHT

ENRICHED YEAST BREADS

CHAPTER NINE

LAMINATED DOUGHS

RECIPES

CHAPTER FIFTEEN

ICE CREAM AND FROZEN DESSERTS

CHAPTER SIXTEEN

HEALTHFUL AND SPECIAL-NEEDS BAKING

RECIPES

ON BAKING

> "The ranks of every profession concerned with the sale or preparation of food, including cooks, caterers, confectioners, pastry cooks, provision merchants and the like, have multiplied in ever-increasing proportions. . . . New professions have arisen; that, for example, of the pastry cook—in his domain are biscuits, macaroons, fancy cakes, meringues. . . . The art of preserving has also become a profession in itself, whereby we are enabled to enjoy, at all times of the year, things naturally peculiar to one or other season.
>
> —Jean-Anthelme Brillat-Savarin,
> French writer, politician and philosopher (1755–1826)"

CHAPTER ONE

PROFESSIONALISM

LIKE ANY FINE ART, GREAT COOKERY REQUIRES TASTE AND CREATIVITY, an appreciation of beauty and a mastery of technique. Like the sciences, successful cookery demands knowledge and an understanding of basic principles. And like any successful leader, today's food service professionals must exercise sound judgment and be committed to achieving excellence in their endeavors.

This book describes foods and baking equipment, explains baking and culinary principles and confectionery techniques and provides formulas using these principles and techniques. No book, however, can provide taste, creativity, commitment and judgment. For these, you must rely on yourself.

BAKERS, CHEFS AND RESTAURANTS

The student studying the baking and pastry arts is entering a world rich in cultural heritage. Knowledge of this heritage is an important part of a culinary education, one that serves as a source of professional pride. Bakers and pastry chefs tap this long history for inspiration for recipes, ingredients and techniques.

Bread Making since Ancient Times

The first bread products humans consumed were firm porridges made from grasses and grains cooked on flat stones heated by an open fire. The earliest form of wheat used for bread making, *Triticum dioccum*, thrived in the fertile basin of the Nile River valley. The use of a stone oven for bread making dates to the Neolithic period (4000 B.C.E.). Remarkably, the ovens discovered in archaeological ruins from that time closely resemble the domed beehive-shaped ovens still used today. It is believed that the Egyptians discovered the effect of wild yeast organisms in leavening bread and perfected bread making to achieve consistent results. (This discovery also led to the development of beer.) What historians interpret as organized bakeries are depicted in hieroglyphics, sculptures and tomb paintings discovered throughout Egypt, where as many as 70 kinds of bread were consumed in the first millennia B.C.E.

Most historians believe that the development of organized societies began with the evolution of agriculture. Once plants and grains could be consistently produced and animals raised systematically, humans were no longer forced to hunt and forage for food. The time saved allowed them to concentrate on perfecting other skills and crafts such as the way food was prepared. Bread making and **confectionery** were the first labor activities organized into specialized trades. Pharaohs employed skilled bakers to provide bread for their private consumption. Among the trades recognized by the highly organized Greek society of the fourth and third centuries B.C.E. were the wafer makers (*oblaten*) and the pastry cooks. The religion of ancient Greece focused on the worship of multiple deities and included the offering of gifts to these gods, especially around critical times, to ensure plentiful harvests, adequate rain and prosperity. As is customary today, certain breads and sweets were eaten to commemorate special occasions. Historians credit the ancient Greeks with spreading the profession of the skilled baker throughout the Mediterranean basin. According to the Greek historian Herodotus, writing in the fourth century B.C.E., bakers accompanied roving Greek armies on their raids. When Roman armies conquered them, Greek soldiers and bakers remained in what is now Italy. Roman occupation then helped spread the techniques for cultivating grains, milling and baking bread products throughout the western world. Bread rapidly became the staple food essential for human survival, a position it held in most western societies until the 20th century.

confectionery transforming sugar into sweets; also refers to the trade of candy making

Ancient Egyptian sculpture depicting kneading bread dough.

19th-century bakery in France.

Bread baking and pastry making found a fertile home on the European continent. In the northern regions including Austria, Germany, the Netherlands, Scandinavia and Great Britain, where a cool, damp climate was inhospitable to wheat growing, rye grain products took hold. In the 17th century, the Dutch and British debuted the use of pans in which to bake bread, paving the way for the development of the sandwich.

Until the process for milling flour was perfected in the 1830s, white flour was expensive and most bread was made from assorted and relatively coarse ground grains. These grains, such as emmer and spelt, baked into rough-textured solid loaves quite unlike their light and crusty descendants eaten today. The milling process was labor intensive, involving grinding the grain between millstones and then sifting the flour manually through cloth to remove the coarse bran. The finest and whitest flour, the smallest quantity produced after many stages of sifting, made the softest products and was available only to the wealthy.

In the mid-19th century, advances were made in the production of a stable form of yeast to leaven bread. Once perfected by a Viennese distiller, this yeast paste popularized the production of a wider variety of breads. Simultaneously, improved mechanical kneading machinery appeared, making the task of large-scale bread mixing possible.

Refined Sugar and the Art of Confectionery

Humans share a strong appetite for sweet foods; it is the only universally innate taste preference. If, for millennia, the consumption of bread ensured sustenance and survival, eating sweet foods ensured satisfaction and pleasure. For much of prehistory, historians assume that fruits were humans' primary source of sweet foods. Sweet pastes made from dates and figs and syrups made from the juices of fruits such as grapes and berries were also used to sweeten foods. Tree sap from maple and birch trees sweetened foods as did syrups from cooked grains such as sorghum. Honey was the first concentrated sweetener to be widely used. In ancient Egypt, Greece and Rome, honey was used to season both savory and sweet dishes and as a preservative. Egyptian hieroglyphs from the 15th century B.C.E. depicting clay beehives document the cultivation of bees for their honey.

Though many candies and sweet confections can be made from honey, not until refined sugar became readily available did the pastry and confectionery trades evolve. Without refined sugar, many of the candies and sweets widely consumed today would not be possible. **Sugarcane** produces a liquid syrup that hardens and crystallizes when boiled. Sugar's ability to be both a liquid and solid, discussed at length in the chapters in this book, makes it indispensable for candy and pastry making.

The process of extracting sugar from a large tropical grass now known as sugarcane began in India around 500 B.C.E. Arabs perfected the cultivation and refining of sugar

sugarcane (*Saccharum officinarum*) a tropical grass native to Southeast Asia; the primary source of sugar

MARIE-ANTOINE (ANTONIN) CARÊME (1783–1833)

Carême, known as the "cook of kings and the king of cooks," was an acknowledged master of French grande cuisine. Abandoned on the streets of Paris as a child, he worked his way from cook's helper in a working-class restaurant to become one of the most prestigious chefs of his (or, arguably, any other) time. During his career, he was chef to the famous French diplomat and gourmand Prince de Talleyrand, the prince regent of England, Tsar Alexander I of Russia and Baron de Rothschild, among others.

His stated goal was to achieve "lightness," "grace" and "order" in the preparation and presentation of food. As a pâtissier, he designed and prepared elaborate and elegant pastry and confectionery creations, many of which were based on architectural designs. He is credited with the invention of croquembouche, millefeuille and pulled sugar work. As a saucier, he standardized the use of roux as a thickening agent and devised a system for classifying sauces. As a culinary professional, he designed kitchen tools, equipment and uniforms.

As an author, he wrote and illustrated important texts on the culinary arts, including *Le Pâtissier royal Parisian* (1825), containing fanciful designs for *les pieces montées*, the great decorative centerpieces that were the crowning glory of grand dinners; and his five-volume masterpiece on the state of his profession, *L'Art de la cuisine au XIXe siècle* (1833). Carême's writings almost single-handedly refined and summarized 500 years of culinary evolution. But his treatises were not mere cookbooks. Rather, he analyzed cooking, old and new, emphasizing procedure and order and covering every aspect of the art known as grande cuisine.

---

around 600 C.E. Arab conquests of the Mediterranean region, international trade and the travels of the crusaders spread the use of refined sugar throughout Europe during the 13th through 15th centuries. (The island of Crete takes its name from the Arabic *quandi*, meaning "crystalized sugar"; it was the site of possibly the world's first sugar refinery, built by the Arabs around 1000 C.E.) Sugar remained an expensive luxury until the ability to extract and refine sugarcane became more common. (See Chapter 4, Bakeshop Ingredients.) Venice was one of the first European cities to set up its own sugar refineries in the 15th century, making refined cane sugar available throughout the region. Many confections from that time, such as sugared fruits, sugared almonds and marzipan, are still prepared in the same manner today.

During his travels to the New World, Columbus carried sugarcane from the Canary Islands to Santo Domingo, where it flourished in the tropical climate of the island that now comprises the Dominican Republic and Haiti. As sugarcane became more dispersed geographically, the cost of production dropped, causing sugar to lose status as a luxury item while increasing its importance as a basic nutrient. During the 16th through 19th centuries sugar confectionery began to take hold in Europe.

Another source of refined sugar is the **sugar beet** (*Beta vulgaris*), the second most important source of sugar in the world. In the 18th century, German chemists discovered how to extract sugar from the root of beets and built a refinery to do this commercially in 1800. When cane sugar supplies were cut off during the Napoleonic Wars, Napoleon ordered the cultivation of sugar beets on a large scale, creating a viable sugar beet industry. Today, much of the sugar consumed in northern countries comes from sugar beets, and about half of the sugar produced in the United States comes from sugar beets.

sugar beet (*Beta vulgaris*) a plant with a high concentration of sucrose in its root; a major source of refined sugar

RESTORATIVES

The word *restaurant* is derived from the French word *restaurer* ("to restore"). Since the 16th century, the word *restorative* has been used to describe rich and highly flavored soups or stews capable of restoring lost strength. Restoratives, like all other cooked foods offered and purchased outside the home, were made by authorized guild members.

The Birth of the Bakery and Restaurant

The culinary crafts evolved during the Middle Ages under the European guild system. The **guild system** was a method of organizing the production and sale of goods produced outside the home. Guilds ensured quality manufacturing methods and consistent pricing. Each guild had a monopoly on preparing certain items. For example, during the reign of Henri IV of

AUGUSTE ESCOFFIER (1846–1935)

Escoffier's brilliant culinary career began at age 13 in his uncle's restaurant and continued until his death at age 89. Called the "emperor of the world's kitchens," he is perhaps best known for defining French cuisine and dining during La Belle Époque (the "Gay Nineties"). Unlike Carême, Escoffier never worked in an aristocratic household. Rather, he exhibited his culinary skills in the dining rooms of the finest hotels in Europe, including the Place Vendôme in Paris and the Savoy and Carlton Hotels in London.

Escoffier did much to enhance the *grande cuisine* that arguably reached its perfection under Carême. Crediting Carême with providing the foundation for great—that is, French—cooking, Escoffier simplified the profusion of flavors, dishes and garnishes typifying Carême's work. He also streamlined some of Carême's overly elaborate and fussy procedures and classifications. For example, he reduced Carême's elaborate system of classifying sauces into the five families of

sauces still recognized today. Some consider his refinement of *grande cuisine* to have been so radical as to credit him with the development of a new cuisine referred to as *cuisine classique* (classic or classical cuisine).

His many writings include *Le Livre des menus* (1912), in which, discussing the principles of a well-planned meal, he analogizes a great dinner to a symphony with contrasting movements that should be appropriate to the occasion, the guests and the season. But his most important contribution is a culinary treatise intended for the professional chef entitled *Le Guide culinaire* (1903). Still in use today, it is an astounding collection of more than 5000 classic cuisine recipes and garnishes. In it, Escoffier emphasizes the mastery of techniques, the thorough understanding of cooking principles and the appreciation of ingredients—attributes he considered the building blocks professional chefs should use to create great dishes. Escoffier's most famous recipe was Peach Melba, created for Australian opera star Nellie Melba (1861–1931) when she was staying at the Savoy in 1893. Dame Nellie also liked her toast made in the way that today bears her name: Melba toast.

France (1553–1610), there were separate culinary guilds for *rôtisseurs* (who cooked *la grosse viande*, the main cuts of meat), *pâtissiers* (who cooked poultry, pies and tarts), *tamisiers* (who baked breads) and *traiteurs* (who made ragoûts). By the end of the 17th century, according to culinary historian Barbara Wheaton, Paris bakeshops sold a remarkable variety: "rye bread and milk rolls, fine bread and coarse bread, soup breads, a variety of little rolls . . . leavened with brewer's yeast (*pain de levure*), others with a sourdough starter (*pain de levain*)."

The French claim that the first modern **restaurant** opened one day in 1765 when a Parisian tavern keeper, a Monsieur Boulanger, hung a sign advertising the sale of his special restorative, a dish of sheep feet in white sauce. Boulanger's establishment differed from the inns and taverns that had existed throughout Europe for centuries. These inns and taverns served foods prepared (usually off premises) by the appropriate guild. The food—of which there was little choice—was offered by the innkeeper as incidental to the establishment's primary function: providing sleeping accommodations or drink. Customers were served family style and ate at communal tables. Boulanger's contribution to the food service industry was to serve a variety of foods prepared on premises to customers whose primary interest was dining.

The French Revolution (1789–1799) had a significant effect on the budding restaurant industry. Along with the aristocracy, guilds and their monopolies were generally abolished. The revolution also allowed the public access to the skills and creativity of the well-trained, sophisticated chefs and **pâtissiers** who had worked in the aristocracy's private kitchens. Although many of the aristocracy's chefs either left the country or lost their jobs (and some their heads), a few opened restaurants catering to the growing urbanized middle class.

As the 19th century progressed, more restaurants opened, serving a greater selection of items and catering to a wider clientele. By midcentury, several large, grand restaurants in Paris were serving elaborate meals, decidedly reminiscent of the **grande cuisine** (also known as *haute cuisine*) of the aristocracy. *Grande cuisine*, which arguably reached its peak of perfection in the hands of Antonin Carême, was characterized by meals consisting of dozens of courses of elaborately and intricately prepared, presented, garnished and sauced

pâtissier French for *pastry chef*; the person responsible for all baked items, including breads, pastries and desserts

grande cuisine the rich, intricate and elaborate cuisine of the 18th- and 19th-century French aristocracy and upper classes. It is based on the rational identification, development and adoption of strict culinary principles. By emphasizing the how and why of cooking, *grande cuisine* was the first to distinguish itself from regional cuisines, which tend to emphasize the tradition of cooking

GASTON LENÔTRE (1920–2009)

Gaston Lenôtre started in the baking trade in the heart of Normandy in the 1930s. By age 15, he had passed his professional exams and set off to work in his hometown. In 1947, he bought the boulangerie/pâtisserie of his boss in Pont Audemer. His bakery became a destination for sophisticated Parisians on their way to their country estates. In 1957 he was enticed to open a shop in Paris at 44 rue d'Auteuil in the 16th arrondissement, one of the city's most stylish sections. It was the first of more than a baker's dozen of locations, plus a vast catering business, which literally catered to "le tout Paris."

Lenôtre chose the village of Plaisir outside Paris for his third location—a vast production kitchen that became the heart of his expanding empire. He saw that to realize his expansion plans, he needed to train workers in his methods, and he began an in-house school, L'École Lenôtre. But here is where Gaston Lenôtre demonstrated his talent as both baker and businessman: There was a crisis in the trade at the time due to a lack of qualified bakers, so Lenôtre opened the school, a few years

later, to the entire professional community. For a fee, even his competitors could come and learn from his *Meilleurs Ouvriers de France*—chefs recognized by the French government as the best artisans in the trade.

As befitting a native of Normandy, the heart of France's dairy industry, Lenôtre's innovations came in the area of Bavarians,

charlottes and fruit mousses. Many of his cakes and tortes became modern classics, copied by pastry chefs worldwide. La Feuille d'Automne, Le Concorde and L'Opéra were ubiquitous in Parisian bakeries in the 1980s. Lenôtre mastered the technique of freezing, using it with respect to protect the quality of his products without adulterating them. He used the latest technology to maintain the integrity of his products. Proper freezing preserves the product, extending its shelf life without having to use chemicals and preservatives common in industrial food production. Many professionals believe that Lenôtre single-handedly saved the pastry profession when it was threatened by mass production.

Lenôtre is considered by many the father of modern French pastry, and his impact is worldwide. By the early 1980s he had 18 stores in Japan as well as outposts in Germany, Switzerland and England. Today, whether you go to Rio de Janeiro, Disney World in Florida, Lebanon or Las Vegas, you will find Lenôtre's name on the marquee.

—ALEX MILES, Pastry Chef and Culinary Educator, Dijon, France

foods. Carême was known for advancing the art of the pâtissier by creating elaborate showpieces made with pastillage and pulled sugar. A great innovator, he is credited with perfecting nougat, meringue, croquembouche and millefeuille.

The Late 19th Century—Escoffier and *Cuisine Classique*

Following the lead set by the French in both culinary style and the restaurant business, restaurants opened in the United States and throughout Europe during the 19th century. Charles Ranhofer (1836–1899) was the first internationally renowned chef of an American restaurant, Delmonico's in New York City. In 1893, Ranhofer published his "franco-american" encyclopedia of cooking, *The Epicurean*, containing more than 3500 recipes including recipes for flannel cakes and brandy snaps.

One of the finest restaurants outside France was the dining room at London's Savoy Hotel, opened in 1898 under the direction of César Ritz (1850–1918) and Auguste Escoffier. Escoffier is generally credited with refining the *grande cuisine* of Carême to create *cuisine classique* or **classic cuisine**. By doing so, he brought French cuisine into the 20th century.

The Mid-20th Century—Point and *Nouvelle Cuisine*

The mid-20th century witnessed a trend toward lighter, more naturally flavored and more simply prepared foods. Fernand Point was a master practitioner of this movement. But this master's goal of simplicity and refinement was carried to even greater heights by a generation of chefs Point trained: principally, Paul Bocuse, Jean and Pierre Troisgros, Alain Chapel, François Bise and Louis Outhier. They, along with Michel Guérard and

classic cuisine a late 19th- and early 20th-century refinement and simplification of French *grande cuisine*. Classic (or classical) cuisine relies on the thorough exploration of culinary principles and techniques and emphasizes the refined preparation and presentation of superb ingredients

LIONEL POILÂNE (1945–2002)

What many bakers don't realize is that good wheat can make bad bread. The magic of bread baking is in the manipulation and the fermentation. What has been lost . . . is this method.

—Lionel Poilâne

Called a true visionary and an ambassador of bread, Lionel Poilâne is credited with elevating the craft of bread baking and the appreciation of traditional artisan ways of making bread in our time. At age 14, he began working in his father's small bakery on a project that would become his life's passion. His father had started making a large dark rustic loaf, like that which was common in Paris before the light baguette-style bread captivated the city in the 1920s. Enchanted by this old-style bread, Poilâne dedicated himself to reviving traditional regional breads. Renowned for his attention to detail and appreciation of the craft of

the baker, in the early 1980s he set out to document regional bread recipes. Captured in his book, *Guide de l'Amateur de Pain*, these breads were fading memories before

he rediscovered them. His book is used as a reference text in schools throughout France to this day.

Thousands of loaves of *pain Poilâne*, the name for his singular crusty round loaf, are made each day in a production bakery outside Paris. This bread is sold in restaurants and shops throughout Paris and flown to the United States and more than a dozen other countries daily. Though the production is large, it is not industrialized. He believed in what he called "retro-innovation," combining the best of the old techniques with modern advances. Two bakers work at each of 24 wood-fired stone ovens, forming the loaves by hand. The original shop at 8 rue du Cherche-Midi is situated on the site of an 18th-century monastery and houses ovens dating from that time. The shop, which still sells fresh *pain Poilâne* and a limited selection of other baked goods, is a Mecca for serious bread lovers from around the world.

Roger Vergé, were the pioneers of **nouvelle cuisine** in the early 1970s. In the world of the pâtissier, Gaston Lenôtre made inroads by taking the classic pastries of *grande cuisine* and adapting them to a brighter, fresher style of pastry making.

Their culinary philosophy was principled on the rejection of overly rich, needlessly complicated dishes. These chefs emphasized healthful eating. The ingredients must be absolutely fresh and of the highest possible quality; the cooking methods should be simple and direct whenever possible. The accompaniments and garnishes must be light and contribute to an overall harmony; the completed plates must be elegantly designed and decorated. Following these guidelines, some traditional cooking methods have been applied to untraditional ingredients, and ingredients have been combined in new and previously unorthodox fashions.

nouvelle cuisine French for "new cooking"; a mid-20th-century movement away from many classic cuisine principles and toward a lighter cuisine based on natural flavors, shortened cooking times and innovative combinations

Return to Craftsmanship and the Artisan Bread Movement

During this period, a number of Parisian bread bakers, notably Lionel Poilâne, sought to return simplicity to quality bread making. The bread most often associated with France—the long, golden-brown baguette with the white fluffy interior—is a 20th-century invention. In the 1920s a new mixing technique was introduced, which produced lighter, softer bread than what had been available previously. During World War II, severe shortages forced bread rationing in France. The scarce bread that was available during the war was made from whole grains extended with inferior ingredients such as ground beans. According to French historian Jérôme Assire, this bread's offensive taste made the longing for pure white bread even more intense. Following the war, the demand for fluffy white bread was greater than ever. New dough-mixing methods and rack ovens capable of handling large numbers of loaves produced plenty of bread to meet this demand.

In the 1960s Lionel Poilâne began working at his father's bakery, where he learned to make an old-style loaf of bread like that sold by bakers in 18th-century Paris. Using a blend of whole-meal flours and long fermentation (rising) times, he learned to bake breads on the stone floor of a wood-fired oven. Following his lead, other bakers in Paris were similarly

artisan a person who works in a skilled craft or trade; one who works with his or her hands. Applied to bread bakers and confectioners who prepare foods using traditional methods

inspired to rediscover traditional ways of making flavorful bread. These bakers inspired an international interest in producing what is called **artisan** bread, bread made in traditional ways with the purest of ingredients.

The Late 20th and Early 21st Century— An American Culinary Revolution

During the last 35 years, broad changes have affected the culinary landscape in the United States. During this period, restaurateurs and chefs began Americanizing the principles of French *nouvelle cuisine*. When Alice Waters opened Chez Panisse in Berkeley, California, in 1971, her goal was to serve fresh food, simply prepared. Rejecting the growing popularity of processed and packaged foods, Waters wanted to use fresh, seasonal and locally grown produce in simple preparations that preserved and emphasized the foods' natural flavors. Chez Panisse and the many chefs who passed through its kitchen launched a new style of cuisine that became known as **new American cuisine**.

new American cuisine a late-20th-century movement that began in California but has spread across the United States; it stresses the use of fresh, locally grown, seasonal produce and high-quality ingredients simply prepared in a fashion that preserves and emphasizes natural flavors

As Waters's culinary philosophy spread across the United States, farmers and chefs began working together to make fresh, locally grown foods available, and producers and suppliers began developing domestic sources for some of the high-quality ingredients that were once available only from overseas. European-style cultured butter from Vermont and goat cheese from Sonoma, California, are just two examples.

Pastry chefs and bakers followed Waters's lead. Those who fell under her direct influence, including Lindsey Shere and Steve Sullivan, and others such as Nancy Silverton, traveled to France to study as Waters had done. They returned with European skills and a desire to serve desserts with freshness and simplicity. Pastry chefs and bakers, exposed on their travels to the work of Lenôtre and Poilâne, brought these influences into kitchens throughout this country. Combining ingredients and/or preparation methods, they created a new American way with pastry.

Others worked to rediscover American cooking and baking traditions. Lacking professional reference texts on the subject, professionals turned to cookbooks written for home consumers for inspiration. Talented pastry chefs such as Maida Heatter, whose 1974 book

PIERRE HERMÉ (1961–)

Pierre Hermé, known as "the Picasso of Pastry," has acquired a reputation as an innovator, revolutionary, provocateur and magician, for his success in transforming traditional French dessert making into a fine art of dazzling excitement. His St-Germain-des-Prés boutique has become an indispensable stop on the Paris gastronomic circuit, and his elegant creations are displayed like fine jewelry. The novelty and fantasy in his creations are always matched by consummate professionalism and perfect technique.

Coming from an Alsatian family of pastry makers, Hermé was apprenticed to Gaston Lenôtre and headed Fauchon's pastry department before setting out on his own, establishing his first outlets in Tokyo. Returning to Paris in 2001, he opened a boutique at 72 rue Bonaparte, just off the Place St-Sulpice, which became an overnight sensation, with long lines of

international admirers waiting to buy his creations. A second boutique in the 15th arrondissement soon followed.

If any delicacy typifies the Hermé phenomenon, it would be the almond macaroon. From the standard flavors of coffee and raspberry, he has extended the repertoire to chestnut and green tea. Like the major fashion houses he has rolled out new "spring-summer" and "fall-winter" lines. His hottest selling creation, the Ispahan ("spring-summer" 1997), consists of rose petal cream, fresh raspberries and lychee nuts, sandwiched between two rose-flavored macaroons and topped by a rose petal.

Chocolate also deserves special mention. Hermé opened a "chocolate bar" in Tokyo in 2005 and treats the medium like a magic potion to stretch the limits of his creativity and the sensory pleasures of his customers. For those who can't get to Paris or Tokyo, Hermé's prolific contributions to the dessert literature, along with a line of "e-gourmandises" from fruitcake to chocolates, are available from the Hermé Web site.

Maida Heatter's Book of Great Desserts became a well-thumbed reference in professional kitchens in the 1970s and 1980s, introduced the restaurant public to homey desserts including Palm Beach Brownies and Sweet Potato Pecan Pie.

By the mid-1980s, American chefs began a period of bold experimentation. They began to combine ingredients or preparation methods of a variety of cuisines. Their work resulted in **fusion cuisine**. With fusion cuisine, ingredients or preparation methods associated with one ethnic or regional cuisine are combined with those of another. French pastry cream flavored with star anise served with a banana spring roll and kiwi Napoleon are examples of fusion-style preparations.

The culinary influences felt since the American food revolution began in the 1970s, now firmly rooted, have intensified. In these early decades of the 21st century, there is a **farm-to-table movement** as chefs work in tandem with farmers to bring fresh flavors while preserving local agriculture and heirloom varieties. The interest in locally raised ingredients has materialized into restaurants where chefs serve seasonal foods such as spring berries or autumn apples found within a few miles of the establishment.

Since 1980, the culinary influences of immigrants from Southeast Asia, India, China, Latin America and other regions are being felt around the country. Restaurants and shops catering to their cuisine have opened in neighborhoods where they have settled. Across the country, chefs are absorbing these influences and incorporating these flavors and techniques as never before. The fluidity of international borders, the accessibility of global travel and the popularity of the Internet have made the larders of the world available to chefs everywhere. With a few clicks chefs can access recipes, menus and stores featuring food from any nation.

Pastry chefs are experimenting in novel ways, defying conventional kitchen wisdom and employing techniques more common in industrial manufacturing than in classic kitchens. Inspired and influenced by modern, experimental cuisine or **molecular gastronomy**, a movement with roots in Spain and France, pastry chefs such as Will Goldfarb, Pierre Hermé and Johnny Iuzzini are reinventing the notion of pastry and dessert, often with the use of dry ice and vacuum machines as well as the freshest local ingredients.

Today, many European and American food writers and pundits now consider American chefs among the best in the world, a fact they often triumph at the same time that they express their concern about the general decline of French cuisine and the exodus of European chefs to America. In addition, the American public has taken food to heart.

The career of professional chef, whether pastry chef, baker or chef de cuisine, is now as respected in the United States as it has been for many years in Europe. Chefs have been elevated to celebrity status; an entire cable television network is devoted to cooking. Broadcasts of pastry and baking competitions occupy prime-time slots. Bookstore and library shelves are jammed with cookbooks, and newspapers and magazines regularly review restaurants or report on culinary trends. With gourmet shops and cookware stores in most malls, cooking has become both a hobby and a spectator sport. All of this has helped inspire a generation of American teenagers to pursue careers behind the stove—and in front of the camera.

THE BAKESHOP AND FOOD SERVICE OPERATION

A professional bakeshop may be a small section within a restaurant kitchen or a separate kitchen composed of many departments with its own staff and operating budget. No matter the size, the organizational concepts are the same. To function efficiently, a bakeshop and pastry operation must be well organized and staffed with appropriate personnel.

Today most food service operations use a simplified version of the kitchen **brigade**, a system created by Auguste Escoffier in the early 20th century. The **executive chef** coordinates kitchen activities and directs the kitchen staff's training and work efforts. The executive chef plans menus and creates recipes. He or she sets and enforces nutrition, safety and sanitation standards and participates in (or at least observes) the preparation and presentation of menu items to ensure that quality standards are rigorously and consistently maintained. He or she also purchases food items and equipment. In some food service

fusion cuisine the blending or use of ingredients and/or preparation methods from various ethnic, regional or national cuisines in the same dish; also known as transnational cuisine

farm-to-table movement an awareness of the source of ingredients with an emphasis on serving locally grown and minimally processed fresh food in season

molecular gastronomy a culinary movement that investigates the use of chemistry, physics and scientific principles in restaurant cooking

brigade a system of staffing a kitchen so that each worker is assigned a set of specific tasks; these tasks are often related by cooking method, equipment or type of foods being produced

THE BUSINESS OF THE BAKESHOP

The Retail Bakers of America, which represents the interests of independent bakeries, estimates that more than 30,000 retail bakeries operate in the United States. Professional trade publications such as *Modern Baking* and *Milling and Baking News* peg the baking industry as a $100 billion business. According to the American Bakers Association, which represents more than 700 baking facilities and baking company suppliers, the commercial baking industry employs close to half a million skilled workers.

Training in the baking and pastry arts can lead to work in myriad establishments such as in-store bakeries in supermarkets, food service bakery-cafés and commercial specialty cake manufacturers as well as in the finest pastry kitchens or independent artisan bakeries.

operations, the executive chef may help design the menu, dining room and kitchen. He or she trains the dining room staff so that they can correctly answer questions about the menu. He or she may also work with food purveyors to learn about new food items and products, as well as with catering directors, equipment vendors, food stylists, restaurant consultants, public relations specialists, sanitation engineers, nutritionists and dietitians.

The executive chef is assisted by a **sous-chef** or executive sous-chef, who participates in, supervises and coordinates the preparation of menu items. His or her primary responsibility is to make sure that the food is prepared, portioned, garnished and presented according to the executive chef's standards. The sous-chef may be the cook principally responsible for producing menu items and supervising the kitchen.

Large hotels and conference centers with multiple dining facilities may have one or more **area or station chefs**, each responsible for a specific facility or function. There could be, for instance, a restaurant chef and a banquet chef. Area chefs usually report to the executive chef. Each area chef, in turn, has a brigade working under him or her. **Assistants** and **apprentices** are assigned where needed to assist and learn the area.

The **pastry chef** (Fr. *pâtissier*) develops recipes for and prepares desserts, pastries, frozen desserts and breads. He or she reports directly to the executive chef and usually purchases the food items used in the bakeshop. In a large operation, an **executive pastry chef** may oversee a staff of pastry specialists. A classic kitchen brigade includes a pastry chef, who supervises the **bread baker** (Fr. *boulanger*) who makes the breads, rolls and baked dough containers used for other menu items (for example, bouchées and feuilletés); the **confectioner** (Fr. *confiseur*), who makes candies and petit fours; the **ice cream maker** (Fr. *glacier*), who makes all chilled and frozen desserts; and the **decorator** (Fr. *décorateur*), who makes showpieces and special cakes. An executive pastry chef possesses the same authority and responsibility within his or her area of expertise as an executive chef.

The independent retail pastry shop or bakeshop is organized into departments according to the tasks required. A **head baker** directs the mixing and baking of all baked goods. He or she may purchase all ingredients and train the staff on preparation. One group of bakers may bake the bread while another group mixes all the yeast dough and laminated dough to make breads and pastries. A cake decorator fills and ices cakes according to the style of the operation.

A bakeshop may employ a **master baker** (Fr. *maître boulanger*, Gr. *Bäckermeister*). This title recognizes the highest level of achievement; only highly skilled and experienced bakers who have demonstrated their professional knowledge in written and practical exams are entitled to use it. This title recalls the European guild tradition still alive in many countries today. In France and Germany, for example, a baker must pursue many years of classroom and job training, work as an apprentice and pass numerous examinations before acquiring the right to call himself or herself a master baker. In the United States, several professional organizations administer programs leading to certification as a master baker. (See Online Resources.)

The Professional Pastry Chef and Baker

Today the job prospects for the skilled baker and pastry chef are wide and varied. The old corner bakery, with the baker in back producing daily batches of bread and sweets and his wife serving the customers, has been reinvented. In major cities and increasingly in rural areas, artisan-style bakeshops inspired by those found in France, Italy and Germany are appearing. Products offered may include luscious pastries and rustic breads as well as coffee and light meals served all day long. Chains of bakery-cafés now dot the national landscape and serve increasingly better-quality products. Skilled personnel are needed to staff hundreds of locations as well as off-site commissary kitchens. In restaurants of every kind, from fast-casual establishments to luxury restaurants, the service of dessert has been elevated to the level of fine cuisine.

Although there is no one recipe for producing a good professional baker or pastry chef, with knowledge, skill, taste, judgment, dedication and pride a student chef will mature into a professional.

WORDS TO SURVIVE IN A PROFESSIONAL KITCHEN

So you want to be a pastry chef and spend your life trying to satisfy the nation's insatiable sweet tooth? No one has more friends than a pastry chef, but getting there is hard work and only for the very dedicated. However, if you are the kind of person who can't fall asleep at night because you're distracted by a new dessert you thought up using figs, crème brûlée base, cheddar cheese ice cream and a port reduction, then this may be the art form for you.

You may have discovered your love for baking at your mom's knee, but she's not coming into the pro kitchen with you. So make sure you chose it for the right reason—because you can't imagine doing anything else. Keep in mind that

everyone has something to teach you, even your chef. As you truss yourself into your apron, feel confident, feel strong, play well with others in the sandbox and teach your hands to work like a surgeon's, in consort with your mind. Constantly try new recipes and solve problems, not make them. Scrape your mixing bowl often, more often than you really want to and check your math twice when scaling up a recipe.

The main thing is to always, always, always wear comfortable shoes. If your feet are happy you'll be happy and you'll be successful at this glorious form of expression called Pastry.

—GALE GAND, Pastry Chef and Co-Owner, Tru, Chicago, IL

KNOWLEDGE

Pastry chefs and bakers must be able to identify, purchase, use and prepare a wide variety of foods. They should be able to train and supervise a safe, skilled and efficient staff. To do all this successfully, professional pastry chefs and bakers must possess a body of knowledge and understand and apply certain scientific and business principles. Schooling helps. A professional baking program should, at a minimum, provide the student with a basic knowledge of foods and baking ingredients, food styles and the methods used to prepare foods. Students should also understand sanitation, nutrition and business procedures such as food costing.

This book attempts to address the core competencies needed for success in the field. The study begins with extensive sections identifying equipment, tools and ingredients. Throughout this book, basic baking principles are discussed while formulas illustrate these principles in action. Whenever possible, whether it be preparing puff pastry or ice cream, the focus of the material is on the general procedure, highlighting fundamental principles and skills, both the hows and whys of baking. Only then are specific applications and sample formulas given. In order for the student to gain a sense of the rich tradition of food and the baking and pastry arts, informative sidebars on culinary history, chef biographies and other topics are scattered throughout the book.

In this way, the materials in this book follow the trail blazed by Escoffier, who wrote in the introduction to *Le Guide culinaire* that his book is not intended to be a compendium of recipes slavishly followed, but rather a tool that leaves his colleagues "free to develop their own methods and follow their own inspiration; . . . the art of cooking . . . will evolve as a society evolves, . . . only basic rules remain unalterable."

As with any profession, an education does not stop at graduation. The acquisition of knowledge continues throughout one's professional career. Look for opportunities to learn advanced skills through additional classes on pastry traditions and techniques, nutrition or business management. Stay abreast of trends by reading some of the many periodicals and books devoted to baking and the pastry arts. Well-rounded food professionals should travel and should try new products to broaden their culinary horizons. Professional organizations (see Online Resources) offer career support, opportunities to exchange ideas with one's peers and the chance to build a network of relationships to last a lifetime.

PASSIONATE FOR PASTRY

Competition kitchens are the extreme version of the professional kitchen. Everything is done with purpose and is probably well rehearsed. It is similar to a well-run professional kitchen where everyone has a job and knows what needs to be done to keep the kitchen running smoothly. Teamwork and understanding each person's role within the group are very similar in both settings. A competition kitchen adds intensity, focus and a common goal: win the event. Competition training taught me to be better organized and time conscious. I am a perfectionist, which is good for a competition. On the one hand, I am aware of all the details and scenarios. It is a balance of artistic skill, efficiency, communication, and grace under pressure. On the other hand, perfectionism can slow the team down. Too much attention to detail and I forget about the big picture. Competition is not for everyone, but it can be a very rewarding experience that builds strength and character.

—EN-MING HSU, Pastry Chef Consultant

—CHEF HSU was captain of the U.S. Pastry Team that won the Gold Medal at the World Pastry Cup in Lyon, France in 2001.

SKILL

Professional training alone does not make a student a pastry chef or baker. Nothing but practical, hands-on experience will provide even the most academically gifted student with the skills needed to produce, consistently and efficiently, quality foods or to organize, train, motivate and supervise a staff.

Many food service and baking operations recognize that new workers, even those who have graduated from culinary programs, need time and experience to develop and hone their skills. Therefore, many graduates start in entry-level positions. Do not be discouraged; advancement will come, and the training pays off in the long run. Learn from those with experience and accept criticism as part of the learning process. Seeking out and working with seasoned professionals will contribute to the student's learning experiences. Today, culinary styles and fashions change frequently. What does not go out of fashion are well-trained, skilled and knowledgeable professionals. They can adapt.

TASTE

No matter how knowledgeable or skilled the baker or pastry chef, he or she must be able to produce foods that taste great, or the consumer will not return. A professional baker or pastry chef can do so only with confidence about his or her own sense of taste.

Our total perception of taste is a complex combination of smell, taste, sight, sound and texture. All senses are involved in the enjoyment of eating; all must be considered in creating or preparing a dish. The baking professional should develop a taste memory by sampling foods, both familiar and unfamiliar. Baking professionals should also think about what they taste, making notes and experimenting with flavor combinations and cooking methods. But one should not be inventive simply for the sake of invention. Rather, a pastry chef must consider how the flavors, appearances, textures and aromas of various foods interact to create a total taste experience.

JUDGMENT

Creating a pastry menu, determining how much of what item to order, deciding whether and how to combine ingredients and approving finished items for service are all matters of judgment. Although knowledge and skill play a role in developing judgment, sound judgment comes only with experience. And real experience is often accompanied by failure. Do not be upset or surprised when a dish does not turn out as expected. One can learn from mistakes as well as from successes; these experiences help develop sound judgment.

DEDICATION

Becoming a pastry chef and baker is hard work; so is being one. The work is often physically taxing; the hours, often in the early morning, are usually long and the pace is frequently hectic. Despite these pressures, the professional is expected to efficiently produce consistently fine products that are properly prepared and presented. To do so requires enthusiastic pastry chefs and bakers who are dedicated to the job.

Dedication means never faltering. The bakery and food service industry is competitive and depends on the continuing goodwill of an often fickle public. One bad dish, one pale loaf or one off night can result in a disgruntled customer and lost business. The pastry chef and baker should always be mindful of the food prepared and the customer served.

The true professional is dedicated to his or her staff. Virtually all bakeries and food service operations rely on teamwork to get the job done well. Good teamwork requires a positive attitude and dedication to a shared goal.

PRIDE

Professional bakers and pastry chefs share a sense of pride in doing their jobs well. Pride should also extend to personal appearance and behavior in and around the kitchen. The professional should be well groomed and in uniform when working.

The pastry chef wears the same uniform as that worn by any professional chef: comfortable shoes, trousers (either solid white, solid black, black-and-white checked or black-and-white striped), a white double-breasted jacket, an apron and a neckerchief usually knotted or tied cravat style. The uniform has certain utilitarian aspects: Checked trousers disguise stains; the double-breasted white jacket can be rebuttoned to hide dirt, and the double layer of fabric protects from scalds and burns; the neckerchief absorbs facial perspiration and the apron protects the uniform and insulates the body.

The professional baker's uniform varies from that of other chefs. Though comfortable shoes are the foundation of any food professional's uniform, the baker may wear white trousers and a short-sleeved white shirt. The choice of white is utilitarian; it does not show the presence of flour as would a dark-colored uniform. The uniform should be worn with pride. Shoes should be polished; trousers and jacket should be pressed.

The crowning element of the uniform is the **toque**. A toque is the tall white hat worn by chefs almost everywhere. Most chefs now wear a standard 6-inch- or 9-inch-high toque, but historically a cook's rank in the kitchen dictated the type of hat worn. Beginners wore flat-topped *calottes*; cooks with more advanced skills wore low toques and the master chefs wore high toques called *dodin-bouffants*. Traditionally, the baker wears a flat-topped baker's cap. Its derivation is quite simple; bending and working close to the bread oven would prevent a tall cap from staying in place.

SAFETY AND SANITATION

Like all food service professionals, pastry chefs and bakeshop workers must have a thorough understanding of sanitation principles and practices. The threat of transmitting food-borne illnesses is of serious concern to all food professionals. Providing consumers with well-prepared and safe food is the primary responsibility of all cooking professionals. (Many people have serious food allergies that affect what they can safely eat. It is critical that food service workers have a knowledge of common food allergies and methods for preventing allergic reactions, which is discussed in Chapter 16, Healthful and Special-Needs Baking.)

Microorganisms that cause food-borne illnesses can be destroyed or their growth severely limited by proper food-handling procedures. Bacteria, molds, yeasts, viruses and fungi are **microorganisms** that thrive on certain foods. These foods are referred to as **potentially hazardous foods (PHF)** which may require time/temperature control for safety (TCS). By observing proper handling and sanitation procedures, kitchen workers can stop the spread or growth of these microorganisms.

Safe Food-Handling Practices

Learning about food contaminants, how they are spread and how they can be prevented or controlled can help ensure customer safety. Temperature is the most important factor in the environment of **pathogenic** bacteria because it is the factor most easily controlled by food service workers. Most microorganisms are destroyed at high temperatures. Freezing slows but does not stop growth, nor does it destroy bacteria.

Most bacteria that cause food-borne illnesses multiply rapidly at temperatures between 70°F and 125°F (21°C and 52°C). Therefore, the broad range of temperatures between

---

POTENTIALLY HAZARDOUS FOODS OR TIME/TEMPERATURE CONTROL FOR SAFETY FOODS

A potentially hazardous food (PHF), which may require time and temperature control for safety (TCS), is any food or food ingredient that will support the rapid growth of infectious or toxigenic microorganisms, or the slower growth of *Clostridium botulinum*. PHF/TCS foods include the following:

- Food from an animal source (for example, meat, fish, shellfish, poultry, milk and eggs)
- Food from a plant that has been heat-treated (for example, cooked rice, beans, potatoes, soy products and pasta)
- Raw seed sprouts
- Cut melons and fresh leafy greens that have been cut, shredded, sliced, chopped or torn
- Cut tomatoes or mixtures of cut tomatoes that are not acidified or otherwise appropriately modified at a processing plant
- Garlic-in-oil mixtures that are not acidified or otherwise appropriately modified at a processing plant
- Foods containing any of the preceding items (for example, custards, sauces and casseroles)

microorganisms single-celled organisms as well as tiny plants and animals that can be seen only through a microscope

pathogen any organism that causes disease; usually refers to bacteria

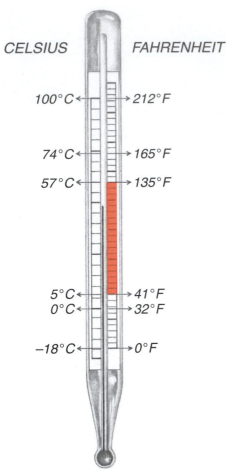

CELSIUS   FAHRENHEIT

100°C ←   → 212°F

74°C ←   → 165°F

57°C ←   → 135°F

5°C ←   → 41°F
0°C ←   → 32°F

−18°C ←   → 0°F

FIGURE 1.1 ▶ The temperature danger zone.

THE TEMPERATURE DANGER ZONE

The temperature danger zone is a broad range of temperatures in which most of the bacteria that cause food-borne illnesses multiply rapidly. The 2009 Model Food Code of the Food and Drug Administration (FDA) indicates that the temperature danger zone begins at 41°F (5°C) and ends at 135°F (57°C). Regulations in some localities and with some organizations may vary, however. Here we use the range recommended by the FDA.

41°F and 135°F (5°C and 57°C) is referred to as the **temperature danger zone**. See Figure 1.1. Keeping foods out of the temperature danger zone decreases the bacteria's ability to thrive and reproduce.

To control the growth of any bacteria that may be present, it is important to maintain the internal temperature of food at 135°F (57°C) or above, or 41°F (5°C) or below. Simply stated: Keep hot foods hot and cold foods cold. Potentially hazardous foods should be heated or cooled quickly so that they are within the temperature danger zone as briefly as possible. This is known as the *time-and-temperature principle*.

Keep hot foods hot. The high internal temperatures reached during proper cooking kill most of the bacteria that can cause food-borne illnesses. Once properly heated, hot foods must be held at temperatures of 135°F (57°C) or above. Foods that are to be displayed or served hot must be heated rapidly to reduce the time within the temperature danger zone. When heating or reheating foods:

▶ Heat small quantities at a time.

▶ Stir frequently.

▶ Heat foods as close to service time as possible.

▶ Use preheated ingredients whenever possible to prepare hot foods.

▶ Never use a steam table for heating or reheating foods. Bring reheated food to an appropriate internal temperature (at least 165°F [74°C]) before placing it in the steam table for holding.

Keep cold foods cold. Foods that are to be displayed, stored or served cold must be cooled rapidly. When cooling foods:

▶ Refrigerate semisolid foods at 41°F (5°C) or below in containers that are less than 2 inches (5 centimeters) deep. (Increased surface area decreases cooling time.)

▶ Avoid crowding the refrigerator; allow air to circulate around foods.

▶ Vent and cool hot foods in an ice-water bath, as illustrated in Chapter 5, Mise en Place.

▶ Prechill ingredients such as pastry cream before preparing cold foods.

▶ Store cooked foods above raw foods to prevent cross-contamination.

Keep frozen foods frozen. Freezing at 0°F (−18°C) or below essentially stops bacterial growth but does not kill the bacteria. Do not place hot foods in a standard freezer. This does not cool the food any faster, and the release of heat can raise the temperature of other foods in the freezer. Only a special blast freezer can be used for chilling hot items. If one is not available, cool hot foods as mentioned earlier before freezing them. When frozen foods are thawed, bacteria that are present begin to grow. Therefore:

▶ Never thaw foods at room temperature.

▶ Thaw foods gradually under refrigeration to maintain the food's temperature at 41°F (5°C) or less. Place thawing foods in a container to prevent cross-contamination from dripping or leaking liquids.

▶ Thaw foods under running water at a temperature of 70°F (21°C) or cooler.

▶ Thaw foods in a microwave only if the food will be prepared and served immediately.

Bacteria need moisture to thrive. Dry foods such as flour, sugar and crackers are rarely subject to bacterial infestations. However, when a dry food such as beans is cooked and moistened it becomes a breeding ground for the growth of any bacteria that may be present. Bacteria do not thrive in foods that are high in acid, such as lemon juice or vinegar. Simply adding acid, however, should not be relied on to destroy bacteria or to preserve foods.

Cross-Contamination

Generally, microorganisms and other contaminants cannot move by themselves. Rather, they are carried to foods and food contact surfaces by humans, rodents or insects. This transfer is referred to as **cross-contamination**. Humans provide the ideal environment for the growth of microorganisms. Everyone harbors bacteria in the nose and mouth.

These bacteria spread easily through sneezing or coughing or not washing hands frequently and properly. Workers who are ill should report the illness promptly to their supervisor, who has the right to ask them to leave work if their illness threatens contamination in the kitchen. The best prevention is not to report to work when sick.

Observing proper cleaning procedures prevents cross-contamination. Kitchen staff can do several things to decrease the risk of an illness being spread by poor personal hygiene:

▶ Wash hands frequently and thoroughly. Gloves are not a substitute for proper hand washing.

▶ Keep fingernails short, clean and neat. Do not bite nails or wear nail polish.

▶ Keep any cut or wound antiseptically bandaged. An injured hand should also be covered with a disposable glove.

▶ Bathe daily, or more often if required.

▶ Keep hair clean and restrained.

▶ Wear work clothes that are clean and neat. Avoid wearing jewelry or watches.

▶ Do not eat, drink, smoke or chew gum in food preparation areas.

PROCEDURE FOR PROPER HAND WASHING

① Using hot water (100°F/38°C), rinse hands and forearms.

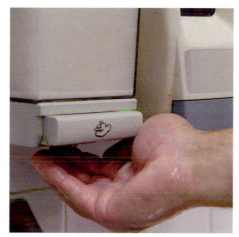

② Apply an antibacterial soap.

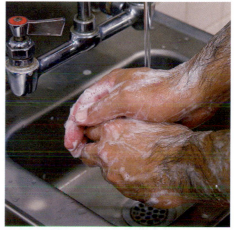

③ Rub hands and arms briskly with soapy lather for at least 20 seconds.

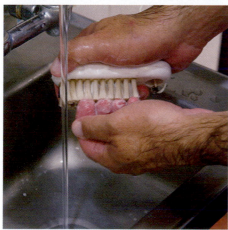

④ Scrub between fingers and clean nails with a clean nail brush.

⑤ Rinse thoroughly under hot running water. Reapply soap and scrub hands and forearms for another 5 to 10 seconds. Rinse again.

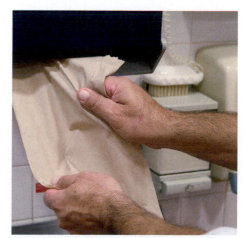

⑥ Dry hands and arms using a single-use towel or appropriate hand dryer; use the towel to turn off the water. Discard the towel in a trash receptacle.

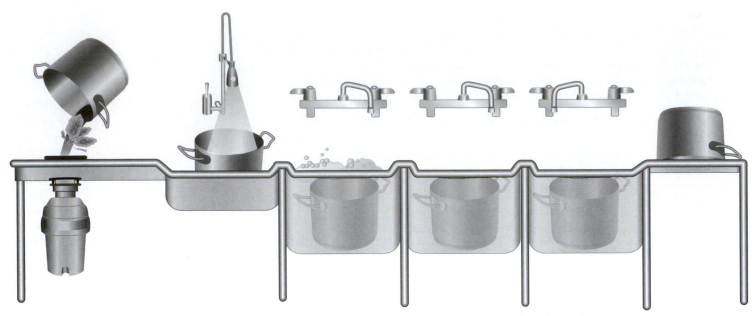

FIGURE 1.2 ▶ The three-compartment sink procedure—scrape, spray, wash, rinse, sanitize and air-dry each item.

Even with proper hand washing, food service workers should strive to minimize direct contact with prepared food by using single-use gloves, clean tongs, tasting spoons, bakery tissue paper and other appropriate tools. Be aware that disposable gloves can prevent cross-contamination only when used properly. Wash hands before putting on disposable gloves because microorganisms on the hands could contaminate the gloves. Gloves, along with proper bandaging, must always be worn if there is a cut or infection on the hand. Wear single-use gloves for only one task; for example, change gloves immediately after handling raw meats and when switching from making sandwiches to making salads. Change gloves as often as necessary, when they are torn or after 4 hours of continual use. Do not wash or try to reuse disposable gloves. To remove a glove, grab the cuff, peel the glove off inside out over the fingers and then throw it away. Check your local regulations because some health departments require the use of disposable gloves when handling any ready-to-eat foods.

Food service workers can prevent cross-contamination by observing proper cleaning and sanitizing procedures. Soiled cutting boards, knives and side towels are major sources of cross-contamination. For example, when a cutting board that has been used to cut raw poultry is used to slice fruit for a salad, the fruit can become exposed to microorganisms present in the poultry. Probe thermometers should be washed before and after each use.

Cleaning refers to removing visible soil and food residue. *Sanitizing* refers to removing harmful substances to safe levels. Something that is clean may not always be sanitary; the visible dirt can be removed but the disease-causing microorganism may remain. The cleaning of dishes, pots, pans and utensils in a food service operation involves both removing soil and sanitizing. Soil can be removed manually or by machine. Sanitizing can be accomplished with heat or chemical disinfectants.

Procedures for manually washing, rinsing and sanitizing dishes and equipment generally follow the three-compartment sink setup shown in Figure 1.2. The dishwasher must do the following:

1. Scrape and spray the item to remove soil.
2. Wash the item in the first sink compartment using an approved detergent. A brush or cloth may be used to remove any remaining soil.
3. Rinse the item in the second sink compartment using clear, hot water.

**SAFETY ALERT
Sanitizing Solution**

Use a clean cloth dipped in sanitizing solution when wiping off knives, utensils or cutting boards during work. An acceptable solution can be made by combining 1 gallon (4 liters) lukewarm water with 1 tablespoon (15 milliliters) chlorine bleach. Replace this solution every 2 hours and store it below work areas to avoid accidental spills.

④ Sanitize the item in the third sink compartment by either
   a. immersing it in 171°F (77°C) water for at least 30 seconds, or
   b. immersing it in an approved chemical sanitizing solution used according to the manufacturer's directions.

⑤ Empty, clean and refill each sink compartment as necessary, and check the water temperature regularly.

Food service items, dishes, silverware and utensils should always be allowed to air-dry, as towel drying may recontaminate them.

Chemical products used to clean and sanitize equipment should be stored well away from clean equipment and foodstuffs to avoid contaminating foodstuffs with these chemicals.

Pest control is of special concern in the bakeshop, as insect and rodent infestation of bulk ingredients such as flour and grains can introduce harmful contaminants to otherwise safe ingredients. An insect or rodent infestation is usually considered a serious health risk and should be dealt with immediately and thoroughly. Pests must be controlled by (1) building them out of the facility, (2) creating an environment in which they cannot find food, water or shelter and (3) relying on professional extermination.

The best defense against pests is to prevent infestations in the first place by building them out. Any crack—no matter how small—in door frames, walls or windowsills should be repaired immediately, and all drains, pipes and vents should be well sealed. Inspect all deliveries thoroughly and reject any packages or containers that contain evidence of pests.

Flies are a perfect method of transportation for bacteria because they feed and breed on human waste and garbage. Use screens or "fly fans" (also known as air curtains) to keep them out in the first place. Controlling garbage is also essential because moist, warm, decaying organic material attracts flies and provides favorable conditions for eggs to hatch and larvae to grow.

Pest management also requires creating an inhospitable environment for pests. Store all food and supplies at least 6 inches (15 centimeters) off the floor and 6 inches (15 centimeters) from walls. Rotate stock often to disrupt nesting places and breeding habits. Provide good ventilation in storerooms to remove humidity, airborne contaminants, grease and fumes. Do not allow water to stand in drains, sinks or buckets, as cockroaches are attracted to moisture. Clean up spills and crumbs immediately and completely to reduce their food supply.

Despite all best efforts to build pests out and maintain proper housekeeping standards, it is still important to watch for the presence of pests. For example, cockroaches leave a strong, oily odor and feces that look like large grains of pepper. Cockroaches prefer to search for food and water in the dark, so seeing any cockroach on the move in the daylight is an indication of a large infestation.

Rodents (mice and rats) tend to hide during the day, so an infestation may be rather serious before any creature is actually seen. Rodent droppings, which are shiny black to brownish gray, may be evident, however. Rodent nests made from scraps of paper, hair or other soft materials may be spotted.

Should an infestation occur, consult a licensed pest control operator immediately. With early detection and proper treatment, infestations can be eliminated. Be very careful in attempting to use pesticides or insecticides yourself. These chemicals are toxic to humans as well as to pests. Great care must be used to prevent contaminating food or exposing workers or customers to the chemicals.

SAFETY ALERT
Tasting Food

To avoid cross-contamination, a two-spoon tasting method should be used when sampling in the professional kitchen. To safely taste food, use a clean spoon to remove some of the food from the pan in which it was made or stored. Pour that food into a second clean spoon before tasting it. This prevents the soiled spoon from going back into the food being prepared. Keep a supply of clean spoons for this purpose near all cooking and preparation stations.

The Safe Worker

Food service professionals are also responsible for their own personal safety as well as that of their customers and fellow workers. Bakeshops and kitchens are filled with objects that can cut, burn, break, crush or sprain the human body. The best ways to prevent work-related injuries are proper training, good work habits and careful supervision.

The federal government enacted legislation designed to reduce hazards in the work area, thereby reducing accidents. The Occupational Safety and Health Act (OSHA) covers a broad range of safety matters. Employers who fail to follow its rules can be severely fined. Unfortunately, human error is the leading cause of accidents, and no amount of legislation can protect someone who doesn't work in a safe manner.

Safe behavior on the job reflects pride, professionalism and consideration for fellow workers. The following list should alert you to conditions and activities aimed at preventing accidents and injuries:

▶ Clean up spills as soon as they occur.

▶ Learn to operate equipment properly; always use guards and safety devices.

▶ Wear clothing that fits properly; avoid wearing jewelry, which may get caught in equipment.

▶ Use knives and other equipment for their intended purposes only.

▶ Walk, do not run.

▶ Keep exits, aisles and stairs clear and unobstructed.

▶ Always assume pots and pans are hot; handle them with dry towels.

▶ Position pot and pan handles out of the aisles so that they do not get bumped.

▶ Get help or use a cart when lifting or moving heavy objects.

▶ Avoid back injury by lifting with your leg muscles; stoop, don't bend, when lifting.

▶ Use an appropriately placed ladder or stool for climbing; do not use a chair, box, drawer or shelf.

▶ Keep breakable items away from food storage or production areas.

▶ Warn people when you must walk behind them, especially when carrying a hot pan.

Some accidents will inevitably occur, and it is important to act appropriately in the event of an injury or emergency. This may mean calling for help or providing first aid. Every food service operation should be equipped with a complete first-aid kit. Municipal regulations may specify the exact contents of the kit. Be sure that the kit is conveniently located and well stocked at all times.

The American Red Cross and local public health departments offer training in first aid, cardiopulmonary resuscitation (CPR) and the Heimlich maneuver used for choking victims. All employees should be trained in basic emergency procedures. A list of emergency telephone numbers should be posted by each telephone.

1 Describe the influences on the baker and pastry chef in the 21st century.

2 Many contemporary confections and pastries are rooted in ancient recipes. Use the Internet and library resources to research an early product such as a cake, cookie or candy and discuss how its taste and preparation technique has evolved over time. www

3 What are the roles of the executive chef and the pastry chef in the modern kitchen brigade?

4 Review the 2009 revised Model Food Code and discuss its impact on sanitary practices in the bakeshop.

5 Numerous professional organizations hold competitions for pastry chefs and bread makers each year. Use the Internet to research recent bread-making and pastry competitions. Discuss the winning entries and the people who succeeded in these competitions. www

QUESTIONS FOR DISCUSSION

Terms to Know

guild system
restaurant
executive chef
sous-chef
area chef
apprentice
executive pastry
 chef
confectioner
decorator
master baker
toque
potentially
 hazardous
 food (PHF)
temperature
 danger zone
cross-
 contamination

> "If the divine creator has taken pains to give us delicious and exquisite things to eat, the least we can do is prepare them well and serve them with ceremony.
> —FERNAND POINT, FRENCH CHEF (1897–1955)

CHAPTER TWO

TOOLS AND EQUIPMENT FOR THE BAKESHOP

HAVING THE PROPER TOOLS AND EQUIPMENT FOR A PARTICULAR TASK MAY MEAN THE DIFFERENCE BETWEEN a job well done and one done carelessly, incorrectly or even dangerously. This chapter introduces most of the tools and equipment typically used in a professional bakeshop. Items are divided into categories according to their function: hand tools, knives, measuring and portioning devices, strainers and sieves, cookware and bakeware, decorating and finishing tools, processing equipment, heavy equipment and safety equipment.

A wide variety of specialized tools and equipment is available to today's baker. Breading machines, dough molders and doughnut glazers are designed to speed production by reducing handwork. Much of this specialized equipment is quite expensive and found only in specialized kitchens or food manufacturing operations; a discussion of it is beyond the scope of this chapter. Other devices—a chocolate tempering machine or madeleine pan, for example—are used only for unique tasks. Brief descriptions of some of these specialized devices are, however, found in the Glossary and in the chapters on yeast breads, chocolate and decorative work.

STANDARDS FOR TOOLS AND EQUIPMENT

NSF International (NSF) promulgates consensus standards for the design, construction and installation of kitchen tools, cookware and equipment. Many states and municipalities require that food service operations use only NSF-certified equipment. Although NSF certification is voluntary, most manufacturers submit their designs to NSF to show that they are suitable for use in professional food service operations. Certified equipment bears the NSF mark shown in Figure 2.1.

NSF standards reflect the following requirements:

1. Equipment must be easily cleaned.
2. All food contact surfaces must be nontoxic (under intended end-use conditions), non-absorbent, corrosion resistant and nonreactive.
3. All food contact surfaces must be smooth, that is, free of pits, cracks, crevices, ledges, rivet heads and bolts.
4. Internal corners and edges must be rounded and smooth; external corners and angles must be smooth and sealed.
5. Coating materials must be nontoxic and easily cleaned; coatings must resist chipping and cracking.
6. Waste and waste liquids must be easily removed.

FIGURE 2.1 ▶ The NSF mark.

SELECTING TOOLS AND EQUIPMENT

In general, only commercial food service tools and equipment should be used in a professional kitchen and bakeshop. Household tools and appliances not NSF-certified may not withstand use in a professional kitchen. Look for tools that are well constructed and up to the rigors of repeated use. For example, joints should be welded, not bonded with solder; handles should be comfortable, with rounded borders; plastic and rubber parts should be seamless. Before using any equipment, study the operator's manual or have someone experienced with the particular item instruct you on proper procedures for its use and cleaning. And remember to always think safety first.

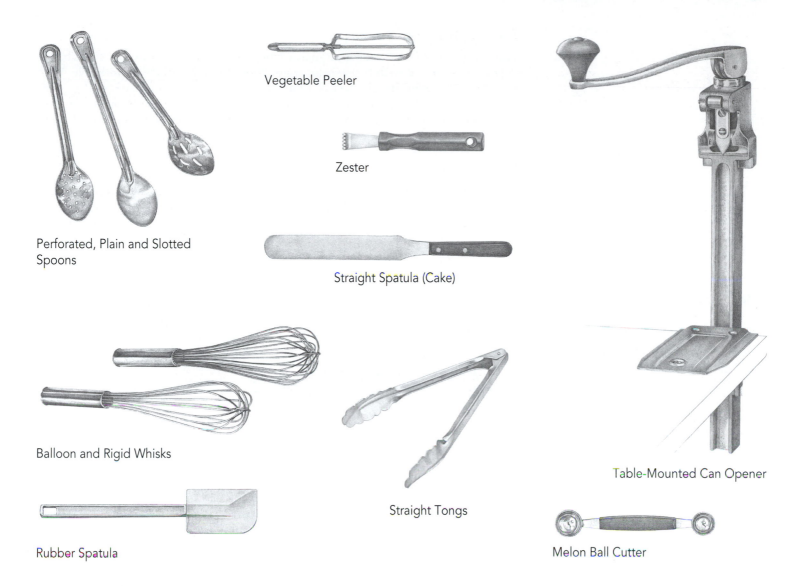

Vegetable Peeler

Zester

Perforated, Plain and Slotted Spoons

Straight Spatula (Cake)

Balloon and Rigid Whisks

Straight Tongs

Table-Mounted Can Opener

Rubber Spatula

Melon Ball Cutter

HAND TOOLS

Hand tools are designed to aid in cutting, shaping, moving or combining foods. They have few, if any, moving parts. The essential hand tools in the bakeshop are the spatulas, dough scrapers, whisks, tongs and specialized cutters used every day for routine preparations. Sturdiness, durability and safety are the watchwords when selecting hand tools. Choose tools that can withstand the heavy use of a professional kitchen and those that are easily cleaned.

Graters

A variety of graters are used to shred ingredients into small uniform pieces so that they will blend or melt easily when baked. The most common grater is the four-sided box grater. This grater is made from tin or stainless steel; each side is punched with small holes of varying sizes. A handle on top secures the grater while the open bottom permits foods to be released. A flat metal grater with tiny, razor-sharp holes resembling a woodworker's rasp is now available for the bakeshop. These graters are especially useful for removing the zest from citrus fruits without any of the bitter pith. Handheld or table-mounted rotary graters are used for grating chocolate and nuts into a fine powder. Graters designed specifically for nutmeg and ginger are widely used.

Rasp-Style Grater

Bench Brush

Textured Rolling Pin

Baker's Peel

Pastry Wheel

Pastry Brushes

Brushes are used in the bakeshop to apply coatings onto bakeware or to glaze foods before or after cooking. A **bench brush** helps remove flour from the bakeshop worktable. With a long-handled **oven brush**, the baker can safely sweep the floor of a pizza or deck oven to prevent bits of flour or cornmeal from burning. Oven brushes must be made from special materials so they don't burn. Natural bristles do not burn as easily as nylon ones, but brushes with synthetic bristles are easier to keep clean and sanitize.

Rolling Pins

Rolling pins help flatten or spread dough to a uniform thickness before cutting and baking. They also help knead and flatten lumps of dough. Common rolling pins are made from hardwoods that resist splitting, such as maple or beechwood, and are mounted on ball bearings with handles at either end. The dowel or **French rolling pin** is a solid piece of wood, straight or slightly tapered at each end. Though durable, wooden rolling pins should never be soaked in water. Teflon-coated rolling pins are handy for rolling marzipan and pastillage for decorative work. Marble rolling pins are useful when working with buttery dough because they may be chilled before using. **Textured rolling pins** are used to emboss cookie dough with a decorative pattern before baking or to transfer patterns onto a sheet of marzipan or fondant icing before it is draped over a cake.

Rolling Pin   French Rolling Pin

Baker's Peel or Transfer Peel

A baker's peel is a flat wooden or metal shovel used to slide breads and pizza onto the floor of the deck oven. It is a necessity when baking breads or pizza on the floor of a hearth oven.

Cutters

Cutting tools help the pastry chef and baker save time and produce uniform products. Most kitchens have a set of round biscuit cutters and a rolling cutter. Made from stainless steel, chrome-plated metal, tin or plastic, pastry cutters come in sets of graduated sizes, with either fluted or smooth edges. A wide variety of shapes are also sold individually. The bottom edge is sharp for cutting and the top edge is reinforced to take pressure. A doughnut cutter is a 4-inch (10 centimeter) round cutter with a smaller circular cutter mounted in the center. On some models, a lever on the cutter releases a small piece of dough, which becomes the doughnut hole once fried. (See page 248.) Rolling cutters consist of one or more round blades mounted in a handle. They are used to portion pizzas, trim edges on pastry before baking or leave a decorative impression on dough. Also known as **pastry wheels**, those with multiple blades cut several strips of dough at one time.

KNIVES

Good-quality knives are expensive but last for many years with proper care. Select easily sharpened, well-constructed knives that are comfortable and balanced in your hand. Knife construction and commonly used knives are discussed here.

Knife Construction

A good knife begins with a single piece of metal, stamped, cut or—best of all—forged and tempered into a blade of the desired shape. Several substances are generally used for knife blades.

    Carbon steel, an alloy of carbon and iron, is traditionally used for blades because it is soft enough to be sharpened easily. It corrodes and discolors easily, however, especially when used with acidic foods.

Stainless steel will not rust, corrode or discolor and is extremely durable. A stainless steel blade is much more difficult to sharpen than a carbon steel one, although once an edge is established, it lasts longer than the edge on a carbon steel blade.

High-carbon stainless steel is an alloy that combines the best features of carbon steel and stainless steel; it neither corrodes nor discolors and can be sharpened almost as easily as carbon steel. It is now the most frequently used metal for blades.

A **ceramic** called zirconium oxide is now used to make knife blades that are extremely sharp, very easy to clean, rustproof and nonreactive. With proper care, ceramic blades remain sharp for years, but when sharpening is needed, it must be done professionally on special diamond wheels. Material costs and tariffs make ceramic-bladed knives very expensive. Although this ceramic is highly durable, it does not have the flexibility of metal, so never use a ceramic knife to pry anything, to strike a hard surface or to cut against a china or ceramic surface.

A portion of the blade, known as the **tang**, fits inside the handle. The best knives are constructed with a full tang running the length of the handle; they also have a bolster where the blade meets the handle (the bolster is part of the blade, not a separate collar).

Knife handles are often made of hard woods infused with plastic and riveted to the tang. Molded polypropylene handles are permanently bonded to a tang without seams or rivets. Stainless steel handles welded directly to the blade are durable but very lightweight. Any handle should be shaped for comfort and ground smooth to eliminate crevices where bacteria can grow.

Knife Shapes

Among the many knives a chef will collect during his or her career, the following are among the more useful in the bakeshop.

PARING KNIFE

A short knife used for detail work or cutting fruits; the most common knife used in the bakeshop. The rigid blade is from 2 to 4 inches (5 to 10 centimeters) long. A tournée or **bird's-beak knife** is similar to a paring knife but with a curved blade; it is used to cut curved surfaces.

Paring Knife

FRENCH OR CHEF'S KNIFE

An all-purpose knife used for chopping and slicing. Its rigid 8- to 14-inch (20- to 35-centimeter) blade is wide at the heel and tapers to a point at the tip.

French or Chef's Knife

UTILITY KNIFE

An all-purpose knife used for cutting and carving. Its rigid 6- to 8-inch (15- to 20-centimeter) blade is shaped like a chef's knife but narrower.

Utility Knife

BREAD KNIFE OR CAKE KNIFE

A knife with a long, serrated blade that cuts easily through bread crust or pastry items. The tip may be round or pointed, and the blade may be flexible or rigid. (A similar knife with a smooth edge is used for slicing cooked meat.)

Bread Knife

LAME OR BREAD SLASHER

The bread baker uses a **lame** or bread slasher to score the surface of bread dough before baking. This knife may have a fixed blade or a holder for a replaceable razor blade.

Lame for Scoring Bread

MEASURING AND PORTIONING DEVICES

Ingredients must be measured precisely, especially in the bakeshop. Batters and doughs should be measured before baking to provide uniform baking times and to control portion size and cost. Accuracy in measurement is key to producing quality and consistent results.

Scales, temperature gauges and measuring devices make up a well-equipped kitchen. The devices used to measure and portion foods are, for the most part, hand tools designed to make food preparation and service easier and more precise. The accuracy they afford prevents the cost of mistakes made when accurate measurements are ignored.

Measurements may be based on weight (for example, grams, ounces, pounds) or volume (for example, teaspoons, cups, gallons) as discussed in Chapter 5, Mise en Place. Therefore, it is necessary to have available several measuring devices, including a variety of scales and liquid and dry measuring cups. Thermometers and timers are also measuring devices discussed here. When purchasing any measuring device, look for quality construction and accurate markings.

Scales

Scales are necessary to determine the weight of an ingredient or a portion of food (for example, individual pieces of dough for dinner rolls). Weighing ingredients in the bakeshop ensures the most accurate results. **Balance scales** (also known as **baker's scales**) use a two-tray and free-weight counterbalance system. A curved hopper holds dry ingredients on one side of the scale. Counterweights graduated in ¼-ounce increments balance the weight on the other side. When both trays are level, the desired quantity has been measured.

Portion scales use a spring mechanism, round dial and single flat tray. They are available calibrated in grams, ounces or pounds. Capacity varies; portion models accommodate up to 2 pounds in ¼-ounce increments, while larger-capacity scales measure in ½-pound increments up to 25 pounds or their metric equivalents. Electronic scales also use a spring mechanism but provide digital readouts in ⅒ or ¼-ounce increments. An automatic **tare** feature allows the user to ignore the weight of any container used to hold loose ingredients on the scale. This feature makes measuring accurately more convenient. A scale's accuracy depends on the model and precision, not its construction. Digital electronic scales, for example, may be readable to 0.1 ounce. This means that the scale can measure in ⅒-ounce increments, more precise than the baker's balance scale, which measures in ¼-ounce increments.

Any scale must be properly used and maintained to provide an accurate reading. Never pick up a scale by its platform, as this can damage the balancing mechanism. Scales must be calibrated or checked periodically for accuracy.

Portion Scale

Electronic Digital Scale

Balance or Baker's Scale

Measuring Spoons

Liquid Measuring Cup

Volume Measures

Ingredients may be measured by volume using **measuring spoons** and **measuring cups**, though most professional bakeshops use scales to measure all but the smallest quantities. Measuring spoons sold as a set usually include ¼-teaspoon, ½-teaspoon, 1-teaspoon and 1-tablespoon units (1.25-, 2.5-, 5- and 15-milliliter units). Liquid measuring cups are available in capacities from 1 cup to 1 gallon (or the metric equivalent). They have a lip or pour spout above the top line of measurement to prevent spills. Though more commonly used in the home kitchen, measuring cups for dry ingredients are sometimes used in the professional kitchen, especially for converting home recipes or measuring small amounts of items such as chopped nuts and spices. They are usually sold in sets of ¼-cup, ⅓-cup, ½-cup and 1-cup units. They do not have pour spouts, so the top of the cup is level with the top measurement specified. To ensure an accurate measurement of dry ingredients, fill the cup and then level off the top with a knife or flat spatula. Glass measuring cups are not recommended because they can break. Avoid using bent or dented measuring cups, as the damage may distort the measurement capacity.

Dry Measuring Cups

Ladles

Long-handled ladles are useful for portioning liquids such as sauces, custards and syrups. The capacity, in ounces or milliliters, is stamped on the handle.

Portion Scoops

Portion scoops (also known as dishers) resemble ice cream scoops. They come in a range of standardized sizes and have a lever-operated blade for releasing their contents. Scoops are useful for **portioning** muffin batters and cookie dough or other soft foods. A number, stamped on either the handle or the release mechanism, indicates the number of level scoopfuls per quart. The higher the scoop number, the smaller the scoop's capacity. See Table 2.1.

Thermometers and Gauges

Various types of **thermometers** and gauges are used in the bakeshop to determine when foods are fully cooked and when working with yeast dough, chocolate, sugar and other ingredients.

Stem-type or probe thermometers, including instant-read models, are inserted into foods to obtain temperature readings. Temperatures are shown on either a dial noted by an arrow or a digital readout. An **instant-read thermometer** is a small stem-type model, designed to be carried in a pocket and used to provide quick temperature readings. An instant-read thermometer should not be left in foods that are cooking because doing so damages the thermometer. Sanitize the stem of any thermometer before use in order to avoid cross-contamination.

Ladles   Portion Scoop

Instant-Read   Candy
Thermometer   Thermometer

SCOOP NUMBER	VOLUME		APPROXIMATE WEIGHT*	
	U.S.	METRIC	U.S.	METRIC
6	⅔ c.	160 ml	5 oz.	160 g
8	½ c.	120 ml	4 oz.	120 g
10	3 fl. oz.	90 ml	3–3½ oz.	85–100 g
12	⅓ c.	80 ml	2½–3 oz.	75–85 g
16	¼ c.	60 ml	2 oz.	60 g
20	1½ fl. oz.	45 ml	1¾ oz.	50 g
24	1⅓ fl. oz.	40 ml	1⅓ oz.	40 g
30	1 fl. oz.	30 ml	1 oz.	30 g
40	0.8 fl. oz.	24 ml	0.8 oz.	23 g
60	½ fl. oz.	15 ml	½ oz.	15 g

TABLE 2.1   PORTION SCOOP CAPACITIES

*Weights are approximate because they vary by food.

Candy and fat thermometers measure temperatures up to 400°F (204°C) using mercury in a column of glass encased in a shatterproof coating. A back clip attaches the thermometer to the pan, keeping the chef's hands free. Many models include helpful notations on their casing to indicate critical stages for cooking candy or fat. Be careful not to subject glass thermometers or gauges to quick temperature changes, as the glass may shatter.

Specialty gauges that look like thermometers are used when making sugar mixtures for candies, syrups and creams. Known as a syrup-density meter or Baumé hydrometer, this tool measures the amount of sugar dissolved in a solution. (See page 72.)

Electronic probe thermometers are now reasonably priced and commonly used in food service facilities. These thermometers provide immediate, clear, digital readouts from a handheld unit attached to a metal probe. Other models can be programmed to beep when a set temperature is reached, which is useful for chocolate and sugar work. A chocolate thermometer is highly calibrated and designed to use while stirring and tempering chocolate. It measures up to 130°F (54°C) in 1-degree gradations.

The latest advancement in thermometers relies on infrared sensors with laser sightings. **Infrared thermometers** can instantly monitor the surface temperature of foods during cooking or holding and the temperature of goods at receiving and in storage. Units can respond to a wide range of temperatures in less than a second without actually touching the food, thus avoiding any risk of cross-contamination. These thermometers are especially useful as maintenance tools to monitor the efficiency of refrigeration equipment.

Digital Infrared Thermometer

Because proper temperatures must be maintained for holding and storing foods, many health departments require the use of oven and refrigerator thermometers. Select thermometers with easy-to-read dials or column divisions.

Timers

Portable kitchen timers are useful for any busy chef. Small digital timers can be carried in a pocket; some even time three functions at once. Select a timer with a loud alarm signal and long timing capability.

STRAINERS AND SIEVES

Round Mesh Strainer

Strainers and sieves are used primarily to aerate and remove impurities from dry ingredients and drain or purée cooked foods. Strainers, colanders, drum sieves and china caps (chinois) are nonmechanical devices with a stainless steel mesh or screen through which food passes. The size of the mesh or screen varies from extremely fine to several millimeters wide; select the fineness best suited for the task at hand.

The **china cap** and the **chinois** are cone-shaped metal strainers. Their conical shape allows liquids to filter through small openings. The body of a china cap is perforated metal; a chinois is made of very fine mesh. Either style is used for straining liquids and sauces, with the fine-screened chinois being particularly useful for removing seeds from fruit purées. A china cap can also be used with a pestle to purée soft foods.

Reinforced Mesh Strainer (Chinois)

Perforated Metal Strainer (China Cap)

Both the **skimmer** and **spider** are long-handled tools used to remove foods or impurities from liquids. The flat, perforated disk of a skimmer is used for removing whole foods such as bagels from poaching liquids. The spider has a finer mesh disk, which makes it better for retrieving items from hot fat.

Cheesecloth is a loosely woven cotton gauze used for straining liquids and sauces and for draining cream and cheese products. Cheesecloth is also indispensable for making sachets to hold spices used to flavor syrups, creams and poaching liquids. Always rinse cheesecloth thoroughly before use; this removes lint and prevents the cheesecloth from absorbing other liquids.

A **food mill** purées and strains food at the same time. Food is placed in the hopper and a hand-crank mechanism turns a blade in the hopper against a perforated disk, forcing the food through the disk. Most models have interchangeable disks with various-sized holes. Choose a mill that can be taken apart easily for cleaning.

A **sifter** is used for aerating, blending and removing impurities from dry ingredients such as flour, cocoa and leavening agents. The 8-cup hand-crank sifter shown here uses four curved rods to brush the contents through a curved mesh screen. The sifter should have a medium-fine screen and a comfortable handle. The French **tamis** is a drum-shaped sieve useful for sifting ingredients as well as for straining thick purées to remove lumps and seeds.

Skimmer

Spider

Food Mill

Drum Sieve (Tamis)

Flour Sifter

COOKWARE AND BAKEWARE

Cookware for the bakeshop includes the saucepans used on the stove top as well as the baking sheets, cake pans and specialty molds used inside the oven. The term *bakeware* is also used to refer to items used inside the oven. Cookware and bakeware should be selected for its size, shape, ability to conduct heat evenly and overall quality of construction.

Materials and Heat Conduction

Cookware and bakeware that fails to distribute heat evenly may cause hot spots that burn foods. Because different metals conduct heat at different rates, and thicker layers of metal conduct heat more evenly than thinner ones, the most important considerations when choosing cookware are the type and thickness (known as the **gauge**) of the material used. Copper, aluminum and stainless steel are the most versatile and useful materials for cookware and bakeware in the bakeshop. No one cookware or material suits every process or need, however; always select the most appropriate material for the task at hand.

gauge the thickness of a material such as aluminum; the lower the gauge number, the thicker the material

Small Cakes Baked in Silicone Molds

COPPER

Copper is an excellent conductor: It heats rapidly and evenly and cools quickly. Indeed, unlined copper pots are unsurpassed for cooking sugar and fruit mixtures. (See the photo on page 74.) But copper cookware is extremely expensive. It also requires a great deal of care and is often quite heavy. Moreover, because copper may react with some foods, copper cookware usually has a tin lining, which is soft and easily scratched. Because of these problems, copper is now often sandwiched between layers of stainless steel or aluminum in the bottom of pots and pans. (One exception is the unlined copper mixing bowl designed for beating eggs; it is believed that egg white foam is more stable when beaten in contact with copper.)

ALUMINUM

Aluminum is the metal used most commonly in commercial utensils. It is lightweight and, after copper, conducts heat best. Aluminum is a soft metal, though, so it should be treated with care to avoid dents. Do not use aluminum containers for storage or for cooking acidic foods because the metal reacts chemically with many foods. Light-colored foods, such as custard sauce, may be discolored when cooked in aluminum, especially if stirred with a metal whisk or spoon. Select heavy-gauge aluminum baking pans to prevent delicate cakes and cookies from browning too quickly. Or put the aluminum baking pan on top of a sheet pan before placing in the oven. This double panning slows down the conduction of heat.

Anodized aluminum has a hard, dark, corrosion-resistant surface that helps prevent sticking and discoloration.

STAINLESS STEEL

Although stainless steel conducts and retains heat poorly, it is a hard, durable metal particularly useful for holding foods and for low-temperature cooking where hot spots and scorching are not problems. Stainless steel pots and pans are available with aluminum or copper bonded to the bottom or with an aluminum-layered core. Though expensive, such cookware combines the rapid, uniform heat conductivity of copper and aluminum with the strength, durability and nonreactivity of stainless steel. Stainless steel is also an ideal material for storage containers because it does not react with foods.

CERAMICS

Ceramics, including earthenware, porcelain and stoneware, are used primarily for baking dishes, soufflé cups, casseroles and baking stones because they conduct heat uniformly and retain temperatures well. Ceramics are nonreactive, inexpensive and generally suitable for use in a microwave oven (provided there is no metal in the glaze). Ceramics are easily chipped or cracked, however, and should not be used over a direct flame. Also, quick temperature changes may cause the cookware to crack or shatter.

OTHER MATERIALS

Cast-iron, glass and enamel cookware are popular for home cooking but have few applications in the professional kitchen. Cast-iron cookware distributes heat evenly and holds high temperatures well. It is often used in griddles and large skillets, but it must be seasoned properly and maintained carefully to prevent rust. Glass retains heat well but conducts it poorly. It does not react with foods. Tempered glass is suitable for microwave cooking provided it does not have any metal band or decoration. But commercial operations rarely use glass cookware because of the danger of breakage. Pans lined with enamel should not be used for cooking; in many areas, law prohibits their use in commercial kitchens. The enamel can chip or crack easily, providing good places for bacteria to grow. Silicone is a newer material used for bakeware. Although it conducts heat poorly, silicone works well for batters and doughs that need to bake and brown slowly.

NONSTICK COATINGS

Without affecting a metal's ability to conduct heat, a polymer (plastic) known as polytetrafluoroethylene (PTFE) and marketed under the trade names Teflon and Silverstone may be applied to many types of cookware and bakeware. It provides a slippery, nonreactive finish that prevents food from sticking and allows the use of less fat in cooking. Cookware with nonstick coatings requires a great deal of care, however, as the coatings can scratch, chip and blister. Do not use metal spoons or spatulas in cookware with nonstick coatings. Some nonstick coatings give pans a charcoal-colored finish. This dark color may affect the browning of cookies or cakes baked on such pans, giving delicate baked goods an unpleasantly dark crust.

Common Cookware

POTS

Pots are large round vessels with straight sides and two loop handles. Available in a range of sizes based on volume, they are used on the stove top for making custards and cooked fillings, or for boiling or simmering foods, particularly when rapid evaporation is not desired. Flat or fitted lids are available. The double boiler, a small pan that sits snugly on top of a pot filled with simmering water, is useful when melting chocolate or cooking delicate creams.

PANS

Pans are round vessels with one long handle and straight or sloped sides. They are usually smaller and shallower than pots. Pans are available in a range of diameters and are used for general stove top cooking, especially sautéing, frying or reducing liquids rapidly. Pans commonly used in the bakeshop include those for making crêpes or sautéing fruit.

Saucepot

Saucepan

Sauteuse (Sloped Sided)

Common Bakeware

Baking pans and molds are used for shaping or holding various batters and dough. Some pans such as baking sheets and hotel pans are standard items in the professional kitchen. Others, such as brioche or savarin molds, are specialty bakeshop items named for the cake or pastry baked in them.

SHEET PANS, SHEET TRAYS OR BAKING SHEETS

Sheet pans are shallow rectangular trays with a 1-inch (2.5-centimeter) lip on all four sides. The most common are made from aluminum and come in two standard sizes: 18 inches × 26 inches (45 centimeters × 65 centimeters) (full size) and 13 inches × 18 inches (32.5 centimeters × 45 centimeters) (half size). Some baking sheets may be rimless or have a rim on one side; this makes it easy to slide items off the sheet after baking. For making cookies, bright shiny baking sheets promote even browning. *Perforated sheet pans* may be used when baking bread and pastries in a convection oven; the holes allow more air to come in direct contact with the dough, resulting in a crisp crust. Adjustable frames, called *pan extenders*, made from stainless steel or ovenproof plastic the same dimension as sheet pans, are available. They protect the edges of the product during baking and increase the height of the pan, so they may be used for baking large sheet cakes.

HOTEL PANS

Hotel pans (also known as steam table pans) are rectangular stainless steel pans designed to hold food for service in steam tables. Hotel pans are also used for baking, roasting or poaching inside an oven. Perforated pans useful for draining, steaming or icing down foods

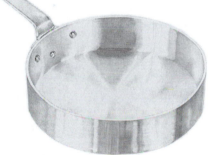
Sautoir (Straight Sides)

Full-Size Sheet Pans

Hotel Pans

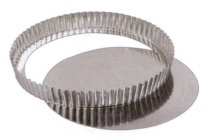

are also available. The standard full-size pan is 12 inches × 20 inches (30 centimeters × 50 centimeters) with pans one-half, one-third, one-sixth and other fractions of this size available. Hotel pan depth is standardized at 2 inches (referred to as a "200 pan"), 4 inches, 6 inches and 8 inches (4, 10, 15 and 20 centimeters).

TART PANS

Tart pans come in individual or large sizes and in round, rectangular or square shapes. Some have fluted edges and removable bottoms, making removing the baked pastry from the pan easier.

Tart Pan (Removable Bottom)

CAKE AND BREAD PANS

Properly designed cake pans heat evenly to allow delicate batters to rise properly. Most cake pans are made from a heavy-gauge aluminum in a variety of sizes. Angel food, Bundt and kugelhopf pans are known as tube pans. They are round pans with a hollow cone in the middle. This design brings heat to the center of the batter and is beneficial when baking heavy batters as well as delicate egg foam cakes.

Most bread pans are made from heavy-gauge aluminum or coated steel in a variety of rectangular shapes. When joined together in a frame, they are called *strap pans* and allow the baker to easily move a large number of pans in and out of the oven at one time.

Springform pans have a removable bottom and sides that release with the flip of a spring mechanism (see page 499). Cheesecakes and fragile desserts that would be difficult to unmold are often best baked in springform pans.

Flan rings or *ring molds* are strips of coated steel curved and formed into rings. They look like bottomless cake pans. When placed on a baking sheet, these rings are used to mold or to contain mousses and ice creams before chilling. Layers of baked cake and filling may be placed in a ring mold to make a European-style torte. Once the ring is removed the mousse or cake maintains its perfect shape.

Assortment of Bread Pans, Strap Pans and Specialty Cake Pans

Muffin pans make it possible to bake a number of individual quick breads or cupcakes at one time. Large sheets or plaques of smaller molds, such as those used to make popovers, tartlets or madeleine cookies, speed the production of these items.

Flan or Ring Molds

MOLDS

Unique shapes give bakeshop products enhanced eye appeal. Buttery yeast dough can take on a totally different appearance and taste when baked in different-shaped molds. Molds are made from a variety of materials including tinned steel, stainless steel, silicone and aluminum. The assortment of molds available to the pastry chef is limitless, from individual baba molds to drum-shaped molds for panettone or charlottes. A creative chef can even improvise molds from many products found at any local hardware store.

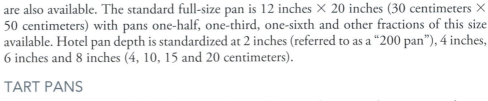

Timbale Molds

Timbale molds are small (about 4 ounces/120 milliliters) metal or ceramic containers used for molding or baking individual portions of mousse or custard. Their slightly flared sides allow the contents to release cleanly when inverted. Oven-baked custards and puddings are usually made in ceramic molds called ramekins, custard cups or soufflé cups.

DECORATING AND FINISHING TOOLS

Like the sculptor, painter or fine woodworker, the pastry and bakeshop artist uses a wide variety of tools to help decorate cakes and pastries. (Many of these tools appear in photographs throughout this book and in Figure 2.2.) **Pastry bags** help the chef dispense fillings, frosting and batters into uniform and decorative patterns. They may be made from plastic-coated cotton, nylon, or disposable heavy-gauge plastic. The **dispensing tips** are stainless steel, plastic or chrome-plated metal cones. Once slipped inside the pastry bag, the tips produce unique shapes when paste or icing is squeezed through them. Pastry tips come in a wide variety of sizes and are numbered according to the size and shape of the piping produced. The most common pastry tips are the plain tip, used to pipe batters for baking or frying, and the open or closed star tip. A pastry chef can pipe icing onto a decorator's nail when making roses or flowers for cake garnishes.

Cake combs are flat metal or stiff plastic tools with teeth cut along each edge. When dragged across the surface of a frosted cake, they leave parallel lines in the icing. The **cake-decorating turntable** is a round metal or plastic platform seated on a heavy stand. It makes applying an even layer of icing or decorative piping on a layer cake fast and easy.

An assortment of disposable paper and other products help put the finishing touches on pastries. Silicone-coated greaseproof paper called parchment paper is used to line baking sheets. Its nonstick surface makes removing baked goods easier. This paper is formed into liners for muffin pans and chocolate work. Special disposable paperboard containers are available for baking in the oven, making the purchase of costly specialized pans unnecessary. Light corrugated cardboard cake rounds and sheets in a wide variety of sizes are used under cakes to make them easy to frost and transport. Clear strips of plastic acetate can line ring molds to protect the edges of layered tortes and pastries and can be used to create chocolate decorations.

PROCESSING EQUIPMENT

Processing equipment includes both electrical and nonelectrical mechanical devices used to chop, purée, slice or grind foods. Before using any such equipment, be sure to review its operating procedures and ask for assistance if necessary. Always turn the equipment off and disconnect the power before disassembling, cleaning or moving the appliance. Any problems or malfunctions should be reported immediately.

Slicer

An electric **slicer** is used to cut bread, cheese, raw fruits, meat and vegetables into uniform slices. It has a circular blade that rotates at high speed. Food is placed in a carrier and then passed (manually or by an electric motor) against the blade. The distance between the blade and the carrier determines slice thickness. Because of the speed with which the blade rotates, foods can be cut into extremely thin slices very quickly.

Mandoline

A **mandoline** is a manually operated slicer made of stainless steel with adjustable slicing blades. Its narrow, rectangular body sits on the work counter at a 45-degree angle. Foods are passed against a blade to obtain uniform slices. It is useful for slicing small quantities of fruits or vegetables when using a large electric slicer would be unwarranted. To avoid injury, always use a hand guard or steel glove when using a mandoline.

FIGURE 2.2 ▶ Clockwise from center back: cake turntable, cake pans, flan ring, tartlet pans, cannoli forms, offset spatulas, flat cake spatula, blade for scoring breads, flower nail, rectangular tartlet pans, piping bag and tips, metal spatula, dough cutter, rolling pin, springform pan, copper sugar pot (on cooling rack), nest of round cutters.

> **SAFETY ALERT**
> **Machinery**
>
> Never place your hand into any machinery when the power is on. Processing equipment is powerful and can cause serious injury.

Mandoline

Food Processor

A food processor has a motor housing with a removable bowl and S-shaped metal blade. It is used, for example, to purée cooked foods, chop nuts, and emulsify sauces. Special disks can be added that slice, shred or julienne foods. Bowl capacity and motor power vary; select a model large enough for your most common tasks.

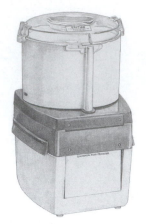

Food Processor

Blender

Though similar in principle to a food processor, a blender has a tall, narrow food container and a four-pronged blade. Its design and whirlpool action is better for processing liquids or liquefying foods quickly. A blender is used to prepare smooth drinks, purée sauces, blend batters and chop ice. A **vertical cutter/mixer (VCM)** operates like a very large, powerful blender. A VCM is usually floor-mounted and has a capacity of 15 to 80 quarts (14 to 75 liters.).

Heavy-Duty Blender

Immersion Blender

An **immersion blender**—as well as its household counterpart called a hand blender or wand—is a long shaft fitted with a rotating blade at the bottom. Operated by pressing a button in the handle, an immersion blender is used to purée a soft food or sauce or blend directly in the container in which it was prepared, eliminating the need to transfer the food from one container to another. This is especially useful when working with hot foods. Small cordless, rechargeable models are convenient for puréeing or mixing small quantities or beverages, but larger heavy-duty electric models are more practical in commercial kitchens.

Immersion Blender

Juicer

Two types of juicers are available: **reamers** and **extractors**. Reamers, also known as citrus juicers, remove juice from citrus fruits. They can be manual or electric. Manual models use a lever arm to squeeze the fruit with increased pressure. They are most often used to prepare small to moderate amounts of juice for beverages and cooking. Juice extractors are electrical devices that create juice by liquefying raw fruits, vegetables and herbs. They use centrifugal force to filter out fiber and pulp.

Reamer

Citrus Juicer

HEAVY EQUIPMENT

Mixing and Dough Handling

MIXER

The electric mixer is indispensable in the commercial kitchen, and several types are found in most professional bakeshops. The selection of a mixer depends on many factors, such as the type of products being mixed and the volume of production required. *Vertical planetary mixers are the most common because they are multipurpose and come in a wide range of sizes. A*

20-Quart Mixer

U-shaped arm holds a metal mixing bowl in place; the selected mixing attachment fits onto the rotating head. The three common mixing attachments are the **whip** (used for whipping eggs or cream), the **paddle** (used for cake batter, dough and general mixing) and the **dough hook** or *dough arm* (used for kneading bread). Most planetary mixers have several operating speeds; depending on the manufacturer, table or bench models may have three to six speeds. Bench models range in capacity from 4.5 to 20 quarts (4 to 18 liters), whereas floor mixers can hold as much as 140 quarts (132 liters.). Some mixers can be fitted with shredder/slicers, meat grinders, juicers or power strainers, making the equipment more versatile.

In larger bakeshops, a **spiral mixer** may be used to mix bread dough. Unlike the planetary mixer, the spiral mixer has both a bowl that rotates and a corkscrew-shaped arm, which twists through the dough. Many artisan bakers prefer the spiral mixer for its rapid and gentle mixing action, which minimizes the introduction of air into the dough and produces less friction during mixing. Spiral mixers come in a range of capacities from 5 to 20 quarts (4.5 to 18 liters) for small models or up to 800 pounds (350 kilograms) for large machines. They may have a fixed or removable bowl. Or the entire machine may tilt to deposit the finished dough into a separate container. Although they are used exclusively for mixing yeast dough, spiral mixers are considered versatile because they can be usable at as little as 20 percent of their capacity.

A *fork mixer* or **oblique mixer** is another type of mixer used, particularly in France, to produce artisan bread dough. An inverted V-shaped dough hook, which resembles two outstretched arms, performs the kneading. As the arms turn in the dough, the bowl moves counterclockwise. The friction of the dough rubbing on the bowl creates the kneading effect, said to mimic the feel of human hands. Fork mixers must be filled to near capacity to perform well, making them less versatile than spiral mixers, although they are praised for their gentle handling of the dough.

Large commercial bakeries may use *horizontal mixers*, large enclosed drums with intensive mixing blades that can mix up to thousands of pounds of ingredients at a time. And bakery manufacturing plants may use continuous batch mixers customized to mix a specific product within the plant's production line.

AUTOMATED MAKE-UP EQUIPMENT

Larger bakeries use machinery to make the workflow more efficient. For bread making, mechanical and electric **dough dividers** portion dough before it is shaped and baked. Such machines may be tabletop models that divide dough for rolls or more sophisticated machinery designed to portion, round and shape many varieties of breads before baking. Other pieces of equipment help form dough into loaves. Industrial bakeries are fully automated with customized production lines that eliminate much of the handwork typically associated with bread baking.

SHEETER

The dough **sheeter** is an electric appliance that mechanically rolls dough and pastry to a uniform thickness. The device consists of a cloth conveyor belt that moves beneath a stationary rolling pin. The height of the pin is adjusted to change the thickness of the product. Table and floor models are available, as are reversible models that automatically move the dough back and forth beneath the roller. Larger bakeshops and bakeries have a sheeter for rolling out cookie, puff pastry and croissant doughs.

Flat Paddle

Whip

Dough Arm or Hook

Spiral Mixer

Dough Sheeter

Semiautomatic Dough Divider

PROOF BOX

Bread dough and yeast-leavened pastries need a warm, moist environment in which to rest before baking. The **proof box** or proofer cabinet is used for this purpose. A simple proof box is a metal cabinet lined with shelves spaced to hold full-size and half-size sheet pans. Heat and humidity are generated from a small pan of water sitting on the bottom, heated by an electric coil. In a hotel bakeshop or small commercial bakery, the proof box may be large enough to accommodate one or more rolling racks, with temperature and humidity automatically controlled. Larger bakeries may invest in entire rooms especially steam-heated for fermenting yeast dough products.

RETARDER

Chilling yeast dough as it proofs slows proofing time allowing dough to develop flavor while controlling production timing. Chilling units, called retarders, perform this function. *Retarder proofers* combine chilling and warming functions in one device.

Work Surfaces, Storage and Organization

In the professional kitchen, stainless steel is the preferred material for all tables and work surfaces. It meets all sanitation standards as it is nontoxic (under intended end-use conditions), nonabsorbent, corrosion resistant, and nonreactive. Wooden-topped tables have a special place in the bakeshop, however. Because wood is a poor heat conductor, it is a great surface for maintaining the optimal dough temperature when handling yeast dough. The somewhat soft surface of a wooden-topped table is preferred for rolling out pastry dough by hand. When kept clean, smooth and free from cracks and crevices, hardwood such as maple or close-grained wood is a sanitary surface approved by the NSF for use in the bakeshop.

Marble or granite tabletops are also used in some pastry kitchens. They stay cool, a useful feature when working with candy and chocolate.

STORAGE CONTAINERS

Proper storage containers are necessary for keeping leftovers and opened packages of food safe for consumption. Proper storage can also reduce the costs incurred by waste or spoilage.

Although stainless steel pans such as hotel pans are suitable and useful for some items, the expense of stainless steel and the lack of airtight lids makes these pans impractical for general storage purposes. Aluminum containers are not recommended because the metal can react with even mildly acidic items. Glass containers are generally not allowed in commercial kitchens because of the hazards of broken glass. The most useful storage containers are those made of high-density food-grade plastics such as polyethylene and polypropylene.

Storage containers must have well-fitting lids and should be available in a variety of sizes, including some that are small enough to hold even minimal quantities of food without allowing too much exposure to oxygen. Round and square plastic containers are widely available. Flat, snap-on lids allow containers to be stacked for more efficient storage. Containers may be clear or opaque white, which helps protect light-sensitive foods. Some storage containers are marked with graduated measurements so that content quantity can be determined at a glance.

Large quantities of dry ingredients, such as flour, sugar and rice, can be stored in rolling ingredient bins. The bins should be seamless with rounded corners for easy cleaning. They should have well-fitting but easy-to-open lids and should move easily on well-balanced casters.

RACKS

Rolling racks, also known as speed racks or Queen Anne's, are metal frames designed to hold a number of pans or trays in a space-saving manner. They are useful for moving multiple pans from one area of the bakery to another efficiently, storing trays of items waiting to be placed in the oven or for receiving hot pans directly from an oven. To retain their distinctive textures, cakes, pastries and breads are often cooled on wire racks. A rolling shelf unit made from wire racks is used for cooling a large quantity of breads after baking.

Heated Proof Box

Storage Containers

Ingredient Bin with Scoop

Baking and Cooking

Though the cook stove is the centerpiece of the professional kitchen, the oven is one of the more significant pieces of cooking equipment in the bakeshop. Most pastries, breads and bakeshop foods, even custards, are baked in some type of oven. The type of products made in the bakeshop determine what types of ovens may be used.

OVENS

An oven is an enclosed space where food is cooked by being surrounded by hot air. **Conventional ovens** are often located beneath a stove top. They have a heating element located at the unit's bottom or floor. Conventional ovens may also be separate, freestanding units or decks stacked one on top of the other. In **stack ovens** or deck ovens, pans are placed directly on the deck or floor and not on wire racks.

Stack Oven

Commercial Deck Oven

Specialty **deck ovens** or **hearth ovens** have floors made from stone or masonry. Bread, pizzas or other items are baked directly on the heated stone surface. Ovens designed for hearth baking of artisan bread and pastries have steam-injecting devices installed. Steam injection ovens use conventional heat flow but allow the baker to automatically add steam to the cooking chamber as needed to produce crisp-crusted breads. Although expensive, steam injection ovens are a necessity for commercial bakeries and larger restaurant and hotel bakeshops. Commercial bakeries may use more specialized ovens including revolving ovens, rotating rack ovens and tunnel conveyor ovens.

Convection ovens use internal fans to circulate hot air over and around foods placed on adjustable wire racks inside the oven's cavity. This tends to cook foods more quickly and evenly. Convection ovens are almost always freestanding units, powered either by gas or electricity. Because convection ovens cook foods more quickly, temperatures may need to be reduced by 25°F–50°F (10°C–20°C) from those recommended for conventional ovens. Convection ovens can reduce cooking time, but the air currents may damage delicate products such as spongecake or puff pastry. Large-scale convection ovens are built so that one or more entire racks of products can simply be rolled inside for baking.

hearth oven an oven whose floor is made from stone or masonry; bread, pizzas or other items are baked directly on its heated stone surface; also known as a deck oven

A NOTE ON BAKING INSTRUCTIONS IN THIS BOOK

Baking instructions in the following chapters are based on the use of a conventional oven. If a convection oven is used instead, remember that the temperatures may need to be reduced by 25°F–50°F (10°C–20°C) from those recommended in these formulas. Watch the baking time as well because convection ovens can cook as much as 20 percent more quickly than conventional ovens.

Convection Oven

Rotating Rack Oven

Wood-Burning Oven

Flat-Top Range

Propane Torch

WOOD-BURNING OVENS

The ancient practice of baking in a retained-heat masonry oven has been revived, with many upscale restaurants and artisan bakeries installing brick or adobe ovens for baking pizzas and breads as well as roasting fish, poultry and vegetables. These ovens have a curved interior chamber that is usually recessed into a wall. Although gas-fired models are available, wood firing is more traditional and provides the aromas and flavors associated with brick ovens. A wood fire is built inside the oven to heat the brick chamber. The ashes are then swept out and the food is placed on the flat oven floor. Breads and pizzas baked in direct contact with the hot masonry rise better than in a conventional oven and develop a unique crisp crust. The combination of high heat and wood smoke adds distinctive flavors to foods.

MICROWAVE OVENS

Microwave ovens are electrically powered ovens used to cook or reheat foods. They are available in a range of sizes and power settings. Microwave ovens do not brown foods unless fitted with special browning elements, however. In the bakeshop, microwave ovens are useful as a convenience device for melting chocolate or butter. Only certain types of cookware can be used in microwave ovens. Tempered glass or plastic made from phenolic resin are the only materials recommended for use in most microwaves.

COOK STOVES

Stove tops or ranges have one or more burners powered by gas or electricity. The burners may be open or covered with a cast-iron or steel plate. Open burners supply quick, direct heat that is easy to regulate. A steel plate, known as a *flat top*, supplies even but less intense heat. Although it takes longer to heat than a burner, the flat top supports heavier weights and makes a larger area available for cooking. Many stoves include both flat tops and open burner arrangements.

BROILER, SALAMANDER AND PROPANE TORCH

A top browning is given to sugar-coated custards and some baked goods before serving. A broiler, salamander or propane torch is used for this purpose. For a broiler, the heat source is above the food. Most broilers are gas powered. A **salamander** is a small overhead broiler primarily used to finish or top-brown foods. A handheld **propane torch** such as that used in the plumbing trade may be used for this purpose. Be sure to select a propane torch with a simple ignition and an easily changed fuel cartridge.

DEEP-FAT FRYERS

Deep-fat fryers are used to cook foods in a large amount of hot fat. Doughnuts are the most common bakeshop items cooked in a deep-fat fryer. Fryers are sized by the amount of fat they hold. Most commercial fryers hold between 2 and 10 gallons (4 and 20 liters). Fryers can be

INDUCTION—A NEW HEAT WAVE

Induction cooking uses special conductive coils called inductors placed below the stove top's surface in combination with flat-bottomed cookware made of cast iron or magnetic stainless steel. The coil generates a magnetic current so that the cookware is heated rapidly with magnetic friction. Heat energy is then transferred from the cookware to the food by conduction. The cooking surface, which is made of a solid ceramic material, remains cool. Only the cookware and its contents get hot. This means that induction systems are extremely efficient with instant response time because power is directed into the cooking utensil, not the surrounding air.

Induction cooking is gaining acceptance in professional kitchens because of the speed with which foods can be heated and the ease of cleanup. Induction burners are useful in the bakeshop where there may be only a limited need for direct-heat cooking; they are portable and maintain a safer, cooler cooking environment.

Induction Cooktop

either gas or electric and are thermostatically controlled for temperatures between 200°F and 400°F (90°C and 204°C).

When choosing a fryer, look for a fry tank with curved, easy-to-clean sloping sides. Some fryers have a cold zone (an area of reduced temperature) at the bottom of the fry tank to trap particles. This prevents them from burning, creating off-flavors and shortening the life of the fryer fat.

Deep fryers usually come with steel wire baskets to hold the food during cooking. Fryer baskets are usually lowered into the fat and raised manually, although some models have automatic basket mechanisms. A doughnut fryer is wide but shallow and includes a submerging screen to hold the doughnuts below the fat so that the batter cooks and browns evenly. Some models include portioning devices that automatically dispense uniform quantities of batter into the fat.

The most important factor when choosing a deep fryer is **recovery time**. Recovery time is the length of time it takes the fat to return to the desired cooking temperature after food is submerged in it. When food is submerged, heat is immediately transferred to the food from the fat. This heat transfer lowers the fat's temperature. The more food added at one time, the greater the drop in the fat's temperature. If the temperature drops too much or does not return quickly to the proper cooking temperature, the food may absorb excess fat and become greasy.

Doughnut Fryer with Dough Depositor and Draining Rack

Refrigeration and Cleaning

REFRIGERATORS AND FREEZERS

Proper refrigeration space is an essential component of any kitchen. Many foods must be stored at low temperatures to maintain quality and safety. Most commercial refrigeration is of two types: walk-in units and reach-in or upright units.

A walk-in is a large, room-sized box capable of holding hundreds of pounds of food on adjustable shelves. A separate freezer walk-in may be positioned nearby or even inside a refrigerated walk-in.

Reach-ins may be individual units or parts of a bank of units, each with shelves approximately the size of a full sheet pan. Reach-in refrigerators and freezers are usually located throughout the kitchen to provide quick access to foods. Small units may also be placed beneath the work counters. Freezers and refrigerators are available in a wide range of sizes and door designs to suit any operation.

Other forms of commercial refrigeration include chilled drawers located beneath a work area that are just large enough to accommodate a hotel pan, and display cases used to show foods to the customer. Large bakeries may include blast freezers and special chill units. In open kitchens and retail bakeries, refrigerated display cases may be required for soft pies and filled pastries.

ICE CREAM FREEZERS

Ice cream freezers or ice cream machines incorporate air while freezing a sweetened cream or fruit mixture. These machines come in two styles, batch and continuous, with a wide range of capacities. The simplest manual machine is the one our grandparents used, a table model with a metal canister for the cream mixture sitting inside a larger container for crushed ice and rock salt. A chilled mixture is poured into the metal container, and then a flat blade called a dasher is inserted and a hand crank is attached. When the crank is turned, the mixture is stirred, adding air and minimizing the formation of ice crystals as the mixture freezes. In commercial-batch ice cream freezers a coolant is sealed in the walls of a metal cylinder and frozen before using. This eliminates the need for crushed ice. These small appliances make batches of ice cream or sherbet ranging in capacity from 1 quart to 1 gallon (1 to 4 liters). Larger commercial ice cream machines may make single batches of ice cream or may be fully automated machines producing continuously. The cylinder may be horizontal or vertical; the style of each affects the texture and amount of air in the finished product. The soft-serve machine, for example, churns, aerates and dispenses the frozen dessert in one continuous process. Continuous-batch ice cream freezers are used in high-volume factory settings.

Batch Ice Cream Freezer

DISHWASHERS

Mechanical dishwashers are available to wash, rinse and sanitize dishware, glassware, cookware and utensils. Small models clean one rack of items at a time, whereas larger models can handle several racks simultaneously on a conveyor belt system. Commercial bakeshops may have a pan washer designed to accommodate full-size sheet trays. Sanitation is accomplished either with extremely hot water (180°F/82°C) or with chemicals automatically dispensed during the final rinse cycle. Any dishwashing area should be carefully organized for efficient use of equipment and employees and to prevent recontamination of clean items.

SAFETY EQUIPMENT

Certain items are critical to the well-being of a food service operation, although they are not used in food preparation. These are safety devices, many of which are required by federal, state or local law. Failing to include safety equipment in a kitchen or failing to maintain it properly endangers workers and customers.

Fire Extinguishers

Fire extinguishers are canisters of foam, dry chemicals (such as sodium bicarbonate or potassium bicarbonate) or pressurized water used to extinguish small fires. They must be placed within sight of and easily reached from the work areas in which fires are likely to occur. Different classes of extinguishers use different chemicals to fight different types of fires. The appropriate class must be used for the specific fire; see Table 2.2. Fire extinguishers must be recharged and checked from time to time. Be sure they have not been discharged, tampered with or otherwise damaged.

Ventilation Systems

Ventilation systems (also called ventilation hoods) are commonly installed over cooking equipment to remove vapors, heat and smoke. Some systems include fire extinguishing agents or sprinklers. A properly operating hood makes the kitchen more comfortable for the staff and reduces the danger of fire. The system should be designed, installed and inspected by professionals, then cleaned and maintained regularly.

Remember the acronym **P.A.S.S.** for the four steps to follow when using any fire extinguisher:

- **Pull**—Pull the safety pin on the extinguisher.
- **Aim**—Aim the extinguisher hose at the base of the fire.
- **Squeeze**—Squeeze the handle to discharge the material.
- **Sweep**—Sweep the hose from side to side across the base of the fire.

TABLE 2.2   FIRE EXTINGUISHERS

CLASS	SYMBOL	USE
Class A		Fires involving wood, paper, cloth or plastic
Class B		Fires involving oil, grease or flammable chemicals
Class C		Fires involving electrical equipment or wiring
Class K		Fires involving cooking oil, fat and grease in commercial cooking equipment

Combination extinguishers—AB, BC and ABC—are also available.

First-Aid Kits

First-aid supplies should be stored in a clearly marked box, conspicuously located near food preparation areas. State and local laws may specify the kit's exact contents. Generally, the kit should include a first-aid manual, bandages, gauze dressings, adhesive tape, antiseptics, scissors, cold packs and other supplies. The kit should be checked regularly and items replaced as needed. In addition, cards with emergency telephone numbers should be placed inside the first-aid kit and near a telephone.

THE PROFESSIONAL BAKESHOP

In France and Italy, the pastry kitchen is called a laboratory (*laboratoire* or *laboratorio*). As its name suggests, the classic bakeshop is a controlled environment where specialized operations take place under exacting conditions and to high standards. The layout of such a structured pastry kitchen ideally includes separate kitchens for each department according to the brigade system discussed in Chapter 1, Professionalism. The mixing of bread and pastry dough would be separate from the hot baking areas. Chocolate and ice cream making would take place in temperature-controlled spaces. But in most small bakeshops or in those that form part of a restaurant, space may be scarce. The pastry department often consists of a small worktable, possibly shared during the hours when meals are served.

When planning the layout of a professional bakeshop, the items to be made and tasks performed must be identified. The goal of designing a bakeshop is the efficient use of space so that each task has a designated area or **work station** where similar tasks are performed. The bakeshop should have an efficient flow. Ideally work stations should be designed to minimize the steps necessary to perform the task. The task of baking is divided into four stages: measuring and mixing of ingredients, make-up of the product before baking, baking and final assembly. Professional bakeshops are arranged to give enough space for each of these stages.

Measuring and mixing requires easy access to ingredients and ample room in which to maneuver large quantities of finished dough. Flour, sugar and other bulk items may be stored in covered rolling bins underneath a worktable. Large bags of unopened ingredients may be stored off the floor on pallets in a secure storeroom near the mixing area. Smaller quantities of items such as spices, flavorings and baking powder may be stored on shelving above a worktable. The scale and mixer should be placed near each other and the entire work station should have easy access to water, an important ingredient in bread dough and other preparations that require mixing. Larger bakeries have a metering device to portion water adjacent to the mixer.

Dough make-up requires a large surface area on which to divide and roll dough. Operations that produce a large volume of Danish and croissant pastries require wide-open tables on which dough is rolled or portioned. These same tables may be used for cutting out doughnuts, forming bagels and assembling cakes as long as the work schedule prevents overlaps when the space is required for multiple tasks. In a small independent bakery, such a worktable or workbench may be positioned in a central location to be shared between different departments throughout the day. Bread dough may be divided into loaves and then rolled and formed on the table early in the morning; cakes may be filled and frosted in the same place in the afternoon.

The baking stage requires ample room for loading and unloading the oven. Because an oven generates intense heat, positioning it away from other bakery activities is desired. Where large quantities of bread, muffins and pastries are baked, the ovens may be in a separate room. Space is also allotted for large wire cooling racks on wheels, which are used to cool the breads before packaging or service.

The final assembly stage includes the filling and frosting of cookies, pastries and cakes. Because of the perishability of many of the creams, icings, custards and fruits used in the bakeshop, pastry assembly should take place in a cool, dry, dust-free environment far from the heat of the oven. Many specialized tools are needed to perform these tasks: piping bags, turntables, decorative stencils and color spray guns, to name a few. Accessible and safe storage for these items must be provided.

In addition to production areas, a typical bakeshop and professional kitchen includes areas dedicated to the following:

Receiving and storing foods and other items. Most bakeshops need freezer, refrigerator and dry-goods storage facilities. Each should have proper temperature, humidity and light controls in

WORK SECTIONS AND THEIR STATIONS

Sections	Stations
Garde-manger section	Salad greens cleaning
	Salad preparation
	Cold food preparation
	Sandwich station
	Showpiece preparation
Bakery section	Mixing station
	Dough holding and proofing
	Dough rolling and forming
	Baking and cooling
	Dessert preparation*
	Frozen dessert preparation*
	Plating desserts*

*These stations are sometimes found in the garde-manger section.

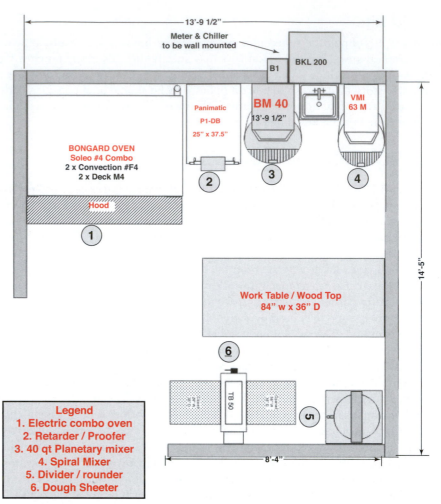

FIGURE 2.3 ▶ Bread bakery equipment layout. (Courtesy FBM Baking Machines, Inc.)

order to properly and safely maintain the stored items. Typically there is a combination of central and section storage, with smaller quantities stored at a work station and bulk storage separate. Additional storage space is needed for cleaning and paper supplies, dishes and other serviceware.

Washing dishes and other equipment. Dish-washing and equipment-washing facilities should have their own sinks. Food preparation and hand-washing sinks must be separate.

Employee use. Restrooms, locker facilities and an office are also found in most food service facilities.

The guiding principle behind good bakeshop design is to maximize the flow of goods and staff from one area to the next and within each area itself. Maximizing flow creates an efficient work environment and helps reduce preparation and service time.

Figure 2.3 shows a compact layout of equipment for a bread and pastry baking work station, which could be in a bakery or within a large hotel kitchen. It includes a lineup of mixing equipment for making dough, an ample worktable on which to prepare breads and pastries and ingredient storage bins underneath. There is make-up equipment such as a sheeter for efficiently rolling dough and both convection and hearth ovens under a ventilation hood in the shaded area. This layout promotes efficiency. There is adequate space for one baker to mix dough, another to work on make-up and a third to load the oven. Racks of cooling baked goods would be rolled directly into a retail sales or packing area. Figure 2.4 shows a compact retail bakeshop that includes mixing and make-up stations to the rear and the deck oven and cooking racks directly behind the customer display case.

Governmental building, health, fire and safety codes dictate, to a degree, certain aspects of a professional kitchen's design. But to make the most of these spaces, the well-designed kitchen should reflect a sound understanding of the tasks to be performed and the equipment necessary to perform them efficiently.

FIGURE 2.4 ▶ Small retail artisan bread bakery. (Courtesy Cream Pan, Tustin, CA)

1. What is NSF International? What is its significance with regard to commercial bakery and kitchen equipment?

2. List four materials used to make cookware and bakeware and describe the advantages and disadvantages of each.

3. Describe the types of equipment used to mix ingredients in the bakeshop.

4. List four classes of fire extinguishers. For each one, describe its designating symbol and identify the type or types of fire it should be used to extinguish.

5. Explain the relationship between work sections and work stations and the kitchen brigade system discussed in Chapter 1, Professionalism.

6. Assume that you have been asked to select a new oven for a small commercial bakery. You must research the industry and find a bakery oven supplier that can provide specialized equipment for your establishment. Find a few Internet sites of companies that can help you with this research. List the questions you must be able to answer in order to purchase the appropriate equipment. **www**

Terms to Know

NSF International	cake-decorating
hand tools	turntable
bench brush	slicer
pastry wheel	mandoline
tang	vertical cutter/
lame	mixer (VCM)
scales	immersion
balance or	blender
baker's scale	whip
portion scale	paddle
tare	dough hook
measuring cup	spiral mixer
portion scoops	oblique mixer
thermometer	sheeter
calibrate	deck oven
chinois	convection oven
silicone	salamander
sheet pan	propane torch
hotel pan	induction
timbale mold	recovery time
pastry bag	P.A.S.S.
dispensing tip	work station
cake comb	

CHAPTER THREE

PRINCIPLES OF BAKING

- understand the various mixing methods used in the bakeshop
- understand how heat affects batters and doughs, the basis of most bakeshop items
- identify and understand the basic baking and cooking methods employed in the bakeshop
- understand the science of taste and basic flavor principles

formula a standard term used throughout the industry for a bakeshop recipe; formulas rely on weighing to ensure accurate measuring of ingredients

emulsify to combine a fat and a liquid into a homogeneous mixture by properly blending ingredients

gluten an elastic network of proteins created when wheat flour is moistened and manipulated; it gives structure and strength to baked goods and is responsible for their volume, texture and appearance

aerate to incorporate air into a mixture through sifting and mixing; to whip air into a mixture to lighten, such as beating egg whites to a foam

BAKING IS A SCIENCE THAT RELIES ON UNDERSTANDING THE BASIC PRINCIPLES of the baking and cooking processes. Once a student understands that the actions that take place when a mixture of flour, fat and water becomes a finished product are a function of scientific principles, he or she will be able to select ingredients and work with **formulas** with greater ease. Though a degree in chemistry or physics is not a prerequisite for working in the bakeshop, a good understanding of the everyday science of the kitchen makes for a well-rounded professional. Throughout this book different aspects of the principles discussed in this chapter are demonstrated and expanded upon.

MIXING METHODS AND TECHNIQUES

The first step in the production of breads, pastries and other bakeshop products is the measuring of ingredients; see Chapter 5, Mise en Place. Once measured, ingredients must be mixed or combined in a manner designed to achieve desired results. The techniques used to mix or combine ingredients affect the baked good's final volume, appearance and texture. Mixing accomplishes some or all of the following:

▶ Even distribution of ingredients

▶ Breakdown of fats and liquids, causing them to blend or **emulsify**

▶ Activation of the proteins in wheat flour, causing the formation of the elastic structure called **gluten**

▶ Incorporation of air into a mixture (**aeration**) to help it rise and develop a light texture when baked.

Mixing methods accomplish many things simultaneously. (See Table 3.1.) **Blending**, **folding**, **sifting** and **stirring** ensure that ingredients are properly combined. But **cutting** also combines ingredients, in this case fat, in a unique way to ensure that a dough bakes into a flaky crust or cookie. **Beating**, **creaming**, **kneading** and **whipping** help incorporate air into a batter, dough or foam during mixing. The creation of pockets of air (*air cells*) gives baked goods their final texture after baking. Air cells are formed by the coagulation of proteins in the mixture. A buttery cake batter has many tiny even air cells, which give the cake a uniform fine texture. These air cells are created exclusively during the mixing process.

Fats do not blend with water. Beating, blending, creaming, kneading and stirring break up fats into particles, allowing them to blend with liquids into a homogenous mixture. Learn the difference in these mixing techniques, then use the designated method with the appropriate equipment or tool to ensure a good-quality finished product. Future chapters in this book explore how using these mixing techniques, combined with different mixing methods and combinations of basic ingredients, creates a variety of distinct baked items.

The Importance of Gluten

Gluten is the tough, rubbery substance created when wheat flour is mixed with water. It's what helps make country bread chewy and pound cake light and tender. Flour does not contain gluten; only a dough or batter can contain gluten. It is formed when the proteins *glutenin* and *gliadin* in wheat flour are moistened or hydrated.

Gluten development is affected by a number of factors, including mixing technique and the presence of fat and moisture. Generally, the longer a substance is mixed, the more gluten will develop. (However, extreme overmixing in industrial equipment can break down the gluten structure.) The type and proportion of ingredients in a formula also affect

TABLE 3.1   MIXING METHODS

METHOD	PURPOSE	EQUIPMENT
Beating	Vigorously agitating foods to incorporate air or develop gluten	Spoon or electric mixer with paddle attachment
Blending	Mixing two or more ingredients until evenly distributed	Spoon, rubber spatula, whisk or electric mixer with paddle attachment
Creaming	Vigorously combining softened fat and sugar while incorporating air	Electric mixer with paddle attachment on medium speed
Cutting	Incorporating solid fat into dry ingredients only until lumps of the desired size remain	Pastry cutters, fingers or electric mixer with paddle attachment
Folding	Very gently incorporating ingredients such as whipped cream or whipped eggs into dry ingredients, a batter or cream	Rubber spatula or balloon whisk
Kneading	Working a dough to develop gluten	Hand or electric mixer with dough hook; if done by hand, the dough must be vigorously and repeatedly folded and turned in a rhythmic pattern
Sifting	Passing one or more dry ingredients through a wire mesh to remove lumps, combine and aerate	Rotary or drum sifter or mesh strainer
Stirring	Gently mixing ingredients by hand until evenly blended	Spoon, whisk or rubber spatula
Whipping	Beating vigorously to incorporate air	Whisk or electric mixer with whip attachment

gluten development. Flour needs to absorb liquid in order for its proteins to bond and form gluten. Fats in a formula coat the fine particles of flour, preventing water from being absorbed into the flour. This inhibits the formation of a strong gluten bond.

A high-fat cookie dough that contains very little liquid bakes into a crumbly product, not a light and chewy one. But the dough for a French baguette contains no fat and bakes into a solid, chewy product. Even the fat in milk will inhibit gluten formation, which is why milk is used in dough for dinner rolls or sandwich bread, two breads that are tender and soft. The protein content of flour also affects the gluten development in a formula. Firm bread dough that can be kneaded and shaped before baking requires a higher-protein flour than a tender cake.

The factors and ingredients that affect gluten development in the bakeshop will be studied throughout this book.

The Importance of Moisture

Moisture in the form of water, milk or other liquids, as well as the moisture in ingredients such as fresh fruits or eggs, is of great importance to the final result in baking. Throughout the mixing process, water and moisture in a formula *dissolves ingredients* such as salt or chemical leavening. Once dissolved, moisture *activates compounds* such as yeast or chemical leavening in the formula. Even when an ingredient does not dissolve completely as would salt or sugar, moisture helps *hydrate ingredients*. Flour or starch, for example, absorbs water, which binds with molecules in these ingredients. Water molecules attach to the starch granules in flour, trapping them in a kind of shell that gives baked goods their structure. Water and other liquids are also important for *adjusting the temperature* in a formula. Using temperature-controlled water when mixing yeast dough, for example, helps the dough reach the ideal temperature for fermentation. Chilled water in pastry dough helps prevent fat in the formula from melting during mixing.

Baked goods are made from doughs and batters; it is the moisture content that distinguishes between the two. A **dough** has a low moisture or water content and a firm **consistency**. The moisture in the formula binds with protein to form gluten, which forms the continuous medium into which other ingredients are embedded. A dough is

consistency the degree of firmness, flow or density

usually prepared by beating, blending, cutting or kneading and is often stiff enough to cut into various shapes. Some common types of dough are yeast bread dough, cookie dough and pie dough.

A **batter** has a thin consistency and generally contains more liquids, fat and sugar than a dough. Gluten development is minimized and liquid forms the continuous medium in which other ingredients are dispersed. A batter bakes into softer, moister products. A batter is usually prepared by blending, creaming, stirring or whipping and is generally thin enough to pour. Some common types of batter are cake batter, muffin batter and pancake batter.

Baking or cooking a dough or batter drives out moisture and creates the final result, whether it be a crusty bread with a fluffy interior or a uniformly crisp cookie.

HEAT TRANSFER AND THE SCIENCE OF BAKING

Once a batter or dough is mixed, the application of heat transforms it into an appealing finished product. Heat is a type of energy. When a substance is heated, its **molecules** absorb energy, which causes the molecules to vibrate rapidly, expand and bounce off one another. As the molecules move, they collide with nearby molecules, causing a transfer of heat energy. The faster the molecules within a substance move, the higher its temperature. This is true whether the substance is air, water, an aluminum pot or an apple pie.

Heat energy may be transferred to foods and baked goods in three primary ways: through conduction, convection and radiation (Figure 3.1).

Conduction

Conduction is the movement of heat from one item to another through direct contact. For example, heat is conducted directly from a pan placed over a burner into foods cooked on the stove top. The pan heats up and the heat is transferred from the pan to the food it contains. Conduction is the primary heat transfer method in stove top cooking, but conduction is important in baking as well. For example, when heat energy hits a cake pan or baking sheet placed in a hot oven, heat is conducted to the pan. The metal of the pan then conducts heat to the batter or dough contained in that pan. When bread dough or pizza dough is placed on the hearth of a wood-fired oven, the oven's heated deck conducts heat directly into the dough during baking.

Some materials conduct heat better than others. Generally metals are good conductors. As discussed in Chapter 2, Tools and Equipment for the Bakeshop, copper and

molecule the smallest physical unit of a substance that retains all of its chemical and physical properties

FIGURE 3.1 ▶ The types of heat energy in an oven: conduction (orange waves), convection (yellow arrows) and radiation (red arrows).

aluminum are the best conductors, conducting heat quickly to foods. Liquids and gases are poor conductors and conduct heat relatively slowly, which can be used to a baker's advantage. Delicate creams and custards, which can curdle or separate when baked at too high a temperature, are baked in a water bath so they cook slowly and evenly. Stone is considered a good conductor for yeast bread baking because it acts as a heat sink, filling up with heat and slowly releasing it back over an extended period of time. The type of material and its gauge or thickness all contribute to the conductivity of cookware and bakeware.

Conduction is a relatively slow method of heat transfer because there must be physical contact to transfer energy from one molecule to adjacent molecules. Consider what happens when a metal spoon is placed in a pot of simmering soup. At first the spoon handle remains cool. Gradually, however, heat travels up the handle, making it warmer and warmer, until it becomes too hot to touch. Water is a better conductor of heat than air. This explains why you cannot place your hand in boiling water at a temperature of 212°F (100°C), but can place your hand, at least very briefly, into a 400°F (200°C) oven.

Conduction is important in all cooking methods because it is responsible for the movement of heat from the surface of a food to its interior. As the molecules near the food's exterior gather energy, they move more and more rapidly. As they move, they conduct heat to the molecules nearby, thus transferring heat through the food (from the exterior of the item to the interior).

In conventional heating methods (nonmicrowave), the heat source causes food molecules to react largely from the surface inward so that layers of molecules heat in succession. This produces a range of temperatures within the food, which means that the outside can brown and form a crust long before the interior is noticeably warmer. That is why a loaf of bread can brown on the outside yet still remain moist and tender inside.

Convection

Convection refers to the transfer of heat through a fluid, which may be liquid or gas. Natural convection occurs because warm gases tend to rise while cooler ones fall, causing a constant natural circulation of heat. In a conventional oven, heated air (a gas) naturally circulates in and around the baking chamber. **Mechanical convection** relies on fans or stirring to circulate heat more quickly and evenly. This explains why foods heat faster and more evenly when stirred. Convection ovens are equipped with fans to increase the circulation of air currents, thus speeding up the baking process.

Radiation

Radiation is the transfer of heat energy through waves that move from the heat source to the food. It does not require physical contact between the heat source and the food being cooked. Think of the heat radiating from the glowing coals of a fire. Heating elements within a conventional oven radiate heat into the oven chamber, the metal walls of which absorb the heat. These heated walls then radiate heat back onto the surface of the foods being baked. For this reason, foods placed closer to the heating element or oven walls will cook more quickly than those farther away. Baking pans also radiate heat. (Place your hand over, but not touching, a sheet pan that has been in a hot oven for a few minutes to feel the heat it radiates.)

Infrared cooking uses an electric or ceramic element heated to such a high temperature that it gives off waves of radiant heat that cook the food. Radiant heat waves travel at the speed of light in any direction (unlike convection heat, which only rises) until they are absorbed by a food. Infrared cooking is commonly used with toasters and broilers.

Microwave ovens also rely on radiation generated by a special oven to penetrate the food, where it agitates water molecules, creating friction and heat. This energy then spreads throughout the food by conduction (and by convection in liquids). Microwave cooking is much faster than other methods because energy penetrates the food up to a depth of several centimeters, setting all water molecules in motion at the same time. Heat is generated quickly and uniformly throughout the food. Microwave cooking does not

BAKING TEMPERATURES

When using a convection oven, reduce the temperatures recommended in the formulas in this book by 25°F–50°F (10°C–20°C). Watch the baking time as well because convection ovens can cook as much as 20 percent more quickly than conventional ovens.

reduction a liquid cooked until a portion of it evaporates, reducing the volume of the liquid; used to concentrate flavor and thicken liquids

brown foods, however, and often gives meats a dry, mushy texture, making microwave ovens an unacceptable replacement for traditional ovens.

Because microwave radiation affects only water molecules, a completely waterless material (such as a plate) will not get hot. Any warmth felt in a plate used when microwaving food results from heat being conducted from the food to the plate.

BAKING AND COOKING METHODS

Most of the heat transfer of concern to the baker and pastry chef takes place in the oven. This is a dry-heat cooking environment where circulating hot air is the medium that cooks the food.

Foods can be cooked in air or fat (dry-heat cooking methods) or in water or steam (moist-heat cooking methods). **Dry-heat cooking methods** using air or fat are the principal methods employed to bake and cook batter and dough. Baking and frying are methods used when preparing many foods including yeast bread, cakes and doughnuts. Dry-heat cooking also includes the cooking methods associated with the savory kitchen—grilling, roasting, sautéing and pan-frying. These are, for the most part, of secondary importance in the bakeshop. (See Table 3.2.)

Moist-heat cooking methods are those using water or steam. They are poaching, simmering and boiling, techniques regularly used to cook fruits and other pastry components, as well as steaming. Moist-heat cooking methods are used to tenderize foods and enhance their natural flavor. They are also used to heat liquids to encourage evaporation, resulting in an intensified flavor or a **reduction**, such as for a syrup or sauce. Moist-heat methods such as simmering are used to gently heat mixtures so that proteins set and the mixture thickens, such as for custards and creams. Detailed procedures and formulas applying these methods to specific foods are found throughout this book.

THE BAKING PROCESS

Many changes occur in a dough or batter as it bakes. A pourable liquid solidifies into a tender, light cake; a sticky mass becomes chewy cookies; a soft, elastic dough becomes firm, crusty French bread. These physical changes are the result of the ingredients used, the mixing methods employed and the effect of heat applied during the baking process. Namely, gases form and are trapped within the dough or batter; starches, proteins and sugars cook; fats melt; moisture evaporates and staling begins.

TABLE 3.2 COMMON BAKESHOP COOKING METHODS

METHOD	MEDIUM	BAKESHOP PRODUCTS	EQUIPMENT
DRY-HEAT COOKING METHODS			
Baking	Air	Doughs, batters for breads, cakes, cookies, pastries, fruits	Oven, convection oven
Broiling	Air	Fruits, glazed custards	Overhead broiler, salamander
Deep-frying	Fat	Doughnuts, fritters	Deep-fat fryer
Pan-frying	Fat	Batters for griddlecakes	Stove top
Sautéing	Fat	Fruit	Stove top
MOIST-HEAT COOKING METHODS			
Boiling	Water or other liquids	Creams, sauces, fruits	Stove top
Poaching	Water or other liquids	Fruits, fresh and dried	Stove top, oven
Simmering	Water or other liquids	Creams, sauces, fruits	Stove top, oven

By learning to control these changes, the baker also learns to control the final product. Control can be exerted in the selection of ingredients and the methods by which those ingredients are combined, as well as by the baking temperature and duration.

Stages of Baking

Batters and dough pass through ten stages during and after the baking process.

1. Fats melt.
2. Gases form.
3. Gases are trapped.
4. Microorganisms are killed.
5. Starches gelatinize.
6. Proteins coagulate.
7. Water evaporates and gases escape.
8. Sugars caramelize.
9. Carryover baking occurs.
10. Staling begins.

FATS MELT

With their low melting point, between 90°F and 130°F (30°C and 55°C), most fats begin to melt as soon as a batter or dough is placed in a heated oven. As fats melt, droplets are dispersed throughout the product. These fat droplets coat the starch (flour) granules, thus moistening and tenderizing the product by keeping the gluten strands short. Any water that is present will turn to steam at higher temperatures. Fats also coat egg proteins, interrupting the development of a baked good's structure. Fats melt at different temperatures. Those that melt at lower temperatures, such as butter, tenderize more than those that melt at higher temperatures, such as vegetable shortening. It is important to select a fat with the proper melting point for the product being prepared. See Chapter 4, Bakeshop Ingredients.

GASES FORM

A baked good's final texture is determined by the amount of leavening or rise that occurs both before and during baking. This rise is caused by the gases present in the dough or batter. These gases are carbon dioxide, air and steam. Air and carbon dioxide are present in doughs and batters before they are heated. (Air may be incorporated during the mixing process. Carbon dioxide is released as a by-product of leaveners, such as yeast, used in the mixture.) The formation of gases begins upon mixing and continues as a product is heated until it reaches a temperature of around 170°F (77°C). Steam is one gas formed when heat is applied. For example, steam is created as the moisture in a dough is heated; yeast and baking powder rapidly release additional carbon dioxide when placed in a hot oven. These gases then expand and leaven the product. (Additional information on the effects of baking powder and baking soda is found in Chapter 6, Quick Breads. Yeast is discussed in detail in Chapter 7, Artisan and Yeast Breads.)

GASES ARE TRAPPED

The stretchable network of proteins created in a batter or dough, either egg proteins or gluten, traps gases in the product. Without an appropriate network of proteins, the gases would just escape without causing the mixture to rise. Proper mixing ensures the appropriate protein development in a batter or dough.

MICROORGANISMS ARE KILLED

A batter or dough may contain beneficial yeast organisms as well as harmful bacteria and molds. Most die at temperatures above 140°F (60°C). The temperature can vary depending on the type of microorganism and the quantity of salt or sugar in the formula.

THE SCIENCE OF BAKING A CAKE, CIRCA 1806

"The heat of the oven is of great importance for cakes, especially those that are large. If not pretty quick, the batter will not rise. Should you fear its catching by being too quick, put some paper over the cake to prevent its being burnt. If not long enough lighted to have a body of heat, or it is become slack, the cake will be heavy. To know when it is soaked, take a broad bladed knife that is very bright, and plunge it into the very center, draw it instantly out, and if the least stickiness adheres, put the cake immediately in, and shut up the oven."

—MARIA ELIZA KETELBY RUNDELL (1745–1828), from *A New System of Domestic Cookery: Formed upon Principles of Economy, and Adapted to the Use of Private Families* (Exeter, NH: Norris & Sawyer, 1808).

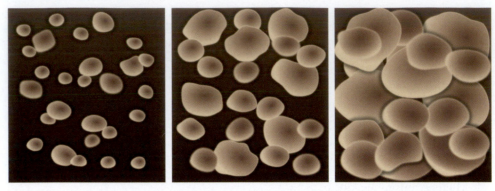

FIGURE 3.2 ▶ Gelatinization of starch. From left: uncooked starch granules floating in a liquid, starch beginning to swell when heated, fully gelatinized starches binding into a solid mass.

STARCHES GELATINIZE

starch complex carbohydrate from plants that is edible and either digestible or indigestible (fiber), consisting of long chains of glucose sugar molecules

Starches are complex **carbohydrates** present in plants and grains such as potatoes, wheat, rice and corn. Flour, which is approximately 70 percent starch, is the primary ingredient in most baked goods. When a mixture of starch and liquid is heated, remarkable changes occur. (See Figure 3.2.) Starches begin to absorb and capture moisture—up to 10 times their own weight—beginning at temperatures as low as 105°F (41°C). When starch granules in a batter or dough reach a temperature of approximately 140°F (60°C), they absorb additional moisture and expand. This process is referred to as **gelatinization**. Properly gelled starches contribute to the baked good's structure. Gelatinization occurs gradually over a range of temperatures—140°F–212°F (60°C–100°C)—depending on the type of starch present. And the amount of water in a formula effects starch gelatinization. Not all starch present in cookie or pie dough gelatinizes because of the low moisture content in such formulas.

carbohydrates a group of compounds composed of oxygen, hydrogen and carbon; the human body's primary source of energy (4 calories per gram); carbohydrates are classified as simple (including certain sugars) and complex (including starches and fiber)

PROTEINS COAGULATE

gelatinization the process by which starch granules are cooked; they absorb moisture when placed in a liquid and heated; as the moisture is absorbed, the product swells, softens and clarifies slightly

Proteins begin to bond and **coagulate** (solidify) when the dough or batter reaches a temperature of 160°F (71°C). Proteins are large, complex molecules found in every living cell, plant as well as animal. They are formed from amino acids that are chemically bonded into long, loosely folded chains. In the presence of heat, the protein chains unfold (**denature**), which allows them to rebond and solidify into a solid mass. In other words, as proteins cook, they lose moisture, shrink and become firm. (See Figure 3.3.) Common examples of coagulation are egg whites changing from a clear liquid to a white solid when heated and the setting of the structure of wheat proteins (gluten) in bread during baking. This process provides most of the baked good's structure.

coagulation the irreversible transformation of proteins from a liquid or semiliquid state to a solid state

Proper baking temperatures are important for controlling the point at which proteins coagulate. If the temperature is too high, proteins solidify before the gases in the product have expanded fully, resulting in a product with poor texture and reduced volume. If the

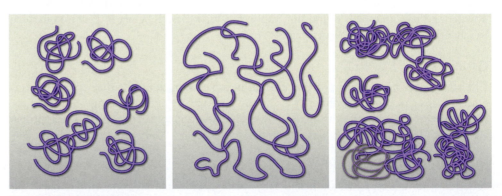

FIGURE 3.3 ▶ Protein coagulation. From left: loosely folded protein chain, denatured protein, coagulated protein.

TABLE 3.3	GASES THAT LEAVEN BAKED GOODS
GAS	**PRESENT IN**
Air	All products, especially those containing whipped eggs or creamed fat
Steam	All products when liquids evaporate or fats melt
Carbon dioxide	Products containing baking soda, baking powder, baking ammonia or yeast

temperature is too low, gases escape before the proteins coagulate, resulting in a product that may collapse. Most proteins complete coagulation at 160°F–185°F (71°C–85°C).

WATER EVAPORATES AND GASES ESCAPE

Throughout the baking process, the water contained in the liquid ingredients will turn to steam and **evaporate**. This steam is a useful leavener; see Table 3.3. During the early stages of baking, starting at around 160°F (72°C), the product is porous, allowing these gases to escape readily. As steam is released the dough or batter dries out, starting from the outside, resulting in the formation of a dry yet pale crust. The loss of moisture also means a product is losing weight; in the case of bread, 10 to 14 percent of weight is lost during baking, although this varies greatly depending on the size of the loaf, its shape and whether it is baked in a pan. Distinctive aromas from gases such as alcohol and carbon dioxide signal this important stage in baking. Pay attention to aromas and smells during baking. Aromas can work as well as a timer to signal when to check a baked good for doneness.

SUGARS CARAMELIZE

As soon as water evaporation slows around 300°F (150°C), the surface temperature of a baking product will rise. As sugars in bake goods are heated above 320°F (160°C), they break down and darken or caramelize. (The process of cooking sugar is known as **caramelization**.) The result is the gradual darkening of the surface of a baked good. Sugars are simple carbohydrates used by all plants and animals to store energy. Sugars are found in eggs, dairy products and other ingredients in a formula, not only in refined sugar and liquid sweeteners. Caramelization of sugars is responsible for most of the flavors associated with baked goods. Because high temperatures are required for caramelization, most foods brown only on the outside and only through the application of dry heat.

caramelization the process of cooking sugars; the browning of sugar enhances the flavor and appearance of food

The **Maillard reaction**, named for the French scientist who discovered this principle, describes the process of sugar breaking down in the presence of protein. Maillard browning results in darkening as well as the development of pleasing, nutty baked flavors. (Some of the aromas and flavors of roasted nuts, chocolate and coffee derive from Maillard browning.)

CARRYOVER BAKING OCCURS

The physical changes in a baked good do not stop when it is removed from the oven. The residual heat contained in the hot baking pan, and within the product itself, continues the baking process as the product cools. This is why a crisp-style cookie or biscuit may be soft and seem a bit underbaked when removed from the oven; it will finish baking as it cools.

As a baked product cools, other noticeable changes take place. At first, these changes yield pleasing characteristics. Fats resolidify, causing the product to firm. Sugars recrystallize, giving a pleasant crunchiness to the crust of a cookie, for example. When these changes become unpleasantly noticeable, a product is considered stale.

STALING BEGINS

Staling is a change in a baked good's texture and aroma caused by both moisture loss and changes in the structure of the starch granules. Stale products have lost their fresh aroma and are firmer, drier and more crumbly than fresh goods. Staling is not just a general loss

starch retrogradation the process whereby starch molecules in a batter or dough lose moisture after baking; the result is baked goods that are dry or stale

of moisture into the atmosphere; it is also a change in the location and distribution of water molecules within the product. This process, known as **starch retrogradation**, occurs as starch molecules cool, becoming denser and expelling moisture.

In breads, this moisture migrates from the interior to the drier crust, causing the crust to become tough and leathery. If the product is not well wrapped, moisture escapes completely into the surrounding air. In humid conditions, the crust on unwrapped bread absorbs moisture from the atmosphere, resulting in the same loss of crispness. The flavor and texture of breads can be revived by reheating them to approximately 140°F (60°C), the temperature at which starch gelatinization occurs. Usually, products can be reheated only once without causing additional quality loss.

The retrogradation process is temperature dependent. It occurs most rapidly at temperatures of approximately 40°F (4°C). Therefore, baked products should not be refrigerated unless they contain perishable components such as cream fillings. It is better to store products frozen or at room temperature, as long as food safety is not of concern.

Products containing fats and sugars, which retain moisture, tend to stay fresh longer. Commercial bakeries usually add chemical emulsifiers, modified shortening or special sweeteners to retard staling, but these additives are not as practical for small-scale production.

SENSORY SCIENCE

Understanding the proper way to mix a batter or dough and gaining expertise in proper mixing and baking techniques goes a long way toward ensuring a delicious product. Part of professional culinary training also involves learning to balance ingredients and present food to create an engaging eating experience. An experienced pastry professional is able to taste and evaluate a dish, adjusting flavorings, ingredients and cooking techniques as needed to maximize the diner's experience.

Sensory science is the study of the ways humans experience the world through our five primary senses—sight, sound, smell, taste and touch. Eating engages all of these senses. Imagine a loaf of bread. First there is its scent while in the oven, perhaps even the sound of its crust crackling as it cools after baking. Then its appearance, a burnished color of the browned crust. With the first bite we experience the texture of the bread. As it is chewed, its taste becomes apparent, whether it is sweet or salty. With chewing, more complex flavors are released. Any consumer can form an opinion of the bread after eating, but the sensory scientist is trained to evaluate a food product at each stage. A basic understanding of sensory science will enhance a food professional's cooking and serving ability.

When we talk about food, we often try to describe the physical perception we have when eating ("it tastes tart or sugary" or "it feels greasy") or the recognition of the flavor ("I can sense the rosemary" or "there is a hint of strawberries"). In either case, the terms *flavor* and *taste* are often confused. Although often used interchangeably, they are not synonymous.

flavor an identifiable or distinctive quality of a food, drink or other substance perceived with the combined senses of taste, touch and smell

To the food scientist, **flavor** is a combination of sensations caused by the presence of a foreign substance in the mouth, the feel, aromas and taste of food. The flavor experience includes **mouthfeel** or the texture of a food. Is it creamy, crunchy, smooth or crumbly? (See Table 3.4.)

mouthfeel the sensation created in the mouth by a combination of a food's taste, smell, texture and temperature

Aromas are the odors that enter the nose or float up through the back of the mouth to activate smell receptors in the nose. Aromas are volatile chemical compounds that travel directly to the limbic center of the brain, the source of all emotional memory. Aroma receptors in the brain interpret these compounds and automatically register the smell, along with visual and emotional clues tied to the experience of smelling and eating. (For many of us, the scent of chocolate chip cookies baking becomes fused with happy childhood moments spent with Mom.) As much as 80 percent of the experience of a flavor comes from its aroma, making the sense of smell an extremely powerful part of the eating experience.

aroma the sensations, as interpreted by the brain, of what we detect when a substance comes in contact with sense receptors in the nose

taste the sensations, as interpreted by the brain, of what we detect when food, drink or other substances come in contact with our taste buds

Tastes are the sensations we detect when a substance comes in contact with the taste buds on the tongue (i.e., sweet, sour, salt, bitter and umami). Some substances irritate nerves on the tongue or embedded in the fleshy areas of the mouth. These nerves respond to sensations of pain, heat or cold, or sensations our brain interprets as spiciness, pungency or astringency.

Whenever a particular taste, sensation and/or aroma is detected, a set of neurons in the brain is excited and, with experience, we learn to recognize these patterns as the flavor of bananas, chocolate, roasted nuts or sour milk. Each person has a unique ability to recognize and appreciate thousands of these patterns. This compendium of flavors and the ability to recognize them is sometimes referred to as the **palate**.

The way humans perceive taste is described more fully in the sidebar on page 58. For many years, western cultures have identified four tastes: sweet, sour, salty and bitter.

palate (1) the complex of smell, taste and touch receptors that contribute to a person's ability to recognize and appreciate flavors; (2) the range of an individual's recognition and appreciation of flavors

Sweet   For most people, sweetness is the most pleasurable and sought-after taste, although, ironically, the fewer sweet-tasting foods we consume, the more enhanced becomes our ability to recognize sweetness. A food's sweetness comes from the naturally occurring sugars it contains (for example, sucrose and fructose) or artificial sweeteners added to it. This sweetness can sometimes be enhanced by adding a small amount of a sour, bitter or salty taste. Adding too much sourness, bitterness or saltiness, however, lessens our perception of the food's sweetness.

Sour   Considered the opposite of sweet, a sour taste is found in acidic foods and, like sweetness, can vary greatly in intensity. Many foods with a dominant sour taste, such as red currants or sour cream, also contain a secondary or slight sweetness. Often a sour taste can be improved by adding a little sweetness or negated by adding a large amount of a sweet ingredient.

Salty   With the notable exception of oysters and other shellfish, celery and seaweed, the presence of a salty taste in a food is the result of the cook's decision to add the mineral sodium chloride (salt) or to use a previously salted ingredient such as salt-cured fish or soy sauce. Salt helps finish a dish, heightening or enhancing its other flavors. Dishes that lack salt often taste flat. For this reason, salt may be added to sweet preparations. Like the taste of sweetness, the less salt consumed on a regular basis, the more saltiness we can detect in foods.

Bitter   Although the bitterness associated with tasting alkaloids and other organic substances may occasionally be appreciated, such as when tasting chocolate, coffee or dark beer, a bitter-flavored ingredient unbalanced by something sour or salty is generally disliked and, as a survival mechanism, is believed to serve as a warning of inedibility or unhealthfulness.

Recently, many western researchers have begun to recognize a fifth taste, akin to the savory taste long recognized as the fifth taste in Japanese cuisine. Called **umami** (from the Japanese word *umai*, meaning "delicious"), this fifth taste does not have a simple English translation. Rather, for some people it refers to a food's savory characteristic; for others to the richness or fullness of a dish's overall taste; and for still others to the meatiness or meaty taste of a dish. Umami is also considered an element that accentuates a taste in a dish, such as when sun-dried tomatoes are added to a pizza or yeast bread.

umami often called the "fifth taste"; refers to the rich, full taste perceived in the presence of the natural amino acid glutamate and its commercially produced counterpart known as monosodium glutamate (MSG); cheese, meats, rich stocks, soy sauce, shellfish, fatty fish, mushrooms, tomatoes and wine are all high in glutamate

Some foods cause a tingling, sharp, dry, cooling or burning sensation when eaten. These sensations are detected by nerve endings embedded in the fleshy part of the mouth. These nerves, when "irritated" by the presence of compounds such as piperine (the active ingredient in black peppercorns) or capsaicin (the active ingredient in chiles), register a burning sensation that the brain translates as the hot and spicy "taste" of Szechuan or Mexican cuisines, for example. This is called the *trigeminal effect*.

Factors Affecting Perception of Flavors

A number of factors affect one's perception of flavor.

Temperature   Foods at warm temperatures offer the strongest tastes. Heating foods releases volatile flavor compounds, which intensifies one's perceptions of odors. This is why fine cheese is served at room temperature to improve its eating quality and flavor. Foods

HOW WE EXPERIENCE TASTE AND SMELL

The smallest functional unit of taste is the taste bud. These specialized sensory organs can be found on the tongue within three different kinds of **papillae** (Figure 3.4) as well as the back of the throat and the roof of the mouth. Each taste bud contains several **taste receptor cells**, and **taste compounds** interact with the tops of these specialized cells, which then transmit taste information through a nerve to the brain. The process of tasting begins when a substance is placed in the mouth and taste compounds begin to dissolve in saliva. Mastication, or chewing, further breaks down the substance and increases the concentration of taste compounds dissolved in the saliva. Once dissolved in saliva, the taste compounds have the potential to stimulate taste receptors and ultimately elicit taste sensations. Because compounds must dissolve in the saliva in order to reach the taste receptors, taste compounds must be water-soluble.

The process of smelling begins when odor compounds reach the olfactory neurons, the specialized sensing organs of smell. Olfactory neurons are located at the top of the nasal cavity and are clustered together in the **olfactory bulb** (Figure 3.5). A separate olfactory bulb rests at the bottom of each hemisphere of the brain and at the top of each nasal cavity. Odor compounds can reach these receptors through two different pathways: orthonasally via the external nares (or **nostrils**) or retronasally via the internal nares. When we sniff or experience odors that are external to our bodies, we are smelling orthonasally. Once we place a substance in our mouths, the aromas we experience are being delivered through the **retronasal path**. Regardless of route, in order for odor compounds to reach the olfactory receptors they must be able to volatilize, or dissolve in air. Because air is hydrophobic, this means most odor compounds do not dissolve well in water, dissolving better in oils.

A pervasive myth (based on misinterpretation of an article written in German in the 1800s) is that you experience certain taste qualities on only certain areas of the tongue (i.e., sweet on the tip, bitter in the back, salt on the front sides and sour on the back sides). In fact, you can taste all taste compounds everywhere on your tongue, and it is easy to prove this to yourself by placing various items representative of sweet, sour, salty, bitter and even umami on the tip of your tongue. You will be able to immediately perceive any taste at the tongue tip (or anywhere else you have taste buds) and will not need to wait for bitter compounds to diffuse to the back, sour to the back sides, or salt to the front sides.

—JEANNINE DELWICHE, PhD, an expert in sensory science and chemosensory psychophysics, is a senior scientist at Firmenich, Inc., as well as an adjunct faculty member of both The Ohio State University and Brock University.

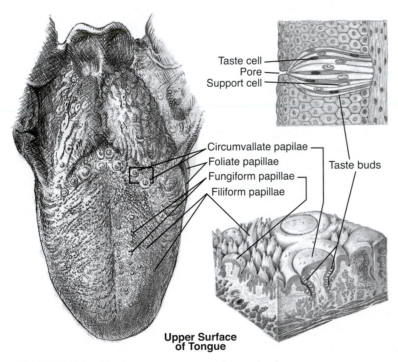

Taste cell
Pore
Support cell

Circumvallate papilae
Foliate papillae
Fungiform papillae
Filiform papillae

Taste buds

Upper Surface of Tongue

FIGURE 3.4 ▶ The human tongue and taste buds.

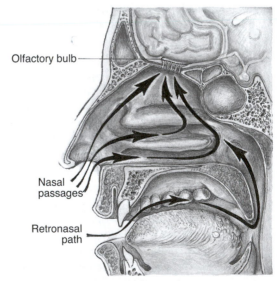

Olfactory bulb

Nasal passages

Retronasal path

FIGURE 3.5 ▶ The human olfactory system.

tend to lose their sour or sweet tastes both the colder and the hotter they become. Therefore serving temperature is important to take into consideration when preparing custard or sorbet mixtures before freezing. Saltiness, however, is perceived differently at extreme cold temperatures; the same quantity of salt in a solution is perceived more strongly when very cold than when merely cool or warm.

Consistency   A food's consistency affects its flavor. Two items with the same amount of taste and smell compounds that differ in texture will differ in their perceived intensity and onset time; the thicker item will take longer to reach its peak intensity and will have a less intense flavor. For example, two batches of sweetened heavy cream made from the same ingredients in the same proportions can taste different if one is whipped and the other is unwhipped; the whipped cream has more volume and therefore a milder flavor. Similarly, the intense sweet and sour tastes of lemonade can be adjusted by adding more water.

Presence of Contrasting Tastes   Sweet and sour are considered opposites, and often adding one to a food dominated by the other enhances the food's overall flavor. For example, sprinkling a grapefruit with a little sugar reduces the fruit's sourness; adding a squeeze of lemon to sautéed peaches reduces their sweetness. But add too much, and the dominant taste is negated. Likewise, something sweet, sour or salty added to a dish with a predominantly bitter flavor cuts the bitterness.

Presence of Fats   Many of the chemical compounds that create tastes and aromas are dissolved in fats occurring naturally in foods or added to foods during cooking. As these compounds are slowly released by evaporation or saliva, they provide a sustained taste sensation. Fat is usually a good carrier of flavor in foods. If, however, there is too little fat, the flavor compounds may not be released efficiently, resulting in a dish with little sustained flavor. The vanilla flavor in a cookie made with butter is more prominent than in a cookie made without fat. Too much fat poses another problem; it can coat the tongue and interfere with the ability of taste receptors to perceive flavor compounds.

Color   A food's color affects how the consumer perceives the food's flavor before it is even tasted. When foods or beverages lack their customary color, they are less readily identified correctly than when appropriately colored. As color level increases to match normal expectations, our perception of taste and flavor intensity increases. A miscue created by the perceived flavor (the flavor associated with the color) can have an adverse impact on the consumer's appreciation of the actual flavor. For example, if the predominant flavor of a dessert is lemon, the dessert or some component of the dessert should be yellow; a green color will trigger an expectation of lime and the possible disappointment of the consumer. Similarly, the dark ruby-red flesh of a blood orange looks different from the bright orange flesh of a Valencia orange. This tonal difference can create the expectation of a different, non-orangey flavor, even though the blood orange's flavor is similar to other sweet orange varieties. Likewise, a sliced apple that has turned brown may suggest an off-flavor, although there is not one.

Lighting has an impact on one's perception of color. Be aware of any differences between lighting in the service area and kitchen when composing a finished plate of food for service.

Compromises to the Perception of Taste

The sense of taste can be challenged by factors both within and beyond one's control. Age and general health can diminish one's perception of flavor, as can fatigue and stress. Bakers and pastry chefs need to be aware of the age and health of their clientele, adjusting the flavoring of foods served according to their needs. Here are some factors, described by Jeannine Delwiche, PhD, that can affect one's taste perceptions.

Age "The bad news is that taste and smell sensitivity does decline as we age. The good news is that it declines at a slower rate than our vision and hearing. The sense of smell tends to decline earlier than the sense of taste. There is a great deal of variance across individuals, with some showing declines earlier than others."

Health "An acute condition, such as a cold, can result in a temporary loss of smell. The presence of mucus can prevent airflow, preventing the odor compounds from reaching the olfactory receptors. In contrast, the sense of taste would remain largely unaffected. Medications can also alter the perception of taste and smell. Some medications suppress the perception of saltiness, while others result in a chronic perception of bitterness. Still other medications alter salivary flow, making it difficult to swallow dry foods. A further complication is the underlying condition for the taking of the medication. If an individual is taking high blood pressure medications, not only may the medication have a direct impact upon perceived taste, but the same individual is likely to be on a sodium-restricted diet."

Smoking "Anecdotal reports from those who quit smoking strongly indicate that smoking diminishes odor sensitivity. This is further supported by evidence that indicates that those who smoke generally are less sensitive to odors than those who do not. In contrast, evidence indicates that if one waits two hours after smoking, the sense of taste is unaltered. Immediately after smoking, however, taste sensitivity is lowered."

Describing Aromas and Flavors in Food

Sensory scientists and professional tasters make their living describing the smell and taste of foods. Many have attempted to standardize the language used to describe both positive and negative aromas and flavors. Frequently they employ flavor wheels or other charts to identify and organize the flavors and tastes found in specific food items. For example, there are flavor wheels devoted to chocolate, coffee, citrus fruits and just about every other category of food and beverage on the market. These charts help food scientists, product developers and quality control tasters speak a common language when describing the flavors they encounter.

Table 3.4 shows words used by sensory scientists to describe the physical aspects of foods. Table 3.5 shows a list used by food chemists to describe sixteen broad categories of tastes and smells that correspond to the major chemicals found in aromas and tastes. Such lists are helpful when trying to analyze and describe the flavors in a dish.

TABLE 3.4 DESCRIPTIVE WORDS FOR SENSORY CHARACTERISTICS OF FOOD
VISUAL CHARACTERISTICS
Color: hue, intensity, chroma
Dimension: thickness, overall size, density
Geometry: square, round, spherical, ovoid, triangular, wedge
Texture: sticky, tacky, rough, smooth, crumbling, congealed, oily, viscous
TACTILE CHARACTERISTICS WHEN CONSUMED
Texture: flaky, grainy, fibrous, lumpy, chalky, gritty
Moisture: moist, juicy, dry, oily, greasy
Resistance: dense, friable, melting, smooth, hard, chewy, spongy, sticky

TABLE 3.5 COMMON FLAVOR DESCRIPTIONS

TYPE OF AROMA OR FLAVOR	FOODS WITH SUCH CHARACTERISTICS
Green, grassy	Green bell peppers, raw apple skins
Fruity, esters	Bananas, apples
Citrus, terpenic	Lemons, limes, juniper
Minty, camphoraceous	Fresh mint, rosemary
Floral, sweet	Roses, orange blossom, honey
Spicy, herbaceous	Allspice, cinnamon, nutmeg, parsley
Woody, smoky	Smoked and grilled foods
Roasted, burnt	Coffee, toasted bread
Caramel, nutty	Toasted nuts, carmelized sugar, molasses
Bouillon, high vegetable protein	Meat stock, beans
Meaty, animalic	Roasted meat
Fatty, rancid	Stale cooking oil, spoiled fish
Alliaceous, sulfurous	Onions, garlic, rotten egg
Mushroom, earthy	Cooked and raw mushrooms, raw potato, yeasty bread
Dairy, buttery	Cream, milk, dairy products
Sour, pungent, acidic	Sour milk, sour cream, vinegar

1 Discuss the various mixing techniques and the tools used for each. Explain how mixing affects gluten development.

2 What are the various cooking methods employed in the bakeshop, and for which products are they commonly used?

3 What elements in baked goods make them rise?

4 List and describe the ten steps in the baking process.

5 Explain what process causes staling. List ways to minimize staling of breads and cakes.

6 List and describe the five basic tastes.

7 Use the Internet to locate a flavor wheel that describes a food such as coffee or chocolate. Use the vocabulary provided to discuss the sensory characteristics of a popular bakeshop preparation such as a pie, cookie or cake. **WWW**

8 What effect does the presence of fat in a cookie formula have on one's perception of its flavor?

QUESTIONS FOR DISCUSSION

Terms to Know

emulsify	gluten
aerate	development
blending	consistency
folding	conduction
sifting	convection
stirring	radiation
cutting	denature
beating	evaporate
creaming	Maillard reaction
kneading	sensory science
whipping	flavor

CHAPTER FOUR

BAKESHOP INGREDIENTS

After studying this chapter, you will be able to:

- identify different types of flours, sweeteners and fats
- understand gluten and its importance in the bakeshop
- identify a variety of fruits
- understand how to purchase and store fruits appropriate for your needs
- understand the function of many bakeshop ingredients

FLOUR, SUGAR, EGGS, MILK, BUTTER, FRUITS AND FLAVORINGS— with this simple list of ingredients a seemingly endless variety of delectable bakeshop sweets are made: breads, sauces, pastries, ice cream. But to produce consistently good brioche, Bavarians, biscuits or the like, the baker must pay careful attention to the character and quantity of each ingredient, the way the ingredients are combined and how heat is applied to them. Although substituting ingredients may have little or no effect on some dishes (carrots may replace turnips in a stew, for instance), this is not the case with baked goods. Different flours, fats, liquids and sweeteners function differently. Bread flour and cake flour are not the same, nor are shortening and butter. When substituting one ingredient for another, the results will be different.

Understanding ingredients, why they function the way they do and how to adjust for their differences will make the baking experience more successful and consistent. This chapter covers most of the ingredients used in the bakeshop, from the most common, flour, to more unusual specialty flavorings. Ingredients are grouped according to the function they perform. Chemical leavening agents, without which there would be neither biscuits nor muffins, are discussed in Chapter 6, Quick Breads. Yeast and natural leaveners are discussed in Chapter 7, Artisan and Yeast Breads. Chocolate is discussed in detail in Chapter 20, Chocolate and Sugar Work.

FLOURS

Flour *provides bulk and structure* to baked goods. Some flours are used to *thicken liquids* in items such as puddings and pie fillings, or to *prevent foods from sticking* during preparation and baking. Flour is produced when grain kernels are milled or ground into a powder. Grains are grasses that bear edible seeds. Corn, rice and wheat are the most significant grains for human consumption, but the most frequently used—and therefore the most important ingredient in the bakeshop—is wheat flour.

Wheat Flour

Wheat flour (Fr. *farine*) is produced by milling wheat kernels or berries from one of numerous varieties of common wheat (*Triticum aestivum*). A wheat kernel has a hard outer covering called **bran**, a valuable source of dietary fiber. Bran is composed of seven layers that envelop and protect the **endosperm**. Composed of 50 to 75 percent starch and 8 to 18 percent protein, the endosperm supplies energy to the plant as it grows. The innermost part is the **germ**, which contains fat and serves as the wheat seed (see Figure 4.1).

During milling, the endosperm is separated from the bran and germ, and it is gradually reduced in particle size. Originally the wheat kernels were ground between two grooved stones. The bran was then removed by sifting or bolting, which produced a fine wheat flour. Although this type of stone ground flour is still available, modern mills are equipped with steel rollers and sophisticated equipment for sifting the different streams of flour, bran and endosperm. First the kernels pass through metal rollers to crack or break them, and then the bran and germ are separated through repeated stages of sifting. The remaining endosperm is then ground into flour. There are three primary commercial grades of flour: patent flour, clear flour and straight flour. **Patent flour** is made from the section of the endosperm closest to the germ. It is finer and whiter in color, the highest quality of

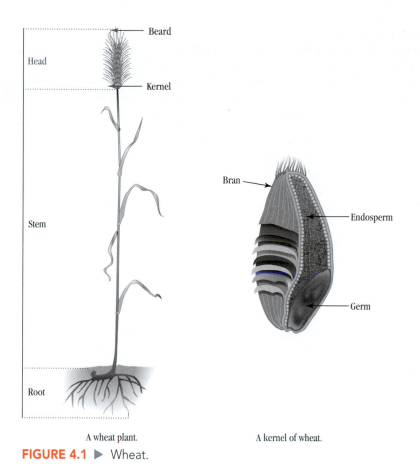

A wheat plant.   A kernel of wheat.

FIGURE 4.1 ▶ Wheat.

commercial-grade flour available. **Clear flour** is made from the portion of the endosperm nearer the bran. Coarser and darker than other flours, it is considered the lowest commercial grade of flour, although it has a high protein content. Flour may also be milled from the entire endosperm. This is **straight flour**. Because it contains bran and germ not easily separated out, straight flour is darker in color than patent or clear flours. Straight flour is used to make bread in France but is less common in the United States. Most flour blends sold in the United States are made from patent flour.

COMPOSITION OF FLOUR

Flour consists primarily of five nutrients: fat, minerals, moisture, starches and proteins. **Fat** and **minerals** each generally account for less than 1 percent of flour's content. Minerals, which are found in higher concentration in the bran and the outer part of the endosperm, contribute to yeast fermentation and add wheat flavor to breads. **Ash** is an indicator of the degree of flour milling. Ash content is determined by burning a sample of flour and weighing what remains. Because minerals resist burning, this process gives a good indication of mineral content. The higher the ash content, the darker the flour. Artisan bakers often seek flours with a higher ash content; conventional bakers look for a lower ash content flour in order to produce baked goods that are white in color.

The **moisture** content of flour is relatively low—when packaged, it cannot exceed 14 percent under government standards. Actual moisture content varies depending on climatic conditions and storage, however. In damp areas, flour absorbs moisture from the atmosphere.

Starches constitute 63 to 77 percent of flour and are necessary for the absorption of moisture during baking. This process, known as gelatinization, occurs primarily at temperatures above 140°F (60°C). Starches that are damaged during milling, although usually a fraction of the starch present, are converted to sugar when moistened, thus providing food for yeast during fermentation.

Gums, primarily *pentosans*, are another component of the carbohydrates in flour. Though gums constitute a small percentage of the flour (2–3 percent), they are important because they can absorb up to 10 times their weight in water, enhancing strength and structure in a batter or dough. Gums are a good source of soluble fiber.

Protein accounts for 6 to 18 percent of flour. These proteins are of crucial importance because of their gluten-forming potential. As discussed in Chapter 3, Principles of Baking, gluten is the tough, rubbery substance created when wheat flour is mixed with water. Flour does not contain gluten; only a dough or batter can contain gluten. The proteins responsible for gluten formation are *glutenin* and *gliadin*; they represent about 80 percent of the protein in flour. Gluten is produced when glutenin and gliadin are moistened and manipulated, as when they are stirred or kneaded. Gluten strands are both plastic (that is, they change shape under pressure) and elastic (they resume their original shape when that pressure is removed). Gluten is responsible for the volume, texture and appearance of baked goods. It provides structure and enables dough to retain the gases given off by leavening agents. Without gluten, there could be no raised breads. The gases created by yeast fermentation or chemical leaveners would simply escape if there were no network of gluten strands to trap them in the dough.

Enzymes such as amylase, lipase and protease are the remaining proteins in flour. Although they represent a fraction of the protein present, enzymes are important for the flour's performance in yeast bread. Enzymes help break down starches into sugars, allowing yeast organisms to form gas.

In general, the higher a flour's protein content, the greater that flour's gluten-forming potential. In some cases, however, flour with, for example, 13 percent protein may perform better than one with 14 percent protein because the proteins in the flour are of superior quality. Patent flour has a higher quality protein than clear flour and the gluten structure formed when it is made into dough will be more elastic and extensible. In order to make a chewy product such as a crusty French loaf, a flour with a high protein content must be used. Lower-protein flours are used for tender soft products such as cakes or muffins.

Other ingredients and mixing methods affect the development of gluten, as discussed in Chapter 3, Principles of the Bakeshop. The factors that affect gluten development in the bakeshop will be studied throughout this book.

CLASSIFICATION OF WHEAT

The character of the wheat determines the character of the flour. Professional bakers pay close attention to flour characteristics, which are printed on bags of flour and on flour specification sheets available from suppliers. Wheat is classified according to the growing season, its color and kernel hardness—*soft* or *hard* depending on the kernel's shape and density. Wheat has two distinct growing seasons—winter and spring. **Winter wheat**, grown where winters are mild, is sown in the fall and harvested in the spring. Flour made from winter wheat usually has a medium gluten strength and a protein content from 10 to 12 percent. **Spring wheat**, grown mainly in the northern plains states and Canada, is sown in the spring and harvested later in the summer. Flour made from spring wheat usually has a high gluten strength and a protein content from 12 to 14 percent.

Different strains of wheat have different color bran. Though a dark color, referred to as **red**, is more common, newer strains of wheat have been developed with a white bran, referred to as *white* wheat, which some believe results in less bitter-tasting whole-grain products. The hardness of the wheat kernel indicates its protein content. The harder the wheat kernel, the higher its protein content. Soft wheat yields soft flour with a low protein content. **Soft flour**, also called **weak flour**, is typically whiter in color and fine grained, packing easily when squeezed. Soft flour is best for tender products such as cakes. Hard wheat yields a **hard flour** with a high protein content. Hard wheat remains somewhat gritty when milled and resists clumping when squeezed. Hard flour, also known as **strong flour**, is used for yeast breads. Table 4.1 shows wheat classifications and their uses.

TREATING FLOUR

Malting and Enrichment

Millers may add minute quantities of malted barley flour to hard wheat flour after blending. Malted barley flour is high in the type of enzyme (alpha-amylase) that helps starch break down into sugars, making the sugars available as yeast food, thus promoting the rise

Squeezing soft, low-protein pastry flour (left) between one's fingers results in clumping. Higher-protein bread flour (right) remains free-flowing.

TABLE 4.1 WHEAT CLASSES	
WHEAT CLASSES	**USES**
Hard red winter	Breads and other yeast-leavened baked goods
Hard red spring	
Hard white	
Soft red winter	Cakes, crackers, cookies and pastries
Soft white	
Durum	Noodles, pasta and some Italian breads

of bread dough. **Malting** also helps dough brown uniformly. Vitamins and minerals lost during milling—thiamin, niacin, riboflavin, folic acid and iron—may be added back to the flour during blending.

Aging and Bleaching

Flour develops better baking qualities if allowed to rest for several weeks after milling. Freshly milled flour produces a sticky dough and products with less volume than those made with aged flour. During aging, flour turns white through a natural oxidation process referred to as bleaching.

Because natural aging and bleaching are somewhat unpredictable, time-consuming processes, chemicals are often used to expedite both. Potassium bromate and chlorine dioxide gas rapidly age flour. Benzoyl peroxide, chlorine dioxide and other chemicals bleach flour by removing yellow pigments in order to obtain a uniform white color. (Chlorine gives cake flour its pure white color.) Bleaching alters the flavor of the flour and destroys small amounts of the flour's naturally occurring vitamin E. Many artisan bakers use unbleached and unbromated flours exclusively. (Potassium bromate has been identified as a possible carcinogen and may not be added to flour milled and sold in Canada or Europe.)

Dough Conditioners

Bakers may add dough conditioners or dough improvers to yeast dough formulas. Dough conditioners, which are a blend of emulsifiers, salts, acids and other chemicals, can perform numerous functions. Sometimes conditioners are used to reduce fermentation time or make doughs perform well under harsh industrial mixing and handling conditions. The use of dough conditioners and other bread additives is regulated. Their use does not necessarily contribute to a quality product.

Vital Wheat Gluten

Vital wheat gluten (gluten flour) is the pure protein extracted from wheat flour. With an average protein content of 75 percent, it is used to boost the protein content of weaker flours such as rye and whole-wheat flour. A dry, creamy powder, it must be blended with other ingredients to form a dough or batter. Additional water may be needed in a formula when it is used.

TYPES OF FLOUR

Various types of flour are created by mixing or blending flours from different classes and varieties of wheat. **Cake flour** is a fine, white flour with a low protein content. It is ground from deep within the endosperm and is treated with bleaching agents to produce its pure color. The bleaching also contributes to the properties of cake flour, which absorbs moisture but develops a weak gluten bond. High-ratio cakes, which contain a high percentage of liquid and sugar, require cake flour in order to rise properly. **Pastry flour** is a low-protein flour usually milled from soft red winter wheat, and not usually bleached. **All-purpose flour**, a blend of hard and soft flours, is designed for use in a wide range of foods. It is readily available in quantities appropriate for small food service operations and is often labeled *Hotel and Restaurant* flour. Sold both bleached and unbleached, all-purpose flour

malting soaking, sprouting and drying barley or other grains to develop enzymes; malted grains may be added to wheat flour to improve its baking qualities

TABLE 4.2   PROTEIN CONTENT OF FLOURS

TYPE OF FLOUR	PERCENT PROTEIN	USES
Cake	6–8	Tender cakes
Pastry	7–9.5	Biscuits, pie crusts
All-purpose	9.5–12	General baking
Artisan bread	11.5–12.5	European-style crusty hearth breads, baguettes
Bread	11.5–14	Yeast breads, pan breads, rolls, laminated dough
Whole-wheat	13–14	Breads
High-gluten	13.5–14.5	Bagels, hard rolls; used to increase protein content of weaker flours such as rye, whole-grain or specialty flours
Durum	12–15	Noodles, pasta and Italian breads
Vital wheat gluten (gluten flour)	40–85	Added to flour to increase protein content of weaker flours such as rye, whole-grain or specialty flours

varies widely by miller. Large bakeshops rarely use all-purpose flour; instead, they choose flours milled and blended for specific characteristics. **Bread flour**, milled from hard red spring or hard red winter wheat, has the higher protein content necessary to produce baked goods with a chewy crumb and crisp crust. **Artisan bread flour**, milled from hard red winter wheat, is somewhat lower in protein than bread flour (11.5–12.5 percent). This blend, now available from many mills in the United States, resembles French flour, which has high-quality protein and develops a good gluten structure so that the dough tolerates a long fermentation time. **High-gluten flour**, as its name implies, is a blend of the highest-protein-content flour and is used to make bagels and hard rolls. **Durum flour** is made from a type of hard wheat (*Triticum turgidum* L. var. *durum*) with an amber germ and high protein content. It is used to make noodles and pasta and blended in some crusty Italian bread formulas.

Table 4.2 lists the protein content and uses for several common flours. Substituting one type of flour for another may be acceptable in some formulas as long as the ratio of fats, moisteners and other ingredients is adjusted accordingly. In many cases, such as substituting cake flour for bread flour in a loaf of crusty bread, substituting one type of flour for another will result in a changed and probably less desirable product. And although many cakes can be made from pastry or bread flour, cake flour is required when making delicate high-ratio cakes to achieve their featherweight texture.

Specialty Flours

Whole-wheat flour is made by milling the entire wheat kernel, including the bran and nutritious germ. Whole-wheat flour, typically made from hard red wheat, has a nutty, sweet flavor and brown, flecked color. Products made with whole-wheat flour will be heavier and denser, with less volume than those made with white flour; bran particles cut through the gluten strands in the dough, resulting in a heavier crumb. The granulation size of whole-wheat flour varies from fine to coarse, depending on the manufacturer. A finer grind will absorb more water; therefore, it is important to adjust formulas according to the type of whole-wheat flour used. A newer strain of white wheat produces a lighter-colored whole-wheat flour with the nutritional benefits of whole wheat. Whole-wheat flour has a reduced shelf life because fats in the germ can become rancid during storage. Whole-wheat pastry and high-gluten flours are available. Graham flour is a type of coarse whole-wheat flour used to add texture to crackers and baked goods.

Though not a flour, **wheat germ** is often used in place of some flour in recipes for flavor and fiber. Wheat germ, preferably toasted, can be used in place of up to one-third of the wheat flour in a dough formula. The finished product will have a denser texture, however.

Whole-Wheat Flour

Self-rising flour is an all-purpose flour to which salt and a chemical leavener, usually baking powder, have been added. It is not recommended for professional use. Chemicals lose their leavening ability over time and may cause inconsistent results. Furthermore, different formulas call for different ratios of salt and leaveners; no commercial blend is appropriate for all purposes.

Nonwheat flours, also referred to as **composite flours**, are made from grains, seeds or beans. Corn, soybeans, rice, oats, buckwheat, potatoes and other items provide flours, but none of them contain the gluten-forming proteins of wheat flour. For this reason they are often used to produce baked goods for those with allergies to wheat proteins, as discussed in Chapter 16, Healthful and Special-Needs Baking. In conventional baking, composite flours are generally blended with a high-protein wheat flour for baking. Substituting composite flour for wheat flour changes the flavor and texture of the product.

Rye flour is commonly used in bread baking. It is milled from the rye berry, much as wheat flour is milled from the wheat berry. Rye flour comes in four grades or colors: *light* or *white*, *medium*, *dark* and *rye meal*. White rye flour is made from only the center of the rye berry. Medium and dark rye flours are made from the whole rye berry after the bran is removed and have the most intense rye flavor. Rye meal is the entire rye berry milled into a flour of different granulations, most often a coarse-textured flour. Some mills refer to their rye meal as *pumpernickel flour*. Others use pumpernickel to describe dark rye flour. All rye flours have a warm, pungent flavor similar to caraway and a gray-brown color. Although rye flour contains proteins, they will not form gluten, so bread made with 100 percent rye flour will be dense and flat. Therefore, rye flour is usually blended with a high-protein wheat flour to produce a more acceptable product. Rye flour is high in the gum pentosan; the gum absorbs water so that dough made with a high percentage of rye flour tends to absorb more water and be sticky. White rye flour can be substituted successfully for up to 40 percent of wheat flour in a recipe without significant loss of volume. Medium and dark rye flours should be limited to no more than 30 percent and 20 percent of the total amount of flour, respectively.

Cornmeal is made by grinding a special type of corn known as dent, which may be yellow, white or blue. (When stone ground, cornmeal may be somewhat coarse in texture.) Cornmeal, which contains no gluten-forming proteins, is often added to breads to lend a crunchy texture. It is also sprinkled on a baker's peel to help pizza and bread slide into a hearth oven.

Oats are one of the most common grains consumed in America, usually in the form of a hot breakfast cereal. Added to bread, oats lend texture, taste and nutrition to many products. An oat groat is the whole oat kernel with only the husk removed. It contains both the bran and germ. *Steel-cut oats* are groats that are toasted and then cut into small pieces with steel blades. *Rolled oats* are groats that have been steamed, then rolled into flat flakes. *Quick-cooking oats* are simply rolled oats that are cut into smaller pieces to reduce cooking time. *Oat flour* is made from whole-grain oats, often mixed into multigrain bread doughs.

Rice flour is made from whole white or brown rice kernels that are finely ground. It contains little protein and forms no gluten. Rice flour is often used to make gluten-free baked goods. Rice flour is also used to dust hearth breads to give them a delicate crunch.

Finely ground almonds, hazelnuts, pistachios and other nuts are called **nut flours** and are used in the bakeshop. Containing no protein-forming gluten, these flours lend a delicate taste and texture to cakes and cookies in which they are added. See Chapter 5, Mise en Place, page 133. Because of their high fat content, nut flours are prone to rancidity. They should be stored under refrigeration.

Purchasing and Storing

Most flours are purchased in 50- and 100-pound bags. They should be stored in a lit, ventilated room at temperatures no higher than 80°F (27°C). Flour can be stored in a refrigerator or freezer if necessary to prevent the onset of rancidity. Refrigeration may cause the flour to absorb moisture, however, which will limit the flour's ability to absorb additional moisture during actual use. An open bag of flour should be transferred to a closed container to prevent contamination. Even unopened bags of flour should not be

Rye Flour

Cornmeal

Oats

Blanched Almond Flour

stored near items with strong odors, as flour readily absorbs odors. Whole grains should be stored in airtight containers in cool, dry, dark conditions. Coolness inhibits insect infestations; dryness prevents mold. Using airtight containers stored in darkness helps prevent nutrient loss.

SUGAR AND SWEETENERS

Sugar (Fr. *sucre*) and other sweeteners serve several purposes in the bakeshop: They *provide flavor and color, tenderize products* by weakening gluten strands, *provide food for yeasts, serve as a preservative* and *act as a creaming or foaming agent* to assist with leavening. (Artificial sweeteners are discussed in Chapter 16, Healthful and Special-Needs Baking.)

Sugar

Sugars are carbohydrates. They are classified as either (1) single or simple sugars (monosaccharides), such as glucose and fructose, which occur naturally in honey and fruits, or (2) double or complex sugars (disaccharides), which may occur naturally, such as lactose in milk, or in refined sugars. See Table 4.3.

sucrose the chemical name for common refined sugar; it is a disaccharide, composed of one molecule each of glucose and fructose

The sugar most often used in the kitchen is **sucrose**, a refined sugar obtained from both the large tropical grass called sugarcane (*Saccharum officinarum*) and the root of the sugar beet (*Beta vulgaris*). Sucrose is a disaccharide, composed of one molecule each of **glucose** and **fructose**.

The chemical composition of beet and cane sugars is identical. The two products taste, look, smell and react the same. Sucrose is available in many forms: white granulated, light or dark brown granulated, molasses and powdered.

SUGAR MANUFACTURING

Common refined or table sugar is produced from sugarcane or sugar beets. The first step in sugar production is to crush the cane or beet to extract the juice. This juice contains tannins, pigments, proteins and other undesirable components that must be removed through refinement. Refinement begins by dissolving the juice in water, then boiling it in large steam evaporators. The solution is then crystallized in heated vacuum pans. The uncrystallized liquid by-product, known as molasses, is separated out in a centrifuge. The remaining crystallized product, known as raw sugar, contains many impurities; the USDA considers it unfit for direct use in food.

Raw sugar is washed with steam to remove some of the impurities. This yields a product known as turbinado sugar. Refining continues as the turbinado is heated, liquefied, centrifuged and filtered. Chemicals may be used to bleach and purify the liquid sugar. Finally, the clear liquid sugar is recrystallized in vacuum pans as granulated white sugar.

Pure sucrose is sold in granulated and powdered forms and is available in several grades. Because there are no government standards regulating grade labels, various manufacturers' products may differ slightly.

TYPES OF SUGAR

Turbinado sugar, sometimes called Demerara sugar, is the closest consumable product to raw sugar. It is partially refined, light brown in color, with coarse crystals and a caramel flavor. It is sometimes used in beverages and certain baked goods. Because of its high and

TABLE 4.3 SUGARS	
MONOSACCHARIDES	**DISACCHARIDES**
Glucose (plant-based sugar)	Lactose (milk sugar) = glucose + galactose
Fructose (fruit sugar)	Maltose (malt sugar) = glucose + glucose
Galactose (part of milk sugar)	Sucrose (table sugar) = glucose + fructose

variable moisture content, turbinado sugar is not recommended as a substitute for granulated or brown sugar.

Sanding sugar has a large, coarse crystal structure that prevents it from dissolving easily. It is used almost exclusively for decorating cookies and pastries.

Pearl sugar (Fr. *sucre grain*) is a type of decorating sugar made by polishing large crystals until they resemble pearls.

Granulated sugar is the all-purpose sugar used throughout the kitchen. The crystals are a fine, uniform size suitable for a variety of purposes. **Sugar cubes** are formed by pressing moistened granulated sugar into molds and allowing it to dry. Most cubes are used for beverage service.

Brown sugar is simply regular refined cane sugar with some of the molasses returned to it. Light brown sugar contains approximately 3.5 percent molasses; dark brown sugar contains about 6.5 percent. Molasses adds moisture and a distinctive flavor. (A brown sugar substitute can be made by combining 1 part molasses by weight with 9 parts granulated sugar.) Brown sugar can be substituted for refined sugar, measure for measure, in any formula where its flavor is desired. Because of the added moisture, brown sugar tends to lump, trapping air into pockets. Always store brown sugar in an airtight container to prevent it from drying and hardening.

Superfine or castor sugar is granulated sugar with a smaller-sized crystal. It can be produced by processing regular granulated sugar in a food processor for a few moments. Superfine sugar dissolves quickly in liquids and produces light and tender cakes.

Powdered sugar (Fr. *sucre en poudre*) or confectioner's sugar is made by grinding granulated sugar crystals through varying degrees of fine screens. Powdered sugar cannot be made in a food processor. It is widely available in various degrees of fineness: 10× is the finest and most common; 6× and 4× are progressively coarser. Because of powdered sugar's tendency to lump, 3 percent cornstarch is added to absorb moisture. Powdered sugar is most often used in icings and glazes and for decorating baked products.

Fructose is a simple sugar (monosaccharide) that occurs naturally in honey, fruits and vegetables. Fructose is normally a liquid; however, a free-flowing crystalized fructose powder can be made from invert sugar or glucose syrup, discussed shortly. Fructose is nearly twice as sweet as sucrose. Fructose attracts more water than does sugar; therefore, fructose-sweetened products tend to be moist. Baked products made with fructose are darker than those made with sucrose.

Clockwise from top left: Demerara sugar cubes, light brown sugar, powdered sugar, sugar cubes, brown sugar crystals, granulated sugar.

Liquid Sweeteners

Except for leavening, liquid sweeteners can be used to achieve the same benefits as sugar in baked goods. Most of these liquids have a distinctive flavor as well as sweetness. Some liquid sweeteners are made from sugarcane; others are derived from other plants, grains or the activities of bees.

Corn syrup is produced by extracting starch from corn kernels and treating it with acid or an enzyme to develop a sweet syrup. This syrup is extremely thick or viscous and less sweet-tasting than honey or refined sugar. Its viscosity gives foods a thick, chewy texture. It stabilizes products made with sugar, preventing them from recrystallization. Corn syrup is available in light and dark forms; the dark syrup has caramel color and flavor added. Corn syrup is a **hygroscopic** (water-attracting) sweetener, which means it will attract water from the air on humid days and lose water through evaporation more slowly than granulated sugar. Thus, it keeps products moister and fresher longer.

Glucose syrup is a thick syrup extracted from the starch in corn, potatoes, rice or wheat in a process known as hydrolysis. Like corn syrup, glucose syrup is less sweet-tasting than sugar and is hygroscopic. It is an invert sugar widely used in the confectionery industry for its ability to prevent sugar crystallization. Light corn syrup may be used interchangeably for glucose syrup in recipes in this book.

Invert sugar is a dense sugar syrup produced by refining sucrose with an acid. When sucrose is heated and combined with an acid, it "inverts" or partially breaks down into glucose and fructose. This inversion makes it more difficult for crystals to form. Invert sugar is about 20 to 30 percent sweeter than regular sucrose, and it is extremely hygroscopic.

hygroscopic describes a food that readily absorbs moisture from the air

Glucose Syrup

Honey

Molasses

Saccharometer or Baumé hydrometer

Using a Baumé hydrometer or saccharometer.

density the relationship between the mass and volume of a substance ($D = m/v$); as more and more sugar is dissolved in a liquid, the heavier or denser the liquid will become; sugar density is measured on the Baumé scale using a saccharometer

Honey and corn syrup are naturally occurring invert sugars, and invert sugar syrup, similar to corn syrup, is available commercially. Like glucose syrup, invert sugar syrup is widely used in the confectionery industry and when making pulled sugar and other decorative sugar work.

Honey (Fr. *miel*) is a strong sweetener consisting of fructose and glucose. Honey is created by honeybees from nectar collected from flowers. Its flavor and color vary depending on the season, the type of flower the nectar came from and its age. Commercial honey is often a blend, prepared to be relatively neutral and consistent. Like corn syrup, honey is highly hygroscopic. Honey is 25 percent sweeter than sugar or sucrose. On average honey is composed of 85 percent solids and 18 percent water, unlike granulated sugar, which contains 100 percent solids. To substitute honey for sugar in a formula, some liquid in a formula must be reduced to compensate for this, keeping in mind the overall sweetening effect of the honey.

Malt syrup is a liquid sweetener produced from germinated barley or wheat grains. The enzymes (called alpha-amylase) in *diastatic* malt aid in the fermentation of many types of bread. (*Nondiastatic* malt has been heated to deactivate the enzymes while retaining the malt color and flavor.) Often European bread formulas, especially those with rye flour, include malt, which acts as a quick yeast food. Malt also enhances the elasticity of bread dough and retains moisture in the crumb. (A powdered form of malt is often used in bread making to enhance browning.)

Maple syrup is made from the sap of sugar maple trees. Sap is collected during the spring, then boiled to evaporate its water content, yielding a sweet brown syrup. One sugar maple tree produces about 12 gallons (45 liters) of sap each season; 30–40 gallons of sap produce 1 gallon of syrup. Pure maple syrup must weigh not less than 11 pounds per gallon; it is graded according to color, flavor and sugar content. The more desirable products, Grades AA and A, have a light amber color and delicate flavor. Pure maple syrup is expensive, but it adds a distinct flavor to baked goods, frostings and, of course, pancakes and waffles. Maple-flavored syrups, often served with pancakes, are usually corn syrups with artificial colorings and flavorings added.

As mentioned earlier, **molasses** (Fr. *mélasse*) is the liquid by-product of sugar refining. Edible molasses is derived only from cane sugar, as beet molasses has an unpleasant odor and bitter flavor. Unsulfured molasses is not a true by-product of sugar making. It is intentionally produced from pure cane syrup and is preferred because of its lighter color and milder flavor. Sulfured molasses is a by-product and contains some of the sulfur dioxide used in secondary sugar processing. It is darker and has a strong, bitter flavor.

The final stage of sucrose refinement yields blackstrap molasses, which is somewhat popular in the American South. Blackstrap molasses is very dark and thick, with a strong, unique flavor that is unsuitable for most purposes.

Sorghum molasses is produced by cooking down the sweet sap of a brown corn plant known as sorghum, which is grown for animal feed. The flavor and appearance of sorghum molasses, a specialty in the Southern United States, are almost identical to unsulfured sugarcane molasses.

Cooking Sugar

Sugar can be incorporated into a prepared item in its dry form or when liquefied into a syrup. Dry granulated sugar and sugar syrups are not used interchangeably, however. Granulated sugar is necessary to create the emulsion necessary for leavening cakes. **Sugar syrups** (not to be confused with liquid sweeteners such as molasses) take two forms: **simple syrups**, which are mixtures of sugar and water, and **cooked syrups**, which are made of melted sugar cooked until it reaches a specific temperature. The making and handling of liquid sugar is discussed in Chapter 13, Cakes and Icings.

Simple Sugar Syrups

Simple or stock syrups are solutions of sugar and water. Often referred to as moistening or dessert syrups, they are used to moisten cakes and to make sauces, sorbets and beverages. The syrup's **density** or concentration is dictated by its intended purpose. Cold water dissolves up to double its weight in sugar; heating the solution forms denser, more concentrated syrups. A saccharometer or hydrometer, which measures specific gravity and shows degrees of concentration from 0° to 50° on the Baumé scale, is the most accurate guide to density. In 58°F (15°C) water a saccharometer should register 0°. The higher the number, the greater the density of the solution.

Simple syrups can be prepared without the aid of a saccharometer, however. To make a simple sugar syrup, specific amounts of water and sugar are combined in a saucepan and brought to a boil. Once the solution boils, it is important not to stir, as this may cause recrystallization or lumping. For successful simple sugar syrups, the following formulas must be followed precisely.

▶ Light syrup—Boil 2 parts water with 1 part sugar by weight for 1 minute. This concentration should measure 17°–20° on the Baumé scale. A light syrup can be used for making sorbet or moistening spongecake.

▶ Medium syrup—Boil 1½ parts water with 1 part sugar by weight for 1 minute. This concentration should measure 21°–24° on the Baumé scale. A medium syrup can be used for candying citrus peel.

▶ Heavy syrup—Boil equal parts water and sugar for 1 minute. This concentration should measure 28°–30° on the Baumé scale, and the solution should be at 220°F (104°C). Heavy syrup is a basic, all-purpose syrup kept on hand in many bakeshops.

PROCEDURE FOR MAKING SIMPLE SYRUP

1 Combine measured amounts of water and sugar in a heavy saucepan. An unlined copper pan may be used.

2 Bring the mixture to a boil without stirring, to prevent the sugar from crystallizing. Boil the syrup for 1 minute or until the syrup reaches the proper density reading required for the type of syrup needed.

3 Remove the syrup from the heat. Fresh mint, tea leaves, ground coffee and other aromatics may be steeped in the syrup to flavor. Or the syrup may be flavored with an emulsion, liqueur or extract. The standard ratio of simple syrup to flavoring is 3 parts syrup to 1 part flavoring.

4 Cool, then store under refrigeration.

SIMPLE SYRUP (HEAVY)

Yield: 28 fl. oz. (840 ml)

| Water | 1 pt. | 480 ml |
| Sugar | 1 lb. | 480 g |

1 Combine the water and sugar in a heavy saucepan. Bring to a full boil.

2 Cook 1 minute or cook to temperature reading for desired syrup.

Approximate values per 1-fl.-oz. (30-ml) serving: **Calories** 80, **Total fat** 0 g, **Saturated fat** 0 g, **Cholesterol** 0 mg, **Sodium** 0 mg, **Total carbohydrates** 20 g, **Protein** 0 g

Concentrated Cooked Sugar Syrups

Meringue, buttercream, candy, caramel sauce and other confections often need liquid sugar that will be firm when cool or have a cooked caramel flavor. For these purposes, sugar needs to be cooked to temperatures far higher than for simple syrups. A small amount of water is generally added at the beginning to help the sugar dissolve evenly. As the mixture boils, the water evaporates, the solution's temperature rises and its density increases. The syrup's concentration depends on the amount of water remaining in the final solution: the less water, the harder the syrup will become when cool.

The sugar's temperature indicates its concentration. If a great deal of water is present, the temperature will not rise much above 212°F (100°C). As water evaporates, however, the temperature rises until it reaches 320°F (160°C), the point at which all water is evaporated. At temperatures above 320°F (160°C), the pure sugar begins to brown or caramelize. As sugar caramelizes, its sweetening power decreases dramatically. At approximately 375°F (191°C), sugar burns, developing a bitter flavor. If allowed to continue cooking, sugar ignites.

Sugar solutions are unstable because of their molecular structure. They can recrystallize because of agitation or uneven heat distribution. Several steps are taken to prevent recrystallization of a concentrated sugar syrup. The solution is never stirred once it comes to a boil. An interferent may be added when the solution begins to boil. Cream of tartar, vinegar, glucose syrup (a monosaccharide) and lemon juice are known as **interferents** because they interfere with the formation of sugar crystals. Some formulas specify which interferent to use, although most are used in such small quantities that their flavor cannot be detected.

Brushing down the sides of the pan with cold water washes off crystals that may be deposited there. These sugar crystals may seed the solution, causing more crystals (lumps) to form if not removed. Instead of using a brush to wash away crystals, you can cover the pan for a few moments as soon as the solution comes to a boil. Steam will condense on the cover and run down the sides of the pan, washing away the crystals.

The concentration of sugar syrup should be determined with a candy thermometer that measures very high temperatures. If a thermometer is not available, use the traditional but less accurate ice-water test: Spoon a few drops of the hot sugar into a bowl of very cold water. Check the hardness of the cooled sugar with your fingertips. Each stage of cooked sugar is named according to its firmness when cool—for example, soft ball or hard crack.

Table 4.4 lists the various stages of cooked sugar and the temperature for each. Each stage is also identified by the ice-water test result. Note that even a few degrees makes a difference in the syrup's concentration.

interferent a substance such as glucose syrup or lemon juice that helps stop sugar from recrystallizing when dissolved in a solution

Preparing cooked sugar syrups and caramel.

Brushing sugar crystals from the side of the pan.

Soft ball stage.

Hard ball stage.

Hard crack stage.

TABLE 4.4 STAGES OF COOKED SUGAR

STAGE	TEMPERATURE	ICE-WATER TEST—ONE DROP:
Thread	236°F (113°C)	Spins a 2-in. (5-cm) thread when dropped
Soft ball	240°F (116°C)	Forms a soft ball
Firm ball	246°F (119°C)	Forms a firm ball
Hard ball	260°F (127°C)	Forms a hard, compact ball
Soft crack	270°F (132°C)	Separates into a hard, but not brittle, thread
Hard crack	300°F (149°C)	Separates into a hard, brittle sheet
Caramel	338°F (170°C)	Liquid turns brown

PROCEDURE FOR PREPARING CONCENTRATED COOKED SUGAR SYRUP

1. Combine granulated sugar and a small amount of water in a heavy saucepan. An unlined copper pan may be used.

2. Stir the solution to make sure all sugar crystals dissolve before it reaches a boil. Cover the pan and bring the mixture to a boil. Do not stir the solution after it begins boiling, however.

3. Once the syrup boils, uncover the pan and add the interferent specified in the formula. Corn syrup, glucose syrup, cream of tartar or lemon juice may be used.

4. Continue cooking the syrup, brushing down the sides of the pan with a clean brush dipped in cold water to wash off crystals that may be deposited there.

5. Cook the syrup to the desired temperature, using a candy thermometer to gauge the syrup's concentration. Wash off the thermometer probe after placing in the syrup; sugar that clings to it can reseed the syrup.

CARAMEL

Sugar that cooks to the caramel stage cools to a hard crack with a distinctive golden hue and smoky flavor. Many pastries, such as croquembouche, are dipped in caramel to give their exterior a pleasing crunch. Hard caramel may be drizzled into decorative shapes on oiled parchment or silicone mats, or over oiled bowls to make a caramel cage. When cooled, the caramel is used as a garnish over custards, puddings or mousses.

When making caramel, the same care must be taken to prevent recrystallization of the syrup. Once it begins to caramelize, the syrup will brown quickly if not removed from the heat. Even removing the caramel from the heat doesn't stop browning of the sugar due to carryover cooking. Placing the pan in ice water helps cool the pan and stop caramelization. The procedure for making caramel is illustrated with the formula for Decorating Caramel (page 727). Caramel syrup, when used to dip pastries such as Merveilleux Pastries (page 422) or cream puffs for croquembouche, may include a high percentage of corn syrup or glucose syrup. These liquid sugars keep the caramel pliable longer, making dipping large numbers of pastries possible.

FATS

Fats are part of a group of natural organic compounds (**lipids**) that do not break down in the presence of water. Fats, cholesterol and lecithin are all lipids, and *fat* is the general term for butter, lard, margarine, shortening and oil. Fats *provide flavor and color, add moisture and richness, assist with leavening, help extend a product's shelf life* and *shorten gluten strands,* producing tender baked goods.

The flavor and texture of a baked good depends on the type of fat used and the manner in which it is incorporated with other ingredients. In pastry doughs, solid fat shortens

GRADING BUTTER

whole butter butter that is not clarified, whipped or reduced-fat

Lard

or tenderizes the gluten strands; in bread doughs, fat increases loaf volume and lightness; in cake batters, fat incorporates air bubbles and helps leaven the mixture. Fats should be selected based on their flavor, melting point and ability to form emulsions.

Most bakeshop ingredients combine completely with liquids; fats do not. Fats will break down into smaller and smaller particles through mixing, but they do not dissolve. With proper mixing, these fat particles are evenly dispersed throughout the other ingredients, causing fat and liquid to blend or emulsify.

Butter

Butter is a fatty substance produced by agitating or churning cream. Its flavor is unequaled in sauces, breads and pastries. Butter contains at least 80 percent milkfat, not more than 16 percent water and 2 to 4 percent milk solids. It may or may not contain added salt. Butter is firm when chilled and soft at room temperature. It melts into a liquid at approximately 93°F (34°C) and reaches the smoke point at 260°F (127°C). Butter is prized in the bakeshop for its flavor; however, its low melting point makes it difficult to handle in certain applications, and it burns easily. Working with butter at the proper temperature during mixing ensures baking success. In most applications, butter performs best between 60°F and 70°F (15°C and 21°C). Unsalted butter is preferred for baking because it tends to be fresher, and additional salt may interfere with product formulas.

Salted butter is butter with up to 2.5 percent salt added. This not only changes the butter's flavor, it also extends its keeping qualities. When salted butter is used, the salt content must be considered in the total recipe.

European-style butter contains more milkfat than regular butter, usually from 82 to 86 percent, and very little or no added salt. It is often churned from cultured cream, giving it a more intense, buttery flavor.

Whipped butter is made by incorporating air into the butter. This increases its volume and spreadability but also increases the speed with which the butter will become rancid. Because of the change in density, whipped butter should not be substituted in recipes calling for regular butter.

Clarified butter is butter that has had its water and milk solids removed by a process called clarification. Although **whole butter** can be used for cooking or sauce making, sometimes a more stable and consistent product will be achieved by using clarified butter. The clarification process is described in Chapter 5, Mise en Place.

STORAGE

Butter should be well wrapped and stored at temperatures between 32°F and 35°F (0°C and 2°C). Unsalted butter is best kept frozen until needed. If well wrapped, frozen butter will keep for up to 9 months at a temperature of 0°F (−18°C).

Lard

Lard (Fr. *saindoux*) is rendered pork fat. It is a solid white product of almost 100 percent pure fat; it contains only a small amount of water. Lard yields flaky, flavorful pastries, such as pie crusts, but it is highly prone to rancidity.

Margarine

Margarine is manufactured from animal or vegetable fats or a combination of such fats. Flavorings, colorings, emulsifiers, preservatives and vitamins are added, and the mixture is firmed or solidified by exposure to hydrogen gas at very high temperatures, a process known as hydrogenation. Generally, the firmer the margarine, the greater the degree of hydrogenation and the longer its shelf life. Like butter, margarine is approximately 80 percent fat and 16 percent water. But even the finest margarine cannot match the flavor of butter. Margarine melts at a slightly higher temperature than butter, making it useful for some rolled-in doughs such as puff pastry or Danish. Because they require higher temperatures to melt, margarine and other vegetable-based shortenings can leave a greasy taste on the tongue.

TABLE 4.5	MELTING POINT OF FATS*
Butter, clarified	92°F–98°F (33°C–36°C)
Butter, whole	92°F–98°F (33°C–36°C)
Cocoa butter	88°F–93°F (31°C–34°C)
Lard	89°F–98°F (32°C–36°C)
Margarine, solid	94°F–98°F (34°C–36°C)
Shortening, all-purpose vegetable	120°F (49°C)
Shortening, emulsified vegetable	115°F (46°C)
Shortening, heavy-duty fryer	102°F (39°C)

*The melting point of any fat depends on its specific ratio of fatty acids. Natural products such as butter and lard vary more from one lot to the next than do manufactured products such as margarine. This information was obtained from a variety of manufacturers and assumes that the fat is pure and previously unused.

Margarine packaged in tubs is softer and more spreadable than solid products and generally contains more water and air. Indeed, diet margarine is approximately 50 percent water. Because of their decreased density, these soft products should not be substituted for regular butter or margarine in baking. Specially formulated and blended margarine is available for commercial use in making puff pastry, croissant doughs, frostings and the like.

Shortenings

Any fat is a **shortening** in baking because it shortens gluten strands and tenderizes the product. What is generally referred to as shortening, however, is a type of solid, white, generally flavorless fat, specially formulated for baking. Shortenings are made from animal fats and/or vegetable oils that are solidified through **hydrogenation**. This process extends the shelf life of a fat, reducing its tendency to go rancid. These products are 100 percent fat with a relatively high melting point (see Table 4.5). Solid shortenings are ideal for greasing baking pans because they are flavorless and odorless. When substituting shortening in a formula calling for butter, additional liquid must be added to compensate for the lack of moisture in the shortening.

Emulsifiers may be added to regular shortening to assist with moisture absorption and retention as well as leavening. **Emulsified shortenings**, also known as high-ratio shortenings, are used in the commercial production of cakes and frostings where the formula contains a large amount of sugar. If a formula calls for an emulsified shortening, use it. If any other fat is substituted, the product's texture suffers.

Oils may be extracted from a variety of plants including corn, cottonseed, grapeseeds, peanuts, rapeseeds (canola), and soybeans by pressure or chemical solvents. Vegetable oils are virtually odorless and have a neutral flavor. Because they contain no animal products they are cholesterol-free. Oils extracted from a variety of nuts, including walnuts and hazelnuts, are prized for their distinctive flavors.

Unlike butter and other fats, oil blends thoroughly throughout a mixture. It therefore coats more of the proteins, and the gluten strands produced are much shorter, a desirable result in fine-textured products such as muffins or chiffon cakes. For baking, select a neutral-flavored oil unless the distinctive taste of olive oil is desired, as in some breads. Never substitute oil in a formula requiring a solid shortening.

MILK AND DAIRY PRODUCTS

Milk *provides texture, flavor, volume, color and nutritional value for cooked or baked items.* Milk in a formula contributes to browning as well as softness in the crust and structure of a baked item. Highly perishable, milk is an excellent bacterial breeding ground. Care must be exercised when handling and storing milk and other dairy products.

hydrogenation the process used to harden oils; hydrogen atoms are added to unsaturated fat molecules, making them partially or completely saturated and thus solid at room temperature

lactose a disaccharide that occurs naturally in mammalian milk; milk sugar

Whole milk—that is, milk as it comes from the cow—consists primarily of water (about 88%). It contains approximately 3.5% milkfat and 8.5% other milk solids (proteins, milk sugar [**lactose**] and minerals).

Whole milk is graded A, B or C according to standards recommended by the U.S. Public Health Service. Grades are assigned based on bacterial count, with Grade A products having the lowest count. Grades B and C, though still safe and wholesome, are rarely available for retail or commercial use. Fresh whole milk is not available raw, but must be processed as we describe shortly.

Processing Techniques

PASTEURIZATION

By law, all Grade A milk must be pasteurized prior to retail sale. Pasteurization is the process of heating something to a sufficiently high temperature for a sufficient length of time to destroy pathogenic bacteria. This typically requires holding milk at a temperature of 161°F (72°C) for 15 seconds. Pasteurization also destroys enzymes that cause spoilage, thus increasing shelf life. Milk's nutritional value is not significantly affected by pasteurization.

ULTRA-PASTEURIZATION

Ultra-pasteurization is a process in which milk is heated to a very high temperature (275°F/135°C) for a very short time (2 to 4 seconds) in order to destroy virtually all bacteria. Ultra-pasteurization is most often used with whipping cream and individual creamers. Although the process may reduce cream's whipping properties, it extends its shelf life dramatically.

ULTRA-HIGH-TEMPERATURE PROCESSING

Ultra-high-temperature (UHT) processing is a form of ultra-pasteurization in which milk is held at a temperature of 280°F–300°F (138°C–149°C) for 2 to 6 seconds. It is then packed in sterile containers under sterile conditions and aseptically sealed to prevent bacteria from entering the container. Unopened UHT milk can be stored without refrigeration for at least three months. Although UHT milk can be stored unrefrigerated, it should be chilled before serving and stored like fresh milk once opened. UHT processing may give milk a slightly cooked taste, but it has no significant effect on milk's nutritional value. Long available in Europe, it is now gaining popularity in the United States.

HOMOGENIZATION

Homogenization is a process in which the fat globules in whole milk are reduced in size and permanently dispersed throughout the liquid. This prevents the fat from clumping together and rising to the surface as a layer of cream. Although homogenization is not required, milk sold commercially is generally homogenized to ensure a uniform consistency, a whiter color and a richer taste.

MILKFAT REMOVAL

Whole milk can also be processed in a centrifuge to remove all or a portion of the milkfat, resulting in reduced-fat, low-fat and nonfat milks. Reduced-fat or less-fat milk is whole milk from which sufficient milkfat has been removed to produce a liquid with 2% milkfat. Low-fat or little-fat milk contains 1% milkfat. Nonfat milk, also referred to as fat-free, no-fat or skim milk, has had as much milkfat removed as possible. The fat content must be less than 0.5%. *Nonfat milk should not be substituted for whole milk in most baked-good formulas without the addition of fat to compensate for that removed.*

Pasteurized milk needs to be heated to 200°F (93°C) to destroy certain milk enzymes that are known to weaken gluten structure, resulting in sticky, difficult-to-handle dough. For convenience, dry milk powder is often used instead because it requires no heating and is easily stored. Yogurt, buttermilk and UHT milk require no preheating to destroy this enzyme.

TRANS FATS

Hydrogenated fat is less prone to rancidity and has a longer shelf life than nonhydrogenated fat. For these reasons, it has been used in abundance in the food manufacturing industry. But the hydrogenation process also results in the formation of *trans* fats, considered a risk factor for heart disease and possibly other diseases such as cancer. The food ingredient industry is working hard to find ways to provide the same functional benefits to fats as hydrogenation without adding the deleterious *trans* fats in the process. Low-*trans*-fat options include tropical fats and oils such as those made from coconut, palm and palm kernels. Vegetable oils that are not hydrogenated typically contain less than 1.5 percent *trans* fat. Manufacturers are working with canola, corn, soybean and other blends to make *trans*-fat-free solid shortenings. Check with major edible oil producers as well as your bakery ingredient supplier for suitable substitutes.

SAFETY ALERT
Milk Storage

Canned milks, aseptically packaged milks and dry milk powders are shelf-stable products needing no refrigeration. After the can or box is opened or the powder is reconstituted with water, however, these become potentially hazardous foods and must be handled just as carefully as fresh milk. Do not store an open can of milk in its original container, and keep all milk products refrigerated at or below 40°F (4°C).

STORAGE

Fluid milk is a potentially hazardous food and should be kept refrigerated at or below 40°F (4°C). Its shelf life is reduced by half for every 5-degree rise in temperature above 40°F (4°C). Keep milk containers closed to prevent absorption of odors and flavors. Freezing is not recommended.

Concentrated Milks

Concentrated milks or condensed milk products are produced by using a vacuum to remove all or part of the water from whole milk. The resulting products have a high concentration of milkfat and milk solids and an extended shelf life.

Evaporated milk is produced by removing approximately 60 percent of the water from whole, homogenized milk. The concentrated liquid is canned and heat-sterilized. This results in a cooked flavor and darker color. Evaporated skim milk, with a milkfat content of 0.5%, is also available. A can of evaporated milk requires no refrigeration until opened, although the can should be stored in a cool place. Evaporated milk can be reconstituted with an equal amount of water and used like whole milk for cooking or drinking.

Sweetened condensed milk is similar to evaporated milk in that 60 percent of the water has been removed. But unlike evaporated milk, sweetened condensed milk contains large amounts of sugar (40 to 45 percent). Sweetened condensed milk is also canned; the canning process darkens the color and adds a caramel flavor. Sweetened condensed milk cannot be substituted for whole milk or evaporated milk because of its sugar content. Its distinctive flavor is most often found in puddings, fudge and other confections.

Dry milk powder is made by removing virtually all the moisture from pasteurized milk. Dry whole milk, nonfat milk and buttermilk are available. The lack of moisture prevents the growth of microorganisms and allows dry milk powders to be stored for extended periods without refrigeration. Powdered milks can be reconstituted with water and used like fresh milk. Milk powder may also be added to foods directly, with additional liquid included in the recipe. This procedure is typical in bread making and does not alter the function of the milk or its flavor in the finished product.

Cream

Cream is a rich, liquid milk product containing at least 18% fat. It must be pasteurized or ultra-pasteurized and may be homogenized. Cream has a slight yellow or ivory color and is more viscous than milk. It is used throughout the kitchen to give flavor and body to sauces, soups and desserts. Cream is marketed in several forms with different fat contents, as described here.

Half-and-half is a mixture of whole milk and cream containing between 10 percent and 18 percent milkfat. It is often served with cereal or coffee but does not contain enough fat to whip into a foam.

Light cream, **coffee cream** and **table cream** are all products with more than 18 percent but less than 30 percent milkfat. These products are often used in baked goods or soups as well as with coffee, fruit and cereal.

Light whipping cream or, simply, whipping cream, contains between 30% and 36% milkfat. It is generally used for thickening and enriching sauces and making ice cream. It can be whipped into a foam and used as a dessert topping or folded into custards or mousses to add flavor and lightness.

Heavy whipping cream or, simply, **heavy cream**, contains not less than 36% milkfat. It whips easily and holds its whipped texture longer than other creams. It must be pasteurized, but is rarely homogenized. Ultra-pasteurized heavy cream has a longer shelf life than regular pasteurized cream but does not whip as easily. Vegetable gums are added to compensate. Heavy cream is used throughout the kitchen in the same ways as light whipping cream.

Clotted cream is a thick spreadable cream with 55% milkfat made from unpasteurized whole milk. The milk is heated, and then the thick cream clumps and floats to the top when the milk cools, and the dense clotted cream is removed. It is served as a spread or filling for scones, cakes and other pastries. Clotted cream is also referred to as Devon or Devonshire cream, named for two English counties where it is made.

BUTTERMILK IN A PINCH

To make a buttermilk substitute when none is available, combine 8 fluid ounces (240 milliliters) whole milk with ½ fluid ounce (15 milliliters) white vinegar or lemon juice. The mixture should begin to curdle in 15 minutes. Stir well before using. Combining 2 fluid ounces (60 milliliters) whole milk with 6 fluid ounces (180 milliliters) plain yogurt also works as a buttermilk substitute.

STORAGE

Ultra-pasteurized cream will keep for 6 to 8 weeks if refrigerated at or below 40°F (4°C). Unwhipped cream should not be frozen. Keep cream away from strong odors and bright lights, as they can adversely affect its flavor.

Cultured Dairy Products

Cultured dairy products such as yogurt, buttermilk and sour cream are produced by adding specific bacterial cultures to fluid dairy products. The bacteria convert the milk sugar lactose into lactic acid, which causes the proteins to coagulate, giving these products their body and tangy, unique flavors. The acid content also retards the growth of undesirable microorganisms; thus cultured products have been used for centuries to preserve milk. With their mild acidity, these products are most often used in baked goods for their distinctive taste.

Buttermilk originally referred to the liquid remaining after cream was churned into butter. Today, buttermilk is produced by adding lactic acid bacteria (*Streptococcus lactis*) to fresh, pasteurized skim or low-fat milk. This results in a tart milk with a thick texture.

Sour cream is produced by adding the lactic acid bacteria to pasteurized, homogenized light cream. The resulting product is a white, tangy gel used to give baked goods a distinctive flavor. Sour cream must have a milkfat content of not less than 18%.

Crème fraîche is a cultured cream popular in French cuisine. Although thinner and richer than sour cream, it has a similar tart, tangy flavor and adds depth of flavor when added to chilled custard sauces and for ice cream base. It is easily prepared using the recipe on this page.

Yogurt is a thick, tart product made from milk (either whole, low-fat or nonfat) cultured with *Lactobacillus bulgaricus* and *Streptococcus thermophilus*. Though touted as a health or diet food, yogurt contains the same amount of milkfat as the milk from which it is made. Yogurt may also contain a variety of sweeteners, flavorings and fruits. Yogurt may be used in baked products and frozen desserts. Greek yogurt is a more creamy and dense style of yogurt, made by straining more of the whey from the product. (Authentic Greek yogurt is often made with sheep's milk.)

CRÈME FRAÎCHE

Yield: 1 pint (500 ml)

Heavy cream	16 fl. oz.	500 ml
Buttermilk, with active cultures	1 fl. oz.	30 ml

1. Heat the cream (preferably not ultra-pasteurized) to approximately 100°F (38°C).
2. Remove the cream from the heat and stir in the buttermilk.
3. Allow the mixture to stand in a warm place, loosely covered, until it thickens, approximately 12 to 36 hours.
4. Chill thoroughly before using. Crème fraîche will keep for up to 10 days in the refrigerator.

Approximate values per 1-oz. (30-g) serving: **Calories** 90, **Total fat** 10 g, **Saturated fat** 6 g, **Cholesterol** 35 mg, **Sodium** 10 mg, **Total carbohydrates** 1 g, **Protein** 1 g, **Vitamin A** 10%, **Claims**—very low sodium

STORAGE

Cultured products are potentially hazardous foods and should be kept refrigerated at or below 40°F (4°C). Under proper conditions, sour cream lasts up to 4 weeks, yogurt up to 3 weeks and buttermilk up to 2 weeks. Freezing is not recommended for these products, but dishes prepared with cultured products generally can be frozen.

Cheeses

Cheese (Fr. *fromage*; It. *formaggio*) is one of the oldest and most widely used foods known to humans. It is ideal served alone with bread or in many bakeshop preparations including cakes, breads and other baked goods. Cheese starts with a mammal's milk; cows, goats and sheep are the most commonly used. The milk proteins (known as **casein**) are coagulated with the addition of an enzyme, usually **rennet**, which is found in calves' stomachs. As the milk coagulates, it separates into solid curds and liquid whey. After draining off the whey, either the curds are made into fresh cheese, such as ricotta or cottage cheese, or the curds are further processed by cutting, kneading and cooking. The resulting substance, known as "green cheese," is packed into molds to drain. Salt or special bacteria may be added to the molded cheeses, which are then allowed to age or ripen under controlled conditions to develop the desired texture, color and flavor.

> **casein** the predominant protein in milk
>
> **rennet** a coagulating enzyme, harvested from the stomachs of calves, used to make cheese; also used to describe any enzyme used for the coagulation of milk

Some cheeses, such as Brie or Camembert, develop a natural rind or surface because of the application of bacteria (bloomy rind) or by repeated washing with brine (washed rind). Most natural rinds may be eaten if desired. Other cheeses, such as Gouda and Cheddar, are coated with an inedible wax rind to prevent moisture loss. Fresh cheeses have no rind whatsoever.

Moisture and fat contents are good indicators of a cheese's texture and shelf life. The higher the moisture content, the softer the product and the more perishable it will be. Low-moisture cheeses such as Parmigiano-Reggiano and pecorino romano may be used for grating and will keep for several weeks if properly stored. (Reduced water activity levels prohibit bacterial growth.) Fat content ranges from low fat (less than 20 percent fat) to double cream (at least 60 percent fat) and triple cream (at least 72 percent fat). Cheeses with a high fat content will be creamier and have a richer flavor and texture than low-fat products.

FRESH OR UNRIPENED CHEESES

Fresh cheeses are uncooked and unripened with many uses in sweet and savory bakeshop preparations. Referred to as *fromage blanc* or *fromage frais* in French, they are generally mild and creamy with a tart tanginess. They should not taste acidic or bitter. Fresh cheeses have a moisture content of 40 to 80 percent and are highly perishable. Fresh cheeses have no rind. A few of the more common fresh cheeses used in the bakeshop are featured here.

Cream cheese is a soft cow's-milk cheese containing approximately 35 percent fat. It is available in various-sized solid white blocks or whipped and flavored. A popular spread for bagels and toast, cream cheese is used in cheesecakes, pastry fillings and icings. Cream cheese and other soft, fresh or unripened cheeses should be gently softened before blending them into fillings, icings and batters. Blend the cheese on low speed with a paddle to soften and remove lumps before adding sugar, eggs or other liquid ingredients.

Farmer's cheese, **baker's cheese**, and **quark** are traditional, fresh soft cheeses made from cow's milk with a light taste and a smooth texture. They may be used interchangeably. Quark, German for "curd," is like a cross between mild cream and cream cheese. If quark is not available, substitute an equal amount of farmer's cheese, baker's cheese, or cream cheese. Add enough milk to soften the cheese to a yogurtlike consistency. Yogurt may also be used in place of quark.

Mascarpone (mas-cahr-POHN-ay) is a soft cow's-milk cheese originally from Italy's Lombard region. It contains 70–75 percent fat and is extremely smooth and creamy. Mascarpone is highly perishable and is available in bulk or in 8- or 16-ounce tubs. With its pale ivory color and rich, sweet flavor, it is useful in sweet sauces, ice creams and fillings.

Ricotta (rih-COH-tah) is a soft Italian cheese, similar to American cottage cheese, made from the whey left when other cow's-milk cheeses are produced. It contains only 4–10 percent fat. It is white or ivory in color and fluffy, with a small grain and sweet flavor. Ricotta is an important ingredient in Italian cheesecake and as a filling for cannoli pastries. It can be made easily with the following recipe.

Mascarpone

RICOTTA CHEESE

THE ART INSTITUTE OF WASHINGTON, ARLINGTON, VA
Chef John Harrison

Yield: 8 oz. (240 g)

| Milk | 1 qt. | 960 ml |
| Fresh lime juice | 3 fl. oz. | 90 ml |

1. Allow the milk to reach room temperature in a covered container.
2. In a stainless steel saucepan slowly heat the milk to 180°F (82°C), stirring often. Hold the heated milk at 180°F (82°C) for 5 minutes.
3. Remove the milk from the heat and gently stir it while adding the lime juice. Continue to stir until curds form.
4. Gently pour the curds into a strainer or china cap lined with new, rinsed cheesecloth. Allow the whey (liquid) to separate and drain away from the curds (solids). Discard the whey.
5. Allow the cheese to rest undisturbed for 1 hour. For a firm, dry ricotta, lift the corners of the cheesecloth and tie them together with twine. Suspend the bag in a tall, covered container, place it in the refrigerator and allow the cheese to drain for 4 hours or overnight.
6. Unwrap the cheese. Season it with salt if desired. Use the cheese as you would use commercially produced ricotta.

Approximate values per 1-oz. (30-g) serving: **Calories** 80, **Total fat** 4 g, **Saturated fat** 2.5 g, **Cholesterol** 15 mg, **Sodium** 60 mg, **Total carbohydrates** 7 g, **Protein** 4 g, **Calcium** 15%

1 Heat the milk to 180°F (82°C).

2 Gently stir in the lime juice.

3 Strain the mixture through cheesecloth.

4 The finished ricotta.

STORAGE

Most cheeses are best kept refrigerated, well wrapped to keep odors out and moisture in. Firm and hard cheeses can be kept for several weeks; fresh cheeses will spoil in 7 to 10 days because of their high moisture content. Some cheeses that have become hard or dry may still be grated for cooking or baking. Freezing is possible but not recommended because it changes the cheese's texture, making it mealy or tough.

EGGS

Eggs *flavor, leaven and thicken items* in the bakeshop. They *enrich and tenderize yeast breads* and *extend the shelf life* of some baked goods.

COMPOSITION

The primary parts of an egg are the shell, yolk and albumen. See Figure 4.2. The **shell**, composed of calcium carbonate, is the outermost covering of the egg. It helps prevent microbes from entering and moisture from escaping and also protects the egg during handling and transport. The shell is somewhat porous, however, and can absorb odors and flavors. The breed of the hen determines shell color; for chickens, it can range from bright white to brown. Shell color has no effect on quality, flavor or nutrition.

The **yolk** is the yellow portion of the egg. It constitutes just over one-third of the egg and contains three-fourths of the calories, most of the minerals and vitamins and all the fat. The yolk also contains *lecithin*, the compound responsible for emulsification in products such as sabayon sauce and French buttercream icing. Egg yolk solidifies (coagulates) at temperatures between 149°F and 158°F (65°C and 70°C). Although the color of a yolk may vary depending on the hen's feed, color does not affect quality or nutritional content.

The **albumen** is the clear portion of the egg and is often referred to as the egg white. It constitutes about two-thirds of the egg and contains more than half of the protein and riboflavin. Consisting of both a thick area closest to the yolk and a thin area closest to the shell, an egg white thins as the egg ages. When cooked, egg white coagulates, becoming firm and opaque, at temperatures between 144°F and 149°F (62°C and 65°C).

An often-misunderstood portion of the egg is the **chalazae cords**. These thick, twisted strands of egg white anchor the yolk in place. They are neither imperfections nor embryos. The more prominent the chalazae, the fresher the egg. Chalazae do not interfere with cooking or with whipping egg whites. Table 4.6 lists the composition of fresh eggs.

Eggs are sold in Jumbo, Extra Large, Large, Medium, Small and Peewee sizes, as determined by weight per dozen. (See Figure 4.3.) Food service operations generally use Large eggs, which weigh 24 ounces per dozen including the shell. Other sizes are based on plus

AVERAGE WEIGHT OF LARGE EGG, SHELLED	
Whole egg	1.6 oz. (50 g)
White	1 oz. (30 g)
Yolk	0.6 oz. (20 g)

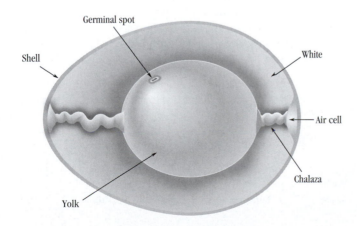

FIGURE 4.2 ▶ An egg.

TABLE 4.6	COMPOSITION OF FRESH EGGS		
	WHOLE EGG	ALBUMEN	YOLK
Moisture	76%	87%	52%
Protein	12%	11%	16%
Fat	10%	<1%	30%
Other components (ash and sugar)	2%	2%	2%

ROAMING POULTRY

Free range refers to chickens that are allowed to roam freely in the farmyard as opposed to living in cages. *Free-range eggs* are produced from such chickens. The USDA has no standards regulating the term *free-range*, however. Some producers may add the term *cage-free* to indicate that the birds were not confined. Though this term is not regulated, companies must apply to the Food Safety and Inspection Service of the USDA for permission to use this term; laying operations are not actually inspected.

Grade AA

Grade A

Grade B

or minus 3 ounces per dozen; Medium eggs weigh 21 ounces per dozen, and Extra Large eggs weigh 27 ounces per dozen. All recipes in this book call for large eggs. The average weight of a large egg once shelled is 1.6 ounces (50 grams). A large egg white weighs 1 ounce (30 grams) and a large egg yolk weighs 0.6 ounce (20 grams).

GRADING

Eggs are **graded** by the USDA or a state agency following USDA guidelines. The grade AA, A or B is given to an egg based on interior and exterior quality, not size. The qualities for each grade are described in Table 4.7. Grade has no effect on nutritional values.

STORAGE

Improper handling quickly diminishes egg quality. Eggs should be stored at temperatures below 45°F (7°C) and at a relative humidity of 70 to 80 percent. Eggs age more during one day at room temperature than during one week under proper refrigeration. As eggs age, the white becomes thinner and the yolk becomes flatter. Although this changes the appearance of poached or fried eggs, age has little effect on nutrition or behavior during cooking procedures.

   Do not use dirty, cracked or broken eggs, as they may contain bacteria or other contaminants. Cartons of fresh, uncooked eggs will keep for at least 4 to 5 weeks beyond the pack date if properly refrigerated. Hard-cooked eggs left in their shells and refrigerated should be used within 1 week. Store eggs away from strongly flavored foods to reduce odor absorption. Rotate egg stock to maintain freshness. Frozen eggs should be thawed in the refrigerator and used only in dishes that will be thoroughly cooked, such as baked products.

SANITATION

Eggs are a potentially hazardous food. Rich in protein, they are an excellent breeding ground for bacteria. Salmonella is of particular concern with eggs and egg products because the bacteria are commonly found in a chicken's intestinal tract. Although shells are cleaned at packinghouses, some bacteria may remain. Therefore, to prevent contamination, it is best to avoid mixing a shell with the liquid egg.

   Inadequately cooking or improperly storing eggs may lead to food-borne illnesses. USDA guidelines indicate that pasteurization is achieved when the whole egg stays at a temperature of 140°F (60°C) for 3½ minutes. Custards thickened with eggs and ice cream

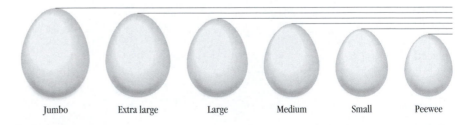

Jumbo   Extra large   Large   Medium   Small   Peewee

FIGURE 4.3 ▶ Egg sizes.

TABLE 4.7 EGG GRADES			
	GRADE AA	**GRADE A**	**GRADE B**
Spread*	Remains compact	Spreads slightly	Spreads over wide area
Albumen	Clear, thick and firm; prominent chalazae	Clear and reasonably firm; prominent chalazae	Clear; weak or watery
Yolk	Firm; centered; stands round and high; free from defects	Firm; stands fairly high; practically free from defects	Enlarged and flattened; may show slight defects
Shell	Clean; of normal shape; unbroken	Clean; of normal shape; unbroken	Slight stains permissible; abnormal shape; unbroken
Use	Any use, especially frying, poaching and cooking in shell		Baking; scrambling, used in bulk egg products

*Spread refers to the appearance of the egg when first broken onto a flat surface.

products are especially fertile breeding grounds for bacteria. Heat these products above 145°F (63°C). Chill these products over an ice bath as soon as they are made and keep them refrigerated below 40°F (4°C).

Egg Products

Bakeries and large food service operations often want the convenience of buying eggs out of the shell in the exact form needed: whole eggs, yolks only or whites only. These processed items are called **egg products** and are subject to strict pasteurization standards and USDA inspections. **Pasteurized eggs** are recommended when the preparation requiring eggs will not be cooked, such as for an unbaked meringue pie topping (see page 374). Egg products offer a consistent product with no loss due to breakage. Because they do not need cracking, they can be labor saving and take up less space than shell eggs.

Egg products are available in frozen, refrigerated or dried forms. Frozen and refrigerated whole eggs and whites may be used interchangeably with fresh eggs and whites weight for weight. Frozen egg yolks contain up to 10 percent sugar or glucose to prevent separation during freezing. It is recommended that the amount of sugar in a formula be reduced when using frozen sugared yolks. For example, when a formula calls for 10 ounces (300 grams) of egg yolks, reduce the sugar in the formula by 1 ounce (30 grams) when using sugared frozen yolks (10 ounces sugared yolks × 10% = 1 ounce). Frozen egg products should be thawed under refrigeration for up to 48 hours, then stirred before using. Plain dried egg products need to be reconstituted in water before use according to the manufacturer's directions, although dried egg whites are often added to liquid egg whites to stabilize egg foams when making meringues. Some dried egg products contain additional ingredients to aid whipping and to compensate for changes to the product during drying. Follow the manufacturer's directions when reconstituting these products. Dried egg product must be stored under refrigeration.

Concerns about the cholesterol content of eggs have increased the popularity of **egg substitutes**. There are two general types of substitutes. The first is a complete substitute made from soy or milk proteins. It should not be used in recipes where eggs are required for thickening. The second substitute contains real albumen, but the egg yolk has been replaced with vegetable or milk products. Egg substitutes have a different flavor from real eggs but may be useful for people on a restricted diet.

Whipped Egg Whites

Egg whites are often whipped into a foam that is then incorporated into cakes, custards, soufflés, pancakes and other products. The air beaten into the egg foam gives products lightness and assists with leavening.

> **SAFETY ALERT**
> **Eggs**
>
> Never leave an egg dish at room temperature for more than 1 hour, including preparation and service time. Never reuse a container after it has held raw eggs without thoroughly cleaning and sanitizing it.

PROCEDURE FOR WHIPPING EGG WHITES

1. Use fresh egg whites that are completely free of egg yolk and other impurities. Warm the egg whites to room temperature before whipping; this helps a better foam to form.

2. Use a clean bowl and whisk. Even a tiny amount of fat can prevent the egg whites from foaming properly.

3. Whip the whites until very foamy, then add salt or cream of tartar as directed.

4. Continue whipping until soft peaks form, then gradually add granulated sugar as directed.

5. Whip until stiff peaks form. Properly whipped egg whites should be moist and shiny; overwhipping will make the egg whites appear dry and spongy or curdled.

6. Use the whipped egg whites immediately. If liquid begins to separate from the whipped egg whites, discard them; they cannot be rewhipped successfully.

1. Egg whites whipped to soft peaks.

2. Egg whites whipped to stiff peaks.

3. Spongy, overwhipped egg whites.

THICKENERS

Starches

Starches are often used as *thickening agents* in bakeshop products. Starches are long complex carbohydrates, chains of sugar molecules, found in most plant materials. Starch molecules are either **amylose**, which forms long straight chains, or **amylopectin**, which forms branched chains. Functionally, starches high in amylose tend to form firm gels that are cloudy when cool. They are thicker when cold than when hot and often break down and "weep" liquid when frozen or stored. Starches high in amylopectin thicken without gelling into relatively clear products. Such products tend to retain their texture without weeping whether hot or cold and do not break down during freezing.

Starch granules, which vary in size and shape, are found or extracted from cereal grains and root vegetables. Grain starches tend to be high in amylose. **Cornstarch** is a grain-based starch. It must be dissolved in cold water, then added to a mixture to be thickened. Once it reaches just below the boiling point, it must be cooked for 3 minutes to thicken into an opaque gel. Cornstarch is used when a firm set is desired, such as for cream pies. Products thickened with cornstarch should not be vigorously stirred once cooled, or they can break down and soften. They also tend to separate when thawed after freezing. **Waxy maize** is a starch made from a special type of corn with desirable qualities. It is usually treated or "modified" so that it is stable whether heated or frozen. Modified food starches may require cooking or may be added directly to cold mixtures. They are generally used in the production of frozen foods.

Root starches come from any number of tuberous plants such as potatoes. Most are higher in amylopectin than cereal starches; therefore they produce a clearer gel with a softer texture. **Arrowroot** is extracted from the root of a tropical herb that is ground into a fine powder. Arrowroot is dissolved in cold water and added to a liquid to thicken it. Used primarily to thicken hot sauces, arrowroot can break down if overcooked, making it most appropriate for thickening sauces that will be served immediately. **Tapioca** is a starch produced from the root of the tropical cassava (manioc or yuca) plant. It is available as a flour or as balls, referred to as pearls. Tapioca flour can be used in the same manner as cornstarch to thicken sauces, fruit pies and fruit mixtures. Pearl tapioca is used to thicken milk for tapioca pudding or to thicken fruit pie fillings. Most pearl tapioca must be soaked in a cold liquid for several hours before cooking. Instant tapioca, which is smaller, needs to soak for only 20 to 30 minutes before cooking.

Starches for pies are discussed in more detail on page 373.

Pearl Tapioca

Gelatin

One of the most commonly used thickeners in the bakeshop is **gelatin**, a natural, water-soluble product derived from collagen, an animal protein. When moistened and then cooled, the protein in gelatin bonds into long strands, which form a web that entraps liquids. Gelatin will either thicken a liquid or, when present in large quantities, bond it into a solid mass. Gelatin is available in two forms: granulated gelatin and sheet (also called leaf) gelatin. A two-step process is necessary to use either form; the gelatin must first be softened in a cold liquid, **bloomed**, then dissolved in a hot liquid. For best results, gelatin should not be added to a liquid above 140°F (60°C) because it may lose gelling strength at higher temperatures.

bloom to soften granulated gelatin in a liquid before melting and using

Gelatin is classified according to bloom rating, a measurement of the gel strength of the product. Most granulated gelatin available to pastry chefs has an average **bloom strength** of 230. The bloom strength of sheet gelatin varies according to the type of sheet, from "platinum" sheets with a bloom rating of 250 to "bronze" sheets with a bloom rating of 130.

Granulated gelatin is available in bulk or in ¼-ounce (7-gram) envelopes (slightly less than 1 tablespoon). One quarter ounce (one envelope) is enough to set 16 fluid ounces (474 milliliters) of liquid into a firm gel for aspic or decorating or 24 fluid ounces (709 milliliters) of liquid into a softer mousse consistency. Granulated gelatin should be softened in six times its weight of cold liquid for at least 5 minutes, then heated gently to dissolve. The initial softening in a cold liquid is necessary to separate the gelatin molecules so that they will not lump together when the hot liquid is added. Melting over a double boiler prevents scorching.

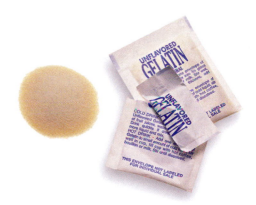

Granulated Gelatin

Sheet or **leaf gelatin** is available in 1-kilogram boxes, sometimes further packaged in envelopes containing five or six sheets. Manufacturers label sheet gelatin platinum, gold, silver or bronze corresponding in descending order to their bloom strength (250 for platinum; 130 for bronze). The thicknesses and weights of sheet gelatin vary according to the bloom strength. Manufacturers have standardized gelatin sheets so that they can be used interchangeably. Four sheets of gelatin is enough to set 16 fluid ounces (474 milliliters) of liquid into a firm gel for aspic or decorating or 24 fluid ounces (709 milliliters) of liquid into a softer mousse consistency. Higher-grade platinum or gold gelatin sheets are preferred because they solidify and set more quickly; a small quantity is required and they have a lighter color and less odor and taste. Before using, leaves of sheet gelatin must be separated and soaked in ice water until very soft, at least 15 minutes. They are then removed from the water, squeezed to remove excess moisture and stirred into a hot liquid until completely dissolved. When sheet gelatin is added to a hot liquid, it is not necessary to melt it first.

Granulated and sheet gelatin can be used interchangeably in any formula. However, it is recommended to test a formula before converting from one type or brand of gelatin to another. Adjustments in the amount of gelatin required for the desired results may be needed. Sheet gelatin, though more expensive, is preferred for its lack of flavor and color. It also tends to dissolve more readily and evenly and has a longer shelf life than the granulated form. Once incorporated into a product such as a Bavarian, gelatin can be frozen, or melted and reset once or twice, without a loss of thickening ability. Because it scorches easily, gelatin and mixtures containing gelatin should not be allowed to boil. Products thickened with gelatin, such as mousse or custard, can become rubbery after a few days in the refrigerator.

TABLE 4.8	GELATIN EQUIVALENCIES
TYPE	QUANTITY
Granulated Gelatin	0.25 oz. (7 g) will set 16 fl. oz. (474 ml) firm for aspic or cutting
	0.25 oz. (7 g) will set 24 fl. oz. (709 ml) soft for mousse, chiffon or creams
Sheet Gelatin	4 Sheets will set 16 fl. oz. (474 ml) firm for aspic or cutting
	4 Sheets will set 24 fl. oz. (709 ml) soft for mousse, chiffon or creams

Note: When substituting granulated gelatin for sheet gelatin:

1. Determine the weight of granulated gelatin called for in the formula.

2. Multiply the quantity of sheet gelatin called for in the formula by 6. This is the amount of water needed to bloom the granulated gelatin.

PROCEDURE FOR USING SHEET GELATIN

❶ Gelatin sheets are submerged in ice water for several minutes to soften.

❷ Softened gelatin sheets are then removed from the ice water and incorporated into a hot liquid.

SUBSTITUTING GRANULATED AND SHEET GELATIN

When sheet gelatin is specified in formulas in this book, the number of sheets is listed. The weight of granulated gelatin to be used is also listed. Additional water in which to bloom the granulated gelatin will be required, however. When substituting sheet gelatin in a formula that calls for granulated gelatin, use the equivalencies in Table 4.8 to determine the number of sheets of gelatin to use. Then simply submerge the sheet gelatin in ice water until it is soft and pliable. Drain the sheets and add them to the warm liquid to melt. Additional water will not be required to bloom the gelatin. To calculate how much water to eliminate from the formula, multiply the weight of granulated gelatin called for by 6. Reduce the liquid in the formula by that amount. For example, if the formula calls for ½ ounce (15 grams) of granulated gelatin, reduce the water by 3 fluid ounces (90 milliliters). [6 × ½ ounce (15 grams) = 3 fluid ounces (90 milliliters).]

To substitute granulated gelatin for sheet gelatin, additional water will be needed to dissolve the gelatin. First determine the weight of granulated gelatin needed using Table 4.8. To calculate how much water will be required to soften the granulated gelatin, multiply the weight of the gelatin by 6. To add the granulated gelatin, first let the granulated gelatin bloom (soften) in that amount of water. Then melt the softened granulated gelatin over very low heat and add it to the recipe. For example, if the recipe calls for "Sheet gelatin, 8 sheets, softened," bloom ½ ounce (15 grams) granulated gelatin in 3 fluid ounces (90 milliliters) water, then melt the gelatin over low heat and continue with the formula.

CONTEMPORARY PASTRY INGREDIENT AND EQUIPMENT TRENDS

Pastry chefs have long been known for their ability with formulas and technical precision. Frequently pastry recipes involve "industrial" ingredients, including many of the family now referred to as hydrocolloids, which help control the flow of water. Pâte de Fruit is a great example of a classic technique that takes advantage of the relationship among pectin, sugar and acid to control texture.

The trends in contemporary cooking, which have favored the continued exploration of these ingredients, are likely to become even more prevalent, just like baking soda, cornstarch and gelatin before them. Some of my favorite ingredients are methylcellulose of various grades, modified tapioca starches, isolated soy proteins, diverse gums, pectin and innovative gelling agents.

For me, this family of ingredients offers a natural solution to flavor enhancement. I am able to deliver flavor with great purity as well as control the texture to influence the finished products' taste, balance and aesthetic. For example, isolated soy protein can be used to create an ultra-flavorful and light "meringue"-type consistency, without the need for any animal product. Further, for consistency and efficiency, as well as economic concerns, the pastry chef would be well advised to learn as much about as many ingredients as possible.

The modern pastry kitchen is similar to the traditional pastry kitchen for the most part. The "toys" that have been developed in recent years are generally for supplemental flourishes. Items like whipping cream canisters, digital jewelers' scales and vacuum sealers are quite prevalent.

The Paco Jet, dehydrators and blast chillers are more frequently found whereas liquid nitrogen, rotary evaporators and the Hold-o-mat are still rare. But what I really can't live without in my kitchen are my quenelle spoons and a small palette knife.

The most important thing in pastry is an understanding of basic technique. Upon achieving a comfort level with traditional methods, the pastry chef may choose to investigate other "contemporary" techniques. It is important to balance the needs of the guest, which include being satisfied and receiving value, with experimentation. I always like to use one very classic item in a dessert with one that features something modern to make sure that I have provided pleasure.

—Will Goldfarb, Owner of Willpowder and Willequipped

Vegetable Gums

Vegetable gums such as pectin, agar and carrageenan bind water and are used to produce thick liquids and solid gels. Like starches, gums are a type of carbohydrate that absorbs large quantities of liquid. **Pectin** is one of the more familiar gums used in the bakeshop. Derived from fruits such as apples and citrus, pectin forms clear, tender gels and is especially useful for setting jams, jellies, glazes and fruit preparations. Naturally occurring pectin is found in such fruits as apples, cranberries, and plums. When combined with sugar, these fruits will gel easily. Pectin requires the presence of an acid and sugar in order to gel. Different types of pectin are used depending on the amount of sugar in a formula. Most of the formulas in this book rely on apple pectin, which works best in formulas with a high sugar content such as sorbet or fruit jellies. (See Raspberry Pâte de Fruit, page 654.)

FRUITS

Fruits add *flavor, moisture, texture, body and taste to baked goods*—and they take center stage in much of what comes out of the bakeshop and pastry kitchen. Fruits are divided here into eight categories: berries, citrus, exotics, grapes, melons, pomes, stone fruits and tropicals, according to either their shape, seed structure or natural habitat. The names given here follow generally accepted custom and usage.

Berries

Berries are small, juicy fruits that grow on vines and bushes. Berries are characterized by thin skins and many tiny seeds that are often so small they go unnoticed. Some of the fruits classified here as berries do not fit the botanical definition (for example, raspberries and strawberries), whereas some fruits that are berries botanically (for example, bananas and grapes) are classified elsewhere.

Berries must be fully **ripened** on the vine, as they will not ripen further after harvesting. Select berries that are plump and fully colored. Avoid juice-stained containers and berries with whitish-gray or black spots of mold. All berries should be refrigerated and used

ripe describes fully grown and developed fruit; the fruit's flavor, texture and appearance are at their peak, and the fruit is ready to eat

Blackberries

Blueberries

Cranberries

White Currants   Red Currants

Raspberries

Strawberries

promptly. Do not wash berries until you are ready to use them, as washing removes some of their aroma and softens them.

BLACKBERRIES

Blackberries resemble raspberries but are larger and shinier, with a deep purple to black color. Thorny blackberry vines are readily found in the wild; commercial production is limited. Their peak season is mid-June through August. Loganberries, Marionberries, olallie berries and boysenberries are blackberry hybrids.

BLUEBERRIES

Blueberries (Fr. *myrtilles*) are small and firm, with a true blue to almost black skin and a juicy, light gray-blue interior. Cultivated berries (high-bush varieties) tend to be larger than wild (low-bush) ones. Blueberries are native to North America and are grown commercially from Maine to Oregon and along the Atlantic seaboard. Their peak season is short, from mid-June to mid-August.

CRANBERRIES

Cranberries, another native North American food, are tart, firm fruit with a mottled red skin. They grow on low vines in cultivated bogs (swamps) throughout Massachusetts, Wisconsin and New Jersey. Rarely eaten raw, they are made into sauce or relish or are used in breads, pies or pastries. Cranberries are readily available frozen or made into a jelly-type sauce and canned. Although color does not indicate ripeness, cranberries should be picked over before cooking to remove those that are soft or bruised. Their peak harvesting season is from Labor Day through October, leading to the association of cranberries with Thanksgiving dinner.

CURRANTS

Currants are tiny, tart fruits that grow on shrubs in grapelike clusters. The most common are a beautiful, almost translucent red, but black and golden (or white) varieties also exist. All varieties are used for jams, jellies and sauces, and black currants are made into a liqueur, *crème de cassis*. Although less commonly grown in the United States, currants are very popular and widely available in Europe, with a peak season during the late summer. (The dried fruits called currants are not produced from these berries; they are a special variety of dried grapes.)

RASPBERRIES

Raspberries (Fr. *framboises*) are perhaps the most delicate of all fruits. They have a tart flavor and velvety texture. Red raspberries are the most common, with black, purple and golden berries available in some markets. When ripe, the berry pulls away easily from its white core, leaving the characteristic hollow center. Because they can be easily crushed and are susceptible to mold, most of the raspberries grown are marketed frozen. They grow on thorny vines in cool climates from Washington State to western New York and are imported from New Zealand and South America. The peak domestic season is from late May through November.

STRAWBERRIES

Strawberries (Fr. *fraises*) are brilliant red, heart-shaped fruits that grow on vines. The strawberry plant is actually a perennial herb. The berry's flesh is covered by tiny black seeds called achenes, which are the plant's true fruits. Select berries with a good red color and intact green leafy hull. (The hulls can be easily removed with a paring knife.) Avoid berries with soft or brown spots. Huge berries may be lovely to look at, but they often have hollow centers and little flavor or juice. Although strawberries are available to some extent all year, fresh California strawberries are at their peak from April through June.

The tiny wild or Alpine berries, known by their French name, *fraises des bois*, have a particularly intense flavor and aroma. They are not widely available in the United States.

PROCEDURE FOR FANNING STRAWBERRIES

Cut thin parallel slices into the base of the strawberry without cutting through the stem. Press lightly to fan out the strawberry, exposing the cut slices.

Citrus

Citrus fruits include lemons, limes, grapefruits, tangerines, kumquats, oranges and several hybrids. They are characterized by a thick rind, most of which is a bitter white pith (albedo) with a thin exterior layer of colored skin known as the **zest**. Their flesh is segmented and juicy. Citrus fruits are acidic, with a strong aroma; their flavors vary from bitter to tart to sweet. Most types of citrus rind can be infused in syrups or alcohol to be used as flavorings.

Citrus fruits grow on trees and shrubs in tropical and subtropical climates worldwide. All citrus fruits are fully ripened on the tree and do not ripen further after harvesting. They should be refrigerated for longest storage. Select fruits that feel heavy and have thin, smooth skins. Avoid those with large blemishes or moist spots. Whenever the rind will be eaten, use organic fruit.

zest the colored outer portion of the rind of citrus fruit; contains the oil that provides flavor and aroma

CITRON

Citrons are lemonlike fruits with a dry pulp and lumpy, yellow to green skin that is candied and used in fruitcakes.

GRAPEFRUITS

Grapefruits (Fr. *pamplemousse*) are large and round with a yellow skin, thick rind and tart flesh. They are an 18th-century hybrid of the orange and pummelo (a large, coarse fruit used mostly in Middle and Far Eastern cuisines). Two varieties of grapefruit are widely available all year: white-fleshed and pink- or ruby-fleshed. White grapefruits produce the finest juice, although pink grapefruits are sweeter.

KUMQUATS

Kumquats are very small, oval-shaped, orange-colored fruits with a soft, sweet skin and slightly bitter flesh. They can be eaten whole, either raw or preserved in syrup, and may be used in jams and preserves.

LEMONS

The most commonly used citrus fruits, lemons (Fr. *citrons*), are oval-shaped, bright yellow fruits available all year. Their strongly acidic flavor makes them unpleasant to eat raw but perfect for flavoring desserts and confections. Lemon zest is candied or used as garnish. Rubbing the skin of a lemon or other citrus fruit with a sugar cube extracts much of the aromatic oil. The cube can then be crushed or dissolved to use in formulas calling for citrus flavor.

Citron

Red Grapefruits

White Grapefruits

Kumquats

Lemons

Limes

Key Limes

LIMES

Limes (Fr. *limons*) are small fruits with thin skins ranging from yellow-green to dark green. Limes are too tart to eat raw and are often substituted for lemons. Their juice adds its distinctive flavor to ices, curds and sorbet. Lime zest can be grated and used to give color and flavor to a variety of dishes. Limes are available all year; their peak season is during the summer. Key lime is a small tart lime variety native to South Florida and used to make key lime pie.

ORANGES

Oranges (Sp. *naranja*) are round fruits with a juicy, orange-colored flesh and a thin, orange skin. They can be either sweet or bitter.

Valencia oranges and navel oranges (a seedless variety) are the most popular sweet oranges. They can be juiced and the flesh may be eaten raw, cooked in desserts or used as a garnish. The zest may be grated or julienned for sauces or garnish. Sweet oranges are available all year; their peak season is from December to April. Blood oranges are also sweet but are small, with a rough, reddish skin. Their flesh is streaked with a blood-red color. Blood oranges are available primarily during the winter months. When selecting sweet oranges, look for fruits that feel plump and heavy, with unblemished skin. The color of the skin depends on weather conditions; a green rind does not affect the flavor of the flesh.

Navel Oranges

Valencia Oranges

Bitter oranges include the Seville and bergamot. They are used primarily for the essential oils found in their zest. Oil of bergamot gives Earl Grey tea its distinctive flavor; oil of Seville is essential to curaçao, Grand Marnier and orange flower water. Seville oranges are also used in marmalades.

TANGERINES

Tangerines, sometimes referred to as mandarins, are small and dark orange. Their rind is loose and easily removed to reveal sweet, juicy, aromatic segments. Tangerines are most often eaten fresh and uncooked but are available canned as mandarin oranges.

Tangelos are a hybrid of tangerines and grapefruits. They are the size of a medium orange with a bulbous stem end and few to no seeds. Clementines are a hybrid of tangerines and Seville oranges. They are small and sweet with a loose, thin rind.

Blood Oranges

Tangerines

PROCEDURE FOR SEGMENTING CITRUS FRUITS

Citrus segments, known as *supremes*, are made by first carefully cutting off the entire peel (including the bitter white pith) in even slices.

Individual segments are then removed by gently cutting alongside each membrane.

PROCEDURE FOR ZESTING CITRUS FRUITS

A five-hole zester is used to remove paper-thin strips of the colored rind.

PROCEDURE FOR CUTTING CITRUS PEELS

Large strips of citrus zest may be cut into julienne strips to be used as a garnish or to flavor custards and sauces.

Yuzu (YOU-zoo) is a sour citrus fruit from Japan. Its aromatic rind is used as a garnish and flavor enhancer. Tart yuzu juice is used by pastry chefs in confections and creams. Both the bottled juice and dried rind are available from specialty producers, although the fresh fruit is rarely available in the United States.

Yuzu

Exotics

Improved transportation has led to the increasing availability (although sporadic in some areas) of exotic or unusual fresh fruits such as figs, persimmons, pomegranates, prickly pears, rhubarb and star fruits. Other exotic fruits, such as breadfruit, durian, feijoa, loquat, mangosteen and rambutan are still available only on a limited basis from specialty purveyors and are less commonly used in the bakeshop. They are not discussed here.

FIGS

Figs (Fr. *figues*) are the fruit of ficus trees. They are small, soft, pear-shaped fruits with an intensely sweet flavor and rich, moist texture made crunchy by a multitude of tiny seeds. Fresh figs can be served on tarts or baked, poached and simmered to make jams, preserves or compotes.

Dark-skinned figs, known as Mission figs, are a variety planted at Pacific Coast missions during the 18th century. They have a thin skin and small seeds and are available fresh, canned or dried. The white-skinned figs grown commercially include the White Adriatic,

Calimyrna Figs

HYBRIDS AND VARIETIES

Several fruits are extremely responsive to selective breeding and crossbreeding and have been toyed with by botanists and growers since at least the time of ancient Rome. Two distinct products are recognized: hybrids and varieties. **Hybrids** result from crossbreeding fruits from different species that are genetically unalike. The result is a unique product. Citrus is particularly responsive to hybridization. **Varieties** result from breeding fruits of the same species that have different qualities or characteristics. Breeding two varieties of apples, for example, produces a third variety with the best qualities of both parents.

Guava

Persimmons

used principally for drying and baking, and the all-purpose Kadota. The most important domestic variety, however, is the Calimyrna. These large figs have a rich yellow color and large nutty seeds. Fresh Calimyrna figs are the finest for eating out of hand; they are also available dried.

For the best flavor, figs should be fully ripened on the tree. Unfortunately, fully ripened figs are very delicate and difficult to transport. Most figs are in season from June through October; fresh Calimyrna figs are available only during June.

GOOSEBERRIES

Several varieties of gooseberry (Fr. *groseille maquereau*) are cultivated for culinary purposes. One prized variety is the European gooseberry, a member of the currant family. Its berries can be relatively large, like a small plum, but are usually less than 1 inch (2.5 centimeters) in diameter. The skin can be green, white, yellow or red. The tart berries contain many tiny seeds. They are eaten fresh or used for jellies, preserves, tarts and other desserts. North American gooseberry varieties are smaller, perfectly round, and pink to deep red at maturity. Cape gooseberries, also known as physalis, are unrelated to European and American gooseberries. Cape gooseberries are covered with a paper-thin husk or calyx. About the size of a cherry, they have a waxy, bright orange skin and many tiny seeds. Their flavor is similar to coconut and oranges, but tarter. Cape gooseberries may be eaten raw, made into jam or used in desserts. Fresh, they make an especially striking garnish and are excellent for dipping in tempered chocolate.

Cape Gooseberries

GUAVA

Guava (GWAH-vah) are a small, oval or pear-shaped fruit with a strong fragrance and a mild, slightly grainy flesh. They are excellent juiced and in jams and preserves. Guava paste, a thick, sliceable gel, is a popular treat throughout Central America and the Caribbean. Guava will ripen if stored at room temperature and should be slightly soft and fully ripened for the best flavor.

LYCHEES

The lychee (LEE-chee), also spelled *litchi* or *leechee*, is the fruit of a large tree native to southern China and Southeast Asia. The fruits, which grow in clusters, are oval to round, red and about 1 inch (2.5 centimeters) in diameter. The tough outer skin encloses juicy, white, almost translucent flesh and one large seed. Neither the skin nor the seed is edible.

Lychees are eaten fresh out of hand or juiced and are widely available canned or dried. Fresh lychees are mild but sweet with a pleasant perfume.

Lychees

PERSIMMONS

Persimmons, sometimes referred to as kaki or Sharon fruits, are a bright orange, acorn-shaped fruit with a glossy skin and a large papery blossom. The flesh is bright orange and jellylike, with a mild but rich flavor similar to honey and plums. Persimmons should be peeled before use; any seeds should be discarded. Select bright orange fruits and refrigerate only after they are completely ripe. When ripe, persimmons will be very soft and the skin will have an almost translucent appearance.

Ripe persimmons are delicious eaten raw, halved and topped with cream or soft cheese or peeled, sliced and added to fruit salads. Persimmon bread, muffins, cakes and pies are also popular. Underripe persimmons are almost inedible, however. They are strongly tannic with a chalky or cottony texture.

Persimmons are tree fruits grown in subtropical areas worldwide, although the Asian varieties—now grown in California—are the most common. Fresh persimmons are available from October through January.

POMEGRANATES

An ancient fruit native to Persia (now Iran), pomegranates (POM-uh-gran-uhtz) are round, about the size of a large orange, with a pronounced calyx. The skin forms a hard shell with a pinkish-red color. The interior is filled with hundreds of small red seeds (which are, botanically, the actual fruits) surrounded by juicy red pulp. An inedible yellow membrane separates the seeds into compartments. Pomegranates are sweet-sour, and the seeds are pleasantly crunchy. The bright red seeds make an attractive garnish. Pomegranate juice is a popular beverage in Mediterranean cuisines, and grenadine syrup is made from concentrated pomegranate juice.

Select heavy fruits that are not rock-hard, cracked or heavily bruised. Whole pomegranates can be refrigerated several weeks. Pomegranates are available from September through December; their peak season is in October.

Pomegranates

PRICKLY PEARS

Prickly pear fruits, also known as cactus pears and barbary figs, are actually the berries of several varieties of cactus. They are barrel- or pear-shaped, about the size of a large egg. Their thick, firm skin is green or purple with small sharp pins and nearly invisible stinging fibers. Their flesh is spongy, sweet and a brilliant pink-red, dotted with small black seeds. Prickly pears have the aroma of watermelon and the flavor of sugar water.

Once peeled, prickly pears can be diced and eaten raw, or they can be puréed for making jams, sauces, custards or sorbets, to which they give a vivid pink color. Prickly pears are especially common in Mexican and southwestern cuisines.

Select fruits that are full-colored, heavy and tender, but not too soft. Avoid those with mushy or bruised spots. Ripe prickly pears can be refrigerated for a week or more. Prickly pears are grown in Mexico and several southwestern states and are available from September through December.

Prickly Pears

PROCEDURE FOR PEELING PRICKLY PEARS

❶ To avoid being stung by a prickly pear, hold it steady with a fork, then use a knife to cut off both ends.

❷ Cut a lengthwise strip through the skin. Slip the tip of the knife into the cut and peel away the skin by holding it down while rolling the fruit away.

RHUBARB

Although botanically a vegetable, rhubarb (ROO-barb) is most often prepared as a fruit. It is a perennial plant that grows well in temperate and cold climates. Only the pinkish-red stems are edible; the leaves contain high amounts of oxalic acid, which is toxic.

Rhubarb stems are extremely acidic, requiring large amounts of sugar to create the desired sweet-sour taste. Cinnamon, ginger, orange and strawberry are particularly compatible with rhubarb. It is excellent for pies, cobblers, preserves or stewing. Young, tender stalks of rhubarb do not need to be peeled. When cooked, rhubarb becomes very soft and turns a beautiful light pink color.

Rhubarb

Fresh rhubarb is sold as whole stalks, with the leaves removed. Select crisp, unblemished stalks. Rhubarb's peak season is during the early spring, from February through May. Frozen rhubarb pieces are readily available and are excellent for pies, tarts or jams.

STAR FRUITS

Star fruits, also known as carambola, are oval, up to 5 inches (12.5 centimeters) long, with five prominent ribs or wings running their length. A cross-section cut is shaped like a star. The edible skin is a waxy orange-yellow; it covers a dry, paler yellow flesh. Its flavor is similar to that of plums, sweet but bland. Star fruits are most often sliced, unpeeled and added to fruit salad or used as a garnish.

Color and aroma are the best indicators of ripeness. The fruits should be a deep golden-yellow and there should be brown along the edge of the ribs. The aroma should be full and floral. Green fruits can be kept at room temperature to ripen, then refrigerated for up to 2 weeks. Fresh fruits are available from August to February.

Star Fruits

Grapes

Grapes (Fr. *raisins*; Sp. *uvas*) are the single largest fruit crop in the world, due, of course, to their use in wine making. This section, however, discusses only table grapes, those grown for eating. Grapes are berries that grow on vines in large clusters. California is the world's largest producer, with more than a dozen varieties grown for table use. Grapes are classified by color as white (which are actually green) or black (which are actually red). White grapes are generally blander than black ones, with a thinner skin and firmer flesh.

The grape's color and most of its flavor are found in the skin. Grapes are usually eaten raw, either alone or in fruit salads. They are also used as a garnish or accompaniment to desserts and cheeses, and they add texture in fruit purées. Dried grapes are known as raisins (Fr. *raisins sec*); they are usually made from Thompson Seedless or muscat grapes, currants (made from Black Corinth grapes and labeled Zante currants) or sultanas (made from sultana grapes).

Grapes are available all year because the many varieties have different harvesting schedules. Look for firm, unblemished fruits that are firmly attached to the stem. A surface bloom or dusty appearance is caused by yeasts and indicates recent harvesting. Wrinkled grapes or those with brown spots around the stem are past their prime. All grapes should be rinsed and drained before use.

RED FLAME GRAPES

Red Flame grapes are a seedless California hybrid, second only in importance to the Thompson Seedless. Red Flame grapes are large and round with a slightly tart flavor and variegated red color.

Red Flame Grapes

THOMPSON SEEDLESS GRAPES

The most commercially important table grapes are a variety known as Thompson Seedless, which are pale green with a crisp texture and sweet flavor. Their peak season is from June to November. Many are dried in the hot desert sun of California's San Joaquin Valley to produce dark raisins. For golden raisins, Thompson Seedless grapes are treated with sulfur dioxide to prevent browning, then dried mechanically.

OTHER TABLE GRAPES

Of the table grapes containing seeds, the most important varieties are the Concord, Ribier and Emperor. They range from light red to deep black, and all three are in season during the autumn. Concord grapes, one of the few grape varieties native to the New World, are especially important for making juices and jellies.

Thompson Seedless Grapes

Concord Grapes

Melons

Like pumpkins and cucumbers, melons are members of the gourd family (*Cucurbitaceae*). The dozens of melon varieties can be divided into two general types: sweet (or dessert) melons and watermelons. Sweet melons have a tan, green or yellow netted or farrowed rind and dense, fragrant flesh. Watermelon has a thick, dark green rind surrounding crisp, watery flesh.

Melons are almost 90 percent water, so cooking destroys their texture, quickly turning the flesh to mush. Most are served simply sliced in fruit salads or puréed and made into sorbet.

Melons should be vine-ripened. A ripe melon should yield slightly and spring back when pressed at the blossom end (opposite the stem). It should also give off a strong aroma and be heavy for its size. Avoid melons that are very soft or feel damp at the stem end. Ripe melons may be stored in the refrigerator, although the flavor will be better at room temperature. Slightly underripe melons can be stored at room temperature to allow flavor and aroma to develop.

CANTALOUPES

American cantaloupes, which are actually muskmelons, are sweet melons with a thick, yellow-green netted rind, a sweet, moist, orange flesh and a strong aroma. As with all sweet melons, the many small seeds are found in a central cavity.

Avoid cantaloupes with the pronounced yellow color or moldy aroma that indicates overripeness. Mexican imports ensure a year-round supply, although their peak season is summer.

HONEYDEW MELONS

Honeydew melons are large oval sweet melons with a smooth rind that ranges from white to pale green. Although the flesh is generally pale green, with a mild, sweet flavor, pink- or gold-fleshed honeydews are also available. Like casaba melons, honeydew melons have little to no aroma. They are available almost all year; their peak season is from June through October.

WATERMELONS

Watermelons are large (up to 30 pounds or 13.5 kilograms) round or oval-shaped melons with a thick rind. The skin may be solid green, green-striped or mottled with white. The flesh is crisp and extremely juicy with small, hard, black seeds throughout. Seedless hybrids are available. Most watermelons have pink to red flesh, although golden-fleshed varieties are becoming more common. Watermelons are of a different genus from the sweet melons described earlier. They are native to tropical Africa and are now grown commercially in Texas and several southern states.

Cantaloupes

Honeydew Melons

Watermelon

Pomes

Pomes are tree fruits with thin skin and firm flesh surrounding a central core containing many small seeds called pips or carpels. Pomes include apples, pears and quince.

APPLES

Apples (Fr. *pommes*), perhaps the most common and commonly appreciated of all fruits, grow on trees in temperate zones worldwide. They are popular because of their convenience, flavor, variety and availability. Apples can be eaten raw out of hand, or they can be used in a wide variety of cooked or baked dishes. Apple juice (cider) produces alcoholic and nonalcoholic beverages and cider vinegar.

Of the hundreds of known apple varieties, only 20 or so are commercially significant in the United States. Several varieties and their characteristics are noted in Table 4.9. Most have a moist, creamy white flesh with a thin skin of yellow, green or red. They range in flavor from very sweet to very tart, with an equally broad range of textures, from firm and crisp to soft and mealy.

In Europe, apples are divided into distinct cooking and eating varieties. Cooking varieties are those that disintegrate to a purée when cooked. American varieties are less rigidly classified. Nevertheless, not all apples are appropriate for all types of cooking. Firm apples that retain their shape better during cooking are the best choices where slices or appearance are important. Varieties with a higher malic acid content break down easily, making them more appropriate for applesauce or juicing. A combination of apples, chosen for their aroma, texture, tartness and sugar content, may be desirable when making pies. Any type may be eaten out of hand, depending on personal preference.

Rome Apple

Red Delicious Apple

Granny Smith Apple

Golden Delicious Apple

McIntosh Apples

Gala Apples

Although not native to North America, apples are now grown commercially in 35 states, with Washington and New York leading in production. Apples are harvested when still slightly underripe, then stored in a controlled atmosphere (temperature and oxygen are greatly reduced) for extended periods until ready for sale. Modern storage techniques make fresh apples available all year, although their peak season is during the autumn.

When selecting apples, look for smooth, unbroken skins and firm fruits, without soft spots or bruises. Badly bruised or rotting apples should be discarded immediately. They emit quantities of ethylene gas that speed spoilage of nearby fruits. Store apples chilled for up to 6 weeks. Apple peels (the skin) may be eaten or removed as desired, but in either case, apples should be washed just before use to remove pesticides and any wax that was applied to improve appearance. Apple slices can be frozen (often with sugar or citric acid added to slow spoilage) or dried.

TABLE 4.9 APPLE VARIETIES

VARIETY	SKIN COLOR	FLAVOR	TEXTURE	PEAK SEASON	USE
Fiji	Yellow-green with red highlights	Sweet-spicy	Crisp	All year	Eating, in salads
Gala	Yellow-orange with red stripes	Sweet	Crisp	Aug.–March	Eating, in salads, sauce
Golden Delicious	Glossy greenish-gold	Sweet	Semifirm	Sept.–Oct.	In tarts, with cheese, in salads
Granny Smith	Bright green	Tart	Firm and crisp	Oct.–Nov.	Eating, in tarts
Jonathan	Brilliant red	Tart to acidic	Tender	Sept.–Oct.	Eating, all-purpose
McIntosh	Red with green background	Tart to acidic	Soft	Fall	Applesauce, in closed pies
Pippin (Newton)	Greenish-yellow	Tart	Semifirm	Fall	In pies, eating, baking
Red Delicious	Deep red	Sweet but bland	Soft to mealy	Sept.–Oct.	Eating
Rome	Red	Sweet-tart	Firm	Oct.–Nov.	Baking, pies, sauces
Winesap	Dark red with streaks	Tangy	Crisp	Oct.–Nov.	Cider, all-purpose

PROCEDURE FOR CORING APPLES

❶ Remove the core from a whole apple with an apple corer by inserting the corer from the stem end and pushing out the cylinder containing the core and seeds.

❷ Alternatively, first cut an apple into quarters, then use a paring knife to cut away the core and seeds.

TABLE 4.10   PEAR VARIETIES

VARIETY	APPEARANCE	FLAVOR	TEXTURE	PEAK SEASON	USE
Anjou (Beurre d'Anjou)	Greenish-yellow skin; egg-shaped with short neck; red variety also available	Sweet and juicy	Firm, keeps well	Oct.–May	Eating, poaching
Bartlett (Williams)	Thin yellow skin; bell-shaped; red variety also available	Very sweet, buttery, juicy	Tender	Aug.–Dec.	Eating, canning, in salads
Bosc	Golden-brown skin; long tapered neck	Buttery	Dry, holds its shape well	Sept.–May	Poaching, baking
Comice	Yellow-green skin; large and chubby	Sweet, juicy	Smooth	Oct.–Feb.	Eating
Sekel	Tiny; brown to yellow skin	Spicy	Very firm, grainy	Aug.–Dec.	Poaching, pickling

PEARS

Pears (Fr. *poires*) are an ancient tree fruit grown in temperate areas throughout the world. Most of the pears marketed in the United States are grown in California, Washington and Oregon.

Although thousands of pear varieties have been identified, only a dozen or so are commercially significant. Several varieties and their characteristics are noted in Table 4.10. Pear varieties vary widely in size, color and flavor. They are most often eaten out of hand but can be baked or poached. Pears are delicious with cheese, especially blue cheeses, and can be used in fruit salads, compotes or preserves.

Asian pears, also known as Chinese pears or apple-pears, are of a different species than common pears. They have the moist, sweet flavor of a pear and the round shape and crisp texture of an apple. They are becoming increasingly popular in the United States, particularly those known as Twentieth Century or Nijisseiki.

When selecting pears, look for fruits with smooth, unbroken skin and an intact stem. Pears do not ripen properly on the tree, so they are picked while still firm and should be allowed to soften before use. Underripe pears may be left at room temperature to ripen. A properly ripened pear should have a good fragrance and yield to gentle pressure at the stem end. Pears can be prepared or stored in the same ways as apples.

Anjou Pears

Asian Pears

Sekel Pears

Bosc Pears

Bartlett Pears

Red d'Anjou Pears

QUINCE

Common quince (kwence; Fr. *coing*) resemble large, lumpy yellow pears. Their flesh is hard, with many pips or seeds, and they have a wonderful fragrance. Too astringent to eat raw, quince develop a sweet flavor and pink color when cooked with sugar. Quince are used in breads, jellies, marmalades and pies. They have a high pectin content and may be added to other fruit jams or preserves to encourage gelling.

Quince

Apricots

Bing Cherries

Remove the stem and place the cherry in the pitter with the indentation facing up. Squeeze the handles together to force out the pit.

Fresh quince, usually imported from South America or southeast Europe, are available from October through January. Select firm fruits with a good yellow color. Small blemishes may be cut away before cooking. Quince will keep for up to a month under refrigeration.

Stone Fruits

Stone fruits, also known as drupes, include apricots, cherries, nectarines, peaches and plums and are related to the almond. They are characterized by a thin skin, soft flesh and one woody stone or pit. Although most originated in China, the shrubs and trees producing stone fruits are now grown in temperate climates worldwide.

The domestic varieties of stone fruits are in season from late spring through summer. They tend to be fragile fruits, are easily bruised and difficult to transport and have a short shelf life. Do not wash them until ready to use, as moisture can cause deterioration. Stone fruits are excellent dried and are often used to make liqueurs and brandies. (The kernel inside the pits of many stone fruits contains amygdalin, a compound that has a bitter almond flavor. Eating the raw kernel can cause digestive discomfort or more serious side effects and should be avoided. When cooked it is harmless and can add flavor to jams and creams.)

APRICOTS

Apricots (Fr. *abricots*) are small, round stone fruits with a velvety skin that varies from deep yellow to vivid orange. Their juicy orange flesh surrounds a dark, almond-shaped pit. Apricots can be eaten out of hand, poached, stewed, baked or candied. Apricots have a short season, peaking during June and July, and do not travel well. Select apricots that are well shaped, plump and fairly firm. Avoid ones that are greenish-yellow or mushy. Fresh apricots will last several days under refrigeration, but the flavor is best at room temperature. If fresh fruits are unavailable, canned apricots are usually an acceptable substitute. Dried apricots and apricot juice (known as nectar) are readily available.

CHERRIES

From the northern states, particularly Washington, Oregon, Michigan and New York, come the two most important types of cherry: the sweet cherry and the sour (or tart) cherry.

Sweet cherries (Fr. *cerises*) are round to heart-shaped, about 1 inch (2.5 centimeters) in diameter, with skin that ranges from yellow to deep red to nearly black. The flesh, which is sweet and juicy, may vary from yellow to dark red. The most common and popular sweet cherries are the dark red Bings. Yellow-red Royal Ann and Rainier cherries are also available in some areas.

Rainier Cherries

Sweet cherries are often marketed fresh, made into maraschino cherries or candied for use in baked goods. Fresh sweet cherries have a very short season, peaking during June and July. Cherries do not ripen further after harvesting. Select fruits that are firm and plump with a green stem still attached. There should not be any brown spots around the stem. A dry or brown stem indicates that the cherry is less than fresh. Once the stem is removed, the cherry will deteriorate rapidly. Store fresh cherries in the refrigerator and do not wash them until ready to use.

Sour cherries are light to dark red and are so acidic that they are rarely eaten uncooked. The most common sour cherries are the Montmorency and Morello. Most sour cherries are canned or frozen, or cooked with sugar and starch (usually cornstarch or tapioca) and sold as prepared pastry and pie fillings. Both sweet and sour varieties are available dried.

PEACHES AND NECTARINES

Peaches (Fr. *pêches*) are moderate-sized, round fruits with a juicy, sweet flesh. Nectarines are a variety of peach with a thin, smooth skin. Peaches have a thin skin covered with fuzz. The flesh of either fruit ranges from white to pale orange. Although their flavors are somewhat different, they may be substituted for each other in most formulas.

Peaches and nectarines are excellent for eating out of hand or in tarts, pastries, ice cream and preserves. Although the skin is edible, peaches are generally peeled before being used. (Peaches are easily peeled if blanched first.) Peaches and nectarines are either freestones or clingstones. With freestones, the flesh separates easily from the stone; freestone fruits are commonly eaten out of hand. The flesh of clingstones adheres firmly to the stone; they hold their shape better when cooked and are the type most often canned.

Peaches

Select fruits with a good aroma, an overall creamy, yellow or yellow-orange color and an unwrinkled skin free of blemishes. Red patches are not an indication of ripeness; a green skin indicates that the fruit was picked too early and it will not ripen further. Peaches and nectarines soften but do not become sweeter after harvesting. The United States, especially California, is the world's largest producer of peaches and nectarines. Their peak season is through the summer months, with July and August producing the best crop. South American peaches are sometimes available from January to May. Canned and frozen peaches are readily available.

Nectarines

PLUMS

Plums (Fr. *prunes*) are round to oval-shaped fruits that grow on trees or bushes. Dozens of plum varieties are known, although only a few are commercially significant. Plums vary in size from very small to 3 inches (7.5 centimeters) in diameter. Their thin skin can be green, red, yellow or various shades of blue-purple. Plums are excellent for eating out of hand. Plums can also be baked, poached or used in pies, cobblers or tarts.

Santa Rosa Plums

Fresh plums are widely available from June through October; their peak season is in August and September. When selecting plums, look for plump, smooth fruits with unblemished skin. Generally, they should yield to gentle pressure, although the green and yellow varieties remain quite firm. Avoid plums with moist, brown spots near the stem. Plums may be left at room temperature to ripen, then stored in the refrigerator. Dried plums (prunes), discussed later, are produced by drying special plum varieties, usually the French Agen.

Damson Plums

Tropicals

Tropical fruits are native to the world's hot, tropical or subtropical regions. Most are now readily available throughout the United States thanks to rapid transportation and distribution methods. All can be eaten fresh, without cooking. Their flavors complement each other and are popular in desserts and pastries.

BANANAS

Common yellow bananas (Fr. *bananes*) are actually the berries of a large tropical herb. Grown in bunches called hands, they are about 7 to 9 inches (17 to 22 centimeters) long, with a sticky, soft, sweet flesh. Their inedible yellow skin is easily removed. Baby bananas (Nino, Ladyfinger or Finger Bananas) measure 4 to 5 inches (10 to 12.5 centimeters) long with yellow or red skin. Their flesh is more dense and sweeter than most larger banana varieties. Properly ripened bananas are excellent eaten out of hand or used in salads. Lightly bruised or overripe fruits are best used for breads or muffins. Bananas blend well with other tropical fruits and citrus. Their unique flavor is also complemented by cinnamon, ginger, honey and chocolate.

Fresh bananas are available all year. Bananas are always harvested when still green, because the texture and flavor will be adversely affected if the fruits are allowed to turn yellow on the tree. Unripe bananas are hard, dry and starchy. Because bananas ripen after harvesting, it is acceptable to purchase green bananas if there is sufficient time for final ripening before use. Bananas should be left at room temperature to ripen. A properly ripened banana has a yellow peel with brown flecks. The tip should not have any remaining green coloring. As bananas continue to age, the peel darkens and the starches turn to sugar, giving the fruits a sweeter flavor. Avoid bananas that have large brown bruises or a gray cast (a sign of cold damage).

Plantains, also referred to as cooking bananas, are larger but not as sweet as common bananas. They are frequently cooked as a starchy vegetable in tropical cuisines.

Common Yellow Bananas

Medjool Dates

Kiwis

Mangoes

DATES

Dates (Fr. *datte*) are the fruit of the date palm tree, which has been cultivated since ancient times. Dates are about 1 to 2 inches (2.5 to 5 centimeters) long, with a paper-thin skin and a single grooved seed in the center. Most are golden to dark brown when ripe.

Although dates appear to be dried, they are actually fresh fruits. They have a sticky-sweet, almost candied texture and rich flavor. Dates provide flavor and moisture for breads, muffins, cookies and tarts. Pitted dates are readily available in several packaged forms: whole, chopped or extruded (for use in baking). Whole unpitted dates are available in bulk. Date juice is also available for use as a natural sweetener in baked goods. Although packaged or processed dates are available all year, peak season for fresh domestic dates is from October through December. When selecting dates, look for those that are plump, glossy and moist.

KIWIS

Kiwis, sometimes known as kiwifruits or Chinese gooseberries, are small oval fruits, about the size of a large egg, with a thin, fuzzy brown skin. The flesh is bright green with a white core surrounded by hundreds of tiny black seeds. A golden-fleshed variety is also now available.

Kiwis are sweet, but somewhat bland. They are best used raw, peeled and sliced for fruit salads or garnish. Although kiwis are not recommended for cooking because heat causes them to fall apart, they are a perfect addition to glazed fruit tarts and can be puréed for sorbets, sauces or mousses. Kiwis contain an enzyme similar to that in fresh pineapple and papaya, which prevents gelling.

MANGOES

Mangoes (Fr. *mangue*) are oval or kidney-shaped fruits that normally weigh between 6 ounces and 1 pound (180 grams and 500 grams). Their skin is smooth and thin but tough, varying from yellow to orange-red, with patches of green, red or purple. As mangoes ripen, the green disappears. The juicy, bright orange flesh clings to a large, flat pit.

A mango's unique flavor is spicy-sweet, with an acidic tang. Mangoes can be puréed for use in drinks or sauces, or the flesh can be sliced or cubed for use in salads, pickles, chutneys or desserts.

Although Florida produces some mangoes, most of those available in the United States are from Mexico. Their peak season is from May through August. Select fruits with good color that are firm and free of blemishes. Ripe mangoes should have a good aroma and should not be too soft or shriveled. Allow mangoes to ripen completely at room temperature, then refrigerate for up to 1 week.

PROCEDURE FOR PITTING AND CUTTING MANGOES

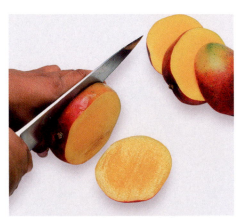

❶ Cut along each side of the pit to remove the two sections.

❷ Each section can then be cubed using the "hedgehog" technique: Make crosswise cuts through the flesh, just to the skin; press up on the skin side of the section, exposing the cubes.

❸ The mango may be served like this or the cubes can be cut off to use in salads or other dishes.

PAPAYAS

The papaya (puh-PIE-yuh) is a greenish-yellow fruit shaped rather like a large pear and weighing 1 to 2 pounds (500 to 1000 grams). The flesh is golden to reddish-pink; its center cavity is filled with round, silver-black seeds resembling caviar. Ripe papayas can be eaten raw, with only a squirt of citrus juice. They can also be puréed for sauces or sorbets. Papayas contain **papain**, which breaks down proteins, making them unsuitable for use in gelatins because it inhibits gelling.

Papaya seeds are edible, with a peppery flavor and slight crunch. They are occasionally used to garnish fruit dishes.

Papayas are grown in tropical and subtropical areas worldwide. Although they are available year-round, their peak season is from April through June. Select papayas that are plump, with a smooth, unblemished skin. Color is a better determinant of ripeness than is softness: The greater the proportion of yellow to green skin color, the riper the fruit. Papayas may be held at room temperature until completely ripe, then refrigerated up to 1 week.

papain an enzyme found in papayas that breaks down proteins; used as the primary ingredient in many commercial meat tenderizers

Papayas

PASSION FRUITS

Passion fruits (Fr. *granadillas*) have a firm, almost shell-like purple skin with orange-yellow pulp surrounding large, black, edible seeds. They are about the size and shape of large hen eggs, with a sweet, rich and unmistakable citrusy flavor. The pulp is used in custards, sauces and ice creams.

Select heavy fruits with dark, shriveled skin and a strong aroma. Allow them to ripen at room temperature, if necessary, then refrigerate. Passion fruits are now grown in New Zealand, Hawaii and California and should be available all year, although their peak season is in February and March. Bottles or frozen packs of purée are readily available and provide a strong, true flavor.

Passion Fruit

Red Papayas

PINEAPPLES

Pineapples (Fr. *ananas*) are the fruit of a shrub with sharp spear-shaped leaves. Each fruit is covered with rough, brown eyes, giving it the appearance of a pinecone. The pale yellow flesh, which is sweet and very juicy, surrounds a cylindrical woody core that is edible but

Pineapples

too tough for most uses. Most pineapples weigh approximately 2 pounds (1 kilogram), but dwarf varieties are also available.

Pineapples are excellent eaten raw or sautéed. Canned or cooked pineapple can be added to gelatin mixtures, but avoid using fresh pineapple; an enzyme (bromelin) found in fresh pineapple breaks down gelatin.

Pineapples do not ripen after harvesting. They must be left on the stem until completely ripe, at which time they are extremely perishable. Most pineapples come from Hawaii. Fresh pineapples are available all year, with peak supplies in March through June. Select heavy fruits with a strong, sweet aroma and rich color. Avoid those with dried leaves or soft spots. Pineapples should be used as soon as possible after purchase. Pineapples are also available canned in slices, in cubes or crushed, dried or candied.

PROCEDURE FOR TRIMMING AND SLICING PINEAPPLES

❶ Slice off the leaves and stem end. Stand the fruit upright and cut the peel off in vertical strips.

❷ Cut the peeled fruit in quarters, then cut away the woody core.

❸ The flesh can then be cut as desired.

Purchasing Fresh Fruits

Fresh fruits have not been subjected to any processing (such as canning, freezing or drying). Fresh fruits may be ripe or unripe, depending on their condition when harvested or the conditions under which they have been stored. In order to use fresh fruits to their best advantage, it is important to make careful purchasing decisions. The size of each piece of fruit, its grade or quality, its ripeness on delivery and its nutritional content may affect your ability to use the fruit in an appropriate and cost-effective manner.

COMMODITY BOARDS: CULINARY ALLIES

How can you find out more about using fruits, nuts, and other important ingredients? The U.S. Department of Agriculture, as well as state grower associations and industry groups, have established commodity boards to promote their products, educate consumers and assist growers and food service professionals. Their well-organized Web sites contain a wide range of recipes, feature noted chefs, provide nutritional data and address key consumer concerns.

The National Honey Board (www .honey.com), for example, draws consumer attention to distinguish pure honey from similarly packaged honey-syrup blends. It also invites culinarians to subscribe to a monthly recipe newsletter. The National Peanut Board (www.nationalpeanutboard. org) devotes special attention to food allergy management, offering access to advice from an international panel of research and medical experts. The most recently established commodity board, the National Mango Board (www.mango.org), in addition to the usual recipes and nutrition information, presents the full range of mango varieties, including peak availability periods and ripening cues, so that less well-known fruit may be used to the best advantage. The Cherry Marketing Institute (www.choosecherries.com) focuses on health benefits—to athletes, arthritis and gout sufferers, and as a source of melatonin, to counter jet lag.

These boards and dozens more offer information and inspiration to the pastry chef and baker to use ingredients more effectively and provide greater variety and enjoyment to their customers.

GRADING

Fresh fruits traded on the wholesale market may be graded under the USDA's voluntary program. The grades, based on size and uniformity of shape, color and texture as well as the absence of defects, are U.S. Fancy, U.S. No. 1, U.S. No. 2 and U.S. No. 3. Most fruits purchased for food service operations are U.S. Fancy. Fruits with lower grades are suitable for processing into sauces, jams, jellies or preserves.

RIPENING

Several important changes take place in a fruit as it ripens. The fruit reaches its full size; its pulp or flesh becomes soft and tender; its color changes. In addition, the fruit's acid content declines, making it less tart, and its starch content converts into the sugars fructose and glucose, which provide the fruit's sweetness, flavor and aroma.

Unfortunately, these changes do not stop when the fruit reaches its peak of ripeness. Rather, they continue, deteriorating the fruit's texture and flavor and eventually causing spoilage.

Depending on the species, fresh fruits can be purchased either fully ripened or unripened. Figs and pineapples, for example, ripen only on the plant and are harvested at or just before their peak of ripeness, then rushed to market. They should not be purchased unripened as they will never attain full flavor or texture after harvesting. On the other hand, some fruits, including bananas and pears, continue to ripen after harvesting and can be purchased unripened.

With most harvested fruits, the ripening time as well as the time during which the fruits remain at their peak of ripeness can be manipulated. For instance, ripening can be delayed by chilling. Chilling slows down the fruit's **respiration rate** (fruits, like animals, consume oxygen and expel carbon dioxide). The slower the respiration rate, the slower the conversion of starch to sugar. For quicker ripening, fruit can be stored at room temperature.

Ripening is also affected by ethylene gas, a colorless, odorless hydrocarbon gas. Ethylene gas is naturally emitted by ripening fruits and can be used to encourage further ripening in most fruits. Apples, tomatoes, melons and bananas give off the most ethylene and should be stored away from delicate fruits and vegetables, especially greens. Fruits that are picked and shipped unripened can be exposed to ethylene gas to induce ripening just before sale. Conversely, if you want to extend the life of ripe fruits a day or two, isolate them from other fruits and keep them well chilled.

respiration rate the speed with which the cells of a fruit use up oxygen and produce carbon dioxide during ripening

BAKING WITH THE SEASONS

What I make for dessert depends on the season. I appreciate what each season has to offer and use it to its maximum potential. When winter comes I am drawn to warm sweets, and spring's annual arrival finds me on the lookout for the first sightings of rhubarb.

As a pastry chef, you can't just look at a calendar to know when a fruit is available. What if you have a very cool spring? The berries will be delayed. You have to see the fruit in the market. Pastry making requires a lot of specific recipes and measurements. With fresh fruit, you can't only rely on a recipe. You have to think like a cook. Once you get in the fruit, you have to taste it. Take strawberries, for example.

How much sun and rain will affect how much sugar they have, which will really affect what you can do with the fruit. Strawberries are often served with poundcakes, which take good juicy berries. Taste the berries to see what to add. Lemon juice and salt brings out the strawberries' flavor and unleashes their juices. Also bake with the fruit. Close your eyes when you taste your dessert, what is your brain telling you? Many times we see the red strawberry and our brain tells us we are eating strawberries even if they have little taste.

Even ingredients available all year round I use differently from one season to the next. In winter, I may serve chocolate in a warm chocolate pudding or hot soufflé. In the summer, you want something cooling such as chocolate ice cream. But a chocolate layer cake works all year round. With nuts I might put them in an almond cake or torte. In summer the cake is served with berries and ice cream, but in winter I might serve it warm with an orange caramel compote. (And even though I could use frozen raspberry for purée, I won't serve it in the winter when it is not in the spirit of the season because the berries are not locally available.)

Regardless of the season, cooking with fresh local ingredients increases the tastes of a dessert.

—EMILY LUCHETTI, Executive Pastry Chef at Farallon and Waterbar Restaurants, San Francisco, CA

Fresh fruits do not ripen further once they are cooked or processed. The cooking or processing method applied, however, may soften the fruits or add flavor.

PURCHASING

Fresh fruits are sold by weight or by count. They are packed in containers referred to as crates, bushels, cartons, cases, lugs or flats. The weight or count packed in each of these containers varies depending on the type of fruit, the purveyor and the state in which the fruits were packed. For example, Texas citrus is packed in cartons equal to $\frac{7}{10}$ of a bushel; Florida citrus is packed in cartons equal to $\frac{4}{5}$ of a bushel. Sometimes fruit size must be specified when ordering. A 30-pound case of lemons, for example, may contain 96, 112 or 144 individual lemons, depending on their size.

Some fresh fruits, especially melons, pineapples, peaches and berries, are available trimmed, cleaned, peeled or cut. Sugar and preservatives may be added. They are sold in bulk containers, sometimes packed in water. These items offer a consistent product with a significant reduction in labor costs. The purchase price may be greater than that for fresh fruits, and flavor, freshness and nutritional qualities may suffer somewhat from the processing.

Purchasing and Storing Preserved Fruits

Preservation techniques are designed to extend the shelf life of fruits in essentially fresh form. These methods include irradiation, acidulation, canning, freezing and drying. Except for drying, these techniques do not substantially change the fruits' texture or flavor. Canning and freezing can also be used to preserve cooked fruits.

ACIDULATION

Apples, pears, bananas, peaches and other fruits turn brown when cut. Although this browning is commonly attributed to exposure to oxygen, it is actually caused by the reaction of enzymes.

Immersing cut fruits in an acidic solution such as lemon or orange juice can retard enzymatic browning. This simple technique is sometimes referred to as **acidulation**. Soaking fruits in water or lemon juice and water (called acidulated water) is not recommended. Unless a sufficient amount of salt or sugar is added to the water, the fruits will just become mushy. But if enough salt or sugar is added to retain texture, the flavor will be affected.

CANNED FRUITS

Almost any type of fruit can be canned successfully; pineapple and peaches are the largest sellers. In commercial canning, raw fruits are cleaned and placed in a sealed container, then subjected to high temperatures for a specific amount of time. Heating destroys the microorganisms that cause spoilage, and the sealed environment created by the can eliminates oxidation and retards decomposition. But the heat required by the canning process also softens the texture of most fruits.

In *solid-pack cans*, little or no water is added. The only liquid is from the fruits' natural moisture. *Water-pack cans* have water or fruit juice added, which must be taken into account when determining costs. *Syrup-pack cans* have a sugar syrup—light, medium or heavy—added. The syrup should also be taken into account when determining food costs, and the additional sweetness should be considered when using syrup-packed fruits. Cooked fruit products such as pie fillings are also available canned.

Canned fruits are purchased in cases of standard-sized cans (see Appendix I). Once a can is opened, any unused contents should be transferred to an appropriate storage container and refrigerated. Cans with bulges should be discarded immediately, without opening.

FROZEN FRUITS

Freezing is a highly effective method for preserving fruits. It severely inhibits the growth of microorganisms that cause fruits to spoil. But freezing can alter the appearance or texture of most fruits because of their high water content. This occurs when ice crystals formed from the water in the cells burst the cells' walls.

Many fruits, especially berries and apple and pear slices, are now individually quick-frozen (IQF). This method employs blasts of cold air, refrigerated plates, liquid nitrogen, liquid air or other techniques to chill the produce quickly, producing better-quality frozen products. Speeding the freezing process can greatly reduce the formation of ice crystals.

Fruits can be trimmed and sliced before freezing and are also available frozen in sugar syrup, which adds flavor and prevents browning. Berries are frozen whole; stone fruits are usually peeled, pitted and sliced. Fruit purées, a bakeshop staple, are also available frozen.

Frozen fruits are graded as U.S. Grade A (Fancy), U.S. Grade B (Choice or Extra Standard), or U.S. Grade C (Standard). The "U.S." indicates that a government inspector has graded the product, but packers may use grade names without an actual inspection if the contents meet the standards of the grade indicated.

IQF fruits can be purchased in bulk by the case. All frozen fruits should be sealed in moisture-proof wrapping and kept at a constant temperature of 0°F (−18°C) or below. Temperature fluctuations can cause freezer burn. Frozen berries such as blueberries and blackberries should not be thawed before adding to batters because their juice can easily discolor the batter.

DRIED FRUITS

Drying is the oldest known technique for preserving fruits, having been used for more than 5000 years. When ripe fruits are dried, they lose most of their moisture. This concentrates their flavors and sugars and dramatically extends shelf life. Although most fruits can be dried, plums (prunes), grapes (raisins, sultanas and currants), apricots and figs are the fruits most commonly dried. The drying method can be as simple as leaving ripe fruits in the sun to dry naturally or the more cost-efficient technique of passing fruits through a compartment of hot, dry air to quickly extract moisture.

Freeze-dried fruit is prepared by heating fruit at low temperatures under a vacuum. The result is a product with approximately 5 percent moisture and a fresh taste and natural color. Though it is often used for portability, freeze-dried fruit, especially in a powdered form, can also be used as a garnish or to boost flavor in fruit preparations.

Dried fruits actually retain 16 to 25 percent residual moisture, which leaves them moist and soft. They are often treated with sulfur dioxide to prevent browning (oxidation) and to extend shelf life. Before use, dried fruits may be softened by steeping them for a short time in a hot liquid such as water, wine, rum, brandy or other liquor. Some dried fruits should be simmered in a small amount of water before use.

Store dried fruits in airtight containers to prevent further moisture loss; keep in a dry, cool area away from sunlight. Dried fruits may mold if exposed to both air and high humidity.

SELECTING FRUIT PURÉES

Frozen fruit purées are a convenient ingredient for making sauces, creams and sorbets. Quality frozen fruit purées are made from ripe fruits that are cleaned, puréed then strained and pasteurized with heat for safety and to prevent enzymatic browning. Sweeteners and stabilizers may be added to improve product consistency and some manufacturers may enhance their products with flavorings. Concentrated purées that have some water removed are also available. Berries, cherries and other stone fruits as well as pineapples and citrus make excellent purées, but some fruit may lose flavor and color during processing. Taste the purée before using it and make the appropriate adjustment to sugar in the formulas as required.

Golden Raisins

Currants

Kiwis

Apricots

Persimmons

Apples

Pears

juice the liquid extracted from any fruit or vegetable

nectar the diluted, sweetened juice of peaches, apricots, guavas, black currants or other fruits, the juice of which would be too thick or too tart to drink straight

cider mildly fermented apple juice; nonalcoholic apple juice may also be labeled cider

SAFETY ALERT
Fruit Sanitation

Remove any labels and wash fruits thoroughly in clean water before using, even if they are to be peeled or juiced. Because fruits are often served uncooked, proper hand washing is especially important when preparing them. Remember that many health departments require single-use gloves to be worn—and changed frequently—whenever working with products that will not be cooked before service.

Rock Salt

Fleur de Sel

Juicing

Fruit juice is used as a beverage, alone or mixed with other ingredients, and as the liquid ingredient in other preparations. Juice can be extracted from fruits in two ways: pressure and blending.

Pressure is used to extract juice from fruits such as citrus that have a high water content. Pressure is applied by hand-squeezing or with a manual or electric reamer. All reamers work on the same principle: A ribbed cone is pressed against the fruit to break down its flesh and release the juice. Always strain juices to remove seeds, pulp or fibrous pieces.

A blender or an electric juice extractor can be used to liquefy less-juicy fruits such as apples and pears. The extractor pulverizes the fruit, then separates and strains the liquid from the pulp with centrifugal force.

Interesting and delicious beverages can be made by combining the juice of one or more fruits: pineapple with orange, apple with cranberry, strawberry with tangerine and papaya with orange. Color should be considered when creating mixed-juice beverages, however. Some combinations can cause rather odd color changes. Although yellow and orange juices are not a problem, those containing red and blue flavonoid pigments (such as Concord grapes, cherries, strawberries, raspberries and blueberries) can create some unappetizing colors. Adding an acid such as lemon juice helps retain the correct red and blue hues.

FLAVORINGS

Many flavoring ingredients are used in the bakeshop. Practically any herb, spice, beverage or extract can be used to give baked goods, creams and confections their characteristic flavors. As with all baking ingredients, select flavoring components for overall quality and freshness, and combine flavorings carefully to achieve a balanced, good-tasting finished product.

Salt

Salt (Fr. *sel*) is the most basic seasoning, used to enhance the flavor and sweetness of other ingredients in food. The presence of salt can be tasted easily but not smelled. Salt suppresses bitter flavors, making the sweet and sour ones more prominent. A little salt added to fresh fruit mixtures can enhance the perception of their flavor and sweetness. When used in chocolate and caramel candies, salt heightens contrasting tastes of bitter and sweet. In yeast dough, salt slows yeast fermentation. Salt also strengthens the gluten structure in bread dough. Omitting or reducing the amount of salt can cause the dough to rise too quickly, adversely affecting the shape and flavor of bread.

Culinary or **table salt** is sodium chloride (NaCl), available from several sources, each with its own flavor and degree of saltiness. Table salt is produced by pumping water through underground salt deposits, then bringing the brine to the surface to evaporate, leaving behind crystals. Chemicals are usually added to prevent table salt from absorbing moisture and thus keep it free flowing. Iodized salt is commonly used in the United States. The iodine has no effect on the salt's flavor or use; it is added simply to provide an easily available source of iodine, an important nutrient, to a large number of people.

For baking, use finely ground salt from whichever source is preferred, as it will dissolve readily in all mixtures. Weighing is the only way to measure salt accurately, as different granulations of salt have different volume measurements.

Rock salt, mined from underground deposits, is available in both edible and nonedible forms. It is used in ice cream churns, for thawing frozen sidewalks and, in edible form, in salt mills.

Sea salt is obtained, not surprisingly, by evaporating seawater. Unlike other table salts, sea salt contains additional mineral salts that give it a stronger, more complex flavor and a grayish-brown color. The region where it is produced can also affect its flavor. Sea salt is considerably more expensive than other table salts and is often reserved for finishing a dish or used as a condiment. *Fleur de sel* and *sel gris* are two distinctive types of unrefined sea salt.

Kosher salt has large, irregular crystals and is used in the "koshering," or curing, of meats. It is purified rock salt that contains no iodine or additives. It can be substituted weight-for-weight with common kitchen salt.

Because it is nonorganic, salt keeps indefinitely. It will, however, absorb moisture from the atmosphere, which prevents it from flowing properly. Salt is a powerful preservative; its presence stops or greatly slows down the growth of many undesirable organisms.

Kosher Salt

Emulsions and Extracts

Emulsions and extracts are liquid flavoring agents derived from various flavoring oils (**essential oils**) taken from fruits, beans, spices or seeds.

Emulsions are flavoring oils mixed into water with the aid of emulsifiers. Lemon and orange are the most common emulsions. Emulsions are much stronger than extracts and should be used carefully and sparingly. **Extracts** are mixtures of flavoring oils or essential oils and ethyl alcohol. Vanilla, almond and lemon are frequently used extracts. An extract may be made with pure flavoring oils or with artificial flavors and colors. Contents are regulated by the FDA, and package labels must indicate any artificial ingredients. Emulsions and extracts are highly volatile. They should be stored in sealed containers in a cool area away from direct light. Mixtures of natural or artificial flavors, sweeteners, stabilizers and other ingredients called **flavoring compounds**, and **aroma pastes** are also sold to use in baked goods, cream and ice creams. Consult the manufacturer before using these products, as their composition varies widely.

essential oils pure oils extracted from the skins, peels and other parts of plants used to give their aroma and taste to flavoring agents in foods, cosmetics and other products

VANILLA

Vanilla (Fr. *vanille*) is the most frequently used flavoring in the bakeshop. It comes from the pod fruit, called a bean, of a vine in the orchid family. Vanilla beans are purchased whole, individually or by the pound. They should be soft and pliable, with a rich brown color and good aroma. The finest vanilla comes from Tahiti and Madagascar.

To use a vanilla bean, cut it open lengthwise with a paring knife. Scrape out the moist seeds with the knife's tip and stir them into the mixture being flavored. The seeds do not dissolve and will remain visible as small black or brown flecks. After all the seeds have been removed, the bean can be stored in a covered container with sugar to create vanilla sugar. Because the intensity of vanilla extract varies, it is difficult to recommend an equivalent in vanilla beans. Generally, ½ fluid ounce (15 milligrams) of vanilla extract can be substituted for one vanilla bean; however, taste should be the ultimate guide.

Scraping the seeds from the interior of a vanilla bean.

Vanilla beans should be stored in an airtight container in a cool, dark place. During storage, the beans may develop a white coating. This is not mold, but rather crystals of vanilla flavor known as vanillin. It should not be removed.

Pure vanilla extract is an easy and less expensive way to give bakeshop products a true vanilla flavor. It is dark brown and aromatic and comes in several strengths referred to as folds. The higher the number of folds, the stronger the flavor of the extract. Any product labeled "vanilla extract" must not contain artificial flavorings and must be at least 35 percent alcohol by volume. Vanilla extract should be stored at room temperature in a closed, opaque container. It should not be frozen.

Artificial or imitation vanilla flavoring is made with synthetic vanillin. Artificial flavoring is available in a clear form, which is useful for white buttercreams where the dark brown color of pure vanilla extract would be undesirable. Although inexpensive, artificial vanilla is, at best, weaker and less aromatic than pure extract. It can also impart a chemical or bitter taste to foods.

Chocolate

Chocolate is one of the most popular flavorings—perhaps the most popular—for candies, cookies, cakes and pastries. Chocolate is also served as a beverage and is an ingredient in the traditional spicy Mexican molé sauce. Chocolate is available in a variety of forms and degrees of sweetness. Chocolate and cocoa are discussed in Chapter 20, Chocolate and Sugar Work.

THE COMPLEXITY OF VANILLA

Thousands of orchids exist in the world, but only one species, *Vanilla planifolia*, gives us the complex, yet versatile, flavor of vanilla. It was discovered and cultivated by the Totonaco Indians in Mexico but spread throughout the world by conquest. Today, the most widely used beans come from Madagascar, followed by Indonesia, Uganda, Mexico, India, Papua New Guinea and Tahiti. Where vanilla is grown, however, determines its flavor characteristics. Beans from Madagascar, for example have a mellow creaminess. Mexican beans, on the other hand, are a marriage of sweet and woody notes, with a spicy character similar to cloves or nutmeg. Indonesian beans have a sharp, woody scent, while those from Tahiti and French Polynesia contain floral and fruity aromas.

More than 300 compounds make up the flavor we identify as vanilla. While vanillin is the most dominant, it actually only constitutes a tiny percentage of the total number of flavor components. This is one reason why artificial vanilla, which features only this one compound, pales in comparison to natural vanilla. Different components run the gamut, featuring such flavor notes as honey, nutty, anise and others, which allow vanilla to be used as a spice in such a wide array of foods, from breads, cakes and pastries to ice cream, chocolate confections and tomato sauce.

As a flavor enhancer, vanilla boosts our ability to taste other flavors such as coffee, nuts and fruits. When used with citrus fruits, vanilla covers the fruits' acidic bite, giving them a creamier taste. And vanilla adds a smoothing influence on chocolate ice cream, cakes, bars and cookies.

—CRAIG NIELSEN, Chief Executive Officer, and DAN FOX, Industrial Sales, Nielsen-Massey Vanillas Inc.

Green Unroasted Coffee Beans

French-Roast Beans

Coffee and Tea

Coffee (Fr. *café*) is equally important for flavoring pastries as it is for accompanying them. Its smoky richness marries well with chocolate, cinnamon, mint and nuts in mousses, candies and ice creams. Ground coffee may be steeped in milk or cream to be used in a formula, then strained. Brewed coffee may be reduced to a potent syrup for use as a flavoring. Commercially prepared coffee extract is also available.

Coffee begins as the fruit of a small tree grown in tropical and subtropical regions throughout the world. The fruit, referred to as a cherry, is bright red with translucent flesh surrounding two flat-sided seeds. These seeds are the coffee beans. When ripe, the cherries are harvested by hand, then cleaned, fermented and hulled, leaving the green coffee beans. The beans are then roasted, blended and ground for brewing.

Tea (Fr. *thé*) is used to flavor creams and custards. The leaves may be steeped in the milk used for ice cream, for example, then strained before chilling and freezing. Tea is the name given to the leaves of *Camellia sinensis*, a tree or shrub that grows at high altitudes in damp tropical regions. Although tea comes from only one species of plant, there are three general types of tea—black, green and oolong. **Black tea** is amber-brown and strongly flavored. Its color and flavor result from fermenting the leaves. Black tea leaves are named or graded by leaf size. Because larger leaves brew more slowly than smaller ones, teas are sorted by leaf size for efficient brewing. *Souchong* denotes large leaves, *pekoe* denotes medium-sized leaves and *orange pekoe* denotes the smallest whole leaves, not a citrus flavor. Broken tea is smaller, resulting in a darker, stronger brew, and is most often used in tea bags. For **green tea** the leaves are not fermented, resulting in a yellowish-green colored beverage with a bitter flavor. **Oolong tea** is partially fermented to combine the characteristics of black and green teas.

Herbs and Spices

Herbs refer to the large group of aromatic plants whose leaves, stems or flowers are used to add flavors to other foods. Most herbs are available fresh or dried. Because drying alters their flavors and aromas, fresh herbs are generally preferred and should be used if possible. Spices are the bark, roots, seeds, buds or berries of plants, most of which grow naturally only in tropical climates. Spices are almost always used in their dried form, rarely fresh, and can usually be purchased whole or ground. Some plants—dill, for example—can be used as both an herb (its leaves) and a spice (its seeds).

TABLE 4.11	BAKESHOP USES FOR SOME COMMON HERBS AND SPICES	
FLAVORING	**FORM**	**SUGGESTED USES**
Allspice	Dry ground	Fruits, quick breads and spice cookies
Anise	Dry, whole or ground	Pastries and breads
Basil	Fresh or dried	Savory bread, pizzas and bagels; sorbet; poached fruit
Caraway	Whole or ground	Rye breads, bagel topping
Cardamom	Ground	Sweet dough, cookies and pastries
Cinnamon	Whole	Infused in syrups and poaching liquid
	Ground	Pies, pastries, breads and ice cream
Cloves	Whole or ground	Poaching liquids for fruit, spice breads and muffins
Dill	Whole seeds or fresh	Breads, bread toppings
Ginger	Fresh root	Infused in syrups, ice cream and custards
	Powder	Cakes, cookies, muffins and gingerbread
Mace	Ground	Spice breads and cookies
Mint	Fresh	Infused in sauces and syrups, garnish
Nutmeg	Ground	Custards, spice breads and cookies
Pepper	Whole	Infused in wine for poaching fruit
	Ground	Spice blends for cakes, custards and cookies such as gingerbread

Most herbs are associated with the savory kitchen. But many, including basil, parsley, chives, oregano and dill, do find a place in savory breads and pizza; pastry chefs are increasingly experimenting with new flavor combinations such as black pepper in ice cream or rosemary and hot pepper in chocolate. When chopped finely, herbs may be added directly to dough or applied as a topping before baking. Spices are more commonly associated with baked goods. Creative pastry chefs are expanding the uses for many herbs and spices, incorporating them or infusing syrups, custards and chocolates with their distinctive aromas. Table 4.11 lists some of the herbs and spices more commonly used in the bakeshop, along with recommendations for bakeshop use.

HERBS

Lavender (Fr. *lavande*) is an evergreen with thin leaves and tall stems bearing spikes of tiny purple flowers. Although lavender is known primarily for its aroma, which is widely used in perfumes, soaps and cosmetics, the flowers are also used as a flavoring, particularly in Middle Eastern and Provençal cuisines. These flowers have a sweet, lemony flavor and can be crystallized and used as a garnish. Lavender is also used in jams and preserves and to flavor custards, teas and tisanes.

Lemon verbena (Fr. *verveine*) is a perennial shrub with thin spiked leaves on woody stems. Verbena contains citral and nerol, which give it a powerful lemon scent that can be used to infuse tea, creams, custards and sorbets.

Mint (Fr. *menthe*), a large family of herbs, includes many species and flavors (even chocolate). **Spearmint** is the most common garden and commercial variety. It has soft, bright green leaves and a tart aroma and flavor. Mint has an affinity for chocolate. It can also be brewed into a beverage or used as a garnish.

Peppermint has thin, stiff, pointed leaves and a sharper menthol flavor and aroma. Fresh peppermint is used less often in cooking or as a garnish than spearmint, but peppermint oil is a common flavoring in sweets and candies.

Lavender

Peppermint

Spearmint

EDIBLE FLOWERS

Many specialty produce growers offer edible pesticide-free blossoms to be used as cake or pastry decorations. (Fresh violets coated in sugar and then dried are sold as candied violets.) Some flowers such as hibiscus, nasturtiums, calendulas and pansies are raised and picked specifically for eating. Others such as roses and violets may be grown for ornament only. Be certain to use only flowers raised for consumption.

Nasturtiums

Calendulas

Pansies

SPICES

Allspice (Fr. *toute-épice*), also known as Jamaican pepper, is the dried berry of a tree that flourishes in Jamaica and one of the few spices still grown exclusively in the New World. Allspice is available whole; in berries that look like large, rough, brown peppercorns; or ground. Ground allspice is not a mixture of spices, although it does taste like a blend of cinnamon, cloves and nutmeg. Allspice gives a distinctive taste to spiced cookies and gingerbread.

Allspice

Anise (Fr. *anis*) is native to the eastern Mediterranean, where it was widely used by ancient civilizations. Today, it is grown commercially in warm climates throughout India, North Africa and southern Europe. The tiny, gray-green egg-shaped seeds have a distinctively strong, sweet flavor, similar to licorice and fennel. When anise seeds turn brown, they are stale and should be discarded. Anise is used in pastries and in alcoholic beverages (for example, Pernod, Sambuca and ouzo).

Anise Seeds

Caraway (Fr. *carvi*) is perhaps the world's oldest spice. Its use has been traced to the Stone Age, and seeds have been found in ancient Egyptian tombs. The caraway plant grows wild in Europe and temperate regions of Asia. It produces a small, crescent-shaped brown seed with the peppery flavor of rye. Seeds may be purchased whole or ground. (The leaves have a mild, bland flavor and are rarely used in cooking.) Caraway is a very European flavor, used extensively in the rye breads of Germany and Austria. It is also used in alcoholic beverages and cheeses. It is said to have preservative qualities extending the shelf life of breads made with it.

Caraway Seeds

Cardamom (Fr. *cardamome*) is one of the most expensive spices, second only to saffron in cost. Its seeds are encased in ¼-inch- (6-millimeter-) long light green or brown pods. Cardamom is highly aromatic. Its flavor, lemony with notes of camphor, is quite strong and is used in both sweet and savory dishes. Cardamom is widely used in India and the Middle East to flavor coffee. Scandinavians use cardamom to flavor breads and pastries. Ground cardamom loses its flavor rapidly, so it is best to purchase whole seeds and grind your own as needed.

Cardamom Seeds

Cinnamon (Fr. *cannelle*) and its cousin cassia are among the oldest known spices: Cinnamon's use is recorded in China as early as 2500 B.C.E., and the Far East still produces most of these products. Both cinnamon and cassia come from the bark of small evergreen trees, peeled from branches in thin layers and dried in the sun. High-quality cinnamon should be pale brown and thin, rolled up like paper into sticks known as quills. Cassia is coarser and has a stronger, less subtle flavor than cinnamon. Consequently, it is cheaper than true cinnamon. Cinnamon is usually purchased ground because it is difficult to grind. Cinnamon sticks are used when long cooking times allow for sufficient flavor to be extracted (for example, in poaching liquids). Cinnamon's flavor is most often associated with pastries and sweets. Labeling laws do not require that packages distinguish between

Ground Cinnamon and Cinnamon Sticks

cassia and cinnamon, so most of what is sold as cinnamon in the United States is actually cassia, blended for consistent flavor and aroma.

Cloves (Fr. *clous de girofles*) are the unopened buds of evergreen trees that flourish in muggy tropical regions. When dried, whole cloves have hard, sharp prongs that can be used to push them into other foods, such as onions or fruit, in order to provide flavor. Cloves are extremely pungent, with a sweet, astringent aroma. A small amount provides a great deal of flavor. Cloves are usually blended with other spices for cakes and cookies. They may be purchased whole or ground.

Cloves

Coriander (Fr. *coriandre*) seeds come from the cilantro plant. They are round and beige, with a distinctive sweet, spicy flavor and strong aroma. Unlike other plants in which the seeds and the leaves carry the same flavor and aroma, coriander and cilantro are very different. Coriander seeds are available whole or ground and are frequently used in sweet dough and cookie recipes.

Coriander Seeds

Ginger (Fr. *gingembre*) is a well-known spice obtained from the root of a tall, flowering tropical plant. Fresh ginger root is known as a "hand" because it looks vaguely like a group of knobby fingers. It has grayish-tan skin and a pale yellow, fibrous interior. Fresh ginger should be plump and firm with smooth skin. It should keep for about a month under refrigeration. Its flavor is fiery but sweet, with notes of lemon and rosemary. Ginger is also available peeled and pickled in vinegar, candied in sugar or preserved in alcohol or syrup. Dried, ground ginger is a fine yellow powder widely used in pastries. Its flavor is spicier and not as sweet as fresh ginger.

Ginger Root

Nutmeg (Fr. *noix de muscade*) and mace come from the yellow plumlike fruit of a large tropical evergreen. These fruits are dried and opened to reveal the seed known as nutmeg. A bright red lacy coating or aril surrounds the seed; the aril is the spice mace. Whole nutmegs are oval and look rather like a piece of smooth wood. The flavor and aroma of nutmeg are strong and sweet, and a small quantity provides a great deal of flavor. Nutmeg should be grated directly into a dish as needed; once grated, flavor loss is rapid. Nutmeg is used in pastries and sweets in many European cuisines.

Whole Nutmegs with Ground Mace (left) and Ground Nutmeg (right)

Mace (Fr. *macis*) is an expensive spice, with a flavor similar to nutmeg but more refined. It is almost always purchased ground and retains its flavor longer than other ground spices. Mace is used primarily in pastry items.

Peppercorns (Fr. *poivre*) are the berries of a vine plant (*Piper nigrum*) native to tropical Asia, not to be confused with chile (capsicum) peppers. Black and white peppercorns are produced from the same plant, but are picked and processed differently. For black peppercorns, the berries are picked when green and simply dried whole in the sun. Black pepper has a warm, pungent flavor and aroma. For white peppercorns, the berries are allowed to ripen until they turn red. The ripened berries are allowed to ferment, and then the outer layer of skin is washed off. White pepper has fewer aromas than black pepper but is useful where the appearance of black speckles is undesirable. Green peppercorns and pink peppercorns, actually the berries of a South American tree, are also available. The floral aroma and flavor of pink peppercorns as well as their decorative color makes them an intriguing contemporary pastry ingredient.

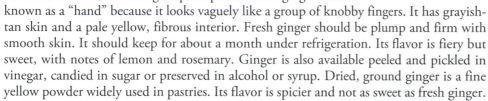

Mace

Black Pepper (left) and White Pepper (right)

Poppy seeds (Fr. *pavot*) are the ripened seeds of the opium poppy, which flourishes in the Middle East and India. (When ripe, the seeds do not contain any of the medicinal alkaloids found elsewhere in the plant.) The tiny blue-gray seeds are round and hard with a sweet, nutty flavor. Poppy seeds are used in pastries and breads, often combined with honey and citrus rind.

Poppy Seeds

Sesame seeds, also known as benne seeds, are native to India. They are small, flat ovals with a creamy white color. Their taste is nutty and earthy, with a pronounced aroma when roasted or ground into a paste (known as tahini). Sesame seeds are the source of sesame oil, which has an intense, smoky flavor and does not go rancid easily. Sesame seeds are often toasted and used in confections and cookies and as a garnish for breads.

Sesame Seeds

Almonds

Brazil Nuts

Cashews

Coconuts

Nuts

Nuts (Fr. *noix*) provide texture and flavor in baked goods and are often substituted for all or part of the wheat flour in a pastry such as dacquoise (page 413). A nut is the edible single-seed kernel of a fruit surrounded by a hard shell. A hazelnut is an example of a true nut. The term is used more generally, however, to refer to any seed or fruit with an edible kernel in a hard shell. Walnuts and peanuts are examples of non-nut "nuts" (peanuts are legumes that grow underground; walnuts have two kernels). Nuts are high in fat, making them especially susceptible to rancidity and odor absorption. Nuts should be stored in nonmetal, airtight containers in a cool, dark place. Most nuts may be kept frozen for up to one year.

Nuts are often roasted in a low (275°F/135°C) oven or in a sauté pan over low heat before being used in order to heighten their flavor. Allowing roasted nuts to cool to room temperature before grinding prevents them from releasing too much oil. Some nuts such as hazelnuts, pistachios, almonds, peanuts and cashews are ground into nut butters used to flavor pastries. When sweetened, nut butter is referred to as a paste and is used to flavor chocolates, ice creams and other baked items.

Almonds (Fr. *amandes*) are the seeds of a plumlike fruit, native to western India, that was first cultivated by the ancient Greeks. It is now a major commercial crop in California. Almonds are available whole, sliced, slivered or ground. Blanched almonds have had their brown, textured skins removed; natural almonds retain their skins. Unless the brown color of natural almond skin is undesirable, the two types can be used interchangeably in recipes. Almonds are frequently used in pastries and candies and are the main ingredient in almond paste and marzipan.

Almond Paste

Brazil nuts (Fr. *noix du Brésil*), sometimes referred to as cream nuts, are the large, oval-shaped seeds of huge trees that grow wild in the rain forests of Central and South America. Their high oil content gives them a rich, buttery flavor and a tender texture. Brazil nuts are available both in-shell and shelled, and are eaten raw, roasted, salted and in ice creams and bakery and confectionery products.

Cashews (Fr. *noix de caju*), native to the Amazon, are actually the seeds of a plant related to poison ivy. Because of toxins in the shell, cashews are always sold shelled. They are expensive and have a pronounced flavor. Cashews make a wonderful addition to cookies and candies.

Chestnuts (Fr. *marrons*) are true nuts that must be cooked before using. Available steamed, dried, boiled or roasted, they are often sold as a canned purée, with or without added sugar. Candied or glazed chestnuts are also available. Most chestnuts are grown in Europe, primarily Italy, but new varieties are beginning to flourish in North America. Their distinctive flavor is found in many sweet dishes and pastries.

Chestnuts

Coconuts (Fr. *noix de coco*) are the seeds from one of the largest of all fruits. They grow on the tropical coconut palm tree. The nut is a dark brown oval, covered with coarse fibers. The shell is thick and hard; inside is a layer of white, moist flesh. The interior also contains a clear liquid known as **coconut water**. (This is not the same as **coconut milk, coconut purée** or **coconut cream**, each of which is prepared from the flesh.) Coconut has a mild aroma, a sweet, nutty flavor and a crunchy, chewy texture. Fresh coconuts are readily available but require some effort to use. Coconut flesh is available shredded or flaked, with or without added sugar. **Macaroon coconut** is a finely ground, unsweetened, dried or dessicated coconut used to make macaroon cookies and candy centers. Coconut purée is sold as a pastry ingredient and in ethnic markets. Coconut is most often used in pastries and candies and is also an important ingredient in East Indian and Caribbean cuisines. A good fresh coconut should feel heavy; you should be able to hear the coconut water sloshing around inside. Avoid cracked, moist or moldy coconuts.

Hazelnuts (Fr. *noisette*) are true nuts that grow wild in the northwestern and upper midwestern states. The cultivated form, known as a filbert, is native to temperate regions throughout the Northern Hemisphere. A bit larger than the hazelnut, the filbert has a weaker flavor than its wild cousin. Both nuts look like smooth brown marbles. Filberts are more abundant, so are generally less expensive. Their distinctive flavor goes well with chocolate and coffee.

Hazelnuts

To remove the hazelnut's skin, roast whole nuts at 275°F (135°C) for 12 to 15 minutes. They should give off a good aroma and just begin to darken. While still hot, rub the nuts in a dry towel or against a mesh sifter to remove the skin.

Hazelnut paste (Fr. *praliné*) is a smooth composition made from finely ground roasted hazelnuts and sugar. It is used to flavor creams, chocolates and icings. Gianduja (zhahn-DOO-yah) refers to chocolate blended with hazelnut paste. It is used as a filling or in candies.

Hazelnut Paste

Macadamia nuts are small, round, creamy white nuts with a sweet, rich flavor and high fat content, native to Australia. The shell is extremely hard and must be removed by machine, so the macadamia is always sold out of the shell. Its flavor blends well with fruit, coconut and white and dark chocolate.

Macadamias

Peanuts (Fr. *arachides*), also known as groundnuts, are actually legumes that grow underground. The peanut is native to South America; it made its way into North America via Africa and the slave trade. They may be eaten raw or roasted and are available shelled or unshelled, with or without their thin red skins. Peanuts are ubiquitous ground with a bit of oil into peanut butter. (Unless otherwise noted, when a formula in this book calls for "peanut butter," use a product that is stabilized such as most widely available commercial brands.)

Peanuts

Pecans (Fr. *noix pacane*), native to the Mississippi River valley, are perhaps the most popular nuts in America. Their flavor is rich and mapley and appears most often in breads, sweets and pastries. They are available whole in the shell or in various standard sizes and grades of pieces.

Pecans

Pine nuts (Fr. *pignon*), also known as piñon nuts and pignole, are the seeds of several species of pine tree. The small, creamy white, teardrop-shaped nuts are commonly used in pastries from Spain, Italy and the American Southwest. They are rarely chopped or ground because of their small size, and need roasting only if being used in a dish that will not receive further cooking.

Pine Nuts

Pistachios (Fr. *pistaches*) are native to central Asia, where they have been cultivated for more than 3000 years. California now produces most of the pistachios marketed in the United States. Pistachios are unique for the green color of their meat. When ripe, the shell opens naturally at one end, aptly referred to as "smiling," which makes shelling the nuts quite easy. Red pistachios are dyed, not natural. Pistachios are sold whole, shelled or unshelled and are used in pastries and confections.

Pistachios

English Walnuts

Walnuts (Fr. *noix*), relatives of the pecan, are native to Asia, Europe and North America. The black walnut, native to Appalachia, has a dark brown meat and a strong flavor. The English walnut, now grown primarily in California, has a milder flavor, is easier to shell and is less expensive. Walnuts are more popular than pecans outside the United States. They are used in baked goods and are pressed for oil.

Alcoholic Beverages

Liquors, liqueurs, wines and brandies are used to either add or enhance flavors in products made in the bakeshop. When these products are added to doughs and pastes that will be baked, most of the alcohol in them evaporates during cooking. Liquors such as rum, bourbon or whiskey can be used for their own distinctive flavors or to blend with other flavors such as chocolate and coffee. Liqueurs are also selected for their specific flavors: for example, kirsch for cherry, amaretto for almond, Kahlúa for coffee, crème de cassis for

TABLE 4.12	LIQUEURS COMMONLY USED AS FLAVORINGS	
LIQUEUR	**ALCOHOL BASE**	**FLAVORINGS**
Amaretto	Grape brandy	Almonds and apricots
B&B	Grape brandy	Benedictine and brandy
Benedictine	Grape brandy	Herbs, spices and citrus peels
Campari	Neutral spirits	130 different herbs, plants, peels and aromatics
Chambord	Grape brandy	Black raspberries
Chartreuse	Grape brandy	More than 125 herbs and other flavorings
Cointreau	Grape brandy	Bitter orange peel
Crème de cacao	Neutral spirits	Chocolate
Crème de café	Neutral spirits	Coffee
Crème de cassis	Neutral spirits	Black currants
Crème de menthe	Neutral spirits	Peppermint
Curaçao	Neutral spirits	Bitter oranges
Drambuie	Scotch whisky	Honey
Frangelico	Neutral spirits	Hazelnuts
Galliano	Neutral spirits	Anise, licorice and vanilla
Grand Marnier	Grape brandy	Bitter oranges
Irish Crème	Irish whiskey	Cream and sugar
Kahlúa	Neutral spirits	Coffee
Kirsch	Neutral spirits	Cherries
Limoncello	Neutral spirits, vodka	Lemons
Malibu	White rum	Coconut
Midori	Neutral spirits	Melons
Nocino	Neutral spirits	Unripened walnuts
Ouzo	Neutral spirits	Anise seed and herbs
Pernod	Neutral spirits	Anise seed and licorice
Pimm's No. 1	Gin	Herbs, botanicals and fruit extracts
Sambuca	Neutral spirits	Anise seed and elderberries
Sloe Gin	Gin, neutral spirits	Sloe berries
Southern Comfort	American whiskey	Peaches and oranges
St-Germain	Grape brandy	Elderflower
Tia Maria	Cask-aged rum	Coffee beans and spices
Triple Sec	Grape brandy	Bitter orange peel

black currant and crème de cacao for chocolate. Wine, both still and sparkling, is used as a flavoring (for example, in sabayon sauce) or as a cooking medium (for example, pears poached in red wine). Brandy, especially the classic orange-flavored Grand Marnier, is another common bakeshop flavoring. Brandy complements fruits and rounds off the flavor of custards and creams.

When selecting an alcoholic beverage for baking, make quality your first concern. Only high-quality products will enhance the flavor and aroma of your baked goods. Table 4.12 lists some popular liqueurs used as flavorings in the bakeshop.

QUESTIONS FOR DISCUSSION

1. What is the importance of protein in flour for bread making? Name the general types of flours available and their different uses in the bakeshop.

2. What is milkfat, and how is it used in classifying milk-based products?

3. Discuss the four functions of sugar and sweeteners in baked goods.

4. Why are eggs pasteurized? What precautions can the pastry cook and baker take to ensure food safety when handling raw egg products?

5. Many varieties of fat and shortening are available to today's baker and pastry chef. Discuss which fats are preferred for various bakeshop applications.

6. Define ripeness and explain why ripe fruits are most desirable. How does the ripening process affect the availability of some fruits? Which fruits emit ethylene gas, and why is this a consideration when storing fruits?

7. Explain why some apple or pear varieties are preferred for baking, while other varieties are preferred for eating without cooking.

8. Why are nuts often roasted before use in baked goods? What functions does roasting accomplish? When is preroasting not recommended?

9. Use the Internet to locate a U.S. producer of European-style pastry ingredients. What type of flavorings and nut products do they produce and market? WWW

Terms to Know

bran	concentrated milk
endosperm	grading
germ	pasteurized eggs
patent flour	amylose
straight flour	amylopectin
ash	bloom strength
enzymes	pectin
soft (weak) flour	ripening
hard (strong) flour	hybrids
malting	varieties
simple syrup	respiration rate
lipids	acidulation
ultra high temperature (UHT)	

CHAPTER FIVE

MISE EN PLACE

After studying this chapter, you will be able to:

- understand measurement systems and how to measure ingredients
- explain the importance of weighing ingredients
- convert formulas and use baker's percentage
- organize and plan your work more efficiently
- understand basic flavoring techniques
- prepare items needed prior to actual cooking

THE FRENCH TERM *MISE EN PLACE* MEANS "PUT IN PLACE." In the professional kitchen it means having everything in place necessary for the successful preparation of a meal. In the bakeshop, mise en place (MEEZ ahn PLAHZ) means accurate selection and measurement of ingredients and preparation of all the components and equipment needed to prepare the final product. Mise en place is as much a mental exercise as it is the physical act of preparing to bake. Anticipating the steps required to prepare a formula, from identifying the tools and ingredients necessary to setting the oven to the proper temperature, saves time and prevents mishaps.

This chapter discusses many of the basics that must be in place before baking begins: measuring ingredients, preparing pans for baking, clarifying butter, toasting nuts and flavoring ingredients. The proper handling and care of knives, often overlooked in the bakeshop, is also discussed.

FORMULAS AND RECIPES

As in the scientific laboratory, many basic recipes in the bakeshop are referred to as *formulas*, perhaps in reference to the scientific nature of what seems like the magic of baking. Using the same preparation method, a product may bake into something entirely different when the ratio of ingredients is altered. For example, if the amount of fat in a formula for pie dough is increased but the type and quantity of other ingredients are not adjusted, the result may be a product that bears no resemblance to what was intended.

The first step when making bakeshop items is to become familiar with the formula and the intended result. Read the formula carefully to identify any special steps that may be required. Locate and prepare all of the equipment needed to complete the task. Select and prepare any ingredients called for in the formula. Often these ingredients, such as butter for creaming into a poundcake, need to be brought to the proper temperature, which requires forethought and planning.

Many finished pastries consist of several components. For example, a lemon meringue pie requires three components—dough for the crust, lemon filling and an egg white meringue topping. The dough must be made and then chilled before rolling so that it will be easier to handle. Because it contains a precooked filling, the pie crust must then be baked before the lemon filling is added. And the meringue topping deflates easily, especially in humid conditions, so it should be prepared and applied close to serving time. Read the entire formula attentively to plan the best order for completing the work. Similarly, a formula for sourdough rye bread requires a sourdough starter, which can take as long as a week to develop. Sourdough bread formulas may deceive if the time to prepare this essential ingredient is overlooked.

It is equally important to follow bakeshop formulas carefully and completely. Unlike other types of cooking, baking mistakes often cannot be discovered until the product is finished, by which time it is too late to correct them. If the salt is omitted when preparing a stew, the mistake can be corrected by adding salt at service time. If the salt is omitted from a loaf of bread, however, the mistake cannot be corrected after the bread has baked, and its texture and flavor may be ruined. It is probably more important to follow a written formula, measure ingredients precisely and combine them accurately in the bakeshop than anywhere else in the kitchen.

PLANNING CHECKLIST

Proper planning helps the baker avoid mishaps. The baker or pastry chef should make special note of these important elements in every formula.

Specific ingredients

Components of a formula that may need advance preparation

Temperature of ingredients

Special equipment required

Equipment preparation

Refrigeration time required

Oven temperatures required

MEASURING INGREDIENTS

The precise, accurate measurement of ingredients is extremely important for bakeshop products. To reproduce products consistently and for the same cost day after day, it is important that the ingredients be measured accurately each time. In a kitchen, measurements may be made in three ways: weight, volume and count.

Weight refers to the mass or heaviness of a substance. It is expressed in terms such as grams, ounces, pounds, kilograms and tons. Weight may be used to measure liquid or dry ingredients (for example, 2 pounds of eggs for a bread recipe) and portions (for example, 3 ounces of hot fudge for a sundae). Weight is the most accurate form of measurement and the one most commonly used in the bakeshop.

Volume refers to the space occupied by a substance. This is mathematically expressed as height × width × length. It is expressed in terms such as cups, quarts, gallons, teaspoons, fluid ounces, bushels and liters. Volume is most commonly used to measure liquids. It may also be used for dry ingredients when the amount is too small to be weighed accurately without specialized equipment (for example, ¼ teaspoon of salt). Formulas in this book include the approximate volume measurements of ingredients that weigh less than ½ ounce (15 grams). Use these measurements when a scale accurate for weighing small quantities is unavailable.

Cooks who assume that 8 ounces of flour is the same as 1 cup of flour commonly make errors in the bakeshop. In fact, 1 cup of flour may weigh from 3 to 5 ounces (90 to 150 grams) depending on the flour and how it was scooped into the measuring cup. Measuring ingredients by weight, commonly referred to as **scaling**, is more accurate; therefore, baking formulas often use weight, even for liquid ingredients.

It is not unusual to see both weight and volume measurements used in a single formula. When a formula ingredient is expressed in weight, weigh it. When it is expressed as a volume, measure it. (Like most rules, however, this one has exceptions. The weight and volume of water, butter, eggs and shortening are nearly identical. In formulas that call for less than 1 pint, weighing yields nearly identical results. When measuring small quantities of these ingredients use whichever measurement is most convenient.) Some common abbreviations for weight and volume measurement appear in Table 5.1.

Because accurate weights are so important, balance scales are commonly employed in the bakeshop. Once the basic procedures are understood, scaling will be faster than measuring by volume.

TABLE 5.1	COMMON ABBREVIATIONS	
teaspoon	=	tsp.
tablespoon	=	Tbsp.
cup	=	c.
pint	=	pt.
quart	=	qt.
gram	=	g
milliliter	=	ml
liter	=	lt
ounce	=	oz.
fluid ounce	=	fl. oz.
pound	=	lb.
kilogram	=	kg

scaling measuring ingredients on a scale before mixing a batter or dough

Liquids can be measured by volume in liquid measuring cups, which may be marked in U.S. and/or metric units.

Small amounts of dry ingredients are measured by overfilling the appropriate measuring spoon, then leveling the ingredient.

PROCEDURE FOR USING A BALANCE SCALE

PREPARING TO BAKE

In order to run efficiently, bakeshops and pastry kitchens rely on planning, coordination and organization to produce the proper variety of baked goods each day. A multi-unit operation may have elaborate procedures and printed forms for what to make daily; a small bakeshop may simply write up a prep list. In any case, the concepts remain the same; bakers and pastry chefs take a physical inventory of preparations on hand from which they create a list of tasks for that day or week. This **production planning** determines what will be produced and who will produce it. By physically counting and weighing the finished cakes, cookies or pies on hand, bakers know what has sold during the previous period. Careful tracking helps identify particular times of the day or the week when certain items are popular.

Not only finished baked goods are scheduled, however. Doughs or batters that can be stored for several days, such as cookie dough or muffin batter, may be mixed at specific times and then frozen to be used as needed. Cakes freeze well and can be thawed and frosted to order. Some bakeshops prepare a time- and space-consuming dough, such as that used to make Danish pastries, once a week. Or chocolate production, which requires cooler temperatures, may be scheduled at a time of the week when the ovens are not in use. Whatever the case, each individual must plan his or her day's activities to meet production needs.

❶ To use a balance scale to weigh an ingredient, place an empty container on the left, then set a counterbalance to that container on the right. Use weights and the sliding beam weight to add an amount equal to the amount of the ingredient needed.

❷ Place the ingredient on the left side of the scale until the two platforms are balanced.

Count refers to the number of individual items. Count is used in formulas (for example, 4 grapefruits) and in portion control (for example, 1 poached pear). Count is also commonly used in purchasing to indicate the size of the individual items. For example, a "96 count" case of lemons means that a 40-pound case contains 96 individual lemons; a "115 count" case means that the same 40-pound case contains 115 individual lemons. So, each lemon in the 96-count case is larger than each lemon in the 115-count case. When placing an order, the chef must specify the desired count.

Measurement Systems

The measurement formats of weight, volume and count are used in both the U.S. and metric measurement systems. Both of these systems are used in modern bakeshops, so today's pastry chef and baker should be able to prepare formulas written in either one.

The **U.S. system** is actually the more difficult system to understand. It uses ounces and pounds for weight and cups for volume.

The **metric system** is the most commonly used system in the world. Developed in France during the late 18th century, it was intended to fill the need for a mathematically rational and uniform system of measurement. The metric system is a decimal system in which the gram, liter and meter are the basic units of weight, volume and length, respectively. Larger or smaller units of weight, volume and length are formed by adding a prefix to the word *gram*, *liter* or *meter*. Some of the more commonly used prefixes in food service operations are *deca-* (10), *kilo-* (1000), *deci-* (1/10) and *milli-* (1/1000). Thus, a kilogram is 1000 grams; a decameter is 10 meters; a milliliter is 1/1000 of a liter. Because the metric system is based on multiples of 10, it is extremely easy to increase or decrease amounts.

Knowledge of the metric system is useful for bakers and pastry chefs interested in European formulas. Luckily, most modern measuring equipment is calibrated in both U.S. and metric increments and there is no need to convert amounts from metric to the U.S. measuring system. The need to convert amounts will arise only if the proper equipment is unavailable. What is most important is to prepare a formula using one set of measurements. If a formula is written in metric units, use metric measuring equipment; if it is written in U.S. units, use U.S. measuring equipment.

TABLE 5.2   COMMON EQUIVALENTS

Dash	=	1/8 teaspoon
3 teaspoons	=	1 tablespoon
2 tablespoons	=	1 fluid ounce
4 tablespoons	=	1/4 cup (2 fluid ounces)
5 1/3 tablespoons	=	1/3 cup (2 2/3 fluid ounces)
16 tablespoons	=	1 cup (8 fluid ounces)
2 cups	=	1 pint (16 fluid ounces)
2 pints	=	1 quart (32 fluid ounces)
4 quarts	=	1 gallon (128 fluid ounces)
2 gallons	=	1 peck
4 pecks	=	1 bushel
1 gram	=	0.035 ounces (1/30 ounce)
1 ounce	=	28.35 grams (often rounded to 30 for convenience)
454 grams	=	1 pound
2.2 pounds	=	1 kilogram (1000 grams)
1 teaspoon	=	5 milliliters
1 tablespoon	=	15 milliliters
1 fluid ounce	=	29.57 milliliters (often rounded to 30 for convenience)
1 cup	=	0.24 liters
1 gallon	=	3.80 liters

CONVERTING GRAMS AND OUNCES

Being familiar with metric conversions allows the baker in the United States to understand, at a glance, the yield and quantities in a metric formula. As you can see from Table 5.2, 1 ounce equals 28.35 grams. Likewise, 1 fluid ounce equals 29.57 milliliters. This number is often rounded to 30 for convenience, however. So, to convert ounces to grams or milliliters, multiply the number of ounces by 30.

$$8 \text{ oz.} \times 30 = 240 \text{ g}$$
$$8 \text{ fl. oz.} \times 30 = 240 \text{ ml}$$

To convert grams or milliliters to ounces or fluid ounces, divide the number of grams or milliliters by 30.

$$240 \text{ g} \div 30 = 8 \text{ oz.}$$
$$240 \text{ ml} \div 30 = 8 \text{ fl. oz.}$$

To develop a framework for judging conversions, remember that:

▶ A kilogram is about 2.2 pounds.
▶ A gram is about $\frac{1}{30}$ ounce.
▶ A pound is about 480 grams.
▶ A liter is slightly more than a quart.
▶ A centimeter is slightly less than ½ inch.
▶ 0°C (32°F) is the freezing point of water.
▶ 100°C (212°F) is the boiling point of water.

NOTE ON MEASUREMENTS

All ingredients in this book are listed in both U.S. and metric measurements. The metric equivalents are rounded off to even, easily measured amounts. Consider these ingredient lists as separate recipes or formulas; do not measure some ingredients according to the metric amounts and other ingredients according to the U.S. amount or the proportions will not be accurate and the intended result will not be achieved.

These approximations are not a substitute for accurate conversions, however. Appendix I contains additional information on equivalents and metric conversions. There is no substitute for knowing this information.

The formulas in this book were developed using the equivalent of 1 ounce equals 30 grams. Although 28.35 is a more mathematically accurate representation of the number of grams in a U.S. ounce, rounding the numeral to 30 produces more usable formulas. If, for example, formulas are converted using 28.35 grams per ounce, then 4 ounces of butter would become 113.4 grams of butter. Likewise, 1000 grams of flour would be 35.27 ounces of flour. In each case, expensive, highly specialized scales would be necessary to measure ingredients. The U.S. and metric formulas in this book may not yield identical amounts. They should each be treated as separate formulas.

Temperature Measurements

Temperature may be expressed in the Fahrenheit temperature scale, which is the standard system used in the United States, or in the Celsius temperature scale, which is used in most of the rest of the world and by the scientific community. In the Fahrenheit scale, the freezing point of pure water is indicated at 32°F and the boiling point is reached at 212°F. Named after the Swedish astronomer who invented it in the 18th century, the Celsius scale measures 100 degrees between the freezing (0°C) and boiling point (100°C) of pure water. The system is sometimes referred to as the centigrade system. To convert Fahrenheit to Celsius, subtract 32 from the Fahrenheit temperature, then multiply the resulting number by 5 and divide that result by 9.

$$140°F - 32 = 108 \times 5 = 540 \div 9 = 60°C$$

FORMULA CONVERSIONS

yield the total amount produced by a formula expressed in total weight, volume or number of units of the product

Whether it produces 6 servings or 60 servings, 3 pounds or 30 pounds of dough, every formula is designed to produce or **yield** a specific amount of product. The yield may be expressed in volume, weight or servings (for example, 1 quart of sauce; 8 pounds of bread dough; 8½-cup servings). The yield for the formulas in this book may be expressed by unit and by weight, such as "60 cookies, ¾ ounce (22 grams) each." If you increase the weight of each piece of dough during scaling, fewer cookies will be obtained. The weight listed is calculated before baking. Remember that the weight of a finished bread, cake or cookie will change because of moisture lost during baking. Formulas for some icings and creams are expressed by volume, such as "2 quarts (2 liters) Bavarian cream." Volume measure is useful when calculating the number of servings of such products, which are normally presented in a mold or cup.

If the stated yield of a formula is not what is needed, the ingredient amounts must be converted (that is, increased or decreased) to produce the desired quantity. Increasing (decreasing) a formula yield is also referred to as **scaling up (down)**.

scale up (down) to increase (decrease) a recipe or formula mathematically

conversion factor (C.F.) the number used to increase or decrease ingredient quantities and recipe yields

It is just as easy to change yields by uneven amounts as it is to double or halve formulas. The mathematical principle is the same: Each ingredient is multiplied by a **conversion factor (C.F.)**. Do not take shortcuts by estimating formula amounts or conversion factors. Inaccurate conversions lead to inedible foods, embarrassing shortages or wasteful excesses. Take the time to learn and apply proper conversion techniques.

Converting Total Yield

$$\frac{\text{New Yield}}{\text{Old Yield}} = \text{C.F.}$$

When portion size is unimportant or remains the same, formula yield is converted by a simple two-step process:

STEP 1   Divide the desired (new) yield by the formula (old) yield to obtain the conversion factor (C.F.).

New Yield ÷ Old Yield = Conversion Factor

Old Quantity × C.F. = New Quantity

STEP 2   Multiply each ingredient quantity by the conversion factor to obtain the new quantity.

Old Quantity × Conversion Factor = New Quantity

EXAMPLE 5.1

You need to convert a formula for grapefruit sorbet. The present formula yields 1½ quarts, but only ¾ quart is needed.

STEP 1   Determine the conversion factor:

$$0.75 \text{ quart} \div 1.5 \text{ quarts} = 0.5$$

Note that any unit can be used, as long as the same unit is used with both the new and the old formula. For example, the same conversion factor would be obtained if the formula amounts were converted to fluid ounces:

$$24 \text{ fluid ounces} \div 48 \text{ fluid ounces} = 0.5$$

STEP 2   Apply the conversion factor to each ingredient in the sorbet formula:

GRAPEFRUIT SORBET

	Old quantity	×	C.F.	=	New quantity
Fresh grapefruit juice	1 qt.	×	0.5	=	½ qt.
Granulated sugar	8 oz.	×	0.5	=	4 oz.
Lemon juice	1 fl. oz.	×	0.5	=	½ fl. oz.
Corn syrup	1 Tbsp.	×	0.5	=	1½ tsp.

Converting Portion Size

Formula conversion is sometimes complicated by portion size conversion. For example, it may be necessary to convert a formula that initially produces 24 2-ounce servings of ice cream into a formula that produces 62 4-ounce servings.

Sometimes the amount of food served as a portion must be changed. For example, a new muffin pan may hold less batter than one it is replacing, or a new plated dessert may require a smaller portion of ice cream than a single serving of ice cream by itself. A few additional steps are necessary to convert formulas when portion sizes must also be changed. This is easy to understand in terms of the total amount of a food item that is needed in relation to the total amount of that item (yield) produced by the current formula. The key is to find a common denominator for the new and old formula: ounces, grams, cups, servings and so on. Any unit can be used, as long as the same unit is used with both the new and the old formula.

STEP 1   Determine the total yield of the existing formula by multiplying the number of portions by the portion size.

Original Portions × Original Portion Size = Total (old) Yield

No. of Portions × Portion Size = Yield

STEP 2   Determine the total yield desired by multiplying the new number of portions by the new portion size.

Desired Portions × Desired Portion Size = Total (new) Yield

STEP 3   Obtain the conversion factor as described earlier.

Total (new) Yield ÷ Total (old) Yield = Conversion Factor

$$\frac{\text{New Yield}}{\text{Old Yield}} = \text{C.F.}$$

STEP 4   Multiply each ingredient quantity by the conversion factor.

Old Quantity × Conversion Factor = New Quantity

Old Quantity × C.F. = New Quantity

EXAMPLE 5.2

Returning to the grapefruit sorbet: The original formula produced 1½ quarts or 24 2-ounce servings. Now you need 36 3-ounce servings.

STEP 1   Total original yield is 24 × 2 = 48 ounces.

STEP 2   Total desired yield is 36 × 3 = 108 ounces.

STEP 3   The conversion factor is calculated by dividing total new yield by total old yield:

$$108 \div 48 = 2.25$$

STEP 4   Old ingredient quantities are multiplied by the conversion factor to determine the new quantities:

GRAPEFRUIT SORBET

	Old quantity	×	C.F.	=	New quantity
Fresh grapefruit juice	1 qt.	×	2.25	=	2.25 qt.
Granulated sugar	8 oz.	×	2.25	=	18 oz.
Lemon juice	1 fl. oz.	×	2.25	=	2.25 fl. oz.
Corn syrup	1 Tbsp.	×	2.25	=	2.25 Tbsp.

Additional Conversion Problems

When making significant changes to a formula's yield—for example, from 5 to 25 portions or 600 to 300 portions—you may encounter additional problems. The mathematical conversions described here do not take into account changes in equipment, evaporation rates, unforeseen formula errors or cooking times. Pastry chefs and bakers learn to use their judgment, knowledge of cooking principles and skills to compensate for these factors.

EQUIPMENT

When the size of a formula changes, the equipment necessary to produce it must change as well. Problems arise, however, when the production techniques previously used no longer work with the new quantity of ingredients. For example, if a small muffin formula can be mixed by hand, an increased batch size may require the use of a mixer. But if mixing time remains the same, the batter may become overmixed, resulting in poor-quality muffins. Trying to prepare a small amount of product in equipment that is too large for the task can also affect its quality.

EVAPORATION

Equipment changes can also affect product quality because of changes in evaporation rates. Increasing a custard formula may require substituting a large, shallow pot for a deep, narrow saucepan. But because the shallow pot provides more surface area for evaporation than does a deep saucepan, reduction time must be decreased to prevent overthickening the cream. The increased evaporation caused by increased surface area may also alter the strength of the flavoring used.

FORMULA ERRORS

A formula may contain errors in ingredients or techniques that are not obvious when it is prepared in small quantities. When increased, however, small mistakes often become big (and obvious) ones, and the final product suffers. The only solution is to test formulas carefully and rely on your knowledge of cooking principles to compensate for unexpected problems.

TIME

Do not multiply time specifications given in a formula by the conversion factor used with the formula's ingredients. All things being equal, cooking time will not change when baking a larger batch. For example, if the pan and portion size remains the same, a muffin requires the same amount of baking time whether you prepare 1 dozen or 14 dozen. Of more significance is the effect that changing equipment has on cooking time. If the muffin pan size is increased, cooking time may increase. Conversely, a smaller pan may take noticeably less time to bake. And an oven filled to capacity may lose more heat, thus slowing the baking time. Cooking time will also be affected by changes in evaporation rate or heat conduction caused by equipment changes. A larger batch of milk for custard cooking in the same size pan will take longer to heat than the original formula. Mixing time may change when formula size is changed. Different equipment may perform mixing tasks more or less efficiently than previously used equipment.

Baker's Percentage

Many commercial formulas, especially those for cookies, cakes and breads, list ingredients as a percentage in addition to, or in place of, a specific weight or volume measurement. Percentages make accurate formula conversions possible, and percentages are also a convenient type of shorthand. At a glance, the baker who is familiar with the function of ingredients can tell how rich, moist or crisp a finished product will be. For example, a cookie dough with a high percentage of fat in relation to flour will bake into a more crumbly pastry than cookie dough containing a lower percentage of fat. The simplest bread dough made with flour, water, salt and yeast will bake into a crusty loaf with a crisp crust. When even a small percentage of fat is added, the loaf will become more tender and the crust will be less crisp. When formulas list ingredients in proportion to other ingredients, the experienced baker can select formulas with the proper ratios for the product desired.

The percentage may represent the true percentage or the baker's percentage. In the **true percentage** method, the percentage of each ingredient is calculated based on the total weight of all ingredients in a formula, with the total being 100%.

The percentage formula most commonly used in the bakeshop is called the **baker's percentage**. When using baker's percentage, the quantity of each ingredient is expressed as a percentage of the total amount of flour used in the formula. The weights of all the ingredients must be in the same unit of measure, such as ounces, grams, pounds, or kilos. The flour in the formula is always 100%. If a formula calls for two or three types of flour, the total of all the flours must equal 100%. Consult the companion DVD, *Math for Bakers*, for additional information on measurement systems, formula conversions and baker's percentage.

baker's percentage a system for measuring ingredients in a formula by expressing them as a percentage of the total flour weight

CALCULATING BAKER'S PERCENTAGE

To calculate the baker's percentage in a formula:

STEP 1   Identify the weight of the flour in the formula. This weight will be 100%.

STEP 2   Assure that the weights of all ingredients are in the same unit of measure.

STEP 3   Divide the weight of each of the other ingredients in the formula by the weight of the flour.

STEP 4   Multiply the number obtained by 100 to calculate the baker's percentage for each ingredient.

$$\text{Weight of Ingredient} \div \text{Weight of Flour} \times 100 = \text{Baker's Percentage of Ingredient}$$

$$\frac{\text{Weight of Ingredient}}{\text{Weight of Flour}} \times 100 = \text{B.P.}$$

EXAMPLE 5.3

The formula for Sugar Cookie Dough shown in Figure 5.2 needs to be converted to baker's percentage so that it can be scaled up.

STEP 1   Determine the weight of the flour, which is 100%.
$$1 \text{ pound (16 ounces) of flour} = 100\%$$

STEP 2   Divide the weight of the sugar by the weight of the flour.
$$6 \div 16 = 0.375$$

STEP 3   Multiply the number obtained by 100 to obtain the baker's percentage for the sugar.
$$0.375 \times 100 = 37.5\%$$

STEP 4   Calculate the baker's percentage for each of the remaining ingredients in the formula as outlined in Steps 1, 2 and 3.
$$\text{Butter: } 7 \div 16 = 0.437 \times 100 = 43.7\%$$
$$\text{Vanilla extract: } 1 \div 16 = 0.062 \times 100 = 6.2\%$$

An experienced baker will know at a glance that this sugar cookie with 44% butter will be more tender and crumbly than one made from a formula with just 20% butter. With 37.5% sugar, this cookie will be sweet and somewhat crisp but not as brittle as a similar cookie with 60% sugar. When one understands baker's percentage it becomes easy to compare formulas.

Sample Baker's Percentage Formula

Here is an example of how a formula written in baker's percentage might look. The column to the right indicates the relationship of all ingredients in this formula to the quantity of total flour in the formula. The total batch weight and baker's percentage are used to scale a formula up or down.

SUGAR COOKIE DOUGH

Yield: 20 Cookies, 1½ oz. each

	Quanity	Baker's Percentage
Flour	1 lb.	100%
Granulated sugar	6 oz.	37.5%
Butter	7 oz.	43.7%
Vanilla extract	1 fl. oz.	6.2%
Total:	1 lb. 14 oz.	187.4%

FIGURE 5.1 ▶ Sample baker's percentage formula.

Compare the Spritz Cookies on page 347 with the Sugar Cookie Dough in Figure 5.1. Simply by reading the formulas, the baker knows that the Spritz Cookies, with 80% butter, will be richer and more buttery than the Sugar Cookies. The baker can also easily customize a formula by using percentages. Seeing that the vanilla extract in the Sugar Cookie Dough is 6.2%, the baker knows that adding 5 or 6 percent of another flavoring, ground nuts or chocolate chips will transform this cookie without significantly altering the texture of the finished product. Note that the total baker's percentage for a formula is always calculated. It is used to scale a formula up or down using the baker's percentages.

CONVERTING A FORMULA USING BAKER'S PERCENTAGE

With baker's percentage the relationship or ratio of ingredients remains unchanged, making it very easy to scale a formula up or down. To convert a formula using baker's percentage, first the new formula yield must be determined. Then the total baker's percentage for the original formula is divided by 100 to obtain a baker's percentage conversion factor. The new formula yield is multiplied by the conversion factor to obtain the quantity of flour needed for the new scaled formula. Once the total amount of flour has been determined, it is easy to calculate the quantities of other ingredients in the formula. The remaining ingredient quantities are determined by multiplying the new flour weight by the baker's percentage for each ingredient.

$$\frac{\text{Total Baker's Percentage}}{100}$$

$$= \text{B.P. Conversion Factor}$$

STEP 1 Determine the new formula yield required. Converting the total yield from pounds (kilograms) to ounces (grams) ensures accuracy.

STEP 2 Divide the total baker's percentage for the original formula by 100 to obtain the baker's percentage (B.P.) conversion factor for the formula.

Total Baker's Percentage ÷ 100 = B.P. Conversion Factor

STEP 3 Divide the new formula yield by the B.P. conversion factor.

New Formula Yield ÷ B.P. Conversion Factor = Quantity of flour for new formula

$$\frac{\text{New Formula Yield}}{\text{B.P. C.F.}}$$

$$= \text{New Flour Quantity}$$

STEP 4 Compute the quantity of other ingredients required by multiplying the baker's percentage for each ingredient by the new flour weight.

EXAMPLE 5.4

The formula for Sugar Cookie Dough yields 20 cookies at 1.5 ounces each (1 pound 14 ounces of dough). You need four dozen cookies weighing 1.5 ounces each (4.5 pounds of dough). See Figure 5.2.

Example of Scaling Using Baker's Percentage
SUGAR COOKIE DOUGH

Yield: 20 Cookies, 1½ oz. each   **New Yield:** 48 Cookies, 1½ oz. each

	Old Quantity	Baker's Percentage	New Quantity	Rounded
Flour	1 lb.	100%	38.5 oz.	39 oz.
Granulated sugar	6 oz.	37.5%	14.4 oz.	14 oz.
Butter	7 oz.	43.7%	16.7 oz.	17 oz.
Vanilla extract	1 fl. oz.	6.2%	2.3 fl. oz.	2 fl. oz.
Total:	1 lb. 14 oz.	187.4%	71.9 oz.	72 oz.
				4 lb. 7.9 oz.	4 lb. 8 oz.

FIGURE 5.2 ▶ Scaling up using baker's percentage.

STEP 1   Calculate the new formula yield.

$$4.5 \text{ lb.} \times 16 \text{ (oz. per lb.)} = 72 \text{ oz.}$$

STEP 2   Divide the total baker's percentage for the original formula by 100 to obtain the baker's percentage conversion factor for the formula.

$$187.4 \div 100 = 1.874$$

STEP 3   Divide the new formula yield by the B.P. conversion factor.

$$72 \div 1.874 = 38.42 \text{ oz. flour}$$

STEP 4   Compute the quantity of other ingredients required by multiplying the new flour weight by the baker's percentage for each ingredient.

$$38.42 \times 37.5\% = 14.4 \text{ oz. sugar}$$
$$38.42 \times 43.7\% = 16.7 \text{ oz. butter}$$
$$38.42 \times 6.2\% = 2.3 \text{ fl. oz. vanilla extract}$$

Note that the weight of ingredients may be rounded to make scaling more efficient.

Baker's percentage is included in formulas in this book when flour is a primary ingredient. In the few formulas for which baker's percentage is provided but flour is not the dominant ingredient, the formula will indicate this. In formulas where baker's percentage is used, the percentages are what dictate the quantity of ingredients in either the U.S. or metric column. The metric ingredient measurements are not always exact equivalents of the U.S. ingredient measurement. Quantities may be rounded to the nearest whole number to make the formulas usable. An exception is made for significant ingredients when their weight is less than 5 percent of the weight of flour, however.

Yield Percentage

Ingredients such as fruits require cleaning and trimming before they are ready for use in a formula. Once an apple is peeled and cored, for example, the peels are discarded and the remaining **edible portion (E.P.)** is what is left. Pastry chefs and bakers conduct a **yield test** to determine the usable portion of an ingredient. **Yield percentage** is calculated to determine how much of an ingredient to order. The edible portion (E.P.) or the weight of the ingredient after it is prepared for use divided by the weight of the ingredient as purchased (A.P.) is the yield percentage for that food item.

STEP 1   Weigh the ingredient as purchased (A.P.) before cleaning, trimming and peeling.

STEP 2   Peel, trim and clean the ingredient as required.

STEP 3   Weigh the cleaned, trimmed product to determine the edible portion (E.P.).

STEP 4   Divide the E.P. weight by the A.P. weight to obtain the yield percentage.

edible portion (E.P.) the amount of a food item available for consumption or use after trimming or fabrication; a smaller, more convenient portion of a larger or bulk unit

yield test measuring and weighing an ingredient before and after trimming to determine the usable portion; used to determine the quantity of an ingredient to purchase as well as actual ingredient cost

yield percentage the ratio of the usable weight of an ingredient after cleaning and trimming to the quantity purchased, calculated by dividing the trimmed weight by the as-purchased weight of the ingredient

E.P. Weight ÷ A.P. Weight =
Yield Percentage

EXAMPLE 5.5

The weight of 5 pounds of apples (A.P.) after peeling and coring is 4 pounds (E.P.). Dividing 4 pounds peeled and cored apples E.P. by 5 pounds unpeeled apples A.P gives an 80% yield percentage:

4 pounds peeled, cored apples (E.P.) ÷ 5 pounds unpeeled apples (A.P.)
= 80% yield percentage

USING YIELD PERCENTAGE TO CALCULATE A.P. QUANTITY

Often formulas are written listing the edible portion of an ingredient. You must then calculate the A.P. quantity required. To find the A.P. quantity needed for a formula, divide the A.P. quantity in the formula by the yield percentage.

E.P. Quantity ÷ Yield Percentage = A.P. Quantity

E.P. Quantity ÷ Yield Percentage =
A.P. Quantity

EXAMPLE 5.6

An apple tart formula requires 12 pounds of peeled and cored apples. Apples have an 80% yield percentage; therefore 15 pounds of apples will be required.

12 pounds E.P. ÷ 0.80 (yield percentage for apples) = 15 pounds A.P.

Yield percentage is also used to determine actual costs of these ingredients. Chefs periodically conduct yield tests on items requiring fabrication and trimming to ensure that they are properly costing ingredients. (Tables listing average yields of common ingredients are also available in books and from produce purveyors.)

KNIFE SKILLS

Basic knife skills are the backbone of the techniques used in a professional kitchen. In the pastry kitchen, dough must be cut, chocolate must be chopped and fruit must be sliced. Sharp knives in skilled hands are just as critical in the bakeshop as they are in other areas of the kitchen. Here we outline some of the basics of safe knife handling.

Using Knives Safely

The first rule of knife safety is to focus on the task at hand. In addition:

1. Use the correct knife for the task at hand.
2. Always cut away from yourself.
3. Always cut on a cutting board. Do not cut on glass, metal or marble. Secure the cutting board by placing a damp towel underneath it to prevent it from sliding.
4. Keep knives sharp; a dull knife is more dangerous than a sharp one.
5. When carrying a knife, hold it point down, parallel and close to your leg as you walk.
6. A falling knife has no handle. Do not attempt to catch a falling knife; step back and allow it to fall.
7. Never leave a knife in a sink of water; anyone reaching into the sink could be injured and other pots and utensils could dent the knife.

Caring for Knives

A sharpening stone called a **whetstone** is used to put an edge on a dull blade. To use a whetstone, place the heel of the blade against the whetstone at a 20-degree angle. Keeping that angle, press down on the blade while pushing it away from you in one long arch, as if to slice off a thin piece of the stone. The entire length of the blade should come in contact with the stone during each sweep. Repeat the procedure on both sides of the blade until sufficiently sharp. With a triple-faced stone, such as that shown here, you progress from the coarsest to the finest surface. Any whetstone can be moistened with either water or mineral oil, but not both. Do not use vegetable oil on a whetstone because it will soon become rancid and gummy.

When sharpening a knife against a three-sided whetstone, go from the coarsest to the finest surface.

Honing a knife against a steel straightens the blade between sharpening.

A **steel** does not sharpen a knife. Rather it is used to hone or straighten the blade immediately after and between sharpenings. To use a steel, place the blade against the steel at a 20-degree angle. Then draw the blade along the entire length of the steel. Repeat the technique several times on each side of the blade.

Do not wash knives in commercial dishwashers. The heat and harsh chemicals can damage the edge and the handle. The blade can also be damaged if it knocks against cookware or utensils. In addition, the knife could injure an unsuspecting worker. Always wash and dry your knives by hand immediately after each use.

PREPARING EQUIPMENT

Getting ready to bake means identifying and readying the equipment necessary. Preheating the oven is a crucial step. Convection ovens generally heat more quickly than conventional and hearth ovens. Racks may need to be adjusted depending on the type of products being baked. When the oven is not going to be filled, plan on baking in the center rack of the oven. The racks should be evenly spaced when you expect to fully load an oven with baking sheets.

Pans, baking sheets and molds require preparation before use. In order to prevent baked goods from sticking, most baking pans are coated with fat, a nonstick baking parchment or both. Disposable paper liners are usually placed in muffin pans before they are filled. It is good practice to lightly coat these pans with vegetable oil, shortening or pan release spray to prevent any overflow from sticking, even when using paper liners. Silicone bakeware also performs best when lightly coated with such pan release sprays. Parchment paper is often used alone or along with pan coatings to line cake pans that will be used to bake butter cakes, especially batters that contain a higher percentage of chocolate, fruit or nuts.

In kitchens where a great deal of baking is done, it may be more convenient to prepare quantities of pan coating to be kept available for use as needed. Pan coating is a mixture of equal parts oil, shortening and flour that can be applied to cake pans with a pastry brush. It is used whenever pans need to be greased and floured. Pan coating will not leave a white residue on a baked crust, as a dusting of flour often does. Apply sparingly as a thick coating may leave a discernible taste. Make small batches so the mixture does not turn rancid before it can be used.

Cutting parchment paper to fit a pie shell for baking blind.

PAN COATING

Yield: 3 lb. (1440 g)

Vegetable oil	1 lb.	480 g
All-purpose shortening	1 lb.	480 g
Bread flour	1 lb.	480 g

1. Place all of the ingredients in the bowl of a mixer fitted with the paddle attachment. Blend on low speed for 5 minutes or until smooth.
2. Store in an opaque airtight container at room temperature for up to 1 month.
3. Apply to baking pans in a thin, even layer using a pastry brush.

PREPARING INGREDIENTS

Ingredient Temperature

Ingredients perform best at certain temperatures. When making yeast dough, for example, the water temperature may need to be adjusted according to a specific formula discussed in Chapter 7, Artisan and Yeast Breads. The temperature of fats is critical as well. Some muffin batters require melted butter. But when making a creamed butter mixture for cake batter, the butter should be softened but not melted. In most applications, butter performs best between 65°F and 75°F (18°C and 23°C), what is often referred to as **room temperature**. Formulas in the book will indicate softened butter or room-temperature butter, which can be easily obtained simply by cutting the butter into smaller pieces; after a few minutes unrefrigerated, the butter should soften. Conversely, butter should be chilled when making pie crust and many cookie doughs. When making egg foam mixtures for cakes, the eggs may also need to be slightly warmed to room temperature before whipping.

Making Bread, Cake or Cookie Crumbs

Pass the crumbs, if desired, through a tamis or sieve so that they will be the same size.

Crumbs are used to make fillings for pastries and crusts for pies and cheesecake. Depending on the application, almost any bread or pastry, including leftover baked Danish and croissant pastries, may be ground and used as a crumb. (Often bakers grind unsold Danish pastries and add them to fillings for the next day's batch.) **Fresh crumbs** are made from fresh bread, plain cookies or plain cake trimmings that are slightly dried out, approximately 2 to 4 days old. If the products are too fresh the crumbs will be gummy and stick together. If the products are stale the crumbs will taste stale. **Dry crumbs** are made from bread, cake trimmings, broken plain cookies or baked pastries that have been dried out in the oven. Ground graham crackers, vanilla cookies, plain butter cookies and spice cookies make excellent crusts for cheesecake (see page 368).

To make crumbs, the product is cubed or torn into pieces and ground in a food processor. Dried crumbs can be processed to a finer consistency than can fresh crumbs. After processing, the crumbs should be passed through a tamis and stored in a tightly closed container in a cool, dry place.

Clarifying Butter

Unsalted whole butter is approximately 80% fat, 16% water and 4% milk solids. When the water and milk solids are removed from butter through a process known as **clarification**, the butter does not burn as quickly and is more stable than whole melted butter. Unsalted or salted butter may be clarified. Clarified butter is often added to egg foam cakes such as genoise (Chapter 13, Cakes and Icings) to add flavor without additional liquid. Clarified butter will keep for extended periods in either the freezer or refrigerator.

PROCEDURE FOR CLARIFYING BUTTER

1 Slowly warm the butter in a saucepan over low heat without boiling or agitation. As the butter melts, the milk solids rise to the top as a foam and the water sinks to the bottom.

2 When the butter is completely melted, skim the milk solids from the top.

3 When all the milk solids have been removed, ladle the butterfat into a clean pan, being careful to leave the water in the bottom of the pan.

4 The clarified butter is now ready to use. One pound (480 grams) of whole butter yields approximately 12 ounces (360 grams) of clarified butter—a yield of 75 percent.

Skimming milk solids from the surface of the melted butter.

Ladling the butterfat into a clean pan.

Toasting Nuts and Spices

Nuts are often toasted lightly before being used in baked goods and confections. Whole spices are sometimes toasted before being ground for a sauce or custard. Toasting not only browns the food, it brings out its flavor and makes it crispier and crunchier. When toasting nuts or spices on the stove top or in the oven, watch them closely as they can develop scorched flavors and burn easily.

Blanching Nuts

The skin on many nuts, especially almonds or hazelnuts, can taste bitter and discolor baked goods such as butter cakes and cookies. Nuts with skins such as almonds and hazelnuts are blanched to remove the skins before using. (They may also be purchased blanched.) To blanch whole almonds, cover the nuts with boiling water and let them soak for 3 to 5 minutes. Drain the nuts and then squeeze each one to remove its skin. Because the moistened skins may discolor the nuts, remove them promptly.

To blanch hazelnuts, place the nuts on a baking sheet. Heat them at 275°F (135°C) for 12 to 15 minutes, just until the nuts start to become fragrant. Remove the nuts from the oven and place them in a clean cloth towel. Briskly rub the nuts in the towel and most of the skin will come off.

Preparing Nut Flour

Finely ground nuts, especially almonds and hazelnuts, are substituted for some or all of the wheat flour in a number of recipes, particularly tortes and egg foam cakes such as dacquoise (page 424), joconde (page 605) and almond *macarons* (page 639). Nut flour may be purchased as an ingredient from a bakery or pastry ingredient supplier; it may also be made in small quantities in most bakeshops. Using a handheld or table model rotary grater makes a finely ground nut flour. The raw nuts, with or without their skins, are placed in the grater and the crank is turned. A food processor may also be used to prepare nut flour, but care must be taken to keep the nuts from overheating and turning into nut butter. When grinding nuts in a food processor, the friction caused by the blade heats the nuts, extracting some of their oil. Freezing the nuts before grinding will help minimize this. Adding some granulated sugar while grinding the nuts and pulsing the machine during processing is also recommended. Sifting the nut flour through a tamis will make a more uniform product.

Toasting sesame seeds in a dry sauté pan on the top of the stove.

Rubbing toasted hazelnuts with a towel to remove the skins.

PROCEDURE FOR GRINDING NUTS INTO FLOUR USING A FOOD PROCESSOR

1. Place whole blanched (skins removed) almonds or hazelnuts in the bowl of a food processor fitted with a metal blade. Add ½ ounce (15 grams) of sugar or 10 percent of the sugar called for in the formula to the nuts.

2. Turn on the machine and grind the nuts for 10 seconds. Turn off the machine, then pulse it on and off at 15- to 20-second intervals during grinding to keep heat from building up.

3. Once the nuts are ground, to obtain finer flour, sift the nut flour through a medium-mesh strainer or tamis.

PREPARING TO BAKE

Ingredients are often flavored before being used in bakeshop formulas. Creams and syrups may be **infused** with the aroma of an herb or spice. Dried fruits and ingredients may be perfumed with an extract or liqueur.

Although most fruits are edible raw and typically served that way, many fruits are enhanced by soaking (**macerating**) them in a flavored syrup or liqueur with added spices and flavorings. When macerating fruits, be certain they are well washed and bruise-free. Drying the fruits after washing prevents diluting the macerating liquid with water.

infuse to flavor a liquid by steeping it with ingredients such as tea leaves, coffee beans, whole spices or herbs

macerate to soak foods in a flavorful liquid, usually alcoholic, to soften them

Steeping

Steeping is the process of soaking dry ingredients in a liquid (usually hot) in order to infuse their flavor into the liquid. Spices, vanilla and coffee beans and nuts are often steeped in hot milk to extract their flavors. The milk is then used to flavor other foods during cooking. For example, coffee beans can be steeped in hot milk and then strained out, with the coffee-flavored milk being used to make a custard sauce.

Note that the steeping mixture is generally covered and removed from the heat to avoid evaporation or reduction of the liquid.

Conditioning Dry Fruit

Dry fruits such as raisins, currants, candied peel and other similar ingredients benefit from a short or overnight soaking in liquid before using in order for them to remain tender once baked in bread and muffin dough. Typically the softened fruits will be used in a formula and the liquid discarded. This is called **conditioning**. To condition dry fruit with water, cover the dry fruit with 80°F (27°C) water and let it sit for 5 minutes. Drain the fruit in a strainer or colander, then let the fruit sit for four hours before using. The last step allows the fruit to plump and absorb any moisture remaining on the outer skin. To condition and flavor dried fruit for certain types of baked products, soak it overnight in sugar syrup, rum, lemon essence or other fruit juice. Drain the fruit before adding it to the dough or batter. The soaking liquid may be used in place of up to 10 percent of the liquid in the formula.

Blanching and Parboiling

blanching very briefly and partially cooking a food in boiling water; used to assist in preparation (for example, to loosen skin from fruit), as part of a combination cooking method or to remove undesirable flavors

parboiling partially cooking a food in boiling or simmering liquid; similar to blanching, but the cooking time is longer

Some foods, especially fruit and herbs such as mint being used in a sauce, are **blanched** or **parboiled**. To do so, they are immersed in a large quantity of boiling unsalted water. This parcooking assists in their preparation (for example, it loosens skins from peaches and other fruit), removes some bitterness, preserves color, softens fruit and shortens final cooking time. The only difference between blanching and parboiling is total cooking time.

Steeping a vanilla bean and cinnamon sticks in warm milk to extract their flavors.

Conditioning raisins in hot water to rehydrate.

Blanching is done quickly, usually only a few seconds. Parboiling lasts longer, usually several minutes. The water may be changed, as when parboiling citrus rind, to remove off-flavors from the cooking liquid. Foods that are blanched or parboiled in water are **shocked** or refreshed in ice water to halt the cooking process.

Making an Ice Bath

Because of the risk of food-borne illness, it is important to cool food quickly to a temperature below 41°F (5°C) before storing it in the refrigerator. An **ice bath** is an easy, efficient way to do so. An ice bath is also necessary for stopping the cooking of delicate mixtures such as custards and for shocking or refreshing blanched or parcooked fruit or herbs. An ice bath is simply a container of ice cubes and cold water. The combination of ice and water chills foods more rapidly than a container of ice alone. The food being chilled also cools faster if it is in a metal container, rather than one made of plastic.

Making a Hot-Water Bath

Custards and fillings made with eggs can curdle when cooked above 185°F (85°C) and chocolate can scorch when melted over direct heat. Water insulates these products for more gentle cooking. These products can be cooked in a pan set over simmering water (a *double boiler*). Individual servings of custard may be baked in a **hot-water bath**, which protects them from the oven's heat. Have available a shallow pan large enough to accommodate the dish or cups in which the custard will bake without touching each other. (When it is time to bake, you will place the filled cups in this pan, then fill it with hot water to within ½ inch (1.2 centimeters) of the tops of the cups.)

shocking also called refreshing; the technique of quickly chilling blanched or parcooked foods in ice water; prevents further cooking and sets colors

Chilling vanilla custard sauce in an ice bath.

1. Why is it so important to weigh ingredients used in the bakeshop? What types of ingredients may be accurately measured by volume?

2. Describe the proper procedures for sharpening a knife.

3. Explain the process used to scale up a formula. Why is it important to follow the procedures described in this chapter when scaling a bakeshop formula up or down?

4. Conduct a yield test for two or three items in your kitchen such as strawberries, pears and oranges. What are the various considerations when testing the yield percentage for these three fruits? Which fruit has the highest yield percentage? Explain why.

5. Discuss what steps are necessary when a formula calls for "room-temperature" butter.

6. Select a formula from Chapter 14, Custards, Creams and Sauces, and describe the mise en place for that item.

Terms to Know

production planning	whetstone
count	steel
metric system	room temperature
yield	clarification
scale up	infuse
conversion factor (C.F.)	macerate
true percentage	ice bath
baker's percentage	hot-water bath

CHAPTER SIX

QUICK BREADS

After studying this chapter, you will be able to:

- understand and use chemical leavening agents properly
- prepare a variety of quick breads using the biscuit method, muffin method and creaming method
- prepare a variety of griddlecakes

BUTTERMILK BISCUITS, BLUEBERRY MUFFINS, BANANA NUT BREAD AND CURRANT SCONES ARE ALL QUICK BREADS. Why they are called quick breads is obvious: They are quick to make and quick to bake. With only a few basic ingredients and no yeast, almost any food service operation can provide its customers with fresh muffins, biscuits, scones and loaf breads.

The variety of ingredients is virtually limitless: cornmeal, whole wheat, fruits, nuts, spices and vegetables all yield popular products. And the use of these products is not limited to breakfast service—they are equally appropriate for lunch, snacks and buffets. This chapter looks at these basic quick breads as well as formulas for griddlecakes such as pancakes and waffles.

CHEMICAL LEAVENING AGENTS

Quick breads are made from soft doughs or batters prepared using chemical leavening agents, principally baking soda and baking powder. This sets them apart from breads that are made with yeast and require additional time for fermentation and proofing, as discussed in Chapter 7, Artisan and Yeast Breads. Understanding how chemical leavening agents operate is essential to successfully producing quick breads.

Chemical leavening agents perform several functions in baked goods. They *leaven batters and dough*. They *tenderize baked goods*. And small amounts of chemical leaving *contribute to the characteristic flavor of quick breads*. Chemical leavening releases gases (primarily carbon dioxide) through chemical reactions between **acids** and **bases** contained in the formula. These gases form bubbles or air pockets throughout the dough or batter. As the product bakes, these gases expand, causing the product to rise. The proteins in the dough or batter then set around these air pockets, giving the quick bread its rise and texture.

Baking Soda

Sodium bicarbonate ($NaHCO_3$) is more commonly known as household baking soda. Baking soda is an alkaline compound (a base), which releases carbon dioxide gas (CO_2) if both an acid and moisture are present. Heat is not necessary for this reaction to occur. Therefore, products made with baking soda must be baked at once, before the carbon dioxide has a chance to escape from the batter or dough. This is especially true when baking soda is mixed into a wet batter. The presence of moisture in a wet batter accelerates the reaction time of the baking soda. Batters made with baking soda are said to have a low **bench tolerance**, which means they will lose much of their leavening action if left on the work bench too long.

Acids commonly used in formulas with baking soda are buttermilk, sour cream, lemon juice, vinegar, honey, molasses and fruits high in acid such as citrus. Generally, the amount of baking soda used in a formula is only the amount necessary to neutralize the acids present. This amount will vary depending on the amount and type of acid in a formula. Vinegar, for example, is a stronger acid that reacts differently from honey; therefore a formula containing honey may require a different ratio of baking soda in the formula. Often if more leavening action is needed, baking powder, not more baking soda, should be used. Too much baking soda causes the product to taste soapy or bitter; it may also cause a yellow color and brown spots to develop.

Baking Powder

Baking powder is a mixture of sodium bicarbonate and one or more acids in the form of an **acid salt**, which releases acid once dissolved in water. Generally cream of tartar ($KHC_4H_4O_6$), which is also called potassium acid tartrate, and/or sodium aluminum sulfate ($Na_2SO_4 \cdot Al_2[SO_4]_3$) are used. Baking powder also contains a starch to prevent lumping and to prevent chemical reactions from taking place in the mixture before use. Because baking powder contains both the acid and the base necessary for the desired chemical reaction, the quick bread formula does not need to contain any acid. Only moisture is necessary to induce the release of gases.

There are two types of baking powder: single-acting and double-acting. An excess of either type produces undesirable flavors, textures and colors in baked products.

Single-acting baking powder requires only the presence of moisture to start releasing gas. The eggs, milk, water or other liquids in the formula supply this moisture. As with baking soda, products using single-acting baking powder must be baked immediately. Single-acting baking powder can be made by combining two parts cream of tartar, one part baking soda and one part cornstarch by volume. This combination can be used measure-for-measure for baking powder in formulas where a fast-reacting leavening is desirable.

Double-acting baking powder is formulated with sodium bicarbonate (baking soda) and one or more acid salts, which react at different speeds. With double-acting baking powder, there is a small release of gas upon contact with moisture and a second, stronger release of gas when heat is applied. Products made with double-acting baking powder need not be baked immediately, but can sit for a short time without loss of leavening ability. All formulas in this book rely on double-acting baking powder.

Both baking soda and baking powder are sometimes used in one formula. This is because baking soda can release CO_2 only to the extent that there is also an acid present in the formula. If the soda/acid reaction alone is insufficient to leaven the product, baking powder is needed for additional leavening. Small amounts of baking soda also contribute to the rich color in products that contain natural cocoa powder or molasses, such as Cocoa Pear Muffins (page 157) or Whoopie Pies (page 348).

Baking Ammonia

Baking ammonia (ammonia bicarbonate or ammonia carbonate) is also used as a leavening agent and to add crispness in some baked goods, primarily cookies and crackers. Baking ammonia releases ammonia and carbon dioxide very rapidly when heated. The strong odor it releases as it bakes dissipates once the product is cooked above 140°F (60°C). It is suitable for low-moisture products (less than 3 percent moisture) with large surface areas that are baked at high temperatures, such as crackers, biscotti and springerle, a cookie with embossed designs. Consequently, it is rarely used in quick breads.

Purchasing and Storing

Purchase chemical leaveners in the smallest unit appropriate for your operation. Although a large can of baking powder may cost less than several small ones, if not used promptly the contents of a larger container can deteriorate, causing waste or unusable baked goods.

Chemical leavening agents should always be kept tightly covered. Not only is there a risk of contamination if left open, they can also absorb moisture from the air and lose their effectiveness. They should be stored in a cool place because heat deteriorates them. A properly stored and unopened container of baking powder or baking soda has a shelf life of several years.

MIXING METHODS

Quick breads are tender products made from soft doughs or batters. Gluten development is minimized to ensure a tender product. Tenderness comes from the mixing method used as well as the type and amount of fat in the formula. Quick breads are generally mixed by the **biscuit method**, the **muffin method** or the **creaming method**. The mixing method employed is directly related to the type and consistency of fat used in the formula. Cold solid fats, such as butter, lard or vegetable shortening, are used in the biscuit method to produce flaky products. Fats that are soft but not liquid are used in the high-fat

---

BAKING POWDER IN A PINCH

To make a fast-acting baking powder when none is available, combine two parts cream of tartar, one part baking soda and one part cornstarch by volume. This is a **fast-acting leavener**, and any batter or dough made with it should be baked immediately after mixing.

DOUGH REACTION RATES

By federal law all baking powders are designed to release a minimum of 12 percent carbon dioxide by weight. This makes baking powders interchangeable in terms of leavening power. But baking powders are composed of different types of acid salts that react at different temperatures and speeds. Bakers consider a baking powder slow- or fast-acting depending on how quickly a dough reacts, the **dough reaction rate** (DRR). Baking powder made solely with cream of tartar, for example, has a fast DRR, releasing as much as 70 percent of its carbon dioxide during mixing. Today all commercially available baking powders are double-acting. They are made with combinations of fast-acting acids salts such as cream of tartar and monocalcium phosphate (MCP) and such slow-acting acid salts as sodium aluminum sulfate (SAS) and sodium acid pyrophosphate (SAPP).

TABLE 6.1	QUICK-BREAD MIXING TECHNIQUES	
MIXING TECHNIQUE	FAT	RESULT
Biscuit method	Solid (chilled)	Flaky dough
Muffin method	Liquid (oil or melted butter)	Soft, tender, cakelike texture
Creaming method	Softened (room temperature)	Rich, tender, cakelike texture

Biscuits

crumb the interior of bread or cake; may be elastic, aerated, fine or coarse grained

creaming method. Liquid fats, such as oil or melted butter, are used in the muffin method to produce very moist, tender products. See Table 6.1.

To achieve tenderness and a soft **crumb**, quick breads are made using wheat flour with a protein content in the range of 8 to 9 percent. Some blends of all-purpose flour fit in this range, as do many blends of pastry flour. For this reason, many recipes in this chapter specify all-purpose or pastry flour. To keep gluten development to a minimum, flour is mixed into quick breads swiftly and gently.

Biscuit Method

The biscuit method is used for biscuits, shortcakes and scones and is very similar to the technique used to make flaky pie doughs discussed in Chapter 11, Pies and Tarts. The goal is to create a baked good that is light, flaky and tender. The cold fat is cut into the flour using a knife and fork, a pastry cutter or a mixer fitted with the paddle attachment. For small batches of dough, it may also be **rubbed in** using the tips of one's fingers. To achieve the desired flakiness in biscuit dough, the fat is cut into visible uniform pieces.

PROCEDURE FOR PREPARING PRODUCTS WITH THE BISCUIT METHOD

1. Preheat the oven. Measure all ingredients.
2. Sift the dry ingredients together.
3. Cut or rub in the fat, which should be in a solid form.
4. Combine the liquid ingredients, including any eggs.
5. Add the liquid ingredients to the dry ingredients. Mix just until the ingredients are combined. Do not overmix, as this causes toughness and inhibits the product's rise.
6. Place the dough on the bench and knead it lightly four or five times (approximately 20 to 30 seconds). The dough should be soft and slightly elastic, but not sticky. Too much kneading toughens the biscuits. Use a slow speed and a short mixing time when kneading biscuit dough in a mixer.

make-up the cutting, shaping and forming of dough products before baking

7. The dough is now ready for **make-up** and baking.

MAKE-UP OF BISCUIT-METHOD PRODUCTS

1. Roll out the dough on a lightly floured surface to a thickness of ½ to ¾ inch (1.2 to 1.8 centimeters). Be careful to roll it evenly. Biscuits should double in height during baking.
2. Cut into the desired shapes. Cut straight down; do not twist the cutters, as this inhibits rise. Space cuts as close together as possible to minimize scraps.
3. Position the biscuits on a lightly greased or paper-lined sheet pan. If placed with sides nearly touching, the biscuits will rise higher and have softer sides. Place farther apart for crusty sides.

4️⃣ Reworking and rerolling the dough may cause tough, misshapen biscuits. See Figure 6.1. Nevertheless, it may be possible to reroll scraps once by pressing the dough together gently without kneading.

5️⃣ Tops may be brushed with egg wash before baking or with melted butter after baking. Bake immediately in a hot oven.

6️⃣ Cool the finished products on a wire rack.

FIGURE 6.1 ▶ Properly made biscuit dough (right) rises more fully and evenly than reworked biscuit dough (left).

COUNTRY BISCUITS

Yield: 36 Biscuits, 2 ¼ oz. (66 g) each   **Method:** Biscuit

All-purpose or pastry flour	2 lb. 8 oz.	1200 g	100%
Salt	0.75 oz.	24 g	2%
Granulated sugar	2 oz.	60 g	5%
Baking powder	2 oz.	60 g	5%
Unsalted butter, cold	14 oz.	420 g	35%
Milk	1 ½ pt.	720 ml	60%
Total dough weight:	5 lb. 2 oz.	2484 g	207%

1️⃣ Sift the dry ingredients together, making sure they are blended thoroughly.
2️⃣ Cut or rub in the butter. The mixture should look mealy; do not overmix.
3️⃣ Add the milk and stir, combining only until the mixture holds together.
4️⃣ Transfer the dough to a lightly floured work surface; knead until it forms one mass, approximately five or six kneadings.
5️⃣ Roll out the dough to a thickness of ½ inch (1.2 centimeters). Cut with a floured 2-inch (5-centimeter) cutter and place the biscuits on a paper-lined sheet pan.
6️⃣ Bake at 425°F (220°C) until the tops are light brown, the sides almost white and the interiors still moist, approximately 10 to 12 minutes. Internal heat will continue to cook the biscuits after they are removed from the oven.
7️⃣ Remove the biscuits to a wire rack to cool.

Approximate values per biscuit: **Calories** 210, **Total fat** 10 g, **Saturated fat** 6 g, **Cholesterol** 25 mg, **Sodium** 240 mg, **Total carbohydrates** 27 g, **Protein** 4 g, **Vitamin A** 10%

MISE EN PLACE

▶ Line a sheet pan with parchment paper.
▶ Preheat oven to 425°F (220°C).

1️⃣ Sifting the dry ingredients together.

2️⃣ Cutting in the fat.

3️⃣ Kneading the dough.

4️⃣ Cutting the biscuits.

FIGURE 6.2 ▶ Properly mixed corn muffins (left) rise evenly and show no signs of tunneling. Improperly mixed corn muffins (right) rise unevenly and have large irregular holes.

Muffin Method

Muffins are any small, cakelike baked good made in a muffin tin (pan). Batters for muffins and loaf quick breads are generally interchangeable. For example, banana muffin batter may be baked in a loaf pan, provided the baking time is altered. Generally batters mixed using the muffin method are less rich and less sweet than the cakelike muffins or breads made using the creaming method.

When preparing baked goods by the muffin method, the goal is to produce a tender product with an even shape and an even distribution of fruits, nuts or other ingredients. The most frequent problem encountered with muffin-method products is overmixing. This causes toughness and may cause holes to form inside the baked product, a condition known as **tunneling** (see Figure 6.2).

tunneling large tubular holes in muffins and cakes, a defect caused by overmixing

PROCEDURE FOR PREPARING PRODUCTS WITH THE MUFFIN METHOD

1 Preheat the oven and prepare the pans. Measure all ingredients.

2 Sift the dry ingredients together.

3 Combine the liquid ingredients, including melted fat or oil. Melted butter or shortening may resolidify when combined with the other liquids; this is not a cause for concern.

4 Add the liquid ingredients to the dry ingredients and stir just until combined. Do not overmix. The batter will be lumpy.

5 The batter is now ready for make-up and baking.

MAKE-UP OF MUFFIN-METHOD PRODUCTS

1 Muffin pans and loaf pans should be greased with butter, shortening or commercial pan grease. Paper liners may be used and will prevent sticking if the batter contains fruits or vegetables. Paper liners, however, inhibit rise.

2 A portion scoop is a useful tool for ensuring uniform-sized muffins. Be careful not to drip or spill batter onto the edge of the muffin cups; it will burn and cause sticking.

3 Allow muffins and loaf breads to cool for several minutes before attempting to remove them from the pan.

4 Cool the finished products on a wire rack.

BLUEBERRY MUFFINS

Yield: 26 Muffins, approximately 3 oz. (90 g) each   **Method:** Muffin

Pastry or all-purpose flour	1 lb. 4 oz.	600 g	100%
Granulated sugar	1 lb. 2 oz.	540 g	90%
Salt	0.5 oz.	15 g	2.5%
Baking powder	0.54 oz. (4 tsp.)	16 g	2.7%
Eggs	5 oz. (3 eggs)	150 g	25%
Buttermilk (1% fat)	10 fl. oz.	300 ml	50%
Vegetable oil	8 oz.	240 g	40%
Vanilla extract	0.15 fl. oz. (1 tsp.)	5 ml	0.075%
Blueberries	1 lb.	480 g	80%
Lemon zest, grated	0.4 oz. (2 Tbsp.)	12 g	2%
Streusel Topping (page 145; optional)	as needed	as needed	
Total batter weight:	4 lb. 14 oz.	2358 g	392%

MISE EN PLACE

▸ Preheat oven to 400°F (200°C).
▸ Grate lemon zest.
▸ Grease or line muffin cups.

❶ Combining the liquid ingredients.

❷ Folding in the blueberries.

❸ Portioning the batter.

1. Sift together the flour, sugar, salt and baking powder.
2. In a separate bowl whisk the eggs until completely smooth. Add the buttermilk, oil, vanilla and lemon zest.
3. Stir the liquid mixture into the dry ingredients. Do not overmix. The batter should be lumpy.
4. Gently fold in the blueberries and lemon zest.
5. Portion into greased and floured, paper-lined or silicone muffin cups. Sprinkle with Streusel Topping (if using). Bake at 400°F (200°C) until the center bounces back when lightly pressed, approximately 18 to 22 minutes.
6. Cool the muffins in the pan for several minutes before removing.

Variations:

Cranberry Orange Muffins—Substitute fresh orange zest for the lemon zest and 8 ounces (240 grams/40%) dried cranberries for the blueberries.

Pecan Spice Muffins—Omit the blueberries and lemon zest. Add 8 ounces (240 grams/40%) chopped pecans, 0.08 oz. (1 teaspoon/2 g/0.4%) cinnamon and 0.04 oz. (½ teaspoon/1 gram/0.4%) each of nutmeg and ground ginger to the batter.

❹ The finished muffins.

Approximate values per muffin: **Calories** 250, **Total fat** 9 g, **Saturated fat** 1 g, **Cholesterol** 20 mg, **Sodium** 290 mg, **Total carbohydrates** 40 g, **Protein** 22 g

Creaming Method

The creaming method is comparable to the mixing method used for many butter cakes. In fact many butter cake formulas may be baked in muffin pans and served as muffins. The softened fat and granulated sugar should be properly creamed to incorporate air, which will help leaven the product as it bakes. The final product will be cakelike, with a fine texture. There is less danger of overmixing with this method because the higher fat content shortens gluten strands and tenderizes the batter. Muffins prepared using the creaming method tend to remain fresh longer than those made using the muffin method.

PROCEDURE FOR PREPARING PRODUCTS WITH THE CREAMING METHOD

1. Preheat the oven and prepare the pans. Measure all ingredients.
2. Sift the dry ingredients together.
3. Combine the softened fat and sugar in a mixer bowl. Cream on low speed until the color lightens and the mixture fluffs.
4. Add eggs gradually, slowly beating well after each addition.
5. Add the dry and liquid ingredients to the creamed fat alternately. In other words, a portion of the flour is added to the fat and incorporated, then a portion of the liquid is added and incorporated. These steps are repeated until all the liquid and dry ingredients are incorporated. By adding the liquid and dry ingredients alternately, you avoid overmixing the batter and prevent the butter-and-sugar mixture from curdling.
6. The batter is now ready for make-up and baking.

MAKE-UP OF CREAMING-METHOD PRODUCTS

Panning and baking procedures are the same as those for quick breads prepared with the muffin method.

SOUR CREAM MUFFINS

MISE EN PLACE

▶ Allow butter and eggs to come to room temperature.
▶ Preheat oven to 350°F (180°C).
▶ Grease or line muffin cups.

Sour Cream Muffins with Streusel Topping.

Yield: 12 Muffins, 3¼ oz. (100 g) each   **Method:** Creaming

All-purpose flour	10 oz.	300 g	100%
Baking powder	0.14 oz. (1 tsp.)	4 g	1.4%
Baking soda	0.14 oz. (1 tsp.)	4 g	1.4%
Salt	0.2 oz. (1 tsp.)	6 g	2%
Unsalted butter, room temperature	8 oz.	240 g	80%
Granulated sugar	8 oz.	240 g	80%
Eggs	3.3 oz. (2 eggs)	100 g	33%
Sour cream	10 oz.	300 g	100%
Vanilla extract	0.15 fl. oz. (1 tsp.)	5 ml	1.5%
Total batter weight:	2 lb. 7 oz.	1199 g	399%

1. Sift the flour, baking powder, baking soda and salt together.
2. Cream the butter and sugar until light and fluffy. Add the eggs gradually.
3. Stir the dry ingredients and sour cream, alternately, into the butter mixture in three additions. Stir in the vanilla.
4. Portion into greased or paper-lined muffin cups and bake at 350°F (180°C) until light brown and set, approximately 20 minutes.
5. Allow the muffins to cool briefly in the pan before removing.

❶ Creaming the butter and sugar.

❷ Adding the sour cream.

❸ Topping the muffins with the streusel.

Variations:

Sour cream muffin batter makes delicious cupcakes. The batter can also be topped with **streusel** or flavored with a wide variety of fruits or nuts by adding approximately 4–6 ounces (1 cup/120–180 grams/40–60%) fresh or frozen drained fruit to the batter. Blueberries, dried cherries, candied fruits, pecans and diced pears yield popular products. To make basic spice muffins, add 0.04 ounces (½ teaspoon/1 gram/0.3%) each of cinnamon and nutmeg.

streusel a crumbly mixture of fat, flour, sugar and sometimes nuts and spices; used to top baked goods

Approximate values per muffin: **Calories** 290, **Total fat** 17 g, **Saturated fat** 10 g, **Cholesterol** 70 mg, **Sodium** 260 mg, **Total carbohydrates** 31 g, **Protein** 4 g, **Vitamin A** 15%

STREUSEL TOPPING

Yield: 4 lb. 11 oz. (2.25 kg)

All-purpose flour	2 lb.	960 g	100%
Cinnamon, ground	0.14 oz. (2 tsp.)	4 g	0.4%
Salt	0.4 oz. (2 tsp.)	12 g	1.25%
Brown sugar	11 oz.	336 g	35%
Granulated sugar	8 oz.	240 g	25%
Whole butter, cold	1 lb. 8 oz.	720 g	75%
Total weight:	4 lb. 11 oz.	2272 g	236%

❶ Combine the dry ingredients. Cut in the butter until the mixture is coarse and crumbly.

❷ Sprinkle on top of muffins or quick breads before baking. Streusel topping will keep for several weeks under refrigeration and may be frozen for longer storage. There is no need to thaw before use.

Approximate values per 1-oz. (30-g) serving: **Calories** 190, **Total fat** 8 g, **Saturated fat** 5 g, **Cholesterol** 20 mg, **Sodium** 45 mg, **Total carbohydrates** 29 g, **Protein** 2 g

TABLE 6.2 TROUBLESHOOTING CHART FOR MUFFINS AND QUICK BREADS

PROBLEM	CAUSE	SOLUTION
Soapy or bitter flavor	Chemical leaveners not properly mixed into batter	Sift chemicals with dry ingredients
	Too much baking soda	Adjust formula
Elongated holes (tunneling)	Overmixing	Do not mix until smooth; mix only until moistened
Crust too thick	Too much sugar	Adjust formula
	Oven temperature too low	Adjust oven
Flat top with only a small peak in center	Oven temperature too low	Adjust oven
Cracked, uneven top	Oven temperature too high	Adjust oven
No rise; dense product	Old batter	Bake promptly
	Damaged leavening agents	Store new chemicals properly
	Overmixing	Do not overmix

Troubleshooting Muffins and Quick Breads

Although tender quick breads are easy to prepare, skilled handling ensures consistent results. Scale ingredients carefully. Use fresh chemical leavening in the proper quantities. (See Figure 6.3.) Preheat the oven to the desired temperature before mixing. Table 6.2 lists some common problems when making quick breads and how to avoid them. Avoid overmixing quick bread batters when panning so as not to toughen the products. Pans for quick breads should be well greased. Muffin pans may also be lined with paper liners to ease removal from the pans. Firm paper cups, which do not require pans, may also be used as well as silicone baking cups. When baking in paper or silicone, oven temperatures may need to be reduced by 25°F–50°F (10°C–20°C) from those recommended. Because equipment varies, experience will determine what temperatures work best under specific conditions.

GRIDDLECAKES

Pancakes and waffles are types of griddlecakes or griddle breads. They are usually leavened with baking soda or baking powder and are quickly cooked on a very hot griddle or waffle iron using very little fat. Griddlecakes should be more than just an excuse for eating butter and maple syrup, however. They should have a rich flavor and a light, tender, moist interior.

Pancake and waffle batters may be flavored with tangy buckwheat flour, fruits, whole grains or nuts. Both pancakes and waffles are usually served with plain or flavored butter and fruit compote or syrup. Waffles must be cooked in a special waffle iron, which gives the cakes a distinctive gridlike pattern and a crisp texture. Electric waffle irons are available with square, round and even heart-shaped grids. The grids should be seasoned well, then never washed. (Follow the manufacturer's directions for seasoning.) Belgian waffles are especially light and crisp because of the incorporation of whipped egg whites and/or yeast. They are often made in a waffle iron with extra deep grids and are served for breakfast or as a dessert, topped with fresh fruit, whipped cream or ice cream.

PROCEDURE FOR MAKING PANCAKES

1. Prepare the batter.
2. Heat a flat griddle or large sauté pan over moderately high heat. Add clarified butter.
3. Portion the pancake batter onto the hot griddle using a portion scoop, ladle or adjustable batter dispenser. Pour the portioned batter in one spot; it should spread into an even circle. Drop the batter so that no two pancakes will touch after the batter spreads.

FIGURE 6.3 ▶ Effects of different amounts of leavening in quick bread (clockwise from left): 150 percent of the amount of leavening recommended in the formula, 100 percent of the amount of leavening recommended and 50 percent of the amount of leavening recommended.

❹ Cook until bubbles appear on the surface and the bottom of the cake is set and golden brown. Flip the pancake using an offset spatula.

❺ Cook the pancake until the second side is golden brown. Avoid flipping the pancake more than once, as this causes it to deflate.

BUTTERMILK PANCAKES

Yield: 24 Pancakes, 2 oz. (60 g) each

All-purpose flour	1 lb.	480 g	100%
Granulated sugar	0.9 oz. (2 Tbsp.)	28 g	6%
Baking powder	0.4 oz. (1 Tbsp.)	12 g	2.5%
Salt	0.3 oz. (1½ tsp.)	9 g	2%
Buttermilk	1½ pt.	720 ml	150%
Unsalted butter, melted	2 oz.	60 g	12.5%
Eggs, beaten	5 oz. (3 eggs)	150 g	31%
Clarified butter	as needed	as needed	
Total batter weight:	3 lb.	1459 g	304%

MISE EN PLACE
- ▶ Preheat griddle.
- ▶ Melt butter.
- ▶ Beat eggs.
- ▶ Clarify butter.

❶ Sift the flour, sugar, baking powder and salt together.

❷ Combine the buttermilk, melted butter and eggs and add them to the dry ingredients. Mix just until the ingredients are combined.

❸ If the griddle is not well seasoned, coat it lightly with clarified butter. Once its temperature reaches 375°F (190°C), drop the batter onto it in 2-fluid-ounce (60-milliliter) portions using a ladle, portion scoop or batter portioner.

❹ When bubbles appear on the pancake's surface and the bottom is browned, flip the pancake to finish cooking.

Variations:

Blueberry Pancakes—Gently stir 1 pound (480 grams/100%) fresh or frozen blueberries into the batter. If using frozen berries, drain them thoroughly, then pat dry with paper towels before adding them to the batter. Serve with blueberry syrup or compote.

Apple-Pecan Pancakes—Gently fold 4 ounces (120 grams/25%) chopped cooked apples, 0.02 ounces (¼ teaspoon/0.5 gram/0.01%) cinnamon and 1 ounce (30 grams/6.2%) finely chopped pecans into the batter.

Approximate values per pancake: **Calories** 120, **Total fat** 4 g, **Saturated fat** 2.5 g, **Cholesterol** 35 mg, **Sodium** 250 mg, **Total carbohydrates** 17 g, **Protein** 4 g

CONVENIENCE PRODUCTS

Prepared quick-bread and muffin mixes and batters are available in a number of formats. Dry powdered muffin mixes or muffin bases require the addition of liquid, some oil and sometimes eggs. Attention to mixing remains the same as for a muffin batter made from scratch. Select mixes with natural ingredients and flavorings and less sugar.

Ready-to-use quick-bread batters are sold in 1- to 5-gallon containers, designed to be scooped out, panned and then baked.

These batters offer the bakeshop the flexibility of baking small batches of muffins as needed. Additionally, the bakeshop can customize a basic batter by adding selected fruits, nuts and seasonings. These batters also come in plastic tubes, designed to be piped directly from their packaging into prepared pans. Prepared batters must be refrigerated or frozen and thawed as directed and leftovers must be stored according to the manufacturer's directions. Improper storage, panning or baking will affect final product quality.

QUESTIONS FOR DISCUSSION

Terms to Know

acid
base
sodium
  bicarbonate
bench tolerance
acid salt
fast-acting
  leavener
baking ammonia
dough reaction
  rate
biscuit method
muffin method
creaming method
rubbing in

❶ Name two chemical leavening agents and explain how they cause batters and doughs to rise. Describe the purpose of leavening agents in baked goods. Explain why baking soda is used with an acid in baked goods.

❷ List three common methods used for mixing quick breads. What is the significance of the type of fat used for each of these mixing methods?

❸ What is the most likely explanation for discolored and bitter-tasting biscuits? What is the solution?

❹ What happens when muffin batter has been overmixed?

❺ Visit the Web sites for King Arthur Flour and White Lily Foods to learn more about the varieties of flours and flavoring ingredients that are available for use in biscuits and muffins. What are each of these companies famous for? How do the products of these two regional flour manufacturers differ? **WWW**

CREAM SCONES

Yield: 24 Scones, 1½ oz. (45 g) each

Method: Biscuit

All-purpose flour	1 lb.	480 g	100%
Granulated sugar	1.5 oz.	45 g	9%
Baking powder	0.4 oz. (1 Tbsp.)	12 g	2.5%
Baking soda	0.14 oz. (1 tsp.)	4 g	0.9%
Salt	0.2 oz. (1 tsp.)	5 g	1%
Unsalted butter, cold	4 oz.	120 g	25%
Egg yolks	1.3 oz. (2 yolks)	40 g	8%
Half-and-half	11 fl. oz.	330 ml	69%
Total dough weight:	2 lb. 2 oz.	1036 g	214%

1. Combine all ingredients using the biscuit method.
2. Roll out the dough to a thickness of approximately ½ inch (1.2 centimeters). Cut as desired.
3. Bake at 400°F (200°C) for approximately 10 minutes.
4. Brush the tops with butter while hot. Serve warm with clotted cream and jam.

VARIATIONS:

Add 4 ounces (120 grams/25%) raisins, sultanas or currants to the ingredients.

Approximate values per scone: **Calories** 130, **Total fat** 6 g, **Saturated fat** 3.5 g, **Cholesterol** 35 mg, **Sodium** 160 mg, **Total carbohydrates** 17 g, **Protein** 3 g

CHOCOLATE CHERRY SCONES

Yield: 24 Scones, approximately 4¼ oz. (130 g) each   **Method:** Biscuit

Unsalted butter, cold	14 oz.	420 g	44%
Granulated sugar	4 oz.	120 g	12.5%
Buttermilk	8 fl. oz.	240 ml	25%
Sour cream	1 lb.	480 g	50%
Salt	0.6 oz. (1 Tbsp.)	18 g	2%
Vanilla extract	0.5 fl. oz. (1 Tbsp.)	15 ml	1.5%
All-purpose or pastry flour	2 lb.	960 g	100%
Baking powder	2 oz.	60 g	6%
Sun-dried cherries	1 lb.	480 g	50%
Chocolate chunks	9 oz.	270 g	28%
Powdered sugar	as needed	as needed	
Total dough weight:	6 lb. 6 oz.	3063 g	319%

1. Chill a mixer bowl and paddle attachment in the freezer for at least 15 minutes before mixing.
2. Cut the butter into ¼-inch (6-millimeter) cubes. Set aside in the refrigerator.
3. Whisk together the sugar, buttermilk, sour cream, salt and vanilla in a bowl until smooth. Set aside in the refrigerator.
4. Put the flour and baking powder in the chilled mixer bowl. Place the butter on top. Mix on low speed using the paddle attachment until the mixture resembles coarse meal.
5. Add the buttermilk mixture to the dry ingredients and mix very briefly, until just combined. Mix in the cherries and chocolate until just combined.
6. Scale the dough into three uniform pieces. On a lightly floured surface, press each piece of dough out into an 8-inch (20.5-centimeter) disk using a metal torte ring or other form as a guide.
7. Cut each disk of dough into eight wedges. Position the wedges of dough spaced 2 inches (5 centimeters) apart on parchment-lined baking sheets. Bake at 375°F (190°C) until light golden brown, approximately 18 to 24 minutes. When cool, dust with powdered sugar if desired.

VARIATION:

Cinnamon Orange Scones—Omit the sun-dried cherries and chocolate chunks. Add 0.5 ounce (15 grams/1.5%) ground cinnamon and 0.2 ounce (6 grams/0.6%) grated orange zest in Step 3. Yield is reduced to 4 pounds 15 ounces (2313 grams).

Approximate values per scone: **Calories** 430, **Total fat** 21 g, **Saturated fat** 13 g, **Cholesterol** 45 mg, **Sodium** 550 mg, **Total carbohydrates** 58 g, **Protein** 6 g, **Vitamin A** 25%, **Calcium** 20%, **Iron** 15%

1. Mixing in the chilled butter.

2. Adding the chilled buttermilk mixture.

3. Placing the portioned dough on baking sheets.

4. The baked scone.

CRANBERRY SOUR CREAM SCONES

Yield: 24 Scones, approximately 4 oz. (120 g) each

Method: Biscuit

Unsalted butter, cold	14 oz.	420 g	44%
Granulated sugar	4 oz.	120 g	12.5%
Buttermilk	8 fl. oz.	240 ml	25%
Sour cream	1 lb.	480 g	50%
Salt	0.6 oz. (1 Tbsp.)	18 g	2%
Vanilla extract	0.5 fl. oz. (1 Tbsp.)	15 ml	1.5%
Orange zest	0.2 oz. (1 Tbsp.)	6 g	0.6%
All-purpose or pastry flour	2 lb.	960 g	100%
Baking powder	2 oz.	60 g	6%
Cinnamon, ground	1 oz.	6 g	3%
Cranberries, chopped coarse	14 oz.	420 g	44%
Total dough weight:	5 lb. 11 oz.	2745 g	388%

1. Chill a mixer bowl and paddle attachment in the freezer for at least 15 minutes before mixing.
2. Cut the butter into ¼-inch (6-millimeter) cubes. Set aside in the refrigerator.
3. Whisk together the sugar, buttermilk, sour cream, salt, vanilla and orange zest in a bowl until smooth. Set aside in the refrigerator.
4. Put the flour, baking powder and cinnamon in the chilled mixer bowl. Place the butter on top. Mix on low speed using the paddle attachment until the mixture resembles coarse meal.
5. Add the buttermilk mixture to the dry ingredients and mix very briefly, until just combined. Mix in the cranberries until just combined.
6. Scale the dough into three uniform pieces. On a lightly floured surface, press each piece of dough out into an 8-inch (20.5-centimeter) disk using a metal torte ring or other form as a guide.
7. Cut each disk of dough into eight wedges. Position the wedges of dough spaced 2 inches (5 centimeters) apart on parchment-lined baking sheets. Bake at 375°F (190°C) until light golden brown, approximately 20 to 25 minutes.

Approximate values per scone: **Calories** 320, **Total fat** 18 g, **Saturated fat** 11 g, **Cholesterol** 45 mg, **Sodium** 550 mg, **Total carbohydrates** 39 g, **Protein** 5 g, **Calcium** 0%, **Iron** 15%

BISCUITS AND SCONES: A GENEALOGY

Biscuit is a French word used to describe any dry, flat cake, whether sweet or savory. It was, perhaps, originally coined to describe twice-baked cakes (*bis* = twice, *cuit* = cooked). Crusader chronicles, for example, mention soldiers eating a "bread called 'bequis' because it is cooked twice" and still, today, the Reims biscuit is returned to the oven for further baking after it is removed from its tin.

Over the centuries, the French began to use the term *biscuit* generically and appended modifiers to identify the particular type of dry, flat cake. For example, a *biscuit de guerre* was the very hard, barely risen product of flour and water used from the time of the Crusades to the era of Louis XIV as an army ration (*guerre* is French for "war"); *biscuit de Savoie* is a savory sponge-cake; *biscuit de pâtisserie* is a sweet biscuit.

To the British, a biscuit is what Americans call a cracker or cookie. Yet there appears to be no British quick bread quite comparable to the American biscuit—the closest relative would be the scone. But because a scone contains eggs and butter, it is much richer than a biscuit.

Elizabeth Alston, in *Biscuits and Scones*, proposes that the biscuit is an American variant of the scone. She theorizes that early British colonists in America brought with them traditional scone recipes. Unable to find or afford the necessary fresh butter and eggs, these practical bakers substituted lard and omitted the eggs. What they created, however, were not mock scones, but rather a new product, different from scones but still delicious. Alston further speculates that French cooks initially called the new American product "biscuit de something" and eventually dropped the "de something."

SHORTCAKES

Yield: 48 Shortcakes, approximately 2¾ oz. (83 g) each

Method: Biscuit

All-purpose flour	4 lb.	1920 g	100%
Baking powder	3.75 oz.	115 g	6%
Salt	0.4 oz. (2 tsp.)	12 g	0.6%
Granulated sugar	13 oz.	385 g	20%
Unsalted butter, cold	1 lb. 12 oz.	845 g	44%
Eggs	11.5 oz. (7 eggs)	345 g	18%
Milk	18 fl. oz.	540 ml	28%
Total dough weight:	8 lb. 10 oz.	4162 g	216%
Whole butter, melted	as needed	as needed	
Granulated sugar	as needed	as needed	

1. Combine all of the ingredients using the biscuit method.
2. Cut into 3-inch (7.5-centimeter) circles and space 2 inches (5 centimeters) apart on a paper-lined sheet pan.
3. Bake at 400°F (200°C) until lightly browned, approximately 12 to 17 minutes.
4. Remove from the oven and brush the tops with melted butter, then sprinkle with granulated sugar. Serve these shortcakes, split in half layered with sliced fresh strawberries and Crème Chantilly (page 502).

Approximate values per shortcake: **Calories** 310, **Total fat** 15 g, **Saturated fat** 9 g, **Cholesterol** 65 mg, **Sodium** 250 mg, **Total carbohydrates** 38 g, **Protein** 5 g, **Vitamin A** 15%

IRISH WHEATEN BREAD

This traditional bread from Ireland is leavened with baking soda. Deep cuts in the dough allow the bread to be broken into four triangular pieces after baking. The type and brand of whole wheat flour used will affect the amount of liquid needed in this formula. Add the buttermilk gradually to determine the amount required.

Yield: 1 Round Loaf, 9 in. (24 cm)

Method: Biscuit

Whole-wheat flour, coarse	12 oz.	360 g	75%
Bread flour	4 oz.	120 g	25%
Sea salt	0.2 oz. (1 tsp.)	6 g	1.25%
Baking soda	0.14 oz. (1 tsp.)	4 g	0.09%
Unsalted butter, diced	2.5 oz.	72 g	15%
Low-fat buttermilk	12 fl. oz.	360 ml	75%
Total dough weight:	1 lb. 14 oz.	922 g	191%

1. Sift the dry ingredients together, making sure they are blended thoroughly.
2. Cut in the butter until the mixture resembles a light meal.
3. Stir in the buttermilk gradually to make a firm batterlike dough that is not sticky.
4. Scrape the dough out onto a work surface and knead lightly a few times to form the dough into a ball. Round the dough into a loaf approximately 8 inches (20 centimeters) in diameter. Flatten the dough with the palm of your hands to a thickness of approximately 2 inches (5 centimeters).
5. Place the dough on a paper-lined baking sheet. Sprinkle the top of the dough with coarse whole-wheat flour, then cut the surface of the dough in a cross pattern approximately ½ inch (1.2 centimeters) deep.
6. Bake the bread at 425°F (220°C) until it is well browned and firm, approximately 35 to 40 minutes. Cool on a wire rack and serve warm.

Approximate values per ½₂-loaf serving: **Calories** 190, **Total fat** 50 g, **Saturated fat** 3.5 g, **Cholesterol** 15 mg, **Sodium** 320 mg, **Total carbohydrates** 29 g, **Protein** 6 g

BASIC BERRY MUFFINS

STOUFFER STANFORD COURT HOTEL, SAN FRANCISCO, CA

Former Executive Chef Ercolino Crugnale

Yield: 60 Muffins, 2½ oz. (75 g) each   **Method:** Muffin

Eggs	13.3 oz. (8 eggs)	400 g	28%
Heavy cream	1 qt.	925 ml	66%
Lemon zest, finely grated	0.2 oz. (1 Tbsp.)	6 g	0.4%
Nutmeg, ground	0.02 oz. (¼ tsp.)	0.5 g	0.04%
Granulated sugar	1 lb. 4 oz.	590 g	42%
Baking powder	2.5 oz. (6 Tbsp.)	70 g	5%
Cake flour	3 lb.	1400 g	100%
Kosher salt	0.5 oz. (1 Tbsp.)	14 g	1%
Fresh berries or nuts*	1–1½ lb.	460–700 g	33–50%
Unsalted butter, melted	1 lb.	460 g	33%
Total batter weight:	9 lb. 4 oz.	4325 g	308%

1. Whisk the eggs, cream and lemon zest together by hand.
2. Sift the dry ingredients together. Add the berries or nuts, tossing to coat them evenly with the flour mixture.
3. Add the dry ingredients to the egg mixture and stir until about two-thirds mixed. Add the melted butter and finish mixing.
4. Portion into greased muffin cups and bake at 375°F (190°C) for approximately 15 to 18 minutes.

*Blueberries, blackberries, raspberries, chopped pecans or walnuts may be used, as desired.

Approximate values per muffin: **Calories** 260, **Total fat** 13 g, **Saturated fat** 8 g, **Cholesterol** 70 mg, **Sodium** 135 mg, **Total carbohydrates** 31 g, **Protein** 3 g, **Vitamin A** 15%, **Claims**—low sodium

MORNING GLORY MUFFINS

Yield: 18 Large Muffins, 5 oz. (150 g) each   **Method:** Muffin

All-purpose flour	1 lb.	480 g	100%
Granulated sugar	18 oz.	540 g	112%
Baking soda	0.6 oz. (4 tsp.)	20 g	4%
Salt	0.6 oz. (1 Tbsp.)	18 g	3.7%
Cinnamon, ground	0.3 oz. (4 tsp.)	10 g	2%
Carrots, grated	14 oz.	420 g	88%
Raisins	6 oz.	180 g	38%
Pecan pieces	4 oz.	120 g	25%
Coconut, shredded	4 oz.	120 g	25%
Apple, unpeeled, grated	6 oz.	180 g	38%
Eggs	10 oz. (6 eggs)	300 g	62%
Corn oil	10.5 oz.	315 g	65%
Vanilla extract	0.6 fl. oz. (4 tsp.)	20 ml	4%
Total batter weight:	5 lb. 10 oz.	2723 g	567%

1. Sift the dry ingredients together and set aside.
2. Combine the carrots, raisins, pecans, coconut and apple.
3. Whisk together the eggs, oil and vanilla.
4. Toss the carrot mixture into the dry ingredients. Then add the liquid ingredients, stirring just until combined.
5. Portion into well-greased large muffin cups and bake at 350°F (180°C) until done, approximately 25 minutes.

Approximate values per muffin: **Calories** 520, **Total fat** 27 g, **Saturated fat** 5 g, **Cholesterol** 70 mg, **Sodium** 310 mg, **Total carbohydrates** 63 g, **Protein** 6 g, **Vitamin A** 45%, **Claims**—good source of fiber

BRAN MUFFINS WITH RAISINS

Yield: 36 Muffins, 3½ oz. (105 g) each   **Method:** Muffin

Buttermilk	1 qt.	960 ml	152%
Wheat bran	10 oz.	300 g	47%
Salt	0.75 oz.	22 g	3.5%
All-purpose flour	1 lb. 5 oz.	630 g	100%
Baking powder	0.6 oz. (4 tsp.)	18 g	3%
Baking soda	0.6 oz. (4 tsp.)	18 g	3%
Cinnamon, ground	0.4 oz. (2 Tbsp.)	12 g	2%
Eggs	6.5 oz. (4 eggs)	195 g	31%
Vegetable oil	12 fl. oz.	360 ml	57%
Brown sugar	1 lb. 8 oz.	720 g	114%
Raisins, conditioned	1 lb.	480 g	75%
Streusel Topping (page 145; optional)	as needed	as needed	
Total batter weight:	7 lb. 11 oz.	3697 g	587%

1 Combine the buttermilk, wheat bran and salt. Set aside for 15 minutes. (The mixture will look deceptively dry.)

2 Sift together the flour, baking powder, baking soda and cinnamon.

3 In a separate bowl whisk the eggs until completely smooth. Add the oil and brown sugar. Stir into the soaked bran mixture.

4 Fold in the conditioned raisins. Then fold in the dry ingredients and combine without overmixing.

5 Portion into greased and floured, paper-lined or silicone muffin cups. Sprinkle with Streusel Topping (if using). Bake at 400°F (200°C) until the center bounces back when lightly pressed, approximately 18 to 22 minutes.

VARIATION:

Up to 6 ounces (180 grams/50%) chopped nuts may be added to the batter if desired.

Approximate values per muffin: **Calories** 290, **Total fat** 11 g, **Saturated fat** 1.5 g, **Cholesterol** 20 mg, **Sodium** 450 mg, **Total carbohydrates** 48 g, **Protein** 5 g, **Claims**—good source of fiber

PUMPKIN MUFFINS

Yield: 29 Muffins, approximately 4½ oz. (135 g) each   **Method:** Muffin

All-purpose flour	1 lb. 10 oz.	780 g	100%
Baking soda	0.2 oz. (1½ tsp.)	6 g	0.08%
Baking powder	0.42 oz. (1 Tbsp.)	12 g	1.6%
Cinnamon, ground	0.75 oz.	22 g	2.9%
Cloves, ground	0.07 oz. (1 tsp.)	2 g	0.03%
Ginger, ground	0.25 oz.	7 g	1%
Cardamom, ground	0.04 oz. (½ tsp.)	1 g	0.02%
Eggs	13 oz. (8 eggs)	380 g	49%
Granulated sugar	2 lb. 10 oz.	1260 g	161.5%
Vegetable oil	8 oz.	242 g	31%
Salt	0.5 oz.	15 g	2%
Pumpkin purée	2 lb.	960 g	123%
Orange juice	12 fl. oz.	360 ml	46%
Streusel Topping (page 145; optional)	as needed	as needed	
Total batter weight:	8 lb. 6 oz.	4047 g	518%

1. Sift the dry ingredients together and set aside.
2. Whip the eggs in the bowl of a mixer fitted with the whip attachment until well beaten. Add the sugar, oil and salt and whip for 5 minutes on medium speed. Add the pumpkin purée and mix until combined. Add the dry ingredients and mix until well blended. Pour in the orange juice and mix until smooth.
3. Scale the batter into greased or paper-lined muffin cups approximately three-quarters full. Sprinkle with Streusel Topping (if using).
4. Bake at 400°F (200°C) until the muffins bounce back when lightly pressed, approximately 18 to 22 minutes.

VARIATION:

Sweet Potato Muffins—Substitute sweet potatoes that have been peeled, cooked and mashed for the pumpkin purée.

Approximate values per muffin: **Calories** 360, **Total fat** 10 g, **Saturated fat** 1.5 g, **Cholesterol** 55 mg, **Sodium** 380 mg, **Total carbohydrates** 65 g, **Protein** 5 g, **Vitamin A** 100%

Sweet potato muffins.

LEMON POPPY SEED MUFFINS

Yield: 48 Muffins, 2¾ oz. (83 g) each

Method: Creaming

Pastry flour	2 lb.	960 g	80%
Bread flour	8 oz.	240 g	20%
Baking soda	0.14 oz. (1 tsp.)	4 g	0.3%
Baking powder	0.42 oz. (1 Tbsp.)	12 g	1%
Poppy seeds	3 oz.	90 g	7.5%
Unsalted butter, room temperature	1 lb.	480 g	40%
Granulated sugar	1 lb. 10 oz.	780 g	65%
Glucose syrup or honey	4 oz.	120 g	10%
Olive oil	4 fl. oz.	120 ml	10%
Eggs	20 oz. (12 eggs)	600 g	50%
Salt	0.4 oz. (2 tsp.)	12 g	1%
Vanilla extract	1 fl. oz.	30 ml	2.5%
Lemon zest, grated	0.5 oz.	15 g	1.25%
Sour cream	1 lb.	480 g	40%
Powdered sugar	as needed	as needed	
Total batter weight:	8 lb. 3 oz.	3935 g	328%

1. Sift the flours, baking soda and baking powder together. Stir in the poppy seeds and set aside.
2. Using a large mixer fitted with the paddle attachment, cream the butter until lump-free and fluffy. Add the sugar, glucose syrup and oil and cream until light.
3. Gradually add the eggs followed by the salt, vanilla, lemon zest and sour cream. Then stir in the sifted dry ingredients.
4. Scale the batter into 5-ounce (150-gram) portions using a scale or #6 scoop and place in greased or paper-lined muffin cups.
5. Bake at 425°F (220°C) until the centers of the muffins bounce back when lightly pressed, approximately 15 to 18 minutes. Dust the cooled muffins with powdered sugar.

Approximate values per muffin: **Calories** 580, **Total fat** 29 g, **Saturated fat** 14 g, **Cholesterol** 155 mg, **Sodium** 310 mg, **Total carbohydrates** 72 g, **Protein** 9 g, **Vitamin A** 15%, **Vitamin C** 15%

MANGO OAT MUFFINS

Yield: 32 Large Muffins, approximately 6 oz. (180 g) each

Method: Muffin

Brown sugar	2 lb. 6 oz.	1140 g	95%
Trimoline or granulated sugar	3 oz.	90 g	7.5%
Bread flour	2 lb. 8 oz.	1200 g	100%
Quick-cooking oats	8 oz.	240 g	20%
Oat bran	8 oz.	240 g	20%
Baking powder	0.3 oz. (2 tsp.)	9 g	0.75%
Baking soda	0.3 oz. (2 tsp.)	9 g	0.75%
Cinnamon, ground	0.75 oz.	24 g	2%
Salt	0.5 oz.	15 g	1.25%
Eggs	1 lb. 10 oz. (16 eggs)	780 g	65%
Light olive or vegetable oil	2 lb.	960 g	80%
Lemon zest, grated	0.5 oz.	15 g	1%
Orange zest, grated	0.5 oz.	15 g	1%
Vanilla extract	0.5 fl. oz	15 ml	1.25%
Mango, cut into ½-inch (6-millimeter) cubes	2 lb. 8 oz.	1200 g	100%
Streusel Topping (page 145, optional)	as needed	as needed	
Total batter weight:	12 lb. 6 oz.	5952 g	495%

trimoline invert sugar syrup used commercially to prevent crystallization in candies and fondant fillings

❶ Combine the brown sugar, trimoline, flour, oats, oat bran, baking powder, baking soda, cinnamon, salt and eggs in the bowl of a large mixer fitted with the paddle and scraper attachments on low speed for 1 minute.

❷ Increase the speed to medium and mix for 4 minutes.

❸ Scrape down the bowl. With the mixer running on low speed, gradually add the oil, lemon and orange zests and vanilla.

❹ Stir in the mango and mix until just combined.

❺ Portion the batter into greased or paper-lined muffin cups. Sprinkle with Streusel Topping (if using).

❻ Bake at 400°F (200°C) until the centers of the muffins bounce back when lightly pressed, approximately 18 to 22 minutes.

VARIATION:

Blackberry Muffins—Increase the bread flour to 3 pounds (1515 grams/100%). Omit the quick-cooking oats. Add 0.5 ounce (15 grams/1%) ground ginger in Step 3. Substitute frozen, unthawed blackberries for the mango cubes in Step 4.

Mango Oat Muffins (foreground) and Blackberry Oat Muffins (rear and right)

Approximate values per muffin: **Calories** 620, **Total fat** 32 g, **Saturated fat** 5 g, **Cholesterol** 95 mg, **Sodium** 320 mg, **Total carbohydrates** 78 g, **Protein** 10 g, **Iron** 20%

COCOA PEAR MUFFINS

Yield: 45 Large Muffins, approximately 5 oz. (150 g) each

Method: Muffin

Canned pear halves, #10 can, in light syrup, drained	3 lb. 12 oz.	1802 g	143%
Brown sugar	2 lb. 6 oz.	1134 g	90%
Bread flour	2 lb. 10 oz.	1260 g	100%
Cocoa powder	10 oz.	302 g	24%
Baking powder	1.25 oz.	38 g	3%
Baking soda	0.75 oz.	22 g	1.8%
Cinnamon, ground	0.75 oz.	22 g	1.8%
Salt	0.5 oz.	15 g	1.2%
Eggs	1 lb. 12 oz. (17 eggs)	840 g	66%
Vanilla extract	1 fl. oz.	30 ml	2.4%
Grapeseed, light olive or vegetable oil	2 lb.	956 g	76%
Walnut pieces	1 lb. 2 oz.	540 g	43%
Chocolate chips	10 oz.	302 g	24%
Total batter weight:	15 lb. 3 oz.	7263 g	578%

> ### YIELD OF CANNED FRUIT
>
> The amount of fruit and packing liquid in canned fruit varies according to its grade. The range of weights for canned pear halves after draining is between 3 pounds 12 ounces (1.7 kilograms) and 4 pounds (1.8 kilograms) per #10 can. The weight of the drained fruit may vary depending on the brand of canned pears used.

1. Cut the drained pears into large dice. Set aside.
2. In the bowl of a large mixer fitted with the paddle attachment, blend the brown sugar, flour, cocoa powder, baking powder, baking soda, cinnamon, salt and eggs on low speed for 1 minute. Scrape down the bowl, then mix on medium speed for 2 more minutes.
3. With the mixer running on low speed, gradually add the vanilla and oil. Scrape the bowl. Gently stir in the diced pears, walnut pieces, and chocolate chips.
4. Scale the batter into 5-ounce (150-gram) portions and place in well-greased or paper-lined muffin cups.
5. Bake at 400°F (200°C) until the centers of the muffins bounce back when lightly pressed, approximately 20 to 25 minutes.

Approximate values per muffin: **Calories** 580, **Total fat** 36 g, **Saturated fat** 5 g, **Cholesterol** 115 mg, **Sodium** 390 mg, **Total carbohydrates** 60 g, **Protein** 9 g, **Iron** 20%

APPLE CRANBERRY SOUR CREAM MUFFINS

Yield: 26 Large Muffins, approximately 6 oz. (150 g) each

Method: Creaming

Bread flour	1 lb. 14 oz.	900 g	100%
Baking soda	0.14 oz. (1 tsp.)	4 g	0.5%
Baking powder	0.14 oz. (1 tsp.)	4 g	0.5%
Cinnamon, ground	0.5 oz.	15 g	1.6%
Unsalted butter, room temperature	1 lb.	480 g	53%
Granulated sugar	1 lb. 10 oz.	780 g	86%
Trimoline or additional granulated sugar	4 oz.	120 g	13%
Grapeseed, light olive or vegetable oil	4 fl. oz.	120 ml	13%
Eggs	19 oz. (12 eggs)	570 g	63%
Salt	0.4 oz. (2 tsp.)	10 g	1.3%
Vanilla extract	1 fl. oz.	30 ml	3.3%
Sour cream	1 lb.	480 g	53%
Quick-cooking oats	10 oz.	300 g	33%
Apples, peeled, diced	1 lb. 4 oz.	600 g	66%
Cranberries, fresh or frozen IQF	12 oz.	360 g	40%
Powdered sugar	as needed	as needed	
Total batter weight:	9 lb. 15 oz.	4773 g	527%

1. Sift the flour, baking soda, baking powder and cinnamon together. Set aside.
2. In the bowl of a large mixer fitted with the paddle attachment, cream the butter until lump-free and fluffy.
3. Add the sugar, trimoline, and oil. Cream until the mixture lightens. Scrape down the bowl.
4. Gradually add the eggs, followed by the salt, vanilla and sour cream. Stir in the oats.
5. Beat in the dry ingredients until well blended. Fold in the apples and cranberries.
6. Scale the batter into 6-ounce (180-gram) portions and place in greased or paper-lined muffin cups.
7. Bake at 400°F (200°C) until the centers of the muffins bounce back when lightly pressed, approximately 20 to 25 minutes. Dust cooled muffins with powdered sugar, if desired.

Approximate values per muffin: **Calories** 470 , **Total fat** 22 g, **Saturated fat** 11 g, **Cholesterol** 125 mg, **Sodium** 250 mg, **Total carbohydrates** 59 g, **Protein** 8 g, **Iron** 15%

ZUCCHINI BREAD

Yield: 2 Loaves, 9 in. × 5 in. (24 cm × 12 cm)　　　**Method:** Muffin

Eggs	5 oz. (3 eggs)	150 g	36%
Corn oil	7 oz.	210 g	50%
Granulated sugar	1 lb. 2 oz.	540 g	128%
Vanilla extract	0.15 fl. oz. (1 tsp.)	5 ml	1.1%
Cinnamon, ground	0.14 oz. (2 tsp.)	4 g	1%
Salt	0.2 oz. (1 tsp.)	6 g	1.4%
Baking soda	0.14 oz. (1 tsp.)	4 g	1%
Baking powder	0.07 oz. (½ tsp.)	2 g	0.5%
All-purpose flour	14 oz.	420 g	100%
Zucchini, coarsely grated	11 oz.	330 g	78%
Pecans, chopped	4 oz.	120 g	28%
Total batter weight:	3 lb. 11 oz.	1791 g	425%

1. Combine all of the ingredients using the muffin method.
2. Bake in two greased loaf pans at 350°F (180°C) until the center bounces back when lightly pressed, approximately 1 hour.

VARIATION:

Zucchini Muffins—Portion the batter into greased or paper-lined 4-fluid-ounce (120-milliliter) muffin cups. Bake at 375°F (190°C) until browned and the centers of the muffins bounces back when pressed, approximately 20 to 25 minutes.

Approximate values per ⅟₁₂-loaf serving: **Calories** 260, **Total fat** 12 g, **Saturated fat** 1.5 g, **Cholesterol** 30 mg, **Sodium** 160 mg, **Total carbohydrates** 35 g, **Protein** 3 g

BASIC CORN MUFFINS

Yield: 20 Muffins, 3¾ oz. (112 g) each　　　**Method:** Muffin

Yellow cornmeal	12 oz.	360 g	50%
All-purpose flour	12 oz.	360 g	50%
Granulated sugar	10 oz.	300 g	42%
Baking powder	0.4 oz. (1 Tbsp.)	12 g	1.6%
Baking soda	0.14 oz. (1 tsp.)	4 g	0.6%
Salt	0.15 oz. (¾ tsp.)	4 g	0.6%
Buttermilk	24 fl. oz.	720 ml	100%
Eggs	10 oz. (6 eggs)	300 g	42%
Unsalted butter, melted	6 oz.	180 g	25%
Total batter weight:	4 lb. 10 oz.	2240 g	311%

1. Combine all of the ingredients using the muffin method.
2. Portion the batter into greased muffin cups, filling them two-thirds full.
3. Bake at 375°F (190°C) until done, approximately 20 to 25 minutes.

VARIATION:

Southern-Style Cornbread—Omit the sugar. Pour the batter into cast-iron skillets or molds that are preheated and well greased with shortening or bacon fat. Bake at 425°F (220°C) until golden.

Approximate values per muffin: **Calories** 100, **Total fat** 6 g, **Saturated fat** 3.5 g, **Cholesterol** 55 mg, **Sodium** 140 mg, **Total carbohydrates** 28 g, **Protein** 4 g

FLAVORFUL CORN BREAD

Corn muffin batter is extremely versatile. Replace some of the cornmeal with blue or white varieties. Fold in fresh corn kernels in season or dried fruit, scallions, other cooked vegetables or shredded basil and herbs. Any type of grated cheese is a welcome addition. Bake the batter in a well-greased cast iron skillet or loaf pans instead of traditional muffin cups. Adjust baking time if needed.

Jalapeño Corn Muffins (left) and Bacon Cheddar Corn Muffins (right)

JALAPEÑO CHEDDAR CORN MUFFINS

Yield: 20 Muffins, 4¼ oz. (130 g) each

Method: Muffin

Yellow cornmeal	12 oz.	360 g	50%
Pastry or all-purpose flour	12 oz.	360 g	50%
Granulated sugar	3 oz.	90 g	12.50%
Baking powder	0.4 oz. (1 Tbsp.)	12 g	1.6%
Baking soda	0.14 oz. (1 tsp.)	4 g	0.6%
Salt	0.21 oz. (1 tsp.)	6 g	0.9%
Buttermilk	24 fl. oz.	720 ml	100%
Eggs	10 oz. (6 eggs)	300 g	42%
Grapeseed, olive or vegetable oil	8 fl. oz.	240 ml	33%
Corn kernels	6 oz.	180 g	25%
Grated Cheddar cheese	6 oz.	180 g	25%
Seeded and diced jalapeño peppers	4 oz.	120 g	16.5%
Total batter weight:	5 lb. 5 oz.	2572 g	356%

❶ Stir together the cornmeal, flour, sugar, baking powder, baking soda and salt.

❷ Stir together the buttermilk, eggs and oil.

❸ Combine the dry and liquid ingredients using the muffin method.

❹ Gently fold in the corn kernels, cheese and jalapeño peppers.

❺ Portion the batter into greased muffin cups, filling them three-quarters full.

❻ Bake at 375°F (190°C) until the centers of the muffins bounce back when lightly pressed, approximately 20 to 25 minutes.

VARIATION:

Bacon Cheddar Corn Muffins—Omit the jalapeño peppers. Fold 12 slices finely chopped crisp-cooked bacon and 1 ounce (30 grams/4%) finely chopped chives into the batter in Step 4.

Approximate values per muffin: **Calories** 310, **Total fat** 17 g, **Saturated fat** 3.5 g, **Cholesterol** 70 mg, **Sodium** 340 mg, **Total carbohydrates** 35 g, **Protein** 9 g, **Calcium** 15%, **Iron** 20%

HUSH PUPPIES (DEEP-FRIED CORNBREAD)

Yield: 60 Pieces, 2 in. (5 cm) each

Method: Muffin

Yellow cornmeal	1 lb.	480 g	66%
All-purpose flour	8 oz.	240 g	34%
Baking powder	0.4 oz. (1 Tbsp.)	12 g	1.6%
Salt	0.6 oz. (1 Tbsp.)	18 g	2.5%
Black pepper	0.2 oz. (1 Tbsp.)	6 g	0.8%
Granulated sugar	2 oz.	60 g	8%
Onions, minced	8 oz.	240 g	34%
Eggs	6.75 oz. (4 eggs)	200 g	28%
Milk	1 pt.	480 ml	66%
Total batter weight:	3 lb. 10 oz.	1736 g	241%

1 Combine all of the ingredients using the muffin method.

2 Drop small scoops (using a #60 or #70 portion scoop) into deep fat at 375°F (190°C), allowing the batter to swim freely in the fat. Deep-fry* until golden brown.

3 Remove from the fat and drain. Serve immediately.

*Deep-fat frying is discussed in Chapter 8, Enriched Yeast Breads.

Approximate values per piece: Calories 70, **Total fat** 3 g, **Saturated fat** 1 g, **Cholesterol** 5 mg, **Sodium** 120 mg, **Total carbohydrates** 10 g, **Protein** 1 g

1 Scooping the hush puppy batter into the deep-fat fryer.

2 Draining the cooked hush puppies.

ORANGE CRANBERRY BREAD

Yield: 2 Loaves, 9 in. × 5 in. (24 cm × 12 cm) each

Method: Muffin

Pastry or all-purpose flour	1 lb.	480 g	100%
Granulated sugar	13 oz.	390 g	81%
Baking soda	0.14 oz. (1 tsp.)	4 g	0.9%
Baking powder	0.4 oz. (1 Tbsp.)	12 g	2.5%
Cinnamon, ground	0.14 oz. (2 tsp.)	4 g	0.9%
Eggs	3.3 oz. (2 eggs)	100 g	20%
Vegetable oil	4 fl. oz.	120 ml	25%
Corn syrup or additional sugar	3 oz.	90 g	18.75%
Salt	0.4 oz. (2 tsp.)	12 g	2.5%
Orange zest, grated	0.6 oz. (3 Tbsp.)	18 g	3.75%
Orange juice	12 fl. oz.	360 ml	75%
Cranberries, fresh or IQF, chopped coarse	1 lb. 4 oz.	600 g	125%
Walnut or pecan pieces	4 oz.	120 g	25%
Total batter weight:	4 lb. 13 oz.	2308 g	480%

1. Sift together the flour, sugar, baking soda, baking powder and cinnamon.
2. In a large mixing bowl whisk together the eggs and oil and then add the corn syrup, salt, orange zest and orange juice.
3. Add the dry ingredients, folding gently, followed by the cranberries and nuts.
4. Divide evenly into two buttered and floured loaf pans. Bake at 350°F (180°C) until the center of the loaves bounces back when lightly pressed, approximately 1 hour.

Approximate values per ½-loaf serving: **Calories** 230, **Total fat** 8 g, **Saturated fat** 1 g, **Cholesterol** 15 mg, **Sodium** 290 mg, **Total carbohydrates** 38 g, **Protein** 3 g, **Vitamin C** 15%

LEMON TEA BREAD

Yield: 12 Muffins, 2½ oz. (75 g) each, or 1 Loaf, 9 in. × 5 in. (24 cm × 12 cm)

Method: Creaming

Unsalted butter, softened	3 oz.	90 g	50%
Granulated sugar	10 oz.	300 g	166%
Eggs	3.3 oz. (2 eggs)	100 g	55%
Milk	4 fl. oz.	120 ml	66%
All-purpose flour	6 oz.	180 g	100%
Baking powder	0.14 oz. (1 tsp.)	4 g	2.3%
Salt	0.1 oz. (½ tsp.)	3 g	1.6%
Lemon zest, grated	0.4 oz. (2 Tbsp.)	12 g	6%
Lemon juice	4 fl. oz.	120 ml	66%
Total batter weight:	1 lb. 14 oz.	929 g	513%

1 Cream the butter with 7 ounces (210 grams) of the sugar until light and fluffy. Add the eggs and milk. Mix well.

2 Sift the flour, baking powder and salt together and add to the butter mixture. Fold in the lemon zest. Portion into lightly greased muffin pans or a greased loaf pan.

3 Bake at 350° (180°C) until a tester comes out clean, approximately 35 to 40 minutes for a large loaf or 12 to 15 minutes for muffins. Remove the bread from the pan(s) and place on a cooling rack.

4 Combine the remaining 3 ounces (90 grams) of sugar with the lemon juice. Heat until the sugar dissolves and the mixture is hot. Slowly pour or brush the glaze over the hot bread.

Approximate values per serving: **Calories** 220, **Total fat** 7 g, **Saturated fat** 4 g, **Cholesterol** 50 mg, **Sodium** 115 mg, **Total carbohydrates** 36 g, **Protein** 3 g

A CUP OF TEA HISTORY

Some believe that the Chinese emperor Shen Nung discovered tea drinking in 2737 B.C.E. Legend holds that the emperor was boiling his drinking water beneath a tree when some leaves fell into the pot. Enchanted with the drink, he began to cultivate the plant. Whether this is myth or truth, it is known that a hot drink made from powdered dried tea leaves whipped into hot water was regularly consumed in China sometime after the fourth century. But it was not until the Ming dynasty (1368–1644) that infusions of tea leaves became commonplace.

By the ninth century, tea drinking had spread to Japan. In both Chinese and Japanese cultures, tea drinking developed into a ritual. For the Chinese, a cup of tea became the mirror of the soul. For the Japanese, it was the drink of immortality.

Tea was first transported from China to Europe by Dutch merchants during the early 1600s. By midcentury, it was introduced into England. In 1669, the British East India Company was granted a charter by Queen Elizabeth I to import tea, a monopoly it held until 1833. To ensure a steady supply, the English surreptitiously procured plants from China and started plantations throughout the Indian subcontinent, as did the Dutch.

Tea drinking became fashionable in England, at least in court circles, through Charles II (raised in exile at The Hague in Holland, he reigned from 1660 to 1685) and his Portuguese wife, Catherine of Braganza. Queen Anne of England (who reigned from 1702 to 1714) introduced several concepts that eventually became part of the English tea custom. For example, she substituted tea for ale at breakfast and began using large silver pots instead of tiny china pots.

The social custom of afternoon tea began in the late 1700s, thanks to Anna, Duchess of Bedford. Historians attribute to her the late-afternoon ritual of snacking on sandwiches and pastries accompanied by tea. She began the practice in order to quell her hunger pangs between breakfast and dinner (which was typically served at 9:30 or 10:00 P.M.).

Eventually, two distinct types of teatime evolved. Low tea was aristocratic in origin and consisted of a snack of pastries and sandwiches, with tea, served in the late afternoon as a prelude to the evening meal. High tea was bourgeois in origin, consisting of leftovers from the typically large middle-class lunch, such as cold meats, bread and cheeses. High tea became a substitute for the evening meal.

GINGERBREAD

Yield: 4 Dozen 2-in. (5-cm) Squares

Method: Creaming

Ingredient	US	Metric	%
Unsalted butter	1 lb.	480 g	57%
Brown sugar	1 lb.	480 g	57%
Molasses	1 lb.	480 g	57%
Eggs	5 oz. (3 eggs)	150 g	18%
Vanilla extract	0.3 fl. oz. (2 tsp.)	10 ml	1%
Salt	0.6 oz. (1 Tbsp.)	15 g	2%
Coffee, brewed, warm	12 fl. oz.	360 ml	43%
Pastry or all-purpose flour	1 lb. 12 oz.	840 g	100%
Baking soda	0.2 oz. (1 ½ tsp.)	6 g	0.75%
Baking powder	0.2 oz. (1 ½ tsp.)	6 g	0.75%
Ginger, ground	0.75 oz.	25 g	3%
Cinnamon, ground	1.5 oz.	42 g	5%
Cardamom or cloves, ground	0.07 oz. (1 tsp.)	2 g	0.25%
Total batter weight:	6 lb.	2896 g	344%

1. Cream the butter in the bowl of a 6 quart (6.5 liter) or larger mixer fitted with the paddle attachment. Add the brown sugar and molasses and continue creaming until lightened. Add the eggs one at a time, scraping down the bowl after each addition. Stir in the vanilla and salt.

2. Add half of the coffee and blend on low speed until the mixture is smooth.

3. Sift the remaining dry ingredients together, then add half to the batter and mix until combined. Add the remaining coffee and, once it is incorporated, add the remaining dry ingredients.

4. Spread the batter on a paper-lined half-sheet pan fitted with a pan extender. (Alternatively, scale the batter into greased loaf pans.) Bake at 375°F (190°C) until the center bounces back when lightly pressed, approximately 40 to 45 minutes.

5. Cool the cake in the pan on a rack. Unmold and cut into 2-inch × 2-inch (5-centimeter × 5-centimeter) squares.

Approximate values per serving: **Calories** 190, **Total fat** 8 g, **Saturated fat** 5 g, **Cholesterol** 35 mg, **Sodium** 200 mg, **Total carbohydrates** 3 g, **Protein** 2 g

SOUR CREAM COFFEECAKE

Yield: 1 Tube Cake, 10 in. (25 cm)

Method: Creaming

Filling:

All-purpose flour	0.4 oz. (1½ Tbsp.)	12 g	5.7%
Cinnamon, ground	0.2 oz. (1 Tbsp.)	6 g	2.8%
Brown sugar	6 oz.	180 g	86%
Pecans, chopped	4 oz.	120 g	57%
Unsalted butter, melted	1 oz.	30 g	14%

Cake:

Unsalted butter	4 oz.	120 g	57%
Granulated sugar	8 oz.	240 g	114%
Eggs	3.3 oz. (2 eggs)	100 g	47%
Sour cream	8 oz.	240 g	114%
Cake flour, sifted	7 oz.	210 g	100%
Salt	0.05 oz. (¼ tsp.)	1 g	0.7%
Baking powder	0.14 oz. (1 tsp.)	4 g	2%
Baking soda	0.14 oz. (1 tsp.)	4 g	2%
Vanilla extract	0.15 fl. oz. (1 tsp.)	5 ml	2.1%
Total batter weight:	2 lb. 10 oz.	1272 g	604%

1. To make the filling, blend all the filling ingredients together in a small bowl. Set aside.
2. To make the cake batter, cream the butter and sugar. Add the eggs one at a time, beating well after each addition. Add the sour cream. Stir until smooth.
3. Sift the sifted flour, salt, baking powder and baking soda together twice. Stir into the batter. Stir in the vanilla.
4. Spoon half of the batter into a greased tube pan. Top with half of the filling. Cover the filling with the remaining batter and top with the remaining filling. Bake at 350°F (180°C) for approximately 35 minutes.

Approximate values per ⅟₁₆-cake serving: **Calories** 240, **Total fat** 13 g, **Saturated fat** 6 g, **Cholesterol** 40 mg, **Sodium** 130 mg, **Total carbohydrates** 29 g, **Protein** 2 g

BANANA BREAD

Yield: 3 Small Loaves, 8½ oz. (255 g) each

Method: Creaming

Unsalted butter, room temperature	2 oz.	60 g	30%
Granulated sugar	2 oz.	60 g	30%
Brown sugar	2.5 oz.	70 g	36%
Egg	1.6 oz. (1 egg)	45 g	23%
Ripe banana	6.5 oz.	180 g	89%
Cake flour	3.5 oz.	100 g	50%
Pastry flour	3.5 oz.	100 g	50%
Baking powder	0.07 oz. (½ tsp.)	2.5 g	1.2%
Baking soda	0.07 oz. (½ tsp.)	2.5 g	1.2%
Salt	0.05 oz. (¼ tsp.)	1 g	1%
Cinnamon, ground	0.04 oz. (½ tsp.)	1 g	0.5%
Buttermilk	2 fl. oz.	55 ml	28%
Walnuts, chopped	1.75 oz.	50 g	24%
Powdered sugar (optional)	as needed	as needed	
Chocolate curls (optional)	as needed	as needed	
Banana slices brushed lightly with lemon juice (optional)	as needed	as needed	
Total batter weight:	1 lb. 9 oz.	727 g	363%

1. Cream the butter and sugars in the bowl of a mixer fitted with the paddle attachment until light, pale and fluffy. Add the egg, then mash the banana and add to the mixture.
2. Sift the flours with the baking powder, baking soda, salt and cinnamon. Add to the banana mixture, alternating with the buttermilk. Stir in the walnuts.
3. Divide the batter among three prepared 5 × 4 × 1½-inch (12.5 × 10 × 3.7-centimeter) loaf pans and bake at 375°F (190°C) until light brown, approximately 25 to 30 minutes.
4. Garnish the cooled loaves with powdered sugar, chocolate curls and banana slices (if using).

VARIATION:

Chocolate Chip Banana Cake—Add 4 ounces (115 grams/57%) chocolate chips to the batter along with the walnuts.

Approximate values per ¼-cake serving: **Calories** 180, **Total fat** 7 g, **Saturated fat** 3 g, **Cholesterol** 30 mg, **Sodium** 130 mg, **Total carbohydrates** 27 g, **Protein** 3 g

WAFFLES

Yield: 20 Waffles, 2¾ oz. (83 g) each

All-purpose flour	18 oz.	540 g	100%
Salt	0.4 oz. (2 tsp.)	12 g	2.2%
Baking powder	0.8 oz. (2 Tbsp.)	24 g	4.4%
Granulated sugar	2 oz.	60 g	11%
Eggs	6.75 oz. (4 eggs)	200 g	37%
Milk, warm	24 fl. oz.	720 ml	133%
Unsalted butter, melted	5 oz.	150 g	28%
Vanilla extract	0.3 fl. oz. (2 tsp.)	9 ml	1.6%
Total batter weight:	3 lb. 9 oz.	1715 g	317%

1. Mix the dry ingredients together in a large bowl.
2. Whisk the eggs together in a separate bowl; add the milk, butter and vanilla.
3. Pour the liquid mixture into the dry ingredients, stirring to blend. Keep refrigerated until ready to use. Batter may be made up to one day in advance.
4. Cook in a preheated waffle iron according to the manufacturer's directions. Serve waffles immediately with your choice of toppings.

VARIATION:

Pecan Waffles—Sprinkle 0.3 ounces (1 tablespoon/9 grams/1.6%) chopped pecans over the batter as soon as it is poured onto the waffle iron. Substitute 0.15 fluid ounces (1 teaspoon/5 milliliters/0.8%) pecan flavoring for the vanilla extract, if desired.

Approximate values per waffle: **Calories** 190, **Total fat** 8 g, **Saturated fat** 4.5 g, **Cholesterol** 65 mg, **Sodium** 480 mg, **Total carbohydrates** 25 g, **Protein** 5 g, **Calcium** 20%

DRIED FRUIT COMPOTE

This dried fruit compote pairs well with many of the muffins and quick breads in this chapter. Serve it as an accompaniment to pancakes or waffles with powdered sugar and Crème Chantilly (page 502).

Yield: 3 lb. (1.4 kg)

Dried apricots	5 oz.	150 g
Prunes, pitted	5 oz.	150 g
Dried pears or apples	5 oz.	150 g
Dried peaches	5 oz.	150 g
Water, hot	24 fl. oz.	720 ml
Cinnamon stick	1	1
Glucose or corn syrup	12 fl. oz.	360 ml
Cointreau	2 fl. oz.	60 ml

1. Coarsely chop the fruits. Place the pieces in a nonreactive saucepan and add the water and cinnamon stick.
2. Bring the mixture to a simmer, cover and cook until tender, approximately 12 to 15 minutes.
3. Add the glucose syrup and Cointreau. Simmer uncovered until thoroughly heated. Remove the cinnamon stick. Serve warm or refrigerate for longer storage.

Approximate values per 1-oz. (30-g) serving: **Calories** 60, **Total fat** 0 g, **Saturated fat** 0 g, **Cholesterol** 0 mg, **Sodium** 15 mg, **Total carbohydrates** 15 g, **Protein** 0 g, **Claims**—fat free; very low sodium

CHAPTER SEVEN

ARTISAN AND YEAST BREADS

- select and use yeast properly
- perform the 10 steps involved in yeast bread production
- understand artisan bread-making techniques
- mix yeast doughs using the straight dough method and the sponge method
- mix yeast doughs using pre-fermentation and sourdough techniques
- prepare artisan breads
- prepare bagels, flatbreads and other specialty breads

BREAD MAKING IS AN ART THAT DATES BACK TO ANCIENT TIMES. Over the centuries, bakers have learned to manipulate the basic ingredients—flour, water, salt and leavening—to produce a vast variety of breads. Thin-crusted baguettes, tender Parker House rolls, crisp flatbreads and chewy bagels derive from careful selection and handling of the same key ingredients. A renewed interest in the traditional craft of baking has seen many new artisan bread bakeries open in recent years. Customers are demanding, and more restaurants are serving, exciting bread assortments to their guests at every meal. Although few baked goods intimidate novice bakers as much as yeast breads, few baked goods are actually as forgiving to prepare. By mastering a few basic procedures and techniques, restaurants and bakeshops can offer their customers delicious, fresh yeast products.

Yeast breads can be divided into two major categories: lean doughs and rich doughs. Lean doughs, such as those used for crusty French and Italian artisan breads, contain little or no sugar or fat. Traditional sourdough and rye breads are lean doughs that require special handling to bring out their unique flavor. Rich doughs, such as brioche and challah, contain significantly more sugar and fat than lean doughs. Rich dough bakes into softer products with a tender crust and interior crumb and is discussed in Chapter 8, Enriched Yeast Breads. A specific type of rich, flaky dough is made by incorporating layers of fat and flour and is covered in Chapter 9, Laminated Doughs.

This chapter covers in detail the basic production techniques for making lean and sourdough bread products. The principles discussed in this chapter apply to working with all types of yeast-raised products, including artisan-style breads also discussed here. Rereading the discussion of the function of ingredients found in Chapter 4, Bakeshop Ingredients, is recommended before beginning this chapter.

YEAST

fermentation the process by which yeast converts sugar into alcohol and carbon dioxide; it also refers to the time that yeast dough is left to rise—that is, the time it takes for carbon dioxide gas cells to form and become trapped in the gluten network

Artisan and other yeast breads are made from dough prepared with yeast, which, over time leavens the dough, causing it to rise and become less dense. Yeast is a living organism: a one-celled fungus. Various strains of yeast are present virtually everywhere. Yeast feeds on carbohydrates present in the starches and sugars in bread dough, converting them to carbon dioxide and ethanol, an alcohol, in an organic process known as **fermentation**:

$$\text{Yeast} + \text{Carbohydrates} = \text{Alcohol} + \text{Carbon Dioxide}$$

When yeast releases carbon dioxide gas during bread making, the gas becomes trapped in the dough's gluten network. (See Chapter 3, Principles of Baking, page 53.) The trapped gas leavens the bread, providing the desired rise and texture. The small amount of alcohol produced by fermentation evaporates during baking.

As with most living things, yeast is very sensitive to temperature and moisture. It prefers temperatures between 75°F and 95°F (24°C and 35°C). At temperatures below 34°F (2°C),

THE RISE OF YEAST BREADS

How and when the first yeast-leavened breads came into being, no one knows. Perhaps some wild yeasts—the world is full of them—drifted into a dough as it awaited baking. Perhaps some ancient baker substituted fermented ale or beer for water one day. In any case, the resulting bread was different, lighter and more appetizing.

Based on models, images and writings found in excavated tombs, historians are fairly certain that the ancient Egyptians saved a bit of fermented dough from one day's baking to add to the next day's. This use of sourdough starter continues today, enjoying widespread popularity.

Other cultures developed their own leavening methods. The Greeks and Romans prepared a wheat porridge with wine, which caused their doughs to ferment. The Gauls and Iberians added the foamy head from ale to their doughs. Both methods resulted in lighter breads that retained their fresh textures longer. Since ancient times, bread baking has been one of the first household tasks readily turned over to professionals. The first cooks to work outside homes during the Greek and Roman empires were bakers. The bakery trade flourished during the Middle Ages, with a wide variety of breads being produced. Yeast-leavened breads remained the exception, not the

norm, until well into the 17th century, however. The first real collection of bread recipes is found in Nicolas Bonnefon's *Les Délices de la campagne*, published in 1654. Bonnefon's instructions, meant for those dissatisfied with commercial products of the time, included the use of beer yeast. By the end of the 17th century, published works included recipes for breads leavened with sourdough starter and the yeasts used in breweries.

Louis Pasteur finally identified yeast as a living organism in 1857. Soon after, a process for distilling or manufacturing baker's yeast was developed. By 1868, commercial baking yeast was available in stores.

it becomes dormant; above 138°F (59°C), it dies. See Table 7.1. Moisture activates the yeast cells, helping the yeast convert carbohydrates in the dough into food.

Salt is used in bread making because it conditions gluten, making it stronger and more elastic. Salt also affects yeast fermentation. Because salt inhibits the growth of yeast, it helps control the dough's rise. Too little salt and not only will the bread taste bland, it will rise too rapidly. Too much salt, however, and the yeast will be destroyed. By learning to control the amount of food for the yeast and the temperatures of fermentation, you can learn to control the texture and flavor of yeast-leavened products.

Types of Yeast

Baker's yeast, *Saccharomyces cerevisiae*, is available in three forms: compressed, active dry and instant. (Do not be confused by a product called brewer's yeast; it is a nutritional supplement with no leavening ability.)

COMPRESSED YEAST

Compressed yeast is a mixture of yeast and starch with a moisture content of approximately 70 percent. Also referred to as fresh yeast, compressed yeast must be kept refrigerated. It should be creamy white and crumbly with a fresh, yeasty smell. Do not use

Compressed Yeast

TABLE 7.1	TEMPERATURE FOR YEAST DEVELOPMENT	
TEMPERATURE		**YEAST DEVELOPMENT**
34°F	(2°C)	Inactive
60°F–70°F	(16°C–21°C)	Slow action
75°F–95°F	(24°C–35°C)	Best temperature for yeast activity
85°F–100°F	(29°C–38°C)	Best water temperature for hydrating instant yeast
100°F–110°F	(38°C–43°C)	Best water temperature for hydrating active dry yeast
138°F	(59°C)	Yeast dies

compressed yeast that has developed a sour odor, brown color or slimy film. Compressed yeast is softened in twice its weight in warm water at 100°F (38°C) before being added to bread dough. Some bakers even add compressed yeast directly to the dry mix.

Compressed yeast is available in 1-pound (500-gram) blocks. Under proper storage conditions, compressed yeast has a shelf life of 2 to 3 weeks. When fresh, it may be frozen and stored for 1 month. Frozen compressed yeast loses about 5 percent of its activity when thawed.

ACTIVE DRY YEAST

Dry Yeast

Active dry yeast differs from compressed yeast in that virtually all the moisture has been removed by hot air. The absence of moisture renders the organism dormant and allows the yeast to be stored without refrigeration for several months. When used in preparing doughs, dry yeast is generally rehydrated in a lukewarm (approximately 110°F [43°C]) liquid before being added to the other ingredients.

Dry yeast is available in ¼-ounce (7-gram) packages and 1- or 2.2-pound (500-gram or 1-kilogram) vacuum-sealed bags. It should be stored in a cool, dry place and refrigerated after opening.

INSTANT DRY YEAST

Instant dry yeast has gained popularity because of its ease of use; it is added directly to the dry ingredients in a bread formula without rehydrating. The water in the formula activates it. Like all yeasts, instant dry yeast is a living organism and is destroyed at temperatures above 138°F (59°C). (See Table 7.1.) Although instant yeast can be added to flour without hydration, some bakers still prefer to hydrate instant yeast before using it in certain types of formulas. When doughs are mixed briefly or are very firm, such as bagel or croissant dough, instant dry yeast may not fully dissolve during mixing. In such cases the yeast is moistened in four to five times its weight of water. Deduct this amount of water from the total water called for in the formula.

SUBSTITUTING YEASTS

The flavors of dry and compressed yeasts are virtually indistinguishable, but dry yeasts are at least twice as strong. Because too much yeast can ruin bread causing it to rise too quickly and collapse during baking, always remember to reduce the specified weight for compressed yeast when substituting dry yeast or active dry yeast in a formula. Likewise, if a formula specifies dry or active dry yeast, increase the quantity specified when substituting compressed yeast. Any type of yeast may be used in the formulas in this book. Use the formulas in Table 7.2 to convert one type of yeast to another.

NATURAL YEAST LEAVENERS—SOURDOUGH STARTER

Prior to commercial yeast production, bakers relied on natural yeast leaveners, also called **starters**, to make bread rise. Early starters were simple mixtures of flour and a liquid (water, potato broth, milk) left to capture wild yeasts and beneficial acid-producing bacteria from the environment. Once the mixture fermented, it was used to leaven bread. Only a

TABLE 7.2 YEAST SUBSTITUTIONS

Use these formulas to convert from one type of yeast to another	Compressed (fresh) yeast	×	0.5	=	Active dry yeast
	Compressed (fresh) yeast	×	0.33	=	Instant yeast
	Active dry yeast	×	2	=	Compressed (fresh) yeast
	Active dry yeast	×	0.75	=	Instant yeast
	Instant yeast	×	3	=	Compressed (fresh) yeast
	Instant yeast	×	1.33	=	Active dry yeast

portion of the starter was used at a time. The rest was kept for later use, refreshed periodically with additional flour and liquid so that the yeast activity could continue. Natural yeast leaveners and sourdough starter are discussed in detail on pages 185–187.

PRODUCTION STAGES FOR YEAST BREADS

The production of yeast breads can be divided into 10 stages:

1. Scaling the ingredients
2. Mixing and kneading the dough
3. Fermenting the dough
4. Punching down the dough
5. Portioning the dough
6. Rounding the portions
7. Make-up: shaping the portions
8. Proofing the products
9. Baking the products
10. Cooling and storing the finished products

Stage 1: Scaling the Ingredients

As with any other bakeshop product, it is important to scale or measure ingredients accurately and to have all ingredients at the proper temperature when making a yeast bread. Liquids such as water, milk and eggs may all be weighed to ensure accuracy in a formula. When a very small quantity of an ingredient is required, such as for salt and spices, a volume measurement may be preferred.

The amount of flour required in yeast bread may vary depending on the humidity level, storage conditions of the flour and the accuracy with which other ingredients are measured. Flour from different mills or from different batch lots may **absorb** more or less water depending on the type of wheat used. Flour with a higher protein content will absorb more liquid than one with a lower protein content. Even switching flour batches will affect the amount of water needed in a formula. Professional bakers will test a formula with their ingredients to determine exactly how much water to use. The amount of flour stated in most formulas is to be used as a guide. Have additional flour available before mixing. Experience will teach when more or less flour is actually needed.

absorption the ability of flour to absorb moisture when mixed into dough, which varies according to protein content and growing and storage conditions

ATTAINING THE PROPER DOUGH TEMPERATURE

Yeast activity is most beneficial when the finished bread dough reaches a temperature range of 75°F to 80°F (24°C to 27°C) after mixing. Having the dough at the proper temperature when mixing is complete is one key to controlling the bread-making process. The final **dough temperature** is important because a higher dough temperature will increase the rate of fermentation. Conversely, a lower temperature will slow yeast activity. The rate of fermentation affects the characteristics and flavor of the finished bread. The temperature of the flour and water, the temperature in the bakeshop and the heat built up by friction during mixing all affect the final dough temperature. The ingredients in the formula must be adjusted to the proper temperature before mixing yeast dough.

Temperatures vary widely in most bakeshops depending on the time of the year, the local climate and the location of hot ovens inside the bakery. Some commercial bakeries are temperature controlled, but in most bakeries the temperature fluctuates frequently. The bakeshop and flour temperature are not easily changed but they can be gauged with a thermometer. The friction produced when the dough is kneaded by machine (**friction factor**) depends on the specific equipment used in the bakeshop. Most equipment user manuals indicate what the friction factor is for the specific equipment.

Of all the variables, the easiest to control is water temperature. Consequently, when scaling water the baker adjusts the water temperature according to a formula. The

friction factor the temperature increase that a mixer generates in bread dough as it is being kneaded

TABLE 7.3	FORMULA FOR ADJUSTING WATER TEMPERATURE FOR YEAST BREAD DOUGH	
FORMULA	**EXAMPLE**	
Multiply the desired dough temperature by 3	77°F × 3 (25°C × 3) =	231°F (75°C)
Subtract the total of the room temperature, the flour temperature and the mixer friction factor	Room temperature	77°F (25°C)
	Flour temperature	68°F (20°C)
	Mixer friction factor	25°F (14°C)
	Less subtotal	170°F (59°C)
Water temperature should be	Ideal water temperature	61°F (16°C)

In this example, for a yeast dough that is to be mixed immediately, the water temperature should be 61°F (16°C).

Note: The friction factor of 25°F (14°C) is different when working in Fahrenheit or Celsius. The difference takes into account the variances between the two measuring systems.

formula is to multiply by 3 the desired dough temperature after mixing. Then the temperature of the flour, the room temperature and the friction factor are subtracted from this number. The result is the temperature to which the water should be adjusted before mixing the dough. See the formula in Table 7.3. The desired dough temperature of 77°F (25°C) is used for most yeast doughs, although some enriched doughs may be mixed to 80°F (27°C) as discussed in Chapter 8, Enriched Yeast Breads. Often in hot weather, cold water will be required and ice cubes will be used to chill water to the desired temperature.

The friction factor is a number that is included in the formula for obtaining the proper water temperature to adjust for the temperature increase during machine mixing. A friction factor of 25°F (or the number 14°C), which is used in Table 7.3, works for many machines. Consult the user guide or test the mixer. To determine the friction factor of a specific mixer, scale the ingredients for a batch of dough. Use a friction factor of 25°F (or the number 14°C) to determine the temperature for the water. Mix the dough 7 to 8 minutes on medium speed. Take the temperature of the dough. If the dough is too cold (hot), reduce (increase) the temperature of the friction factor by 5°F (1°C) and test again on another batch of dough. Repeat testing as required to determine the friction factor for that equipment.

The formulas in this book requiring water that is adjusted by using this formula are indicated as "temperature controlled."

Stage 2: Mixing and Kneading the Dough

The way ingredients are combined affects the outcome of the bread. Yeast dough must be mixed and kneaded properly in order to combine the ingredients uniformly, distribute the yeast and develop the gluten. If the dough is not mixed properly, the bread's texture and shape suffer.

Yeast breads are usually mixed by either the **straight dough method** (direct method) or one of several *pre-fermentation methods* (indirect method) in which the dough is mixed in several stages: the **sponge method**, the **old dough method** and the **sourdough method**. Old dough and sourdough methods are more commonly used in artisan production and are discussed later in that section of this chapter. (Another method used for rich, flaky doughs, the lamination or rolling-in method, is discussed in Chapter 9, Laminated Doughs.)

Once the ingredients are combined, the dough must be kneaded to develop gluten, the network of proteins that gives bread its shape and texture. **Kneading** achieves certain key results. It helps the proteins hydrate, ensuring development of the gluten web in the bread dough, and it warms the dough to a temperature conducive to keeping the yeast active. Kneading can be done by hand or by an electric mixer fitted with a dough hook. The goal is to create a dough that is smooth and moderately elastic.

PROCEDURE FOR KNEADING DOUGH BY HAND

① First, bring a portion of the dough toward you.

② Then push the dough away with your fist.

③ Repeat, turning the dough 90° each time until the dough is properly kneaded.

Mixing is done in two stages. In the first stage (**pickup stage**) the ingredients are combined on low speed until a rough dough is formed, approximately 2 to 3 minutes. At this point, the baker makes any required adjustments to the formula, adding more liquid or flour if necessary depending on the flour's absorption. When the dough appears too soft, additional flour may be added; when the mixture seems dry and will not form a dough, more water can be added. Be warned, however, that dough hydrates and softens during mixing. What appears to be a dry dough at the outset may be a perfect supple dough once kneaded. The baker uses his or her experience with mixing dough and with the particular formula to determine whether to add more flour or liquid.

Once the ingredients are combined, the dough is kneaded (**mixing stage**) on medium speed approximately 5 to 10 minutes. The goal is to properly develop the gluten structure in the dough and to warm the dough to the ideal temperature. The dough should look smooth. In many cases, the dough will clear away from the machine bowl toward the end of the kneading process.

PROCEDURE FOR KNEADING DOUGH BY MACHINE

Combining ingredients in the pickup stage.

Dough coming together during mixing.

The kneaded dough.

Bakers can check to see when bread dough is properly kneaded and its gluten structure is fully developed by performing the **windowpane test**. To do this, turn off the mixer and take a small piece of dough from the bowl. Using both hands, gently stretch the dough apart. If it stretches without tearing and becomes nearly translucent (like bubble gum or a latex glove), the dough has reached its optimum development. The windowpane test is used on dough made with wheat flours that contain enough protein to form gluten; bread dough with a high percentage of rye and other low-protein flours may not achieve this

windowpane test a procedure to check that yeast dough has been properly kneaded; a piece of the kneaded dough is pulled to see if it stretches without breaking apart

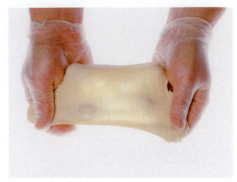

FIGURE 7.1 ▶ The windowpane test.

sponge a thick flour-and-water batter, which may or may not contain some yeast, used to improve the flavor and texture of yeast breads

stage of elasticity. Figure 7.1 shows the windowpane test being used on bread dough that has been properly mixed.

MIXING METHODS

Straight Dough Method

The simplest and most common method for mixing yeast doughs is known as the straight dough method. With this method, all ingredients are simply combined and mixed. Once the ingredients are combined, the dough is kneaded until it is smooth and elastic. Kneading time varies according to the kneading method used and the type of dough being produced. The straight dough method is illustrated by Soft Yeast Dinner Rolls (page 190).

Pre-Fermentation Methods

A number of mixing methods employ a two-step process often referred to as a pre-fermentation technique. First a batter, dough or starter is prepared to allow the yeast to begin fermentation. Then this mixture is turned into a finished dough. Pre-fermentation helps improve the flavor, texture, crust and color of the finished loaf and is discussed more fully in the section on fermentation (page 177).

Sponge Method   The sponge method of mixing yeast dough has two stages. During the first stage the yeast, the liquid and approximately half the flour are combined to make a thick batter known as a **sponge**. The sponge is allowed to rise until bubbly and doubled in size. During the second stage, the remaining ingredients are added. The dough is kneaded and allowed to rise again. These two fermentations give sponge method breads a somewhat different flavor and a lighter texture than breads made with the straight dough method.

The sponge method is often used to improve the texture of heavy doughs such as rye and some enriched yeast doughs as discussed in Chapter 8, Enriched Yeast Breads. The first-stage sponge is usually prepared only for the specific formula and is not reserved for later use. In a high-volume or commercial bakery, however, an all-purpose sponge may be made to streamline production, as long as it is used within a short time period as illustrated on page 190. The sponge method is illustrated by Light Rye Bread (page 191).

KNEADING

Mixing and kneading times given in formulas should be used only as a guide. Reaching the correct dough temperature and creating dough that passes the windowpane test are the goals of proper mixing and kneading. Care should be taken not to overknead the dough. Overkneading results in dough that is, at best, difficult to shape and, in extreme cases, sticky and inelastic.

When the desired dough temperature is not reached after mixing the dough, the baker has several options. If the temperature is too low by a few degrees, knead the dough another minute to increase the dough temperature. If the dough is still too cool after the additional mixing, flatten the dough and let it rise in a warm area. When the dough temperature is 2 or 3 degrees higher than desired after kneading, flatten the dough and place it in a cool area to rise. (Increased surface area helps the dough warm up or cool down more quickly.) When the dough temperature is more than 5 degrees higher than required, it may have been overkneaded. Overkneaded dough will become wet and sticky because the gluten breaks down, causing water that was absorbed during mixing to be released. Discard overkneaded dough or use it for Old Dough (page 199).

Ingredients such as raisins, nuts and other add-ins should be incorporated after the dough has fully developed in order to maintain their integrity in the finished bread.

Stage 3: Fermenting the Dough

As mentioned earlier, fermentation is the natural process by which yeast converts sugar into alcohol and carbon dioxide. Fermentation begins the moment the dough is finished mixing and continues until the dough is baked and reaches a temperature high enough to kill the yeast cells—138°F (59°C). Fermentation also refers to the period when yeast dough is left to rise—that is, the time it takes carbon dioxide gas to form and become trapped in the gluten network. Fermentation is divided into two stages. **Bulk fermentation** refers to the rise given to the entire mass of yeast dough before the dough is shaped, and **proofing** refers to the rise given to shaped yeast products just prior to baking.

Dough develops characteristics during fermentation that will enhance the taste and texture of the finished bread. As it feeds on the sugars and starches in the dough, the yeast converts them to flavorful enzymes and bacteria. The gluten strengthens during fermentation, ensuring a bread that will hold its structure when baked. For fermentation, place the kneaded dough into a container large enough to allow the dough to expand, or scrape the dough onto a floured workbench. The surface of the dough may be oiled to prevent drying. Cover the dough and place it in a draft-free place at a temperature between 75°F and 85°F (24°C and 29°C).

Fermentation is complete when the dough has approximately doubled in size and no longer springs back when pressed gently with two fingers. The time necessary varies depending on the type of dough, the temperature of the room and the temperature of the dough. Generally lean dough will ferment 1 to 3 hours until it is roughly doubled in bulk. Longer fermentation times at cool temperatures are recommended for flavor development in lean bread doughs and certain enriched doughs. Bread doughs that rely on a starter for leavening (see page 185) may require even longer fermenting because natural yeast may be less concentrated than commercially prepared yeast.

CONTROLLING FERMENTATION

The ingredients in the formula, the dough temperature and the temperature of the environment in which the dough ferments will affect the total fermentation time. Bakers use different strategies to regulate fermentation time to achieve desired results.

Ingredients

Dough with more yeast and more yeast food will ferment more quickly. Increasing the yeast in a formula will increase the rate of fermentation, thus speeding production time. Adding sugar, malt, honey or other yeast food will speed fermentation also, although too much sugar can actually slow yeast's activity; enriched dough formulas often include a higher percentage of yeast for this reason.

No-time dough refers to formulas in which the quantity of yeast is increased to such an extent that fermentation time is reduced significantly. **Dough conditioners** are added to these formulas to ensure that the dough ferments properly in the brief time allotted.

Dough Temperature

Using warmer water in the dough and fermenting it in a warm environment will speed up the fermentation process. Conversely, kneading the dough to the proper dough temperature and then letting it ferment in a cool environment will slow down this process. Wintertime baking in colder climates must take this into consideration.

Room Temperature

Bakeries often extend the fermentation time of certain doughs in a specially designed refrigerator called a retarder. **Retardation** describes the stage when dough is put in a cool place, usually between 38°F and 50°F (3°C and 10°C), for anywhere from 2 to 36 hours. The cool temperature slows down the yeast activity, giving the dough the maximum opportunity to develop its flavor. The cool temperature inhibits or retards the yeast activity, yet leaves it with enough strength for the final proofing stage after the loaves are formed. Formed bread dough may also be retarded before proofing, which can be extremely helpful in scheduling production and baking.

Stage 4: Punching Down the Dough

After fermentation, the dough is gently folded down to expel and redistribute the gas pockets with a technique known as punching down. The procedure reactivates the yeast cells, encouraging more yeast activity. **Punching down** dough also helps even out the dough's temperature and relaxes the gluten. Punching down the dough involves gently folding the dough to expel the gas before placing it seam side down onto the workbench or into a container before make-up or a second fermentation.

bulk fermentation the rise given to the entire mass of yeast dough before the dough is shaped

proofing the rise given to shaped yeast products just before baking

no-time dough dough formulated with more yeast to speed fermentation

dough conditioner enzymes, emulsifiers and yeast foods added to bread dough to improve gluten development or to soften the dough for faster mixing and shorter fermentation times; available as a powdered blend

retardation chilling a yeasted dough product under refrigeration to slow yeast activity and to extend fermentation or proofing time

PROCEDURE FOR PUNCHING DOWN DOUGH

① Scrape fermented dough onto the workbench.

② Use a dough scraper to fold over one side of the dough.

③ Fold over the other side of dough into a uniform shape.

Scaling bread dough.

Rounding bread dough.

rounding the process of shaping dough into smooth, round balls; used to stretch the outside layer of gluten into a smooth coating

bench rest allowing bread dough, usually covered, to ferment in bulk on a worktable for a short time

Stage 5: Portioning the Dough

The dough is now ready to be divided into portions. For loaves, the dough is scaled to the desired weight. For individual rolls, the dough can be rolled into an even log from which portions are cut with a chef's knife or dough cutter. Weighing the cut dough pieces on a portion scale ensures even-sized portions. When portioning, work quickly and keep the dough covered to prevent it from drying out.

Stage 6: Rounding the Portions

The portions of dough must be shaped into smooth, round balls in a technique known as **rounding** or preshaping. Rounding stretches the outside layer of gluten into a smooth coating. This helps hold in gases and makes it easier to shape the dough. Unrounded rolls rise unevenly and have a rough, lumpy surface. At this stage some breads may be left on the worktable for a short period of **bench rest**. This relaxes the gluten, making the shaping process easier.

Stage 7: Make-Up: Shaping the Portions

Lean doughs and some rich doughs can be shaped into a variety of forms: large loaves, small loaves, free-form or country-style rounds or individual dinner rolls. An important consideration when shaping dough is its texture. As a general rule, when shaping a soft dough, a tighter shaping is preferred. When shaping a firm, elastic dough, the dough may be shaped more gently. When making free-form loaves, the molded dough is often placed between the floured folds of heavy linen canvas (**couche**) to hold their shape while proofing. Or these loaves may be placed in linen-lined baskets (**bannetons**) or coiled willow or plastic baskets (**brotforms**). These baskets hold the loaves' shape and leave a distinctive imprint on the loaves when they are removed from them before baking.

Placing bread in a canvas couche before proofing.

Loaves in a brotform.

banneton (BAN-tahn) a traditional willow basket, often lined with canvas, in which yeast bread is placed to rise before baking

brotform (BROT-form) a traditional woven basket in which yeast bread is placed to rise before baking. The basket leaves marks in the dough. Heavy plastic versions are available for commercial food service use

Some common shaping techniques are shown here. Other doughs, particularly brioche, croissant and Danish, are usually shaped in very specific ways. Those techniques are discussed and illustrated in Chapter 8, Enriched Yeast Breads, and Chapter 9, Laminated Doughs.

PROCEDURE FOR FORMING AN OBLONG LOAF

1 Round a portion of dough into a ball by rolling it under cupped hands across the surface of the workbench.

2 Flatten the rounded dough into a disk.

3 Fold up the bottom edge of the dough two-thirds of the way, then fold the top edge down. Press to seal.

4 Rotate the dough 180° and fold again in the same manner as in Step 3.

5 Flatten the dough into a rectangle.

6 Fold the right and left edges over, then roll the dough into a tight cylinder.

7 Place the dough with the seam facing up into a flour-dusted brotform or banneton. Or place the dough seam side down on a cornmeal-dusted sheet pan.

Taking a rounded piece of dough, molding it and placing it in a brotform.

PROCEDURE FOR FORMING A TWISTED KNOT ROLL OR LOAF

1 Roll a portion of dough into a long rope. Form a loop by attaching the left end to the middle of the rope. Pinch to seal the dough.

2 Pass the right end of the rope through the loop.

3 Fold down the top of the loop and twist slightly.

4 Thread the loose end of the loaf through the loop.

Forming a twisted knot loaf.

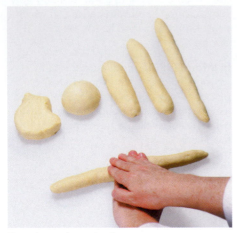

Forming a long loaf.

PROCEDURE FOR ROLLING A LONG LOAF OR BAGUETTE

1 Round a portion of dough into a ball by rolling it under cupped hands across the surface of the workbench.
2 Roll out the ball of dough into a short cylinder.
3 With both hands together, roll the dough until it gradually begins to lengthen.
4 Roll to the desired length.

Forming a bow knot roll.

PROCEDURE FOR FORMING A BOW KNOT ROLL

1 Roll a portion of dough into a short rope.
2 Pick up one end of the dough. Cross it over the other end of the dough.
3 Tie a simple knot in the dough.
4 Tuck the end of the dough underneath and pinch to seal it.

PROCEDURE FOR FORMING A STAR LOAF

1 Divide the dough into one 5-ounce (150-gram) and nine 2½-ounce (76-gram) portions. Round the dough and bench rest, covered, for 5 minutes.
2 Place one of the smaller portions of dough in the center of a flour-dusted sheet pan. Moisten the surface of four more portions of dough, then dip them in grated cheese or sesame, caraway or other seeds. Place them evenly around the small portion of dough

Scoring a Star Loaf with scissors before proofing.

Star Loaf

on the sheet pan without touching. Roll the four remaining smaller portions of dough into ovals. Moisten them with water, then dip them in poppy seeds, sea salt or other seeds of a contrasting color or texture. Position them evenly between the rounds.

3 Slightly flatten the remaining larger portion of dough with a rolling pin, then place it in the center of the star-shaped bread. Score the star loaf with scissors before proofing. The loaf may be left plain. The decorative scoring will create a pattern on the bread once the loaf bakes.

PROCEDURE FOR MAKING A THREE-STRAND BRAIDED LOAF

1 Divide the dough into three equal pieces. Roll the pieces into three long ropes of equal length. Press the three strands together at one end.

2 Cross the left strand over the center strand. Then cross the right strand over the new center strand.

3 Repeat this pattern until the strands are all braided. Tuck the ends underneath and pinch to seal the braid.

1 Pressing the three strands together.

2 Crossing the strips one over the other to make the braid.

3 Rolling the ends together to seal the braid.

PANNING DOUGH

Doughs can also be scaled and placed in pans. First the scaled dough piece must be rounded and shaped to fit the selected pan. Filling a pan two-thirds full is usually recommended. Table 7.4 lists common bread pan sizes and quantities of dough each can hold.

TABLE 7.4	PAN SIZE	
PAN	**APPROXIMATE SIZE**	**WEIGHT OF DOUGH***
Sandwich loaf	16 in. × 4 in. × 4½ in (40 cm × 10 cm × 11.2 cm)	4 lb. (1920 g)
Pullman	13 in. × 4 in. × 3 in. (32.5 cm × 10 cm × 7.5 cm)	3 lb. (1440 g)
Large	9 in. × 5 in. × 3 in. (22.5 cm × 12.5 cm × 7.5 cm)	2 lb. (960 g)
Medium	8 in. × 4 in. × 2 in. (20 cm × 10 cm × 5 cm)	1 lb. 8 oz. (720 g)
Small	7 in. × 3 in. × 2 in. (17.5 cm × 7.5 cm × 5 cm)	1 lb. (480 g)
Miniature	5 in. × 3 in. × 2 in. (12.5 cm × 7.5 cm × 5 cm)	8 oz. (240 g)

*Weights given are approximate; variations may occur based on the type of dough used as well as the temperature and length of proofing.

Stage 8: Proofing the Products

Proofing is the final rise of shaped or panned yeast products before baking. For most bread, the temperature should be between 80°F and 115°F (27°C and 46°C), slightly higher than the temperature for fermentation. Some humidity is also desirable to prevent the dough from drying or forming a crust. Temperature and humidity can be controlled with a special cabinet known as a proofer or **proof box**.

Most products are proofed until the dough doubles in size and springs back slowly when lightly touched. Underproofing results in poor volume and texture. Overproofing results in a sour flavor, poor volume and a paler color after baking. Some doughs made with low-protein flours such as rye or multigrains and some enriched yeast doughs may be proofed less, until expanded only 50 to 70 percent in volume. The weaker gluten structure and the heavier weight of the ingredients in such doughs makes them fragile. Proofing these doughs until doubled in volume can result in loaves that collapse in the oven.

proof box a heat- and humidity-controlled cabinet in which yeast-leavened dough is placed to rise immediately before baking

Pressing proofed dough gently.

Properly proofed bread dough.

Stage 9: Baking the Products

As yeast breads bake, a variety of chemical and physical changes turn the dough into an edible product. These changes are discussed in Chapter 3, Principles of Baking. Because of the expansion of gases, yeast products experience a sudden rise, referred to as **oven spring**, when first placed in a hot oven. As the dough's temperature increases, the yeast dies, the gluten fibers become firm, the starches gelatinize, the moisture evaporates and, finally, the crust forms and turns brown due to the caramelization of the sugars. To assist the rise during baking and to improve their appearance when baked, loaves may be brushed with a wash and/or scored before baking.

oven spring the rapid rise of yeast goods when first placed in a hot oven resulting from the temporary increase of yeast activity and the expansion of trapped gases

Rolls baked with various washes: egg yolk and water, egg yolk and cream, egg white, egg white and milk (top row from left to right); whole egg and salt, whole egg and milk, whole egg and water (bottom row from left to right).

WASHES

The appearance of yeast breads can be altered by applying a glaze or wash to the dough before baking. The crust is made shiny or matte, hard or soft, darker or lighter by the proper use of washes. Washes are also used to attach seeds, wheat germ, oats or other toppings to the dough's surface.

The most commonly used wash is an egg wash, composed of whole egg and water, usually one part water to three parts egg. Yeast products can also be topped with plain water, a mixture of egg and milk, plain milk or richer glazes containing sugar and flavorings. Even a light dusting of white flour can be used to top dough. (This is commonly seen with potato rolls.) Rye breads are often coated with a starch wash (see online resources), made from cornstarch cooked in water, which produces a dark shiny crust. (See Table 7.5.)

Washes may be applied before or after proofing. Delicate doughs that may collapse easily are best washed before proofing. If applied after proofing, be extremely careful not

TABLE 7.5	WASHES FOR YEAST PRODUCTS
WASH	**USE**
Whole egg and water	Shine and color
Whole egg and milk	Shine and color with soft crust
Egg white and water	Shine with firm crust
Egg yolk and cream or milk	Shine and color with soft crust
Milk or cream	Color with soft crust
Water	Crisp crust
Flour	Texture and contrast
Starch wash	Shine and color

docker a hand tool designed to pierce holes in the surface of bread, cracker, pastry and pizza dough before baking to release air bubbles so the product bakes evenly

to deflate the product. Avoid using too much wash, as it can burn or cause the product to stick to the pan. Puddles or streaks of egg wash on the dough will cause uneven browning.

Occasionally, a formula will specify that melted butter or oil be brushed on the product after baking. Do not, however, apply egg washes to already baked products, as the egg will remain raw and the desired effect will not be achieved.

SCORING AND DOCKING

The shape and appearance of some breads can be improved by cutting their tops with a sharp knife or razor (lame) just before baking. (A lame is pictured in the photograph on page 27.) This is referred to as **scoring** or slashing. Hard-crusted breads are usually scored to allow for continued rising and the escape of gases after the crust has formed. Breads that are not properly scored will burst or break along the sides. Scoring can also be used to make an attractive design on the product's surface. Some flatbreads such as pizza and crackers may be docked, or pricked with small holes to prevent the formation of irregular air bubbles in the finished product. A tool called a **docker** is used for this purpose. By contrast, pita bread is not docked so that its distinctive pocket will form. Even a hard-crusted loaf of bread can be gently docked after proofing to create an attractive design on the crust.

Dipping bread in seeds and coatings before baking.

Scoring a round loaf with a lame.

Docking a risen loaf of raisin bread with a docker before baking.

Unmolding a loaf from a brotform onto a sheet pan (in the foreground) and a scored loaf (at the top).

OVEN STEAM

The crisp crust desired for certain breads and rolls is achieved by introducing moisture into the oven during baking. Steam revitalizes the yeast in the dough and keeps the surface of the dough soft so that it can rise fully in the oven. The steam also contributes to the

Loading bread into a deck oven.

chemical changes of the starch and sugar on the surface of the dough, producing a thin crust and brown color. Steam is introduced into the oven in the early baking stages only. Excessive steam will produce a crust that is pale and thick. Professional bakers' ovens have built-in steam injection jets to provide moisture as needed. Steam must not be present during the final stages of baking so the bread can brown.

To create steam, spray the bread with water several times during baking, or place a pan on the oven's lowest rack to receive water. Then pour ½ to ¾ cup (120 to 180 milliliters) of water into the pan just before placing the bread in the oven. This creates a burst of steam during the first few minutes of baking. (Slightly open the oven door or the vent in a deck oven during the last few minutes of baking to let condensed steam escape.) Rich doughs, which do not form crisp crusts, may be baked without steam.

Many artisan bakeries bake their breads directly on the flat heated surface of a deck oven. Usually made from masonry material, the hearth or deck traps heat and conducts it directly to the bread dough. Bakers slide the bread onto the hearth using a flat wooden or metal peel.

DETERMINING DONENESS

Baking time is determined by many factors: the product's size, the oven thermostat's accuracy and the desired crust color. Larger items require a longer baking time than smaller ones. Lean dough products bake faster and at higher temperatures than enriched dough products.

Fully baked lean bread dough should reach an internal temperature of 190°F to 210°F (88°C to 99°C). Rich bread dough is fully baked when it reaches an internal temperature of 180°F to 190°F (82°C to 88°C). The internal temperature can be gauged with great accuracy using an instant-read thermometer. However, bread loaves are commonly tested for doneness by tapping them on the bottom and listening for a hollow sound. This indicates that air, not moisture, is present inside the loaf. If the bottom is damp or heavy, the loaf probably needs more baking time. The texture and color of the crust are also a good indication of doneness, particularly with individual rolls. Browning (caramelization) on the outside of bread flavors the entire loaf. A pale loaf will have less flavor than a well-browned one. The baking times indicated in formulas are estimates only and may vary depending on the equipment used. Experience will teach how to determine doneness without strict adherence to elapsed time.

GUIDELINES FOR DETERMINING BREAD DONENESS

- Uniform, rich, burnished gold to brown crust color
- Hollow sound when bottom of loaf is tapped
- Lean dough—Internal temperature 190°F to 210°F (88°C to 99°C)
- Rich dough—Internal temperature 180°F to 190°F (82°C to 88°C)

Stage 10: Cooling and Storing the Finished Products

The quality of even the finest yeast products suffers if they are cooled or stored improperly. Yeast products should be cooled on racks at room temperature and away from drafts. Yeast breads and rolls should be removed from their pans for cooling unless indicated otherwise. Cool completely before slicing. This allows the internal structure to settle and evaporates any excess moisture remaining. Once cool, yeast products should be stored at room temperature or frozen for longer storage. Do not refrigerate yeast breads, as refrigeration promotes staling. Do not wrap crisp-crusted breads such as Italian or French loaves, as this causes the crust to soften.

ARTISAN BREAD

An artisan is a person who works with his or her hands, a skilled craftsperson in a trade, whether it be cheese making, ceramics or butchery. When it comes to yeast breads, the term *artisan* refers to many things: a style of bread making as well as specific production techniques. Since the 1970s, there has been an interest in traditional techniques employed in European bakeries. As discussed in Chapter 1, Professionalism, the spread of automated baking machinery led to deterioration in the quality of bread, especially in France, where bread is an important symbol of pride and national identity. Combined with the deprivations surrounding World War II, the quality of bread in France suffered greatly during the mid-twentieth century, leading bakers such as Lionel Poilâne to search out and reemploy neglected ingredients and techniques. Now in the United States and globally, "artisan baking" is part of a larger food movement away from large scale commercial production back to small-scale, hands-on production techniques.

ARTISAN YEAST BREAD

The term *artisan bread* is not easily defined because it has been adopted by small-scale independent bakers as well as industrial producers. Some generally-recognized characteristics of artisan bread are hand-crafted products made with high-quality, traditional ingredients without additives or preservatives. Unbleached, unbromated and organic flours are preferred, and doughs generally contain natural starters mixed using pre-fermentation methods. Mixers may be used to prepare the dough, but rounding and forming is usually done by hand. And artisan breads are often baked without pans, directly on the heated stone deck of a hearth oven. Some specific ingredients and techniques used to make artisan bread are discussed here, although they may apply to any type of bread being made.

Breads baked at an artisan bread competition.

Ingredients for Artisan Bread

The selection of ingredients for artisan breads is significant. Artisan bakers look for high-quality, all-natural unbleached, unbromated flours. Seeking to emulate traditional bread from Europe, bakers choose lower-protein flours with a high ash content such as those used abroad. (See page 65.) Ash content indicates the bran contained in the flour; higher-ash-content flour tends to be slightly darker with distinctive flavors. Minerals in the bran are nutritious and enhance yeast activity during fermentation. But a high bran content can also weaken the gluten bond in doughs. Artisan-style bread flour may absorb less water than conventional bread flour. This means that water quantities may have to be adjusted when using artisan-style flour as when changing any type of flour used in a formula.

The type of flour used impacts dough-handling techniques employed by artisan bakers. Organic flour from a small producer may behave somewhat differently from its conventional counterpart. There may be less consistency from bag to bag requiring the need to test-bake a batch of bread with each delivery of flour. Stone-ground flours, which are coarse, tend to absorb less water than flours milled on steel rollers. Flours milled from whole grains, which are often an important component in artisan breads, tend to absorb more water. Bread dough may need longer fermentation or different make-up techniques when made with lower-protein flours. Bakers need to understand and pay close attention to the impact of each ingredient when preparing an artisan dough.

NATURAL YEAST STARTERS, SOURS AND PREFERMENTS

Artisan bakers prefer to limit or eliminate the use of commercial yeast in order to bring out the best qualities of their flour. They accomplish this by using natural starters and preferments for leavening.

Natural starters contribute a distinctive flavor, from mild and buttery to sharp and tangy, to the finished product. A natural yeast starter, known as a natural starter, sour, mother or a *chef* in French, is made when wild yeasts such as *Candida milleri* and bacteria are captured in a dough. During the fermentation process bacteria, such as lactobacilli, convert sugars into acids that lend distinctive flavors to bread. Two types of acid are produced during fermentation, lactic and acetic acid. **Lactic acid** is mild and **acetic acid** is strong with the tang of vinegar. Generally a cool fermentation favors the development of lactic acid, whereas a shorter, warmer fermentation will favor the development of acetic acids.

Wild yeasts, unlike their commercial counterparts, can tolerate a higher level of acidity. Natural starters are essential to make sourdough and many types of artisan bread. Because thousands of strains of wild yeast and bacteria thrive in the various geographic regions, starters vary widely. Over time and in different regions, bakers developed numerous strategies for using natural yeast starters to create regionally desirable flavors and textures in bread. Although the term *sourdough* implies that the bread will have a distinctive sharpness, European breads made with natural starters do not usually have a strongly sour flavor because of the way in which the dough is handled, balancing fermentation temperature and time.

Starter activity at three stages: just mixed (lower right), 3 hours after mixing (left) and 12 hours later (upper right).

Making a Natural Starter

To make a natural starter, begin by combining equal parts flour and water into a wet mixture. Using organic flour will increase yeast activity, as will using equal parts by weight of rye flour, which ferments quickly, and white flour in the initial starter mixture. A small

AN HONEST LOAF

It is astonishing that the word *artisan* as it applies to bread baking remains so challenging to define. "I know it when I see it," "Bread made all by hand," "Bread made by hand except for mechanical mixing and an oven," and "Bread made from the soul of the baker" all have been presented by various spokespeople. I once heard someone call artisan bread "an honest loaf" and it made me think of all the implications of our craft—not the inference of the word but the impact of a lifelong quest for the bread they call "honest."

To today's artisanal baker, the creation of an honest loaf goes beyond man versus machine. It's about respect. Respect for everything that occurs before the baker creates the loaf and respect for everything that the loaf means after it leaves the bakery. Today's baker knows the source of the wheat, sometimes the name of the farmer who planted it, and has respect for the methodology used to sustain the wheat field. Today's artisanal baker knows where the wheat was milled and has a good understanding of complicated scientific tests that predict the quality of the grain. To bake an honest loaf the baker maintains the integrity of the bread-baking process, facing day-to-day challenges without taking shortcuts. The baker realizes that his or her art is on display not in a museum but in a home, around the family dinner table sharing all the joy and pain of reality. Finally, being a prideful sort, today's artisanal baker realizes that unselfishly teaching others, sharing information, and setting an example of professional discipline are the cornerstones of sustaining the honest loaf.

A famous singer once compared herself to Rembrandt. "It's not easy to be a performing artist. Rembrandt only had to paint *Return of the Prodigal Son* once. I have to paint it every time I perform." The same could be said about the artisanal baker. The quest for the honest loaf is eternal.

—GREG MISTELL, owner, Delphina's Bakery and Pearl Bakery, Portland, OR; past chairman, Bread Bakers Guild of America

CHARACTERISTICS OF ARTISAN BREAD

- made from all natural ingredients
- made using natural yeast starters and preferments rather than commercial yeast
- produced in small batches
- fermented slowly, perhaps under retardation to develop flavor
- formed by hand and baked in a deck oven

amount of grapes, apple peels or orange rinds may be added to introduce natural yeasts to the mixture. Some bakers also add a small amount of prepared yeast to initiate fermentation. After several hours covered at room temperatures (60°F–80°F/15°C–26°C), bubbles will appear on the surface, indicating that yeast activity has begun. Within 12 to 24 hours, yeast activity should be noticeable and the mixture will double or triple in volume. Over time, the starter will develop a mellow flavor with some noticeable acidity. A quantity of starter is then used as an ingredient in various bread dough formulas. Starters can be kept and used for literally years if properly maintained. To maintain a natural starter, frequently **refresh** or feed it with more flour and water. Yeast is more active in a wet starter than a dry one; add more flour when the starter will not be used for an extended period of time. A drier starter—more like a dough than a batter—will ferment more slowly and develop more sour flavors under refrigeration. When preparing to make sourdough bread for production, feed the starter as often as every 8 hours to keep the yeast active. A starter is ready to use when it doubles in volume in 8 to 12 hours after feeding. (Another test some bakers use is to place a small piece of dry starter in warm water. If it floats, the starter has the strength to leaven bread dough.) The amount of flour and water necessary to feed a starter varies, but never add more flour and water than would double the mixture at one time. More water can be added to speed fermentation in the starter on the day when it will be used. Recipes for starters appear on page 194 and page 198. Learning to build and maintain a starter is an essential baking skill that takes time and experience to master.

Using a Natural Starter

When using a natural starter to leaven bread, certain procedures must be followed to ensure a viable rise. The true sourdough starter method of mixing bread has three stages. First a sourdough culture or mother (Fr. *chef*) is prepared. Because natural yeasts may be less concentrated in the starter, a second-stage mixture called a **levain** is prepared to add more yeast food and encourage yeast activity. In the third stage, the final dough is mixed. The three-stage sourdough mixing method is illustrated by Pain au Levain (Traditional French Sourdough Bread) (page 219).

Authentic sourdough bread contains no commercially prepared yeast. Today, however, many bread doughs made with starters are often fortified with commercial yeast to provide consistency and reliability. The starter provides flavor and other qualities to the dough, while the yeast ensures timely bread production. A sourdough bread made with starter and some commercial yeast is illustrated by Italian Country Sourdough Loaves (page 194). Bread dough with a high percentage of rye flour benefits from the inclusion of a starter.

levain the French term for leavening; it refers to a dough made from a sourdough culture that forms the basis for French-style sourdough bread

The acidity in the starter inactivates enzymes in rye flour allowing starches in the dough to gelatinize and give the bread its structure.

PREFERMENTS

A **preferment** is a batter or dough mixed as a first step in making artisan bread. Preferments are mixed from a portion of the water and flour in the bread formula. Commercial yeast and, sometimes, salt are included. This dough or batter is allowed to ferment for a time before it is incorporated into the remaining ingredients of the formula. The use of preferments offers several benefits. The bread's flavor and aroma is enhanced, and the acids created in the preferment help strengthen gluten proteins and extend the bread's shelf life. Production time is also shortened because bulk fermentation time decreases.

Many types of these pre-fermented mixtures are used by artisan bakers, although the terms are not standardized. Among the most basic is **old dough** (Fr. *pâte fermentée*). Old dough is nothing more than a piece of dough saved from a previous batch of bread and added to a new batch to improve the aroma and flavor of the bread. Because the old dough has already fermented, a bakery may use this method to add flavor without compromising a production schedule. Up to an equal amount of old dough can be added to a new batch of dough. Because old dough contains salt, which retards fermentation, additional yeast may be needed. Because the old dough is fully developed, it is added near the end of the mixing and kneading period.

An all-purpose bread dough formula is provided to use as old dough in formulas listing it as an ingredient. (See page 199.) But any similar dough may be used for this purpose. Old dough may be omitted in any formula that calls for it. Yield on the finished dough will be that much less, however. Old dough keeps for at least 3 days under refrigeration. The old dough method is illustrated by Traditional French Baguettes with Old Dough (page 192).

Poolish is the French term for a type of sponge. Its invention is attributed to Polish bakers of the 19th century. Breads made with poolish have a lighter texture and a less sour flavor than traditional sourdough. Poolish is made from equal parts water and flour by weight plus a small quantity of commercial yeast. This mixture will be very liquid and should ferment at room temperature until it doubles in volume. The goal is to have a long slow fermentation of at least 2 to 3 hours at cool temperatures. This helps the bread develop complex aromas and flavors. The poolish is mature and ready to use when it just begins to crest and sink back slightly.

The quantity of yeast used in a poolish depends on the fermentation time in the baking schedule and on the temperature of the room in which it is maturing. For longer fermentation, decrease the quantity of yeast so that the preferment isn't at its optimum fermentation point too soon. Likewise, when the temperature is warmer decrease the amount of yeast; a cooler temperature may require more yeast. It is important to use the poolish while it is still active and bubbling. Once it collapses, harsh acetic acids will dominate. Bread dough that calls for poolish is mixed using the sponge method illustrated with the recipe for Light Rye Bread (page 191).

Biga is the Italian term for a yeasted starter, one that is generally a dry mixture made with only 30 to 35 percent water by weight. A biga and bread dough made from it require a long fermentation.

Production Stages for Artisan Breads

Artisan breads are prepared following the same procedures as all yeast bread dough. Special attention is paid at certain steps, however. Most artisan breads are mixed using the sponge, old dough or sourdough starter methods illustrated on pages 190 and 193–194. Artisan bakers select machinery and mixing methods designed to minimize the friction and oxidation of the dough during mixing. When hand kneading is not feasible, artisan bakers select their mixers carefully. Spiral mixers are popular with artisan bakers because of the gentle way they knead bread dough. (See page 37.)

AUTOLYSE

Many artisan bakers use a resting technique during kneading that improves the dough's baking and handling qualities. Created by French artisan baker Raymond Calvel, this simple technique, called *autolyse*, requires kneading only the flour and water briefly before resting the dough for 20 minutes. After resting, the yeast or starter and salt are added and the dough is kneaded until it is fully developed. The resting period allows the flour to

Old Dough

Active Poolish Sponge

absorb all of the water in the formula, enhancing starch and gluten expansion. Yeast and salt are held back so that nothing inhibits gluten development and enzyme activity in the dough. The total kneading time is shortened, and the dough becomes easier to handle. Dough that has rested before the final kneading will be stretchy and rise more fully when baked. The autolyse technique can be used for any yeast bread dough.

PROCEDURE FOR KNEADING DOUGH USING AUTOLYSE TECHNIQUE

1. Scale the ingredients. Adjust the water temperature.
2. Knead the flour and water until the dough just comes together, approximately 2 to 3 minutes.
3. Cover and let the dough rest for 20 minutes.
4. Hydrate the yeast if necessary.
5. Add the yeast and salt to the dough. Knead the dough on medium speed until it is fully developed, approximately 2 to 5 minutes.

Adding the yeast and salt to bread dough that has rested.

Dough that has rested after the second kneading.

FERMENTATION, MAKE-UP AND BAKING ARTISAN BREADS

The use of starters and preferments impacts the techniques artisan bakers use when fermenting bread dough. Preferments add flavor to bread dough, as does a long, cool fermentation. Artisan breads may be left to ferment at temperatures from approximately 65°F to 75°F (18°C to 23°C). But as dough ferments, more acids will develop, giving the bread a strong flavor profile, which may or may not be desirable. Experienced artisan bakers pay attention to fermentation conditions, which will vary depending on the equipment and ingredients used as well as the season, to ensure a desirable flavor profile in their starter and doughs. Artisan breads are usually hand molded and baked in a hearth or deck oven, which promotes the development of a thick, dark blistered crust.

PROCEDURES FOR PREPARING YEAST BREADS

The following formulas illustrate each of the basic mixing methods used to produce contemporary and artisan yeast breads discussed in this chapter. Additional formulas appear at the end of this chapter.

FORMULAS FOR ARTISAN BREADS

As Greg Mistell writes on page 186, artisan bread is "an honest loaf," not a separate category of products. Consumers often think of artisan bread as bread made with organic ingredients, whole grains, fruit and nuts, or other specialty ingredients, however. In actual practice, many of the formulas in this book will produce artisan bread when made with time and care by those attentive to the craft of bread making.

PROCEDURE FOR YEAST BREAD: STRAIGHT DOUGH METHOD

1. Scale the ingredients. Adjust water temperature and rehydrate yeast if necessary.
2. Combine all ingredients in the bowl of a mixer fitted with a dough hook on low speed to moisten; this is the pickup stage.
3. Adjust mixture with water or flour if needed to correct dough consistency.
4. Knead the dough on medium speed to properly develop the dough, approximately 5 to 10 minutes.

⑤ Ferment the dough until double in bulk, then punch down to release gases.

⑥ Scrape the dough onto the workbench, then divide and scale into uniform pieces. Round each piece into a smooth ball, then rest before rolling into desired shapes. Pan the formed dough as desired.

⑦ Proof the dough. Brush with egg wash and score the dough, if necessary.

❶ Mixing the soft yeast dough: (a) Combining the ingredients in the bowl of a mixer fitted with a dough hook.

(b) Adding the yeast-and-water mixture.

❷ Kneading the dough.

❸ The dough before fermenting.

❹ Punching down the risen dough: (a) Pressing down on the center of the dough with your fist.

(b) Folding the edges of the dough in toward the center.

❺ Scaling the dough for rolls.

❻ Rounding the rolls.

❼ Brushing the rolls with egg wash.

SOFT YEAST DINNER ROLLS

Yield: 64 Rolls, approximately 1 ¼ oz. (38 g) each

Method: Straight dough

Fermentation: 1 hour

Proofing: 30 to 45 minutes

Active dry yeast	2 oz.	60 g	4.5%
Water (temperature controlled)	1 lb. 8 oz.	720 ml	54.5%
Bread flour	2 lb. 12 oz.	1320 g	100%
Salt	1 oz.	30 g	2.3%
Granulated sugar	4 oz.	120 g	9%
Nonfat dry milk powder	2 oz.	60 g	4.5%
Shortening	2 oz.	60 g	4.5%
Unsalted butter, softened	2 oz.	60 g	4.5%
Eggs	3.2 oz. (2 eggs)	100 g	7.5%
Egg wash	as needed	as needed	
Total dough weight:	5 lb. 4 oz.	2530 g	191%

1. Dissolve the yeast in the water in a bowl. Combine the flour, salt, sugar, milk powder, shortening, butter and eggs in the bowl of a mixer fitted with a dough hook.
2. Add the water-and-yeast mixture to the mixer bowl; stir to combine.
3. Knead on medium speed 10 minutes or until the dough reaches 77°F (25°C).
4. Transfer the dough to a lightly greased bowl, cover and place in a warm spot. Ferment until doubled, approximately 1 hour.
5. Punch down the dough. Let it rest a few minutes to allow the gluten to relax.
6. Divide the dough into 1 ¼-ounce (38-gram) portions and round. Shape as desired and arrange on paper-lined sheet pans. Proof until doubled in size.
7. Carefully brush the proofed rolls with egg wash. Bake at 400°F (200°C) until medium brown, approximately 12 to 15 minutes.

Approximate values per roll: **Calories** 90, **Total fat** 1.5 g, **Saturated fat** 0.5 g, **Cholesterol** 10 mg, **Sodium** 160 mg, **Total carbohydrates** 15 g, **Protein** 3 g, **Claims**—low fat; low saturated fat; low cholesterol

PROCEDURE FOR YEAST BREAD: SPONGE METHOD

1. Scale ingredients. Adjust water temperature and rehydrate yeast if necessary.
2. Mix the sponge from a portion of the flour, the water and the yeast. Usually half the total flour weight is used.
3. Ferment the sponge until bubbly and approximately double in bulk.
4. Add the remaining ingredients, then knead the dough on medium speed until properly developed, approximately 5 to 10 minutes.
5. Ferment the dough until double in bulk, then punch down to release gases.
6. The dough is now ready for scaling, shaping, proofing and baking.

LIGHT RYE BREAD

Yield: 2 Large Loaves

Method: Sponge

Fermentation: Sponge, 1 hour. Final dough, 45 minutes to 1 hour

Proofing: 45 minutes

Unbleached wheat flour	1 lb.	480 g	66%
Medium rye flour	8 oz.	240 g	34%
Dark molasses	3 oz.	90 g	12.5%
Water (temperature controlled)	14 fl. oz.	420 ml	58%
Active dry yeast	0.5 oz.	15 g	2%
Nonfat dry milk powder	1.5 oz.	45 g	6%
Caraway seeds, crushed	0.6 oz.	20 g	3%
Kosher salt	0.5 oz.	15 g	2%
Unsalted butter, melted	0.5 oz.	15 g	2%
Cornmeal or oil	as needed	as needed	
Egg wash	as needed	as needed	
Total dough weight:	2 lb. 12 oz.	1340 g	185%

MISE EN PLACE

- ▶ Adjust water temperature.
- ▶ Crush caraway seeds.
- ▶ Melt butter.
- ▶ Prepare the egg wash.
- ▶ Dust a sheet pan with cornmeal while the dough ferments.

1. Stir the flours together and set aside.
2. To make the sponge, combine the molasses, water and yeast. Add 8 ounces (240 grams) of the flour mixture. Stir vigorously for 3 minutes. Cover the bowl and set aside to ferment until doubled and very bubbly, approximately 1 hour.
3. Stir the milk powder, caraway seeds, salt and butter into the sponge.
4. Transfer the dough to the bowl of a mixer fitted with a dough hook.
5. Gradually add the remaining flour to the sponge. Mix on low speed and continue adding flour until the dough is stiff but slightly tacky. Knead 5 minutes on low speed until the dough reaches 77°F (25°C).
6. Transfer the dough to a lightly greased bowl, cover and place in a warm place until doubled, approximately 45 to 60 minutes.
7. Punch down the dough and divide into two equal pieces. Shape each piece into a round loaf and place on a sheet pan that has been dusted with cornmeal or lightly oiled. Brush the loaves with egg wash and let rise until doubled, approximately 45 minutes.
8. Score the tops with a razor or knife. Bake at 375°F (190°C) until golden brown and crusty, approximately 35 to 45 minutes.

Approximate values per ⅒-loaf serving: **Calories** 160, **Total fat** 1.5 g, **Saturated fat** 0 g, **Cholesterol** 15 mg, **Sodium** 370 mg, **Total carbohydrates** 31 g, **Protein** 6 g, **Claims**—low fat; no saturated fat; low cholesterol

1. Rye bread sponge.

2. Mixing the rye dough.

3. Shaping the rye loaves.

PROCEDURE FOR YEAST BREAD: OLD DOUGH METHOD

1. Prepare the old dough and ferment. (If using old dough that has been refrigerated, bring it to room temperature before using.)

2. Scale other ingredients. Adjust water temperature and rehydrate yeast if necessary.

3. Combine the flour, yeast, salt and water and mix until moistened, then knead on medium speed until the dough is almost fully developed. Divide the old dough into small pieces and add to the new dough in the mixer. Knead another 1 or 2 minutes until the old dough is fully incorporated.

4. Ferment the dough until double in bulk.

TRADITIONAL FRENCH BAGUETTES WITH OLD DOUGH

MISE EN PLACE

▶ Prepare old dough.
▶ Adjust water temperature.
▶ Dust a canvas couche with flour while dough ferments.

Yield: 4 Loaves, 12 oz. (360 g) each

Method: Old dough

Fermentation: Old dough, 4 to 6 hours. Final dough, 1 to 2 hours.

Proofing: 30 to 45 minutes.

Old Dough (page 199), room temperature	8.5 oz.	255 g	35.5%
Bread flour	1 lb. 8 oz.	720 g	100%
Instant yeast	0.2 oz. (1¼ tsp.)	6 g	0.8%
Water (temperature controlled)	15.25 fl. oz.	457 ml	63.5%
Salt	0.5 oz.	15 g	2%
Rice flour or bread flour	as needed	as needed	
Total dough weight:	3 lb.	1453 g	202%

1. Prepare the Old Dough and allow it to ferment at least 4 hours. Or remove the Old Dough from the refrigerator and bring it to room temperature 2 to 4 hours before mixing.

2. Place the flour, yeast, water and salt in the bowl of a mixer fitted with a dough hook. Mix on low speed until blended. Then knead on medium speed until the dough is almost fully developed and reaches 75°F (24°C), approximately 7 to 10 minutes. Add the Old Dough in small pieces. Continue kneading until the dough is fully developed and reaches approximately 77°F (25°C).

3. Place the dough on a floured surface or in a large bowl. Cover the dough and ferment until doubled in size, approximately 1 to 2 hours.

4. Punch down the dough and divide into four equal pieces. Round the dough, cover and bench rest 10 minutes.

5. Shape each piece of dough into a 10-inch (25-centimeter) cylinder. Cover the dough and rest several minutes before rolling it into 24-inch- (60-centimeter-) long baguettes.

6. Place the rolled dough seam side down onto a canvas couche lightly dusted with rice flour or bread flour or in prepared baguette pans. Proof until the loaves increase 55 to 65 percent in volume, approximately 30 to 45 minutes.

7. Remove the proofed loaves from the proof box and let the bread's surface dry for 5 minutes. Use the canvas to roll the bread onto sheet pans or leave in the baguette pans. Score several diagonal cuts in each piece of dough.

8. Bake at 450°F (230°C), with steam injected into the oven during the first few minutes of baking, until golden brown, approximately 20 to 22 minutes.

Variation:

Olive Bread—Once the dough is mixed, knead in 0.25 ounce (8 grams/1.3%) finely chopped fresh oregano and 12 ounces (360 grams/63%) pitted and finely chopped Kalamata olives. Knead only to incorporate the ingredients. Ferment, then divide and shape the dough as desired.

Approximate values per ⅓-loaf serving: **Calories** 100, **Total fat** 0 g, **Saturated fat** 0 g, **Cholesterol** 0 mg, **Sodium** 280 mg, **Total carbohydrates** 20 g, **Protein** 3 g

❶ The dough is portioned, then rolled into baguettes in two stages.

❷ The proofed loaves are scored to allow steam to escape.

❸ The finished baguettes.

PROCEDURE FOR YEAST BREAD: SOURDOUGH STARTER METHOD

❶ Prepare a sourdough starter: Combine approximately equal parts flour and water with a source of natural yeast such as grapes or fruit peel. (A small amount of commercial yeast may be used to initiate a starter). Allow the yeast to grow at room temperature for 8 to 12 hours. (If using a prepared sourdough starter that has been refrigerated, allow it to come to room temperature before using.)

❷ Replenish the yeast food by adding no more than half the starter weight in flour and water. Allow the yeast to grow at room temperature for at least 4 hours before using. The starter is ready to use when it doubles in volume in 8 to 12 hours after refreshing.

❸ To make the sourdough bread: Scale ingredients. Adjust water temperature and rehydrate yeast if necessary.

❹ Combine all ingredients in the bowl of a mixer fitted with a dough hook on low speed to moisten; this is the pickup stage. Knead the dough on medium speed to properly develop the dough, approximately 5 to 10 minutes.

❺ Ferment the dough until double in bulk.

❻ The dough is now ready for scaling, shaping, proofing and baking.

NATURAL SOURDOUGH STARTER
(CHEF)

Active starter (front) and underdeveloped starter (rear).

Yield: 1 lb. 5 oz. (630 g)

Spring water, 70°F (21°C)	9 fl. oz.	270 ml	100%
Organic grapes	3 oz.	90 g	33%
Bread flour	9 oz.	270 g	100%
Total weight:	1 lb. 5 oz.	630 g	233%

1. Combine 3 fluid ounces (90 milliliters) of the water and the grapes. Add 3 ounces (90 grams) of the flour and mix together using a rubber spatula. The dough will be somewhat firm. Transfer the mixture to a container with a tight-fitting lid or cover tightly with plastic wrap.
2. Store at room temperature, 70°F to 75°F (21°C to 24°C), 24 hours.
3. Remove the grapes. Stir in 3 ounces (90 grams) of the flour and 3 fluid ounces (90 milliliters) of the water and mix energetically.
4. Cover tightly and store at room temperature until the starter is bubbling, 24 hours.
5. Add the remaining flour and water to the bubbly dough and mix energetically.
6. Cover well and store at room temperature 24 hours.
7. By the third day, the starter should be ready to use to make Pain au Levain (page 219). The *chef* may be refrigerated for 2 to 3 days, and then may be made into a levain or used in any formula calling for a sourdough starter.
8. To keep the starter alive and fresh over a long period of time, every 2 to 4 days remove it from the refrigerator. Feed the starter with 3 fluid ounces (90 milliliters) water and 3 ounces (90 grams) flour. Mix, then let the starter sit at room temperature 6 to 8 hours. Use the starter at that time or refrigerate it.

Note: If liquid rises to the top of the starter, it can be drained off or stirred back into the mixture. If the starter develops a pink or yellow film, it has been contaminated and must be discarded.

Approximate values per 1-oz. (30-g) serving: **Calories** 50, **Total fat** 0 g, **Saturated fat** 0 g, **Cholesterol** 0 mg, **Sodium** 0 mg, **Total carbohydrates** 10 g, **Protein** 2 g

---

ITALIAN COUNTRY SOURDOUGH LOAVES

MISE EN PLACE

▶ Feed the starter.
▶ Dust canvas or sheet pans with flour while dough ferments.

Yield: 2 Loaves, approximately 15 oz. (450 g) each

Method: Sourdough starter

Fermentation: 3 to 5 hours

Proofing: 30 to 45 minutes

Simple Sourdough Starter (page 198)	6.5 oz.	195 g	43%
Bread flour	11 oz.	330 g	73%
Rye flour	1.5 oz.	45 g	10%
Whole-wheat flour	2.5 oz.	75 g	17%
Fine sea salt	0.5 oz.	15 g	3%
Instant yeast	0.09 oz. (½ tsp.)	3 g	0.6%
Water (temperature controlled)	10 fl. oz.	300 ml	66%
Rice flour, coarse cornmeal or bread flour	as needed	as needed	
Total dough weight:	1 lb. 15 oz.	963 g	213%

1. Two to 4 hours before mixing the dough, refresh the Simple Sourdough Starter. Allow the starter to sit at room temperature until it is frothy, bubbly and visibly active.

2. Measure the correct amount of starter. Place the starter, bread flour, rye flour, whole-wheat flour, salt, yeast and water in the bowl of a mixer fitted with a dough hook. Mix on low speed until blended. Increase the speed to medium and knead until the dough is smooth and fully developed and reaches 77°F (25°C).

3. Cover the dough and ferment 3 to 5 hours at room temperature.

4. Punch down the dough and divide into two equal pieces. Shape into oblong loaves, then place the dough seam side down on a flour-dusted canvas or a sheet pan lightly dusted with rice flour, coarse cornmeal or bread flour. Proof until the loaves increase 55 to 65 percent in volume, approximately 30 to 45 minutes.

5. Remove the dough from the proof box and uncover the loaves to allow the surface of the bread to dry slightly. Use the canvas to roll the bread onto sheet pans if necessary. Score the loaves.

6. Bake at 450°F (230°C), with steam injected into the oven during the first few minutes of baking, until the crust is a deep dark brown, approximately 25 to 30 minutes.

Approximate values per ⅑-loaf serving: **Calories** 100, **Total fat** 0 g, **Saturated fat** 0 g, **Cholesterol** 0 mg, **Sodium** 280 mg, **Total carbohydrates** 20 g, **Protein** 3 g

QUALITIES OF BREAD

Bread is judged by its external and internal appearance, flavor, aroma and keeping properties. Well-crafted bread has a pleasing uniform brown surface color. When properly proofed, the bread rises and bakes evenly. (See Figures 7.2 and 7.3.) The crust is neither too thick nor too thin, depending on the type of formula. The crust is crisp or tender without being leathery and excessively thick. With the exception of long-fermented sourdough, the crust should be uniform and free from surface blisters. The interior (crumb) of a tender-crusted bread or enriched-dough product should be even and moist without being sticky. A long-fermented country bread or sourdough may contain an irregular cell structure characteristic of this type of bread. Well-crafted bread has good keeping properties; improperly made bread will stale in a matter of hours. Use Table 7.6 to troubleshoot yeast bread dough mixing and baking.

FIGURE 7.2 ▶ Overproofed bread (left) flattens when baked. Underproofed bread (right) rises unevenly and has a dense crumb.

FIGURE 7.3 ▶ Properly proofed yeast bread rises evenly and has a uniform crumb.

TABLE 7.6 TROUBLESHOOTING CHART

PROBLEM	CAUSE	SOLUTION
Dense, leaden dough	Too much flour forced into the dough	Gradually add water; adjust formula
Crust too pale	Oven temperature too low	Adjust oven
	Dough overproofed	Proof only until almost doubled, then bake immediately
	Too much steam	Adjust steam
	Underbaked	Bake longer
Crust too dark	Oven too hot	Adjust oven
	Too much sugar in the dough	Adjust formula or measure sugar carefully
Top crust separates from loaf	Dough improperly shaped	Shape dough carefully
	Crust not scored properly	Score dough to a depth of ½ in. (1.2 cm)
	Dough dried out during proofing	Cover dough during proofing; increase humidity in proof box
Sides of loaf are cracked	Bread expanded after crust formed in oven	Score top of loaf before baking
	Bread underproofed	Proof until loaf almost doubled
Dense texture	Not enough yeast	Adjust formula or measure yeast carefully
	Not enough fermentation time	Let dough rise until doubled or as directed
	Improper molding technique	Handle dough gently
	Too much salt	Adjust formula or measure salt carefully
Ropes of undercooked dough running through product	Insufficient kneading	Knead dough until smooth and elastic and passes window-pane test, or as directed
	Insufficient rising time	Allow adequate time for proofing
	Oven too hot	Adjust oven
Free-form loaf spreads and flattens	Dough too soft	Adjust formula or measure carefully
Large holes in bread	Too much yeast	Adjust formula or measure yeast carefully
	Overkneaded	Knead only as directed
	Inadequate punch-down	Punch down properly to knead out excess air before shaping
Blisters on crust	Too much liquid	Measure ingredients carefully
	Improper shaping	Knead out excess air before shaping
	Too much steam in oven	Reduce amount of steam or moisture in oven

CONVENIENCE PRODUCTS

The popularity of freshly baked bread has led to the introduction of many products designed to make fresh bread within the reach of all types of food service establishments. Bread mixes are dry blends of flours, salt and other ingredients. In the bakeshop, yeast and water are added, then the product is mixed and fermented as for scratch dough. Mixes allow the baker to prepare a variety of breads with few additional ingredients. Bread mixes may be made from all-natural ingredients, or they can include dough conditioners and additives to speed mixing and fermentation times and ease shaping.

Bread bases are dry blends of specialty ingredients that must be added to a scratch bread formula or a mix. Bases are added to a formula in a ratio of from 25 to 50 pounds of base for each 50 pounds of flour. Bread bases come in varieties such as multigrain, cracked wheat, oatmeal, potato and herb among countless others. A small bakery that would otherwise offer a scratch product might use a base to expand the variety of breads offered. Waste is avoided because large bags of unusual flours, grains or nuts that might not be used quickly are replaced by smaller quantities of bases. Check the ingredient label to determine whether the mix or base meets the requirements of your bakeshop. With bread mixes and bases, careful measuring and temperature control of water is still a skill required to achieve the best results. Consult the manufacturer's recommendations because mixing and fermentation times may be different for breads prepared from these products. Forming, proofing and baking, however, are the same as for scratch products.

Powdered sourdough starters give breads the tangy flavor of sourdough without the effort of preparing and nurturing natural yeast. Made from a starter mixture that has been dried and pulverized, these prepared starters are simply added to the dry ingredients in a yeast dough formula. Commercial yeast leavens the dough while the starter lends its tangy flavor.

Frozen bread dough enables the restaurant operator or smaller bakeshop to offer freshly baked bread even when time, space or staff are limited. The dough comes already fermented. It needs only thawing, proofing and baking. Frozen bread dough may be purchased in bulk; 10- and 20-pound cases are common. Once thawed, the dough is portioned, shaped, proofed and baked. Nuts, seeds, herbs, spices, dried fruit or other flavoring ingredients can be kneaded into the dough to customize the product. From the same dough, a restaurant can offer dinner rolls, bread sticks, pizza and sandwich bread. Fresh refrigerated bread dough is also available. Frozen dough also comes portioned and formed into loaves and rolls. It requires panning and then careful thawing, usually under refrigeration.

Much of the guesswork in the proofing and baking process has been removed with parbaked bread. This is bread dough that has been formed and then baked only long enough to stop all yeast activity and solidify the starches without browning the crust. The parbaked bread is then flash-frozen. The restaurant operator simply pans and thaws the parbaked loaves or rolls, then finishes the baking. With parbaked bread it is essential to bake at the temperatures and for the time indicated by the manufacturer. Fully baked frozen breads, rolls, bread sticks and other products are the ultimate convenience, if not the ultimate in flavor. Inattentive reheating and cooling will destroy the flavor, texture and appearance of these yeast breads, however.

1. Explain the differences among active dry yeast, instant dry yeast and compressed yeast. Describe the correct procedures for working with these yeasts.
2. Explain the differences between a sponge and a sourdough starter. How is each of these items used?
3. Describe the straight dough mixing method and give two examples of products made with this procedure.
4. List the 10 production stages for yeast breads. Which of these production stages would also apply to quick bread production? Explain your answer.
5. Locate a professional organization for bread bakers. What services are available to its members? WWW
6. Locate two recipes each for typical French, German and Italian yeast breads and determine whether they are made with the straight dough, sponge or other pre-fermentation method. WWW

QUESTIONS FOR DISCUSSION

Terms to Know

leavening
active dry yeast
instant dry yeast
starter
dough temperature
straight dough method
sponge method
sourdough method
old dough method
kneading
windowpane test
pickup stage
punching down
rounding
proofing
scoring
refresh
lactic acid
acetic acid
poolish
biga

The formulas provided here are grouped according to bread types: Tender-Crusted Breads; Hard-Crusted Breads; Multigrain, Rye and Sourdough Breads; and Specialty Breads. To help production planning, guidelines at the beginning of each formula indicate approximate times for fermentation, proofing and baking. Be aware that times may need to be adjusted according to the conditions in the bakeshop. Adjusting the quantity of yeast used, the temperature of the water and other ingredients in the formulas and changing the mixing time will all affect production. As discussed in this chapter, fermentation and proofing may be accelerated or slowed to accommodate a particular schedule. Using old dough gives many types of bread a full flavor; however, it may be omitted when called for in formulas in this book. The first formulas in this section are for a sourdough starter, basic sponge and old dough, which may be required in later formulas.

SIMPLE SOURDOUGH STARTER

Yield: 3 lb. 12 oz. (1850 g)

Active dry yeast	0.15 oz. (1 tsp.)	5 g	0.5%
Water, warm	4 fl. oz.	120 ml	12%
Water, room temperature	24 fl. oz.	720 ml	75%
All-purpose flour	2 lb.	960 g	100%
Total weight:	3 lb. 12 oz.	1805 g	187%

1. Combine the yeast and warm water. Let stand until foamy, approximately 10 minutes.
2. Stir in the room-temperature water, then add the flour, 2 ounces (60 grams) at a time.
3. Blend by hand or with the paddle attachment of an electric mixer on low speed 2 minutes.
4. Place the starter in a warmed bowl and cover with plastic wrap. Let stand at room temperature 8 to 12 hours. The starter should triple in volume but still be wet and sticky. Refrigerate until ready to use.
5. Each time a portion of the starter is used, it must be refreshed and activated. Remove the starter from the refrigerator several hours before using. Refresh the starter to activate the yeast cells. To refresh the starter, stir in equal amounts by volume of flour and warm water. Then allow the mixture to ferment at room temperature for several hours or overnight before using again or refrigerating. The starter is ready to use when it doubles in volume in 8 to 12 hours after refreshing.

Note: If liquid rises to the top of the starter, it can be drained off or stirred back into the mixture. If the starter develops a pink or yellow film, it has been contaminated and must be discarded.

Approximate values per fluid ounce (30 ml): **Calories** 100, **Total fat** 0 g, **Saturated fat** 0 g, **Cholesterol** 0 mg, **Sodium** 0 mg, **Total carbohydrates** 22 g, **Protein** 3 g

POOLISH

To streamline production, larger bakeries may use an all-purpose poolish or sponge for a variety of formulas. When this poolish is refrigerated after fermentation, it may be kept up to 24 hours before using.

Yield: 1 lb. 4 oz.

Fermentation: 4 to 6 hours

Bread flour, room temperature	10 oz.	300 g	100%
Water, 70°F (21°C)	10 fl. oz.	300 ml	100%
Instant yeast	0.07 oz. (½ tsp.)	2 g	0.7%
Total weight:	1 lb. 4 oz.	602 g	200%

1. Combine all ingredients. Mix until thoroughly blended, approximately 2 minutes. Lightly dust the surface of the dough with flour and then cover it with plastic film.
2. Ferment the dough at room temperature until doubled in volume, bubbling on the surface and the dough just begins to deflate, approximately 4 to 6 hours. Use immediately or refrigerate the sponge overnight and use it within 24 hours.
3. To use the sponge, remove from the refrigerator 2 hours before needed, so that it reaches room temperature before use. Or cut the dough into small pieces and place on a well-floured sheet pan in a warm area or proof box to speed warming.

Poolish at optimum fermentation.

Approximate values per 1-oz. (30-g) serving: **Calories** 50, **Total fat** 0 g, **Saturated fat** 0 g, **Cholesterol** 0 mg, **Sodium** 0 mg, **Total carbohydrates** 10 g, **Protein** 2 g

PÂTE FERMENTÉE (OLD DOUGH)

Yield: 1 lb. 1 oz. (507 g)

Fermentation: 4 to 6 hours

Bread flour	10 oz.	300 g	100%
Instant yeast	0.15 oz. (1 tsp.)	4.5 g	1.5%
Water, 70°F (21°C)	6.5 fl. oz.	195 ml	65%
Salt	0.25 oz. (1¼ tsp.)	7.5 g	2.5%
Total weight:	1 lb. 1 oz.	507 g	169%

1. Combine the ingredients in the bowl of a mixer fitted with a dough hook. Knead on medium speed until a perfect windowpane has been reached, approximately 8 minutes. Lightly dust the dough with flour and cover it with plastic film.
2. Ferment the dough until fully doubled, approximately 4 to 6 hours.
3. Use the dough immediately or retard it in the refrigerator up to 4 days.
4. Remove the dough from the refrigerator 2 hours before needed so that the dough warms to room temperature, approximately 70°F (21°C), before use.

Approximate values per 1-oz. (30-g) serving: **Calories** 60, **Total fat** 0 g, **Saturated fat** 0 g, **Cholesterol** 0 mg, **Sodium** 170 mg, **Total carbohydrates** 13 g, **Protein** 2 g

TENDER-CRUSTED BREADS

WHITE SANDWICH BREAD

Panning the dough for cloverleaf rolls.

Yield: 2 Large Loaves

Method: Straight dough

Fermentation: 1 to 1½ hours

Proofing: 30 minutes to 1 hour

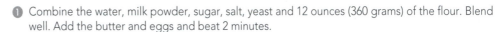

Water (temperature controlled)	12 fl. oz.	360 ml	50%
Nonfat dry milk powder	1.25 oz.	35 g	5%
Granulated sugar	1 oz.	30 g	4%
Salt	0.5 oz.	15 g	2%
Active dry yeast	0.5 oz.	15 g	2%
Bread flour	1 lb. 8 oz.	720 g	100%
Unsalted butter, softened	1 oz.	30 g	4%
Eggs	3.2 oz. (2 eggs)	100 g	14%
Egg wash	as needed	as needed	
Total dough weight:	2 lb. 11 oz.	1305 g	181%

1. Combine the water, milk powder, sugar, salt, yeast and 12 ounces (360 grams) of the flour. Blend well. Add the butter and eggs and beat 2 minutes.
2. Stir in the remaining flour, 2 ounces (60 grams) at a time. Knead 8 minutes or until the dough reaches 77°F (25°C).
3. Place the dough in a lightly greased bowl, cover and ferment at room temperature until doubled, approximately 1 to 1½ hours.
4. Divide the dough into two uniform pieces. Shape into loaves, place the dough into greased loaf pans and proof until doubled.
5. Brush the dough with egg wash. Bake at 375°F (190°C) until brown and hollow-sounding, approximately 50 minutes.

VARIATIONS:

Whole-Wheat Sandwich Bread—Substitute up to 12 ounces (360 grams/50%) whole-wheat flour for an equal amount of the bread flour.

Cloverleaf Rolls—Divide the dough into 1-ounce (30-gram) pieces. Roll each piece of dough into a tight ball. Place three balls of dough into each greased muffin tin. Proof, egg wash and bake at 375°F (190°C) until lightly browned and cooked through, approximately 20 to 25 minutes.

Approximate values per 2-oz. (60-g) serving: **Calories** 150, **Total fat** 2 g, **Saturated fat** 1 g, **Cholesterol** 25 mg, **Sodium** 250 mg, **Total carbohydrates** 28 g, **Protein** 6 g, **Vitamin A** 4%

PULLMAN LOAVES

Yield: 3 Loaves, approximately 2 lb. (970 g) each

Method: Straight dough

Fermentation: Bench rest, 25 minutes

Proofing: 30 minutes to 1 hour

Dry milk powder	1 oz.	30 g	1.85%
Bread flour	1 lb. 11 oz.	810 g	50%
High-gluten flour	1 lb. 11 oz.	810 g	50%
Water (temperature controlled)	34 fl. oz.	1020 ml	63%
Compressed yeast	2.5 oz.	75 g	4.6%
Granulated sugar	1.25 oz.	37 g	2.3%
Salt	1 oz.	30 g	1.85%
Dough conditioner (optional)	1 oz.	30 g	1.85%
Unsalted butter, room temperature	2.75 oz.	82 g	5%
Total dough weight:	6 lb. 1 oz.	2924 g	180%

Pullman refers to a long loaf of white bread, resembling a railroad car, baked in a lidded pan so that the slices are perfectly square. The loaves are usually sold unsliced so they can be cut horizontally for making many canapés or vertically into thinner slices for club sandwiches and the like. The connection to the Pullman Railroad is more than a physical resemblance. Nineteenth-century railroad entrepreneur George Pullman invented a covered loaf pan as a space-saving feature in his railroad dining car. (With his pan, the equivalent of 3 loaves of bread could fit in the same space where only two fit previously.) According to Andrew Smith in the Oxford Companion to America Food and Drink, *Pullman's compact railroad kitchen influenced kitchen apartment design in the 20th century.*

1. Stir the milk powder into the flours in the bowl of a mixer fitted with a dough hook. Add the remaining ingredients and mix on low speed to combine. Stop the machine and scrape down the bowl. The dough should be soft and smooth. Add more water if the dough appears to be dry. Increase the speed to medium and knead the dough until it is fully developed and passes the windowpane test, approximately 7 minutes. The dough should reach 77°F (25°C).

2. Scrape the dough onto a lightly floured work bench and cover. Bench rest 10 minutes. Punch down the dough, then cover and bench rest another 5 minutes.

3. Divide the dough into three equal pieces, then round them, cover with plastic and bench rest 10 minutes. Shape the dough into long loaves and place the dough into greased 13 × 4 × 3-inch (32.5 × 10 × 7.5-centimeter) Pullman or loaf pans. Or divide the dough into six equal pieces, shape into long loaves and twist two pieces together before placing them in greased pans.

4. Grease the interior of the Pullman pan lids or the bottoms of three half-sheet pans. Place the lids on the pans or the greased sheet pans on top of the loaves. Proof the dough until it is 1 inch (2.5 centimeters) away from the top of the pan.

5. Bake at 375°F (190°C) until well browned, approximately 60 to 65 minutes.

Approximate values per 1/17-loaf serving: **Calories** 120, **Total fat** 1.5 g, **Saturated fat** 1 g, **Cholesterol** 5 mg, **Sodium** 250 mg, **Total carbohydrates** 23 g, **Protein** 4 g

1. Twisting the Pullman dough before placing in the pan.

2. Pullman loaf after proofing.

3. Fully baked Pullman loaves.

OATMEAL BREAD

Yield: 2 Large Loaves, approximately 2 lb. (960 g) each

Method: Straight dough

Fermentation: 2 to 3 hours

Proofing: Approximately 45 minutes

Water, boiling	12 fl. oz.	340 ml	40%
Quick-cooking oats	5 oz. (1 ½ cups)	135 g	16%
Unsalted butter	2 oz.	60 g	7%
Honey	1.5 oz.	42 g	5%
Water, 70°F (21°C)	1 pt.	450 ml	53%
Instant yeast	0.3 oz.	9 g	1.1%
Bread flour	1 lb. 14 oz.	850 g	100%
Salt	0.6 oz. (1 Tbsp.)	18 g	2.2%
Rolled oats	as needed	as needed	
Total dough weight:	4 lb. 3 oz.	1904 g	224.3%

1. Pour the boiling water over the quick-cooking oats in a small bowl, then stir in the butter and honey. Let cool to 80°F to 90°F (26°C to 32°C), very warm to the touch but not so hot as to kill the yeast.
2. Place the oatmeal mixture, water, yeast, flour and salt in the bowl of a stand mixer fitted with a dough hook. Knead on low speed until the dough comes together, approximately 2 minutes. Scrape down the bowl and let the mixture rest 5 minutes.
3. Knead on low speed until the soft dough is smooth, approximately 6 to 8 minutes.
4. Cover and ferment the dough until double, approximately 2 to 3 hours.
5. Punch down the dough and divide into two pieces. Mold the dough into two plump ovals. Pan the dough in greased loaf pans sprinkled with rolled oats. Sprinkle the tops of the loaves with more rolled oats. Proof the loaves until increased approximately 75 percent in volume, approximately 45 minutes.
6. Score the loaves, then bake at 425°F (220°C), with steam injected during the first few seconds of baking, until the crust is golden brown, approximately 45 to 50 minutes.

Approximate values per 1-oz. (30-g) serving: **Calories** 70, **Total fat** 1.5 g, **Saturated fat** 0.5 g, **Cholesterol** 0 mg, **Sodium** 115 mg, **Total carbohydrates** 12 g, **Protein** 2 g

AMERICAN HAMBURGER OR HOT DOG ROLLS

Yield: 20 Rolls, approximately 3½ oz. (105 g) each

Method: Straight dough

Fermentation: Bench rest, 25 minutes

Proofing: 20 to 30 minutes

Compressed yeast	3.5 oz.	100 g	10%
Water (temperature controlled)	17 fl. oz.	485 ml	48.5%
Salt	0.75 oz.	21 g	2%
Bread flour	2 lb. 3 oz.	1000 g	100%
Dough conditioner (optional)	0.5 oz.	15 g	1.5%
Vegetable shortening or butter	3.5 oz.	100 g	10%
Granulated sugar	3.5 oz.	100 g	10%
Dry milk powder	1 oz.	25 g	2.5%
Vital wheat gluten	0.5 oz.	15 g	1.5%
Eggs	3.3 oz. (2 eggs)	100 g	10%
Egg wash or melted butter	as needed	as needed	
Sesame seeds	as needed	as needed	
Total dough weight:	4 lb. 4 oz.	1961 g	196%

❶ The formed rolls before baking.

1. Dissolve the yeast in half of the water and set aside.
2. Dissolve the salt in the remaining water in the bowl of a mixer fitted with a dough hook. Add the flour, dough conditioner (if using), shortening, sugar, milk powder, gluten and eggs. Stir in the yeast mixture and mix 3 minutes on low speed to combine the ingredients. Stop the machine and scrape down the bowl. Add more flour or water to make a soft dough. Increase the speed to medium and knead the dough until fully developed, approximately 7 to 9 minutes. The dough should reach 77°F (25°C).
3. Scrape the dough onto a lightly floured work bench and cover. Bench rest 10 minutes. Punch down the dough, cover and bench rest another 5 minutes.
4. Divide the dough into 2-ounce (60-gram) pieces. Bench rest another 10 minutes. Round the rolls, then bench rest another 10 minutes.
5. Make up the dough into rolls for hamburger buns, then flatten slightly with a rolling pin and place them on paper-lined sheet pans. For hot dog rolls, roll the dough into oblongs 6 inches (15 centimeters) long.
6. Brush with egg wash or melted butter, sprinkle with sesame seeds (if using), then proof the rolls until doubled, 20 to 30 minutes. Bake at 450°F (230°C), with steam injected into the oven during the first few seconds of baking, until golden brown, approximately 9 to 12 minutes.

❷ The baked rolls.

bun any of a variety of small, round yeast rolls; can be sweet or savory

Approximate values per roll: **Calories** 160, **Total fat** 4 g, **Saturated fat** 1 g, **Cholesterol** 15 mg, **Sodium** 180 mg, **Total carbohydrates** 27 g, **Protein** 5 g

POTATO HERB ROLLS

Yield: 35 Rolls, 2 oz. (60 g) each

Method: Straight dough

Fermentation: Approximately 1 hour

Proofing: 30 minutes to 1 hour

Bread flour	2 lb. 2 oz.	1020 g	92%
Potato flour	3 oz.	90 g	8%
Instant yeast	1 oz.	30 g	3%
Water (temperature controlled)	21 fl. oz.	630 ml	57%
Eggs	3.3 oz. (2 eggs)	100 g	9%
Dry milk powder	1.5 oz.	45 g	4%
Granulated sugar	2.5 oz.	75 g	7%
Salt	0.75 oz.	22 g	2%
Olive oil	3 fl. oz.	90 ml	8%
Fresh parsley, chopped fine	1 oz.	30 g	3%
Fresh rosemary, chopped fine	0.14 oz. (2 tsp.)	4 g	0.4%
Black pepper	0.07 oz. (1 tsp.)	2 g	0.2%
Egg wash	as needed	as needed	
Onion slices, ⅛ inch (3 millimeters) thick (optional)	35	35	
Kosher salt	as needed	as needed	
Total dough weight:	4 lb. 7 oz.	2138 g	194%

1. Place the flours, yeast, water, eggs, milk powder, sugar, salt and oil in the bowl of a mixer fitted with a dough hook. Mix on low speed to combine. Knead on medium speed until a perfect windowpane has been reached and the dough reaches 77°F (25°C), approximately 7 to 9 minutes. Mix in the herbs and pepper just until evenly distributed in the dough.
2. Cover the dough and ferment until doubled in bulk, approximately 1 hour.
3. Punch down the dough and divide into 2-ounce (60-gram) pieces. Round and place on paper-lined sheet pans.
4. Proof until the rolls increase 70 to 80 percent in volume.
5. Brush the proofed rolls carefully with egg wash and place a slice of onion on top of each roll (if using). Sprinkle with kosher salt.
6. Bake without steam at 375°F (190°C) until golden brown, approximately 16 to 18 minutes.

VARIATION:

Potato Herb Pull-Apart Loaf—Place 4 rounded rolls touching each other in the center of a paper-lined half-sheet pan in Step 3. Position 10 rounded rolls around the perimeter of the rolls on the sheet pan. Repeat with the remaining rolls to make 2 loaves. (Make individual rolls with any dough that remains.) Omit the egg wash and kosher salt. Dust the proofed rolls lightly with sifted flour before baking in Step 5.

Approximate values per roll: **Calories** 150, **Total fat** 3.5 g, **Saturated fat** 0.5 g, **Cholesterol** 10 mg, **Sodium** 250 mg, **Total carbohydrates** 26 g, **Protein** 5 g

POTATO CHEDDAR CHEESE BREAD

STOUFFER STANFORD COURT HOTEL, SAN FRANCISCO, CA
Former Executive Chef Ercolino Crugnale

Yield: 7 Loaves, 1 lb. 4 oz. (600 g) each

Method: Straight dough

Fermentation: Approximately 2 hours

Proofing: 45 minutes

Active dry yeast	2 oz.	60 g	2.7%
Water, warm (100°F/38°C)	8 fl. oz.	240 ml	11%
Potatoes, Russet, boiled and peeled	2 lb.	950 g	44%
Bread flour	4 lb. 8 oz.	2160 g	100%
Kosher salt	1.5 oz.	45 g	2%
Black pepper, table grind	0.5 oz.	15 g	0.7%
Unsalted butter, melted	3 oz.	90 g	4%
Cheddar cheese, grated	1 lb.	475 g	22%
Water, room temperature	22 fl. oz.	658 ml	30%
Total dough weight:	9 lb. 7 oz.	4525 g	209%

1. Dissolve the yeast in the warm water and set aside.
2. Pass the potatoes through a ricer. Place the riced potatoes and the flour, salt, pepper, butter and cheese in the bowl of a large mixer fitted with the dough hook. Blend on low speed 2 to 3 minutes. Add the room-temperature water and the yeast mixture. Knead on medium speed 8 to 10 minutes adding additional water should the dough appear too dry after 2 or 3 minutes of mixing.
3. Allow the dough to ferment in a warm spot until doubled, approximately 2 hours. Punch down the dough and divide into seven equal loaves.
4. Round each piece of dough, then form into an oval. Place them in flour-dusted bannetons and proof until doubled in size, approximately 45 minutes. Remove the proofed dough from the bannetons. Dust them with additional flour, then score the loaves and bake at 350°F (180°C) until brown, approximately 20 to 30 minutes.

Approximate values per 1½-oz. (45-g) serving: **Calories** 100, **Total fat** 3 g, **Saturated fat** 1.5 g, **Cholesterol** 5 mg, **Sodium** 220 mg, **Total carbohydrates** 15 g, **Protein** 4 g

JALAPEÑO CHEESE BREAD

This zesty bread has many uses. Serve it layered with shaved cold cuts or grilled vegetables. Or use it when making grilled cheese panini. Fold 3 cups well-drained cooked corn kernels into the dough along with the jalapeños. Use this dough to make dinner rolls, the ideal accompaniment to chili or red beans and rice.

Yield: 4 Loaves, approximately 1 lb. 6 oz. (660 g) each

Method: Straight dough

Fermentation: 1 to 1½ hours

Proofing: 30 to 45 minutes

Bread flour	2 lb. 3 oz.	1050 g	100%
Water (temperature controlled)	13 fl. oz.	380 ml	37%
Eggs	6.75 oz. (4 eggs)	200 g	19%
Instant yeast	1 oz.	30 g	3%
Dry milk powder	1 oz.	30 g	3%
Granulated sugar	3 oz.	90 g	9%
Salt	0.75 oz.	22 g	2%
Olive oil	3 fl. oz.	90 ml	9%
Jalapeño peppers, seeded and chopped, small dice	10 oz.	300 g	29%
Cilantro, chopped fine	1.5 oz.	45 g	4%
Onion, fine dice	2 oz.	60 g	6%
Cheddar cheese, large dice	10 oz.	300 g	29%
Total dough weight:	5 lb. 7 oz.	2607 g	250%

1. Place the flour, water, eggs, yeast, milk powder, sugar, salt and oil in the bowl of a 6 quart (6.5 liter) or larger mixer fitted with a dough hook. Mix on low speed until the ingredients are combined into a firm dough. Increase the speed to medium and knead until the dough is fully developed, approximately 7 to 9 minutes. Add the jalapeños, cilantro, onion and cheese and mix just until blended into the dough. The dough should reach 80°F (27°C) after kneading.

2. Cover the dough and ferment until doubled, approximately 1 to 1½ hours.

3. Punch down the dough and divide into four equal pieces. Round the dough, cover and bench rest 10 minutes.

4. Roll the dough into cylinders and place them seam side down into greased or paper-lined loaf pans.

5. Proof until the formed loaves have increased 75 to 80 percent in volume, approximately 30 to 45 minutes.

6. Brush with egg wash and bake at 375°F (190°C) until golden brown, approximately 50 minutes. Cool the loaves in their pans for 30 minutes to prevent the loaves from collapsing.

Approximate values per 1½-oz. (45-g) serving: **Calories** 110, **Total fat** 3.5 g, **Saturated fat** 1.5 g, **Cholesterol** 15 mg, **Sodium** 170 mg, **Total carbohydrates** 14 g, **Protein** 4 g

CARROT BREAD WITH HERBS

Yield: 3 Loaves, approximately 1 lb. 8 oz. (720 g) each

Method: Straight dough or old dough

Fermentation: Old dough, 4 to 6 hours. Final dough, 1 hour

Proofing: 35 to 40 minutes

Water (temperature controlled)	17 fl. oz.	510 ml	53%
Olive oil	1.5 fl. oz.	45 ml	5%
Salt	0.75 oz.	22 g	2.3%
Granulated sugar	0.75 oz.	22 g	2.3%
Bread flour	2 lb.	960 g	100%
Instant yeast	0.5 oz.	15 g	1.5%
Old Dough (page 199), room temperature (optional)	1 lb.	480 g	50%
Fresh parsley, chopped fine	2 oz.	60 g	6%
Fresh thyme, chopped fine	0.5 oz.	5 g	1.5%
Onion, chopped fine	5 oz.	150 g	16%
Carrots, grated coarse	8 oz.	240 g	25%
Total dough weight:	5 lb. 4 oz.	2509 g	262%

1. Place the water, oil, salt and sugar in the bowl of a 6 quart (6.5 liter) or larger mixer fitted with a dough hook. Add the flour and yeast. Blend on low speed to combine. Knead at medium speed until the dough is almost fully developed.
2. Add the Old Dough in small pieces (if using) and continue mixing until the dough is smooth and elastic. The dough should reach 77°F (25°C) and pass the windowpane test. Knead in the herbs and vegetables on low speed just to incorporate.
3. Cover the dough and ferment until doubled, approximately 1 hour.
4. Punch down the dough, divide into three equal pieces and shape as desired.
5. Proof at 80°F (25°C) until the loaves increase 50 percent in volume, approximately 30 to 45 minutes.
6. Score the loaves. Bake at 400°F (200°C), with steam injected into the oven during the first few minutes of baking, until well browned, approximately 40 to 45 minutes.

Approximate values per 2-oz. (60-g) serving: **Calories** 120, **Total fat** 1.5 g, **Saturated fat** 0 g, **Cholesterol** 0 mg, **Sodium** 250 mg, **Total carbohydrates** 22 g, **Protein** 4 g, **Vitamin A** 40%

1. Adding the old dough.

2. Adding the herbs and vegetables.

3. The finished bread.

TIGER BREAD

This light wheat bread takes its name from the distinctive crackled pattern its coating gives the finished loaf. The coating may be used on any tender-crust, mild wheat bread.

① Spreading topping over proofed bread.

② The finished tiger bread.

Yield: 4 Loaves, approximately 13 oz. (390 g) each

Method: Straight dough

Fermentation: Approximately 2 hours

Proofing: Approximately 25 minutes

Dough:

Bread flour	2 lb. 3 oz.	1000 g	100%
Dough conditioner (optional)	0.75 oz.	20 g	2%
Shortening	0.3 oz. (2 tsp.)	10 ml	1%
Salt	0.75 oz.	20 g	2%
Compressed yeast	0.75 oz.	20 g	2%
Granulated sugar	0.3 oz. (2 tsp.)	10 g	1%
Water (temperature controlled)	18 fl. oz.	520 ml	52%
Total dough weight:	3 lb. 7 oz.	1600 g	160%

Topping:

Water	8 fl. oz.	240 ml	
Compressed yeast	0.5 oz.	15 g	
Granulated sugar	0.5 oz.	15 g	
Bread flour	1 oz.	30 g	
Rice flour	9 oz.	270 g	
Vegetable oil	0.5 fl. oz.	15 ml	
Salt	0.25 oz.	7.5 g	
Total weight:	1 lb. 3 oz.	592 g	

① Prepare the dough by combining all the dough ingredients in the bowl of a mixer fitted with a dough hook. Mix on low approximately 3 minutes. Stop the machine and scrape down the bowl. Add additional flour to make a firm dough if needed. Increase speed to high and knead approximately 6 to 7 minutes. The dough will be smooth yet somewhat firm and should reach 77°F (25°C).

② Cover the dough and ferment 1 hour.

③ Divide the dough into four equal pieces. Round the dough, cover and bench rest 45 minutes.

④ Form the dough into short baguettes 12 inches (30 centimeters) long. Proof on a parchment-lined sheet pan until loaves have increased 75 percent in volume.

⑤ While the dough is proofing, prepare the topping. Place all the topping ingredients in the bowl of a mixer fitted with the paddle attachment. Mix until well blended, approximately 2 to 3 minutes. The mixture should be somewhat wet and sticky but not loose. Cover the topping and ferment in a warm place 30 minutes.

⑥ Place the topping in a piping bag fitted with a medium plain tip. Pipe the topping over the proofed loaves, then use an offset spatula to spread it smoothly over the bread, covering the entire surface of each loaf down to the parchment paper. Resume proofing the loaves until the topping begins to crack, approximately 10 to 15 minutes.

⑦ Bake at 450°F (230°C) with steam injected into the oven during the first few seconds of baking. Immediately reduce the oven temperature to 375°F (190°C) and bake until crisp and browned, approximately 30 to 35 minutes.

Approximate values per ⅑-loaf serving: **Calories** 110, **Total fat** 1 g, **Saturated fat** 0 g, **Cholesterol** 0 mg, **Sodium** 230 mg, **Total carbohydrates** 22 g, **Protein** 3 g

HARD-CRUSTED BREADS

KAISER OR VIENNA ROLLS

Yield: 28 Rolls, 2 oz. (60 g) each

Method: Straight dough

Fermentation: Bench rest, 30 minutes

Proofing: 35 to 45 minutes

Bread flour	2 lb. 3 oz.	1000 g	100%
Dough conditioner (optional)	0.75 oz.	20 g	2%
Vegetable shortening	1 oz.	30 g	3%
Salt	0.75 oz.	20 g	2%
Compressed yeast	1.75 oz.	50 g	5%
Water (temperature controlled)	22 fl. oz.	630 ml	63%
Vegetable oil	as needed	as needed	
Poppy seeds	as needed	as needed	
Sesame seeds	as needed	as needed	
Caraway seeds	as needed	as needed	
Coarse salt	as needed	as needed	
Total dough weight:	3 lb. 13 oz.	1745 g	175%

Kaiser roll a large round yeast roll with a crisp crust and a curved pattern stamped on the top; used primarily for sandwiches

1. Combine the flour, dough conditioner (if using), shortening, salt, yeast and water in the bowl of a mixer fitted with a dough hook. Mix on low speed 3 to 4 minutes, until blended. Stop the machine and scrape down the bowl. The dough should be somewhat soft and smooth. Add more water if the dough appears dry. Increase the speed to medium and knead until the dough is fully developed and reaches 77°F (25°C), approximately 7 to 9 minutes.

2. Scrape the dough onto a lightly floured workbench and cover. Ferment 10 minutes. Punch down the dough and fold over to release gases. Cover and bench rest another 10 minutes.

3. Divide the dough into 2-ounce (30-gram) pieces. Round the dough, cover and bench rest another 10 minutes. Place the formed dough onto paper-lined sheet pans, spaced 2 inches (5 centimeters) apart. Brush the tops of the dough with oil and proof until doubled in size, approximately 20 to 30 minutes.

4. Dip a Kaiser roll stamp in flour and press into each proofed roll. Spray the rolls lightly with water and sprinkle them with poppy, sesame or caraway seeds combined with no more than 10 percent coarse salt. Proof another 15 minutes.

5. Bake at 450°F (230°C), with steam injected into the oven during the first few minutes of baking, until golden brown, approximately 12 to 14 minutes.

Approximate values per roll: **Calories** 130, **Total fat** 1.5 g, **Saturated fat** 0 g, **Cholesterol** 0 mg, **Sodium** 280 mg, **Total carbohydrates** 24 g, **Protein** 4 g

ONION RING LOAVES

❶ Coating the onion ring in flour before proofing.

❷ The finished onion ring loaves.

Yield: 6 Loaves, 10 oz. (300 g) each

Method: Straight dough

Fermentation: Bench rest, approximately 35 minutes

Proofing: 20 to 30 minutes

Bread flour	2 lb. 2 oz.	950 g	95%
Light rye flour	1.75 oz.	50 g	5%
Water (temperature controlled)	22 fl. oz.	620 ml	62%
Compressed yeast	0.7 oz.	25 g	2%
Toasted onion flakes	3.5 oz.	100 g	10%
Salt	0.6 oz.	18 g	1.8%
Dough conditioner (optional)	0.3 oz. (2 tsp.)	10 g	1%
Vegetable shortening	0.5 oz.	15 g	1.5%
Rye flour	as needed	as needed	
Total dough weight:	3 lb. 15 oz.	1788 g	178%

❶ Combine the bread and light rye flours, water, yeast, onion flakes, salt, dough conditioner (if using) and shortening in the bowl of a mixer fitted with a dough hook. Mix on low speed to combine. Stop the machine and scrape down the bowl. Add more water if the dough appears dry. Increase speed to medium and knead until the dough is fully developed and reaches 77°C (25°C), approximately 7 to 8 minutes.

❷ Scrape the dough onto a lightly floured workbench and cover. Rest 15 minutes. Punch down the dough and fold over to release gases. Cover and bench rest another 10 minutes.

❸ Divide the dough into 10-ounce (300-gram) pieces. Round, cover and bench rest another 10 minutes.

❹ Roll the dough pieces into 12-inch- (30-centimeter-) long ropes as for baguettes. Moisten each end of a piece of dough lightly with water. Press the ends together to form a ring.

❺ Place the rings, top side down, onto a sheet pan lined with a very wet, clean towel. Then dip each moistened ring in rye flour and place flour side up on paper-lined sheet pans. Cover and proof until doubled in size, approximately 20 to 30 minutes.

❻ Score each ring four times in a crosshatch pattern.

❼ Bake at 420°F (215°C), with steam injected into the oven during the first 2 minutes of baking, until well browned, approximately 15 to 20 minutes. Open the oven door slightly during the last 5 minutes of baking to remove any trace of steam.

Approximate values per ⅙-loaf serving: **Calories** 120, **Total fat** 1 g, **Saturated fat** 0 g, **Cholesterol** 0 mg, **Sodium** 260 mg, **Total carbohydrates** 23 g, **Protein** 4 g

ONION WALNUT BREAD

Yield: 4 Loaves, 1 lb. 6 oz. (660 g) each

Method: Sponge and old dough

Fermentation: Sponge and old dough, 4 to 6 hours. Final dough, approximately 1 hour.

Proofing: 45 minutes to 1 hour

Topping:

Onions, peeled	12 oz.	360 g	
Powdered sugar	as needed	as needed	
Kosher salt	as needed	as needed	

Dough:

Poolish (page 199), room temperature	1 lb. 4 oz.	600 g	62%
Bread flour	1 lb. 8 oz.	720 g	75%
Dark rye flour	4 oz.	120 g	12.5%
Whole-wheat flour	4 oz.	120 g	12.5%
Instant yeast	0.75 oz.	22 g	2.3%
Water (temperature controlled)	16 fl. oz.	480 ml	50%
Salt	1 oz.	30 g	3%
Old Dough (page 199), room temperature (optional)	1 lb.	480 g	50%
Walnuts, chopped	6 oz.	175 g	19%
Total dough weight:	5 lb. 11 oz.	2747 g	286%

1. Cut the onions into ⅛-inch- (3-millimeter-) thick slices. Place them on paper-lined sheet pans. Lightly dust with powdered sugar and sprinkle with kosher salt. Bake the onions at 375°F (190°C) until lightly browned. Set aside.

2. Place the Poolish, flours, yeast, water and salt in the bowl of a 6 quart (6.5 liter) or larger mixer fitted with a dough hook. Mix on low speed to combine the ingredients. Then knead on medium speed until the dough is smooth and elastic and reaches 77°F (25°C), approximately 7 to 10 minutes.

3. Add the Old Dough in small pieces (if using). Continue kneading until the dough is fully developed. Mix in 8 ounces (240 grams) of the cooked onions and the walnuts until combined.

4. Ferment the dough until doubled, approximately 1 hour.

5. Punch down the dough and divide into four equal pieces. Shape into loaves and place seam side down on a floured canvas, banneton or sheet pan. Proof in a warm area until the loaves increase 50 percent in volume, approximately 45 minutes to 1 hour.

6. Flip the loaves onto a baking sheet or peel, if necessary. Score the top and then garnish with the remaining onions. Bake at 425°F (220°C), with steam injected into the oven during the first few minutes of baking, until golden brown, 40 to 45 minutes.

Approximate values per 2-oz. (60-g) serving: **Calories** 140, **Total fat** 3.5 g, **Saturated fat** 0 g, **Cholesterol** 0 mg, **Sodium** 290 mg, **Total carbohydrates** 24 g, **Protein** 5 g, **Iron** 10%

ARTISAN BAGUETTES

Yield: 7 Loaves, approximately 12.5 oz. (375 g) each

Method: Sponge

Fermentation: Sponge, 15 to 20 hours. Final dough, approximately 2 hours

Proofing: 45 minutes to 1 hour

Poolish (page 199)	2 lb.	960 g	89%
Artisan bread flour or all-purpose flour	2 lb. 4 oz.	1080 g	100%
Instant yeast	0.3 oz.	10 g	1%
Salt	1.3 oz.	40 g	3.7%
Water (temperature controlled)	1 lb. 4 oz.	600 g	55.5%
Rice or bread flour	as needed	as needed	
Total dough weight:	5 lb. 9 oz.	2690 g	250%

1 Combine the Poolish, flour, yeast, salt and water in the bowl of a 6 quart (6.5 liter) or larger mixer fitted with a dough hook. Mix on low speed to blend the ingredients. Knead on medium speed until a windowpane is reached and the temperature measures 75°F (23°C), approximately 8 to 9 minutes.

2 Cover and allow the dough to ferment 1 hour.

3 Fold the dough over, then cover and allow the dough to ferment until it feels spongy and alive, for an additional 45 to 60 minutes.

4 Punch down the dough, cover and bench rest 15 minutes.

5 Scale the dough into 13-ounce (390-gram) pieces. Round each piece of dough.

6 Preshape the dough before rolling into baguettes. Flatten each dough piece into a rectangle. Fold in the ends of each long side. Fold over the flattened dough piece into a tight cylinder, using your thumb to create tension on its surface. Seal using the ball of your palm or fingertips.

7 Roll out each dough piece into a long loaf. Place the rolled dough seam side down onto a canvas couche lightly dusted with rice or bread flour. Proof until the loaves increase 40 to 50 percent in volume, approximately 45 to 60 minutes.

8 Use the canvas to roll the bread onto sheet pans or onto a floured oven peel. Score the loaves, then bake at 450°F (232°C), with steam injected into the oven during the first few minutes of baking. Bake until the loaves are evenly browned, approximately 18 to 20 minutes.

Approximate values per 1-oz. (30-g) serving: **Calories** 60, **Total fat** 0 g, **Saturated fat** 0 g, **Cholesterol** 0 mg, **Sodium** 170 mg, **Total carbohydrates** 12 g, **Protein** 2 g

1 Creating tension on a round of dough.

2 Folding in the sides of the dough piece.

3 Folding over the dough piece.

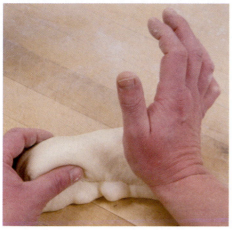

④ Sealing the dough piece before rolling.

⑤ Rolling the dough into a long shape before placing it in floured canvas.

FRENCH OR ITALIAN BREAD

This dough lends itself to the autolyse resting method described on page 187. For improved flavor when time permits, reduce the yeast by half and extend the fermentation time to 4 to 5 hours. This versatile dough can be formed into many shapes from small **club rolls** *to boules, baguettes or large rustic loaves.*

Yield: 4 Loaves, approximately 1 lb. 9 oz. (750 g) each

Method: Straight dough

Fermentation: 1 to 3 hours

Proofing: 30 to 45 minutes

Water (temperature controlled)	39 fl. oz.	1170 ml	65%
Active dry yeast	1 oz.	28 g	1.6%
Bread flour	3 lb. 12 oz.	1.8 kg	100%
Salt	1.25 oz.	36 g	2%
Total dough weight:	6 lb. 5 oz.	3026 g	168%

club roll a small oval-shaped roll made of crusty French bread

① Combine the water and yeast in the bowl of a mixer, 6 quart (6.5 liter) or larger, fitted with a dough hook. Add the remaining ingredients and mix on low speed until all the flour is incorporated.

② Increase the speed to medium and knead the dough until it is smooth and elastic.

③ Ferment the dough until doubled, approximately 1 to 3 hours. Punch down, divide and shape as desired. Proof the loaves until doubled.

④ Score the loaves then bake them at 425°F (218°C), with steam injected during the first few minutes of baking, until the crust is well developed and golden brown and the bread is baked through, approximately 12 minutes for rolls and 20 minutes for small loaves.

Approximate values per 1½-oz. (45-g) serving: **Calories** 80, **Total fat** 0 g, **Saturated fat** 0 g, **Cholesterol** 0 mg, **Sodium** 135 mg, **Total carbohydrates** 16 g, **Protein** 3 g

MULTIGRAIN, RYE AND SOURDOUGH BREADS

This category of breads requires special handling. The low protein and coarse texture of whole grains cuts into the gluten strands that develop when kneading dough. Higher-protein flours such as high-gluten flour as well as vital wheat gluten (see Chapter 4, Bake-shop Ingredients) are added to strengthen multigrain and rye doughs.

Rye grows well in colder northern climates and was for centuries the primary grain available for bread making in Europe. German, Austrian and other central European bakers have mastered working with this challenging grain. The protein in rye flour is not usable to form the gluten structure necessary to make rye loaves rise; bread formulas with more than 40 percent rye flour will be dense, flat and uneven when baked. Combining rye with higher-protein flour compensates for this while preserving rye flavor. Sourdough starters add flavor to rye breads and their chemical properties help rye ferment, something rye flour does rapidly. Rye doughs are mixed and baked relatively quickly and can overproof easily.

  ## MULTIGRAIN SOURDOUGH BREAD

Yield: 2 Loaves, 9 in. × 5 in. (22 cm × 13 cm)

Method: Straight dough

Fermentation: 2 to 3 hours

Proofing: 30 to 45 minutes

Cracked wheat	4.5 oz.	135 g	22%
Water, hot	8 fl. oz.	240 ml	40%
Whole butter, melted	2 oz.	60 g	10%
Molasses	1.5 oz.	45 g	7.5%
Honey	1.5 oz.	45 g	7.5%
Salt	0.2 oz. (1 tsp.)	6 g	1%
Nonfat dry milk powder	2 oz.	60 g	10%
Flax seeds	2 oz.	60 g	10%
Sunflower seeds, roasted	2 oz.	60 g	10%
Sourdough starter	1 lb. 6 oz.	660 g	110%
Active dry yeast	0.15 oz. (1 tsp.)	4.5 g	0.7%
Whole-wheat flour	10 oz.	300 g	50%
Bread flour	10 oz.	300 g	50%
Egg wash	as needed	as needed	
Total dough weight:	4 lb. 1 oz.	1975 g	328%

❶ Combine the cracked wheat and hot water in the bowl of an electric mixer. Add the butter, molasses, honey, salt and milk powder. Set aside to cool.

❷ When the mixture has cooled to lukewarm, stir in the flax seeds, sunflower seeds, starter and yeast. Stir in the whole-wheat flour, then gradually add the bread flour. When the dough begins to stiffen, attach the bowl to a 6 quart (6.5 liter) or larger mixer fitted with a dough hook and continue adding the bread flour. Knead until the dough is smooth and elastic, approximately 5 minutes.

❸ Place the dough in a lightly oiled bowl, cover and ferment until doubled.

❹ Punch down the risen dough, cover and ferment again.

❺ After the second rise, punch down the dough and divide into two equal portions. Place the dough into two well-greased loaf pans, cover and proof the dough until doubled again.

❻ Brush the surface of each loaf with egg wash and make two or three cuts across the top of each loaf. Bake at 375°F (190°C) until done, approximately 30 minutes.

Approximate values per ¹⁄₁₆-loaf serving: **Calories** 150, **Total fat** 3.5 g, **Saturated fat** 1 g, **Cholesterol** 5 mg, **Sodium** 90 mg, **Total carbohydrates** 26 g, **Protein** 5 g, **Iron** 10%, **Claims**—good source of fiber and iron

NINE-GRAIN BREAD

Nine-grain mix is a blend of various grains including cracked wheat, barley, cornmeal, millet, rolled oats, rye, triticale, brown rice, soy flour and flax seeds. Many bakery suppliers carry a similar combination of grains and seeds to use in bread. Any combination of these grains will work in this formula.

Nine-Grain Mix

Yield: 3 Loaves, 1 lb. 9 oz. (750 g) each

Method: Straight dough or old dough

Fermentation: Old dough, 4 to 6 hours. Final dough, 1 to 1½ hours

Proofing: 30 to 45 minutes

Nine-grain mix	8 oz.	240 g	33%
Water, room temperature	10 fl. oz.	300 ml	42%
High-gluten flour	1 lb. 8 oz.	720 g	100%
Vital wheat gluten	1.25 oz.	36 g	5%
Instant yeast	0.75 oz.	22 g	3%
Salt	0.75 oz.	22 g	3%
Water (temperature controlled)	16 fl. oz.	485 ml	67%
Old Dough (page 199), room temperature (optional)	1 lb.	480 g	66%
Total dough weight:	4 lb. 12 oz.	2305 g	319%

Nine-Grain Bread

1. Soak the nine-grain mix in the room-temperature water in a mixer bowl for 1 hour.
2. Sift the flour and gluten into the soaked grains. Add the yeast, salt and temperature-controlled water to the flour mixture. Mix on low speed to combine, then knead on medium speed until the dough is smooth and pulls away from the sides of the bowl and reaches 77°F (25°C).
3. Add the Old Dough in small pieces (if using) and continue mixing until a perfect windowpane is reached.
4. Ferment the dough until doubled in bulk, 1 to 1½ hours.
5. Punch down the dough and divide into 26-ounce (780-gram) pieces. Mold the dough into plump oval loaves. Place them on paper-lined sheet pans or on floured canvas. Proof the dough in a warm area until the loaves increase 50 percent in volume, approximately 30 to 45 minutes.
6. Gently use the canvas to turn the loaves onto a floured peel or baking sheet. Score the loaves.
7. Bake at 400°F (200°C), with steam injected during the first few seconds of baking, until the crust is a deep dark brown, approximately 40 to 45 minutes.

Approximate values per 2-oz. (60-g) serving: **Calories** 120, **Total fat** 1 g, **Saturated fat** 0 g, **Cholesterol** 0 mg, **Sodium** 290 mg, **Total carbohydrates** 24 g, **Protein** 5 g, **Claims**—good source of fiber

ARTISAN WHEAT BREAD

Whole-wheat flours differ greatly in how much water they can absorb. It may be necessary to adjust the dough using additional water or flour, depending on the specific whole-wheat flour used. This dough will absorb additional moisture during fermentation and therefore will become less sticky to the touch after the initial rise.

Yield: 6 Loaves, 1 lb. 12 oz. (840 g) each

Method: Sponge

Fermentation: Sponge, overnight, 15 to 20 hours. Final dough, 80 minutes

Proofing: 45 minutes

Poolish (page 199)	2 lb. 4 oz.	1080 g	45%
Whole-wheat flour	2 lb. 8 oz.	1200 g	50%
Bread flour	2 lb. 8 oz.	1200 g	50%
Instant yeast	1 oz.	30 g	1.25%
Salt	2 oz.	60 g	2.5%
Granulated sugar	2 oz.	60 g	2.5%
Water (temperature controlled)	3 lb. 3 oz.	1530 g	63.75%
Flour or rice flour	as needed	as needed	
Total dough weight:	10 lb. 12 oz.	5160 g	215%

1. Combine the Poolish, flours, yeast, salt, sugar and water in the bowl of a large mixer fitted with a dough hook. Mix on low speed to blend the ingredients. Knead on medium speed until a windowpane is reached and the temperature measures 77°F (25°C), approximately 8 minutes.
2. Remove the dough from the machine. Cover and ferment it until doubled in bulk, approximately 60 to 80 minutes.
3. Punch down the dough, cover and allow it to rest 15 minutes.
4. Scale the dough into 29-ounce (870-gram) pieces. Round each piece of dough.
5. Shape each round into an oval loaf. Place each loaf seam side down on a floured canvas or sheet pan. Proof the loaves until they have increased 50 percent in volume, approximately 45 minutes.
6. Use the canvas to turn the loaves onto a floured oven peel. (Or carefully invert each proofed loaf onto paper-lined sheet pans.) Dust them lightly with flour.
7. Score the loaves. Bake at 425°F (220°C) with steam injected into the oven during the first few minutes of baking, until well browned, approximately 40 to 45 minutes.

Approximate values per ⅟₁₆-loaf serving: **Calories** 100, **Total fat** 0.5 g, **Saturated fat** 0 g, **Cholesterol** 0 mg, **Sodium** 230 mg, **Total carbohydrate**s 21 g, **Protein** 4 g

❶ Scoring loaves before baking.

❷ The finished loaves.

PLIÉ BRETON
(BRITTANY FRENCH RYE)

Yield: 4 Loaves, approximately 1 lb. (480 g) each

Method: Sourdough starter

Fermentation: Sourdough sponge, overnight, 15 to 20 hours. Final dough, bench rest 30 minutes

Proofing: 25 to 30 minutes

Sponge:

Sourdough starter	1.75 oz.	50 g	5%
Water, cool	2.75 fl. oz.	80 ml	8%
Light rye flour	3 oz.	100 g	10%

Dough:

Bread flour	2 lb.	900 g	90%
Dough conditioner (optional)	0.75 oz.	20 g	2%
Compressed yeast	0.75 oz.	20 g	2%
Salt	0.6 oz.	18 g	1.8%
Quark, farmer's cheese or baker's cheese	2.5 oz.	75 g	7.5%
Water (temperature controlled)	20.5 fl. oz.	580 ml	58%
Total dough weight:	4 lb.	1843 g	184%

❶ Brittany rye bread folded before proofing and baking.

❶ The day before making the finished bread, make the sourdough sponge. Combine the starter, cool water and rye flour. Mix to combine the ingredients. Cover the sponge and ferment at room temperature approximately 15 to 20 hours.

❷ Combine the sponge with the remaining ingredients in the bowl of a mixer fitted with a dough hook. Mix 3 minutes on low speed to combine the ingredients. Stop the machine and scrape down the bowl. Knead on medium speed until smooth and elastic, approximately 5 to 7 minutes. The dough should reach 77°F (25°C) after kneading.

❸ Cover the dough and ferment 15 minutes.

❹ Punch down the dough and divide into four equal pieces. Round the dough, cover and bench rest 15 minutes.

❺ Flatten each piece of dough with a rolling pin into a 10-inch (25-centimeter) oval approximately 1 inch (2.5 centimeters) thick. Brush the tops of the ovals with water and fold them in half. Place each loaf on lightly floured sheet pans. Proof until doubled in size, approximately 25 to 35 minutes.

❻ Dust the loaves lightly with rye flour. Bake at 450°F (230°C), with steam injected into the oven during the first few seconds of baking. Immediately reduce the temperature to 375°F (190°C) and bake until well browned and cooked through, approximately 30 to 35 minutes.

❷ The finished plié Breton.

Approximate values per ⅛-loaf serving: **Calories** 100, **Total fat** 0.5 g, **Saturated fat** 0 g, **Cholesterol** 0 mg, **Sodium** 250 mg, **Total carbohydrates** 20 g, **Protein** 3 g

SAN FRANCISCO SOURDOUGH BREAD

STOUFFER STANFORD COURT HOTEL, SAN FRANCISCO, CA
Former Executive Chef Ercolino Crugnale

Since the days of the California Gold Rush, San Francisco has been identified with sourdough bread. This noticeably tangy product sustained prospectors and their cooks who carried the starter culture from camp to camp. To try to replicate the puckery taste of bread made in San Francisco, make sure that the starter used is quite sour in taste. Alternately, allow the dough to ferment under refrigeration for anywhere from 3 to 6 hours. These steps will help develop a sour flavor in the bread after baking. Authentic San Francisco sourdough bread, however, can be prepared only in that city, where the local bacterium that gives the bread its distinctive flavor—
Lactobacillus sanfrancisco—*thrives.*

Yield: 1 Loaf

Method: Sourdough starter

Fermentation: 1 to 3 hours

Proofing: 1 to 2 hours

Active dry yeast	0.5 oz.	15 g	3%
Water (temperature controlled)	8 fl. oz.	240 ml	50%
Sourdough starter	6 oz.	180 g	37%
Bread flour	1 lb.	480 g	100%
Kosher salt	0.5 oz.	15 g	3%
Cornmeal	as needed	as needed	
Egg white, beaten	1 oz. (1 white)	30 g	
Total dough weight:	2 lb.	930 g	193%

1. Sprinkle the yeast over 2 fluid ounces (60 milliliters) of the water and set aside until dissolved and foamy.
2. In the bowl of a mixer fitted with a dough hook, combine the starter and the remaining water. Add 6 ounces (180 grams) of the flour.
3. Stir until a dough forms, then add the yeast mixture. Knead 5 minutes on medium speed.
4. Add the remaining flour and the salt. Knead until the dough is smooth and elastic, approximately 10 minutes.
5. Place the dough in a lightly greased bowl and cover with a damp cloth. Ferment in a warm place, approximately 80°F to 90°F (27°C to 32°C), until doubled.
6. Punch down the dough and shape it into a round loaf. Place the loaf on a greased and cornmeal-dusted sheet pan.
7. Proof the dough in a warm place, covered with a damp cloth, until it has risen to 2½ times its original size. This may take 1 to 2 hours, depending on the vitality of the original starter.
8. Brush the risen loaf with the beaten egg white and score the top of the loaf with a sharp knife.
9. Bake at 450°F (230°C), with steam injected into the oven during the first 4 minutes of baking.
10. Reduce the oven temperature to 375°F (190°C) and continue baking until the loaf is well browned, approximately 35 to 45 minutes.

Approximate values per 2-oz. (60-g) serving: **Calories** 135, **Total fat** 0.5 g, **Saturated fat** 0 g, **Cholesterol** 0 mg, **Sodium** 355 mg, **Total carbohydrates** 27 g, **Protein** 4 g

PAIN AU LEVAIN (TRADITIONAL FRENCH SOURDOUGH BREAD)

Yield: 3 Loaves, approximately 1 lb. 6 oz. (660 g) each

Method: Sourdough starter

Fermentation: Levain, 8 to 12 hours. Final dough, approximately 2 hours

Proofing: 1 to 2 hours

Levain:

Natural Sourdough Starter (page 194)	1 lb. 2 oz.	540 g	360%
Bread flour	5 oz.	150 g	100%
Total levain weight:	1 lb. 7 oz.	690 g	460%

Dough:

Levain	1 lb. 7 oz.	690 g	88%
Bread flour	1 lb. 10 oz.	780 g	100%
Water (temperature controlled)	18 fl. oz.	540 ml	69%
Salt	0.75 oz.	22 g	3%
Total dough weight:	4 lb. 3 oz.	2032 g	260%

Pain au Levain

1. To make the levain, combine the starter and flour in the bowl of a mixer fitted with a dough hook. Knead on medium speed until combined.
2. Scrape the mixture into a large bowl or plastic container and cover. Store at room temperature 8 to 12 hours.
3. To make the dough, place the levain mixture in the bowl of a mixer fitted with a dough hook. Add the flour, water and salt. Mix on low speed until well combined. Increase speed to medium and knead until the dough is smooth, elastic and fully developed, approximately 7 to 8 minutes.
4. Cover the dough and ferment 2 hours.
5. Punch down the dough and divide into three equal pieces. Round the dough, cover and bench rest 10 minutes.
6. Shape the dough into plump oval loaves slightly tapered at each end. Place the loaves seam side down on paper-lined sheet pans or in flour-dusted bannetons.
7. Proof until the loaves increase 70 percent in volume. This may take 1 to 2 hours, depending on the vitality of the original starter.
8. Unmold the loaves from the bannetons (if using) and then score them lengthwise with three slashes. Bake at 425°F (220°C), with steam injected into the oven during the first few minutes of baking, until the crust is a deep dark brown, approximately 40 to 45 minutes.

Pain au Levain with Walnuts and Cranberries

VARIATIONS:

Pain au Levain with Nuts—Add 3 ounces (90 grams/11%) walnuts, 3 ounces (90 grams/11%) whole toasted almonds and 3 ounces (90 grams/11%) whole toasted hazelnuts to the dough once it has been fully kneaded. Mix just to distribute the nuts throughout the dough.

Pain au Levain with Garlic and Herbs—Bake 3 whole heads of garlic, wrapped in aluminum foil, at 350°F (180°C), approximately 1 hour. Cool, then peel the baked garlic. Add the baked garlic cloves and 0.05 ounce (15 grams/2%) finely chopped fresh rosemary to the dough once it has been fully kneaded.

Pain au Levain with Three Cheeses—Dice 8 ounces (240 grams/30%) each of Parmesan, mozzarella and Gruyère cheese into 5/8-inch (1.5-centimeter) cubes and add to the dough once it has been fully kneaded.

Pain au Levain with Walnuts and Cranberries—Add 10 ounces (300 grams/38%) walnuts and 10 ounces (300 grams/38%) dried cranberries to the dough once it has been fully kneaded.

Approximate values per 1/12-loaf serving: **Calories** 100, **Total fat** 0 g, **Saturated fat** 0 g, **Cholesterol** 0 mg, **Sodium** 220 mg, **Total carbohydrates** 20 g, **Protein** 3 g

SPECIALTY BREADS

ENGLISH MUFFINS

KENDALL COLLEGE SCHOOL OF CULINARY ARTS, EVANSTON, IL
Chef Instructor Mike Artlip, CEC, CCE

Yield: 18 Muffins, approximately 3¼ oz. (95 g) each

Method: Sponge

Fermentation: Sponge, 15 minutes. Dough, 1 to 2 hours

Proofing: Approximately 45 minutes

Milk	12 fl. oz.	337 ml	37.5%
Instant yeast	0.25 oz. (2 tsp.)	7 g	0.8%
Pastry flour	1 lb.	450 g	50%
Bread flour	1 lb.	450 g	50%
Baking powder (optional)	0.4 oz. (1 Tbsp.)	12 g	1.25%
Granulated sugar	1.5 oz.	42 g	4.7%
Salt	0.6 oz.	18 g	2%
Unsalted butter, room temperature	1.5 oz.	42 g	4.7%
Water (temperature controlled)	12 fl. oz.	337 ml	37.5%
Rice flour or fine cornmeal	as needed	as needed	
Total dough weight:	3 lb. 11 oz.	1695 g	188%

1. Heat the milk to 75°F (24°C). Stir the yeast into the milk until it dissolves. Mix in 10 ounces (300 grams) of the pastry flour. Cover the sponge and ferment 15 minutes.

2. Warm the remaining flour in a 250°F (120°C) oven until it reaches 120°F (49°C).

3. Place the sponge, warmed flour, baking powder, sugar, salt, butter and water in the bowl of a mixer fitted with a dough hook. Mix 3 minutes on low speed to moisten the ingredients, then beat on high speed another 7 minutes. The dough will be very soft and sticky.

4. Cover the dough and ferment 1 to 2 hours at room temperature.

5. Line a baking sheet with parchment paper. Sprinkle evenly and generously with rice flour or fine cornmeal. Grease two 3-inch (7.5-centimeter) round cutters or tart rings and place them 2 inches (5 centimeters) apart on the prepared baking sheet.

6. Scrape the dough out onto a clean damp worktable or silicone mat. Using a dough scraper, divide the dough into 3 to 3¼-ounce (90 to 97-gram) pieces. Place a portion of the dough into one ring. Press it lightly into shape. Remove the ring and proceed with the remaining dough alternating between the two rings. Dust the tops lightly with more rice flour.

7. Proof at 80°F (25°C) until visibly risen, approximately 45 minutes.

8. Bake the muffins on a lightly greased griddle heated to medium low, approximately 325°F (160°C), until golden brown, approximately 10 to 12 minutes per side.

Approximate values per muffin: **Calories** 210, **Total fat** 3.5 g, **Saturated fat** 1.5 g, **Cholesterol** 5 mg, **Sodium** 410 mg, **Total carbohydrates** 41 g, **Protein** 6 g, **Iron** 15%

GRISSINI
(DRY ITALIAN-STYLE BREAD STICKS)

Yield: 4½ Dozen Bread Sticks, approximately 1 oz. (30 g) each

Method: Straight dough

Fermentation: 1 to 1½ hours

Proofing: 15 to 20 minutes

Bread flour	2 lb. 3 oz.	1050 g	100%
Instant yeast	0.5 oz.	15 g	1.4%
Salt	1.3 oz.	40 g	3.8%
Water (temperature controlled)	15 fl. oz.	450 ml	43%
Olive oil	4 fl. oz.	120 ml	11.4%
Unsalted butter, softened	4 oz.	120 g	11.4%
Olive oil (optional)	as needed	as needed	
Kosher salt, sesame seeds and fresh herbs, chopped (optional)	as needed	as needed	
Total dough weight:	3 lb. 11 oz.	1795 g	171%

1. Combine the flour, yeast, salt, water, oil and butter in the bowl of a mixer fitted with a dough hook. Mix on low speed to blend the ingredients. Increase the speed to medium and knead the dough until it is smooth but firm and fully developed and the temperature reaches 75°F (23°C), approximately 6 to 8 minutes.

2. Remove the dough from the bowl. Cover and let the dough ferment until nearly doubled, approximately 45 to 60 minutes.

3. Punch down the dough. Cover and bench rest 15 minutes.

4. Roll the dough out ¼-inch (3-millimeters) thick into a rectangle approximately 12 inches (30 centimeters) wide. Cut the dough into ¼-inch (3-millimeter) strips.

5. Roll each strip lightly. Position the strips spaced ½ inch (1.2 centimeters) apart on paper-lined sheet pans.

6. Proof until the dough increases 25 percent in volume, approximately 15 minutes.

7. Brush the dough lightly with olive oil and sprinkle it with salt, sesame seeds and/or herbs, if desired.

8. Bake at 375°F (180°C) until golden brown, approximately 10 to 12 minutes.

Approximate values per bread stick: Calories 33, **Total fat** 1.25 g, **Saturated fat** 0.5 g, **Cholesterol** 1 mg, **Sodium** 90 mg, **Total carbohydrates** 4.5 g, **Protein** 0.5 g

1. Cutting the dough into strips.

2. Rolling the strips of dough.

3. The baked bread sticks.

PLAIN BAGELS

Forming a bagel by wrapping dough around one hand.

Assortment of Plain and Flavored Bagels

Bagels develop their distinctive shine because of their brief dip in boiling water. Surface starch gelatinizes into a smooth film that reflects light after baking.

Yield: 14 Bagels, approximately 2¾ oz. (80 g) each

Method: Straight dough

Fermentation: 30 minutes to 1 hour

Proofing: Approximately 25 minutes

Dough:

High-gluten flour	1 lb. 8 oz.	720 g	100%
Vital wheat gluten	1.25 oz.	36 g	5%
Water (temperature controlled)	16 fl. oz.	475 ml	66%
Instant yeast	0.75 oz.	22 g	3%
Barley malt or honey	0.5 oz.	15 g	2%
Salt	0.5 oz.	15 g	2%
Sesame, poppy or caraway seeds, chopped onions, kosher salt (optional)	as needed	as needed	
Total dough weight:	2 lb. 11 oz.	1283 g	178%

Poaching liquid:

Water	1 gal.	4 lt
Honey or barley malt	3 oz.	90 g
Baking soda	1 oz.	30 g

1. Combine all dough ingredients in the bowl of a mixer fitted with a dough hook. Mix on low speed to blend the ingredients. Increase the speed to medium and knead the dough until it is smooth but firm and fully developed. The dough should reach 77°F (25°C).

2. Place the dough on an unfloured workbench. Cover and ferment until not quite doubled, approximately 30 minutes.

3. Flatten the dough into a large rectangle. Cut the dough into 5-inch- (12.5-centimeter-) wide strips the length of the rectangle. Divide each strip of dough into 3-ounce (90-gram) pieces.

4. Roll the portioned dough into 10-inch- (25-centimeter-) long ropes. Wrap one rope of dough around one hand, overlapping the ends 1 inch (2.5 centimeters) to form a ring. Pinch the ends to seal the dough. Roll the dough back and forth on the workbench to even the shape and thickness of the bagel.

5. Place the formed bagels on a lightly floured canvas or paper-lined sheet pans. Proof until the bagels have increased 20 percent in volume.

6. Combine the water, honey or barley malt and baking soda in a wide shallow pot for the poaching liquid. Bring it to a full rolling boil. Just before adding the bagels to the liquid, reduce the heat so that the water simmers. Add as many bagels as the pot will comfortably hold.

7. Poach each batch of bagels 45 seconds to 1 minute. Flip the bagels with a skimmer and poach them another 45 seconds on the other side. Remove them from the liquid with the skimmer and drain them in a colander. Place the poached bagels on paper-lined sheet pans, leaving enough space between each bagel for further expansion. Sprinkle with toppings, if desired.

8. Bake at 450°F (230°C) until amber-colored, approximately 18 to 20 minutes.

VARIATIONS:

Long-Fermented Bagels—Form the bagels, then place them on sheet pans generously sprinkled with flour or cornmeal. Retard the formed bagels covered in the refrigerator or retarder overnight, then bring them to room temperature before proofing, boiling and baking. Or retard the bagels after poaching, then let them sit 90 minutes at room temperature before baking.

Tomato Basil Bagels—Add 6 ounces (180 grams/25%) sun-dried tomatoes cut in small dice and 0.75 ounce (22 grams/3%) finely chopped fresh basil to the dough toward the end of the kneading process. Garnish each poached bagel with a thin slice of fresh tomato. Brush with olive oil and sprinkle with salt before baking.

Onion Walnut Bagels—Cut 8 ounces (240 grams/33%) peeled onions into ⅛-inch- (3-millimeter-) thick slices. Place on a sheet pan. Dust lightly with powdered sugar and bake at 375°F (190°C) until lightly browned. Cool, then add to the dough near the end of the kneading process along with 8 ounces (240 grams/33%) chopped walnuts. Slice 2 more peeled onions thinly and place on top of the poached bagels. Sprinkle with kosher salt, black pepper and poppy seeds, then bake immediately.

Cinnamon Raisin Bagels—Increase the instant yeast to 1 ounce (30 grams/4%). Add 2 ounces (60 grams/8%) granulated sugar to the dough in the first step. Add 0.25 ounce (8 grams/1%) ground cinnamon and 8 ounces (240 grams/33%) raisins to the dough toward the end of the kneading process. Remove from the mixer when the dough is still streaked with cinnamon. When the bagels come out of the oven, brush them with melted butter and dip in cinnamon sugar.

Approximate values per bagel: **Calories** 190, **Total fat** 0.5 g, **Saturated fat** 0 g, **Cholesterol** 0 mg, **Sodium** 400 mg, **Total carbohydrates** 39 g, **Protein** 9 g, **Iron** 15%

Cinnamon Raisin Bagel

❶ Dividing the dough into rectangles.

❷ Stretching the dough.

❸ Sliding the loaves into the deck oven.

❹ The sliced ciabatta loaf.

CIABATTA

Ciabatta *means "slipper" in Italian. This chewy loaf, full of large elongated holes, takes its name from its characteristic shape formed by gentle handling after fermentation.*

Yield: 7 Loaves, 1 lb. (480 g) each

Method: Sponge

Fermentation: Poolish, 15 to 20 hours. Final dough, 2 hours.

Proofing: 30 to 45 minutes

Poolish:

Bread flour	1 lb. 4 oz.	600 g	100%
Water, room temperature	1 lb. 4 oz.	600 g	100%
Instant yeast	0.07 oz. (½ tsp.)	2 g	0.35%
Total poolish weight:	2 lb. 8 oz.	1202 g	200%

Final dough:

Poolish	2 lb. 8 oz.	1200 g	91%
Bread flour	2 lb. 12 oz.	1320 g	100%
Water (temperature controlled)	1 lb. 11 oz.	705 g	61.3%
Salt	1.5 oz.	45 g	3.5%
Instant yeast	0.5 oz.	15 g	1%
Rice flour or bread flour	as needed	as needed	
Total dough weight:	7 lb. 1 oz.	3392 g	257%

❶ To make the poolish, combine the flour, water and yeast in the bowl of a large mixer fitted with the paddle attachment and mix until smooth, approximately 2 minutes. Cover and allow it to ferment at room temperature 15 to 20 hours.

❷ To make the final dough, combine the poolish with the remaining ingredients in the bowl of a mixer fitted with the dough hook. Mix on low speed until well combined. Knead on medium speed until the dough reaches 77°F (23°C). The batterlike dough will be extraordinary soft, wet and sticky and the windowpane will not be fully developed.

❸ Scrape the dough onto a floured workbench. Cover and let the dough ferment 1 hour. Punch down the dough, then let the dough ferment another hour.

❹ Gently gather and shape the dough into a rectangle approximately 1½ inches (3.7 centimeters) thick.

❺ Using a dough scraper or knife, divide the dough into 1-pound (450-gram) rectangular pieces. Stretch each piece of dough into 9-inch- (22-centimeter-) long loaves. Place on sheet pans lined with well-floured canvas or clean cotton towels.

❻ Proof until the dough increases 25 percent in volume, approximately 30 to 45 minutes.

❼ Use the canvas to gently roll the loaves onto an oven peel dusted with rice flour or onto flour-dusted paper-lined sheet pans.

❽ Bake at 450°F (230°C) with steam injected into the oven during the first few seconds of baking, until dark brown, approximately 40 to 45 minutes.

VARIATION:

Black Olive Ciabatta—After the dough is mixed in Step 3, add 1 pound 5 ounces (630 grams/105%) well-drained pitted black olives.

Approximate values per 1-oz. (30-g) serving: **Calories** 60, **Total fat** 0 g, **Saturated fat** 0 g, **Cholesterol** 0 mg, **Sodium** 150 mg, **Total carbohydrates** 12 g, **Protein** 2 g

FOCACCIA
(ROMAN FLATBREAD)

Yield: 1 Half-Sheet Pan, 12 in. × 18 in. (30 cm × 45 cm)

Method: Straight dough

Fermentation: 1 to 2 hours

Proofing: 15 minutes

Topping the flatbread dough with crushed rosemary.

Granulated sugar	0.4 oz. (1 Tbsp.)	11 g	2%
Active dry yeast	0.4 oz. (1 Tbsp.)	11 g	2%
Water (temperature controlled)	12 fl. oz.	350 ml	66%
All-purpose flour	1 lb. 2 oz.	540 g	100%
Kosher salt	0.3 oz. (2 tsp.)	10 g	1.7%
Onion, chopped fine	3 oz.	90 g	17%
Olive oil	0.5 fl. oz.	15 ml	3%
Fresh rosemary, crushed	0.2 oz. (2 Tbsp.)	5 g	1%
Total dough weight:	2 lb. 2 oz.	1032 g	193%

1 Combine the sugar, yeast and water. Stir to dissolve the yeast. Stir in the flour, 4 ounces (120 grams) at a time.

2 Stir in 1½ teaspoons (7 milliliters) of the salt and the onion. Mix well, then knead on a lightly floured board or in the bowl of a mixer fitted with a dough hook until smooth.

3 Place the dough in an oiled bowl, cover and ferment until doubled.

4 Punch down the dough, then flatten it onto an oiled sheet pan. It should be no more than 1 inch (2.5 centimeters) thick. Brush the top of the dough with the olive oil. Let the dough proof until doubled, approximately 15 minutes.

5 Sprinkle the crushed rosemary and the remaining ½ teaspoon (2 milliliters) salt on top of the dough. Bake at 400°F (200°C) until lightly browned, approximately 20 minutes.

Approximate values per 1-oz. (30-g) serving: **Calories** 100, **Total fat** 0.5 g, **Saturated fat** 0 g, **Cholesterol** 0 mg, **Sodium** 230 mg, **Total carbohydrates** 21 g, **Protein** 3 g

PIZZA DOUGH

Yield: 1 Large Pizza or 8 Individual Pizzas

Method: Straight dough

Fermentation: 30 minutes

The formed pizza before baking.

Active dry yeast	0.4 oz. (1 Tbsp.)	12 g	3%
Water, hot (90°F/32°C)	2 fl. oz.	60 ml	14%
Bread flour	14 oz.	420 g	100%
Water, cool	6 fl. oz.	180 ml	43%
Salt	0.2 oz. (1 tsp.)	6 g	1.4%
Olive oil	1 fl. oz.	30 ml	7%
Honey	0.75 oz.	20 g	5%
Total dough weight:	1 lb. 8 oz.	728 g	173%

❶ Stir the yeast into the hot water to dissolve. Add the flour.

❷ Stir the remaining ingredients into the flour mixture. Knead with a dough hook or by hand until smooth and elastic, approximately 5 minutes.

❸ Place the dough in a lightly greased bowl and cover. Ferment the dough in a warm place 30 minutes. Punch down the dough and divide into portions. The dough may be wrapped and refrigerated up to 2 days.

❹ On a lightly floured surface, roll the dough into very thin rounds and top as desired. Bake at 400°F (200°C) until crisp and golden brown, approximately 8 to 12 minutes.

Approximate values per 2-oz. (60-g) serving: **Calories** 220, **Total fat** 4 g, **Saturated fat** 0.5 g, **Cholesterol** 0 mg, **Sodium** 290 mg, **Total carbohydrates** 41 g, **Protein** 6 g, **Claims**—low saturated fat; no cholesterol

PITA BREAD

Yield: 18 Individual Pitas

Method: Straight dough

Fermentation: Bench rest, 45 minutes

Proofing: 25 to 30 minutes

Compressed yeast	2.75 oz.	80 g	8%
Water (temperature controlled)	19 fl. oz.	530 ml	53%
Bread flour	2 lb. 4 oz.	1000 g	100%
Salt	0.75 oz.	20 g	2%
Vegetable oil	3 fl. oz.	85 ml	8.5%
Total dough weight:	3 lb. 13 oz.	1715 g	171%

❶ Rolling the dough.

❶ Dissolve the yeast in the water in the bowl of a mixer fitted with a dough hook. Add the remaining ingredients and mix on low speed 3 minutes. Scrape down the bowl. Add more flour, if necessary, to make a stiff dough. Knead the dough on high speed until it is smooth and comes away from the sides of the bowl, approximately 7 more minutes. The dough should reach 77°F (25°C).

❷ Cover the dough and rest 15 minutes. Punch down the dough and rest another 10 minutes.

❸ Divide the dough into 3-ounce (90-gram) pieces. Round and lightly oil each piece. Cover the oiled dough and bench rest 20 minutes. Flatten each dough ball into a 6-inch (15-centimeter) circle. Place the dough on paper-lined sheet pans. Proof the dough in a warm, dry place until doubled in size, approximately 25 to 30 minutes.

❹ Bake at 475°F (250°C) until puffed and lightly browned, approximately 8 to 10 minutes. Cool on racks to preserve the pocket in the dough.

Approximate values per pita: **Calories** 250, **Total fat** 6 g, **Saturated fat** 0.5 g, **Cholesterol** 0 mg, **Sodium** 410 mg, **Total carbohydrates** 42 g, **Protein** 1 g, **Iron** 15%

❷ The baked pitas.

ROASTED RED PEPPER AND ALMOND BUTTER TAPENADE

Yield: 1 lb. 12 oz. (840 g)

Roasted red peppers, canned	24 oz.	720 g
Garlic cloves, peeled	4	4
Salt	0.6 oz. (3 tsp.)	18 g
Roasted almond butter	3 oz.	180 g
Cumin, ground	0.04 oz. (½ tsp.)	1 g
Black pepper, ground	0.04 oz. (½ tsp.)	1 g
Fresh cilantro sprigs	as needed	as needed
Pita bread or naan	as needed	as needed

❶ Drain the roasted red peppers in a colander, then blot with clean paper towels. Set aside.

❷ In the bowl of a food processor fitted with a metal blade, grind the garlic and half of the salt into a paste. Add the almond butter and 1 fluid ounce (2 tablespoons/30 milliliters) water. Process until the mixture turns into a smooth dry paste, approximately 10 seconds. Add the drained roasted red peppers, cumin and black pepper. Process until smooth, approximately 30 seconds. Adjust the seasonings with the remaining salt, if needed. Garnish with cilantro. Serve with flatbreads such as fresh pita or naan.

Approximate values per 1-fl.-oz. (30-ml) serving: **Calories** 80, **Total fat** 8 g, **Saturated fat** 1 g, **Cholesterol** 0 mg, **Sodium** 0 mg, **Total carbohydrates** 2 g, **Protein** 1 g, **Vitamin A** 15%, **Vitamin C** 50%

TURKISH PIDE BREAD

Chef Klaus Tenbergen, CMB, CEPC, ASBPB

Yield: 3 Loaves

Method: Sponge

Fermentation: Sponge, 3 hours. Final dough, bench rest 50 minutes

Proofing: 35 minutes

Compressed yeast	0.75 oz.	20 g	2%
Water, cool	3.5 fl. oz.	100 ml	10%
Bread flour	2 lb.	900 g	90%
Light rye flour	3.5 oz.	100 g	10%
Dough conditioner (optional)	0.3 oz. (2 tsp.)	10 g	1%
Salt	0.6 oz.	20 g	2%
Water (temperature controlled)	20.5 fl. oz.	580 ml	58%
Cornmeal	as needed	as needed	
Egg wash	as needed	as needed	
Sesame seeds	as needed	as needed	
Total dough weight:	4 lb. 6 oz.	2000 g	200%

① Make the sponge by dissolving the yeast in the cool water in the bowl of a 6 quart (6.5 liter) or larger mixer fitted with a dough hook. Add 7 ounces (210 grams) of the bread flour. Mix 5 minutes at medium speed. Cover the sponge and ferment at room temperature until active and bubbling, approximately 3 hours.

② Add the remaining bread flour, light rye flour, dough conditioner (if using), salt and temperature-controlled water to the sponge. Mix on low speed to combine all the ingredients, approximately 3 to 4 minutes. Stop the machine and scrape down the bowl. Knead the dough on medium speed until fully developed, 7 to 10 minutes, to make a soft, pliable dough.

③ Scrape the dough onto a lightly floured workbench. Cover the dough and ferment 30 minutes. Divide the dough into three equal pieces. Round the dough, cover and bench rest another 20 minutes.

④ Flatten the portioned dough on a cornmeal-dusted workbench into a 12-inch (30-centimeter) circle. Press a thin rolling pin or dowel, measuring approximately 1 inch (2.5 centimeters) in diameter, into the dough, making rows of parallel lines. Repeat in the opposite direction to create a diamond pattern on the surface of the bread.

⑤ Place the dough on paper-lined sheet pans. Brush or spray the bread with egg wash. Sprinkle the loaves with sesame seeds. Proof until doubled in bulk, approximately 30 to 40 minutes.

⑥ Bake at 450°F (230°C) until dark golden brown, 12 to 15 minutes. Cool on racks.

Approximate values per ⅟₁₄-loaf serving: **Calories** 90, **Total fat** 0.5 g, **Saturated fat** 0 g, **Cholesterol** 5 mg, **Sodium** 180 mg, **Total carbohydrates** 18 g, **Protein** 3 g

① Pressing dowel into Turkish pide bread.

② Spraying egg wash on Turkish pide bread. The commercial sprayer uses an aerosol canister of egg wash solution.

③ The finished Turkish pide bread.

PRETZELS

The characteristic shiny brown surface of a pretzel is created by dipping the proofed dough in a bath of sodium hydroxide, commonly referred to as lye or caustic soda. This caustic chemical causes the surface of the dough to become alkaline, accelerating the gelatinization of starches on the crust. After the shaped dough is drained, the pretzels are baked until richly glistening brown. Working with lye requires great care, as it is a dangerous poison. A reasonable substitute can be made using baking soda and water, the same type of liquid in which bagels are poached before baking.

Yield: 21 Pretzels, approximately 3 oz. (90 g) each

Method: Old dough

Fermentation: Old dough, 6 hours or overnight. Final dough, 1½ hours

Proofing: Approximately 40 minutes

Dough:

Old Dough (page 199), room temperature	8.5 oz.	255 g	26.5%
Bread flour	2 lb.	960 g	100%
Instant yeast	0.5 oz.	15 g	1.5%
Water (temperature controlled)	19.5 fl. oz.	585 ml	61%
Salt	0.5 oz.	15 g	1.5%
Unsalted butter	1.5 oz.	45 g	4.7%
Coarse salt	as needed	as needed	
Total dough weight:	3 lb. 14 oz.	1875 g	195%

Poaching liquid:

Water	1 gal.	4 lt
Baking soda	2 oz.	60 g

❶ Forming a pretzel (counterclockwise from left): forming a loop, twisting the ends of the loop, and folding the twisted ends to make the pretzel shape.

❶ Prepare the Old Dough and allow it to ferment 6 to 12 hours.

❷ Place the flour, yeast, water, salt and butter in the bowl of a mixer fitted with a dough hook. Mix on low speed until well combined. Increase the speed to medium and knead until the dough reaches 75°F (23°C). Add the Old Dough in small pieces, kneading until the dough is incorporated.

❸ Scrape the dough onto a floured surface or into a large bowl. Cover the dough and ferment 1 hour.

❹ Punch down the dough, cover and ferment another 30 minutes.

❺ Divide the dough into 3-ounce (90-gram) pieces and round. Cover to prevent drying. Roll each piece into 18- to 20-inch (45- to 50-centimeter) ropes, pressing to taper the ends.

❻ To form each pretzel, cross over the ends of a rope of dough to form a 4-inch (10-centimeter) loop. Twist the ends two times. Lift the twisted ends and fold them back onto the loop to make the pretzel shape.

❼ Transfer the formed dough onto lightly oiled sheet pans. Proof covered until the pretzels have increased 50 percent in volume. Uncover, then place the proofed dough into the refrigerator until the dough develops a light crust, approximately 40 minutes or as long as overnight.

❽ While the dough is proofing, prepare the poaching liquid. Bring the water to a full rolling boil in a large wide pot. Gradually stir in the baking soda. Reduce the heat to a simmer and add as many proofed pretzels as the pot will hold in one layer.

❾ Poach each batch of pretzels 20 to 30 seconds. Flip and poach them another 15 seconds. Remove the pretzels from the liquid with a skimmer and drain them in a colander.

❿ Transfer the pretzels onto an oven peel or a perforated sheet pan. Sprinkle them with the coarse salt. Bake at 450°F (230°C) until evenly browned, approximately 15 to 20 minutes.

❷ The finished pretzel.

Approximate values per pretzel: **Calories** 200, **Total fat** 2.5 g, **Saturated fat** 1 g, **Cholesterol** 5 mg, **Sodium** 330 mg, **Total carbohydrates** 36 g, **Protein** 6 g

NAAN
(INDIAN FLATBREAD)

Yield: 6 Loaves, approximately 10 oz. (300 g) each

Method: Sponge

Fermentation: Sponge, 3 hours. Final dough, 3½ hours

Proofing: 1 hour

Compressed yeast	0.18 oz. (1 tsp.)	5 g	0.5%
Water (temperature controlled)	17 fl. oz.	470 ml	47%
Bread flour	1 lb. 8 oz.	670 g	67%
Whole-wheat flour	12 oz.	330 g	33%
Yogurt	10.5 oz.	300 g	30%
Olive oil	1 fl. oz.	30 ml	3%
Baking powder	0.07 oz. (½ tsp.)	2 g	0.2%
Baking soda	0.07 oz. (½ tsp.)	2 g	0.2%
Salt	0.7 oz.	20 g	2%
Vegetable or olive oil	as needed	as needed	
Black sesame seeds	as needed	as needed	
Fresh parsley, chopped	as needed	as needed	
Total dough weight:	4 lb. 1 oz.	1829 g	182%

1. To prepare the sponge, dissolve 0.04 ounce (1 gram/0.1%) of the yeast in 6 fluid ounces (160 milliliters/16%) of the water in the bowl of a mixer fitted with a dough hook. Add 8 ounces (220 grams/22%) of the bread flour and mix until well incorporated. Cover and set aside. Ferment at room temperature until cracks appear on the surface of the starter, approximately 3 hours.

2. Place the sponge and the remaining bread flour and water, the whole-wheat flour, yogurt, olive oil, baking powder and baking soda in the bowl of a mixer fitted with a dough hook. Mix on low speed 3 minutes. Stop the mixer and scrape down the bowl. Add the remaining 0.14 ounce (4 grams/0.4%) of the yeast and mix on high speed another 3 minutes. Add the salt, then mix until the dough is fully developed and reaches 77°F (25°C), approximately 5 more minutes.

3. Cover the dough and ferment 3 hours.

4. Punch down the dough and divide into six equal pieces. Round the portioned dough. Cover and bench rest 30 minutes.

5. Stretch each piece of dough out until it measures 12 inches (30 centimeters) long. Place the dough on flour-dusted sheet pans and proof until doubled, approximately 50 minutes.

6. Dimple the surface of the dough with your fingertips. Brush the dough with oil and sprinkle it with black sesame seeds or chopped fresh parsley. Place the dough directly on the heated surface of a deck oven at 500°F (260°C) or place the sheet pan of dough on a rack in the oven. Bake until the bread is well browned and crisp, approximately 10 to 12 minutes. To prevent a soggy crust, open the oven door or vent during the last 2 minutes of baking to remove any excess steam that may build up in the oven.

Approximate values per 1½-oz. (45-g) serving: **Calories** 100, **Total fat** 1 g, **Saturated fat** 0 g, **Cholesterol** 0 mg, **Sodium** 230 mg, **Total carbohydrates** 19 g, **Protein** 4 g

FOUGASSE WITH OLIVES

Yield: 12 Loaves, approximately 1 lb. (450 g) each

Method: Old dough

Fermentation: Old dough, 4 to 6 hours. Final dough, approximately 1 hour

Bread flour	5 lb. 8 oz.	2640 g	100%
Water (temperature controlled)	3 lb. 6 oz.	1620 g	61%
Olive oil	4 fl. oz.	120 ml	4.5%
Salt	2 oz.	60 g	2.2%
Instant yeast	1 oz.	30 g	1.1%
Old Dough (page 199)	1 lb. 1 oz.	510 g	19%
Kalamata olives, pitted, chopped coarse	2 lb.	960 g	36%
Fresh oregano, chopped fine	0.5 oz.	15 g	0.5%
Total dough weight:	12 lb. 6 oz.	5955 g	225%

❶ Scoring the fougasse dough with a rolling pastry wheel.

1. Combine the flour, water, olive oil, salt and yeast in the bowl of a large mixer fitted with a dough hook. Mix on low speed well combined. Increase the speed to medium and knead until the dough reaches 75°F (23°C). Add the Old Dough in small pieces. Continue kneading until the dough is fully developed and reaches 77°F (25°C).

2. Mix in the olives and oregano on low speed until just incorporated.

3. Scrape the dough onto a floured surface. Cover loosely and ferment 1 hour, or until doubled. Punch the dough.

4. Divide the dough into 1-pound (450-gram) pieces. Round each piece and place them on a floured surface. Let the dough rest, lightly covered, 10 to 15 minutes.

5. With a floured rolling pin, flatten each piece of dough into a teardrop shape measuring approximately 11 inches (28 centimeters) high and 8½ inches (21.5 centimeters) wide. Place the shaped dough pieces onto a floured canvas couche or pieces of parchment paper.

6. Proof until pieces have increased 40 to 50 percent in volume.

7. Flip the proofed pieces of dough from the floured canvas onto a floured peel, or slide the loaves on the parchment paper gently onto a peel. (The fougasse may also be baked on parchment-lined baking sheets.)

8. Cut several vents into each piece of dough using a dough scraper, then open the vents slightly by pulling them with your hands.

9. Bake at 440°F (226°C) with steam in the oven for the first 5 minutes. Continue baking until the crust is uniformly browned, approximately 27 to 30 minutes. Cool the fougasse on wire racks before serving or bagging.

❷ The finished flatbread.

VARIATION:

Plain Fougasse—Omit the olives and oregano.

Approximate values per loaf: **Calories** 200, **Total fat** 2.5 g, **Saturated fat** 1 g, **Cholesterol** 5 mg, **Sodium** 330 mg, **Total carbohydrates** 36 g, **Protein** 6 g

DECORATING DOUGH

This simple dough is used to make decorative plaques or add ornamentation to yeast bread. Because there is no yeast in the formula, the dough retains its shape after baking. The milk powder, sugar and eggs in the formula make the dough pliable and help it develop color when baked. Commemorative plaques made from decorating dough such as that shown here make impressive displays on a bread buffet for the holidays or other special occasions. The dough can also be rolled and cut into shapes to embellish yeast loaves; large, round country loaves work best for this purpose. When making a decorative piece, dusting sections of the work with grains, rye flour or seeds before baking adds to the piece's visual appeal. To enhance the color of the finished piece, chefs often paint sections of bread showpieces with coffee extract after baking. (Reheat the piece for a few minutes to dry the surface.)

Yield: 11 lb. 10 oz. Dough

Method: Straight dough

Bread flour	6 lb. 8 oz.	3120 g	100%
Dry milk powder	4 oz.	120 g	4%
Water, room temperature	2 lb. 8 oz.	1200 g	38.5%
Granulated sugar	7 oz.	210 g	7%
Salt	1 oz.	30 g	1%
Eggs	9.5 oz. (6 eggs)	285 g	9%
Shortening, butter or margarine	1 lb. 4 oz.	600 g	19.2%
Sesame seeds (optional)	as needed	as needed	
Edible food lacquer (optional)	as needed	as needed	
Total dough weight:	11 lb. 9 oz.	5565 g	179%

1. Sift together the flour and milk powder. Set aside.
2. Blend the water, sugar, salt and eggs in the bowl of a large mixer fitted with the paddle attachment. When the mixture is smooth, add the shortening, blending until the shortening is evenly dispersed.
3. Switch to the dough hook. Add the flour mixture and knead only until a smooth, firm dough is formed, approximately 2 to 3 minutes. Let the dough rest for 15 minutes before using. (The dough can be wrapped tightly and held overnight in the refrigerator before using. Or it can be stored in the freezer for up to 2 weeks. Let the dough come to room temperature before using.)
4. To obtain a smooth and homogeneous surface, use one solid piece of dough that has not been reworked. For the featured plaque, scale a 4-pound (1.8-kilogram) piece of dough. Working on a lightly floured surface, roll the dough out into a 16-inch (40-centimeter) square approximately ¼ inch (6 millimeters) thick. Square off the edges of the dough using a ruler and a sharp knife.
5. Transfer the rolled dough onto a paper-lined sheet pan.
6. To decorate the surface, scale a 2-pound (1-kilogram) piece of decorating dough. Roll out the dough ⅛ inch (3 millimeters) thick on a lightly floured surface. Cut a portion of the dough into twenty-eight 1-inch (2.5-centimeter) squares using a sharp paring knife.

7 To attach the cut-out dough squares to the decorative piece, brush them lightly on each side with water. Dip each piece into sesame seeds (if using) and then position the pieces, sesame-coated side up, evenly around the edges of the large rolled square of dough.

8 Using letter-shaped cookie cutters, cut out the desired message in the remaining dough, rolling out additional dough if necessary. Brush each letter on the reverse side lightly with water and position the letters to form the message in the center of the showpiece.

9 Scale a 2-pound (1-kilogram) piece of decorating dough. Roll out the dough ⅛ inch (3 millimeters) thick on a lightly floured surface. Cut out approximately twenty-five 2-inch (5-centimeter) leaf shapes with a sharp paring knife. Press the knife lightly onto one side of the cut-outs to create veining. Brush each leaf on the reverse side lightly with water and position them to form a garland surrounding the message.

10 Cut out a 1-inch- (2.5-centimeter-) wide strip of dough approximately 32 inches (81 centimeters) long from the remaining dough. Divide the strip of dough into four 8-inch (20-centimeter) pieces. Form the two loops and the two tails of the ribbon with the dough, brushing the sides of the cut pieces lightly with water before attaching each piece to the showpiece. Scatter the center design with small balls of dough rolled from the scraps and moistened lightly with water.

11 Bake the showpiece at 300°F (150°C) until it is well dried, at least 80 to 90 minutes; total time will depend on the total thickness of the piece. Check the piece every 10 minutes for the first 20 minutes of baking to ensure that no unwanted bubbles develop. If bubbles develop, prick them with a toothpick as soon as they appear.

12 Once well dried, remove the piece from the oven. Increase the heat to 400°F (200°C). Return the piece to the oven to brown lightly for approximately 10 to 20 minutes.

13 Once cooled, spray the work with edible lacquer to enhance the sheen, if desired. Store the cooled showpiece lightly covered in a cool, dry place. It will keep for several weeks.

CHAPTER EIGHT

ENRICHED YEAST BREADS

After studying this chapter, you will be able to:

- understand the mixing and handling requirements for making enriched yeast breads
- prepare brioche, challah, doughnuts and a variety of enriched yeast dough products
- prepare a variety of specialty breakfast pastries made from sweet dough
- understand the basic principles of deep-frying sweet dough

ENRICHED YEAST BREADS, AS THE NAME INDICATES, HAVE A HIGHER PERCENTAGE OF FAT, EGGS, MILK AND/OR SWEETENERS than traditional yeast breads. Fats and sweeteners interfere with the development of gluten in these types of dough, resulting in breads, rolls and pastries with a soft crust and tender crumb. Because they are usually softer and stickier than lean yeast bread dough, enriched yeast doughs are handled somewhat differently. But a good understanding of the techniques and terms covered in Chapter 7, Artisan and Yeast Breads, is necessary for successful preparation of these breads as well.

In many parts of the world, breakfast includes some version of the breads and pastries discussed in this chapter. Buns, babka and coffeecake, as well as croissants and Danish pastries, discussed in Chapter 9, Laminated Doughs, are all considered enriched yeast dough products. Popular breakfast items such as sticky buns and brioche rely on large quantities of butter to make these flavorful crusty yet tender pastries.

ENRICHED YEAST DOUGH

Enriched yeast dough, also referred to as sweet dough, bakes into popular breakfast pastries such as sticky buns, coffeecake, sweet rolls and doughnuts. Among the breads featured in this chapter are stollen, panettone and challah, festive breads served around the world to mark holidays and celebratory occasions. Enriched yeast doughs are made with a good proportion of fat and sugar, though not all are sweet.

The ingredients used to make enriched yeast breads are the same as those used in any yeasted bread product. It is the quantity of the ingredients that differs. Enriched yeast doughs may be made with all-purpose, bread or high-gluten flour. As the amount of fat and sweeteners in the formula increases, a higher-protein flour may be needed. Fats added while the dough is mixing will coat the flour, inhibiting the development of gluten. A stronger flour compensates for this. In some enriched yeast dough products, such as brioche, the amount of eggs and fat makes the dough quite heavy. Higher-protein flour develops the gluten structure needed to support the weight of these ingredients.

Dairy products, butter, shortening, oil and eggs may be added in varying proportion according to the specific formula. Pasteurized milk contains enzymes that can weaken gluten, resulting in a sticky dough that is difficult to handle. For best results, heat milk to 200°F (93°C) to destroy these enzymes. Because dry milk powder requires no heating, it is frequently used in place of liquid milk in bread formulas for convenience. Yogurt, buttermilk and UHT milk require no preheating to destroy this enzyme. Butter is the preferred fat in these products because of its flavor and browning ability. To make up for the large amount of eggs in many enriched dough formulas, the quantity of liquid is reduced.

As discussed in Chapter 7, Artisan and Yeast Breads, sugar is a yeast food that, when present in large quantities, can slow yeast activity and gluten formation. Fats in enriched dough coat flour, inhibiting yeast access to carbohydrates in the flour. To compensate, enriched yeast dough formulas may contain slightly higher amounts of yeast than normally used in leaner bread doughs. (Commercial bakeries may use *osmotolerant* yeast, a type specially formulated for enriched doughs.) Barley malt, honey or other sweeteners are often used in enriched yeast dough formulas along with or in place of sugar. Beneficial enzymes in these liquid sweeteners aid fermentation without overfeeding the yeast.

Some bakers prefer to hydrate instant dry yeast before it is used in an enriched yeast dough formula because dry yeast may not fully dissolve during mixing. Instant dry yeast may be dissolved in a portion of the water called for in the formula before adding it to the dry ingredients.

Dried fruits, especially raisins and currants, enhance many enriched yeast doughs. In order for dried fruit to remain tender after the dough is baked, the fruit should be softened or **conditioned** to increase its moisture content before being mixed into the dough. This technique is described in Chapter 5, Mise en Place.

conditioning soaking dried fruit in liquid before use so that it remains tender after baking

Mixing Enriched Yeast Doughs

Enriched yeast doughs are mixed using either the *straight dough method*, the *sponge method* or the *enriched dough method*. The **straight dough method** is used for enriched bread dough where the percentage of fat and sugar is not so great as to interfere with gluten development. See Challah (page 240), Jumbo Cinnamon Buns (page 258) or Hot Cross Buns (page 256). The **sponge method** works well in formulas with the highest percentage of fat and eggs, such as Stollen (page 266), Parisian Brioche (page 263) and Sweet Bun Dough (page 242). The **sponge** improves the texture of enriched doughs and enhances the flavor of bread made from these doughs. Fermentation begins in the sponge before the fat inhibits access to the yeast food in the flour. Some enriched doughs, whether made with or without sponge, such as Rum Babas (page 265) and brioche are kneaded until the gluten is developed before the fat is added. This **enriched dough method** of mixing is unique to high-fat yeast doughs.

When mixing the enriched doughs in this chapter, the temperature of the water is adjusted according to the method discussed in Chapter 7, Artisan and Yeast Breads. To accelerate yeast activity, enriched dough may be mixed to a slightly warmer dough temperature than lean bread dough, approximately 80°F (27°C). Any butter or fat should be at room temperature so that it blends easily into the dough during kneading. Because fat and sugar slow gluten development, enriched doughs often require longer kneading for the gluten to fully develop. Use the windowpane test to judge when these doughs have been kneaded sufficiently. Long cool fermentation, often in a refrigerator or retarder, brings out the flavor of these bread doughs. Chilling the dough before forming also makes these soft, sticky doughs easier to handle.

Forming Enriched Yeast Doughs

Most enriched dough products are divided and formed using the methods described in Chapter 7, Artisan and Yeast Breads, pages 178 to 181. Braiding is a commonly used technique because it helps the rich and soft dough hold its shape during baking. Elaborate shapes using four or more strands of dough are part of the sweet dough tradition throughout the world. See Challah (page 240). Multitiered braided loaves signify the baker's skill and are served for festive occasions. Once braided, the dough can be shaped into a horseshoe, oval or wreath for special occasions.

PROCEDURE FOR MAKING A FOUR-STRAND BRAIDED LOAF

❶ Divide the dough into two equal pieces. Roll each piece into a long strand.

❷ Lay out the two strands of dough perpendicular to each other. Twist the two ends of the horizontal strand, bringing the right end up and the left end down.

❸ Repeat this motion with the vertical strand. Continue crossing the strands until the dough forms a tight loaf. Tuck the ends underneath and pinch to seal the braid.

❶ Forming a cross with two strands of dough.

❷ Twisting the ends of the dough.

❸ Tucking the ends of the dough underneath to form a tight loaf.

PROCEDURE FOR MAKING A TURBAN BRAIDED LOAF

❶ Divide the dough into six equal pieces. Roll the pieces into six narrow ropes. Make two thick ropes by laying three narrow ropes side by side and pinching the ends together to seal.

❷ Place one thick dough rope perpendicular to the other. Fold one end of A down, crossing over the horizontal strip of dough. Bring D under B and over A.

❸ Repeat the pattern, bringing C over D and under A.

❹ Tuck the ends underneath and pinch to seal the braid.

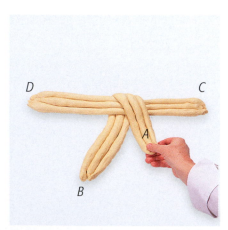

❶ Crossing the two ropes of dough and folding one end down.

❷ Bringing the left end D under B and over A.

❸ The finished turban braided loaf.

Because they are tender and delicate, many types of sweet doughs are molded and baked in pans to hold their shape. **Brioche, babas, kugelhopf, panettone, savarin, stollen** and many breads in this chapter are associated with special shapes and molds. Pans should be well greased and lined with parchment paper when possible, before using. Dried fruit, nuts and other fillings can easily burn, causing the dough to stick, when making these breads.

Proofing and Baking Enriched Yeast Dough

Care must be taken to properly proof enriched yeast doughs. These fragile doughs collapse easily if overproofed. In many cases—Kugelhopf (page 264) and Stollen (page 266), for example—a slight underproofing ensures that enough yeast energy remains to leaven these heavy doughs. Brushing with egg wash before proofing keeps the dough moist so that it expands fully during baking. Proofing in a hot environment, above 85°F (29°C), may melt the butter in sticky bun or brioche dough and is not recommended. As the sugar rapidly caramelizes during baking, enriched dough browns easily. Bake these doughs at moderate temperatures, 350°F to 375°F (180°C to 190°C), to ensure fully baked bread without a burnt crust.

Cooling, Finishing and Storing Enriched Yeast Dough Products

Cool these breads thoroughly before unmolding to help keep their soufflé-like texture intact. Rest the baked bread in the pan on a wire rack for 10 to 30 minutes, then unmold and cool to room temperature before slicing or packaging. After baking, sweet and decorative icings will enhance the appearance of many types of bread made from enriched dough. A dusting with powdered sugar or a drizzle of Basic Sugar Glaze (page 456) or Royal Icing (page 457) puts a finishing touch on the cooled loaves.

PROCEDURES FOR PREPARING ENRICHED YEAST DOUGH

The procedure for mixing an enriched yeast dough using the straight dough method is illustrated by Challah (page 240). The procedure for mixing an enriched yeast dough using the straight dough method with fat added later in the mixing is illustrated by Sweet Bun Dough (page 242).

brioche (BREE-osh) a rich yeast bread containing large amounts of eggs and butter

baba a small, light yeast cake soaked in rum syrup; traditionally baked in individual cylindrical molds, giving the finished product a mushroom shape

kugelhopf (KOO-guhl-hopf) a light, buttery yeast cake studded with nuts and raisins and baked in a special fluted mold; a specialty of Germany, the Alsace region of France and other central European countries

panettone (pan-eh-TONE-nay) a sweet Italian yeast bread filled with raisins, candied fruits, anise seeds and nuts; traditionally baked in a rounded cylindrical mold and served as a breakfast bread or dessert during the Christmas holidays

savarin (SA-va-ran) a rich, yeasted cake prepared from baba dough baked into a small round ring, the center of which may be filled with whipped cream and candied fruit

stollen (STOH-lunn) a sweet German yeast bread filled with dried fruit and marzipan, shaped into a folded oval and coated with powdered sugar

PROCEDURE FOR PREPARING ENRICHED YEAST DOUGH: STRAIGHT DOUGH METHOD

1 Scale ingredients. Adjust water to proper temperature and rehydrate yeast if necessary.

2 Combine all ingredients in the bowl of a mixer fitted with a dough hook on low speed to moisten. The flour may be added a small amount at a time in order to form a soft dough. Scrape down the bowl.

3 Knead on medium speed to properly develop the dough, approximately 5 to 10 minutes.

4 Ferment the dough until double in bulk, then punch down to release gases.

5 Scrape the dough onto a workbench, then divide and scale into uniform pieces. Round each piece into a smooth ball, then rest before rolling into desired shapes. Pan the formed dough as desired.

6 Proof the dough. Brush with egg wash and score the dough, if necessary, then bake.

MISE EN PLACE

▶ Adjust water temperature.
▶ Melt butter.
▶ Prepare the egg wash and line sheet pans with parchment while the dough ferments.

❶ Braiding the challah loaf.

❷ Assorted baked challah loaves.

CHALLAH

Challah (HAH-la) is the traditional bread for Jewish Sabbath and holiday celebrations, rich with eggs and flavored with honey. Time-honored tradition dictates that challah be braided or formed into a turban-shaped loaf as described on page 238. Topped with poppy or sesame seeds, challah is excellent for toast or sandwiches.

Yield: 2 Large Loaves

Method: Straight dough

Fermentation: 1 to 1½ hours

Proofing: 45 minutes

Active dry yeast	0.5 oz.	15 g	1.8%
Water, hot (90°F/32°C)	2 fl. oz.	60 ml	7%
Honey	3 fl. oz.	92 ml	11%
Water (temperature controlled)	5 fl. oz.	210 ml	25%
Unsalted butter, melted	4 oz.	120 g	14%
Eggs	6.75 oz. (4 eggs)	200 g	24%
Bread flour	1 lb. 12 oz.	840 g	100%
Salt	0.6 oz.	18 g	2%
Egg wash	as needed	as needed	
Sesame or poppy seeds	as needed	as needed	
Total dough weight:	3 lb. 3 oz.	1555 g	185%

❶ Dissolve the yeast in the hot water. Stir in the honey.

❷ Place the remaining water, butter, eggs, 8 ounces (240 grams) of the flour and the salt in the bowl of a mixer fitted with a dough hook. Add the yeast mixture. Stir until smooth.

❸ Knead the dough on medium speed, adding the remaining flour 2 ounces (60 grams) at a time, until smooth, elastic and fully developed, approximately 5 minutes.

❹ Place the dough in a lightly greased bowl, cover and ferment until doubled, approximately 1 to 1½ hours.

❺ Punch down the dough and divide into six equal portions. Form the dough into two three-strand braided loaves (page 181). Place the loaves on a paper-lined sheet pan.

❻ Brush the loaves with egg wash and sprinkle with sesame or poppy seeds. Proof until doubled, approximately 45 minutes.

❼ Bake at 350°F (180°C) until the loaves are golden brown and sound hollow when thumped, approximately 40 minutes.

Approximate values per 2-oz. (30-g) serving: **Calories** 156, **Total fat** 4 g, **Saturated fat** 2 g, **Cholesterol** 44 mg, **Sodium** 145 mg, **Total carbohydrates** 25 g, **Protein** 6 g

Sweet Dough or Bun Dough

For many years in the United States and Great Britain, a small yeast roll or **bun** was a staple item in every bakeshop. The dough used to prepare this slightly sweet, deeply browned roll is referred to as "sweet dough" or **bun dough** by many bakers. Although there is no single formula for sweet dough, all formulas are sweeter and richer than that used to make dinner rolls or Pullman loaves but with less fat than brioche. Most sweet dough has fewer eggs than challah but a higher percentage of fat. Sweet dough is more tender and less elastic than challah when baked. Sweet dough is often kneaded into a fully developed dough before the fat is added.

Sweet dough bakes into aromatic bread with a golden color and buttery taste. Raisins, candied fruit or chopped nuts can be kneaded into the dough before fermentation. The dough is firm enough to be formed easily into knot or twist roll shapes, as described on page 179. Sweet dough or bun dough works equally well when formed into plain rolls or decorative pastries. The dough can be rolled out flat with a rolling pin, then spread with chopped nuts, streusel, fruit preserves, poppy seeds or any of the following fillings:

Almond Paste Filling (page 296)

Almond Cream (page 296)

Apricot Filling (page 297)

Cinnamon Roll Paste (page 307)

Cream Cheese Filling (page 295)

Frangipane (page 295)

Ricotta Cheese Filling (page 297)

Once coated with filling, the dough can be rolled up and baked in a loaf or cake pan. See Sweet Dough Coffeecakes (page 255). The dough may also be made up as for the braided Danish coffeecake illustrated on page 293 in Chapter 9, Laminated Doughs.

bun any of a variety of small, round yeast rolls; can be sweet or savory

PROCEDURE FOR PREPARING ENRICHED YEAST DOUGH: ENRICHED DOUGH METHOD

1. Scale ingredients. Adjust water to proper temperature and rehydrate yeast if necessary.
2. Combine all ingredients except the fat in the bowl of a mixer fitted with a dough hook on low speed to moisten. The flour may be added a small amount at a time in order to form a soft dough. Scrape down the bowl.
3. Knead on medium speed to properly develop the dough, approximately 5 to 10 minutes.
4. Add the fat, a small amount at a time, and mix until it is fully incorporated into the dough.
5. Ferment the dough until double in bulk, then punch down to release gases.
6. Portion, shape and proof the dough.
7. Brush with egg wash and score the dough, if necessary, then bake.

MISE EN PLACE

- ▶ Adjust water temperature.
- ▶ Soften butter.
- ▶ Prepare the egg wash and line sheet pans with parchment while the dough proofs.
- ▶ Prepare the Basic Sugar Glaze while the dough bakes.

SWEET BUN DOUGH

This dough can be used to make any of the following breads and pastries: pan loaves, rolls or braided bread; sticky buns or cinnamon rolls; braided Danish coffeecake, pretzel Danish or turnovers.

BENNISON BAKERY, EVANSTON, IL
Chef Jory Downer

Yield: 36 Buns, approximately 2 oz. (60 g) each

Method: Enriched dough

Fermentation: 12 to 24 hours under refrigeration

Proofing: 20 to 30 minutes

Compressed yeast	2 oz.	50 g	5%
Water (temperature controlled)	15 fl. oz.	420 ml	42%
Dry milk powder	2 oz.	55 g	5.5%
Bread flour	1 lb. 11 oz.	750 g	75%
Pastry flour	9 oz.	250 g	25%
Granulated sugar	7.5 oz.	210 g	21%
Baking powder	0.5 oz.	14 g	1.4%
Salt	0.5 oz.	14 g	1.4%
Eggs	3.3 oz. (2 eggs)	100 g	10%
Unsalted butter, room temperature	3.6 oz.	100 g	10%
Vegetable shortening or butter	3.6 oz.	100 g	10%
Egg wash	as needed	as needed	
Total dough weight:	4 lb. 10 oz.	2063 g	206%
Pearl sugar or chocolate sprinkles (optional)	as needed	as needed	
Basic Sugar Glaze (page 456)	as needed	as needed	
Nuts, chopped (optional)	as needed	as needed	

1. Soften the yeast in the water in the bowl of a mixer fitted with a dough hook.
2. Stir the milk powder into the flours. Add the flour mixture to the bowl along with the sugar, baking powder, salt and eggs. Mix the dough 2 minutes at low speed until the ingredients are moistened. Stop the machine and scrape down the bowl. Add additional flour if needed to make a firm yet sticky dough. (The dough will soften as it kneads.) Increase the speed to medium and knead the dough 3 more minutes.
3. Add the butter and shortening (or additional butter) and mix until the soft dough is smooth and fully developed, approximately 3 more minutes. The dough should reach 77°F (25°C) after kneading.
4. Cover the dough and bench rest 45 minutes.
5. Divide the dough into two equal pieces. Round them and place on a paper-lined sheet pan. Cover the rounded dough and refrigerate a minimum of 12 hours, but no longer than 24 hours.
6. Remove the dough from the refrigerator and rest at room temperature 20 minutes. Divide each piece of dough into 18 portions to make a total of 36 portions. Form into smooth rolls and place the rounded rolls on paper-lined sheet pans.
7. Proof until doubled in size, approximately 20 to 30 minutes.
8. Brush the rolls with egg wash. Dip the rolls in pearl sugar or chocolate sprinkles, if desired. Bake at 350°F (180°C), with a short burst of steam at the beginning of baking, until golden brown and baked through, approximately 18 to 20 minutes.
9. Brush the hot rolls with Basic Sugar Glaze. Rolls may also be sprinkled with chopped nuts after glazing, if desired. Cool on a cooling rack.

Variations:

Quick Fermented Sweet Bun Dough—For shorter fermentation times, increase the amount of yeast to 3 ounces (75 grams/8%). Ferment the dough until doubled, approximately 45 minutes. Shape, proof and bake.

Cardamom Sweet Bun Dough—Add 0.07 ounce (1 teaspoon/2 grams/0.2%) ground cardamom to the flour before mixing. Mix, ferment, proof and bake.

Approximate values per 2-oz. (60-g) serving: **Calories** 190, **Total fat** 6 g, **Saturated fat** 2.5 g, **Cholesterol** 15 mg, **Sodium** 210 mg, **Total carbohydrates** 29 g, **Protein** 4 g

Brioche

Brioche (bree-OHSH) is a rich, tender bread made with a generous amount of eggs and butter. The high ratio of fat makes this dough difficult to work with, but the flavor is well worth the extra effort.

Brioche dough is mixed using the two-stage enriched dough method. First, the flour, liquid, yeast and eggs are kneaded into a soft bread dough. Then the softened butter is added. This unique kneading process allows the protein structure to be developed in the dough before the fat can interfere. Once kneaded, the dough is fermented, then stored in the refrigerator overnight (retarded) before make-up, proofing and baking. Brioche may also be mixed using the sponge method. See Parisian Brioche (page 263).

Brioche is traditionally baked in fluted pans and has a cap or topknot of dough; this shape is known as brioche à tête. The molded dough is washed with beaten egg or egg yolks and milk or cream before and after proofing. It is important to keep the wash from touching the sides of the pan, where it could coagulate and prevent the dough from rising when baked. The dough may also be baked in a loaf pan, making it perfect for toast or canapés. Savory brioche dough is popular as a casing for pâté and **coulibiac**, the stuffed salmon dish of Russian origin.

coulibiac a creamy mixture of salmon fillet, rice, hard-cooked eggs, mushrooms, shallots and dill enclosed in a pastry envelope usually made of brioche dough

PROCEDURE FOR MIXING BRIOCHE DOUGH

1 Have all ingredients at room temperature.

2 Hydrate the yeast, then combine it with the flour, salt, sugar and eggs. Mix until a soft dough is formed.

3 Knead the dough on medium speed for 15 to 20 minutes until it is smooth and shiny.

4 Add the butter in small increments, kneading until the butter is incorporated before adding more. Continue this process until all of the butter has been absorbed into the dough, approximately 8 to 15 minutes.

5 Cover the dough and ferment at room temperature until doubled.

6 Punch down the dough, then cover and refrigerate overnight.

7 Divide the chilled brioche dough and mold it into desired shapes. Brush with egg wash or cover lightly and proof until doubled in volume. Do not proof brioche in a very warm place; the butter may melt out of the dough before proofing is complete.

8 Bake in a moderate oven until the crust is deep golden brown. Cool in pans on racks for 10 minutes to prevent the loaves from collapsing, then remove the bread from the pans and finish cooling on racks.

BRIOCHE

MISE EN PLACE

▶ Adjust temperature of the water.
▶ Allow butter to come to room temperature.
▶ Prepare egg wash and butter pans while dough ferments.

❶ Combining the ingredients for brioche.

❷ Adding the yeast-and-water mixture to the dough.

Yield: 7 Large Loaves or 60 Rolls, approximately 3 oz. (90 g) each

Method: Enriched dough

Fermentation: 1 to 2 hours at room temperature, then overnight under refrigeration

Proofing: 30 minutes to 1½ hours

All-purpose flour	4 lb. 7 oz.	2130 g	100%
Eggs	2 lb. 6 oz. (24 eggs)	1130 g	53%
Salt	1.75 oz.	50 g	2.5%
Granulated sugar	7 oz.	210 g	10%
Active dry yeast	1.75 oz.	50 g	2.5%
Water (temperature controlled)	7 fl. oz.	210 ml	10%
Unsalted butter, room temperature	3 lb.	1430 g	67%
Egg wash	as needed	as needed	
Total dough weight:	10 lb. 14 oz.	5210 g	245%

❶ Place the flour, eggs, salt and sugar into the bowl of a large mixer fitted with a dough hook. Stir the ingredients together.

❷ Combine the yeast and water and add to the dough.

❸ Knead approximately 20 minutes on medium speed. The dough will be smooth, shiny and moist. It should not form a ball.

❹ Slowly add the butter to the dough. Knead only until all the butter is incorporated. Remove the dough from the mixer and place it into a bowl dusted with flour. Cover the dough and ferment at room temperature until doubled.

❺ Punch down the dough, cover tightly with plastic wrap and refrigerate overnight.

❻ Portion and shape the chilled dough as desired. For large brioche à tête, divide the dough into 4¾-ounce (142-gram) pieces and round. Generously butter seven large brioche pans. Fill each brioche pan with five rounded pieces of dough. First position four rounded pieces of dough in the bottom of each pan and then taper one side of the fifth piece of dough and place it in the center on top of the other four pieces, tapered end down.

❼ Proof at 85°F (30°C), until the loaves have increased 70 percent in volume, approximately 1 hour. (Proofing will be longer if the dough has been retarded.)

❽ Gently brush the loaves with egg wash. Bake at 375°F (190°C) until deeply browned, approximately 38 to 40 minutes for large brioche loaves.

Variations:

Raisin Brioche—Gently warm 3 fluid ounces (90 milliliters/4%) rum with 6 ounces (180 grams/8%) raisins. Set aside until the raisins are plumped. Drain off the remaining rum and add the raisins to the dough after the butter is incorporated.

Brioche for Sandwiches or Coulibiac—Reduce the sugar to 3 ounces (90 grams/4%). Ferment the dough, then retard it overnight. Mold in a rectangular loaf pan for slicing, or use the dough to wrap salmon and fillings for coulibiac.

Savory Cheese and Herb Brioche—Reduce the sugar to 3 ounces (90 grams/4%). Add 4 ounces (120 grams/5%) grated Parmesan and 4 ounces (120 grams/5%) grated Gruyère cheese, 0.02 ounce (¼ teaspoon/0.5 grams) black pepper, and 0.02 ounce (¼ teaspoon/ 0.5 grams) dried thyme to the dough with the flour. Mold in rectangular or conical pans. Serve sliced thinly with smoked salmon, pâté or other savory spreads.

Approximate values per 4-oz. (120-g) serving: **Calories** 475, **Total fat** 30 g, **Saturated fat** 17 g, **Cholesterol** 192 mg, **Sodium** 138 mg, **Total carbohydrates** 43 g, **Protein** 9 g, **Vitamin A** 30%, **Iron** 16%

③ Brioche dough after kneading for 20 minutes.

④ Adding the butter to the brioche dough.

⑤ The finished brioche dough ready for fermentation.

⑥ Shaping brioche à tête.

⑦ A finished brioche and slices.

DEEP-FRYING ENRICHED YEAST DOUGH AND SPECIALTY SWEET GOODS

Deep-frying is a popular cooking method for yeast dough and other bakeshop specialties such as beignets, fritters and churros. Small portions of dough or batter are submerged in hot fat until the surface browns and the interior cooks.

The most popular deep-fried pastry is the ring-shaped doughnut, which is made either from sweet yeast dough (yeast-raised) or a rich batter (cake style). The dough for yeast-raised doughnuts is mixed using the straight dough or enriched dough method discussed in this chapter. The dough should not be overly rich to prevent rapid browning before the interior cooks. Cake doughnuts are made from a batter that is mixed using the creaming method (page 435). French *beignets* and Mexican *buñelos* are yeast-raised doughnuts made from dough cut into rounds, rectangles or squares. Some doughnut-like pastries such as churros are made from a rich egg batter discussed in Chapter 12, Pastry and Dessert Components.

Although deep-frying is a dry-heat cooking method, it resembles boiling. In deep-frying, dough is submerged in hot fat until the surface browns and the interior cooks. A key difference between boiling and deep-frying is the temperature of the cooking medium. The boiling point, 212°F (100°C), is the hottest temperature at which food can be cooked in water. At this temperature, most foods require a long cooking period and surface sugars cannot caramelize. With deep-frying, temperatures up to 400°F (200°C) are used. These high temperatures cook the dough more quickly and allow the surface to brown rapidly.

recovery time the length of time it takes a cooking medium such as fat or water to return to the desired cooking temperature after food is submerged in it

Although small quantities of dough can be deep-fried in a saucepan, this can be both impractical and dangerous. **Recovery time** is usually very slow, and temperatures are difficult to control. Also, the fat can spill easily, leading to injuries or creating a fire hazard.

Most bakeshops use specially designed commercial fryers that have built-in thermostats, making temperature control more precise. Doughnut fryers (see page 41) are wide and shallow to accommodate the shape of the product. The portioned dough pieces are placed on flat screens, which are lowered into the hot fat. The fryer may be designed with a second screen, which keeps the dough submerged in the fat while it cooks. Otherwise the dough will float on the surface and need to be flipped to finish frying on the top. Deep fryers for cake doughnuts, which are made with a quick-bread batter, have built-in depositors for dropping the batter into the fat.

Clean fat for frying (left) is clear, free from off-odors and light in color. Fat that has darkened (right) should be discarded.

Fats for Deep-Frying

Many types of fats can be used for deep-frying sweet dough, other foods and bakery products. By far the most common fats used for deep-frying are vegetable oils such as soybean, peanut and canola oil, all of which have high smoke points and are relatively inexpensive. *Smoke point* is the temperature at which the fat breaks down and smokes.

Specially formulated deep-frying compounds are also available. These are usually composed of a vegetable oil or oils to which antifoaming agents, antioxidants and preservatives have been added. These additives increase the oil's usable life and raise its smoke point. Deep-fryer fats may also be hydrogenated. **Hydrogenation** is a chemical process that adds hydrogen to oil, turning the liquid oil into a solid (margarine is hydrogenated vegetable oil). Hydrogenated fats are more resistant to oxidation and chemical breakdown.

Liquid oils are best for fried items that are to be consumed immediately. Sweet dough products such as doughnuts, which are not usually cooked to order, are fried in fats that are solid at room temperature. If liquid oil is used, the dough may become soggy as it cools. And the liquid fat may leech out after frying, staining the packaging in which the product is shipped.

Other considerations when choosing the right fat are flavor, smoke point and resistance to chemical breakdown. High-quality frying fat should have a clean or natural flavor and a high smoke point and, when properly maintained, should be resistant to chemical breakdown. See Table 8.1.

Properly maintaining deep-fryer fat will greatly extend its useful life. To do so:

1 Store the fat in tightly sealed containers away from strong light; cover the deep fryer when not in use. Prolonged exposure to air and light turns fat rancid.

2 Skim and remove food particles from the fat's surface during frying. Food particles cause fat to break down; if they are not removed, they will accumulate in the fryer and burn.

3 Do not overheat the fat (turn the fryer down or off if not in use). High temperatures break down the fat.

4 Filter the fat each day or after each shift if the fryer is heavily used. Best results are obtained by using a filtering machine designed specifically for this purpose. Many large commercial fryers even have built-in filter systems. Less well-equipped operations can simply pour the hot fat through a paper filter.

Considerations When Deep-Frying Enriched Sweet Breads

Yeast dough for doughnuts should not be overly rich. Dough with a large quantity of sugar or fat tends to brown too quickly in the hot oil. Although lowering the temperature of the fat is an option, more oil will be absorbed, resulting in an unpleasantly greasy product. Unlike other enriched sweet doughs, doughnuts are proofed at room temperature or cooler. This keeps the doughs somewhat firm, making the proofed pieces easier to transfer into the heated fat. Hold dough for subsequent batches in the refrigerator so it will not overproof.

SAFETY ALERT
Cooking with Hot Oil

When hot oil comes into contact with liquid, it can spatter, causing severe burns. Use caution when placing foods into hot fat.

Oil heated to its flash point can ignite, causing burns or a serious kitchen fire. When oil is heated to its smoke point, it begins to break down, creating acreolin, a harsh-smelling chemical compound. This offensive smell is a good warning that hot oil may be close to its flash point. Turn off the heat and carefully remove the pan of oil from its heat source. Allow the oil to cool completely before discarding.

Doughnuts and other deep-fried sweet goods should be of a size and shape that allows them to float freely in the fat. They should not be deep-fried in the same fat used for more strongly flavored foods such as fish or onions, as the doughnuts could develop an odd taste from residual flavors left in the fat.

To deep-fry doughnuts and other sweet goods, first heat the fat or oil to a temperature between 365°F and 385°F (185°C and 196°C). The fat must be hot enough to quickly seal the surface of the dough so that it does not become greasy, yet it should not be so hot that the dough's surface burns before the interior is cooked. Fried dough absorbs between 5 and 25 percent of its weight in fat during frying. Select the highest temperature that is appropriate to minimize oil absorption. The temperature must be adjusted according to the formula, however. Dough with a high percentage of eggs, fat and sugar will require lower temperatures.

Most doughnuts initially sink to the bottom when placed in hot fat, then rise to the top as they cook. When the surface that is in contact with the fat is properly browned, the doughnuts are turned over with a spider, a wooden doughnut stick or a pair of tongs so they can cook evenly on both sides. When done, they are removed from the fat and drained.

TABLE 8.1
FRYER FAT CAN BE DAMAGED BY:
Salt
Water
Overheating
Food particles
Oxygen
CHANGE FRYER FAT WHEN IT:
Becomes dark
Smokes
Foams
Develops off-flavors

PROCEDURE FOR DEEP-FRYING DOUGHNUTS

1. Prepare the dough and allow it to ferment.

2. Cut out individual doughnuts and proof until they have increased 75 percent in volume.

3. Heat the oil or fat to the desired temperature, 365°F to 385°F (185°C to 196°C).

4. Carefully place as many pieces of the proofed dough in the fryer as will fit without crowding. (Hold dough for subsequent batches in the refrigerator to keep from over-proofing.) Maintain the temperature of the fat.

5. Fry the doughnuts until the surface is well colored without browning, approximately 2 to 3 minutes. Flip and continue cooking on the other side until done. Doneness is usually determined by timing, surface color or sampling.

6. Remove the doughnuts from the fryer with a skimmer and hold them over the cooking fat, allowing the excess fat to drain off. Place the doughnuts on a wire rack to cool.

YEAST-RAISED DOUGHNUTS

MISE EN PLACE

▶ Adjust water temperature.

❶ Cutting the dough into round doughnut shapes.

❷ Frying the doughnuts and doughnut holes.

Yield: 40 Doughnuts, 2½ oz. (75 g) each

Method: Straight dough

Fermentation: 1½ to 2 hours

Proofing: 30 minutes to 1 hour

Granulated sugar	8 oz.	240 g	14%
Salt	1 oz.	30 g	1.8%
Bread flour	3 lb. 8 oz.	1680 g	100%
Dry milk powder	3 oz.	90 g	5.5%
Cinnamon, ground	0.04 oz. (½ tsp.)	1 g	0.07%
Mace, ground	0.25 oz. (3½ tsp.)	7 g	0.4%
Shortening	6 oz.	180 g	11%
Eggs	10 oz. (6 eggs)	300 g	18%
Buttermilk	6 fl. oz.	180 ml	11%
Vanilla extract	1 fl. oz.	30 ml	1.8%
Instant yeast	1 oz.	30 g	1.8%
Water, warm (95°F/35°C)	1 pt.	470 ml	28%
Total dough weight:	6 lb. 12 oz.	3238 g	193%
Topping:			
Granulated sugar	6 oz.	180 g	
Cinnamon, ground	0.2 oz. (1 Tbsp.)	6 g	

❶ Combine the sugar, salt, flour, milk powder, cinnamon, mace and shortening in the bowl of a 6 quart (6.5 liter) or larger mixer fitted with a dough hook. Mix briefly to blend the spices throughout the dry mixture. Beat the eggs lightly and then add them to the flour mixture along with the buttermilk and vanilla.

❷ Dissolve the yeast in the water and add to the flour. Mix on low speed about 2 to 3 minutes, adding additional flour if needed to make a soft dough. Scrape down the bowl and increase the speed to medium. Knead the dough 5 to 7 minutes until it is smooth, soft and elastic.

❸ Ferment the dough until doubled, approximately 1½ to 2 hours.

❹ Divide the dough into four equal pieces. Place three portions of the dough on a lightly floured sheet pan, cover and refrigerate while making up the first piece of dough. Roll the dough out into a rectangle ½ inch (1.2 centimeters) thick. Cut out individual pieces with a doughnut cutter and place them on paper-lined or lightly-floured sheet pans.

❺ Portion the remaining dough, then cover and proof until it has increased 75 percent in volume.

❻ Fry the doughnuts in batches in deep fat heated to 385°F (196°C). Cook until puffed and browned, approximately 1 or 2 minutes. Flip the doughnuts using a long wooden skewer and cook another minute until browned. Remove from the fat and drain on absorbent paper.

❼ Combine the sugar and cinnamon. Toss the hot doughnuts in this mixture. Alternatively, the cooled doughnuts may be dipped in flat icing (page 456).

Variations:

Jelly-Filled Doughnuts—Divide the fermented dough into 2½-ounce (75-gram) pieces. Round, proof and fry. Cool the doughnuts before filling. Place doughnut filling in the bowl of a mixer fitted with the paddle attachment and mix on medium speed to soften. Scrape the jelly into a doughnut pump or pastry bag fitted with a small plain tip. Pierce a hole in each doughnut with a skewer. Insert the tip into the doughnut. Fill each with jelly. Dust with powdered sugar.

Bismarcks—Prepare the doughnuts as for jelly doughnuts. Cut the cooled doughnuts three-quarters of the way through horizontally. Fill with Crème Chantilly (page 502) or Pastry Cream (page 492). Dust with powdered sugar.

Approximate values per doughnut: **Calories** 320, **Total fat** 15 g, **Saturated fat** 3 g, **Cholesterol** 25 mg, **Sodium** 300 mg, **Total carbohydrates** 41 g, **Protein** 7 g, **Iron** 10%

ENRICHED YEAST BREADS **249**

CONVENIENCE PRODUCTS

As with the yeast dough discussed in Chapter 7, Artisan and Yeast Breads, many varieties of prepared mixes for enriched yeast dough are available. Most manufacturers sell mixes that are formulated for making a generic sweet dough, which can be used to make everything from rolls to sticky buns to filled coffee cake. The baker adds yeast and water, then mixes, forms, proofs and bakes the products. Better flavors can be achieved from mixes that call for the addition of fresh eggs and butter according to the manufacturer's recommendation.

Mixes are formulated to perform well under specific mixing and baking conditions. The combination of ingredients in a doughnut mix, for example, is selected to withstand cooking in hot oil without burning. The amount and type of fat and sweeteners is adjusted to produce evenly browned products when fried. Do not be tempted to use a sweet dough mix to make doughnuts unless it is recommended by the manufacturer. Similarly, adding eggs to a sweet dough mix will not necessarily produce challah dough, a product recognized by the subtle sweetness of honey, eggs and fats.

Frozen brioche dough is sold in 2- to 12-pound blocks, rolled into sheets or portioned into individual pastries. Some manufacturers use pure butter, others vegetable shortening. As with other frozen doughs, care must be taken to thaw frozen brioche dough, usually under refrigeration overnight. If thawed at room temperature, the exterior of the dough will be warm while the center remains frozen. Yeast activity will be uneven, affecting the quality of the finished bread made from the dough.

Frozen sweet dough usually comes portioned and formed into filled or plain rolls, buns or pastries. The dough requires panning and then careful thawing, usually under refrigeration, before proofing and baking. The baker applies toppings and glazes after baking the dough. Frozen fully baked sweet dough products such as sticky buns, rum babas and doughnuts are also available. These products are simply defrosted and then glazed or iced as desired. As with similar products, the advantages of convenience and time savings must be weighed against the flavor and quality of freshly made products.

1. Describe the kinds of flour used to make enriched and sweet yeast doughs such as brioche or challah. What characteristics of flour are important to consider when making these doughs?

2. Discuss the mixing methods used to make enriched and sweet yeast doughs.

3. What effect will using firm butter have on the mixing of enriched yeast doughs such as brioche?

4. What issues does the baker face when making brioche or other enriched sweet yeast doughs in a hot and humid climate? Discuss techniques that the baker can employ under such working conditions.

5. Discuss the principles of deep-frying enriched dough. What are the most important considerations when frying doughnuts?

6. Using the Internet, research the history of one of the traditional breads discussed in this chapter, such as baba, kugelhopf or savarin. What are the unique characteristics of the specialty bread you have selected? WWW

QUESTIONS FOR DISCUSSION

Terms to Know

brioche
bun dough
sponge method
enriched dough
  method

challah
doughnuts
recovery time

CINNAMON SWIRL RAISIN BREAD

Yield: 3 Loaves, 1 lb. 14 oz. (840 g) each

Method: Enriched dough

Fermentation: Approximately 45 minutes to 1 hour

Proofing: Approximately 45 minutes

Bread flour	1 lb. 11 oz.	810 g	100%
Potato flour	2 oz.	60 g	7.4%
Dry milk powder	1.25 oz.	37 g	4.6%
Water (temperature controlled)	13 fl. oz.	390 ml	48%
Eggs	4 oz. (2 ½ eggs)	120 g	15%
Vanilla extract	0.15 fl. oz. (1 tsp.)	4 ml	0.5%
Granulated sugar	4.5 oz.	135 g	16.7%
Salt	0.75 oz.	22 g	2.8%
Instant yeast	1 oz.	30 g	3.7%
Water, warm	2 fl. oz.	60 ml	7.4%
Unsalted butter, softened	6.5 oz.	195 g	24%
Raisins	1 lb. 6 oz.	660 g	81.5%
Cinnamon Sugar (recipe follows)	8 oz.	240 g	29.6%
Egg wash	as needed	as needed	
Total dough weight:	5 lb. 12 oz.	2763 g	341%

1. Sift together the flours and milk powder. Set aside.
2. In the bowl of a 6 quart (6.5 liter) or larger mixer fitted with the paddle attachment, combine the temperature-controlled water, eggs and vanilla. Add the flour mixture, sugar and salt. Blend well.
3. Dissolve the yeast in the warm water. Add to the dough. Switch to a dough hook.
4. Knead until the dough reaches 75°F (24°C), then gradually add the butter. Knead until the dough is fully developed and passes the windowpane test. Mix the raisins gently into the dough.
5. Cover and ferment until doubled, approximately 45 to 60 minutes.
6. Punch down the dough and divide it into three equal pieces. Round and bench rest 5 minutes.
7. Roll each piece of dough into a rectangle measuring 10 inches × 6 inches (25 centimeters × 15 centimeters). Sprinkle each piece of dough with Cinnamon Sugar. Roll up tightly and place the dough, seam side down, into buttered or paper-lined loaf pans.
8. Proof at 80°F (25°C) until the loaves have increased 75 percent in volume, approximately 45 minutes. Brush with egg wash.
9. Bake at 375°F (190°C) until browned, approximately 40 to 45 minutes. Cover the loaves with aluminum foil if they begin to brown too quickly.
10. Cool the loaves in the pans for approximately 30 minutes before unmolding to prevent them from collapsing.

Approximate values per 1-oz. (30-g) serving: **Calories** 90, **Total fat** 2 g, **Saturated fat** 1 g, **Cholesterol** 10 mg, **Sodium** 95 mg, **Total carbohydrates** 16 g, **Protein** 2 g

CINNAMON SUGAR

Yield: 8 oz. (240 g)

Cinnamon, ground	1 oz.	30 g
Granulated sugar	7 oz.	210 g

1. Combine the cinnamon and sugar. Keep covered and use as needed.

QUARK STUTEN
(GERMAN SWEET SPICE AND RAISIN BREAD)

Yield: 5 Loaves, 1 lb. (480 g) each

Method: Straight dough

Fermentation: Bench rest, 40 minutes

Proofing: 30 to 45 minutes

Compressed yeast	2 oz.	60 g	6%
Water (temperature controlled)	13.75 fl. oz.	390 ml	39%
Bread flour	2 lb. 3 oz.	1000 g	100%
Dough conditioner (optional)	0.3 oz. (2 tsp.)	10 g	1%
Granulated sugar	5.25 oz.	150 g	15%
Cardamom, ground	0.17 oz. (2½ tsp.)	5 g	0.5%
Salt	0.7 oz.	20 g	2%
Shortening or margarine	3.5 oz.	100 g	10%
Quark, farmer's cheese or baker's cheese	10.5 oz.	300 g	30%
Orange zest, grated fine	3.5 oz.	100 g	10%
Golden raisins, conditioned	10.5 oz.	300 g	30%
Total dough weight:	5 lb. 5 oz.	2435 g	243%
Clarified unsalted butter	as needed	as needed	
Granulated sugar	as needed	as needed	

① Dissolve the yeast in the water in the bowl of a 6 quart (6.5 liter) or larger mixer fitted with a dough hook. Mix in the flour, dough conditioner (if using), sugar, cardamom, salt, shortening, quark and orange zest. Mix at low speed until the ingredients are combined, approximately 3 minutes. Knead on medium speed until fully developed, approximately 7 minutes. Add the raisins and knead just until incorporated.

② Scrape the dough onto a lightly floured workbench. Cover the dough and bench rest 20 minutes. Punch down the dough and bench rest another 10 minutes.

③ Divide the dough into five uniform pieces and round. Cover and bench rest another 10 minutes. Shape each piece of dough into an oval and place the loaves on paper-lined sheet pans.

④ Cover and proof until doubled, approximately 30 to 45 minutes. Dock the surface of the loaves. Bake at 400°F (200°C), with steam injected into the oven during the first few seconds of baking, until the loaves are golden brown and baked through, approximately 35 to 40 minutes.

⑤ Brush the baked loaves with clarified butter and roll in sugar. Cool on racks.

Approximate values per 2-oz. (60-g) serving: **Calories** 160, **Total fat** 3.5 g, **Saturated fat** 1 g, **Cholesterol** 0 mg, **Sodium** 220 mg, **Total carbohydrates** 29 g, **Protein** 4 g

PAIN DE MIE
(SANDWICH BREAD)

More tender than a Pullman loaf, pain de mie is an even-crumbed loaf baked in a rectangular pan with lid.

Yield: 2 Loaves, 1 lb. 14 oz. (900 g) each

Method: Straight dough

Fermentation: 45 minutes

Proofing: Approximately 30 to 45 minutes

Instant yeast	0.7 oz.	20 g	2%
Water (temperature controlled)	19 fl. oz.	570 ml	56%
Bread flour	2 lb. 2 oz.	1020 g	100%
Dry milk powder	1 oz.	30 g	3%
Granulated sugar	1.3 oz.	40 g	4%
Salt	0.7 oz.	20 g	2%
Unsalted butter, room temperature	4 oz.	120 g	12%
Egg wash	as needed	as needed	
Total dough weight:	3 lb. 12 oz.	1820 g	179%

1. Moisten the yeast in the water in the bowl of a mixer fitted with a dough hook. Mix in the flour, milk powder, sugar and salt on medium speed. Mix until a soft dough is formed, approximately 3 minutes. Cut the butter into eight pieces and add it to the dough. Mix until the dough is smooth and elastic and passes the windowpane test, approximately 5 minutes.

2. Place the dough in a lightly oiled bowl. Cover and ferment at room temperature until doubled in size, approximately 45 minutes.

3. Punch down the dough and divide into two uniform pieces. Round the portions, cover and bench rest 5 minutes.

4. Shape the dough into cylinders and place the formed dough into buttered loaf pans with lids (Pullman pans). (When no lids are available, grease a half-sheet pan and place it over the loaves.)

5. Proof until the loaves have increased 70 to 80 percent in volume, approximately 30 to 45 minutes. Brush with egg wash. Close the lids or set the greased sheet pans on top of the loaves.

6. Bake at 375°F (190°C) until golden brown, approximately 40 minutes. Remove the lids and cool the loaves in their pans for 10 minutes before unmolding.

Approximate values per 1½-oz. (45-g) serving: **Calories** 120, **Total fat** 2.5 g, **Saturated fat** 1.5 g, **Cholesterol** 5 mg, **Sodium** 190 mg, **Total carbohydrates** 19 g, **Protein** 3 g

MILK BREAD

Milk bread dough may be baked in many forms, including loaves for slicing or individual rolls (see Chapter 7, Artisan and Yeast Breads). The make-up method illustrated in this formula produces small loaves composed of several individual rolls that stick together during proofing and baking. After baking, the loaves may be served intact or the segments pulled apart into individual rolls after cooling.

Yield: 7 Loaves, approximately 10 oz. (300 g) each

Method: Straight dough

Fermentation: Bench rest, 20 minutes

Proofing: 30 minutes

Milk	20 fl. oz.	550 ml	55%
Compressed yeast	2.25 oz.	60 g	6%
Bread flour	1 lb. 2 oz.	500 g	50%
Pastry flour	1 lb. 2 oz.	500 g	50%
Shortening	4.5 oz.	120 g	12%
Granulated sugar	3.6 oz.	100 g	10%
Dough conditioner (optional)	0.5 oz.	15 g	1.5%
Salt	0.75 oz.	20 g	2%
Eggs	3.3 oz. (2 eggs)	100 g	10%
Egg wash	as needed	as needed	
Sliced almonds	as needed	as needed	
Pearl sugar	as needed	as needed	
Total dough weight:	4 lb. 6 oz.	1965 g	196%

1. Warm the milk to 200°F (93°C), then cool it to room temperature.
2. Dissolve the yeast in the milk in the bowl of a mixer fitted with a dough hook. Mix in the flours, shortening, sugar, dough conditioner (if using), salt and eggs on low speed until combined, approximately 3 minutes.
3. Stop the mixer, scrape down the bowl and check the dough consistency. Add more flour if necessary to make a soft dough. Increase the speed to medium and knead until the dough is fully developed and reaches 80°F (27°C), approximately 7 minutes.
4. Scrape the dough onto a lightly floured workbench and cover. Bench rest 15 minutes. Punch down the dough, then cover and bench rest another 5 minutes.
5. Divide the dough into 2-ounce (60-gram) pieces. Round the rolls, cover and bench rest 5 minutes. Shape each piece of dough into a small oval. Place five pieces of the formed dough side by side on a paper-lined sheet pan with their long sides touching. Repeat until seven loaves have been formed. Brush the dough with egg wash.
6. Proof until doubled in size, approximately 30 minutes. Score the loaves and sprinkle them with sliced almonds or pearl sugar.
7. Bake at 375°F (190°C) until golden brown, approximately 8 to 10 minutes. The loaves can be served intact or pulled apart into individual rolls after cooling.

Approximate values per 1½-oz. (45-g) serving: **Calories** 130, **Total fat** 4 g, **Saturated fat** 1 g, **Cholesterol** 10 mg, **Sodium** 140 mg, **Total carbohydrates** 21 g, **Protein** 4 g

Milk bread rolls.

Milk bread dough baked into various loaf shapes.

pearl sugar large-grain sugar formed into opaque pellets for decorating cookies and breads

❶ Rolling the dough into a cylinder.

❷ Twisting the two pieces of dough together.

CINNAMON BABKA TWIST LOAF

Yield: 3 Loaves, approximately each 2 lb. (960 g) each

Method: Straight dough

Proofing: Approximately 1 hour

Sweet Bun Dough (page 242), fermented	4 lb. 10 oz.	2220 g
Cinnamon Roll Paste (page 307)	1 lb. 8 oz.	720 g
Walnuts, chopped	8 oz.	240 g
Powdered sugar	as needed	as needed

❶ Grease three 10-inch (25-centimeter) loaf pans and line the bottom and sides with parchment paper. Set aside.

❷ Roll the dough out into a rectangle measuring 24 × 18 inches (60 × 45 centimeters). Trim the edges of the dough evenly with a rolling cutter.

❸ Spread the Cinnamon Roll Paste evenly over the dough, leaving a ½-inch (1.2-centimeter) border along one edge. Sprinkle the walnuts evenly over the dough. Roll the dough up into a tight cylinder.

❹ Chill the filled dough until firm enough to cut, approximately 30 minutes. Divide the cylinder of dough into three 8-inch (20-centimeter) pieces.

❺ Working with one section of dough at a time, cut the dough in half lengthwise, then twist the two halves together, exposing the cut side. Position the twist of dough in one of the prepared pans. Repeat with the remaining dough.

❻ Proof the dough until doubled in volume, approximately 1 hour. Bake at 350°F (180°C), with a short burst of steam at the beginning of baking, until golden brown and baked through, approximately 45 minutes to 1 hour.

❼ Remove the babkas from their pans and cool on a cooling rack. Dust the cooled loaves generously with powdered sugar.

Approximate values per 2-oz. (60-g) serving: **Calories** 240, **Total fat** 17 g, **Saturated fat** 8 g, **Cholesterol** 35 mg, **Sodium** 115 mg, **Total carbohydrates** 19 g, **Protein** 4 g

❸ The finished babka.

SWEET DOUGH COFFEECAKES

Yield: 3 Coffeecakes, approximately 2 lb. (960 g) each

Method: Straight dough

Proofing: Approximately 1 hour

Cardamom Sweet Bun Dough (page 242), fermented	4 lb. 10 oz.	2220 g
Unsalted butter, melted	4 oz.	120 g
Cocoa Streusel (page 398)	1 lb.	480 g
Fondant Glaze (page 483)	as needed	as needed
Basic Sugar Glaze (page 456)	as needed	as needed
Nuts, chopped	as needed	as needed

1 Grease three 8-inch (20-centimeter) cake pans and line with parchment paper. Set aside.

2 Roll the dough out into a rectangle measuring 24 × 18 inches (60 × 45 centimeters). Trim the edges of the dough evenly with a rolling cutter. Brush the dough with the melted butter and sprinkle with 6 ounces (180 grams) of the Cocoa Streusel.

3 Roll up the dough into a cylinder. Cut into 1-inch- (2.5-centimeter-) thick slices. Place seven slices around the outside edge and one in the center of each prepared pan. Sprinkle the dough with the remaining Cocoa Streusel.

4 Proof the cakes until doubled in volume, approximately 1 hour. Bake at 350°F (180°C), with a short burst of steam at the beginning of baking, until golden brown and baked through, approximately 25 to 30 minutes.

5 Remove the coffeecakes from their pans. Brush the hot cakes with Fondant Glaze. Cool the cakes on a cooling rack. Decorate the cooled cakes with Basic Sugar Glaze and chopped nuts.

Approximate values per 2-oz. (60-g) serving: **Calories** 290, **Total fat** 18 g, **Saturated fat** 11 g, **Cholesterol** 50 mg, **Sodium** 160 mg, **Total carbohydrates** 29 g, **Protein** 4 g, **Vitamin A** 10%

HOT CROSS BUNS

Bread often plays a major role in holiday and religious observances. The hot cross bun is traditional Lenten bread, its exact origins unknown. Some say that it has pagan origins, the cross representing the moon and its four quarters. Anglo-Saxons ate the sacramental buns in honor of their goddess Eastore. When the Romans arrived in Britain, the clergy tried to stop the use of the sacramental buns, but could not. So they blessed them and gave the cross on the buns a Christian meaning.

Traditionally these buns are decorated with dough piped across the top before baking, not a sweet icing as is commonly seen. A thin glaze brushed over the hot buns provides the added sweetness.

Yield: 30 Rolls, approximately 3½ oz. (105 g) each

Method: Straight dough

Fermentation: 45 minutes

Proofing: 1 hour

Dough:

Golden raisins, conditioned	10 oz.	300 g	30%
Dark raisins, conditioned	10 oz.	300 g	30%
Candied orange peel	3 oz.	80 g	8%
Bread flour	2 lb. 4 oz.	1000 g	100%
Unsalted butter or shortening	4 oz.	120 g	12%
Granulated sugar	3.5 oz.	100 g	10%
Dough conditioner (optional)	0.3 oz. (2 tsp.)	10 g	1%
Dry milk powder	2 oz.	50 g	5%
Compressed yeast	2.75 oz.	80 g	8%
Salt	0.6 oz. (1 Tbsp.)	18 g	1.8%
Eggs	3.2 oz. (2 eggs)	100 g	10%
Vanilla extract	0.15 fl. oz. (1 tsp.)	5 ml	0.5%
Cardamom, ground	0.07 oz. (1 tsp.)	2 g	0.2%
Allspice, ground	0.07 oz. (1 tsp.)	2 g	0.2%
Ginger, ground	0.14 oz. (2 tsp.)	4 g	0.4%
Cinnamon, ground	0.2 oz. (1 Tbsp.)	6 g	0.6%
Water	19 fl. oz.	520 ml	52%

Cross dough:

Pastry flour	8 oz.	220 g	22%
Unsalted butter or shortening	1.5 oz.	40 g	4%
Milk	7 fl. oz.	190 ml	19%
Total dough weight:	6 lb. 15 oz.	3147 g	314%
Bun Glaze (recipe follows)	5 fl. oz.	150 ml	

1 Place the raisins and orange peel in a small bowl and cover with hot water. Let soften in the water for 5 minutes. Drain the water and let the fruit condition 2 to 4 hours before using. Set aside.

2 Place the flour, butter, sugar, dough conditioner (if using), milk powder, yeast, salt, eggs, vanilla and spices in the bowl of a 6 quart (6.5 liter) or larger mixer fitted with a dough hook. Add the water and mix the dough on low speed 3 minutes until moistened. Stop the machine and scrape down the bowl. Add additional flour if necessary to create a soft dough. Mix the dough on medium speed 6 to 7 minutes until it is soft and pliable.

3 Add the conditioned fruit and mix the dough on low speed until the fruit is well distributed in the dough. If necessary, dust the dough lightly with more flour to help the fruit incorporate.

4 Scrape the dough onto a flour-dusted workbench. Cover and ferment 30 minutes. Deflate the dough and fold it into thirds, then bench rest another 15 minutes.

5 Divide the dough into 3½-ounce (105-gram) pieces. Round the dough into tight rolls with a smooth top surface. Place the formed rolls seam side down on a paper-lined half-sheet pan. Position them in rows on the tray, five rolls by six rolls, so that the rolls touch when fully proofed.

6 Proof the rolls with low humidity until doubled in size, approximately 50 minutes.

7 While the rolls proof, prepare the cross dough. Combine the flour, butter and milk in the bowl of a mixer fitted with the paddle attachment. Mix on medium speed until the shortening is well blended and the dough is lump-free.

8 When the rolls have proofed, scoop the cross dough into a pastry bag fitted with a plain tip. Quickly pipe a cross over the surface of each roll.

9 Bake at 375°F (190°C) until the rolls are a rich brown color, approximately 15 minutes.

10 Brush the hot rolls generously with the chilled Bun Glaze, making certain they are well coated so that no dry spots appear when the glaze dries.

BUN GLAZE

Yield: 5 fl. oz. (150 ml)

Water	1.75 fl. oz.	50 ml
Granulated sugar	3.5 oz.	100 g
Ginger, ground	0.02 oz. (¼ tsp.)	0.5 g
Lemon juice	0.15 fl. oz. (1 tsp.)	5 ml
Lemon zest, finely grated	0.07 oz. (1 tsp.)	2 g
Cream of tartar	1 pinch	1 pinch

1 Place all ingredients in a heavy saucepan. Bring the mixture to a boil, stirring until the sugar dissolves. Continue boiling 5 minutes until the mixture reduces into a light syrup.

2 Strain the glaze into a bowl and allow it to cool, then refrigerate the glaze until it is well chilled.

Approximate values per bun: **Calories** 280, **Total fat** 6 g, **Saturated fat** 1.5 g, **Cholesterol** 15 mg, **Sodium** 260 mg, **Total carbohydrates** 53 g, **Protein** 6 g, **Iron** 15%

JUMBO CINNAMON BUNS

Yield: 24 Large Rolls, approximately 3 oz. (120 g) each

Method: Straight dough

Fermentation: 1 to 2 hours

Proofing: Approximately 1 hour

Dough:

Buttermilk	12 fl. oz.	360 ml	37.5%
Instant yeast	2 oz.	60 g	6%
Egg	1.6 oz. (1 egg)	48 g	5%
Egg yolks	2 oz. (3 yolks)	60 g	6%
Vanilla extract	0.15 fl. oz. (1 tsp.)	5 ml	0.5%
Pastry or all-purpose flour	1 lb.	480 g	50%
Bread flour	1 lb.	480 g	50%
Granulated sugar	5 oz.	150 g	15.6%
Salt	0.75 oz.	22 g	2.3%
Unsalted butter, softened	18 oz.	540 g	56%
Total dough weight:	4 lb. 9 oz.	2205 g	229%

Filling:

Unsalted butter, melted	6 oz.	180 g
Cinnamon, ground	0.5 oz.	15 g
Brown sugar	6 oz.	180 g
Pecans, chopped	12 oz.	360 g
Raisins (optional)	12 oz.	360 g
Powdered Sugar Glaze (recipe follows)	as needed	as needed

❶ Brushing the buns with glaze.

❷ A finished cinnamon bun.

❶ In the bowl of a 6 quart (6.5 liter) or larger mixer fitted with a dough hook, combine the buttermilk, yeast, egg, egg yolks and vanilla. Add the pastry and bread flours, sugar and salt. Mix on medium speed until well blended into a soft dough, approximately 3 to 4 minutes. Then add the softened butter and mix until a windowpane has been obtained and the dough reaches approximately 75°F–80°F (24°C–26°C).

❷ Ferment the dough until doubled, approximately 1 hour. Meanwhile, prepare the filling.

❸ Whisk together the melted butter, cinnamon and brown sugar. Set aside.

❹ Roll the fermented dough into a rectangle measuring 18 inches × 30 inches (45 centimeters × 75 centimeters).

⑤ Spread the filling evenly over the entire surface of the dough. Sprinkle with the pecans and raisins (if using).

⑥ Starting with the longer side, roll the dough into a spiral. Cut into 24 pieces, each approximately 1½ inches (3.7 centimeters) thick. Place the rolls close together, cut side up, on a paper-lined sheet pan and allow them to rise until the rolls have increased 70 percent in volume.

⑦ Bake at 350°F (180°C) until golden brown, approximately 20 to 25 minutes.

⑧ Cool slightly, then top with Powdered Sugar Glaze.

VARIATION:

Cream Cheese Glazed Cinnamon Buns—Omit the Powdered Sugar Glaze. Blend 12 ounces (360 grams) softened cream cheese, 3 ounces (90 grams) softened butter, 6 ounces (180 grams) powdered sugar, 0.01 ounce (0.03 gram/1 teaspoon) grated lemon zest and 0.5 fluid ounce (15 milliliters/1 tablespoon) vanilla extract until smooth and lump-free. Coat the cooled buns with the cream cheese topping.

Approximate values per roll: **Calories** 510, **Total fat** 35 g, **Saturated fat** 16 g, **Cholesterol** 100 mg, **Sodium** 370 mg, **Total carbohydrates** 45 g, **Protein** 8 g, **Vitamin A** 15%, **Iron** 15%

POWDERED SUGAR GLAZE

Yield: 18 fl. oz. (530 ml)

Powdered sugar, sifted	1 lb.	450 g
Vanilla extract	0.3 fl. oz. (2 tsp.)	10 ml
Lemon juice	0.3 fl. oz. (2 tsp.)	10 ml
Water, warm	2 fl. oz.	60 ml

① Combine all ingredients in a small bowl. Stir to blend thoroughly and dissolve any lumps. Cover and store at room temperature.

Approximate values per 1-fl.-oz. (30-ml) serving: **Calories** 160, **Total fat** 0 g, **Saturated fat** 0 g, **Cholesterol** 0 mg, **Sodium** 0 mg, **Total carbohydrates** 41 g, **Protein** 0 g

PECAN STICKY BUNS

Sweet dough filled with a cinnamon-and-nut filling and a sticky topping is one of the most popular forms of sweet dough preparations. Almost any sweet dough can be used to form the dough for this pastry, including Sweet Bun Dough (page 242) or Brioche (page 244). The dough in this formula is rich and buttery. Buttermilk, lemon zest and lemon juice give it a pleasant tang to contrast with the gooey filling.

Yield: 12 to 15 Buns

Method: Straight dough

Fermentation: 1 to 2 hours. Bench rest, 10 minutes

Proofing: 20 minutes

Dough:

Active dry yeast	1 oz.	30 g	6.25%
Granulated sugar	2 oz.	60 g	12.5%
Milk	0.5 fl. oz.	15 ml	3%
Buttermilk	5.5 fl. oz.	163 ml	34%
Vanilla extract	0.15 fl. oz. (1 tsp.)	5 ml	1%
Lemon zest, grated	0.2 oz. (1 Tbsp.)	6 g	1.25%
Lemon juice	0.15 fl. oz. (1 tsp.)	5 ml	1%
Egg yolks	1.2 oz. (2 yolks)	36 g	8%
Salt	0.4 oz. (2 tsp.)	12 g	2.5%
All-purpose flour	1 lb.	480 g	100%
Unsalted butter, very soft	8 oz.	240 g	50%
Total dough weight:	2 lb. 3 oz.	1052 g	219%

Topping:

Honey	3 fl. oz.	90 ml
Brown sugar	3 oz.	90 g
Pecans, chopped	2 oz.	60 g

Filling:

Cinnamon, ground	0.07 oz. (1 tsp.)	2 g
Pecans, chopped	3 oz.	90 g
Brown sugar	4 oz.	120 g
Unsalted butter, melted	3 oz.	90 g

① Brushing melted butter over the sticky bun dough.

② Rolling up the filling in the sticky bun dough.

③ Cutting and panning the sticky buns.

1. To make the dough, stir the yeast, sugar and milk together in a small bowl. Set aside.

2. Stir the buttermilk, vanilla, lemon zest and lemon juice together and add to the yeast mixture.

3. Add the egg yolks, salt, flour and butter to the liquid mixture. Knead until the butter is evenly distributed and the dough is smooth and fully developed, approximately 6 minutes. Cover and ferment until doubled.

4. Prepare the topping and filling mixtures while the dough is fermenting. To make the topping, cream the honey and sugar together. Stir in the pecans. This mixture will be very stiff. To make the filling, stir the cinnamon, pecans and sugar together.

5. Lightly grease muffin cups, then distribute the topping mixture evenly, about 1 tablespoon (15 milliliters) per muffin cup. Set the pans aside at room temperature until the dough is ready.

6. Punch down the dough and bench rest 10 minutes. Roll out the dough into a rectangle measuring 12 inches × 18 inches (30 centimeters × 45 centimeters) and approximately ¼ inch (6 millimeters) thick. Brush with the melted butter and top evenly with the filling mixture.

7. Starting with either long edge, roll up the dough. Cut into slices about ¾ to 1 inch (1.8 to 2.5 centimeters) thick. Place a slice in each muffin cup over the topping.

8. Proof the buns until doubled, approximately 20 minutes. Bake at 325°F (160°C) until very brown, approximately 25 minutes. Immediately invert the muffin pans onto paper-lined sheet pans to let the buns and their topping slide out.

Approximate values per bun: **Calories** 480, **Total fat** 26 g, **Saturated fat** 11 g, **Cholesterol** 75 mg, **Sodium** 100 mg, **Total carbohydrates** 55 g, **Protein** 5 g, **Vitamin A** 15%, **Iron** 15%

CONCHAS

LA PETITE PASTRY SHOP, CHICAGO, IL
Chef Bill Goebel, Owner

These sweet rolls are a Mexican specialty, popular at breakfast. The plump rolls are usually topped with a brightly colored sugar paste that, when baked, cracks open to resemble a seashell.

Yield: 40 Rolls, 2 oz. (60 g) each

Method: Straight dough

Fermentation: Bench rest, 3 hours

Proofing: 30 minutes to 1 hour

Dough:

Compressed yeast	3.6 oz.	100 g	10%
Water (temperature controlled)	9 fl. oz.	250 ml	25%
Bread flour	2 lb. 4 oz.	1000 g	100%
Eggs	1 lb. (10 eggs)	450 g	45%
Granulated sugar	9.75 oz.	270 g	27%
Unsalted butter or lard, room temperature	6.5 oz.	180 g	18%
Vanilla extract	0.25 fl. oz. (1 ½ tsp.)	7.5 ml	0.7%
Salt	0.15 oz. (¾ tsp.)	5 g	0.5%
Total dough weight:	5 lb. 1 oz.	2262 g	226%

Topping:

Bread flour	1 lb.	450 g	100%
Powdered sugar	10 oz.	280 g	63%
Shortening or lard	10 oz.	280 g	63%
Water	1 fl. oz.	30 ml	7%
Cocoa powder or food coloring (optional)	as needed	as needed	
Total topping weight:	2 lb. 5 oz.	1040 g	233%
Melted shortening or lard	1.5 oz.	45 g	
Granulated sugar	as needed	as needed	

1. To prepare the dough, soften the yeast in the water in the bowl of a mixer fitted with a dough hook. Add the remaining dough ingredients and mix 3 minutes on low speed. Scrape down the bowl. Restart the mixer on medium speed and knead until the dough is soft and smooth, approximately 7 more minutes. The dough should reach 80°F (27°C) after kneading.
2. Place the dough on a lightly floured workbench, cover and bench rest 30 minutes.
3. Punch down the dough. Bench rest another 30 minutes. Repeat this process two more times for a total of 3 hours bench rest.
4. While the dough is resting, prepare the topping. Combine the flour, sugar, shortening or lard and water in the bowl of a mixer fitted with the paddle attachment. Beat to combine the ingredients into a smooth paste. Add enough cocoa powder or food coloring (if using) to tint the topping to the desired shade. Set aside.
5. Scale the dough into 2-ounce (60-gram) pieces. Shape each piece into a round ball and place on a paper-lined sheet pan. Brush each piece with melted shortening or lard.
6. Divide the topping into ½-ounce (15-gram) pieces. Spread each ball of dough with a piece of the topping. Dip a concha cutter, pizza wheel or Kaiser roll stamp in flour. Use it to stamp a series of five lines into the dough in a pattern resembling a shell. Sprinkle the rolls with sugar.
7. Proof at 80°F (25°C) until the rolls triple in volume, approximately 1 hour.
8. Bake the rolls at 375°F (190°C), with steam injected into the oven during the first few minutes of baking, until golden brown, approximately 8 to 10 minutes.

Approximate values per roll: **Calories** 340, **Total fat** 15 g, **Saturated fat** 5 g, **Cholesterol** 60 mg, **Sodium** 60 mg, **Total carbohydrates** 45 g, **Protein** 6 g, **Iron** 10%

PARISIAN BRIOCHE

Using high-gluten flour in the final dough makes it easier to shape this brioche dough; however, bread flour can be used instead. This brioche formula may be prepared without retarding, but for improved flavor development, retard the fermented dough for several hours or overnight before forming, proofing and baking.

Yield: 3 Loaves, approximately 1 lb. 8 oz. (720 g) each

Method: Sponge

Fermentation: Sponge, 2 hours. Final dough, 1 hour at room temperature

Proofing: 1 hour

Sponge:

Instant yeast	0.5 oz.	15 g	6.25%
Water, warm	4 fl. oz.	120 ml	50%
Bread flour	8 oz.	240 g	100%
Eggs	8 oz. (5 eggs)	240 g	100%
Granulated sugar	1 oz.	30 g	12.5%
Total sponge weight:	1 lb. 5 oz.	645 g	269%

Dough:

Instant yeast	0.25 oz. (1½ tsp.)	8 g	1%
Water, warm	1 fl. oz.	30 ml	4%
Sponge	1 lb. 5 oz.	645 g	80%
High-gluten flour	1 lb. 10 oz.	780 g	100%
Granulated sugar	4 oz.	120 g	15%
Eggs, lightly beaten	8 oz. (5 eggs)	235 g	30%
Salt	0.75 oz.	23 g	3%
Unsalted butter, softened but still pliable	13 oz.	390 g	50%
Egg wash	as needed	as needed	
Total dough weight:	4 lb. 10 oz.	2231 g	283%

❶ The formed loaves before proofing.

❷ The finished loaf.

❶ Prepare the sponge by combining the yeast, water, flour, eggs and sugar in the bowl of a mixer fitted with the paddle attachment. Mix on low speed, scraping down the bowl frequently, until well combined and very smooth, approximately 5 minutes. Cover with plastic and ferment 2 hours, or until doubled.

❷ To prepare the dough, dissolve the yeast in the water. Add it to the sponge along with the flour, sugar, 6 ounces (180 grams) of the eggs and the salt. Mix on low speed until a soft, smooth and shiny dough forms, approximately 3 to 5 minutes.

❸ Add the remaining eggs.

❹ Add the butter in six increments, waiting for the butter to be fully incorporated before adding more to the dough.

❺ Cover the dough and ferment 45 minutes to 1 hour. (Retard the dough after fermentation for 1 to 2 hours to make it easier to handle, if desired.)

❻ Punch down the dough, divide and shape as desired. For pull-apart loaves, divide the dough into three 1-pound, 8-ounce (720-gram) pieces and round. Divide each piece into six even pieces and round.

❼ Generously butter three 8-inch (20-centimeter) loaf pans. Position six pieces of dough in each pan.

❽ Proof at 85°F (30°C), until the loaves have increased 70 percent in volume, approximately 1 hour. (Proofing will be longer if the dough has been retarded.)

❾ Gently brush the loaves with egg wash. Bake at 375°F (190°C) until deeply browned, approximately 45 to 50 minutes.

❸ The texture of the baked bread.

Approximate values per 1½-oz. (45-g) serving: **Calories** 130, **Total fat** 7 g, **Saturated fat** 4 g, **Cholesterol** 55 mg, **Sodium** 170 mg, **Total carbohydrates** 14 g, **Protein** 4 g

KUGELHOPF

This brioche-style bread, rich with raisins, is a specialty of Alsace, France, and regions to the east. Its name refers to both the bread and the mold in which it is baked. Traditional turban-shaped kugelhopf molds are made from terra cotta, copper or tin. Kugelhopf is served with coffee as a breakfast bread or afternoon snack.

Yield: 4 Loaves, approximately 1 lb. 9 oz. (750 g) each

Method: Enriched dough

Fermentation: 1 to 1½ hours

Proofing: Approximately 1 hour

Milk	10 fl. oz.	300 ml	29.5%
Instant yeast	2 oz.	60 g	6%
Eggs	1 lb. (10 eggs)	480 g	47%
Vanilla extract	0.15 fl. oz. (1 tsp.)	5 ml	0.5%
Bread flour	2 lb. 2 oz.	1020 g	100%
Granulated sugar	5 oz.	150 g	15%
Salt	0.75 oz.	22 g	2.2%
Unsalted butter, softened	18 oz.	540 g	47%
Raisins, conditioned	1 lb.	480 g	81.5%
Total dough weight:	6 lb. 5 oz.	3057 g	300%

1. In the bowl of a 6 quart (6.5 liter) or larger mixer fitted with the paddle attachment, combine the milk, yeast, eggs and vanilla. Add the flour, sugar and salt. Mix on medium speed until well blended.

2. Switch to a dough hook. Knead until the dough reaches 75°F (24°C). Gradually add the butter. Knead until the soft dough is fully developed and passes the windowpane test. Add the raisins and gently mix them into the dough.

3. Ferment the dough, covered, until doubled, approximately 1 to 1½ hours. Punch down the dough, cover and bench rest 15 minutes.

4. Divide the dough into four equal pieces. Round the dough. Make an indentation in the center of each round of dough using your thumbs. With floured hands, gently stretch the dough so that the hole fits over the tube in the kugelhopf mold. Place each piece of formed dough into a buttered kugelhopf mold. Proof until the loaves have increased 70 percent in volume, approximately 1 hour.

5. Bake at 350°F (180°C) for approximately 45 minutes. If the loaves brown too quickly, cover them with lightly buttered aluminum foil.

6. Cool the loaves in the pans for approximately 30 minutes before unmolding to prevent them from collapsing.

Approximate values per 1-oz. (30-g) serving: **Calories** 100, **Total fat** 5 g, **Saturated fat** 3 g, **Cholesterol** 30 mg, **Sodium** 90 mg, **Total carbohydrates** 12 g, **Protein** 2 g

RUM BABAS WITH CRÈME CHANTILLY

Yield: 18 Babas, approximately 2½ oz. (75 g) each

Method: Enriched dough

Fermentation: 45 minutes to 1 hour

Proofing: Approximately 1 hour

Dough:

Instant yeast	0.5 oz.	15 g	3%
Water (temperature controlled)	12 fl. oz.	360 ml	75%
Granulated sugar	1 oz.	30 g	6%
Salt	0.3 oz. (1½ tsp.)	10 g	2%
Vanilla extract	0.15 fl. oz. (1 tsp.)	5 ml	1%
Bread flour	1 lb.	480 g	100%
Eggs	8.3 oz. (5 eggs)	250 g	52%
Unsalted butter, room temperature	6 oz.	180 g	37%
Total dough weight:	2 lb. 12 oz.	1330 g	276%
Simple Syrup (page 73)	3 qt.	3 lt	
Dark rum	2 fl. oz.	60 ml	
Crème Chantilly (page 502)	1 pt.	480 ml	
Toasted Coconut Curls (page 672)	18	18	
Strawberry Coulis (page 512)	as needed	as needed	
Strawberries, fresh, sliced	1 lb. 4 oz.	600 g	

❶ Piping baba dough into buttered molds.

❷ The finished babas with garnishes.

❶ Dissolve the yeast in the water in the bowl of a mixer fitted with the paddle attachment. Add the sugar, salt, vanilla and flour and mix on low speed until the dough is smooth, approximately 6 to 10 minutes. Add the eggs one at a time, waiting until each egg is incorporated before adding the next. Mix until the dough is smooth and elastic, approximately 5 to 7 minutes.

❷ Break the butter up into several pieces and place it on top of the dough. Mix the dough about 20 to 30 seconds on low speed, just enough to distribute the butter throughout the dough without completely incorporating it into the dough.

❸ Ferment the dough in the bowl of the mixer, covered, until it doubles in size, approximately 45 minutes.

❹ Return the bowl of dough to the mixer and knead on medium speed for 2 to 3 minutes to completely mix the butter into the dough. The dough will be very soft, smooth and elastic when fully kneaded.

❺ Place the dough in a pastry bag fitted with a large plain tip. Pipe buttered baba or savarin molds one-third to one-half full with the dough. Use scissors to cut the dough away from the pastry tip.

❻ Proof until doubled in size. Bake at 375°F (190°C) until golden brown, approximately 15 minutes. Cool to room temperature.

❼ Bring the Simple Syrup to a boil in a large saucepan. Reduce the heat to a low simmer. Place the babas in the simmering syrup, allowing ample room for them to expand. After 1 minute flip the pastries, then leave them to soak up the syrup for 1 minute on the other side. When fully soaked, the babas will expand by approximately 25 percent.

❽ Remove the babas from the syrup using a slotted spoon and place them on a serving plate. (Strain any leftover syrup and reserve for another use.) Sprinkle or brush each baba with the dark rum. Babas may be served warm or at room temperature. Decorate with Crème Chantilly and Toasted Coconut Curls. Garnish each plate with strawberry coulis and fresh strawberry slices.

Approximate values per baba: **Calories** 340, **Total fat** 20 g, **Saturated fat** 11 g, **Cholesterol** 105 mg, **Sodium** 230 mg, **Total carbohydrates** 34 g, **Protein** 5 g, **Vitamin C** 30%

STOLLEN

Yield: 4 Loaves, approximately 1 lb. 4 oz. (600 g) each

Method: Enriched dough

Fermentation: Sponge, 2 hours. Final dough, 1 hour

Proofing: 45 minutes to 1 hour

Sponge:

Bread flour	7 oz.	210 g	100%
Water	7 fl. oz.	210 ml	100%
Instant yeast	0.25 oz. (1½ tsp.)	7.5 g	3.5%
Total sponge weight:	14 oz.	427 g	203%

Dough:

Sponge	14 oz.	427 g	140%
Bread flour	10 oz.	300 g	100%
Water (temperature controlled)	3 fl. oz.	90 ml	30%
Instant yeast	0.5 oz.	15 g	5%
Granulated sugar	2 oz.	60 g	20%
Glucose or corn syrup	0.75 oz.	22 g	0.7%
Salt	0.5 oz.	15 g	5%
Egg	1.6 oz. (1 egg)	50 g	16%
Egg yolk	0.6 oz. (1 yolk)	20 g	6%
Dry milk powder	1 oz.	30 g	10%
Vanilla extract	0.15 fl. oz. (1 tsp.)	5 ml	0.2%
Unsalted butter, softened	6 oz.	180 g	60%
Hazelnuts, toasted and chopped	5 oz.	150 g	50%
Dried cherries	3 oz.	90 g	30%
Raisins, soaked in rum 12 hours	1 lb.	480 g	160%
Candied orange peel	2.5 oz.	75 g	25%
Pistachios, chopped	5.5 oz.	165 g	55%
Marzipan	6 oz.	180 g	60%
Egg wash	as needed	as needed	
Total dough weight:	4 lb. 14 oz.	2354 g	773%
Unsalted butter, melted	as needed	as needed	
Powdered or granulated sugar	as needed	as needed	

❶ Placing the log of marzipan on the flattened stollen dough.

❷ The finished stollen: undecorated (left), dusted with powdered sugar (back) and dusted with granulated sugar (front).

❶ To make the sponge, combine the flour, water and yeast. Cover and ferment 2 hours.

❷ Place the sponge in the bowl of a mixer fitted with a dough hook. Add the flour, water, yeast, sugar, glucose, salt, egg, egg yolk, milk powder and vanilla. Once incorporated, mix on medium speed until the dough is fully developed, approximately 7 to 8 minutes. The dough should reach 77°F (25°C).

❸ Gradually knead in the butter on medium speed until the dough is completely smooth. Add the hazelnuts, cherries, raisins, orange peel and pistachios, kneading just until combined.

❹ Cover the dough and ferment until doubled in bulk, approximately 1 hour.

❺ Divide the dough into four equal pieces. Round the dough and place it seam side up on a lightly floured workbench. Cover and bench rest 15 minutes.

❻ Scale the marzipan into 1½-ounce (45-gram) pieces. Roll each piece into an 8-inch (20-centimeter) cylinder. Set aside.

❼ Flatten each piece of dough into an oval. Place a log of marzipan in the middle of each piece of flattened dough. Fold the dough lengthwise to cover the marzipan. Press the dough together with a dowel placed parallel to the marzipan. Transfer the formed loaves to paper-lined sheet pans and proof at 85°F (30°C) until the loaves have increased 60 to 70 percent in volume, 45 minutes to 1 hour.

❽ Brush with egg wash and bake at 375°F (190°C) until well browned, approximately 40 minutes. While still warm, brush each loaf generously with melted butter. Dust the cooled loaves with powdered sugar.

Approximate values per 2-oz. (60-g) serving: Calories 190, **Total fat** 9 g, **Saturated fat** 2.5 g, **Cholesterol** 20 mg, **Sodium** 150 mg, **Total carbohydrates** 26 g, **Protein** 4 g

PANETTONE

Yield: 3 Loaves, 2 lb. 2 oz. (968 g) each

Method: Enriched dough

Fermentation: Sponge, 1½ hours. Final dough, approximately 1 hour

Proofing: 45 minutes to 1 hour

Sponge:

Bread flour	8 oz.	240 g	100%
Water, 80°F (27°C)	12 fl. oz.	360 ml	150%
Instant yeast	0.25 oz. (1½ tsp.)	7.5 g	3.2%
Total sponge weight:	1 lb. 4 oz.	607 g	253%

Dough:

Sponge	1 lb. 4 oz.	607 g	71%
Water	4 fl. oz.	120 ml	14%
Instant yeast	1 oz.	30 g	3.6%
Egg yolks	4 oz. (6 yolks)	120 g	14%
Bread flour	1 lb. 12 oz.	840 g	100%
Granulated sugar	8 oz.	240 g	28.5%
Salt	0.75 oz.	22 g	2.7%
Lemon zest, grated	0.14 oz. (2 tsp.)	4 g	0.5%
Orange zest, grated	0.21 oz. (1 Tbsp.)	6 g	0.7%
Vanilla extract	0.5 fl. oz. (1 Tbsp.)	15 ml	1.8%
Unsalted butter, softened	12 oz.	360 g	43%
Raisins, conditioned	6 oz.	180 g	22%
Golden raisins, conditioned	6 oz.	180 g	22%
Candied orange peel, diced	6 oz.	180 g	22%
Egg wash	as needed	as needed	
Total dough weight:	5 lb. 13 oz.	2904 g	346%

1. Prepare the sponge by combining the flour, water and yeast in a bowl until smooth. Cover with plastic and ferment 1½ hours, or until doubled.
2. To prepare the dough, place the sponge in the bowl of a 6-quart (6.5-lilter) or larger mixer fitted with a dough hook. Add the water, yeast and egg yolks. Cover with the flour, sugar, salt, lemon and orange zest and vanilla. Mix on medium speed until the soft dough is nearly developed and reaches 77°F (25°C).
3. With the machine running, add the butter a little at a time until the soft dough is completely smooth. Add the raisins and orange peel to the dough, mixing only until combined.
4. Cover the dough and ferment until doubled in volume, approximately 1 hour.
5. Punch down the dough and bench rest 10 minutes. Divide the dough into three pieces.
6. Generously butter three panettone molds. Round the dough and place it into the greased pans.
7. Proof until the dough has increased 60 to 70 percent in volume, 45 minutes to 1 hour.
8. Gently brush the proofed loaves with egg wash. Bake at 350°F (180°C) until the loaves are well browned, approximately 43 to 48 minutes. Cover the loaves with aluminum foil if they begin to brown too quickly.
9. Cool the loaves in the pans for approximately 15 minutes before unmolding.

Approximate values per 1-oz. (30-g) serving: **Calories** 90, **Total fat** 3 g, **Saturated fat** 2 g, **Cholesterol** 20 mg, **Sodium** 85 mg, **Total carbohydrates** 14 g, **Protein** 2 g

BIENENSTICH
(BEE STING PASTRY)

❶ Portioning the pastry.

❷ The finished bee sting pastry.

Yield: 40 Pastries, 3 inch (7.5 centimeters) each

Method: Straight dough

Proofing: 45 minutes

Sweet Bun Dough (page 242), fermented	4 lb. 10 oz.	2220 g
Topping:		
Heavy cream	8 oz.	240 g
Honey	3 oz.	90 g
Unsalted butter	10 oz.	300 g
Granulated sugar	10 oz.	300 g
Salt	0.02 oz. (⅛ tsp.)	0.5 g
Sliced almonds	10 oz.	300 g
Pastry Cream (page 492)	4 lb.	1920 g

❶ Grease two half-sheet pans with melted butter and line them with parchment paper. Set aside.

❷ Combine the heavy cream, honey, butter, granulated sugar and salt in a heavy saucepan over medium high heat. Bring to a boil, stirring constantly and cook for 5 minutes. Add the almonds and boil for another 5 minutes. The mixture should be thick like honey. Remove from heat and set aside.

❸ Divide the dough into two equal pieces. On a lightly floured surface, roll out each piece of dough into an even rectangle the size of a half-sheet pan. Press the dough into the pans,

❹ Divide the almond topping evenly between the two sheets and spread it over the surface of the dough. If the topping has cooled too much and is too difficult to spread, reheat it until lukewarm.

❺ Proof the dough until nearly doubled in volume, approximately 45 minutes.

❻ Bake at 375°F (190°C) until the topping is light golden brown and the dough is baked through, approximately 16 to 18 minutes.

❼ Cool the bread. Split each sheet of bread horizontally using a serrated knife. To make two two-layer pastries, spread the bottom layer of each bread with half of the Pastry Cream. Place the remaining layer of bread on top.

❽ Cut the dough into 3 inch (7.5 centimeter) squares.

Approximate values per pastry: **Calories** 390, **Total fat** 20 g, **Saturated fat** 9 g, **Cholesterol** 105 mg, **Sodium** 210 mg, **Total carbohydrates** 46 g, **Protein** 7 g

APPLE FRITTERS

Yield: 100 Fritters, 2 in. (5 cm) each

Egg yolks	4 oz. (6 yolks)	120 g	25%
Milk	16 fl. oz.	480 ml	100%
All-purpose flour	1 lb.	480 g	100%
Baking powder	0.4 oz. (1 Tbsp.)	12 g	2.5%
Salt	0.2 oz. (1 tsp.)	6 g	1.2%
Granulated sugar	2 oz.	60 g	12.5%
Cinnamon, ground	0.04 oz. (½ tsp.)	1 g	0.25%
Apples, peeled and cored, medium dice	1 lb. 8 oz.	700 g	150%
Egg whites	6 oz. (6 whites)	180 g	37.5%
Total weight:	4 lb. 4 oz.	2059 g	429%
Powdered sugar	as needed	as needed	

Deep-fried batter-coated fresh fruit makes a delectable dessert or a garnish on a complex plated presentation. Apples, bananas, pears, pineapples and firm peaches mixed in or coated with batter work best for deep-frying. These fruits should be peeled, cored, seeded and cut into evenly sized slices or chunks. They may also need to be dried with paper towels so that the batter or coating can adhere. Fritters are spooned or dropped directly into the hot fat; they form a crust as they cook. Once cooked and drained, they may be served sprinkled with powdered or granulated sugar or accompanied by ice cream or whipped cream.

1. Combine the egg yolks and milk.
2. Sift together the flour, baking powder, salt, sugar and cinnamon. Add the flour mixture to the milk-and-egg mixture; mix until smooth.
3. Allow the batter to rest 1 hour.
4. Stir the apples into the batter.
5. Just before the fritters are to be cooked, whip the egg whites to soft peaks and fold into the batter.
6. Scoop the fritters into deep fat at 350°F (180°C). Once browned on one side, flip the fritters in the fat to cook until done.
7. Dust with powdered sugar and serve hot.

VARIATION:

Banana Fritters—Omit the cinnamon and apples. Add 0.6 ounce (18 grams) finely grated orange zest, 4 fluid ounces (120 milliliters) orange juice and 2 large bananas, peeled and diced (not puréed).

Approximate values per fritter: **Calories** 60, **Total fat** 4 g, **Saturated fat** 1 g, **Cholesterol** 15 mg, **Sodium** 5 mg, **Total carbohydrates** 6 g, **Protein** 1 g

1. Adding the dry ingredients to the liquids.

2. Folding the egg whites into the batter.

3. Dropping the fritters into the deep fat.

4. Dusting the fritters with powdered sugar.

BUÑUELOS
(MEXICAN-STYLE DOUGHNUTS)

Yield: 4½ Dozen Doughnuts, approximately 4 in. (10 cm) each

Method: Straight dough

Fermentation: 1½ to 2 hours. Bench rest, 15 minutes

Milk	12 fl. oz.	360 ml	46%
Butter	2 oz.	60 g	8%
Instant yeast	0.6 oz. (4 tsp.)	15 g	2%
Water, 90°F (32°C)	4 fl. oz.	120 ml	15%
All-purpose flour	26 oz.	780 g	100%
Salt	0.4 oz. (2 tsp.)	12 g	1.5%
Granulated sugar	6 oz.	180 g	23%
Eggs	3.2 oz. (2 eggs)	94 g	12%
Total dough weight:	3 lb. 6 oz.	1621 g	207%
Honey	as needed	as needed	

1. Bring the milk to a boil over medium heat. Add the butter and let the mixture cool to 100°F (38°C).
2. Dissolve the yeast in the water. Set aside.
3. Combine the flour, salt and sugar in the bowl of a mixer fitted with a dough hook. Add the cooled milk mixture, the yeast mixture and the eggs. Stir briefly to combine the ingredients, then knead on medium speed until a smooth soft dough forms.
4. Ferment the dough until doubled in size, approximately 1 to 1½ hours.
5. Punch down the dough and then knead it briefly on a lightly floured surface. Bench rest 15 minutes.
6. Roll the dough out into a rectangle ½ inch (1.2 centimeters) thick. Cut it into 2-inch (5-centimeter) rounds. Lightly stretch out each round of dough into 4-inch (10-centimeter) disks.
7. Fry the dough in batches in deep fat heated to 350°F (180°C). Cook until puffed and browned, approximately 1 or 2 minutes. Flip the doughnuts and cook another minute until browned. Remove from the fat and drain on absorbent paper. Serve warm with honey for dipping.

Approximate values per doughnut: **Calories** 126, **Total fat** 60 g, **Saturated fat** 1 g, **Cholesterol** 10 mg, **Sodium** 86 mg, **Total carbohydrates** 14 g, **Protein** 2 g

CHOCOLATE BEIGNETS

HERBSAINT BAR AND RESTAURANT, NEW ORLEANS, LA
Chef Donald Link

Beignets (ben-YEA) are leavened, deep-fried doughnutlike pastries smothered in powdered sugar. They are served piping hot 24 hours a day in New Orleans' French Quarter. Chef Link has added chocolate to the traditional formula for this dessert presentation.

Yield: 60 Pieces

Method: Enriched dough

Fermentation: 30 minutes

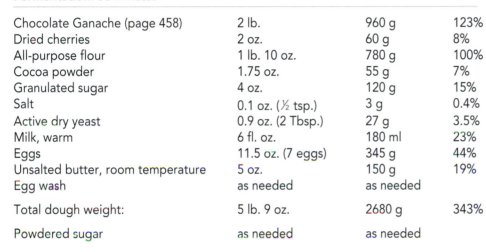

Chocolate Ganache (page 458)	2 lb.	960 g	123%
Dried cherries	2 oz.	60 g	8%
All-purpose flour	1 lb. 10 oz.	780 g	100%
Cocoa powder	1.75 oz.	55 g	7%
Granulated sugar	4 oz.	120 g	15%
Salt	0.1 oz. (½ tsp.)	3 g	0.4%
Active dry yeast	0.9 oz. (2 Tbsp.)	27 g	3.5%
Milk, warm	6 fl. oz.	180 ml	23%
Eggs	11.5 oz. (7 eggs)	345 g	44%
Unsalted butter, room temperature	5 oz.	150 g	19%
Egg wash	as needed	as needed	
Total dough weight:	5 lb. 9 oz.	2680 g	343%
Powdered sugar	as needed	as needed	

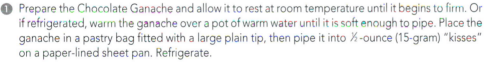

1. Prepare the Chocolate Ganache and allow it to rest at room temperature until it begins to firm. Or if refrigerated, warm the ganache over a pot of warm water until it is soft enough to pipe. Place the ganache in a pastry bag fitted with a large plain tip, then pipe it into ½-ounce (15-gram) "kisses" on a paper-lined sheet pan. Refrigerate.

2. Steep the cherries in hot water for 5 minutes, then drain and chop.

3. Sift the flour with the cocoa powder, then stir in the sugar and salt.

4. Combine the yeast with the milk. Add the yeast and milk to the dry ingredients in the bowl of a mixer fitted with a dough hook. Mix the ingredients at low speed, adding the eggs a small amount at a time. Mix the dough until the gluten develops, approximately 7 to 10 minutes.

5. Rest the dough 5 minutes. Then mix the dough on medium speed, adding the butter a small piece at a time. Let the butter mix in after each addition. When all of the butter has been added and the dough is pulling away from the sides of the bowl, add the cherries and mix until incorporated. Rest the dough in the refrigerator 30 minutes before using.

6. Roll a portion of the dough into a long rectangle, approximately 2 inches (5 centimeters) wide and ⅛ inch (3 millimeters) thick. Mark a centerline down the length of the dough with the back of a chef's knife. Brush the dough with egg wash. Place a row of ganache kisses on the lower half of the dough, spaced approximately 2 inches (5 centimeters) apart. Fold the upper half of the dough over the ganache. Press the dough together around the ganache kisses, ravioli-style. Cut the dough between the ganache kisses to form individual pillows. Place the beignets on a paper-lined sheet pan and freeze.

7. Place several frozen beignets in a deep-fryer basket. Place another deep-fryer basket over the beignets to keep them submerged in the fat as they cook. Deep-fry the frozen beignets at 325°F (160°C), approximately 3 to 4 minutes. Drain, toss in powdered sugar and serve.

Approximate values per 3-piece serving: **Calories** 870, **Total fat** 54 g, **Saturated fat** 30 g, **Cholesterol** 225 mg, **Sodium** 170 mg, **Total carbohydrates** 93 g, **Protein** 17 g, **Vitamin A** 30%, **Calcium** 10%, **Iron** 35%

CHAPTER NINE

LAMINATED DOUGHS

- understand the steps and techniques for preparing and baking laminated dough
- prepare puff pastry
- prepare croissants and Danish pastries
- prepare a variety of pastries using these doughs and other components

FEW PRODUCTS DISTINGUISH A FINE BAKESHOP more than those made from the types of dough presented in this chapter. Forms of these flaky pastries appear on many continents—the croissant and mille feuille in France, the crescent roll in the United States, the flaky custard-filled sfogliatelle in Italy. Formal pâtisseries and humble bakeries are united in the scent of melting butter and crisping pastry from an oven load of flaky croissants. These doughs are produced by lamination, a technique that sandwiches layers of fat between layers of dough. Careful handling of ingredients and repeated rolling and folding produces delicate layers of crisp pastry when baked. Though the techniques necessary to make these products require some practice to master, the results are worth the effort.

This chapter covers the techniques for mixing, laminating, handling and baking a variety of rolled-in doughs and pastries. An understanding of the principles for preparing yeast dough covered in Chapter 7, Artisan and Yeast Breads, is recommended before working with the techniques discussed here.

PREPARING LAMINATED DOUGH

Puff pastry, croissant and Danish dough are called **rolled-in doughs** or **laminated doughs**. These pastries are so named because the fat is incorporated into the dough through a process of rolling and folding. Laminating produces alternating layers (laminates) of dough and fat, which creates layers when baked and helps leaven the dough. Products made with laminated dough have a distinctive flaky texture created by the many layers of fat within the dough. Although the formulas for making these products may differ, the techniques for laminating and shaping these doughs are similar.

Laminated dough develops its flavor characteristics by the way in which it is prepared, leavening action and ingredients.

There are four basic stages in the production of a laminated dough:

1. Preparing the dough.
2. Selecting and preparing the fat for lamination.
3. Enclosing the fat inside the dough.
4. Flattening, rolling and folding the dough to develop the proper layers.

Preparing the Dough for Laminated Products

The dough for laminated baked goods may be a simple mixture of flour, fat and water as for puff pastry dough, or it may also contain yeast as for **croissants** and **Danish pastry**. All-purpose flour produces a tender flakiness in laminated dough but insufficient gluten strength to keep the dough from tearing. A higher-protein flour such as bread flour produces a dough with the strength needed to withstand rolling and prevent the fat from breaking through the dough. A flour with protein between 11 and 12.5 percent is preferred for both strength and tenderness. A combination of all-purpose and bread flour can produce the desired results.

The dough for puff pastry and yeast-raised laminated dough is relatively dry because soft dough can stretch out and tear when rolled and folded. Additional fat is added to the dough in order to add flavor. The fat also helps lubricate the gluten strands and aids in dough stretching and extensibility. Salt is added for flavor and to toughen the gluten structure.

The dough for laminated pastry is not kneaded excessively because the gluten will continue to develop during the rolling and folding in of the fat. Yeast-raised laminated dough, discussed later in this chapter, must be fermented before laminating with fat. The dough for puff pastry is customarily chilled overnight in the refrigerator to relax any gluten development and allow the starches in the flour to absorb the water before laminating.

Selecting and Preparing the Fats for Lamination

When making laminated dough, a minimum of one third of the dough's weight is from the **roll-in** fat, with especially rich products containing up to 80 percent fat. Although commercially produced roll-in fats are acceptable, and shortening or margarine can be used, unsalted butter is the preferred choice. Butter produces a better flavor and color in the finished product and it has better eating qualities; butter melts at body temperature, unlike shortening, which tends to coat the tongue with a layer of grease. Most professional bakers prefer a dry butter with a least an 82 percent butterfat content. Because butter lacks **plasticity** and becomes brittle when cold, a small amount of flour may be mixed in with the butter before using it. (The flour also helps absorb any moisture in the butter.) Shortening and margarine are more flexible when cold and somewhat easier to handle than butter, however. For this reason, some bakers prefer margarine and special laminating shortenings. Each has a higher melting point and more plasticity than butter, but neither offers the flavor or browning qualities of butter.

To create a uniform shape of butter to lock into the dough, the butter is manually softened. It can be softened with a dough scraper before being formed into a uniform block. Or the butter can be placed between layers of parchment or plastic film, where it is pounded to soften and then flattened with a rolling pin into a shape to match the size of the dough.

Enclosing the Fat into the Base Dough

Once prepared and allowed to rest or ferment, the ball of base dough must be flattened to encase the fat. Customarily, the dough is rounded and then scored to help flatten it before rolling into a uniform rectangle. The dough is rolled out into an even thickness just large enough to enclose the block of roll-in fat. Then the dough is wrapped around the fat and sealed or locked in, as shown here. Dough and fat should be at the same temperature and consistency. If the dough is too soft and the butter too cold, the dough could tear. If the dough is too cold and firm and the butter too soft, the butter could ooze out from between the layers and laminate unevenly during rolling.

Rolling and Folding the Dough to Develop Layers

In order to ensure that puff pastry and other laminated dough rises properly, the fat must be evenly distributed through the dough. Specific folding techniques help ensure proper fat distribution and the maximum number of layers in the baked pastry. Equally important, the fat should be neither absorbed by the dough nor broken up into small lumps by the pulling force of the rolling motion with either the rolling pin or pastry sheeter. To achieve this, the roll-in fat must be the same consistency as the dough. Keeping the dough cool, around 40°F–60°F (4°C–16°C), during rolling prevents the dough from absorbing the fat.

Numerous methods can be used to roll laminated dough. All methods depend on the proper layering of fat and dough through a series of **turns** to give the pastry its characteristic flakiness and rise. The number of turns is determined by the product being made. In this chapter two methods for folding and rolling in the fat—the **three fold** or **single book fold** method and the **four fold** or **double book fold** method—are illustrated next.

Using flour when rolling prevents tearing and shredding, but excess flour should be brushed off before folding so that layers adhere to one another. Work rapidly to keep the dough cool. It should be firm yet pliable like clay. Refrigerating between turns relaxes the gluten, making the dough easier to roll, and chills the dough and fat layers so they will remain separate. If the dough has been rolled more in one direction than another, shrinkage and distortion can occur in the finished pieces. Maintaining square edges helps ensure

roll-in shorthand for the butter or other fat used in layering laminated dough; also referred to as lock-in fat

plasticity a physical characteristic of fat; its capability of being shaped or molded

turns the number of times that laminated dough is rolled and folded

Rolling the fat between plastic into a uniform rectangle to be locked into laminated dough.

The roll-in fat is wrapped in the dough.

Use the tips of your fingers to seal the edges of the dough and to secure the roll-in fat.

proper lamination of the dough. Roll in one direction only with each turn. Although laminated dough may be rolled by hand, most commercial establishments will use an electric dough sheeter as illustrated next.

Rolling-In Laminated Dough

Most bakeshops where puff pastry, croissant and Danish dough are made regularly use an electric **sheeter** to speed the process and ensure consistent results. Rolling-in the fat using the single and double book fold is illustrated on the following pages.

PROCEDURE FOR THINNING LAMINATED DOUGH ON A SHEETER

❶ Place a block of dough on the bed of a sheeter. Pass the dough under the rollers to thin the dough.

❷ Decrease the height of the roller setting on the sheeter. Pass the dough under the rollers to thin the dough. Continue decreasing the height of the rollers on the sheeter and passing the dough under the rollers until the dough is the desired thickness.

❸ Thinned dough ready for use.

PROCEDURE FOR MAKING A SINGLE BOOK FOLD

SAFETY ALERT
Sheeters

Training on how to operate a mechanical sheeter is recommended before attempting to use it. The movement of the canvas arms and the pressure between the rollers can cause severe injury.

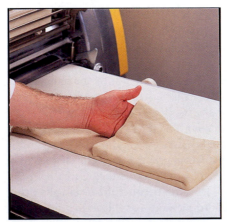

❶ Lift the right side of the dough and fold it over, covering one-third of the dough.

❷ Lift the left side of the dough and fold it over to create three uniform layers of dough. Align the edges into a neat packet. This procedure completes one turn.

PROCEDURE FOR **MAKING A DOUBLE BOOK FOLD**

① Lift the right side of the dough and fold it over, covering three-quarters of the dough. Pick up the left side of the dough and fold it until the edges touch.

② Fold both ends of the dough in toward the center again to make four layers. The folded package will resemble a book. This procedure completes one turn.

Shaping Laminated Dough for Baking

Laminated dough is not rounded or molded to shape for baking. Rather it is cut using a sharp knife or cutting tool to preserve the layers. The procedures customarily used for shaping puff pastry appear on pages 281 to 284. The procedures for shaping yeasted laminated dough appear on pages 291 to 293. Many of the shaping techniques can be used with either type of dough, however.

PUFF PASTRY

Puff pastry is one of the bakeshop's most elegant and sophisticated products. Also known as **pâte feuilletée** or **mille feuille**, it is a rich, buttery dough that bakes into hundreds of light, crisp layers. The classic way of making puff pastry produces more than one thousand layers in the finished dough; hence its name in French is *mille feuille*, meaning "one thousand leaves."

Puff pastry is used for both sweet and savory preparations. It can be baked and then filled, or filled first and then baked. Puff pastry may be used to wrap beef (for beef Wellington), pâté (for pâté en croûte) or almond cream (for an apple tart). It can be shaped into shells or cases known as vol-au-vents or bouchées and filled with shellfish in a cream sauce or berries in a pastry cream. Puff pastry is essential for Napoleons, pithiviers and tartes tatin. The Italian pastry *sfogliatelle* is a type of cream-filled puff pastry shaped like a shell. Spanish *holadres* are made from puff pastry dough.

Puff pastry does not contain any yeast or chemical leavening agents, unlike croissants and Danish, discussed later in this chapter. Fat is rolled into the dough in horizontal layers; when baked, the fat melts, separating the dough into layers. The fat's moisture turns into steam, which causes the dough to rise and the layers to further separate. The bubbling of the fat as the steam escapes also leavens the pastry, as does steam escaping from the moisture in the dough. To ensure that it rises properly, puff pastry must be baked at high temperatures, usually around 400°F (204°C), to convert the moisture to steam before the fat melts.

To produce puff pastry, a relatively firm dough base (**détrempe**) is made using flour and water. Often an acid such as cream of tartar, lemon juice or vinegar is added to the dough to make the gluten more elastic and extensible during lamination. Sweeteners are not usually added to the détrempe for puff pastry dough, although a small amount will assist the dough in browning.

feuilletage (fuh-yuh-TAHZH) French for "flakiness"; used to describe puff pastry or the process for making puff pastry

détrempe (day-trup-eh) a paste made with flour and water during the first stage of preparing pastry dough, especially rolled-in doughs

Visible layers in a finished French pastry.

The procedures described here for making and folding puff pastry dough are just two of several. All methods, however, depend on the proper layering of fat and dough through a series of turns to give the pastry its characteristic flakiness and rise. A minimum of five turns ensures that puff pastry rises properly, which is six to eight times its initial volume.

Some chefs prefer to prepare a dough called **blitz** or **quick puff pastry**. It does not require the extensive rolling and folding procedure used for true puff pastry. Blitz puff pastry is less delicate and flaky and it does not rise as much as traditional puff pastry, but may be perfectly acceptable for some uses. A formula for it is given on page 299.

PROCEDURE FOR PREPARING PUFF PASTRY

1. Prepare the dough base (détrempe) by combining the flour, water, salt and a small amount of fat. Do not overmix. Overmixing results in greater gluten formation, and too much gluten can make the pastry undesirably tough.

2. Wrap the détrempe and chill for several hours or overnight. This allows the gluten to relax and the flour to absorb the liquid.

3. Shape the butter into a rectangle of even thickness; wrap and chill until ready to use.

4. Allow the détrempe and butter to sit at room temperature until slightly softened and of the same consistency. Butter should be firm, and cold, but pliable like clay.

5. Roll out the détrempe into a rectangle of even thickness large enough to completely cover the butter rectangle.

6. Position the butter on the dough. Fold the dough over the butter to completely encase it in the dough. Press the dough to seal the edges and **lock in** the butter.

7. Roll out the block of dough and butter into a long, even rectangle. Roll only at right angles so that the layered structure is not destroyed.

8. Fold the dough like a business letter: Fold the bottom third up toward the center so that it covers the center third, then fold the top third down over the bottom and middle thirds. This is the single book fold. This completes the first turn, the expression used to describe the rolling and folding of the dough. Wrap the dough and chill approximately 1 hour.

9. Rotate the block of dough one quarter turn (90 degrees) on the work surface. Roll out again into a long, even rectangle.

10. Fold the dough in thirds again, like a business letter. This completes the second turn. Wrap the dough and chill approximately 1 hour. The resting period allows the gluten to relax; the chilling prevents the butter from becoming too soft.

11. Repeat the rolling and folding process, chilling between every one or two turns, until the dough has been turned a total of five times. (Some prefer a total of six turns, but five ensures an energetic rise in the dough during baking.)

Layers of butter visible in chocolate puff pastry after second turn.

12. Wrap well and chill overnight. Raw dough may be refrigerated for a few days or frozen for 2 to 3 months.

13. Shape and bake as needed. Baked, unfilled puff pastry can be stored at room temperature for 2 to 3 days.

CONVENIENCE PRODUCTS

In bakeshops where space and time does not permit the making of laminated dough, frozen prepared products may be preferred. Frozen puff pastry dough is available in 2- to 10-pound blocks. The dough is thawed in the refrigerator, then rolled, portioned and baked as needed. Frozen sheets of puff pastry dough rolled to a ¼-inch (3-millimeter) thickness and separated by pieces of parchment paper make preparing fresh bouchées, feuilletées, cheese straws and other items possible in even the smallest restaurant kitchen. These sheets thaw quickly under refrigeration. Once the required number of sheets is thawed, they are ready to be portioned and baked. Some bakers thin the sheets further with a rolling pin before portioning and baking.

Manufacturers also sell frozen croissant and Danish dough in bulk blocks or sheets. Because of the yeast, croissant and Danish dough require proofing as well as baking. Croissant and Danish dough is also available portioned and formed into individual pastries before freezing. The pastries are sold filled or to be filled by the baker after baking. Many manufacturers include separate packets of fruit and cheese filling or sugar glazes, designed to be piped directly from their packaging onto the pastries once they are baked.

Bakers can choose products at every stage in the process: formed and frozen; formed, frozen and fully proofed; or formed, frozen, proofed and baked. When handling frozen croissant and Danish dough products, follow the manufacturer's instructions. It is generally recommended that the frozen dough units be placed on paper-lined sheet pans. The pans need to be covered with a plastic poly bag or rolling rack cover. The dough can be thawed and proofed at room temperature until it doubles in size and bounces back when gently touched. Or it can be refrigerated to thaw and begin proofing slowly overnight. The following day, the pans are left at room temperature, away from direct heat, until the products double in size. The exact length of time, as with any proofed product, will depend on kitchen temperatures.

As with scratch laminated doughs, these frozen products must be glazed with egg wash before baking. For the best flavor and color after baking, select products that are made from pure butter.

MISE EN PLACE

- ▶ Chill water.
- ▶ Chill flours.
- ▶ Soften butter for the détrempe.

❶ Scoring the ball of dough (upper left). Flattening it into a neat rectangle (upper right). Wrapping the fat in the dough (lower right).

❷ Rolling out the dough.

❸ Folding the dough in thirds.

PUFF PASTRY (PÂTE FEUILLETÉE)

Yield: 3 lb. 3 oz. (1530 g)

Salt	0.5 oz.	15 g	2.4%
Water, chilled	10.5 fl. oz.	315 ml	51%
Bread flour, chilled or frozen	10 oz.	300 g	49%
All-purpose flour, chilled or frozen	10.5 oz.	315 g	51%
Unsalted butter, very soft	4.5 oz.	135 g	22%
Unsalted butter, cold	15 oz.	450 g	73%
Total dough weight:	3 lb. 3 oz.	1530 g	248%

❶ In the bowl of a mixer fitted with a dough hook, dissolve the salt in the chilled water. Add the bread flour, all-purpose flour and soft butter. Knead just until a smooth dough forms, approximately 1 to 2 minutes.

❷ Wrap the dough tightly in plastic and chill 1 hour or overnight.

❸ To roll-in the butter, first prepare the cold butter by placing it between two sheets of parchment paper or plastic film. Use a rolling pin to soften the butter so that it remains firm yet pliable like clay. Shape the butter into a 7.5-inch × 10.5-inch (20-centimeter × 27-centimeter) rectangle. It is important that the détrempe and butter be of almost equal consistency. If necessary, allow the détrempe to sit at room temperature to soften slightly or chill the butter briefly to harden.

❹ On a lightly floured board, roll the détrempe into a rectangle approximately 12 inches × 18 inches (30 centimeters × 46 centimeters) long. Lift and rotate the dough as necessary to prevent sticking.

❺ Use a dry pastry brush to brush away any flour from the dough's surface. Loose flour can cause gray streaks and can prevent the puff pastry from rising properly when baked.

❻ Peel one piece of parchment or plastic wrap from the butter. Position the butter, which should have the same consistency as the dough, on the left side of the dough rectangle. Fold the right side of the dough over the butter and press on all sides to seal. Stretch the dough if necessary; it is important that none of the butter be exposed.

❼ Press the dough several times with a rolling pin. Use a rocking motion to create ridges in the dough. Place the rolling pin in each ridge and slowly roll back and forth to widen the ridge. Repeat until all the ridges are doubled in size.

❽ Starting from the seamless side, roll the dough out into a smooth even rectangle approximately 10 inches × 24 inches (25 centimeters × 60 centimeters). Be careful to keep the corners of the dough at right angles.

❾ Use a dry pastry brush to remove any loose flour from the dough's surface. Fold the dough in thirds, like a business letter, the single book fold. If one end is damaged or in worse condition, fold it in first; otherwise, start at the bottom. This completes the first turn. Wrap in plastic and chill at least 1 hour.

❿ Rotate the block of dough 90 degrees so that the folded edge is on your left and the dough faces you like a book. Roll out the dough again into a smooth, even rectangle, approximately 10 inches × 24 inches (25 centimeters × 60 centimeters).

⓫ Fold the dough in thirds again, completing the second turn. Cover the dough with plastic wrap and chill at least 30 minutes.

⓬ Repeat the rolling, folding and chilling technique until the dough has had a total of five turns. Cover the dough completely and chill overnight before shaping and baking.

Note: The détrempe can be made in a food processor. To do so, combine the flour, salt and pieces of soft butter in the bowl of a food processor fitted with the metal blade. Process until a coarse meal is formed. With the processor running, add the water all at once. Turn the machine off as soon as the dough comes together to form a ball. Proceed with the remainder of the recipe.

Approximate values per 1-oz. (30-g) serving: **Calories** 120, **Total fat** 9 g, **Saturated fat** 6 g, **Cholesterol** 25 mg, **Sodium** 110 mg, **Total carbohydrates** 9 g, **Protein** 1 g, **Vitamin A** 8%

Bouchée filled with fruit and pastry cream.

Cheese straws.

Shaping Puff Pastry

Once puff pastry dough is prepared, it can be shaped into containers of various sizes and shapes. **Bouchées** are small puff pastry shells usually used for hors d'oeuvre or appetizers. **Vol-au-vents** are larger, deeper shells, often filled with savory mixtures for a main course. Although they may be simply round or square, special vol-au-vent cutters are available in the shape of fish, hearts or petals. **Feuilletées** are square, rectangular or diamond-shaped puff pastry boxes. They can be filled with a sweet or savory mixture.

It is not necessary to work with the entire block of dough when making bouchées, cookies or the like. Cut the block into thirds or quarters and work with one of these portions at a time, keeping the rest chilled until needed. Roll out the dough on a workbench dusted lightly with flour. After rolling puff pastry but before cutting it into portions, refrigerate the dough for 30 minutes. This ensures that the cut pieces retain their shape after baking. Use a pastry or rolling cutter to make straight cuts in puff pastry. When a knife must be used, press its tip into the dough and cut by pressing down on the handle. Do not drag the knife through the dough or the layers will be crushed, preventing the dough from rising properly. Sheets of puff pastry to be baked into layers for Napoleons (page 303) are docked before baking, as are the centers of vol-au-vents and bouchées. Docking with a fork or docker ensures an even rise. The pastry can also be baked covered with parchment paper and a perforated sheet pan so that it bakes into flat and level layers.

Puff pastry scraps cannot be rerolled and used for products needing a high rise. The additional rolling destroys the layers. Scraps (known as **rognures**), however, can be used for palmiers (page 302), turnovers, decorative crescents (fleurons), tart shells, Napoleons (page 303) or any item for which rise is less important than flavor and flakiness. For best results, press the dough scraps into a 1-inch- (2.5-centimeter-) thick stack to maintain the integrity of the layers. Roll the dough out into an even rectangle. Fold the dough into thirds and refrigerate overnight. The next day, roll, cut and bake as required.

Care should be taken when applying egg wash to puff pastry products. Any wash that drips down the cut sides can prevent rise. For a shiny brown surface, five minutes before it finishes baking, brush the puff pastry with simple syrup and return it to the oven.

bouchées (boo-SHAY) small puff pastry shells that can be filled and served as bite-size hors d'oeuvre or petit fours

vol-au-vents (vul-oh-vanz) deep, individual portion-sized puff pastry shells, often shaped as a heart, fish or fluted circle; they are filled with a savory mixture and served as an appetizer or main course

feuilletées (fuh-yuh-TAY) square, rectangular or diamond-shaped puff pastry boxes; may be filled with a sweet or savory mixture

rognures French for "trimmings" or "scraps"; ususally refers to scraps of uncooked dough

PROCEDURE FOR CUTTING UNIFORM PIECES OF PUFF PASTRY DOUGH

1. Roll out the puff pastry dough into an even rectangle, approximately ⅛ to ¼ inch (3 to 6 millimeters) thick. Square off the edges of the dough using a pastry cutter and a straightedge, reserving the scraps for other uses.

2. Measure horizontally along the top edge of the dough and mark the dough, without cutting through it, with the tip of a knife or pastry cutter spaced every 4 inches (10 centimeters) from the left to right, to use as cutting guides.

3. Repeat this step, measuring the same amount vertically across the dough. Use the straightedge to connect the guides and cut the dough into uniform squares.

PROCEDURE FOR SHAPING VOL-AU-VENTS AND BOUCHÉES

1. Roll out the puff pastry dough to a thickness of approximately ¼ inch (6 millimeters).
2. Cut the desired shape and size using a vol-au-vent cutter or rings.
3. Place the vol-au-vent or bouchée on a paper-lined sheet pan. If you used rings, place the base on the paper-lined sheet pan, brush lightly with water, then top it with the dough ring; score the edge with the back of a paring knife. Chill 20 to 30 minutes to allow the dough to relax before baking.
4. Brush with egg wash if desired and dock the center with a fork.

1. A vol-au-vent cutter looks like a double cookie cutter with one cutter about 1 inch (2.5 centimeters) smaller than the other. To cut the pastry, simply position the cutter and press down.

2. To shape with rings, use two rings, one approximately 1 inch (2.5 centimeters) smaller than the other. The larger ring is used to cut two rounds. One will be the base and is set aside. Use the smaller ring to cut out an interior circle from the second round, leaving a border ring of dough.

PROCEDURE FOR SHAPING MEDALLIONS

1. Roll out the puff pastry dough approximately ⅛ to ¼ inch (3 to 6 millimeters) thick and cut it into even 4-inch (10-centimeter) squares (upper left). Fold each square in half diagonally. Cut through two sides of the dough, about ½ inch (1.2 centimeters) from the edge. Cut a V, being careful not to cut through the corners (upper right). Pull the sides of the dough out (lower left) and bring the sides of the dough together to form a loop, pinching them together to seal (lower right).
2. Chill the dough 20 to 30 minutes before baking. Brush with egg wash if desired.
3. Bake the medallion until golden and well risen. Fill the baked medallion with cream filling or jam. Brush the baked pastry with glaze.

PROCEDURE FOR SHAPING FEUILLETÉES

1. Roll out the puff pastry dough into an even rectangle, approximately ⅛ to ¼ inch (3 to 6 millimeters) thick. Square off the edges of the dough using a pastry cutter and a straightedge, reserving the scraps for other uses.

2. Using a sharp paring knife or chef's knife, cut squares that are about 2 inches (5 centimeters) larger than the desired interior of the finished feuilletée.

3. Fold each square in half diagonally. Cut through two sides of the dough, about ½ inch (1.2 centimeters) from the edge. Cut a V, being careful not to cut through the corners at the center fold.

4. Open the square and lay it flat. Brush water on the edges to seal the dough. Lift opposite sides of the cut border at the cut corners and cross them.

5. Place the feuilletées on a paper-lined sheet pan.

6. Score the edges with the back of a paring knife. Chill 20 to 30 minutes to allow the dough to relax before baking.

7. Brush with egg wash if desired and dock the center with a fork.

PROCEDURE FOR MAKING CHEESE STRAWS

1. Roll out the puff pastry dough approximately ⅛ to ¼ inch (3 to 6 millimeters) thick. The length is not important, but the width should be at least 7 inches (17.5 centimeters). Brush off any flour that clings to the dough. Brush the dough with egg wash or flavored butter and sprinkle with grated hard cheese such as Parmesan, Cheddar or Gruyère.

2. Cut the dough into thin strips measuring approximately ¾ inch (2 centimeters) wide and 7 inches (17 centimeters) long using a rolling cutter. Pick up each strip and twist both ends three or four times, then place on paper-lined sheet pans.

3. Bake at 400°F (200°C) until the twists are evenly browned, approximately 8 to 12 minutes.

PROCEDURE FOR SHAPING CREAM HORNS

① Cut puff pastry into narrow strips. Wrap one strip around a cream horn form, overlapping each piece slightly. Press one side into pearl sugar.

② The finished cream horns are filled with crème Chantilly.

YEAST-RAISED LAMINATED DOUGH

Viennoiserie the term applied to the category of enriched pastry doughs, which includes brioche, croissants, Danish pastries and other laminated dough products

Croissant and Danish doughs are made from an enriched yeast dough that, like puff pastry, is laminated with fat. This category of luscious pastry is referred to as **Viennoiserie**. Unlike many sweet doughs discussed in Chapter 8, Enriched Yeast Breads, most of the fat in Danish and croissant dough is incorporated through the lamination process. Danish dough contains eggs and more sugar than croissant dough, making it richer and sweeter. Virtually all of the fat in croissant dough is incorporated by lamination, making it flakier. These enriched doughs are prepared following most of the 10 production stages for making yeast breads discussed in Chapter 7, Artisan and Yeast Breads. The principal differences are that (1) butter is incorporated through the turning process described earlier in this chapter after the dough base is fermented and punched down; (2) rolled-in doughs are portioned somewhat differently from other yeast doughs; and (3) the portions are shaped without rounding.

The enriched yeast doughs used for croissant and Danish pastries are leavened by the yeast in the dough, the steam escaping from the moisture in the layered fat, and eggs, if present, in the formula. These products bake into tender soft-crusted pastries with a distinctive flakiness. The quantity of fat in these doughs is very high, as much as 50 percent of the total dough weight. Because fat and sugar inhibits gluten development, these formulas often use higher-protein flour. Careful handling of the dough in all stages ensures a tender flaky product.

Production Stages for Yeast-Raised Rolled-In Doughs

The production of yeast-raised rolled-in dough can be divided into 10 stages:

① Scaling the ingredients.

② Mixing and kneading the dough.

③ Fermenting the dough.

④ Preparing the roll-in fat.

⑤ Laminating the fat in the dough.

⑥ Make-up: portioning the dough.

⑦ Filling the dough.

⑧ Proofing the products.

⑨ Baking the products.

⑩ Glazing, cooling and storing.

Fruit-filled Danish pastries.

STAGE 1: SCALING THE INGREDIENTS

As with all bakeshop preparations, careful measuring of ingredients helps ensure accurate results. The temperature of the dough should be cool yet not so cold as to harden the fat.

STAGE 2: MIXING AND KNEADING THE DOUGH

Croissant and Danish dough may be mixed using a straight dough or sponge mixing method. The dough base should not be kneaded too much, as gluten will continue to develop during the rolling and folding process. If the dough is fully developed during kneading, it may be difficult to roll.

STAGE 3: FERMENTING THE DOUGH

Dough for croissants and Danish is fermented until it doubles in bulk, approximately 1 to 3 hours. Better results are obtained, however, when the dough is retarded overnight before laminating; it enhances the flavor development in the dough and relaxes the gluten, making the dough easier to handle. Retard the dough overnight to relax the gluten before laminating the next day.

STAGE 4: PREPARING THE ROLL-IN FAT

The roll-in fat used in croissant and Danish dough is softened (conditioned) in a mixer or on a workbench with a dough scraper before use. It should be kept cool during lamination. The fat should be the same consistency as the dough. As with puff pastry, croissant and Danish dough are best laminated with butter. However, specially formulated shortenings may be used for ease of handling and cost savings.

STAGE 5: LAMINATING THE FAT IN THE DOUGH

The dough is rolled out and topped with the roll-in fat prepared earlier. The fat may be spread evenly over the dough or, when formed into a block, wrapped in the dough. The turning and folding process used for croissant and Danish dough is the same as that used to laminate puff pastry illustrated on pages 275 to 277. The number of turns and type of folds used is according to preference; generally croissant and Danish dough get fewer turns than puff pastry, however. Special attention should be paid to the temperature of the dough during roll-in; because yeasted doughs are softer than the détrempe used for puff pastry, it is essential to chill the dough thoroughly in the refrigerator or freezer between turns.

   An electric dough sheeter is common in bakeshops where these products are made, saving time and ensuring product consistency. Croissants and Danish pastries can be made from start to finish in one day, but a two-day process eases the organization schedule of the workplace. Yeasted laminated dough may also be retarded after lamination, a technique used by artisan bakers for added flavor development as well as for convenience.

STAGE 6: MAKE-UP: PORTIONING THE DOUGH

Laminated yeast dough is not rolled and rounded like the yeast doughs in Chapter 7, Artisan and Yeast Breads. Instead, to preserve the layers in the dough, it is flattened with a rolling pin or sheeter to an even thickness. The dough is then cut into portions to be formed into shapes such as the croissant.

STAGE 7: FILLING THE DOUGH

Laminated doughs are frequently filled with custard, fruit or nut fillings. Uncooked fillings that contain eggs, such as **frangipane** (an almond cream filling; see page 295), must be added before the pastries bake. Fillings are added before proofing when the shaping of the dough requires it, such as for bear claws or filled croissants. Some bakers prefer, when possible, to add fillings after the dough is proofed to allow the dough to rise more fully.

THE CULTURED CROISSANT

A croissant brings to mind a Parisian sidewalk café and a steaming cup of café crème. It is, however, a truly international delicacy. According to historian Jim Chevalier in *Dictionnaire Universel du Pain*, crescent-shaped bread existed since ancient times and was popular in Vienna as early as the 13th century. August Zang introduced *kipferl* (crescent) bread to France in 1829 when he opened his Viennese Bakery. His success inspired imitators among French bakers who adopted the rich bread delicacy. But it was not until the early 20th century that the croissant was made from laminated dough. The first machine for mass-producing croissants was designed by a Japanese firm and manufactured in Italy. Although croissants became popular in the United States only during the late 20th century, Americans now consume millions of croissants each year.

STAGE 8: PROOFING THE PRODUCTS

Laminated yeast doughs are proofed at a low temperature, 80°F (27°C) with high humidity (80 percent) if using a proof box, to keep the butter from melting during proofing. Slight underproofing, until the dough expands 70 to 75 percent in volume, ensures a fully risen product after baking. The amount of fat weakens the gluten, making these pastries fragile when fully proofed.

Many bakeshops prepare croissants and Danish pastries once a week. The unbaked products are frozen as soon as they are shaped. Then daily, the raw frozen pastries are removed from the freezer (usually in the afternoon) and thawed overnight under refrigeration. The next morning the croissants or Danish pastries are proofed and baked.

STAGE 9: BAKING THE PRODUCTS

Laminated doughs are carefully brushed with egg wash before baking. Croissants and Danish pastries are baked at 375°F to 400°F (190°C to 200°F) to ensure a good rise.

STAGE 10: GLAZING, COOLING AND STORING

Once they are baked, Danish pastries are often coated with thin glazes or icings such as those discussed in Chapter 13, Cakes and Icings. A light wash with a sugar syrup or fondant glaze when the Danish pastries are still hot from the oven sweetens the crust without softening it. Pastries made from laminated yeast dough should cool before packaging to preserve their crisp crust. They may be stored loosely covered in plastic under refrigeration or in the freezer.

A formula for a rich Parisian croissant using a fully developed direct dough illustrates the mixing, rolling and folding technique for croissant dough. Later in this chapter (on page 304), a variation is offered, a formula with short fermentation times that is retarded overnight after lamination.

PROCEDURE FOR PREPARING YEAST-RAISED ROLLED-IN DOUGHS

1. Mix the dough and allow it to rise.

2. Prepare the butter or shortening for lamination.

3. Roll out the dough evenly, then top it with the butter. The butter may be formed into a rectangle to be enclosed in the dough, or it may be softened and spread on the dough.

4. Fold the dough around the butter, enclosing it completely.

5. Roll out the dough into a rectangle, approximately ¼ to ½ inch (0.6 to 1.2 centimeters) thick. Always be sure to roll at right angles; do not roll haphazardly or in a circle as for other pastry doughs.

6. Fold the dough as directed. Be sure to brush off any excess flour from between the folds. Chill the dough 20 to 30 minutes.

7. Roll out the dough and fold it in the same manner a second and third time, allowing the dough to rest between each turn. After completing the third turn, wrap the dough carefully and allow it to rest, refrigerated, several hours or overnight before shaping and baking. (Additional turns may be given to this dough, although four are common.)

PARISIAN CROISSANTS

Yield: 60 Rolls

Method: Rolled-in dough

Fermentation: Approximately 1 hour, chill overnight

Proofing: 45 minutes

Bread flour	2 lb. 4 oz.	1080 g	100%
Salt	1 oz.	30 g	3%
Granulated sugar	6 oz.	180 g	17%
Milk	21 fl. oz.	625 ml	58%
Active dry yeast	1 oz.	30 g	3%
Unsalted butter, softened	1 lb. 8 oz.	720 g	67%
Egg wash	as needed	as needed	
Total dough weight:	5 lb. 9 oz.	2665 g	248%

MISE EN PLACE

▶ Soften butter.
▶ Prepare the egg wash before shaping the dough.

1. Stir the flour, salt and sugar together in the bowl of a 6 quart (6.5 liter) or larger mixer fitted with a dough hook.
2. Warm the milk to approximately 90°F (32°C). Stir in the yeast.
3. Add the milk-and-yeast mixture to the dry ingredients. Stir until combined, then knead on medium speed 10 minutes.
4. Place the dough in a large floured bowl, cover and let rise until doubled in size, approximately 1 hour.
5. Prepare the butter while the dough is rising. Place the butter in an even layer between two large pieces of plastic wrap and roll into a flat rectangle, approximately 8 inches × 11 inches (20 centimeters × 27.5 centimeters) and chill.
6. After the dough has risen, punch it down. Roll out the dough into a large rectangle, approximately ½ inch (1.2 centimeters) thick and large enough to enclose the rectangle of butter. Place the unwrapped butter in the center of the dough and fold the dough around the butter, enclosing it completely.
7. Roll out the block of dough into a long rectangle, approximately 1 inch (2.5 centimeters) thick. Fold the dough in thirds, a single book fold. This completes the first turn. Wrap the dough in plastic and chill approximately 20 to 30 minutes.
8. Repeat the rolling and folding process two more times, chilling the dough between each turn. When finished, wrap the dough well and chill it overnight before shaping and baking.
9. To shape the dough into croissant rolls, cut off one-quarter of the block at a time, wrapping the rest and returning it to the refrigerator. Roll each quarter of dough into a large rectangle, approximately ¼ inch (6 millimeters) thick.
10. Cut the dough into uniform triangles. Starting with the large end, roll each triangle into a crescent and place on paper-lined sheet pans.
11. Brush lightly with egg wash. Proof until doubled, but do not allow the dough to become so warm that the butter melts.
12. Bake at 375°F (190°C) until golden brown, approximately 12 to 15 minutes.

Approximate values per roll: Calories 200, **Total fat** 12 g, **Saturated fat** 7 g, **Cholesterol** 40 mg, **Sodium** 230 mg, **Total carbohydrates** 19 g, **Protein** 3 g, **Vitamin A** 10%

① Rolling out the butter between two sheets of plastic wrap.

② Folding the dough around the butter, which has been placed in the center.

③ Brushing the excess flour from the rolled-out dough.

④ Folding the dough in thirds.

⑤ The finished croissant dough.

⑥ Cutting the dough intro triangles.

⑦ Baked croissants.

Shaping Croissants

PROCEDURE FOR FORMING CROISSANTS USING A ROLLING CUTTER

Trim the edges of the flattened croissant dough to an even rectangle using a ruler. Use the croissant cutter (upper right) to mark cutting guides on the dough. With a rolling cutter, divide the dough into even triangles using the marks made by the croissant cutter as guidelines. Reserve scraps to be reworked.

PROCEDURE FOR FORMING A FILLED CROISSANT

Cut a ½-inch (1.2-centimeter) slit in the short end of the triangle of croissant dough (upper left). Place a few strips of cooked bacon, ham, cheese or other filling along the scored edge (upper right). Roll up the dough starting from the filled end (lower left). Finish rolling with the pointed end of the dough tucked under the croissant before baking (lower right).

PROCEDURE FOR FORMING A CHOCOLATE-FILLED CROISSANT

Cut the flattened croissant dough into 3-inch × 4-inch (7.5-centimeter × 10-centimeter) rectangles (center left). Place a chocolate bâtonnet along the bottom edge of the dough (center) and roll once until the chocolate is covered (center right). Place another bâtonnet (bottom left) and continue rolling until the chocolate is completely covered. Place the rolled dough with the seam tucked underneath (bottom center). Use a dowel to even the edges of the dough (bottom right).

Danish Pastry

According to baking lore, Danish pastry was actually created by a French baker more than 350 years ago. He forgot to knead butter into his bread dough and attempted to cover the mistake by folding in softened butter. This rich, flaky pastry is now popular worldwide for breakfasts, desserts and snacks. The dough may be shaped in a variety of ways and is usually filled with jam, fruit, cream or marzipan. Applying a sugar syrup wash to the pastries when they are hot from the oven adds sheen and flavor.

The butter used to create the flakiness in the layers of Danish pastry may be locked in using the same technique as for croissants, illustrated on page 275. Alternately, the butter may be softened and spread on the dough.

MISE EN PLACE

▶ Adjust the temperature of the water and milk.

▶ Prepare the lock-in butter while the dough ferments.

❶ Rolling out the dough.

❷ Folding the dough in thirds to complete a turn.

DANISH PASTRY DOUGH

Yield: 36 Pastries

Method: Rolled-in dough

Fermentation: Dough, 1 to 1½ hours. During lamination, 3 hours

Proofing: 15 to 20 minutes

Active dry yeast	0.5 oz.	15 g	2.5%
Bread flour	10 oz.	300 g	50%
All-purpose flour	10 oz.	300 g	50%
Granulated sugar	4 oz.	120 g	20%
Water (temperature controlled)	4 fl. oz.	120 ml	20%
Milk (temperature controlled)	4 fl. oz.	120 ml	20%
Eggs, room temperature	3.3 oz. (2 eggs)	100 g	16%
Salt	0.2 oz. (1 tsp.)	6 g	1%
Vanilla extract	0.15 fl. oz. (1 tsp.)	4 ml	0.7%
Cinnamon, ground	0.04 oz. (½ tsp.)	1 g	0.2%
Unsalted butter, melted	1.5 oz.	45 g	7.5%
Unsalted butter, cold	1 lb.	480 g	80%
Egg wash	as needed	as needed	
Granulated sugar (optional)	as needed	as needed	
Total dough weight:	3 lb. 5 oz.	1611 g	268%

❶ In a large bowl, stir together the yeast and 12 ounces (360 grams) of the combined flours. Add the sugar, water, milk, eggs, salt, vanilla, cinnamon and melted butter. Stir until well combined.

❷ Add the remaining flour gradually, kneading the dough by hand or with a mixer fitted with a dough hook. Knead until the dough is smooth and only slightly tacky to the touch, approximately 2 to 3 minutes.

❸ Place the dough in a bowl that has been lightly dusted with flour. Cover and refrigerate for 1 to 1½ hours.

❹ Prepare the lock-in butter while the dough is chilling. First place the cold butter between two sheets of parchment paper or plastic film. Use a rolling pin to soften the butter so that it remains firm yet pliable like clay. Shape the butter into a 10-inch × 9-inch (25-centimeter × 22-centimeter) rectangle. The butter should still be cold. If it begins to melt, refrigerate it until firm. Keep the butter chilled until the dough is ready.

❺ On a lightly floured surface, roll the dough out into a rectangle about 12 inches × 18 inches (30 centimeters × 45 centimeters). Brush away any excess flour.

❻ Peel off the parchment or plastic and place the chilled butter on the left side of the dough. Fold the dough over, enclosing the butter. Press the edges together to seal in the butter.

❼ Roll the dough into a rectangle about 12 inches × 18 inches (30 centimeters × 45 centimeters). Fold the dough using the single book fold method. This rolling and folding (called a turn) must be done a total of six times. Chill the dough between turns as necessary. After the final turn, wrap the dough well and retard for at least 4 hours or overnight.

❽ Shape and fill the Danish dough as desired. Place the shaped pastries on paper-lined baking sheets and proof for approximately 15 to 20 minutes.

❾ Brush the pastries with egg wash and sprinkle lightly with sugar, if desired. Bake at 400°F (200°C) for 5 minutes. Decrease the oven temperature to 350°F (170°C) and bake until light brown, approximately 12 to 15 minutes.

Approximate values per pastry, without filling: **Calories** 85, **Total fat** 1.5 g, **Saturated fat** 0 g, **Cholesterol** 15 mg, **Sodium** 65 mg, **Total carbohydrates** 15.5 g, **Protein** 2 g

FORMING AND FILLING DANISH PASTRIES

Danish pastries may be rolled and cut into many of the same shapes as for puff pastry illustrated on pages 282 to 284. (Puff pastry may also be rolled and formed into many of the following shapes.) For best results, roll the dough out to a thickness of ¼ inch (6 millimeters) then cut and fold into various shapes before proofing. Allow the pastries to increase 70 to 75 percent in volume before baking.

Assortment of Danish pastries.

PROCEDURE FOR MAKING FRUITBASKETS AND TURNOVERS

For fruitbaskets, divide the rolled Danish dough into even 4-inch (10-centimeter) diamonds (upper left). Fold the right and left points into the center of the dough (center left). Fold the top and bottom points into the center (lower left). Proof, bake and fill. For turnovers, divide the Danish dough into 4-inch (10-centimeter) diamonds (upper right). Place a small amount of almond paste, frangipane or cheese filling on the dough (center right). Bring together two points of the dough to cover the filling (lower right), pinching them to seal.

PROCEDURE FOR MAKING SNAIL DANISH

Cut the rolled Danish dough into strips measuring 10 inches (25 centimeters) long and ½ inch (1.2 centimeters) wide. Sprinkle each strip generously with cinnamon and sugar. Twist the strip of dough several times so that the sugar mixture is caught inside the dough. Then twist the strip. Coil the dough into a tight circle (snail) shape.

PROCEDURE FOR SHAPING PINWHEELS OR WINDMILLS

Roll out the puff pastry or Danish dough approximately ⅛ to ¼ inch (3 to 6 millimeters) thick and cut it into even 4-inch (10-centimeter) squares (upper left). Starting at each corner, make four diagonal cuts 1 inch (2.5 centimeters) long in the dough without cutting the dough in half (upper right). Fold one point in each triangular section of dough down toward the center to form the pinwheel shape (lower left and right).

PROCEDURE FOR SHAPING BEAR CLAWS

Roll out the puff pastry or Danish dough approximately ⅛ to ¼ inch (3 to 6 millimeters) thick and cut it into even 4-inch (10-centimeter) squares (upper left). Place approximately 2 ounces (30 grams) almond paste, frangipane or other filling in the center of the dough (lower left). Moisten the edges of the dough with water, then fold the dough over to enclose the filling (upper right). Seal the edges of the pastry. With a pastry cutter or knife, cut short incisions along one edge of the pastry spaced ½ inch (1.2 centimeters) apart (center right). Curve the pastry slightly before placing it on the baking sheet (lower left).

PROCEDURE FOR MAKING TWISTED FRUIT DANISH

Cut the rolled Danish dough into rectangles measuring 2 inches × 4 inches (5 centimeters × 10 centimeters) (top left). Cut a short slit in the center of the dough (top center). Tuck one end of the dough through the opening. Grab it from the other side and pull it through the opening (top right). Flatten slightly. Repeat with the other side (bottom left). Pipe a small amount of pastry cream onto the dough (bottom center) and top with fruit preserves (bottom right).

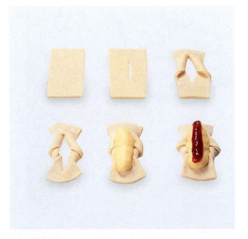

PROCEDURE FOR MAKING CANDIED FRUIT STRIPS

From the left, cut the rolled Danish dough into a rectangle measuring 12 inches × 18 inches (30 centimeters × 45 centimeters). Spread half of the dough with fruit preserves. Sprinkle it with finely chopped candied cherries, lemon peel or other fruit. Cut the dough into strips 1½ inches (3.8 centimeters) wide. Fold the dough over to cover the jam and fruit. Press lightly to seal, then apply egg wash.

PROCEDURE FOR MAKING SNAIL AND PRETZEL DANISH

From the left, cut the rolled Danish dough into strips measuring 10 inches (25 centimeters) long and ¾ inch (2 centimeters) wide. Spread half of each strip with fruit preserves. Fold the dough over so that the preserves are covered between two layers of dough. Then twist the strip. Coil the dough into a tight circle (snail) or pretzel shape.

PROCEDURE FOR MAKING A BRAIDED DANISH COFFEECAKE

Cut the rolled Danish dough into a rectangle measuring 14 inches × 8 inches (35 centimeters × 20 centimeters). Fold the dough over a narrow rolling pin. With a pastry cutter or sharp knife, make incisions along the overlapping edges of the dough spaced ¾ inch (1.8 centimeters) apart (left). Carefully unroll the dough. Cut a piece of spongecake to fit in the center of the pastry dough. Pipe alternating rows of pastry cream and fruit preserves on top of the spongecake. Fold the dough strips over the filling in a crisscross pattern (right).

TABLE 9.1 TROUBLESHOOTING CHART FOR ROLLED-IN DOUGH

PROBLEM	CAUSE	SOLUTION
Dough tears when rolling	Weak flour	Use higher-protein flour
	Gluten too elastic	Rest dough longer before rolling
Fat breaks through when rolling	Dough too warm	Chill dough properly
	Dough too soft	Use higher-protein flour
	Fat too cold	Make certain fat and dough are the same temperature when rolling
Lacks volume when baked	Improper proofing	Proof correctly
	Crust formed before product was baked	Proofer needs more moisture; egg wash before proofing
Product greasy	Too much fat in formula	Adjust formula
	Fat too soft during roll-in	Chill roll-in fat
	Insufficient chilling time between folds	Chill dough longer
	Proofed at too high temperature	Adjust proofing temperature
Product not flaky	Insufficient fat; improper fat used	Adjust formula; use proper fat
	Dough and fat too warm at outset; insufficient chilling time between folds	Prechill dough and fat; chill dough longer
	Proofed at too high temperature	Adjust proofing temperature
Product tough	Fat leaks out of product during baking	Proof at proper temperature
Product flattens, spreads during baking	Overproofed	Proof at proper temperature
Puff pastry rises unevenly	Improper distribution of fat during lamination	Chill lock-in fat properly
		Form lock-in fat evenly into block before rolling
	Dough cut improperly	Use sharp knife or dough cutters
		Do not drag the knife through the dough when portioning

FILLINGS FOR DANISH PASTRIES

Danish pastries may be filled with fruit preserves, cream cheese, sweetened farmer's cheese or custard fillings before or after baking. Fillings containing raw eggs must be baked with the dough, however. A light glaze or drizzle of fondant icing may be added after baking to complete the presentation.

CREAM CHEESE FILLING

Yield: 2 lb. 4 oz. (1091 g)

Cream cheese	1 lb. 8 oz.	720 g
Granulated sugar	4 oz.	120 g
Eggs	4.8 oz. (3 eggs)	144 g
Vanilla extract	0.5 fl. oz.	15 ml
Lemon zest, grated fine	0.07 oz. (1 tsp.)	2 g
Pastry or all-purpose flour	3 oz.	90 g

1. In the bowl of a mixer fitted with the paddle attachment, blend the cream cheese and sugar on low speed until smooth. Scrape down the bowl and gradually add the eggs, scraping the bowl between each addition.
2. Stir in the vanilla and lemon zest. Fold in the flour.
3. Fill pastries with this mixture before baking.

Approximate values per 1-oz. (30-g) serving: **Calories** 100, **Total fat** 6 g, **Saturated fat** 4 g, **Cholesterol** 25 mg, **Sodium** 75 mg, **Total carbohydrates** 10 g, **Protein** 1 g

MISE EN PLACE
▶ Grate the lemon zest.

Piping cream cheese filling onto rectangles of Danish dough.

FRANGIPANE

Yield: 2 lb. 2 oz. (1010 g)

Almond paste	1 lb.	480 g
Granulated sugar	2 oz.	60 g
Unsalted butter, softened	7 oz.	210 g
Eggs	6.75 oz. (4 eggs)	200 g
Vanilla extract	0.5 fl. oz.	15 ml
Cake flour	1.5 oz.	45 g

1. In the bowl of a mixer fitted with the paddle attachment, blend the almond paste and sugar on low speed until lump-free with a sandy texture.
2. Gradually add the butter in small amounts, waiting for each addition of butter to be incorporated before adding more.
3. Add in the eggs one at a time, waiting for each to be fully incorporated before adding the next one. Scrape down the bowl between each addition. Mix on medium speed 5 minutes or until the mixture is light and airy. Stir in the vanilla, then add the flour, blending until the mixture is smooth and pipeable.
4. Fill pastries with this mixture before baking.

Approximate values per 1-oz. (30-g) serving: **Calories** 120, **Total fat** 9 g, **Saturated fat** 3.5 g, **Cholesterol** 35 mg, **Sodium** 10 mg, **Total carbohydrates** 9 g, **Protein** 2 g

MISE EN PLACE
▶ Soften butter.

ALMOND PASTE FILLING

Yield: Approximately 2 lb. (973 g)

Almond paste, room temperature	20 oz.	600 g
Unsalted butter, softened	8 oz.	240 g
Salt	0.1 oz. (½ tsp.)	3 g
Vanilla extract	0.3 fl. oz. (2 tsp.)	10 ml
Egg whites	3 oz. (3 whites)	90 g

1. Blend the almond paste until smooth in the bowl of a mixer fitted with the paddle attachment. Add in the butter in four increments, waiting for the butter to be fully incorporated before adding more. Add the salt and vanilla, and then the egg whites. Blend well.
2. Fill pastries with this mixture before baking.

Variation:

Pistachio Almond Paste Filling—Combine 6 ounces (180 grams) pistachios and 1.5 ounces (45 grams) pistachio compound in a food processor and blend until smooth. Combine the pistachio mixture with the almond paste, butter, salt and 10 ounces (300 grams) sugar. Omit the vanilla. Moisten with 7 to 8 ounces (210 to 240 grams) egg whites.

Approximate values per 1-oz. (30-g) serving: **Calories** 130, **Total fat** 11 g, **Saturated fat** 4 g, **Cholesterol** 15 mg, **Sodium** 45 mg, **Total carbohydrates** 9 g, **Protein** 2 g, **Claims**—gluten free

---

ALMOND CREAM

VINCENT ON CAMELBACK, PHOENIX, AZ
Chef Vincent Guerithault

Yield: 3 lb. (1480 kg)

Unsalted butter, softened	8 oz.	240 g
Granulated sugar	1 lb.	480 g
Eggs	8.3 oz. (5 eggs)	250 g
All-purpose flour	5 oz.	150 g
Almonds, ground	12 oz.	360 g

1. Cream the butter and sugar. Slowly add the eggs, scraping down the bowl as necessary.
2. Stir the flour and almonds together, then add to the butter mixture. Blend until no lumps remain.
3. Almond cream may be stored under refrigeration up to 3 weeks.
4. Fill pastries with this mixture before baking.

Approximate values per 1-oz. (30-g) serving: **Calories** 140, **Total fat** 8 g, **Saturated fat** 3 g, **Cholesterol** 30 mg, **Sodium** 5 mg, **Total carbohydrates** 13 g, **Protein** 2 g

RICOTTA CHEESE FILLING

Yield: 2 lb. 14 oz. (1395 g)

Cream cheese, softened	1 lb. 8 oz.	720 g
Ricotta	10 oz.	300 g
Granulated sugar	5 oz.	150 g
Eggs	3.3 oz. (2 eggs)	100 g
Vanilla extract	0.15 fl. oz. (1 tsp.)	5 ml
Pastry or all-purpose flour	4 oz.	120 g

MISE EN PLACE
▶ Soften cream cheese.

1. In the bowl of a mixer fitted with the paddle attachment, combine the cream cheese and ricotta on low speed until no lumps remain.
2. Add the sugar, gradually add the eggs and scrape down the bowl between additions.
3. Add the vanilla, followed by the flour, and combine well.
4. Fill pastries with this mixture before baking.

Approximate values per 1-oz. (30-g) serving: **Calories** 90, **Total fat** 6 g, **Saturated fat** 4 g, **Cholesterol** 25 mg, **Sodium** 50 mg, **Total carbohydrates** 6 g, **Protein** 2 g

THICKENED CHERRIES

Yield: 2 lb. 8 oz. (1200 g)

Cherries, IQF	2 lb.	960 g
Granulated sugar	8 oz.	240 g
Cornstarch	1.5 oz.	45 g
Water	3 fl. oz.	90 ml
Almond extract	0.04 fl. oz (¼ tsp.)	1 ml

1. Defrost the cherries, reserving their juices. Add water to the juice to obtain a total of 8 fluid ounces (240 milliliters).
2. In a nonreactive saucepan, bring the juice and sugar to a boil.
3. Combine the cornstarch and water and pour into the boiling juice. Whisk until thickened.
4. Remove from heat; fold in the cherries and almond extract. Cool before using.

Approximate values per 1-oz. (30-g) serving: **Calories** 45, **Total fat** 0 g, **Saturated fat** 0 g, **Cholesterol** 0 mg, **Sodium** 0 mg, **Total carbohydrates** 11 g, **Protein** 0 g

APRICOT FILLING

Yield: 2 lb. (961 g)

Dried apricots	8 oz.	240 g
Orange juice	1 pt.	480 ml
Granulated sugar	6 oz.	180 g
Salt	0.05 oz. (¼ tsp.)	1.5 g
Unsalted butter	2 oz.	60 g

1. Place the apricots and orange juice in a small saucepan. Cover and simmer until the apricots are very tender, approximately 25 minutes. Stir in the sugar and salt. When the sugar is dissolved, add the butter and remove from the heat.
2. Purée the mixture in a blender until smooth. Cool completely before using.

Approximate values per 1-oz. (30-g) serving: **Calories** 60, **Total fat** 1.5 g, **Saturated fat** 1 g, **Cholesterol** 5 mg, **Sodium** 20 mg, **Total carbohydrates** 13 g, **Protein** 0 g, **Vitamin A** 20%, **Vitamin C** 15%, **Claims**—gluten free, low fat; low sodium; good source of vitamins A and C

MISE EN PLACE

▸ Soften butter.

COCONUT CREAM FILLING

Yield: 1 lb. 1 oz. (521 g)

Unsalted butter, softened	4 oz.	120 g
Granulated sugar	5 oz.	150 g
Salt	0.2 oz. (1 tsp.)	6 g
Eggs	4 oz. (2½ eggs)	120 g
Vanilla extract	0.15 fl. oz. (1 tsp.)	5 ml
Macaroon coconut	4 oz.	120 g

1. In the bowl of a mixer fitted with the paddle attachment, cream the butter and sugar until smooth. Scrape down the bowl. Add the remaining ingredients on low speed and mix until well combined.
2. Fill pastries with this mixture before baking.

Approximate values per 1-oz. (30-g) serving: **Calories** 140, **Total fat** 10 g, **Saturated fat** 7 g, **Cholesterol** 40 mg, **Sodium** 140 mg, **Total carbohydrates** 10 g, **Protein** 2 g, **Claims**—gluten free

QUESTIONS FOR DISCUSSION

Terms to Know

rolled-in doughs	sheeter
laminated doughs	puff pastry
	pâte feuilletée
croissants	mille feuille
Danish pastry	blitz (quick puff
single book fold	pastry)
turns	lock in
double book fold	frangipane

1. Briefly describe the procedure for making a rolled-in dough, and give two examples of products made from rolled-in doughs.

2. Name the leaveners used in laminated dough.

3. Describe the effect that docking has on puff pastry and why this technique would be used.

4. What can happen if croissants and Danish pastries are proofed at high temperatures?

5. Explain the difference between *pâte feuilletée* and croissant dough. Which dough benefits from proofing?

6. Viennoiserie is an important category of breads prepared by bakers in international competitions. Use the Internet to research some formulas for Viennoiserie used by bakers competing in events such as the World Cup of Bread Baking (Coupe du Monde du Pain). Describe the types of dough and fillings used in these competitions. **WWW**

QUICK PUFF PASTRY

Adapted from Nick Malgieri's Perfect Pastry

Yield: 1 lb. 3 oz. (591 g)

Unbleached all-purpose flour	6.25 oz.	190 g	100%
Cake flour	1.25 oz.	38 g	20%
Unsalted butter	8 oz.	240 g	128%
Salt	0.1 oz. (½ tsp.)	3 g	1.6%
Water, very cold	4 fl. oz.	120 ml	64%
Total dough weight:	1 lb. 3 oz.	591 g	313%

1. To mix the dough, place the all-purpose flour in a 2-quart (2-liter) mixer bowl and sift the cake flour over it. Thoroughly stir the two flours together.

2. Slice 1 ounce (30 grams) of the butter into thin pieces and add to the bowl. Rub in the butter by hand, tossing and squeezing in the butter until no visible pieces remain.

3. Cut the remaining butter into ½-inch (1.2-centimeter) cubes. Add the butter cubes to the flour mixture. Toss with a rubber spatula just to separate and distribute the butter. Do not rub the butter into the flour.

4. Dissolve the salt in the water. Make a well in the flour-and-butter mixture and add the water. Toss gently with the spatula until the dough is evenly moistened. Add drops of water, if necessary, to complete the moistening. Press and squeeze the dough in a bowl to form a rough cylinder.

5. To turn the dough, first lightly flour the work surface and the dough. Using the palm of your hand, press down on the dough three or four times to shape the dough into a rough rectangle.

6. Press and pound the dough with a rolling pin to form an even rectangle about ½ inch (1.2 centimeters) thick. Roll the dough back and forth along its length once or twice until it is an even rectangle about ¼ inch (6 millimeters) thick. At this stage, pieces of butter are likely to stick to the work surface. If the dough does stick, loosen it with a long spatula or scraper. Clean the surface to minimize further sticking.

7. Fold both ends of the dough in toward the center, then fold them in toward the center again to make four layers, the double book fold. Position the package of dough so that the "spine" is on the left.

8. Lightly flour the work surface and the dough and repeat the pressing as before. Roll the dough along its length as before, then roll several times along its width to form a rectangle, approximately 6 inches × 18 inches (15 centimeters × 45 centimeters). Fold the dough into the double book fold as before. Repeat the process once more so that the dough will have three double turns.

9. Wrap the dough well in plastic and chill at least 1 hour before using.

10. The dough can be refrigerated about 3 days or frozen up to 1 month. Defrost frozen dough in the refrigerator overnight before using it.

Approximate values per 3-oz. (90-g) serving: **Calories** 480, **Total fat** 37 g, **Saturated fat** 23 g, **Cholesterol** 100 mg, **Sodium** 240 mg, **Total carbohydrates** 31 g, **Protein** 5 g, **Vitamin A** 35%

1. Adding water to the flour and butter cube mixture.

2. Pressing and gathering the dough into a uniform shape.

3. Rolling the dough into a rectangle.

❶ Filling the dough with the cherries.

❷ The finished turnovers.

CHERRY TURNOVERS

Yield: 18 Turnovers

Puff pastry	3 lb. 3 oz.	1530 g
Egg wash	as needed	as needed
Thickened Cherries (page 297)	2 lb. 8 oz.	1245 g
Simple Syrup (page 73)	as needed	as needed

❶ Position the dough with the seamless side parallel to the edge of the workbench and roll it into a rectangle 15 inches (38 centimeters) wide, 30 inches (76 centimeters) long and ⅛ inch (3 millimeters) thick.

❷ Cut the dough into uniform 5-inch (13-centimeter) squares using a pastry wheel.

❸ Lightly brush the dough with egg wash. Spoon some Thickened Cherries in the center of each square. Fold over one corner of each square of dough to form triangles and place them on a paper-lined baking sheet.

❹ Lightly brush the pastries with egg wash. Using scissors, cut a vent hole in the center of each pastry. Let the pastries rest for 15 minutes at room temperature, then bake them at 400°F (205°C) until golden. Reduce the heat to 360°F (183°C) and continue baking until baked through, approximately 30 to 40 more minutes.

❺ Brush the hot turnovers with Simple Syrup.

Approximate values per turnover: **Calories** 400, **Total fat** 25 g, **Saturated fat** 16 g, **Cholesterol** 65 mg, **Sodium** 310 mg, **Total carbohydrates** 41 g, **Protein** 4 g, **Vitamin A** 25%

INDIVIDUAL PUFF PASTRY FRUIT TARTS

Yield: 12 Tarts, 2½ in. (7.5 cm) each

Puff pastry, shaped into bouchées (page 282) and baked	12 bouchées	12 bouchées
Crème Brûlée for Tarts (page 518)	2 lb.	960 g
Strawberries	1 pt.	0.5 lt
Neutral glaze, flavored with raspberry purée	as needed	as needed
Raspberries	1 pt.	0.5 lt
Red currants	0.5 pt.	0.25 lt
Powdered sugar	as needed	as needed

❶ Fill the bouchées two-thirds full with the Crème Brûlée for Tarts.

❷ In a circular fashion, place the strawberries cut side up, overlapping one another.

❸ Using a pastry brush, glaze the strawberries with the raspberry glaze.

❹ Randomly sprinkle the raspberries and red currants on the strawberries.

❺ Dust the edges of the tarts with powdered sugar.

Approximate values per tart: **Calories** 520, **Total fat** 40 g, **Saturated fat** 24 g, **Cholesterol** 250 mg, **Sodium** 250 mg, **Total carbohydrates** 35 g, **Protein** 6 g, **Vitamin A** 25%, **Vitamin C** 60%

GATEAU PITHIVIERS

Yield: 1 Cake, 9 in. (22 cm)

Puff pastry	1 lb. 3 oz.	600 g
Frangipane (page 295)	10 oz.	300 g
Rum	1 fl. oz.	30 ml
Egg wash	as needed	as needed
Simple Syrup (page 73)	as needed	as needed

1. Roll out the puff pastry into a sheet 11 inches (28 centimeters) wide, 22 inches (56 centimeters) long and ⅛ inch (3 millimeters) thick.
2. Place the dough on a parchment-lined sheet pan. Cover with plastic. Refrigerate for 30 minutes.
3. Cut two 11-inch (28-centimeter) circles with the aid of a metal ring or a cake board. Return one puff pastry round to the refrigerator.
4. Combine the Frangipane with the rum. Using a piping bag fitted with a medium plain tip, pipe the filling into a tight spiral starting from the center of the puff pastry. Leave a generous 1.5-inch (4.5-centimeter) border along the edge of the dough.
5. Brush the edge with egg wash and place the remaining layer of puff pastry on top pressing gently to seal. Invert an 8- or 9-inch (19- or 22-centimeter) cake pan or pie tin over the cake. Using the pan as a guide, cut the edge into a scallop pattern with a sharp knife. (Refrigerate the dough if it seems too soft to cut easily.)
6. Brush the pastry with egg wash, then refrigerate the pastry for 30 minutes.
7. Brush with egg wash once more. Using a sharp knife or blade, incise the surface of the dough in a series of curved parallel lines forming a spoke pattern that radiates from the top center of the dough.
8. Bake at 375°F (190°C) until golden brown, approximately 50 minutes.
9. Brush the hot pastry with a thin coating of Simple Syrup. Return the pastry to the oven for 2 minutes. Cool to room temperature before serving.

Approximate values per ½₂-cake serving: **Calories** 300, **Total fat** 22 g, **Saturated fat** 12 g, **Cholesterol** 65 mg, **Sodium** 180 mg, **Total carbohydrates** 21 g, **Protein** 4 g

❶ Folding the dough toward the center from both edges.

❷ Slicing the log of dough into individual cookies.

PALMIERS

Puff pastry	as needed	as needed
Granulated sugar	as needed	as needed

❶ Roll out the puff pastry into a very thin rectangle. The length is not important, but the width should be at least 7 inches (17 centimeters).

❷ Using a rolling pin, gently press the sugar into the dough on both sides.

❸ Make a 1-inch (2.5-centimeter) fold along the long edges of the dough toward the center. Sprinkle on additional sugar.

❹ Make another 1-inch (2.5-centimeter) fold along the long edges of the dough toward the center. The two folds should almost meet in the center. Sprinkle on additional sugar.

❺ Fold one side on top of the other. Press down gently with a rolling pin or your fingers so that the dough adheres. Chill 1 hour.

❻ Cut the log of dough in thin slices. Place the cookies on a paper-lined sheet pan and bake at 400°F (200°C) until the edges are brown, approximately 8 to 12 minutes.

Approximate values per 1-oz. (30-g) serving: **Calories** 130, **Total fat** 5 g, **Saturated fat** 1 g, **Cholesterol** 0 mg, **Sodium** 35 mg, **Total carbohydrates** 19 g, **Protein** 1 g

❶ Assembling layers of puff pastry for fans.

❷ Puff Pastry Fans (top) and Palmiers (bottom).

PUFF PASTRY FANS

Yield: 24 to 28 Pastries

Granulated sugar, extra fine	14 oz.	420 g
Speculaas Spices (page 341; optional)	as needed	as needed
Puff pastry	3 lb. 8 oz.	1680 g

❶ Generously coat a work surface with granulated sugar. Sprinkle with Speculaas Spices (if using).

❷ Roll out the puff pastry in the sugar into a rectangle ⅛ inch (3 millimeters) thick. The length is not important, but the width should be at least 20 inches (50 centimeters).

❸ Cut the dough lengthwise into three strips, two strips measuring 8 inches (20 centimeters) wide and one strip measuring 4 inches (10 centimeters) wide.

❹ Fold each 8-inch strip of dough as for the Palmiers, above: Make a 2-inch (5-centimeter) fold along the long edges of each strip of the dough toward the center. Sprinkle on additional sugar.

❺ Place one folded 8-inch strip of dough on the work surface. Place the second folded 8-inch strip of dough directly on top of the first folded strip of dough.

❻ Fold the 4-inch (10-centimeter) strip of dough in half to make one 2-inch (5-centimeter) strip of dough. Position this strip of dough on top of the stack of dough strips, lining up the folded edge. Fold over the entire assembly to form one log of 10 layers of puff pastry.

❼ Press down firmly on the pastry log with your fingers or a rolling pin so that the dough adheres. Chill 1 hour.

❽ Cut the log of dough into ⅜-inch- (1-centimeter-) thick slices. Press the slices, cut side down, into additional granulated sugar. Place the slices spaced 2 inches (5 centimeters) apart onto buttered or paper-lined sheet pans. Let the dough rest for 30 minutes before baking.

❾ Bake at 400°F (200°C) until the edges of the pastries turn light golden brown, approximately 8 to 12 minutes. Using a wide spatula, flip over the pastries. Reduce the oven temperature to 375°F (190°C) and bake until golden, approximately 5 additional minutes.

Approximate values per pastry: **Calories** 310, **Total fat** 170 g, **Saturated fat** 12 g, **Cholesterol** 50 mg, **Sodium** 210 mg, **Total carbohydrates** 33 g, **Protein** 3 g

CREAM-FILLED NAPOLEONS

Yield: 12 to 14 Pastries

Puff pastry (scraps may be used)	1 lb. 14 oz.	900 g
Grand Marnier or rum (optional)	1.5 fl. oz.	45 ml
Pastry Cream (page 492)	2 lb.	960 g
Granulated sugar, extra fine	as needed	as needed
Powdered sugar	as needed	as needed

❶ Sheet of baked puff pastry.

❶ Roll the puff pastry $\frac{1}{12}$ inch (2 millimeters) thick into a rectangle measuring 13 inches × 24 inches (33 centimeters × 61 centimeters). Dock the dough and let it rest 30 minutes at room temperature.

❷ Bake at 375°F (190°C) for 12 to 14 minutes, then place a sheet of parchment paper over the dough. Cover the parchment paper with an icing screen or perforated sheet pan.

❸ Return the dough to the oven and bake until it is light golden brown, approximately 15 to 20 minutes. Remove the parchment paper. Replace the icing screen and reduce the temperature to 350°F (180°C). Bake until the dough is evenly baked through and golden brown, approximately 30 additional minutes. The total baking time will be nearly 1 hour.

❹ Let the pastry cool. Trim the edges and then cut it lengthwise into three equal strips. Set aside the flattest strip to use for the top of the finished dessert.

❺ Fold the Grand Marnier (if using) into the Pastry Cream. Using a pastry bag fitted with a large plain tip, pipe four rows of pastry cream lengthwise on one strip of baked puff pastry. Cover with another strip of puff pastry and top with the remaining pastry cream. Place the reserved strip of puff pastry on last.

❻ Using a sharp serrated knife, gently cut the assembled pastry into 1½-inch- (4-centimeter-) wide portions. Sprinkle the top of each pastry with a thin layer of extra fine granulated sugar. Using a blowtorch, melt the sugar until it lightly caramelizes.

❷ The finished Napoleon pastry.

❼ Mask half of each Napoleon with a strip of parchment paper. Sprinkle the exposed surfaces with powdered sugar. Serve within 2 hours of preparation.

Note: The puff pastry can also be caramelized in the oven; however, the final assembled pastry may be more difficult to slice. Cut one sheet of the baked puff pastry dough into three equal strips. Sprinkle with a thin layer of extra fine granulated sugar. Bake the pastry at 425°F (220°C) until well caramelized. Proceed from Step 5, then cut the assembled pastry carefully with a serrated knife.

Approximate values per 4½-oz. (135-g) serving: **Calories** 420, **Total fat** 29 g, **Saturated fat** 18 g, **Cholesterol** 195 mg, **Sodium** 280 mg, **Total carbohydrates** 36 g, **Protein** 5 g

CROISSANTS

The flakiest croissants are made with the highest percentage of butter. This artisan-style formula is among the richest, with nearly 30 percent more butter than Parisian Croissants (page 287). To complete the layering in only three turns, this formula uses a combination of the single book fold and the double book fold. For the best flavor development and to ease handling, retard this dough overnight before proofing and baking the finished products.

Yield: 35 Croissants, approximately 2½ oz. (75 g) each

Method: Rolled-in dough

Fermentation: 12 to 15 hours under retardation

Proofing: Approximately 1 hour

Dough:

Granulated sugar	4 oz.	120 g	12%
Salt	1 oz.	30 g	3%
Dry milk powder	1 oz.	30 g	3%
Egg	1.6 oz. (1 egg)	50 g	5%
Water, ice cold	18 fl. oz.	540 ml	56%
Vanilla extract	0.15 fl. oz. (1 tsp.)	5 ml	0.5%
Instant yeast	1 oz.	30 g	3%
Bread flour	2 lb.	960 g	100%
Unsalted butter, softened	1 lb. 14 oz.	900 g	94%
Total dough weight:	5 lb. 8 oz.	2665 g	276%

Egg wash:

Heavy cream	2 fl. oz.	60 ml
Eggs, lightly beaten	3.2 oz. (2 eggs)	100 g

1 Combine the sugar, salt, milk powder, egg, water and vanilla in the bowl of a 6 quart (6.5 liter) or larger mixer fitted with a dough hook. Stir until blended.

2 Add the yeast, the flour and 2 ounces (60 grams) of the butter to the mixing bowl. Mix 3 to 4 minutes on medium speed to make a smooth but soft dough.

3 Place the dough on a paper-lined sheet pan and refrigerate to chill thoroughly, approximately 30 minutes to 1 hour.

4 Mix the remaining butter in the bowl of a mixer fitted with the paddle attachment on low speed until pliable and lump-free, but still firm. Roll the butter into a 10-inch (25-centimeter) square between two sheets of plastic wrap or parchment paper. Keep the butter cold.

5 After the dough has chilled, place it on a lightly floured work surface and roll it into a rectangle, 11 inches × 21 inches (28 centimeters × 53 centimeters). Place the butter, which should have the same consistency as the dough, on the left side of the dough rectangle. Fold the right side of the dough over the butter and press on the ends to seal them closed.

6 Place the dough with a folded edge parallel to the edge of the table and roll the dough lengthwise until it is ½ inch (1.2 centimeters) thick. Fold the dough into thirds, making a single book fold.

7 Refrigerate until the dough is cold and firm, approximately 30 minutes to 1 hour. Roll the dough out into a rectangle approximately ½ inch (1.2 centimeters) thick, then fold into a double book fold. Cover well with plastic wrap and refrigerate.

8 Roll out and fold the dough into thirds, making a single book fold again. Refrigerate 1 hour.

9 Position the dough with the seamless side toward you and roll lengthwise to 15 inches (38 centimeters) wide and ⅛ inch (3 millimeters) thick.

10 Using a pastry wheel, cut the dough lengthwise in half to obtain two strips. Cut the strips into uniform triangles approximately 7½ inches (19 centimeters) long with a base width of 4½ inches (11 centimeters).

11 Roll the croissants from base to point, with the point tucked underneath the croissant, and bend the ends toward the center. Place the croissants on paper-lined sheet pans. Cover the croissants and retard in the refrigerator overnight.

12 Remove the croissants from the refrigerator and proof them until increased 70 percent in volume. Place the croissants in a proof box set to a maximum temperature of 80°F (27°C) with 80 percent humidity.

13 Combine the heavy cream and beaten eggs. Brush the proofed croissants with the egg wash. Bake at 425°F (220°C) until golden, approximately 18 to 20 minutes.

Approximate values per croissant: **Calories** 310, **Total fat** 22 g, **Saturated fat** 13 g, **Cholesterol** 80 mg, **Sodium** 330 mg, **Total carbohydrates** 23 g, **Protein** 5 g, **Vitamin A** 15%

ALMOND ORANGE CROISSANTS

Yield: 35 Croissants

Croissant dough, chilled	5 lb. 8 oz.	2640 g
Almond Paste Filling (page 296)	as needed	as needed
Orange marmalade	as needed	as needed
Eggs, beaten	3.3 oz. (2 eggs)	100 g
Heavy cream	3 fl. oz.	90 ml
Simple Syrup (page 73)	6 fl. oz.	180 ml
Orange Fondant Glaze (page 483)	as needed	as needed
Sliced almonds, toasted	8 oz.	240 g

Almond Orange Croissants

1 Roll out the croissant dough and cut into triangles.

2 Fill a pastry bag fitted with a medium plain tip with the Almond Paste Filling. Pipe a line of paste across the widest part of each dough triangle.

3 Fill another pastry bag fitted with a medium plain tip with the orange marmalade. Pipe a small mound of orange marmalade next to the almond paste.

4 Roll the croissants from base to tip. Place the formed croissants on paper-lined sheet pans without curving.

5 Proof the formed croissants until increased 70 percent in volume or retard them, covered, up to 24 hours.

6 Combine the eggs and heavy cream. Brush the proofed croissants with the egg wash.

7 Bake at 425°F (220°C) without steam until golden, approximately 18 to 20 minutes.

8 Brush the hot croissants with Simple Syrup. Cool, then brush them with the Orange Fondant Glaze. Sprinkle with the toasted sliced almonds.

VARIATIONS:

Macadamia and Ginger Jam Croissants—Substitute Sugar-Free Mango Ginger Jam (page 590) for the orange marmalade. Sprinkle some chopped macadamia nuts over the jam before rolling the croissants. Sprinkle more chopped macadamia nuts over the proofed croissants before baking. Omit the sliced almonds. Brush the hot croissants with Simple Syrup. Cool, then brush them with the Orange Fondant Glaze.

Chocolate Pistachio Croissants—Substitute Pistachio Almond Paste Filling (page 296) for the Almond Paste Filling. Omit the orange marmalade and the almonds. Pipe a line of paste on each dough triangle. Press a chocolate bâtonnet into the paste, then roll the dough into a straight log shape. Proof, brush with egg wash and sprinkle with chopped pistachios before baking.

Ham and Cheese Croissants—Slice ham and Gruyère cheese into thin strips (bâtonnets) and position approximately 1 ounce (30 grams) ham and ¾ ounce (22 grams) Gruyère cheese at the widest part of each of the dough triangles. Roll, proof and brush with egg wash as for filled croissants. Sprinkle additional grated Gruyère on the surface of the croissants before baking. Omit the Orange Fondant Glaze and Simple Syrup.

Ham and Cheese Croissant

Approximate values per croissant: **Calories** 350, **Total fat** 26 g, **Saturated fat** 14 g, **Cholesterol** 80 mg, **Sodium** 330 mg, **Total carbohydrates** 26 g, **Protein** 6 g, **Vitamin A** 15%

EUROPEAN DANISH DOUGH

The best lamination is achieved when working with dough at the proper temperature. In this artisan-style Danish dough formula, the dough is chilled at precise intervals. When time permits, an overnight retarding is recommended.

Yield: 5 lb. 1 oz. (2453 g) Dough

Method: Rolled-in dough

Fermentation: Dough, 30 minutes. During lamination, 2 to 3 hours

Proofing: 1 hour

Instant yeast	1 oz.	30 g	3%
Water (temperature controlled)	14 fl. oz.	420 ml	44%
Bread flour	2 lb.	960 g	100%
Granulated sugar	4 oz.	120 g	12%
Dry milk powder	1.25 oz.	38 g	4%
Vanilla extract	0.5 fl. oz.	15 ml	1.5%
Eggs	3.2 oz. (2 eggs)	100 g	10%
Unsalted butter, softened	3 oz.	90 g	9%
Salt	0.6 oz.	20 g	2%
Unsalted butter, cold	1 lb. 6 oz.	660 g	69%
Total dough weight:	5 lb. 1 oz.	2453 g	254%

1. Dissolve the yeast in the water in the bowl of a 6 quart (6.5 liter) or larger mixer fitted with a dough hook. Add the flour, sugar, milk powder, vanilla, eggs, softened butter and salt. Mix on low speed until the dough is uniform and smooth, approximately 4 minutes.

2. Flatten the dough onto a paper-lined sheet pan and place in the freezer or refrigerator until thoroughly chilled, approximately 30 minutes to 1 hour.

3. Beat the cold butter in the bowl of a mixer fitted with the paddle attachment on low speed until pliable and lump-free, but still firm.

4. Roll out the dough into a rectangle ½ inch (1.2 centimeters) thick. Spread the butter over half of the dough and fold the dough over to completely cover the buttered dough. Press the edges of the dough with a rolling pin to seal. Place the dough with the seamless side toward you and roll out the dough lengthwise ½ inch (1.2 centimeters) thick. Fold dough into thirds, making a single book fold.

5. Refrigerate until dough is cold and firm, approximately 30 minutes to 1 hour. Roll the dough, fold into a double book fold, and then wrap in plastic and refrigerate 1 hour to complete this second turn.

6. Give the dough a third turn using a single book fold. Wrap in plastic and refrigerate at least 1 hour before using. Dough may be stored in the refrigerator overnight before using. Form, proof and bake as desired.

Approximate values per 2-oz. (60-g) serving: **Calories** 220, **Total fat** 15 g, **Saturated fat** 9 g, **Cholesterol** 45 mg, **Sodium** 190 mg, **Total carbohydrates** 20 g, **Protein** 4 g, **Vitamin A** 10%

CINNAMON ROLLS

Yield: 45 Pastries

Danish dough, chilled	5 lb. 4 oz.	2520 g
Cinnamon Roll Paste (recipe follows)	3 lb.	1440 g
Pecans	1 lb.	480 g
Orange Fondant Glaze (page 483)	1 lb. 5 oz.	630 g
Pecan pieces	as needed	as needed

1 Roll the dough into a rectangle measuring 14 inches (35 centimeters) wide.

2 Spread the Cinnamon Roll Paste evenly over the rectangle, leaving ½ inch (1 centimeter) of each long edge clear. Sprinkle evenly with pecans.

3 Tightly roll the dough up from the bottom edge into a long tube. Cut ½-inch- (1.2-centimeter-) wide pieces from the dough with a sharp chef's knife.

4 Lay each cut piece flat on paper-lined sheet pans, tucking the end of the dough spiral underneath the center of each roll.

5 Proof the rolls until increased 90 percent in volume, or cover and retard the pastries.

6 Bake at 400°F (200°C) until evenly browned, approximately 18 to 20 minutes.

7 Cool the rolls, then brush liberally with Orange Fondant Glaze. Roll the edges of each pastry in pecan pieces.

Approximate values per pastry: **Calories** 430, **Total fat** 29 g, **Saturated fat** 12 g, **Cholesterol** 80 mg, **Sodium** 230 mg, **Total carbohydrates** 39 g, **Protein** 6 g, **Vitamin A** 15%

CINNAMON ROLL PASTE

Yield: 3 lb. (1452 g)

Unsalted butter, softened	8 oz.	240 g
Granulated sugar	9 oz.	270 g
Salt	0.2 oz. (1 tsp.)	6 g
Cinnamon, ground	2 oz.	60 g
Vanilla extract	0.5 fl. oz.	15 ml
Orange oil	5 drops	5 drops
Almond extract	0.04 fl. oz. (¼ tsp.)	1 ml
Eggs	6.75 oz. (4 eggs)	200 g
Almond flour	9 oz.	270 g
Cake flour	1 oz.	30 g
Pastry Cream (page 492)	12 oz.	360 g

1 In the bowl of a mixer fitted with the paddle attachment, mix the butter until creamy. Add the sugar, salt, cinnamon, vanilla, orange oil and almond extract. Scrape down the bowl and add the eggs, beating to combine.

2 Stir in the flours. Scrape down the bowl and fold in the Pastry Cream.

3 Use immediately or refrigerate for later use.

Approximate values per 1-oz. (30-g) serving: **Calories** 110, **Total fat** 8 g, **Saturated fat** 3 g, **Cholesterol** 40 mg, **Sodium** 55 mg, **Total carbohydrates** 10 g, **Protein** 2 g

CUSTARD CHERRY ROLL

Yield: 42 Pastries

Danish dough, chilled	5 lb. 4 oz.	2520 g
Pastry Cream (page 492)	3 lb.	1440 g
Dried cherries	1 lb.	480 g
Egg wash	as needed	as needed
Simple Syrup (page 73)	10 fl. oz.	300 ml
Fondant Glaze (page 483)	1 lb. 4 oz.	600 g
Toasted almonds	8 oz.	240 g

Custard Cherry Rolls (upper left) and Apricot Pistachio Pinwheels (right).

1. Position the dough with the seamless side parallel to the edge of the workbench and roll it into a rectangle 14 inches (35 centimeters) wide and ⅛ inch (3 millimeters) thick.
2. Spread the Pastry Cream over the entire surface of the dough, leaving a ½-inch (1.2-centimeter) border around each edge. Evenly sprinkle with the dried cherries.
3. Starting from one long edge, tightly roll the dough into a spiral toward the center. Repeat, starting from the other long edge, tightly rolling the dough into a spiral. The two rolls should meet in the center.
4. Slice the dough into ½-inch- (1.2-centimeter-) wide pieces using a sharp French knife. Place the dough cut side up on paper-lined sheet pans.
5. Retard overnight or proof immediately until almost doubled in size.
6. Carefully brush the rolls with egg wash and bake at 400°F (200°C) until well browned, approximately 20 minutes.
7. Brush the hot rolls with a thin coat of Simple Syrup. Cool, then glaze the pastries with a thin coat of Fondant Glaze. Sprinkle immediately with toasted almonds.

VARIATION:

Almond Raspberry Bear Claws—Roll out the Danish dough and cut it into rectangles measuring 4½ inches (11 centimeters) long and 2½ inches (6.5 centimeters) wide. Brush with egg wash. Omit the Pastry Cream and dried cherries. Pipe a strip of Frangipane (page 295) lengthwise in the center of each dough cutout. Sprinkle with four or five fresh raspberries and a tablespoon of raspberry jam. Fold the dough in half lengthwise to make a long tube of filled dough. Using a knife or a pastry cutter, make five ½-inch (1.2-centimeter) slits along the seam, as illustrated on page 292. Transfer the pastry to a paper-lined sheet pan, curving slightly to open the cut sides.

Approximate values per pastry: **Calories** 400, **Total fat** 21 g, **Saturated fat** 11 g, **Cholesterol** 110 mg, **Sodium** 200 mg, **Total carbohydrates** 49 g, **Protein** 7 g, **Vitamin A** 15%

APRICOT PISTACHIO PINWHEELS

Yield: 40 Pastries

Danish dough, chilled	5 lb. 4 oz.	2520 g
Pistachio Almond Paste Filling (page 296)	3 lb.	1440 g
Apricot halves, fresh or canned and drained	44	44
Egg wash	as needed	as needed
Simple Syrup (page 73)	8 fl. oz.	240 ml
Fondant Glaze (page 483)	12 oz.	360 g
Pistachios, coarsely chopped	8 oz.	240 g

1. Roll out the dough and cut it into 3½-inch (9-centimeter) squares.
2. Form into fruitbasket shapes (page 291) and place them on paper-lined baking sheets.
3. Using a piping bag fitted with a medium piping tip, fill the center of each pastry with Pistachio Almond Paste Filling. Top with an apricot half.
4. Proof until almost doubled in size, carefully brush with egg wash and bake at 400°F (200°C), 18 to 20 minutes.
5. Remove from the oven and immediately brush with Simple Syrup. Set aside to cool at room temperature.
6. Brush the pastries with a thin coat of Fondant Glaze and immediately sprinkle with chopped pistachios.

Approximate values per pastry: **Calories** 420, **Total fat** 28 g, **Saturated fat** 13 g, **Cholesterol** 60 mg, **Sodium** 230 mg, **Total carbohydrates** 39 g, **Protein** 7 g, **Vitamin A** 20%

STRAWBERRY CREAM DANISH

In this formula, the Danish dough is formed and baked before it is filled.

Yield: 40 Pastries

Danish dough, chilled	5 lb. 4 oz.	2520 g
Egg wash	as needed	as needed
Crème Brûlée for Tarts (page 518)	3 lb. 4 oz.	1560 g
Strawberries	2 qt.	2 lt.
Powdered sugar	as needed	as needed

1. Roll out the dough and cut it into 3½-inch (9-centimeter) squares. Place them on paper-lined sheet pans.
2. Proof until doubled, or cover and retard the dough overnight. Brush the squares of dough with egg wash and bake at 400°F (200°C) until evenly browned, approximately 18 to 20 minutes.
3. Let cool. Slice the pastries in half horizontally. Place the Crème Brûlée for Tarts in a pastry bag with a medium plain tip. Pipe the filling on the bottom half of each pastry.
4. Top the filling with strawberries, then replace the top half of the pastry. Dust with powdered sugar.

Approximate values per pastry: **Calories** 360, **Total fat** 26 g, **Saturated fat** 15 g, **Cholesterol** 145 mg, **Sodium** 210 mg, **Total carbohydrates** 27 g, **Protein** 5 g, **Vitamin A** 20%, **Vitamin C** 20%

CHAPTER **TEN**

COOKIES AND BROWNIES

After studying this chapter, you will be able to:

- prepare a variety of cookie doughs and batters
- understand the various make-up methods for cookies, biscotti and brownies
- assemble a variety of decorated cookies and brownies

COOKIES NEED NO INTRODUCTION. These portable sweets are an American favorite. Brought here by early Dutch settlers—*koekje* means "little cake" in Dutch—sweet, dry biscuits have been assimilated and adapted by generations of immigrants. Sugar cookies, Italian biscotti, gingersnaps and other varieties from around the world are common in bakeshops across the country. With a good profit margin and all-around customer appeal, these products are a bakeshop staple.

This chapter examines the fundamental techniques for making a wide variety of basic cookies and all-American brownies. More elaborate and specialty cookies are discussed in further detail in Chapter 18, Petits Fours and Confections.

COOKIES

Cookies are small, flat pastries usually eaten alone (although not singularly) as a snack or with coffee at the end of a meal. They are one of America's best-loved foods, enjoyed frequently because of their versatility.

Cookies may be eaten as a midmorning snack or as a component on a modern plated dessert. Inventive cookie plates, often baked to order, appear on contemporary dessert menus alongside more traditional desserts. Cookies also provide the finishing touch to a serving of ice cream, custard or fruit. Flavors are limited only by the baker's imagination: chocolate, oatmeal, cornmeal, fresh and dried fruit and nuts all find their way into several types of cookies.

Most cookie doughs are made using pastry or all-purpose flours, which have enough protein to add structure without toughening the cookies. Cookies can be leavened with baking soda, baking powder or just air and steam. Most cookies are high in fat, which contributes flavor and tenderness and extends shelf life. Butter, shortenings and egg yolks contribute tenderness as well as color in cookie dough.

Mixing Methods

Most cookies are made from a rich dough that is mixed by the **creaming method** used for quick breads and cake batters. (See Chapter 6, Quick Breads, and Chapter 13, Cakes and Icings.) However, because most cookie dough contains less liquid than these batters, the liquid and flour need not be added alternately.

Proper creaming of the cookie dough determines its final texture and the amount it spreads during baking. When thoroughly creamed, granulated sugar begins to dissolve and fat is properly aerated. Thoroughly creamed sugar and fat produce a cookie with maximum spread. When less spread is desired, less creaming is recommended. For cookie dough with a very high proportion of fat, such as Traditional Shortbread (page 329), too much creaming produces a cookie that crumbles easily.

In cookie formulas with a high percentage of fat and low moisture content, overdevelopment of gluten is usually not a problem. However, careless mixing can produce tough and dense cookies. Scraping down the bowl frequently ensures that all of the butter and sugar gets evenly incorporated into the batter. When there are eggs or liquid in the dough, the flour is blended in gently and rapidly to minimize gluten development. Add-ins such as chopped nuts, chocolate and pieces of fruit are stirred into the dough for this same reason.

Assortment of Cookies

PROCEDURE FOR **MIXING COOKIE DOUGHS BY THE CREAMING METHOD**

1. Cream the fat and sugar together to make a lump-free mixture and to blend the ingredients completely.
2. Add the eggs gradually, scraping down the bowl frequently as needed.
3. Stir in the liquid ingredients.
4. Stir in the flour, salt, spices and leaveners.
5. Fold in any nuts, chocolate chips or chunky ingredients by hand or in a mixer on slow speed, taking care not to overmix the dough.

Equal weights of butter increase in volume when creamed thoroughly (right) and expand very little in volume when creamed insufficiently (left).

CHOCOLATE CHUNK COOKIES

Yield: 50 Cookies, approximately 2 oz. (60 g) each

Method: Drop cookies

Unsalted butter, softened	1 lb.	480 g	80%
Granulated sugar	8 oz.	240 g	40%
Brown sugar	12 oz.	360 g	60%
Eggs	5 oz. (3 eggs)	150 g	25%
Vanilla extract	0.3 fl. oz. (2 tsp.)	9 ml	1.5%
Salt	0.4 oz. (2 tsp.)	12 g	2%
Pastry flour	1 lb. 4 oz.	600 g	100%
Baking soda	0.14 oz. (1 tsp.)	4 g	0.7%
Pecans or walnut pieces, chopped	8 oz.	240 g	40%
Chocolate chunks or chips	2 lb.	960 g	160%
Total dough weight:	6 lb. 5 oz.	3055 g	509%

1. Cream the butter and the sugars in the bowl of a 6 quart (6.5 liter) or larger mixer fitted with the paddle attachment. Beat until light, approximately 5 minutes at medium speed.
2. Add the eggs to the creamed mixture one at a time. Add the vanilla.
3. Stir the salt, flour and baking soda together and add to the creamed mixture.
4. Stir in the pecans or walnuts and chocolate chips.
5. Portion the dough using a #20 scoop onto a paper-lined sheet pan and bake at 350°F (180°C) until the cookies are golden brown and cooked through, approximately 10 to 12 minutes.

Approximate values per 2-oz. (60-g) cookie: **Calories** 310, **Total fat** 20 g, **Saturated fat** 7 g, **Cholesterol** 20 mg, **Sodium** 160 mg, **Total carbohydrates** 35 g, **Protein** 3 g

MISE EN PLACE

▸ Allow butter to come to room temperature.
▸ Chop nuts.
▸ Line sheet pan with parchment paper.
▸ Preheat the oven to 350°F (180°C).

Some cookies are made from an egg batter that is mixed by the **egg foam or sponge method** used for some cake batters. (See Chapter 13, Cakes and Icings.) These batters are fragile and should be mixed in small batches to be used as needed. Examples of such batters are Tuile Batter (page 354), Madeleines (page 647), and other petits fours discussed in Chapter 18, Petits Fours and Confections. A **one-stage method** is also used to mix some chewy, home-style cookie doughs. With this method, overmixing can be a problem, however.

Drop Cookies

Make-Up Methods

Cookie varieties are usually classified by the way in which the individual cookies are prepared once the dough has been made. This section describes eight preparations or make-up techniques: **drop**, **icebox**, **bar**, **sheet**, **cut-out**, **piped**, **rolled** or **molded** and **wafer**.

DROP COOKIES

Drop cookies are made from a soft dough that is spooned or scooped into mounds for baking. Chunky cookies such as Chocolate Chunk Cookies (page 313), Oatmeal Cookies (page 323) and Snickerdoodles (page 326) are common examples. Although a uniform appearance is not as important for drop cookies as for other types, uniform size and placement results in uniform baking time. Position the dough in even rows on the baking sheet so that they bake evenly. Space the dough to allow room for the dough to spread, which is common with drop cookies. A portion scoop is recommended for portioning the dough. See page 752 for recommended scoops and sizes. Rolling the ball of dough between moistened palms will make a more uniform shape in the finished cookie. (Many doughs for drop cookies can also be rolled into a log and sliced before baking.) Often the surface of a drop cookie is flattened slightly with a fork before baking. Moistening the fork with water or dipping it in sugar before pressing is helpful. The tines of a fork give peanut butter cookies, for example, their distinctive surface pattern. Drop cookies tend to be thick with a soft or chewy texture.

ICEBOX COOKIES

Icebox cookies are made from dough that is shaped into logs or rectangles, chilled thoroughly, then sliced into individual pieces and baked as needed. Logs of icebox cookies are often rolled in sugar or nuts before slicing, giving a flavorful decorative edge to the cookie once it bakes. Icebox cookies can be as simple as a log of chocolate chip dough or as sophisticated as elegant pinwheel and checkerboard cookies assembled with two colors of short dough. This method usually produces uniform, waferlike cookies with a crisp texture.

To create cookies of a uniform thickness, mark the roll of dough using a portioning device or knife to indicate where to cut the dough.

The formed dough freezes nicely and can be stored when well wrapped with plastic for up to 1 month before using. Because it can easily be stored in the freezer, the dough can be sliced and baked anytime fresh cookies are needed. Thaw this type of dough in the refrigerator overnight before using as directed. Checkerboard Cookies (page 328) and Traditional Shortbread (page 329) illustrate the procedures for making icebox cookies.

Bar Cookies

❶ Portioning icebox cookie dough with a rolling cutter.

❷ Slicing icebox cookie dough that was rolled in nuts.

BAR COOKIES

Bar cookies are made from a stiff dough that is rolled into a log, then baked. The bars are then cut into thick slices. Biscotti (page 356) are a type of bar cookie that is baked a second time after the log has been baked. This produces a dry cookie with a long shelf life.

SHEET COOKIES

Sheet cookies are made from a dough or batter that is pressed, poured or layered in shallow pans and cut into portions after baking, usually in squares or rectangles to avoid waste or scraps. This category contains a wide variety of layered or fruit-filled products. Often a short dough such as that used for a fruit tart or shortbread cookie forms the base of the sheet cookies, and then a topping is layered on the cookie before or after baking. See Mirror Cookies (page 338) and Lemon or Lime Bars (page 334). Brownies, often considered a sheet cookie, are discussed later in this chapter. Other sheet cookies can be produced by baking a traditional pastry in a shallow sheet pan and then cutting it into bite-sized portions. Graham-cracker-crust cheesecake, Linzer tarts and ganache tarts are good examples of this technique.

The eye appeal of sheet cookies is enhanced by precise and uniform portioning. For best results, the sheets of baked dough are cooled then chilled or frozen before cutting.

Sheet Cookies

Using a rolling cutter to mark sheet cookies before cutting.

Using a two-handled cheese knife to portion sheet cookies evenly.

CUT-OUT COOKIES

Cut-out cookies are made from a firm dough that is chilled thoroughly, then rolled out into a sheet. Various shapes are cut out of the dough before baking. Many of the rich tart doughs in Chapter 11, Pies and Tarts, can be used as cut-out cookie dough. Dough for rolled or cut-out cookies freezes well and can be stored well wrapped in the freezer for up to 1 month. This dough should be thawed in the refrigerator overnight before using as directed in the formulas. See Sugar Cookies (page 339) and Gingerbread Cookies (page 340).

A light dusting of flour on the work surface and rolling pin helps keep the dough from sticking when making cut-out cookies. A sprinkling of granulated or powdered sugar may also be used with some formulas. When the dough is especially high in fat, rolling on silicone baking mats or between layers of parchment paper or plastic film is advised. For best results, cut-out cookie dough is rolled to a thickness of between ⅛ and ¼ inch (3 and 6 millimeters).

Cut-Out Cookies

A seemingly infinite selection of cookie cutters is available, or a paring knife or pastry wheel can be used to cut the dough into the desired shape. Dipping the cutter or knife in flour helps keep the dough from sticking to the cutting tool. Always start cutting cookies from the edge of the dough, working inward. Cut the cookies as close to each other as possible to avoid scraps. Although scraps of dough can sometimes be reworked and rerolled, often this results in a tougher dough and a tougher baked cookie.

Sliced nuts, coarse granulated sugar or other garnishes can be pressed into the cookie dough before baking. Doing this as soon as the cookies are rolled helps ensure that the ingredients adhere to the surface. Cut-out cookies are usually baked on an ungreased pan to keep the dough from spreading. After baking, cut-out cookies are sometimes decorated with sugar glaze or colored frostings, an especially popular bakery offering during holiday seasons. See Sugar Cookies and Decorative Cookie Icing (page 339). Ice cookies only after they have cooled completely. Decorative icing should not be applied to cookies that will be frozen; it is best to ice those closer to service.

cookie press also known as a cookie gun; a hollow tube fitted with a plunger and an interchangeable decorative tip or plate; soft cookie dough is pressed through the tip to create shapes or patterns

Piped Cookie

Wafer Cookies

PIPED COOKIES

Also referred to as bagged, pressed or **spritz** cookies, piped cookies are made with a soft dough that is forced through a pastry tip or **cookie press**. For ease of preparation, pipe the dough as soon as it is made. Piped cookies are usually small with a distinct, decorated shape. Dough for cookies that must retain their shape is generally drier and firmer than dough for piped cookies, where spread is not of concern.

The task of piping out dozens of identical cookies may seem daunting, but the skill can be mastered with practice and an understanding of doughs. Doughs for piped cookies often use eggs as their only liquid. Eggs, which are a toughener, contribute body and help the cookies retain their shape. Using too much fat or too soft a flour (that is, one low in protein) can cause the cookies to spread and lose their shape. Overcreaming can also result in dough that will not retain distinctive piping marks in a piped cookie. See Spritz Cookies (page 347).

ROLLED OR MOLDED COOKIES

Rolled or molded cookies are made from a stiff dough that is hand-shaped into spheres, crescents or other traditional shapes. See Swedish Yule Logs (page 345). Often shortbread cookie dough is pressed into decorative carved molds before baking. The impression remains in the dough after baking. Dough for molding is firm and dry so that it holds its shape and keeps the impression intact during baking. Traditional European gingerbread and Scandinavian springerle cookies are molded cookies.

WAFER COOKIES

Wafer cookies are extremely thin and delicate. They are made with a thin egg batter that is poured or spread onto a baking sheet and baked. Then while still hot, the wafer is molded into a variety of shapes. The most popular shapes are the tightly rolled cigarette and the cup-shaped tulipe also known as the tuile. Wafer batter, also known as **stencil batter**, is sweet and buttery and is often flavored with citrus zest or ground nuts. Often a stencil is used to contain the batter into a desired shape as it is spread onto the baking sheet. See Tuile Batter and Russian Cigarette Cookies (page 354). When the baked wafer cookies are still warm, they can also be trimmed with a cutter to make a uniform shape.

Panning and Baking

Proper panning and baking ensures that cookies will bake to the proper texture and color. For consistent results, roll cookie dough to a uniform thickness. Use a tablespoon measure or small scoop to evenly portion drop cookie dough. With practice and a steady hand, piped cookies will be easy to pipe uniformly. Leave the same amount of space between cookies on the baking sheet to allow heat and air to circulate so cookies will brown evenly. For some cookies such as Biscotti (page 356), doubling the sheet pans protects the cookies from burning on the bottom. A filled sheet pan is simply placed on top of a clean pan before baking. The extra pan and the air trapped between them insulates the bottom of the cookies. Depending on the equipment used, sheets of cookies may require rotation during baking to ensure even browning. Most cookies should be removed from their pans once baked and cooled on a rack. Carryover cooking may cause them to burn, and they may stick once cooled. However, some fragile cookies may need to be briefly cooled on their pans before moving so that they set, to prevent breaking. Wafer cookies must be formed while still hot. Test baking times with a small batch of cookies in your equipment until you achieve the desired results.

Cookie Formula Balance

A great deal of the pleasure and taste in a cookie comes from its distinctive texture. The textures associated with cookies—crispness, softness, chewiness and **spread**—are affected by various factors, including the ingredients used and their ratio in the formula or **formula balance**—the oven's temperature during baking and the pan's coating. Understanding these factors allows you to adjust formulas or techniques to achieve the desired results. See Table 10.1.

TABLE 10.1   COOKIE TEXTURES

DESIRED TEXTURE	FAT	SUGAR	LIQUID	FLOUR	SIZE OR SHAPE	BAKING
Crispness	High	High; use granulated sugar	Low	Strong	Thin dough	Well done; cool on baking sheet
Softness	Low	Low; use hygroscopic sugars	High	Weak	Thick dough	Use parchment-lined pan; underbake
Chewiness	High	High; use hygroscopic sugars	High	Strong	Not relevant; chilled dough	Underbake; cool on rack
Spread	High	High; use coarse granulated sugar	High; especially from eggs	Weak	Not relevant; room-temperature dough	Use greased pan; low temperature

CRISPNESS

Crisp cookies are made from firm dough made with a high fat and sugar content and a low moisture content. Crisp cookies are usually portioned so that they dry out thoroughly during baking. Cookie dough that spreads during baking results in a thinner product. When baked through, cookies that spread are usually crisper than those with less spread. Using a coarse granulated sugar in a formula will increase the spread in cookie dough. Powdered sugar in a cookie dough will produce cookies that spread less.

Flour with a higher protein content creates a firm and crisp cookie. Low oven temperatures increase baking time, making cookies drier and crisper. An extreme example of this is baked meringue. Smaller and thinner cookies can usually be baked more crisp than thick cookies. If more or less crispness is desired, examine the options described in Table 10.1. A cookie that spreads more is usually crisper.

Cookie dough that is thoroughly creamed (left column) spreads more than dough that is minimally creamed (right column). Moderately mixed cookie dough (center column) rises evenly with a small amount of spread.

SOFTNESS AND CHEWINESS

Soft cookies are made from a dough or a batter with a high moisture content and a lower proportion of fat and sugar. Eggs in the dough contribute to making a chewier cookie. The proteins in the eggs bind and firm during baking. The moisture in the eggs helps develop gluten in the flour. Using granulated sugar, not powdered sugar, helps make a chewier cookie. For even softer, chewier cookies, replace 10 to 15 percent of the sugar with invert sugar, glucose, honey or corn syrup. These sugars act as **humectants**, absorbing moisture and resulting in a softer baked cookie. Bake at slightly higher temperatures and underbake the cookies slightly to ensure a chewy texture. Wrap cookies or the entire sheet pans with food film while still warm. This helps the cookies retain moisture and stay soft. Spreading has a large effect on tenderness or chewiness; cookies that have spread too much are usually not tender or chewy.

SPREAD

Ingredients play a major role in increasing or decreasing spread. If more spread is desired, add additional baking soda or baking powder. For less spread, reduce the leaveners. Choosing flour with a lower protein content will increase spread; flour with a higher protein content will have the opposite effect. Substituting cornstarch for a portion of the flour in a cookie dough formula will produce a firmer cookie that spreads less. Powdered sugar decreases spread; granulated sugar increases it. Mixing methods also affect spread. Insufficient creaming of the batter will reduce spread; overcreaming will increase it. Buttering the sheet pan or parchment paper will aid spreading.

Baking temperatures also affect spread. If the oven temperature is too low, the cookies will spread more because gelatinization takes longer. If the temperature is too high, the exterior crust will form before the dough can spread appropriately.

Use Table 10.2 to troubleshoot mixing, forming and baking cookie dough.

Finishing

Once cookies are baked, the further possibilities for embellishing them are endless. Sandwich cookies are made with two identical cookies spread with a thin layer of filling or ice cream and pressed together. Icebox and cut-out cookies lend themselves to being sandwiched with fillings such as thick jam, melted chocolate, buttercream, ganache, nut butter or fruit curd. Some piped cookies are indented before baking and filled with jam, chocolate or fruit purée.

Baked, cooled cookies may be garnished with a thin drizzle or a thick dipping of melted dark or white chocolate. Fondant, royal icing or glaze can be piped, poured or spread on, provided that the color and flavor selected offers an appropriate contrast to the cookie itself. For best results, ice cookies only after they have cooled completely. When freezing cookies for longer storage, it is best to ice them after they thaw because the icing can become damaged when frozen.

humectant a substance such as corn syrup, glucose or honey that absorbs moisture, making baked goods soft and tender

Creaming the butter thoroughly and baking on a greased baking sheet increases spread (top) in high-fat cookie dough.

PROCEDURE FOR DECORATING COOKIES WITH ICING

Icing sugar cookies.

❶ Place thinned fondant or decorative icing in a pastry bag fitted with a thin tip.

❷ Outline the edge of the cookie with the icing. Pipe the outlines of any designs to be filled in with colored icing. Allow the icing to set or dry, approximately 10 to 20 minutes.

❸ Thin some of the remaining icing with just enough water so that it flows easily. Fill a piping bag or plastic squeeze bottle with the icing. Fill in the outlined shapes with the icing, allowing it to flow smoothly and evenly. Garnish with colored or pearl sugar or other edible decorations if desired.

TABLE 10.2   TROUBLESHOOTING CHART FOR COOKIES

PROBLEM	CAUSE	SOLUTION
Cookies too dense or hard	Too little liquid in the dough	Adjust formula or measure carefully; add more eggs
	Too little fat in the dough	Adjust formula or measure fat carefully
	Too much flour in the dough	Adjust formula or measure flour carefully
	Dough overmixed	Cream properly; avoid overmixing after adding dry ingredients
	Cookies overbaked	Remove cookies from oven promptly
Cookies tough	Improper flour used	Use lower-protein flour
	Too much flour in the dough	Adjust formula or measure flour carefully
	Too little fat in the dough	Adjust formula or measure fat carefully
	Too little sugar in the dough	Adjust formula or measure sugar carefully
	Dough overmixed	Avoid overmixing after adding dry ingredients
	Dough reworked during rolling	Roll dough carefully; do not re-roll scrap dough
Cookies too crumbly	Dough lacks gluten development	Mix longer; use higher-protein flour
	Too much chemical leavening, fat or sugar used in the dough	Adjust formula or measure carefully
	Too few eggs in the dough	Adjust formula
	Dough too thin	Roll or cut dough thicker
Cookies flatten and spread too much	Wrong type of flour used	Use higher-protein flour
	Too little flour in the dough	Adjust formula or measure flour carefully
	Too much chemical leavening, fat or liquid in the dough	Adjust formula or measure ingredients carefully
	Too much grease on baking sheets	Grease equipment carefully
	Dough too warm before baking	Chill dough thoroughly before using
	Oven too cool	Adjust oven
Cookies do not spread	Incorrect flour used	Use lower-protein flour
	Too much flour in the dough	Adjust formula or measure flour carefully
	Incorrect type of fat used	Replace shortening with butter or oil
	Too little sugar, chemical leavening or liquid used	Adjust formula or measure ingredients carefully
	Dough improperly mixed	Cream fat and sugar thoroughly
	Dough too thick	Roll or cut dough thinner; bake cookies longer
	Oven too hot	Adjust oven
Cookies too pale	Too little sugar in the dough	Adjust formula or measure sugar carefully
	Oven too cool	Adjust oven
	Cookies underbaked	Bake cookies longer
Cookies burned or too dark	Too much sugar in the dough	Adjust formula or measure sugar carefully
	Oven too hot	Adjust oven
	Cookies overbaked	Remove cookies from oven promptly
	Uneven oven heat	Rotate pans in oven to prevent burning
Poor flavor	Poor ingredients	Check aroma, flavor and freshness of all ingredients
	Unclean pans	Do not grease pans with rancid fats; do not reuse parchment paper

Storing

Most cookies can be stored up to 1 week in a cool dry place when packed in an airtight container. Do not store crisp cookies with soft cookies in the same container, however. The crisp cookies will absorb moisture from the soft cookies, ruining the texture of both. Do not store strongly flavored cookies, such as spice, with those that are milder, such as shortbread. Most baked cookies freeze well if wrapped airtight to prevent moisture loss or freezer burn. Raw dough can also be frozen, either in bulk or shaped into individual portions.

BROWNIES

Where do you draw the line between cakes and brownies? The decision must be a matter of texture and personal preference, for the preparation methods are nearly identical. Brownies are generally chewy and fudgy, sweeter and denser than even the richest butter cakes. Brownies are a relatively inexpensive and easy way for a food service operation to offer its customers a fresh-baked dessert. Although not as sophisticated as an elaborate gâteau, a well-made brownie can always be served with pride (and a scoop of ice cream).

Mixing Methods

Brownies are prepared using the same procedures as those for high-fat cakes. Eggs and air incorporated during the mixing process are usually the only leaveners in a traditional brownie formula. Good brownies are achieved with a proper balance of ingredients: A high percentage of butter to flour and not too many eggs produces a dense, fudgy brownie. The fat coats the flour, preventing the protein from developing into gluten. Less butter produces a more cakelike brownie. Increasing the eggs produces a brownie with a crumb structure that more closely resembles a true cake.

Likewise, the higher the ratio of sugar, the gooier the finished brownie will be. In some formulas, the fat is creamed to incorporate air, as with butter cakes. In others, the fat is first melted and combined with other liquid ingredients. Brownies are rarely made with whipped egg whites, however, as this makes their texture too light and cakelike.

PROCEDURE FOR PREPARING BROWNIES

1. Melt unsweetened or bittersweet chocolate and butter over a double boiler.
2. Whip eggs and sugar until light and aerated.
3. Stir in the melted chocolate mixture.
4. Stir in flour and nuts or other add-ins.
5. Bake until the batter is set but not dry. Cool the brownies completely in the pan before cutting. Freezing before portioning helps ensure that the brownies will cut cleanly.

FUDGE BROWNIES

Yield: 4 Dozen Brownies, approximately 2 in. (5 cm) each, 1 Half-Sheet Pan

Method: Sheet cookies

Unsalted butter, room temperature	18 oz.	535 g	112%
Unsweetened chocolate	1 lb.	480 g	100%
Eggs	1 lb. (10 eggs)	480 g	100%
Granulated sugar	2 lb. 8 oz.	1200 g	250%
Salt	0.2 oz. (1 tsp.)	6 g	1.2%
Vanilla extract	1 fl. oz.	30 ml	6.2%
Coffee extract (optional)	0.5 fl. oz.	15 ml	3%
Pastry or all-purpose flour	1 lb.	480 g	100%
Pecan pieces	8 oz.	240 g	50%
Total batter weight:	7 lb. 3 oz.	3466 g	722%
Powdered sugar (optional)	as needed	as needed	

① Melt the butter and chocolate over a double boiler to 120°F (49°C). Hold the chocolate at this temperature.

② While the chocolate is melting, beat the eggs and granulated sugar in the bowl of a large mixer fitted with the paddle attachment on medium speed for 10 minutes. Add the salt and extracts. Scrape down the bowl, then add the melted chocolate, blending until well combined. Add the flour and mix until combined. Fold in the nuts.

③ Spread the batter evenly onto a paper-lined half-sheet pan. The pan will be very full. Bake at 325°F (160°C) until the center is set, approximately 40 minutes.

④ Cool completely before cutting. (Refrigerating or freezing brownies before cutting ensures a clean edge.) Dust the brownies with powdered sugar, if desired.

Approximate values per 2-in. (5-cm) square: **Calories** 343, **Total fat** 18 g, **Saturated fat** 9 g, **Cholesterol** 70 mg, **Sodium** 16 mg, **Total carbohydrates** 41 g, **Protein** 4 g

MISE EN PLACE

▶ Allow butter to come to room temperature.

▶ Line a half-sheet pan with parchment paper.

▶ Preheat the oven to 325°F (160°C).

Flavoring Brownies

Everyone has their own idea of the quintessential brownie. Some prefer a cloyingly sweet brownie, with a creamy texture and an abundance of chocolate; others prefer a bitter and crisp brownie. Whatever style, once the batter is made, brownies may be flavored in a number of ways to please many palates. See German Chocolate Layered Brownies (page 360). The techniques for flavoring brownies illustrates the many ways in which a basic brownie can be customized. It is not necessary to use all these techniques for each brownie; sometimes a dusting of powdered sugar is all that's necessary to make a simple brownie sensational.

TECHNIQUES FOR FLAVORING BROWNIES

▶ Prepare the brownie batter. Flavor the brownie batter with an extract, liqueur or flavoring oil. Almond, anise, cherry, chilli pepper, coffee, hazelnut, lemon and orange work especially well with chocolate.

▶ Fold nuts, chunks of white or dark chocolate, raisins, dried fruit, coconut or diced pieces of almond paste into the batter before panning. Diced pieces of toffee, broken candy bars or miniature marshmallows all make excellent additions to brownies.

▶ Once panned, place large spoonfuls of jam over the surface of the batter. Marbleize the batter with the jam. Raspberry or strawberry jam, orange marmalade, peanut or almond butter or softened cream cheese complement many chocolate brownie batters.

▶ Layer the panned brownie batter with a toffee or coconut filling, as for German Chocolate Layered Brownies (page 360).

Two styles of layered brownies.

▶ Once baked and cooled, ice the brownies with flavored cream cheese icing, buttercream or melted chocolate. Select a topping that contrasts with the sweetness and texture of the brownie. The slight sourness of a cream cheese icing balances what otherwise might be a cloying sweetness.

▶ Garnish iced brownies with nuts, streusel or toasted coconut.

▶ Cut the brownies into bars, squares or triangles.

Storing

For short-term storage, brownies should be wrapped airtight and kept at room temperature. Baked brownies can be frozen 2 to 3 months if well wrapped.

CONVENIENCE PRODUCTS

Prepared dry mixes and prepared dough are common convenience products to assist in making cookies or brownies. Dry mix, especially for brownies, requires the addition of water, and frequently oil and eggs.

Cookie dough comes packaged in bulk 2- and 5-gallon buckets, refrigerated or frozen. This offers the bakeshop the convenience of a premixed dough to which additional items may be added to customize the mix. Frozen dough is also sold in portioned units, in bulk or already positioned on parchment paper ready for placing on a baking sheet and baking.

Select products with quality ingredients. Pure butter, nuts, natural flavorings, a high percentage of fruit and chocolate and few preservatives are good indications of quality. Refrigerated and frozen products must be properly stored and thawed according to manufacturer's recommendations, usually under refrigeration. Once thawed, these dough products perform much like a scratch product. You must pan, bake and cool using the same care as you would a scratch product.

QUESTIONS FOR DISCUSSION

1 Discuss the effect that changing ingredients has on cookie products. What results can you expect when cake flour is used instead of all-purpose flour in an icebox cookie, for example?

2 Describe the different effect that creaming will have on cookie dough after it is baked.

3 Describe three garnishing techniques for icebox cookies, before and after baking.

4 What are the proper cooling methods for various types of cookies? How does proper cooling affect the qualities and characteristics of these different types of cookies?

5 Design a cookie plate to be included on a restaurant dessert menu. Include at least five different cookies and explain the reason for your selection. www

Terms to Know

creaming method
egg foam
   or sponge
   method
one-stage
   method
drop cookies
icebox cookies
bar cookies

sheet cookies
cut-out cookies
piped cookies
rolled cookies
wafer cookies
spritz cookies
stencil batter
spread
formula balance

OATMEAL COOKIES

Yield: 32 Cookies, approximately 2 oz. (60 g) each   **Method:** Drop cookies

All-purpose or pastry flour	10.5 oz.	315 g	100%
Baking soda	0.14 oz. (1 tsp.)	4 g	1.3%
Cinnamon, ground	0.2 oz. (1 Tbsp.)	6 g	2%
Quick-cooking oats	9 oz.	270 g	86%
Unsalted butter, softened	9 oz.	270 g	86%
Granulated sugar	9 oz.	270 g	86%
Brown sugar	9 oz.	270 g	86%
Eggs	3.2 oz. (2 eggs)	95 g	30%
Orange juice concentrate	1.5 fl. oz.	45 ml	14%
Vanilla extract	0.5 fl. oz.	15 ml	4.7%
Salt	0.2 oz. (1 tsp.)	5 g	1.9%
Raisins	12 oz.	360 g	114%
Total dough weight:	4 lb.	1925 g	612%

1. Sift together the flour, baking soda and cinnamon. Stir in the oats and set aside.
2. Cream the butter until light and fluffy. Add the sugars and continue creaming until the mixture is lightened. Add the eggs one at a time, scraping down the bowl frequently and mixing well after each addition. Add the orange juice concentrate, vanilla extract and salt.
3. Fold in the flour mixture and the raisins. Portion the dough onto paper-lined sheet pans.
4. Bake at 375°F (190°C) until golden, approximately 10 to 12 minutes.

Approximate values per cookie: **Calories** 220, **Total fat** 7 g, **Saturated fat** 4.5 g, **Cholesterol** 30 mg, **Sodium** 110 mg, **Total carbohydrates** 38 g, **Protein** 3 g

CHOCOLATE CHEWIES

Yield: 2 Dozen Cookies, approximately 3¾ oz. (112 g) each

Method: Drop cookies

		Sugar at 100%	
Powdered sugar	2 lb. 14 oz.	1300 g	100%
Cocoa powder	6 oz.	170 g	13%
Salt	0.5 oz.	15 g	1%
Vanilla extract	0.5 fl. oz.	15 ml	1%
Egg whites	12 oz. (12 whites)	340 g	26%
Walnuts, chopped coarse	1 lb. 12 oz.	795 g	61%
Total batter weight:	5 lb. 13 oz.	2635 g	202%

1. In the bowl of a 6 quart (6.5 liter) or larger mixer fitted with the paddle attachment, combine the sugar, cocoa powder, salt, vanilla and egg whites. Mix 2 minutes on medium speed, then add the nuts.
2. Using a #8 portion scoop, portion the batter onto paper-lined sheet pans. Space 3 inches (7.5 centimeters) apart to allow room for the cookies to spread.
3. Bake at 400°F (200°C) until the centers of the cookies are just set, approximately 12 to 14 minutes. When perfectly baked, the cookies will be chewy yet crisp.

Approximate values per cookie: **Calories** 450, **Total fat** 23 g, **Saturated fat** 2.5 g, **Cholesterol** 0 mg, **Sodium** 250 mg, **Total carbohydrates** 63 g, **Protein** 8 g, **Claims**—gluten free

CARROT CAKE "COOKIES"

Yield: 48 Cookies, approximately 2½ oz. (75 g) each

Method: Drop cookies

Pastry or all-purpose flour	1 lb. 4 oz.	600 g	100%
Baking soda	0.3 oz. (2 tsp.)	9 g	1.5%
Baking powder	0.3 oz. (2 tsp.)	9 g	1.5%
Cinnamon, ground	0.2 oz. (1 Tbsp.)	6 g	1%
Ginger, ground	0.14 oz. (2 tsp.)	4 g	0.7%
Unsalted butter, softened	1 lb.	480 g	80%
Granulated sugar	1 lb.	480 g	80%
Brown sugar	14 oz.	420 g	70%
Eggs	6.4 oz. (4 eggs)	195 g	32%
Vanilla extract	0.5 fl. oz.	15 ml	2.5%
Salt	0.2 oz. (1 tsp.)	6 g	1%
Quick-cooking oats	13 oz.	390 g	65%
Carrots, finely grated	1 lb. 6 oz.	660 g	110%
Raisins, conditioned	12 oz.	360 g	60%
Total dough weight:	7 lb. 9 oz.	3634 g	605%
Cream Cheese Icing (page 482)	2 lb. 6 oz.	1140 g	

1. Sift together the flour, baking soda, baking powder, cinnamon and ginger. Set aside.
2. In the bowl of a 6 quart (6.5 liter) or larger mixer fitted with the paddle attachment, cream the butter and sugars until light and fluffy, approximately 5 to 7 minutes.
3. Add the eggs one at a time, scraping down the bowl frequently and mixing well after each addition. Add the vanilla extract, salt and oats.
4. Stir in the flour mixture, mixing until just combined. Fold in the carrots and raisins.
5. Portion the dough onto paper-lined sheet pans using a #30 scoop.
6. Bake at 375°F (190°C) until golden brown around the edges, approximately 12 to 14 minutes. Cool cookies a few minutes in their pans. Then transfer them to cooling racks to cool completely before filling.
7. Pipe a rounded mound of Cream Cheese Icing on the flat side of half of the cookies. Top with the remaining cookies.

Approximate values per cookie: **Calories** 280, **Total fat** 11 g, **Saturated fat** 6 g, **Cholesterol** 45 mg, **Sodium** 160 mg, **Total carbohydrates** 47 g, **Protein** 4 g, **Vitamin A** 45%

LIME AND PINEAPPLE COCONUT MACAROONS

Yield: 40 Cookies, approximately 1¾ oz. (52 g) each

Method: Drop cookies

			Sugar at 100%
Pineapple slices, canned or fresh	12 oz. (8 slices)	360 g	37.5%
Egg whites	12 oz. (12 whites)	360 g	37.5%
Granulated sugar	2 lb.	960 g	100%
Macaroon coconut	1 lb. 2 oz.	540 g	56%
Dark rum (optional)	1 fl. oz.	30 ml	3%
Vanilla extract	0.3 fl. oz. (2 tsp.)	10 ml	1%
Lime zest, grated	0.4 oz. (2 Tbsp.)	12 g	1.25%
Total batter weight:	4 lb. 11 oz.	2272 g	236%

Macaroon Coconut

1. Cut each slice of pineapple into five pieces. Set aside.
2. In a double boiler over low heat, stir together the egg whites, sugar and coconut using a rubber spatula. Cook, stirring constantly, until the mixture reaches 130°F (54°C).
3. Remove the mixture from the heat. Stir in the rum (if using), vanilla extract and lime zest. Allow the batter to stand for 45 minutes to cool and firm.
4. Drop the batter in 1¾-ounce (52-gram) mounds using a small ice cream scoop onto buttered, paper-lined sheet pans. With gloved hands, indent the center of each cookie. Place a piece of pineapple in the center of each cookie.
5. Bake at 400°F (200°C) until golden brown, approximately 18 to 20 minutes.

VARIATIONS:

Chocolate Drizzled Coconut Macaroons—Fill a parchment paper cone with melted chocolate and drizzle over the cooled cookies.

Coconut Raspberry Macaroons—Omit the lime zest and pineapple. With gloved hands, indent the center of each cookie, then fill it with raspberry jam in Step 4.

Chocolate Coconut Macaroons—Omit the lime zest and pineapple. With gloved hands, indent the center of each cookie, then fill it with chocolate chips in Step 4.

Approximate values per cookie: **Calories** 100, **Total fat** 7 g, **Saturated fat** 6 g, **Cholesterol** 35 mg, **Sodium** 15 mg, **Total carbohydrates** 12 g, **Protein** 2 g, **Claims**—gluten free

Assorted coconut macaroons (from left): Coconut Raspberry Macaroons, Chocolate Coconut Macaroons and Lime and Pineapple Coconut Macaroons

SNICKERDOODLES
(CINNAMON BUTTER COOKIES)

Yield: 40 Cookies, 1 oz. (30 g) each

Method: Drop cookies

Dough:

Pastry or all-purpose flour	14 oz.	420 g	100%
Baking powder	0.14 oz. (1 tsp.)	4 g	1%
Cinnamon, ground	0.25 oz. (3½ tsp.)	8 g	2%
Unsalted butter, softened	8 oz.	240 g	57%
Granulated sugar	6 oz.	180 g	43%
Brown sugar	8 oz.	240 g	57%
Eggs	3.3 oz. (2 eggs)	100 g	23%
Vanilla extract	0.5 fl. oz.	15 ml	4%
Salt	0.4 oz. (2 tsp.)	12 g	3%
Total dough weight:	2 lb. 8 oz.	1219 g	290%

Topping:

Granulated sugar	2 oz.	60 g	
Cinnamon, ground	0.14 oz. (2 tsp.)	4 g	

1 To prepare the dough, sift together the flour, baking powder and cinnamon. Set aside.

2 Cream the butter and sugars until light and fluffy. Beat in the eggs, one at a time, then add the vanilla extract and salt. Gradually add the flour mixture, beating just until well combined.

3 Combine the sugar and cinnamon in a large bowl. Using a #30 portion scoop, drop the dough in 1-ounce (30-gram) mounds in the mixture. Coat the pieces of dough in the sugar mixture, round them, then place on paper-lined sheet pans. Flatten the dough using the bottom of a cup to ½ inch (1.2 centimeters).

4 Bake at 400°F (200°C) until golden brown but still moist, approximately 9 to 11 minutes.

Approximate values per cookie: **Calories** 90, **Total fat** 4 g, **Saturated fat** 2.5 g, **Cholesterol** 15 mg, **Sodium** 100 mg, **Total carbohydrates** 14 g, **Protein** 1 g

PEANUT BUTTER SANDIES

Yield: 4½ Dozen Cookies, 1⅓ oz. (40 g) each

Method: Rolled cookies

Pastry or all-purpose flour	1 lb. 8 oz.	720 g	100%
Baking soda	0.14 oz. (1 tsp.)	4 g	0.6%
Baking powder	0.14 oz. (1 tsp.)	4 g	0.6%
Unsalted butter, softened	1 lb.	475 g	66%
Granulated sugar	1 lb.	475 g	66%
Eggs	3.3 oz. (2 eggs)	100 g	14%
Peanut butter	10 oz.	300 g	42%
Salt	0.4 oz. (2 tsp.)	12 g	1.7%
Granulated sugar	as needed	as needed	
Peanut halves (optional)	2 oz.	60 g	8%
Total dough weight:	4 lb. 8 oz.	2150 g	299%

1. Sift together the flour, baking soda and baking powder. Set aside. Cream the butter. Add the sugar and continue creaming. Gradually add the eggs, followed by the peanut butter and salt.
2. Add the dry ingredients to the butter mixture and mix to make a firm dough.
3. Scale the dough into 1-pound (480-gram) pieces. Roll the dough into 12-inch (30-centimeter) logs. Cut into 1-inch (2.5-centimeter) pieces.
4. Roll each cookie into a ball and place on a paper-lined sheet pan. Press each ball down using the bottom of a measuring cup to slightly less than ½ inch (1.2 centimeters). The edges of the cookies will develop some cracks, which is a desired look.
5. Using a fork, press crisscross markings on the surface of each cookie. Lightly brush the cookies with water. Sprinkle lightly with granulated sugar and press one peanut half into each cookie, if using.
6. Bake at 400°F (200°F) until golden brown, approximately 12 minutes.

Approximate values per cookie: **Calories** 190, **Total fat** 12 g, **Saturated fat** 5 g, **Cholesterol** 20 mg, **Sodium** 160 mg, **Total carbohydrates** 22 g, **Protein** 3 g

CHECKERBOARD COOKIES

Yield: 160 Cookies, approximately ¾ oz. (25 g) each

Method: Icebox cookies

Vanilla dough:

Unsalted butter, softened	1 lb.	475 g	66%
Powdered sugar	13 oz.	390 g	54%
Eggs	6.75 oz. (4 eggs)	200 g	28%
Salt	0.4 oz. (2 tsp.)	12 g	1.6%
Vanilla extract	0.5 fl. oz.	15 ml	2%
Almond extract	0.15 fl. oz. (1 tsp.)	5 ml	0.6%
Almond flour	6 oz.	180 g	25%
Pastry or all-purpose flour	24 oz.	720 g	100%
Total dough weight:	4 lb. 2 oz.	1997 g	277%

Chocolate dough:

Unsalted butter, softened	1 lb.	480 g	70%
Powdered sugar	15 oz.	450 g	65%
Eggs	6.75 oz. (4 eggs)	200 g	29%
Salt	0.4 oz. (2 tsp.)	12 g	1.7%
Vanilla extract	0.5 fl. oz.	15 ml	2%
Almond extract	0.15 fl. oz. (1 tsp.)	5 ml	0.6%
Almond flour	3 oz.	90 g	13%
Cocoa powder	3 oz.	90 g	13%
Pastry or all-purpose flour	1 lb. 7 oz.	690 g	100%
Total dough weight:	4 lb. 3 oz.	2032 g	294%

❶ Marking the layered block of chocolate and vanilla dough for slicing.

❷ Cutting the dough into narrow strips to reveal alternating layers of dough.

❶ For the vanilla dough, cream the butter and sugar until light and fluffy. Add the eggs one at a time, scraping well between additions. Beat in the salt, extracts and almond flour. Add the pastry flour and beat until just combined.

❷ Wrap tightly and chill the dough until firm.

❸ Prepare the chocolate dough following the same procedure used for the vanilla dough. Add the cocoa powder with the almond flour. Wrap tightly and chill the dough until firm.

❹ On a well-floured surface, roll the vanilla and chocolate doughs into rectangles ¼ inch (6 millimeters) thick. Cut the dough into 2-inch- (5-centimeter-) wide strips.

❺ Brush a strip of chocolate dough lightly with water; place a vanilla strip on top. Repeat with a second chocolate strip and end with a strip of vanilla dough. Refrigerate until firm.

❻ Using a long French knife, cut the block of dough lengthwise into four equal strips.

❼ Place a cut strip flat side down on a paper-lined sheet pan. Lightly moisten with water. Place another cut strip onto the first, making certain that the chocolate and vanilla bands are touching. Repeat with two more strips for a total of four. This block of dough may be wrapped in a ⅛-inch- (3-millimeter-) thick sheet of dough, if desired.

❽ Freeze until hard. Cut crosswise in ¼-inch (6-millimeter) slices. Place on a paper-lined sheet pan. Bake at 375°F (190°C) until golden brown, about 14 to 16 minutes.

Approximate values per cookie: **Calories** 120, **Total fat** 7 g, **Saturated fat** 3.5 g, **Cholesterol** 25 mg, **Sodium** 70 mg, **Total carbohydrates** 14 g, **Protein** 2 g

3 Stacking the striped layers of dough to form a checkerboard pattern.

4 Wrapping a layer of chocolate dough around the log of checkerboard dough.

5 Slicing the block of checkerboard dough into cookies before baking.

TRADITIONAL SHORTBREAD

Yield: 7 Dozen Cookies, approximately ½ oz. (15 g) each

Method: Icebox cookies

Unsalted butter, softened	1 lb.	480 g	84%
Powdered sugar	8 oz.	240 g	42%
Vanilla extract	0.5 fl. oz.	15 ml	3%
Salt	0.2 oz. (1 tsp.)	5 g	1%
Pastry or all-purpose flour	1 lb. 3 oz.	570 g	100%
Egg wash	as needed	as needed	
Total dough weight:	2 lb. 11 oz.	1310 g	230%

1 Blend the butter and powdered sugar in a mixing bowl without creaming. Stir in the vanilla and salt, mixing thoroughly. Add the flour and mix until just combined.

2 Divide the dough into four equal portions. Roll each piece of dough into 8-inch (20-centimeter) disks. Wrap in plastic. Freeze until hard, approximately 30 minutes.

3 Remove from the freezer and unwrap, then lightly brush each disk with egg wash. Cut each disk into eight wedges. Dock the wedges with a fork.

4 Bake at 375°F (190°C) until pale golden brown, approximately 15 to 20 minutes.

VARIATIONS:

Bergamot Shortbread—Add 12 drops of oil of bergamot with the vanilla in Step 1. Divide the dough into four equal portions. Roll each piece into a 10-inch- (25-centimeter-) long cylinder. Freeze until hard, approximately 30 minutes. Brush each cyclinder with egg wash. Roll each cyclinder in granulated sugar. Cut the cylinders into ½-inch- (1.2-centimeter-) thick slices, then place the slices cut side down on paper-lined sheet pans. Dock the cookies with a fork and bake.

Pecan Shortbread—Add 7 ounces (210 grams/37%) of finely chopped pecans to the dough in Step 1.

Approximate values per cookie: **Calories** 70, **Total fat** 4.5 g, **Saturated fat** 3 g, **Cholesterol** 10 mg, **Sodium** 30 mg, **Total carbohydrates** 8 g, **Protein** 1 g

Bergamot Shortbread

Pecan Shortbread

TEA-SCENTED CHERRY COOKIES

Yield: 7 Dozen Cookies, approximately ⅔ oz. (20 g) each

Method: Icebox cookies

Unsalted butter, softened	1 lb. 2 oz.	540 g	95%
Powdered sugar	10 oz.	300 g	53%
Vanilla extract	0.5 fl. oz.	15 ml	2.7%
Almond extract	0.3 fl. oz. (2 tsp.)	10 ml	1.6%
Salt	0.2 oz. (1 tsp.)	6 g	1%
Earl Grey tea bags, single-serving size	3	3	
Dried cherries, chopped coarse	6 oz.	180 g	32%
Pastry or all-purpose flour	1 lb. 3 oz.	570 g	100%
Egg wash	as needed	as needed	
Almonds, chopped	as needed	as needed	
Three Red Fruit Jam (recipe follows)	as needed	as needed	
Total dough weight:	3 lb. 6 oz.	1621 g	285%

1. Blend the butter and sugar in the bowl of a mixer fitted with the paddle attachment. Thoroughly mix in the extracts, salt, and the contents of the tea bags. Add the cherries and flour and mix until just combined.
2. Divide the dough into four equal portions, approximately 12½ ounces (375 grams) each. Roll each piece into a 10-inch- (25-centimeter-) long cylinder. Freeze until hard, approximately 30 minutes.
3. Remove from the freezer and lightly brush the dough with egg wash. Roll the dough in chopped almonds and cut into ⅜-inch- (1-centimeter-) thick slices.
4. Place the cookies on paper-lined sheet pans. Indent the center of each cookie with the back of a spoon and fill the indentation with Three Red Fruit Jam.
5. Bake at 375°F (190°C) until the cookies are golden brown, approximately 18 minutes.

THREE RED FRUIT JAM

Yield: 2 lb. 8 oz. (1200 g)

Strawberries, fresh or IQF	8 oz.	240 g
Raspberries, fresh or IQF	8 oz.	240 g
Cherries, fresh or IQF	8 oz.	240 g
Granulated sugar	1 lb.	480 g
Pectin	0.3 oz. (2 tsp.)	10 g
Citric acid (optional)	as needed	as needed

1. Heat the fruits in a stainless steel pan to 120°F (49°C). Using an immersion blender, chop the softened fruit into small pieces.
2. Blend the sugar with the pectin and add to the fruit. Bring to a boil while stirring constantly. Boil about 10 minutes. Remove from the heat. Add a small amount of citric acid (if using). Store this jam in the refrigerator because of its reduced sugar content.

Approximate values per cookie: **Calories** 110, **Total fat** 5 g, **Saturated fat** 3 g, **Cholesterol** 15 mg, **Sodium** 30 mg, **Total carbohydrates** 16 g, **Protein** 1 g

BLUEBERRY-FILLED GINGER COOKIES

Yield: 7 Dozen Cookies, approximately ½ oz. (15 g) each

Method: Icebox cookies

Bread flour	1 lb. 1 oz.	510 g	100%
Baking powder	0.2 oz. (1½ tsp.)	6 g	1.2%
Baking soda	0.07 oz. (½ tsp.)	2 g	0.4%
Unsalted butter, softened	8 oz.	240 g	47%
Granulated sugar	1 lb.	480 g	94%
Glucose or corn syrup	1 oz.	30 g	6%
Eggs	3.3 oz. (2 eggs)	100 g	19%
Vanilla extract	0.3 fl. oz. (2 tsp.)	10 ml	2%
Ginger, ground	0.3 oz. (1½ Tbsp.)	10 g	2%
Lemon oil	3 drops	3 drops	
Orange oil	3 drops	3 drops	
Egg wash	as needed	as needed	
Granulated sugar	as needed	as needed	
Total dough weight:	2 lb. 14 oz.	1388 g	271%
Blueberry, mango or ginger jam	1 lb. 14 oz.	900 g	
Powdered sugar	as needed	as needed	

1. Sift together the flour, baking powder and baking soda. Set aside.
2. Cream the butter, granulated sugar and syrup until light and fluffy. Gradually add the eggs, vanilla, ginger and oils. Add the flour mixture, beating just until well combined.
3. Divide the dough into 11-ounce (330-gram) pieces. Roll each piece into a 10-inch- (25-centimeter-) long log. Freeze until hard, approximately 30 minutes.
4. Remove from the freezer and unwrap, then lightly brush the cylinders with egg wash and roll them in granulated sugar. Cut into ¼-inch- (6-millimeter-) thick slices and place them cut side down on paper-lined sheet pans.
5. Bake at 400°F (200°C) until the cookies are crisp, approximately 15 to 18 minutes. Cool the cookies on a wire rack.
6. Turn over half of the cookies. Using a piping bag fitted with a plain tip, fill the center of each cookie with the blueberry jam. Top each with another cookie.
7. To create a half-moon-shaped garnish, rest a teaspoon over the edge of a sandwiched cookie. Using a fine sifter or tea strainer, sift powdered sugar over the exposed area of each cookie.

VARIATION:

Chewy Ginger Cookies—Cut the dough into ½-inch- (1.2-centimeter-) thick slices in Step 4. Indent the center of each sliced cookie. Bake the cookies until lightly browned, approximately 15 minutes.

Approximate values per cookie: **Calories** 90, **Total fat** 2.5 g, **Saturated fat** 1.5 g, **Cholesterol** 10 mg, **Sodium** 20 mg, **Total carbohydrates** 16 g, **Protein** 1 g

HAWAIIAN MACADAMIA COOKIES

Yield: 40 Cookies, approximately 1 ¼ oz. (37 g) each

Method: Icebox cookies

Macadamia nuts, whole	8 oz.	240 g	50%
Brown sugar	4 oz.	120 g	25%
Semisweet chocolate	2 oz.	60 g	12.5%
Vegetable oil	0.5 fl. oz.	15 ml	3%
Unsalted butter	12 oz.	360 g	75%
Powdered sugar	6 oz.	180 g	37.5%
Egg	1.6 oz. (1 egg)	48 g	10%
Vanilla extract	0.5 fl. oz.	15 ml	3%
Salt	0.2 oz. (1 tsp.)	6 g	1.25%
Pastry or all-purpose flour, sifted	1 lb.	480 g	100%
Macadamia nuts, chopped fine	8 oz.	240 g	50%
Total dough weight:	3 lb. 10 oz.	1764 g	367%

1. Place the whole macadamia nuts and the brown sugar in the bowl of a food processor fitted with the metal blade. Grind until the mixture becomes smooth and resembles peanut butter. Set aside.
2. Melt the chocolate and oil in a bowl over simmering water. Set aside.
3. In the bowl of a mixer fitted with the paddle attachment, cream the butter until softened. Add the powdered sugar and cream until lightened. Blend in the macadamia mixture.
4. Scrape down the bowl, then gradually add the egg, followed by the vanilla and salt. Stir in the flour and chopped macadamia nuts and mix until just combined. Divide the dough into three uniform, 18-ounce (540-gram) pieces.
5. Place a silicone baking mat or piece of parchment on a work surface. Using an offset spatula, spread out one-third of the dough into a 6-inch × 10-inch (15-centimeter × 25-centimeter) rectangle. Level the surface evenly.
6. Spread half of the chocolate mixture onto the cookie dough. Freeze the chocolate-coated dough until the chocolate sets, approximately 3 to 5 minutes.
7. Spread another third of dough onto the chocolate-coated dough, leveling the surface evenly. Coat with the remaining melted chocolate. Freeze the layered dough until the chocolate sets, approximately 3 to 5 minutes.
8. Spread the remaining dough onto the chocolate-coated dough, leveling the surface evenly. Cover and chill the dough 1 hour or overnight in the freezer.
9. Cut the block of layered dough in half lengthwise. Mark the dough at ½-inch (1.2-centimeter) intervals, then portion the dough using a sharp knife. Place the cookies flat onto paper-lined baking sheets.
10. Bake at 375°F (190°C) until the cookies are golden, approximately 14 to 18 minutes.

Approximate values per cookie: **Calories** 220, **Total fat** 17 g, **Saturated fat** 6 g, **Cholesterol** 25 mg, **Sodium** 60 mg, **Total carbohydrates** 18 g, **Protein** 2 g

CUCCIDATI
(SICILIAN FIG COOKIES)

Yield: 12 Dozen Cookies

Method: Icebox cookies

Dough:

Pastry flour or all-purpose flour	2 lb. 4 oz.	1080 g	100%
Granulated sugar	1 lb. 2 oz.	540 g	50%
Baking powder	0.4 oz. (1 Tbsp.)	12 g	1.1%
Salt	0.6 oz. (1 Tbsp.)	17 g	1.6%
Unsalted butter, cold, cut in ¼-in. (6-mm) cubes	1 lb.	480 g	44.5%
Orange zest, grated	0.14 oz. (2 tsp.)	4 g	0.4%
Eggs	6.4 oz. (4 eggs)	194 g	18%
Buttermilk	8 fl. oz.	240 ml	22%
Vanilla extract	0.5 fl. oz.	15 ml	1.4%

Filling:

Dried figs, conditioned	1 lb.	480 g	44.5%
Raisins	8 oz.	240 g	22%
Honey	9 fl. oz.	270 ml	22%
Rum	2 fl. oz.	60 ml	5.5%
Lemon zest, grated	0.07 oz. (1 tsp.)	2 g	0.2%
Orange zest, grated	0.07 oz. (1 tsp.)	2 g	0.2%
Almonds, toasted, chopped coarse	10 oz.	300 g	28%
Walnuts, chopped coarse	5 oz.	150 g	14%
Cinnamon, ground	0.4 oz. (2 Tbsp.)	12 g	1.1%
Total dough weight:	8 lb. 8 oz.	4098 g	377%
Powdered sugar	as needed	as needed	

1. To prepare the dough, place the flour, sugar, baking powder, salt and butter in the chilled bowl of a large mixer fitted with the paddle attachment. Blend on low speed until the mixture resembles coarse cornmeal, approximately 3 to 4 minutes.

2. In a separate bowl, whisk together the orange zest, eggs, buttermilk and vanilla until smooth. Add the liquid mixture to the flour mixture. Mix on low speed until just combined.

3. Divide the dough into two uniform pieces. On a lightly floured surface, roll each piece of dough into a uniform 12-inch (30-centimeter) square. (Chill the dough before rolling, if necessary.) Wrap the rolled dough in plastic and freeze until firm, approximately 30 to 50 minutes.

4. Prepare the filling while the dough chills. Grind the figs, raisins, honey, rum and lemon and orange zests in the bowl of a food processor fitted with the metal blade until the fruit is chopped coarse. Scrape down the bowl, then continue blending until the mixture comes together into a coarse paste.

5. Scrape the fruit paste into a bowl. Fold in the chopped nuts and cinnamon.

6. Spread the fruit and nut paste evenly over one square of the frozen dough. Place the second dough square on top of the filling, pressing firmly to level it evenly. Wrap the layered dough in plastic and freeze until firm.

7. Cut the layered dough into 2-inch- (5-centimeter-) wide strips. Portion each frozen strip into ½-inch- (1.2-centimeter-) thick slices. Lay out each slice of dough, cut side down, on paper-lined sheet pans. Bake at 375°F (190°C) until light golden, approximately 15 to 18 minutes.

8. Cool the cookies, then dust lightly with powdered sugar before serving.

Approximate values per cookie: Calories 100, **Total fat** 4.5 g, **Saturated fat** 2 g, **Cholesterol** 10 mg, **Sodium** 60 mg, **Total carbohydrates** 15 g, **Protein** 2 g

OAT CHOCOLATE CHIP BAR COOKIES

Yield: 3 Dozen Bars, approximately 2 in. × 3 in. (5 cm × 7.5 cm), 1 Half-Sheet Pan

Method: Sheet cookies

Pastry or all-purpose flour	12 oz.	360 g	100%
Baking soda	0.14 oz. (1 tsp.)	4 g	1.1%
Cinnamon, ground	0.14 oz. (2 tsp.)	4 g	1.1%
Unsalted butter, softened	12 oz.	360 g	100%
Brown sugar	12 oz.	360 g	100%
Granulated sugar	6 oz.	180 g	50%
Eggs	5 oz. (3 eggs)	150 g	42%
Buttermilk	2 fl. oz.	60 ml	17%
Salt	0.2 oz. (1 tsp.)	5 g	1.4%
Vanilla extract	0.3 fl. oz. (2 tsp.)	9 ml	2.7%
Quick-cooking oats	14 oz.	420 g	116%
Chocolate chunks	12 oz.	360 g	100%
Walnuts, chopped	6 oz.	180 g	50%
Total dough weight:	5 lb. 1 oz.	2452 g	681%

1. Sift together the flour, baking soda and cinnamon. Set aside. Cream the butter and sugars. Gradually add the eggs, then mix in the buttermilk, salt, vanilla and oats. Add the flour mixture, beating just until well combined. Stir in the chocolate chunks and nuts.

2. Spread the batter on a greased and floured half-sheet pan and bake at 375°F (190°C) until golden, approximately 45 minutes.

3. After cooling, slide the sheet of cookies onto a workbench, then cut into 2-inch × 3-inch (5-centimeter × 7.5-centimeter) bars.

Approximate values per cookie: **Calories** 410, **Total fat** 23 g, **Saturated fat** 11 g, **Cholesterol** 50 mg, **Sodium** 150 mg, **Total carbohydrates** 51 g, **Protein** 6 g

LEMON OR LIME BARS

Yield: Approximately 80 Cookies, 1½ in. (4 cm) Square, 1 Half-Sheet Pan

Method: Sheet cookies

Sweet Tart Dough (page 368), chilled	2 lb. 8 oz.	1200 g
Egg wash	as needed	as needed
Filling:		
Granulated sugar	1 lb. 6 oz.	640 g
Eggs	13.3 oz. (8 eggs)	400 g
Pastry or all-purpose flour	2 oz.	60 g
Lemon or lime juice	11 fl. oz.	330 ml
Milk	5 fl. oz.	150 ml
Salt	0.1 oz. (½ tsp.)	3 g
Powdered sugar	4 oz.	120 g

1. Roll the chilled Sweet Tart Dough out on parchment paper to fit the sides and bottom of a half-sheet pan. Flip the parchment-covered dough onto a half-sheet pan. Remove the parchment. Trim uneven edges and reserve dough scraps. Prick the surface of the dough with a fork and bake at 350°F (180°C) until the dough is light golden and baked through, approximately 15 minutes. If cracks develop during the baking process, patch with the leftover dough and return briefly to the oven.

2 Brush the baked dough with egg wash and return to the oven for 3 minutes or until the egg wash has set.

3 To prepare the filling, whip the sugar and eggs just until smooth. Whisk in the flour until well combined, then add the lemon juice, milk and salt.

4 Pour the lemon filling into the prebaked shell.

5 Bake at 325°F (160°C) until set, approximately 25 to 30 minutes.

6 Cool, then cut into 1½-inch × 1½-inch (4-centimeter × 4-centimeter) squares. Dust liberally with powdered sugar.

Approximate values per cookie: **Calories** 140, **Total fat** 6 g, **Saturated fat** 3 g, **Cholesterol** 40 mg, **Sodium** 80 mg, **Total carbohydrates** 21 g, **Protein** 2 g

---

CLASSIC PECAN BARS

Yield: 8 Dozen Cookies, approximately 2 in. (5 cm) each, 1 Half-Sheet Pan

Method: Sheet cookies

Sweet Tart Dough (page 368)	2 lb. 8 oz.	1200 g
Filling:		
Brown sugar	15 oz.	450 g
Unsalted butter	8 oz.	240 g
Honey	14 oz.	420 g
Granulated sugar	3.5 oz.	105 g
Pecans, chopped	2 lb.	960 g
Heavy cream	4 fl. oz.	120 ml

1 Roll the chilled Sweet Tart Dough out on parchment paper to fit the sides and bottom of a half-sheet pan. Flip the parchment-covered dough onto a half-sheet pan. Remove the parchment. Trim uneven edges and reserve dough scraps. Prick the surface of the dough with a fork and bake at 350°F (180°C) until the dough is light golden, approximately 15 minutes. If cracks develop during the baking process, patch with the leftover dough and return briefly to the oven.

2 To prepare the filling, stir the brown sugar, butter, honey and granulated sugar together in a large saucepan. Bring the mixture to a full rolling boil. Boil the filling 3 minutes.

3 Remove the pan from the heat and stir in the pecans and cream. Pour the filling into the baked crust.

4 Bake at 350°F (180°C) until light brown and bubbling, approximately 15 to 20 minutes.

5 Cool on a wire rack completely before cutting. Cut into 2-inch (5-centimeter) squares, then cut each bar in half on the diagonal to make a triangle shape.

Approximate values per cookie: **Calories** 220, **Total fat** 11 g, **Saturated fat** 4.5 g, **Cholesterol** 50 mg, **Sodium** 105 mg, **Total carbohydrates** 28 g, **Protein** 3 g

GRANOLA BARS

Yield: 6 Dozen Bars, approximately 2 in. × 3 in. (5 cm × 7.5 cm) each, 1 Full-Sheet Pan

Method: Sheet cookies

			Sugar at 100%
Rolled oats	3 lb. 8 oz.	1680 g	255%
Coconut flakes, sweetened	1 lb. 4 oz.	600 g	91%
Slivered almonds	1 lb. 4 oz.	600 g	91%
Oat bran	10 oz.	300 g	46%
Sesame seeds	1 lb.	480 g	73%
Maple syrup	14 fl. oz.	420 ml	64%
Unsalted butter, melted	2 lb. 14 oz.	1380 g	209%
Honey	1 lb.	480 g	73%
Brown sugar	1 lb. 6 oz.	660 g	100%
Raisins or dried cranberries	1 lb.	480 g	73%
Total weight:	14 lb. 12 oz.	7080 g	1075%

1. Combine the oats, coconut, almonds, oat bran, sesame seeds, maple syrup and 1 pound 4 ounces (600 grams) of the butter in a large bowl. Toss well.

2. Divide the mixture evenly among four paper-lined sheet pans. Bake at 375°F (190°C), frequently tossing the mixture until the ingredients are light golden brown and fragrant, approximately 30 to 45 minutes in the oven. Remove the mixture from the oven and immediately transfer it into a large bowl.

3. Combine the honey, the remaining 1 pound 10 ounces (780 grams) of the butter and the brown sugar. Mix well. Pour over the warm toasted oat mixture. Stir in the raisins or cranberries.

4. Press the mixture into a paper-lined full-sheet pan fitted with a pan extender. Press down energetically and firmly on the mixture using a small cutting board to ensure that the ingredients will hold together.

5. Refrigerate until thoroughly chilled. Invert the pan onto a cutting board covered with a clean sheet of parchment paper and cut into 2-inch × 3-inch (5-centimeter × 7.5-centimeter) bars, rectangles or squares.

Approximate values per cookie: **Calories** 510, **Total fat** 32 g, **Saturated fat** 15 g, **Cholesterol** 45 mg, **Sodium** 10 mg, **Total carbohydrates** 57 g, **Protein** 9 g, **Calcium** 15%, **Iron** 20%

DULCE DE LECHE COOKIES

Yield: 60 Cookies, approximately ¾ oz. (22 g) each

Method: Cut-out cookies

Unsalted butter, cold, cut into ¼-in. (6-mm) dice	1 lb. 2 oz.	540 g	112%
Powdered sugar	7 oz.	210 g	44%
Salt	0.2 oz. (1 tsp.)	6 g	1.3%
Pastry flour, chilled	1 lb.	480 g	100%
Rice flour (or additional pastry flour)	4 oz.	120 g	25%
Vanilla extract	0.15 fl. oz. (1 tsp.)	5 ml	0.1%
Cinnamon, ground	0.2 oz. (1 Tbsp.)	6 g	1.2%
Total dough weight:	2 lb. 13 oz.	1367 g	284%
Dulce de leche	as needed	as needed	
Powdered sugar	as needed	as needed	

dulce de leche (DUL-say de LAY-chay) a thick, caramel-like syrup made by slowly heating sweetened milk; used as a sauce or spread especially in Latin American, Spanish and South American cooking

1. Place the butter, sugar, salt, flours, vanilla and cinnamon in the bowl of a mixer fitted with the paddle attachment. Blend the ingredients until the dough just barely comes together. (Or blend in the bowl of a food processor fitted with the metal blade.)

2. Remove the dough from the machine. Gather the dough together into a smooth ball. Flatten the dough onto a paper-lined sheet pan. Cover and chill until the dough is firm, approximately 1 hour.

3. On a lightly floured surface, roll out the dough to a thickness of ⅛ inch (3 millimeters). Cut out the dough with a 2-inch (5-centimeter) round floured cutter. Place on paper-lined sheet pans.

4. Bake at 375°F (190°C) until the cookies are light golden brown, approximately 8 to 10 minutes. Cool the cookies completely.

5. Turn over half of the cookies. Using a piping bag fitted with a plain tip, fill the center of each cookie with dulce de leche. Top each with another cookie.

6. To garnish, arrange the sandwich cookies in rows on clean sheet pans. Position 1-inch- (2.5-centimeter-) wide, long strips of parchment paper down the center of each row of cookies. Lightly sift powdered sugar over the exposed sections of the cookies.

Approximate values per cookie: Calories 170, **Total fat** 11 g, **Saturated fat** 5 g, **Cholesterol** 25 mg, **Sodium** 75 mg, **Total carbohydrates** 21 g, **Protein** 2 g

MIRROR COOKIES

Yield: 4 Dozen Cookies, 2½ in. (6 cm) each

Method: Cut-out cookies

Shortbread Tart Dough (page 382), made with hazelnuts, chilled	4 lb. 7 oz.	2.1 kg
Almond Macaronnade (recipe follows)	1 lb. 3 oz.	570 g
Red currant jam	1 lb.	480 g

Piping macaronnade on dough.

❶ On a well-floured surface, roll the chilled hazelnut Shortbread Tart Dough ¼ inch (6 millimeters) thick.

❷ Cut the dough into 2½-inch (6-centimeter) circles. Place the dough circles on paper-lined sheet pans and bake at 375°F (190°C) until pale blond in color, approximately 8 to 10 minutes.

❸ Using a pastry bag fitted with a small star tip, pipe a border of Almond Macaronnade along the edge of the baked cookie. Fill the center with red currant jam.

❹ Return to the oven and bake until the macaronnade is golden brown, approximately 12 to 14 minutes.

The finished cookies.

VARIATIONS:

Raspberry Streusel Squares—Omit the Almond Macaronnade. Roll the chilled hazelnut Shortbread Tart Dough into a ¼-inch- (6-millimeter-) thick rectangle and place on paper-lined half-sheet pans. Bake at 400°F (200°C) until blond in color, approximately 10 to 12 minutes. Coat with raspberry jam and top with Streusel Topping (page 145). Return to the oven. Reduce the temperature to 350°F (180°C) and bake another 10 to 12 minutes, until the jam is bubbling and the streusel is browned. Cool completely, then cut into bars.

Luxembergers—Substitute Coconut Almond Tart Dough (page 383). Roll the chilled dough into a rectangle ³⁄₁₆ inch (5 millimeters) thick. Cut into 12-inch- (30-centimeter-) long strips, 2 inches (5 centimeters) wide. Bake on paper-lined sheet pans at 400°F (200°C) until pale blond in color. Pipe three lines of Almond Macaronnade along the entire length of the strips, one down the center and one along each edge. Pipe a strip on both 2-inch (5-centimeter) ends to contain the jam. Substitute raspberry jam for the red currant jam. Return to the oven and bake until golden brown. Cool, then cut into ¾-inch (2-centimeter) squares.

ALMOND MACARONNADE

Yield: 1 lb. 3 oz. (585 g)

			Almond paste at 100%
Almond paste	12 oz.	360 g	100%
Granulated sugar	5 oz.	150 g	41%
Egg whites	2.5 fl. oz. (2.5 whites)	75 g	20%
Total weight:	1 lb. 3 oz.	585 g	161%

Luxembergers

❶ Blend the almond paste and sugar in the bowl of a mixer fitted with the paddle attachment. Add a quarter of the egg whites. Mix until the dough becomes completely homogenous. Scrape down the bowl and paddle. Gradually add the remaining egg whites until the dough is firm but soft enough to pipe.

❷ Scrape the dough into a pastry bag fitted with a small plain or star tip. Pipe a border of this dough onto a prebaked cookie or tart crust and bake as directed. Or pipe the dough into 1-inch (2.5-centimeter) circles on paper-lined sheet pans. Bake at 375°F (190°C) until the cookies are golden brown, approximately 12 to 14 minutes.

Approximate values per cookie: **Calories** 200, **Total fat** 15 g, **Saturated fat** 7 g, **Cholesterol** 65 mg, **Sodium** 75 mg, **Total carbohydrates** 24 g, **Protein** 4 g

SUGAR COOKIES

Scraps from this cookie dough can be carefully rerolled one time and used to make cookies. Once it has been reworked more than this, the dough will toughen noticeably. It can be used to line tart shells or rolled, baked then crumbled for topping.

Yield: 20 Cookies, approximately 1 oz. (30 g) each

Method: Cut-out cookies

Pastry or all-purpose flour	8 oz.	240 g	100%
Baking powder	0.07 oz. (½ tsp.)	2 g	0.9%
Unsalted butter, softened	6 oz.	180 g	75%
Granulated sugar	4 oz.	120 g	50%
Powdered sugar	2 oz.	60 g	25%
Salt	0.1 oz. (½ tsp.)	3 g	1.25%
Egg	1.6 oz. (1 egg)	48 g	20%
Vanilla extract	0.15 fl. oz. (1 tsp.)	5 ml	1.9%
Total dough weight:	1 lb. 5 oz.	658 g	274%
Decorative Cookie Icing (recipe follows)	as needed	as needed	

1. Sift together the flour and baking powder and set aside.
2. Cream the butter and sugars until light and fluffy. Blend in the salt, egg and vanilla. Add the flour mixture, beating just until combined.
3. Wrap the dough in plastic and refrigerate until firm, approximately 1 to 2 hours.
4. Work with half of the dough at a time, keeping the remainder refrigerated. On a lightly floured board, roll out the dough to a thickness of approximately ⅛ inch (3 millimeters). Cut as desired with cookie cutters approximately 3 inches (7.5 centimeters) in diameter. Carefully transfer the cookies to paper-lined or lightly buttered baking sheets.
5. Bake at 325°F (160°C) until set and pale golden in color, approximately 10 to 12 minutes. Let the cookies stand 1 minute, then transfer them to wire racks to cool.
6. To decorate the cookies, use a pastry bag fitted with a small plain tip to pipe a fine outline of Decorative Cookie Icing around the edge of each cookie. Allow the icing outline to set for 5 minutes. Thin the remaining icing with water until it has the texture of thick cream. Tint if desired. Fill the center of each cookie with additional decorative icing.

Approximate values per cookie: Calories 140, **Total fat** 7 g, **Saturated fat** 4.5 g, **Cholesterol** 30 mg, **Sodium** 150 mg, **Total carbohydrates** 17 g, **Protein** 1 g

DECORATIVE COOKIE ICING

Yield: 1 lb. 6 oz. (665 g)

Powdered sugar	1 lb.	480 g
Lemon juice or water	4 fl. oz.	120 ml
Corn syrup	2 fl. oz.	60 ml
Vanilla extract	0.15 fl. oz. (1 tsp.)	5 ml
Food coloring	as needed	as needed

1. Combine the sugar, lemon juice or water, corn syrup and vanilla in the bowl of a mixer fitted with the paddle attachment. Blend on low speed until the sugar dissolves and the mixture is smooth. Adjust the consistency of the icing by adding more water if necessary. Color as desired.
2. Apply the icing to cookies and let them air-dry until the icing hardens. Cover leftover icing and store it in the refrigerator, where it will keep about 3 weeks.

Approximate values per ¾-oz. (20-g) serving: Calories 60, **Total fat** 0 g, **Saturated fat** 0 g, **Cholesterol** 0 mg, **Sodium** 0 mg, **Total carbohydrates** 16 g, **Protein** 0 g

LINZER COOKIES

Yield: 2 Dozen Cookies, 2½ in. (6 cm) each

Method: Cut-out cookies

Shortbread Tart Dough (page 382), made with hazelnuts, chilled	4 lb. 7 oz.	2.1 kg
Raspberry jam	1 lb.	480 g

1. On a well-floured surface, roll the chilled hazelnut Shortbread Tart Dough ¼ inch (6 millimeters) thick.
2. Cut the dough with a floured cutter into 2½-inch (6-centimeter) circles or ovals. Place the dough cut-outs on paper-lined sheet pans.
3. Using a slightly smaller cookie cutter, remove the center from half of the dough cut-outs. These will be the cookie tops for the sandwich cookies. (Save the dough scraps for more cookies.)
4. Bake at 375°F (190°C) until pale blond in color, approximately 8 to 10 minutes. Cool the cookies completely.
5. Melt 3 ounces (90 grams) of the raspberry jam. Brush the solid cookies with the melted jam. Place the cookie tops on the jam-coated cookies. Using a pastry bag fitted with a small plain tip, fill the center of each cookie with the remaining raspberry jam.

Approximate values per cookie: **Calories** 200, **Total fat** 15 g, **Saturated fat** 7 g, **Cholesterol** 65 mg, **Sodium** 75 mg, **Total carbohydrates** 24 g, **Protein** 4 g

 ## GINGERBREAD COOKIES

Yield: 1 Dozen Cookies, 2⅓ oz. (70 g) each

Method: Cut-out cookies

Unsalted butter, softened	4 oz.	120 g	33%
Brown sugar	4 oz.	120 g	33%
Molasses, dark	6 fl. oz.	180 ml	50%
Egg	1.6 oz. (1 egg)	50 g	13%
All-purpose flour	12 oz.	360 g	100%
Baking soda	0.14 oz. (1 tsp.)	4 g	1%
Salt	0.1 oz. (½ tsp.)	3 g	0.8%
Ginger, ground	0.14 oz. (2 tsp.)	4 g	1%
Cinnamon, ground	0.07 oz. (1 tsp.)	2 g	0.6%
Nutmeg, ground	0.03 oz. (½ tsp.)	1 g	0.2%
Cloves, ground	0.03 oz. (½ tsp.)	1 g	0.2%
Total dough weight:	1 lb. 12 oz.	845 g	233%
Royal Icing (page 457)	as needed	as needed	

1. Cream the butter and sugar until light and fluffy. Add the molasses and egg and beat to blend well; set aside.
2. Stir together the remaining ingredients. Gradually add the flour mixture to the butter mixture, beating until just blended. Gather the dough into a ball and wrap in plastic wrap; refrigerate at least 1 hour.
3. On a lightly floured board, roll out the gingerbread to a thickness of ¼ inch (6 millimeters). Cut out the cookies with a floured cutter and transfer to greased baking sheets.
4. Bake at 325°F (160°C) until the cookies are lightly browned around the edges and feel barely firm when touched, approximately 10 minutes. Transfer to wire racks to cool, then decorate as desired with Royal Icing.

Approximate values per cookie: **Calories** 260, **Total fat** 8 g, **Saturated fat** 5 g, **Cholesterol** 40 mg, **Sodium** 220 mg, **Total carbohydrates** 41 g, **Protein** 4 g, **Vitamin A** 8%

SPECULAAS
(BELGIAN SPICE COOKIES)

Yield: 11 Dozen Cookies, approximately ⅔ oz. (20 g) each

Method: Cut-out cookies

Unsalted butter, softened	1 lb. 2 oz.	540 g	53%
Brown sugar	1 lb. 13 oz.	870 g	85%
Eggs	4.5 oz. (3 eggs)	135 g	13%
Milk	2 fl. oz.	60 ml	6%
Salt	0.2 oz. (1 tsp.)	6 g	0.6%
Cinnamon, ground	0.25 oz. (3½ tsp.)	8 g	0.7%
Speculaas Spices (recipe follows)	0.5 oz.	15 g	1.4%
Baking soda	0.75 oz.	20 g	2%
Pastry flour, sifted	2 lb. 2 oz.	1020 g	100%
Egg wash	as needed	as needed	
Sliced almonds	as needed	as needed	
Total dough weight:	5 lb. 9 oz.	2674 g	262%

1 Cream the butter and the sugar. Add the eggs, one at a time. Then add the milk, salt, cinnamon, Speculaas Spices and baking soda. Blend in the flour and mix until incorporated. Wrap the dough in plastic and refrigerate overnight.

2 On a lightly floured surface, roll the dough ⅛ inch (3 millimeters) thick. Cut into 3-inch × 1½-inch (7.5-centimeter × 4-centimeter) rectangles. Place on paper-lined sheet pans spaced 1 inch (2.5 centimeters) apart. Lightly brush with egg wash and sprinkle with sliced almonds.

3 Bake at 350°F (180°C) until the surface of the cookies bounces back when lightly pressed, approximately 18 minutes. Cool, then store in airtight containers. Speculaas will last several weeks.

SPECULAAS SPICES

Yield: 7¾ oz. (232 g)

Cinnamon, ground	4.5 oz.	135 g
Cloves, ground	1.25 oz.	37 g
Ginger, ground	1 oz.	30 g
Cardamom, ground	0.5 oz.	15 g
White pepper	0.5 oz.	15 g

1 Stir the ingredients together. Store in an airtight container in a dark cool place.

Approximate values per cookie: **Calories** 60, **Total fat** 3 g, **Saturated fat** 1.5 g, **Cholesterol** 10 mg, **Sodium** 50 mg, **Total carbohydrates** 10 g, **Protein** 1 g

Three savory crackers: Dijon Mustard Black Pepper Crackers (left), Whole Wheat Crackers (center), Parmesan Sun-Dried Tomato Crackers (right).

DIJON MUSTARD BLACK PEPPER CRACKERS

Yield: 10 Dozen Crackers, approximately ¼ oz. (7 g) each

Method: Cut-out cookies

Dijon mustard	2 oz.	60 g	20%
White wine	2 fl. oz.	60 ml	20%
Pastry or all-purpose flour	10 oz.	300 g	100%
Quick-cooking oats	4 oz.	120 g	40%
Baking powder	0.14 oz. (1 tsp.)	4 g	1.4%
Baking soda	0.28 oz. (2 tsp.)	8 g	2.8%
Salt	0.4 oz. (2 tsp.)	12 g	4%
Granulated sugar	1 oz.	30 g	10%
Black pepper, table grind	0.5 oz.	15 g	5%
Unsalted butter, cold, diced	6 oz.	180 g	60%
Black sesame seeds	as needed	as needed	
Total dough weight:	1 lb. 10 oz.	789 g	263%

1 Combine the mustard and wine in a small bowl. Set aside.

2 In the bowl of a mixer fitted with the paddle attachment, combine the flour, oats, baking powder, baking soda, salt, sugar, black pepper and butter. Mix on low speed until the butter is pea size.

3 Add the mustard mixture and blend on low speed until smooth. Gather the mixture into a ball of dough.

4 Divide the dough into four pieces. Working with one piece of dough at a time, roll the dough ⅛ inch (3 millimeters) thick. Cut into 2-inch (5-centimeter) rounds with a cookie cutter and place on paper-lined sheet pans. Sprinkle with black sesame seeds.

5 Bake at 400°F (200°C) until golden, approximately 8 to 10 minutes.

Approximate values per cracker: **Calories** 25, **Total fat** 1.5 g, **Saturated fat** 0.5 g, **Cholesterol** 5 mg, **Sodium** 70 mg, **Total carbohydrates** 3 g, **Protein** 0 g

PARMESAN SUN-DRIED TOMATO CRACKERS

Yield: 10 Dozen Crackers, approximately ¼ oz. (7 g) each

Method: Cut-out cookies

Pastry or all-purpose flour	12 oz.	360 g	100%
Unsalted butter, cold, diced	6 oz.	180 g	50%
Parmesan cheese, grated	8 oz.	240 g	67%
Sun-dried tomatoes, chopped fine	3 oz.	90 g	25%
Fresh basil, chopped fine	0.3 oz. (3 Tbsp.)	9 g	2.5%
Fresh oregano, chopped fine	0.2 oz. (2 Tbsp.)	6 g	1.7%
Salt	0.3 oz. (1½ tsp.)	9 g	2.5%
Garlic powder	0.1 oz. (1 Tbsp.)	3 g	0.1%
Balsamic vinegar	2 fl. oz.	60 ml	17%
Total dough weight:	1 lb. 15 oz.	957 g	265%

1. In the bowl of a mixer fitted with the paddle attachment, combine the flour, butter, cheese, tomatoes, basil, oregano, salt and garlic powder. Mix on low speed until the butter is pea size and still visible.

2. Add the vinegar and mix until a soft dough is formed. Wrap the dough in plastic and chill until firm, at least 1 hour.

3. On a lightly floured surface, roll the dough ⅛ inch (3 millimeters) thick. Cut into 1-inch (2.5-centimeter) squares with a cookie cutter and place on paper-lined sheet pans.

4. Bake at 375°F (190°C) until light golden brown, approximately 12 to 14 minutes.

Approximate values per cracker: **Calories** 30, **Total fat** 1.5 g, **Saturated fat** 1 g, **Cholesterol** 5 mg, **Sodium** 70 mg, **Total carbohydrates** 3 g, **Protein** 1 g

WHOLE-WHEAT CRACKERS

Yield: 10 Dozen Crackers, approximately ¼ oz. (7 g) each

Method: Cut-out cookies

Whole-wheat flour, stone ground	10 oz.	300 g	100%
Quick-cooking oats	6 oz.	180 g	60%
Baking powder	0.14 oz. (1 tsp.)	4 g	1.4%
Granulated sugar	0.5 oz.	15 g	5%
Black pepper	0.2 oz. (1 Tbsp.)	6 g	2%
Cayenne pepper, ground	0.14 oz. (2 tsp.)	4 g	1.4%
Sesame seeds	1 oz.	30 g	1%
Salt	0.4 oz. (2 tsp.)	12 g	4.2%
Unsalted butter, cold, diced	10 oz.	300 g	100%
Balsamic vinegar	2 fl. oz.	60 ml	20%
Total dough weight:	1 lb. 14 oz.	911 g	304%

1. In the bowl of a mixer fitted with the paddle attachment, combine all the ingredients except the vinegar. Mix on low speed until the butter is pea size.

2. Add the vinegar and mix until a dough forms.

3. Roll the dough ⅛ inch (3 millimeters) thick. Cut into 1-inch (2.5-centimeter) diamonds with a cookie cutter and place on paper-lined sheet pans.

4. Bake at 375°F (190°C) until light golden brown, approximately 12 to 14 minutes.

Approximate values per cracker: **Calories** 35, **Total fat** 2 g, **Saturated fat** 1.5 g, **Cholesterol** 5 mg, **Sodium** 40 mg, **Total carbohydrates** 3 g, **Protein** 1 g

RUGELACH

Yield: 3 Dozen Cookies, approximately 1½ oz. (45 g) each

Method: Rolled cookies

Pastry flour	15 oz.	450 g	100%
Baking soda	0.07 oz. (½ tsp.)	2 g	0.5%
Cream cheese, room temperature	9 oz.	270 g	60%
Granulated sugar	7 oz.	210 g	46%
Lemon zest, grated fine	0.14 oz. (2 tsp.)	4 g	1%
Unsalted butter, softened	8 oz.	240 g	53%
Salt	0.2 oz. (1 tsp.)	6 g	1.3%
Red currant or apricot jam	12 oz.	360 g	80%
Dried cherries, finely chopped	4 oz.	120 g	26%
Walnuts, chopped coarse	4 oz.	120 g	26%
Cinnamon, ground	as needed	as needed	
Egg wash	as needed	as needed	
Total dough weight:	3 lb. 11 oz.	1782 g	394%
Powdered sugar	as needed	as needed	

1. Sift together the flour and baking soda. Set aside.
2. Blend the cream cheese, sugar and lemon zest on low speed until homogenous. Add the butter and salt and blend well. Mix in the flour mixture until combined. Chill the dough 2 hours.
3. Divide the dough into 12-ounce (360-gram) pieces. On a lightly floured surface, roll each piece of dough into a strip ¼ inch (6 millimeters) thick and 6 inches (15 centimeters) wide. Trim the edges. Spread 4 ounces (120 grams) of jam on each strip of dough. Lightly sprinkle with cherries and walnuts, followed by cinnamon.
4. Cut the dough into 2½-inch (6-centimeter) triangles. Roll each piece as for filled croissants (see the photo on page 289). Place on paper-lined sheet pans and brush with egg wash.
5. Bake at 375°F (190°C) until golden, approximately 12 to 14 minutes.
6. Lightly dust with powdered sugar.

Approximate values per cookie: **Calories** 160, **Total fat** 10 g, **Saturated fat** 5 g, **Cholesterol** 20 mg, **Sodium** 105 mg, **Total carbohydrates** 17 g, **Protein** 2 g

1. Spreading jam on rugelach dough.

2. Cutting jam-and-nut-topped rugelach dough into triangles.

3. Rolling the rugelach before placing on a sheet pan and baking.

SWEDISH YULE LOGS

This cookie goes by a number of names depending upon its shape, the type of nuts and spices used and where it is served. The dough may be rolled into a ball as for Russian Tea Cakes and Mexican Wedding Cookies (Polvorones). Or it may be curved into a crescent shape as for these Swedish-style cookies. Finely ground hazelnuts, pecans or walnuts may be used in the formula or nuts may be omitted entirely. The ground cardamom gives this dough its Scandinavian flavor profile. Omit it or add another ground spice such as powdered ginger or cinnamon in its place.

Yield: 1 ½ Dozen Cookies, approximately 1 ½ oz. (45 g) each

Method: Molded cookies

Unsalted butter, softened	10 oz.	300 g	83%
Powdered sugar	2 oz.	60 g	16%
Vanilla extract	0.25 fl. oz. (1½ tsp.)	7.5 ml	2%
Sherry or vanilla extract	1 fl. oz.	30 ml	8%
Cardamom, ground	0.04 oz. (½ tsp.)	1 g	0.3%
All-purpose flour	12 oz.	360 g	100%
Pecans or walnuts, chopped fine	3.75 oz.	112 g	31%
Total dough weight:	1 lb. 13 oz.	870 g	240%
Powdered sugar	as needed	as needed	

1 Cream the butter and sugar together until smooth. Stir in the vanilla, sherry and cardamom.

2 Stir the flour and pecans together, then add to the creamed butter mixture, blending well. Cover and chill 30 minutes.

3 Portion the dough into uniform 1½-ounce (45-gram) pieces. Shape each piece into a log, then bend the ends to create a crescent shape. Place on an ungreased baking sheet and bake at 375°F (190°C) until set and very lightly browned, approximately 12 minutes.

4 Sift powdered sugar onto a pan or plate. Cool the baked cookies 5 to 6 minutes, then carefully roll them in the sugar, coating thoroughly. After the cookies are completely cool they may be rerolled in powdered sugar if necessary to form a solid coating.

Approximate values per cookie: **Calories** 240, **Total fat** 17 g, **Saturated fat** 8 g, **Cholesterol** 35 mg, **Sodium** 0 mg, **Total carbohydrates** 18 g, **Protein** 3 g, **Vitamin A** 10%

CHINESE ALMOND COOKIES

Yield: 40 Cookies, approximately ¾ oz. (20 g) each

Method: Rolled cookies

Granulated sugar	8 oz.	240 g	66%
All-purpose or pastry flour	12 oz.	360 g	100%
Baking soda	0.07 oz. (½ tsp.)	2 g	0.06%
Unsalted butter, chilled	8 oz.	240 g	66%
Egg	1.6 oz. (1 egg)	48 g	13%
Almond extract	0.15 fl. oz. (1 tsp.)	5 ml	1.25%
Almond halves	40	40	
Egg whites, lightly beaten	as needed	as needed	
Granulated sugar	as needed	as needed	
Total dough weight:	1 lb. 13 oz.	895 g	247%

1. Combine the sugar, flour and baking soda in the bowl of a mixer fitted with the paddle attachment. Grate the butter over the small holes of a box grater directly into the flour mixture.
2. Combine the ingredients just until the butter is evenly coated with the flour and the mixture is crumbly.
3. Whisk together the egg and almond extract. Add it to the flour mixture and mix until the dough is just combined without any pieces of butter being visible.
4. Divide the dough into four equal portions. Roll each piece into a 10-inch- (25-centimeter-) long cylinder.
5. Cut the cylinders into 1-inch- (2.5-centimeter-) thick slices. Roll each piece into a ball and place onto paper-lined sheet pans. Press each ball down using the bottom of a measuring cup to ½ inch (1.2 centimeters) thick.
6. Press an almond half into each cookie. Brush lightly with egg white and sprinkle lightly with granulated sugar.
7. Bake at 350°F (180°C) until golden and the edges are crisp, approximately 18 to 20 minutes.

Approximate values per cookie: **Calories** 100, **Total fat** 5 g, **Saturated fat** 3 g, **Cholesterol** 15 mg, **Sodium** 15 mg, **Total carbohydrates** 12 g, **Protein** 1 g

SPRITZ COOKIES

Yield: 4 Dozen Cookies, approximately ½ oz. (15 g) each

Method: Piped cookies

Unsalted butter, softened	8 oz.	240 g	80%
Granulated sugar	4 oz.	120 g	40%
Salt	0.05 oz. (¼ tsp.)	1.5 g	0.5%
Vanilla extract	0.15 fl. oz. (1 tsp.)	5 ml	1.5%
Egg	1.6 oz. (1 egg)	50 g	16%
Cake flour, sifted	10 oz.	300 g	100%
Fruit preserves	as needed	as needed	
Total dough weight:	1 lb. 7 oz.	716 g	238%

1. Cream the butter and sugar until light and fluffy. Add the salt, vanilla extract and egg; beat well.
2. Add the flour, beating until just blended. The dough should be firm but neither sticky nor stiff.
3. Press or pipe the dough onto an ungreased sheet pan, using a cookie press or a piping bag fitted with a large star tip. Indent each mound of dough with a gloved finger dipped in water. Pipe fruit preserves onto each cookie.
4. Bake at 350°F (180°C) until lightly browned around the edges, approximately 10 minutes. Transfer to wire racks to cool.

VARIATIONS:

Citrus Spritz Cookies—Add 0.21 ounces (1 tablespoon/6 grams/2%) grated lemon zest to the butter in Step 1.

Cinnamon Spritz Cookies—Add 0.04 ounces (½ teaspoon/1.2 grams/0.4%) ground cinnamon with the flour in Step 2. Sprinkle the piped cookies with cocoa nibs before baking in Step 3 if desired.

Approximate values per cookie: **Calories** 70, **Total fat** 4 g, **Saturated fat** 2.5 g, **Cholesterol** 15 mg, **Sodium** 15 mg, **Total carbohydrates** 7 g, **Protein** 1 g

1. Indenting the piped cookie dough.

2. Filling the dough with fruit preserves before baking.

WHOOPIE PIES

As with many foods, tracing the origins of the Whoopie Pie is a delicious mystery. It's been a favorite in the Northeast for years, yet the Whoopie Pie is neither a cookie nor a pie, but something else entirely. Two states and one city claim ownership, but first a definition.

Whoopie Pies are two dark chocolate cakes with a creamy vanilla center. They're squishy, sticky and soft, and kids of all ages love them.

In Maine, the story is that a commercial baker plopped some leftover batter onto a baking sheet, added some frosting and pressed the two halves together, creating a sandwich concoction that was an immediate hit with customers. Amish farmers in Pennsylvania also take credit for creating the black-and-white treat. The story is that Amish mothers would pack the portable cake in their children's lunch pails. When kids saw the treat, they'd shout, "Whoopie!" In Boston, some say the Berwick Baking Company started making them during the Great Depression. Some food historians have traced them to the shores of Europe. What seems more likely is that imaginative bakers working independently in various places developed a baked confection people would love.

❶ Piping buttercream on the cooked cookies.

❷ The finished cookie.

Yield: 20 Sandwiched cookies

Method: Piped cookies

All-purpose flour	10 oz.	300 g	100%
Baking soda	0.14 oz. (1 tsp.)	4 g	1.45%
Cream of tartar	0.07 oz. (½ tsp.)	2 g	0.7%
Cocoa powder	2.5 oz.	75 g	25%
Granulated sugar	8 oz.	240 g	80%
Salt	0.2 oz. (1 tsp.)	6 g	2%
Egg	1.6 oz. (1 egg)	48 g	16%
Vegetable oil	3 fl. oz.	90 ml	30%
Vanilla extract	0.2 fl. oz. (1 tsp.)	6 ml	2%
Buttermilk (1% fat), shaken	12 fl. oz.	360 ml	120%
Total batter weight:	2 lb. 5 oz.	1131 g	377%
Simple Buttercream (page 451) or other icing	1 lb. 4 oz.	600 g	

❶ Sift together the flour, baking soda, cream of tartar, cocoa powder, sugar and salt and set aside.

❷ In a separate bowl, whisk the egg and oil together until completely blended. Add the vanilla and buttermilk.

❸ Stir in the dry ingredients using a firm whisk, just until blended, without overmixing.

❹ Using a pastry bag fitted with a large plain tip, pipe the batter into even mounds, allowing space for spreading.

❺ Bake at 375°F (190°C) until the center of the cakes bounce back when lightly pressed for approximately 11 to 13 minutes.

❻ Cool the cakes on a wire rack. Pipe a ring of Simple Buttercream around the perimeter of the flat side of half of the cakes. Top with another cake.

Approximate values per serving: **Calories** 150, **Total fat** 5 g, **Saturated fat** 1 g, **Cholesterol** 10 mg, **Sodium** 190 mg, **Total carbohydrates** 24 g, **Protein** 3 g

GINGERSNAPS

Yield: 150 Cookies, approximately ⅓ oz. (9 g) each

Method: Piped cookies

All-purpose flour	2 lb. 4 oz.	1080 g	100%
Baking soda	0.5 oz. (4 tsp.)	16 g	1.5%
Unsalted butter	1 lb.	480 g	44.5%
Granulated sugar	2 lb.	960 g	89%
Honey	16 fl. oz.	480 ml	44.5%
Eggs	6.4 oz. (4 eggs)	190 g	18%
Salt	0.2 oz. (1 tsp.)	6 g	0.5%
Ginger, ground	1 oz.	30 g	3%
Cinnamon, ground	0.27 oz. (4 tsp.)	8 g	0.07%
White pepper, ground	0.07 oz. (1 tsp.)	2 g	0.02%
Allspice, ground	0.27 oz. (4 tsp.)	8 g	0.07%
Granulated sugar, for topping	0.6 oz. (3 Tbsp.)	18 g	1.5%
Total weight:	6 lb. 13 oz.	3278 g	303%

1. Sift together the flour and baking soda. Set aside.
2. Cream the butter in the bowl of a mixer fitted with the paddle attachment. Add the sugar and honey and cream until light and fluffy.
3. Beat in the eggs one at a time, mixing well after each addition.
4. Add the salt and spices and mix well. Add the flour mixture all at once mixing until just combined.
5. Using a plain tip, pipe the dough into 1-inch (2.5-centimeter) mounds with space for spreading. Sprinkle with granulated sugar.
6. Bake at 350°F (180°C) until the cookies have just collapsed, approximately 12 to 14 minutes. (For a slightly chewy cookie, remove the cookies from the oven while still pale and soft.)
7. Transfer to wire racks to cool.

Approximate values per ¾-oz. (22-g) serving: **Calories** 90, **Total fat** 2.5 g, **Saturated fat** 1.5 g, **Cholesterol** 10 mg, **Sodium** 45 mg, **Total carbohydrates** 15 g, **Protein** 1 g

NEW ORLEANS PRALINE COOKIES

Yield: 80 Cookies, approximately 1 oz. (30 g) each

Method: Piped cookies

Pastry flour	1 lb. 12 oz.	840 g	100%
Baking powder	0.4 oz. (1 Tbsp.)	12 g	1.5%
Unsalted butter, softened	12 oz.	360 g	43%
Brown sugar	2 lb. 4 oz.	1085 g	128%
Eggs	4.8 oz. (3 eggs)	145 g	17%
Vanilla extract	0.5 fl. oz.	15 ml	1.8%
Salt	0.4 oz. (2 tsp.)	10 g	1.4%
Total dough weight:	5 lb. 2 oz.	2467 g	293%
Pecan Praline (recipe follows)	1 lb. 6 oz.	660 g	

1. Sift together the flour and baking powder. Set aside.
2. In the bowl of a mixer fitted with the paddle attachment, cream the butter. Add the sugar and mix until combined and lump-free. Add the eggs gradually, followed by the vanilla and salt, mixing only until the dough comes together. Blend in the flour mixture just until a soft dough is formed.
3. Using a large plain tip, pipe the dough into 1-ounce (30-gram) rounds spaced 2 inches 5 (centimeters) apart onto paper-lined sheet pans. (Or portion the dough using a #30 portion scoop.)
4. Bake at 380°F (195°C) until the cookies are golden brown, approximately 10 to 12 minutes.
5. Warm the Pecan Praline in a double boiler over simmering water.
6. Spoon a tablespoon of the Pecan Praline onto each cookie. Allow the praline to cool slightly and set before packaging or serving.

Approximate values per cookie: **Calories** 150, **Total fat** 5 g, **Saturated fat** 2.5 g, **Cholesterol** 20 mg, **Sodium** 90 mg, **Total carbohydrates** 25 g, **Protein** 1 g

PECAN PRALINE

Yield: 1 lb. 6 oz. (660 g)

Heavy cream	4 fl. oz.	120 ml
Brown sugar	7 oz.	210 g
Powdered sugar	5 oz.	150 g
Maple syrup	2 fl. oz.	60 ml
Vanilla bean, halved and seeded	½	½
Salt	1 pinch	1 pinch
Pecan pieces, small	4 oz.	120 g
Total weight:	1 lb. 6 oz.	660 g

1. Bring the cream, sugars, maple syrup, vanilla bean and salt to a boil in a nonreactive saucepan, stirring frequently with a heat-resistant spatula. Boil for 2 to 3 minutes, stirring if necessary. Remove the mixture from heat. Remove the vanilla bean. Stir in the pecans.
2. Use to fill cookies or top cakes when slightly warm. Reheat as needed in a microwave oven or over a double boiler.

BUTTER COOKIES

Yield: 2 Dozen Cookies, approximately 1 ¼ oz. (37 g) each

Method: Piped cookies

Unsalted butter, softened	9 oz.	270 g	82%
Powdered sugar	6 oz.	180 g	54%
Egg	1.6 oz. (1 egg)	50 g	15%
Vanilla extract	0.5 fl. oz.	15 ml	5%
Orange oil	5 drops	5 drops	
Almond oil	0.15 fl. oz. (1 tsp.)	5 ml	1%
Salt	0.2 oz (1 tsp.)	6 g	2%
Pastry flour	11 oz.	330 g	100%
Pistachios	as needed	as needed	
Dried cherries	as needed	as needed	
Almonds, slivered	as needed	as needed	
Candied orange or grapefruit peel	as needed	as needed	
Total dough weight:	1 lb. 12 oz.	856 g	259%

1. Cream the butter and sugar. Gradually add the egg, vanilla, oils and salt. Blend in the flour just until combined.
2. Using a piping bag and a medium-size star tip, pipe 1-inch (2.5-centimeter) rosettes on parchment-lined sheet pans. Place a pistachio, dried cherry, almond sliver and piece of candied peel on each cookie.
3. Bake at 375°F (190°C) until golden, approximately 10 to 12 minutes.

Approximate values per cookie: **Calories** 150, **Total fat** 9 g, **Saturated fat** 5 g, **Cholesterol** 30 mg, **Sodium** 100 mg, **Total carbohydrates** 17 g, **Protein** 2 g

ALMOND HORNS

tempering a process of melting chocolate during which the temperature of the cocoa butter is carefully stabilized; this keeps the chocolate smooth and glossy

Yield: 3 Dozen Cookies, ¾ oz. (20 g) each

Method: Piped cookies

			Almond paste at 100%
Almond paste	1 lb.	480 g	100%
Granulated sugar	8 oz.	240 g	50%
Grapefruit zest, grated fine	0.4 oz. (2 Tbsp.)	12 g	2.5%
Vanilla extract	0.5 fl. oz.	15 ml	3%
Egg whites	4 oz. (4 whites)	120 g	25%
Almonds, sliced	as needed	as needed	
Egg whites, beaten	as needed	as needed	
Granulated sugar	as needed	as needed	
Total dough weight:	1 lb. 12 oz.	867 g	180%
Semisweet chocolate, **tempered**	as needed	as needed	

1. In the bowl of a mixer fitted with the paddle attachment, blend the almond paste, sugar and grapefruit zest on low speed until lump-free. Add the vanilla.
2. Beat in the egg whites gradually in four steps, waiting for each addition to be completely incorporated and then scraping down the bowl before adding the next. Add only enough egg whites to make a firm yet pipeable batter.
3. Spread a thick layer of sliced almonds in a hotel pan. With a large plain tip, pipe the dough into 2-inch (5-centimeter) strips, each weighing about ¾ ounce (20 grams). Pipe the dough directly onto the sliced almonds, then roll the dough into the almonds to coat. Shape each piece of dough into a small crescent, then place the cookie on a clean paper-lined baking sheet.
4. Lightly brush the cookies with beaten egg whites and sprinkle with sugar.
5. Bake at 375°F (190°C) for approximately 15 minutes. Cool completely, then dip the ends of the cookies in tempered semisweet chocolate.

Approximate values per cookie: **Calories** 80, **Total fat** 3.5 g, **Saturated fat** 0 g, **Cholesterol** 0 mg, **Sodium** 5 mg, **Total carbohydrates** 12 g, **Protein** 1 g

BRANDY SNAPS

Yield: 4 Dozen Cookies, approximately ⅓ oz. (10 g) each

Method: Wafer cookies

Unsalted butter	4 oz.	120 g	100%
Granulated sugar	4 oz.	120 g	100%
Glucose or corn syrup	2.5 fl. oz.	75 ml	62.5%
Brandy	1 fl. oz.	30 ml	25%
Salt	0.05 oz. (¼ tsp.)	1.5 g	0.1%
Lemon zest, grated	0.14 oz. (2 tsp.)	4 g	3.5%
Ginger, ground	0.14 oz. (2 tsp.)	4 g	3.5%
All-purpose or pastry flour	4 oz.	120 g	100%
Total dough weight:	15 oz.	474 g	395%
Crème Chantilly (optional)	as needed	as needed	

1. Combine the butter, sugar and syrup in a saucepan and stir over medium heat until melted. Do not boil the mixture. Remove from the heat.
2. Add the brandy, salt, lemon zest and ginger and combine. Stir in the flour.
3. Using a piping bag fitted with a plain medium tip, pipe the mixture into teaspoon-sized mounds well apart on silicone- or parchment-lined sheet pans.
4. Bake at 350°F (180°C) until evenly golden brown, approximately 9 minutes. Lift the cookies using a metal spatula and roll onto a cannoli form or narrow metal cylinder. Allow to cool.
5. Fill with brandy-flavored Crème Chantilly (page 502) if desired.

Approximate values per cookie: Calories 40, **Total fat** 2 g, **Saturated fat** 1 g, **Cholesterol** 5 mg, **Sodium** 15 mg, **Total carbohydrates** 5 g, **Protein** 0 g

1. Piping the batter.

2. Rolling the warm cookie onto the form.

❶ Spreading the batter into circles on a sheet pan lined with a silicone mat.

❷ Shaping the baked wafer cookies into cups while still hot.

TUILE BATTER (TULIPE COOKIES)

Yield: 2 Dozen Cookies, approximately 6 in. (15 cm) in diameter, approximately ¾ oz. (22 g) each

Method: Wafer cookies

Unsalted butter	4 oz.	120 g	100%
Powdered sugar	4 oz.	120 g	100%
Egg whites, room temperature	4 oz.	120 g	100%
All-purpose flour	4 oz.	120 g	100%
Total batter weight:	1 lb.	480 g	400%
Butter, melted	as needed	as needed	

❶ Cream the butter and sugar in the bowl of a mixer fitted with the paddle attachment. Gradually add the egg whites. Blend in the flour without overmixing.

❷ Coat several sheet pans with melted butter or line with silicone mats. Spread the batter into 6-inch (15-centimeter) circles on the pans. Bake at 400°F (200°C) until the edges are brown and the batter is dry, approximately 4 to 6 minutes.

❸ To shape into cups, lift the hot cookies off the sheet pan one at a time with an offset spatula. Immediately place over an inverted glass bowl and top with a ramekin or small bowl. The cookies cool very quickly, becoming firm and crisp. (If the cookies have cooled before the shaping process, reheat them until they are very soft, about 3 minutes, and then resume the shaping process.) The cookie bowls can be used for serving ice cream, crème brûlée, fruit or other items.

VARIATION:

Russian Cigarette Cookies—Spread the batter into 3-inch (7.5-centimeter) circles on a silicone baking mat or buttered sheet pans. Bake at 425°F (220°C) until golden and the edges are lightly brown, approximately 4 to 6 minutes. Lift the cookies off the sheet pan one at a time with an offset spatula. Immediately roll each cookie around a ¼-inch (6-millimeter) dowel. After cooling, dip the ends in tempered chocolate.

Approximate values per cookie: **Calories** 240, **Total fat** 12 g, **Saturated fat** 8 g, **Cholesterol** 35 mg, **Sodium** 40 mg, **Total carbohydrates** 37 g, **Protein** 4 g, **Vitamin A** 10%

Rolling baked wafer batter around a dowel to make cigarette cookies

Russian Cigarettes

ALMOND TUILES

Yield: 48 Cookies, approximately 3 in. (7.5 cm) in diameter

Method: Wafer cookies

Granulated sugar	6 oz.	180 g	400%
Egg whites	4 oz. (4 whites)	120 g	266%
Vanilla extract	0.15 fl. oz. (1 tsp.)	5 ml	10%
Salt	0.05 oz. (¼ tsp.)	1.5 g	3%
Cake or all-purpose flour	1.5 oz.	45 g	100%
Unsalted butter, melted	2.25 oz.	67 g	150%
Almonds, sliced, toasted, coarsely chopped	6 oz.	180 g	400%
Orange zest, grated	0.07 oz.	2 g	4.5%
Total dough weight:	1 lb. 4 oz.	600 g	1333.5%
Melted butter for pans	2 fl. oz.	60 ml	

❶ The cookies cooling in a tuile sheet.

❶ Whisk together the sugar, egg whites, vanilla and salt until thick, approximately 2 to 3 minutes. Add the flour and mix well.

❷ Add the melted butter, almonds and orange zest. Refrigerate 1 hour or overnight.

❸ Coat several sheets of parchment paper with melted butter. Alternatively, use clean silicone pan liners.

❹ Working on a flat surface, spread the batter into 3-inch (7.5-centimeter) circles onto one sheet of the buttered paper. Transfer the paper to a baking sheet. Bake at 400°F (200°C) until golden brown, approximately 6 to 8 minutes.

❺ Remove the pan from the oven. Working quickly using a metal spatula, lift each cookie off the paper. Drape them over a small rolling pin or place them upside down in a tuile sheet.

❻ Cool, then store the cookies in airtight containers.

Approximate values per cookie: Calories 50, **Total fat** 3.5 g, **Saturated fat** 1 g, **Cholesterol** 5 mg, **Sodium** 15 mg, **Total carbohydrates** 5 g, **Protein** 1 g

❷ The finished cookies.

BISCOTTI

Italian in origin, biscotti are twice-baked cookies served with coffee, wine or other beverages. The dough is mixed and shaped into a log. The log of dough is baked, then cut on a diagonal into individual cookies, which are returned to the oven to bake further. This twice-baked process ensures that the cookies will have a long-lasting firm, crisp texture.

Yield: 3 Dozen Biscotti, 2 oz. (60 g) each

Method: Bar cookies

Cinnamon, ground	0.2 oz. (1 Tbsp.)	4 g	1%
Ammonium carbonate or baking powder	0.3 oz. (2 tsp.)	8 g	1.8%
Hazelnut flour	10 oz.	300 g	62%
Almond flour	3 oz.	90 g	19%
Pastry flour	1 lb.	480 g	100%
Eggs	8.3 oz. (5 eggs)	250 g	52%
Salt	0.2 oz. (1 tsp.)	6 g	1.25%
Granulated sugar	1 lb.	480 g	100%
Unsalted butter, melted	8 oz.	240 g	50%
Whole hazelnuts	10 oz.	300 g	62%
Total dough weight:	4 lb. 8 oz.	2152 g	448%
Chocolate, melted and tempered (optional)	as needed	as needed	

❶ Biscotti dough rolled into a log before the first baking.

❷ Slicing biscotti before the second baking.

❸ The finished biscotti.

❶ Sift together the cinnamon and ammonium carbonate or baking powder. Stir in the flours. Set aside.

❷ In a large bowl, whisk together the eggs, salt and sugar until thick, pale and at least doubled in volume, approximately 3 minutes. Add the butter. Stir in the flour mixture with a rubber spatula, then stir in the hazelnuts.

❸ Divide the dough into three equal pieces. Refrigerate until cold.

❹ Roll each piece of dough into a 12-inch (30-centimeter) log. Place on a paper-lined sheet pan, leaving at least 3 inches (7.5 centimeters) of space between each log.

❺ Bake at 350°F (180°C) until golden brown, approximately 20 minutes. Cool the logs, then slice them into 1-inch- (2.5-centimeter-) thick slices.

❻ Place the sliced cookies upright on paper-lined sheet pans. Place each sheet pan on top of a clean sheet pan to insulate the cookies.

❼ Reduce heat to 325°F (160°C) and bake until the biscotti are thoroughly crisp, approximately 40 minutes.

❽ Once cool, the biscotti may be dipped in tempered chocolate, if desired.

VARIATIONS:

Orange Biscotti—Add 0.5 oz. (15 grams/3%) grated orange zest to the flour mixture.

Anise Biscotti—Add 0.25 ounce (7 grams/1.5%) chopped anise seeds to the flour mixture.

Chocolate Biscotti—Replace 5 ounces (150 grams/31%) of the pastry flour with cocoa powder. Add 0.3 fluid ounces: (9 milligrams/2%) coffee extract and 0.3 ounce (9 grams/2%) ground cinnamon to the flour mixture.

Approximate values per cookie: **Calories** 260, **Total fat** 17 g, **Saturated fat** 4 g, **Cholesterol** 45 mg, **Sodium** 30 mg, **Total carbohydrates** 26 g, **Protein** 5 g

BLONDIES

Yield: 4 Dozen Bars, approximately 2 in. (5 cm) each, 1 Half-Sheet Pan

Method: Sheet cookies

All-purpose flour	1 lb. 1 oz.	510 g	100%
Baking soda	0.14 oz. (1 tsp.)	4 g	0.08%
Cream of tartar	0.02 oz. (⅛ tsp.)	0.5 g	0.01%
Unsalted butter, softened	12 oz.	360 g	70.5%
Brown sugar	1 lb. 2 oz.	540 g	106%
Corn syrup or honey	3 oz.	90 g	17.5%
Eggs	5 oz. (3 eggs)	150 g	29%
Vanilla extract	0.5 fl. oz. (1 Tbsp.)	15 ml	3%
Salt	0.21 oz. (1 tsp.)	5 g	1.2%
Walnut pieces	14 oz.	420 g	82%
Dark chocolate chips	5 oz.	150 g	29%
White chocolate chips	5 oz.	150 g	29%
Total batter weight:	4 lb. 15 oz.	2394 g	467%

1. Sift together the flour, baking soda and cream of tartar. Set aside.
2. Blend the butter until very creamy in the bowl of a mixer fitted with the paddle attachment. Add the sugar and the corn syrup or honey. Add the eggs one at a time, scraping down the bowl between each addition. Add the vanilla and salt.
3. Blend in the flour mixture without overmixing. Add the remaining ingredients and blend until just incorporated.
4. Spread the batter onto a paper-lined half-sheet pan. Bake at 350°F (180°C) until the center of the batter is set, approximately 35 to 40 minutes.
5. Cool in the pan to room temperature, then refrigerate or freeze until firm.
6. Using a stiff plastic scraper, cut around the edges of the blondies to loosen them from the pan. Invert the blondies onto a cutting board covered with a clean sheet of parchment paper. Cut into 2-inch (5-centimeter) squares or the desired size.

Approximate values per square: **Calories** 220, **Total fat** 13 g, **Saturated fat** 5 g, **Cholesterol** 25 mg, **Sodium** 85 mg, **Total carbohydrates** 24 g, **Protein** 3 g

Chocolate Peanut Butter Brownies (left) and Cream Cheese Sun-Dried Cherry Brownies (right)

CHOCOLATE PEANUT BUTTER BROWNIES

Yield: 4 Dozen Brownies, approximately 2 in. (5 cm) each, 1 Half-Sheet Pan

Method: Sheet cookies

Pastry or all-purpose flour	1 lb.	480 g	100%
Baking powder	0.3 oz. (2 tsp.)	8 g	1.8%
Eggs	8.3 oz. (5 eggs)	250 g	52%
Granulated sugar	12 oz.	360 g	75%
Brown sugar	12 oz.	360 g	75%
Peanut butter	12 oz.	360 g	75%
Vanilla extract	0.5 fl. oz.	15 ml	3%
Unsalted butter, melted	3 oz.	90 g	19%
Peanuts, toasted	6 oz.	180 g	38%
Semisweet chocolate chunks	6 oz.	180 g	38%
Total batter weight:	6 lb. 4 oz.	3003 g	627%
Chocolate Ganache (page 458)	1 lb. 8 oz.	720 g	150%
Chocolate Decorations (page 699)	as needed	as needed	
Peanut halves	as needed	as needed	

1 Sift together the flour and baking powder. Set aside.
2 In the bowl of a large mixer fitted with the paddle attachment, blend the eggs and sugars. Add the peanut butter and vanilla. Mix until well combined, then beat in the butter. Stir in the flour mixture, peanuts and chocolate chunks.
3 Spread the batter on a paper-lined half-sheet pan. Bake at 350°F (180°C) until set, approximately 35 to 38 minutes.
4 Let cool completely, turn over onto the back of a clean sheet pan and frost the surface with ganache heated to 110°F (43°C).
5 Cut into 2-inch × 2-inch (5-centimeter × 5-centimeter) squares and top with chocolate decorations and peanuts.

Approximate values per brownie: **Calories** 230, **Total fat** 12 g, **Saturated fat** 5 g, **Cholesterol** 30 mg, **Sodium** 55 mg, **Total carbohydrates** 27 g, **Protein** 4 g

CREAM CHEESE SUN-DRIED CHERRY BROWNIES

Yield: 4 Dozen Brownies, approximately 2 in. (5 cm) each, 1 Half-Sheet Pan

Method: Sheet cookies

Pastry or all-purpose flour	10 oz.	300 g	100%
Cocoa powder	1.5 oz.	45 g	15%
Baking powder	0.07 oz. (½ tsp.)	2 g	0.7%
Unsalted butter, cubed	6 oz.	180 g	60%
Chocolate, semisweet or bittersweet, chopped fine	14 oz.	420 g	140%
Eggs	9 oz. (5½ eggs)	270 g	90%
Granulated sugar	14 oz.	420 g	140%
Vanilla extract	0.5 fl. oz.	15 ml	5%
Almond extract	0.15 fl. oz. (1 tsp.)	4 ml	1.5%
Salt	0.1 oz. (½ tsp.)	3 g	1%
Cream Cheese Topping (recipe follows)	3 lb. 4 oz.	1560 g	520%
Sun-Dried Cherry Jam (recipe follows)	8 oz.	240 g	80%
Total weight:	7 lb. 3 oz.	3459 g	1153%

1. Sift together the flour, cocoa and baking powder. Set aside.
2. Melt the butter and chocolate in a double boiler until it reaches 110°F (43°C). Set aside, holding the mixture at this temperature over a warm-water bath.
3. While the chocolate is melting, whip the eggs, sugar, extracts and salt in the bowl of a large mixer fitted with the whip attachment.
4. Add the melted butter-and-chocolate mixture. Scrape down the bowl and add the flour mixture to the chocolate.
5. Spread the batter onto a paper-lined half-sheet pan. Spread the Cream Cheese Topping evenly over the surface of the batter.
6. Pipe swirls of Sun-Dried Cherry Jam over and into the cheese topping using a piping bag fitted with a medium plain tip.
7. Bake at 325°F (160°C) until the brownies are set and bounce back when lightly pressed, approximately 50 to 55 minutes.
8. Cool in the pan to room temperature, then refrigerate or freeze until firm.
9. Using a stiff plastic scraper, cut around the edges of the brownies to loosen them from the pan. Invert the brownies onto a cutting board covered with a clean sheet of parchment paper. (If the brownies do not release easily, hold the pan briefly over a heat source to release.)
10. Cut into 2-inch × 2-inch (5-centimeter × 5-centimeter) squares.

Approximate values per brownie: **Calories** 260, **Total fat** 8 g, **Saturated fat** 8 g, **Cholesterol** 70 mg, **Sodium** 95 mg, **Total carbohydrates** 28 g, **Protein** 4 g

CREAM CHEESE TOPPING

Yield: 3 lb. 4 oz. (1572 g)

Cream cheese	2 lb.	960 g
Granulated sugar	7 oz.	210 g
Unsalted butter, soft and lump-free	4 oz.	120 g
Eggs	6.4 oz. (4 eggs)	192 g
Vanilla extract	0.5 fl. oz.	15 ml
Cake flour, sifted	2.5 oz.	75 g

1. In the bowl of a mixer fitted with the paddle attachment, blend the cream cheese on the lowest speed.
2. Add the sugar and mix until completely smooth. Add the butter and eggs and mix to combine.
3. Stir in the vanilla and sifted cake flour.

Approximate values per 1-oz. (30-g) serving: **Calories** 100, **Total fat** 8 g, **Saturated fat** 5 g, **Cholesterol** 40 mg, **Sodium** 55 mg, **Total carbohydrates** 5 g, **Protein** 2 g

SUN-DRIED CHERRY JAM

Yield: 1 lb. 8 oz. (722 g)

Tart red cherries	12 oz.	360 g
Granulated sugar	9 oz.	270 g
Sun-dried cherries	3 oz.	90 g
Apple pectin	0.2 oz. (2 tsp.)	2 g
Total weight:	1 lb. 8 oz.	722 g

1. Combine the tart cherries and 8 ounces (240 grams) of the sugar in a saucepan. Bring to a boil, then add the sun-dried cherries. Boil for 5 minutes.
2. Using an immersion blender, purée until the cherries are broken up but some pulp remains.
3. Stir the pectin and remaining sugar together in a bowl, then add it to the cherry mixture. Bring to a boil. Cook for 5 minutes.
4. Chill before using.

Approximate values per 1-oz. (30-g) serving: **Calories** 90, **Total fat** 0 g, **Saturated fat** 0 g, **Cholesterol** 0 mg, **Sodium** 0 mg, **Total carbohydrates** 24 g, **Protein** 0 g, **Vitamin A** 15%

GERMAN CHOCOLATE LAYERED BROWNIES

Yield: 8 Dozen Brownies, approximately 2 in. (5 cm) each, 1 Full-Sheet Pan

Method: Sheet cookies

❶ Placing coconut topping on brownie batter spread in the sheet pan.

❷ Spreading topping on layered brownies before baking.

❸ The finished brownies.

Batter:

Semisweet chocolate	1 lb.	480 g	114%
Unsalted butter	1 lb. 4 oz.	600 g	143%
Vanilla extract	0.5 fl. oz.	15 ml	4%
Eggs	20 oz. (12 eggs)	600 g	143%
Salt	0.1 oz. (½ tsp.)	3 g	0.7%
Granulated sugar	2 lb.	960 g	228%
Cocoa powder	2 oz.	60 g	14%
All-purpose flour	14 oz.	420 g	100%
Pecans, chopped	1 lb.	480 g	114%

Topping:

Unsalted butter	12 oz.	360 g	86%
Shredded coconut	12 oz.	360 g	86%
Coconut flavoring	0.6 fl. oz. (4 tsp.)	20 ml	5%
Vanilla extract	0.6 fl. oz. (4 tsp.)	20 ml	5%
Powdered sugar	1 lb. 4 oz.	600 g	143%
Cream cheese, softened	1 lb. 8 oz.	720 g	171%
Total weight:	11 lb. 13 oz.	5698 g	1356%

❶ Melt the chocolate and butter together and set aside. Stir in the vanilla.

❷ Beat the eggs, salt and granulated sugar together in another bowl.

❸ In a large bowl stir together the cocoa powder, flour and pecans. Add the egg mixture to the flour, then stir in the melted chocolate.

❹ Pour the batter into a greased and floured sheet pan, spreading evenly. (Freeze the batter if desired for 15 minutes to firm before spreading it with the coconut topping.)

❺ To make the topping, melt the butter in a large saucepan, and then stir in the shredded coconut, coconut flavoring, vanilla and powdered sugar. Cook over low heat until the sugar has dissolved and the mixture is creamy.

❻ Cream the cream cheese in a mixer or food processor. Add the hot butter mixture and blend until no lumps of cheese remain.

❼ Immediately spoon the topping over the unbaked chocolate batter. Spread the topping into a thin layer using an offset spatula.

❽ Bake at 300°F (150°C) until the center has set and the surface is golden brown, approximately 1 hour. Cool, then wrap and chill completely overnight before cutting into 2-inch × 2-inch (5-centimeter × 5-centimeter) squares.

Approximate values per brownie: **Calories** 220, **Total fat** 15 g, **Saturated fat** 8 g, **Cholesterol** 50 mg, **Sodium** 45 mg, **Total carbohydrates** 22 g, **Protein** 2 g

APPLESAUCE BROWNIES

This formula offers much of the delicious taste of a great brownie with less fat. The applesauce mimics the fat, creating fudginess. This is the formula to use when a healthier alternative to a classic brownie is required.

Yield: 8 Dozen Brownies, approximately 2-in. (5-cm) each, 1 Full-Sheet Pan

Method: Sheet cookies

Unsweetened chocolate	4 oz.	120 g	25%
Cake flour, sifted	1 lb.	480 g	100%
Cocoa powder	9 oz.	270 g	56%
Salt	0.4 oz. (2 tsp.)	12 g	2.5%
Egg whites	12 oz. (12 whites)	360 g	75%
Whole eggs	13.3 oz. (8 eggs)	400 g	83%
Granulated sugar	2 lb. 2 oz.	1020 g	212%
Light corn syrup	2 lb.	960 g	200%
Unsweetened applesauce	1 lb. 8 oz.	720 g	150%
Canola oil	7 oz.	210 g	44%
Vanilla extract	1 fl. oz.	30 ml	6%
Total batter weight:	9 lb. 8 oz.	4582 g	953%

1. Coat a sheet pan lightly with vegetable oil.
2. Melt the chocolate over a bain marie and set aside.
3. Sift the flour, cocoa powder and salt together and set aside.
4. Whisk the egg whites and eggs together in a large bowl. Add the sugar, corn syrup, applesauce, oil and vanilla. Whisk in the chocolate.
5. Fold the flour mixture into the egg mixture. Pour into the prepared pan and bake at 350°F (180°C) until a cake tester comes out clean, approximately 25 minutes.
6. Cool in the pan, then cut into squares and dust with powdered sugar.

Approximate values per brownie: **Calories** 120, **Total fat** 3.5 g, **Saturated fat** 1 g, **Cholesterol** 15 mg, **Sodium** 65 mg, **Total carbohydrates** 24 g, **Protein** 2 g

> "The pie is an English institution which, planted on American soil, forthwith ran rampant and burst forth into an untold variety of genera and species.
>
> —HARRIET BEECHER STOWE, AMERICAN NOVELIST (1811–1896)"

CHAPTER ELEVEN

PIES AND TARTS

- prepare a variety of pie crusts and fillings
- form and bake a variety of pies and tarts
- prepare a variety of dessert and pastry items, incorporating components from other chapters

pastry may refer to a group of doughs made primarily with flour, water and fat; pastry can also refer to foods made with these doughs or to a large variety of fancy baked goods

PERHAPS THE MOST IMPORTANT (AND VERSATILE) BUILDING BLOCK IN PASTRY MAKING IS THE DOUGH. The next two chapters examine the different doughs used to form pastries. This chapter focuses on the basic doughs used to make pies and tarts. This chapter demonstrates how to make, fill, bake and garnish a variety of pies and tarts. The cream, custard and mousse fillings used in some of the formulas at the end of this chapter are discussed in Chapter 14, Custards, Creams and Sauces. Additional doughs used to make particular kinds of pastry are discussed in Chapter 12, Pastry and Dessert Components, which covers éclair paste, meringues and phyllo dough, and in Chapter 9, Laminated Doughs, which details the methods for making puff pastry, croissant and Danish dough.

A pie is composed of a sweet or savory filling in a baked crust. It can be made without a top crust or, more typically, topped with a full crust or a **lattice crust**. A pie is generally made in a round, slope-sided pan and cut into wedges for service. A tart is similar to a pie except it is made in a shallow, straight-sided pan, often with fluted edges. A tart can be almost any shape; round, square, rectangular and petal shapes are the most common. It is usually open-faced garnished with an attractive arrangement of glazed fruit, piped cream or chocolate decorations.

CRUSTS

Pie crusts and tart shells can be made from several types of doughs or crumbs. Flaky pie dough, mealy pie dough and crumbs are best for pie crusts; such sweet tart doughs as **pâte sucrée** and **pâte sablée** are usually used for tart shells. What distinguishes them is the texture of the crust once the dough is baked. The texture of pie and tart dough is affected by the ingredients used, the proportions of the ingredients in the formula, the way the fat is incorporated and the way the doughs are mixed. See Table 11.1. A pie crust or tart shell can be shaped and completely baked before filling (known as *baked blind*) or filled and baked simultaneously with the filling.

Flaky and Mealy Pie Doughs

Dough for pie and tart crust may be made with or without sugar. Because of its low moisture and high fat content, dough for pie crust is usually made with low-protein flour, which ensures a tender product after baking. Most pies are made using an unsweetened pie dough that may be flaky or mealy depending on how it is mixed.

Flaky pie dough takes its name from its final baked texture. It is best for pie top crusts and lattice coverings and may be used for prebaked shells that will be filled with a cooled filling shortly before service. **Mealy pie dough** takes its name from its raw texture. It is used whenever a soggy crust would be a problem (for example, as the bottom crust of a custard or fruit pie) because it is sturdier and resists sogginess better than flaky dough. Both flaky and mealy doughs are too delicate for tarts that will be removed from the pan for service. The sweet tart doughs pâte sucrée and pâte sablée, described later, are better for these types of tarts.

Flaky and mealy doughs can be prepared from the same formula with only a slight variation in mixing method. For both types of dough, a cold fat such as butter or shortening is cut into the flour. The amount of flakiness in the baked crust depends on the size of the fat particles in the dough. The larger the pieces of fat, the flakier the crust will be. This is because the flakes are actually the sides of fat pockets created during baking by the melting

TABLE 11.1	CLASSIFICATION OF PIE AND TART DOUGHS	
DOUGH	**CHARACTERISTICS AFTER BAKING**	**USE**
Flaky pie dough	Very flaky; not sweet	Prebaked pie shells; pie top crusts
Mealy pie dough	Moderately flaky; not sweet	Custard, cream or fruit pie crusts; quiche crusts
Pâte brisée	Moderately flaky; not sweet; rich	Pies; tart and tartlet shells
Sweet tart dough (pâte sucrée)	Very rich; crisp; not flaky	Tart and tartlet shells
Shortbread tart dough (pâte sablée)	Very rich; fragile; not flaky	Tart and tartlet shells; cookies

fat and steam. When preparing flaky dough, the fat is left in larger pieces, about the size of peas or peanuts. When preparing mealy dough, the fat is blended in more thoroughly, until the mixture resembles coarse cornmeal. Because the resulting fat pockets are smaller, the crust is less flaky.

The type of fat used affects both the dough's flavor and flakiness. Butter contributes a delicious flavor and is preferred by most artisan bakers but does not produce as flaky a crust as other fats. Butter is also more difficult to work with than other fats because of its lower melting point and its tendency to become brittle when chilled. Hydrogenated vegetable shortening produces a flaky crust but contributes nothing to its flavor. The flakiest pastry is made with lard. Because some people dislike its flavor for sweet pies or do not eat pork products, lard is more often used for pâté en croûte or other savory preparations. Some chefs prefer to use a combination of butter with either shortening or lard. Oil is not an appropriate substitute as it disperses too thoroughly throughout the dough; when baked, the crust will be extremely fragile but without any flakiness.

After the fat is cut into the flour, water or milk is added to form the dough. Less water is needed for mealy dough because more flour is already in contact with the fat, reducing its ability to absorb liquid. Cold water is normally used for both flaky and mealy doughs. The water should be well chilled to prevent softening the fat. Milk may be used to increase richness and nutritional value. It will produce a darker, less crisp crust, however. If dry milk powder is used, it should be dissolved in water first. Mixing should be brief, especially when making flaky dough, so as not to develop the gluten and toughen the dough.

Hand mixing is best for small to moderate quantities of dough. You retain better control over the procedure when you can feel the fat being incorporated. Mixing flaky dough with an electric mixer or food processor requires more care, as the machine tends to cut the fat in too thoroughly. When using machines, mixing should be brief. Overmixing develops too much gluten, making the dough elastic and difficult to use. If an electric mixer must be used for large quantities, use the paddle attachment at the lowest speed and be sure the fat is well chilled, even frozen. Refrigerating pie dough after mixing is recommended to allow the moisture to evenly distribute through the mixture and to firm the fat for ease of handling. It relaxes the gluten preventing shrinkage during baking. The recipe for Basic Pie Dough on page 366 as well as the recipe for Pâte Brisée (page 384), a type of French dough for pies and tarts, may be mixed using the following procedure.

When properly prepared, flaky dough bakes into many visible layers.

PROCEDURE FOR PREPARING FLAKY AND MEALY DOUGHS BY HAND

1 Sift flour onto work surface or into a large bowl.

2 Cut the fat into the flour.

3 Dissolve salt and sugar, if using, in the cold liquid. Add the mixture to the flour, mixing gently until the dough holds together. Do not overmix.

4 Cover the dough with plastic wrap and chill thoroughly before using.

5 Remember that rerolled scraps will be tough and elastic.

BASIC PIE DOUGH

Yield: 2 lb. 10 oz. (1267 g) Dough; 3–4 Shells

Unsalted butter, chilled	1 lb.	475 g	76%
Pastry or all-purpose flour	1 lb. 5 oz.	630 g	100%
Buttermilk or water	4 fl. oz.	120 ml	19%
Salt	0.4 oz. (2 tsp.)	12 g	1.9%
Granulated sugar	0.5 oz.	15 g	2.3%
Vanilla extract (optional)	0.5 fl. oz. (1 Tbsp.)	15 ml	2.3%
Total dough weight:	2 lb. 10 oz.	1267 g	201%

1. Cut the butter into medium dice ⅜ inch (9 millimeters) square. Sift the flour onto a work surface or into a large bowl.
2. Cut the butter into the flour mixture until the desired consistency (flaky or mealy) is reached.
3. Combine the buttermilk or water, salt, sugar and vanilla (if using) in a bowl with a whisk. Gradually add the buttermilk to the flour mixture. Mix gently until the dough holds together. Do not overmix or add too much liquid.
4. Cover the dough with plastic wrap and chill thoroughly before using.
5. When ready to use, roll out the chilled dough on a lightly floured board to a thickness of ⅛ to ¼ inch (3 to 6 millimeters). Line a pie or tart pan with the dough following the procedures on pages 370 to 372.
6. To bake blind, cover the dough with parchment or foil. Fill with pie weights. Bake at 350°F (180°C) for 10 to 15 minutes. Remove the weights and paper. Bake until golden brown and fully cooked, approximately 10 to 15 minutes. Cool, then fill as desired.

Approximate values per 1-oz. (30-g) serving: **Calories** 130, **Total fat** 9 g, **Saturated fat** 6 g, **Cholesterol** 25 mg, **Sodium** 110 mg, **Total carbohydrates** 11 g, **Protein** 2 g

1. Using a handheld chopper to cut the fat into the flour coarsely for flaky dough.

2. Using a handheld chopper to cut the fat into the flour finely for mealy dough.

3. The finished dough.

The preceding basic pie dough recipe may be mixed by machine using the following procedure.

PROCEDURE FOR PREPARING FLAKY AND MEALY DOUGHS BY MACHINE

1. Chill a mixer bowl and paddle attachment for at least 30 minutes in the refrigerator.
2. Sift the flour into the mixer bowl. Add the cold diced butter.
3. Gently blend the butter with the flour on low speed until the mixture resembles coarse meal or fine meal, depending on the desired consistency of the finished dough.
4. Dissolve the salt and sugar, if using, in the cold liquid. Add the mixture to the flour. Blend on low speed until the dough just comes together without overmixing, approximately 12 to 20 seconds. Do not overmix.
5. Cover the dough with plastic wrap and chill thoroughly before using.

INSPIRATION—THE ZEN OF APPLE PIE

I am sitting at a small table sipping Japanese tea at Café Matsunosuke in Kyoto. Wafting from the kitchen is the unmistakable aroma of apple pie. This American icon is being served to women dressed in kimonos who utter astonished whispers of praise secreted behind delicate hands.

I am here to teach Japanese students how to make apple pie. As I go through the steps of making a pie, the process becomes a meditation. I see, through the eyes of my students, a ritual unfolding. I become an extension of the dough as I rapidly move my fingertips through the flour and shortening to achieve the perfect texture. The class breathes a collective sigh of knowing as the slow drizzle of ice water miraculously fuses flour and shortening into the promise of a pie. Use your senses. Touch your earlobe. The dough should feel the same. Keep everything cold. Handle the dough with respect. Biological forces are at work. Glutens need to relax. Roll it out with a light touch, just a sprinkling of flour. Carefully fold the circle of dough into quarters and transport it to a waiting pie tin. Fill the crust to heaping with thinly sliced apples, the perfect blend of spices, and crown with slivers of sweet butter. Add a top crust and begin the ritual of "crimping" the edges. Your fingertips coax the dough into waves lapping to a shore of apples. The pie is ceremoniously carried to the waiting oven. For a few moments, this humble pie becomes the center of the universe, a tranquility meditation, and a link that connects two cultures.

—CHERYL JEAN, culinary educator, Germantown, NY

Sweet Tart Dough (Pâte Sucrée) and Shortbread Tart Dough (Pâte Sablée)

Tarts are usually made with sweet tart dough (pâte sucrée) or shortbread tart dough (pâte sablée). Sweet tart dough (pâte sucrée) is a rich, nonflaky dough used for sweet tart shells. It is sturdier than flaky or mealy dough because it contains egg yolks and the fat is blended in thoroughly. Because more fat coats the flour, less gluten is formed, making for a tender dough when baked. It is also more cookielike than classic pie dough and has the rich flavor of butter. It creates a crisp but tender crust and is excellent for tartlets as well as for straight-sided tarts that will be removed from their pans before service. Shortbread tart dough (pâte sablée) is sweet tart dough with a high percentage of fat, also used, as its name implies, for rich butter cookies. Pâte sablée bakes into a delicate, crumbly and rich crust. It may contain a small amount of cooked egg yolk, and finely ground almond flour may be used in addition to the wheat flour in the formula for flavor and texture. Pâte sablée is more fragile and difficult to handle than pâte sucrée. (Recipes for pâte sablée are on page 382.)

Because of the amount of fat and sugar, pâte sucrée and pâte sablée need stronger flour such as all-purpose flour or a low-protein bread flour to create enough structure in the dough. The type of sugar used affects the final product. Powdered sugar produces a finer texture in the dough than granulated sugar. Pâte sucrée and pâte sablée are mixed using the creaming method. This mixing technique produces dough that is not flaky when baked. Eggs are used to moisten, flavor and leaven these doughs. A small amount of baking powder may be added to lighten the texture. These raw sweet doughs may be kept refrigerated up to 2 weeks or frozen up to 3 months.

PROCEDURE FOR PREPARING SWEET TART DOUGH (PÂTE SUCRÉE) AND SHORTBREAD TART DOUGH (PÂTE SABLÉE)

1. Cream softened butter and sugar. Beat until the mixture is smooth and lump-free.
2. Slowly add eggs, blending well.
3. Add flour, mixing only until incorporated. Overmixing toughens the dough.
4. Cover the dough with plastic wrap and chill thoroughly before using.
5. Scraps may be rerolled once or twice, provided the dough is still cool, nongreasy and pliable. If too much gluten develops, the crust will shrink and toughen.

MISE EN PLACE

▶ Soften butter.

❶ Mixing sweet dough.

❷ The finished sweet dough.

SWEET TART DOUGH
(PÂTE SUCRÉE)

Yield: 2 lb. 7 oz. (1180 g) Dough; approximately 3 Shells, 9 in. (22 cm) each

Unsalted butter, softened	10 oz.	300 g	52.5%
Powdered sugar	6.5 oz.	195 g	34%
Eggs	3.3 oz. (2 eggs)	100 g	17%
Salt	0.2 oz. (1 tsp.)	6 g	1%
Vanilla extract	0.15 fl. oz. (1 tsp.)	5 ml	0.8%
All-purpose or pastry flour	1 lb. 3 oz.	570 g	100%
Baking powder (optional)	0.14 oz. (1 tsp.)	4 g	0.7%
Total dough weight:	2 lb. 7 oz.	1180 g	206%

❶ Cream the butter and powdered sugar in the bowl of a mixer fitted with the paddle attachment.

❷ Blend in one egg. Scrape down the bowl, add the remaining egg and mix until well blended. Add the vanilla and salt.

❸ Sift together the flour and baking powder (if using). Add it to the creamed butter. Then blend on low speed until the dough comes together without overmixing.

❹ Press the dough onto a parchment-lined half-sheet pan. Cover with plastic wrap. Chill in the refrigerator for at least 1 hour before using.

❺ When ready to use, roll out the chilled dough on a lightly floured board to a thickness of ⅛ to ¼ inch (3 to 6 millimeters). The dough may be crumbly and difficult to work with, which is normal. Simply press the dough back together with your fingertips. Line a pie or tart pan with the dough following the procedures on pages 370 to 372.

❻ To bake blind, cover the dough with parchment or foil. Fill with pie weights. Bake at 350°F (180°C) for 10 to 15 minutes. Remove the weights and paper. Bake until golden brown and fully cooked, approximately 10 to 15 minutes. Cool, then fill as desired.

Approximate values per 1-oz. (30-g) serving: **Calories** 120, **Total fat** 5 g, **Saturated fat** 3 g, **Cholesterol** 15 mg, **Sodium** 0 mg, **Total carbohydrates** 16 g, **Protein** 2 g, **Vitamin A** 4%

Crumb Crusts

A quick and tasty bottom crust can be made from finely ground cookie crumbs moistened with melted butter. Crumb crusts can be used for unbaked pies such as those with cream or chiffon fillings, or they can be baked with their fillings, as with cheesecakes.

Chocolate cookies, graham crackers, gingersnaps, vanilla wafers and macaroons are popular choices for crumb crusts. Some breakfast cereals such as corn flakes or bran flakes are also used. Ground nuts and spices can be added for flavor. Whatever cookies or other ingredients are used, be sure they are ground to a fine, even crumb. If packaged crumbs are unavailable, a food processor, blender or rolling pin can be used.

The typical ratio for a crumb crust is one part melted butter, two parts sugar and four parts crumbs. The amount of sugar may need to be adjusted depending on the type of crumbs used, however; for example, chocolate sandwich cookies need less sugar than graham crackers. If the mixture is too dry to stick together, gradually add more melted butter. Press the mixture into the bottom of the pan and chill or bake it before filling.

PROCEDURE FOR PREPARING A CRUMB CRUST

1. Select firm, dry cookies or crackers for the crust. Graham crackers, gingersnaps, vanilla wafers or biscotti alone or in combination with ground nuts are often used.
2. Crush the cookies or crackers into fine crumbs using a rolling pin or food processor.
3. Blend the crumbs with sugar and spices as needed. Add melted butter to bind the crumbs. The amount will vary depending on the type of crumbs used.
4. Press the crumb mixture evenly into the bottom of a lightly greased pie shell or spring-form pan.
5. Bake the crumb mixture briefly before filling, if desired.

BASIC CRUMB CRUST

Yield: 1 lb. 12 oz. (844 g) Crumbs; 2 Shells, 9 in. (22 cm) each

			Crumbs at 100%
Graham crackers, crushed	16 oz.	480 g	100%
Granulated sugar	8 oz.	240 g	50%
Cinnamon, ground	0.14 oz. (2 tsp.)	4 g	0.9%
Unsalted butter, melted	4 oz.	120 g	25%
Total weight:	1 lb. 12 oz.	844 g	176%

1. Combine the crushed graham crackers, sugar and cinnamon in a mixing bowl.
2. Drizzle in the melted butter, stirring until the crumbs are evenly moistened.
3. Press the crumb mixture evenly in the bottom of two 9-inch (22-centimeter) pie pans.
4. Bake the shells at 350°F (190°C) until the crumbs have toasted slightly and the crust has firmed, approximately 10 to 12 minutes. Fill the parbaked shells as desired.

Approximate values per 1¾-oz. (50-g) serving: **Calories** 230, **Total fat** 9 g, **Saturated fat** 4 g, **Cholesterol** 15 mg, **Sodium** 170 mg, **Total carbohydrates** 36 g, **Protein** 2 g

MISE EN PLACE

▶ Crush crackers.
▶ Melt butter.
▶ Preheat oven to 350°F (190°C).

Shaping Crusts

Crusts are shaped by rolling out the dough to fit into a pie pan or tart shell (mold) or to sit on top of fillings. Mealy, flaky and sweet doughs are all easier to roll out and work with if well chilled, as chilling keeps the fat firm and prevents stickiness. Although an electric dough sheeter (see Chapter 2, Tools and Equipment for the Bakeshop) will roll out doughs quickly and evenly, sheeters are not available in every kitchen. So any good pastry cook should be comfortable working with all types of dough by hand.

When rolling and shaping the dough, work on a clean, flat surface (wood or marble is best, but a metal workbench can be chilled before using). Rolling dough on parchment paper or a silicone mat is also recommended. Lightly dust the work surface, rolling pin and dough with bread flour or all-purpose flour before starting to roll the dough. (Cake or pastry flour tends to clump and is not recommended.) Also, work only with a manageable amount at a time: usually one crust's worth for a pie or standard-sized tart or enough for 10 to 12 tartlet shells.

Roll out the dough from the center, working toward the edges. Periodically lift the dough gently and rotate it. This keeps the dough from sticking and helps produce an even thickness. If the dough sticks to the rolling pin or work surface, sprinkle on a bit more flour. Too much flour, however, makes the crust dry and crumbly and causes gray streaks.

Chilling a work surface with ice before rolling fragile dough for pie or tart crust.

PROCEDURE FOR ROLLING AND SHAPING DOUGH FOR DOUBLE-CRUST PIES

❶ A typical pie crust or tart shell should be rolled to a thickness of approximately ⅛ inch (3 millimeters); it should also be at least 2 inches (5 centimeters) larger in diameter than the baking pan.

❷ Carefully roll the dough up onto a rolling pin. Position the pin over the pie or tart pan and unroll the dough, easing it into the pan.

❸ Press the dough into the pan and trim the edges as needed.

❹ When making a double-crust pie, roll the dough out as before, making the circle large enough to hang over the pan's edge. The dough may be lifted into place by rolling it onto the rolling pin, as with the bottom crust. Slits or designs can be cut from the top crust to allow steam to escape.

❺ Seal the top crust to the bottom crust with egg wash or water. Crimp as desired.

PROCEDURE FOR ROLLING AND SHAPING DOUGH FOR LATTICE CRUSTS

❶ Roll the dough out as before. Using a ruler as a guide, cut even strips of the desired width, typically ½ inch (1.2 centimeters).

❷ Using an over-under-over pattern, weave the strips together on top of the filling. Be sure the strips are evenly spaced for an attractive result. Crimp the lattice strips to the bottom crust to seal.

PROCEDURE FOR ROLLING AND SHAPING DOUGH FOR TARTLET SHELLS

❶ A typical crust for tartlets should be approximately ⅛ inch (3 millimeters) thick.

❷ Roll the dough out as described earlier. Then roll the dough up onto the rolling pin.

❶ Lay out a single layer of tartlet shells. Unroll the dough over the shells, pressing the dough gently into each one.

❷ Roll the rolling pin over the top of the shells. The edge of the shells will cut the dough. Be sure the dough is pressed against the sides of each shell. Bake or fill as desired.

Baking Pies and Crusts

Pie crusts can be filled and then baked, or baked and then filled. Filled pie crusts are baked near the bottom of the oven to ensure that the bottom crust cooks thoroughly. Using mealy pie dough for the bottom crust helps prevent sogginess. Pies may also be placed on preheated sheet pans before loading the oven. As filled pies bake, if the crust browns too quickly, cover them with foil, then continue baking. Lowering the temperature during baking can help prevent pie crust from browning too quickly.

Pie crusts that are baked before being filled are said to be **baked blind**. To retain their shape, small holes are pricked in the pie shell dough with a fork or paring knife, a technique known as **docking**. The unbaked pie shell is then lined with parchment or buttered foil and filled with baking (or pie) weights, dry rice or beans. An empty pie pan may be used as a baking weight when making prebaked pie shells. The unbaked pie shell is then baked at 350°F (180°C) until the crust has baked long enough to set so it will not puff up, 10 to 15 minutes or longer depending on the size of the pan and the thickness of the dough. Then the weights are removed, the dough is docked and the shell is returned to the oven to finish baking for approximately 10 to 15 more minutes. To help retain crispness once filled, the crust may be coated with a thin layer of egg wash during the final minutes of baking. A baked crust can also be brushed with a thin layer of caramel or melted chocolate for the same effect. Note that dry rice or beans may be reused several times for future pies or tarts, but may not be used for consumption. Unfilled baked crusts can be stored at room temperature 2 to 3 days or wrapped in plastic wrap and frozen as long as 3 months.

bake blind to bake a pie shell or tart shell unfilled, using baking weights or beans to support the crust as it bakes

docking pricking small holes in an unbaked dough or crust to allow steam to escape and to prevent the dough from rising when baked

Cutting the edges of parchment paper to fit an unbaked pie shell.

Removing pie weights from a baked pie shell.

PROCEDURE FOR ROLLING AND BAKING UNFILLED TART CRUSTS (BAKED BLIND)

❶ Roll the dough out to the desired thickness and line the pie pan or tart ring with the dough.

❷ Place a tart ring on a paper-lined sheet pan. Carefully roll the dough up onto a rolling pin. Position the pin over the tart ring and unroll the dough.

❸ Ease the dough into the tart ring, pressing to make a smooth edge.

❹ Run a rolling pin over the edge of the tart ring to remove excess dough and produce a level edge to the tart. Dock the tart dough with a fork.

❺ Cover the dough with heat-resistant plastic, parchment paper or greased aluminum foil (greased side down). Press the plastic, paper or foil against the walls of the shell, allowing a portion of it to extend above the pan. Fill the pan with baking weights or dry rice or beans.

❻ Bake the weighted crust at 350°F (180°C) 10 to 15 minutes. Remove the weights and paper.

❼ Brush the baked crust with egg wash, then return the crust to the oven. Bake until golden brown and fully cooked, approximately 10 to 15 minutes. Cool, then fill as desired.

FILLINGS

Fillings make pies and tarts distinctive and flavorful. Four types of fillings are discussed here: *cream, fruit, custard* and *chiffon*. (Chapter 14, Custards, Creams and Sauces, includes more custard and cream fillings in detail.) There is no one correct presentation or filling-and-crust combination. The apples in an apple pie, for example, may be sliced, seasoned and topped with streusel; caramelized, puréed and blended with cream; chopped and covered with a flaky dough lattice; or poached, arranged over pastry cream and brushed with a shiny glaze. Only an understanding of the fundamental techniques for making fillings—and some imagination—ensures success.

Starches for Pies

A variety of pie fillings rely on starches for stability and thickening. Even custard fillings, which include eggs for thickening and flavor, may contain starch to keep the filling from separating. The type of starch depends on the desired results.

Although flour is somewhat unreliable as a thickener, it can be used in traditional baked fruit pies in which the fruit is not excessively juicy, such as Pippin apples or Bosc pears. Cornstarch is preferred for custard and fruit fillings because it sets up into a somewhat firm, clear gel. Dissolving the cornstarch in some liquid before adding it to the formula ensures that it will gelatinize properly. Cooking the filling so that the starches gelatinize fully is also essential to ensure that the filling is firm enough to stand up when the pie is sliced. (Be aware that cornstarch loses its potency when combined with sugar or an acid such as lemon juice.)

When a pie is to be frozen, cornstarch is not recommended as a thickener, however. The gel formed by cornstarch when cooking breaks down during freezing. Use tapioca or tapioca starch instead. Tapioca is a good choice for fruit fillings because it thickens at a lower temperature than cornstarch, withstands freezing and cooks into a clear gel. Instant tapioca can be measured and then ground into a powder before using. Grinding makes it easier to disperse.

Modified starch, usually derived from a type of corn called waxy maize, can also be used for pies that must be frozen. This type of starch, also referred to as *pregelatinized starch*, is made by cooking and then drying the starch. It bakes into a clear, somewhat soft gel.

Cream Fillings

A **cream filling** is really nothing more than a flavored pastry cream. Pastry cream is a type of starch-thickened egg custard discussed in Chapter 14, Custards, Creams and Sauces. When used as a pie filling, pastry cream should be thickened with cornstarch or a combination of cornstarch and flour so that it is firm enough to hold its shape when sliced. (Cornstarch provides sheen while the flour ensures firmness.) In either case, the custard must be cooked long enough for the starch to fully gelatinize. Popular cream filling flavors are chocolate, banana and coconut.

A cream filling is fully cooked on the stove top, so a prebaked or crumb crust is needed. The crust can be filled while the filling is still warm, which makes for fewer air pockets and a more attractive slice. Or the filling can be chilled and piped into the crust later. A cream pie is often topped with meringue, which is then browned quickly in an oven or under a broiler.

MISE EN PLACE

▶ Bake flaky pie shells.

tempering heating gently and gradually; slowly adding a hot liquid to eggs or other foods to raise their temperature without causing them to curdle

❶ Tempering the eggs.

❷ Stirring the cream as it comes to a boil.

Banana Cream Pies (bottom) and Coconut Cream Pies (top)

BASIC CREAM PIE

Yield: 3 Pies, 9 in. (22 cm) each

Method: Cream filling

Filling:

Granulated sugar	14 oz.	420 g
Milk	44 fl. oz.	1320 ml
Heavy cream	20 fl. oz.	600 ml
Egg yolks	4.8 oz. (8 yolks)	144 g
Cornstarch	4.25 oz.	128 g
Unsalted butter	4 oz.	120 g
Vanilla extract	1 fl. oz.	30 ml
Flaky or sweet tart dough pie shells, baked	3 shells	3 shells
Crème Chantilly (page 502)	as needed	as needed
Bittersweet chocolate shavings	as needed	as needed

❶ In a heavy saucepan, dissolve 7 ounces (210 grams) of the sugar in the milk. Add the heavy cream and bring to a boil.

❷ Meanwhile, whisk the egg yolks and the remaining sugar together in a small bowl. Add the cornstarch and whisk until smooth.

❸ **Temper** the egg mixture with approximately one-fourth of the boiling milk. Stir the warmed egg mixture back into the remaining milk and return it to a boil, whisking constantly.

❹ Whisking constantly and vigorously, allow the cream to boil until thick, approximately 2 minutes. Remove from the heat and stir in the butter and vanilla. Stir until the butter is melted and incorporated.

❺ Pour the cream into the pie shells. Chill the pie.

❻ The pies can be topped with Crème Chantilly once the filling is very cold. Decorate the pies with chocolate shavings.

Variations:

Banana Cream Pie—Layer 12 ounces (360 grams) sliced bananas (approximately 3 medium bananas) into the baked shell with the warm cream filling. Garnish with piped Crème Chantilly and chocolate decorations (page 698).

Coconut Cream Pie I—Substitute 12 fluid ounces (360 milliliters) coconut milk for 12 fluid ounces (360 milliliters) of the milk. If desired, add 0.5 fluid ounce (15 milliliters) coconut extract or the amount recommended by the extract manufacturer, as this can vary. Prepare slices of fresh coconut with a vegetable peeler, leaving some of the brown skins intact. Garnish the pie with the coconut slices and some chocolate decorations (page 698).

Coconut Cream Pie Ii—Stir 8 ounces (240 grams) toasted coconut into the warm cream.

Meringue-Coated Cream Pie—While the filling is still warm, coat the top of the pie with Italian Meringue (page 413). Place the pie in a 425°F (220°C) oven until the meringue is lightly browned. The meringue topping can also be browned using a propane torch, as shown on page 395.

Approximate values per ⅛-pie serving: **Calories** 220, **Total fat** 9 g, **Saturated fat** 5 g, **Cholesterol** 130 mg, **Sodium** 55 mg, **Total carbohydrates** 29 g, **Protein** 5 g, **Vitamin A** 10%

Fruit Fillings

A fruit filling is a mixture of fruit, fruit juice, spices and sugar thickened with a starch. Apple, cherry, blueberry and peach are traditional favorites. The fruit can be fresh, frozen or canned. (See Chapter 4, Bakeshop Ingredients, pages 104 to 107, for comments on selecting the best fruits for fillings.) When selecting fresh fruits, they should be at their seasonal peak. Frozen fruit should be completely thawed and drained well before using. The juices can be added to the liquid in a cooked juice filling. The starch can be flour, cornstarch, tapioca or a packaged commercial instant or pregelatinized starch. The amount of fruit determines the quality of the filling. A ratio of three to four parts fruit to one part gelled filling ensures the highest-quality filling.

The ingredients for a fruit filling are most often combined using one of three methods: **cooked fruit**, **cooked juice** or **baked fruit**.

COOKED FRUIT FILLINGS

The cooked fruit filling method is often used when the fruits need to be softened by cooking (for example, apples or rhubarb) or are naturally rather dry, such as dried apricots or raisins. Dried fruits should be conditioned before using. Canned fruits should not be used in cooked fruit fillings as they have already been cooked and would break down in the process. A cooked fruit filling should be combined with a prebaked or crumb crust.

PROCEDURE FOR PREPARING COOKED FRUIT FILLINGS

1. Combine the fruit, sugar and some juice or liquid in a heavy, nonreactive saucepan and bring to a boil.
2. Dissolve the starch (usually cornstarch) in a cold liquid, then add to the boiling fruit.
3. Stirring constantly, cook the fruit-and-starch mixture until the starch is clear and the mixture is thickened.
4. Add any other flavorings and any acidic ingredients such as lemon juice. Stir to blend.
5. Remove from the heat and cool before filling a prebaked pie or crumb crust.

APPLE-CRANBERRY PIE

Yield: 1 Pie, 9 in. (22 cm)

Method: Cooked fruit filling

Filling:

Fresh tart apples such as Granny Smiths, peeled, cored and cut in 1-in. (2.5-cm) cubes	1 lb.	480 g
Brown sugar	4 oz.	120 g
Granulated sugar	4 oz.	120 g
Orange zest, grated fine	0.2 oz. (1 Tbsp.)	6 g
Cinnamon, ground	0.07 oz. (1 tsp.)	2 g
Salt	0.05 oz. (¼ tsp.)	1.5 g
Cornstarch	0.18 oz. (2 tsp.)	6 g
Orange juice	3 fl. oz.	90 ml
Fresh cranberries, rinsed	1 pt.	500 ml
Mealy dough pie shell, 9 in. (22 cm), partially baked	1 shell	1 shell
Streusel Topping (page 145)	7 oz.	210 g

MISE EN PLACE

▶ Peel, core and cut apples.
▶ Sort and rinse cranberries.
▶ Prepare and partially bake pie shell.
▶ Preheat oven to 400°F (200°C).

1. Combine the apples, sugars, orange zest, cinnamon and salt in a large, nonreactive saucepan.
2. Dissolve the cornstarch in the orange juice and add it to the apples.
3. Cover and simmer until the apples begin to soften, stirring occasionally. Add the cranberries, cover and continue simmering until the cranberries just begin to soften, approximately 2 minutes.
4. Place the apple-cranberry mixture in the pie shell and cover with the prepared Streusel Topping. Bake at 400°F (200°C) until the filling is bubbling hot and the topping is lightly browned, approximately 20 minutes.

Variation:

Apple-Rhubarb Pie—Substitute cleaned rhubarb, cut into 1-inch (2.5-centimeter) chunks, for the cranberries. Add 0.01 ounce (⅛ teaspoon/0.3 gram) nutmeg.

Approximate values per ⅛-pie serving: **Calories** 430, **Total fat** 18 g, **Saturated fat** 11 g, **Cholesterol** 45 mg, **Sodium** 310 mg, **Total carbohydrates** 67 g, **Protein** 2 g, **Vitamin C** 15%, **Claims**—good source of fiber

COOKED JUICE FILLINGS

The cooked juice filling method is used for soft, juicy fruits such as berries, especially when they are canned or frozen. This method is also recommended for delicate fruits that cannot withstand cooking, such as strawberries, pineapple and blueberries. Because only the juice is cooked, the fruit retains its shape, color and flavor better. A cooked juice filling should be combined with a prebaked or crumb crust.

PROCEDURE FOR PREPARING COOKED JUICE FILLINGS

1. Drain the juice from the fruit. Measure the juice and add water if necessary to create the desired volume.
2. Combine the liquid with sugar in a nonreactive saucepan and bring to a boil.
3. Dissolve the starch in cold water, then add it to the boiling liquid while whisking constantly to prevent lumps from forming. Boil until the starch is clear and the juice is thickened, about 3 minutes.
4. Add any other flavoring ingredients.
5. Pour the thickened juice over the fruit and stir gently.
6. Cool the filling before placing it in a precooked pie shell.

CHERRY PIE

MISE EN PLACE

▶ Bake mealy pie shell.

1. The thickened cherry juice.

2. Filling the baked pie shell with the cherries.

Yield: 1 Pie, 9 in. (22 cm)

Method: Cooked fruit filling

Canned tart cherries, 14.5-oz. (411-g) cans, packed in juice	2 cans	2 cans
Salt	1 pinch	1 pinch
Granulated sugar	10 oz.	300 g
Cornstarch	2 oz.	60 g
Almond extract	0.04 fl. oz. (¼ tsp.)	1.25 ml
Unsalted butter	1.5 oz.	45 g
Mealy dough pie shell, 9 in. (22 cm), fully baked	1 shell	1 shell
Crème Chantilly (page 502)	as needed	as needed
Bittersweet chocolate shavings	as needed	as needed
Almonds, sliced and toasted	as needed	as needed

1. Drain the juice from the canned cherries, reserving both the fruit and the juice.
2. Measure the juice and, if necessary, add enough water to provide 12 fluid ounces of liquid. Bring 9 fluid ounces (270 milliliters) of the juice, the salt and 7 ounces (210 grams) of the sugar to a boil.
3. Dissolve the cornstarch in the remaining 3 fluid ounces (90 milliliters) of cherry juice.
4. Add the cornstarch to the boiling juice. Whisk vigorously and boil until the mixture thickens and clears. Remove from the heat.
5. Whisk in the almond extract and butter and the remaining 3 ounces (90 grams) of sugar. Gently fold in the cherries.
6. Chill the cherry filling.
7. Pour the chilled filling into the pie shell. Chill the pie.
8. The pie can be topped with Crème Chantilly once the filling is very cold. Decorate the pie with chocolate shavings and toasted almonds.

Approximate values per ⅟₁₀-pie serving: **Calories** 390, **Total fat** 21 g, **Saturated fat** 10 g, **Cholesterol** 110 mg, **Sodium** 200 mg, **Total carbohydrates** 46, **Protein** 6 g, **Vitamin A** 15%

BAKED FRUIT FILLINGS

The baked fruit filling method is a traditional technique in which the fruit, sugar, flavorings and flour or starch are combined in an unbaked shell. The dough and filling are then baked simultaneously. Results are not always consistent with this technique, however, as thickening is difficult to control. Tapioca pearls are not recommended to thicken a baked fruit filling to be topped with a lattice crust. The tapioca pearls may not properly gelatinize when exposed to air. Use instant tapioca instead.

PROCEDURE FOR PREPARING BAKED FRUIT FILLINGS

1. Peel, core, cut and drain the fruit as desired or as directed in the recipe.
2. Toss the fruit with the flour or starch, sugar and spices, coating well. Let stand for 15 minutes.
3. Fill an unbaked shell with the fruit mixture to just below the rim. Take care not to spill filling on the edge of the pie shell. This can prevent the top crust from sealing properly.
4. Add small lumps of butter on top of the fruit.
5. Cover with a top crust, lattice or streusel and bake.

BLUEBERRY PIE WITH LATTICE CRUST

Yield: 1 Pie, 9 in. (22 cm)

Method: Baked fruit filling

Blueberries, fresh or IQF, thawed	1 lb. 6 oz.	660 g
Granulated sugar	4 oz.	120 g
Lemon zest, grated	0.14 oz. (2 tsp.)	4 g
Lemon juice	1 fl. oz.	30 ml
Salt	0.02 oz. (⅛ tsp.)	1 g
Instant tapioca	1.25 oz.	37 g
Cinnamon, ground	0.02 oz. (¼ tsp.)	0.5 g
Unsalted butter	0.5 oz.	15 g
Mealy pie dough	1 lb. 1 oz.	510 g

MISE EN PLACE

► Grate lemon zest.
► Prepare mealy pie dough.
► Preheat oven to 375°F (180°C) while the filling rests.

1. Combine the blueberries, sugar, lemon zest, lemon juice, salt, tapioca and cinnamon in a bowl. Allow the filling to stand for 15 minutes. (If using frozen berries, allow the filling to stand for 45 minutes.)
2. Using 11 ounces (330 grams) of the pie dough, roll a circle just large enough to fill the pie dish.
3. Gently place the filling in the unbaked shell and dot with the butter.
4. Roll the remaining pie dough ⅛ inch (3 millimeters) thick and form a lattice over the fruit.
5. Bake at 375°F (180°C) until the filling is bubbly and the crust is well browned, approximately 50 minutes.

Approximate values per ⅛-pie serving: **Calories** 390, **Total fat** 21 g, **Saturated fat** 13 g, **Cholesterol** 55 mg, **Sodium** 260 mg, **Total carbohydrates** 54 g, **Protein** 4 g, **Vitamin A** 15%, **Vitamin C** 15%

Custard Fillings

A **custard pie** has a soft filling that bakes along with the crust. Popular examples include pumpkin, egg custard and pecan pies. As explained in Chapter 14, Custards, Creams and Sauces, custards are liquids thickened by coagulated egg proteins. To make a custard pie, an uncooked liquid containing eggs is poured into a pie shell. When baked, the egg proteins coagulate, firming and setting the filling.

The procedure for making custard pies is simple: Combine the ingredients and bake. But there is often a problem: baking the bottom crust completely without overcooking the filling.

For the best results, start baking the pie near the bottom of a hot oven at 400°F (200°C). After 10 minutes, reduce the heat to 325°F–350°F (160°C–180°C) to finish cooking the filling slowly.

To determine the doneness of a custard pie:

❶ Shake the pie gently. It is done if it is no longer liquid. The center should show only a slight movement.

❷ Insert a thin knife approximately 1 inch (2.5 centimeters) from the center. The filling is done if the knife comes out clean.

MISE EN PLACE

▶ Beat eggs.
▶ Prepare and shape pie shells.
▶ Preheat oven and sheet pan to 400°F (200°C) while filling rests.

❶ Indenting leaf-shaped dough cutouts with the back of a knife.

❷ A slice of the finished pie.

PUMPKIN PIE

Yield: 2 Pies, 9 in. (22 cm) each; approximately 4 lb. 10 oz. (2254 g) Filling

Method: Custard filling

Filling:

Eggs, beaten slightly	6.75 oz. (4 eggs)	200 g
Pumpkin purée	2 lb.	960 g
Granulated sugar	12 oz.	360 g
Salt	0.2 oz. (1 tsp.)	6 g
Nutmeg, ground	0.04 oz. (½ tsp.)	1 g
Cloves, ground	0.04 oz. (½ tsp.)	1 g
Cinnamon, ground	0.14 oz. (2 tsp.)	4 g
Ginger, ground	0.07 oz. (1 tsp.)	2 g
Evaporated milk	24 fl. oz.	720 ml
Flaky dough pie shells, 9 in. (22 cm), unbaked	4 shells	4 shells
Flaky pie dough (optional)	8 oz.	240 g
Crème Chantilly (optional) (page 502)	as needed	as needed

❶ Combine the eggs and pumpkin. Blend in the sugar.

❷ Add the salt and spices, and then the evaporated milk. Whisk until completely blended and smooth.

❸ Allow the filling to rest 15 to 20 minutes before filling the pie shells. This allows the starch in the pumpkin to begin absorbing liquid, making it less likely to separate after baking.

❹ Pour the filling into the unbaked pie shells. Place in the oven on a preheated sheet pan at 400°F (200°C). Bake 15 minutes. Lower the oven temperature to 350°F (180°C) and bake until a knife inserted near the center comes out clean, approximately 40 to 50 minutes.

❺ While the pies bake, roll the flaky pie dough ⅛ inch (3 millimeters) thick. Cut the dough into leaf shapes with a paring knife. Using the back of the knife, indent the leaves to simulate veins. Bake the cutouts until golden brown. Garnish the cooled pie with Crème Chantilly and the baked pie dough garnishes if desired.

Approximate values per ⅛-pie serving: **Calories** 210, **Total fat** 10 g, **Saturated fat** 2.5 g, **Cholesterol** 30 mg, **Sodium** 230 mg, **Total carbohydrates** 25 g, **Protein** 4 g, **Vitamin A** 6%

Chiffon Fillings

A **chiffon filling** is created by adding gelatin to a stirred custard or a fruit purée. Whipped egg whites are then folded into the mixture. The filling is placed in a prebaked crust and chilled until firm. These preparations are the same as those for chiffons, mousses and Bavarians discussed in Chapter 14, Custards, Creams and Sauces.

ASSEMBLING PIES AND TARTS

The various types of pie fillings can be used to fill almost any crust or shell provided the crust is prebaked as necessary. Any of the chiffons, mousses or Bavarians in Chapter 14, Custards, Creams and Sauces, can be used as a pie filling in a prebaked crust. The filling can then be topped with meringue or whipped cream as desired. Garnishes such as toasted coconut, cookie crumbs and chocolate curls are often added for appearance and flavor.

TABLE 11.2	SUGGESTIONS FOR ASSEMBLING PIES		
FILLING	**CRUST**	**TOPPING**	**GARNISH**
Vanilla or lemon cream	Prebaked flaky dough or crumb	None, meringue or whipped cream	Crumbs from the crust
Chocolate cream	Prebaked flaky dough or crumb	None, meringue or whipped cream	Crumbs from the crust or shaved chocolate
Banana cream	Prebaked flaky dough	Meringue or whipped cream	Dried banana chips
Coconut cream	Prebaked flaky dough	Meringue or whipped cream	Shredded coconut
Fresh fruit	Unbaked mealy dough, or sweet tart dough if shallow tart	Lattice, full crust or streusel	Sanding sugar or cut-out designs if lattice or top crust is used
Canned or frozen fruit	Unbaked mealy dough	Lattice, full crust or streusel	Sanding sugar or cut-out designs if lattice or top crust is used
Chiffon or mousse	Crumb or prebaked sweetened flaky dough	None or whipped cream	Crumbs, fruit or shaved chocolate
Custard	Unbaked mealy dough	None	Whipped cream, cinnamon
Vanilla pastry cream	Prebaked sweet tart dough	Fresh fruit	Glaze
Lemon or citrus curd	Prebaked sweet tart dough	Fresh fruit, berries	Glaze, Italian meringue

Brushing the inside of a baked-blind tart shell with melted chocolate or a complementary jam adds extra flavor. A thin layer of absorbent spongecake soaked with flavored simple syrup may be placed in the bottom of a baked tart shell to prevent the baked crust from softening. The sponge can then be topped with a cream filling and fruit topping. Table 11.2 offers some suggestions for pie and tart filling and topping combinations.

PROCEDURE FOR ASSEMBLING A FRUIT TART

1 Line tart shells with prepared sweet dough. Bake blind and cool completely.

2 Prepare pastry cream, curd or other filling. Pour filling into prepared crust.

3 Refrigerate or freeze filled tart shells until filling is set.

4 Arrange fresh fruit decoratively over filled tart shell.

5 Warm tart glaze according to manufacturer's directions. Cool it slightly, then brush it over the surface of the fresh fruit. Small tartlets may be placed on an icing screen set over a sheet pan. Ladle or brush the glaze over the tartlets. Excess glaze captured by the pan may be reheated and reused.

FRESH FRUIT TART

Yield: 1 Tart, 9 in. (22 cm)

Sweet Tart Dough (page 368) tart shell, 9 in. (22 cm), fully baked	1 shell	1 shell
Pastry Cream (page 492)	1 pt.	0.5 lt
Fresh cut fruit and berries such as apples, cherries, strawberries, blackberries, blueberries or raspberries	3 pt.	1.5 lt
Apricot glaze	as needed	as needed

1 Fill the cool tart shell with Pastry Cream.

2 Arrange the fruit and berries over the Pastry Cream in an even layer. Be sure to place the berries so that the Pastry Cream is covered.

3 Heat the apricot glaze and brush over the fruit to form a smooth coating.

Approximate values per ⅙-tart serving: **Calories** 135, **Total fat** 3 g, **Saturated fat** 1 g, **Cholesterol** 2 mg, **Sodium** 62 mg, **Total carbohydrates** 26 g, **Protein** 2 g

Neutral Glaze

Tart Glaze (Mirror Glaze)

Tart glaze is a shiny coating applied to tarts, mousse-filled tortes and small pastries. It is spooned over the surface of the product. Once chilled, the product has a mirrorlike smooth surface that protects and enhances the pastry's appearance. Tart glaze may be made with gelatin, simple syrup and flavorings or from a prepared **neutral glaze**. It should flow easily but not be so thin that it would drip off a tart. To test the glaze, pour a few tablespoons of it on a small plate and refrigerate. Check in 5 minutes. It should set without being rubbery. Neutral glaze may be flavored with fruit juice, fruit purée, coffee or another liquid. Use about 40 percent liquid to 60 percent glaze. Although a glaze can be heated to soften it to the desired consistency, warm glaze can damage the fresh fruits it coats. Tart glaze can easily be softened without heating; add a small amount of fruit juice or purée to the glaze, then use an immersion blender to make the glaze spreadable. Fruit preserves may be melted for tart glaze but are not as stable.

CONVENIENCE PRODUCTS

Preformed pie and tart shells in disposable pans are available in a range of sizes and styles, ready to be filled and baked as needed. These are frozen products that, once thawed, must be filled and baked with the same care that scratch pies and tarts require. Deep-dish and double-crust styles are offered as well as products made with pure butter or all-vegetable shortening. The texture of these crusts once baked may be flaky or mealy; manufacturer's specifications indicate the style of the final product. Fully baked ready-to-use pie and tart shells are also available. Most are made with hydrogenated shortenings, though some European manufacturers offer products made with pure butter. These prebaked products have a long shelf life when stored in cool, dry conditions. Once filled, however, they require refrigeration and can become soggy. Like a freshly made tart, these prepared products should be served within 1 or 2 days of preparation.

Prepared or canned pie fillings are available in a variety of fruit and custard flavors. These products offer convenience, consistency and the ability to serve fruit pies out of season. The ratio of fruit to pregelled liquid varies greatly from brand to brand, however. Most commercial fillings are stabilized to permit additional baking that may be needed to assemble the final product. Shelf life tends to be extremely long, often without the need for refrigeration. Dry custard mixes are also available, needing only the addition of water or milk to produce a cream pie filling.

Prepared tart glaze is available as a neutral or flavored product. These glazes can easily be softened to use to dress fresh fruit tarts and other pastries. Depending on the brand and its composition, fresh fruit purée can be added to these products at a level of 30 to 60 percent of the weight of the purée. This allows the pastry chef to create a flavor profile in the glaze to match a specific dessert.

STORING PIES AND TARTS

Pies and tarts filled with cream or custard must be kept refrigerated to retard bacterial growth. Unbaked fruit pies or unbaked pie shells may be frozen up to 2 months. Freezing baked fruit pies is not recommended, but they may be stored 2 to 3 days in the refrigerator. Custard, cream and meringue-topped pies should be stored in the refrigerator no more than 2 to 3 days. They should not be frozen, as the eggs will separate, making the product runny. See Table 11.3 for troubleshooting pie making.

TABLE 11.3	TROUBLESHOOTING CHART FOR PIES	
PROBLEM	**CAUSE**	**SOLUTION**
Crust shrinks	Overmixing	Adjust mixing technique
	Overworking dough	Adjust rolling technique
	Not enough fat	Adjust formula
	Did not let dough rest after mixing; dough was stretched or rolled incorrectly	Refrigerate dough after mixing; improve handling technique
Soggy crust	Wrong dough used	Use mealier dough
	Oven temperature too low	Adjust oven
	Not baked long enough	Adjust baking time
	Filling too moist	Adjust formula
Crumbly crust	Not enough liquid	Adjust formula
	Not enough fat	Adjust formula
	Improper mixing	Adjust mixing technique
Tough crust	Not enough fat	Adjust formula
	Overmixing	Adjust mixing technique
Runny filling	Insufficient starch	Adjust formula
	Starch insufficiently cooked	Cook longer
Lumpy cream filling	Starch not incorporated properly	Blend starch with sugar before adding liquid; stir filling while cooking
	Filling overcooked	Adjust cooking time
Custard filling "weeps" or separates	Too many eggs	Reduce egg content or add starch to the filling
	Eggs overcooked	Reduce oven temperature or baking time

1 How does the type of pie filling influence the selection of a pie crust? What type of crust would be best for a pie made with fresh, uncooked fruit? Explain your answer.

2 Why doesn't sweet tart dough (which contains a high ratio of butter) produce a flaky crust?

3 Explain the difference between a cream pie filling and a custard pie filling. Give two examples of each type of filling.

4 List and describe three ways of preparing fruit fillings for pies.

5 Plan a dessert buffet where four different fruit tarts will be offered. List the combination of fillings and toppings to be used. Describe the fruits you will use and how they will be sourced if they are out of season. WWW

QUESTIONS FOR DISCUSSION

Terms to Know

lattice crust	cooked fruit
pâte sucrée	cooked juice
pâte sablée	baked fruit
flaky pie dough	custard pie
mealy pie dough	chiffon filling
baked blind	neutral glaze
cream filling	pâte brisée

Several of the formulas given in the following pages are combinations of the pies and tarts presented in this chapter and the creams, custards and other dessert products covered in other chapters. For example, the Lemon Curd Tart is made with the Coconut Almond Tart Dough discussed in this chapter, plus the Italian Meringue discussed in Chapter 12, Pastry and Dessert Components, and the Lemon Curd discussed in Chapter 14, Custards, Creams and Sauces. As a student, you should first learn to prepare a variety of pastry components. You can then combine and assemble them appropriately into both classic and modern desserts.

SHORTBREAD TART DOUGH (PÂTE SABLÉE)

Yield: 4 lb. 7 oz. (2139 g) Dough; approximately 7 Tart Shells, 8 in. (20 cm) each, or 46 Tartlet Shells, 2½ in. (7.5 cm) each

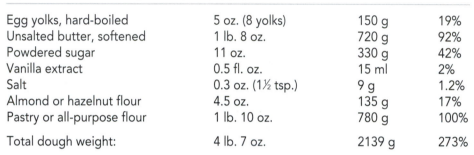

Egg yolks, hard-boiled	5 oz. (8 yolks)	150 g	19%
Unsalted butter, softened	1 lb. 8 oz.	720 g	92%
Powdered sugar	11 oz.	330 g	42%
Vanilla extract	0.5 fl. oz.	15 ml	2%
Salt	0.3 oz. (1½ tsp.)	9 g	1.2%
Almond or hazelnut flour	4.5 oz.	135 g	17%
Pastry or all-purpose flour	1 lb. 10 oz.	780 g	100%
Total dough weight:	4 lb. 7 oz.	2139 g	273%

1. Press the egg yolks through a sieve using a plastic pastry scraper. Set aside.
2. In the bowl of a mixer fitted with the paddle attachment, cream the butter. Add the powdered sugar, combining well.
3. Add the vanilla, salt and nut flour, then the sieved egg yolks, and mix until combined.
4. Add the pastry flour and mix on low speed just until combined. Do not overmix.
5. Wrap the dough in plastic and chill several hours or overnight.
6. When ready to use, roll out the chilled dough on a lightly floured board to a thickness of ⅛ to ¼ inch (3 to 6 millimeters). The dough may be crumbly and difficult to work with, which is normal. Simply press the dough back together with your fingertips.
7. To bake blind, cover the dough with parchment or foil. Fill with pie weights. Bake at 350°F (180°C) for 10 to 15 minutes. Remove the weights and paper. Bake until golden brown and fully cooked, approximately 10 to 15 minutes. Cool, then fill as desired.

Approximate values per 2-oz. (60-g) serving: **Calories** 227, **Total fat** 19 g, **Saturated fat** 10 g, **Cholesterol** 93 mg, **Sodium** 103 mg, **Total carbohydrates** 25 g, **Protein** 4 g

COCONUT SHORTBREAD TART DOUGH (COCONUT PÂTE SABLÉE)

Yield: 3 lb. 3 oz. (1535 g) Dough; approximately 5 Shells, 8 in. (20 cm) each

Unsalted butter	1 lb.	480 g	89%
Powdered sugar	7 oz.	210 g	39%
Eggs	2.5 oz. (1½ eggs)	75 g	14%
Salt	0.2 oz. (1 tsp.)	5 g	1%
Vanilla extract	0.5 fl. oz.	15 ml	3%
Macaroon coconut	7 oz.	210 g	39%
Pastry or all-purpose flour	1 lb. 2 oz.	540 g	100%
Total dough weight:	3 lb. 3 oz.	1535 g	285%

1. In the bowl of a mixer fitted with the paddle attachment, cream the butter. Add the powdered sugar and combine well. Scrape down the bowl.
2. Add the eggs a small amount at a time, then add the salt, vanilla and coconut. Mix until combined.
3. Add the pastry flour and mix on low speed just until combined. Do not overmix.
4. Wrap the dough in plastic and chill several hours or overnight before using.
5. When ready to use, roll out the chilled dough on a lightly floured board to a thickness of ⅛ to ¼ inch (3 to 6 millimeters). The dough may be crumbly and difficult to work with, which is normal. Simply press the dough back together with your fingertips. Line a pie or tart pan with the dough following the procedures on pages 370 to 372.
6. To bake blind, cover the dough with parchment or foil. Fill with pie weights. Bake at 350°F (180°C) for 10 to 15 minutes. Remove the weights and paper. Bake until golden brown and fully cooked, approximately 10 to 15 minutes. Cool, then fill as desired.

Approximate values per 1-oz. (30-g) serving: **Calories** 140, **Total fat** 10 g, **Saturated fat** 7 g, **Cholesterol** 25 mg, **Sodium** 50 mg, **Total carbohydrates** 13 g, **Protein** 2 g

SWEET ALMOND TART DOUGH (ALMOND PÂTE SUCRÉE)

Yield: 3 lb. 15 oz. (1887 g) Dough; approximately 6 Tarts, 8 in. (20 cm) each, or 30 Tartlets, 2½ in. (7.5 cm) each

Unsalted butter, softened	1 lb.	480 g	59%
Powdered sugar	10 oz.	300 g	37%
Eggs	5 oz. (3 eggs)	150 g	19%
Salt	0.4 oz. (2 tsp.)	12 g	1.5%
Vanilla extract	0.5 fl. oz.	15 ml	2%
Almond flour	4 oz.	120 g	15%
Pastry or all-purpose flour	1 lb. 11 oz.	810 g	100%
Total dough weight:	3 lb. 15 oz.	1887 g	234%

1. In the bowl of a mixer fitted with the paddle attachment, cream the butter. Add the powdered sugar and combine well. Scrape down the bowl.
2. Add the eggs a small amount at a time, then add the salt, vanilla and almond flour and mix until combined.
3. Add the pastry flour and mix on low speed just until combined. Do not overmix.
4. Wrap the dough in plastic and chill several hours or overnight before using.
5. When ready to use, roll out the chilled dough on a lightly floured board to a thickness of ⅛ to ¼ inch (3 to 6 millimeters). The dough may be crumbly and difficult to work with, which is normal. Simply press the dough back together with your fingertips. Line a pie or tart pan with the dough following the procedures on pages 370 to 372.
6. To bake blind, cover the dough with parchment or foil. Fill with pie weights. Bake at 350°F (180°C) for 10 to 15 minutes. Remove the weights and paper. Bake until golden brown and fully cooked, approximately 10 to 15 minutes. Cool, then fill as desired.

VARIATION:

Coconut Almond Tart Dough—Reduce the powdered sugar to 7 ounces (210 grams/26%). Reduce the eggs to 2.5 ounces (75 grams/9%). Reduce the salt to 0.2 oz. (1 teaspoon/6 grams/0.8%). Reduce the pastry flour to 1 pound 2 ounces (510 grams/66%) and add 7 ounces (210 grams/26%) macaroon coconut with the flour.

Approximate values per 1½-oz. (45-g) serving: **Calories** 180, **Total fat** 11 g, **Saturated fat** 6 g, **Cholesterol** 35 mg, **Sodium** 115 mg, **Total carbohydrates** 21 g, **Protein** 3 g

CHOCOLATE TART DOUGH (CHOCOLATE PÂTE SUCRÉE)

Yield: 3 lb. 5 oz. (1614 g) Dough; approximately 5 Shells, 8 in. (20 cm) each

Unsalted butter	1 lb.	480 g	100%
Granulated sugar	10 oz.	300 g	62.5%
Salt	0.1 oz. (½ tsp.)	3 g	0.6%
Vanilla extract	0.5 fl. oz.	15 ml	3%
Eggs	3.2 oz. (2 eggs)	96 g	20%
Hazelnut or almond flour	3 oz.	90 g	19%
Pastry or all-purpose flour	1 lb.	480 g	100%
Cocoa powder	5 oz.	150 g	31%
Total dough weight:	3 lb. 5 oz.	1614 g	336%

1. In the bowl of a mixer fitted with the paddle attachment, cream the butter until light.
2. Cream in the sugar, salt and vanilla. Scrape down the bowl.
3. Add the eggs one at a time, waiting for the previous egg to be fully incorporated. Add the nut flour.
4. Sift together the pastry flour and cocoa powder. Add it to the butter mixture. Blend on low speed until just combined. Do not overmix.
5. Chill the dough until firm, approximately 30 minutes.
6. When ready to use, roll out the chilled dough on a lightly floured board to a thickness of ⅛ to ¼ inch (3 to 6 millimeters). The dough may be crumbly and difficult to work with, which is normal. Simply press the dough back together with your fingertips. Line a pie or tart pan with the dough following the procedures on pages 370 to 372.
7. To bake blind, cover the dough with parchment or foil. Fill with pie weights. Bake at 350°F (180°C) for 10 to 15 minutes. Remove the weights and paper. Bake until golden brown and fully cooked, approximately 10 to 15 minutes. Cool, then fill as desired.

Approximate values per 1-oz. (30-g) serving: **Calories** 130, **Total fat** 9 g, **Saturated fat** 4.5 g, **Cholesterol** 25 mg, **Sodium** 25 mg, **Total carbohydrates** 14 g, **Protein** 2 g

PÂTE BRISÉE

Pâte brisée is similar to pie dough except that it usually contains eggs. There are wide variations among formulas for pâte brisée; some use water, some use only eggs and some contain a small amount of sugar depending on the intended use. What is important is knowing the end result and selecting the right formula and mixing method for the desired end product. This dough is often used for making **quiche**.

Yield: 2 lb. 10 oz. (1260 g) Dough; approximately 3 Shells, 9 in. (22 cm) each

Unsalted butter, chilled	1 lb.	480 g	76%
All-purpose or pastry flour	1 lb. 5 oz.	630 g	100%
Egg	1.6 oz. (1 egg)	48 g	7.6%
Salt	0.4 oz. (2 tsp.)	12 g	2%
Water, ice cold	3 fl. oz.	90 ml	14%
Total dough weight:	2 lb. 10 oz.	1260 g	199%

quiche a savory tart filled with custard and other ingredients such as cheese, ham and vegetables

1. Cut the butter into medium dice ⅜ inch (9 millimeters) square. Sift the flour onto the work surface or into a large bowl.
2. Cut the butter into the flour until a flaky or mealy consistency is reached.
3. Whisk together the egg, salt and water in a bowl. Add the liquid mixture and combine until the dough just holds together. Do not overmix.

4. Cover the dough with plastic wrap and chill thoroughly before using.
5. When ready to use, roll out the chilled dough on a lightly floured board to a thickness of ⅛ to ¼ inch (3 to 6 millimeters). The dough may be crumbly and difficult to work with, which is normal. Simply press the dough back together with your fingertips. Line a pie or tart pan with the dough following the procedures on pages 370 to 372.
6. To bake blind, cover the dough with parchment or foil. Fill with pie weights. Bake at 350°F (180°C) for 10 to 15 minutes. Remove the weights and paper. Bake until golden brown and fully cooked, approximately 10 to 15 minutes. Cool, then fill as desired.

Approximate values per 1-oz. (30-g) serving: **Calories** 120, **Total fat** 7 g, **Saturated fat** 4 g, **Cholesterol** 35 mg, **Sodium** 140 mg, **Total carbohydrates** 12 g, **Protein** 2 g

LEMON MERINGUE PIE

Yield: 2 Pies, 9 in. (22 cm) each; approximately 4 lb. (1890 g) Filling

Method: Cream filling

Filling:

Granulated sugar	1 lb. 4 oz.	600 g
Cornstarch	3 oz.	90 g
Salt	1 pinch	1 pinch
Water, cold	24 fl. oz.	720 ml
Egg yolks	6 oz. (10 yolks)	180 g
Lemon juice, fresh	8 fl. oz.	240 ml
Lemon zest, grated	0.4 oz. (2 Tbsp.)	12 g
Unsalted butter	1 oz.	30 g
Flaky dough pie shells, 9 in. (22 cm), baked	2 shells	2 shells
Egg whites, pasteurized	8 oz. (8 whites)	240 g
Granulated sugar	8 oz.	240 g

1. To make the filling, combine the sugar with the cornstarch, salt and water in a heavy saucepan. Cook over medium-high heat, stirring constantly, until the mixture becomes thick and almost clear, approximately 3 to 5 minutes.
2. Remove from the heat and pour approximately 1 cup of the filling into a small bowl. Whisk in the egg yolks to temper them. Whisk the egg yolk mixture back into the filling. Return to the heat and cook, stirring constantly, until thick and smooth.
3. Stir in the lemon juice and zest. Remove the filling from the heat. Add the butter and stir until melted.
4. Set the filling aside to cool briefly. Fill the pie shells with the lemon filling.
5. To prepare the meringue, whip the egg whites until soft peaks form. Slowly add 8 ounces (240 grams) sugar while whisking constantly. The meringue should be stiff and glossy, not dry or spongy-looking.
6. Mound the meringue over the filling, creating decorative patterns with a spatula. Be sure to spread the meringue to the edge of the crust so that all of the filling is covered with the meringue.
7. Bake the pies at 400°F (200°C) until the meringue browns, approximately 5 to 8 minutes. Let cool, then refrigerate. Serve the same day.

Approximate values per ⅛-pie serving: **Calories** 400, **Total fat** 12 g, **Saturated fat** 4 g, **Cholesterol** 135 mg, **Sodium** 310 mg, **Total carbohydrates** 67 g, **Protein** 5 g, **Vitamin C** 10%

CHOCOLATE CREAM PIE

Yield: 3 Pies, 9 in. (22 cm) each

Method: Cream filling

Filling:

Brown sugar	14 oz.	420 g
Milk	2 qt.	1920 ml
Cocoa powder	1 oz.	30 g
Egg yolks	4.8 oz. (8 yolks)	144 g
Cornstarch	3 oz.	90 g
Bittersweet chocolate (64% cacao), chopped fine	14 oz.	420 g
Unsalted butter	4 oz.	120 g
Vanilla extract	1 fl. oz.	30 ml
Mealy or sweet tart dough pie shells, 9 in. (22 cm), baked	3 shells	3 shells
Crème Chantilly (page 502)	as needed	as needed
Chocolate shavings (page 700)	as needed	as needed

❶ Filling a baked pie shell with chocolate custard.

❷ Topping with whipped cream.

❶ In a heavy saucepan, dissolve 7 ounces (210 grams) of the brown sugar in the milk. Add the cocoa powder and bring to a boil.

❷ Meanwhile, whisk the egg yolks, the remaining sugar and cornstarch until smooth.

❸ Temper the egg mixture with approximately one-fourth of the boiling milk. Stir the warmed egg mixture back into the remaining milk and return to a boil, whisking constantly.

❹ Whisking constantly and vigorously, allow the cream to boil until thick, approximately 2 minutes. Remove from the heat and stir in the chocolate, butter and vanilla. Stir until the ingredients are melted and incorporated.

❺ Pour the cream through a sieve into the pie shells and place in a refrigerator.

❻ Top the pies with Crème Chantilly once the filling is very cold. Decorate the pies with chocolate shavings.

VARIATION:

Meringue-Coated Chocolate Cream Pie—While the filling is still warm, coat the top of the pie with Italian Meringue (page 413). Place the pie in a 425°F (220°C) oven until the meringue is lightly browned. The meringue topping can also be browned using a propane torch, as shown on page 395.

Approximate values per ⅛-pie serving: **Calories** 480, **Total fat** 270 g, **Saturated fat** 17 g, **Cholesterol** 125 mg, **Sodium** 220 mg, **Total carbohydrates** 5 g, **Protein** 8 g, **Vitamin A** 15%, **Calcium** 15%

PEANUT BUTTER PIE

Yield: 1 Pie, 9 in. (22 cm)   **Method:** Cream filling

Milk	1 pt.	480 ml
Granulated sugar	6 oz.	180 g
Eggs	6.4 oz. (4 eggs)	200 g
Cornstarch	1.25 oz.	37 g
Peanut butter	9 oz.	270 g
Heavy cream	12 fl. oz.	360 ml
Chocolate Tart Dough (page 384), 9 in. (22 cm) pie shell, baked	1 shell	1 shell
Crème Chantilly (page 502)	as needed	as needed
Chocolate shavings (page 700)	as needed	as needed
Powdered sugar	as needed	as needed

1. In a heavy saucepan, bring the milk and 3 ounces (90 grams) of the sugar to a boil.
2. Meanwhile, whisk the eggs and add the remaining 3 ounces (90 grams) of sugar until smooth. Whisk in the cornstarch until smooth.
3. Temper the egg mixture with approximately one-fourth of the boiling milk. Stir the warmed egg mixture back into the remaining milk and return to a boil, whisking constantly.
4. Whisking constantly and vigorously, allow the cream to boil until thick, approximately 2 minutes. Remove from the heat and whisk in the peanut butter.
5. Let the mixture cool to 110°F (43°C).
6. Whip the cream to a soft ribbon, then fold it into the peanut mixture. Pour the cream into the pie shell and place in a refrigerator.
7. Garnish the pie with Crème Chantilly, chocolate shavings and powdered sugar.

Approximate values per ⅛-pie serving: **Calories** 690, **Total fat** 49 g, **Saturated fat** 22 g, **Cholesterol** 185 mg, **Sodium** 260 mg, **Total carbohydrates** 55, **Protein** 35 g, **Vitamin A** 25%, **Calcium** 15%, **Iron** 15%

FRESH STRAWBERRY PIE

Yield: 2 Pies, 9 in. (22 cm) each   **Method:** Cooked juice filling

Filling:

Granulated sugar	1 lb. 7 oz.	690 g
Water	8 fl. oz.	240 ml
Cornstarch	2.5 oz.	75 g
Water, cold	12 fl. oz.	360 ml
Salt	0.1 oz. (½ tsp.)	3 g
Lemon juice	2 fl. oz.	60 ml
Red food coloring	as needed	as needed
Fresh strawberries, rinsed and sliced in half	2 qt.	2 lt
Flaky dough pie shells, 9 in. (22 cm), baked	2 shells	2 shells
Crème Chantilly (page 502)	as needed	as needed

1. Bring the sugar and 8 fluid ounces (240 milliliters) water to a boil.
2. Dissolve the cornstarch in the cold water and add to the boiling liquid. Cook over low heat until clear, approximately 5 minutes.
3. Stir in the salt and lemon juice and enough red food coloring to produce a bright red color.
4. Pour this glaze over the strawberries and toss gently to coat them. Spoon the filling into the prepared pie shells. Chill thoroughly and top with Crème Chantilly for service.

Approximate values per ⅛-pie serving: **Calories** 330, **Total fat** 8 g, **Saturated fat** 2 g, **Cholesterol** 0 mg, **Sodium** 200 mg, **Total carbohydrates** 63 g, **Protein** 2 g, **Vitamin C** 80%

❶ Cutting vents into the pie crust with a cookie cutter.

❷ The finished pie.

STRAWBERRY RHUBARB PIE

Yield: 1 Pie, 9 in. (22 cm)

Method: Baked fruit filling

Strawberries	14 oz.	420 g
Rhubarb, fresh or IQF, cut in ½-in. (1-cm) pieces	1 lb.	480 g
Granulated sugar	8 oz.	240 g
Instant tapioca	1.25 oz.	37 g
Cinnamon, ground	0.07 oz. (1 tsp.)	2 g
Vanilla extract	0.15 oz. (1 tsp.)	5 g
Salt	0.04 oz. (¼ tsp.)	1 g
Unsalted butter	0.5 oz.	15 g
Basic Pie Dough (page 366)	1 lb. 4 oz.	600 g
Egg white, beaten, or water	as needed	as needed
Granulated sugar	as needed	as needed

❶ Quarter the strawberries and combine in a bowl with the rhubarb, sugar, tapioca, cinnamon, vanilla and salt. Allow the filling to stand for 15 minutes. (If using frozen rhubarb, allow the filling to stand for 45 minutes.)

❷ Using 11 ounces (330 grams) of the pie dough, roll a circle just large enough to fill the pie dish.

❸ Gently place the filling in the unbaked shell and dot with the butter.

❹ Roll the remaining pie dough ⅛ inch (3 millimeters) thick. Cut out vents in the dough with a cookie cutter. Place over the filling. Crimp to seal. Brush with egg whites or water and sprinkle with granulated sugar.

❺ Bake at 400°F (200°C) for 15 minutes. Lower the oven temperature to 375°F (180°C) and bake until the filling is bubbly, an additional 60 to 75 minutes.

Approximate values per ⅛-pie serving: **Calories** 480, **Total fat** 24 g, **Saturated fat** 15 g, **Cholesterol** 60 mg, **Sodium** 270 mg, **Total carbohydrates** 67 g, **Protein** 5 g, **Vitamin A** 15%, **Vitamin C** 60%

A cobbler is a home-style baked fruit dessert, usually made with a top crust of flaky pie dough, biscuit dough or streusel topping. The finished product will be slightly runny and is often served warm in a bowl or rimmed dish, accompanied by whipped cream or ice cream.

BLACKBERRY COBBLER

Yield: 10 Servings

Method: Baked fruit filling

Blackberries, IQF	2 qt.	2 lt
Granulated sugar	8 oz.	240 g
Instant tapioca	2 oz.	60 g
Water	10 fl. oz.	300 ml
Unsalted butter	2 oz.	60 g
Lemon zest, grated	0.2 oz. (1 Tbsp.)	6 g
Streusel Topping (page 145)	16 oz.	480 g

❶ Combine the berries, sugar, tapioca, water, butter and lemon zest, tossing the berries gently until well coated with the other ingredients.

❷ Transfer to a lightly buttered half-size hotel pan, then set aside at least 30 minutes before baking.

❸ Cover the top of the cobbler with an even layer of Streusel Topping.

❹ Bake at 350°F (180°C) until the berry mixture bubbles and the crust is appropriately browned, approximately 40 to 50 minutes.

Approximate values per 6-oz. (180-g) serving: **Calories** 210, **Total fat** 5 g, **Saturated fat** 3 g, **Cholesterol** 20 mg, **Sodium** 10 mg, **Total carbohydrates** 39 g, **Protein** 1 g, **Vitamin C** 45%

PEACH BLACKBERRY MINT CRISP

Yield: 6 Servings

Method: Baked fruit filling

Instant tapioca	0.75 oz. (1½ Tbsp.)	22 g
Orange juice	3 fl. oz.	90 ml
Peaches, peeled	1 lb. 8 oz.	720 g
Blackberries, fresh or IQF	8 oz.	240 g
Granulated sugar	6 oz.	180 g
Vanilla extract	0.15 fl. oz. (1 tsp.)	5 ml
Fresh mint leaves, chopped fine	30	30
Baked Streusel for Crumble (recipe follows)	as needed	as needed
Powdered sugar	as needed	as needed

1. Place the tapioca in a small bowl. Cover it with the orange juice. Set aside for 20 minutes.
2. Cut the peeled peaches into eight uniform slices each and combine with the blackberries in a medium bowl. Add the sugar, vanilla, mint leaves and moistened tapioca. Fold the ingredients together with a spatula.
3. Divide the mixture among six 8-ounce (240-gram) ramekins. Place the ramekins on a half-sheet pan. Cover it with foil and cut a small hole for steam to escape.
4. Bake at 375°F (190°C) until thick bubbles appear on the surface, approximately 40 to 45 minutes.
5. Remove the foil. Sprinkle with Baked Streusel for Crumble and dust with powdered sugar before serving.

Approximate values per serving: **Calories** 190, **Total fat** 0.5 g, **Saturated fat** 0 g, **Cholesterol** 0 mg, **Sodium** 0 mg, **Total carbohydrates** 48 g, **Protein** 2 g

BAKED STREUSEL FOR CRUMBLE

Yield: 1 lb. 4 oz. (617 g)

Pastry or all-purpose flour	8 oz.	240 g	100%
Brown sugar	5 oz.	150 g	62.5%
Unsalted butter, cold, cut in small cubes	7 oz.	210 g	87.5%
Salt	0.2 oz. (1 tsp.)	6 g	2.5%
Cinnamon, ground	0.2 oz. (1 Tbsp.)	6 g	2.5%
Vanilla extract	0.15 fl. oz. (1 tsp.)	5 ml	1.9%
Total weight:	1 lb. 4 oz.	617 g	257%

1. Blend all of the ingredients together in the bowl of a mixer fitted with the paddle attachment until the mixture resembles coarse meal and lumps form; do not mix until it forms a smooth dough.
2. Scatter the mixture in small clumps onto a paper-lined sheet pan. (If the mixture is too firm to crumble, chill the dough and then press it through the large holes of a grater or sieve into clumps onto the sheet pan.) Bake at 375°F (190°C) until light golden brown, approximately 8 to 10 minutes. Baking time will vary depending on how thickly the mixture was spread.
3. Sprinkle over the top of baked fruit desserts or use to decorate iced cakes, cheesecakes and tortes.

Approximate values per 1-oz. (30-g) serving: **Calories** 140, **Total fat** 5 g, **Saturated fat** 5 g, **Cholesterol** 20 mg, **Sodium** 120 mg, **Total carbohydrates** 16 g, **Protein** 1 g

PEACH PIE WITH DECORATIVE CRUST

Yield: 1 Pie, 8 in. (20 cm)

Method: Baked fruit filling

Instant tapioca	2 oz.	60 g
Lemon or lime juice	1 fl. oz.	30 ml
Water	1 fl. oz.	30 ml
Peaches, sliced, frozen, defrosted, drained	1 lb. 4 oz.	600 g
Vanilla extract	0.15 fl. oz. (1 tsp.)	5 ml
Granulated sugar	3 oz.	90 g
Honey	1 oz.	30 g
Fresh ginger, grated fine	0.07 oz. (1 tsp.)	2 g
Basic Pie Dough (page 366)	1 lb. 4 oz.	600 g

1. Mix the tapioca with the lemon or lime juice and water. Set aside at least 5 minutes.
2. Combine the peaches, vanilla, sugar, honey and ginger in a bowl. Add the moistened tapioca. Allow the filling to stand at least 30 minutes.
3. Roll out 10 ounces (300 grams) of the pie dough into a circle on a surface lightly dusted with bread flour. Line an 8-inch (20-centimeter) pie pan with the dough.
4. Fill the pie shell with the peach filling. Roll the remaining dough ⅛ inch (3 millimeters) thick. Cut the dough into leaf shapes with a paring knife. Using the back of the knife, indent the leaves to simulate veins.
5. Arrange the leaves on the fruit, starting in the center and working to the outside edges. Brush the leaves with water and sprinkle lightly with granulated sugar.
6. Place on a sheet pan and bake at 350°F (180°C) until the crust is golden brown and the filling makes thick bubbles, approximately 70 to 80 minutes.

Approximate values per ⅛-pie serving: **Calories** 420, **Total fat** 22 g, **Saturated fat** 14 g, **Cholesterol** 55 mg, **Sodium** 270 mg, **Total carbohydrates** 55 g, **Protein** 4 g, **Vitamin A** 15%, **Vitamin C** 120%

FREEFORM APPLE TARTS

LINCOLN CULINARY INSTITUTE, HARTFORD, CT
Chef Jamie Roraback

Yield: 4 Pies, 6 in. (15 cm) each   **Method:** Baked fruit filling

Dough:

Unsalted butter	8 oz.	240 g	100%
All-purpose flour	8 oz.	240 g	100%
Salt	0.2 oz. (1 tsp.)	6 g	2.5%
Water, ice cold	3 fl. oz.	90 ml	37.5%
Total dough weight:	1 lb. 3 oz.	576 g	240%

Filling:

Apples, peeled, cored, large dice	1 lb.	480 g
Unsalted butter	1 oz.	30 g
Granulated sugar	2 oz.	60 g
Cinnamon, ground	0.02 oz. (¼ tsp.)	0.5 g
Vanilla extract	0.5 fl. oz.	15 ml
Apple brandy	2 fl. oz.	60 ml

Egg wash:

Egg	1.6 oz. (1 egg)	50 g
Milk	1 fl. oz.	30 ml
Sanding sugar	as needed	as needed
Powdered sugar	as needed	as needed
Ice cream or whipped cream	as needed	as needed

1 To prepare the dough, cut the butter into medium dice and place it in the freezer 5 minutes. Sift the flour with the salt. Toss the butter with the flour and salt, then place the mixture in the bowl of a food processor. Pulse until the butter chunks are the size of very small peas. Then, in a continuous stream, drizzle in the ice water and pulse just until the dough barely comes together. Do not overmix.

2 Turn the dough out onto a work surface. Knead it gently and quickly. Divide the dough into four small rounds. Place the rounds on a sheet pan, cover them with plastic wrap and refrigerate approximately 20 minutes before rolling out.

3 To prepare the filling, heat a sauté pan over high heat, add the apples and let them brown slightly. Add the butter and let it melt so that it loosens and frees the apples from the bottom of the pan. Then cook approximately 1 minute, add the sugar and let it brown, stirring occasionally. Add the cinnamon and vanilla. Remove from the heat, add the apple brandy, return to the heat and flambé. Cool the filling before assembling the pies.

4 Prepare the egg wash by whipping the egg together with the milk.

5 On a floured surface, roll out each round of dough into a circle approximately 8 inches (20 centimeters) wide. Place an appropriate-size plate or other circular object on top of the rolled-out dough and cut out a circle.

6 Place one-quarter of the apple filling in the center of each dough round, leaving exposed 1½ inches (3.7 centimeters) of dough along the edges. Fold this border over the filling in approximately five or six folds, each fold slightly overlapping the previous one. Place the tarts on a sheet pan and, using a pastry brush, glaze each tart (dough only) with egg wash. Sprinkle sanding sugar over the tarts after glazing.

7 Place the tarts in the freezer until frozen. (Freezing will help prevent the butter running from the high-butter-content crust during baking.)

8 Preheat the oven to 400°F (200°C). While the tarts are baking, rotate them occasionally. Bake until the apples are tender and the crust is evenly browned, approximately 20 minutes. Serve at room temperature, dusted with powdered sugar and accompanied by whipped cream or ice cream.

Approximate values per ½-tart serving: **Calories** 420, **Total fat** 27 g, **Saturated fat** 16 g, **Cholesterol** 95 mg, **Sodium** 300 mg, **Total carbohydrates** 36 g, **Protein** 4 g, **Vitamin A** 20%

SAFETY ALERT
Cooking with Alcohol

When alcohol comes into contact with a flame, it can ignite. In order to avoid singed eyebrows and kitchen fires, please be careful when adding wine, brandy, liqueurs or liquor to a dish on or near the stove. Often a dish will require flaming or **flambéing**, which means igniting the brandy, rum or other liquor so that the alcohol burns off and the flavor of the liquor is retained. When a dish calls for flambéing, follow these procedures. Stand away from the pan being flamed. Tilt the pan away from you before putting a match to the liquid, as the flames can leap from the pan, igniting anything they contact.

flambé (flahm-BAY) to ignite brandy, rum or other liquor so that the alcohol burns off and the flavor of the liquor is retained

❶ Slice of apple crumb pie.

❷ Whole apple crumb pie with pastry leaf and sliced apple garnish.

APPLE CRUMB PIE

Yield: 1 Pie, 9 in. (22 cm)	**Method:** Baked fruit filling	
Basic Pie Dough (page 366)	15 oz.	450 g
Filling:		
Golden Delicious apples, peeled and cored	2 lb.	960 g
Granny Smith apples, peeled and cored	1.5 lb.	720 g
Granulated sugar	9 oz.	270 g
Lemon juice	0.5 fl. oz. (1 Tbsp.)	15 ml
Vanilla extract	0.5 fl. oz. (1 Tbsp.)	15 ml
Pastry or all-purpose flour	1 oz.	30 g
Cinnamon, ground	0.3 oz. (1½ Tbsp.)	9 g
Unsalted butter, diced fine	2 oz.	60 g
Streusel Topping (page 145)	7 oz.	210 g
Granulated sugar, for topping	as needed	as needed
Green apple slice (optional)	1	1
Powdered sugar	as needed	as needed

❶ Roll out 11 ounces (330 grams) of the pie dough into a circle ⅛ inch (3 millimeters) thick and line a 9-inch (22-centimeter) pie pan with the dough. Set aside.

❷ Cut the apples into 12 uniform wedges each. Toss the apple wedges in a large bowl with the sugar, lemon juice and vanilla.

❸ Sift together the flour and cinnamon. Stir the mixture into the apples.

❹ Fill the crust with the apple filling. Dot with the butter. Sprinkle the surface evenly with the Streusel Topping.

❺ Bake the pie at 375°F (190°C) until the filling is bubbling and looks like thick honey, approximately 1 hour and 20 minutes.

❻ While the pie bakes, roll the remaining dough ⅛ inch (3 millimeters) thick. Cut leaf shapes out of the dough. Using a paring knife, indent the dough to simulate leaf veins. Brush the dough cutouts with water and sprinkle them with granulated sugar. Place them on a paper-lined sheet pan and bake at 375°F (390°C) until golden brown, approximately 8 to 12 minutes.

❼ Decorate the top of the baked pie with the pastry dough leaf garnish and the slice of green apple, if using. Dust the edges of the pie with powdered sugar.

Approximate values per ⅛-pie serving: **Calories** 600, **Total fat** 30 g, **Saturated fat** 18 g, **Cholesterol** 75 mg, **Sodium** 300 mg, **Total carbohydrates** 85 g, **Protein** 5 g

PECAN PIE

Yield: 4 Pies, 9 in. (22 cm) each	**Method:** Custard filling	
Filling:		
Eggs	16 oz. (10 eggs)	480 g
Brown sugar	10 oz.	300 g
Unsalted butter, barely melted	8 oz.	240 g
Vanilla extract	0.5 fl. oz. (1 Tbsp.)	15 ml
Salt	0.2 oz. (1 tsp.)	6 g
Maple syrup or dark corn syrup	1 pt.	480 ml
Glucose or light corn syrup	1 pt.	480 ml
Pecan pieces	1 lb.	480 g
Pecan halves	12 oz.	360 g
Mealy dough pie shells, 9 in. (22 cm), unbaked	4 shells	4 shells
Powdered sugar	as needed	as needed

❶ Positioning the pecan halves on top of the pie.

① Whisk together the eggs, brown sugar and melted butter. Add the vanilla and salt. Whisk in the syrups until well combined.

② Evenly divide the pecan pieces among the pie shells. Pour the egg-and-syrup mixture evenly over the pecans in each pie shell. Position the pecan halves evenly on top of the pecan pieces.

③ Bake at 325°F (160°C) until the centers of the pies have set, approximately 35 to 40 minutes.

④ Dust the edges of the crust with powdered sugar. Serve the cooled pie with ice cream, if desired.

Approximate values per 1/8-pie serving: **Calories** 700, **Total fat** 47 g, **Saturated fat** 19 g, **Cholesterol** 135 mg, **Sodium** 390 mg, **Total carbohydrates** 70 g, **Protein** 8 g

② A slice of the Pecan Pie.

SWEET POTATO PIE

Yield: 2 Pies, 9 in. (22 cm) each

Method: Custard filling

Filling:

Sweet potatoes, peeled and cubed	1 lb.	480 g
Brown sugar	10 oz.	300 g
Salt	0.2 oz. (1 tsp.)	6 g
Cinnamon, ground	0.07 oz. (1 tsp.)	2 g
Ginger, ground	0.14 oz. (2 tsp.)	4 g
Allspice, ground	0.14 oz. (2 tsp.)	4 g
Vanilla extract	0.3 fl. oz. (2 tsp.)	10 ml
Eggs	6.75 oz. (4 eggs)	200 g
Buttermilk	8 fl. oz.	240 ml
Heavy cream	10 fl. oz.	300 ml
Mealy dough or sweet tart dough pie shells, 9 in. (22 cm), baked	2 shells	2 shells
Crème Chantilly (page 502)	as needed	as needed

① Boil the sweet potatoes in lightly salted water until tender. Drain thoroughly. Pass the sweet potatoes through a food mill or ricer. Transfer the sweet potatoes to a mixing bowl and whip until smooth.

② Add the sugar, salt, cinnamon, ginger, allspice and vanilla.

③ Add the eggs and whisk until smooth, followed by the buttermilk and cream.

④ Divide the filling evenly between the two pie shells. Bake at 400°F (200°C) for 15 minutes. Reduce the oven temperature to 325°F (160°C). Bake until the filling is set, approximately 30 more minutes.

⑤ Garnish the cooled pie with Crème Chantilly and pastry dough leaf garnish, if desired.

Approximate values per ⅛-pie serving: **Calories** 310, **Total fat** 16 g, **Saturated fat** 7 g, **Cholesterol** 80 mg, **Sodium** 320 mg, **Total carbohydrates** 37 g, **Protein** 4 g, **Vitamin A** 130%

CHESS PIE

A traditional American pie, especially in the South, chess pie is a type of custard pie. Its origins are not clear, but some say "chess" refers to the cheeselike texture of the eggy filling. Others claim that when a southern woman was complimented on the deliciousness of her pie, she would reply, "Oh, it's just pie." With a southern accent, "just" becomes "jess."

Yield: 2 Pies, 9 in. (22 cm) each		Method: Custard filling
Filling:		
Unsalted butter, melted	4 oz.	120 g
Granulated sugar	1 lb. 3 oz.	570 g
Eggs	6.75 oz. (4 eggs)	200 g
Evaporated milk	8 fl. oz.	240 ml
Lemon juice	0.08 fl. oz. (½ tsp.)	2.5 ml
Vanilla extract	0.15 fl. oz. (1 tsp.)	5 ml
All-purpose flour	0.5 oz.	15 g
Mealy dough pie shells, 9 in. (22 cm), unbaked	2 shells	2 shells
Nutmeg, ground	1 pinch	1 pinch

1. Beat the butter, sugar, eggs, milk, lemon juice, vanilla and flour together. Pour into the pie shells and sprinkle the top of each pie lightly with nutmeg.
2. Bake at 325°F (160°C) until set and the crust is brown, approximately 40 minutes.

Approximate values per ⅛-pie serving: **Calories** 350, **Total fat** 16 g, **Saturated fat** 7 g, **Cholesterol** 75 mg, **Sodium** 160 mg, **Total carbohydrates** 47 g, **Protein** 4 g, **Vitamin A** 6%

LEMON CURD TART

**SAFETY ALERT
Caramelizing Sugar**

Caramelizing sugar can cause serious burns. Use rubber gloves and take proper precautions to avoid hot sugar coming into direct contact with your skin.

St. Honoré patron saint of the pastry chef; name for a light crisp pastry composed of puff pastry topped with cream puffs filled with custard and coated with hard caramel; also refers to a piping tip that produces a wedge-shaped design, which is often used to pipe in the filling

Yield: 1 Tart, 8 in. (20 cm)		Method: Cream filling
Raspberry jam	as needed	as needed
Coconut Almond Tart Dough (page 383) tart shell, 8 in. (20 cm), fully baked	1 shell	1 shell
Lemon or Lime Curd (page 493)	1 lb. 4 oz.	600 g
Italian Meringue (page 413)	10 oz.	300 g
Lemon juice	1.5 fl. oz.	45 ml
Fresh raspberries	2 oz.	60 g
Neutral glaze	as needed	as needed

1. Spread the raspberry jam on the base of the cooled tart shell.
2. Fill with Lemon Curd.
3. Refrigerate or freeze the tart until the curd is firm, about 1 hour.
4. Prepare the Italian Meringue and flavor it with the lemon juice. Using a piping bag fitted with a **St. Honoré** tip, pipe parallel rows of meringue to cover the surface of the tart.
5. Using a propane torch, brown the surface of the meringue.
6. Scatter the meringue with fresh raspberries. Heat the neutral glaze until flowing. Pour it into a parchment paper cone, then pipe a few drops of glaze on each berry to resemble dewdrops.

Approximate values per ⅛-tart serving: **Calories** 520, **Total fat** 30 g, **Saturated fat** 18 g, **Cholesterol** 125 mg, **Sodium** 95 mg, **Total carbohydrates** 61 g, **Protein** 5 g, **Vitamin A** 20%, **Vitamin C** 20%

① Spreading raspberry jam in the baked tart shell with an offset spatula.

② Pouring the lemon curd into the tart shell.

③ Piping the Italian meringue with a St. Honoré tip in a freeform pattern over the lemon curd.

④ Browning the surface of the meringue with a propane torch.

⑤ Piping drops of neutral tart glaze on the raspberries.

PURPLE FIG TART WITH MINTED CHEESE MOUSSE

Yield: 12 Tarts, 2½ in. (7.5 cm) each

Shortbread Tart Dough (page 382), made with almond flour	24 oz.	720 g
Egg wash	as needed	as needed
Minted Cheese Mousse (recipe follows)	1 lb. 10 oz.	780 g
Fresh purple figs	30	30
Neutral glaze	2.5 oz.	75 g
Orange juice	1.5 fl. oz.	45 ml

1. Roll out the almond Shortbread Tart Dough to a thickness of ⅛ inch (3 millimeters). Using a round cutter, cut circles slightly wider than the tart pans. Line the tart pans with the dough, gently pressing the dough into place.

2. Place paper and pie weights in the shells and bake at 375°F (190°C) until the edges of the tarts are lightly golden, approximately 6 minutes. Remove the paper and weights from the shells, brush the shells with egg wash and bake until golden brown, approximately 12 to 15 minutes.

3. Using a pastry bag fitted with a medium plain tip, pipe the Minted Cheese Mousse into the tart shells. Chill until the filling has set.

4. Slice the figs in half and arrange in pyramid style on the tarts.

5. Combine the neutral glaze with the orange juice and brush the fruit with the glaze.

Approximate values per tart: **Calories** 440, **Total fat** 27 g, **Saturated fat** 16 g, **Cholesterol** 110 mg, **Sodium** 140 mg, **Total carbohydrates** 50 g, **Protein** 5 g, **Vitamin A** 25%

MINTED CHEESE MOUSSE

Yield: 1 lb. 10 oz. (795 g)

Cream cheese or mascarpone	10 oz.	300 g
Granulated sugar	4 oz.	120 g
Water	2 fl. oz.	60 ml
Mint compound (or 20 mint leaves)	0.5 fl. oz.	15 ml
Heavy cream	10 fl. oz.	300 ml

1. Cut the cream cheese into medium cubes, place in a bowl and soften in a microwave oven until the cheese is 90°F (32°C).

2. Boil the sugar and water for 1 minute. Remove from the heat and cool, then use a spatula to incorporate into the softened cheese.

3. Whip the mint compound and cream to soft peaks. (Or cut the mint leaves into fine strips, add to the cream and whip to soft peaks.) Fold the cream into the cheese mixture and use immediately.

Approximate values per 1-oz. (30-g) serving: **Calories** 110, **Total fat** 9 g, **Saturated fat** 5 g, **Cholesterol** 70 mg, **Sodium** 10 mg, **Total carbohydrates** 5 g, **Protein** 2 g

INDIVIDUAL KEY LIME MANGO TARTS

Yield: 12 Tarts, 2½ in. (7.5 cm) each

Lemon or Lime Curd (page 493)	1 lb. 4 oz.	600 g
Coconut Almond Tart Dough (page 383), 2½-in. (7.5-cm) tart shells, fully baked	12 shells	12 shells
Mangoes, peeled	6	6
Neutral glaze	5 oz.	150 g
Mango purée	2.5 oz.	75 g
Lime juice	0.5 fl. oz.	15 ml
White chocolate decorations (page 703)	as needed	as needed

1 Using a pastry bag fitted with a medium plain tip, pipe the Lime Curd into the tart shells, filling to the rim of the tarts. Refrigerate or freeze the tarts until the curd is firm, about 1 hour.

2 Cut the mangoes into small dice, ¼ inch (6 millimeters) square. Arrange the mango cubes over the surface of the curd.

3 Dissolve the neutral glaze with the mango purée and the lime juice in a small saucepan over low heat. Cool to lukewarm, then brush the fruit with the glaze. (Or blend the glaze, mango purée and lime juice using an immersion blender.)

4 Garnish with white chocolate decorations.

Approximate values per tart: **Calories** 430, **Total fat** 26 g, **Saturated fat** 16 g, **Cholesterol** 95 mg, **Sodium** 75 mg, **Total carbohydrates** 51 g, **Protein** 4 g, **Vitamin A** 100%, **Vitamin C** 60%

INDIVIDUAL STRAWBERRY CREAM TARTS

Yield: 18 Tartlets, 2½ in. (7.5 cm) each

Minted Cheese Mousse (page 396), made without the mint	1 lb. 10 oz.	780 g
Shortbread Tart Dough (page 382), made with hazelnut flour, 2½-in. (7.5-cm) tart shells, fully baked	18 shells	18 shells
Fresh strawberries	2 pt.	1 lt
Neutral glaze	5 oz.	150 g
Strawberry purée	3 oz.	90 g
Pistachios, chopped fine	as needed	as needed

1 Using a pastry bag fitted with a large plain tip, pipe the Minted Cheese Mousse in large mounds into the tart shells.

2 Slice the strawberries in half lengthwise. Press the strawberries into the cream with the cut side facing in, pyramid style, on the tarts.

3 In a small saucepan over low heat, dissolve the neutral glaze with the strawberry purée. Cool to lukewarm, then brush the fruit with the glaze.

4 Sprinkle chopped pistachios on the neutral glaze along the rim of the tarts.

Approximate values per tart: **Calories** 350, **Total fat** 29 g, **Saturated fat** 17 g, **Cholesterol** 115 mg, **Sodium** 140 mg, **Total carbohydrates** 28 g, **Protein** 5 g, **Vitamin A** 15%, **Vitamin C** 20%

FLEMISH PEAR TARTS

Yield: 10 Tarts, 3 in. (7.5 cm) each

Sweet Almond Tart Dough (page 383)	1 lb. 4 oz.	600 g
Ripe pears, such as Bosc	6–7	6–7
Filling:		
Eggs	3.2 oz. (2 eggs)	95 g
Brown sugar	3.25 oz.	100 g
Almond extract	0.3 fl. oz. (2 tsp.)	10 ml
Vanilla extract	0.15 fl. oz. (1 tsp.)	5 ml
Orange zest, grated fine	0.7 oz. (1 tsp.)	2 g
Salt	0.1 oz. (½ tsp.)	3 g
Cake or potato flour	0.5 oz.	15 g
Cinnamon, ground	0.1 oz. (1½ tsp.)	3 g
Unsalted butter, melted	2.5 oz.	75 g
Cocoa Streusel (recipe follows)	8 oz.	240 g
Ginger Ice Cream (page 554)	1 pt	480 ml
Caramelized Dried Pear Slices (recipe follows; optional)	10 slices	10 slices

1. Roll out the Sweet Almond Tart Dough to a thickness of ⅛ inch (3 millimeters) and line ten 3-inch (7.5-centimeter) tart rings or pans, gently pressing the dough in place.
2. Peel and core the pears and cut into medium dice, ⅜ inch (9 millimeters) square. Divide the fruit evenly among the tart pans.
3. Whisk the eggs and brown sugar in a mixing bowl until well combined. Stir in the extracts, orange zest, salt, flour and cinnamon. Cool the melted butter to approximately 130°F (54°C) and whisk it into the egg mixture.
4. Immediately divide the filling among the tart pans, pouring it evenly over the pear cubes. Top with the Cocoa Streusel.
5. Bake at 375°F (190°C) until the filling has set, approximately 30 minutes.
6. Remove the tarts from the pans. Top with Ginger Ice Cream and a Caramelized Dried Pear Slice (if using).

Note: *Potato flour, not to be confused with potato starch, is found in health food stores. It makes a tender custard. Cake flour may be used in its place.*

VARIATION:

Pear Ginger Tart—Cut 2 ounces (60 grams) candied ginger into small dice, ⅛ inch (3 millimeters) square, and toss with the pears.

Approximate values per tart: **Calories** 320, **Total fat** 18 g, **Saturated fat** 10 g, **Cholesterol** 95 mg, **Sodium** 220 mg, **Total carbohydrates** 39 g, **Protein** 4 g, **Vitamin A** 15%

COCOA STREUSEL

Yield: 1 lb. 8 oz. (747 g)

Unsalted butter, cold	5 oz.	150 g
Brown sugar	7 oz.	210 g
Vanilla extract	0.5 fl. oz.	15 ml
Salt	0.2 oz. (1 tsp.)	6 g
Pastry flour	5 oz.	150 g
Cocoa powder	1 oz.	30 g
Cinnamon, ground	0.2 oz. (1 Tbsp.)	6 g
Hazelnut flour	6 oz.	180 g

1. In the bowl of a mixer fitted with the paddle attachment, blend the butter, brown sugar, vanilla and salt until combined but not creamed.

❷ Sift together the pastry flour, cocoa and cinnamon. Stir in the hazelnut flour and add the flour mixture to the butter mixture. Mix very briefly until the mixture resembles coarse meal and lumps form; do not mix until it forms a smooth dough.

❸ Sprinkle the streusel on top of custard tarts, butter cakes, coffeecakes or brownies before baking. When refrigerated, this topping keeps 1 month.

Approximate values per 1-oz. (30-g) serving: **Calories** 140, **Total fat** 9 g, **Saturated fat** 3.5 g, **Cholesterol** 15 mg, **Sodium** 200 mg, **Total carbohydrates** 15 g, **Protein** 2 g

CARAMELIZED DRIED PEAR SLICES

Yield: 10 slices

Granulated sugar	as needed	as needed
Pears	1–2	1–2
Lemon juice	1 fl. oz.	30 ml
Caramel:		
Glucose or corn syrup	4 oz.	120 g
Granulated sugar	6 oz.	180 g

❶ Spread some granulated sugar out in a thin layer on a half-sheet pan. Set aside.

❷ Thinly slice the unpeeled pears using a mandoline or an electric meat slicer. Dip the slices in lemon juice, shaking off any extra juice that clings to the slices.

❸ Dip each slice in granulated sugar, coating them lightly. Transfer the coated slices to a sheet pan lined with a silicone baking mat.

❹ Bake at 175°F (180°C) until the pear slices are dry and crisp, at least 2 to 4 hours. (Pear slices can be made ahead to this point. Store them tightly sealed in a covered plastic container in a cool dry place for up to 1 week.)

❺ Prepare a paper cone with a small hole, not larger than 1⁄16 inch (2 millimeters) in diameter. Set aside.

❻ To make the caramel, bring the syrup to a boil. Add half of the sugar and cook until it dissolves. Brush any sugar crystals from the sides of the pan using a pastry brush dipped in cold water. Add the remaining sugar and stir until it dissolves.

❼ Cook the sugar until it is light golden brown and remove it from heat. To stop the cooking process, place the pan in a bowl filled with room-temperature water for 15 seconds.

❽ Holding the paper cone with a dry towel, fill it half full with caramel. On one side of each slice, pipe lines of caramel horizontally and vertically to form an inconspicuous support grid. Flip over each pear slice, then pipe a thin line of caramel around it to form a pear-shaped silhouette.

❾ Store these pear slices in single layers on parchment paper in a cool dry place for up to 2 days before using.

> **SAFETY ALERT**
> **Caramelizing Sugar**
>
> Caramelizing sugar can cause serious burns. Use rubber gloves and take proper precautions to avoid hot sugar coming into direct contact with your skin.

INDIVIDUAL BLACK AND BLUE BERRY TARTS

Yield: 12 Tartlets, 2½ in. (7.5 cm) each

Crème Brûlée for Tarts (page 518)	2 lb.	960 g
Shortbread Tart Dough (page 382), made with almond flour, 2½-in. (7.5-cm) tart shells, fully baked	12 shells	12 shells
Blackberries	2 pt.	1 lt
Blueberries	1 pt.	0.5 lt
Powdered sugar	as needed	as needed

❶ Using a pastry bag fitted with a medium plain tip, pipe the Crème Brûlée for Tarts into each tart shell.

❷ Scatter the surface of the cream with the berries. Dust with powdered sugar to garnish.

Approximate values per tart: **Calories** 430, **Total fat** 33 g, **Saturated fat** 19 g, **Cholesterol** 260 mg, **Sodium** 95 mg, **Total carbohydrates** 36 g, **Protein** 6 g, **Vitamin A** 20%, **Vitamin C** 25%

INDIVIDUAL ORANGE MILK CHOCOLATE RUBY RED GRAPEFRUIT TARTS

Yield: 18 Tartlets, 2½ in. (7.5 cm) each

Orange Milk Chocolate Ganache (page 485)	2 lb. 2 oz.	1020 g
Shortbread Tart Dough (page 382), made with hazelnut flour, 2½-in. (7.5-cm) tart shells, fully baked	18 shells	18 shells
Ruby red grapefruits	3–4	3–4
Neutral glaze	5 oz.	150 g
Grapefruit juice	3 fl. oz.	90 ml
Red currants or raspberries	as needed	as needed

1. Using a pastry bag fitted with a medium plain tip, pipe the Orange Milk Chocolate Ganache into the tart shells.
2. Segment the grapefruits, saving the juice, and position three to four overlapping segments on top of each tart.
3. Dissolve the neutral glaze with the grapefruit juice and brush evenly over each tart. Garnish each tart with a few currants or raspberries.

Approximate values per tart: **Calories** 370, **Total fat** 27 g, **Saturated fat** 14 g, **Cholesterol** 80 mg, **Sodium** 85 mg, **Total carbohydrates** 41 g, **Protein** 5 g, **Vitamin C** 40%

FRENCH APPLE TART

The amount of each ingredient, the yield and the baking time will depend on the capacity and number of tart molds used. This procedure can be used for individual tartlets or large round, rectangular or daisy-shaped tart pans.

Sweet Tart Dough (page 368)	as needed
Almond Cream (page 296)	as needed
Tart apples, peeled, cored and sliced thin	as needed
Unsalted butter, melted	as needed
Granulated sugar	as needed
Apricot glaze	as needed

1. Line the tart pans with Sweet Tart Dough. Do not prick the dough.
2. Pipe in an even layer of Almond Cream.
3. Arrange the apples in overlapping rows, covering the Almond Cream completely.
4. Brush the top of the apples with melted butter and sprinkle lightly with granulated sugar.
5. Bake at 375°F (190°C) until the crust is done and the apples are light brown.
6. Allow the tart to cool to room temperature. Brush the top with apricot glaze.

Approximate values per 4-oz. (120-g) serving: **Calories** 395, **Total fat** 17 g, **Saturated fat** 7 g, **Cholesterol** 234 mg, **Sodium** 98 mg, **Total carbohydrates** 56 g, **Protein** 7 g, **Vitamin A** 12%

LINZER TART

Chefs Susan Feniger and Mary Sue Milliken

Yield: 8–10 Servings

Dough:

Unsalted butter, softened	8 oz.	240 g	73%
Granulated sugar	8 oz.	240 g	73%
Egg yolks	1.3 oz. (2 yolks)	40 g	12%
Orange zest, grated fine	0.4 oz. (2 Tbsp.)	12 g	3.6%
Lemon zest, grated fine	0.2 oz. (1 Tbsp.)	6 g	1.8%
All-purpose flour	11 oz.	330 g	100%
Hazelnuts, ground fine	6 oz.	180 g	54%
Baking powder	0.14 oz. (1 tsp.)	4 g	1.2%
Cinnamon, ground	0.14 oz. (2 tsp.)	4 g	1.2%
Cloves, ground	0.04 oz. (½ tsp.)	1 g	0.3%
Salt	0.05 oz. (¼ tsp.)	1.5 g	0.5%
Total dough weight:	2 lb. 3 oz.	1058 g	320%
Raspberry preserves	14 oz.	420 g	

1 To make the dough, cream together the butter and sugar until light and fluffy. Add the egg yolks and the orange and lemon zest. Beat until well combined.

2 In another bowl, mix together the flour, hazelnuts, baking powder, cinnamon, cloves and salt. Add the dry mixture all at once to the creamed mixture and mix briefly, until just combined. (This dough looks more like cookie dough than pastry.) Wrap in plastic and chill until firm, at least 4 hours or overnight.

3 Divide the dough in half. On a generously floured board, briefly knead one piece of dough and flatten it with the palm of your hand. Gently roll the dough out 1/4 inch (6 millimeters) thick and use it to line a 9- or 10-inch (22- or 25-centimeter) tart pan with a removable bottom. This rich dough patches easily. Chill approximately 10 minutes.

4 Roll out the second piece of dough to form a 12-inch × 4-inch (30-centimeter × 10-centimeter) rectangle. Using a sharp knife or pastry wheel, cut lengthwise strips, approximately ½ inch (1.2 centimeters) wide. (Reserve any leftover dough for making additional tarts or cookies.)

5 Remove the lined tart shell from the refrigerator and spread the raspberry preserves evenly over it. To create the lattice pattern with the pastry strips, first lay some strips in parallel lines, ½ inch (1.2 centimeters) apart. Then lay a second row of strips at a 45-degree angle to the first. Press the strips to the edge of the crust to seal.

6 Bake at 350°F (180°C) until the crust is golden brown and the filling is bubbly in the center, approximately 45 minutes. Set aside to cool.

Approximate values per ¹⁄₁₀-tart serving: **Calories** 300, **Total fat** 29 g, **Saturated fat** 12 g, **Cholesterol** 90 mg, **Sodium** 65 mg, **Total carbohydrates** 7 g, **Protein** 4 g, **Vitamin A** 20%, **Claims**—low sodium; good source of fiber

CHOCOLATE TART WITH FRESH BERRIES

Yield: 2 Tarts, 8 in. (20 cm) each

Shortbread Tart Dough (page 382), made with hazelnut flour	20 oz.	600 g
Egg wash	as needed	as needed
Flourless Chocolate Spongecake (recipe follows), 7-inch (17-centimeter) rounds	2 rounds	2 rounds
Raspberry Ganache (page 585)	1 lb. 7 oz.	690 g
Fresh raspberries and strawberries	4–5 pt.	2–2.4 lt
Neutral glaze	1 oz.	30 g

1. Roll out the hazelnut Shortbread Tart Dough to a thickness of ⅛ inch (3 millimeters) and line two 8-inch (20-centimeter) tart rings or pans with it, gently pressing the dough into place.
2. Place paper and pie weights in the shells. Bake at 375°F (190°C) until the edges are lightly golden, approximately 8 minutes. Remove the paper and weights from the shells, brush them with egg wash and bake until golden brown, approximately 12 to 15 minutes. Set aside to cool.
3. Place a 7-inch (17-centimeter) round of Flourless Chocolate Spongecake in the bottom of each cooled tart shell.
4. Using a ladle, fill each tart to the rim with Raspberry Ganache. Refrigerate until set.
5. Cover the entire surface of the tart with fresh berries.
6. Place the neutral glaze in a parchment paper piping and pipe a drop of glaze on each berry to resemble dew drops.

Approximate values per ⅛-tart serving: **Calories** 420, **Total fat** 24 g, **Saturated fat** 13 g, **Cholesterol** 145 mg, **Sodium** 95 mg, **Total carbohydrates** 50 g, **Protein** 6 g, **Vitamin A** 15%, **Vitamin C** 70%, **Iron** 15%

FLOURLESS CHOCOLATE SPONGECAKE

Yield: 3 Rounds, 7 in. (17 cm) each

			Sugar at 100%
Egg whites	6 oz. (6 whites)	180 g	92%
Granulated sugar	6.5 oz.	195 g	100%
Egg yolks	4 oz. (6 yolks)	120 g	61%
Vanilla extract	0.15 fl. oz. (1 tsp.)	5 ml	2%
Cocoa powder, sifted	2 oz.	60 g	30%
Total batter weight:	1 lb. 3 oz.	560 g	285%

1. In the bowl of a mixer fitted with the whip attachment, beat the egg whites to soft peaks. Add the sugar and continue whipping to stiff peaks.
2. In a separate bowl, whip the egg yolks to a thick ribbon.
3. When both mixtures have reached the proper consistency, add one-third of the whipped yolks to the egg whites, folding them together using a balloon whisk. Heavy streaks may remain in the batter.
4. Add the remaining egg yolks and gently fold together. Some streaks may remain in the batter.
5. Add the vanilla and cocoa powder and gently fold together until no streaks remain in the batter.
6. Using a piping bag fitted with a large plain tip, pipe the batter onto parchment-lined sheet pans in a tight spiral pattern in order to form three 7-inch- (17-centimeter-) diameter rounds.
7. Bake at 350°F (180°C) until the cake springs back when gently touched, approximately 25 minutes. Cool completely. Any unneeded cake rounds can be wrapped tightly in plastic wrap and frozen for later use.

Approximate values per round: **Calories** 470, **Total fat** 16 g, **Saturated fat** 6 g, **Cholesterol** 545 mg, **Sodium** 115 mg, **Total carbohydrates** 73 g, **Protein** 17 g, **Vitamin A** 15%, **Iron** 25%, **Claims** gluten free

ZUPPA INGLESE TART

Trifle, the national dessert of the British Isles, is a spongecake soaked with wine or spirits and then layered with candied fruit or jam and thick custard topped with whipped cream. The Italian version, Zuppa Inglese, is not an "English soup" but a génoise spongecake flavored with rum and filled with pastry cream. Its curious name suggests how popular the dessert was among homesick Britons vacationing in coastal cities including Genoa and Naples, where this dish originated in the late 19th century. Here the trifle ingredients are contained in a pastry shell coated with a thin layer of white chocolate to retain a crisp crust.

Yield: 2 Tarts, 8 in. (20 cm) each

Shortbread Tart Dough (page 382), tart shells, 8 in. (20 cm), fully baked	2 shells	2 shells
White chocolate, melted	6 oz.	120 g
Classic Génoise (page 440), 7-in. (17-cm) round	1 round	1 round
Simple Syrup (page 73)	4 fl. oz.	120 ml
Rum	1 fl. oz.	30 ml
Vanilla extract	0.15 fl. oz. (1 tsp.)	5 ml
Pastry Cream (page 492)	2 pt.	1 lt
Fresh strawberries, sliced in half	1 pt.	0.5 lt
Raspberry jam	as needed	as needed
Crème Chantilly (page 502)	as needed	as needed
Almonds, sliced and toasted	as needed	as needed

1. Brush the inside of the baked and cooled tart shells with the melted white chocolate.
2. Split the Classic Génoise in half and fit one layer in each tart shell.
3. Combine the Simple Syrup, rum and vanilla in a small bowl. Moisten the génoise layer with the syrup.
4. Place the Pastry Cream in a pastry bag fitted with a plain tip. Pipe a ¾-inch (1-centimeter) layer of Pastry Cream over the génoise layer in each tart shell.
5. Cover the entire surface of the Pastry Cream with the sliced strawberries, then spread them with raspberry jam.
6. Using a pastry bag with a star tip, pipe rosettes of Crème Chantilly over each tart.
7. Sprinkle the tarts with toasted sliced almonds.

Approximate values per ⅛-tart serving: **Calories** 540, **Total fat** 31 g, **Saturated fat** 15 g, **Cholesterol** 235 mg, **Sodium** 120 mg, **Total carbohydrates** 65 g, **Protein** 10 g

CHAPTER TWELVE

PASTRY AND DESSERT COMPONENTS

- prepare a variety of pastries using éclair paste
- prepare a variety of meringues
- prepare a variety of specialty pastries using phyllo dough
- prepare crêpes
- prepare a variety of dessert and pastry items, incorporating components from other chapters

ONE OF THE ENTICEMENTS OF A GREAT BAKESHOP is the array of different pastries and cakes on display. The secret to such variety is the baker's ability to use a limited number of preparations to make a wide variety of delights. The doughs and preparations in this chapter are quick and easy to prepare, with great versatility. Éclair paste can be baked, poached or deep-fried. When baked, éclair paste becomes its namesake cream-filled pastry as well as sweet puffs, savory appetizers and elaborate cakes such as Paris-Brest and **croquembouche**. Other doughs, such as thin, flaky phyllo and tender, pancake-like crêpes, can be shaped and filled in numerous ways to create classic and contemporary pastry and dessert items. Egg white meringues, although not a dough in the traditional sense of the word, are included here because they can be baked into crisp shells or layers, then filled or topped with cream, custard, ganache and other products to create many sophisticated pastries and tortes (see Table 12.1).

croquembouche a pyramid of small puffs, each filled with pastry cream; a French tradition for Christmas and weddings, it is held together with caramelized sugar and decorated with spun sugar or marzipan flowers

profiteroles small baked rounds of éclair paste filled with ice cream and topped with chocolate sauce

éclairs baked fingers of éclair paste filled with pastry cream; the top is then coated with chocolate glaze or fondant

Paris-Brest rings of baked éclair paste cut in half horizontally and filled with light pastry cream and/or whipped cream; the top is dusted with powdered sugar or drizzled with chocolate glaze

beignets squares or strips of éclair paste deep-fried and dusted with powdered sugar

churros a Mexican and Spanish pastry in which sticks of éclair paste flavored with cinnamon are deep-fried and rolled in sugar while still hot

crullers a Dutch pastry in which a loop or strip of twisted éclair paste is deep-fried

gougère éclair paste flavored with cheese or herbs, baked and served as a savory hors d'oeuvre

ÉCLAIR PASTE

Éclair paste, also known as **pâte à choux**, bakes up into golden brown, crisp pastries. Inside these light pastries are mostly air pockets with a bit of moist dough. They can be filled with sweet cream, custard, fruit or even savory mixtures. The dough is most often piped into rounds for **cream puffs**, **profiteroles**, fingers for **éclairs** or rings for **Paris-Brest**. Éclair paste may also be piped or spooned into specific shapes and deep-fried for doughnut-type products known as **beignets**, **churros** and **crullers**. And this dough may be flavored with herbs, spices and cheese and made into savory puffs known as **gougères**. Seasoned éclair paste even becomes a savory casserole when pieces of the dough are poached and baked with cheese or a cream sauce.

Making Éclair Paste

Éclair paste is unique among doughs because it is cooked before baking. The cooking occurs when the flour is added to a boiling mixture of water, milk and butter. This process breaks down the starches in the flour, allowing them to absorb the liquid, speeding gelatinization. Strong flour is used to give structure to the finished products. Eggs are added to the flour mixture for leavening. (The quantity of eggs will vary depending on the size of the eggs used, the type of flour used and the moisture content of the flour mixture.) The dough produced is batterlike with a smooth, firm texture. Without this technique, the dough would not puff up and develop the desired large interior air pockets when baked. Steam is a key leavening agent in baked goods with a large proportion of moisture such as éclair paste, popovers and other pourable batters. To activate the steam before the dough sets, these products are baked at relatively high temperatures, around 400°F (200°C). At this temperature, steam is produced before the egg and other proteins in the formula coagulate.

Products made with éclair paste can develop deep unwanted cracks on the surface, however. A cooler baking temperature creates less aggressive oven expansion and thus curbs the development of these deep cracks. Steam buildup in the oven also contributes to uneven baking and the development of surface cracks on the baked choux pastries. Open the steam escape valve of the oven if it is equipped with one, or open the oven door slightly during the second half of the baking period to allow steam to be released.

TABLE 12.1	CLASSIFICATION OF PASTRY DOUGHS		
DOUGH	FRENCH NAME	CHARACTERISTICS AFTER BAKING	USE
Éclair paste	Pâte à choux	Hollow with crisp exterior	Cream puffs; éclairs; savory products
Puff pastry	Pâte feuilletée	Rich but not sweet; hundreds of light, flaky layers	Tart and pastry cases; cookies; layered pastries; savory products
Meringue	Meringue	Sweet; light; crisp or soft depending on preparation	Topping or icing; baked as a shell or component for layered desserts, cookies and pastries
Phyllo	Phyllo	Very thin, crisp, flaky layers; bland	Middle Eastern pastries and savory dishes, especially hors d'oeuvre; baklava
Crêpes	Crêpes	Very thin, flexible pancake-like layers; eggy, buttery flavor	Filled as plated desserts or savory dishes

PROCEDURE FOR PREPARING ÉCLAIR PASTE

1. Combine the liquid ingredients and butter cut into small cubes. Bring to a boil.

2. As soon as the water-and-butter mixture comes to a boil, add all the flour to the saucepan. If the liquid is allowed to boil, evaporation occurs; this can create an imbalance in the liquid-to-flour ratio.

3. Stir vigorously until the liquid is absorbed. Continue cooking the dough until it forms a ball that comes away from the sides of the pan, leaving only a thin film of dough on the sides of the pan.

4. Transfer the dough to a mixing bowl. Allow the dough to cool slightly, then add the eggs one at a time, beating well after each addition. (This may be done in the bowl of a mixer fitted with the paddle attachment or by hand.) The number of eggs used varies depending on the size of each egg and the moisture content of the flour mixture. Stop adding eggs when the dough just begins to fall away from the beaters.

5. The finished dough should be smooth and pliable enough to pipe through a pastry bag; it should not be runny.

6. Pipe the dough as desired and bake immediately. Do not open the oven door during the first half of the baking period.

7. Allow the dough to bake until completely dry. If the products are removed from the oven too soon, they will collapse. Test doneness by breaking open one pastry. If the interior is moist and eggy, continue baking.

8. Baked éclair paste can be stored, unfilled, several days at room temperature or frozen for several weeks. Once filled, the pastry should be served within 2 or 3 hours, as it quickly becomes soggy.

MISE EN PLACE

▶ Preheat oven to 400°F (200°C).
▶ Line sheet pans with parchment paper.

❶ Heating the butter and milk.

❷ Adding the flour to the hot liquid.

❸ Stirring the dough to dry it.

ÉCLAIR PASTE
(PÂTE À CHOUX)

Yield: 3 lb.–3 lb. 2 oz. (1479–1527 g) Dough

Milk*	8 fl. oz.	240 ml	80%
Water	8 fl. oz.	240 ml	80%
Salt	0.3 oz. (1½ tsp.)	9 g	3%
Unsalted butter	7 oz.	210 g	70%
Bread flour	10 oz.	300 g	100%
Eggs	16–17.6 oz. (10–11 eggs)	480–528 g	160–176%
Total dough weight:	3 lb. 1 oz.–3 lb. 2 oz.	1479–1527 g	493–509%

❶ Place the milk, water, salt and butter in a saucepan. Bring to a boil. Make sure the butter is fully melted.

❷ Remove from the heat and immediately add all the flour. Vigorously beat the dough by hand. Put the pan back on the heat and continue beating the dough until it comes away from the sides of the pan. The dough should look relatively dry and should just begin to leave a film on the saucepan.

❸ Transfer the dough to the bowl of a mixer fitted with the paddle attachment and beat it for a few seconds at medium speed. Then begin to beat in the eggs one at a time.

❹ Continue to add the eggs one by one until the mixture is shiny but firm. It may not be necessary to use all of the eggs. The dough should pull away from the sides of the bowl in thick threads; it will not clear the bowl.

❺ Put a workable amount of dough into a pastry bag fitted with a large plain tip and pipe onto the sheet pans in the desired shapes at once. (Spraying the inside of the pastry bag with vegetable cooking spray will help keep the sticky éclair paste from clinging to the inside of the bag and make cleanup easier.)

❻ Bake immediately at 400°F (200°C) for 15 minutes. Reduce the heat to 350°F (180°C) and bake until the pastries are dry and crisp, approximately 35 minutes for éclairs. To test for doneness, when the éclair paste seems to be baked through, remove one unit and let it sit for 1 to 2 minutes. If it does not collapse, the product is sufficiently baked.

❼ Cool completely, then fill as desired. Leftovers can be frozen or stored at room temperature.

*For a crisper product, replace the milk with water.

Approximate values per 1-oz. (30-g) serving: **Calories** 70, **Total fat** 4.5 g, **Saturated fat** 2.5 g, **Cholesterol** 50 mg, **Sodium** 0 mg, **Total carbohydrates** 4 g, **Protein** 2 g

❹ The finished batter after the eggs are incorporated.

❺ Piping éclairs.

MERINGUE

Meringue refers to both a basic mixture of egg whites whipped with sugar and a confection or cake baked from this preparation. (See Chapter 4, Bakeshop Ingredients, page 86, for the proper technique for whipping egg whites.) The texture—hard or soft—depends on the ratio of sugar to egg whites. A low sugar content relative to the egg whites creates a **soft meringue**. Soft meringue can be folded into a mousse or Bavarian to lighten it, or it can be used in a spongecake or soufflé. Meringue with only a small amount of sugar will always be soft; it will not become crisp no matter how it is used.

Hard meringue is made with egg whites and an equal part or more, by weight, of sugar. It can be incorporated into a buttercream or pastry cream or used to top a pie or Baked Alaska. These toppings are usually placed briefly under a broiler to caramelize the sugar, creating an attractive brown surface.

With twice as much sugar, by weight, as egg whites, hard meringue can be piped into disks or other shapes and dried in an oven. A low oven temperature evaporates the eggs' moisture, leaving a crisp, sugary, honeycomb-like structure. Weather conditions affect meringues. When humid, the meringue may remain soft for a longer period of time. Additional drying time may be necessary. Disks of baked meringue can be used as layers in a torte or cake. Cups or shells of baked meringue can be filled with cream, mousse, ice cream or fruit.

Meringue Preparations

There are three methods for making meringue: **common (French) meringue**, **Swiss meringue** and **Italian meringue** (see Table 12.2). Egg whites need to be free of any traces of yolk to foam properly. The whites foam best at room temperature, 70°F to 80°F (21°C to 27°C). Dried egg whites or an acid such as cream of tartar are often added to stabilize the egg whites when making common meringue. (Swiss and Italian meringue do not need stabilizers because the way in which they are prepared ensures stability.) The formula is 0.3 ounce (10 grams/2 teaspoons) cream of tartar for 1 pound (480 grams) of egg whites. Beating the whites in an unlined copper bowl also helps stability; however, stainless steel will work equally well with the addition of an acid. Aluminum will discolor the product. Regardless of which preparation method is used, the final product should be smooth, glossy and moist. Meringue should never be dry or spongelike (see Table 12.3).

COMMON (FRENCH) MERINGUE

Common meringues are made by first beating egg whites until a soft foam capable of holding soft peaks is achieved. Granulated sugar is then slowly beaten or folded into the egg whites. The final product may be hard or soft, depending on the ratio of sugar to

TABLE 12.2 CLASSIFICATION OF MERINGUES

TYPE	RATIO OF SUGAR TO EGG WHITES BY WEIGHT	PREPARATION	USE
Common (French)—hard	Twice as much or more	Whip or fold sugar into whipped egg whites	Baked
Common (French)—soft	Equal parts or less	Whip or fold sugar into whipped egg whites	Pie topping; soufflé; cake ingredient
Swiss	Varies	Warm egg whites to 100°F (38°C) with sugar, then whip	Buttercream; pie topping; baked
Italian	Varies	Hot sugar syrup poured into whipped egg whites	Buttercream; frosting; crème Chiboust; mousse; baked

egg whites. When baked, this is considered the finest meringue because of its lightness and melt-in-the-mouth quality. Common meringue is less stable than other varieties and should be used as soon as it is made.

PROCEDURE FOR PREPARING COMMON MERINGUE

1. Place the egg whites in a clean stainless steel or copper bowl; whip on medium speed until foamy.
2. Gradually add no more than half of the total amount of sugar to the foamy egg whites. Continue whipping on medium speed until very stiff and glossy.
3. Remove from the mixer and fold in the remaining sugar and any flavorings by hand.
4. Spread or pipe the meringue into desired shapes for baking.
5. Bake immediately at a low temperature, 225°F to 250°F (110°C to 120°C), until the meringue is crisp through without browning, approximately 1 to 2 hours. Break a baked meringue to test for doneness; if the interior is sticky and moist, return the meringue to the oven.
6. When pasteurized egg whites are used, common meringue can be used to garnish pies such as Lemon Meringue Pie (page 385) or Chocolate Cream Pie (page 386).

 ## COMMON (FRENCH) MERINGUE

MISE EN PLACE

▶ Preheat oven to 225°F (110°C).
▶ Line sheet pans with parchment paper.

Yield: 6 Disks, 8 in. (20 cm) each, 1 lb. 8 oz. (733 g) Meringue

Egg whites	8 oz. (8 whites)	240 g
Granulated sugar	1 lb.	480 g
Dried egg whites (optional)	0.3 oz. (2 tsp.)	8 g
Vanilla extract	0.15 fl. oz. (1 tsp.)	5 ml

1. Place the liquid egg whites in the bowl of a mixer fitted with the whip attachment and whip on medium speed until foamy and the mixture holds soft peaks.
2. Sift 8 ounces (240 grams) of the sugar with dried egg whites (if using), then add gradually to the whipped egg whites. Continue to whip the egg whites on medium speed until very stiff and glossy.
3. Remove from the mixer. Fold in the remaining sugar and the vanilla without overmixing.
4. Spread or pipe the meringue into desired shapes on parchment-lined sheet pans.
5. Bake at 225°F (110°C) 1 to 2 hours. Break off a small piece of a baked meringue disk to verify doneness if necessary. Check the interior after 30 seconds; if the interior is still sticky and moist, return the meringue to the oven. The baked meringue should be firm, crisp and dry inside but not browned.
6. Once cooled, the baked meringues may be stored, unrefrigerated, in tightly closed plastic bags. Properly wrapped, they will have a long shelf life.

Piping common (French) meringue into individual disks before baking.

Disks of baked meringue.

Variations:

Chocolate Meringue—Substitute 8 ounces (240 grams) powdered sugar for the 8 ounces (240 grams) granulated sugar in Step 3. Sift it with 2 ounces (60 grams) cocoa powder.

Coffee Meringue—Substitute 0.5 ounce (15 grams) instant coffee powder and 0.5 fluid ounce (15 milliliters) coffee extract for the vanilla. Coffee crystals will be visible in the meringue.

Lemon or Orange Meringue—Omit the vanilla extract. Add 0.14 ounce (4 grams/ 2 teaspoons) lemon or orange zest to the meringue at the end of the whipping.

Coconut Meringue—Fold in 6 ounces (180 grams) macaroon coconut along with the remaining sugar in Step 3.

Almond Meringue—Fold 4 ounces (120 grams) almond flour and 8 ounces (240 grams) toasted chopped almonds into the whipped egg whites with the remaining sugar in Step 3.

Approximate values per 1-oz. (30-g) serving: **Calories** 80, **Total fat** 0 g, **Saturated fat** 0 g, **Cholesterol** 0 mg, **Sodium** 15 mg, **Total carbohydrates** 19 g, **Protein** 1 g, **Claims**—fat free; no cholesterol; low sodium; gluten free

SWISS MERINGUE

Swiss meringue is made by combining unwhipped egg whites with sugar and warming the mixture over a bain marie to a temperature of approximately 100°F (38°C) until the sugar is dissolved. The syrupy solution is then whipped until cool and stiff. The final product may be hard or soft, depending on the ratio of sugar to egg whites. Swiss meringue is extremely stable but rather difficult to prepare. If the mixture gets too hot, it will not whip properly; the result will be syrupy and runny. Another test for Swiss meringue is to feel whether all of the sugar has dissolved. Once it loses all of its graininess, remove the whites from the double boiler and whip. When baked, Swiss meringue does not expand as much as common meringue, making it ideal for decorations. Swiss meringue is often used as a topping or in buttercream (see Chapter 13, Cakes and Icings).

PAVLOVA, LIGHT AS AIR

As apple pie is to America, **pavlova** is to Australia and New Zealand: the classic dessert. Both countries claim its invention, but what appears certain is that it came into being in the early 1930s after the second Pacific tour of the famed Russian ballerina Anna Pavlova. It is said that Herbert Sachse, the chef at the Esplanade Hotel, where Pavlova stayed during her performances in Perth, created the dish in her honor.

Basically a fruit tart with a meringue base, the classic pavlova is filled with whipped cream decorated with strawberries and/or kiwifruit, usually topped with a passion fruit purée. When the meringue is garnished with a shell border of whipped cream, the dessert resembles a ballerina's frilled skirt. There are now countless variations of fillings: fruit, mousse, even ice cream. The meringue base should be crisp on the outside, chewy and not too soft inside. Small, individual pavlovas can also be created. The guiding principle is that the pavlova, like its namesake, should be as light as air.

PROCEDURE FOR PREPARING SWISS MERINGUE

1. Combine the egg whites and sugar in a clean stainless steel or copper bowl.
2. Place the bowl over a bain marie of barely simmering water. Whisk until the sugar has dissolved and the egg mixture reaches 100°F (38°C).
3. Remove from the heat and whip until the egg whites are stiff and glossy.
4. Spread or pipe the meringue into desired shapes for baking. Bake immediately as for Common Meringue.

MISE EN PLACE

▶ Preheat oven to 250°F (120°C).
▶ Line sheet pans with parchment paper.

SWISS MERINGUE

Yield: 2 lb. 12 oz. (1320 g)

Egg whites, room temperature	1 lb. (16 whites)	480 g
Granulated sugar	28 oz.	840 g

1. Combine the egg whites and sugar in a stainless steel bowl.
2. Place the bowl over a pan of barely simmering water and whip until the mixture reaches 100°F (38°C).
3. Remove from the heat and whip the mixture until stiff on medium speed.
4. Pipe or spread into desired shapes on parchment-lined sheet pans.
5. Bake at 250°F (120°C) 1½ to 2 hours, checking for doneness as for Common Meringue.

Approximate values per 1-oz. (30-g) serving: **Calories** 70, **Total fat** 0 g, **Saturated fat** 0 g, **Cholesterol** 0 mg, **Sodium** 15 mg, **Total carbohydrates** 18 g, **Protein** 1 g, **Claims**—fat free; no cholesterol; low sodium; gluten free

ITALIAN MERINGUE

Italian meringue is made by slowly pouring hot sugar syrup into whipped egg whites. The heat from the syrup cooks the egg whites, adding stability. Hot sugar syrup that is poured on egg whites that were whipped to stiff peaks rather than soft-medium peaks may partially cook the egg whites, resulting in tiny white pieces in the meringue. Be sure that the sugar syrup reaches the correct temperature and that it is added to the egg whites in a slow, steady stream. Italian meringue is used in buttercream or may be flavored and used as a cake filling and frosting called boiled icing. It is indispensable in the aeration of mousses and creams such as crème Chiboust (see Chapter 14, Custards, Creams and Sauces). Furthermore, the human tongue perceives the texture of Italian meringue as velvety and rich; it is therefore an excellent substitute for high-fat whipped cream in reduced-fat preparations.

For many mousses used as torte and tart fillings, Italian meringue may be stabilized with gelatin. (See Chapter 17, Tortes and Specialty Cakes, and Chapter 14, Custards, Creams and Sauces.) The amount of gelatin varies with the application. The softened or melted gelatin is added to the finished meringue when it reaches 120°F (49°C).

PROCEDURE FOR PREPARING ITALIAN MERINGUE

1. Prepare a sugar syrup.
2. Place the egg whites in the bowl of a mixer fitted with the whip attachment.
3. While the syrup is cooking and the temperature approaches 220°F (104°C), begin to whip the egg whites. When soft peaks form, add additional granulated sugar to stabilize the egg foam. Reduce the mixer speed to low.
4. When the sugar syrup reaches the soft ball stage (240°F/116°C), slowly pour the syrup over the egg whites, being careful that no syrup touches the whip.
5. Once all the syrup has been added, whip the eggs 1 minute on high speed. Then reduce the speed to medium and whip until the mixture is cool.
6. Spread or pipe the meringue into desired shapes for baking. Bake immediately as for Common Meringue. Or use the Italian meringue to top pies or Baked Alaska (page 562) or as an ingredient in mousses, as discussed in Chapter 14, Custards, Creams and Sauces.

ITALIAN MERINGUE

Yield: Approximately 1 lb. 7 oz. (690 g)

Granulated sugar	13 oz.	390 g
Glucose or corn syrup	2 oz.	60 g
Water	3 fl. oz.	90 ml
Egg whites, room temperature	8 oz. (8 whites)	240 g

1 Place 12 ounces (360 grams) of the sugar in a heavy saucepan with the syrup and water. Attach a candy thermometer to the pan and bring the sugar to a boil over high heat.

2 Place the egg whites in the bowl of a mixer fitted with the whip attachment. As the temperature of the boiling sugar approaches 220°F (104°C), begin whipping the egg whites. When the whites form soft peaks, gradually add the remaining 1 ounce (30 grams) of sugar. Reduce the mixer speed and continue whipping.

3 When the sugar reaches the soft ball stage (240°F/116°C), remove it from the heat. Pour it into the whites, with the mixer running at high speed. Pour in a steady stream between the side of the bowl and the beater. Once all the sugar is incorporated, whip 1 more minute at high speed, then reduce to medium speed and whip until the meringue is cool.

Approximate values per 1-oz. (30-g) serving: **Calories** 70, **Total fat** 0 g, **Saturated fat** 0 g, **Cholesterol** 0 mg, **Sodium** 20 mg, **Total carbohydrates** 17 g, **Protein** 1 g, **Claims**—fat free; no cholesterol; low sodium; gluten free

Browning Meringue

As discussed previously, meringue makes a stable light coating for numerous finished pastries such as Baked Alaska (page 562), Lemon Meringue Pie (page 385) or Passion Fruit Tart (page 582). To give an appealing browned appearance to the meringue, the meringue-topped product can be placed briefly in a hot oven or under a broiler. The meringue can also be browned using a handheld propane torch. To use a torch to brown the surface of meringue, carefully light the device. Hold it several inches from the surface of the meringue topping. Move the lit torch back and forth over the surface so that it browns evenly.

Nut Meringue Preparations

Often ground nuts and starch, usually cake flour, are folded into meringue before baking to make various preparations used for pastries and tortes. Because ground nuts can be oily, a small amount of flour helps absorb the oil and makes the meringue more stable. Although the names for these preparations vary—dacquoise, progrès, succès and japonais—the formulas are similar. Small changes in the ratio of ingredients create subtle differences in the textures of the finished products. Formulas for two nut meringue cakes—Dacquoise and Succès—appear at the end of this chapter.

MISE EN PLACE

▶ Bring egg whites to room temperature.

SAFETY ALERT
Propane Torch

Training on how to operate a propane torch is recommended before using it to brown meringue or other dessert preparations. Use extreme caution and follow appropriate safety procedures when using a torch. Keep the gas bottle away from sources of heat. Do not leave the torch unattended. Rest the bottle on a stable surface away from any flammable materials.

Browning a tart decorated with Italian meringue.

TABLE 12.3	TROUBLESHOOTING CHART FOR MERINGUES	
PROBLEM	**CAUSE**	**SOLUTION**
Weeps or beads of sugar syrup are released	Old eggs	Use fresher eggs or add starch or stabilizer
	Egg whites overwhipped	Whip only until stiff peaks form
	Not enough sugar	Increase sugar
	Not baked long enough	Increase baking time
	Browning too rapidly	Do not dust with sugar before baking; reduce oven temperature
	Moisture in the air	Increase baking time
Fails to attain any volume or stiffness	Fat present	Start over with clean bowls and utensils
	Sugar added too soon	Allow egg whites to reach soft peaks before adding sugar
Lumps	Not enough sugar	Add additional sugar gradually or start over
	Overwhipping	Whip only until stiff peaks form
Not shiny	Not enough sugar	Add additional sugar gradually or start over
	Overwhipping	Whip only until stiff peaks form

Kataifi (shredded phyllo dough)

PHYLLO DOUGH

Phyllo (fee-low), also spelled *filo* or *fillo*, is from the Greek *phyllon*, meaning "thin sheet or leaf." Although its name is Greek, its origin is unknown. Indians, Turks, Syrians, Yugoslavs and Austrians all claim it as their own. Somewhat blandly flavored, phyllo sheets are brushed with melted butter or oil, stacked and then used in many Mediterranean, Middle Eastern and Central Asian dishes as a tart crust or a wrapper for various sweet or savory fillings. Shredded phyllo, called *kataifi*, is also used for some Mediterranean and Middle Eastern specialties.

Phyllo dough is made from flour, water, a bit of oil and eggs. The dough must be stretched tissue-paper thin, using techniques that can take years to master. Fortunately, excellent commercially prepared phyllo is available in frozen sheets of varying thickness. Sheets of phyllo can stick together if thawed too quickly, so thaw frozen dough slowly for a day or so in the refrigerator. Then allow the package of dough to sit at room temperature at least 1 hour before opening. (Unused phyllo should not be refrozen; it will keep several days in the refrigerator if tightly wrapped.)

When ready to use, open the package and unfold the stack of leaves. Place them flat on a sheet pan or work surface and cover with a sheet of plastic wrap topped with a damp towel. Remove one leaf at a time from the stack, keeping the remainder well covered to prevent them from drying out. Brush melted butter or oil over the sheet's entire surface. Chopped nuts, sugar, cocoa powder or bread crumbs can be dusted over the butter or oil for additional flavor. Repeat with additional leaves until the desired number of layers have been prepared and stacked together. The number of layers will depend on the thickness of the sheets and their use. Cut the stacked phyllo with scissors or a very sharp knife and use as directed in the formula.

BAKLAVA PASTRIES

Yield: approximately 3 Dozen; 1 Quarter-Sheet Pan

Pastry:

Unsalted butter, melted	14–16 oz.	420–480 g
Walnuts, almonds or pistachios, chopped coarse	1½ lb.	720 g
Granulated sugar	4 oz.	120 g
Cinnamon, ground	0.07 oz. (1 tsp.)	2 g
Cloves, ground	0.04 oz. (½ tsp.)	1 g
Phyllo dough sheets, 9 in. × 14 in. (23 cm × 35.5 cm)	1 lb.	480 g

Syrup:

Granulated sugar	12 oz.	360 g
Honey	2 fl. oz.	60 ml
Water	12 fl. oz.	360 ml
Cinnamon stick	1	1
Lemon juice	0.5 fl. oz.	15 ml

MISE EN PLACE

▶ Melt butter.
▶ Chop walnuts.
▶ Preheat oven to 350°F (180°C).

1. Brush the bottom and sides of a quarter-sheet pan generously with some of the melted butter. Set aside. Mix the walnuts, sugar, ground cinnamon and cloves together in a bowl. Set aside.

2. Lay out one sheet of phyllo dough on the bottom of the prepared sheet pan. Brush it with melted butter. Place another sheet of phyllo dough on top, brush with more of the butter and repeat until there is a stack of eight sheets.

3. Sprinkle the stack of sheets with one quarter of the nut filling mixture.

4. Add eight more layers of phyllo dough, brushing each with butter. Sprinkle with one quarter of the nut filling.

5. Repeat these steps two more times so that there are four alternating layers of pastry and nut filling, each composed of eight sheets of phyllo dough.

6. Cover the last layer of nuts with eight sheets of phyllo dough, brushing each with butter. Brush the top layer of the pastry generously with butter. Refrigerate at least 30 minutes.

7. Before baking, score the pastry into 1½-inch (4-centimeter) diamond shapes. Using a sharp knife, cut three-fourths of the way through the pastry without touching the bottom layer.

8. Bake at 350°F (180°C) for 15 minutes. Reduce the heat to 325°F (160°C) and continue baking until light golden, approximately 15 to 20 additional minutes.

9. While the pastry bakes, prepare the syrup. Bring the sugar, honey, water and cinnamon to boil over medium high heat. Simmer the syrup until it thickens slightly, approximately 4 to 6 minutes. Add the lemon juice. Remove the cinnamon stick.

10. Pour the hot syrup over the warm baklava. Allow it to stand to absorb the syrup before serving.

Approximate values per serving: **Calories** 190, **Total fat** 14 g, **Saturated fat** 5 g, **Cholesterol** 20 mg, **Sodium** 445 mg, **Total carbohydrates** 16 g, **Protein** 2 g

CRÊPES

Crêpes are thin, delicate, unleavened pancakes. They are made with a very liquid egg batter cooked in a small, very hot sauté pan or crêpe pan. Crêpe batter can be flavored with buckwheat flour, cornmeal or other grains. Crêpes are not eaten as is, but are usually filled and garnished with sautéed fruits, creams or fruit preserves. A crêpe may be filled with any type of soufflé mixture, baked in the oven and served warm. Crêpes can be prepared in advance, then filled and reheated as needed.

A traditional way to serve a number of crêpe desserts is in a preparation known as **crêpes flambées**. The prepared crêpes are reheated in full view of the customer, then flamed with a flavored brandy before plating and serving them. Crêpes Suzette is the most famous of these preparations. A waiter well skilled in tableside service reheats the crêpes

SAFETY ALERT
Cooking with Alcohol

When alcohol comes into contact with a flame, it can ignite. In order to avoid singed eyebrows and kitchen fires, please be careful when adding wine, brandy, liqueurs or liquor to a dish on or near the stove. Often a dish will require flaming or **flambéing**, which means igniting the brandy, rum or other liquor so that the alcohol burns off and the flavor of the liquor is retained. When a dish calls for flambéing, follow these procedures. Stand away from the pan being flamed. Tilt the pan away from you, allowing the fumes to be ignited by the open flame. Be careful, as the flames can leap from the pan.

crêpes flambées (krayp flahm-BAY) a dessert preparation consisting of thin pancakes filled with fruit, jam or other fillings served flaming; produced by igniting brandy, rum or other liquor so that the alcohol burns off and the flavor of the liquor is retained

with butter and sugar in a decorative sauté pan. Once the sugar begins to caramelize, orange juice and zest are added. An orange-scented liqueur or brandy is added, then carefully ignited. As the alcohol burns off, flames leap from the sauté pan. Then the waiter skillfully folds the crêpes into quarters, placing one or two on each plate. Variations on this type of hot crêpe dish are popular for dessert menus as well as buffet presentations. See Flambéed Pineapple in Crêpes with Blackberry Sorbet (page 682).

Blintzes are crêpes that are cooked on only one side, then filled with cheese, browned in butter and served with sour cream, fruit compote or preserves. A formula for cheese blintzes is provided with the online resources.

PROCEDURE FOR PREPARING CRÊPES

1 Prepare the batter.

2 Heat a well-seasoned crêpe pan or small sauté pan over moderately high heat. Add a small amount of clarified butter.

3 Ladle a small amount of batter into the pan. Tilt the pan so that the batter spreads and coats the bottom evenly.

4 Cook until the crêpe is set and the bottom begins to brown, approximately 1 minute. Flip the crêpe over with a quick flick of the wrist or by lifting it carefully with a spatula.

5 Cook the crêpe for an additional 30 seconds. Slide the finished crêpe from the pan. Crêpes can be stacked between layers of parchment paper for storage.

1 Coating the bottom of the pan evenly with the batter.

2 Flipping the crêpe. Notice the proper light brown color.

CRÊPES

Yield: 30 Crêpes, 6 in. (15 cm) each

Eggs	10 oz. (6 eggs)	300 g	71%
Egg yolks	4 oz. (6 yolks)	120 g	28%
Water	12 fl. oz.	360 ml	86%
Whole milk	18 fl. oz.	540 ml	129%
Granulated sugar	6 oz.	180 g	43%
Salt	0.2 oz. (1 tsp.)	6 g	1.4%
All-purpose flour	14 oz.	420 g	100%
Unsalted butter, melted	5 oz.	150 g	36%
Total batter weight:	4 lb. 5 oz.	2076 g	494%
Clarified butter	as needed	as needed	

1 Whisk together the eggs, egg yolks, water and milk. Add the sugar, salt and flour; whisk together. Stir in the melted butter. Cover and set aside to rest at least 1 hour before cooking.

2 Heat a small sauté or crêpe pan; brush lightly with clarified butter. Pour in 1–1½ fluid ounces (30–45 milliliters) of batter; swirl to coat the bottom of the pan evenly.

3 Cook the crêpe until set and light brown, approximately 60 seconds. Flip it over and cook 30 seconds longer. Remove from the pan.

4 Cooked crêpes may be used immediately or covered and held briefly in a warm oven. Crêpes can also be wrapped well in plastic wrap and refrigerated for 2 to 3 days or frozen for several weeks.

Variation:

Savory Crêpes—Reduce the sugar to 0.45 ounce (13 grams/1 tablespoon/0.3%). Substitute up to 5 ounces (150 grams/36%) buckwheat flour or whole-wheat flour for an equal amount of the all-purpose flour if desired.

Approximate values per 2-oz. (60-g) serving: **Calories** 140, **Total fat** 7 g, **Saturated fat** 3.5 g, **Cholesterol** 95 mg, **Sodium** 100 mg, **Total carbohydrates** 17 g, **Protein** 4 g

CONVENIENCE PRODUCTS

Various mixes and powders are sold to make many of the products discussed in this chapter. The addition of water and eggs turns powdered éclair mix into batter for éclairs, puffs or profiteroles. Although mixes remove the guesswork from measuring and mixing, no mix can make up for a lack of skill in the forming and baking of these products. Éclairs made from a mix tend to bake into drier products than those made from scratch.

Meringue powder is made from dried egg whites and may contain sugar, gums and other additives. When water is added, the product may be whipped to make baked meringue or to use in any preparation calling for meringue. Meringue powder bakes into a sweet, dense meringue with less of the lightness associated with a scratch product. Because it is very stable, meringue powder is frequently added to liquid egg whites when whipping them for icings and mousses, as discussed in Chapter 13, Cakes and Icings, and Chapter 14, Custards, Creams and Sauces. Fully cooked meringues come in many sizes, from small cookies to whole tart shells. When stored under dry conditions, these products will keep for several months.

It is the rare bakeshop where phyllo dough is made by hand. Quality fresh or frozen dough is standard.

Powdered crêpe batter to which eggs, water or milk is added is available. Some operations purchase frozen cooked crêpes, using the time saved to prepare fresh fruit and cream fillings.

QUESTIONS FOR DISCUSSION

1. Why is it said that éclair paste is the only dough that is cooked before it is baked? Why is this step necessary? List three ways of using éclair paste in making classic desserts.

2. Explain the process by which products made from éclair paste are leavened.

3. Explain the differences and similarities among common, Swiss and Italian meringues.

4. Discuss ways in which phyllo dough may be used to make tart or pie products.

5. In which ways might crêpes be served as a hot plated dessert?

Terms to Know

pâte à choux	Swiss meringue
cream puffs	Italian meringue
meringue	pavlova
soft meringue	phyllo dough
hard meringue	crêpe
common (French) meringue	flambé

Many of the formulas in this section use components that appear in other chapters in this book. For example, Individual St. Honoré Pastries uses puff pastry dough, discussed in Chapter 9, Laminated Doughs. Your first goal as a student should be to learn to prepare a variety of pastry components. You can then combine and assemble them appropriately into both classic and modern desserts.

CHOCOLATE ÉCLAIRS

Yield: 20 Éclairs

Baked éclair shells, 4 in. (10 cm) long, made from Éclair Paste (page 408)	20	20
Pastry Cream (page 492)	1 qt.	1 lt
Chocolate Glaze (page 456), warm	as needed	as needed
White chocolate, melted (optional)	as needed	as needed

❶ Using a pastry bag to fill the éclairs with pastry cream.

① Use a paring knife or skewer to cut a small hole in the end of each baked, cooled éclair shell.

② Pipe the Pastry Cream into each shell using a piping bag fitted with a small plain tip. Be sure that the cream fills the full length of each shell. Refrigerate the filled éclairs.

③ In a single, smooth stroke, drag the top of each filled éclair through the warm Chocolate Glaze. Only the very top of each pastry should be coated with chocolate.

④ Melted white chocolate (if using) may be piped onto the wet glaze, then pulled into patterns using a toothpick. Keep the finished éclairs refrigerated and serve within 8 to 12 hours.

VARIATION:

Raspberry Cream and Fruit-Filled Éclairs—Prepare the éclairs. Dip the bottom of the cooled pastry shells in Decorating Caramel (page 727). Slice each éclair in half horizontally. Reserve the caramelized half. With a medium plain tip, fill the other half with Diplomat Cream Filling (page 514) and garnish with fresh raspberries, blackberries or strawberries. Top with the caramelized side on top. Dust with powdered sugar.

Approximate values per éclair: **Calories** 410, **Total fat** 31 g, **Saturated fat** 17 g, **Cholesterol** 110 mg, **Sodium** 230 mg, **Total carbohydrates** 27 g, **Protein** 5 g, **Vitamin A** 20%

❷ Dipping the éclairs in chocolate glaze.

PROFITEROLES WITH CHOCOLATE SAUCE

Yield: 6 Servings

Baked profiterole shells, 2 in. (5 cm), made from Éclair Paste (page 408)	30	30
Pistachio or other ice cream	1 qt.	1 lt
Chocolate Caramel Sauce (page 538), warm	12 oz.	360 g

① Cut the profiterole shells horizontally in half. Reheat them briefly at 350°F (180°C) until crisp, approximately 10 minutes.

② Fill each warm shell with ice cream. To serve, place five filled profiteroles on each plate. Pour warm Chocolate Caramel Sauce over the profiteroles. Serve at once.

Approximate values per serving: **Calories** 710, **Total fat** 46 g, **Saturated fat** 20 g, **Cholesterol** 250 mg, **Sodium** 270 mg, **Total carbohydrates** 61 g, **Protein** 13 g, **Vitamin A** 25%, **Calcium** 20%

PARIS-BREST

Named for a famed 19th-century bicycle race between the city of Paris and the country town of Brest, France, the Paris-Brest resembles a puffed bicycle tire. It is filled with a hazelnut pastry cream and may be sprinkled with Hazelnut Crunch (see online resources).

Yield: 12 Individual Pastries

Éclair Paste (page 408)	2 lb.	1 kg
Egg wash	as needed	as needed
Sliced almonds	1 oz.	30 g
Paris-Brest Cream (recipe follows)	2 lb. 8 oz.	1200 g
Powdered sugar	1 oz.	30 g

1. Using a pastry bag with a large star tip, pipe the Éclair Paste into rings 3½ inches (9 centimeters) in diameter onto a paper-lined sheet pan.
2. Brush the rings lightly with egg wash and then sprinkle with sliced almonds.
3. Bake in a 375°F (190°C) oven until golden brown and the rings' interiors are well dried, approximately 30 minutes. Let cool, then slice the rings in half horizontally.
4. Pipe the Paris-Brest Cream on the bottom half of the baked rings in a connecting chain of rosettes using a medium star tip and pastry bag.
5. Replace the top halves. Dust with powdered sugar.

Approximate values per serving: **Calories** 630, **Total fat** 52 g, **Saturated fat** 29 g, **Cholesterol** 330 mg, **Sodium** 500 mg, **Total carbohydrates** 36 g, **Protein** 9 g, **Vitamin A** 25%

PARIS-BREST CREAM

Yield: 2 lb. 8 oz. (1200 g)

Unsalted butter, softened	12 oz.	360 g
Hazelnut paste, smooth and lump-free	4 oz.	120 g
Pastry Cream (page 492)	1 lb. 8 oz.	720 g

1. In the bowl of a mixer fitted with the paddle attachment, cream the butter until light and fluffy. Add the hazelnut paste and continue the creaming process. Add the Pastry Cream in one step and mix until well combined.

Approximate values per 1-oz. (30-g) serving: **Calories** 110, **Total fat** 10 g, **Saturated fat** 5 g, **Cholesterol** 50 mg, **Sodium** 10 mg, **Total carbohydrates** 5 g, **Protein** 1 g

INDIVIDUAL ST. HONORÉ PASTRIES

Yield: 8 Pastries

Puff Pastry (page 280) (scraps can be used)	10 oz.	300 g
Decorating Caramel (page 727)	as needed	as needed
Baked cream puff shells, 2 in. (5 cm), made from Éclair Paste (page 408)	32 shells	32 shells
Raspberry Liqueur or Grand Marnier (optional)	1 fl. oz.	30 ml
Pastry Cream (page 492)	14 oz.	420 g
Crème Chantilly (page 502)	10 fl. oz.	300 ml
Fresh raspberries	as needed	as needed

1. Roll out the Puff Pastry ⅛ inch (3 millimeters) thick. Cut out eight 3½-inch (8.75-centimeter) rounds. Place the rounds on a paper-lined sheet pan. Set aside at room temperature for 30 minutes.

2. Bake the rounds at 375°F (190°C) until the pastry has risen and the surface is no longer moist to the touch, approximately 10 to 12 minutes. Place an icing screen on top of the sheet pan to ensure that the pastry rises evenly. Continue baking until the rounds are light golden brown, approximately 15 to 20 minutes longer.

3. Cool the rounds on a wire rack.

4. Line several sheet pans with silicone baking mats or parchment paper. Prepare the Decorating Caramel. Dip the bottom of each baked cream puff in the caramel, then place immediately on the prepared sheet pans. Let cool.

5. Fill a paper cone with additional Decorating Caramel and pipe decorative oval shapes that will garnish the finished pastries onto the prepared pans. Set aside.

6. Stir the liqueur (if using) into the Pastry Cream.

7. Using the point of a paring knife, poke a small round opening on the bottom of each cream puff, large enough to accommodate a medium piping tip. Fill a pastry bag fitted with a medium plain tip with the Pastry Cream. Quickly pipe the filling into each cream puff.

8. To assemble each pastry, pipe a ring of Pastry Cream in the center of each baked Puff Pastry round and top with three of the filled cream puffs.

9. Using a large star tip, pipe rows of Crème Chantilly from the bottom to top next to each cream puff, meeting in the center at the top. Place a fourth cream puff on top of each pastry. Decorate each pastry with the raspberries and decorative caramel pieces.

Approximate values per serving: **Calories** 500, **Total fat** 31 g, **Saturated fat** 18 g, **Cholesterol** 220 mg, **Sodium** 290 mg, **Total carbohydrates** 52 g, **Protein** 7 g, **Vitamin A** 15%

SAFETY ALERT
Caramelizing Sugar

Caramelizing sugar can cause serious burns. Use rubber gloves and take proper precautions to avoid hot sugar coming into direct contact with your skin.

POPOVERS

Popovers are crisp hollow muffins made from a rich egg batter. The steam released from the eggs and milk as the popovers bake is trapped in the gluten web of the batter, causing it to rise. Popovers and other products that rely on steam for leavening are baked at a high temperature so that the steam forms quickly before the gluten bond sets. Yorkshire pudding, a popular accompaniment to roasted rib of beef, is made from this same batter. These pastries resemble products baked from éclair paste.

LINCOLN CULINARY INSTITUTE, HARTFORD, CT
Chef Jamie Roraback

Yield: 20 Popovers

Beef fat or vegetable oil	10 fl. oz.	360 ml
All-purpose flour	8 oz.	240 g
Salt	0.2 oz. (1 tsp.)	6 g
Eggs	10 oz. (6 eggs)	300 g
Whole milk	1 pt.	480 ml
Whole butter, melted	3 oz.	90 g

1 Place twenty 4-ounce (120-milliliter) greased ramekins or popover tins on a sheet pan and drop 0.5 fluid ounce (15 milliliters) beef fat or vegetable oil in the bottom of each ramekin. Place the ramekins in a 425°F (220°C) oven until the fat smokes.

2 Sift the flour and salt together into a large bowl. In a separate bowl, whisk together the eggs, milk and butter. Pour the liquid ingredients into the dry ingredients and whip until smooth.

3 Remove the ramekins from the oven and fill each approximately two-thirds full with batter. Bake at 425°F (220°C) 20 minutes without opening the oven door. After 20 minutes, reduce the heat to 375°F (190°C) and bake approximately 10 more minutes.

4 Remove the popovers from the oven, unmold and serve.

5 For crisper popovers, slit the sides of the unmolded popovers to allow the steam to escape. Place on a sheet pan and return them to the oven until the tops are firm, crisp and brown, approximately 10 minutes.

VARIATION:

Onion Popovers—Sauté 2 ounces (60 grams) finely chopped onion in 0.5 ounce (15 grams) butter until tender. Sprinkle the onion over the batter just before baking.

Approximate values per popover: **Calories** 250, **Total fat** 21 g, **Saturated fat** 11 g, **Cholesterol** 95 mg, **Sodium** 150 mg, **Total carbohydrates** 10 g, **Protein** 4 g

CHURROS
(FLUTED MEXICAN DOUGHNUT STICKS)

Yield: 30–35 Pastries

Cinnamon, ground	0.5 oz.	15 g
Granulated sugar	4 oz.	120 g
Water	1 pt.	480 ml
Salt	0.17 oz. (1 tsp.)	5 g
Pastry flour	8 oz.	240 g
Egg whites	3 oz. (3 whites)	90 g
Vanilla extract	0.15 fl. oz. (1 tsp.)	5 ml
Chocolate Fudge Sauce (page 538)	as needed	as needed

1. Combine the cinnamon and sugar in a quarter-size hotel pan. Set aside.
2. Bring the water and salt to a boil in a heavy saucepan.
3. Remove the boiling salted water from the heat. Add the flour all at once. Stir vigorously with a firm spatula until a soft dough forms.
4. Transfer the dough immediately to the bowl of a mixer fitted with the paddle attachment. On medium to high speed, add one-third of the egg whites. Mix until completely combined. Scrape down the bowl. Repeat the process until all of the egg whites are incorporated. Add the vanilla.
5. Pipe the batter using a medium star tip into 6- to 8-inch (15- to 20-centimeter) strips on very lightly oiled parchment paper.
6. Slide the piped batter into oil heated to 375°F (190°C). Fry in batches until crisp, approximately 3 to 5 minutes. Drain briefly on paper towels, then roll in the cinnamon sugar. Serve warm with Chocolate Fudge Sauce.

Approximate values per serving: **Calories** 100, **Total fat** 7 g, **Saturated fat** 1 g, **Cholesterol** 0 mg, **Sodium** 65 mg, **Total carbohydrates** 9 g, **Protein** 1 g

---

MERVEILLEUX PASTRIES

Yield: 15 Individual Pastries

Crème Chantilly (page 502)	1 qt.	1 lt
Common (French) Meringue (page 410), baked into 2¼-in (6-cm) disks	30 disks	30 disks
Raspberries or wild strawberries	10 oz.	300 g
Chocolate shavings	9 oz.	270 g
Cocoa powder	0.5 oz.	15 g

1. Using a pastry bag fitted with a medium tip, pipe a large rosette of the Crème Chantilly on half of the meringue disks.
2. Place a few berries on the cream and top with an inverted meringue disk.
3. Ice the sides and top of the merveilleux with the remaining Crème Chantilly.
4. Roll the merveilleux, sides and top, in chocolate shavings.
5. Dust lightly with cocoa powder and garnish with more berries.

Approximate values per serving: **Calories** 350, **Total fat** 18 g, **Saturated fat** 11 g, **Cholesterol** 45 mg, **Sodium** 40 mg, **Total carbohydrates** 48 g, **Protein** 3 g, **Vitamin C** 15%

① Filling each meringue disk.

② Spreading cream on the edge of the pastry.

③ Rolling the pastry in chocolate.

ROCHERS (MERINGUE COOKIES)

Rochers ("rocks" in French) are crunchy cookies made from baked meringue. They are baked in a warmer oven than most other meringues to ensure that caramelization takes place so that the pastries develop their light golden color.

Yield: 24 Cookies

Egg whites	8 oz. (8 whites)	240 g
Granulated sugar	8 oz.	240 g
Vanilla extract	0.15 oz. (1 tsp.)	5 ml
Salt	0.02 oz. (⅛ tsp.)	0.5 g
Powdered sugar, sifted	8 oz.	240 g
Slivered almonds, toasted and chopped	3 oz.	90 g

① Whip the egg whites in the bowl of a mixer fitted with the whip attachment on medium speed until foamy. Gradually add the granulated sugar and whip to stiff peaks. Add the vanilla and salt and remove the bowl from the mixer.

② Using a rubber spatula, fold in the sifted powdered sugar and toasted slivered almonds.

③ Drop the mixture into mounds on parchment-lined sheet pans using two soup spoons.

④ Bake at 225°F (110°C) until crisp and the cookies release easily from the parchment paper, approximately 60 to 75 minutes.

VARIATIONS:

Chocolate-Dipped Rochers—Dip the cooled meringues in melted tempered chocolate.

Chocolate Nib Rochers—Omit the slivered almonds. Fold in 1.5 ounces (45 grams) cocoa nibs.

Mocha Rochers—Replace the vanilla extract with coffee extract. Fold in 3 ounces (90 grams) finely chopped dark chocolate in place of the almonds.

Approximate values per cookie: **Calories** 100, **Total fat** 2 g, **Saturated fat** 0 g, **Cholesterol** 0 mg, **Sodium** 25 mg, **Total carbohydrates** 20 g, **Protein** 2 g, **Claims**—low fat; no cholesterol; low sodium; gluten free

Rochers

Chocolate Nib Rochers

DACQUOISE

Yield: 6 Rounds, 7 or 8 in. (17 or 20 cm) each, or 1 Full-Sheet Pan, or approximately 35 Individual Rounds, 3 in. (7.5 cm) each

Egg whites	8 oz. (8 whites)	240 g	800%
Dried egg whites (optional)	0.3 oz. (2 tsp.)	10 g	30%
Granulated sugar	9.5 oz.	285 g	950%
Vanilla extract	0.5 fl. oz.	15 ml	50%
Almond flour	7 oz.	210 g	700%
Cake flour	1 oz.	30 g	100%
Total batter weight:	1 lb. 10 oz.	790 g	2630%

1. Whip the liquid egg whites in the bowl of a mixer fitted with the whip attachment on medium speed until foamy. If using the dried egg whites, sift them with 4 ounces (120 grams) of the sugar and add to the foamy egg whites. Whip the egg whites until they hold a firm peak. Fold in the vanilla.

2. Stir the remaining 5.5 ounces (165 grams) of sugar into the flours. Fold this mixture into the whipped egg whites with a rubber spatula.

3. Place the mixture in a pastry bag fitted with a medium to large tip. Pipe it into three or four 7-inch (17-centimeter) discs on a paper-lined sheet pan. (Or spread it into torte rings placed on a paper-lined half-sheet pan.)

4. Bake at 350°F (180°C) until done, approximately 30 minutes. Check for doneness by removing part of the crust using a paring knife; the interior should spring back when lightly pressed.

5. This cake is a component in Lemon Dacquoise Cake (page 425). Or it may be filled with whipped cream or any of the buttercream fillings in Chapter 13, Cakes and Icings.

VARIATIONS:

Nougatine Dacquoise—Chop 8 ounces (240 grams/800%) Basic Nougatine (page 724) into fine pieces. Fold into the dacquoise mixture along with the dry ingredients. Because the nougatine may clog a pastry tip, pipe using a pastry bag without a tip.

Dried Apricot and Pistachio Dacquoise—Finely chop 5 ounces (150 grams/500%) dried apricots and 5 ounces (150 grams/500%) pistachios. Fold into the dacquoise mixture along with the dry ingredients. Because the fruit and nuts may clog a tip, pipe using a pastry bag without a tip.

Pistachio Dacquoise—Replace half of the almond flour with pistachio flour.

Chocolate or Macadamia Nut Dacquoise—Fold 10 ounces (300 grams/1000%) finely chopped chocolate chunks or 8 ounces (240 grams/800%) finely chopped macadamia nuts into the dacquoise mixture with the dry ingredients.

Approximate values per 1-oz. (30-g) serving: **Calories** 90, **Total fat** 4 g, **Saturated fat** 0 g, **Cholesterol** 0 mg, **Sodium** 15 mg, **Total carbohydrates** 13 g, **Protein** 3 g

Spreading the meringue into torte rings.

A finished Dacquoise pastry filled with Paris-Brest Cream and garnished with candied almonds.

SCHAUM TORTE
(AUSTRIAN BAKED MERINGUE PASTRIES)

Yield: 4 Servings

Pastry Cream (page 492)	10 oz.	300 g
Baked meringue shells, 3 in. (7.5 cm), made from Common Meringue (page 410)	4 shells	4 shells
Fresh blueberries	4 oz.	120 g
Fresh raspberries	4 oz.	120 g
Crème Chantilly (page 502)	10 fl. oz.	300 ml

1. For each pastry, pipe the Pastry Cream in an even layer in the bottom of the baked meringue shells. Scatter half of the blueberries and strawberries over the shells.

2. Using a large star tip, dot the surface of the filled shells with rows of Crème Chantilly. Decorate with the remaining blueberries and raspberries. Refrigerate the pastries and serve the same day.

Approximate values per pastry: **Calories** 388, **Total fat** 27 g, **Saturated fat** 16 g, **Cholesterol** 215 mg, **Sodium** 51 mg, **Total carbohydrates** 35 g, **Protein** 4 g

1. Filling the shell with pastry cream.

2. The finished pastry.

LEMON DACQUOISE CAKE

Yield: 6 Cakes, 7 in. (17.5 cm) each

Vegetable oil	as needed	as needed
Granulated sugar	as needed	as needed
Lemon-Lime Mousse (page 530)	2 lb. 14 oz.	1380 g
Dacquoise (page 424), 7-in. (17.5-cm) disks	12 disks	12 disks
Powdered sugar	as needed	as needed
Edible gold leaf (optional)	as needed	as needed

1. Oil and sugar six 6¼-inch (16-centimeter) torte rings. Place the rings on paper-lined sheet pans.

2. Prepare the Lemon-Lime Mousse. Evenly divide it among the six rings. Freeze until firm, at least 2 hours.

3. Unmold each frozen ring of Lemon-Lime Mousse onto one baked Dacquoise disk. Top with the remaining Dacquoise disks.

4. Dust the top of each cake with powdered sugar and decorate with gold leaf (if using).

Approximate values per serving: **Calories** 270, **Total fat** 14 g, **Saturated fat** 4 g, **Cholesterol** 20 mg, **Sodium** 45 mg, **Total carbohydrates** 32 g, **Protein** 7 g

SUCCÈS
(NUT MERINGUE CAKE)

❶ A disk of the pastry filled with Crème Chantilly and fruit.

❷ Garnishing the finished pastry.

Yield: 4 Pastries, 8 Rounds, approximately 3 in. (7.5 cm) each

Egg whites	8 oz. (8 whites)	240 g	400%
Dried egg whites (optional)	0.3 oz. (2 tsp.)	9 g	15%
Granulated sugar	12 oz.	360 g	600%
Vanilla extract	0.15 fl. oz. (1 tsp.)	5 ml	7.5%
Almond or hazelnut flour or combination	8 oz.	240 g	400%
Cake flour	2 oz.	60 g	100%
Total batter weight:	1 lb. 14 oz.	914 g	1523%
Crème Chantilly (page 502), buttercream, or icing	as needed	as needed	
Fresh raspberries or other fruit	as needed	as needed	
Neutral glaze (optional)	as needed	as needed	

❶ Whip the liquid egg whites in the bowl of a mixer fitted with the whip attachment on medium speed until foamy. If using the dried egg whites, sift them with 5 ounces (150 grams) of the sugar and add to the whipped egg whites.

❷ Whip the egg whites to firm peaks. Fold in the vanilla.

❸ Stir the remaining 7 ounces (210 grams) of sugar into the nut and cake flours. Fold the nut-and-flour mixture into the whipped egg whites using a rubber spatula.

❹ Pipe the mixture onto a paper-lined sheet pan in eight 3-inch (7.5-centimeter) rounds using a medium-large tip.

❺ Bake at 350°F (180°C) until golden and crisp, approximately 30 minutes.

❻ Cool the cakes. Pipe a ring of Crème Chantilly, buttercream or other icing around the edge of four of the disks. Fill with berries. Top with the remaining disks. Dust with powdered sugar and garnish with a fresh berry topped with neutral glaze if desired.

Approximate values per 1-oz. (30-g) serving: **Calories** 100, **Total fat** 4 g, **Saturated fat** 0 g, **Cholesterol** 0 mg, **Sodium** 15 mg, **Total carbohydrates** 14 g, **Protein** 3 g

APPLE STRUDEL

Yield: 2 Rolls, 12 in. (30 cm) each

Apples, peeled, cored and slivered	1 lb. 8 oz.	720 g
Lemon juice	0.5 fl. oz.	15 ml
Granulated sugar	8 oz.	240 g
Raisins	2 oz.	60 g
Orange zest, grated	0.2 oz. (1 Tbsp.)	6 g
Cinnamon, ground	0.07 oz. (1 tsp.)	2 g
Phyllo dough, 12-in. × 17-in. (30-cm × 42-cm) sheets	12 sheets	12 sheets
Clarified butter, melted	4 fl. oz.	120 ml
Ground almonds	0.6 oz.	18 g

❶ Brushing phyllo sheets with clarified butter.

❶ Toss the apples with the lemon juice and half of the sugar in a medium bowl. Let stand 30 minutes, then drain off the liquid that forms.

❷ Gently combine the drained apples with the raisins, orange zest, cinnamon and the remaining sugar.

❸ Prepare the phyllo dough for each roll by laying one sheet out on a piece of parchment paper. Brush lightly with clarified butter and top with a second sheet of phyllo. Brush this sheet lightly with butter and sprinkle with about 0.1 ounce (1 teaspoon/3 grams) ground almonds. Top with a third sheet of dough, more butter and nuts and repeat until six sheets of phyllo are stacked.

❹ Place half of the apple mixture along the short edge of each stack of assembled phyllo dough sheets. For each roll, using the paper to assist with rolling the dough, roll the phyllo around the filling tightly.

❺ Place each strudel seam side down on a baking sheet. Brush the surface lightly with melted butter. Bake at 375°F (190°C) until golden brown and crisp, approximately 18 minutes.

❷ Sprinkling phyllo with chopped nuts before adding another layer of phyllo.

Approximate values per ⅙-roll serving: **Calories** 260, **Total fat** 10 g, **Saturated fat** 6 g, **Cholesterol** 20 mg, **Sodium** 0 mg, **Total carbohydrates** 42 g, **Protein** 2 g

❸ Topping the phyllo sheets with the apples.

❹ Rolling up the strudel.

❺ The finished strudel.

PEACH AND BLUEBERRY NAPOLEON

PESCE RESTAURANT, HOUSTON, TX

Former Pastry Chef Milan Villavicencio

Yield: 10 Servings

Fresh peaches	2 lb.	960 g
Fresh blueberries	2 pt.	1 lt
Orange Muscat wine	8 fl. oz.	240 ml
Phyllo Crisps (recipe follows)	30	30
Muscat Mousseline (page 514)	as needed	as needed
Powdered sugar	as needed	as needed
Raspberry Sauce (page 533)	1 pt.	480 ml

1. Split the peaches in half and discard the pits. Cut each half into six wedges.
2. Macerate the peach wedges and blueberries in the wine.
3. To assemble each napoleon, place a Phyllo Crisp in the center of a plate. Pipe Muscat Mousseline along the edges of the crisp. Arrange four peach wedges and approximately six blueberries on the crisp and pipe a dollop of mousseline on top of the fruit. Place another crisp on top of the mousseline and fruit, pipe more mousseline and add more fruit to this second layer. Top with a third crisp and dust with powdered sugar.
4. Drizzle Raspberry Sauce around the napoleon on the plate and garnish with additional blueberries and peaches.

Approximate values per serving: **Calories** 790, **Total fat** 31 g, **Saturated fat** 17 g, **Cholesterol** 355 mg, **Sodium** 170 mg, **Total carbohydrates** 111 g, **Protein** 10 g, **Vitamin A** 35%, **Vitamin C** 20%, **Calcium** 15%

PHYLLO CRISPS

Yield: 10 Servings

Whole butter, melted	4 oz.	120 g
Powdered sugar	8 oz.	240 g
Phyllo dough, 12-in. × 17-in. (30-cm × 42-cm) sheets	8 sheets	8 sheets

1. Line a full-sheet pan with parchment paper and brush with melted butter. Dust with powdered sugar and place two sheets of phyllo dough side by side on the pan.
2. Brush the phyllo sheets with butter and dust with powdered sugar. Place a second phyllo sheet on top of each of the first sheets, brush them with butter and dust with powdered sugar. Continue until there are two stacks of phyllo dough, each four layers high.
3. Using a pastry wheel, cut each stack of phyllo into four columns and four rows, creating 16 small rectangular stacks of phyllo dough from each large stack.
4. Cover the phyllo stacks with parchment paper and another sheet pan. Bake at 325°F (160°C) until brown, approximately 15 minutes. Remove and cool.

Approximate values per crisp: **Calories** 70, **Total fat** 3 g, **Saturated fat** 2 g, **Cholesterol** 10 mg, **Sodium** 25 mg, **Total carbohydrates** 10 g, **Protein** 0 g

STRAWBERRY CRÊPES FITZGERALD

BRENNAN'S RESTAURANT, New Orleans, LA
Chef Michael Roussel (1938–2005)

Yield: 8 Servings

Cream cheese, room temperature	1 lb.	480 g
Sour cream	2.5 oz.	75 g
Vanilla extract	0.5 fl. oz.	15 ml
Granulated sugar	5 oz.	150 g
Crêpes (page 416)	16	16
Whole butter	0.5 oz.	15 g
Fresh strawberries, sliced	1 lb. 8 oz.	720 g
Fresh lemon juice	0.5 fl. oz.	15 ml
Maraschino liqueur	1 fl. oz.	30 ml

1. Combine the cream cheese, sour cream, vanilla and 1 ounce (30 grams) of the sugar in a mixing bowl and beat until smooth.
2. Place 3 tablespoons (45 milliliters) of the filling on one end of each crêpe; roll the crêpes around the filling and then refrigerate them while preparing the topping.
3. To make the topping, heat the butter and the remaining sugar in a large saucepan. Cook over medium heat, stirring until the sugar dissolves. Add the strawberries and lemon juice.
4. Bring the mixture to a boil, then reduce the heat and simmer until the liquid thickens, approximately 10 to 12 minutes. Add the maraschino liqueur and flambé.
5. To serve, place two crêpes on each plate and spoon approximately 6 fluid ounces (180 milliliters) warm strawberry topping over the crêpes.

Approximate values per serving: **Calories** 630, **Total fat** 37 g, **Saturated fat** 22 g, **Cholesterol** 260 mg, **Sodium** 380 mg, **Total carbohydrates** 65 g, **Protein** 13 g, **Vitamin A** 20%, **Vitamin C** 100%

SAFETY ALERT
Cooking with Alcohol

When alcohol comes into contact with a flame, it can ignite. In order to avoid singed eyebrows and kitchen fires, please be careful when adding wine, brandy, liqueurs or liquor to a dish on or near the stove. Often a dish will require flaming or flambéing, which means igniting the brandy, rum or other liquor so that the alcohol burns off and the flavor of the liquor is retained. When a dish calls for flambéing, follow these procedures. Stand away from the pan being flamed. Tilt the pan away from you, allowing the fumes to be ignited by the open flame. Be careful, as the flames can leap from the pan.

> "Once in a young lifetime one should be allowed to
> have as much sweetness as one can possibly want and hold."
>
> —JUDITH OLNEY, AMERICAN COOKBOOK WRITER

CHAPTER THIRTEEN

CAKES AND ICINGS

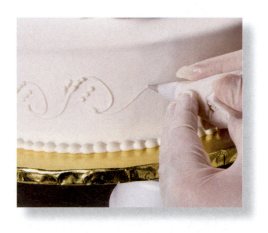

- prepare a variety of cakes
- prepare a variety of icings
- assemble cakes using basic finishing and decorating techniques
- describe the functions of ingredients used to make cakes
- prepare a variety of cakes using creamed fat and whipped egg mixing methods
- explain basic cake finishing and decorating techniques

CAKES ARE POPULAR IN MOST BAKESHOPS because a wide variety of finished products can be created from only a few basic cake, filling and icing formulas. Many of these components can even be made in advance and assembled into finished desserts as needed. Cakes are also popular because of their versatility: They can be served as unadorned sheets in a high-volume cafeteria or as the elaborate centerpiece of a wedding buffet.

Cake making need not be difficult or intimidating, but it does require an understanding of ingredients and mixing methods. This chapter begins by explaining how typical cake ingredients interact. Each of the traditional mixing methods is then explained and illustrated with a specific formula. Information on panning batters, baking temperatures, determining doneness and cooling methods follows. The second portion of this chapter presents methods for assembling and decorating a variety of cakes using many of the icing formulas discussed in the chapter. An array of creams and mousses suitable for filling certain cakes and tortes are discussed in Chapter 14, Custards, Creams and Sauces. A selection of cake and icing formulas, which can be used throughout this book, concludes the chapter.

CAKES

Most cakes are created from liquid batters with high fat and sugar content. The baker's job is to combine all the ingredients to create a structure that will support these rich ingredients yet keep the cake as light and delicate as possible. As with other baked goods, it is impossible to taste a cake until it is fully cooked and too late to alter the formula. Therefore, it is extremely important to study any formula before beginning and to follow it with particular care and attention to detail.

Ingredients

Good cakes begin with high-quality ingredients (see Chapter 4, Bakeshop Ingredients); however, even the finest ingredients must be combined in the proper balance. Too much flour and the cake may be dry; too much egg and the cake will be tough and hard. Changing one ingredient may necessitate a change in one or more of the other ingredients.

Each ingredient performs a specific function and has a specific effect on the final product. Cake ingredients can be classified by function as **tougheners, tenderizers, moisteners, driers, leaveners** and **flavorings**. Some ingredients fulfill more than one of these functions. For example, eggs contain water, so they are moisteners, and they contain protein, so they are tougheners. By understanding the function of various ingredients, you should be able to understand why cakes are made in particular ways and why a preparation sometimes fails. With additional experience, you should be able to recognize and correct flawed formulas and develop your own cake formulas.

TOUGHENERS

Flour, milk and eggs contain protein. Protein provides structure and strengthens the cake once it is baked. Too little protein and the cake may collapse; too much protein and the cake may be tough and coarse.

TENDERIZERS

Sugar, fats and egg yolks interfere with the development of the gluten structure when cakes are mixed. They shorten the gluten strands, making the cake tender and soft. These ingredients also improve the cake's keeping qualities.

MOISTENERS

Liquids such as water, milk, juice and eggs bring moisture to the mixture. Moisture is necessary for gluten formation and starch gelatinization, as well as for improving a cake's keeping qualities.

DRIERS

Flour, starches and milk solids absorb moisture, giving body and structure to the cake.

LEAVENERS

Cakes rise because gases in the batter expand when heated. Cakes are leavened by the air trapped when fat and sugar are creamed together, by carbon dioxide released from baking powder and baking soda and by air trapped in beaten eggs. All cakes rely on natural leaveners—steam and air—to create the proper texture and rise. Because baking soda and baking powder are also used in some cake formulas, reviewing the material on chemical leaveners in Chapter 6, Quick Breads, is recommended.

FLAVORINGS

Flavorings such as extracts, cocoa, chocolate, spices, salt, sugar and butter provide cakes with the desired flavors. Acidic flavoring ingredients such as sour cream, chocolate and fruit also provide the acid necessary to activate baking soda.

Cake ingredients should be at room temperature, approximately 70°F (21°C), before mixing begins. If one ingredient is too cold or too warm, it may affect the batter's ability to trap and hold the gases necessary for the cake to rise.

Mixing Methods

Even the finest ingredients will be wasted if the cake batter is not mixed correctly. When mixing any cake batter, the goals are to combine the ingredients uniformly, incorporate air cells and develop the proper texture.

All mixing methods can be divided into two categories: high fat (those that create a structure that relies primarily on **creamed fat**) and egg foam (those that create a structure that relies primarily on **whipped eggs**). Within these broad categories are several mixing methods or types of cakes. Creamed-fat cakes include **butter cakes** (also known as **creaming-method cakes**) and **high-ratio cakes**. Whipped-egg cakes include **genoise, spongecakes, angel food cakes** and **chiffon cakes**. See Table 13.1. Although certain general procedures are used to prepare each cake type, there are, of course, numerous variations. Certain European-style cake formulas include both creaming and egg foam mixing techniques. Sacher Torte (page 614), for example, is made from a creamed-fat batter into which whipped egg whites are folded before baking. Follow specific formula instructions precisely.

CREAMED FAT

Creamed-fat/high-fat cakes include most of the popular American-style cakes: poundcakes, layer cakes, coffeecakes and even brownies (see Chapter 10, Cookies and Brownies). All are based on high-fat formulas, most containing chemical leaveners. A good high-fat cake has a fine grain, cells of uniform size and a crumb that is moist rather than crumbly. Crusts should be thin and tender.

Creamed-fat/high-fat cakes can be divided into two classes: butter cakes and high-ratio cakes.

POUNDCAKES

Poundcakes are the original high-fat, creaming-method cake. They are called poundcakes because early formulas specified one pound each of butter, eggs, flour and sugar. Poundcakes should have a close grain and compact texture but still be very tender. They should be neither heavy nor soggy.

As bakers experimented with poundcake formulas, they reduced the amount of eggs and fat, substituting milk instead. These changes led to the development of the modern butter cake.

TABLE 13.1 CAKES

CATEGORY	TYPE OF CAKE/MIXING METHOD	KEY FORMULA CHARACTERISTICS	TEXTURE
Creamed fat (high fat)	Butter (creaming method)	High-fat formula; chemical leavener used	Fine grain; air cells of uniform size; moist crumb; thin and tender crust
	High-ratio (two-stage)	Emulsified shortening; two-part mixing method	Very fine grain; moist crumb; relatively high rise
Whipped eggs	Genoise (egg foam)	Whole eggs are whipped with sugar; no chemical leaveners	Dry and spongy
	Sponge (egg foam)	Egg yolks are mixed with other ingredients, then whipped egg whites are folded in	Moister and more tender than genoise
	Angel food (egg foam)	No fat; large quantity of whipped egg whites; high percentage of sugar	Tall, light and spongy
	Chiffon (egg foam)	Vegetable oil used; egg yolks mixed with other ingredients, then whipped egg whites folded in; baking powder may be added	Tall, light and fluffy; moister and richer than angel food

Butter Cakes

Butter cakes, also known as creaming-method cakes, begin with softened butter or shortening creamed to incorporate air cells. Because of their high fat content, these cakes usually need the assistance of a chemical leavener to achieve the proper rise.

Modern-day butter cakes—the classic American layer cakes, popular for birthdays and special occasions—are made with the creaming method. These cakes are tender yet sturdy enough to handle rich buttercreams or fillings. High-fat cakes are too soft and delicate, however, to use for roll cakes or to slice into extremely thin layers.

Creaming fat mechanically leavens the cake and creates a mixture in which fats and liquid are suspended. Air cells are trapped in the fat, lightening the mixture (see the photograph below). As eggs are mixed into the creamed fat, the mixture emulsifies. Fats and liquids, which normally would not blend, are held in suspension, ensuring that the batter will hold the additional liquids and flour necessary to produce a delectable cake.

Equal weights of butter increase in volume when creamed thoroughly (right) and expand very little in volume when creamed insufficiently (left).

FIGURE 13.1 ▶ Properly mixed butter cake (right) rises evenly, has a fine, even crumb and shows no signs of tunneling. Improperly mixed butter cake (left) lacks volume and has large irregular holes.

Creaming-method cake formulas specify whether to use butter or shortening. Because butter contains approximately 15 percent moisture, when shortening is substituted for butter, additional liquid must be added to replace the liquid lost. An emulsion made with butter cannot support the same quantity of sugar, liquids and flour as one made with shortening. Substituting butter for shortening in a creaming-method cake will require adjustments to the formula.

For butter cakes, the fat should be creamed at low to moderate speeds to prevent raising its temperature. An increased temperature could cause a loss of air cells. All ingredients should be at room temperature, 70°F (21°C), for effective creaming. When the butter is too warm, the soft fat will resist forming air cells. Eggs should be added slowly to maintain the emulsion formed when the sugar and butter were creamed. Properly emulsifying the ingredients in a butter cake is essential to obtain a perfect texture. A poorly emulsified batter will curdle and will not hold the air cells that are required for proper leavening, resulting in a dense and dry cake. See Figure 13.1. Flour is added gradually, alternating with the liquid. This allows the flour and liquid to be absorbed and prevents overdevelopment of gluten. The emulsion is preserved when these ingredients are blended or folded in properly.

Improperly emulsified creaming mixture separates and curdles.

PROCEDURE FOR PREPARING BUTTER CAKES (CREAMING METHOD)

1. Preheat the oven and prepare the pans.
2. Sift the dry ingredients together and set aside.
3. Cream the butter or shortening until it is light and fluffy. Add the sugar and cream until the mixture is fluffy and smooth. Scrape down the bowl frequently to make certain the entire mixture is well creamed.
4. Add the eggs slowly, beating well after each addition. Scrape down the bowl after each addition.
5. Add the dry and liquid ingredients alternately. In other words, a portion of the flour is added to the fat and incorporated, then a portion of the liquid is added and incorporated. These steps are repeated until all the liquid and dry ingredients are incorporated.
6. Divide the batter into prepared pans and bake immediately.
7. Cool the cakes in their pans on a wire rack for 10 minutes. Unmold and cool completely before filling and icing.

POUNDCAKE

MISE EN PLACE

▶ Allow the butter, eggs and buttermilk to come to room temperature.
▶ Zest the lemon and orange.
▶ Grease pans.
▶ Preheat oven to 400°F (200°C).

Yield: 3 Loaves, 9 in. × 5 in. (22 cm × 12 cm) each

Method: Creaming

Cake flour	1 lb. 5 oz.	630 g	100%
Baking powder	0.37 oz.	11 g	1.8%
Unsalted butter, room temperature	15 oz.	450 g	71%
Granulated sugar	1 lb. 7 oz.	690 g	109%
Corn syrup or additional granulated sugar	1 oz.	30 g	5%
Salt	0.37 oz.	11 g	1.8%
Eggs, room temperature	1 lb. (16 eggs)	480 g	76%
Vanilla extract	0.25 fl. oz. (1½ tsp.)	7 ml	1.2%
Almond extract (optional)	0.25 fl. oz. (1½ tsp.)	7 ml	1.2%
Lemon zest, grated	0.04 oz. (½ tsp.)	1 g	0.2%
Orange zest, grated	0.04 oz. (½ tsp.)	1 g	0.2%
Buttermilk, room temperature	8 fl. oz.	240 ml	38%
Total batter weight:	5 lb. 5 oz.	2558 g	405%

1. Sift the flour and baking powder together. Set aside.
2. Cream the butter until light and lump-free. Add the sugar, corn syrup and salt. Cream on medium speed until light and fluffy. Add the eggs a few at a time, allowing them to be completely incorporated before adding more eggs. Scrape down the bowl after each addition.
3. Add the vanilla and almond extract (if using) and the lemon and orange zest.
4. Fold in the dry ingredients alternately with the buttermilk in three additions each.
5. Divide the batter evenly into three 9-inch × 5-inch (22-centimeter × 12-centimeter) greased loaf pans. Bake at 400°F (200°C) for 15 minutes, then reduce the oven temperature to 350°F (180°C). Bake until the centers of the cakes bounce back when lightly pressed, approximately 45 to 55 minutes. If the cakes begin to darken, cover them loosely with aluminum foil.
6. Cool the cakes in their pans on a wire rack for 10 minutes. Unmold and cool completely.

VARIATIONS:

Chocolate Poundcake—Reduce the flour to 1 pounds 2 ounces (530 grams/85%). Sift 3 ounces (90 grams/14%) cocoa powder with the flour.

French-Style Fruitcake—Add 9 ounces (270 grams/43%) finely diced nuts, raisins and candied fruit into the batter. Add 2.25 fluid ounces (67.5 milliliters/10%) rum to the batter. After baking, brush the cake with additional rum.

Approximate values per ¹⁄₁₂-cake serving: **Calories** 240, **Total fat** 11 g, **Saturated fat** 7 g, **Cholesterol** 80 mg, **Sodium** 170 mg, **Total carbohydrates** 132 g, **Protein** 3 g

1. Creaming the butter.

2. Folding in the flour.

3. Panning the batter.

4. The finished cake.

High-Ratio Cakes

Commercial bakeries often use a special **two-stage mixing method** to prepare large quantities of a very liquid cake batter with high sugar content. These formulas require special emulsified shortenings to help give the cake its structure. They are known as two-stage cakes because the liquids are added in two stages or portions. If emulsified shortenings are not available, do not substitute all-purpose shortening or butter, as those fats cannot absorb the large amounts of sugar and liquid in the formula.

Because they contain a high ratio of sugar and liquid to flour, these cakes are often known as high-ratio cakes. They have a very fine, moist crumb and relatively high rise. High-ratio cakes can be used interchangeably with modern butter cakes and are most common in high-volume bakeries.

PROCEDURE FOR PREPARING HIGH-RATIO CAKES

1. Preheat the oven and prepare the pans.
2. Place all of the dry ingredients and emulsified shortening in a mixer bowl. Blend on low speed for several minutes.
3. Add approximately half of the liquid ingredients and blend.
4. Scrape down the bowl and add the remaining liquid ingredients. Blend into a smooth batter, scraping down the bowl as necessary.
5. Pour the batter into prepared pans using liquid measurements to ensure uniform division.

HIGH-RATIO YELLOW CAKE

Yield: 1½ to 2 Full-Sheet Pans

Method: Two-stage

Cake flour	2 lb. 8 oz.	1200 g	100%
Granulated sugar	2 lb. 10 oz.	1260 g	105%
Emulsified shortening	1 lb. 4 oz.	600 g	50%
Salt	1 oz.	30 g	2.5%
Baking powder	2 oz.	60 g	5%
Dry milk powder	4 oz.	120 g	10%
Light corn syrup	6 oz.	180 g	15%
Water, cold	36 fl. oz.	1080 ml	90%
Eggs	1 lb. 4 oz.	600 g	50%
Lemon extract	0.5 fl. oz.	15 ml	1.2%
Total batter weight:	10 lb. 11 oz.	5145 g	428%

MISE EN PLACE
- Grease pans.
- Preheat oven to 340°F (170°C).

1. Combine the flour, sugar, shortening, salt, baking powder, milk powder, corn syrup and 16 fluid ounces (480 milliliters) of the cold water in the large bowl of a large mixer fitted with the paddle attachment. Beat 5 minutes on low speed.
2. Combine the remaining ingredients in a separate bowl. Add these liquid ingredients to the creamed-fat mixture in three additions. Scrape down the bowl after each addition.
3. Beat 2 minutes on low speed.
4. Divide the batter into greased and floured pans. Pans should be filled only halfway. One gallon of batter is sufficient for an 18-inch × 24-inch × 2-inch (45-centimeter × 60-centimeter × 5-centimeter) sheet pan. Bake at 340°F (170°C) until a cake tester comes out clean and the cake springs back when lightly touched, approximately 12 to 18 minutes.

Approximate values per 3-oz. (90-g) serving: **Calories** 390, **Total fat** 16 g, **Saturated fat** 5 g, **Cholesterol** 60 mg, **Sodium** 320 mg, **Total carbohydrates** 57 g, **Protein** 5 g, **Calcium** 10%

SPECIFIC GRAVITY

The amount of air in cake batter relates directly to the quality of the finished cake. Too much air creamed into the batter and the grain may be coarse. Too little air creamed into the batter and the grain will be tight, creating a cake with poor volume. In the commercial bakeshop, tracking **specific gravity** can ensure consistent, uniform results in preparation of cakes, fillings and icings.

Specific gravity refers to the weight of an ingredient or a mixture in relation to the weight of water. One pint (16 fluid ounces) of water weighs 1 pound. But other liquids may be lighter than or heavier than water. Specific gravity is calculated by dividing the weight of a volume of an ingredient or mixture by the weight of an equal volume of water.

$$\text{weight of ingredient} \div \text{weight of water} = \text{specific gravity}$$

For example, a pint of water weighs 16 ounces, but a pint of honey weighs 24 ounces. Therefore the specific gravity of honey is 1.5 (24/16 = 1.5).

A simple test can be used to determine the specific gravity of a cake batter. Once the specific gravity of a formula has been recorded, it can be used to track future batches. Place a small container on a scale and turn the scale to zero. Fill the container with water to the very top and record the weight. Discard the water and fill the container with the cake batter being tested. Record the weight of the batter. Divide the weight of the cake batter by the weight of water. The result is the specific gravity of the batter. For example, if the container holds 8 ounces of water and 10 ounces of cake batter, the specific gravity of the cake batter is 1.25.

In general, butter/high-fat cakes have a higher specific gravity than egg foam cakes. However, specific gravity of cake batter varies with each formula according to the ingredients and equipment used. Adding ingredients such as diced fruit, chocolate, nuts or seeds to a cake batter will alter its specific gravity. A particular brand of butter may contain more liquid, just as a particular type of cake flour may absorb more moisture. For this reason, when developing formulas, bakeshops record the specific gravity for each type of cake in their repertoire and then use these figures to monitor each batch of cake produced thereafter. Each baker will then know what the desired specific gravity of each formula should be. When a butter cake batter has a lower specific gravity, the baker will know that the batter had too much air whipped into it. When a spongecake batter has a higher specific gravity, the baker will know that the batter was deflated during the mixing process. Batters that do not match the desired specific gravity may have to be discarded should consistent results be desired. Specific gravity calculations may also be used to monitor consistency in icing and cream formulas.

WHIPPED EGGS

Cakes based on whipped-egg foams include European-style genoise as well as spongecakes, angel food cakes and chiffon cakes. Some formulas contain chemical leaveners, but the air whipped into the eggs (whether whole or separated) is the primary leavening agent. Weak or low-protein flour is generally preferred when making egg foam cakes to minimize toughening. (A blend of flour and cornstarch may also be used when making egg foam cakes.) Because egg foams are fragile, fold the dry ingredients into an egg foam cake batter with great care. Sift the flour over the batter and fold gently but quickly using a rubber spatula or wire whisk. These techniques will help disperse the flour without deflating the egg foam. When improperly mixed, egg foam cakes lack volume and have a tough tight crumb. See Figure 13.2.

Egg foam cakes contain little or no fat. Genoise and spongecake are pliable; moisture in the eggs develops the protein in the flour, making these cakes springy and elastic. Unlike butter cakes, they resist crumbling. For this reason these cakes are well suited for rolling, as for Swiss Jelly Roll (page 478) or Yule Log (page 476), or for cutting into thin layers, lining a torte ring and so on.

FIGURE 13.2 ▶ Properly prepared egg foam cake (right) has a light even crumb and rises vigorously. Improperly prepared egg foam cake (left) has a dense, compact crumb, shows tunneling and does not rise properly.

Genoise

Genoise is the classic European-style cake. It is based on whole eggs whipped with sugar until very light and fluffy. Chemical leaveners are not used. Slightly warming the egg mixture helps improve the volume of the egg foam. For flavor and moisture a small amount of oil or melted butter is sometimes added to the batter after mixing. Genoise formulas containing fat will bake into cakes that are more tender than plain genoise because the fat helps shorten gluten strands. Learning to incorporate melted butter into the batter takes practice, however. Often genoise is baked in a thin sheet and layered with buttercream, puréed fruit, jam or chocolate filling to create multilayered specialty desserts, sometimes known as torten. Because genoise is rather dry, it is usually soaked with a flavored sugar syrup (see page 73) or liqueur for additional flavor and to increase shelf life. A basic genoise formula, which may be baked in round, square or sheet pans, is included here. Formulas for a richer almond version and the joconde variation are included in Chapter 17, Tortes and Specialty Cakes.

> ## CAKE COMBINATIONS
>
> Any fine grained butter cake lends itself to customization. Use a fruit liqueur such as Chambord (raspberry) or crème de cassis (red currant) in place of the vanilla in the formula. Or add citrus notes by blending in a few drops of lemon or orange oil. Chocolate buttercream is a perfect complement to a butter cake but don't overlook coffee or caramel flavors, which combine well with chocolate as an accent. When finely diced ripe berries, cocoa nibs, ground toasted almonds or chocolate chips are folded into plain buttercream, it becomes a delicious filling for a butter cake. Consider plain butter cake a blank canvas for creating custom specialities.

PROCEDURE FOR PREPARING GENOISE

1. Preheat the oven and prepare the pans.
2. Sift the flour with any additional dry ingredients.
3. Combine the whole eggs and sugar in a large bowl and warm over a double boiler to 105°F–113°F (40°C–45°C).
4. Whip the egg-and-sugar mixture until very light and tripled in volume.
5. Fold the sifted flour into the whipped eggs carefully but quickly.
6. Fold in oil or melted butter if desired.
7. Divide into pans and bake immediately.

MISE EN PLACE

▶ Melt butter, if using.
▶ Line pan with parchment paper.
▶ Preheat oven to 425°F (220°C).

CLASSIC GENOISE

Yield: 1 Full-Sheet Pan or 2 Rounds, 8 in. (20 cm) each

Method: Egg foam

Eggs	1 lb. (10 eggs)	480 g	178%
Granulated sugar	8 oz.	240 g	89%
Unsalted butter, melted (optional)	1.5 oz.	45 g	17%
Vanilla extract	0.3 fl. oz. (2 tsp.)	10 ml	3%
Cake flour	9 oz.	270 g	100%
Total batter weight:	2 lb. 2 oz.	1045 g	387%

1. Whisk the eggs and sugar together in a large mixer bowl. Place the bowl over a bain marie and whisk the mixture continuously to warm the eggs to approximately 105°F–113°F (40°C–45°C).
2. When the eggs are warm, remove the bowl from the bain marie and attach it to a mixer fitted with the whip attachment. Whip the egg-and-sugar mixture at medium speed until the mixture is cool and forms thick ribbons, approximately 12 to 15 minutes.
3. Remove approximately one-eighth of the batter. Place it in a small bowl and mix it with the melted butter (if using) and vanilla extract. Set aside.
4. Using a rubber spatula or balloon whisk, delicately fold the flour into the remaining genoise batter. Carefully fold in the reserved butter-genoise mixture.
5. Spread the batter immediately onto a paper-lined sheet pan. Bake at 425°F (220°C) until light brown and springy to the touch, approximately 10 minutes.

VARIATIONS:

Chocolate Genoise—Reduce the cake flour to 7 ounces (210 grams/78%). Sift 2 ounces (60 grams/22%) of cocoa powder with the flour.

Genoise Rounds—Grease two 8-inch (20-centimeter) round cake pans. Pan the batter into the prepared pans. Bake at 375°F (190°C) until light brown and springy to the touch, approximately 20 minutes.

Approximate values per 1-oz. (30-g) serving: **Calories** 75, **Total fat** 1 g, **Saturated fat** 0.5 g, **Cholesterol** 50 mg, **Sodium** 20 mg, **Total carbohydrates** 13 g, **Protein** 2 g

1 Whipped eggs.

2 Folding in the flour.

3 Adding the melted butter to a portion of the genoise batter.

4 Panning the batter.

Spongecakes

Spongecakes (Fr. *biscuits*) are made with separated eggs. A batter is prepared with egg yolks and other ingredients, and then egg whites are whipped with a portion of the sugar to firm but not dry peaks and folded into the batter. Spongecakes are primarily leavened with air, but baking powder may be included in the formula. As with genoise, oil or melted butter may be added if desired.

Within a few seconds after being whipped, egg whites start to set and become difficult to fold into a spongecake batter. This can result in overfolding and deflating of the batter. To prevent this, when working with whipped egg whites, briefly stir the whipped whites with a hand whisk to recream them right before folding them into the spongecake batter. This restores a smooth and uniform texture to the whites, making them easier to fold into the batter. (See page 506.)

Spongecakes are extremely versatile. They can be soaked with sugar syrup or a liqueur and assembled with butter cream as a traditional layer cake. Or they can be sliced thinly and layered, like genoise, with a jam, custard, chocolate or cream filling.

PROCEDURE FOR PREPARING SPONGECAKES

1. Preheat the oven and prepare the pans.
2. Separate the eggs. Whip the egg yolks with some of the sugar to the **ribbon stage**, that is, until they fall from the beater in thick ribbons that slowly disappear into the surface. Whip in any flavorings.
3. In a separate bowl of a mixer fitted with a clean whip attachment, whip the egg whites with a portion of the sugar until glossy and stiff but not dry.
4. Carefully fold the whipped egg whites into the batter. Then gently fold the sifted dry ingredients into the egg foam in two or three additions.
5. Pour the batter into the pans and bake immediately.

MISE EN PLACE

▸ Preheat oven to 350°F (180°C).
▸ Sift flour.

CLASSIC SPONGECAKE

Yield: 2 Rounds, 9 in. (22 cm) each   **Method:** Egg foam

Eggs	13 oz. (8 eggs)	390 g	185%
Granulated sugar	7.5 oz.	225 g	107%
Vanilla extract	0.3 fl. oz. (2 tsp.)	10 ml	4%
All-purpose flour, sifted	7 oz.	210 g	100%
Total batter weight:	1 lb. 11 oz.	835 g	396%

❶ Butter the bottom and sides of two 9-inch (22-centimeter) cake pans. Let the butter cool, then flour the pans. Set aside.

❷ Separate the eggs, placing the yolks and the whites in separate mixing bowls. Whip the egg yolks and 5½ ounces (60 grams) of the sugar on medium speed until thick, pale and at least doubled in volume, approximately 3 to 5 minutes. The yolks should be whipped until ribbons form.

❸ Place the bowl of egg whites on a mixer fitted with a clean whip attachment and beat on medium speed until foamy. Gradually add the remaining sugar and vanilla. Whip at medium speed until the whites are glossy and hold firm peaks but are not dry.

❹ Pour the egg yolks onto the whipped whites. Quickly fold the two mixtures together.

❺ Sprinkle one-third of the sifted flour over the batter and delicately fold in. Repeat the procedure until all the flour is incorporated. Do not overmix; fold just until incorporated.

❻ Pour the batter into the prepared pans, smoothing the surface as needed. Bake at 350°F (180°C) until the cakes are golden brown and bounce back when lightly pressed in the center, approximately 25 minutes.

❼ Allow the cakes to cool on a wire rack for 10 to 15 minutes before unmolding.

❽ To remove the cakes from their pans, run a thin metal spatula around the edge of each pan if necessary. When the cake is completely cool, it can be frosted or wrapped in plastic and frozen for 2 to 3 months.

VARIATION:

Chocolate Spongecake—Reduce the flour to 5.5 ounces (165 grams/78%). Sift it together with 1.75 ounces (50 grams/25%) cocoa powder and 1.75 ounces (50 grams/25%) powdered sugar. Fold in as described in Step 5.

Approximate values per 2-oz. (60-g) serving: **Calories** 130, **Total fat** 2.5 g, **Saturated fat** 1 g, **Cholesterol** 105 mg, **Sodium** 30 mg, **Total carbohydrates** 23 g, **Protein** 4 g, **Claims**—low fat; low saturated fat; very low sodium

❶ The egg yolks whipped to the ribbon stage.

❷ Folding the flour into the batter.

❸ Panning the batter.

❹ The finished cake.

HIGH-ALTITUDE BAKING

Altitude affects the temperatures at which foods cook. The decreased atmospheric pressure at altitudes above 3000 feet affects the creation of steam and the expansion of hot air in dough and cake batters. These factors must be considered when making breads and cakes. Because gases expand more easily at higher altitudes, breads and cakes may rise so much that their structure cannot support the weight and the bread or cake collapses.

Therefore, the amount of leavening should be decreased at higher altitudes. Chemical leaveners should usually be reduced by one-third at 3500 feet and by two-thirds at altitudes over 5000 feet. Eggs should be underwhipped to avoid incorporating too much air, which would also create too much rise. For yeast-leavened products, bake them before they are fully proofed or reduce the yeast by 20 percent when baking over 5000 feet. In general, oven temperatures should also be increased by 25°F (4°C) at altitudes over 3500 feet to help set the product's structure rapidly.

Because the boiling point decreases at higher altitudes, more moisture will evaporate from baked goods in the oven. This may cause dryness and an excessive proportion of sugar, which shows up as white spots on a cake's surface. Correct this by reducing every 8 ounces (240 grams) of sugar by ½ ounce (15 grams) at 3000 feet and by 1½ ounces (45 grams) at 7000 feet.

Attempting to adjust typical (that is, sea-level) formulas for high altitudes is somewhat risky, especially in a commercial operation. Furthermore, different types of baked goods will need different adjustment techniques. Cake batters may require additional flour and eggs to help maintain their structure. Try to find and use formulas developed especially for your area, or contact the local offices of your state's department of agriculture or the agricultural extension service for detailed assistance. Ingredient manufacturers are another source of information on adjusting formulas for use under high-altitude conditions.

Angel Food Cakes

Angel food cakes are tall, light cakes made without fat and leavened with a large quantity of whipped egg whites. As discussed in Chapter 4, Bakeshop Ingredients, egg whites will not foam properly if grease or egg yolk is present in the mixing bowl. Angel food cakes are traditionally baked in ungreased tube pans, but large loaf pans can also be used. The pans are left ungreased so that the batter can cling to the sides as it rises. The cakes should be inverted as soon as they are removed from the oven and left in the pan to cool. This technique allows gravity to keep the cakes from collapsing or sinking as they cool.

Although they contain no fat, angel food cakes are not low in calories, as they contain a high percentage of sugar. The classic angel food cake is pure white, but flavorings, ground nuts or cocoa powder may be added for variety. Although angel food cakes are usually not frosted, they may be topped with a fruit-flavored or chocolate glaze. They are often served with fresh fruit, fruit compote or whipped cream.

PROCEDURE FOR PREPARING ANGEL FOOD CAKES

1. Preheat the oven.
2. Combine the dry ingredients, including a portion of the sugar, in a bowl and set aside.
3. Whip the egg whites with a portion of the sugar until glossy and stiff but not dry.
4. Gently fold the dry ingredients into the egg whites.
5. Spoon the batter into an ungreased pan and bake immediately.
6. Allow the cake to cool inverted in its pan.

MISE EN PLACE

▸ Sift flour.
▸ Preheat oven to 350°F (180°C).

❶ Folding in the flour.

❷ Panning the batter.

❸ The finished cake.

 ## ANGEL FOOD CAKE

Yield: 1 Tube Cake, 10 in. (25 cm)   **Method:** Egg foam

			Sugar at 100%
Granulated sugar	12 oz.	360 g	100%
Cake flour, sifted	3.5 oz.	105 g	29%
Salt	0.05 oz. (¼ tsp.)	1.5 g	0.4%
Egg whites	12 oz. (12 whites)	360 g	100%
Cream of tartar	0.3 oz. (2 tsp.)	9 g	2.5%
Vanilla extract	0.5 fl. oz. (1 Tbsp.)	15 ml	4%
Total batter weight:	1 lb. 12 oz.	850 g	235%

❶ Combine 5 ounces (150 grams) of the sugar in a bowl with the flour and salt. Set aside.

❷ Whip the egg whites until foamy; add the cream of tartar and beat to soft peaks. Stir in the vanilla. Gradually beat in the remaining sugar. Continue beating until the egg whites are stiff but not dry.

❸ Sift the dry ingredients over the whites and fold in quickly but gently.

❹ Pour the batter into an ungreased tube pan and smooth the top with a spatula. Bake immediately at 350°F (180°C) until the cake springs back when lightly touched and a cake tester comes out clean, approximately 40 to 50 minutes. The cake's surface will have deep cracks.

❺ Remove the cake from the oven and immediately invert the pan onto the neck of a bottle. Allow the cake to rest upside down until completely cool.

❻ To remove the cake from the pan, run a thin knife or spatula around the edge of the pan and the edge of the interior tube. If a two-piece tube pan was used, lift the cake and tube portion out of the pan. Use a knife or spatula to loosen the bottom of the cake, and then invert it onto a cake cardboard or serving platter. (To portion angel food cake without crushing, gently cut the cake with a long serrated knife using a sawing motion.)

VARIATIONS:

Chocolate Angel Food Cake—Combine 1 ounce (30 grams/8%) cocoa powder with 2 fluid ounces (60 milliliters/16%) water and 0.3 fluid ounces (9 milliliters/2.5%) vanilla extract in a bowl. Set aside. Whisk a very large spoonful of the whipped egg white into the cocoa mixture folding it into the remaining egg whites at the end of Step 2.

Lemon Angel Food Cake—Add 0.14 ounce (2 teaspoons/4 grams/1%) fresh lemon zest to the sugar-and-flour mixture. Add 0.15 fluid ounce (1 teaspoon/5 milliliters/1%) lemon extract, folding it and the vanilla extract in at the end of Step 5.

Approximate values per ⅒-cake serving: **Calories** 210, **Total fat** 0.5 g, **Saturated fat** 0 g, **Cholesterol** 0 mg, **Sodium** 150 mg, **Total carbohydrates** 44 g, **Protein** 7 g, **Claims**—low fat; no saturated fat; no cholesterol

Chiffon Cakes

Although chiffon cakes are similar to angel food cakes in appearance and texture, the addition of egg yolks and vegetable oil makes them moister and richer. Chiffon cakes are usually leavened with whipped egg whites but may contain baking powder as well. Like angel food cakes, chiffon cakes are baked in an ungreased pan to allow the batter to cling to the pan as it rises. Chiffon cakes can be frosted with a light buttercream or whipped cream or topped with a glaze. Lemon and orange chiffon cakes are the most traditional, but formulas containing chocolate, nuts or other flavorings are also common.

PROCEDURE FOR PREPARING CHIFFON CAKES

❶ Preheat the oven.

❷ Sift the dry ingredients together. Add the liquid ingredients, including oil.

❸ Whip the egg whites with a portion of the sugar until almost stiff.

❹ Fold the whipped egg whites into the batter.

⑤ Spoon the batter into an ungreased pan and bake immediately.

⑥ Allow the cake to cool inverted in its pan.

ORANGE CHIFFON CAKE

Yield: 1 Tube Cake, 10 in. (25 cm)		**Method:** Egg foam	
Cake flour, sifted	8 oz.	240 g	100%
Granulated sugar	12 oz.	360 g	150%
Baking powder	0.4 oz. (1 Tbsp.)	12 g	5%
Salt	0.2 oz. (1 tsp.)	6 g	2.5%
Vegetable oil	4 fl. oz.	120 ml	50%
Egg yolks	4 oz. (6 yolks)	120 g	50%
Water, cool	2 fl. oz.	60 ml	25%
Orange juice	4 fl. oz.	120 ml	50%
Orange zest, grated fine	0.2 oz. (1 Tbsp.)	6 g	2.5%
Vanilla extract	0.5 fl. oz.	15 ml	6%
Egg whites	8 oz. (8 whites)	240 g	100%
Total batter weight:	2 lb. 11 oz.	1299 g	541%
Glaze:			
Powdered sugar, sifted	3 oz.	90 g	
Orange juice	1 fl. oz.	30 ml	
Orange zest, grated fine	0.14 oz. (2 tsp.)	4 g	

① Sift together the flour, 6 ounces (180 grams) of the sugar and the baking powder and salt.

② In a separate bowl mix the oil, egg yolks, water, orange juice, orange zest and vanilla. Add the liquid mixture to the dry ingredients.

③ In a clean bowl, beat the egg whites until foamy. Slowly beat in the remaining sugar. Continue beating until the egg whites are stiff but not dry.

④ Stir one-third of the egg whites into the batter to lighten it. Fold in the remaining egg whites.

⑤ Pour the batter into an ungreased 10-inch (25-centimeter) tube pan. Bake at 325°F (160°C) until a toothpick comes out clean, approximately 1 hour.

⑥ Immediately invert the pan over the neck of a wine bottle. Allow the cake to hang upside down until completely cool, and then remove from the pan.

⑦ Stir the glaze ingredients together in a small bowl and drizzle over the top of the cooled cake.

VARIATIONS:

Lemon Chiffon Cake—Substitute 2 fluid ounces (60 milliliters/25%) fresh lemon juice and 2 fluid ounces (60 milliliters/25%) water for the orange juice in the batter. Substitute lemon zest for the orange zest. Top with Basic Sugar Glaze (page 456).

Gluten-Free Orange Chiffon Cake—Substitute 6 ounces (180 grams) blanched almond flour and 3½ ounces (105 grams) potato starch for the cake flour in the batter. Omit the water. Reduce the sugar to 7 ounces (210 grams).

Approximate values per ⅒-cake serving: **Calories** 370, **Total fat** 15 g, **Saturated fat** 2.5 g, **Cholesterol** 130 mg, **Sodium** 280 mg, **Total carbohydrates** 54 g, **Protein** 6 g, **Vitamin C** 10%

MISE EN PLACE

▸ Sift flour.
▸ Grate orange zest.
▸ Preheat oven to 325°F (160°C).

① Folding the whipped egg whites into the cake batter.

② The glazed orange chiffon cake.

A HOLLYWOOD CLASSIC

Chiffon cake is one of the few desserts whose history can be traced with absolute certainty. According to Gerry Schremp in her book *Kitchen Culture: Fifty Years of Food Fads*, a new type of cake was invented by Henry Baker, a California insurance salesman, in 1927. Dubbed chiffon, it was as light as angel food and as rich as poundcake. For years he kept the formula a secret, earning fame and fortune by selling his cakes to Hollywood restaurants. The cake's secret ingredient—vegetable oil—became public knowledge in 1947 when Baker sold the formula to General Mills, which promoted it on packages of cake flour. Chiffon cakes, in a variety of flavors, became extremely popular nationwide.

TABLE 13.2   PAN PREPARATIONS

PAN PREPARATION	USED FOR
Ungreased	Angel food and chiffon cakes
Greased or ungreased sides; paper on bottom	Genoise layers
Greased and papered	High-fat cakes, sponge sheets
Greased and coated with flour	High-fat cakes, chocolate cakes, anything in a Bundt or shaped pan
Greased, floured and lined with paper	Cakes containing melted chocolate, fruit chunks or fruit or vegetable purées

Panning, Baking and Cooling

PREPARING PANS

To prevent cakes from sticking, pans may be greased or lined with parchment paper or both before baking. (See Chapter 5, Mise en Place.) Pans must be prepared before the cake is finished mixing to prevent air trapped in the emulsion from deflating while pans are being prepared. See Table 13.2. For a bakeshop that frequently needs to grease pans, an all-purpose pan coating suitable for any cake pan requiring greasing and flouring can be made from the formula on page 131.

Pan coating is not appropriate for all cakes, however. Those containing chocolate, raisins or fruit should still be baked in pans lined with parchment paper in order to prevent sticking.

Angel food and chiffon cakes are baked in ungreased, unlined pans because these fragile cakes need to cling to the sides of the pan as they rise. Spongecakes and genoise are often baked in pans with a paper liner on the bottom and ungreased sides. Although the ungreased sides give the batter a surface to cling to, the paper liner makes removing the cake from the pan easier. Flexible silicone pans require little if any greasing.

FILLING PANS

Pans should be filled no more than one-half to two-thirds full. This allows the batter to rise during baking without spilling over the edges. Pans should be filled to uniform depths. High-fat and egg foam cake batters can be ladled into each pan according to weight. High-ratio cake batter is so liquid that it can be measured by volume and poured into each pan (see Table 13.3). Filling the pans uniformly prevents both uneven layers and overfilled or underfilled pans. When baking multiple layers to be stacked for one presentation with a different amount of batter in each pan, the baking times will vary and the final product will be uneven.

Cake batter should always be spread evenly in the pan. Use an offset spatula. Do not work the batter too much, however, as this destroys air cells and prevents the cake from rising properly.

Scaling butter cake batter.

Evenly filling cupcake pans with batter.

TABLE 13.3 CAKE PAN SIZES

PAN SHAPE AND SIZE	VOLUME OF BATTER	WEIGHT— BUTTER/HIGH-FAT	WEIGHT— EGG FOAM	NO. OF SERVINGS FOR TWO-LAYER CAKE
ROUND, 2 IN. DEEP				
6 in.	1 pt.	8–10 oz.	5–6 oz.	6
8 in.	3 c.	12–16 oz.	8–10 oz.	12
10 in.	1½ qt.	24–32 oz.	16–18 oz.	20
12 in.	1 qt. + 3½ c.	32–36 oz.	18–22 oz.	30
14 in.	2½ qt.	40–48 oz.	24–30 oz.	40
SQUARE, 2 IN. DEEP				
8 in.	1 qt.	16–18 oz.	10–12 oz.	16
10 in.	1½ qt.	24–30 oz.	16–18 oz.	20
12 in.	2½ qt.	40–48 oz.	26–30 oz.	36
14 in.	3 qt. + 1½ c.	48–52 oz.	32–40 oz.	48
RECTANGULAR, 2 IN. DEEP				
6 in. × 8 in.	2½ c.	10–12 oz.	6–8 oz.	12
9 in. × 13 in.	2 qt.	32–36 oz.	20–24 oz.	24
18 in. × 13 in.	2 qt. + 3 c.	3.5–4 lb.	28–32 oz.	48
18 in. × 26 in.	5 qt.	6–8 lb.	2.5–3 lb.	96
CUPCAKES, 2 IN. DEEP	¼–⅓ cup	1½–2 oz.	¾–1 oz.	

*Quantities given are approximate and are based on filling the pans two-thirds full of batter. The weight of cake batter needed to properly fill a pan will vary depending on the type of batter, additional flavor ingredients and the amount of air incorporated during mixing.

BAKING

Temperatures

Always preheat the oven before preparing the batter. If the finished batter must wait while the oven reaches the correct temperature, valuable leavening will be lost and the cake will not rise properly.

Most butter cakes are baked at temperatures between 325°F and 375°F (160°C and 190°C). The temperature must be high enough to create steam within the batter and cause that steam and other gases in the batter to expand and rise quickly. If the temperature is too high, however, the cake may rise unevenly and the crust may burn before the interior is completely baked. The temperature must also be low enough so that the batter can set completely and evenly without drying out. If the temperature is too low, however, the cake will not rise sufficiently and may dry out before baking completely. Delicate egg foam cakes and spongecakes may be baked at slightly higher temperatures when panned in thin layers.

If no temperature is given in a formula or you are altering the dimensions of the baking pan from those specified, use common sense in setting the oven temperature. The larger the surface area, the higher the temperature can usually be. Tall cakes, such as Bundt or tube cakes, should be baked at a lower temperature than thin layer or sheet cakes. Tube or loaf cakes take longer to bake than thin sheet cakes; butter cakes, because they contain more liquid, take longer to bake than genoise or spongecake.

Determining Doneness

In addition to following the baking time suggested in a formula, several simple tests can be used to determine doneness. Whichever tests are used, avoid opening the oven door to check the cake's progress. Cold air or a drop in oven temperature can cause the cake to fall. Use a timer to note the minimum suggested baking time. Then, and only then, should you use the following tests to evaluate the cake's doneness:

▶ Appearance—The cake's surface should be a light to golden brown. Unless noted otherwise in the formula, the edges should just begin to pull away from the pan. The cake should not jiggle or move beneath its surface.

▶ Touch—Touch the cake lightly with your finger. It should spring back quickly without feeling soggy or leaving an indentation.

▶ Cake tester—If appearance and touch indicate that the cake is done, test the interior by inserting a toothpick, bamboo skewer or metal cake tester into the cake's center. With most cakes, the tester should come out clean. If wet crumbs cling to the tester, the cake probably needs to bake a bit longer.

If a formula provides particular doneness guidelines, they should be followed. For example, some flourless cakes are fully baked even though a cake tester will not come out clean.

TABLE 13.4 TROUBLESHOOTING CHART FOR CAKES

PROBLEM	CAUSE	SOLUTION
Butter curdles during mixing	Ingredients too warm or too cold	Eggs must be at room temperature and added slowly
	Incorrect fat is used	Use correct ingredients
	Fat inadequately creamed before liquid was added	Add a portion of the flour, then continue adding the liquid
Cake lacks volume	Flour too strong	Use a weaker flour
	Old chemical leavener	Replace with fresh leavener
	Egg foam underwhipped	Use correct mixing method; do not deflate eggs during folding
	Oven too hot	Adjust oven temperature
Crust burst or cracked	Too much flour or too little liquid	Adjust formula; scale accurately
	Oven too hot	Adjust oven temperature
Cake shrinks after baking	Weak internal structure	Adjust formula
	Too much sugar or fat for the batter to support	Adjust formula
	Cake not fully cooked	Test for doneness before removing from oven
Texture is dense or heavy	Too little leavening	Adjust formula
	Too much fat or liquid	Adjust formula
	Improper mixing	Cream fat or whip eggs properly
	Oven too cool	Adjust oven temperature
Texture is coarse with an open grain	Overmixing	Alter mixing method
	Oven too cool	Adjust oven temperature
Poor flavor	Poor ingredients	Check flavor and aroma of all ingredients
	Unclean pans	Do not grease pans with rancid fats
Uneven shape	Butter not incorporated evenly	Incorporate fats completely
	Batter spread unevenly	Spread batter evenly
	Oven rack not level	Adjust oven racks
	Uneven oven temperature	Adjust oven temperature

COOLING

Generally, a cake is allowed to cool 10 to 15 minutes in its pan set on a cooling rack after taking it out of the oven. This helps prevent the cake from cracking or breaking when it is removed from its pan.

To remove the partially cooled cake from its pan, run a thin knife or spatula blade between the pan and the cake to loosen it. Place a wire rack, cake cardboard or sheet pan over the cake and invert. Then remove the pan. The cake can be left upside down to cool completely or inverted again to cool top side up. Wire racks are preferred for cooling cakes because they allow air to circulate, speeding the cooling process and preventing steam from making the cake soggy.

Angel food and chiffon cakes should be turned upside down immediately after they are removed from the oven. They are left to cool completely in their pans to prevent the cake from collapsing or shrinking. The top of the pan should not touch the countertop, so that air can circulate under the inverted pan.

All cakes should be left to cool away from drafts or air currents that might cause them to collapse. Cakes should not be refrigerated to speed the cooling process, as rapid cooling can cause cracking. Prolonged refrigeration also causes cakes to dry out. Table 13.4 lists some common problems when making cakes and how to avoid them.

ICINGS

Icing, also known as **frosting**, is a sweet decorative coating used as a filling between the layers or as a coating over the top and sides of a cake. It is used to add flavor and to improve a cake's appearance. Icing can also extend a cake's shelf life by forming a protective coating.

There are seven general types of icing: **buttercream**, **foam**, **fudge**, **fondant**, **glaze**, **royal icing** and **ganache**. See Table 13.5. Each type can be produced with a number of formulas and in a range of flavorings.

Because icing is integral to the flavor and appearance of many cakes, it should be made carefully using high-quality ingredients and natural flavors and colors. A good icing is smooth; it is never grainy or lumpy (see Figure 13.3 and Table 13.6). It should complement the flavor and texture of the cake without overpowering it.

TABLE 13.5   ICINGS

ICING	PREPARATION	TEXTURE/FLAVOR
Simple buttercream (American)	Mixture of sugar and fat (usually butter); can contain egg yolks or egg whites	Rich but light; smooth; fluffy
Foam	Meringue made with hot sugar syrup	Light, fluffy; very sweet
Fudge	Cooked mixture of sugar, butter and water or milk; applied warm	Heavy, rich and candylike
Fondant	Cooked mixture of sugar and water; applied warm	Thick, opaque; sweet
Glaze	Powdered sugar with liquid	Thin; sweet
Royal icing	Uncooked mixture of powdered sugar and egg whites	Hard and brittle when dry; chalky
Ganache	Blend of melted chocolate and cream; may be poured or whipped	Rich, smooth; intense chocolate flavor

TABLE 13.6 TROUBLESHOOTING CHART FOR ICINGS

PROBLEM	CAUSE	SOLUTION
Icing breaks or curdles	Fat added too slowly or eggs too hot when fat was added	Add shortening or sifted powdered sugar
	Butter too cold when added	Soften butter before adding
Icing is lumpy	Powdered sugar not sifted	Sift dry ingredients
	Ingredients not blended	Use softened fats
	Sugar syrup lumps in icing	Add sugar syrups carefully
Icing is too stiff	Not enough liquid	Adjust formula; add small amount of water or milk to thin the icing
	Too cold	Bring icing to room temperature; heat gently over simmering water
Icing will not adhere to cake	Cake too hot	Cool cake completely
	Icing too thin	Adjust icing formula
	Icing too stiff	Adjust icing formula
	Icing too cold	Soften icing at room temperature before using

Buttercream

A buttercream is a light, smooth, fluffy mixture of sugar and fat (butter, margarine or shortening). It may also contain egg yolks for richness or whipped egg whites for lightness. Pasteurized eggs must always be used in buttercreams to ensure food safety. A good buttercream will be sweet, but not cloying; buttery, but not greasy.

Buttercreams are popular and useful for most types of cakes and may be flavored or colored as desired. They may be stored, covered, in the refrigerator for several days but must be softened before use. The three most popular styles of buttercream, which are discussed here, are **simple**, **Italian** and **French**.

SIMPLE BUTTERCREAM

Simple buttercream, sometimes known as **American-style buttercream**, is made by creaming butter and powdered sugar together until the mixture is light and smooth. Cream, pasteurized eggs and flavorings may be added as desired. Simple buttercream requires no cooking and is quick and easy to prepare.

If cost is a consideration, hydrogenated all-purpose shortening can be substituted for a portion of the butter, but the flavor and mouth feel will be different. Buttercream made with shortening tends to feel greasier and heavier because shortening does not melt on the tongue like butter. It will be more stable than buttercream made with pure butter, however, and is necessary when a pure white icing is desired.

FIGURE 13.3 ▶ Properly prepared buttercream (left) is smooth, shiny and silken. Improperly prepared buttercream (right) separates, is lumpy and loses its emulsion.

PROCEDURE FOR PREPARING SIMPLE BUTTERCREAMS

1. Cream softened butter or shortening until the mixture is light and fluffy.
2. Beat in pasteurized egg, if desired.
3. Beat in sifted powdered sugar, scraping down the bowl as needed.
4. Beat in the flavoring ingredients.

SIMPLE BUTTERCREAM

Yield: 3 lb. 2 oz. (1510 g)

Lightly salted butter, softened	1 lb.	480 g
Pasteurized egg (optional)	2 oz.	60 g
Powdered sugar, sifted	2 lb.	960 g
Vanilla extract	0.3 fl. oz. (2 tsp.)	10 ml

1. In the bowl of a mixer fitted with the paddle attachment, cream the butter until light and fluffy.
2. Beat in the egg (if using). Gradually add the sugar, frequently scraping down the bowl.
3. Add the vanilla and continue beating until the icing is smooth and light.

VARIATIONS:

Light Chocolate Buttercream—Dissolve 1 ounce (30 grams) sifted cocoa powder in 2 fluid ounces (60 milliliters) cool water. Add to the buttercream along with the vanilla.

Lemon Buttercream—Decrease the vanilla extract to 0.15 fluid ounce (1 teaspoon/ 5 milliliters). Add 0.15 fluid ounce (1 teaspoon/5 milliliters) lemon extract and 0.2 ounce (6 grams/1 tablespoon) finely grated lemon zest.

Approximate values per 1-oz. (30-g) serving: **Calories** 170, **Total fat** 6 g, **Saturated fat** 4 g, **Cholesterol** 25 mg, **Sodium** 70 mg, **Total carbohydrates** 28 g, **Protein** 0 g, **Vitamin A** 10%

MISE EN PLACE

▶ Soften butter.
▶ Sift powdered sugar.

Light Chocolate Buttercream

ITALIAN BUTTERCREAM

Italian buttercream, also known as meringue buttercream, is based on an Italian meringue, which is whipped egg whites cooked with hot sugar syrup. (See Chapter 12, Pastry and Dessert Components.) Softened butter is then whipped into the cooled meringue, and the mixture is flavored as desired. This type of buttercream is extremely soft and light. It can be used on most types of cakes and is particularly popular for multilayered genoise and spongecakes.

PROCEDURE FOR PREPARING ITALIAN BUTTERCREAM

1. Whip the egg whites until soft peaks form.
2. Beat granulated sugar into the egg whites and whip until firm and glossy.
3. Meanwhile, combine additional sugar with water and cook to the soft ball stage (240°F/116°C).
4. With the mixer on medium speed, pour the sugar syrup into the whipped egg whites. Pour slowly and carefully to avoid splatters.
5. Continue whipping the egg-white-and-sugar mixture until completely cool.
6. Whip softened, but not melted, butter into the cooled egg-white-and-sugar mixture.
7. Add flavoring ingredients as desired.

ITALIAN BUTTERCREAM

MISE EN PLACE

▶ Bring all ingredients to room temperature.

▶ Soften butter.

Yield: 5 lb. 5 oz. (2400 g)

Egg whites	14 oz. (14 whites)	400 g
Granulated sugar	1 lb. 11 oz.	750 g
Water	as needed	as needed
Lightly salted butter, softened but not melted	2 lb. 12 oz.	1250 g

1. All ingredients should be at room temperature before beginning.
2. Place the egg whites in a mixer bowl. Have 9 ounces (270 grams) of the sugar nearby.
3. Place 1 pound 2 ounces (540 grams) of the sugar in a heavy saucepan with enough water to moisten. Bring to a boil over high heat.
4. As the sugar syrup's temperature approaches the soft ball stage (240°F/116°C), begin whipping the egg whites. Watch the sugar closely so that the temperature does not exceed 240°F (116°C).
5. When soft peaks form in the egg whites, gradually add the 9 ounces (270 grams) of sugar to them. Reduce the mixer speed to medium and continue whipping the egg whites to stiff peaks.
6. When the sugar syrup reaches the soft ball stage, immediately pour it into the whites while the mixer is running. Pour the syrup in a steady stream between the side of the bowl and the beater. If the syrup hits the beater, it will splatter and cause lumps. Continue beating at medium speed until the egg whites are completely cool. At this point, the product is known as Italian meringue.
7. Gradually add the softened butter to the Italian meringue. When all the butter is incorporated, add flavoring ingredients as desired.

VARIATIONS:

Chocolate Italian Buttercream—Add 0.5 fluid ounces (15 milliliters) vanilla extract to the buttercream, then stir in 10 ounces (300 grams) melted and cooled bittersweet chocolate.

Lemon Italian Buttercream—Add 2 fluid ounces (60 milliliters) lemon extract and 0.4 ounce (2 tablespoons/12 grams) grated lemon zest to the buttercream.

Coffee Italian Buttercream—Add 2 fluid ounces (60 milliliters) coffee extract or strong coffee to the buttercream.

Approximate values per 1-oz. (30-g) serving: **Calories** 175, **Total fat** 13 g, **Saturated fat** 8 g, **Cholesterol** 34 mg, **Sodium** 140 mg, **Total carbohydrates** 16 g, **Protein** 1 g, **Vitamin A** 10%

1. Adding the sugar syrup to the whipped egg.

2. Adding the softened butter to the cooled Italian buttercream.

3. The finished Italian buttercream.

FRENCH BUTTERCREAM

French buttercream, also known as **mousseline buttercream**, is similar to Italian buttercream except that the hot sugar syrup is whipped into beaten egg yolks (not egg whites). This egg yolk meringue, referred to as *pâte à bombe*, is also used to leaven cakes and mousses, especially those used in still-frozen desserts, discussed in Chapter 14, Custards, Creams and Sauces, and in Chapter 15, Ice Cream and Frozen Desserts. Softened butter and flavorings are added when the sweetened egg yolks are fluffy and cool. An Italian meringue such as the one created in the preceding formula is sometimes folded in for additional body and lightness. French buttercream is perhaps the most difficult type of buttercream to master, but it has the richest flavor and smoothest texture. Like a meringue buttercream, mousseline buttercream may be used on almost any type of cake.

PROCEDURE FOR PREPARING FRENCH BUTTERCREAM

1 Prepare a sugar syrup and cook to soft ball stage (240°F/116°C).

2 Beat egg yolks to a thin ribbon.

3 Slowly beat the sugar syrup into the egg yolks.

4 Continue beating until the yolks are pale, stiff and cooled to approximately 78°F–88°F (25°C–31°C).

5 Gradually add softened butter to the cooled yolks.

6 Fold in Italian meringue (if using).

7 Stir in flavoring ingredients.

FRENCH MOUSSELINE BUTTERCREAM

Yield: 6 lb. (3 kg)

Granulated sugar	1 lb. 10 oz.	780 g
Water	8 fl. oz.	240 ml
Egg yolks	9.6 oz. (16 yolks)	288 g
Lightly salted butter, softened but not melted	3 lb.	1440 g
Italian Meringue (page 413)	1 lb.	480 g
Vanilla, coffee, lemon or other flavoring extract	2 fl. oz.	60 ml

MISE EN PLACE

▶ Soften butter.

1 Combine the sugar and water in a small saucepan and bring to a boil. Continue boiling until the syrup reaches 240°F (116°C).

2 Meanwhile, beat the egg yolks in the bowl of a 6 quart (6.5 liter) or larger mixer fitted with the whisk attachment on low speed. When the sugar syrup reaches 240°F (116°C), pour it slowly into the egg yolks, gradually increasing the speed at which they are whipped. Continue beating at medium-high speed until the mixture is very pale, stiff and cooled to approximately 78°F (25°C).

3 Gradually add the softened butter to the egg mixture, frequently scraping down the bowl.

4 Fold in the Italian Meringue with a spatula. Fold in the flavoring extract just until well distributed throughout the buttercream.

VARIATION:

Chocolate Mousseline Buttercream—Add 2 fluid ounces (60 milliliters) vanilla extract to the buttercream, then stir in 10 ounces (300 grams) melted and cooled bittersweet chocolate.

Approximate values per 1-oz. (30-g) serving: **Calories** 230, **Total fat** 20 g, **Saturated fat** 12 g, **Cholesterol** 105 mg, **Sodium** 190 mg, **Total carbohydrates** 12 g, **Protein** 1 g, **Vitamin A** 20%

Foam Icing

Foam icing or **boiled icing** is simply an Italian meringue (made with hot sugar syrup). Foam icing is light and fluffy but very sweet. It may be flavored with extract, liqueur or melted chocolate. It is frequently used to ice layer cakes and complements lemon, coconut or chocolate cakes especially well.

Foam icing is rather unstable. It should be used immediately and served the day it is prepared. Refrigeration often makes the foam weep beads of sugar. Freezing causes it to separate or melt. An easy foam icing can be made by following the formula for Italian Meringue (page 413). As soon as the meringue has cooled to room temperature, it can be flavored as desired with an extract or emulsion.

Fudge Icing

A fudge icing is a warmed mixture of sugar, butter and water or milk. It is heavy, rich and candylike. It is also stable and holds up well. A fudge icing should be applied warm and allowed to dry on the cake or pastry. When dry, it will have a thin crust and a moist interior. A fudge icing can be vanilla- or chocolate-based and is used on cupcakes, layer cakes and sheet cakes.

PROCEDURE FOR PREPARING FUDGE ICING

1. Place sifted powdered sugar into a mixer bowl.
2. Bring corn syrup, shortening and liquids to a boil.
3. Blend the hot liquids into the sugar with the machine running. Add extracts or flavorings.
4. Use fudge icing while still warm.

BASIC FUDGE ICING

Yield: 2 lb. 11 oz. (1295 g)

Powdered sugar, sifted	2 lb.	960 g
Unsalted butter	3 oz.	90 g
Shortening	2 oz.	60 g
Corn syrup or glucose	2 oz.	60 g
Water	4 fl. oz.	120 ml
Salt	0.03 oz. (⅛ tsp.)	0.5 g
Vanilla extract	0.15 fl. oz. (1 tsp.)	5 ml

1. Place the powdered sugar in the bowl of a mixer fitted with the whisk attachment.
2. Bring the butter, shortening, corn syrup, water and salt to a boil in a saucepan over medium-high heat. Remove the pan from heat.
3. With the machine running, pour the hot mixture over the powdered sugar. Whip until the mixture is smooth and fluffy. Stir in the vanilla.
4. The icing can be used immediately.

Approximate values per 1-oz. (30-g) serving: **Calories** 110, **Total fat** 3 g, **Saturated fat** 1.5 g, **Cholesterol** 5 mg, **Sodium** 10 mg, **Total carbohydrates** 22 g, **Protein** 0 g

COCOA FUDGE ICING

Yield: 3 lb. (1460 g)

Unsalted butter, room temperature	12 oz.	360 g
Cocoa powder, unsweetened	12 oz.	360 g
Glucose or corn syrup	8 fl. oz.	240 ml
Water	8 fl. oz.	240 ml
Vanilla extract	0.5 fl. oz. (1 Tbsp.)	15 ml
Salt	0.2 oz. (1 tsp.)	5 g
Powdered sugar, sifted	8 oz.	240 g

❶ Blend the butter with the cocoa powder in the bowl of a mixer fitted with the paddle attachment. Beat until smooth. Scrape down the bowl. Add the glucose and mix until smooth.

❷ Bring the water to a boil. With the mixer running, gradually add the water to the butter mixture. Scrape down the bowl. Add the vanilla and salt.

❸ Add the powdered sugar. Beat for 2 minutes on high speed, until the icing is thick enough to spread.

Approximate values per 1-oz. (30-g) serving: **Calories** 110, **Total fat** 7 g, **Saturated fat** 4 g, **Cholesterol** 15 mg, **Sodium** 55 mg, **Total carbohydrates** 14 g, **Protein** 1 g

MISE EN PLACE

▶ Bring butter to room temperature.
▶ Sift the powdered sugar.

Fondant

Fondant is a thick, opaque sugar paste commonly used for glazing Napoleons, petit fours and other pastries as well as some cakes. It is a cooked mixture of sugar and water, with glucose or corn syrup added to encourage the correct type of sugar crystallization. Poured over the surface being coated, fondant quickly dries to a shiny, nonsticky coating. It is naturally pure white and can be tinted with food coloring. Fondant can also be flavored with melted chocolate.

Fondant is rather tricky to make, so it is usually purchased prepared either as a ready-to-use paste or a powder to which water is added. To use prepared fondant, thin it with water or simple syrup and carefully warm to 100°F (38°C). Watch the temperature; when overheated, the fondant will lose its opacity and will dry with an uneven appearance. Commercially prepared fondant comes in several forms—a soft paste used for glazing cakes and pastry as well as a firm confectionary fondant used for candy centers, discussed in Chapter 20, Chocolate and Sugar Work. When purchasing fondant, select the proper type for your needs. Commercially prepared fondant will keep for several months at room temperature in an airtight container. The surface of the fondant should be coated with simple syrup, however, to prevent a crust from forming.

Rolled fondant is a very stiff doughlike type of fondant that is used for covering cakes and for making flowers and other decorations. As the name implies, it is rolled out to the desired thickness, then draped over a cake or torte to create a very smooth, flat coating. After the fondant dries, the cake may be decorated with royal icing or buttercream according to the procedures discussed on pages 464–465. Rolled fondant is available in a ready-to-use form. It can be flavored or colored if desired. Be sure to keep the rolled fondant tightly wrapped in plastic and stored in an airtight container to prevent it from drying out and cracking.

Celebration cake covered with rolled fondant.

rolled fondant a cooked mixture of sugar, glucose and water with the consistency of a dough; draped over cakes to create a perfectly smooth plasterlike surface

Glaze

A glaze is a thin coating meant to be brushed, poured or drizzled onto a cake or pastry. The typical glaze is a simple mixture made from sugar, water and flavorings, such as the Basic Sugar Glaze that follows. (Glaze can also be made using melted fondant.) A glaze is usually too thin to apply with a knife or spatula. It is used to add moisture and flavor to cakes on which a heavy icing would be undesirable—for example, a chiffon or angel food cake. Glaze is often tinted with food coloring, the color chosen to reflect the flavor of the cake.

A **thread glaze** is a mixture of sugar and water cooked to 236°F (113°C), the thread stage. This type of glaze is used to create a crystallized coating on gingerbread cookies and other pastries. Brushing the thread glaze over cooled pastries helps it crystallize, developing an opaque sweet coating with a subtle texture.

Flat icing or water icing is a specific type of glaze used on Danish pastries and coffeecakes. It is pure white and dries to a firm gloss. A glaze made from fondant (see the recipe on page 483) is also used for this purpose. The invert sugar in fondant prevents it from crystallizing.

BASIC SUGAR GLAZE

MISE EN PLACE

▶ Sift powdered sugar.
▶ Melt butter.

Yield: 12 oz. (385 g)

Powdered sugar, sifted	9.5 oz.	285 g
Light cream or milk	2 fl. oz.	60 ml
Unsalted butter, melted	1 oz.	30 g
Vanilla, lemon or almond extract	0.3 fl. oz. (2 tsp.)	10 ml

1. Stir all the ingredients together in a small bowl until smooth.
2. Adjust the consistency by adding more cream or milk to thin the glaze if necessary.
3. Adjust the flavor as necessary.
4. Use immediately, before the glaze begins to dry.

VARIATION:

Flavored Sugar Glaze—Stir 0.04 fluid ounce (¼ teaspoon/1 milliliter) lemon or orange oil into the glaze. Fruit juice and other flavorings may be substituted for the vanilla.

Approximate values per 1-oz. (30-g) serving: **Calories** 110, **Total fat** 2 g, **Saturated fat** 1.5 g, **Cholesterol** 5 mg, **Sodium** 0 mg, **Total carbohydrates** 23 g, **Protein** 0 g, **Claims**—low fat; low cholesterol; no sodium

CHOCOLATE GLAZE

Yield: 13 oz. (390 g)

Unsweetened chocolate	4 oz.	120 g
Semisweet chocolate	4 oz.	120 g
Unsalted butter	4 oz.	120 g
Light corn syrup	1 oz. (4 tsp.)	30 g

1. Melt all the ingredients together over a bain marie. Remove from the heat and allow to cool until slightly thickened, stirring occasionally.
2. Use immediately, before the glaze begins to dry.

Approximate values per 1-oz. (30-g) serving: **Calories** 130, **Total fat** 12 g, **Saturated fat** 7 g, **Cholesterol** 15 mg, **Sodium** 0 mg, **Total carbohydrates** 8 g, **Protein** 1 g

Royal Icing

Royal icing, also known as **decorator's icing**, is similar to flat icing except it is much stiffer and becomes hard and brittle when dry. It is an uncooked mixture of powdered sugar and egg whites and can be dyed with food coloring pastes.

Royal icing is used for making decorations, particularly intricate flowers or lace patterns. Prepare royal icing in small quantities, and always keep any unused portion well covered with a damp towel and plastic wrap to prevent hardening.

PROCEDURE FOR PREPARING ROYAL ICING

1 Combine pasteurized egg white and lemon juice, if using.

2 Beat in sifted powdered sugar until the correct consistency is reached.

3 Beat until very smooth and firm enough to hold a stiff peak.

4 Color as desired with food coloring paste.

5 Store covered with a damp cloth and plastic wrap.

ROYAL ICING

Yield: 7 oz. (210 g)

Powdered sugar	6 oz.	180 g
Egg white, pasteurized, room temperature	1 oz. (1 white)	30 g
Lemon juice	0.04 fl. oz. (¼ tsp.)	1 ml

1 Sift the sugar and set aside.

2 Place the egg white and lemon juice in a stainless steel bowl.

3 Add 4 ounces (120 grams) of the sugar and beat with an electric mixer or metal spoon until blended. The mixture should fall from a spoon in heavy globs. If it pours, it is too thin and will need the remaining 2 ounces (60 grams) of sugar.

4 Once the consistency is correct, continue beating 3 to 4 minutes. The icing should be white, smooth and thick enough to hold a stiff peak. Food coloring paste can be added at this time if desired.

5 Cover the icing with a damp towel and plastic wrap to prevent it from hardening.

Approximate values per 1-oz. (30-g) serving: **Calories** 120, **Total fat** 0 g, **Saturated fat** 0 g, **Cholesterol** 0 mg, **Sodium** 10 mg, **Total carbohydrates** 28 g, **Protein** 1 g, **Claims**—fat free; no saturated fat; no cholesterol; very low sodium

Ganache

Ganache is a sublime blending of pure chocolate and cream. It can also include butter, liqueur or other flavorings. Any bittersweet, semisweet or dark chocolate may be used; the choice depends on personal preference and cost considerations.

Depending on its consistency, ganache may be used as a candy (see Chapter 20, Chocolate and Sugar Work) or as a filling, icing or glaze-type coating on cakes, cookies, brownies or pastries. The ratio of chocolate to cream determines how thick the cooled ganache will be. Equal parts by weight of chocolate and cream generally are best for icings and fillings. Increasing the percentage of chocolate produces a thicker ganache. Warm ganache can be poured over a cake or pastry and allowed to harden as a thin glaze, or it can be cooled and whipped to create a rich, smooth icing. If it becomes too firm, ganache can be remelted over a bain marie.

Properly prepared ganache for coating cakes is smooth and shiny and holds its shape.

PROCEDURE FOR PREPARING GANACHE

❶ Melt finely chopped chocolate with cream in a double boiler. Alternatively, bring cream just to a boil, then pour it over finely chopped chocolate and allow the cream's heat to gently melt the chocolate. Do not attempt to melt chocolate and then add cool cream. This will cause the chocolate to resolidify and lump.

❷ Stir the ganache with a rubber spatula or an immersion blender to emulsify the cream and chocolate. (Whisking the ganache using a whip may be quicker, but the ganache will be grainy and less creamy.)

❸ Whichever method is used, cool the cream and chocolate mixture over an ice bath, stirring frequently. For poured ganache, cool the cream to 120°F (48°C), then pour the ganache over the chilled cake or pastry to be iced. (Cool the ganache to 130°F (54°C) if pouring it over a frozen cake or pastry.) For whipped ganache, cool the ganache completely, then incorporate air into the mixture by beating or whipping.

CHOCOLATE GANACHE

Yield: Approximately 2 lb. (990 g)

Bittersweet chocolate (58–68% cacao)	1 lb.	480 g
Heavy cream	1 pt.	480 ml
Almond or coffee liqueur	1 fl. oz.	30 ml

❶ Chop the chocolate into small pieces and place it in a large metal bowl.

❷ Bring the cream just to a boil, then immediately pour it over the chocolate, stirring with a rubber spatula or immersion blender to blend. Stir gently until all the chocolate has melted.

❸ Stir in the liqueur.

❹ Allow the mixture to cool, stirring frequently with a rubber spatula until the desired consistency is achieved.

Approximate values per 1-oz. (30-g) serving: **Calories** 130, **Total fat** 10 g, **Saturated fat** 6 g, **Cholesterol** 20 mg, **Sodium** 5 mg, **Total carbohydrates** 8 g, **Protein** 1 g, **Vitamin A** 6%

❶ Pouring the hot cream over the chopped chocolate.

❷ Blending the ganache with an immersion blender.

❸ Cool, firm ganache.

PROCEDURE FOR GLAZING A CAKE WITH GANACHE

1 Prepare the ganache to the proper consistency and temperature. Place a cake on a cake screen set over a clean baking sheet.

2 Pour the ganache evenly around the edge of the cake.

3 Pour the ganache over the center of the cake.

4 Spread the ganache with a spatula, allowing the excess to run down the sides of the cake.

ASSEMBLING AND DECORATING CAKES

Much of a cake's initial appeal lies in its appearance. This is true whether the finished cake is a simple sheet cake topped with swirls of buttercream or an elaborate wedding cake with intricate garlands and bouquets of marzipan roses. Any cake assembled and decorated with care and attention to detail is preferable to a carelessly assembled or garishly overdecorated one.

Thousands of decorating styles and designs are possible, of course. This section describes a few simple options that can be prepared by beginning pastry cooks using a minimum of specialized tools. In planning a cake's design, consider the flavor, texture and color of the components used as well as the number of guests or portions that must be served. Consider who will be cutting and eating the cake and how long the dessert must stand before service.

Assembling Cakes

Before a cake can be decorated, it must be assembled and coated with icing or frosting. First the cake is placed on a cake cardboard or round, the same size as the cake. Most cakes can be assembled in a variety of shapes and sizes; sheet cakes, round layer cakes and rectangular layer cakes are the most common. When assembling any cake, the goal is to fill and stack the cake layers evenly and to apply an even coating of icing that is smooth and free of crumbs. (A thin underlayer of icing called a **crumb coat** may be spread on an assembled cake to seal loose surface crumbs before a final decorative layer of icing is applied.)

Many of the photographs used in this section show the assembly and decoration of the celebration cake shown in the photograph at right.

crumb coat a thin layer of icing applied to a cake to seal loose surface crumbs before a final decorative layer of icing is applied

PROCEDURE FOR FILLING AND ICING A CAKE

① Split the cake horizontally into thin layers if desired. Use cake boards to support each layer as it is removed. Brush away any loose crumbs with a dry pastry brush or your hand.

② Position the bottom layer on a cake board. Place the layer on a revolving cake stand, if available. Pipe a border of buttercream around the cake, then top the layer with a mound of filling. Use a cake spatula to spread it evenly.

③ Position the next cake layer over the filling and continue layering and filling the cake as desired.

④ Place a mound of icing in the center of the cake top. Push it to the edge of the cake with a cake spatula. Do not drag the icing back and forth or lift the spatula off the icing, as these actions tend to pick up crumbs.

⑤ Smooth a thin layer of icing (the crumb coat) over the top of the cake. Cover the sides with excess icing from the top. Chill the cake.

⑥ Place another mound of icing in the center of the cake top. Frost the cake with a second layer of icing. Hold the spatula upright against the side of the cake and, pressing gently, turn the cake stand slowly. This smooths and evens the sides.

Simple Decorating Techniques

An extremely simple yet effective way to decorate an iced cake is with a garnish of chopped nuts, fruit, toasted coconut, shaved chocolate or other foods arranged in patterns or sprinkled over the cake. Be sure to use a garnish that complements the cake and icing flavors or reflects one of the cake's ingredients. For example, finely chopped pecans would be an appropriate garnish for a carrot cake that contains pecans; shaved chocolate would not.

Side masking is the technique of coating only the sides of a cake with garnish. Be sure to apply the garnish while the icing is still moist enough for it to adhere. The top may be left plain or decorated with icing designs or a message.

Stencils can be used to apply patterns of finely chopped garnishes, powdered sugar or cocoa powder to the top of a cake. A design can be cut from cardboard, or thin plastic forms can be purchased. Even simple strips of parchment paper can be used to create an attractive pattern. If using a stencil on an iced cake, allow the icing to set somewhat before laying the stencil on top of it. After the garnishes have been sprinkled over the stencil, carefully lift the stencil to avoid spilling the excess garnish and messing the pattern.

A cake or baker's comb or a serrated knife can be used to create patterns on a cake iced with buttercream, fudge or ganache. Hold the comb against the side of an iced cake and rotate the cake turntable slowly and steadily to create horizontal lines in the icing.

Side masking—coating the sides of a carrot cake with chopped pistachios.

Stencils—creating a design with powdered sugar and strips of parchment paper.

Cake comb—creating a pattern on an iced cake.

PROCEDURE FOR MAKING A PARCHMENT-PAPER CONE

❶ Begin with an equilateral triangle of uncreased paper. Shape it into a cone.

❷ Fold the top edges together to hold the shape.

❸ Cut the tip of the filled parchment cone.

PROCEDURE FOR FILLING A PIPING BAG

❶ Select the proper size piping bag for your task. Insert the desired tip.

❷ Fold down the top of the bag, then fill approximately half full with icing. Do not overfill the bag.

❸ Be sure to close the open end tightly before you start piping. Hold the bag firmly in your palm and squeeze from the top. Do not squeeze from the bottom or you may force the contents out the wrong end. Use the fingers of your other hand to guide the bag.

Piping Techniques

Piping designs made with a star tip.

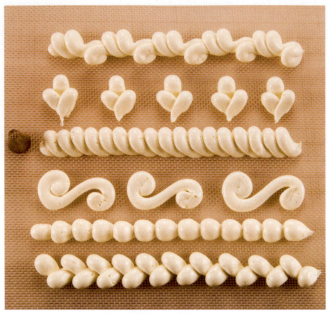

Piping designs made with a plain tip.

More elaborate and difficult decorations can be produced with the aid of a piping bag and an assortment of pastry tips. With these tools, buttercream or royal icing can be used to create borders, flowers and messages. Before applying any decorations, however, plan a design or pattern that is appropriate for the size and shape of the item being decorated.

When used properly, colored icings can bring cake decorations to life. Buttercream, royal icing and fondant are easily tinted using paste food coloring. Liquid food colorings are not recommended as they may thin the icing too much. Always add coloring gradually with a toothpick. Icing colors tend to darken as they sit. It is easy to add more later to darken the color if necessary, but it is difficult to lighten the color if too much is added.

Piping bags made from plastic, nylon or plastic-coated canvas are available in a range of sizes. A disposable piping cone can also be made from parchment paper.

Applying a vine and leaf border onto a celebration cake.

Most decorations and designs are made by using a piping bag fitted with a pastry tip. Pastry tips are available with dozens of different openings and are referred to by standardized numbers. Some common designs piped using a star and a plain tip are pictured above. You can produce a variety of borders and designs by changing the pressure, the angle of the bag and the distance between the tip and the cake surface.

PIPED-ON DECORATING TECHNIQUES

Instead of leaving the sides of an iced cake smooth or coating them with chopped nuts or crumbs, you can pipe on icing designs and patterns. A simple but elegant design is the basket weave, shown on page 463. Normally, a border pattern will be piped around the base of the cake and along the top edge. Borders should be piped on after nuts or any other garnishes are applied.

Each slice or serving of cake can be marked with its own decoration. For example, a rosette of icing or a whole nut or piece of fruit could be used as shown on page 463. This makes it easier to portion the cake evenly. Delicate flowers such as roses can be piped, allowed to harden, then placed on the cake in attractive arrangements. Royal icing is particularly useful for making decorations in advance because it dries very hard and lasts indefinitely.

Applying a bead border onto a celebration cake.

The key to success with a piping bag is practice, practice, practice. Use plain all-purpose shortening piped onto parchment paper to practice and experiment with piping techniques. Once you are comfortable using a piping bag, you can apply these newfound skills directly to cakes and pastries.

Applying a basket weave pattern to the sides of a celebration cake.

Applying a shell border to a celebration cake.

Placing royal icing flowers onto cake portions.

PROCEDURE FOR PIPING BUTTERCREAM ROSES

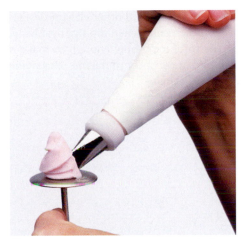

❶ Using a #104 tip, pipe a mound of icing onto a rose nail.

❷ Pipe a curve of icing around the mound to create the center of the rose.

❸ Pipe three overlapping petals around the center.

❹ Pipe five more overlapping petals around the first three petals.

❺ Use a small palette knife or spatula to place a finished rose on the cake.

Royal icing falling from a piping cone in a continual line.

Royal icing scrollwork patterns.

PIPING WITH ROYAL ICING

Delicate lines of royal icing can be piped on the top and sides of cakes that are iced smoothly with buttercream or coated with fondant. Scrollwork and other elegant designs add visual texture when piped in the same color. For best results when piping royal icing, use a plain tip or a parchment-paper cone. Thin the royal icing only enough to make it flow smoothly. The icing should fall from the tip of the cone in a continual line. Practicing on parchment paper or a silicone mat will improve your skills.

Additional piping designs can be found in Appendix IV.

PROCEDURE FOR FILLING CUPCAKES

Using an apple corer or paring knife, remove a small core from the cupcake. Pipe with filling, then cover with buttercream icing.

PROCEDURES FOR ICING CUPCAKES

Place a mound of icing in the center of the cupcake. Push it to the edge with a spatula. Holding the spatula upright against the side of the cupcake, push the icing against the edge to smooth. Dip in chocolate pieces, sprinkles or nuts, if desired.

Dip the top of the cupcake into warm glaze, holding it upside down until excess glaze drips off. Garnish immediately with shaved chocolate, if desired, before the glaze sets.

Using a pastry bag fitted with a star tip, pipe a swirl of icing onto plain or glazed cupcakes.

Covering and Decorating a Cake with Rolled Fondant

Rolled fondant gives cakes an elegant, smooth finish, popular for wedding and special-occasion cakes. Although it is not an easy technique, applying rolled fondant is easily mastered. Because it resembles clay, rolled fondant is versatile; it can easily be rolled like pie crust and cut out to drape over cakes. The fondant holds a pattern and can be embossed with a patterned rolling pin. Cutouts of rolled fondant can be used to create patterns, ribbons and other shapes to embellish the finished design. Rolled fondant can be tinted in any color, one reason for its popularity for specialty cakes. The fondant may be left plain or decorated with piped royal icing according to the procedures discussed in this chapter.

Rolled fondant does not hold up under humid conditions; therefore, cakes covered with rolled fondant should not be stored in the refrigerator. (Moisture from the cake and the refrigerator can condense, marring the appearance and texture of the fondant coating.) Nor should a fondant-covered cake be frozen. Choose a cake that can safely be stored unrefrigerated under cool, dry conditions or frost the cake close to service. Butter cakes, poundcakes and fruitcakes are good choices. Rolled fondant is not suitable as a covering on egg foam cakes because these delicate cakes will sink under its weight. Baking the cakes in pans with rounded edges (contour pans) will make it easier to press the fondant evenly over the cake without tearing.

When using rolled fondant, work quickly to keep it from drying out. Coat the cake with a light layer of icing or thinned preserves to help the fondant adhere to the cake. Roll the fondant to a thickness of approximately ¼ inch (2.5 centimeters), as thinly as suitable to cover the cake without crumbs showing through. (A thick coating of this sweet and chewy icing may not appeal to everyone.) Work on a surface dusted lightly with cornstarch or powdered sugar to keep the icing from sticking. A nonstick rolling pin is a useful tool, although fondant can be rolled with a wooden rolling pin.

Because a patch would be unsightly, roll out as much fondant as needed to cover the cake layer in one piece. See Table 13.7. Drape the fondant over the rolling pin to transfer it to the cake. Trim off the excess fondant with a sharp paring knife.

Piping royal icing scrollwork onto the sides of a fondant-covered cake.

PROCEDURE FOR COVERING A CAKE WITH ROLLED FONDANT

1 Ice the cake with a light coating of buttercream, icing or thinned fruit preserves.

2 Roll out the fondant using a nonstick rolling pin on a smooth clean surface lightly dusted with cornstarch or powdered sugar.

3 Transfer the rolled fondant, draped over a rolling pin, onto the cake. Allow the sheet of fondant to fall evenly from the rolling pin onto the cake.

4 Starting from the center of the cake and working toward the sides, press the fondant gently to remove air pockets and help the fondant stick to the cake.

5 Trim any excess fondant with a paring knife.

1 Rolled out fondant (foreground). Brushing the surface of the cake with melted fruit preserves.

2 Lifting the fondant and draping it over the cake.

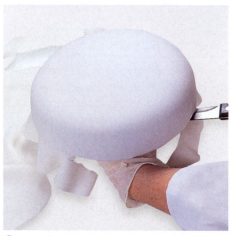

3 The finished cake layer coated with rolled fondant.

Cutting and Portioning Cakes

Cakes must be cut into uniform slices without crushing the cake or destroying its decorative icing. For even slices, a clean metal kitchen ruler may be gently pressed into the surface of the cake to serve as a cutting guide. A long serrated knife can serve the same purpose. Portioning tools, which mark the surface of round cakes, help when cutting an irregular number of slices from a round cake. Large sheet cakes can be cut into many shapes and portion sizes. (See the cutting guidelines in Appendix IV.) Whichever tool is used, cut cakes only at service time to keep them fresh. Do not simply cut one slice out of a cake without making sure of that slice's impact on the total number of cuts to be produced from the whole dessert. All portions should be at least scored uniformly so that future cuts will all be the same size.

Although they may be portioned when chilled, allow buttercream cakes to come to room temperature for 15 to 20 minutes before serving. Iced cakes should be cut with a sharp or serrated knife that has been dipped in hot water, then wiped clean between each cut. Heating helps the knife glide easily through the cake. Wiping prevents crumbs and fillings stuck to the knife blade from marring the surface of the next slice.

Storing Cakes

Plain cake layers or sheets can be stored at room temperature 2 or 3 days if well covered, although they may be easier to handle when chilled. Iced or filled cakes are usually refrigerated to prevent spoilage. Simple buttercreams or sugar glazes made without eggs or dairy products, however, can be left at room temperature 1 or 2 days. Any cake containing custard filling, mousse or whipped cream must be refrigerated. Cakes made with foam-type icing should be eaten the day they are prepared.

TABLE 13.7	QUANTITIES OF ICING AND FONDANT		
CAKE SHAPE AND SIZE	VOLUME OF ICING	WEIGHT OF ICING	WEIGHT OF FONDANT
ROUND, 2 IN. DEEP			
6 in.	1 c.	6–7 oz.	0.75 lb.
8 in.	1½ c.	8–10 oz.	1 lb.
10 in.	2½ c.	16–17 oz.	1.25 lb.
12 in.	3 c.	18–22 oz.	1.5 lb.
14 in.	4 c.	24–28 oz.	2 lb.
SQUARE, 2 IN. DEEP			
6 in.	1½ c.	8–10 oz.	1 lb.
8 in.	2 c.	12–16 oz.	1.25 lb.
10 in.	3½ c.	21–26 oz.	1.5 lb.
12 in.	4½ c.	27–32 oz.	2 lb.
14 in.	6 c.	36–42 oz.	2.5 lb.
CUPCAKES, 2 IN.	2–3 Tbsp.	1–1½ oz.	3–4 oz.

*Quantities given are approximate and are based on a light coating of a buttercream-type icing. The weight of the icing needed to properly cover a cake will vary depending on the type of icing, additional flavorings added and the amount of air incorporated during mixing. Icing for piped decorating is not included. Quantities of fondant given are based on rolling it to a thickness of ¼ inch (6 millimeters).

Cakes can usually be frozen with great success; this makes them ideal for baking in advance. Unfrosted layers or sheets should be well covered with plastic wrap and frozen at 0°F (–18°C) or lower. High-fat cakes will keep up to 6 months; egg foam cakes begin to deteriorate after 2 or 3 months.

Icings and fillings do not freeze particularly well, often losing flavor or changing texture when frozen. Buttercreams made with egg whites or sugar syrups tend to develop crystals and graininess. Foam icings weep, expelling beads of sugar and becoming sticky and deflating or shrinking. Fondant will absorb moisture and separate from the cake. If you must freeze a filled or iced cake, it is best to freeze it unwrapped first, until the icing is firm. The cake can then be covered with plastic wrap without damaging the icing design. Leave the cake wrapped until completely thawed. It is best to thaw cakes in the refrigerator; do not refreeze a thawed cake.

Well-organized pastry shops choose designated times to bake cake and torte components and freeze them until needed for assembly. Baking several batches of cake during one shift saves time and costly mistakes. In a smaller bakeshop, assembly can take place when the oven is not in use, providing a cooler work environment, which is crucial for creams and mousses.

CONVENIENCE PRODUCTS

Packaged cake mixes are a tremendous time-saver for commercial food service operations. Almost any operation can serve a variety of cakes made by relatively unskilled employees using prepared mixes. The results are consistent and the texture and flavor are acceptable to most consumers. Indeed, a well-prepared packaged cake mix is preferable to a poorly prepared cake made from scratch. Most packaged cake mixes can be adapted to include flavorings, nuts, spices or fruits, which can improve the product's overall quality. The convenience of mixes is not without cost, however. Packaged cake mixes are often more expensive than the ingredients needed for an equal number of cakes made from scratch. Cakes made from mixes are also softer and more cottony than scratch cakes, and their flavor tends to be more artificial.

Cake mixes are blends of flour, shortening, emulsifiers, chemical leavening and flavorings that are moistened with water or other liquid. Some mixes require the addition of eggs, fats and flavorings. Mixing techniques vary, so follow package directions carefully. Most cake mixes are not creamed but simply blended with a paddle. To aerate the batter in an angel food cake mix, a whip may be specified. Some mixes require the addition of liquids in two stages. As with any cake batter, scraping down the bowl frequently in the early stages of mixing ensures that the dry mix is properly moistened. Once the batter is mixed, panning, baking and assembly techniques are the same as for scratch preparations.

A wide selection of prepared icings, glazes and toppings are available. Often, chocolate and vanilla fudge-based icings are purchased and then flavored or colored as needed. Foam icings can be purchased in powder form, to which you simply add water and whip. Ready-to-use glazes and flat icings are formulated for many types of applications—brushing over cakes, sweet dough pastries or doughnuts in particular. Even prepared "buttercreams" are available in shelf-stable or frozen forms, although they contain little or no real butter. Prepared fondant, on the other hand, is a convenience. Its expense is outweighed by consistency and savings in labor cost.

Prepared icings are often exceedingly sweet and overpowered by artificial flavors and chemical preservatives. These products save time and offer consistent results but often cost more than their counterparts made from scratch. They should be used only after balancing the disadvantages against the benefits for your particular operation.

QUESTIONS FOR DISCUSSION

Terms to Know

creamed fat (creaming method)	icing
	buttercream
	royal icing
whipped eggs	ganache
butter cake	mousseline
genoise	buttercream
angel food cake	boiled icing
chiffon cake	thread glaze
two-stage mixing method	crumb coat
	side masking

1 Cake ingredients can be classified into six categories according to the function they perform. List them and give an example of each.

2 What is the primary leavening agent in cakes made with the egg foam method? How is this similar to or different from cakes made with the creaming method?

3 What is the difference between a spongecake and a classic genoise?

4 Explain why butter should be softened before preparing buttercream icing.

5 List the steps employed in assembling and icing a three-layer cake.

6 Wedding cakes vary greatly from one region or culture to another. Investigate the various types or styles of cakes traditionally served at weddings in three or four different cultures. Which formulas in this book would be appropriate for a wedding cake? WWW

YELLOW CAKE

Yield: 4 Rounds, 9 in. (22 cm) each

Method: Creaming

Cake flour	1 lb. 2 oz.	540 g	100%
Baking powder	0.6 oz. (4 tsp.)	17 g	3%
Unsalted butter, softened	1 lb.	480 g	89%
Granulated sugar	1 lb. 4 oz.	600 g	111%
Corn syrup, glucose or additional sugar	3 oz.	90 g	16%
Salt	0.2 oz. (1 tsp.)	6 g	1%
Egg yolks	10 oz. (16 yolks)	300 g	55%
Vanilla extract	1 fl. oz.	30 ml	5%
Almond extract (optional)	0.2 fl. oz. (1 tsp.)	65 ml	1%
Buttermilk	12 fl. oz.	360 ml	66%
Total batter weight:	5 lb.	2428 g	447%

1. Sift together the flour and baking powder. Set aside.
2. Cream the butter until light and lump-free in the bowl of a 6 quart (6.5 liter) mixer fitted with the paddle attachment. Add the granulated sugar, corn syrup and salt. Blend just until no lumps remain. The mixture will be stiff.
3. Gradually add the egg yolks, allowing them to fully incorporate before adding more yolks. Scrape down the bowl after each addition. Add the vanilla and almond extract (if using).
4. Mix the batter on medium speed until light. Then continue mixing another 5 to 6 minutes.
5. Fold in the flour mixture alternately with the buttermilk in three additions, ending with the flour and scraping well in between.
6. Scale 1 pound 4 ounces (600 grams) of batter into four buttered and floured 9-inch (22-centimeter) pans. Bake at 350°F (180°C) until the center of the cake bounces back when lightly pressed, approximately 28 minutes.
7. Allow to cool for 15 minutes before unmolding onto paper-lined sheet pans.

Approximate values per ⅛-cake serving: **Calories** 270, **Total fat** 14 g, **Saturated fat** 8 g, **Cholesterol** 125 mg, **Sodium** 140 mg, **Total carbohydrates** 33 g, **Protein** 3 g

CARROT CAKE

Yield: 8 Layer Cakes, 9 in. (22 cm) each   **Method:** Two-stage

Granulated sugar	3 lb. 5 oz.	1590 g	132%
Cake flour	2 lb. 8 oz.	1200 g	100%
Baking powder	1.25 oz.	37 g	3.1%
Baking soda	0.75 oz.	22 g	1.9%
Cinnamon, ground	0.75 oz.	22 g	1.9%
Salt	0.5 oz.	15 g	1.25%
Light olive, grapeseed or vegetable oil	3 lb.	1440 g	120%
Eggs	1 lb. 12 oz.	840 g	70%
Vanilla extract	0.5 fl. oz.	15 ml	1.25%
Carrots, grated fine	2 lb. 5 oz.	1110 g	92.5%
Walnuts, chopped	1 lb.	480 g	40%
Crushed pineapple, drained	1 lb. 5 oz.	625 g	52%
Coconut, shredded	12 oz.	360 g	30%
Total batter weight:	16 lb. 2 oz.	7756 g	646%
Cream Cheese Icing (page 482)	as needed	as needed	
Walnuts, chopped	as needed	as needed	
Fondant or marzipan, tinted (optional)	as needed	as needed	

1. In the bowl of a large mixer fitted with the paddle attachment, blend the sugar, flour, baking powder, baking soda, cinnamon, salt and oil on low speed for 1 minute.
2. Increase the speed to medium and mix for 4 additional minutes.
3. Reduce the speed to low and gradually add the eggs and vanilla. Add the carrots, walnuts, drained pineapple and coconut and mix until just combined.
4. Divide the batter into greased and floured pans.
5. Bake at 375°F (190°C) until the centers of the cakes bounce back when lightly pressed, approximately 30 to 35 minutes.
6. Allow the cakes to cool completely. When cooled, slice each cake into three equal layers. Each filled and iced cake requires three layers.
7. For each cake, place one cake layer on a cake board. Evenly coat it with Cream Cheese Icing. Place a second layer on top and repeat with the same amount of icing. Top with the third layer.
8. Apply a thin coating of Cream Cheese Icing to the top and sides of each cake. Refrigerate until the icing is firm and then apply a final even coating of icing.
9. Pipe 8 rosettes of icing, evenly spaced, on the top of each cake. Tint the marzipan and form it into carrot garnishes for the cakes, if desired. Side mask the bottom edge of each cake with chopped walnuts.

Approximate values per $\frac{1}{12}$-cake serving: **Calories** 795, **Total fat** 46 g, **Saturated fat** 12 g, **Cholesterol** 94 mg, **Sodium** 400 mg, **Total carbohydrates** 88 g, **Protein** 7 g, **Vitamin A** 80%, **Iron** 10%

MARBLE CAKE

Yield: 1 Sheet Cake, 18 in. × 24 in. (45 cm × 60 cm)

Method: Creaming

Cake flour, sifted	1 lb. 11 oz.	810 g	100%
Baking powder	1 oz.	30 g	4%
Salt	0.5 oz.	15 g	2%
Unsalted butter, softened	12 oz.	360 g	44%
Granulated sugar	1 lb. 11 oz.	810 g	100%
Milk	24 fl. oz.	720 ml	89%
Vanilla extract	0.15 fl. oz. (1 tsp.)	5 ml	0.5%
Dark chocolate, melted	4.5 oz.	130 g	16%
Baking soda	0.04 oz. (¼ tsp.)	1 g	0.1%
Coffee extract*	0.3 fl. oz. (2 tsp.)	8 ml	1%
Egg whites	12 oz. (12 whites)	360 g	44%
Total batter weight:	6 lb. 12 oz.	3249 g	400%
Cocoa Fudge Icing (page 455)	as needed	as needed	

1. Sift the flour, baking powder and salt together. Set aside.
2. Cream the butter and sugar in the bowl of a large mixer until light and fluffy.
3. Combine the milk and vanilla.
4. Add the dry ingredients alternately with the milk to the creamed butter. Stir the batter only until smooth.
5. Separate the batter into two equal portions. Add the chocolate, baking soda and coffee extract to one portion.
6. Whip the egg whites until stiff but not dry. Fold half of the whites into the vanilla batter and half into the chocolate batter.
7. Spoon the batters onto a greased sheet pan, lined with a pan extender, alternating the two colors. Pull a paring knife through the batter to swirl the colors together.
8. Bake at 350°F (180°C) until a tester comes out clean, approximately 25 minutes.
9. Allow the cake to cool, then cover the top with Cocoa Fudge Icing.

The coffee extract is added to round out the chocolate flavor, not to impart a "coffee" flavor.

Approximate values per 2-oz. (60-g) serving: **Calories** 170, **Total fat** 7 g, **Saturated fat** 4 g, **Cholesterol** 15 mg, **Sodium** 180 mg, **Total carbohydrates** 27 g, **Protein** 2 g

CHOCOLATE ALMOND FLOUR CAKE

Yield: 1 Full-Sheet Pan, 18 in. × 24 in. (45 cm × 60 cm)

Method: Creaming

			Sugar at 100%
Unsalted butter, softened	14 oz.	420 g	78%
Granulated sugar	1 lb. 2 oz.	540 g	100%
Vanilla extract	0.15 fl. oz. (1 tsp.)	5 ml	0.8%
Cocoa powder	2 oz.	60 g	11%
Egg yolks	8 oz. (12 yolks)	240 g	44%
Eggs	6.75 oz. (4 eggs)	200 g	37%
Semisweet or bittersweet chocolate, melted and held at 110°F (43°C)	1 lb.	480 g	89%
Almond flour	6 oz.	180 g	33%
Egg whites	1 lb. 8 oz.	720 g	133%
Total batter weight:	5 lb. 14 oz.	2845 g	525%

1. Cream the butter and 8 ounces (240 grams) of the sugar in the bowl of a mixer fitted with the paddle attachment. Add the vanilla and cocoa powder.

2. Add the egg yolks and eggs one at a time, scraping down the bowl well after each addition. Make certain the chocolate is warmed to 110°F (43°C). (This will keep the batter light. Colder chocolate will firm the batter, making it impossible to fold in the whipped egg whites.) Pour in the melted chocolate and mix until well combined. Add the almond flour. Set aside.

3. In a separate mixing bowl, use a clean whip to whip the egg whites and remaining 10 ounces (300 grams) of sugar to medium peaks. Quickly fold the whites into the cake batter in three steps.

4. Spread the mixture on a paper-lined sheet pan. Bake at 350°F (180°C) until the top surface of the cake is dry and the interior of the cake is soft but set, approximately 35 to 40 minutes. Test for doneness by removing a bit of the crust and pressing the cake underneath. The crust will be firm but the interior crumb will be soft but not sticky. If the cake is still wet, return it to the oven for a few more minutes.

5. Cool the cake in the pan on a wire rack. Cut the cake to line torte rings as needed. (See Eros Torte, page 622.) Remove the parchment paper after the cake is cut to keep the cake intact.

VARIATIONS:

White Chocolate Chunk Flourless Chocolate Cake—Fold 10 ounces (300 grams/55%) white chocolate chips or chunks into the batter before panning.

Pistachio or Hazelnut Flourless Chocolate Cake—Fold 10 ounces (300 grams/55%) coarsely chopped pistachios or hazelnuts into the batter before panning.

Approximate values per 1-oz. (30-g) serving: **Calories** 100, **Total fat** 7 g, **Saturated fat** 3.5 g, **Cholesterol** 50 mg, **Sodium** 15 mg, **Total carbohydrates** 9 g, **Protein** 2 g, **Claims**–Gluten free

GERMAN CHOCOLATE CAKE

Yield: 1 Layer Cake, 9 in. (22 cm)   **Method:** Creaming

Sweet baking chocolate	8 oz.	240 g	80%
Water, boiling	4 fl. oz.	120 ml	40%
Unsalted butter, softened	8 oz.	240 g	80%
Granulated sugar	1 lb.	480 g	160%
Egg yolks	2.4 oz. (4 yolks)	80 g	24%
Vanilla extract	0.15 fl. oz. (1 tsp.)	5 ml	1.5%
Cake flour	10 oz.	300 g	100%
Baking soda	0.14 oz. (1 tsp.)	4 g	1.4%
Salt	0.1 oz. (½ tsp.)	3 g	1%
Buttermilk	8 fl. oz.	240 ml	80%
Egg whites	4 oz. (4 whites)	120 g	40%
Total batter weight:	3 lb. 13 oz.	1862 g	618%
Coconut Pecan Icing (recipe follows)	1 lb. 3 oz.	900 g	
Silky Ganache Deluxe (page 485; optional)	as needed	as needed	

1. Chop the chocolate and melt it with the boiling water over a bain marie.
2. In the bowl of a mixer fitted with the paddle attachment, cream together the butter and sugar until light and fluffy.
3. Add the egg yolks, one at a time, to the butter, then stir in the vanilla and the melted chocolate.
4. Sift the flour, baking soda and salt together and add them alternately with the buttermilk to the batter, beating well after each addition.
5. Whip the egg whites to stiff peaks and fold into the batter.
6. Divide the batter into three 9-inch (22-centimeter) round pans that have been greased and lined with parchment paper.
7. Bake at 350°F (180°C) until set and just beginning to pull away from the sides, approximately 30 to 40 minutes. When the cake has cooled completely, spread the Coconut Pecan Icing between each layer and on top. The sides of this cake may be iced with Silky Ganache Deluxe or left plain.

Approximate values per ¹⁄₁₂-cake serving: **Calories** 840, **Total fat** 47 g, **Saturated fat** 24 g, **Cholesterol** 210 mg, **Sodium** 240 mg, **Total carbohydrates** 101 g, **Protein** 10 g, **Vitamin A** 25%, **Calcium** 15%, **Iron** 20%

COCONUT PECAN ICING

Yield: 1 lb. 14 oz. (905 g) Icing, enough for 1 three-layer cake

Evaporated milk	8 fl. oz.	240 ml
Granulated sugar	8 oz.	240 g
Egg yolks	2 oz. (3 yolks)	60 g
Unsalted butter	4 oz.	120 g
Vanilla extract	0.15 fl. oz. (1 tsp.)	5 ml
Coconut, flaked	4 oz.	120 g
Pecans, chopped	4 oz.	120 g

1. Combine the milk, sugar, egg yolks and butter in a saucepan over medium heat. Cook, stirring constantly, until the mixture reaches 195°F (90°C) and thickens, approximately 12 minutes.
2. Remove from the heat and add the vanilla, coconut and pecans. Beat until cool and spreadable.

Approximate values per 1-oz. (30-g) serving: **Calories** 140, **Total fat** 11 g, **Saturated fat** 7 g, **Cholesterol** 25 mg, **Sodium** 10 mg, **Total carbohydrates** 10 g, **Protein** 1 g, **Vitamin A** 8%

DEVIL'S FOOD CAKE

Yield: 2 Layer Cakes, 9 in. (22 cm) each   **Method:** Creaming

Pastry flour	1 lb. 1 oz.	510 g	100%
Cocoa powder	8 oz.	240 g	47%
Baking powder	0.3 oz. (2 tsp.)	8 g	1.7%
Baking soda	0.3 oz. (2 tsp.)	8 g	1.7%
Unsalted butter, melted	10 oz.	300 g	59%
Eggs	9.6 oz. (6 eggs)	290 g	56%
Buttermilk	16 fl. oz.	480 ml	94%
Vanilla extract	0.5 fl. oz. (1 Tbsp.)	15 ml	3%
Granulated sugar	1 lb. 14 oz.	900 g	176%
Salt	0.2 oz. (1 tsp.)	6 g	1.2%
Brewed coffee, hot	16 fl. oz.	480 ml	94%
Total batter weight:	6 lb. 11 oz.	3237 g	633%
Silky Ganache Deluxe (page 485)	3 lb.	1460 g	
Baked Streusel for Crumble (page 389) or chocolate shavings	as needed	as needed	

1. Sift together the flour, cocoa powder, baking powder and baking soda. Set aside.

2. Whip the butter and eggs in the bowl of a 6 quart (6.5 liter) or larger mixer fitted with the whip attachment until well blended. Add the buttermilk, vanilla, sugar and salt. Whip until smooth.

3. On low speed, stir in the sifted dry ingredients. Scrape down the bowl well and add the brewed coffee, mixing until just blended.

4. Divide the batter into four greased and floured 9-inch (22-centimeter) round cake pans, measuring 1 pound 11 ounces (810 grams) of batter into each pan. Bake at 350°F (180°C) until the centers of the cakes bounce back when lightly pressed and a cake tester comes out clean, approximately 38 to 43 minutes.

5. Cool the cakes completely on wire racks. Unmold the cooled cakes onto a paper-lined sheet pan.

6. Cut each cake horizontally into two layers. To make two four-layer cakes, spread the bottom layer of two of the cakes with Silky Ganache Deluxe. Place a second layer on top and repeat with the same amount of icing. Top with the third layer and repeat with the same amount of icing. Place the remaining cake layer on top.

7. Apply a generous layer of icing to the top and sides of each cake. Pipe a rosette border along the top edge of each cake. Garnish the sides of each cake with pieces of Baked Streusel for Crumble or chocolate shavings.

Approximate values per 1/12-cake serving: **Calories** 534, **Total fat** 25 g, **Saturated fat** 15 g, **Cholesterol** 10 mg, **Sodium** 374 mg, **Total carbohydrates** 83 g, **Protein** 8 g, **Vitamin A** 20%, **Calcium** 15%, **Iron** 35%

ITALIAN CREAM CAKE

Moist cakes filled with cream, ricotta, candied fruits and nuts such as the Sicilian cassata are popular in Italy and were no doubt a source of inspiration for this dessert. Despite its name, this is an American layer cake commonly found in the Southern states. Buttermilk and pecans give it a decidedly American flavor.

Yield: 4 Layer Cakes, 9 in. (22 cm) each   **Method:** Creaming

Cake flour	1 lb. 8 oz.	720 g	100%
Baking powder	0.28 oz. (2 tsp.)	8 g	1%
Baking soda	0.21 oz. (1½ tsp.)	6 g	0.09%
Unsalted butter, softened	1 lb. 8 oz.	720 g	100%
Granulated sugar	2 lb. 2 oz.	1020 g	141.5%
Salt	0.5 oz.	15 g	2%
Eggs, room temperature	8 oz. (5 eggs)	240 g	33%
Vanilla extract	1 fl. oz.	30 ml	4%
Buttermilk	1 lb. 4 oz.	600 g	83%
Pecans, chopped	8 oz.	240 g	33%
Coconut flakes, sweetened	8 oz.	240 g	33%
Egg whites	14 oz. (14 whites)	420 g	58%
Total batter weight:	8 lb. 13 oz.	4230 g	588%
Cream Cheese Icing (page 482)	4 lb. 8 oz.	2160 g	
Toasted coconut	as needed	as needed	
Pecan halves	32	32	

1. Sift together the flour, baking powder and baking soda. Set aside.
2. Cream the butter, sugar and salt until light and lump-free in the bowl of a large mixer fitted with the paddle attachment.
3. Gradually add the eggs one at a time, waiting for the previous egg to be fully incorporated before adding more. Add the vanilla. Mix until light and creamy.
4. Add one-third of the dry ingredients on low speed. Mix just until incorporated. Scrape down the bowl and paddle. On low speed, add half of the buttermilk and mix until just combined.
5. Repeat with another third of the flour mixture, followed by the remaining buttermilk and then the remaining flour, scraping down the bowl between additions. Fold in the chopped pecans and coconut flakes.
6. Whip the egg whites to medium peaks. Fold them into the batter in three additions.
7. Divide the batter into eight buttered and floured 9-inch (22-centimeter) cake pans. Bake at 350°F (180°C) until the center of each cake bounces back when lightly pressed, approximately 30 minutes.
8. Cool the cakes in their pans for 5 minutes. Unmold them onto paper-lined sheet pans. Allow the cakes to cool completely. (The cakes may be frozen at this point for finishing at a later time.)
9. For each cake, level the surface, then place it on a cake board. Evenly coat it with a layer of Cream Cheese Icing. Level a second cake and place it, trimmed side down, on top of the Cream Cheese Icing. Apply a crumb coat of icing to the top and sides of each cake. Refrigerate until the icing is firm and then apply a final even coating of icing.
10. Press toasted coconut onto the sides of each cake. Pipe Cream Cheese Icing rosettes on the surface and decorate with pecan halves.

Approximate values per ¹⁄₁₂-cake serving: **Calories** 480, **Total fat** 19 g, **Saturated fat** 6 g, **Cholesterol** 5 mg, **Sodium** 210 mg, **Total carbohydrates** 76 g, **Protein** 4 g

BÛCHE DE NOËL (YULE LOG)

❶ Rolling the cake filled with ganache.

Yield: 16 to 18 Servings

Vanilla Spongecake (page 478), freshly baked	1 full sheet	1 full sheet
Simple Syrup (page 73)	9 fl. oz.	270 ml
Raspberry liqueur	3 fl. oz.	90 ml
Raspberry Ganache (page 585)	2 lb. 2 oz.	1125 g
Cocoa Gelée (page 608)	14 oz.	420 g
Chocolate cutouts, chocolate curls, baked meringue cookies and other garnishes	as needed	as needed

❶ Prepare the Vanilla Spongecake, making certain to bake it properly so that the cake remains flexible. Once the cake has cooled, remove the parchment paper. Transfer the cake to a clean sheet of parchment paper.

❷ Combine the Simple Syrup and raspberry liqueur. Moisten the entire surface of the cake with the syrup.

❸ Set aside one-fifth of the Raspberry Ganache. Spread the remaining ganache, which should be the consistency of peanut butter, over the entire surface of the cake.

❹ Cut a ¼-inch- (6-millimeter-) wide strip from the long side of the cake. (This strip will become the center of the Yule log when it is cut.) Place the strip back along one long edge of the cake, then roll up the cake tightly in a spiral.

❺ Wrap the cake tightly in parchment paper. Store the cake seam side down on a sheet pan. Freeze at least 2 hours or until needed.

❻ Unwrap the cake and place it seam side down on a cake board. Spread the reserved soft ganache evenly and smoothly over the entire surface of the cake, covering the bottom as well as the sides of the cake.

❷ The finished Yule log.

❼ Place the cake on an icing screen. Freeze or refrigerate until the outer ganache layer is firm.

❽ Place the icing screen and cake on a full-size sheet pan. Warm the Cocoa Gelée to 115°F (46°C). Pour the warmed gelée in a steady stream from left to right over the cake to coat the log evenly. Refrigerate the cake.

❾ To serve, cut a small slice from each end of the log. Decorate the cake with chocolate cutouts, spirals, meringue cookies and other appropriate garnish.

VARIATIONS:

Mocha Rum Yule Log—Prepare a chocolate spongecake. Substitute coffee buttercream for the ganache. Substitute rum for the raspberry liqueur.

Passion Fruit Yule Log—Substitute Passion Fruit Curd (page 493) for the ganache filling. Substitute Grand Passion liqueur for the raspberry liqueur. Ice the cake with Chocolate Ganache (page 458).

Approximate values per ⅟₁₈-cake serving: **Calories** 430, **Total fat** 16 g, **Saturated fat** 9 g, **Cholesterol** 185 mg, **Sodium** 60 mg, **Total carbohydrates** 63 g, **Protein** 8 g

ALMOND GENOISE

Yield: 2 Rounds, 7 in. (17 cm) each

Method: Egg foam

Almond paste	3 oz.	90 g	37%
Granulated sugar	6 oz.	180 g	75%
Egg yolk	0.6 oz. (1 yolk)	20 g	8%
Eggs	13 oz. (8 eggs)	390 g	162%
Vanilla extract	0.5 fl. oz.	15 ml	6%
Cake flour, sifted	8 oz.	240 g	100%
Unsalted butter, melted	2.5 oz.	75 g	31%
Total batter weight:	2 lb. 1 oz.	1010 g	419%

1. In the bowl of a mixer fitted with the paddle attachment, beat the almond paste and the sugar. Add the egg yolk. When fully incorporated, add the eggs and vanilla.
2. Remove the paddle from the mixer and replace it with a whip. Whip the mixture on medium speed 20 minutes.
3. Remove the bowl from the machine and carefully fold in the flour.
4. Remove one-eighth of the batter and mix it with the melted butter in a small bowl. Fold this mixture into the cake batter.
5. Divide the batter between two buttered and floured 7-inch (17-centimeter) cake pans. Bake at 375°F (190°C) until the cake bounces back when lightly pressed, approximately 40 minutes.
6. Cool, then fill and ice as desired.

VARIATION:

Pistachio Almond Genoise—Carefully fold in 2 ounces (60 grams/25%) pistachio compound paste and 2 ounces (60 grams/25%) finely chopped pistachios after the butter is added in Step 4.

Approximate values per ⅛-cake serving: **Calories** 190, **Total fat** 8 g, **Saturated fat** 3.5 g, **Cholesterol** 130 mg, **Sodium** 35 mg, **Total carbohydrates** 25 g, **Protein** 5 g

VANILLA SPONGECAKE

Yield: 1 Full-Sheet Pan, 18 in. × 24 in. (45 cm × 60 cm)

Method: Egg foam

Eggs	11.5 oz. (7 eggs)	345 g	209%
Egg yolks	4.2 oz. (7 yolks)	125 g	76%
Granulated sugar	10 oz.	300 g	181%
Vanilla extract	1.5 fl. oz.	45 ml	27%
Cake flour, sifted	5.5 oz.	165 g	100%
Egg whites	7 oz. (7 whites)	210 g	127%
Powdered sugar, sifted	2 oz.	60 g	36%
Total batter weight:	2 lb. 9 oz.	1250 g	756%

Swiss Jelly Roll

1. Line a full-sheet pan with parchment. Lightly butter and flour the paper.
2. Whip the eggs, egg yolks, sugar and vanilla in a mixing bowl on medium high speed until the mixture forms thick ribbons.
3. Remove the yolk mixture from the machine and delicately fold in the flour. Set aside.
4. In a separate bowl, use a clean whip to whip the egg whites and powdered sugar to medium-soft peaks.
5. Lighten the yolk mixture with one-third of the whipped egg whites, then fold in the remaining whites.
6. Spread the spongecake batter evenly on the prepared sheet pan, using an offset spatula. Bake at 425°F (220°C) until the cake springs back when lightly touched, approximately 7 to 8 minutes.

VARIATIONS:

Swiss Jelly Roll—Invert the cake onto a piece of parchment dusted with powdered sugar. Carefully remove the paper on which the cake baked. Spread the cake with 2 pounds (960 grams/580%) seedless raspberry or other jam. Roll the cake tightly. Cut into two rolls. Trim the ends and dust with more sugar before serving.

Pistachio Spongecake—Add 1.5 ounces (45 grams/27%) pistachio compound to the yolk mixture once it is whipped. Add 3 ounces (90 grams/54%) pistachio flour to the dry ingredients. Fold 5 ounces (150 grams/91%) coarsely chopped pistachios into the batter.

Approximate values per 1-oz. (30-g) serving: **Calories** 70, **Total fat** 2 g, **Saturated fat** 0.5 g, **Cholesterol** 70 mg, **Sodium** 20 mg, **Total carbohydrates** 11 g, **Protein** 2 g, **Claims**—low fat

LADYFINGERS

Ladyfingers are made from a spongecake batter that is piped into finger-length strips. After baking, these soft cakes may be eaten plain or filled as a cookie or petit four. They are equally good when dried out in the oven, like biscotti. These versatile cakes are used to line the mold for a Bavarian dessert. For convenience, the batter may be piped close together to form a strip after baking and used to line a mold or torte ring. See Tiramisu Torte (page 628).

When the flour is overmixed into the fragile batter, it will become runny; the ladyfingers will not hold their shape and will lose their delicate texture after baking. Dusting the piped batter twice with powdered sugar creates appealing and delicate pearls on the surface of the ladyfingers after baking.

Plain baked ladyfingers.

Yield: 2 lb. 3 oz. (1080 g); approximately 95 Cookies, 4 in. (10 cm) each

Method: Egg foam

Bread flour	5 oz.	150 g	100%
Cornstarch	4 oz.	120 g	80%
Egg yolks	7 oz. (12 yolks)	210 g	140%
Vanilla extract	0.15 fl. oz. (1 tsp.)	5 ml	3%
Egg whites	12 oz. (12 whites)	360 g	240%
Granulated sugar	7.5 oz.	235 g	150%
Total batter weight:	2 lb. 3 oz.	1080 g	713%
Powdered sugar for dusting	as needed	as needed	

1. Sift the flour and cornstarch together. Set aside.
2. Whip the egg yolks and vanilla together in the bowl of a 6 quart (6.5 liter) mixer fitted with the whip attachment until the mixture is thick and creamy.
3. Simultaneously in the bowl of a second mixer fitted with the whip attachment, whip the egg whites and granulated sugar until the mixture holds stiff peaks.
4. Using a balloon whisk, gently stir the egg whites to restore a smooth appearance. Add the whipped yolks all at once into the egg whites. Gently fold the two together using a rubber spatula or a balloon whisk until the mixture is streaked in appearance and is not completely combined. Gently fold in the flour, taking care not to deflate the batter.
5. Place the batter into a pastry bag fitted with a medium plain tip. Pipe 4-inch- (10-centimeter-) long cookies onto paper-lined sheet pans.
6. Sprinkle the surface of the piped batter with powdered sugar. Let it sit for a few minutes until the powdered sugar dissolves. Sprinkle a second time with more powdered sugar.
7. Bake at 410°F (210°C) until the cookies bounce back when lightly pressed, approximately 9 to 11 minutes.

Filling ladyfingers with buttercream.

VARIATION:

Ladyfinger Bands—Pipe ladyfingers 4 inches (10 centimeters) long, spaced so that they touch and form a strip the length of a sheet pan. Bake and use the band of ladyfingers to line pans for tortes or Bavarians.

Approximate values per cookie: **Calories** 20, **Total fat** 0 g, **Saturated fat** 0 g, **Cholesterol** 15 mg, **Sodium** 0 mg, **Total carbohydrates** 4 g, **Protein** 1 g, **Claims**—fat free; no saturated fat; low cholesterol; no sodium; low calorie

TRES LECHES CAKE

Yield: 2 Cakes, 8 in. (20 cm) each		**Method:** Egg foam	

Cake:

Pastry flour	6 oz.	180 g	100%
Baking powder	0.5 oz.	15 g	8%
Egg yolks	5 oz. (8 yolks)	150 g	83%
Granulated sugar	5 oz.	150 g	83%
Egg whites	8 oz. (8 whites)	240 g	133%
Cream of tartar	0.04 oz. (⅛ tsp.)	1.2 g	0.7%
Total batter weight:	1 lb. 8 oz.	736 g	408%

Syrup:

Sweetened condensed milk	14 fl. oz.	420 ml	
Evaporated milk*	12 fl. oz.	360 ml	
Heavy cream or crème fraîche	1 pt.	480 ml	
Vanilla extract	0.3 fl. oz. (2 tsp.)	10 ml	
Rum, dark	2 fl. oz.	60 ml	
Crème Chantilly (page 502)	1 qt.	1 lt	
Common French Meringue (page 410) or Italian Meringue (page 413), piped in teardrop shapes, sprinkled with desiccated coconut, dusted with cocoa powder, baked	40 meringues	40 meringues	
Mango, ripe, cut in cubes	1 lb.	480 g	
Strawberries	1 pt.	0.5 lt	
Neutral glaze	as needed	as needed	

1 Sift the flour and the baking powder together and set aside.

2 Whip the egg yolks with half of the sugar on high speed until they reach the ribbon stage, approximately 2 minutes.

3 In a separate bowl, use a clean whip to beat the egg whites until foamy. Add the cream of tartar and the remaining sugar. Whip on medium speed until the whites are glossy and stiff but not dry.

4 Fold one-third of the egg whites into the whipped yolks, then fold in the remaining whites.

5 Sprinkle one-third of the sifted flour over the batter and fold in. Repeat until all the flour is incorporated.

6 Divide the batter between two greased and floured 8-inch (20-centimeter) pans. Bake at 350°F (180°C) until the cake is golden brown and spongy, approximately 30 minutes.

7 Stir the condensed milk, evaporated milk, cream, vanilla, and rum together in a bowl. Invert the hot cakes onto serving platters. Remove the parchment paper. Ladle the milk syrup over the hot cakes. (If necessary, poke holes in the cakes with a toothpick to allow the cakes to absorb more of the milk syrup.) Let the cakes soak at least 3 hours before serving.

8 Ice each moistened cake with Crème Chantilly. Place the cakes on cake boards. Surround the bottom edge of each cake with the baked meringues.

9 Using a piping bag fitted with a medium plain pastry tip, pipe a teardrop-shaped border of Crème Chantilly along the top edge of each cake. Top each cake with the cubed mango and strawberries. Coat the fruit lightly with neutral glaze.

*For this classic Latin American dish, media crèma is often used in the syrup that moistens the cake. It is a canned milk available in the ethnic food section of many markets and can be used in place of some or all of the evaporated milk.

Approximate values per ¹⁄₁₀-cake serving: **Calories** 370, **Total fat** 14 g, **Saturated fat** 8 g, **Cholesterol** 130 mg, **Sodium** 220 mg, **Total carbohydrates** 47 g, **Protein** 11 g, **Calcium** 35%

COCONUT LEMON CAKE

Yield: 2 Layer Cakes, 7–8 in. (17–20 cm) each

Method: Egg foam

Lemon or Lime Curd (page 493), chilled until firm	2 lb. 8 oz.	1200 g
Coconut Macadamia Cake (page 620), prepared without nuts	4 rounds	4 rounds
Crème Chantilly (page 502)	as needed	as needed
Toasted coconut	as needed	as needed

1. Set aside one-quarter of the Lemon Curd for the final decoration of the cakes.
2. Working with two cake rounds at a time, cut each Coconut Macadamia Cake round in half horizontally into two layers using a serrated knife. Place one layer of cake onto a cake board.
3. Pipe a ring of Crème Chantilly around the edge of the cake using a medium piping tip. Spread an even layer of Lemon Curd in the center of the cake using an offset spatula.
4. Set another cake layer over the Lemon Curd. Repeat the process in Step 3 twice more. Then set the fourth and final cake layer on top.
5. Repeat Steps 2 through 4 with the other two cake rounds.
6. Ice the cakes with a thin layer of Crème Chantilly, then finish icing the cakes with a slightly thicker, smooth coating of Crème Chantilly. Mask the bottom sides of each cake with toasted coconut. Decorate with a ring of Crème Chantilly piped around the edge of each cake.
7. Stir the remaining Lemon Curd well to loosen it, warming it slightly if necessary to make it more fluid. Pour the curd into the center of each ring of piped cream.

Approximate values per 1/10-cake serving: **Calories** 500, **Total fat** 34 g, **Saturated fat** 18 g, **Cholesterol** 220 mg, **Sodium** 80 mg, **Total carbohydrates** 46 g, **Protein** 6 g, **Vitamin A** 20%

1. Piping a ring of icing around the edge of the cake before filling it with lemon curd.

2. The finished cake.

CHOCOLATE FLOURLESS CAKE

VINCENT ON CAMELBACK, PHOENIX, AZ

Chef Vincent Guerithault

Yield: 21 Servings

Method: Egg foam

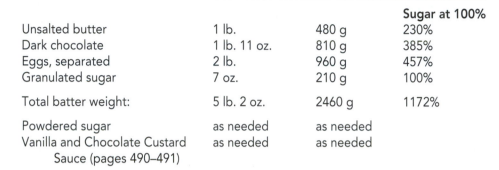

			Sugar at 100%
Unsalted butter	1 lb.	480 g	230%
Dark chocolate	1 lb. 11 oz.	810 g	385%
Eggs, separated	2 lb.	960 g	457%
Granulated sugar	7 oz.	210 g	100%
Total batter weight:	5 lb. 2 oz.	2460 g	1172%
Powdered sugar	as needed	as needed	
Vanilla and Chocolate Custard Sauce (pages 490–491)	as needed	as needed	

1. Melt the butter and chocolate in a large bowl over a bain marie.
2. Whisk the egg yolks into the melted chocolate.
3. Whip the egg whites until shiny. Add the granulated sugar and whip until very stiff. Fold into the chocolate. Pour the batter into a full-size hotel pan lined with buttered parchment.
4. Bake at 400°F (200°C) for 10 minutes. Lower the oven temperature to 350°F (180°C) and continue baking until done, approximately 40 minutes. A cake tester will not come out clean, even though the cake is done.
5. Invert the cake onto the back of a sheet pan. Cool completely, and then dust with powdered sugar. Serve garnished with Vanilla and Chocolate Custard Sauce.

Approximate values per 4-oz. (120-g) serving: **Calories** 470, **Total fat** 35 g, **Saturated fat** 20 g, **Cholesterol** 250 mg, **Sodium** 65 mg, **Total carbohydrates** 32 g, **Protein** 8 g, **Vitamin A** 25%

CREAM CHEESE ICING

Yield: 4 lb. 8 oz. (2295 g)

Cream cheese, softened	3 lb.	1440 g
Powdered sugar, sifted	1 lb. 4 oz.	600 g
Unsalted butter, softened	8 oz.	240 g
Vanilla extract	0.5 fl. oz.	15 ml

1. Blend the cream cheese on low speed in the bowl of a mixer fitted with the paddle attachment. Add the powdered sugar in four increments stirring well between additions and scraping down the bowl frequently.
2. Add the softened butter and vanilla. Blend on low speed until smooth, scraping down the bowl frequently.

Approximate values per serving: **Calories** 130, **Total fat** 6 g, **Saturated fat** 3 g, **Cholesterol** 15 mg, **Sodium** 45 mg, **Total carbohydrates** 17 g, **Protein** 1 g, **Vitamin A** 6%

TRADITIONAL FRENCH BUTTERCREAM

Yield: 3 lb. 12 oz. (1800 g)

Granulated sugar	1 lb. 3 oz.	570 g
Corn syrup or glucose	3 oz.	90 g
Water	6 fl. oz.	180 ml
Eggs	5 oz. (3 eggs)	150 g
Egg yolks	6 oz. (10 yolks)	180 g
Unsalted butter, room temperature	1 lb. 10 oz.	780 g
Vanilla extract	1 fl. oz.	30 ml

1. Combine the sugar, corn syrup and water in a small saucepan and bring to a boil.
2. Meanwhile, place the eggs and egg yolks in the bowl of a mixer fitted with the whip attachment; start whipping the mixture on medium speed the moment the sugar solution begins to boil.
3. Continue boiling until the syrup reaches 250°F (120°C). When the syrup is ready, increase the mixer speed to high and carefully pour the sugar syrup in a steady even stream down the inside of the bowl.
4. Continue whipping until the mixture is mousselike and cools to approximately 78°F (25°C).
5. Reduce the speed to medium and gradually add the butter; whip until light and aerated.
6. Add the vanilla and blend until combined.

VARIATIONS:

Mocha French Buttercream—Omit the vanilla extract. Add 1 fluid ounce (30 milliliters) coffee extract to the buttercream, then stir in 8 ounces (240 grams) melted and cooled bittersweet chocolate.

Citrus French Buttercream—Omit the vanilla extract. Add 0.5 fluid ounce (15 milliliters) orange extract and 0.5 fluid ounce (15 milliliters) lemon extract to the buttercream.

Approximate values per 1-oz. (30-g) serving: **Calories** 140, **Total fat** 11 g, **Saturated fat** 6 g, **Cholesterol** 70 mg, **Sodium** 5 mg, **Total carbohydrates** 10 g, **Protein** 1 g

FONDANT GLAZE

Yield: 12 oz. (365 g)

Fondant	9 oz.	270 g
Water	3 fl. oz.	90 ml
Vanilla extract	0.15 fl. oz. (1 tsp.)	5 ml

1. Combine the fondant and water in a bowl and set it over a pan of simmering water. Heat the fondant to 120°F (49°C), stirring occasionally to ensure even softening of the fondant.
2. Remove the fondant from heat. Stir in the vanilla. Add additional water if needed to obtain the desired consistency.
3. Use this glaze when it is between 110°F and 120°F (43°C and 49°C).

VARIATIONS:

Orange Fondant Glaze—Combine 1 pound (480 grams) fondant with 3 fluid ounces (90 milliliters) orange juice concentrate. Heat as directed. Add 2 fluid ounces (60 milliliters) additional orange juice concentrate and vanilla extract.

Raspberry Fondant Glaze—Substitute 3 ounces (90 grams) raspberry purée for the water. Omit the vanilla extract.

Approximate values per 1-oz. (30-g) serving: **Calories** 80, **Total fat** 0 g, **Saturated fat** 0 g, **Cholesterol** 0 mg, **Sodium** 10 mg, **Total carbohydrates** 20 g, **Protein** 0 g

WHITE CHOCOLATE BUTTERCREAM

Yield: Approximately 5 lb. (2400 g)

Granulated sugar	1 lb. 14 oz.	900 g
Water	8 fl. oz.	240 ml
Egg whites	9 oz. (9 whites)	270 g
Unsalted butter, softened	2 lb. 6 oz.	1140 g
White crème de cacao	3 fl. oz.	90 ml
White chocolate, melted	8 oz.	240 g

1. Cook the sugar and water to 242°F (117°C), then pour into a measuring container with a handle for easier pouring.
2. Place the egg whites in the bowl of a 6 quart (6.5 liter) mixer fitted with the whip attachment. Start whipping the egg whites when the sugar reaches 235°F (113°C).
3. When the whites are whipped to firm peaks, add the hot sugar syrup slowly while continuing to whip at low speed. Whip until completely cool.
4. Add the butter and whip until smooth.
5. Add the crème de cacao to the white chocolate. Whip until smooth, and then add the chocolate to the buttercream.

Approximate values per 1-oz. (30-g) serving: **Calories** 140, **Total fat** 11 g, **Saturated fat** 7 g, **Cholesterol** 25 mg, **Sodium** 10 mg, **Total carbohydrates** 10 g, **Protein** 1 g, **Vitamin A** 8%

CARAMEL NUT FILLING OR ICING

Use this filling in a cake or torte or as a topping on cheesecake.

Yield: 1 lb. 9 oz. (750 g)

Granulated sugar	6 oz.	180 g
Glucose or corn syrup	1.5 oz.	45 g
Water	3 fl. oz.	90 ml
Honey	2 oz.	60 g
Heavy cream, heated	6 fl. oz.	180 ml
Walnuts	5 oz.	150 g
Pecans	4 oz.	120 g
Vanilla extract	0.5 fl. oz.	15 ml

1. In a deep saucepan, bring the sugar, glucose and water to a boil.
2. Wash down any crystals that cling to the sides of the pan with a brush dipped in water. Cook the mixture without stirring until it turns a golden caramel color, approximately 350°F (177°C).
3. Add the honey and cream; be aware that the caramel mixture will rise when these ingredients are added. Reboil the mixture until it darkens to a medium amber color, approximately 3 to 4 minutes.
4. Remove from heat and add the walnuts and pecans. Let cool to room temperature, then stir in the vanilla. Use immediately to fill or ice a cake or torte (see Eros Torte, page 622) or store in the refrigerator. The filling or icing will keep 2 weeks when refrigerated.
5. Reheat the caramel filling to room temperature in a microwave oven or over a bain marie when it will be used to fill a torte. To use for icing, reheat to approximately 130°F (54°C), then spread on a cooled cheesecake or other cake layers. Let the caramel icing set before cutting.

Approximate values per 1-oz. (30-g) serving: **Calories** 140, **Total fat** 10 g, **Saturated fat** 2.5 g, **Cholesterol** 10 mg, **Sodium** 5 mg, **Total carbohydrates** 12 g, **Protein** 1 g

SAFETY ALERT
Caramelizing Sugar

Caramelizing sugar can cause serious burns. Use rubber gloves and take proper precautions to avoid hot sugar coming into direct contact with your skin.

SILKY GANACHE DELUXE

Some ganache formulas add only butter to the chocolate and cream mixture; however, the addition of an invert sugar makes a ganache unsurpassed in resilience and sheen.

Yield: 3 lb. 2 oz. (1500 g)

Heavy cream	1 pt.	480 ml
Granulated sugar	5 oz.	150 g
Corn syrup or glucose	5 oz.	150 g
Semisweet or bittersweet chocolate (58–68% cacao)	1 lb. 3 oz.	570 g
Unsalted butter	5 oz.	150 g

❶ In a large saucepan, bring the cream, sugar and corn syrup to a boil.

❷ Chop the chocolate and butter into walnut-size pieces and place them in a large mixing bowl.

❸ When the cream mixture boils, pour one-sixth of it over the chocolate-and-butter mixture. Stir the chocolate with a rubber spatula. Add the remaining cream in five increments, stirring well between additions to emulsify the ganache.

❹ Use immediately to glaze cakes or pastries or refrigerate. Heat refrigerated ganache over a bain marie to 120°F–130°F (48°C–54°C), depending on the coldness of the cake being iced.

Approximate values per 1-oz. (30-g) serving: **Calories** 120, **Total fat** 80 g, **Saturated fat** 6 g, **Cholesterol** 20 mg, **Sodium** 10 mg, **Total carbohydrates** 12 g, **Protein** 1 g

ORANGE MILK CHOCOLATE GANACHE

Yield: 2 lb. 2 oz. (1020 g)

Heavy cream	8 fl. oz.	240 ml
Milk	6 fl. oz.	180 ml
Glucose or corn syrup	2 oz.	60 g
Unsalted butter	2 oz.	60 g
Milk chocolate	14 oz.	420 g
Bittersweet chocolate	2 oz.	60 g
Orange oil (not extract)	2–3 drops	2–3 drops

❶ Bring the cream and milk to a boil in a large saucepan. Remove from the heat, then whisk in the glucose and butter.

❷ Chop the chocolate into walnut-size pieces and place it in a large mixing bowl. Add the orange oil. Pour one-fifth of the boiled cream over the chocolate. Stir with a rubber spatula. Add the remaining cream in four increments, stirring well between additions to emulsify the ganache.

Approximate values per 1-oz. (30-g) serving: **Calories** 110, **Total fat** 8 g, **Saturated fat** 5 g, **Cholesterol** 15 mg, **Sodium** 15 mg, **Total carbohydrates** 9 g, **Protein** 1 g

CHAPTER FOURTEEN

CUSTARDS, CREAMS AND SAUCES

- explain the function of eggs in custards and creams

- prepare a variety of custards and creams

- prepare a variety of mousses and other fillings

- prepare a variety of hot dessert soufflés and cheesecakes

- prepare a variety of dessert sauces

- use these products in preparing and serving other pastry and dessert items

THE SWEET CREAMS AND CUSTARDS FEATURED IN THIS CHAPTER are stand-alone desserts as well as the foundation of many tortes, pastries and frozen dessert preparations. Sweet custards are cooked mixtures of eggs, sugar and a liquid; flour or cornstarch may be added for thickening. Sweet custards can be flavored in a variety of ways and eaten hot or cold. Some are served alone as a dessert or used as a filling, topping or accompaniment for pies, pastries or cakes. Creams include whipped cream and mixtures lightened with whipped cream such as Bavarians, chiffons and mousses.

This chapter also covers the elegant sauces that put the finishing touch on plated desserts, adding finesse and refinement. Sauces may be based on fruit, custard, caramel or wine. What guides the pastry chef when making these custards, creams and sauces is creating a harmonious balance of sweetness, flavor, aroma and appearance.

SAFETY ALERT
Eggs

Eggs are high-protein foods that are easily contaminated by bacteria such as salmonella that cause food-borne illnesses. Because custards cannot be heated to temperatures high enough to destroy these bacteria without first curdling the eggs, it is especially important that sanitary guidelines be followed in preparing the egg products discussed in this chapter.

1. Cleanliness is important: Wash your hands thoroughly before beginning; be sure to use clean, sanitized bowls, utensils and storage containers.
2. When breaking or separating eggs, do not allow the exterior of the eggshell to come into contact with the raw egg.
3. Heat the milk to just below a boil before combining it with the eggs. This reduces the final cooking time.
4. Chill the finished product quickly in a shallow container set over an ice bath and refrigerate immediately.
5. Do not store any custard mixture, cooked or uncooked, at room temperature.

CUSTARDS

A **custard** is any liquid thickened by the coagulation of egg proteins. As discussed in Chapter 3, Principles of Baking, proteins coagulate, forming a network of tight bonds, when heated. Undiluted, egg proteins solidify into a tight mass at 160°F (71°C). The proportion of eggs to the other ingredients in the mixture affects egg coagulation; cream, milk and sugar interrupt the formation of these bonds, slowing coagulation so that the mixture thickens into a creamy sauce or a tender **pudding**. A custard's consistency depends on the ratio of eggs to liquid, whether whole eggs or just yolks are used, and the type of liquid used. The more eggs used, the thicker and richer the final product will be. The richer the liquid (cream versus milk, for example), the thicker the final product.

A custard can be stirred or baked. A **stirred custard** tends to be soft, rich and creamy. A **baked custard**, typically prepared in a water bath in the oven, is usually firm enough to unmold and slice.

Stirred Custards

A stirred custard is cooked on the stove top either directly in a saucepan or over a double boiler. It must be stirred throughout the cooking process to stabilize the eggs and prevent curdling. Curdling occurs when the egg proteins are overheated and overcoagulate, which forces any liquid trapped within the protein bonds to separate out of the mixture.

A stirred custard can be used as a dessert sauce, incorporated into a complex dessert or eaten alone. The stirred custards most commonly used in food service operations are **vanilla custard sauce (crème anglaise)** and **pastry cream (crème pâtissière)**. Other popular stirred custards are **curd fillings** (page 493) and **sabayon** (page 494).

VANILLA CUSTARD SAUCE (CRÈME ANGLAISE)

Vanilla custard sauce (Fr. *crème anglaise*) is made with egg yolks, sugar and milk or half-and-half. Usually flavored with vanilla bean or pure vanilla extract, a custard sauce can also be flavored with liqueur, chocolate, ground nuts or extracts.

Custard sauce is prepared on the stove top over direct heat in a nonreactive saucepan. (Custard sauce can also be prepared in a bowl over a bain marie of simmering water. This method, although time-consuming, can help prevent the custard from overcooking.) A small portion of the heated milk mixture is stirred into the yolks. Then the yolk mixture is stirred into the heated milk. This step, called **tempering**, helps keep the egg yolks from setting. When making a custard sauce, be extremely careful to stir the mixture continually and do not allow it to boil, or it will curdle. Do not allow the temperature to exceed 190°F (88°C) or the custard will break. Use a thermometer to monitor the custard as it cooks, removing it from the heat when it reaches 185°F (85°C). Carryover cooking will bring the custard to the proper temperature before the mixture overcooks and curdles. A properly made custard sauce should be smooth and thick enough to lightly coat the back of a spoon. It should not contain any noticeable bits of cooked egg.

A custard sauce can be served with cakes, pastries, fruits and soufflés and is often used for decorating dessert plates. It may be served hot or cold. It is also used as the base for many ice creams.

A very thick version of custard sauce, more like a **pudding**, can be made using heavy cream and additional egg yolks. This custard is often served over fruit in a small ramekin and then topped with caramelized sugar for a dessert known as **crème brûlée** ("burnt cream"). See the formula on page 497.

PASTRY CREAM (CRÈME PÂTISSIÈRE)

Pastry cream (Fr. *crème pâtissière*) is a stirred custard made with egg yolks, sugar and milk and thickened with starch (flour, cornstarch or a combination of the two). Because the starch protects the egg yolks from curdling, pastry cream can be boiled. In fact, it must be boiled to fully gelatinize the starch and eliminate its raw taste. Butter is added to enrich pastry cream and soften its texture.

Pastry cream can be flavored with chocolate, liqueurs, extracts or fruits. (Pudding is nothing more than a flavored pastry cream.) It is used for filling éclairs, cream puffs, Napoleons, fruit tarts and other pastries. Pastry cream thickened with cornstarch is also the filling for cream pies (see Chapter 11, Pies and Tarts). Pastry cream is thick enough to hold its shape without making pastry doughs soggy.

Pastry cream can be rather heavy. Folding in whipped cream to produce a **mousseline** can lighten it, or Italian meringue can be folded in to produce a **crème Chiboust**.

tempering heating gently and gradually; refers to the process of slowly adding a hot liquid to eggs or other foods to raise their temperature without causing them to curdle

pudding a thick, spoonable dessert custard, usually made with eggs, milk, sugar and flavorings and thickened with flour or another starch

crème brûlée (krehm broo-LAY) French for "burnt cream"; used to describe a rich dessert custard topped with a crust of caramelized sugar

mousseline (moos-uh-LEEN) a cream or sauce lightened by folding in whipped cream

crème Chiboust (krehm chee-BOOS) a vanilla pastry cream lightened by folding in Italian meringue; traditionally used in a gâteau St. Honoré

PROCEDURE FOR PREPARING VANILLA CUSTARD SAUCE

1. Place milk and/or cream in a heavy, nonreactive saucepan; add a vanilla bean to **steep** in the cream if desired.

2. In a mixing bowl, whisk together the egg yolks and sugar. Start whisking as soon as the egg yolks come into contact with the sugar. If allowed to stand, the yolks and sugar will form lumps in the finished preparation. Do not use an electric mixer, as it incorporates too much air.

3. Bring the liquid just to a boil. Temper the egg mixture with approximately one-third of the hot liquid.

4. Pour the tempered eggs into the remaining hot liquid and return the mixture to the heat. The stove's temperature can be as hot as you dare: the lower the temperature, the longer the custard will take to thicken; the higher the temperature, the greater the risk of curdling. The sauce will lightly coat the back of a spoon.

5. Cook, stirring constantly, until thickened. Custard sauce should reach a temperature of 185°F (85°C).

6. Immediately remove the cooked custard from the hot saucepan to avoid overcooking. Butter or other flavorings can be added at this time.

7. Immediately pour the custard through a fine mesh strainer into a clean bowl set over an ice bath. Cool the custard. Store it in a clean, shallow container.

MISE EN PLACE

▸ Split vanilla bean in half.
▸ Set up an ice bath.

❶ Tempering the eggs.

❷ The properly cooked sauce lightly coats the spatula.

❸ Straining the sauce into a bowl.

VANILLA CUSTARD SAUCE (CRÈME ANGLAISE)

Yield: Approximately 40 fl. oz. (1200 ml)   **Method:** Stirred custard

Half-and-half	1 qt.	1 lt
Vanilla bean, split	1	1
Egg yolks	8 oz. (12 yolks)	240 g
Granulated sugar	10 oz.	300 g

❶ In a heavy nonreactive saucepan, bring the half-and-half and vanilla bean just to a boil.

❷ Whisk the egg yolks and sugar together in a mixing bowl. Temper the egg mixture with approximately one-third of the hot half-and-half, then return the entire mixture to the saucepan with the remaining half-and-half.

❸ Cook the sauce over medium heat, stirring constantly, until it is thick enough to lightly coat the back of a spoon. Do not allow the mixture to go above 185°F (85°C) or the mixture will curdle. Do not allow the sauce to boil.

❹ As soon as the sauce thickens, remove it from the heat and pour it through a fine mesh strainer into a clean bowl. Chill the sauce over an ice bath, then cover and keep refrigerated. The sauce should last 3 to 4 days.

VARIATIONS:

Chocolate Custard Sauce—Stir 6 ounces (180 grams) finely chopped dark chocolate into the strained custard while it is still warm. The heat of the custard will melt the chocolate.

Coffee Custard Sauce—Add 1 fluid ounce (30 milliliters) coffee extract or compound to the warm custard.

Earl Grey Crème Anglaise—Omit the vanilla bean. Steep four Earl Grey tea bags 4 minutes in the half-and-half. Remove the tea bags, then prepare the sauce as directed.

Frangelico Custard Sauce—Omit the vanilla bean. Stir in 0.08 fluid ounce (2.5 milliliters/ ½ teaspoon) vanilla extract and 1 to 1.5 fluid ounces (30 to 45 milliliters) Frangelico, to taste.

Ginger Custard Sauce—Omit the vanilla bean. Steep 3 ounces (90 grams) chopped fresh ginger 10 minutes in the half-and-half. Reheat and continue preparing the sauce as directed. The chopped ginger will be strained out in Step 4.

Pistachio Custard Sauce—Omit the vanilla bean. Place 4 ounces (120 grams) finely chopped pistachio nuts in the saucepan with the barely boiling half-and-half. Remove from the heat, cover and steep up to 1 hour. Uncover the mixture, reheat and continue preparing the sauce as directed. The ground nuts will be strained out in Step 4. One fluid ounce (30 milliliters) pistachio compound may be added to intensify the flavor.

Saffron Custard Sauce—Omit the vanilla bean. Steep ⅛ teaspoon (0.5 milliliter) saffron with the half-and-half.

Approximate values per 1-fl.-oz. (30-ml) serving: **Calories** 80, **Total fat** 4.5 g, **Saturated fat** 2.5 g, **Cholesterol** 75 mg, **Sodium** 15 mg, **Total carbohydrates** 8 g, **Protein** 2 g, **Vitamin A** 6%

PROCEDURE FOR SALVAGING CURDLED VANILLA CUSTARD SAUCE

1 Strain the sauce into a bowl. Place the bowl over an ice bath and whisk vigorously.

2 If this does not smooth out the overcooked sauce, place the sauce in a blender and process for a few moments.

While these steps may reincorporate the curdled eggs, the resulting sauce will be thin and less creamy than a properly prepared vanilla custard sauce.

Use Table 14.2 to troubleshoot preparing custards and creams.

PROCEDURE FOR PREPARING PASTRY CREAM

1 Place milk and/or cream and some of the sugar in a heavy, nonreactive saucepan; add a vanilla bean to steep in the cream if desired.

2 In a mixing bowl, whisk the egg yolks. Combine the remaining sugar and starch in a separate bowl to help starch disperse evenly. Then add the dry ingredients to the yolks. Start whisking as soon as the egg yolks come into contact with the mixture. If allowed to stand, the yolks and sugar will form lumps in the finished preparation. Do not use an electric mixer, as it incorporates too much air.

3 Bring the liquid just to a boil. Temper the egg mixture with approximately one-third of the hot liquid.

4 Pour the tempered eggs into the remaining hot liquid and return the mixture to the heat.

5 Cook, stirring constantly, until the pastry cream comes to a true boil, and begins to thicken slightly. Boil for up to 2 minutes to thicken.

6 Immediately remove the cooked pastry cream from the hot saucepan to avoid overcooking. Do not strain as this will thin out the custard. Stir in any butter or other flavorings without overmixing.

7 Cool over an ice bath. Store in a clean, shallow container. Cover with plastic wrap to prevent the pastry cream from developing a thick skin and refrigerate.

MISE EN PLACE

▶ Split vanilla bean in half.
▶ Set up an ice bath.

❶ Stirring the pastry cream as it comes to a boil.

❷ Folding butter into the cooked pastry cream.

PASTRY CREAM
(CRÈME PÂTISSIÈRE)

Yield: Approximately 3 lb. (1440 g)   **Method:** Stirred custard

Milk	1 qt.	1 lt
Vanilla bean, split	1	1
Granulated sugar	7.5 oz.	225 g
Egg yolks	6 oz. (10 yolks)	180 g
Cornstarch	2.5 oz.	75 g
Unsalted butter	2 oz.	60 g

❶ Bring the milk, vanilla bean and 3 ounces (120 grams) of the sugar to a boil in a large nonreactive saucepan.

❷ Whisk the egg yolks in a mixing bowl. In a separate bowl, combine the remaining sugar and the cornstarch. Whisk the sugar mixture into the egg yolks.

❸ Temper the yolk mixture with one-quarter of the boiling milk. Return the yolk mixture to the pan and cook, whisking vigorously, until the cream boils and is well thickened. Allow the pastry cream to boil approximately 2 minutes, stirring constantly.

❹ Remove the pastry cream from heat and immediately pour it into a clean mixing bowl.

❺ Fold in the butter until melted. Do not overmix, as this will thin the custard.

❻ Cover by placing plastic wrap on the surface of the custard. Chill over an ice bath. Remove the vanilla bean just before using the pastry cream.

Note: When flour or a combination of flour and cornstarch is used to thicken pastry cream, it will need to be boiled longer for the starch to gelatinize and thicken properly. For a firm pastry cream, add an additional 0.5 ounces (15 grams) cornstarch to this formula.

VARIATIONS:

Chocolate Pastry Cream—Stir 4 ounces (120 grams) finely chopped dark chocolate into the strained custard while it is still warm. The heat of the custard will melt the chocolate.

Coffee Pastry Cream—Add 1 fluid ounce (30 milliliters) coffee extract or compound to the warm custard.

Coconut Pastry Cream—Replace 16 fluid ounces (480 milliliters) of the milk with an equal amount of unsweetened canned coconut milk.

Mousseline Pastry Cream—Whip 12 fluid ounces (360 milliliters) heavy cream to stiff peaks. Fold into the chilled pastry cream. Yield: 3 pounds 12 ounces (1800 grams)

White Chocolate Mousseline Pastry Cream—Remove the pastry cream from the heat in Step 3 and stir in 10 ounces (300 grams) finely chopped white chocolate and 0.5 fluid ounce (15 milliliters) vanilla extract. Chill the cream to 80°F (27°C), then fold in 8 fluid ounces (360 milliliters) heavy cream whipped to medium peaks. Cover and chill until needed. Yield: 3 pounds 11 ounces (1775 grams)

Chocolate Buttercream Filling—Whip 1 pound (480 grams) butter, 10 ounces (300 grams) powdered sugar and 1 fluid ounce (30 milliliters) vanilla extract in a mixing bowl until light. Add 1 pound 8 ounces (720 grams) cold pastry cream and mix until combined. Turn off the machine and add 14 ounces (420 grams) semisweet chocolate, melted and cooled to 88°F (31°C). Whip until well blended. Yield: 4 pounds (1950 grams)

Approximate values per 1-fl.-oz. (30-ml) serving: **Calories** 50, **Total fat** 2.5 g, **Saturated fat** 1.5 g, **Cholesterol** 55 mg, **Sodium** 10 mg, **Total carbohydrates** 6 g, **Protein** 1 g

CURD FILLINGS

Curd is a type of stirred custard made with eggs, sugar, butter and fruit juice, usually citrus. It is a popular filling for tarts, cakes, tortes and sandwich cookies. Because of the quantity of sugar used to form the egg-and-butter emulsion, curd is usually flavored with an acid such as lemon or lime juice. A light curd formula follows. A one-step lemon curd formula, which produces a thicker product, appears on page 526.

PROCEDURE FOR PREPARING A FRUIT CURD FILLING

1 Combine sugar and fruit juice in a saucepan. Bring to a boil.

2 Whisk eggs in a nonreactive saucepan, then temper with the boiling sugar mixture. Bring to a boil, whisking constantly. Boil 1 minute.

3 Remove from the heat and whisk over an ice bath to cool to 120°F (49°C). If the mixture is too hot, the butter will separate and the curd will not set properly.

4 Add butter in several increments, stirring to combine. Immediately pour into pie or tart shells or chill, cover and refrigerate. Curd will keep refrigerated several days.

LEMON OR LIME CURD

Yield: 1 lb. 4 oz. (619 g) **Method:** Stirred custard

Lemon or lime juice	4 fl. oz.	120 ml
Granulated sugar	6.5 oz.	195 g
Lemon or lime zest, grated fine	0.14 oz. (2 tsp.)	4 g
Eggs	4 oz. (2 eggs)	120 g
Unsalted butter, room temperature	6 oz.	180 g

1 Combine the lemon or lime juice, 3 ounces (90 grams) of the sugar and the zest in a nonreactive saucepan. Bring to a boil.

2 Place the eggs and the remaining sugar in a nonreactive bowl. Mix well without aerating.

3 Temper the egg mixture with one-quarter of the boiling juice. Add the remaining juice and return to the stove.

4 Bring the mixture to a boil while whisking vigorously. Continue mixing and boil 1 minute.

5 Remove from the heat and chill over an ice bath until the mixture reaches 120°F (49°C).

6 Add the butter in five parts, beating well with a spatula after each addition.

7 Use immediately to fill a pie or tart shell or chill, cover and refrigerate. This formula makes enough curd to fill one 8-inch (20-centimeter) shell.

VARIATIONS:

Orange Bergamot Curd—Reduce the lemon juice to 3 fluid ounces (90 milliliters). Add 3 fluid ounces (90 milliliters) orange juice concentrate. Increase the total sugar to 9.5 ounces (285 grams). Omit the lemon zest. Increase the eggs to 6 ounces (180 grams) and the butter to 9 ounces (270 grams). Combine the orange juice concentrate, lemon juice and 5 ounces (150 grams) sugar. Bring to a boil and proceed as in Step 2. Add 10 drops essential oil of bergamot to the finished curd. Yield: 1 pound 14 ounces (915 grams)

Passion Fruit Curd—Reduce the lemon juice to 0.5 fluid ounce (15 milliliters). Increase the total sugar to 8 ounces (240 grams). Increase the eggs to 10 ounces (300 grams/ 6 eggs). Combine the lemon juice with 5 ounces (150 grams) passion fruit purée and 4 ounces (120 grams) of the sugar. Bring to a boil. Mix the eggs with the remaining 4 ounces (120 grams) sugar. Temper with the passion fruit mixture. Beat in 8 ounces (240 grams) butter. Yield: 2 pounds (945 grams)

Approximate values per 1-oz. (30-g) serving: **Calories** 110, **Total fat** 7 g, **Saturated fat** 4.5 g, **Cholesterol** 40 mg, **Sodium** 5 mg, **Total carbohydrates** 10 g, **Protein** 1 g

MISE EN PLACE

▶ Grate lemon or lime zest.
▶ Bring butter to room temperature.

1 Checking the temperature of the curd.

2 The finished curd.

SABAYON

Sabayon (sah-bay-OWN; It. *zabaglione*) is a foamy, stirred custard sauce made by whisking eggs, sugar and wine over low heat. The egg proteins coagulate, thickening the mixture, while the whisking incorporates air to make it light and fluffy. Usually a sweet wine such as Marsala or champagne is used. The mixture can be served warm, or it can be chilled and lightened with whipped cream or whipped egg whites. Sabayon may be served alone or as a sauce or topping with fruit or pastries such as spongecake or ladyfingers.

PROCEDURE FOR PREPARING SABAYON

1. Combine egg yolks, sugar and wine in the top of a double boiler.
2. Place the double boiler over low heat and whisk constantly until the sauce is foamy and thick enough to form a ribbon when the whisk is lifted.
3. Remove from the heat and serve immediately, or whisk over an ice bath until cool. If allowed to sit, the hot mixture may separate.
4. Whipped egg whites or whipped cream may be folded into the cooled sabayon.

MISE EN PLACE

▶ Set up a bain marie over simmering water.

The thickened sabayon.

flan a firm custard baked over a layer of caramelized sugar and inverted for service

CHAMPAGNE SABAYON

Yield: 1 qt. (1 lt)		**Method:** Stirred custard
Egg yolks	4.8 oz. (8 yolks)	144 g
Granulated sugar	4 oz.	120 g
Salt	0.05 oz. (¼ tsp.)	1.5 g
Marsala wine	2 fl. oz.	60 ml
Dry champagne	6 fl. oz.	180 ml
Heavy cream (optional)	8 fl. oz.	240 ml

1. Combine the egg yolks, sugar and salt in a stainless steel bowl.
2. Add the Marsala and champagne to the egg mixture.
3. Place the bowl over a pan of barely simmering water. Whisk vigorously until the sauce is thick and pale yellow, approximately 10 minutes. Serve immediately.
4. To prepare a sabayon mousseline, place the bowl of sabayon over an ice bath and continue whisking until completely cold. Whip the cream to soft peaks and fold it into the cold sabayon.

Approximate values per 1-fl.-oz. (30-ml) serving: **Calories** 50, **Total fat** 4 g, **Saturated fat** 2 g, **Cholesterol** 60 mg, **Sodium** 25 mg, **Total carbohydrates** 4 g, **Protein** 1 g, **Vitamin A** 6%

Baked Custards

A baked custard is based on the same principle as a stirred custard: a liquid thickened by the coagulation of egg proteins. However, with a baked custard, the thickening occurs in an oven. The container of custard is usually placed in a water bath (bain marie) to help the custard cook evenly and protect the eggs from curdling. Even though the water bath's temperature will not exceed 212°F (100°C), care must be taken not to bake the custards for too long or at too high a temperature. An overbaked custard will be watery or curdled; a properly baked custard should be smooth-textured and firm enough to slice.

Baked custards include simple mixtures of whole eggs or yolks, sugar and milk such as crème caramel, called **flan** in Spain and Mexico. Baked custards also include mixtures in which other ingredients are suspended—for example, cheesecake, rice pudding, bread pudding and quiche.

The texture and flavor of these custards will vary depending on the quantity and types of ingredients used. Whole eggs are used in a simple egg custard such as flan to provide both richness from the fat in the yolk and structure from the protein in the white. This is important in order for the flan to maintain its shape when unmolded. Using heavy cream and additional egg yolks such as in the crème brûlée on page 520 provides added richness and a soft, velvety texture; because the dessert is served in a ramekin, protein strength is not required.

CRÈME CARAMEL

Crème caramel, crème renversée and flan all refer to an egg custard baked over a layer of caramelized sugar and inverted for service. The caramelized sugar produces a golden-brown surface on the inverted custard and a thin caramel sauce. The procedure for preparing crème caramel is illustrated with the formula for Toffee Caramel Flan.

> ### SAFETY ALERT
> ### Caramelizing Sugar
>
> Caramelizing sugar can cause serious burns. Use rubber gloves and take proper precautions to avoid hot sugar coming into direct contact with your skin.

TOFFEE CARAMEL FLAN

Yield: 10 Ramekins, 6 oz. (180 ml) each   **Method:** Baked custard

Granulated sugar	1 lb. 4 oz.	600 g
Water	8 fl. oz.	240 ml
Milk	24 fl. oz.	720 ml
Heavy cream	24 fl. oz.	720 ml
Cinnamon sticks	2	2
Vanilla bean, split	1	1
Eggs	13 oz. (8 eggs)	390 g
Egg yolks	2.4 oz. (4 yolks)	72 g
Brown sugar	6 oz.	180 g
Molasses	0.75 oz.	22 g
Amaretto liqueur	1 fl. oz.	30 ml
Fresh fruit (optional)	as needed	as needed
Caramelized almonds (optional)	as needed	as needed

1 Combine the granulated sugar with the water in a small heavy saucepan; bring to a boil. Cook until the sugar reaches a deep golden brown. Immediately pour approximately 2 tablespoons (30 milliliters) of the sugar into each of the ramekins. Tilt each ramekin to spread the caramel evenly along the bottom. Arrange the ramekins in a 2-inch- (5-centimeter-) deep hotel pan and set aside.

2 Combine the milk, cream, cinnamon sticks and vanilla bean in a large saucepan. Bring just to a boil, cover and remove from the heat. Allow this mixture to steep approximately 30 minutes.

3 Whisk the eggs, egg yolks, brown sugar, molasses and amaretto together in a large bowl.

4 Uncover the milk mixture and return it to the stove top. Bring just to a boil. Temper the egg-and-sugar mixture with approximately one-third of the hot milk. Whisk in the remaining hot milk.

5 Strain the custard through a fine mesh strainer. Pour into the caramel-lined ramekins, filling to just below the rim.

6 Pour enough warm water into the hotel pan to reach halfway up the sides of the ramekins. Bake at 325°F (160°C) approximately 30 to 40 minutes. The custards should be almost set, but still slightly soft in the center.

7 Completely chill the baked custards before serving. To unmold, run a small knife around the edge of the custard, invert onto the serving plate and give the ramekin a firm sideways shake. Garnish with fresh fruit, caramelized almonds, caramel decorations or chocolate decorations, if desired.

Approximate values per serving: **Calories** 670, **Total fat** 33 g, **Saturated fat** 19 g, **Cholesterol** 355 mg, **Sodium** 120 mg, **Total carbohydrates** 82 g, **Protein** 10 g, **Vitamin A** 40%, **Calcium** 20%

MISE EN PLACE

▶ Gather the ramekins and hotel pan.
▶ Preheat oven to 325°F (160°C).
▶ Split vanilla bean in half.

1 Filling the ramekins for flans.

2 The baked flan garnished with fresh fruit, caramel and chocolate decorations.

CRÈME BRÛLÉE

Crème brûlée (krehm broo-LAY) can be made as either a stirred or a baked custard. (It is basically a thick version of custard sauce.) Neither version should be considered superior, however; they are simply different. The stirred or stove top method is quicker but requires constant attention and a practiced feel for the custard's consistency. The finished custard will be heavier, creamier and softer than its baked counterpart. The baked version is served in the ramekin or bowl in which it was baked. Unlike crème caramel or flan, baked crème brûlée is not inverted or removed from its baking dish for service.

Gentle heat is important for both methods. Overcooked stirred custard will curdle, turning into scrambled eggs. Overcooked baked custard will become watery, its texture marred with small bubbles.

Additional flavors and textures can be added to the custard in several ways:

▶ Placing a layer of fresh berries or fruit compote under the custard

▶ Incorporating fruit, nuts or liqueurs directly into the custard

▶ Adding flavoring compounds and extracts to the custard

▶ Infusing the heavy cream with nuts, herbs, spices, tea or other flavorings before making the custard

If fruit purées or other liquids are used, the quantity of cream will have to be adjusted or the custard may be too watery or unable to set properly. A formula for the baked version follows; a stirred version appears on page 520.

A variation of crème brûlée on page 518 is used as a tart filling. Freezing the baked mixture allows it to be removed from its mold and placed in a tart or torte.

PROCEDURE FOR PREPARING BAKED CRÈME BRÛLÉE

1. Heat cream or half-and-half and flavorings in a saucepan just until warm. Infuse the cream with any flavorings. Reheat the cream if necessary.
2. Blend egg yolks and sugar. Stir in the heated cream.
3. Strain the cream into a pitcher or large measuring cup.
4. Pour the hot cream into the ramekins. They may be partially filled with fresh berries, fruit or nuts.
5. Bake the custards in a water bath until set, barely jiggling in the center.
6. Cool the ramekins, then cover and refrigerate them until chilled.
7. Sprinkle the surface of the ramekins with a thin layer of sugar. Brown the sugar with a propane torch or salamander without heating the custard.

CLASSIC CUSTARD

James Beard called crème brûlée "one of the greatest desserts in the realm of cooking." The secret to crème brûlée's success probably lies in its comfort-food familiarity. It is a rich, creamy concoction of egg yolks, sugar and cream served very cold and topped with a crisp, crunchy layer of deeply caramelized sugar. The contrast of textures and flavors satisfies multiple taste desires.

Despite its French name, crème brûlée (literally, "burnt cream") is most likely a product of Great Britain. Perhaps the earliest recipe for burnt cream appears in a 17th-century cookbook from Dorset, England. Numerous sources credit a member of the faculty at Trinity College in Cambridge, England, with successfully introducing this caramelized custard to his peers in the mid-1800s.

Burnt cream was also popular in America, with recognizable versions appearing in Thomas Jefferson's personal recipe collection and in several cookbooks from the 1800s.

Considered a trendy dessert for upscale American restaurants in the 1980s, crème brûlée now appears on all types of menus and is equally at home in neighborhood diners and four-star, white-tablecloth eateries.

BAKED CRÈME BRÛLÉE

Yield: 10 Servings, approximately 4 oz. (120 g) each   **Method:** Baked custard

Milk	8 fl. oz.	240 ml
Heavy cream	24 fl. oz.	720 ml
Vanilla bean, split	½	½
Granulated sugar	7 oz.	210 g
Egg yolks	6 oz. (10 yolks)	180 g
Granulated sugar for garnish	as needed	as needed

1. Heat the milk, cream and vanilla bean in a medium saucepan over medium-high heat until bubbles appear along the sides of the pan.
2. Quickly whisk the sugar into the egg yolks.
3. When the cream is hot, slowly pour it into the yolk mixture. Whisk until well combined.
4. Strain the mixture through a fine sieve into a pitcher or large measuring cup. Scrape the vanilla bean with the tip of a paring knife to remove the remaining seeds; stir the seeds into the custard.
5. Preheat the oven to 325°F (160°C). Arrange the ramekins in a 2-inch- (5-centimeter-) deep hotel pan or baking dish. Pour the custard into the ramekins. Set the pan of ramekins inside the preheated oven, and then carefully pour enough water into the pan to come two-thirds of the way up the sides of the ramekins. Bake until just set, approximately 45 to 50 minutes. Start checking the custards early; baking time will depend on the thickness and depth of your ramekins. The custard should be set, not soupy, with only a small area of jiggle in the center.
6. When the custards are done, carefully remove the baking dish from the oven and allow the ramekins to cool in the water bath. When the ramekins are cool enough to handle, remove them from the water, cover with plastic wrap, and refrigerate at least 4 hours or up to 2 days before service.
7. At service, sprinkle the tops of the custards with an even layer of granulated sugar, then immediately caramelize the sugar with a propane torch or broiler.

VARIATION:

Chocolate Crème Brûlée—When the milk and cream are hot, whisk in 2 ounces (60 grams) cocoa powder and 6 ounces (180 grams) finely chopped semisweet chocolate and remove from the heat. Replace the granulated sugar with 7 ounces (210 grams) brown sugar. Gradually pour the chocolate-cream mixture into the sugar mixture. Add 0.08 ounce (5 milliliters/¼ teaspoon) coffee extract.

Approximate values per serving: **Calories** 430, **Total fat** 40 g, **Saturated fat** 24 g, **Cholesterol** 345 mg, **Sodium** 45 mg, **Total carbohydrates** 14 g, **Protein** 5 g, **Vitamin A** 35%

MISE EN PLACE

▶ Split vanilla bean in half.
▶ Preheat oven to 325°F (160°C).

SAFETY ALERT
Propane Torch

Training on how to operate a propane torch is recommended before using it to caramelize sugar or other dessert preparations. Use extreme caution and follow appropriate safety procedures. Keep the gas bottle away from sources of heat. Do not leave the torch unattended. Rest the bottle on a stable surface away from any flammable materials.

CHEESECAKE

Cheesecake is a baked custard that contains a smooth cheese, usually a soft, fresh cheese such as cream, ricotta, cottage or farmer's cheese. (See Chapter 4, Bakeshop Ingredients.) It is important to work with cheese at room temperature and to mix it on low speed. Mixing or whipping a cheesecake batter on high speed breaks down the cheese, destroying the emulsion of fat and liquid, and will result in a dry-textured cheesecake. A cheesecake may be prepared without a crust, or it may have a base or sides of short dough, cookie crumbs, ground nuts or spongecake. The filling can be dense and rich (New York style, made with cream cheese) or light and fluffy (Italian style, made with ricotta cheese). Fruit, nuts and flavorings may also be included in the filling. Cheesecakes are often topped with fruit or sour cream glaze. Formulas for both dense and light cheesecakes are at the end of this chapter.

Some cheesecakes are unbaked and rely on gelatin for thickening; others are frozen. These are not really custards, however, but are more similar to the chiffons or mousses discussed later.

PROCEDURE FOR MAKING CHEESECAKE

1. Butter springform pans or line the bottom and sides of the pans with a crumb crust, if desired.

2. Soften the cream cheese by gently beating it in the bowl of a mixer fitted with the paddle attachment.

3. Scrape down the bowl, then, on low speed, beat in the sugar and any thickeners (if using). Mix until the cheese is softened but not warm, approximately 4 to 6 minutes.

4. Add the eggs, a small amount at a time, scraping down the bowl frequently to prevent lumps from forming.

5. Stir in additional cream, sour cream or other ingredients and flavorings. Additional ingredients such as dried fruit, nuts or chocolate may be folded into the batter at this time. Divide the batter evenly between the pans.

6. Bake the cheesecakes. A water bath may be used for gentle, even heat; if using a water bath, bake the cheesecakes in regular pans or wrap the bottom of pans in aluminum foil to prevent water from leaking into the cheesecake.

7. Cool the cheesecakes completely at room temperature, then refrigerate overnight before serving.

NEW YORK CHEESECAKE

MISE EN PLACE

- Crush graham crackers.
- Bring cream cheese to room temperature.
- Grate lemon zest.
- Melt butter.

The finished cheesecake garnished with raspberries, raspberry sauce and chocolate.

Yield: 2 Cakes, 8 in. (20 cm) each, 6 lb. 1 oz. (2922 g) Batter

Method: Baked custard

Crust:

Graham crackers, crushed	16 oz.	480 g
Unsalted butter, melted	6 oz.	180 g

Batter:

Cream cheese, room temperature	3 lb. 6 oz.	1620 g
Granulated sugar	14 oz.	420 g
Eggs	12.8 oz. (8 eggs)	384 g
Cake flour or cornstarch	2 oz.	60 g
Vanilla extract	0.5 fl. oz.	15 ml
Lemon zest, grated fine	0.1 oz. (1½ tsp.)	3 g
Heavy cream	14 fl. oz.	420 ml

1. Wrap the bottom of two 8-inch (20-centimeter) round springform pans with foil.

2. Combine the graham cracker crumbs with the melted butter. Press the mixture into the bottom of the springform pans. Bake for 12 to 15 minutes at 375°F (190°C) until the crust is dry to the touch. Set aside.

3. Blend the cream cheese and sugar on low speed in the bowl of a mixer fitted with the paddle attachment until no lumps remain. Scrape down the bowl often.

4. Add the eggs one at a time, waiting for each egg to be fully incorporated before adding more. Scrape down the bowl and paddle after each addition.

5. Add the flour and mix until combined. Add the remaining ingredients and mix to blend.

6. Divide the cheesecake batter evenly between the two pans. Wrap the bottom and sides of each pan in several layers of aluminum foil and place them in a hotel pan.

7. Preheat the oven to 300°F (150°C). Place the batter-filled pans in a hotel pan and set the hotel pan in the preheated oven. Pour enough warm water into the hotel pan to come halfway up the sides of the pans. Bake until the batter is set and no longer trembles, approximately 75 to 90 minutes.

8. Cool the cakes on a wire rack in their pans, then refrigerate overnight. Remove the cakes from the pans. Portion the chilled cheesecakes. Serve garnished with raspberry sauce and chocolate, if desired.

Approximate values per ⅛-cake serving: **Calories** 770, **Total fat** 57 g, **Saturated fat** 34 g, **Cholesterol** 265 mg, **Sodium** 500 mg, **Total carbohydrates** 53 g, **Protein** 13 g, **Vitamin A** 40%, **Iron** 15%

① Pressing crumb mixture into pan. ② Panning the creamy filling.

Cheesecakes should be cut when cold and firm. Use a knife dipped in clean hot water, wiped after each cut to prevent buildup on the knife and the surface of the cake. Clean pieces of thin thread, held taut, can also be used to make neat uniform portions in a soft cake.

BREAD PUDDING

Bread pudding is a home-style dessert in which chunks of bread, flavorings and raisins or other fruit are mixed with an egg custard and baked. The result is somewhat of a cross between a cake and a pudding. It is often served with custard sauce, ice cream, whipped cream or a whiskey-flavored butter sauce. Bread pudding is a delicious way to use stale or leftover bread or overripe fruit. In fact, croissants, brioche, gingerbread, spongecake or a savory product such as cornbread can be used to make sweet or savory bread puddings. A formula for Bread Pudding with Bourbon Sauce appears on page 523.

Soufflés

A **soufflé** is made with a custard base, often thickened with a starch, that is lightened with whipped egg whites and then baked. When heated, air in the egg whites expands to create a light, fluffy texture and tall rise. During baking, the egg proteins set, giving some structure to the finished soufflé. A soufflé is very unstable, however, and will collapse quickly as the air inside it cools.

Soufflés can be prepared in a wide variety of sweet and savory flavors. The flavorings can be incorporated into the custard, as in the following formula. Alternatively, an unflavored pastry cream can be used as the base; the liqueur, fruit or chocolate is then added to each portion separately.

When making a soufflé, the custard base and egg whites should be at room temperature. First, the egg whites will whip to a better volume, and second, if the base is approximately the same temperature as the egg whites, the two mixtures can be more easily incorporated. The egg whites are whipped to stiff peaks with a portion of the sugar for stability. The whipped egg whites are then gently folded into the base immediately before baking.

A soufflé is baked in a straight-sided mold or individual ramekin. Keep the mixture from touching the top edge of the mold so it will rise evenly. The finished soufflé should be puffy with a lightly browned top. It should rise well above the rim of the baking dish. A soufflé must be served immediately, before it collapses. A warm custard sauce (crème anglaise) is often served as an accompaniment to a sweet soufflé.

A frozen soufflé is not a true soufflé. Rather, it is a creamy custard mixture thickened with eggs or gelatin, lightened with whipped egg whites or whipped cream and then frozen before serving. (Frozen dessert soufflés are discussed in Chapter 15, Ice Cream and Frozen Desserts.)

PROCEDURE FOR PREPARING BAKED SOUFFLÉS

1. Butter the mold or ramekins and dust with granulated sugar. Preheat the oven to approximately 425°F (220°C).

2. Prepare the custard base. Add flavorings as desired. Keep warm or reheat before using.

3. Whip the egg whites and sugar to stiff peaks. Fold the whipped egg whites into the base, recreaming the whites as needed to keep the mixture smooth.

4. Pipe or pour the mixture into the prepared mold or ramekins and bake immediately.

CHOCOLATE SOUFFLÉS

MISE EN PLACE

▶ Separate eggs.
▶ Chop chocolate finely.
▶ Melt butter.

Yield: 8 Servings

Orange juice	1 pt.	500 ml
Egg yolks	4.8 oz. (8 yolks)	144 g
Granulated sugar	4 oz.	120 g
All-purpose flour	3 oz.	90 g
Bittersweet chocolate, chopped fine	8 oz.	240 g
Orange liqueur	2 fl. oz.	60 ml
Butter, melted	as needed	as needed
Granulated sugar	as needed	as needed
Egg whites	12 oz. (12 whites)	360 g
Powdered sugar (optional)	as needed	as needed

1. To prepare the base, heat the orange juice to lukewarm in a heavy saucepan.

2. Whisk the egg yolks with 3 ounces (90 grams) of the sugar in a large mixing bowl. Whisk in the flour and warm orange juice, then return the mixture to the saucepan.

3. Cook over medium-low heat, stirring constantly, until the custard is thick. Do not allow it to boil. Remove from the heat.

4. Stir in the chocolate until completely melted. Stir in the liqueur. Cover this base mixture with plastic wrap to prevent a skin from forming. Hold for use at room temperature. (Unused base can be kept overnight in the refrigerator; it should be brought to room temperature before mixing with the egg whites.)

1. Folding the whipped egg whites into the chocolate base.

2. Filling the ramekins.

3. The finished soufflé, ready for service.

⑤ To prepare the soufflés, brush 4-fluid-ounce (120-milliliter) ramekins with melted butter and dust with granulated sugar.

⑥ Preheat the oven to 425°F (220°C). Place a sheet pan in the oven, onto which you will place the soufflés for baking. (This makes it easier to remove the hot soufflé cups from the oven.)

⑦ Whip the egg whites to stiff peaks with the remaining 1 ounce (30 grams) of the sugar. Fold the whites into the chocolate base, recreaming them with a whisk to keep them smooth if necessary. Pipe or spoon the mixture into the prepared ramekins. The ramekins should be filled to within ¼ inch (6 millimeters) of the rim. Smooth the top of each soufflé with a spatula and bake immediately.

⑧ The soufflés are done when well risen and golden brown on top and the edges appear dry, approximately 12 minutes. Do not touch a soufflé to test doneness.

⑨ Sprinkle the soufflés with powdered sugar (if desired) and serve immediately.

Approximate values per serving: **Calories** 350, **Total fat** 15 g, **Saturated fat** 8 g, **Cholesterol** 210 mg, **Sodium** 65 mg, **Total carbohydrates** 48 g, **Protein** 10 g, **Vitamin A** 10%, **Vitamin C** 50%

CREAMS

Creams (Fr. *crèmes*) include light, fluffy or creamy-textured dessert items made with whipped egg whites or whipped cream. Some, such as **Bavarian creams** and **chiffons**, are thickened with gelatin. Others, such as **mousses** and **crème Chantilly**, are softer and lighter. See Table 14.1. The success of all, however, depends on properly whipping and incorporating egg whites or heavy cream.

Review the material on whipping cream in Chapter 4, Bakeshop Ingredients. When preparing any whipped cream, be sure that the cream, the mixing bowl and all utensils are well chilled and clean. A warm bowl can melt the butterfat, destroying the texture of the cream. Properly whipped cream should increase two to three times in volume.

Crème Chantilly

Crème Chantilly is simply heavy cream whipped to soft peaks and flavored with sugar and vanilla. It can be used for garnishing pastry or dessert items.

When making crème Chantilly it is essential that the cream and all equipment are well chilled. Cream that is too warm resists whipping and can curdle. Whip the cream by hand or in a mixer with the whip attachment at medium speed. At higher speeds, the cream will not achieve the same volume and may curdle.

The butterfat content of the cream used to make whipped cream will affect the cream's stability; heavy cream with a butterfat content of approximately 36% will be more stable than whipped cream made with whipping cream, which has a butterfat content of 30%. The vanilla extract and sugar should be added after the cream begins to thicken. Either granulated or powdered sugar may be used; there are advantages and disadvantages to both. Granulated sugar assists in forming a better foam than powdered sugar, but it may cause the cream to feel gritty. Powdered sugar dissolves more quickly and completely than granulated sugar but does nothing to assist with foaming. Whichever sugar is used, it should be added just before the whipping is complete to avoid interfering with the cream's volume and stability.

When properly whipped, heavy cream expands two to two and a half times in volume. Whipped cream that is to be folded into a mousse should be whipped only until soft peaks form; the additional folding into the mousse could cause stiffly whipped cream to break. Whipped cream may be stabilized with gelatin to help prevent it from collapsing in warm humid conditions.

Cream whipped to soft peaks for folding into mousse.

Cream whipped to stiff peaks.

Overwhipped cream loses volume, curdles and separates.

TABLE 14.1	CREAM (CRÈME) COMPONENTS		
FOR A:	**BEGIN WITH A BASE OF:**	**THICKEN WITH:**	**THEN FOLD IN:**
Bavarian	Custard	Gelatin	Whipped cream
Chiffon	Custard or starch-thickened fruit	Gelatin	Whipped egg whites
Mousse	Melted chocolate, puréed fruit or custard	Nothing or gelatin	Whipped cream, whipped egg whites, whipped egg yolks or all three

CRÈME CHANTILLY (CHANTILLY CREAM)

MISE EN PLACE

▶ Chill cream, mixing bowl and whisk.

Properly whipped Crème Chantilly.

Yield: 2–2½ qt. (2–2½ lt)

Heavy cream, chilled	1 qt.	1 lt
Powdered sugar	2 oz.	60 g
Vanilla extract	0.3 fl. oz. (2 tsp.)	10 ml

1 Place the cream in a chilled mixing bowl. Using a balloon whisk, whisk the cream until slightly thickened.

2 Add the sugar and vanilla and continue whisking to the desired consistency. The cream should be smooth and light, not grainy. Do not overwhip.

3 Crème Chantilly may be stored in the refrigerator several hours. If the cream begins to soften, gently rewhip as necessary.

VARIATIONS:

Chocolate Chantilly—Place 6 ounces (180 grams) finely chopped bittersweet chocolate in a medium bowl. Bring 1 quart (960 milliliters) heavy cream, 4 fluid ounces (120 milliliters) milk and 3 ounces (90 grams) sugar to boil. Pour half of the boiled mixture onto the chopped chocolate. Whisk until smooth. Add the remaining cream and cover. Refrigerate overnight before whipping.

Stabilized Whipped Cream—Soften 0.25 ounce (7 grams/2¾ teaspoons) granulated gelatin in 2 fluid ounces (60 milliliters) cold water. Melt the gelatin. Add to the cream just as it begins to form soft peaks. Whip to the desired consistency.

Note: Cream that breaks can be turned into butter. Continue whipping until the mixture decreases in volume and separates into lumps of butter and watery liquid called whey. Place the mixture in a cheesecloth-lined strainer set over a bowl. Knead it briefly to extract as much liquid as possible. Discard the liquid and use the remaining butter for sautéing foods or greasing pans.

Approximate values per 1-fl.-oz. (30-ml) serving: **Calories** 60, **Total fat** 6 g, **Saturated fat** 3.5 g, **Cholesterol** 20 mg, **Sodium** 5 mg, **Total carbohydrates** 2 g, **Protein** 0 g

Bavarian Cream

A Bavarian cream (Fr. *bavarois*) is prepared by first thickening custard sauce with gelatin, then folding in whipped cream. The final product is poured into a mold and chilled until firm enough to unmold and slice. Although a Bavarian cream can be molded into individual servings, it is often poured into a round mold lined with spongecake or ladyfingers to create the classic dessert known as a **charlotte**.

Bavarians can be flavored by adding chocolate, puréed fruit, chopped nuts, extracts or liquors to the custard sauce base. Layers of fruit or liqueur-soaked spongecake can also be added for flavor and texture.

When thickening a dessert cream with gelatin, it is important to use the correct amount of gelatin. If not enough gelatin is used or it is not incorporated completely, the cream will not become firm enough to unmold. If too much gelatin is used, the cream will be tough and rubbery. Refer to Chapter 4, Bakeshop Ingredients, for information on using gelatin. Fresh fruits such as figs, guava, kiwi, mango and pineapple contain bromelain, an enzyme that interferes with the setting of gelatin-thickened creams. The cream may not set properly when these fruits are added to a Bavarian cream. These fruits can be used if they are first heated or poached to 180°F (80°C) or higher before using.

PROCEDURE FOR PREPARING BAVARIAN CREAMS

1 Prepare a custard sauce of the desired flavor.

2 While the custard sauce is still quite warm, stir in softened sheet gelatin. (Or bloom the granulated gelatin in cold water 5 minutes. Melt the gelatin, then pour the melted gelatin into the warm custard sauce.) Make sure the gelatin is completely incorporated.

3 Chill the custard until almost thickened, stirring it from time to time to prevent lumps from forming, then fold in the whipped cream.

4 Pour the Bavarian into a mold or charlotte form. Chill until set.

BAVARIAN CREAM

Yield: Approximately 2 qt. (2 lt)

Milk	14 fl. oz.	420 ml
Heavy cream	14 fl. oz.	420 ml
Granulated sugar	6 oz.	180 g
Vanilla bean, split	1	1
Egg yolks	4.8 oz. (8 yolks)	144 g
Sheet gelatin, softened	8 sheets (0.5 oz.)	15 g
Heavy cream, whipped to soft peaks	1 qt.	960 ml

1 To prepare a custard sauce, combine the milk, cream, 2 ounces (60 grams) of the sugar and the vanilla bean in a heavy saucepan. Bring to a boil.

2 Whisk the egg yolks and remaining 4 ounces (120 grams) of sugar together to the ribbon stage. Temper the yolk mixture with one-quarter of the heated milk, whisking constantly.

3 Pour the yolk mixture into the saucepan with the rest of the milk. Stir constantly with a rubber spatula until the custard reaches 185°F (85°C).

4 Remove from the heat and pour through a fine mesh strainer into a clean bowl.

5 Add the softened sheet gelatin to the hot custard. Chill until thick in an ice bath, stirring regularly to prevent lumps from forming, until the custard reaches 75°F (24°C) or slightly cooler. Fold in the whipped cream.

6 Pour the Bavarian Cream immediately into serving dishes or a mold.

Approximate values per 1-oz. (30-g) serving: **Calories** 120, **Total fat** 7 g, **Saturated fat** 4.5 g, **Cholesterol** 0 mg, **Sodium** 10 mg, **Total carbohydrates** 3 g, **Protein** 1 g

MISE EN PLACE

▶ Split vanilla bean in half.
▶ Soften gelatin.
▶ Whip the cream.

1 Adding gelatin to the custard base.

2 Folding in the whipped cream.

CHARLOTTE, SWEET CHARLOTTE

The original charlotte was created during the 18th century and named for the wife of King George III of England. It consisted of an apple compote baked in a round mold lined with toast slices. A few decades later, the great French chef Carême adopted the name but altered the concept in response to a kitchen disaster. When preparing a grand banquet for King Louis XVIII, he found that his gelatin supply was insufficient for the Bavarian creams he was making, so Carême steadied the sides of his sagging desserts with ladyfingers. The result became known as charlotte russe, probably due to the reigning fad for anything Russian. A fancier version, known as charlotte royale, is made with pinwheels or layers of spongecake and jam instead of ladyfingers. The filling for either should be a classic Bavarian cream.

CHARLOTTE

Yield: 3 Charlottes, 1.5 qt. (1 ½ lt) each

Ladyfinger batter (page 479)	2 lb. 3 oz.	1050 g
Simple Syrup (page 73)	6 fl. oz.	180 ml
Brandy or fruit liqueur	2 fl. oz.	60 ml
Bavarian Cream (page 503)	2 qt.	2 lt
Fresh cherries or other berries, pitted	1½ pt.	750 ml
Crème Chantilly (page 502)	as needed	as needed

1. Using a large plain piping tip, pipe a portion of the Ladyfinger batter into a strip of 5-inch- (12.5-centimeter-) long cookies. Pipe the remaining batter into three 5-inch (12.5-centimeter) disks. Bake according to the recipe on page 479.

2. Lightly oil and sugar the charlotte molds. Line each mold with a strip of baked Ladyfingers, allowing the Ladyfingers to extend out above the mold if necessary. Trim the Ladyfingers to an even height.

3. Combine the Simple Syrup with the brandy. Moisten the Ladyfinger disks with the syrup and set aside.

4. Prepare the Bavarian Cream. Allow the cream to thicken slightly before filling the mold, in order to keep the cream from seeping through the Ladyfingers.

5. Divide one-third of the Bavarian Cream among the three cake-lined molds, filling each mold one-third of the way. Scatter one-third of the fruit over the cream. Fill each mold with another third of the Bavarian Cream and add more fruit. Evenly divide the remaining Bavarian Cream among the molds. Place one Ladyfinger disk on top of each charlotte.

6. Wrap and refrigerate the charlottes at least 2 hours or overnight.

7. To serve, invert each charlotte onto a serving platter. Wrap a decorative ribbon around each cake. Garnish with Crème Chantilly and additional fruit.

Approximate values per ⅙-cake serving: **Calories** 120, **Total fat** 5 g, **Saturated fat** 4 g, **Cholesterol** 33 mg, **Sodium** 6 mg, **Total carbohydrates** 47 g, **Protein** 10 g, **Vitamin A** 20%

Chiffon

A chiffon is similar to a Bavarian except that whipped egg whites instead of whipped cream are folded into the thickened base. The base may be a custard or a fruit mixture thickened with cornstarch. Although a chiffon may be molded like a Bavarian, it is most often used as a pie or tart filling.

PROCEDURE FOR PREPARING CHIFFONS

1. Prepare the base, which is usually a custard or a fruit mixture thickened with cornstarch.
2. Add gelatin to the warm base.
3. Fold in whipped egg whites.
4. Pour into a mold or prebaked pie shell and chill.

LIME CHIFFON

Yield: 1 Pie, 10 in. (25 cm), 8 Servings

Granulated gelatin	0.25 oz. (2½ tsp.)	7.5 g
Water	5 fl. oz.	150 ml
Granulated sugar	7 oz.	210 g
Fresh lime juice	3 fl. oz.	90 ml
Lime zest, grated fine	0.2 oz. (1 Tbsp.)	6 g
Egg yolks, pasteurized	2.4 oz. (4 yolks)	72 g
Egg whites, pasteurized	4 oz. (4 whites)	120 g
Crumb or other baked pie crust (optional)	1	1

1. Bloom the granulated gelatin in 1 fluid ounce (30 milliliters) of the water.
2. Combine 4 ounces (120 grams) of the sugar, the remaining water, lime juice, lime zest and egg yolks in a bowl over a pan of simmering water.
3. Whisk the egg-and-lime mixture together vigorously until it begins to thicken. Melt the gelatin, then add it to the egg-and-lime mixture. Continue whipping until very thick and foamy.
4. Remove from the heat, cover and refrigerate until cool and as thick as whipping cream.
5. Meanwhile, whip the egg whites to soft peaks. Whip in the remaining sugar and continue whipping until stiff but not dry.
6. Fold the whipped egg whites into the egg-and-lime mixture. Pour into a prepared pie crust or serving dishes and chill for several hours, until firm.

VARIATIONS:

Lemon Chiffon—Substitute lemon juice and lemon zest for the lime juice and lime zest.

Orange Chiffon—Substitute orange juice for the lime juice and for 4 fluid ounces (120 milliliters) of the water. Substitute orange zest for the lime zest. Reduce the amount of sugar in the egg yolk mixture to 1 ounce (30 grams).

Approximate values per serving: **Calories** 140, **Total fat** 2.5 g, **Saturated fat** 1 g, **Cholesterol** 105 mg, **Sodium** 35 mg, **Total carbohydrates** 26 g, **Protein** 4 g, **Claims**—low fat; low saturated fat; low sodium

MISE EN PLACE

▸ Grate lime zest.
▸ Prepare pie crust, if using.

Lime Chiffon served in a glass.

SAFETY ALERT
Egg Products in Uncooked Mousses

Pasteurized egg products are recommended for most mousse formulas because the eggs are uncooked and any bacteria will remain viable.

Mousse

The term *mousse* applies to an assortment of dessert creams not easily classified elsewhere. A mousse is similar to a Bavarian or chiffon in that it is lightened with whipped cream, whipped egg whites, whipped egg yolks cooked into a bombe mixture (*pâte à bombe*) or all three. A mousse is generally softer than a Bavarian, however, and is generally too soft to mold. A mousse may be served alone as a dessert or used as a filling in pies, cakes, tortes or pastry items. Plan on serving 4 to 6 fluid ounces (120 to 360 milliliters) of mousse per serving as a stand-alone dessert. Sweet mousses can be based on a custard sauce, melted chocolate or puréed fruit. When making mousse, it is important that the cream be whipped to soft peaks. Any firmer and the cream may separate when it is folded into the mousse base.

PROCEDURE FOR PREPARING MOUSSES

Recreaming whipped egg whites before adding them to mousse.

❶ Prepare the base, which is usually a custard sauce, melted chocolate or puréed fruit.

❷ If using gelatin, soften it first, then dissolve it in the warm base.

❸ Fold in whipped egg whites (if using), whisking them gently to recream them before using. If the base is slightly warm when the egg whites are added, their proteins will coagulate, making the mousse firmer and more stable.

❹ Allow the mixture to cool completely, then fold in whipped cream (if using). Note that the egg whites are folded in before any whipped cream. Although the egg whites may deflate somewhat during folding, if the cream is added first it may become over-whipped when the egg whites are added, creating a grainy or coarse product.

 CLASSIC CHOCOLATE MOUSSE

Yield: 1½–2 qt. (1½–2 lt)

Bittersweet chocolate (60–64% cacao)	15 oz.	450 g
Unsalted butter	9 oz.	270 g
Egg yolks, pasteurized	4.2 oz. (7 yolks)	126 g
Egg whites, pasteurized	11 oz. (11 whites)	330 g
Granulated sugar	2.5 oz.	75 g
Heavy cream	8 fl. oz.	240 ml

❶ Melt the chocolate and butter in a double boiler over low heat. Stir until no lumps remain.

❷ Allow the mixture to cool slightly to 120°F (49°C), then whisk in the egg yolks, a small amount at a time.

❸ Beat the egg whites until soft peaks form. Slowly beat in the sugar and continue beating until stiff peaks form. Fold the whipped egg whites into the chocolate mixture.

❹ Whip the cream to soft peaks. Allow the mousse to cool to 95°F (35°C), then fold in the whipped cream. Make sure no streaks of egg white or cream remain.

❺ Spoon the mousse into serving bowls or chill completely and pipe into bowls or baked tartlet shells. The mousse may be used as a cake or pastry filling.

Approximate values per 3-fl.-oz. (90-ml) serving: **Calories** 370, **Total fat** 31 g, **Saturated fat** 18 g, **Cholesterol** 215 mg, **Sodium** 50 mg, **Total carbohydrates** 16 g, **Protein** 7 g, **Vitamin A** 25%

❶ Adding the whipped egg whites to the chocolate.

❷ Folding in the whipped egg whites.

❸ Adding the whipped cream.

❹ Folding in the whipped cream.

MOUSSE MADE WITH A BOMBE MIXTURE (PÂTE À BOMBE)

A bombe mixture is made by warming eggs and/or egg yolks and sugar over a bain marie of simmering water, then whipping the mixture into a light foam. Heating sets the egg proteins so that the mousse is more stable. Making mousses with a bombe mixture ensures a light, silky mousse. The bombe also ensures a stable product; because the egg proteins are cooked before being added to the base, there is no chance of making a grainy or lumpy finished product. (A bombe mixture used for frozen desserts made with sugar syrup, similar to Italian meringue, is discussed on pages 549–550.)

The procedure for making a mousse with a bombe mixture is illustrated with the formula for Contemporary Chocolate Mousse on page 508.

PROCEDURE FOR PREPARING MOUSSES WITH A BOMBE MIXTURE

❶ Prepare the base, which is usually a custard sauce, melted chocolate or puréed fruit, holding it at required temperatures.

❷ If using gelatin, soften it first, then dissolve it in the warm base. If using whipped cream, whip it to soft peaks and keep it chilled.

❸ Prepare the bombe mixture: Whip the eggs, egg yolks, water and sugar in a bain marie until the mixture reaches 165°F (74°C). Pour the bombe mixture into the bowl of a mixer fitted with the whip attachment. Whip on medium-high speed until the mixture forms thick ribbons and feels cool to the touch.

❹ Lighten the mousse base by folding in a small amount of the whipped cream. Working swiftly, fold in the bombe mixture, then the remaining whipped cream. Fold gently until no streaks remain.

MISE EN PLACE

▶ Chop the chocolate.
▶ Set up a bain marie over simmering water.

PREPARING CHOCOLATE MOUSSE

When made correctly, chocolate mousse has a smooth, velvety texture. Different brands of chocolate produce different results, however. If the mousse is too dense, select chocolate with a higher cocoa butter content. Add additional butter when melting the chocolate or increase the amount of whipped heavy cream used. Keeping the melted chocolate warm before adding whipped eggs or cream preserves the mousse's light, smooth texture. If the chocolate is too cool when the whipped cream is added, the mixture will start setting before all the ingredients are folded together, resulting in a dense, grainy product. See Chapter 20, Chocolate and Sugar Work, for more information.

CONTEMPORARY CHOCOLATE MOUSSE

Yield: 2 lb. 2 oz. (972 g)

Bittersweet chocolate couverture (64% cacao), chopped*	9 oz.	270 g
Unsalted butter	2 oz.	60 g
Heavy cream	12 fl. oz.	360 ml
Eggs	4.8 oz. (3 eggs)	144 g
Egg yolk	0.6 oz. (1 yolk)	18 g
Water	1 fl. oz.	30 ml
Granulated sugar	4 oz.	120 g
Chocolate curved triangles (page 699)	as needed	as needed
Fresh berries	as needed	as needed

❶ Melt the chocolate and butter to 125°F (52°C). Hold the mixture at this temperature by placing it over a bowl of water at 125°F (52°C). Set aside.

❷ Whip the cream to a thick yet soft consistency in a chilled mixing bowl. Set aside.

❸ To prepare the bombe mixture, whip the eggs, egg yolk, water and sugar in a bain marie until the mixture reaches 165°F (74°C). Pour the bombe mixture into the bowl of a mixer fitted with the whip attachment. Whip on medium-high speed until the mixture forms thick ribbons and feels cool to the touch.

❹ Rewarm the melted chocolate, if necessary, so that it is at 125°F (52°C). Fold one-fifth of the whipped cream into the melted chocolate and whisk until smooth.

❶ Whisking the eggs and sugar over simmering water.

❷ The properly whipped bombe mixture.

❸ Adding cream to the chocolate mousse.

❹ Adding the bombe mixture and whipped cream to the chocolate mousse.

⑤ Folding the bombe mixture and whipped cream into the melted chocolate.

⑥ The final folded chocolate mousse.

⑦ The finished dessert.

⑤ Add the bombe mixture to the chocolate, folding it gently together using a rubber spatula. Fold in the remaining whipped cream gently until no streaks remain.

⑥ Divide the mousse evenly among 8 to 10 serving glasses. Garnish with chocolate curved triangles and fresh berries.

Note: Chocolate with a lower cocoa content contains a higher percentage of sugar and will have a less intense chocolate flavor and color. If using chocolate with a lower cocoa content, the following change is suggested: For every 4 percent less cocoa mass, use 1 ounce (30 grams) additional chocolate in this formula.

VARIATION:

Flavored Chocolate Mousse—Add 1–2 fluid ounces (30–60 milliliters) liqueur, coffee extract or other extract to the finished mousse.

Approximate values per 1-oz. (30-g) serving: **Calories** 110, **Total fat** 9 g, **Saturated fat** 5 g, **Cholesterol** 40 mg, **Sodium** 10 mg, **Total carbohydrates** 7 g, **Protein** 1 g

MOUSSE FILLINGS

When a mousse serves as a filling in a layered torte (see Chapter 17, Tortes and Specialty Cakes), it may contain a small amount of gelatin to stabilize the mousse. Italian meringue is also used in place of some of the heavy cream. Because it contains no fat, Italian meringue does not interfere with the delicate flavor of a fruit purée.

To ensure the lightest and creamiest mousse, the fruit purée should be slightly warm when folded into the warm Italian meringue. This keeps the mousse light and prevents the gelatin from setting as soon as the cold whipped cream is added in the last step. When made with gelatin, a mousse should be used immediately in its desired application before it cools and sets. The formula for Apricot Mousse (page 510) illustrates the procedure for making a mousse with Italian meringue.

PROCEDURE FOR PREPARING A MOUSSE WITH ITALIAN MERINGUE

❶ Prepare the base, which is usually a fruit purée. Make certain the fruit purée is slightly warm, approximately 95°F–115°F (35°C–46°C). (Overheating the fruit purée may damage its flavor.) This makes for the lightest mousse.

❷ Soften and melt gelatin, if necessary.

❸ Prepare an Italian meringue. Whip the Italian meringue until it cools down to 120°F (49°C). Add the gelatin to the warm fruit purée.

❹ Fold the slightly warm purée into the Italian meringue in two stages using a balloon whisk. This may require transferring the meringue to a larger bowl.

❺ Whip heavy cream to soft peaks. Fold the whipped cream into the meringue. Use the mousse immediately before the gelatin begins to set.

APRICOT MOUSSE

Reduce the amount of gelatin by half if the mousse will not need to be sliced, as in a torte or tart.

MISE EN PLACE
▶ Soften gelatin.
▶ Whip cream.

Yield: 4 lb. 9 oz. (2155 g)

Apricot purée	2 lb. 3 oz.	1 kg
Egg whites	4 oz. (4 whites)	120 g
Granulated sugar	8 oz.	240 g
Water	3 fl. oz.	90 ml
Sheet gelatin, softened	8 sheets (0.5 oz.)	15 g
Heavy cream, whipped to soft peaks	26 oz.	780 g

1. In a heavy saucepan over low heat, warm the apricot purée to approximately 115°F (46°C).
2. Prepare an Italian meringue with the egg whites, sugar and water according to the method on page 413.
3. Add the softened sheet gelatin to the apricot purée.
4. Transfer the Italian meringue from the mixer into a large bowl.
5. Delicately fold one-quarter of the apricot purée into the Italian meringue with a balloon whisk or rubber spatula. Gradually fold in the remaining apricot purée. Gently fold in the whipped cream, being careful not to overmix.
6. Use immediately. Pipe into serving dishes, tart shells or tortes.

Approximate values per 1-oz. (30-g) serving: **Calories** 60, **Total fat** 4 g, **Saturated fat** 2.5 g, **Cholesterol** 15 mg, **Sodium** 10 mg, **Total carbohydrates** 5 g, **Protein** 1 g, **Vitamin A** 10%

DESSERT SAUCES

Pastries and desserts are often accompanied by sweet sauces. Dessert sauces provide moisture, flavor and texture and enhance plate presentation. Sauces may be based on milk and cream, such as Vanilla Custard Sauce (page 490), the principal dessert sauce. Like any master sauce, it can be flavored and colored with chocolate, coffee extract, liquor or fruit compound as desired. Other dessert sauces include fruit, caramel, butter and wine sauces and chocolate syrup. Sauces should be selected to contrast or complement the dessert or pastry with which they are served. For example, a raspberry soufflé can be complemented by an intense raspberry purée or contrasted with a rich chocolate sauce. Plan on 1 to 2 ounces (30 to 60 milliliters) of sauce per plated dessert.

Fruit Purées

Many types of fruit can be puréed for dessert sauces; strawberries, raspberries, blackberries, apricots, mangoes and papayas are popular choices. They produce thick sauces with strong flavors and colors. Ripe, fresh or individually quick-frozen (IQF) fruits are recommended. Several commercial brands of prepared fruit purées are available. The best use only natural fruits and are excellent for making sauces and sorbets. They provide consistent flavor and color, reduce preparation time, and make out-of-season or hard-to-obtain tropical fruits available at a reasonable price.

Puréed fruit sauces are known as **coulis**. Minimal processing of the best-quality fruit produces pure fresh-tasting sauce. Should thickening be desired, keep in mind that starches require boiling, which can alter the fresh fruit flavor. A thick caramel can be added to tart fruit purées such as raspberry or citrus for sweetening and thickening. Gelatin may be added to a fruit coulis so that it sets once chilled. This fruit gelée can then be used as a filling in a cake or torte, as discussed in Chapter 17, Tortes and Specialty Cakes.

TABLE 14.2 TROUBLESHOOTING CHART FOR CUSTARDS AND CREAMS

PROBLEM	CAUSE	SOLUTION
Custard sauce watery	Custard overcooked	Adjust temperature; remove from heat promptly; cook over a bain marie; chill over ice bath
Custard sauce lumpy	Improper mixing of sugar and yolks	Whisk yolks and sugar together properly
Baked custard curdled, lumpy or watery	Custard overcooked	Adjust oven temperature; remove from oven promptly
	Insufficient water in bain marie	Use sufficient water in bain marie
Custard greasy	Too much fat	Adjust formula; use a combination of heavy cream and milk; use more whole eggs than yolks
Pastry cream lumpy	Starch not incorporated properly	Blend starch with sugar before adding liquid; stir cream while cooking
Pastry cream runny	Insufficient starch	Adjust formula; measure ingredients properly
	Undercooked starch	Cook longer
	Wrong starch used	Adjust formula
	Overstirred after pastry cream has set	Avoid stirring once pastry cream has set
Whipped cream watery	Cream overmixed	Whip properly; stop whisking before cream is fully whipped
	Too warm	Chill cream; use chilled bowl and whisk
Cheesecake grainy	Batter overcooked	Adjust oven temperature
	Batter overmixed	Soften cream cheese before using; blend batter on low speed
Cheesecake cracks	Cake cooled too quickly	Cool slowly
	Batter overmixed	Soften cream cheese before using; blend batter on low speed
Mousse rubbery	Used too much gelatin	Adjust formula
Mousse lumpy	Mixture set before cream added	Mix promptly; have ingredients at recommended temperatures

To make a fruit coulis, most berries as well as apricots, peaches and other tree fruits are puréed, then mixed with sugar and glucose or corn syrup. A ratio of 20 percent sugar to fruit is recommended, though the amount depends on the fruit's natural sweetness and personal preference. The relatively small amount of sweetener interacts with the fruit acids to enhance the true fruit flavor. Glucose syrup is less sweet than sugar and provides body and an attractive sheen. A small amount of lemon juice or citric acid may be added to enhance fruit flavor. For stone fruits, as much as 2 ounces (60 grams) total weight can be lost per pound of fruit after puréeing. For a seedless berry purée, 28 ounces (840 grams) of whole berries produce approximately 16 ounces (480 grams) of seedless purée. When using purchased fruit purée, taste the product before adding all the sugar in the formula. Adjust the quantity of sugar as needed.

PROCEDURE FOR PREPARING A FRUIT COULIS

1. Wash, peel and chop the fruit if necessary.
2. Purée the fruit in a food mill, blender or food processor. Strain to remove seeds.
3. Combine the purée with flavorings and sweeteners, if using.

FRUIT COULIS

MISE EN PLACE

▶ Prepare fruit purée.

Use apricots, blackberries, blueberries, mangoes, peaches, plums, raspberries or strawberries in this formula. Neither citrus fruit nor pineapples are suitable.

Yield: 1 lb. 4 oz. (600 g)

Fruit purée, strained	1 lb.	480 g
Granulated sugar	2.5 oz.	75 g
Glucose or corn syrup	1 oz.	30 g
Lemon juice	0.5 fl. oz.	15 ml

1. Combine the fruit purée with the sugar and glucose syrup. Add as much lemon juice as needed to balance the flavor of the sauce.
2. Serve warm or cold.

Approximate values per 1-oz. (30-g) serving: **Calories** 35, **Total fat** 0 g, **Saturated fat** 0 g, **Cholesterol** 0 mg, **Sodium** 5 mg, **Total carbohydrates** 8 g, **Protein** 0 g, **Claims**—no fat; no cholesterol; very low sodium; low calorie

Caramel Sauce

Caramel sauce is a mixture of caramelized sugar and heavy cream. A liqueur or citrus juice may be used for added flavor. Review the material on caramelizing sugar in Chapter 4, Bakeshop Ingredients, and Chapter 20, Chocolate and Sugar Work. Great care must be taken when caramelizing the sugar and adding the cold cream to the caramel. The sugar can easily spatter and boil over, causing severe burns.

CARAMEL SAUCE

MISE EN PLACE

▶ Warm cream.
▶ Cut butter into pieces.

Yield: 1 qt. (1 lt)

Granulated sugar	1 lb. 2 oz.	540 g
Water	4 fl. oz.	120 ml
Lemon juice	0.5 fl. oz.	15 ml
Heavy cream, room temperature	8 fl. oz.	240 ml
Unsalted butter, cut into pieces	1.5 oz.	45 g

1. Combine the sugar and water in a heavy gauge, medium heavy saucepan. Stir to moisten the sugar completely. Place the saucepan on the stove top over high heat and bring to a boil. Brush down the sides of the pan with water to remove any sugar granules.
2. When the sugar comes to a boil, add the lemon juice. Do not stir the sugar, as this may cause lumping. Continue boiling until the sugar caramelizes, turning a dark golden brown and producing a rich aroma.
3. Remove the saucepan from heat. Gradually add the cream. Be extremely careful, as the hot caramel may splatter. Whisk in the cream to blend.
4. Add the pieces of butter. Stir until the butter melts completely. If necessary, return the sauce to the stove to reheat enough to melt the butter.
5. Strain the sauce and cool completely at room temperature. The sauce may be stored several weeks under refrigeration. Stir before using.

Approximate values per 1-fl.-oz. (30-ml) serving: **Calories** 130, **Total fat** 7 g, **Saturated fat** 4 g, **Cholesterol** 25 mg, **Sodium** 5 mg, **Total carbohydrates** 16 g, **Protein** 0 g, **Vitamin A** 8%

Chocolate Syrup

Chocolate syrup or sauce can be prepared by adding finely chopped chocolate to warm vanilla custard sauce. A darker syrup can also be made with unsweetened chocolate or cocoa powder. Fudge-type sauces, such as Chocolate Fudge Sauce (page 538), are really just variations on ganache (page 458).

DARK CHOCOLATE SYRUP

Yield: 1 pt. (500 ml)

Cocoa powder	2 oz.	60 g
Water	12 fl. oz.	360 ml
Granulated sugar	8 oz.	240 g
Unsalted butter	3 oz.	90 g
Heavy cream	1 fl. oz.	30 ml

1. Mix the cocoa powder with just enough water to make a smooth paste.
2. Bring the sugar and remaining water to a boil in a small, heavy saucepan. Immediately add the cocoa paste, whisking until smooth.
3. Simmer for 15 minutes, stirring constantly, then remove from the heat.
4. Stir the butter and cream into the warm cocoa mixture. Serve warm or at room temperature.

Approximate values per 1-fl.-oz. (30-ml) serving: **Calories** 120, **Total fat** 6 g, **Saturated fat** 3 g, **Cholesterol** 15 mg, **Sodium** 0 mg, **Total carbohydrates** 16 g, **Protein** 1 g, **Vitamin A** 6%.

CONVENIENCE PRODUCTS

Commercially prepared powders and mixes can be used to make a wide assortment of puddings, custards, mousses, gelatin desserts and creams. The advantages of these products are speed, quality control and reduced labor costs. Packaged mixes are simply prepared according to the directions provided by the manufacturer. For most mousses, gelatin desserts or creams, milk or other liquid is added to the powder, and then it is whipped until the desired consistency is obtained. Cooking is not usually required. The pastry cook can often improve on the final product by adding whipped cream, fruit or an appropriate garnish. Flan, pudding and baked custard mixes may require cooking before serving. As with other convenience products, quality varies from merely adequate to very good. Sample and experiment with several brands to select the best for your operation.

Popular sauces such as caramel, butterscotch, hot fudge and strawberry have been available for many years, usually sold for use at ice cream stands. With the broad appeal of plated desserts, more varieties of sauces and products containing less sugar and more natural ingredients are now available. Ready-to-use cream sauce bases allow easy customization with the addition of spices or chocolate. Convenience reached a new level when fruit sauces for plated desserts became available in ready-to-use plastic applicator bottles.

1. Eggs and dairy products are susceptible to bacterial contamination. What precautions should be taken to avoid food-borne illnesses when preparing custards?
2. Explain why pastry cream should be boiled and why custard sauce should not be boiled.
3. Identify three desserts that are based on baked custard.
4. Compare a classically prepared Bavarian, chiffon, mousse and soufflé. How are they similar? How are they different?
5. Why should the oven door be kept closed the entire time that a soufflé bakes?
6. Identify three fruits suitable for making into a fruit coulis and describe the procedure to make them.

QUESTIONS FOR DISCUSSION

Terms to Know

stirred custard	sabayon
baked custard	soufflé
vanilla custard sauce (crème anglaise)	Bavarian cream
	chiffon
pastry cream (crème pâtissière)	mousse
	crème Chantilly
	charlotte
curd fillings	coulis
	clafouti

MUSCAT MOUSSELINE

PESCE RESTAURANT, HOUSTON, TX

Yield: 10 Servings, 5 fl. oz. (150 ml) each   **Method:** Stirred custard

Milk	1 pt.	500 ml
Vanilla bean, seeded	½	½
Cornstarch	2 oz.	60 g
Granulated sugar	8 oz.	240 g
Salt	0.03 oz. (⅛ tsp.)	1 g
Eggs	3.2 oz. (2 eggs)	96 g
Egg yolks	2.4 oz. (4 yolks)	72 g
Orange Muscat or other sweet dessert wine	2 fl. oz.	60 ml
Heavy cream, cold	12 fl. oz.	360 ml

1. Reserve 2 fluid ounces (60 milliliters) of the milk. Place the remaining milk in a saucepot and add the vanilla bean and its seeds. Scald the milk.

2. Combine the cornstarch with 7 ounces (210 grams) of the sugar, the salt and the reserved milk and whisk until smooth. Add the eggs and egg yolks and mix until they are incorporated and the mixture is smooth.

3. Temper the cornstarch mixture with some of the scalded milk and return the mixture to the saucepot with the remaining scalded milk. Whisk and cook over medium heat until the mixture has thickened and begins to boil.

4. Remove the pastry cream from the heat and pour into a hotel pan. Remove the vanilla bean. Lay plastic wrap over the surface of the pastry cream and refrigerate until completely cold.

5. Whip the chilled pastry cream until smooth, approximately 1 minute. Add the wine and whip to combine.

6. Whip the cream with the remaining sugar to stiff peaks. Combine the whipped pastry cream and the whipped cream and whip together, scraping down the bowl as necessary. Refrigerate until ready to use.

Approximate values per 5-fl.-oz. (150-ml) serving: **Calories** 370, **Total fat** 22 g, **Saturated fat** 11 g, **Cholesterol** 330 mg, **Sodium** 90 mg, **Total carbohydrates** 36 g, **Protein** 8 g, **Vitamin A** 20%, **Calcium** 10%

DIPLOMAT CREAM FILLING

Yield: 5 qt. (5 lt)

Pastry Cream, chilled (page 492)	1 gal.	4 lt
Raspberry liqueur	4 fl. oz.	120 ml
Granulated gelatin	1.5 oz.	45 g
Water	6 fl. oz.	180 ml
Whipped cream	1 qt.	1 lt

1. Place the Pastry Cream in a large mixer bowl and whip on high speed until smooth. Add the raspberry liqueur.

2. Bloom the granulated gelatin in the water, then place over a low flame and heat to dissolve.

3. Add one-quarter of the raspberry-flavored Pastry Cream to the gelatin. Place over a low flame and whip by hand until smooth and the gelatin is incorporated. Add this mixture to the rest of the Pastry Cream.

4. Fold in the whipped cream.

Approximate values per 1-oz. (30-g) serving: **Calories** 40, **Total fat** 2 g, **Saturated fat** 1 g, **Cholesterol** 30 mg, **Sodium** 10 mg, **Total carbohydrates** 5 g, **Protein** 1 g

CRÈME CHIBOUST

Yield: 1 pt. (500 ml) **Method:** Stirred custard

Milk	6 fl. oz.	180 ml
Vanilla bean	½	½
Egg yolks	1.8 oz. (3 yolks)	54 g
Granulated sugar	7.5 oz.	225 g
Cornstarch	0.6 oz. (2 Tbsp.)	18 g
Sheet gelatin, softened	3 sheets (0.2 oz.)	6 g
Water	1.5 fl. oz.	45 ml
Egg whites	3 oz. (3 whites)	90 g
Cream of tartar	0.02 oz. (⅛ tsp.)	0.6 g

1. Prepare a pastry cream by heating the milk and vanilla bean just to a boil. Whisk the egg yolks, 1.5 ounces (45 grams) of the sugar and the cornstarch together. Temper with one-third of the hot milk, then return the mixture to the saucepan and cook over moderate heat until thick. The pastry cream should be allowed to boil briefly to properly gelatinize the starch. Remove the cream from the heat and transfer to a clean bowl. Remove the vanilla bean.

2. Stir the softened sheet gelatin into the hot cream. Cover and set aside, but do not chill or allow the cream to set while preparing the Italian meringue.

3. Prepare an Italian meringue using the remaining 6 ounces (180 grams) of sugar and the water, egg whites and cream of tartar. Bring the sugar and water to a boil. Place the egg whites and cream of tartar in the bowl of a mixer fitted with the whip attachment. As the temperature of the boiling sugar approaches 220°F (104°C), begin whipping the egg whites. When the whites reach soft peaks, reduce the mixer speed and continue whipping.

4. When the sugar reaches the firm ball stage (246°F/119°C), remove it from the heat. Pour it into the whites with the mixer running at high speed. Pour in a steady stream between the side of the bowl and the beater. Whip the meringue just until the hot syrup is incorporated, approximately 1 minute.

5. Quickly and thoroughly incorporate one-third of the hot meringue into the warm pastry cream with a spatula. Gently fold in the remaining meringue.

6. Use the Chiboust immediately to fill tarts or tortes. Or pour it into a clean bowl, cover and refrigerate until firm.

Approximate values per 1-fl.-oz. (30-ml) serving: **Calories** 80, **Total fat** 1.5 g, **Saturated fat** 0.5 g, **Cholesterol** 40 mg, **Sodium** 20 mg, **Total carbohydrates** 14 g, **Protein** 3 g, **Claims**—low fat; low saturated fat; very low sodium

PASSION FRUIT CHIBOUST TARTS

Yield: 15 Tarts, 4.75 in. (12 cm) each

Coconut Almond Tart Dough (page 383), 4.75-in. (12-cm) tart shells, fully baked	15 shells	15 shells
Mangoes, ripe, peeled	3	3
Passion Fruit Crème Chiboust (recipe follows)	1 lb. 10 oz.	797 g
Granulated sugar	as needed	as needed
Chocolate decorations (page 696)	15	15
Cape gooseberries or dried mango slices	15	15

❶ Arrange the tart shells on sheet pans, spacing them a few inches apart. Set aside. Cut the mangoes into ¼-inch (6-millimeter) dice. Set aside.

❷ Prepare the Passion Fruit Crème Chiboust. Fill a piping bag fitted with a large plain tip with the crème Chiboust. Fill each tart shell half full. Sprinkle the mango cubes evenly among the half-filled tart shells. Cover with the remaining crème Chiboust. Slightly dome the surface of the filling with a metal spatula.

❸ Refrigerate 2 hours.

❹ Sprinkle a thin even layer of fine granulated sugar on the surface of each crème Chiboust tart. Brown the surface of each tart using a propane torch.

❺ Garnish each tart with a chocolate decoration and a cape gooseberry or a slice of dried mango.

Approximate values per serving: **Calories** 550, **Total fat** 34 g, **Saturated fat** 20 g, **Cholesterol** 130 mg, **Sodium** 160 mg, **Total carbohydrates** 58 g, **Protein** 8 g, **Vitamin A** 20%, **Iron** 15%

PASSION FRUIT CRÈME CHIBOUST

Yield: Approximately 1 lb. 10 oz. (784 g)   **Method:** Stirred custard

Passion fruit juice	6 fl. oz.	180 ml
Heavy cream	3 fl. oz.	90 ml
Egg yolks	3 oz. (5 yolks)	90 g
Granulated sugar	8 oz.	240 g
Cornstarch	1 oz.	30 g
Sheet gelatin, softened	2 sheets (0.12 oz.)	4 g
Powdered sugar	as needed	as needed
Egg whites	5 oz. (5 whites)	150 g
Water	2 fl. oz.	60 ml

❶ Prepare a pastry cream by bringing the juice and cream to a boil in a large stainless steel saucepan.

❷ Whisk the egg yolks and 3 ounces (90 grams) of the sugar to a ribbon, then add the cornstarch. Temper with half of the hot cream.

❸ Return the tempered egg mixture to the saucepan and bring to a boil while vigorously whisking. Once the custard has come to a boil and thickened, remove from the heat and pour into a clean bowl.

❹ Stir the softened sheet gelatin into the cream until it is dissolved and smooth. Scrape down the bowl and lightly dust the surface with powdered sugar to prevent a crust from forming. Do not chill the cream.

❺ Meanwhile, prepare an Italian meringue with the egg whites, the remaining 5 ounces (150 grams) of sugar and the water according to the method on page 413. Delicately fold the Italian meringue into the hot passion fruit cream.

❻ Use immediately. Pour the cream into a serving container or torte or other mold before it sets. This will keep refrigerated several days.

Approximate values per 1-oz. (30-g) serving: **Calories** 90, **Total fat** 2.5 g, **Saturated fat** 1 g, **Cholesterol** 45 mg, **Sodium** 15 mg, **Total carbohydrates** 16 g, **Protein** 2 g

RASPBERRY CREAM FILLING

This formula is used in the Fraisier Torte on page 621.

Yield: 2 lb. (960 g)   **Method:** Stirred custard

Traditional French Buttercream (page 453)	14 oz.	420 g
Pastry Cream (page 492)	12 oz.	360 g
Raspberry purée	5 oz.	150 g
Raspberry compound	1 oz.	30 g

1 Cream the Traditional French Buttercream until light and fluffy. Set aside.

2 Combine the Pastry Cream, raspberry purée and raspberry compound.

3 Delicately fold the Pastry Cream into the Traditional French Buttercream. Use immediately.

Approximate values per 1-oz. (30-g) serving: **Calories** 90, **Total fat** 60 g, **Saturated fat** 3.5 g, **Cholesterol** 55 mg, **Sodium** 10 mg, **Total carbohydrates** 8 g, **Protein** 1 g

APRICOT FLAN

Yield: 2 lb. 9 oz. (1245 g)   **Method:** Baked custard

Eggs	10 oz. (6 eggs)	300 g
Granulated sugar	5 oz.	150 g
Sour cream	2 fl. oz.	60 ml
Heavy cream	6 fl. oz.	180 ml
Vanilla extract	0.5 fl. oz.	15 ml
Apricot purée	1 lb. 2 oz.	540 g
Fresh fruit (optional)	as needed	as needed
Candied Almonds (page 604; optional)	as needed	as needed

1 Whisk the eggs and sugar in a mixing bowl until combined. Add the sour cream, heavy cream, vanilla and apricot purée.

2 Brush individual ramekins with melted butter and arrange in a 2-inch- (5-centimeter-) deep hotel pan. Pour the mixture into the prepared ramekins, filling to just below the rim.

3 Pour enough warm water into the hotel pan to reach halfway up the sides of the ramekins. Bake at 325°F (160°C) until the flan no longer makes ripples in the center and is set, approximately 1 hour.

4 Chill thoroughly in refrigerator before unmolding.

5 To unmold, run a small knife around the edge of the custard, invert onto the serving plate and give the ramekin a firm sideways shake. Garnish with fresh fruit or Candied Almonds.

Note: This flan and others may be baked in a variety of containers. Baking time will vary depending on the container used.

Approximate values per 1-fl.-oz. (30-ml) serving: **Calories** 50, **Total fat** 3 g, **Saturated fat** 1.5 g, **Cholesterol** 40 mg, **Sodium** 10 mg, **Total carbohydrates** 5 g, **Protein** 1 g, **Vitamin A** 10%

CHERRY CLAFOUTI

Clafouti is a country-style dessert from the Loire region of France and is similar to a quiche. Stone fruits such as cherries, peaches or plums are baked in an egg custard, then served piping hot or at room temperature.

Yield: 1 Cake, 10 in. (25 cm)		Method: Baked custard
Dark cherries, fresh or canned, pitted	1 lb.	480 g
Eggs	6.75 oz. (4 eggs)	200 g
Milk	12 fl. oz.	360 ml
Granulated sugar	2 oz.	60 g
Vanilla extract	0.15 fl. oz. (1 tsp.)	5 ml
All-purpose flour	2 oz.	60 g
Powdered sugar	as needed	as needed

1. Drain the cherries and pat them completely dry with paper towels. Arrange them evenly on the bottom of a buttered 10-inch (25-centimeter) pan. Do not use a springform pan or removable-bottom tartlet pan.
2. Make the custard by whisking the eggs and milk together. Add the sugar, vanilla and flour and continue whisking until all the lumps are removed.
3. Pour the custard over the cherries and bake at 325°F (160°C) for 1 to 1½ hours. The custard should be lightly browned and firm to the touch when done.
4. Dust with powdered sugar and serve the clafouti while still warm.

Approximate values per ⅒-cake serving: **Calories** 170, **Total fat** 3.5 g, **Saturated fat** 1.5 g, **Cholesterol** 90 mg, **Sodium** 4.5 mg, **Total carbohydrates** 30 g, **Protein** 5 g, **Vitamin A** 6%

CRÈME BRÛLÉE FOR TARTS

This mixture can be prepared in silicone molds and unmolded as shown in the photo on page 610.

Yield: Approximately 3 lb. (1520 g)		Method: Baked custard
Egg yolks	6 oz. (10 yolks)	180 g
Eggs	3.2 oz. (2 eggs)	100 g
Brown sugar	7 oz.	210 g
Heavy cream	1 qt.	1 lt
Vanilla extract	1 fl. oz.	30 ml

1. Lightly butter a shallow half-size hotel pan or other container and place it on a sheet pan.
2. Combine the egg yolks and eggs in a mixing bowl. Gently whisk in the brown sugar just to blend. Stir in the cream and vanilla. Mix as little as possible to avoid creating a foamy layer on top of the cream.
3. Pour the mixture into the prepared pan to a height of 1½ inches (4 centimeters).
4. Place the sheet pan in a 325°F (160°C) oven. Fill the sheet pan with water to create a water bath. Bake until set, approximately 30 to 40 minutes.
5. Chill completely before using. Cover and keep refrigerated. This filling will keep 3 days in the refrigerator.

Approximate values per 1-oz. (30-g) serving: **Calories** 100, **Total fat** 8 g, **Saturated fat** 5 g, **Cholesterol** 75 mg, **Sodium** 15 mg, **Total carbohydrates** 5 g, **Protein** 1 g

WARM DOUBLE CHOCOLATE SUN-DRIED CHERRY DIPLOMAT

Yield: 1 Mold, 2 qt. (2 lt) **Method:** Baked custard

Butter, melted	as needed	as needed
Granulated sugar	as needed	as needed
Classic Spongecake (page 442)	as needed	as needed
Sun-dried cherries	12 oz.	360 g

Flan:

Eggs	8 oz. (5 eggs)	240 g
Egg yolks	3 oz. (5 yolks)	90 g
Granulated sugar	7 oz.	210 g
Vanilla extract	0.5 fl. oz.	15 ml
Milk	24 fl. oz.	720 ml
Heavy cream	1 pt.	480 ml
Cocoa powder	2 oz.	60 g
Semisweet or bittersweet chocolate, chopped fine	4 oz.	120 g
Vanilla Custard Sauce (page 490)	as needed	as needed

1. Brush a shallow 2-quart (2-liter) mold with melted butter and sprinkle with granulated sugar.
2. Cut the Classic Spongecake in large dice ⅝ inch × ⅝ inch × ⅝ inch (1.5 cm × 1.5 cm × 1.5 cm) and place in the mold, alternating with sun-dried cherries.
3. Prepare the flan mixture. Whisk the eggs, egg yolks, sugar and vanilla in a mixing bowl until combined.
4. Heat the milk and heavy cream to 180°F (82°C) in a large saucepan. Add gradually to the egg mixture. Whisk in the cocoa powder and chocolate.
5. Pour the flan mixture into the mold, covering the spongecake cubes completely.
6. Bake at 325°F (160°C) until set, approximately 60 to 70 minutes. Cooking time will vary depending on the dimensions of the selected mold.
7. Completely chill the mold before serving. To unmold, run a knife around the inner edge of the mold and then invert the flan onto a platter.
8. Slice and serve with Vanilla Custard Sauce.

Approximate values per ⅒-flan serving: **Calories** 780, **Total fat** 42 g, **Saturated fat** 23 g, **Cholesterol** 530 mg, **Sodium** 150 mg, **Total carbohydrates** 95 g, **Protein** 18 g, **Vitamin A** 50%

CRÈME BRÛLÉE

VINCENT ON CAMELBACK, PHOENIX, AZ
Chef Vincent Guerithault

Yield: 3½ qt. (3½ lt)		Method: Stirred custard
Heavy cream	2 qt.	2 lt
Vanilla beans, split	2	2
Egg yolks	1 lb. 14 oz. (50 yolks)	900 g
Granulated sugar	1 lb. 4 oz.	600 g
Fresh berries	as needed	as needed
Tuile Batter cups (page 354)	as needed	as needed
Granulated sugar	as needed	as needed

1. Place the cream and the vanilla beans in a large, heavy saucepan. Heat just to a boil.
2. Whisk the egg yolks and sugar together until smooth and well blended.
3. Temper the egg mixture with one-third of the hot cream. Return the egg mixture to the saucepan and cook, stirring constantly with a whisk, until very thick. Do not allow the custard to boil.
4. Remove from the heat and strain into a clean bowl. Cool over an ice bath, stirring occasionally.
5. To serve, place fresh berries in the bottom of each Tuile Batter cup. Top with several spoonfuls of custard.
6. Sprinkle granulated sugar over the top of the custard and caramelize with a propane torch. Serve immediately.

VARIATIONS:

Passion Fruit Crème Brûlée—Replace ½ quart (500 milliliters) of the cream with ½ quart (500 milliliters) frozen, thawed passion fruit purée.

Coffee Crème Brûlée—Omit the vanilla bean. Add 1–1.5 fluid ounces (30–45 milliliters) coffee extract or compound to the finished custard.

Ginger Crème Brûlée—Omit the vanilla bean. Peel and coarsely chop a 2-inch (5-centimeter) piece of fresh ginger. Steep the ginger in the warm cream 30 minutes, and then proceed with the formula. The ginger will be strained out in Step 4.

Approximate values per 5-fl.-oz. (150-ml) serving: **Calories** 460, **Total fat** 36 g, **Saturated fat** 20 g, **Cholesterol** 480 mg, **Sodium** 135 mg, **Total carbohydrates** 26 g, **Protein** 7 g, **Vitamin A** 50%

CHOCOLATE POTS DE CRÈME

Yield: 8 Servings, 4 fl. oz. (120 ml) each		Method: Baked custard
Milk	1 pt.	500 ml
Bittersweet chocolate	8 oz.	240 g
Granulated sugar	7 oz.	210 g
Vanilla extract	0.15 fl. oz. (1 tsp.)	5 ml
Coffee liqueur	1 fl. oz.	30 ml
Egg yolks	4.2 oz. (7 yolks)	126 g
Whipped cream and chocolate shavings	as needed	as needed

1. Heat the milk just to a simmer. Add the chocolate and sugar. Stir constantly until the chocolate melts; do not allow the mixture to boil. Remove from the heat and add the vanilla and liqueur.
2. Whisk the egg yolks together, then slowly whisk them into the chocolate mixture.
3. Pour the custard into ramekins. Place the ramekins in a hotel pan and add enough hot water to reach halfway up the sides of the ramekins.

④ Bake at 325°F (160°C) until the custards are almost set in the center, approximately 30 minutes. Remove from the water bath and refrigerate until thoroughly chilled. Serve garnished with whipped cream and chocolate shavings.

Approximate values per serving: **Calories** 360, **Total fat** 16 g, **Saturated fat** 9 g, **Cholesterol** 195 mg, **Sodium** 40 mg, **Total carbohydrates** 46 g, **Protein** 6 g, **Vitamin A** 10%, **Calcium** 10%

TURTLE CHEESECAKE

Yield: 2 Cakes, 8 in. (20 cm.) each	**Method:** Baked custard	
New York Cheesecake (page 498), batter, unbaked	6 lb. 1 oz.	2910 g
Coconut Shortbread Tart Dough (page 382) or Speculaas (page 341) dough	1 lb. 8 oz.	720 g
Caramel Nut Filling or Icing (page 484)	1 lb. 9 oz.	750 g
Crème Chantilly (page 502)	as needed	as needed

① Place two 8-inch (20-centimeter) silicone molds into a hotel pan. Divide the cheesecake batter evenly between the molds. Fill the hotel pan with enough warm water to come halfway up the sides of the molds. Bake at 300°F (150°C) until the cakes no longer tremble, approximately 75 to 90 minutes.

② Remove the cakes from the water bath. Cool to room temperature, then chill overnight in a refrigerator.

③ Roll out the tart or cookie dough ¼ inch (6 millimeters) thick. Cut out two 8-inch (20-centimeter) rounds of dough. Place the dough cutouts on paper-lined sheet pans and bake at 375°F (190°C) until light golden brown and baked through, approximately 14 to 18 minutes. Cool.

④ To assemble each cheesecake, place one baked round of dough on top of each cheesecake in the silicone mold. Invert the pan of cheesecake and crust onto a cake round. Remove the silicone mold from each dough-covered cheesecake.

⑤ Warm the Caramel Nut Filling or Icing in a microwave or in a double boiler over gently simmering water until spreadable. Spread the warmed icing over the cheesecakes. Once the caramel topping has cooled, decorate with Crème Chantilly if desired.

Approximate values per ¹⁄₁₂-cake serving: **Calories** 660, **Total fat** 114 g, **Saturated fat** 63 g, **Cholesterol** 442 mg, **Sodium** 615 mg, **Total carbohydrates** 103 g, **Protein** 22 g, **Vitamin A** 45%, **Iron** 15%

① Placing a round of crust on top of the cooled baked cheesecake.

② Removing the silicone mold from the baked cheesecake.

③ The finished cheesecake.

INDIVIDUAL VANILLA CHEESECAKES

Yield: 12 Servings		**Method:** Baked custard
Cream cheese, room temperature	1 lb. 6 oz.	660 g
Granulated sugar	10 oz.	300 g
Eggs	8 oz. (5 eggs)	240 g
Sour cream	1 lb. 7 oz.	700 g
Vanilla extract	0.3 fl. oz. (2 tsp.)	10 ml
Shortbread Tart Dough (page 382), baked into 2½-in. (7-cm) discs	as needed	as needed
Fresh fruit	as needed	as needed
Chocolate Caramel Sauce (page 538)	as needed	as needed

1. Butter twelve 2½-inch (7-centimeter) ramekins and set them on a sheet pan.
2. Blend the cream cheese and sugar in the bowl of a mixer fitted with the paddle attachment on low speed until thoroughly combined. Scrape down the bowl and blend on low 1 more minute until well blended.
3. Add the eggs a small amount at a time, scraping down the bowl and paddle after each addition. Add the sour cream and vanilla.
4. Pour the batter into the prepared ramekins.
5. Place the sheet pan in a 325°F (160°C) oven. Fill the sheet pan with water to create a water bath. Bake until set but not cracked on the surface, approximately 45 minutes.
6. Remove from the water bath and chill immediately after removal from the oven.
7. To serve, unmold each cheesecake onto a disc of Shortbread Tart Dough. Serve them garnished with fresh fruit and Chocolate Caramel Sauce.

VARIATION:

Cappuccino Cheesecakes—Butter eight 2½-inch (7-centimeter) ramekins. Make the cheesecake batter using 1 pound (480 grams) cream cheese, 4 ounces (120 grams) granulated sugar, 3.3 ounces (100 grams/2 eggs) eggs, 4 ounces (120 grams) sour cream, 1 fluid ounce (30 milliliters) coffee extract and 0.15 fluid ounce (1 teaspoon/5 milliliters) vanilla extract. Dust the unmolded cheesecakes with cocoa powder and powdered sugar before serving.

Approximate values per serving: **Calories** 430, **Total fat** 32 g, **Saturated fat** 19 g, **Cholesterol** 170 mg, **Sodium** 210 mg, **Total carbohydrates** 28 g, **Protein** 8 g, **Vitamin A** 25%

BREAD PUDDING WITH BOURBON SAUCE

Yield: 20 Servings   **Method:** Baked custard

Raisins	8 oz.	240 g
Brandy	4 fl. oz.	120 ml
Unsalted butter, melted	2 oz.	60 g
White bread, day-old	1 lb. 8 oz.	720 g
Heavy cream	2 qt.	2 lt
Eggs	10 oz. (6 eggs)	300 g
Granulated sugar	1 lb. 10 oz.	780 g
Vanilla extract	1 fl. oz.	30 ml
Bourbon Sauce (recipe follows)	as needed	as needed

1. Combine the raisins and brandy in a small saucepan. Heat just to a simmer, cover and set aside.
2. Use a portion of the butter to thoroughly coat a 2-inch- (5-centimeter-) deep hotel pan. Reserve the remaining butter.
3. Tear the bread into chunks and place in a large bowl. Pour the cream over the bread and set aside until soft.
4. Beat the eggs and sugar until smooth and thick. Add the vanilla, the remaining melted butter and the raisins and brandy.
5. Toss the egg mixture with the bread gently to blend. Pour into the hotel pan and bake at 350°F (180°C) until browned and almost set, approximately 45 minutes.
6. Serve warm with 1–1½ fluid ounces (30–45 milliliters) of Bourbon Sauce per portion.

VARIATION:

Chocolate Bread Pudding—Omit the brandy, raisins and melted butter. Melt 6 ounces (180 grams) unsalted butter and 12 ounces (360 grams) bittersweet chocolate together. Add the chocolate and butter to the egg mixture in Step 4. Serve with Vanilla Custard Sauce (page 490).

Approximate values per serving: **Calories** 700, **Total fat** 44 g, **Saturated fat** 26 g, **Cholesterol** 270 mg, **Sodium** 260 mg, **Total carbohydrates** 67 g, **Protein** 9 g, **Vitamin A** 50%, **Calcium** 10%, **Iron** 10%

BOURBON SAUCE

Yield: 1 qt. (1 lt)

Unsalted butter	8 oz.	240 g
Granulated sugar	1 lb.	480 g
Eggs	3.2 oz. (2 eggs)	90 g
Bourbon	8 fl. oz.	240 ml

1. Melt the butter; stir in the sugar and eggs and simmer to thicken.
2. Add the bourbon and hold in a warm place for service.

Approximate values per 1-fl.-oz. (30-ml) serving: **Calories** 150, **Total fat** 8 g, **Saturated fat** 5 g, **Cholesterol** 40 mg, **Sodium** 50 mg, **Total carbohydrates** 19 g, **Protein** 1 g, **Vitamin A** 8%

RICE CREAM WITH CHERRY GELÉE

Reduce the gelatin by 20 percent for a softer-setting gelée.

Yield: 8–10 Servings

Cherry Gelée (page 613)	1 lb.	480 g
Water	1 qt.	1 lt
Rice, short or medium grain, rinsed in cold water	6 oz.	180 g
Granulated sugar	4 oz.	120 g
Milk	28 fl. oz.	840 ml
Vanilla bean, split	12	12
Vanilla Custard Sauce (page 490)	13 fl. oz.	390 ml
Almond extract (optional)	0.15 fl. oz. (1 tsp.)	5 ml
Heavy cream, whipped to soft peaks (optional)	6 fl. oz.	180 ml
Chocolate decorations	as needed	as needed
Fresh cherries	as needed	as needed

1. Position 8 to 10 serving glasses on a muffin pan or other mold so that each glass is tilted. Prepare the Cherry Gelée and divide it evenly among the glasses. Refrigerate until set, about 1 hour.

2. Bring the water to a boil in a small saucepan. Add the rice, cover and remove the pan from the heat. Let the rice swell for 10 minutes, then strain.

3. Bring the sugar and milk to a boil in a small saucepan. Add the swelled rice. Scrape the seeds of the vanilla bean into the saucepan. Cook, covered, on low heat until the rice is tender and all of the milk is absorbed. (Check the pan as the rice cooks and add additional milk if necessary until the rice is tender.) Let cool.

4. Add a small amount of Vanilla Custard Sauce to the cooled rice. Blend well, then fold in the remaining custard sauce and almond extract (if using). Fold in the whipped cream (if using).

5. Fill each serving glass with enough of the rice mixture to come to the top edge of the chilled gelée. Refrigerate until set.

6. To serve, balance a thin strip of chocolate decoration and fresh cherries on top of each glass.

VARIATIONS:

Cinnamon Raisin Rice Cream with Strawberry Gelée—Prepare Strawberry Gelée (page 613) instead of Cherry Gelée. Simmer 1 cinnamon stick with the milk and rice in Step 3. Stir in 2 ounces (60 grams) raisins with the Vanilla Custard Sauce in Step 4.

Rice Pudding—Omit the Cherry Gelée. Prepare the rice cream, evenly dividing it among four or five serving glasses. Garnish with diced fresh pineapple and ground cinnamon.

Approximate values per 11-oz. (330-g) serving: **Calories** 380, **Total fat** 15 g, **Saturated fat** 9 g, **Cholesterol** 135 mg, **Sodium** 65 mg, **Total carbohydrates** 54 g, **Protein** 8 g, **Vitamin A** 15%, **Vitamin C** 15%

HOT GRAND MARNIER SOUFFLÉ

Yield: 16 Servings

Milk	1 pt.	480 ml
Vanilla bean paste or extract	0.2 oz. (1 tsp.)	5 ml
Salt	0.03 oz. (⅛ tsp.)	0.5 g
Orange zest, grated	0.2 oz. (1 Tbsp.)	6 g
Egg yolks	7.2 oz. (12 yolks)	216 g
Granulated sugar	8 oz.	240 g
Cornstarch	2.25 oz.	27 g
All-purpose or pastry flour, sifted	1.5 oz.	45 g
Grand Marnier	3 fl. oz.	90 ml
Egg whites	8 oz. (8 whites)	240 g
Powdered sugar	as needed	as needed

Hot Grand Marnier Soufflé

1. Prepare a pastry cream by combining the milk, vanilla, salt and orange zest in a nonreactive saucepan. Bring to a boil.

2. In a mixing bowl, whisk 2.5 ounces (75 grams) of the egg yolks and 4 ounces (120 grams) of the sugar until foamy. Whisk in a few tablespoons of the heated milk, then whisk in the cornstarch and flour until well blended.

3. Temper the egg mixture with one-quarter of the boiled milk. Return the egg mixture to the saucepan. Bring the mixture to a boil, whisking constantly. Remove from the heat when very thick. Scrape into a large bowl and cover with plastic wrap. Set aside until the cream cools to 150°F (65°C).

4. Vigorously whisk the remaining egg yolks one by one into the cream. Whisk in the Grand Marnier. Cover with plastic wrap.

5. Whip the egg whites on medium speed until foamy, then add the remaining sugar gradually. Whip the mixture until stiff but not dry.

6. Whisk the cream base until smooth. Fold one-quarter of the whites into the base. Continue folding in the whipped whites one quarter at a time, recreaming as needed to keep the mixture smooth. Pipe the mixture into 16 individual 5.5-ounce (165-gram) buttered and sugared ramekins. Fill to the rim then level with a metal spatula.

7. Bake immediately at 400°F (200°C) for 10 minutes. Reduce the temperature to 375°F (190°C) and bake until well puffed and lightly browned, approximately 10 to 15 additional minutes.

8. Sift powdered sugar over the tops of the soufflés and serve immediately.

Coffee Soufflé

VARIATION:

Coffee Soufflé—Omit the orange zest and replace the Grand Marnier with 1.5 fluid ounces (45 milliliters) coffee liqueur and 1.5 fluid ounces (45 milliliters) coffee extract.

Approximate values per serving: **Calories** 230, **Total fat** 11 g, **Saturated fat** 6 g, **Cholesterol** 125 mg, **Sodium** 70 mg, **Total carbohydrates** 29 g, **Protein** 5 g, **Vitamin A** 10%, **Vitamin C** 20%

ONE-STEP LEMON CURD

Yield: 1 ½ qt. (1 ½ lt), approximately 5 lb. (2500 g)

Method: Stirred custard

Eggs	1 lb. 4 oz. (12 eggs)	600 g
Egg yolks	2.4 oz. (4 yolks)	72 g
Granulated sugar	2 lb.	960 g
Unsalted butter, cubed	1 lb.	480 g
Lemon zest, grated	1 oz.	30 g
Fresh lemon juice	12 fl. oz.	360 ml

1 Whisk all of the ingredients together in a large bowl.

2 Place the bowl over a pan of simmering water and cook, stirring frequently, until very thick, approximately 20 to 25 minutes.

3 Strain, cover and chill completely. Serve with scones or use as a filling for tartlets or layer cakes.

Approximate values per 1-fl.-oz. (30-ml) serving: **Calories** 170, **Total fat** 9 g, **Saturated fat** 5 g, **Cholesterol** 90 mg, **Sodium** 20 mg, **Total carbohydrates** 20 g, **Protein** 2 g, **Vitamin A** 10%

WHITE CHOCOLATE FRANGELICO BAVARIAN

Yield: 4 qt. (4 lt)

Heavy cream	2 qt.	2 lt
White chocolate, chopped	2 lb.	1 kg
Frangelico (hazelnut liqueur)	10 fl. oz.	300 ml
Sheet gelatin, softened	8 sheets (0.5 oz.)	15 g
Vanilla extract	0.3 fl. oz. (2 tsp.)	10 ml

1 Bring 1 quart (1 liter) of the cream just to a boil. Immediately pour over the chopped chocolate. Stir until the chocolate melts.

2 Gently heat the Frangelico just to a simmer. Remove from the heat and stir in the softened sheet gelatin.

3 Add the softened gelatin mixture to the chocolate. Stir to blend well. Cool over an ice bath, stirring frequently.

4 Whip the remaining cream with the vanilla to stiff peaks.

5 Fold the whipped cream into the cold white chocolate mixture. Chill until ready to use.

Approximate values per 4-fl.-oz. (120-ml) serving: **Calories** 400, **Total fat** 32 g, **Saturated fat** 21 g, **Cholesterol** 90 mg, **Sodium** 50 mg, **Total carbohydrates** 22 g, **Protein** 5 g, **Vitamin A** 25%

CHOCOLATE CHIFFON PIE

Yield: 2 Pies, 9 in. (22 cm) each

Milk	20 fl. oz.	600 ml
Unsweetened chocolate	4 oz.	120 g
Granulated sugar	6 oz.	180 g
Salt	0.05 oz. (¼ tsp.)	1.5 g
Egg yolks	3.6 oz. (6 yolks)	108 g
Sheet gelatin, softened	8 sheets (0.5 oz.)	15 g
Egg whites	6 oz. (6 whites)	180 g
Vanilla extract	0.3 fl. oz. (2 tsp.)	10 ml
Crumb-crust pie shells, 9 in. (22 cm) each	2 shells	2 shells
Whipped cream	as needed	as needed
Chocolate shavings	as needed	as needed

1. Combine the milk and chocolate in a heavy saucepan and warm over low heat until the chocolate melts.
2. Add 4 ounces (120 grams) of the sugar, the salt and the egg yolks. Continue cooking, stirring constantly, until the mixture thickens. Do not boil.
3. Remove from the heat and add the softened sheet gelatin, stirring until completely dissolved. Pour the mixture into a bowl and chill until very thick.
4. Whip the egg whites to soft peaks. Add the vanilla and the remaining sugar and whip to stiff peaks. Fold the whites into the chocolate.
5. Mound the chiffon into the pie shells and chill several hours before serving. Garnish with unsweetened whipped cream and chocolate shavings.

Approximate values per ⅒-pie serving: **Calories** 210, **Total fat** 12 g, **Saturated fat** 4.5 g, **Cholesterol** 70 mg, **Sodium** 160 mg, **Total carbohydrates** 21 g, **Protein** 5 g

MILK CHOCOLATE EARL GREY MOUSSE

Yield: 16 Servings, approximately 5 lb. (2400 g) Mousse

Milk	5 fl. oz.	150 ml
Heavy cream	5 fl. oz.	150 ml
Earl Grey tea leaves	1 oz.	30 g
Orange or bergamot essential oil	0.04 fl. oz. (¼ tsp.)	1 ml
Egg yolks	6 oz. (10 yolks)	180 g
Eggs	8 oz. (5 eggs)	240 g
Granulated sugar	4.5 oz.	135 g
Heavy cream, softly whipped	1 qt.	1 lt
Milk chocolate, melted and held at 130°F (54°C)	1 lb. 2 oz.	540 g

This formula is used in the Bergamot Torte on page 625.

1. Bring the milk and cream to a boil. Add the tea leaves and steep 3 to 4 minutes only, or else a bitter taste may develop. Strain out the tea leaves and add the orange or bergamot oils. Set aside.
2. Place the egg yolks, eggs and sugar in a mixer bowl over a pan of simmering water. Whisk until the mixture reaches 158°F (70°C) and is thickened. Set aside.
3. Stir one-third of the softly whipped cream into the melted chocolate in a large mixing bowl until smooth. Add the tea–cream mixture and combine well.
4. Add the whipped-egg mixture and the remaining tea cream in one step; fold delicately using a balloon whisk.

Approximate values per serving: **Calories** 490, **Total fat** 39 g, **Saturated fat** 23 g, **Cholesterol** 290 mg, **Sodium** 75 mg, **Total carbohydrates** 29 g, **Protein** 7 g, **Vitamin A** 25%, **Calcium** 15%

ORANGE MILK CHOCOLATE MOUSSE

This formula is used in the illustrations on composing a plated dessert on page 676.

Yield: 3 lb. 5 oz. (1601 g)

Egg yolks	4 oz. (6 yolks)	120 g
Water	4 fl. oz.	120 ml
Granulated sugar	4 oz.	120 g
Sheet gelatin, softened	6 sheets (0.37 oz.)	12 g
Cointreau or Grand Marnier	0.75 fl. oz.	22 ml
Milk chocolate	1 lb.	480 g
Orange essential oil	0.04 fl. oz. (¼ tsp.)	1 ml
Heavy cream, whipped to soft peaks	28 fl. oz.	840 ml

1. Prepare a bombe mixture. Whip the egg yolks, water and sugar in a bowl over simmering water until the mixture reaches 165°F (74°C).

2. Add the softened gelatin to the bombe mixture. Stir in the liqueur.

3. Meanwhile, melt the milk chocolate in a bain marie over simmering water until it reaches 100°F (38°C). Stir in the orange oil.

4. Fold the bombe mixture into the melted chocolate with a balloon whisk.

5. Gently fold in the whipped cream using a balloon whisk. Use immediately.

Approximate values per 1-oz. (30-g) serving: **Calories** 120, **Total fat** 9 g, **Saturated fat** 5 g, **Cholesterol** 50 mg, **Sodium** 15 mg, **Total carbohydrates** 8 g, **Protein** 2 g

---

RASPBERRY MOUSSELINE

Yield: 3 lb. 8 oz. (1680 g)

Raspberry purée	1.5 lb.	720 g
Raspberry liqueur (optional)	1.5 fl. oz.	45 ml
Granulated sugar	9 oz.	270 g
Water	3 fl. oz.	90 ml
Egg whites	5 oz. (5 whites)	150 g
Sheet gelatin, softened	8 sheets (0.5 oz.)	15 g
Heavy cream, whipped to soft peaks	1 pt.	480 ml

1. Warm the raspberry purée to approximately 115°F (46°C). Add the liqueur (if using).

2. Prepare an Italian meringue with the sugar, water and egg whites. Bring the sugar and water to a boil. Place the egg whites in the bowl of a mixer fitted with the whip attachment. As the temperature of the boiling sugar approaches 220°F (104°C), begin whipping the egg whites. When the whites reach soft peaks, reduce the mixer speed and continue whipping.

3. When the sugar reaches the firm ball stage (246°F/119°C), remove it from the heat. Pour it into the whites, with the mixer running at high speed. Pour in a steady stream between the side of the bowl and the beater. Once all the sugar is incorporated, whip 1 more minute at high speed, then reduce to medium speed and whip until the meringue cools to approximately 120°F (49°C).

4. Add the softened sheet gelatin to the warm raspberry purée. Stir a few seconds to dissolve the gelatin.

5. Add one-quarter of the raspberry purée to the Italian meringue to temper. Then fold in the remaining purée.

6. Fold in the whipped cream. Use immediately.

Approximate values per 1-oz. (30-g) serving: **Calories** 60, **Total fat** 3 g, **Saturated fat** 2 g, **Cholesterol** 10 mg, **Sodium** 10 mg, **Total carbohydrates** 6 g, **Protein** 1 g

WHITE CHOCOLATE MOUSSE

If the mousse is used for petit fours that may be left at room temperature for 30 minutes or longer, it may be necessary to add gelatin to the custard sauce. Adding 0.33 ounce (10 grams) should be sufficient to hold the mousse for service.

Yield: Approximately 5 lb. (2440 g)

White chocolate, chopped fine	1 lb. 11 oz.	810 g
Heavy cream	12 fl. oz.	360 ml
Egg yolks	2.4 oz. (4 yolks)	72 g
Granulated sugar	2 oz.	60 g
Heavy cream, whipped to soft peaks	38 fl. oz.	1140 ml

1 Place the white chocolate in a large stainless steel bowl. Set aside.

2 Prepare a custard sauce by heating the heavy cream in a saucepan. Beat the egg yolks and sugar together in a bowl. Temper the yolk mixture with some of the hot cream. Pour it back into the remaining hot liquid and cook, stirring constantly, until the mixture reaches 165°F (75°C).

3 Pour the custard sauce over the white chocolate and stir with a spatula until the chocolate melts and the mixture is smooth. Place the bowl over gently simmering water and heat the chocolate mixture until it reaches 110°F (43°C).

4 Using a balloon whisk or rubber spatula, delicately fold in the whipped cream.

5 Use immediately.

VARIATION:

White Chocolate Mousse Bars—Line a half-sheet pan with a piece of food-grade acetate or plastic wrap. Set aside. Prepare the White Chocolate Mousse and spread it out onto the prepared sheet pan. Freeze the mousse until set and firm. Flip the sheet of frozen mousse onto a sheet of clean parchment paper. Remove the sheet pan, using a propane torch to gently heat the edges of the pan if necessary. Lift away the sheet pan. Peel off the acetate. Trim the edges, then cut the sheet of frozen mousse into the desired size. Refrigerate the portioned mousse until ready for plating.

Approximate values per 1-oz. (30-g) serving: **Calories** 150, **Total fat** 12 g, **Saturated fat** 8 g, **Cholesterol** 45 mg, **Sodium** 20 mg, **Total carbohydrates** 8 g, **Protein** 1 g

White Chocolate Mousse served in a glass over a layer of raspberry coulis, garnished with fruits and chocolate curls.

SAFETY ALERT
Propane Torch

Training on how to operate a propane torch is recommended before using it to brown meringue or other dessert preparations. Use extreme caution and follow appropriate safety procedures. Keep the gas bottle away from sources of heat. Do not leave the torch unattended. Rest the bottle on a stable surface away from any flammable materials.

RASPBERRY MOUSSE

This formula is used in the torte assembly pictured on page 609.

Yield: 1 qt. (1 lt)

Raspberries, puréed	12 oz.	360 g
Granulated sugar	3 oz.	90 g
Raspberry brandy	1 fl. oz.	30 ml
Sheet gelatin, softened	6 sheets (0.37 oz.)	12 g
Heavy cream	8 fl. oz.	240 ml

1 Place the raspberry purée, sugar and brandy in a nonreactive saucepan and warm to approximately 115°F (46°C) to dissolve the sugar. Remove from the heat and strain through a fine chinois.

2 Add the softened sheet gelatin, stirring until it is dissolved. Chill the mixture until thick but not set.

3 Whip the cream to soft peaks and fold it into the raspberry mixture.

Approximate values per 3-fl.-oz. (90-ml) serving: **Calories** 180, **Total fat** 11 g, **Saturated fat** 7 g, **Cholesterol** 40 mg, **Sodium** 15 mg, **Total carbohydrates** 16 g, **Protein** 5 g, **Vitamin A** 10%

1 Adding the softened gelatin sheets to the warm raspberry purée.

2 Folding the softly whipped cream into the chilled raspberry purée.

LEMON-LIME MOUSSE

This formula is used in the plated dessert on page 677. Reduce the amount of gelatin by half if the mousse will not need to be sliced, as in a torte or tart.

Yield: Approximately 2 lb. 14 oz. (1400 g)

Lemon juice	4 fl. oz.	120 ml
Lime juice	4 fl. oz.	120 ml
Sheet gelatin, softened	4 sheets (0.25 oz.)	7 g
Grand Marnier	1 fl. oz.	30 ml
Egg whites	4 oz. (4 whites)	120 g
Granulated sugar	7 oz.	210 g
Water	3 fl. oz.	90 ml
Heavy cream, whipped to soft peaks	26 fl. oz.	780 ml

1 Bring the lemon and lime juices to a boil in a nonreactive saucepan to break down the enzyme in the citrus, which might interfere with the gelatin. Let cool to 140°F (60°C) and add the softened sheet gelatin. Stir in the Grand Marnier. Set aside.

2 Prepare an Italian meringue by placing the egg whites in the bowl of a mixer fitted with the whip attachment. Bring the sugar and water to a boil. As the temperature of the boiling sugar approaches 220°F (104°C), begin whipping the egg whites. When the whites form soft peaks, reduce the mixer speed and continue whipping.

3 When the sugar reaches the firm ball stage (246°F/119°C), remove it from the heat. Pour it into the whites with the mixer running at high speed. Pour in a steady stream between the side of the bowl and the beater.

4 Whip until the Italian meringue mixture cools to 120°F (49°C). Then fold it into the juice mixture. Fold in the whipped cream. Use immediately.

Approximate values per 1-oz. (30-g) serving : **Calories** 80, **Total fat** 6 g, **Saturated fat** 3.5 g, **Cholesterol** 20 mg, **Sodium** 10 mg, **Total carbohydrates** 6 g, **Protein** 2 g

---

MASCARPONE CREAM MOUSSE

Omit the gelatin if this mousse is to be served alone as a finished dessert in a serving glass.

Yield: 3 lb. 3 oz. (1537 g)

Egg yolks	6 oz. (10 yolks)	180 ml
Water	5 fl. oz.	150 ml
Granulated sugar	8 oz.	240 g
Sheet gelatin, softened	4 sheets (0.25 oz.)	7 g
Mascarpone, warm, 40°F–50°F (4°C–10°C)	1 lb. 5 oz.	630 g
Heavy cream, whipped to very soft peaks	1 pt.	480 ml

The mousse garnished with ladyfingers, chocolate sauce and chocolate decorations.

1 Prepare a bombe mixture. Whip the egg yolks and water together in a large bowl, then add the sugar. Place the bowl over a bain marie of simmering water. Whip constantly until the mixture reaches 165°F (74°C).

2 Remove the bowl from the heat. Immediately add the softened sheet gelatin.

3 Add the warm mascarpone to the bombe batter and whisk until smooth.

4 Fold in the soft whipped cream, mixing only until the cream is just blended.

5 Use immediately.

Approximate values per 1-oz. (30-g) serving: **Calories** 110, **Total fat** 9 g, **Saturated fat** 5 g, **Cholesterol** 70 mg, **Sodium** 10 mg, **Total carbohydrates** 5 g, **Protein** 2 g

1 Adding the gelatin to the bombe mixture.

2 Adding the mascarpone to the bombe mixture.

3 Folding in the whipped cream.

FIGS WITH BERRIES AND HONEY MOUSSE

GREENS, SAN FRANCISCO, CA

Chef Annie Somerville

Yield: 4 Servings

Fresh raspberries or blackberries	1 pt.	0.5 lt
Fresh figs such as Black Mission, Kadota or Calimyrna	1 pt.	0.5 lt
Fresh mint	as needed	as needed
Honey Mousse (recipe follows)	1 lb.	480 g

1. Pick through the berries, rinse them and then allow them to drain completely.
2. Rinse the figs and cut them in half, leaving the stem attached.
3. Loosely arrange the figs on a platter, sprinkle with the berries, garnish with mint and serve with the Honey Mousse.

Approximate values per serving: **Calories** 680, **Total fat** 47 g, **Saturated fat** 28 g, **Cholesterol** 370 mg, **Sodium** 200 mg, **Total carbohydrates** 57 g, **Protein** 6 g, **Vitamin A** 60%, **Vitamin C** 25%

VARIETAL HONEY

More than three hundred types of varietal honey are available in the United States. Each nectar source contributes a distinct color and flavor to the honey. Use this to advantage when selecting honey to use in ice cream, mousses and custards. From the rich buttery flavor of avocado honey to the delicate floral taste of tupelo honey, alternating honeys will change the flavor profile of a dish. Do taste these honeys before using them. The pronounced taste of buckwheat or heather blossom honey may be better suited to baked goods or chocolate desserts. Edible honeycomb makes an attractive garnish, as do granules of dried honey.

HONEY MOUSSE

Yield: Approximately 2 lb. (997 g)

Egg whites	4 oz. (4 whites)	120 g
Granulated sugar	2 oz.	60 g
Honey	6 oz.	180 g
Water	3 fl. oz.	90 ml
Sheet gelatin, softened	4 sheets (0.25 oz.)	7 g
Vanilla extract	1 fl. oz.	30 ml
Grand Marnier	1 fl. oz.	30 ml
Candied citrus rind, diced (optional)	3 oz.	90 g
Heavy cream, whipped to soft peaks	1 pt.	480 ml

1. Prepare an Italian meringue with the egg whites, sugar, honey and water. Place the egg whites in the bowl of a mixer fitted with the whip attachment. Bring the sugar, honey and water to a boil. As the temperature of the boiling sugar approaches 220°F (104°C), begin whipping the egg whites. When the whites form soft peaks, reduce the mixer speed and continue whipping.
2. When the sugar reaches the firm ball stage (246°F/119°C), remove it from the heat. Pour it into the whites with the mixer running at high speed. Pour in a steady stream between the side of the bowl and the beater. Whip the meringue just until the hot syrup is incorporated, approximately 1 minute.
3. Add the softened sheet gelatin to the Italian meringue. Transfer it to a large mixing bowl. Fold in the vanilla, Grand Marnier and candied citrus rind (if using).
4. Fold in the whipped cream and use immediately.

Approximate values per 1-oz. (30-g) serving: **Calories** 90, **Total fat** 6 g, **Saturated fat** 3.5 g, **Cholesterol** 20 mg, **Sodium** 10 mg, **Total carbohydrates** 7 g, **Protein** 3 g

HAZELNUT CREAM FILLING

This formula is used in the Nobilis Torte on page 626.

Yield: 4 lb. 12 oz. (2295 g)

Traditional French Buttercream (page 483)	2 lb.	960 g
Hazelnut paste, lump-free, creamed	12 oz.	360 g
Sheet gelatin, softened	8 sheets (0.5 oz.)	15 g
Heavy cream, whipped to soft peaks	1 qt.	960 ml

1. Combine the Traditional French Buttercream and hazelnut paste in a mixing bowl. Place over a bain marie of simmering water and whisk constantly to slightly soften the mixture without melting the buttercream. The mixture should be as soft as mayonnaise and approximately 100°F (38°C).
2. Melt the softened sheet gelatin and fold it into the hazelnut mixture.
3. Remove from the heat and fold in the whipped cream. (If the buttercream mixture is too firm or the heavy cream is whipped too stiff, the cream will curdle.) Use immediately.

Approximate values per 1-oz. (30-g) serving: **Calories** 120, **Total fat** 11 g, **Saturated fat** 6 g, **Cholesterol** 50 mg, **Sodium** 10 mg, **Total carbohydrates** 7 g, **Protein** 1 g

RASPBERRY SAUCE

Yield: Approximately 1 qt. (1 lt)

Raspberries, fresh or IQF	2 lb.	1 kg
Granulated sugar	14 oz.	420 g
Lemon juice	1 fl. oz.	30 ml

1. Purée the berries and strain through a fine chinois.
2. Stir in the sugar and lemon juice. Adjust the flavor with additional sugar if necessary.

Approximate values per 1-fl.-oz. (30-ml) serving: **Calories** 70, **Total fat** 0 g, **Saturated fat** 0 g, **Cholesterol** 0 mg, **Sodium** 0 mg, **Total carbohydrates** 17 g, **Protein** 0 g, **Claims**—fat free; no saturated fat; no cholesterol; no sodium

MINTED PEACH COULIS

Yield: 1½ pt. (750 ml)

Peach purée	20 fl. oz.	600 ml
Granulated sugar	5 oz.	150 g
Mint leaves	10	10

1. Blend the ingredients in a blender and process until smooth. Strain if desired.

Approximate values per 1-fl.-oz. (30-ml) serving: **Calories** 35, **Total fat** 0 g, **Saturated fat** 0 g, **Cholesterol** 0 mg, **Sodium** 0 mg, **Total carbohydrates** 9 g, **Protein** 0 g, **Claims**—fat free; no saturated fat; no cholesterol; no sodium

PINEAPPLE SAUCE

Yield: Approximately 1 pt. (480 ml)

Ripe pineapple, peeled and cored	1 lb.	480 g
Unsalted butter	4 oz.	120 g
Granulated sugar	4 oz.	120 g
Cider vinegar	0.6 fl. oz.	20 ml
Vanilla bean	1	1

1. Cut the pineapple into pieces and blend in a food processor until finely puréed. Strain the purée through a chinois or sieve. Set aside.
2. Melt the butter in a nonreactive saucepan over low heat without browning. Add the sugar and whisk the mixture while it comes to a boil. Add the vinegar and boil 2 minutes. Remove the pan from the heat.
3. Add the pineapple purée. Scrape the seeds from the vanilla bean and add the bean and the seeds to the pan. Let the sauce sit at least 30 minutes to infuse it with the vanilla flavor. Remove the vanilla bean before serving.

Approximate values per 1-fl.-oz. (30-ml) serving: **Calories** 90, **Total fat** 6 g, **Saturated fat** 3.5 g, **Cholesterol** 15 mg, **Sodium** 0 mg, **Total carbohydrates** 11 g, **Protein** 0 g

RHUBARB SAUCE

Yield: Approximately 1 pt. (480 ml)

Rhubarb, fresh or frozen, medium dice	1 lb.	480 g
Granulated sugar	8 oz.	240 g
Orange juice	4 fl. oz.	120 ml
Almond extract	0.8 fl. oz. (½ tsp.)	2.5 ml

1. Combine the rhubarb, sugar and orange juice in a nonreactive saucepan. Cook over medium heat, stirring frequently, until rhubarb is soft and sauce is slightly thickened, approximately 15 to 20 minutes.
2. Remove from the heat and add the almond extract. (For a smooth texture, purée the sauce in a blender.) Serve warm or chilled.

Approximate values per 1-fl.-oz. (30-ml) serving: **Calories** 60, **Total fat** 0 g, **Saturated fat** 0 g, **Cholesterol** 0 mg, **Sodium** 0 mg, **Total carbohydrates** 16 g, **Protein** 0 g, Claims—fat free, no sodium, no cholesterol

WARM WINE SAUCE

Yield: Approximately 1 pt. (480 ml)

Sweet dessert wine	12 fl. oz.	360 ml
Orange zest	0.4 oz. (2 Tbsp.)	12 g
Lemon zest	0.14 oz. (2 tsp.)	4 g
Mint leaves	10	10
Vanilla bean, split	1	1
Corn or tapioca starch	0.3 oz. (1 Tbsp.)	10 g
Granulated sugar	6 oz.	180 g
Water	2 fl. oz.	60 ml

1. In a nonreactive saucepan, bring the wine to a boil. Remove from the heat and add the orange and lemon zest, mint leaves and vanilla bean. Cover with plastic film. Infuse 2 hours or overnight.
2. Strain the infusion. Add the starch and bring the mixture to a boil.
3. Cook the sugar and water to a light golden caramel.
4. Carefully pour the heated wine into the caramel. Whisk and reboil the mixture. Remove from the heat and chill before serving.

Note: If made with tapioca starch instead of cornstarch, the sauce will be clearer.

VARIATION:

Cold Wine Sauce—Omit the starch. In step 4, dissolve 0.1 ounce (3 grams) softened sheet gelatin in with the sauce.

Approximate values per 1-fl.-oz. (30-ml) serving: **Calories** 70, **Total fat** 0 g, **Saturated fat** 0 g, **Cholesterol** 0 mg, **Sodium** 0 mg, **Total carbohydrates** 12 g, **Protein** 0 g, **Claims**—fat free; no saturated fat; no cholesterol; no sodium

BUTTERSCOTCH SAUCE

Yield: Approximately 2 qt. (2 lt)

Granulated sugar	1 lb. 8 oz.	720 g
Light corn syrup	2 lb. 4 oz.	1080 g
Unsalted butter	4 oz.	120 g
Heavy cream	10 fl. oz.	300 ml
Scotch whisky	4 fl. oz.	120 ml

1. Cook the sugar to a dark brown caramel. Add the corn syrup.
2. Remove the sugar from the heat and slowly add the butter and the cream, stirring until the butter is completely melted.
3. Stir in the Scotch and cool.

Approximate values per 1-fl.-oz. (30-ml) serving: **Calories** 120, **Total fat** 3 g, **Saturated fat** 2 g, **Cholesterol** 23 mg, **Sodium** 20 mg, **Total carbohydrates** 23 g, **Protein** 0 g, **Vitamin A** 4%

CLEAR CARAMEL SAUCE

Yield: Approximately 1 qt. (900 ml)

Granulated sugar	1 lb.	480 g
Glucose or corn syrup	3 fl. oz.	90 ml
Water	19 fl. oz.	570 ml
Orange juice	2 fl. oz.	60 ml
Vanilla bean	1	1

1. Cook the sugar, glucose syrup and 7 fluid ounces (210 milliliters) of the water to a golden-brown caramel.
2. Meanwhile, boil the remaining water with the orange juice and vanilla bean. Add the orange mixture to the caramel.
3. Return to a boil, whisk until homogenous, and remove from the heat. Remove the vanilla bean before serving.

Approximate values per 1-fl.-oz. (30-ml) serving: **Calories** 70, **Total fat** 0 g, **Saturated fat** 0 g, **Cholesterol** 0 mg, **Sodium** 0 mg, **Total carbohydrates** 17 g, **Protein** 0 g, **Claims**—fat free; no saturated fat; no cholesterol; no sodium

FRUIT CARAMEL SAUCE

Yield: Approximately 20 fl. oz. (600 ml)

Granulated sugar	6 oz.	180 g
Water	3 fl. oz.	90 ml
Glucose or corn syrup	3 fl. oz.	90 ml
Lemon, mandarin orange, passion fruit or pineapple juice, strained	12 fl. oz.	360 ml
Pectin	0.2 oz. (2 tsp.)	2 g
Fruit-flavored liqueur (optional)	1 fl. oz.	30 ml

1. Cook the sugar, water and glucose syrup to a golden caramel.
2. Meanwhile, in a nonreactive saucepan, heat the fruit juice to 120°F (49°C) and whisk in the pectin. Bring to a boil.
3. Pour the boiling juice into the caramel; carefully whisk to homogenize and reboil the mixture.
4. Remove from the heat and let cool. Add the fruit liqueur (if using).

Approximate values per 1-fl.-oz. (30-ml) serving: **Calories** 60, **Total fat** 0 g, **Saturated fat** 0 g, **Cholesterol** 0 mg, **Sodium** 10 mg, **Total carbohydrates** 15 g, **Protein** 0 g, **Claims**—fat free; no saturated fat; no cholesterol

BURNT BLOOD-ORANGE SAUCE

THE BROWN PALACE HOTEL, DENVER, CO
Former Pastry Chef Sky Globe

Yield: Approximately 9 fl. oz. (270 ml)

Granulated sugar	4 oz.	120 g
Corn syrup	1.5 oz.	45 g
Water	0.5 fl. oz.	15 ml
Fresh lemon juice	0.04 fl. oz. (¼ tsp.)	1 ml
Whole butter	1 oz.	30 g
Blood-orange purée	3 oz.	90 g

❶ Combine the sugar, corn syrup, water and lemon juice over low heat until the sugar is dissolved. Turn the heat to high and boil the mixture, occasionally brushing the sides of the pan with the liquid to prevent crystals from forming. Cook the sugar to a caramel stage.

❷ Add the butter. Carefully add the blood-orange purée. Stir until well combined and set aside to cool.

Approximate values per 1-fl.-oz. (30-ml) serving: **Calories** 80, **Total fat** 2.5 g, **Saturated fat** 1.5 g, **Cholesterol** 5 mg, **Sodium** 0 mg, **Total carbohydrates** 16 g, **Protein** 0 g

KUMQUAT SAUCE

Yield: Approximately 10 oz. (300 g)

Fresh kumquats	3 oz.	90 g
Granulated sugar	4 oz.	120 g
Orange juice	5 fl. oz.	150 ml
Lemon or lime juice	0.5 fl. oz.	15 ml
Orange liqueur (optional)	0.5 fl. oz.	15 ml
Cardamom, ground (optional)	0.02 oz. (¼ tsp.)	0.5 g
Vanilla bean paste	0.1 oz. (½ tsp.)	3 g

❶ Slice the kumquats crosswise into thin slices. Remove the seeds. Set aside.

❷ Stir the sugar over medium-high heat in a heavy saucepan until it turns a golden caramel color. Add the orange and lemon juices, stirring to loosen the caramel.

❸ Return the sauce to a boil and add the kumquat slices. Simmer for 3 minutes. Stir in the liqueur, cardamom (if using) and vanilla bean paste until blended.

Approximate values per 1-oz. (30-g) serving: **Calories** 60, **Total fat** 0 g, **Saturated fat** 0 g, **Cholesterol** 0 mg, **Sodium** 0 mg, **Total carbohydrates** 14 g, **Protein** 0 g, **Vitamin C** 15%, **Claims**—fat free; no saturated fat; no cholesterol; no sodium

CHOCOLATE CARAMEL SAUCE

Yield: 1 lb. 11 oz. (810 g)

Granulated sugar	3 oz.	90 g
Milk, scalded and kept warm	10 fl. oz.	300 ml
Semisweet chocolate (58% cacao), chopped fine	14 oz.	420 g

1. In a heavy 2-quart (2-liter) saucepan over medium-high heat, stir the sugar until it turns a golden caramel color. Add the warm milk all at once. Stirring constantly, bring the mixture back to a boil and cook 1 minute.
2. Remove from the heat. Whisk in the chocolate. Stir until the mixture is smooth.
3. Store well covered and refrigerated. Gently rewarm over a bain marie if desired.

Note: For a velvety texture and brilliant shine, stir in the chocolate using an immersion blender. Keep the blade of the immersion blender submerged in the sauce as much as possible to retain an intense dark color and sheen in the finished sauce.

Approximate values per 1-oz. (30-g) serving: **Calories** 100, **Total fat** 6 g, **Saturated fat** 6 g, **Cholesterol** 0 mg, **Sodium** 0 mg, **Total carbohydrates** 12 g, **Protein** 1 g

CHOCOLATE FUDGE SAUCE

Yield: Approximately 1 gal. (4 lt)

Heavy cream	2 qt.	2 lt
Light corn syrup	6 fl. oz.	180 ml
Granulated sugar	8 oz.	240 g
Bittersweet chocolate	4 lb.	2000 g

1. Combine the cream, corn syrup and sugar in a saucepan and bring just to a boil, stirring frequently.
2. Chop the chocolate and place in a large bowl.
3. Pour the hot cream over the chocolate and stir with a whisk until completely melted.
4. Store well covered and refrigerated. Gently rewarm over a bain marie if desired.

VARIATION:

Mint Chocolate Fudge Sauce—Bring the cream to a boil and steep 1 ounce (30 grams) finely chopped fresh mint leaves in the cream 10 minutes. Strain and proceed with the formula.

Approximate values per 1-fl.-oz. (30-ml) serving: **Calories** 130, **Total fat** 9 g, **Saturated fat** 6 g, **Cholesterol** 20 mg, **Sodium** 10 mg, **Total carbohydrates** 10 g, **Protein** 1 g, **Vitamin A** 6%

ESPRESSO SAUCE

CHRISTOPHER'S FERMIER BRASSERIE AND PAOLA'S WINE BAR, PHOENIX, AZ
Chef-Owner Christopher Gross

Yield: Approximately 1½ pt. (700 ml)

Egg yolks	3.5 oz. (6 yolks)	105 g
Granulated sugar	3.5 oz.	105 g
Half-and-half	1 pt.	480 ml
Espresso beans, ground coarse*	1.5 oz.	45 g
Vanilla bean	½	½

1. Whisk the egg yolks and sugar together in a medium bowl.
2. Bring the half-and-half, espresso beans and vanilla bean to a simmer in a heavy saucepan.
3. Add a portion of the hot half-and-half to the egg yolks, then return the mixture to the saucepan. Cook over low heat, stirring constantly, until the sauce is thick enough to coat the back of a spoon. Do not allow the mixture to go above 185°F (85°C) or the mixture will curdle. Strain through a fine mesh sieve and cool over an ice bath.

Note: To prepare the whole espresso beans, use the coarse setting on a coffee grinder or crush them on a work-table with a rolling pin.

Approximate values per 1-fl.-oz. (30-ml) serving: **Calories** 60, **Total fat** 4 g, **Saturated fat** 2 g, **Cholesterol** 75 mg, **Sodium** 10 mg, **Total carbohydrates** 5 g, **Protein** 2 g, **Vitamin A** 6%

COCONUT SAUCE

Yield: Approximately 20 fl. oz. (600 ml)

Coconut purée or unsweetened coconut milk	1 pt.	480 ml
Heavy cream	4 fl. oz.	120 ml
Vanilla extract	0.3 fl. oz. (2 tsp.)	10 ml

1. Combine the coconut purée, cream and vanilla in a small bowl. Blend well with a whisk. Chill before serving.

Approximate values per 1-fl.-oz. (30-ml) serving: **Calories** 60, **Total fat** 7 g, **Saturated fat** 6 g, **Cholesterol** 5 mg, **Sodium** 0 mg, **Total carbohydrates** 1 g, **Protein** 1 g

CHAPTER FIFTEEN

ICE CREAM AND FROZEN DESSERTS

- recognize and evaluate commercially prepared ice cream and frozen products
- understand the churning method for making ice creams and sorbets
- understand the still-freezing method for preparing frozen desserts
- prepare a variety of ice creams, sorbets and frozen desserts
- prepare a variety of frozen soufflées, mousses, tortes and bombes

baked Alaska ice cream set on a layer of spongecake and encased in meringue, then baked until the meringue is warm and golden

bombe two or more flavors of ice cream, or ice cream and sherbet, shaped in a spherical mold; each flavor is a separate layer that forms the shell for the next flavor

overrun a measure of the air churned into an ice cream; it is expressed as a percentage, which reflects the increase in volume of the ice cream greater than the amount of the base used to produce the product

coupe an ice cream sundae, especially one served with a fruit topping

parfait ice cream served in a long, slender glass with alternating layers of topping or sauce; also the name of the mousselike preparation that forms the basis for some still-frozen desserts

FROZEN DESSERTS PROVIDE A PLEASING COLD AND CREAMY CONTRAST at the end of a meal. It is no wonder that ice cream is the world's best-selling dessert or that residents of the United States consume more than 4 gallons a year per person. Ice creams and sorbets are important components in the complex desserts served in restaurants discussed in Chapter 19, Restaurant and Plated Desserts. This chapter covers the most popular varieties of frozen desserts and the methods for producing them. With or without an ice cream freezer, frozen desserts can be made in any restaurant equipped with a standard freezer. No matter the season, the cool and comforting texture of ice cream and frozen desserts is welcomed by virtually every diner.

ICE CREAM AND FROZEN DESSERTS

Frozen desserts are categorized by the freezing method employed, either churned or still-frozen. **Churned** frozen desserts may be dairy based, made from milk or custard, or nondairy, made from fruit, chocolate or other flavorings combined with sugar. Ice cream, gelato, sorbet and sherbet are all churned. **Still-frozen** desserts, known as **semifreddi**, are made from custards or mousses that are frozen without churning. These include frozen soufflés and parfaits as well as desserts assembled with ice cream such as **baked Alaska** and vacherin or **bombes**, molds lined with cake and filled with ice cream, sorbets and frozen mousses and parfaits. Granita is a grainy type of frozen dessert made with fruit juice, wine or other liquids and sugar.

The character of a frozen dessert is determined by the freezing method used and the selection and ratio of ingredients.

Churn-Frozen Desserts

Ice cream, gelato, sorbet and sherbet are churn-frozen desserts made from a custard base or a fruit juice and sugar syrup. One hallmark of good ice cream, gelato and sorbet is smoothness. The ice crystals that would normally form during freezing are reduced when the mixture is constantly stirred or churned during freezing. The motion of the churn breaks up the crystals while adding air to the mixture. The air causes the mixture to expand in volume and lighten.

Overrun is a way to indicate the amount of air churned into a churn-frozen product. Overrun is expressed as a percentage, which reflects the increase in volume of the ice cream greater than the amount of the base used to produce the product. For example, if 1 quart of ice cream base produces 1½ quarts of churned ice cream, the volume has increased 50 percent. The overrun is 50 percent. Good-quality ice creams and sorbets have enough air to make them light; inferior products often contain excessive overrun. Premium ice creams may have an overrun of up to 20 percent, while an inexpensive product may have 100 percent overrun. The difference becomes obvious when equal volumes are weighed. The type of equipment used to churn the ice cream and the amount placed in the freezer will affect overrun. Horizontal and continuous batch freezers used in commercial production tend to incorporate more air. The amount of milkfat and eggs in a formula will also affect overrun.

The higher fat content of ice cream and gelato as compared to sorbet gives the former a smoother **mouthfeel** than the fruit- and sugar-based sorbet. The proper ratio of sugar in frozen mixtures ensures that the product will freeze; too much sugar and the mixture will be slushy. Sugar prevents large crystals from forming, resulting in a smoother product.

ICE CREAM: FROM ANCIENT CHINA TO DOUBLE-FUDGE-BROWNIE-CHOCOLATE-CHIP WITH COOKIE DOUGH AND TOASTED ALMOND SLIVERS

Despite claims to the contrary, it is impossible to identify any one country as having invented ice cream. More likely, it was invented in several places around the world at various times.

Early ancestors of today's ice creams were flavored water ices, which have been popular in China since prehistoric times. They have also been popular in the Mediterranean and Middle East since the Golden Age of Greece. In fact, Alexander the Great had a penchant for wine-flavored ices, made with ice brought down from the mountains by runners. The Roman emperor Nero served his guests mixtures of fruit crushed with snow and honey. The Saracens brought their knowledge of making flavored ices with them when they migrated to Sicily in the 9th century. And 12th-century Crusaders returned to Western Europe with memories of Middle Eastern sherbets.

The Italians are said to have developed gelato from a recipe brought back from China by Marco Polo in the 13th century. Somehow the dish spread to England by the 15th century, where it was recorded that King Henry V served it at his coronation banquet. Catherine de Medici brought the recipe with her when she married the future king of France in 1533. A different flavor was served during each of the 34 days of their marriage festivities.

Ice cream was first sold to the public in Paris during the late 17th century. It was available at fashionable cafés serving another new treat: coffee. French chefs quickly developed many elaborate desserts using ice creams, including bombes, coupes and parfaits.

Many of this country's founders—Thomas Jefferson, Alexander Hamilton and James and Dolley Madison—were confirmed ice cream addicts. George Washington spent more than $200, a very princely sum, for ice cream during the summer of 1790.

The mechanized ice cream freezer was invented in 1846, setting the stage for mass production and wide availability. By the late 19th century, ice cream parlors were popular gathering places. (Some of today's ice cream parlors still take their décor from "Gay Nineties" motifs.)

Despite the disappearance of most ice cream wagons, soda fountains and lunch counters, all of which were popular ice cream purveyors for much of the 20th century, ice cream sales have never waned. Today, more than 80 percent of all ice cream is sold in supermarkets or convenience stores. The public's demand for high-fat, homemade-style "super-premium" ice creams with rich and often-elaborate flavor combinations shows no sign of declining.

When making any frozen mixture, remember that cold dulls flavors. Although perfect at room temperature, flavors seem weaker when the mixture is cold. Increased overrun weakens the concentration of flavor. Thus, it may be necessary to oversweeten or overflavor creams, custards or syrups that will be frozen for service. Although liquors and liqueurs are common flavoring ingredients, alcohol drastically lowers a liquid mixture's freezing point. Too much alcohol will prevent the mixture from freezing; thus any liqueurs or liquors must be used in moderation.

Liquid flavorings and purées are added to ice cream or sorbet mixtures before freezing. Solids—diced fresh fruit, chocolate chips and nuts—are mixed in when the mixture is nearly frozen, yet still soft enough to stir. Otherwise these pieces would disintegrate during churning. Fresh and dried fruits and nuts may be conditioned by poaching in sugar syrup to adjust their moisture content, making them remain tender when frozen. Fudge and fruit swirls are folded into ice cream after churning is completed in order to maintain their integrity and visibility in the finished product.

marquise a frozen mousselike dessert, usually chocolate

neapolitan a three-layered loaf or cake of ice cream; each layer is a different flavor and a different color, a typical combination being chocolate, vanilla and strawberry

ICE CREAM AND GELATO

Ice cream and gelato are custards that are churned during freezing. The procedure for making an ice cream or gelato base is the same as the procedure for making custard sauce discussed in Chapter 14, Custards, Creams and Sauces. These custards can be made with milk and/or cream and whole eggs or egg yolks. Milkfat contributes richness and body to the ice cream. High-quality ice creams may contain as much as 24 percent milkfat, resulting in a dense rich product. (A higher fat content could result in a product so dense that it may have difficulty emulsifying and incorporating air during churning, thus limiting its overrun.)

The USDA has established standards for the labeling of frozen products. They require that products labeled "ice cream" contain at least 10 percent milkfat and 20 percent milk solids. USDA standards also dictate that "ice cream" cannot weigh less than 4½ pounds per gallon. French-style ice creams (frozen custards) contain a higher percentage of egg yolks and cream than standard ice cream. **Gelato** is an Italian-style ice cream made with milk. Although it has a low milkfat content—from 4 to 9 percent—it is denser than American-style products because less air is incorporated during churning. High-quality gelato is made with a 10 to 20 percent overrun, unlike ice cream, which can have as much as a 100 percent overrun. The flavor of gelato is more concentrated, although it may be lower in fat and calories.

Ice milk refers to products that do not meet the standards for ice cream. Low-fat products made without cream or egg yolks are also available for the calorie-conscious. Frozen yogurt uses yogurt as its base. Although touted as a nutritious substitute for ice cream, frozen yogurt may have whole milk or cream added for richness and smoothness. Alternative ingredients including soy and rice milk make creamy frozen desserts available to those allergic to dairy. A formula for a soy milk–based frozen dessert is provided in Chapter 16, Healthful and Special-Needs Baking.

Stabilizers

In frozen mixtures, some water often remains that does not freeze during churning. **Stabilizers** bind the water and increase the mixture's ability to trap air and expand during churning. Commercially, stabilizers are added to ice creams, sorbets and sherbets to improve their texture and freezing abilities. Stabilizers include the eggs used in a formula as well as gums (guar or locust bean), carageenan, gelatin, pectin and other vegetable-derived ingredients. Inexpensive and mass-produced ice cream products often rely on excessive amounts of stabilizers or gelatin to create texture and aid in the overrun process. Stabilizers are less commonly used in the restaurant industry, where frozen products are made more frequently and in small batches.

Churning

Regardless of the formula, cooling an ice cream base before freezing is essential to ensure a smooth texture in the finished product. The longer a mixture takes to freeze in the machine, the more time it has to develop large ice crystals. A properly chilled ice cream base freezes quickly. An ice cream base that contains eggs should be refrigerated for 24 hours before processing to help it achieve a smooth, creamy texture. This period allows the milk and egg proteins to bond with water molecules in the ice cream base, thus inhibiting the formation of ice crystals after freezing and improving the ice cream's texture.

Many food service operations use ice cream makers that have internal freezing units to chill the mixture while churning it. Most commercial machines are suitable for churning either ice cream or sorbet. Follow the manufacturer's directions for using and cleaning any ice cream maker. (Some machines require that the frozen mixture be hardened in a freezer before serving.) **Inclusions**, those tasty and visible ingredients in ice cream such as toasted nuts, pieces of fruit or chocolate, are added near the end of the churning so that they retain their size and shape. Once churned, hold ice cream and sorbet in a freezer set to between 0°F and 6°F (–18°C and –15°C) so that it hardens quickly, then store frozen desserts in a freezer set to between 6°F and 14°F (–15°C and –11°C).

SAFETY ALERT
Ice Cream

It is important to exercise extra care when preparing ice cream products because ice cream contains several potentially hazardous foods, such as cream, milk and eggs. Cooking ice cream bases properly using pasteurized egg products helps ensure a safe product. Ice cream freezers have many grooves and crevices where bacteria can hide and grow. Always break down and clean an ice cream maker after each use, and sanitize all pieces according to the manufacturer's directions. Never store frozen ice cream products in a container that held raw or unprocessed custard without first cleaning and sanitizing the container. And, of course, wash your hands thoroughly and wear gloves when working with ice cream products.

PROCEDURE FOR PREPARING ICE CREAMS

1. Prepare a custard sauce. Place the milk and/or cream in a heavy saucepan. Add flavorings such as vanilla beans or ground coffee to infuse the cream at this time.
2. Whisk the egg yolks and sugar together in a mixing bowl.
3. Bring the liquid just to a boil. Temper the egg mixture with approximately one-third of the hot liquid.
4. Pour the tempered eggs into the remaining hot liquid and return the mixture to the heat.

⑤ Cook, stirring constantly, until warmed to 180°F to 186°F (82°C to 85°C) and slightly thickened.

⑥ Remove the cooked custard sauce from the hot saucepan immediately. If left in the hot saucepan, it will overcook. Flavorings may be added at this time.

⑦ Cool the custard sauce over an ice bath to 40°F (4°C). Store the ice cream base covered and refrigerated at 36°F (2°C) 24 hours before using.

⑧ Process according to the machine manufacturer's directions. Add any pieces of chocolate, fruit or nuts near the end of churning to retain their shape and size.

ICE CREAM BASE

Yield: 2½ qt. (2.5 lt)	**Method:** Churned	
Whole milk	1½ qt.	1.5 lt
Heavy cream	1 pt.	480 ml
Vanilla bean, split (optional)	1	1
Egg yolks	10 oz. (16 yolks)	300 g
Granulated sugar	1 lb. 4 oz.	600 g

① Combine the milk, cream and vanilla bean (if using) in a heavy saucepan and bring to a boil.

② Whisk the egg yolks and sugar together in a mixing bowl.

③ Temper the eggs with one-third of the hot milk. Return the egg mixture to the saucepan.

④ Cook over medium heat, stirring constantly, until the custard reaches 180°F–185°F (82°C–85°C) and is slightly thickened. Pour through a fine mesh strainer into a clean bowl.

⑤ Chill the cooked ice cream base completely over an ice bath before processing.

⑥ Pour the mixture into an ice cream/sorbet machine and process according to the manufacturer's directions.

VARIATIONS:

Chocolate Ice Cream—Add approximately 9 ounces (270 grams) finely chopped bittersweet chocolate per quart (liter) of ice cream base. Add the chocolate to the hot mixture after it has been strained. Stir until completely melted.

Cappuccino Ice Cream—Steep the hot milk and cream with the vanilla bean and two or three cinnamon sticks. After the ice cream base is made, stir in 0.5 fluid ounce (30 milliliters) coffee extract.

Brandied Cherry Ice Cream—Drain the liquid from one 16-ounce (480-gram) can of tart, pitted cherries. Soak the cherries in 1.5 fluid ounces (45 milliliters) brandy. Prepare the ice cream base as directed, omitting the vanilla bean. Add the brandy-soaked cherries to the cooled custard before processing.

Approximate values per 6-fl.-oz. (180-ml) serving: **Calories** 370, **Total fat** 20 g, **Saturated fat** 11 g, **Cholesterol** 270 mg, **Sodium** 65 mg, **Total carbohydrates** 41 g, **Protein** 7 g, **Vitamin A** 25%

SORBET AND SHERBET

Sorbet is a churned mixture of sugar, water and fruit juice, wine, liqueurs or other flavorings. (Even some herb and vegetable flavorings are suitable for sorbet.) It is served as a first course, a palate refresher between courses or a dessert.

Sorbet may be made with fresh, frozen or canned fruit. A wide variety of quality, all-natural frozen purées are available for sorbet making. Granulated sugar or sugar syrup is added for flavor and body. Pasteurized egg whites may also be added during churning for improved texture; the protein in the whites coats the water crystals as the sherbet freezes. Often an invert sugar such as glucose or corn syrup replaces some of the granulated sugar to prevent graininess. **Sherbet** is an Americanization of the French word *sorbet*, which has taken on a slightly different meaning on this side of the

MISE EN PLACE

▶ Set up an ice bath.

① The ice cream in the early stages of churning.

② The finished ice cream.

Atlantic. When it contains fruit juice and sugar, sherbet is identical to sorbet. But milk is often added to the mixture before churning, making it somewhat richer than sorbet and better served at the end of a meal.

The ratio of sugar to fruit purée or juice depends to some extent on the natural sweetness of the specific fruit as well as personal preference. If too much sugar is used, however, the mixture will be soft and syrupy. If too little sugar is used, the sorbet will be very hard and grainy. Following the formula carefully helps avoid this problem. A saccharometer can also be used to measure the concentration of sugar in the mixture before freezing to ensure consistent results.

Measuring Sugar Concentrations

To achieve consistent texture and sweetness, use of a saccharometer is recommended when making sorbet, sherbet or granita. A saccharometer, shown at left, shows the sugar content (**sugar density**) in a liquid mixture.

The saccharometer is a hollow glass tube calibrated with either a density scale, Baumé scale or both. The density reading (D) is obtained where the instrument meets the surface level of the liquid; when a saccharometer is placed in 58°F (14°C) water, it will float exactly at the position marked 1.000 D (0° Baumé). As the percentage of sugar to water increases, the density reading will climb. For example, a simple syrup made from equal amounts of sugar and water will measure 1.2407 D (28° Baumé). Higher temperatures can produce a lower reading, so always measure liquids at room temperature (65°F/19°C).

Fruit sorbet tastes best when the mixture has a density between 1.1333 and 1.1425 D (17° and 18° Baumé). Wine, alcohol, tea, coffee and aromatic plant sorbets should have a density reading between 1.1074 and 1.1333 D (13° and 17° Baumé). A sorbet mixture made with too little sugar and a lower-than-ideal density will be grainy and icy. Adding more of the basic sugar syrup called for in the formula will correct this. Water is added when the density reading is too high, thus preventing an overly sweet product. When a saccharometer is not available, follow the formula exactly, cooking the syrup as indicated. Should problems arise, remelt the sorbet, adding more water or sugar syrup as needed. (When making sorbet, having additional sugar syrup on hand is useful.) Use Table 15.1 to troubleshoot making ice cream and sorbet.

Using a Baumé hydrometer or saccharometer.

TABLE 15.1   TROUBLESHOOTING CHURNED FROZEN DESSERTS

PRODUCT	PROBLEM	CAUSE	SOLUTION
Ice cream	Grainy	Custard too warm before freezing	Chill base thoroughly before churning
		Insufficient milkfat	Adjust formula
		Insufficient egg yolk	Adjust formula
		Custard overcooked	Cook properly
	Too dense	Too many eggs; insufficient air incorporated during churning	Adjust formula; churn a smaller volume of custard or sorbet at one time
	Watery	Too few eggs; not enough cream	Adjust formula
		Improperly prepared custard	Cook custard properly to 180°F to 185°F (82°C to 85°C)
Sorbet or sherbet	Too soft when frozen	Too much sugar; too much fruit pulp, too much alcohol added	Remelt and adjust formula, adding water
	Grainy or icy	Too little sugar	Remelt and adjust formula, adding sugar syrup
	Separation	Too much sugar; not enough stabilizer; too much overrun	Remelt and adjust formula, adding stabilizer and/or water

PROCEDURE FOR PREPARING SHERBET OR SORBET

1. Make a base syrup by combining the water, sugar, invert sugar and stabilizers (if using). Boil 1 minute. Cool completely.

2. Combine the fruit purée or flavorings with the sugar syrup. Check the density. Add more water to reduce the density or add more base syrup to increase the density.

3. Churn according to the manufacturer's directions.

MANGO SORBET

Yield: 1 qt. (1 lt)	**Method:** Churned	
Granulated sugar	3 oz.	90 g
Pectin or stabilizer (optional)	0.1 oz. (1 tsp.)	3 g
Water	6 fl. oz.	180 ml
Glucose or corn syrup	2 oz.	60 g
Mango purée	17 oz.	510 g
Lemon or lime juice	0.5 fl. oz.	15 ml

1. Whisk together the sugar and pectin (if using). Place the sugar, water and glucose syrup in a large saucepan. Whisk until well combined. Bring the syrup to a full rolling boil and boil 1 minute.

2. Remove from the heat and let cool completely, then refrigerate, preferably overnight.

3. Combine the mango purée and lemon juice with the syrup. Check the density. Add water or more sugar syrup to the sorbet base if needed to adjust it to 1.1333 D (17° Baumé).

4. Pour the mixture into an ice cream or sorbet machine and process according to the manufacturer's directions.

5. Remove the sorbet from the machine and freeze at 0°F (–18°C) until needed for service.

VARIATION:

Coconut Sorbet—Use coconut purée in place of the mango purée. Adjust the sorbet mixture to a density reading of 1.1425 D (18° Baumé).

Approximate values per 2½-fl.-oz. (75-ml) serving: **Calories** 100, **Total fat** 0 g, **Saturated fat** 0 g, **Cholesterol** 0 mg, **Sodium** 10 mg, **Total carbohydrates** 26 g, **Protein** 0 g, **Vitamin A** 45%, **Vitamin C** 30%, **Claims**—no fat; no cholesterol; very low sodium; low calorie

1 Churning Mango Sorbet in a batch ice cream machine.

2 Scraping the finished Mango Sorbet from the machine.

GRANITA

Granita (Fr. *granité*), which is very similar to an Italian ice, is made with fruit or other flavorings but with less sugar than sorbet. This produces a mixture that will freeze harder than sorbet. Instead of being churned, the granita mixture is frozen in a shallow stainless steel container, then scraped with a fork or spoon to obtain grainy flakes. Or, as the mixture freezes and ice crystals form, the mixture is periodically stirred until granulation is complete.

Granita made with thick fruit purées, such as mango or raspberry, or with wine and liqueurs requires very cold temperatures to obtain proper granulation. The density reading of a properly prepared granita mixture ranges from 1.0745 to 1.1074 D (10° to 14° Baumé).

PROCEDURE FOR PREPARING GRANITA

1. Make a base syrup by combining the water and sugar. Boil 1 minute. Cool completely.
2. Stir in the fruit juice, coffee, wine or other flavoring liquid. Check the density. Add more water to reduce the density or add more base syrup to increase the density.
3. Pour the mixture into a shallow pan and place in a freezer.
4. Stir the granita mixture with a fork or spoon every 30 minutes as it freezes. The edges of the container will freeze first. As they form, the crystals are stirred into the unfrozen liquid in the center of the pan. This process is repeated until the granulation is complete.
5. Once the granita is completely frozen, scrape the surface of the mixture with a fork to separate the crystals and serve.

MISE EN PLACE

▶ Grind coffee.

COFFEE GRANITA

Yield: 1½ pt. (720 ml)

Water	20 fl. oz.	600 ml
Granulated sugar	5 oz.	150 g
Coffee, ground	0.75 oz.	22 g

1. Bring 4 fluid ounces (120 milliliters) of the water and the sugar to a boil. Stir to dissolve the sugar. Remove the syrup from the heat and let cool.
2. Bring the remaining 1 pint (480 milliliters) of the water to a boil. Add the ground coffee and steep 5 minutes. Strain the mixture and set aside to cool.
3. Combine the sugar syrup with the coffee liquid.
4. Check the density. Add water or more sugar syrup to the sorbet base if needed to adjust it to 1.1074 D (14° Baumé). Pour into a shallow stainless steel pan and freeze until the granita begins to harden, approximately 3 hours.
5. Scrape the surface of the granita with a metal fork or spoon to break up the ice crystals. Return the granita to the freezer until firm.
6. Scrape the surface of the frozen granita to loosen the ice crystals. Scoop into serving dishes and serve immediately.

VARIATION:

Green Tea Granita—Omit the ground coffee. Substitute loose green tea leaves for the ground coffee.

Approximate values per 4-fl.-oz. (120-ml) serving: **Calories** 100, **Total fat** 0 g, **Saturated fat** 0 g, **Cholesterol** 0 mg, **Sodium** 0 mg, **Total carbohydrates** 26 g, **Protein** 0 g, **Vitamin C** 15%, **Claims**—no fat; no cholesterol; very low sodium; low calorie

1. When the mixture has begun to freeze, scrape the ice crystals as they form in the granita.

2. Spoon the finished granita into a serving dish and serve immediately.

Sundae with raspberry sauce, Chantilly cream and nuts.

Mango sorbet on slices of kiwi with chocolate decoration.

Assorted sorbets in a nougatine cup.

SERVING SUGGESTIONS FOR ICE CREAMS AND SORBETS

Ice creams and sorbets are usually served by the scoop, often in cookie cones or bowls. Toppings and sauces can be added to create coupes, parfaits or sundaes. Many of the sauces in Chapter 14, Custards, Creams and Sauces, such as Caramel Sauce (page 512), Chocolate Fudge Sauce (page 538), Espresso Sauce (page 539) or any of the fruit sauces, work well as ice cream toppings. Crumbled Basic Nougatine (page 724) and Hazelnut Crisps (page 748) as well as toasted nuts, broken bits of candy and chocolate can be blended into churned ice creams to add texture and enhance flavor.

Ice creams and sorbets play an important part in restaurant desserts, as discussed in Chapter 19, Restaurant and Plated Desserts. When accompanying a slice of pie or as part of a dessert presentation, figure on 1½ to 2 fluid ounces (45 to 60 milliliters) per person. For a single serving of ice cream or sorbet, figure on 4 to 6 fluid ounces (120 to 180 milliliters) per person.

Serving frozen desserts at the proper temperature improves their flavor and mouthfeel. Ice creams are tempered before serving; that is, they are allowed to warm slightly. In a large operation, ice cream and frozen desserts are transferred from a storage freezer to one set to a slightly warmer temperature. Tempering the desserts at 6°F to 14°F (−15°C to −11°C) for 24 hours makes them soft enough to scoop and cut easily. Special ice cream serving cases used in restaurants or pastry shops keep ice cream at these softer temperatures for easy scooping. Placing a frozen dessert into the refrigerator for 15 to 30 minutes before serving achieves similar results.

Still-Frozen Desserts

Still-frozen desserts (It. *semifreddi*) are based on a **bombe mixture**, which is a mousse or a custard mixed with meringue or whipped cream. The bombe mixture (Fr. *pâte à bombe*) is made by stabilizing whipped egg yolks with sugar syrup cooked to the soft ball stage. Because these mixtures are still-frozen without churning, air must be incorporated by folding in relatively large amounts of whipped cream or meringue. The air in these foams helps keep the mixture smooth and prevents it from becoming too hard. Because of their air content, these desserts feel less cold than ice creams when frozen.

Frozen soufflés, parfaits, marquise, mousses, neapolitans and spumoni are some popular frozen desserts. Layers of spongecake and/or fruit may be added for flavor and texture. The word *bombe* also refers to a finished dessert composed of a frozen cream or sorbet molded and layered with meringue or cake layers. If the terminology seems confusing, it is simply because the components for many of these specialty desserts are the creams, mousses and custards discussed in Chapter 14.

sundae a great and gooey concoction of ice cream, sauces (hot fudge, marshmallow and caramel, for example), toppings (nuts, candies and fresh fruit, to name a few) and whipped cream

bombe mixture (Fr. *pâte à bombe*) egg yolks cooked with sugar syrup and whipped, used as a base for still-frozen desserts and cakes

PARFAITS AND FROZEN MOUSSES

In the United States a parfait is the name for a serving of ice cream layered with sauce and served in a tall slender glass. In France and in the pastry kitchen, a parfait is a mixture of cooked whipped egg yolks (bombe mixture) into which whipped cream and flavorings are folded and then frozen. Frozen soufflés or **soufflés glacés** are simply frozen mousses molded to resemble baked soufflés.

PROCEDURE FOR PREPARING PARFAIT AND FROZEN MOUSSE MIXTURES BASED ON A BOMBE

① Prepare a bombe mixture. Beat the egg yolks in the bowl of a mixer fitted with the whip attachment. Prepare a sugar syrup and cook to the soft ball stage (240°F/116°C). Pour the hot syrup over the frothed egg yolks. Beat until the bombe mixture cools. Fold in flavorings.

② Whip heavy cream.

③ Prepare an Italian meringue, if needed.

④ Fold the whipped cream into the bombe mixture, alternating with the Italian meringue.

⑤ Pour the mixture into molds that have been greased and dusted with granulated sugar. Layer with spongecake, fruits and other fillings if desired.

COFFEE RUM PARFAIT

MISE EN PLACE

▶ Whip cream.
▶ Chop chocolate.

Yield: 22 Servings   **Method:** Still-frozen

Granulated sugar	7 oz.	210 g
Glucose or corn syrup	2 oz.	60 g
Water	4 fl. oz.	120 ml
Egg yolks	5.4 oz. (9 yolks)	162 g
Vanilla extract	0.3 fl. oz. (2 tsp.)	10 ml
Rum	1 fl. oz.	30 ml
Coffee extract	2 fl. oz.	60 ml
Heavy cream, whipped to soft peaks	1 qt.	1 lt
Chocolate shavings, chopped fine	6 oz.	180 g
Powdered sugar	as needed	as needed

① Folding the meringue, cream and chocolate shavings into the parfait mixture.

② Leveling the parfait mixture in the ramekin before freezing.

③ Removing the collar and dusting the finished parfait with powdered sugar before serving.

1 Cut 22 strips of parchment paper or acetate 2 inches (5 centimeters) wide and long enough to wrap around the ramekins. Fasten the paper or acetate around the top of each ramekin with adhesive tape to form a collar. Lightly oil the ramekins and their collars. Sprinkle with granulated sugar.

2 Make the bombe batter. Place the sugar, glucose syrup and water in a heavy saucepan. Attach a candy thermometer to the pan and bring the sugar to a boil over high heat. Boil until the syrup reaches the soft ball stage (240°F/116°C).

3 Whip the egg yolks in the bowl of a mixer fitted with the whip attachment until doubled in volume. With the mixer running on slow speed, pour the cooked syrup along the inner wall of the bowl in a slow steady stream. Whip until the yolk mixture cools, approximately 4 to 5 minutes.

4 Add the vanilla, rum and coffee extract and whip on low speed. Remove the bowl from the machine.

5 Using a spatula or balloon whisk, carefully fold in the whipped cream and chocolate shavings.

6 Fill the ramekins to the rim of their collars and level the cream using a metal spatula. Freeze until hardened, approximately 4 to 6 hours.

7 Remove the collars. Lightly dust with powdered sugar.

Approximate values per serving: **Calories** 260, **Total fat** 20 g, **Saturated fat** 12 g, **Cholesterol** 145 mg, **Sodium** 25 mg, **Total carbohydrates** 18 g, **Protein** 2 g, **Vitamin A** 15%

FROZEN TORTES AND BOMBES

Frozen tortes and bombes are filled with ice cream, sorbet and parfait mixtures alone or in combination. Spongecake or genoise, which absorbs some of the cream as the dessert melts, or baked meringue layers are used to support the cakes. Frozen tortes are assembled in the same manner as described in Chapter 17, Tortes and Specialty Cakes (pages 608–610). Ring molds are lined with cake, then layered with ice cream or parfait mixtures. Or silicone molds are filled with an ice cream, sorbet or parfait mixture, then topped with a disk of cake, meringue or crust. The traditional bombe is made in a decorative oval mold and shaped like a melon, or in a tube pan with a tight-fitting lid. One or more flavors of ice cream, sorbet or parfaits, selected for color and flavor contrast, are packed into the mold, and then the mold is sealed before freezing. Handles on the mold facilitate unmolding the frozen bombe by allowing the pastry chef to easily dip the mold into warm water to help release the bombe.

Classic desserts such as Baked Alaska (page 562) are always popular and make exciting alternatives to traditional celebration cakes. Individual serving sizes are easy to construct in ramekins, small timbale molds or disposable plastic cups. These desserts may be made ahead and iced with Chantilly cream or Italian meringue before service. The formula for Pistachio Apricot Bombe (page 552) illustrates the procedure for preparing a frozen torte or bombe. As with all frozen products, frozen desserts taste better when slightly softened or tempered before serving.

PROCEDURE FOR PREPARING A FROZEN TORTE OR BOMBE

1 Lightly oil a spherical bombe mold. Pack the mold with churned ice cream or sorbet.

2 Cut a layer of spongecake the same diameter as the bombe mold. Top the ice cream with the cake. Seal the mold tightly with its lid or with plastic wrap.

3 To serve, invert the bombe mold onto a serving platter. Remove the mold and garnish the bombe with crème Chantilly, candied fruit and nuts, chocolate decorations or nougatine. Serve immediately.

Unmolding a frozen bombe.

PISTACHIO APRICOT BOMBE

MISE EN PLACE

▸ Prepare the Dacquoise.
▸ Prepare the Pistachio Ice Cream.
▸ Prepare and churn the Apricot Sorbet.
▸ Whip the cream.
▸ Prepare the Cocoa Gelée.

Yield: 3 Bombes, 1 qt. (1 lt) each

Dacquoise (page 424)	1 half sheet	1 half sheet
Pistachio Ice Cream (page 554)	1½ qt.	1.5 lt
Apricot Sorbet (page 556)	1 qt.	1 lt
Heavy cream, whipped to soft peaks	1½ qt.	1.5 lt
Cocoa Gelée (page 608)	as needed	as needed
Chocolate cutouts (page 698)	as needed	as needed
Chocolate combed curls (page 701)	as needed	as needed
Pistachios	as needed	as needed

1. Chill the bombe molds in the freezer at least 30 minutes.

2. Cut the Dacquoise into three pieces trimmed to fit the opening of the molds. Set aside.

3. Using a plastic scraper, spread the freshly churned Pistachio Ice Cream to line the molds to a thickness of ¾ inch (2 centimeters). Freeze until hardened.

4. Pack the molds with the Apricot Sorbet, leaving enough space for the Dacquoise to fit level with the rim of the mold.

5. Press the Dacquoise into place. Cover the molds and freeze until hardened.

6. To serve, run the molds briefly under warm water. Unmold them onto icing screens and then return them to the freezer.

7. In order for the Cocoa Gelée to adhere to the bombes, coat each bombe with a thin layer of whipped cream. Return them to the freezer.

8. Heat the Cocoa Gelée until it reaches approximately 130°F (54°C). Pour the Cocoa Gelée over the bombes to cover evenly. Shake the icing screen to remove excess Cocoa Gelée. Transfer the bombes to cake boards.

9. Surround the base of each bombe with a row of chocolate cutouts. Decorate the top of the bombes with chocolate combed curls and pistachios.

Approximate values per ⅛-bombe serving: **Calories** 480, **Total fat** 26 g, **Saturated fat** 9 g, **Cholesterol** 120 mg, **Sodium** 65 mg, **Total carbohydrates** 54 g, **Protein** 11 g, **Vitamin A** 25%

CONVENIENCE PRODUCTS

Commercially prepared ice cream, gelato, sherbet and sorbet can be a significant convenience item for the pastry chef. These products are available in 1- to 3-gallon containers in a range of quality grades and flavors. As always, the costs should be evaluated against the cost and effort of producing frozen products in-house. Contemporary pastry chefs often seek unique ice cream flavors that are not available commercially, however. Ice cream mixes allow a variety of different flavored ice creams to be freshly made from one basic preparation. The ingredients in frozen dessert mixes vary by manufacturer. Mixes may be made from milk or cream, eggs and sweeteners and may contain stabilizers, gelatin, gums, flavorings or other additives. Some mixes require the addition of fresh milk, cream or other liquid, however. Most are sold as a refrigerated or frozen liquid in a range of different milkfat contents. Nondairy mixes are also available, usually in a powdered form to which water or fruit juice is added. The mix is simply placed in an ice cream machine and frozen as needed.

Mixes also come in a neutral flavor to which the pastry chef adds flavorings or fruit purées to customize the ice cream before churning. Prepared flavoring bases are also available in flavors such as French vanilla, butter pecan, pistachio or green tea. The base may contain additional milkfat and fruit pieces. Mixes and bases are formulated for different styles of ice cream, either hard or soft, and for use in different types of ice cream–making machinery, either in a batch freezer or a continuous-process soft ice cream machine. (See Chapter 2, Tools and Equipment for the Bakeshop.) Packaging is designed to make one batch of ice cream for the standard-size 20-quart commercial ice cream machine. When purchasing an ice cream mix or base, select products with the fewest additives and the highest milkfat content appropriate for the equipment in your bakeshop. *Variegates* are specially formulated mixtures designed to be swirled into ice cream after it is frozen. These variegates remain soft when frozen and come in popular flavors such as fudge, caramel, marshmallow and strawberry.

Nondairy neutral bases for making sorbet and sherbet are also available. Fresh fruit purées or juices are added as needed. Purchasing prepared high-quality ice creams and sorbets lets the pastry chef offer frozen desserts such as baked Alaska or frozen tortes with less preparation time. The pastry chef's creativity can be applied to the flavor combinations and the presentation of the dessert. Some manufacturers will even prepare custom-flavored ice cream and sorbet for a small minimum order.

1. Describe the types of ice creams based on frozen custards and their differences.
2. What can be done to ensure that a sorbet mixture will freeze properly?
3. Consider the types of cookie and cake formulas that are available to the pastry chef. Using cookie or cake formulas discussed in previous chapters of this book, create three new frozen desserts that combine a cake or cookie and a frozen mixture from this chapter.
4. Discuss the function of whipped cream and Italian meringue when making frozen parfaits and bombes.
5. From *paletas* to *kulfi*, the types of ice creams and frozen desserts available around the world seems limitless. Research the various types of ice creams and frozen desserts made in several countries. Identify which formulas in this book might be used to make any of these specialties. Describe how to go about preparing two or three of these specialties using what you have learned in this chapter.

QUESTIONS FOR DISCUSSION

Terms to Know

churned	inclusion
still-frozen	sorbet
semifreddi	sherbet
gelato	sugar density
ice milk	soufflé glacée
stabilizer	

FRENCH ICE CREAM BASE

Yield: 1½ qt. (1½ lt)   **Method:** Churned

Whole milk	20 fl. oz.	600 ml
Heavy cream	14 fl. oz.	420 ml
Egg yolks	4 oz. (6 yolks)	120 g
Granulated sugar	7 oz.	210 g
Glucose or corn syrup	1 oz.	30 g
Ice cream stabilizer (optional)	0.3 oz. (2 tsp.)	10 g

1. Bring the milk and cream to a boil in a nonreactive saucepan.
2. Whip the egg yolks, sugar, glucose and ice cream stabilizer (if using) in the bowl of a mixer fitted with the whip attachment until pale and slightly thickened, approximately 3 minutes. Stir one-third of the boiled milk into the yolk mixture.
3. Return the yolk mixture to the saucepan and heat, stirring constantly with a rubber spatula, until it reaches 180°F to 185°F (82°C to 85°C). Remove from the heat and strain into a clean bowl.
4. Quickly chill the ice cream base over an ice bath until it reaches 40°F (4°C). Refrigerate the ice cream base overnight.
5. Pour the mixture into the container of an ice cream machine and process according to the manufacturer's directions.

VARIATIONS:

Anise Ice Cream—Add 0.5 ounce (15 grams) chopped anise seeds and 2 **star anise** seeds to the milk and cream. Prepare the custard, then strain out the seeds before cooling and churning. One fluid ounce (30 milliliters) anise liqueur may be added before churning.

Banana-Nut Ice Cream—Fold in 8 ounces (240 grams) ripe, puréed bananas and 5 ounces (150 grams) crushed nougatine (page 748) when the ice cream is frozen but still soft enough to stir.

Chestnut Ice Cream—Add 1 pound (480 grams) sweetened chestnut purée to the chilled mixture before churning.

Coconut Ice Cream—Add 8 ounces (240 grams) fresh grated or frozen unsweetened coconut to the milk. Strain the custard before churning or place it in a blender and blend until the coconut shavings are small, and leave them in the ice cream. If desired, add 2 fluid ounces (60 milliliters) dark Jamaican rum.

Coffee Ice Cream—Add 1 fluid ounce (30 milliliters) coffee extract to the chilled mixture before churning.

Ginger Ice Cream—Add 3 ounces (90 grams) chopped fresh ginger to the milk and cream.

Hazelnut Ice Cream—Add 6 ounces (180 grams) hazelnut paste to the chilled mixture before churning.

Indian Cardamom and Pistachio Ice Cream—Steep 10 crushed cardamom pods in the milk and cream 10 minutes. Strain and proceed to make the custard. Stir in 2 ounces (60 grams) finely ground pistachios and 0.04 ounce (0.5 teaspoon/1 gram) ground cardamom before churning.

Mint Ice Cream—Steep 40 fresh mint leaves in the milk and cream. Strain and proceed to make the custard.

Pistachio Ice Cream—Add 8 ounces (240 grams) chopped pistachio nuts and 1 ounce (30 grams) natural pistachio compound to the custard before churning.

STAR ANISE

Star anise, also known as Chinese anise, is the dried, star-shaped fruit of a Chinese magnolia tree. Although it is botanically unrelated, its flavor is similar to anise seeds but more bitter and pungent. It lends a licorice-like flavor to aromatic liquids for poaching fruits and for exotic sauces.

Star Anise

Roasted Peach Ice Cream—Toss 1 pound (480 grams) sliced, peeled ripe peaches with 1 ounce (30 grams) brown sugar. Roast at 400°F (200°C) until softened and lightly browned. Cool and add to the ice cream near the end of churning.

Spiced Chocolate Ice Cream—Increase the milk to 28 fluid ounces (840 milliliters). Place 8 ounces (240 grams) chopped bittersweet or milk chocolate into a bowl. Pour the hot cooked custard base over the chocolate and whisk until the chocolate has melted. Add a pinch of ground white pepper and 0.5 fluid ounce (15 milliliters) coffee extract.

Vanilla Ice Cream—Steep 2 split vanilla beans in the milk and cream.

Approximate values per 4-fl.-oz. (120-ml) serving: **Calories** 250, **Total fat** 17 g, **Saturated fat** 10 g, **Cholesterol** 160 mg, **Sodium** 45 mg, **Total carbohydrates** 22 g, **Protein** 4 g, **Vitamin A** 15%

CHOCOLATE ICE CREAM

CHRISTOPHER'S FERMIER BRASSERIE AND PAOLA'S WINE BAR, PHOENIX, AZ

Chef-Owner Christopher Gross

Yield: 10 Servings   **Method:** Churned

Egg yolks	3 oz. (5 yolks)	90 g
Granulated sugar	5 oz.	150 g
Cocoa powder	1.5 oz.	45 g
Milk	1 pt.	480 ml
Heavy cream	3 fl. oz.	90 ml
Semisweet chocolate, chopped	4 oz.	120 g

1. Whisk the egg yolks, sugar and cocoa powder together.
2. Combine the milk and cream and bring to a boil. Temper the egg mixture with a portion of the hot milk; return the mixture to the saucepan and continue cooking, stirring constantly, until the custard thickens and reaches 180°F–185°F (82°C–85°C).
3. Remove from the heat and add the chocolate. Stir until the chocolate melts, then strain and chill.
4. Process the custard in an ice cream machine according to the manufacturer's directions.

Approximate values per 3-oz. (90-g) serving: **Calories** 210, **Total fat** 11 g, **Saturated fat** 7 g, **Cholesterol** 125 mg, **Sodium** 40 mg, **Total carbohydrates** 27 g, **Protein** 4 g

---

STRAWBERRY ICE CREAM

Yield: 1 qt. (1 lt)   **Method:** Churned

Water	8 fl. oz.	240 ml
Granulated sugar	5 oz.	150 g
Pectin-based ice cream stabilizer (optional)	0.07 oz. (½ tsp.)	2 g
Glucose or corn syrup	8 oz.	240 g
Strawberry purée	1 pt.	480 ml
Heavy cream	6 fl. oz.	180 ml

1. Pour the water into a heavy saucepan. Stir together the sugar and the pectin (if using), then add it to the water. Stir in the glucose syrup and bring the mixture to a boil over medium-high heat. Remove this base from the heat and allow it to cool completely.
2. Pour the cooled syrup, strawberry purée and heavy cream into the container of an ice cream machine and process according to the manufacturer's directions.

Approximate values per 8-oz. (240-g) serving: **Calories** 370, **Total fat** 13 g, **Saturated fat** 8 g, **Cholesterol** 45 mg, **Sodium** 65 mg, **Total carbohydrates** 68 g, **Protein** 1 g, **Vitamin C** 90%

HONEY ICE CREAM

Yield: 1 qt. (1 lt)		Method: Churned
Heavy cream	1 pt.	480 ml
Light cream	1 pt.	480 ml
Egg yolks	4.8 oz. (8 yolks)	144 g
Honey	4 fl. oz.	120 ml

1. In a nonreactive saucepan, combine the heavy and light cream and heat just to a simmer.
2. In a large mixing bowl, beat the egg yolks and honey together until pale, slightly thickened and at the ribbon stage. Slowly add the heated cream, whisking continuously, so as not to cook the yolks.
3. Return the mixture to the saucepan and cook over low heat, stirring constantly, until the mixture coats the back of a spoon and reaches 180°F–185°F (82°C–85°C).
4. Remove from the heat and cool over an ice bath. Pour into the container of an ice cream machine and process according to the manufacturer's directions.

Approximate values per 3½-fl.-oz. (105-ml) serving: **Calories** 275, **Total fat** 22 g, **Saturated fat** 13 g, **Cholesterol** 210 mg, **Sodium** 48 mg, **Total carbohydrates** 15 g, **Protein** 6 g, **Vitamin A** 30%, **Calcium** 10%

Mandarin Sorbet layered between tuiles.

APRICOT, PEACH, PEAR OR PINEAPPLE SORBET

Yield: 1 qt. (1 lt)		Method: Churned
Water	5 fl. oz.	150 ml
Granulated sugar	4 oz.	120 g
Glucose or corn syrup	2.5 oz.	75 g
Pectin-based ice cream stabilizer (optional)	0.07 oz. (½ tsp.)	2.1 g
Apricot, peach, pear or pineapple purée	17 fl. oz.	500 ml

1. Place the water, sugar, glucose syrup and stabilizer (if using) in a large saucepan. Whisk until well combined, then bring to a full rolling boil.
2. Remove from the heat and cool in a refrigerator several hours or overnight.
3. Combine the fruit purée with the base syrup. Check the density. Add more water or sugar syrup to adjust to 1.1333 D (17° Baumé).
4. Pour the mixture into the container of an ice cream/sorbet machine and process according to the manufacturer's directions.

VARIATIONS:

Lemon or Lime Sorbet—Make the base syrup from 22 fluid ounces (665 milliliters) water, 12 ounces (360 grams) sugar, 3.5 ounces (105 grams) glucose or corn syrup and 0.4 ounce (2⅔ teaspoons/12 grams) stabilizer (if using). Add 17 fluid ounces (0.5 liter) lemon or lime juice.

Basil Lemon Sorbet—Add 20 finely minced basil leaves to the lemon sorbet before churning.

Banana or Kiwi Sorbet—Make the base syrup from 22 fluid ounces (665 milliliters) water, 12 ounces (360 grams) granulated sugar, 3.5 ounces (105 grams) glucose or corn syrup and 0.4 ounce (2⅔ teaspoons/12 grams) stabilizer (if using). Add 17 fluid ounces (0.5 liter) banana or kiwi juice.

Raspberry, Cherry, Blackberry or Three Red Fruit Sorbet—Make the base syrup from 7 fluid ounces (210 milliliters) water, 3.5 ounces (105 grams) granulated sugar, 2.5 ounces (75 grams) glucose or corn syrup and 0.25 ounce (1¾ teaspoons/7.5 grams) stabilizer (if using). Add 17 fluid ounces (0.5 liter) raspberry, cherry, blackberry or any combination fruit purée.

Raspberry sorbet in a tuile cup with fresh fruit and sugar garnish.

Green Apple or Wild Strawberry Sorbet—Make the base syrup from 8 fluid ounces (240 milliliters) water, 5 ounces (150 grams) sugar, 2.5 ounces (75 grams) glucose or corn syrup and 0.25 ounce (1¾ teaspoons/7.5 grams) stabilizer (if using). Add 17 fluid ounces (0.5 liter) green apple or wild strawberry purée.

Blueberry, Red Currant or Black Currant Sorbet—Make the base syrup from 10 fluid ounces (300 milliliters) water, 6.5 ounces (195 grams) sugar, 2.5 ounces (75 grams) glucose or corn syrup and 0.14 ounce (1 teaspoon/5 grams) stabilizer (if using). Add 17 fluid ounces (0.5 liter) blueberry, red currant or black currant purée.

Passion Fruit Sorbet—Make the base syrup from 20 fluid ounces (600 milliliters) water, 8 ounces (240 grams) sugar, 5 ounces (150 grams) glucose or corn syrup and 0.14 ounce (1 teaspoon/5 grams) stabilizer (if using). Add 17 fluid ounces (0.5 liter) passion fruit purée. Adjust to 1.1425 D (18° Baumé).

Mandarin or Orange Sorbet—Make the base syrup from 6 fluid ounces (180 milliliters) water, 5 ounces (150 grams) sugar, 2 ounces (60 grams) glucose or corn syrup and 0.14 ounce (1 teaspoon/5 grams) stabilizer (if using). Add 17 fluid ounces (0.5 liter) mandarin or orange juice. Adjust to 1.1425 D (18° Baumé).

Champagne Sorbet—Make the base syrup from 7 fluid ounces (210 milliliters) water, 6 ounces (180 grams) granulated sugar, 1 ounce (30 grams) glucose or corn syrup, 1 ounce (30 grams) orange zest, 1 ounce (30 grams) lemon zest and 0.25 ounce (1¾ teaspoons/7.5 grams) stabilizer (if using). Chill, then add 12 fluid ounces (375 milliliters) champagne. Adjust to 1.1247 D (16° Baumé).

Approximate values per 4-fl.-oz. (120-ml) serving (based on apricot sorbet): **Calories** 110, **Total fat** 0 g, **Saturated fat** 0 g, **Cholesterol** 0 mg, **Sodium** 10 mg, **Total carbohydrates** 28 g, **Protein** 1 g, **Vitamin A** 30%, **Claims**—no fat; no cholesterol; very low sodium; low calorie

CHAMPAGNE-ROSE SORBET

This formula is used in the plated dessert on page 684.

Yield: Approximately 28 fl. oz. (840 ml)   **Method:** Churned

Water	8 fl. oz.	240 ml
Granulated sugar	6 oz.	180 g
Glucose or corn syrup	2 oz.	60 g
Rose petals, organic	10 petals	10 petals
Rose liqueur	1 fl. oz.	30 ml
Champagne	12.5 fl. oz.	375 ml

1. Bring the water, sugar and glucose syrup to boil in a small saucepan. Remove from the heat and add the rose petals. Let cool.
2. Pour the mixture into a blender and purée until the petals are finely chopped. Add the liqueur and champagne. If necessary, adjust the mixture to 1.1074 D (14° Baumé). Chill the mixture completely, then process in an ice cream machine according to the manufacturer's directions.
3. Once the sorbet has been churned, pack it in a clean container and freeze until firm. Or pack it in individual 2-ounce (60-gram) molds. Freeze until firm.

Approximate values per ½ cup serving: **Calories** 100, **Total fat** 0 g, **Saturated fat** 0 g, **Cholesterol** 0 mg, **Sodium** 10 mg, **Total carbohydrates** 26 g, **Protein** 0 g, **Claims**—no fat; no cholesterol; very low sodium; low calorie

① Using a small spoon to hollow out the lemon pulp.

② The lemons filled with sorbet.

LEMON SORBET

VINCENT ON CAMELBACK, PHOENIX, AZ
Chef Vincent Guerithault

Yield: 1½ qt. (1½ lt)		Method: Churned
Lemon juice	1 pt.	500 ml
Water	1 pt.	500 ml
Granulated sugar	1 lb.	500 g
Lemons (optional)	8–12	8–12

① Combine the lemon juice, water and sugar in a large bowl. Stir until the sugar dissolves completely.

② Pour the mixture into the container of an ice cream/sorbet machine and process according to the manufacturer's directions.

③ The finished sorbet will be rather soft. Pack it into a storage container and freeze at a temperature of 0°F (–18°C) or lower until firm.

④ To serve, hold each lemon lengthwise on a flat surface. Using a sharp paring knife, make a shallow cut through the rind about 1 inch (2.5 centimeters) from the top. Carefully peel off the rind. Set aside the rind, then hollow out the fruit with a serrated knife. Pack each lemon with some of the sorbet and top with the reserved rind.

Approximate values per 1½-fl.-oz. (45-ml) serving: **Calories** 25, **Total fat** 0 g, **Saturated fat** 0 g, **Cholesterol** 0 mg, **Sodium** 0 mg, **Total carbohydrates** 6 g, **Protein** 0 g, **Claims**—fat free; no sodium; low calorie

---

STRAWBERRY SORBET

THE RITZ-CARLTON, CHICAGO, IL
Former Executive Chef George Bumbaris and Chef Sarah Stegner

Yield: 8 Servings		Method: Churned
Granulated sugar	4 oz.	120 g
Pectin or stabilizer (optional)	0.14 oz. (1 tsp.)	5 g
Medium sugar syrup (page 73)	8 fl. oz.	240 ml
Strawberries, puréed	1 lb.	480 g
Fresh lemon juice	0.5 fl. oz.	15 ml

① Mix the sugar and pectin together, add the syrup and bring to a boil. Remove from the heat and cool completely.

② Add the puréed berries and lemon juice; strain. Adjust the flavor with additional sugar or lemon juice as needed.

③ Pour the mixture into the container of an ice cream/sorbet machine and process according to the manufacturer's directions.

Approximate values per 4-fl.-oz. (120-ml) serving: **Calories** 196, **Total fat** 0 g, **Saturated fat** 0 g, **Cholesterol** 0 mg, **Sodium** 1.5 mg, **Total carbohydrates** 48 g, **Protein** 0 g, **Vitamin C** 54%, **Claims**—no fat; no cholesterol; very low sodium; high fiber

GRAPEFRUIT SORBET

Yield: 1½ qt. (1½ lt)   **Method:** Churned

Fresh grapefruit juice	1 qt.	1 lt
Granulated sugar	8 oz.	240 g
Lemon leaves (optional)	as needed	as needed
Grapefruit supremes (optional)	as needed	as needed
Grapefruit zest, cut into strips (optional)	as needed	as needed

1. Combine the juice and sugar.
2. Process in an ice cream machine according to the manufacturer's directions.
3. Pack into a clean container and freeze until firm.
4. Using a #8 portion scoop, place the sorbet into serving dishes. Garnish with lemon leaves, grapefruit segments and grapefruit zest if desired.

VARIATION:

Raspberry Sorbet—Combine 2.2 pounds (1 kilogram) puréed, strained raspberries with 1 pound (480 grams) granulated sugar and 1 fluid ounce (30 milliliters) lemon juice.

Approximate values per 3-fl.-oz. (90-ml) serving: **Calories** 94, **Total fat** 0 g, **Saturated fat** 0 g, **Cholesterol** 0 mg, **Sodium** 1 mg, **Total carbohydrates** 23 g, **Protein** 0.5 g, **Vitamin C** 36%, **Claims**—no fat; no cholesterol; very low sodium; low calorie

The sorbet garnished with grapefruit zest and segments.

SORBET SANDWICHES

Yield: 16 Sandwiches

Raspberry or other sorbet (page 556)	2 qt.	2 lt
Chocolate Tart Dough (page 384)	1 lb. 6 oz.	660 g

1. Place an 8-inch × 12-inch (20-centimeter × 30-centimeter) sheet of bright-colored paper on a flat half-size sheet pan. Cover it with plastic. Freeze until well chilled.
2. Spread out the raspberry sorbet into a rectangle on the chilled sheet pan using the paper as a guide. Freeze until very firm, at least 4 hours or overnight.
3. Roll the Chocolate Tart Dough out into a rectangle measuring approximately 8 inches × 12 inches (20 centimeters × 30 centimeters). Trim the edges and cut the dough in half lengthwise. Then cut each half into 1.5-inch- (3.8-centimeter-) wide strips.
4. Place the cut dough on a parchment-lined sheet pan. Bake at 350°F (180°C) until the dough feels firm and easily lifts up from the tray, approximately 14 minutes. (If the dough appears underbaked after cooling, return it briefly to the oven.)
5. Quickly cut the firm frozen sorbet sheet lengthwise in half. Then divide the sorbet into strips the same dimensions as the tart dough.
6. Position each piece of portioned sorbet onto a baked tart dough strip. Top with another piece of baked tart dough. Serve immediately. Or wrap tightly in plastic and keep in the freezer for up to 1 week before serving.

Approximate values per serving: **Calories** 300, **Total fat** 12 g, **Saturated fat** 6 g, **Cholesterol** 35 mg, **Sodium** 35 mg, **Total carbohydrates** 49 g, **Protein** 3 g

COFFEE SHERBET

Yield: 1¾ qt. (1¾ lt)	Method: Churned	
Water	1 pt.	480 ml
Granulated sugar	1 lb. 4 oz.	600 g
Glucose or corn syrup	4 oz.	120 g
Coffee, ground	1 oz.	30 g
Coffee extract	1 fl. oz.	30 ml
Heavy cream	3.5 fl. oz.	105 ml

1 Bring the water, sugar and glucose syrup to a boil. Boil 1 minute and remove from the heat.

2 Add the ground coffee and coffee extract and let the mixture steep 4 minutes. Strain through cheesecloth and discard the grounds.

3 Add the cream to the coffee syrup and then quickly cool the mixture over an ice bath.

4 Check the density of the mixture. Adjust the syrup to 1.1425 D (18° Baumé) by adding more base syrup or water as needed.

5 Pour the mixture into the container of an ice cream/sorbet machine and process according to the manufacturer's directions.

Approximate values per 4-fl.-oz. (120-ml) serving: **Calories** 210, **Total fat** 3 g, **Saturated fat** 1.5 g, **Cholesterol** 10 mg, **Sodium** 15 mg, **Total carbohydrates** 48 g, **Protein** 0 g

CHAMPAGNE SPOOM

A spoom is a type of sherbet, usually made from champagne or a sweet white wine to which Italian meringue is added after the churning process.

Yield: 2½ qt. (2½ lt)	Method: Churned	
Granulated sugar	14 oz.	420 g
Water	14 fl. oz.	420 ml
Glucose or corn syrup	2 oz.	60 g
Whole milk	8 fl. oz.	240 ml
Vanilla bean, split	1	1
Champagne or sparkling wine	24 fl. oz.	750 ml
Italian Meringue (page 413)	12 oz.	360 g

1 Combine the sugar, water, glucose syrup, milk and vanilla bean in a nonreactive saucepan. Boil 1 minute, then chill.

2 Combine the champagne with the chilled base syrup. Check the density of the mixture. Adjust the syrup to 1.1159 D (15° Baumé) by adding more base syrup or water as needed. Remove the vanilla bean.

3 Pour the mixture into the container of an ice cream machine and process according to the manufacturer's directions.

4 Fold the Italian Meringue into the sherbet as soon as it is churned but still soft enough to stir. Pack it in a storage container and freeze until firm.

Approximate values per 4-fl.-oz. (120-ml) serving: **Calories** 180, **Total fat** 0 g, **Saturated fat** 0 g, **Cholesterol** 0 mg, **Sodium** 25 mg, **Total carbohydrates** 35 g, **Protein** 1 g, **Claims**—fat free; no cholesterol

PINEAPPLE GRANITA

Yield: 1½ qt. (1½ lt)   **Method:** Scraped

Water	2 fl. oz.	60 ml
Granulated sugar	6 oz.	180 g
Pineapple juice	1 qt.	1 lt

1. Combine the water and sugar in a saucepan. Bring to a full boil and boil 1 minute. Remove from the heat and add the pineapple juice. Chill, then check the density. Add water or more sugar syrup to the granita base if needed to adjust it to 1.0907 D (12° Baumé).
2. Pour into a shallow stainless steel pan and freeze until the granita begins to harden, approximately 6 to 8 hours.
3. Scrape the surface of the granita with a metal fork or spoon to break up the ice crystals. Return the granita to the freezer until firm.
4. Scrape the surface of the frozen granita to loosen the ice crystals. Scoop into serving dishes and serve immediately.

Approximate values per 4-fl.-oz. (120-ml) cup serving: **Calories** 100, **Total fat** 0 g, **Saturated fat** 0 g, **Cholesterol** 0 mg, **Sodium** 0 mg, **Total carbohydrates** 26 g, **Protein** 0 g, **Vitamin C** 15%, **Claims**–no fat; no cholesterol; very low sodium; low calorie

FROZEN ORANGE SOUFFLÉ

Yield: 15 Servings, 3½-in. (9-cm) ramekins   **Method:** Still-frozen

Egg yolks	5 oz. (8 yolks)	90 g
Granulated sugar	4 oz.	120 g
Water	3 fl. oz.	90 ml
Cointreau or orange liqueur	2 fl. oz.	60 ml
Orange or bergamot essential oil	10 drops	10 drops
Italian Meringue (page 413)	1 lb. 8 oz.	720 g
Heavy cream, whipped	28 fl. oz.	840 ml
Basic Nougatine (page 724)	as needed	as needed
Powdered sugar	as needed	as needed

1. Cut 15 strips of parchment paper or acetate 2 inches (5 centimeters) wide and long enough to wrap around the top of the ramekins. Fasten the paper or acetate around each ramekin with adhesive tape to form a collar. Lightly oil the ramekins and their collars. Sprinkle with granulated sugar.
2. Prepare a bombe mixture. Beat the egg yolks in the bowl of a mixer fitted with the whip attachment until light and foamy.
3. While the egg yolks whip, bring the sugar and water to a boil in a small saucepan, brushing down the sides of the pan with cold water to wash off crystals that may be deposited there. Cook the syrup to the soft ball stage (240°F/116°C). With the machine running on medium speed, pour the hot syrup into the whipped egg yolks. Increase the speed to high and beat until the bombe mixture cools to room temperature.
4. Remove the bombe mixture from the machine; fold in the Cointreau and orange oil.
5. In two steps, delicately fold in the Italian Meringue, followed by the whipped cream.
6. Using a ladle, deposit the mixture into the ramekins, leveling it with a metal spatula to the rim of the collar.
7. Freeze until hard.
8. To serve, remove the paper or acetate collars. Garnish with Basic Nougatine or powdered sugar.

Approximate values per serving: **Calories** 300, **Total fat** 16 g, **Saturated fat** 9 g, **Cholesterol** 170 mg, **Sodium** 20 mg, **Total carbohydrates** 38 g, **Protein** 2 g, **Vitamin A** 15%

BANANAS FOSTER

BRENNAN'S RESTAURANT, NEW ORLEANS, LA
Chef Michael Roussel (1938–2005)

Bananas Foster was created in 1951 by Brennan's chef Paul Blangé to promote New Orleans' role as the major port of entry for bananas arriving from Central and South America. The dish was named for Richard Foster, chair of the New Orleans Crime Commission, a civic group working to clean up the French Quarter. Foster was a good friend to Owen Edward Brennan and a frequent customer at his restaurant. Today Brennan's flambés some 35,000 pounds of bananas each year for this world-famous dessert.

Yield: 4 Servings

Whole butter	2 oz.	60 g
Brown sugar	8 oz.	240 g
Cinnamon, ground	0.04 oz. (½ tsp.)	1 g
Banana liqueur	2 fl. oz.	60 ml
Bananas, cut into quarters	4	4
White rum	2 fl. oz.	60 ml
Vanilla ice cream	4 scoops	4 scoops

1 Combine the butter, sugar and cinnamon in a sauté or flambé pan. Cook over low heat, stirring until the sugar dissolves.

2 Stir in the banana liqueur, then place the bananas in the pan. When the bananas soften and begin to brown, carefully add the rum.

3 Place one scoop of ice cream on each serving plate. Continue to cook the bananas until the rum is hot, then tip the pan slightly to ignite the rum. When the flames subside, lift the bananas out of the pan and place four pieces over each portion of ice cream. Spoon the warm sauce over the ice cream and serve immediately.

Approximate values per serving: **Calories** 640, **Total fat** 23 g, **Saturated fat** 14 g, **Cholesterol** 70 mg, **Sodium** 65 mg, **Total carbohydrates** 103 g, **Protein** 4 g, **Vitamin A** 20%, **Vitamin C** 20%, **Calcium** 15%, **Iron** 10%, **Claims**—good source of fiber, vitamins A and C, calcium and iron

SAFETY ALERT
Cooking with Alcohol

Care must be taken when adding alcoholic flavorings to a dish on or near the stove. Often a dessert requires flaming or flambéing, which means igniting the brandy, rum or other liquor so that the alcohol burns off and the flavor of the liquor is retained. To flambé, stand away from the pan being flamed. Tilt the pan away from you, allowing the fumes to be ignited by the open flame. Be careful, as the flames can leap from the pan.

BAKED ALASKA

Baked Alaska always includes spongecake and Italian meringue, but the flavor of ice cream and sorbet is a personal choice. When prepared with spongecake or baked meringue and sorbet, this becomes a low-fat and relatively healthy dessert option. Serve baked Alaska with a sauce or fruit coulis and garnishes that complement the ice cream or sorbet.

Yield: 20 Servings, 1 Cake

Vanilla Spongecake (page 478)	1 half sheet	1 half sheet
Simple Syrup (page 73)	4 fl. oz.	120 ml
Raspberry liqueur	0.5 fl. oz.	15 ml
Vanilla Ice Cream (page 555), churned	1½ qt.	1.5 lt
Red Currant Sorbet (page 557)	1 qt.	1 lt
Italian Meringue (page 413)	1 lb. 8 oz.	690 g

1 Cut the Vanilla Spongecake into two ovals measuring 6 inches × 11 inches (15 centimeters × 28 centimeters); place the first piece directly on an ovenproof serving tray. Combine the Simple Syrup and the raspberry liqueur. Moisten the cake with half of the raspberry syrup. Place in the freezer 30 minutes.

Individual Baked Alaska.

2 Spread the Vanilla Ice Cream evenly over the chilled cake layer using a plastic scraper. Cover with the second piece of Vanilla Spongecake and moisten with the remaining raspberry syrup. Freeze until hard.

3 Spread the Red Currant Sorbet on the top cake layer using a plastic scraper. Freeze hard.

4 Place the Italian Meringue in a pastry bag fitted with a St. Honoré tip. Pipe vertical lines on the sides and a swirl pattern over the top of the frozen dessert, making certain it is completely covered with Italian Meringue. Return the cake, uncovered, to the freezer. Once it has frozen, cover the cake with plastic wrap. The iced dessert can stay in the freezer up to 1 week before serving.

5 To serve, remove the plastic, place the Baked Alaska in a 500°F (260°C) oven and bake until the meringue is browned, approximately 6 to 9 minutes. Serve immediately.

VARIATION:

Individual Baked Alaska—Cut the Vanilla Spongecake into twenty 3-inch (7.5-centimeter) rounds in Step 1. Mound the Vanilla Ice Cream evenly over the chilled cake cutouts.

Approximate values per ¹⁄₂₀-cake serving: **Calories** 110, **Total fat** 12 g, **Saturated fat** 6 g, **Cholesterol** 170 mg, **Sodium** 75 mg, **Total carbohydrates** 64 g, **Protein** 6 g

CHOCOLATE HAZELNUT MARQUISE WITH FRANGELICO SAUCE

Yield: 12 Servings	**Method:** Still-frozen	
Melted butter	as needed	as needed
Dark chocolate	1 lb.	480 g
Unsalted butter	4 oz.	120 g
Hazelnuts, roasted, skinned and chopped coarse	4 oz.	120 g
Egg yolks	4 oz. (6 yolks)	120 g
Frangelico (hazelnut liqueur)	2 fl. oz.	60 ml
Egg whites	6 oz. (6 whites)	180 g
Salt	0.03 oz. (⅛ tsp.)	1 g
Frangelico Custard Sauce (page 490)	as needed	as needed
Hazelnuts, roasted and chopped coarse	as needed	as needed
Fresh raspberries	as needed	as needed
Fresh mint	as needed	as needed

1 Brush a terrine mold with melted butter and line it with parchment paper.

2 Melt the chocolate and unsalted butter over a bain marie. Remove from the heat and stir in the nuts, egg yolks and Frangelico. Set aside to cool to room temperature. Do not use an ice bath, as the chocolate will solidify.

3 Whip the egg whites with the salt until stiff but not dry. Fold the whipped whites into the chocolate mixture.

4 Pour the mixture into the terrine mold and freeze overnight.

5 Remove the marquise from the mold and peel off the paper. (Work quickly because this melts quickly.) While the marquise is still frozen, use a hot knife to slice the loaf into ⅓-inch- (8-millimeter-) thick slices. Return the marquise to freeze until just before service.

6 Serve two slices on a pool of Frangelico Custard Sauce. Garnish with coarsely chopped hazelnuts, fresh raspberries and fresh mint.

Approximate values per serving: **Calories** 380, **Total fat** 28 g, **Saturated fat** 14 g, **Cholesterol** 125 mg, **Sodium** 35 mg, **Total carbohydrates** 25 g, **Protein** 6 g, **Vitamin A** 10%

CHAPTER SIXTEEN

HEALTHFUL AND SPECIAL-NEEDS BAKING

- recognize dietary conditions that affect today's consumers
- be familiar with allergies and food intolerances and the foods that trigger them
- understand and explain how to adapt bakeshop formulas to meet dietary needs

allergens substances that may cause allergic reactions in some people

ALTHOUGH AMERICANS ARE BECOMING INCREASINGLY HEALTH CONSCIOUS, the pleasures of the dessert table still call to them. Because of national health concerns about overconsumption leading to obesity, cardiovascular disease and diabetes, Americans are looking for baked goods and desserts to satisfy their sweet tooth in a healthier way. At the same time, people with certain health conditions that require them to limit their intake of sugar, fat or wheat are looking for foods that will taste good and meet their diet regimens.

Modifying or adapting formulas for those with special dietary needs presents a challenge even to the most experienced professional because of the exacting nature of baking. In baking more than in any other form of cooking, many of the ingredients provide an important function other than flavor. Healthy baking demands a thorough knowledge of the principles of baking to ensure an appealing product.

Rather than being a complete primer, this chapter is designed to introduce the pastry chef to a variety of healthful baking options and illustrate ways a small bakeshop or restaurant can offer products for those with special dietary requirements.

For a variety of personal and medical reasons, many consumers are concerned about avoiding certain foods or foods containing certain ingredients or additives. For some, it is a matter of preference: They would rather eat a lower-fat cookie or a food prepared with organic ingredients. For others, avoiding a particular ingredient is not a choice but a necessity because consuming or even touching the ingredient can be a matter of life and death. People who are allergic to peanuts, for instance, can develop a life-threatening reaction after eating or touching even a minute amount of peanuts or peanut products such as peanut oil. The concern is not why customers require a special product. The goal is to provide tasty products that meet their dietary needs.

Professional chefs and bakers must be aware of these needs and be willing and able to prepare products that are suitable for customers with special requirements. The challenge is that many of the ingredients that raise concerns are widely used in bakeshop products, including wheat flour (gluten), sugar, fats, eggs, soy products, dairy products and flavorings such as peanuts, tree nuts, alcoholic beverages and chocolate. Customers who are concerned about ingredients will usually ask how a dish is prepared. Waiters, cooks, and other food service workers should take the guest's inquiries seriously. Failure to do so could result in severe illness or death.

Chefs, bakers, managers and restaurateurs can improve customer relations and build a new clientele by developing and promoting strategies that adequately address the health concerns of their patrons. To do so requires a two-phase program. In the first phase, all the staff who come in contact with the public must be made aware of, or have access to, a list of all ingredients in all products. (The 2009 Model Food Code of the Food and Drug Administration [FDA] recommends that foodservice staff be trained in allergen awareness.) Post notices or label products appropriately if peanuts or other potential **allergens** (substances that may cause allergic reactions in some people) are present. For instance, know when alcohol has been used to prepare a dish; learn whether the chocolate used contains a soy-based emulsifier; be aware of where peanuts have been used in the kitchen and if the oil used in a formula is peanut, soy or other vegetable-based oil.

In the second phase, build a repertoire of products that have a reduced fat, sugar, wheat or dairy content. The baker should not expect to be able to adjust all formulas based on a reading of this chapter but should become more aware of potential issues. The pastry chef should also be able to offer customers an alternative bread or dessert on a regular basis, or at least when a special request is made. Finally, chefs and bakers should be familiar with some of the newer products available that can be used to alter or modify baking formulas. These include alternative sweeteners, low-fat and nonfat dairy products, nongluten flours and fruit and vegetable purées. Most manufacturers of commercial products have valuable information on their Web sites. In researching techniques for healthier baking, the Internet is a good place to start.

SPECIAL DIETARY CONCERNS

For many people, personal conviction drives their desire for a modified version of a favorite dessert: weight control, avoiding additives or eating less-processed foods, for example. Weight loss regimens in vogue today run the gamut from high-protein, low-**carbohydrate** diets to the long-established reduced-calorie diets. For others, specific physical conditions prevent them from enjoying a traditional bakeshop item. Many Americans are on low-**cholesterol** and low-fat diets as well as sodium- (salt-) controlled diets to treat cardiovascular disease. Others must pay attention to their intake of calories and carbohydrates because they have diabetes.

Food allergies to wheat, dairy, nuts, eggs and soy are widespread, affecting millions of consumers. The challenge for the pastry chef is to know the function of the ingredient in the bakeshop formula and understand how to alter the formula to meet dietary needs. In the case of peanut allergy, mise en place should be considered as well as removing peanuts from a given formula. No peanuts or peanut products should even be near the area where the preparation is taking place. Avoiding peanut oil or peanut oil–containing products means that pans must be prepared with an alternative oil, and utensils may not come in contact with peanut products or even peanut dust.

In addition to allergies, some people experience some sort of digestive discomfort or **food intolerance** when eating certain foods. One common food component that many consumers cannot tolerate is lactose. **Lactose** is a natural sugar found in milk and dairy products. People who are lactose intolerant have a digestive problem that causes intestinal discomfort if the milk sugar is consumed, sometimes even in small amounts. Because many bakeshop products use dairy products, finding a suitable substitute is important.

Other consumers are looking for lower-fat or lower-calorie items. Also, a growing number of people just want to eat healthier food. These individuals may want a dessert that offers more fiber or is higher in certain vitamins or minerals or antioxidants or lower in sugar because they perceive these foods to be healthier. Many people are trying to avoid eating processed foods containing chemical additives. They may prefer to choose foods prepared with all natural or organic ingredients. Meeting their needs requires creativity and as much vigilance as preparing foods for those with special health conditions.

carbohydrates a group of compounds composed of oxygen, hydrogen and carbon; the human body's primary source of energy (4 calories per gram); carbohydrates are classified as simple (including certain sugars) and complex (including starches and fiber)

cholesterol a substance found only in foods of animal origin; because the human body produces adequate cholesterol for its own needs, consumption of excess cholesterol is discouraged

food allergy a reaction by the immune system to foods; symptoms include digestive problems, hives, swollen airways or the life-threatening reaction known as anaphylaxis

food intolerance an abnormal physical response to food that is not immune-mediated

lactose a kind of naturally occurring sugar found in mammalian milk; milk sugar

DEVELOPING AND MODIFYING FORMULAS

When conceiving and creating healthier bread, pastry and dessert formulas, begin by selecting naturally healthy ingredients. Choose ingredients that are naturally lower in calories, fat, cholesterol and sugar and higher in fiber, vitamins and minerals. For example, a fruit salad or fruit compote garnished with a fruit sorbet might be offered in place of a more traditional item such as a fruit pie garnished with ice cream. This book includes many formulas for desserts and baked goods that are naturally healthy, indicated by our adaptation of the USDA's MyPlate icon, shown to the right.

When modifying a traditional formula, there are three principles to be followed: Reduce, Replace or Eliminate.

▶ *Reduce* the quantity of an ingredient when using less will have little or no effect on the taste, texture or appearance of the final product but will result in a healthier profile for the product.

▶ *Replace* the ingredient or the cooking method with an alternative that will do the least to change the flavor, texture or appearance of the final product.

▶ *Eliminate* an ingredient if doing so does not appreciably change the product.

SHARON B. SALOMON, MS, RD

This chapter was written and researched by Sharon Salomon, a registered dietitian with a Master of Science degree in clinical nutrition. Ms. Salomon has also studied at La Varenne Cooking School in Burgundy, France, and attended the Culinary Institute of America at Greystone for certification in nutritional cuisine. She has taught nutrition and culinary education courses and has worked as a caterer as well as a spokesperson for a variety of food trade organizations. Salomon, who is a freelance writer specializing in nutrition, food and lifestyle issues, has contributed to culinary arts textbooks, Web sites, magazines and newspapers.

lecithin a substance found in egg yolks; a natural emulsifier; also lecithin granules

saturated fats fats found mainly in animal products such as milk, butter, cheese, eggs and meat as well as in tropical oils such as coconut and palm; usually solid at room temperature. Research suggests that high-fat diets, especially those high in saturated fat, may be linked to heart disease, obesity and certain forms of cancer

hydrogenated fats fats that have been chemically altered to increase shelf life and make them more solid at room temperature, such as solid shortening or margarine

Chefs use these concepts when developing more healthy alternatives to traditional pastry and dessert offerings. In other cases a chef may alter a basic formula by reducing the amount of one or more ingredients, often with little significant change to the taste or quality of the finished product. The formulas at the end of this chapter illustrate the various ways that formulas may be changed to meet the needs of certain types of dietary conditions. Some use alternative ingredients; others use substitutes to produce items that meet nutritional guidelines.

Alternative Ingredients and Substitutes

In choosing ingredients for healthful desserts, the flavor, appearance and texture of the final product should be the guiding criteria. It is important to know the function an ingredient serves in a formula before choosing a substitute or alternative. Does the ingredient affect flavor, structure, texture or appearance? When eggs are used as a binder, for example, ground flax seeds, tofu, puréed fruits or commercial egg replacers may be substituted. On the other hand, if the eggs are acting as leaveners, then baking powder mixed with oil and water may be preferable. If the egg is serving as an emulsifier, adding commercially available liquid or granular **lecithin** will substitute for the emulsification properties of the egg.

The successful substitution of many commonly used bakeshop ingredients may require changing the method of preparation used. You may need to increase or decrease the amount of mixing or beating, vary the order in which the ingredients are combined or decrease the temperature for baking as well as the time the product is baked. Here are some suggestions for ingredient substitutions or formula modifications to create healthier and alternative baked goods.

FAT

Some desserts are naturally fat-free or low in fat. Angel food cake (page 444), meringues (page 410) and meringue cake layers are naturally fat-free because they are made with egg whites, sugar and white flour, all fat-free ingredients. Fruit cobblers can be low in fat, especially if the topping is made with a high-fiber cereal and a small amount of melted butter or oil, with fruit juice to substitute for some of the fat. Reduced-fat and fat-free substitutes for such common bakeshop ingredients as milk, buttermilk, sour cream and yogurt can work well in many applications. (See Table 16.1.)

Fats tenderize baked goods. Reducing fats can result in tougher products. In many cases, the fat content of a formula can be reduced by up to 30 percent. But if the formula calls for flour, switch to cake flour to ensure a tender result. Most quick-bread formulas can be reduced to 1 ounce (30 grams) of fat per 4 ounces (120 grams) of flour and still produce good results. If butter is being used for flavor and nothing else, then substituting powdered butter-flavored granules for the butter may work.

There are many choices for replacing fat in formulas; some will affect the flavor, appearance and texture of the finished product. Moisture-retaining ingredients, such as fruit and bean purées, help reduced-fat baked goods remain tender. But some fruit purées will affect the flavor in a negative way while others will enhance the flavor. Prune and black bean purée seems to blend well with chocolate desserts, while applesauce does not. Applesauce does, however, work well in "neutral" cakes, muffins and quick breads. Mashed bananas make an excellent substitute for fat and/or eggs but will add a distinct banana flavor. Other fruit and vegetable substitutes include puréed cooked pumpkin, puréed cooked yellow or orange squash, puréed cooked apricots and mashed ripe bananas. Pumpkin and squash will not affect the flavor as much as the apricots and banana will. Fruit purées also change the texture and color of the baked good. Using a fruit purée to replace some or all of the fat results in a moister, stickier baked good that will get moister during storage.

If butter is crucial to the product's structure, then reducing the amount of butter and replacing some of it with a fruit purée will usually work well. Some bakers substitute low-fat cream cheese in place of some of the butter in cookies and cakes. Be wary of using margarines in place of butter. Substituting margarine for butter in a formula will reduce the **saturated fat** but will not reduce the calories. Choose a margarine that does not contain **hydrogenated fats** or **trans fats** because hydrogenated fats are not considered a healthy alternative to butter. Fat-free margarines usually do not perform well in baked goods.

Using a vegetable oil to substitute for butter will not reduce the amount of fat in a formula, either. Liquid and solid fats have similar amounts of fat and calories; only their composition is different. Solid fats have more saturated fat. Liquid fats have more **unsaturated** components. Using a vegetable oil for some or all of the butter in a formula will also reduce the amount of saturated fat in the product but will not decrease the calories. Substituting liquid oil for a solid fat may alter the texture and appearance of a baked product.

Replacing melted butter or melted shortening with a more healthy liquid fat such as olive oil or canola oil is one simple way to reduce the amount of saturated fat in baked goods. Oils made from nuts, including almonds, hazelnuts and walnuts, will also add a unique flavor and can work well in muffin and cookie formulas. Using vegetable oil in place of melted butter such as in a crêpe batter or for sautéing will only slightly alter the taste. Substituting a liquid oil in a formula that requires a solid fat, however, will alter the product dramatically. Piecrust made with olive oil, for instance, may be difficult to roll out and will bake into a mealy tough crust. For piecrusts, margarine may make a suitable substitute.

DAIRY PRODUCTS

Dairy products add color, texture and flavor to baked goods. They may be the basic liquid in a mixture, such as milk in a cake batter. Dairy products such as cream cheese or sour cream may add body, fat and texture to baked goods. To find an appropriate substitute, first determine whether the fat in the dairy food is necessary for the success of the end product. If it is, try a low-fat or fat-free substitute combined with additional ingredients to substitute for some of the fat lost by using a fat-free dairy product. If the formula calls for whole milk, cream, sour cream, cream cheese or other cheese, a low-fat dairy alternative will usually work.

Reduced-fat milk such as 2%, 1% or skim milk can usually be substituted on an equal basis for whole or regular milk. In some instances, evaporated skim milk may be a better choice, although it could add an off-flavor. Evaporated milk often imparts a "burnt" flavor because of the way it is processed. Light cream cheese (Neufchâtel) can be undetectable in baked goods when it replaces full-fat cream cheese. Using it to replace mascarpone cheese may require some other manipulation such as beating until light and fluffy with the addition of milk and and/or a small amount of sour cream. Plain fat-free cream cheese is not usually a suitable substitute for full-fat cream cheese.

Buttermilk, a by-product of churning cream into butter, is a naturally low-fat dairy product and a good substitute for other full-fat dairy products. Keep in mind that buttermilk is acidic, so using it may require some alteration in leavening ingredients. Low-fat and fat-free sour cream make suitable substitutions for full-fat sour cream in most preparations. Plain fat-free yogurt, made without gelatin, can be drained to remove excess liquid and used in place of sour cream. A better substitute might be Greek yogurt, which is naturally thicker than the conventional yogurt Americans are accustomed to eating. If the mixture is to be heated for a sauce or custard, adding a small amount of cornstarch will prevent curdling. Low-fat cottage cheese that has been blended in a food processor until smooth and creamy can be substituted for some of the full-fat cream cheese in a cheesecake formula. Use low-fat cream cheese for the remainder.

EGGS

Eggs add flavor and color; contribute to structure; incorporate air when beaten; provide liquid, fat and protein; and emulsify fat with liquid ingredients. Egg yolks contain fat, especially cholesterol. (Egg whites are fat-free, however.) Determine how much fat and cholesterol the eggs are adding to each serving of the finished product before deciding to modify the formula. If a cake formula that will serve 8 to 10 people requires 3 ounces (120 grams) or two eggs, it may not be necessary to make any changes, as the per-serving impact of the fat and cholesterol from this small amount of eggs will be low. Two ounces (60 grams) or two egg whites can substitute for one whole egg in a formula. It is best, however, to include some whole eggs for both color and texture. Commercial egg substitutes may not be lower in fat. Read the label to determine the suitability of the egg substitute.

unsaturated fats fats that are normally liquid (oils) at room temperature; they may be monounsaturated (from plants such as olives and avocados) or polyunsaturated (from grains and seeds such as corn, soybeans and safflower as well as from fish)

Fresh fruit desserts such as lemon sorbet are naturally fat-free and healthful dessert options.

When the eggs are used as a binder, certain combinations of ingredients can provide a similar structural component. For one egg, some possible substitutes include the following:

▸ 1 tablespoon (15 milliliters) ground flax seeds with 1.5 fluid ounces (45 milliliters) warm water

▸ 3.5 ounces (105 grams) mashed soft tofu

▸ 1.5 ounces (45 grams) puréed fruit

▸ 2 ounces (60 grams) puréed unflavored cooked beans

▸ unflavored mashed potatoes thinned a bit with warm water

LACTOSE

Those who are lactose intolerant lack a digestive enzyme to properly digest the sugar in milk and other dairy products. Commercially available lactose-free dairy products will work well in most preparations. Lactose is not usually necessary for the successful outcome of a formula. Some lactose-reduced and lactose-free dairy products may taste a bit sweeter to the sensitive palate when consumed plain but will usually substitute well in cooked foods.

Soy milk, either unflavored or flavored, may be substituted for milk, although there may be a detectable flavor difference. Soy milk tends to brown prematurely; therefore, baking temperatures should be reduced and baking times shortened when soy milk is used. A milky substance can be made from nuts such as almonds or walnuts that are ground in water. However, those with a nut allergy would not be able to consume this product. The ratio of nuts to water is 3 ounces (90 grams) nuts ground in 8 fluid ounces (240 milliliters) water.

GLUTEN

Wheat flour is the basis for many bakeshop products. Without it, making cookies, muffins, cakes and bread poses specific challenges. Baked goods will be less elastic and may crumble. Developing formulas that do not use gluten-forming flours involves making a number of changes to basic formulas. Alternative flours made from non-gluten-forming proteins combined with starches can make satisfactory gluten-free baked goods. The addition of

Millet and Amaranth Flours

Buckwheat Flour

SENSITIVITY TO GLUTEN

Gluten intolerance is the umbrella term for any adverse reaction to gluten, which is found in wheat, rye, barley, triticale, kamut and spelt. Gluten intolerance includes wheat allergies, gluten sensitivity (an inability to digest gluten) and **celiac disease**, an inherited autoimmune disease that makes it impossible for a person to eat any gluten-containing foods. People with wheat allergies can often safely consume other grains containing gluten, whereas gluten-sensitive people and those with celiac disease must avoid all gluten-containing foods.

By removing all wheat, rye and barley from the diet, people with celiac disease return to living a normal, healthy life. However, the minutest amount of gluten can cause symptoms to return. Staying gluten-free is quite a challenge and

requires a thorough education about foods and ingredients. Gluten is hidden in many places, including soy sauce (fermented with wheat), sauces, malted milk powder, imitation bacon bits, soups and even some spice blends.

Many flours other than wheat flour are safe for people with celiac disease: rice flour, corn flour, cornstarch, potato flour and potato starch, tapioca starch, quinoa, soy, sorghum, bean flours, buckwheat, millet and amaranth. Teff and oats can be safe as long as the source is free of cross-contamination from wheat. Baking without gluten defies most of the principles of food chemistry. It's best to use a blend of two to three different gluten-free flours and starches, usually rice flour, sorghum, buckwheat or millet with the addition of at least 30 percent starch—corn,

potato or tapioca. Some of the protein and elasticity of gluten can be replaced with gums—xanthan, guar or locust bean gum. Usually 1 teaspoon (5 milliliters) per cup (250 milliliters) is used for pastries and 1 tablespoon (15 milliliters) per cup (250 milliliters) is recommended for creating a blend that is used for bread flour. The addition of eggs helps build up the protein in the mixture. Also, adding a small amount of a flour that is high in protein (amaranth, soy or other bean flour) helps produce moisture in the final product.

Although gluten-free baking takes a bit of extra effort, the rewards outweigh the challenges, as gluten-free consumers are very appreciative and will remain customers for life!

—BETH HILSON, founder,
the Gluten-Free Pantry

stabilizers such as starches and gums, as discussed in Chapter 15, Ice Cream and Frozen Desserts, binds the batters into a homogeneous baked product. Available in powdered forms, gums and pectin can be adapted for use in the commercial kitchen. Because fruits are sources of gums and pectin, the addition of fruit purée to a formula for a gluten-free baked product is worth trying. For best results, mix several gluten-free flours together.

Gluten-free substitutes for wheat flour include flours made from arrowroot, **buckwheat**, corn, potato, rice, tapioca, soy, **amaranth**, **beans** such as chickpea, **flax** meal, **millet**, **quinoa**, **sorghum** and ground nuts. Commercially available gluten-free baking blends ease the preparation of suitable gluten-free products. In addition to the gluten-free formulas at the end of this chapter, a number of the formulas in this book, such as Chiffon Cake (page 445), include a gluten-free variation.

SUGAR

Sugar and other sweeteners add structure, texture and volume to baked goods. They retain moisture, contribute to a product's shelf life and help in the caramelization and browning of baked items. Because sugar provides flavor, color and tenderness to baked goods, finding an alternative that can provide all functions may be difficult. Most of the suitable substitutes for white table sugar are simply other kinds of sugar (such as fructose, which is fruit sugar). Using another kind of sugar will not reduce calories or carbohydrate content.

For consumers who simply prefer not to consume refined white table sugar, natural sweeteners from other sources may be used. Date and maple sugars can be used in baking and desserts but will impart a distinct flavor, which may actually be preferable to the sweetness of white table sugar. Date sugar works especially well as a sweetener when sprinkled on top of a baked good before baking.

Honey, **agave** and brown rice syrups are other natural sweeteners that may be used to replace some or all of the sugar in a formula. But these are liquid sweeteners with varying degrees of sweetness. If the formula calls for a small amount of granulated sugar, no adjustments to the liquid ingredients should be necessary when substituting liquid sweetener. But if granulated sugar represents a large proportion of the ingredients, some of the liquid in the formula will have to be reduced to compensate for the extra liquid. Liquid sugars will not cream mixtures, so formulas may have to be adjusted. Using the muffin mixing method may work instead. Also, be aware of the sweetening power of these different ingredients. Brown rice syrup is less sweet than table sugar, while agave and honey are between 25 and 50 percent sweeter than sugar. Often reducing the amount of white table sugar instead of attempting to find an alternative may be the best solution. Most desserts and baked goods will not be affected when the total sugar in the formula is reduced by up to one-third. To compensate for the reduced sweetness in these formulas, add additional flavor with extracts or spices such as nutmeg, mace, allspice and cinnamon.

The more challenging aspect of reducing the granulated sugar in formulas is replacing the calorie-containing carbohydrate sugar with a noncaloric sweetener. In baking, such sugar substitutes as **aspartame** (sold under the brand names NutraSweet and Equal), **saccharin** (sold under the brand name Sweet'N Low) or **sucralose** (sold under the name Splenda) may not always be good substitutes for white table sugar. Although they will sweeten the dessert, none of them can provide structure to baked goods. And they are chemical products with no nutritional value. Aspartame loses its sweetness when heated, so it can be used only in cold foods.

When a noncaloric sweetener is needed, sucralose may be the best substitute because it can be used measure for measure—by volume, not weight—as for white table sugar. And it stands up well to heat. But cakes and cookies baked with sucralose will not brown because it does not caramelize. It is best to consult usage recommendations provided by the manufacturers of these sugar substitutes before using them. And as when making any formula modification, test for doneness before the stated baking time has elapsed.

SALT

Reducing or eliminating added salt or sodium is usually successful in baked goods. Although chocolate desserts benefit from a dash of salt, most people will not notice that it is

buckwheat flour dark, nutty-tasting flour milled from the seeds of the buckwheat plant and used for centuries in Middle Eastern and Asian countries to make bread, cereals and baked goods

amaranth tiny oval seeds of a type of annual herb plant native to South America; used as a cooked grain and flour

bean flour cooked beans, including chickpeas, soybeans and white beans, that are dried, then ground into a fine powder; many bean flours, especially soy with its 50 percent protein content, are added to wheat flour mixtures to boost protein content

flax a grain plant also known as linseed, rich in omega-3 fatty acids; flax hulls and seeds are crushed into a meal or flour to release beneficial compounds

millet high-protein cereal grain cooked and eaten like rice; ground and used in combination with wheat flour in conventional baking

quinoa (KEEN-wa) tiny, spherical seeds of a plant native to South America, cooked like grain or ground and used like flour

sorghum grain harvested from a plant that resembles corn, used primarily for animal feed and food processing applications; also called milo; when ground, sorghum may be blended with other flours to make gluten-free preparations

agave a type of succulent plant native to the Southwest and the Americas; a syrup made from its thick pointed leaves is used as a natural sweetener

TABLE 16.1 COMMON INGREDIENT SUBSTITUTES AND ALTERNATIVES

INSTEAD OF	USE	IN THESE APPLICATIONS
Butter	Powdered butter-flavored granules plus liquid (either fat-free milk or water)	Muffins, quick bread, and in place of melted butter in batters
	Butter-flavored or vegetable oil sprays	Pan coating, sautéing
	Vegetable and nut oils	In place of melted butter in batters and piecrusts (mealy dough, not flaky); may affect taste and texture
	Dried fruit or cooked vegetable purées	Quick breads, cookies and general baking; may affect color, taste and texture
Chocolate	Cocoa powder (vegetable oil may be added as needed)	General baking, icings; not suitable as a substitute in ganache or for coating chocolate
Cream cheese	Reduced-fat cream cheese or fat-free cream cheese	Cheesecake, icings
Granulated sugar	Other natural, granular sugars; date sugar; unrefined cane sugar	All applications; may darken cakes
	Liquid sugar, honey, rice syrup	All applications; reduce liquid in formula to balance additional moisture
	Sugar substitutes such as aspartame, saccharin or sucralose	For sweetening syrups, custards, creams, compotes
	Sucralose	In baked goods, cakes, quick breads, muffins where granulated sugar would provide structure
Light cream	Equal portions of low-fat milk and fat-free evaporated milk	Custards, creams, frozen desserts, general baking
Milk	Low-fat or skim milk	Most applications
	Soy or other grain- or nut-based beverage	Sauces, custards, frozen desserts; general baking; reduce baking temperatures
Salt	Ground spices including allspice, cinnamon, nutmeg; citrus juice and extracts	Any formula where salt is not needed to assist leavening
Sour cream	Reduced-fat or nonfat sour cream; drained reduced-fat or nonfat plain yogurt without gelatin	Topping, icings, in cakes, quick breads and muffins and for general baking
Whole eggs	Liquid egg substitutes; use 1 egg white for every third whole egg called for in formula	Batters
	Fruit purées alone or combined with starches	Batters when eggs are used to moisten; other binder may be necessary
Whipped cream	Whipped chilled evaporated fat-free milk; the milk and beaters need to be very cold (needs to be stabilized with gelatin)	Topping
	Italian meringue	To aerate mousses, frozen soufflés and creams
Wheat flour	Blends of non-gluten-forming flours and starches, including rice flour, corn flour, cornstarch, potato flour and potato starch, tapioca starch, quinoa, soy, sorghum, bean flours, buckwheat, millet and amaranth	Quick breads, yeast breads, muffins, cookies, cakes and brownies; mix gently

gone. Keep in mind that some leavening agents contain sodium, but there are sodium-free alternatives. Salt substitutes impart a bitter off-flavor and are not recommended. Be aware that skim milk has slightly higher sodium content than regular milk.

fiber also known as dietary fiber; indigestible carbohydrates found in the seeds and cell walls of fruits, vegetables and cereal grains; fiber aids digestion

FIBER

Many Americans do not consume adequate fiber, an important component of a healthy diet. Fiber is found in such plant foods as whole grains, fruits and vegetables. Adding fiber to baked goods may make them more appealing to people concerned about health. Ways in which additional fiber may be added to bakeshop formulas include the following:

- Replace some of the white flour (1 to 2 ounces/30 to 60 grams) per ½ pound (240 grams) with whole-wheat flour. Use whole-wheat pastry flour if substituting more than 2 ounces (60 grams). (Whole white wheat, a variety with a pale hull, can often be used interchangeably with regular flour in bread, cookie, muffin, pastry and quick bread formulas.)
- Add ground flax seeds to any bakeshop formula in small amounts.
- Replace up to 2 ounces (60 grams) white flour per ½ pound (240 grams) with oat bran, oatmeal or bran cereal.
- Add a portion of fruit or vegetable purée to the formula to increase the fiber content.

Table 16.1 lists a number of ingredients and some common substitutions. Use it as a general guide. Appropriate substitutions depend on the function of the ingredient in the specific formula. Experimentation is the key to success.

VEGETARIAN PREPARATIONS

Vegetarianism, eating a plant-based diet, continues to gain in popularity. Lacto-ovo vegetarians eat eggs and dairy products. Some people are strict vegetarians, or **vegans**, and they will not eat any animal product, including gelatin (made from cow's hooves) or honey (made by bees, an "animal" by-product). Use the plant-based substitutes in each category when developing a formula for a vegan. Often vegetarians are particularly concerned with food additives and consuming processed foods. Their foods of choice are often organically grown, minimally processed foods.

Raw foodists, who are also vegans, present a more difficult challenge, especially because preparing raw foods that are appealing can be time-consuming, although the results are often palatable. (Raw foodists believe in eating only foods that have never been heated above 100°F–118°F [38°C–48°C.]) Equipment such as dehydrators are valuable for preparing "raw" desserts.

WEIGHT LOSS DIETS

As waistlines expand, so does the glut of fad diets promising quick and permanent weight loss. Alas, most of them offer nothing more than an unbalanced, unpalatable eating regimen that rarely results in anything other than hunger and headaches. Still, the dining public is easily seduced by the promise of no carbohydrates or raw foods or some combination of ingredients as a way to magically melt away the pounds.

Many Americans are following very low-carbohydrate diets for weight loss. Both flour and sugar are strictly controlled on these diets, as are fruits, but fat is usually not restricted. Suitable desserts for people on these diets include cakes made with ground nut flours, sucralose as the sweetener, and egg whites and/or whole eggs. Cheesecake and meringue-type cookies made with sucralose would also conform to a low-carbohydrate diet.

Whatever the diet regimen, the chef must be creative to find ways to offer sweet endings to a meal.

> **vegetarianism** eating a plant-based diet. Ovo vegetarians will eat eggs; lacto vegetarians will eat some dairy; ovo-lacto vegetarians will eat eggs and dairy; vegans will consume no animal products of any kind; raw foodists eat only raw unprocessed organic foods that have not been heated above 100°F–118°F (38°C–48°C).

1. Select a formula from those at the end of this chapter and compare it with a similar formula from one of the previous chapters. Note the nutritional differences. Discuss the ingredients that may account for these differences.

2. Using a traditional chocolate chip cookie formula, make suggestions for reducing fat and for increasing fiber.

3. Suggest ways to make a cheesecake for someone who must avoid lactose; for someone who is a vegan; for someone who must reduce the saturated fat in his or her diet.

4. You have been hired to develop a menu for a school cafeteria where some of the students have nut and gluten allergies. Use the Internet to obtain information on these two conditions. Then develop a week's worth of dessert menu items that can be offered in a school setting. **www**

Terms to Know

carbohydrates	saccharine
cholesterol	sucralose
celiac disease	vegan
antioxidants	raw foodist
aspartame	

The formulas in this chapter were created specifically to address certain dietary requirements. The formula title or headnote indicates for which application such a dish would be used. Formulas throughout this book that conform to recommended dietary guidelines are indicated with the MyPlate icon.

PEARS POACHED IN RED WINE

Yield: 8 Servings

Ripe pears, Anjou or Bartlett	8	8
Zinfandel wine	52 fl. oz.	1560 ml
Whole black peppercorns	8–10	8–10
Vanilla bean	1	1
Granulated sugar	12 oz.	360 g
Fresh basil, chopped	1 oz.	30 g
Orange zest	from 1 orange	from 1 orange

1. Peel and core the pears, leaving the stems intact.
2. Combine the remaining ingredients in a large nonreactive saucepan. Arrange the pears in the liquid in a single layer.
3. Place the pears on the stove top over a medium-high flame. Bring to just below a boil, then immediately reduce the heat and allow the liquid to simmer gently. Cover with a round of parchment paper if necessary to keep the pears submerged.
4. Continue poaching the pears until tender, approximately 1 to 1½ hours. Remove the saucepan from the stove and allow the pears to cool in the liquid.
5. Remove the pears from the poaching liquid. Strain the poaching liquid, then return it to the stove top. Reduce until the liquid is thick enough to coat the back of a spoon, then strain.
6. Serve the pears chilled or at room temperature in a pool of the reduced wine syrup.

Approximate values per 7-oz. (210-g) serving: **Calories** 410, **Total fat** 1.5 g, **Saturated fat** 0 g, **Cholesterol** 0 mg, **Sodium** 35 mg, **Total carbohydrates** 91 g, **Protein** 6 g, **Vitamin A** 40%, **Calcium** 90%, **Iron** 110%, **Claims**—low fat; no cholesterol; low sodium; high fiber

COINTREAU CHERRIES

Yield: Approximately 2½ lb. (1200 g)

Fresh pitted cherries	1 lb.	480 g
Granulated sugar	12 oz.	360 g
Cointreau or brandy	12–14 fl. oz.	360–420 ml

1. Select one or two narrow deep stainless steel containers such as a quarter-size hotel pan. Sterilize the pans by placing them in a large pot of boiling water. Remove the pans after 2 minutes.
2. Place the pitted cherries in the sterilized containers.
3. Combine the sugar and Cointreau. Pour this mixture over the cherries, making certain that the fruit is completely covered by the liquid, adding more liqueur as needed to completely cover the fruit. Cover with plastic wrap and macerate the cherries at least 1 week in the refrigerator. The cherries are then ready to use as a topping on ice cream and in cakes and tortes. They will keep 6 months.

Approximate values per 1-oz. (30-g) serving: **Calories** 70, **Total fat** 0 g, **Saturated fat** 0 g, **Cholesterol** 0 mg, **Sodium** 0 mg, **Total carbohydrates** 14 g, **Protein** 0 g, **Claims**—fat free; no sodium

FRESH RASPBERRY JAM

Although made with frozen berries, this is a fresh jam because it contains approximately 30 percent less sugar than a normal jam and must be refrigerated to maintain freshness. Use it in any formula calling for raspberry jam.

Yield: Approximately 6 lb. (2.8 kg)

Raspberries, IQF, defrosted	3 lb.	1440 g
Apples, cored, unpeeled, chopped	1 lb. 6 oz.	630 g
Granulated sugar	2 lb.	960 g
Lemon juice	2 fl. oz.	60 ml
Apple pectin	1.5 oz.	45 g
Citric acid	0.6 oz. (1 Tbsp.)	18 g
Water	0.5 fl. oz.	15 ml

1. Drain the raspberries, reserving the juice. Set aside the raspberries. Combine the raspberry juice with the apple pieces and purée the mixture until fine. Purée the raspberries and strain the seeds, if desired, and then add the strained raspberry purée to the apple purée.
2. Place the fruit mixture in a nonreactive pan with 1 pound 14 ounces (900 grams) of the sugar and the lemon juice. Heat to 120°F (49°C).
3. Mix the pectin with the remaining sugar and add to the warm fruit mixture.
4. Bring the mixture to a boil and cook 3 minutes, stirring constantly.
5. Remove from the heat. Combine the citric acid and water and add to the jam. Cool, then refrigerate. This jam keeps 2 to 3 weeks under refrigeration.

Approximate values per 1-oz. (30-g) serving: **Calories** 50, **Total fat** 0 g, **Saturated fat** 0 g, **Cholesterol** 0 mg, **Sodium** 0 mg, **Total carbohydrates** 12 g, **Protein** 0 g, **Claims**—fat free, no sodium, no cholesterol

BRAISED RHUBARB AND APPLES

Yield: Approximately 10 lb. (4.8 kg)

Tart green apples, peeled and cubed	2 lb. 8 oz.	1.1 kg
Rhubarb, IQF pieces	7 lb.	3.2 kg
Unsalted butter	4 oz.	120 g
Sweet white wine	8 fl. oz.	240 ml
Brown sugar	14 oz.	420 g
Vanilla extract	0.3 fl. oz. (2 tsp.)	10 ml
Cinnamon, ground	0.2 oz. (1 Tbsp.)	6 g
Nutmeg, ground	0.02 oz. (¼ tsp.)	0.5 g
Orange juice	2 fl. oz.	60 ml
Salt	0.1 oz. (½ tsp.)	3 g

1 Sauté the apples and rhubarb in the butter until they begin to soften.

2 Add the wine and reduce by half. Add the remaining ingredients. Simmer until the rhubarb is very tender.

3 Serve at room temperature in prebaked pastry cups, topped with reduced-fat sour cream, or serve warm over sorbet.

Approximate values per 1-oz. (30-g) serving: **Calories** 60, **Total fat** 2 g, **Saturated fat** 0.5 g, **Cholesterol** 0 mg, **Sodium** 25 mg, **Total carbohydrates** 11 g, **Protein** 0 g, **Claims**—low fat; no cholesterol; very low sodium

WARM BAKED PEACHES OR NECTARINES

Yield: 8 Servings

Freestone peaches or nectarines	4	4
Vanilla bean	1	1
Granulated sugar	2 oz.	60 g
Lemon	1	1
Unsalted butter	2 oz.	60 g

1 Cut the peaches or nectarines in half. Remove the pits. Place them cut side up in a well-buttered half-size hotel pan or an ovenproof dish.

2 Split the vanilla bean and scrape the seeds into the sugar. Juice the lemon and sprinkle the fruit with the sugar and lemon juice.

3 Place a small piece of the butter in the center of each fruit half and bake at 350°F (180°C) until tender and lightly browned, approximately 20 minutes. Serve warm with ice cream, sorbet or custard.

Approximate values per serving: **Calories** 100, **Total fat** 6 g, **Saturated fat** 3.5 g, **Cholesterol** 15 mg, **Sodium** 0 mg, **Total carbohydrates** 13 g, **Protein** 0 g, **Vitamin A** 10%, **Vitamin C** 10%, **Claims**—low calorie, no sodium

BERRY COMPOTE

Yield: 1 pt. (480 ml)

Berries, fresh or frozen	1 pt.	0.5 lt
Granulated sugar	4 oz.	120 g
Oranges, juiced	2	2
Honey	3 fl. oz.	90 ml
Cinnamon stick	1	1
Brandy	1.5 fl. oz.	45 ml

1. Select an assortment of fresh or frozen berries—strawberries, blueberries, raspberries, blackberries and cherries can be used, depending on availability.
2. Place the fruits and sugar in a nonreactive saucepan. Add the juice from the two oranges. Bring to a simmer over low heat; cook until the fruits are soft but still intact.
3. Strain the mixture, reserving both the fruits and the liquid. Return the liquid to the saucepan. Add the finely grated zest from one orange and the honey, cinnamon stick and brandy.
4. Bring to a boil and reduce until the mixture thickens enough to coat the back of a spoon. Remove from the heat and cool to room temperature. Remove the cinnamon stick.
5. Gently stir the reserved fruits into the sauce, cover and chill. Serve with sorbet, angel food cake or cheesecake.

VARIATION:

Sweet Red Wine Berry Compote—Combine the assortment of fruits in a saucepan with 4 fluid ounces (120 milliliters) sweet red wine. Omit the oranges and simmer over low heat to cook the fruits. Strain the mixture, reserving the fruits. Add the seeds scraped from one vanilla bean. Bring to a boil and cook until the mixture thickens. Stir in the reserved fruits, cover and chill.

Approximate values per 1-oz. (30-g) serving: **Calories** 70, **Total fat** 0 g, **Saturated fat** 0 g, **Cholesterol** 0 mg, **Sodium** 0 mg, **Total carbohydrates** 16 g, **Protein** 0 g, **Vitamin C** 15%, **Claims**—fat free; no sodium

GRATIN OF FRESH BERRIES WITH CRÈME FRAÎCHE

Yield: 1 Serving

Assorted fresh berries, such as raspberries, strawberries and blackberries	4 oz.	120 g
Crème fraîche	2 fl. oz.	60 ml
Orange liqueur	0.15 fl. oz. (1 tsp.)	5 ml
Brown sugar	0.5 oz.	15 g

1. Arrange the berries in an even layer in a shallow, heatproof serving dish.
2. Stir the crème fraîche and orange liqueur together. Spoon this mixture over the berries.
3. Sprinkle the brown sugar over the crème fraîche. Place under a broiler or salamander just until the sugar melts. Serve immediately.

Approximate values per serving: **Calories** 210, **Total fat** 7 g, **Saturated fat** 4 g, **Cholesterol** 20 mg, **Sodium** 30 mg, **Total carbohydrates** 33 g, **Protein** 3 g, **Vitamin C** 40%, **Claims**—very low sodium; high fiber

GRILLED FRUIT KEBABS

Like many desserts based on fresh fruit, these kebabs are fat free.

Yield: 8 Skewers

Cantaloupe	½	½
Honeydew melon	¼	¼
Pineapple	½	½
Fresh strawberries	8	8
Brown sugar	2 oz.	60 g
Lime juice	4 fl. oz.	120 ml
Cinnamon, ground	0.02 oz. (¼ tsp.)	0.5 g

1. Remove the rind and cut the melons and pineapple into 1-inch (2.5-centimeter) cubes. Hull the strawberries and leave whole.
2. Make a sugar glaze by combining the sugar, lime juice and cinnamon, stirring until the sugar dissolves.
3. Heat the grill and clean the grate thoroughly.
4. Thread the fruits onto kebab skewers, alternating colors for an attractive appearance.
5. Brush the fruits with the sugar glaze. Grill, rotating the skewers frequently to develop an evenly light brown surface.
6. Serve immediately.

Approximate values per skewer: **Calories** 70, **Total fat** 0 g, **Saturated fat** 0 g, **Cholesterol** 0 mg, **Sodium** 10 mg, **Total carbohydrates** 16 g, **Protein** 1 g, **Vitamin C** 50%, **Claims**—fat free; very low sodium

APRICOT SOUFFLÉ

This dessert has fewer calories and less fat than a traditional soufflé.

Yield: 8 Servings

Dried apricots, pitted	8 oz.	240 g
Water	18 fl. oz.	540 g
Granulated sugar	8 oz.	240 g
Egg whites	6 oz. (6 whites)	180 g
Lemon juice	1.5 fl. oz. (1½ Tbsp.)	45 ml
Powdered sugar	as needed	as needed

1. Place the apricots and water in a heavy saucepan over medium high heat. Bring the water to a boil, reduce the heat and simmer until the apricots are soft, approximately 20 minutes.
2. Transfer the apricots and remaining water to a food processor fitted with a metal blade. Process until the mixture is smooth, approximately 1 minute. Add 7 ounces (210 grams) of the sugar and half the lemon juice and process to combine. Let the purée cool. Cover and hold for use at room temperature.
3. To prepare the soufflés, brush 8-fluid-ounce (240-milliliter) ramekins with oil and dust with granulated sugar. Preheat the oven to 375°F.
4. Whip the egg whites to stiff peaks with the remaining 1 ounce (30 grams) of sugar and lemon juice. Stir one-quarter of the egg whites into the apricot purée. Fold in the remaining whites and spoon the mixture into the prepared ramekins. Smooth the top of each soufflé with a spatula.
5. Place the soufflés in a shallow hotel pan and set the hotel pan in the preheated oven. Pour enough hot water to come halfway up the sides of the ramekins. Bake until the soufflés are well risen and lightly browned, approximately 25 to 30 minutes. Dust with powdered sugar before serving.

Approximate values per serving: **Calories** 190, **Total fat** 0 g, **Saturated fat** 0 g, **Cholesterol** 0 mg, **Sodium** 40 mg, **Total carbohydrates** 47 g, **Protein** 3 g, **Vitamin A** 20%, **Claims**—fat free, no cholesterol

SPICED POACHED PEARS

Yield: 15 Poached Pears

Pears	15	15
Water	48 fl. oz.	1440 ml
White wine	36 fl. oz.	1080 ml
Granulated sugar	2 lb. 12 oz.	1320 g
Cinnamon, ground	0.5 oz.	15 g
Star anise pods	3	3
Ground cardamom	0.07 oz. (1 tsp.)	2 g
Anise seeds	0.5 oz.	15 g
Lemon zest, grated fine	0.4 oz. (2 Tbsp.)	12 g
Orange zest, grated fine	0.6 oz. (3 Tbsp.)	18 g
Mint leaves	30	30
Vanilla beans	1½	1½

1. Peel the pears, leaving the stems intact. Set aside.
2. Bring the remaining ingredients to a boil in a large stainless steel saucepan.
3. Add the peeled pears to the mixture. Cut a piece of parchment to fit inside the pan on top of the pears. Place the paper over the pears, then fit a lid inside the saucepan so that it weighs down the fruit, keeping it submerged in the liquid.
4. Reduce the heat to very low. Cook the pears in the barely simmering liquid until tender, approximately 45 minutes to 1 hour 15 minutes depending on the variety of pear.
5. Remove the pears from the poaching liquid and return the liquid to the stove top. Reduce until the liquid is thick enough to coat the back of a spoon, then strain.

VARIATION:

Poached Pears in Exotic Syrup—Omit the cinnamon, star anise, cardamom and anise seeds and replace with 4 fluid ounces (120 milliliters) passion fruit juice.

Approximate values per serving: **Calories** 480, **Total fat** 1 g, **Saturated fat** 0 g, **Cholesterol** 0 mg, **Sodium** 0 mg, **Total carbohydrates** 110 g, **Protein** 1 g, **Vitamin C** 15%, **Claims**—low fat, no cholesterol, no sodium, good source of fiber

NONFAT MANGO MOUSSE

Compared with the formula for Apricot Mousse (page 510), this Mango Mousse has half of the calories and none of the fat. To retain a light texture, a larger proportion of Italian meringue is used here than in the Apricot Mousse. This adds some of the lightness that is lost when yogurt is substituted for whipped cream.

Yield: 10 Servings, approximately 3¾ oz. (115 g) each, 2 lb. 6 oz. (1155 g) Mousse

Angel Food Cake (page 444), lemon variation, baked in a half-sheet pan	½ sheet	½ sheet
Yogurt, nonfat, unsweetened	14 oz.	420 g
Mango purée	1 lb.	480 g
Egg whites	3 oz. (3 whites)	90 g
Granulated sugar	5 oz.	150 g
Water	2 fl. oz.	60 ml
Sheet gelatin, softened	8 sheets (0.5 oz.)	15 g
Neutral glaze	as needed	as needed
Italian Meringue (page 413)	as needed	as needed
Fresh mango slices and black currants	as needed	as needed
Isomalt Lace (page 729)	as needed	as needed

1. Place five 2½-inch- (6-centimeter-) wide deep torte rings on a half-sheet pan lined with plastic wrap. Cut the lemon-flavored Angel Food Cake into five 2½-inch (6-centimeter) rounds and five 2-inch (5-centimeter) rounds. Place one 2½-inch (6-centimeter) cake round in the bottom of each torte ring. Reserve the remaining rounds and set aside.

2. Place the yogurt in a cheesecloth-lined strainer set over a bowl to collect the liquid. Drain the yogurt 2 to 3 hours in the refrigerator before using. Discard the liquid.

3. Combine the mango purée and the drained yogurt in a bowl. Lightly warm the mixture over a bain marie to 85°F (29°C). Set aside.

4. Prepare an Italian meringue with the egg whites, sugar and water. Melt the gelatin and add it to the meringue.

5. Fold one-quarter of the mango-yogurt mixture into the meringue using a balloon whisk. Add another one-quarter of the mixture and combine well. Fold in the remaining meringue.

6. Before the gelatin sets, spoon the mousse into the cake-lined torte rings, filling each ring halfway. Place one cake round on top of the mousse in each ring. Top with the remaining mousse. Refrigerate or freeze until the mousse is firm, preferably overnight.

7. Coat the tops of the mousse with neutral glaze. Refrigerate until the glaze sets.

8. Unmold the mousse from the rings. Garnish with Italian Meringue, the fruits and Isomalt Lace. Cut each molded dessert in half to serve.

Approximate values per 3¾-oz. (115-g) serving: **Calories** 120, **Total fat** 0 g, **Saturated fat** 0 g, **Cholesterol** 0 mg, **Sodium** 50 mg, **Total carbohydrates** 25 g, **Protein** 5 g, **Vitamin A** 35%, **Vitamin C** 20%, **Claims**—fat free, low sodium

PIE OR TART DOUGH MADE WITH OLIVE OIL

This crust has no cholesterol and less saturated fat than one made with animal fat or hydroge-nated shortening.

Yield: 1 lb. 4 oz. (598 g) Dough for one 8-in. (20-cm) double-crust pie

Olive oil	5.25 fl. oz.	158 ml	58%
Vanilla extract	0.15 fl. oz. (1 tsp.)	4 ml	1.5%
Molasses	1 oz.	30 g	11%
Almond extract	0.15 fl. oz. (1 tsp.)	4 ml	1.5%
Pastry flour	9 oz.	270 g	100%
Quick-cooking oats	4 oz.	120 g	44%
Salt	0.2 oz. (1 tsp.)	6 g	2%
Cinnamon, ground	0.2 oz. (1 Tbsp.)	6 g	2%
Total dough weight:	1 lb. 4 oz.	598 g	220%

1. Combine the olive oil, vanilla, molasses and almond extract in a measuring cup. Set aside.
2. Place the flour, oats, salt and cinnamon in the bowl of a food processor. With the machine running, pour in the olive oil mixture. Mix until the dough forms a ball, approximately 30 to 40 seconds. Wrap the dough and refrigerate approximately 1 hour before using.

Approximate values per 1-oz. (30-g) serving: **Calories** 140, **Total fat** 8 g, **Saturated fat** 1 g, **Cholesterol** 0 mg, **Sodium** 115 mg, **Total carbohydrates** 15 g, **Protein** 2 g, **Claims**—no cholesterol

PASSION FRUIT TART

This tart represents a lower-calorie dessert when compared with many cream-filled fruit tarts.

❶ Browning the Italian Meringue.

❷ The finished tart.

Yield: 2 Tarts, 7 in. (17 cm) each

Orange juice	1 pt.	480 ml
Passion fruit juice	8 fl. oz.	240 ml
Lemon juice	2 fl. oz.	60 ml
Fructose or granulated sugar	8 oz.	240 g
Eggs	6.75 oz. (4 eggs)	202 g
Egg yolks	1.2 oz. (2 yolks)	36 g
Granulated sugar	6 oz.	180 g
Cornstarch	2.25 oz.	68 g
Unsalted butter, softened	2 oz.	60 g
Nut Tart/Pie Dough (recipe follows), 7-in. (17-cm) shells, fully baked	2 shells	2 shells
Italian Meringue (page 413)	as needed	as needed
Fresh papaya, cubed	8 oz.	240 g
Neutral glaze	5 oz.	150 g
Passion fruit purée	3 oz.	90 g
Dried pineapple slices (page 670)	as needed	as needed
Vanilla bean, split	1	1
Edible gold leaf (optional)	as needed	as needed

❶ Combine the orange juice, passion fruit juice, lemon juice and fructose in a large saucepan. Bring to a boil.

❷ Meanwhile whisk together the eggs, egg yolks and granulated sugar. Stir in the cornstarch.

❸ Temper the egg batter with one-quarter of the boiling fruit juice. Pour the tempered egg mixture into the remaining boiling juice. Whisk vigorously until the mixture boils and is well thickened.

❹ Remove from the heat and stir in the butter, then pour the filling into the baked tart shells. Let cool.

❺ Pipe two borders of Italian Meringue in teardrop shapes around the edge of each tart. Brown the Italian Meringue using a propane torch.

❻ Fill the center of each tart with the diced papaya. Melt the neutral glaze with the passion fruit purée. Cool slightly, then brush the glaze over the papaya. Garnish each tart with a slice of dried pineapple, a split vanilla bean and edible gold leaf (if using). Chill.

Approximate values per ⅛-tart serving: **Calories** 390, **Total fat** 15 g, **Saturated fat** 4.5 g, **Cholesterol** 105 mg, **Sodium** 210 mg, **Total carbohydrates** 59 g, **Protein** 8 g, **Vitamin A** 15%, **Vitamin C** 60%, **Iron** 10%

NUT TART/PIE DOUGH

This crust has less saturated fat than one made with animal fats or hydrogenated shortening.

Yield: 1 lb. 9 oz. (871 g) Dough

Pastry flour, sifted	4 oz.	120 g	66%
White whole-wheat flour	2 oz.	60 g	33%
Almond flour	4 oz.	120 g	66%
Hazelnut flour	4 oz.	120 g	66%
Brown sugar	6 oz.	180 g	100%
Reduced-fat cream cheese	6 oz.	180 g	100%
Egg	1.6 oz. (1 egg)	50 g	26%
Egg white	1 oz. (1 white)	30 g	16%
Vanilla extract	0.15 fl. oz. (1 tsp.)	5 ml	2.5%
Salt	0.2 oz. (1 tsp.)	6 g	3%
Total dough weight:	1 lb. 12 oz.	871 g	478%

1. Combine the pastry, whole-wheat, almond and hazelnut flours. Set aside.
2. Cream the brown sugar and cream cheese until fluffy.
3. Gradually add the egg and egg white, then the vanilla and salt to the creamed mixture.
4. Mix in the flour mixture until just combined.
5. Chill the dough before using.

Approximate values per 1-oz. (30-g) serving: **Calories** 110, **Total fat** 6 g, **Saturated fat** 1 g, **Cholesterol** 10 mg, **Sodium** 105 mg, **Total carbohydrates** 12 g, **Protein** 3 g

EGG- AND CHOLESTEROL-FREE CHOCOLATE RASPBERRY TORTE

Yield: 3 Layer Cakes, 8 in. (20 cm) each   **Method:** Muffin

Pastry or all-purpose flour	1 lb. 11 oz.	810 g	100%
Cocoa powder	7 oz.	210 g	26%
Baking soda	0.5 oz.	15 g	2%
Granulated sugar	2 lb.	960 g	118%
Salt	0.4 oz. (2 tsp.)	12 g	1.5%
Water	1 lb. 8 oz.	720 g	88%
Corn or vegetable oil	1 pt.	480 ml	59%
Vanilla extract	1 fl. oz.	30 ml	4%
Vinegar (apple cider or red wine)	4 fl. oz.	120 ml	15%
Almond extract	0.5 fl. oz.	15 ml	2%
Total batter weight:	7 lb.	3372 g	415.5%
Fresh Raspberry Jam (page 575)	2 lb. 4 oz.	1080 g	
Raspberry Ganache (recipe follows), made without butter	2 lb. 10 oz.	1260 g	
Sliced blanched almonds, toasted	as needed	as needed	
Fresh raspberries	as needed	as needed	
Powdered sugar	as needed	as needed	

1. Sift together the flour, cocoa powder, baking soda, granulated sugar and salt. Set aside.
2. Whisk together the water, oil, vanilla, vinegar and almond extract in a separate large bowl.
3. Add the dry ingredients and stir until smooth.
4. Divide the batter evenly among six buttered and floured 8-inch (22-centimeter) cake pans. Bake at 375°F (190°C) until the center of the cakes bounce back when lightly pressed, approximately 30 minutes.
5. Allow the cakes to cool for 5 minutes in the pans. Invert them onto paper-lined sheet pans. (The cakes may be frozen at this point for finishing at a later time.)
6. Working with two cake rounds at a time, cut each cake in half horizontally into two layers using a serrated knife. Place one layer of cake onto a cake board.
7. Using an offset spatula, spread an even layer of Fresh Raspberry Jam in the center of the cake approximately ½ inch (1.2 centimeters) from the edge.
8. Set another cake layer over the raspberry jam. Repeat the process in Step 7 twice more. Then set the fourth and final cake layer on top.
9. Repeat from Step 6 with the other four cake rounds.
10. Frost each cake with room-temperature Raspberry Ganache. While the ganache is still moist, sprinkle the surface with the almonds. Garnish with fresh raspberries and powdered sugar.

Approximate values per ½₂-torte serving: **Calories** 480, **Total fat** 18 g, **Saturated fat** 0 g, **Cholesterol** 0 mg, **Sodium** 210 mg, **Total carbohydrates** 77 g, **Protein** 4 g

❶ Spreading the raspberry jam over the cut cake.

❷ The finished cake.

RASPBERRY GANACHE

Most ganache formulas call for heavy cream. Raspberry purée takes on the role of the heavy cream in this ganache. The tartness of the fresh berries balances the richness of the chocolate. The butter adds richness but may be omitted in reduced-fat preparations.

Yield: 2 lb. 14 oz. (1353 g)

Semisweet chocolate, chopped	1 lb. 2 oz.	540 g
Raspberry purée, unsweetened, seedless	20 fl. oz.	600 ml
Pectin	0.1 oz. (1 tsp.)	3 g
Granulated sugar	3 oz.	90 g
Unsalted butter, melted (optional)	4 oz.	120 g

1. Place the chopped chocolate in a bowl and set aside.
2. Heat the raspberry purée to 120°F (49°C) in a nonreactive pan.
3. Thoroughly mix the pectin and sugar. Whisk it into the raspberry purée and bring to a boil.
4. Pour approximately 2 fluid ounces (60 milliliters) of the hot purée into the bowl of chocolate. Combine with a spatula, adding the remaining purée in four increments.
5. Stir in the butter (if using). If lumps form or if the chocolate fails to melt completely, place the bowl over a bain marie until completely melted and smooth. Use immediately.

Approximate values per 1-oz. (30-g) serving: **Calories** 86, **Total fat** 4 g, **Saturated fat** 0 g, **Cholesterol** 0 mg, **Sodium** 0 mg, **Total carbohydrates** 11 g, **Protein** 1 g

REDUCED-FAT CARROT CAKE SQUARES

Yield: 4 Dozen Squares, 2 in. (5 cm) each; 1 Half-Sheet Pan

Method: Muffin

All-purpose or pastry flour	1 lb.	480 g	100%
Baking soda	0.4 oz. (1 Tbsp.)	12 g	2.5%
Cinnamon, ground	0.2 oz. (1 Tbsp.)	6 g	1.25%
Grapeseed oil or vegetable oil	4 fl. oz.	120 ml	25%
Vanilla extract	0.3 fl. oz. (2 tsp.)	10 ml	1.9%
Salt	0.4 oz. (2 tsp.)	10 g	2.5%
Eggs	6.4 oz. (4 eggs)	195 g	40%
Granulated sugar	1 lb. 4 oz.	600 g	125%
Invert sugar (or additional granulated sugar)	3 oz.	90 g	19%
Orange zest, grated fine	0.21 oz. (1 Tbsp.)	6 g	1.3%
Carrots, finely grated	1 lb.	480 g	100%
Crushed pineapple, drained	12 oz.	360 g	75%
Low-fat buttermilk	4 fl. oz.	120 ml	25%
Total batter weight:	5 lb. 2 oz.	2489 g	518%
Reduced-Fat Cream Cheese Icing (page 597)	1 lb. 8 oz.	720 g	

1. Sift together the flour, baking soda and cinnamon and set aside.
2. In the bowl of a 6 quart (6.5 liter) or larger mixer fitted with the paddle attachment, blend the oil, vanilla, salt, eggs, sugars and orange zest for 2 minutes on medium speed. Mix in the carrots, pineapple and buttermilk. Add the flour mixture and mix until just combined.
3. Spread the batter onto a paper-lined half-sheet pan fitted with a pan extender.
4. Bake at 350°F (180°C) until the cake bounces back when lightly pressed in the center, approximately 40 minutes. Cool the cake completely on a wire rack.
5. Spread the Reduced-Fat Cream Cheese Icing on the cooled cake. Cut the cake into 2-inch (5-centimeter) squares.

Approximate values per bar: **Calories** 160, **Total fat** 4 g, **Saturated fat** 1 g, **Cholesterol** 20 mg, **Sodium** 200 mg, **Total carbohydrates** 31 g, **Protein** 2 g, **Vitamin A** 35%, **Claims**—reduced fat

REDUCED-FAT THREE BERRY TORTE

This dessert has less total fat and less saturated fat when compared with a traditional cream-filled cake.

Yield: 2 Tortes, 7 in. × 2½ in. (17 cm × 6 cm) each

Dacquoise (page 424), 7-in. (17-cm) disks	4 disks	4 disks
Reduced-Fat Vanilla Cream (recipe follows)	3 lb. 11 oz.	1770 g
Fresh raspberries	6 oz.	180 g
Fresh blueberries	6 oz.	180 g
Fresh blackberries	6 oz.	180 g
Italian Meringue (page 413)	1 lb. 8 oz.	720 g
Red Fruit Gelée (recipe follows)	1 lb.	480 g

1. Lightly oil and sugar two 7-inch (17-centimeter) torte rings, or line the rings with strips of clear acetate. Place on a paper-lined sheet pan.
2. Place one Dacquoise disk in each torte ring.

3 Cover each Dacquoise disk with a 1-inch- (2.5-centimeter-) thick layer of Reduced-Fat Vanilla Cream. Scatter half of the berries over the cream.

4 Trim the two remaining Dacquoise disks slightly to fit inside the torte rings. Place them on top of the cream, then top them with another 1-inch- (2.5-centimeter-) thick layer of the cream and the remaining berries. Cover the berries with the remaining cream, leveling it off with a long metal spatula. Refrigerate the tortes until set, approximately 2 hours.

5 Gently heat the sides of the rings using a propane torch to facilitate the removal of the rings. Place the tortes on a cake board.

6 Ice the tortes with a thin layer of Italian Meringue. Using a pastry bag fitted with a medium star tip or a St. Honoré tip, pipe a connecting meringue border along the edge of the torte. Brown the meringue using a propane torch.

7 Prepare the Red Fruit Gelée and pour it inside the meringue border.

Approximate values per ⅛-cake serving: **Calories** 510, **Total fat** 10 g, **Saturated fat** 1.5 g, **Cholesterol** 5 mg, **Sodium** 240 mg, **Total carbohydrates** 91 g, **Protein** 18 g, **Vitamin C** 25%, **Calcium** 15%

REDUCED-FAT VANILLA CREAM

Yield: 3 lb. 11 oz. (1770 g)

Fat-free cottage cheese	1 lb. 8 oz.	720 g
Fat-free sour cream	10 oz.	300 g
Low-fat sweetened condensed milk	13 fl. oz.	390 ml
Vanilla extract	0.5 fl. oz.	15 ml
Sheet gelatin, softened	8 sheets (0.5 oz.)	15 g
Fresh raspberries	4 oz.	120 g
Fresh blueberries	3 oz.	90 g
Fresh blackberries	4 oz.	120 g

1 Blend the cottage cheese, sour cream, sweetened condensed milk and vanilla in a food processor until smooth.

2 Scrape the mixture into a bowl set over simmering water and warm to 95°F (35°C). Set aside.

3 Melt the gelatin and whisk it into the cheese mixture. Fold in the berries and use immediately.

Approximate values per 1-oz. (30-g) serving: **Calories** 35, **Total fat** 0 g, **Saturated fat** 0 g, **Cholesterol** 0 mg, **Sodium** 45 mg, **Total carbohydrates** 5 g, **Protein** 2 g

RED FRUIT GELÉE

Yield: Approximately 1 lb. (480 g)

Raspberry purée	5 oz.	150 g
Blueberry purée	5 oz.	150 g
Blackberry purée	5 oz.	150 g
Granulated sugar	5 oz.	150 g
Sheet gelatin, softened	8 sheets (0.5 oz.)	15 g

1 In a nonreactive saucepan, combine and heat the fruit purées to 110°F (43°C). Whisk in the sugar. Melt the gelatin and add to the fruit purée.

2 Use immediately to coat the top of a tart or torte.

Approximate values per 1-oz. (30-g) serving: **Calories** 50, **Total fat** 0 g, **Saturated fat** 0 g, **Cholesterol** 0 mg, **Sodium** 5 mg, **Total carbohydrates** 11 g, **Protein** 1 g

REDUCED-FAT LEMON POUNDCAKE

This cake has less total fat and less saturated fat when compared with a traditional poundcake. Butter and egg yolks aid in emulsifying cake batters. Because this cake batter is low in both, it is essential to properly cream the mixture to create a proper emulsion. The higher proportion of egg whites in this formula adds structure to the cake.

Yield: 1 Loaf, 9 in. × 5 in. (22 cm × 12.5 cm)

Method: Creaming

All-purpose or pastry flour	8.5 oz.	255 g	100%
Baking soda	0.4 oz. (¼ tsp.)	1 g	0.05%
Baking powder	0.15 oz. (1 tsp.)	4 g	1.7%
Unsalted butter, room temperature	3 oz.	90 g	35%
Granulated sugar	5.5 oz.	165 g	65%
Corn syrup, glucose or honey	1.5 oz.	45 g	17%
Egg	1.6 oz. (1 egg)	48 g	19%
Egg whites	2 oz. (2 whites)	60 g	23.5%
Lemon zest, grated	0.4 oz. (2 Tbsp.)	12 g	5%
Vanilla extract	0.15 fl. oz. (1 tsp.)	5 ml	1.7%
Salt	0.1 oz. (½ tsp.)	2 g	1%
Buttermilk, low-fat	6 oz.	180 ml	70.5%
Total batter weight:	1 lb. 12 oz.	867 g	340%

Glaze:

Powdered sugar, sifted	3 oz.	90 g	
Lemon juice	1 fl. oz.	30 ml	
Lemon zest, grated fine	0.14 oz. (2 tsp.)	4 g	

1. Sift together the flour, baking soda and baking powder. Set aside.
2. Cream the butter in the bowl of a mixer fitted with the paddle attachment until light and fluffy. Add the sugar and corn syrup. Cream well.
3. Add the egg and egg whites one at a time, waiting for the previously added amount to be fully incorporated. Stir in the lemon zest, vanilla and salt.
4. Fold in the flour mixture alternately with the buttermilk in three additions.
5. Spread the batter into a greased 9-inch × 5-inch (22-centimeter × 12.5-centimeter) loaf pan. Bake at 350°F (180°C) until the cake bounces back when lightly pressed, approximately 1 hour.
6. Stir the glaze ingredients together in a small bowl and drizzle over the top of the cooled cake.

Approximate values per ¹⁄₁₂-cake serving: **Calories** 200, **Total fat** 6 g, **Saturated fat** 4 g, **Cholesterol** 30 mg, **Sodium** 420 mg, **Total carbohydrates** 32 g, **Protein** 4 g

REDUCED-FAT STRAWBERRY AND MANGO TRIFLE

Yield: 12 Servings

Fresh strawberries, quartered	12 oz.	360 g
Granulated sugar	2 oz.	60 g
Mangoes, cubed	12 oz.	360 g
Reduced-Fat Trifle Cream (recipe follows)	1 lb. 3 oz.	570 g
Reduced-Fat Lemon Poundcake (page 588)	1 cake	1 cake
Dried strawberries (page 670), formed into rings	12 rings	12 rings
Chocolate rings (page 703)	12	12
Isomalt Lace (page 729)	as needed	as needed

1. Purée 4 ounces (120 grams) of the strawberries with 1 ounce (30 grams) of the sugar. Fold in the remaining strawberries and set aside.
2. Purée 4 ounces (120 grams) of the mangoes with 1 ounce (30 grams) of the sugar. Fold in the remaining mango cubes and set aside.
3. Spoon approximately ½ ounce (15 grams) of the Reduced-Fat Trifle Cream into the bottom of each of 12 tall parfait glasses.
4. Cut the Reduced-Fat Lemon Poundcake into 12 thin slices. Cut each slice in half and fit one half in each parfait glass.
5. Evenly divide the strawberry mixture among the 12 parfait glasses. Top with ½ ounce (15 grams) of the Reduced-Fat Trifle Cream.
6. Place the remaining pieces of Reduced-Fat Poundcake in each parfait glass, covering the Reduced-Fat Trifle Cream.
7. Evenly divide the mango mixture among the 12 parfait glasses.
8. Fill the glasses with the remaining Reduced-Fat Trifle Cream. Garnish each glass with the dried strawberries, a chocolate ring and some Isomalt Lace.

Approximate values per serving: **Calories** 420, **Total fat** 14 g, **Saturated fat** 4 g, **Cholesterol** 50 mg, **Sodium** 250 mg, **Total carbohydrates** 67 g, **Protein** 10 g, **Vitamin A** 30%, **Vitamin C** 40%

REDUCED-FAT TRIFLE CREAM

Yield: 1 lb. 3 oz. (579 g)

Fat-free ricotta cheese	8 oz.	240 g
Low-fat cottage cheese	6 oz.	180 g
Low-fat sweetened condensed milk	5 fl. oz.	150 ml
Vanilla extract	0.15 fl. oz. (1 tsp.)	5 ml
Peppermint oil (optional)	0.04 fl. oz. (¼ tsp.)	1 ml
Sheet gelatin, softened	1 sheet (0.06 oz.)	2 g

1. Combine the ricotta cheese, cottage cheese, sweetened condensed milk, vanilla and peppermint oil (if using) in the bowl of a food processor. Blend until smooth.
2. Warm the mixture in a double boiler or microwave to 100°F (38°C). Stir in the softened sheet gelatin. Use immediately.

Approximate values per 1-oz. (30-g) serving: **Calories** 40, **Total fat** 0.5 g, **Saturated fat** 0 g, **Cholesterol** 0 mg, **Sodium** 85 mg, **Total carbohydrates** 5 g, **Protein** 3 g

NO-SUGAR-ADDED HAZELNUT SHORTBREAD

Yield: 24 Cookies, 1¾ oz. (50 g) each   **Method:** Icebox

Unsalted butter, softened	8 oz.	240 g	80%
Sucralose	0.75 oz.	22 g	7.5%
Salt	0.2 oz. (1 tsp.)	6 g	2%
Fat-free sour cream	4 oz.	120 g	40%
Orange zest, grated fine	0.2 oz. (1 Tbsp.)	6 g	2%
Hazelnuts, toasted and chopped coarse	5 oz.	150 g	50%
Pastry flour	8 oz.	240 g	80%
Rice flour	2 oz.	60 g	20%
Total dough weight:	1 lb. 12 oz.	844 g	281%

1. Cream the butter, sucralose and salt.
2. Add the sour cream, orange zest and hazelnuts. Mix well.
3. Add the flours and mix until just combined. Form the dough into a long bar measuring 2 inches × 2 inches (5 centimeters × 5 centimeters) square. Chill the bar in the freezer until hard.
4. When ready to bake, cut the bars into ½-inch- (1.2-centimeter-) thick slices.
5. Position the slices on a paper-lined sheet pan and bake at 375°F (190°C) until golden brown, approximately 25 minutes.

Approximate values per cookie: **Calories** 150, **Total fat** 12 g, **Saturated fat** 5 g, **Cholesterol** 20 mg, **Sodium** 100 mg, **Total carbohydrates** 12 g, **Protein** 2 g

---

 ## SUGAR-FREE MANGO GINGER JAM

Yield: 14 oz. (420 g)

Ginger, grated	0.4 oz. (1 Tbsp.)	12 g
Orange juice concentrate	2 fl. oz.	60 ml
Mango, cubed	14 oz.	420 g
Sucralose	0.14 oz. (2 Tbsp.)	4 g
Citric acid, powdered (optional)	1 pinch	1 pinch

citric acid acid found in citrus fruit juice, used to enhance flavor in foods and to prevent crystallization of sugar syrups; available in liquid or powdered form

1. Boil the ginger and orange juice concentrate in a nonreactive pan. Remove from the heat, cover and let sit 10 minutes. Add the remaining ingredients. Bring the mixture to a boil, stirring constantly. Cook 3 to 5 minutes until the mixture thickens.
2. Remove from the heat and let cool.

Approximate values per 1-oz. (30-g) serving: **Calories** 25, **Total fat** 0 g, **Saturated fat** 0 g, **Cholesterol** 0 mg, **Sodium** 0 mg, **Total carbohydrates** 7 g, **Protein** 0 g, **Vitamin A** 20%, **Vitamin C** 20%, **Claims**—low calorie, fat free, sodium free

NO-SUGAR-ADDED REDUCED-FAT APPLE-ALMOND POUNDCAKE

Yield: 2 Cakes, 9 in. × 4 in. (22 cm × 10 cm)   **Method:** Egg foam

Cake flour	8 oz.	240 g	100%
Baking powder	0.3 oz. (2 tsp.)	8 g	3.7%
Baking soda	0.14 oz. (1 tsp.)	4 g	1.2%
Cinnamon, ground	1 oz.	30 g	12%
Ginger, ground	0.14 oz. (2 tsp.)	4 g	1.2%
Dry buttermilk powder	1 oz.	30 g	12%
Almond flour	4.5 oz.	135 g	56%
Fat-free sour cream	10 oz.	300 g	125%
Sucralose	1.5 oz.	45 g	18%
Salt	0.2 oz. (1 tsp.)	6 g	2.5%
Olive oil	10 fl. oz.	300 ml	125%
Vanilla extract	0.15 fl. oz. (1 tsp.)	5 ml	2%
Almond extract	0.3 fl. oz. (2 tsp.)	10 ml	3.7%
Eggs	5 oz. (3 eggs)	150 g	62%
Golden Delicious apples, medium dice	3	3	
Walnut pieces	6 oz.	180 g	75%
Egg whites	4 oz. (4 whites)	120 g	50%
Total batter weight:	3 lb. 4 oz.	1567 g	649%

1. Sift together the cake flour, baking powder, baking soda, cinnamon, ginger and milk powder. Add the almond flour and set aside.
2. In the bowl of a mixer fitted with the paddle attachment, blend the sour cream, sucralose and salt until well combined. Gradually add the olive oil, then the vanilla and almond extract.
3. Add the eggs one at a time, waiting for the previous egg to be fully incorporated before adding the next one. Fold in the dry ingredients. Stir in the apples and walnut pieces.
4. In a separate clean bowl, whip the egg whites to soft peaks. Fold one-third of the whipped egg whites into the cake batter, then fold in the remaining whipped egg whites.
5. Divide the cake batter evenly between two greased 9-inch × 4-inch (22-centimeter × 10-centimeter) pans.
6. Bake at 375°F (190°C) until the cake bounces back when lightly pressed, approximately 20 to 22 minutes.

Approximate values per 2-oz. (60-g) serving: **Calories** 190, **Total fat** 14 g, **Saturated fat** 2 g, **Cholesterol** 20 mg, **Sodium** 150 mg, **Total carbohydrates** 12 g, **Protein** 4 g

GLUTEN-FREE FLAXSEED BREAD

Yield: 1 Loaf

Method: Muffin method

Proofing: Approximately 1 hour

			Rice flour at 100%
Rice flour	9 oz.	270 g	100%
Tapioca starch	6 oz.	180 g	66%
Flax seed meal	2 oz.	60 g	22%
Xanthan gum	0.4 oz. (1 Tbsp.)	12 g	4%
Granulated sugar	1 oz.	30 g	11%
Salt	0.4 oz. (2 tsp.)	12 g	4%
Egg	1.6 oz. (1 egg)	48 g	18%
Olive or grape seed oil	1 fl. oz.	30 ml	11%
Milk at 106°F (41°C)	12 fl. oz.	360 ml	133%
Instant yeast	0.5 oz.	15 g	5%
Vinegar	0.15 fl. oz. (1 tsp.)	5 ml	1.6%
Total batter weight:	2 lb. 2 oz.	1022 g	375%

1. Mix the rice flour, tapioca starch, flax seed meal, xanthan gum, sugar and salt in the bowl of a mixer fitted with the paddle attachment.

2. In a separate bowl, whisk together the egg, oil, milk and yeast. Add the liquid mixture to the dry ingredients. Mix on low speed until blended. Scrape down the bowl. Add the vinegar and mix 4 minutes on medium speed.

3. Scrape the batter into a greased and paper-lined loaf pan measuring 8½ inches × 4½ inches × 4 inches (21 centimeters × 11 centimeters × 10 centimeters). Press the batter evenly into the pan using a wetted hand.

4. Proof the dough in a proof box, allowing it to rise until the loaf has increased 30 to 40 percent in volume.

5. Bake at 375°F (190°C) until the loaves are baked through and evenly risen, approximately 60 to 70 minutes. Do not underbake the loaves or they may collapse. Allow the bread to cool completely in the pans before unmolding.

Approximate values per 2-oz. (60-g) serving: **Calories** 150, **Total fat** 4 g, **Saturated fat** 1 g, **Cholesterol** 15 mg, **Sodium** 290 mg, **Total carbohydrates** 28 g, **Protein** 3 g, **Claims**—Gluten free

xanthan gum a stabilizer produced by fermenting the sugars in corn; it is used to thicken, stabilize and emulsify prepared sauces, dairy products, ice creams and baked goods

GLUTEN-FREE FUDGE BROWNIES

This formula uses rice flour and cornstarch in place of the wheat flour used in the Fudge Brownie formula on page 321. A larger percentage of chocolate adds structure, as does the use of cocoa powder. The result is a more cakelike brownie.

Yield: 4 Dozen Brownies, 2 in. (5 cm) each; 1 Half-Sheet Pan

Method: Sheet cookie

			Rice flour at 100%
Rice flour	6 oz.	180 g	100%
Tapioca flour	2 oz.	60 g	33%
Cornstarch	2 oz.	60 g	33%
Cocoa powder	1 oz.	30 g	16%
Baking powder	0.14 oz. (1 tsp.)	4 g	2%
Unsalted butter	8 oz.	240 g	133%
Semisweet or bittersweet chocolate	1 lb.	480 g	266%
Maple syrup	6 oz.	120 g	100%
Eggs	8.3 oz. (5 eggs)	250 g	138%
Granulated sugar	1 lb.	480 g	266%
Vanilla extract	0.5 fl. oz.	15 ml	8%
Almond extract	0.15 fl. oz. (1 tsp.)	5 ml	2%
Salt	0.2 oz. (1 tsp.)	6 g	3%
Walnuts, chopped	12 oz.	360 g	200%
Total batter weight:	4 lb. 14 oz.	2290 g	1300%
Silky Ganache Deluxe (page 485)	1 lb.	480 g	
Cocoa powder	as needed	as needed	
Walnut halves	48	48	

1 Sift together the rice flour, tapioca flour, cornstarch, cocoa powder and baking powder. Set aside.

2 Combine the butter and chocolate in a bowl over simmering water. Melt the mixture to 110°F (43°C). Set aside.

3 Whip the maple syrup, eggs, sugar, vanilla, almond extract and salt until well combined. Stir in the melted chocolate mixture, the sifted rice flour mixture and then the walnuts.

4 Spread the mixture on a greased and paper-lined half-sheet pan.

5 Bake at 350°F (180°C) until the brownies are just set and bounce back when lightly pressed, approximately 30 to 35 minutes. (Cooking less will produce a chewier brownie.)

6 Cool the brownies, then refrigerate or freeze until firm.

7 Loosen the edge of the brownies from the pan with a plastic scraper. Invert the pan onto the back side of a sheet pan. If the brownies stick, hold the pan briefly over a heat source to release. Remove the paper.

8 Heat the Silky Ganache Deluxe to 110°F (43°C) and spread it over the brownies. Let firm, then cut into 2-inch × 2-inch (5-centimeter × 5-centimeter) squares.

9 Dust the brownies with cocoa powder and place a walnut half in the center of each square.

Approximate values per 2-in. (5-cm) square: **Calories** 260, **Total fat** 17 g, **Saturated fat** 7 g, **Cholesterol** 40 mg, **Sodium** 65 mg, **Total carbohydrates** 27 g, **Protein** 4 g, **Claims**—Gluten free

❶ Cutting steam vents in the pie.

❷ The finished pie.

GLUTEN-FREE APPLE PIE

Yield: 2 Pies, 9 in. (22 cm) each | **Method:** Baked fruit filling

Gluten-Free Pie Dough (recipe follows)	2 lb. 10 oz.	1260 g
Filling:		
Golden Delicious apples, peeled and cored	2 lb.	960 g
Granny Smith apples, peeled and cored	1.5 lb.	720 g
Granulated sugar	9 oz.	270 g
Lemon juice	0.5 fl. oz. (1 Tbsp.)	15 ml
Vanilla extract	0.5 fl. oz. (1 Tbsp.)	15 ml
Instant tapioca	0.75 oz.	22.5 g
Cinnamon, ground	0.3 oz. (1½ Tbsp.)	9 g
Unsalted butter, diced fine	2 oz.	60 g
Sanding sugar	as needed	as needed

❶ For each pie, roll out 10 ounces (300 grams) of the pie dough into a circle ⅛ inch (3 millimeters) thick and line a 9-inch (22-centimeter) pie pan with the dough. Set aside.

❷ Cut the apples into 12 uniform wedges each. Toss the apple wedges in a large bowl with the sugar, lemon juice and vanilla.

❸ Sift together the tapioca and cinnamon. Stir the mixture into the apples. Allow the filling to stand 30 minutes.

❹ Divide the filling evenly between the pie shells. Dot the filling with the butter.

❺ Roll out the remaining pie dough into two rounds. Place the top crust over the filling; seal and flute the edges. Cut several slits in the dough to allow steam to escape. Brush the top crust thinly with water. Sprinkle with sanding sugar.

❻ Bake at 375°F (190°C) until the filling is bubbling and looks like thick honey, approximately 75 minutes.

Approximate values per ⅛-pie serving: **Calories** 450, **Total fat** 21 g, **Saturated fat** 13 g, **Cholesterol** 80 mg, **Sodium** 300 mg, **Total carbohydrates** 64 g, **Protein** 3 g, **Vitamin A** 15%, **Claims**—gluten free

GLUTEN-FREE PIE DOUGH

Yield: 1 lb. 5 oz. (630 g) Dough, for one 8-in. (20-cm) double-crust pie

			Rice flour at 100%
Buttermilk	1.5 fl. oz.	45 ml	21%
Egg	1.6 oz. (1 egg)	50 g	23%
Salt	0.2 oz. (1 tsp.)	6 g	3%
Brown sugar	1 oz.	30 g	14%
Vanilla extract	0.15 fl. oz. (1 tsp.)	5 ml	2%
Almond extract	0.15 fl. oz. (1 tsp.)	5 ml	2%
Rice flour	7 oz.	210 g	100%
Cornstarch	2 oz.	60 g	28%
Tapioca flour	2 oz.	60 g	28%
Xanthan gum	0.05 oz. (½ tsp.)	1 g	7%
Unsalted butter, cold	6 oz.	180 g	88%
Total dough weight:	1 lb. 5 oz.	652 g	316%

❶ Whisk together the buttermilk, egg, salt, sugar, vanilla and almond extract. Set aside.

❷ Combine the rice flour, cornstarch, tapioca flour and xanthan gum in a large bowl. Cut the butter into medium dice, ⅜ inch × ⅜ inch (9 millimeters × 9 millimeters), then cut it into the flour mixture until the pieces are the size of a pea.

❸ Add the buttermilk mixture and mix just until the dough comes together. Wrap the dough in plastic and chill at least 1 hour before using.

Approximate values per 1-oz. (30-g) serving: **Calories** 120, **Total fat** 7 g, **Saturated fat** 4 g, **Cholesterol** 25 mg, **Sodium** 110 mg, **Total carbohydrates** 13 g, **Protein** 1 g, **Claims**—gluten free

GLUTEN-FREE PEANUT BUTTER COOKIES

Sugar gives this simple cookie its structure and makes this more of a candylike treat. Standard peanut butter, which is stabilized and may have some sweetener added, works well in this formula. But the sweetness of the cookie will depend on the brand used.

Yield: 24 Cookies

Method: Drop cookies

			Sugar at 100%
Peanut butter	9 oz.	270 g	112.5%
Brown sugar	8 oz.	240 g	100%
Egg	1.6 oz. (1 egg)	50 g	20%
Peanut halves	as needed	as needed	
Total dough weight:	1 lb. 2 oz.	560 g	232.5%

1. Blend the peanut butter and brown sugar in the bowl of a mixer fitted with the paddle attachment.
2. Beat the egg, then add it to the peanut butter mixture. Blend on low speed just until the mixture comes together.
3. Using a #40 portion scoop, portion the dough onto paper-lined sheet pans. Press each ball of cookie dough down using the bottom of a measuring cup to flatten slightly. Press a few peanut halves into the surface of each portion of dough.
4. Bake at 375°F (180°C) until set, approximately 8 to 11 minutes. Allow the cookies to cool completely before removing them from the pans.

Approximate values per cookie: **Calories** 100, **Total fat** 21 g, **Saturated fat** 1 g, **Cholesterol** 5 mg, **Sodium** 55 mg, **Total carbohydrates** 11 g, **Protein** 3 g, **Claims**—gluten free

GLUTEN-FREE ITALIAN CREAM CAKE

Yield: 2 Cakes, 8 in. (20 cm) each

Method: Creaming

			Rice flour at 100%
Rice flour	10 oz.	300 g	100%
Tapioca flour	2 oz.	60 g	20%
Potato starch	2 oz.	60 g	20%
Cornstarch	1 oz.	30 g	10%
Baking soda	0.3 oz. (2 tsp.)	8 g	3%
Baking powder	0.14 oz. (1 tsp.)	4 g	1.4%
Xanthan gum	0.15 oz. (1½ tsp.)	1.5 g	1.5%
Unsalted butter, softened	5 oz.	150 g	50%
Granulated sugar	10 oz.	300 g	100%
Salt	0.2 oz. (1 tsp.)	6 g	2%
Egg yolks	2.4 oz. (4 yolks)	72 g	24%
Olive oil	2 fl. oz.	60 ml	20%
Buttermilk	4 fl. oz.	120 ml	40%
Vanilla extract	0.5 fl. oz.	15 ml	5%
Pecan pieces	8 oz.	240 g	80%
Coconut flakes	7 oz.	210 g	70%
Egg whites	4 oz. (4 whites)	120 g	40%
Granulated sugar	2 oz.	60 g	20%
Total batter weight:	3 lb. 2 oz.	1816 g	606%
Reduced-Fat Cream Cheese Icing (recipe follows)	2 lb.	960 g	
Walnut halves	8	8	

1. Combine and sift together the rice flour, tapioca flour, potato starch, cornstarch, baking soda, baking powder and xanthan gum. Set aside.

2. In the bowl of a mixer fitted with the paddle attachment, cream the butter and sugar. Add the salt, then add the egg yolks in two additions. Stir in the olive oil, buttermilk and vanilla.

3. Stir in the dry ingredients just until mixed, then stir in the pecan pieces and 3 ounces (120 grams) of the coconut flakes.

4. In a separate clean bowl, whip the egg whites and sugar to soft peaks and fold one-third of the whipped whites into the batter using a rubber spatula. Fold in another third and then the remaining whipped whites.

5. Pour the batter into two 8-inch (20-centimeter) greased pans. Bake at 375°F (190°C) until the cake bounces back when lightly pressed, approximately 35 minutes.

6. Cool the cakes completely, then slice each one into three equal layers. Spread each layer with a thin coating of Reduced-Fat Cream Cheese Icing.

7. Ice the cakes with the remaining icing and surround the bottom edge of the cake with the remaining coconut flakes. Decorate the top with rosettes of icing topped with the walnut pieces.

Approximate values per ⅛-cake serving: **Calories** 710, **Total fat** 44 g, **Saturated fat** 15 g, **Cholesterol** 95 mg, **Sodium** 510 mg, **Total carbohydrates** 73 g, **Protein** 10 g, **Vitamin A** 15%, **Calcium** 10%, **Iron** 10%, **Claims**—gluten free

REDUCED-FAT CREAM CHEESE ICING

Yield: Approximately 2 lb. (990 g)

Reduced-fat cream cheese, room temperature	1 lb. 8 oz.	720 g
Powdered sugar	9 oz.	270 g
Lemon zest, grated fine	0.07 oz. (1 tsp.)	2 g
Orange zest, grated fine	0.14 oz. (2 tsp.)	4 g
Vanilla extract	0.5 fl. oz.	15 ml

1. In the bowl of a mixer fitted with the paddle attachment, mix the cream cheese on low speed until smooth.
2. Add the powdered sugar and mix until well combined.
3. Add the lemon zest, orange zest and vanilla. Blend just until combined.

Approximate values per ounce (30 g): **Calories** 80, **Total fat** 4 g, **Saturated fat** 2.5 g, **Cholesterol** 10 mg, **Sodium** 65 mg, **Total carbohydrates** 10 g, **Protein** 2 g

VARIATION:

No-Sugar-Added Reduced-Fat Cream Cheese Icing—Substitute 0.5 ounce (15 grams) sucralose for the powdered sugar. Add 4 fluid ounces (120 milliliters) buttermilk in Step 2.

Approximate values per ounce (30 g): **Calories** 60, **Total fat** 4 g, **Saturated fat** 2.5 g, **Cholesterol** 15 mg, **Sodium** 75 mg, **Total carbohydrates** 2 g, **Protein** 3 g

LACTOSE-FREE CRÈME BRÛLÉE

Yield: 4 Servings

Method: Baked custard

Egg yolks	2 oz. (3 yolks)	60 g
Eggs	3.2 oz. (2 eggs)	96 g
Brown sugar	4 oz.	120 g
Vanilla bean	1	1
Soy milk creamer	1 pt.	480 ml
Granulated raw sugar	2 oz.	60 g

1. Whisk together the egg yolks, eggs and brown sugar in a bowl until smooth. Scrape the seeds of the vanilla bean into the mixture and add the soy milk creamer.
2. Strain through a chinois and pour into shallow ceramic ramekins.
3. Place the ramekins in a hotel pan and fill with hot water halfway up the sides of the ramekins. Bake at 325°F (160°C) until set, approximately 30 minutes.
4. Let cool in a refrigerator.
5. To serve, sprinkle the crème brûlée with the sugar and caramelize the sugar with a propane torch.

Approximate values per serving: **Calories** 390, **Total fat** 16 g, **Saturated fat** 4.5 g, **Cholesterol** 265 mg, **Sodium** 125 mg, **Total carbohydrates** 56 g, **Protein** 6 g

SAFETY ALERT
Propane Torch

Training on how to operate a propane torch is recommended before using it to caramelize sugar or other dessert preparations. Use extreme caution and follow appropriate safety procedures. Keep the gas bottle away from sources of heat. Do not leave the torch unattended. Rest the bottle on a stable surface away from any flammable materials.

LACTOSE-FREE SOY CHOCOLATE SILK PIE

Yield: 1 Pie, 7 in. (17 cm)

Soy milk	1 pt.	480 ml
Cocoa powder	1.5 oz.	45 g
Brown sugar	5 oz.	150 g
Egg	1.6 oz. (1 egg)	48 g
Egg whites	2 oz. (2 whites)	60 g
Cornstarch	1 oz.	30 g
Vanilla extract	0.15 fl. oz. (1 tsp.)	5 ml
Bitter or semisweet chocolate, chopped	3 oz.	90 g
Lactose-Free Pie Dough (recipe follows), 7-in. (17-cm) shell, fully baked	1 shell	1 shell
Combed chocolate curls (page 701)	2 oz.	60 g
Nougatine (page 724)	as needed	as needed

Lactose-Free Soy Chocolate Silk Pie (left) and individual tart (right).

1. Combine the soy milk, cocoa powder and 2 ounces (60 grams) of the brown sugar in a large saucepan. Bring to a boil.
2. In a separate bowl, whisk together the egg and egg whites. Add the remaining brown sugar and mix to form a smooth batter. Stir in the cornstarch.
3. Temper the egg batter with one-quarter of the boiling soy milk.
4. Add the tempered egg mixture to the remaining boiling milk. Whisk vigorously over medium high heat until the cream boils and is well thickened.
5. Remove from the heat. Add the vanilla and chocolate, stirring until the chocolate is melted. Pour the filling into the baked shell.
6. Cool until set, then sprinkle with chocolate curls and nougatine pieces.

Approximate values per ⅛-pie serving: **Calories** 390, **Total fat** 20 g, **Saturated fat** 6 g, **Cholesterol** 25 mg, **Sodium** 320 mg, **Total carbohydrates** 50 g, **Protein** 10 g, **Vitamin A** 10%, **Iron** 15%

LACTOSE-FREE PIE DOUGH

Yield: 1 lb. 5 oz. (641 g) Dough, for one 8-in. (20-cm) double-crust pie

Soy milk, chilled	2 fl. oz.	60 ml	66%
Egg white	1 oz. (1 white)	30 g	33%
Salt	0.2 oz. (1 tsp.)	6 g	6%
Brown sugar	0.5 oz.	15 g	16%
Vanilla extract	0.15 fl. oz. (1 tsp.)	5 ml	5%
Vinegar	0.5 fl. oz.	15 ml	16%
White whole-wheat flour	3 oz.	90 g	100%
Oat flour or oats ground into flour	6 oz.	180 g	200%
Soy flour	1 oz.	30 g	33%
Soy margarine, cold	7 oz.	210 g	233%
Total dough weight:	1 lb. 5 oz.	641 g	708%

1. Whisk together the soy milk, egg white, salt, brown sugar, vanilla and vinegar. Set aside.
2. Combine the wheat, oat and soy flours in a large bowl. Cut the margarine into medium dice, ⅜ inch × 3/8 inch (9 millimeters × 9 millimeters), then cut it into the flour until the pieces are the size of peas.
3. Add the soy milk mixture. Mix just until combined.
4. Wrap the dough in plastic and chill at least 1 hour before using.

Approximate values per 1-oz. (30-g) serving: **Calories** 130, **Total fat** 9 g, **Saturated fat** 1.5 g, **Cholesterol** 0 mg, **Sodium** 200 mg, **Total carbohydrates** 10 g, **Protein** 3 g

LACTOSE-FREE PECAN ICE CREAM

Yield: 1 ½ pt. (¾ lt)

Soy milk creamer	1 pt.	480 ml
Egg yolks	2.4 oz. (4 yolks)	72 g
Maple syrup	4 oz.	120 g
Caramelized Pecans (recipe follows)	4 oz.	120 g

1. Bring the soy milk creamer to a boil.
2. In a separate bowl, whisk together the egg yolks and the maple syrup. Temper the egg mixture with one-quarter of the soy milk creamer.
3. Pour the tempered egg yolk mixture into the soy milk creamer and heat to 183°F (83°C) while constantly stirring with a rubber spatula.
4. Strain through a chinois and chill in an ice bath. Refrigerate overnight.
5. Process in an ice cream machine. Once the ice cream starts to firm, add the Caramelized Pecans.

Approximate values per 3 ½-oz. (109-g) serving: **Calories** 260, **Total fat** 16 g, **Saturated fat** 3 g, **Cholesterol** 120 mg, **Sodium** 45 mg, **Total carbohydrates** 26 g, **Protein** 3 g

CARAMELIZED PECANS

Yield: 6 oz. (180 g)

Granulated sugar	2 oz.	60 g
Water	1 fl. oz.	30 ml
Vanilla extract	0.15 fl. oz. (1 tsp.)	5 ml
Pecan pieces	4 oz.	120 g

1. Bring the sugar and the water to a full boil. Add the vanilla and pecans. Stir until the sugar coats the pecans and becomes grainy.
2. Reduce the heat to low and stir the pecans until the sugar starts to caramelize. Cool, then store in an airtight container until ready to use.

Approximate values per 1-oz. (30-g) serving: **Calories** 170, **Total fat** 14 g, **Saturated fat** 1 g, **Cholesterol** 0 mg, **Sodium** 0 mg, **Total carbohydrates** 12 g, **Protein** 4 g

CHAPTER SEVENTEEN

TORTES AND SPECIALTY CAKES

After studying this chapter, you will be able to:

- prepare a variety of tortes
- prepare a variety of specialty torte fillings
- assemble tortes using basic and advanced icing techniques
- understand how to assemble and decorate a variety of specialty cakes

A DISPLAY OF TORTES IN AN ARRAY OF COLORS, TEXTURES AND GARNISHES ENTICES CUSTOMERS TO ENTER A BAKESHOP.
Delicious to eat and exciting to prepare, these dazzling creations are the hallmark of an accomplished and skilled pastry chef. Even though the components that go into tortes are not difficult to make, the number of elements can overwhelm a beginner. As with any task in the professional kitchen, success starts with organization. When making modern tortes, pastry chefs also need to be skilled at making cake, cookie and meringue preparations. They must know how to prepare mousses and creams that will hold their shape; understanding the proper use of gelatin is key. (Familiarity with Chapter 14, Custards, Creams and Sauces, and the discussion of gelatin on page 607 is recommended.) And the most refined tortes use appropriate garnishes, such as those discussed in Chapter 20, Chocolate and Sugar Work, many easily mastered by an attentive pastry student.

This chapter emphasizes the special formulas and procedures used for making contemporary tortes and specialty cakes. Many of the tortes in this chapter use cake formulas found in Chapter 13, Cakes and Icings, and the creams and mousses discussed in Chapter 14, Custards, Creams and Sauces. In order to help visualize the construction of these tortes, an illustration of the cross-section of each torte accompanies many of the formulas in this chapter. A selection of torte and specialty cake formulas concludes the chapter.

TORTES

What distinguishes many classic European-style tortes from American-style cakes is that the latter generally have most of the fat baked into the cake. The European-style torte consists of layers of relatively low-fat cake such as genoise and spongecake that may be moistened with a flavored simple syrup (page 73). These layers are then sandwiched with

OF TARTS AND TORTES

The names given to desserts can be rather confusing. One country or region may call an item a *torte*, while another region calls the same item a *gâteau*. The following definitions are based on classic terms. You will, no doubt, encounter variations depending on your location and the training of those with whom you work.

Cake—In American and British usages, *cake* refers to a broad range of pastries, including layer cakes, coffeecakes and gâteaux. *Cake* may refer to almost everything that is baked, tender, sweet and sometimes frosted. But to the French, *le cake* is a loaf-shaped fruitcake, similar to an American poundcake with the addition of fruit, nuts and rum.

Entremet—In France, *entremet* describes a modern dessert torte made with layers of spongecake, mousse and other fillings. This is a contemporary use of the term, which historically refers to a dish served in between courses or on the side.

Gâteau—(pl. *gâteaux*) To the French, *gâteau* refers to various pastry items made with puff pastry, éclair paste, short dough or sweet dough. In America, *gâteau* often refers to any cake-type dessert.

Torte—In Central and Eastern European countries, a *torte* (pl. *torten*) is a rich cake in which all or part of the flour is replaced with finely chopped nuts or bread crumbs. Other cultures refer to any round sweet cake as a torte.

creams, mousses, Bavarians or other fillings discussed in Chapter 14, Custards, Creams and Sauces. To achieve a well-balanced composition, different types of cake layers may be combined to make an individual torte. The formula for a basic mocha torte, genoise filled with mocha buttercream, a popular item on a **Viennese table**, illustrates a classic torte preparation.

Viennese table a dessert buffet comprising a variety of layered tortes, small pastries, fruit tarts, mousses and puddings

---

MOCHA TORTE

Yield: 3 Tortes, approximately 8½ inches × 5½ inches (21 centimeters × 13 centimeters) each

Vanilla Spongecake (page 478)	1 full sheet	1 full sheet
Simple Syrup (page 73)	9 fl. oz.	270 ml
Coffee liquor	3 fl. oz.	90 ml
Italian Buttercream (page 452) or other type	2 lb. 6 oz.	1140 g
Coffee extract	1 fl. oz.	1 ml
Candied Almonds (recipe follows)	12 oz.	360 g

MISE EN PLACE

▶ Prepare the Vanilla Spongecake, Simple Syrup, Italian Buttercream and Candied Almonds.

1. Trim the edges of the Vanilla Spongecake. Cut it into three 16½-inch × 8½-inch (41-centimeter × 21-centimeter) strips. Place one strip on a paper-lined sheet pan.

2. Flavor the Simple Syrup with the coffee liquor and moisten the cake with 4 fluid ounces (120 milliliters) of the coffee syrup.

3. Combine the Italian Buttercream with the coffee extract. Place slightly more than one-third of the coffee buttercream on the cake and spread evenly using an offset spatula.

4. Set another cake layer over the buttercream. Moisten it with one-third of the syrup. Spread another one-third of the buttercream over the cake.

5. Set another cake layer over the buttercream. Moisten with the remaining syrup.

6. Spread the remaining buttercream evenly on the surface of the torte.

7. Refrigerate the cake until the buttercream sets. Once the icing is firm, divide the torte into three equal pieces. Place each piece on a cake board. Garnish the tortes with Candied Almonds.

Approximate values per ⅒-torte serving: **Calories** 390, **Total fat** 21 g, **Saturated fat** 10 g, **Cholesterol** 110 mg, **Sodium** 200 mg, **Total carbohydrates** 46 g, **Protein** 6 g, **Vitamin A** 15%

1. Moistening the cake with the coffee syrup.

2. Spreading buttercream over the moistened cake.

3. Garnishing the finished torte with almonds.

MISE EN PLACE

▶ Preheat oven to 325°F (160°C).

CANDIED ALMONDS

Yield: 8 oz. (240 g)

Egg whites	2 oz. (2 whites)	60 g
Granulated sugar	2 oz.	60 g
Sliced almonds	8 oz.	240 g

1. Whisk the egg whites and sugar together. Add the almonds. Toss with a rubber spatula to coat the nuts completely.
2. Spread the nuts in a thin layer on a lightly greased baking sheet. Bake at 325°F (160°C) until lightly toasted and dry, approximately 15 to 20 minutes. Watch closely to prevent burning.
3. Stir the nuts with a metal spatula every 5 to 7 minutes during baking.
4. Cool completely. Store in an airtight container up to 10 days.

Approximate values per serving: **Calories** 160, **Total fat** 10 g, **Saturated fat** 1 g, **Cholesterol** 0 mg, **Sodium** 10 mg, **Total carbohydrates** 10 g, **Protein** 6 g, **Claims**—gluten free, no saturated fat; no cholesterol; very low sodium

Torte made in a teardrop-shaped form.

FIGURE 17.1 ▶ Assortment of individual and miniature-sized tortes attractively displayed in a refrigerated pastry case.

MODERN TORTES

Although the elements in pastry making have not changed—genoise and butter cakes have been made for many years—new decorating tools have inspired inventive ways of presenting and assembling the dessert torte. Ring or torte molds of various sizes, flexible silicone forms and patterned baking mats give tortes a new look, inviting customers to try new desserts. And the task of preparing individual-sized tortes is streamlined with these new tools. Many of the inventive petit fours featured in Chapter 18, Petits Fours and Confections, are actually miniature tortes. Figure 17.1 shows a variety of miniature tortes.

Cakes for Contemporary Tortes

Sponge, genoise, ladyfinger, meringue and other cake batters may be baked and then cut to fit the ring molds in which modern tortes are prepared. In the European tradition, finely ground nut flours may be added with or in place of wheat flour to make a spongecake with a moist texture and delicate flavor. This type of cake can be baked in a round, square or oval cake pan, or it can be baked in sheets and then cut to fit a torte ring of any size or shape.

JOCONDE CAKE

A **joconde cake** batter is used to prepare many contemporary tortes because it bakes into a moist, flexible cake. The cake batter may be tinted or marbleized for further decorative effect. Thanks to silicone baking materials, this batter can be baked on a patterned baking mat, retaining the imprint of the mat when unmolded. The designs baked into this light spongecake provide an elegant finish to tortes formed in ring molds.

The batter is whipped extensively to build the emulsion during mixing. The joconde sponge requires attentive baking so that it remains flexible to easily conform to the contours of a torte mold. If underbaked, it will stick to the baking mat. If overbaked, it will dry out. Once cooled, the sponge may be cut into strips to line any shape ring mold. Once unmolded, the sides of the torte need no further embellishment.

JOCONDE SPONGECAKE

Yield: 1 Full-Sheet Pan, 18 in. × 24 in. (45 cm × 60 cm)   **Method:** Egg foam

Almond flour	5 oz.	150 g	333%
Granulated sugar	6 oz.	180 g	400%
Cake flour	1.5 oz.	45 g	100%
Eggs	7 oz. (5 eggs)	210 g	466%
Egg whites	3.5 oz. (3½ whites)	105 g	233%
Unsalted butter, slightly melted	1.5 oz.	45 g	100%
Total batter weight:	1 lb. 8 oz.	735 g	1632%

1 In the bowl of a mixer fitted with the whip attachment, combine the almond flour, 5 ounces (150 grams) of the sugar, the cake flour and half of the eggs. Whip the mixture 2 minutes. Stop the machine, scrape down the bowl, then whip 3 more minutes.

2 Gradually add the remaining whole eggs in three increments, whipping for 4 to 5 minutes between each addition to build the egg emulsion.

3 In a clean mixing bowl, whip the egg whites and remaining sugar to medium peaks.

4 Remove the bowl of almond mixture from the machine and fold in the melted butter using a spatula.

5 Fold in one-third of the whipped egg whites to lighten the batter, then fold in the remaining whipped egg whites. Do not overmix.

6 Spread the batter over a silicone baking mat placed on a sheet pan. Level it carefully with a long offset spatula. Bake at 450°F (230°C) until the joconde bounces back when lightly pressed, approximately 6 to 8 minutes.

Note: For a slightly thicker cake, scale up this formula using a 1.5 conversion factor and spread the batter into one full-sheet pan. Increase baking time slightly to approximately 8 to 10 minutes.

VARIATION:

Fruit and Nut Joconde—Before baking, sprinkle the surface of the joconde batter with a total of 2 ounces (60 grams/133%) of one or more of the following ingredients: chopped pistachios, chopped apricots, macaroon-type coconut, sun-dried cherries or dried cranberries.

Approximate values per 1-oz. (30-g) serving: **Calories** 90, **Total fat** 4 g, **Saturated fat** 1.5 g, **Cholesterol** 35 mg, **Sodium** 15 mg, **Total carbohydrates** 11 g, **Protein** 2 g

MISE EN PLACE

▶ Melt butter.
▶ Preheat oven to 450°F (230°C).

1 The properly whipped egg batter.

2 Folding in the melted butter.

3 Folding in the whipped egg whites.

4 Spreading the joconde batter.

PATTERNED JOCONDE CAKE

A rich batter called **décor paste** is used to create distinct designs on the surface of the baked joconde cake. For this visual effect, the décor paste is tinted with a contrasting color or cocoa powder as needed. The décor paste is then spread in a random pattern or stenciled onto a silicone baking mat. After the paste is frozen to ensure that the pattern stays in place, the lighter-weight joconde sponge is spread over the décor paste. Then the cake is baked with care to ensure a flexible cake. Once cooled, the cake is peeled from the baking mat, revealing the distinct pattern. For Bergamot Torte (page 625), a silicone baking mat is finger-painted with cocoa décor paste, then topped with joconde batter before baking.

PATTERNED JOCONDE CAKE

MISE EN PLACE

- ▶ Soften butter.
- ▶ Preheat oven to 450°F (230°C).

Yield: 1 Full-Sheet Pan, 18 in. × 24 in. (45 cm × 60 cm)   **Method:** Egg foam

Unsalted butter, softened	5.5 oz.	165 g	110%
Granulated sugar	5.5 oz.	165 g	110%
Egg whites	5 oz. (5 whites)	150 g	100%
Pastry flour, sifted	5 oz.	150 g	100%
Food coloring, paste or liquid (optional)	as needed	as needed	
Total paste weight:	1 lb. 5 oz.	630 g	420%
Joconde batter (page 605)	1 lb. 8 oz.	720 g	480%
Total weight:	2 lb. 13 oz.	1350 g	900%

1. Cream the butter and sugar until light and fluffy.
2. Gradually add the egg whites. Fold in the flour. Tint the décor paste with food coloring (if using).
3. Spread a thin layer of décor paste approximately $\frac{1}{16}$ inch (1 millimeter) thick onto a silicone baking mat using an offset spatula. Pattern the décor paste into lines, woodgrain or other patterns as desired.
4. Slide the silicone mat onto a flat sheet pan and freeze until hard.
5. Prepare the joconde batter. Remove the mat from the freezer. Transfer the décor paste–coated baking mat to a room-temperature sheet pan. (A cold sheet pan prevents the cake from baking properly.) Quickly pour the joconde batter over the design. Spread the joconde batter evenly with an offset spatula to completely cover the baking mat.
6. Bake at 450°F (230°C) until the joconde bounces back when slightly pressed, approximately 6 to 8 minutes.

VARIATION:

Cocoa Décor Paste—Reduce the pastry flour to 3 ounces (90 grams). Add 2 ounces (60 grams) cocoa powder. Sift the cocoa powder with the flour before using.

Approximate values per 1-oz. (30-g) serving: **Calories** 100, **Total fat** 5 g, **Saturated fat** 2.5 g, **Cholesterol** 25 mg, **Sodium** 15 mg, **Total carbohydrates** 12 g, **Protein** 2 g

① Spreading tinted décor paste.

② Spreading joconde batter over the tinted décor paste.

③ The finished patterned joconde spongecake.

Fillings for Modern Tortes

A classic torte such as **Black Forest Cherry Torte** can simply be filled with whipped cream. But ganache, buttercream, fruit curd or mousse that is stabilized with gelatin can be used to fill a modern torte. Look for a balance between the ingredients in the torte, selecting fillings according to their flavor and mouthfeel. Too many soft, creamy layers can be overly rich or cloying in a torte. Preparing a cream or mousse properly affects the appeal of the finished preparation. Only use just enough gelatin to allow the cream to hold its shape when cut, or the torte will have an unpleasant rubbery mouthfeel. Fresh fruit, cookies and meringue layers all add to the textural interest.

FRUIT GELÉE

Layers of fruit preserves or fruit coulis that are firmed with gelatin are called **gelées**. They provide flavor and color contrast between the cake layers and soft fillings in modern tortes. See the formulas for Mango Mascarpone Torte (page 618), Palomo Torte (page 624) and Rubies Torte (page 623). Enough gelatin is added to a warm fruit juice or purée so that the liquid is firm enough to hold its shape once chilled. The mixture is poured into a container the same shape as the torte or cake. After it sets in the refrigerator or freezer, the fruit gelée is unmolded and placed on top of the mousse or filling in a multilayered torte. The procedure for making a fruit gelée is illustrated by the formula for Raspberry or Mango Gelée.

Black Forest Cherry Torte
(*Schwarzwalder Kirschtorte*) A multilayered chocolate cake flavored with Kirsch, sour cherries and whipped cream, garnished with chocolate shavings

---

RASPBERRY OR MANGO GELÉE

Yield: 2 lb. 9 oz. (1230 g)

Seedless raspberry or mango purée	2 lb.	960 g
Granulated sugar	8 oz.	240 g
Sheet gelatin, softened	16 sheets (1 oz.)	30 g

1. Heat the purée to 120°F (49°C). Add the sugar and stir until it dissolves.
2. Add the softened sheet gelatin to the warm purée. Stir the mixture until the gelatin dissolves. Immediately pour the mixture into the appropriate silicone mat or mold required as indicated in the formula. Chill or freeze until firm.

MISE EN PLACE
▶ Soften gelatin.

VARIATIONS:

Apricot, Black Currant, Blueberry or Peach Gelée—Substitute apricot, black currant, blueberry or peach purée for the raspberry or mango purée.

Approximate values per 1-oz. (30-g) serving: **Calories** 35, **Total fat** 0 g, **Saturated fat** 0 g, **Cholesterol** 0 mg, **Sodium** 5 mg, **Total carbohydrates** 8 g, **Protein** 1 g, **Claims**—fat free; no cholesterol

1 Pouring the purée onto a silicone mat.

2 The finished mango gelée.

COCOA GELÉE

Related to ganache, this luxurious, ebony chocolate glaze incorporates gelatin to give it shine and great covering ability. Use it to glaze the surface of chocolate mousse–filled tarts or tortes, as discussed in Chapter 11, Pies and Tarts, and the tortes discussed in this chapter.

MISE EN PLACE

▸ Sift cocoa powder.
▸ Soften gelatin.

COCOA GELÉE

Yield: Approximately 5 lb. (2400 g)

Water	1 pt.	480 ml
Granulated sugar	2 lb.	960 g
Heavy cream	21 fl. oz.	630 ml
Cocoa powder, sifted	10 oz.	300 g
Sheet gelatin, softened	16 sheets (1 oz.)	30 g
Vanilla extract	1.25 fl. oz.	40 ml

1. In a large saucepan bring the water, sugar and cream to a boil.
2. Whisk in the cocoa powder. Bring the mixture back to a boil and cook 4 minutes, whisking constantly.
3. Remove from the heat and cover the pan with plastic film. Let the mixture cool to 180°F (82°C).
4. Stir the softened sheet gelatin into the warm cocoa mixture. Combine well; re-cover the pan with plastic film and let cool.
5. Add the vanilla.
6. Refrigerate a minimum of 12 hours before using. Heat to 120°F (49°C) for coating tortes, cakes and tarts. Cocoa gelée keeps two weeks when stored, covered in the refrigerator.

Approximate values per 1-oz. (30-g) serving: **Calories** 80, **Total fat** 3.5 g, **Saturated fat** 2 g, **Cholesterol** 10 mg, **Sodium** 5 mg, **Total carbohydrates** 14 g, **Protein** 1 g

Assembling Tortes

Contemporary tortes are constructed by layering components in a torte ring or mold, cake frame or silicone form. Once the torte is assembled and set, the form is removed, revealing a finished cake that may be coated or iced with glaze, buttercream, Italian meringue or other garnishes. The forms may be lined with strips of flexible spongecake or joconde. (See the photos on page 609.) Ladyfingers, trimmed on one end, are another attractive option for lining a torte ring. Or the forms may be filled with alternating layers of cake, baked meringue, baked cookie dough and fillings. This type of assembly leaves the layers of filling visible. (Lining the form with clear **acetate strips** helps preserve the smooth finish on the latter.)

Preparing tortes in these forms allows lighter, fresh mousses, fruits and creams to be used. The formulas in this chapter specify the size and shapes of the forms to be used, but these tortes can be made in any size or shape. When making these layered tortes, time the preparation of the cream or mousse fillings; those thickened with gelatin must be poured into the molds before the gelatin sets.

The procedure for assembling a contemporary torte is illustrated using the Empress Torte (page 627), which consists of spongecake and dacquoise meringue layered with Raspberry Mousseline.

Lining a torte ring with a strip of fruit and nut joconde cake.

Lining a torte ring with trimmed ladyfingers surrounding a disk of spongecake.

PROCEDURE FOR ASSEMBLING A TORTE

1. Prepare the sponge, meringue, ladyfingers or other cake components.
2. Prepare the filling components. Mousses and any fillings that contain gelatin should be made right before filling the molds, as they set quickly.
3. Prepare the flavored simple syrup and finishing glaze or mousse.
4. Line the necessary torte rings with strips of clear acetate, or brush the rings with vegetable oil and dust with granulated sugar. Place the rings on cake cardboards or paper-lined sheet pans. Sheet pan extenders may also be used when making a square or rectangular cake.
5. Trim the cake, meringue or other components to fit inside the chosen torte ring or mold. Moisten the cake layer with flavored simple syrup, if desired.
6. Spread a portion of the filling over the cake, leveling it with an offset cake spatula.
7. Top the filling with additional layers of cake and filling as desired.
8. Pour the glaze over the finished torte, spreading to smooth and level. Chill or freeze the torte several hours or overnight before unmolding.
9. Remove the cake ring and acetate strip (if using). If the torte has been frozen or thoroughly chilled, a propane torch may be used to heat the ring for easy removal. Garnish the torte before serving.

1 Placing the sponge inside the ring.

2 Spreading raspberry mousse over the sponge with an offset spatula.

3 Spreading raspberry glaze over the surface of the finished torte.

4 Removing the ring from the finished torte.

Tortes may also be formed in full- or individual-sized silicone molds. First the flexible molds are placed on a flat sheet pan for support. Then the molds are filled with the selected mousse or cream. A disk of cake or other base, cut to just fit the diameter of the mold, is placed on top of the filling and then pressed until it is level with the edge of each mold.

The assembled tortes are then frozen. For service, the tortes are inverted and popped from their molds before garnishing. Only as many tortes as are needed should be unmolded and garnished at one time. Keep the remaining tortes frozen until needed.

PROCEDURE FOR ASSEMBLING A TORTE IN A SILICONE MOLD

❶ Prepare the cake and filling components. Mousses and any fillings that contain gelatin should be made right before filling the molds, as they set quickly.

❷ Evenly portion the mousse or cream into the molds using a ladle or piping bag.

❸ Press a disk of cake that has been trimmed slightly smaller than the mold into the filling so that it is level with the edge of the mold.

❹ Freeze the filled molds until the filling is firm before unmolding them for service.

❶ Evenly filling the molds.

❷ Pressing a base into the filling.

❸ Unmolding the individual torte.

NAME THAT TORTE

Pastry chefs express themselves in the naming of their desserts. They have commemorated places (Pithivier, a town in France), famous people (Anna Pavlova) and events (the Paris-Brest bicycle race) in their names. In recent years, bestowing inventive names on tortes, pastries and chocolates has become fashionable. Some newer creations, such as the Opéra cake created by Gaston Lenôtre, are made in pastry shops around the world. This chapter includes some well known tortes—the Caraibe, Longchamps and Fraisier have been popular for a number of years—as well as unique combinations that may one day become classics.

Garnishing and Portioning the Modern Torte

Once lined with cake and then filled, modern tortes possess a tailored appearance, requiring little further embellishment, although garnishing them with fresh fruits, chocolate decorations or Italian meringue is common. Often these tortes are coated with neutral glaze to seal the surface and add an appealing shine. Glaze also protects the surface of the torte from drying out. More elaborate decorations such as those discussed in Chapter 20, Chocolate and Sugar Work, are ideal for completing the appearance of a torte.

When cut open, the modern torte reveals a mosaic of colors and textures hidden inside. To portion a torte, remove it from the freezer and let it sit to temper in the refrigerator for 15 to 20 minutes. A clean ruler will help mark the torte so that portions are cut evenly. Dip a long chef's knife in hot water. Wipe it, then use it to make the first cut. Again dip the knife in hot water, wipe the knife and continue cutting, heating and then wiping the knife clean before each cut. For cut portions that are to be sold from a refrigerated display case, wrap each piece in clear acetate; it will keep the torte slice fresh and allow the customer to see the interior layers.

Storing Tortes

Once assembled but before garnishing, modern tortes are usually frozen to retain freshness. Freezing also helps during assembly, making the piece easy to handle and trim neatly. And freezing also makes it easier to cut a torte made in a large sheet pan into several smaller tortes or into individual portions (see Caraibe Torte, page 619). For best results, wrap tortes well with plastic wrap and freeze at 0°F (−18°C) or lower. Tortes filled with mousses can be frozen several weeks. Leave the torte wrapped until completely thawed. It is best to thaw tortes in the refrigerator. Do not refreeze a thawed torte.

SPECIALTY CAKES

Special occasion meals often call for special desserts. Birthdays, christenings, holiday parties and, of course, weddings feature beautifully decorated cakes or tortes. Special-occasion cakes and tortes are an ideal opportunity for a pastry chef to demonstrate his or her creativity.

Once a pastry chef has mastered many of the components and techniques covered in this book, it is time to explore the ways in which this knowledge can be demonstrated to please and impress customers and clients. Special-occasion cakes can be made using a wide variety of cakes and fillings, from a simple carrot cake with cream cheese icing (page 482) to a multilayered torte filled with white chocolate mousse. What concerns the pastry chef is how many people the cake must serve and how long it will be displayed at room temperature before service. The number of people being served determines the number and diameter of cake tiers or the size of torte mold used. The amount of time it must be at room temperature will influence the type of cake or torte selected. For example, a wedding cake filled with basic buttercream can easily be held at room temperature for 2½ to 3 hours. But a custard-filled Fraisier Torte can be left out of the refrigerator for only 1½ hours.

Exterior decorations are an important feature of special occasion cakes and tortes. Decorations should always complement the flavors and textures of the cake and fillings within. For example, chocolate fondant would be inappropriate over a lemon mousse cake, but perfect for a German chocolate cake with pecan-coconut filling. Keep the overall sweetness and richness of the cake in mind when designing the perfect combination. Rolled fondant can create an elegant canvas for further decoration, but is cloyingly sweet and not appropriate for all cake combinations. Often a traditional layer cake can be enhanced with an elaborate garnish when serving it for a special occasion. The carrot cake shown here remains the same under its coating of cream cheese icing. It is the dramatic topping of dried carrot slices that gives the cake a special-occasion feel.

The selection of cakes and tortes at the end of this chapter reflects modern approaches to cake decorating using elements discussed throughout this book.

Portioning a torte.

Carrot cake garnished for a special occasion with chocolate cutouts and dried carrot crisps.

1 List and discuss the types of cake batters suitable for making torte layers.

2 What is the difference between a spongecake and a joconde cake batter?

3 Based on the materials presented in this and previous chapters, which cake and filling components may be used to make a European-style torte?

4 List the steps employed in assembling and garnishing a torte that includes the following components: sponge cake, Italian meringue, chocolate mousse and candied almonds.

5 Pastry competitions require entrants to compete in numerous categories, including tortes and entremets. Use the Internet to research national and international pastry competitions to learn about the types of tortes prepared by the winning competitors. **www**

QUESTIONS FOR DISCUSSION

Terms to Know

entremet	décor paste
gâteau	gelée
torte	acetate strips
joconde cake	

This section provides a wide variety of formulas, some for complete tortes and others for different types of cakes suitable for baking in many shapes and molds. Most of the finished cakes and tortes rely on formulas for fillings and icings discussed in Chapter 13, Cakes and Icings, and Chapter 14, Custards, Creams and Sauces. Some of the advanced decorating techniques referred to here, such as pastillage, are discussed in detail in Chapter 20, Chocolate and Sugar Work.

ALMOND BISCUIT

Yield: 1 Full-Sheet Pan, 18 in. × 24 in. (45 cm × 60 cm)   **Method:** Egg foam

Almond flour	8 oz.	240 g	160%
Powdered sugar	8 oz.	240 g	160%
Eggs	5 oz. (3 eggs)	150 g	100%
Egg yolks	3 oz. (5 yolks)	90 g	60%
Vanilla extract	0.3 fl. oz. (2 tsp.)	9 ml	6%
Cake flour	5 oz.	150 g	100%
Egg whites	10 oz. (10 whites)	300 g	200%
Granulated sugar	4.5 oz.	135 g	90%
Almonds, slivered	8 oz.	240 g	160%
Total batter weight:	3 lb. 4 oz.	1554 g	1036%

biscuit a French word used to describe any dry, flat cake, whether sweet or savory, usually a spongecake

1. Place the almond flour, powdered sugar, eggs, egg yolks and vanilla in the bowl of a 6 quart (6.5 liter) or larger mixer fitted with the whip attachment. Whip until the batter forms thick ribbons, approximately 10 to 15 minutes.
2. Remove the bowl from the machine. Fold in the cake flour and set aside.
3. Place the egg whites and granulated sugar in a clean bowl and whip them with a clean whip attachment to medium peaks.
4. Quickly fold the whipped egg whites into the batter.
5. Spread the batter onto a paper-lined sheet pan. Sprinkle the surface of the batter with the slivered almonds. Bake at 375°F (190°C) until lightly browned, approximately 18 to 20 minutes.

VARIATIONS:

Almond Biscuit with Hazelnuts—Sprinkle the panned cake batter with 12 ounces (360 grams/240%) coarsely chopped hazelnuts instead of slivered almonds.

Pistachio Biscuit—Reduce the almond flour to 6 ounces (180 grams/120%). Add 3 ounces (90 grams/60%) pistachio flour and 2 ounces (60 grams/40%) pistachio paste to the ingredients in Step 1. Sprinkle the panned cake batter with 8 ounces (240 grams/160%) pistachios before baking.

Approximate values per 1-oz. (30-g) serving: **Calories** 100, **Total fat** 5 g, **Saturated fat** 0.5 g, **Cholesterol** 35 mg, **Sodium** 15 mg, **Total carbohydrates** 11 g, **Protein** 3 g

STRAWBERRY GELÉE

Yield: 1 lb. 13 oz. (888 g)

Strawberry purée	1 lb. 8 oz.	720 g
Granulated sugar	5 oz.	150 g
Sheet gelatin, softened	12 sheets (0.75 oz.)	18 g

1 Heat the purée to 120°F (49°C). Stir in the sugar, mixing until it dissolves.

2 Add the gelatin to the purée, stirring until the gelatin dissolves completely. Immediately pour the mixture into the appropriate mold required as indicated in the formula. Chill or freeze until firm.

Approximate values per 1-oz. (30-g) serving: **Calories** 30, **Total fat** 0 g, **Saturated fat** 0 g, **Cholesterol** 0 mg, **Sodium** 5 mg, **Total carbohydrates** 7 g, **Protein** 1 g, **Claims**—fat free

CHERRY GELÉE

Yield: 4 lb. (1920 g)

Cherry purée	3 lb.	1440 g
Granulated sugar	15 oz.	450 g
Sheet gelatin, softened	16 sheets (1 oz.)	30 g

1 Combine the purée and sugar in a nonreactive saucepan and heat the mixture until it reaches 110°F (43°C).

2 Add the gelatin to the purée. Stir until the gelatin dissolves completely. Immediately pour the mixture into the appropriate mold required as indicated in the formula. Chill or freeze until firm.

Approximate values per 1-oz. (30-g) serving: **Calories** 50, **Total fat** 0 g, **Saturated fat** 0 g, **Cholesterol** 0 mg, **Sodium** 5 mg, **Total carbohydrates** 10 g, **Protein** 1 g, **Claims**—fat free

SACHER TORTE

A specialty of the famed Sacher Hotel in Vienna since 1832, this torte exemplifies the simple elegance of a well-crafted torte. A relatively rich chocolate batter is lightened with whipped egg whites. Ground hazelnut flour adds flavor and moisture to the cake. Apricot jam acts as the filling, adhering the two layers and further moistening the cake, which has an extended shelf life. According to the hotel, more than 360,000 Sacher tortes are produced annually, using the exact same formula kept secret for more than 175 years.

Yield: 2 Cakes, 9 in. (22 cm)   **Method:** Creaming

All-purpose flour	10 oz.	300 g	100%
Cocoa powder, alkalized	3 oz.	90 g	30%
Unsalted butter, softened	12.5 oz.	375 g	125%
Granulated sugar	1 lb. 2 oz.	540 g	180%
Egg yolks	8.4 oz. (14 yolks)	255 g	85%
Hazelnuts, toasted and ground	3 oz.	90 g	30%
Egg whites	14 oz. (14 whites)	420 g	140%
Total batter weight:	4 lb. 5 oz.	2070 g	690%
Apricot jam	1 lb. 2 oz.	540 g	
Apricot glaze	as needed	as needed	
Chocolate Glaze (page 456) or Silky Ganache Deluxe (page 485)	as needed	as needed	

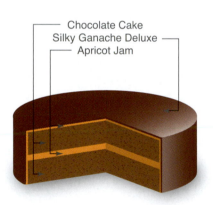

- Chocolate Cake
- Silky Ganache Deluxe
- Apricot Jam

1. Grease two 9-inch (22-centimeter) springform pans lightly with butter and line with parchment paper.
2. Sift the flour and cocoa powder together twice. Set aside.
3. Cream the butter and 7 ounces (210 grams) of the sugar together until light and fluffy. Gradually add the egg yolks and beat well.
4. Fold in the sifted flour and cocoa powder and the hazelnuts by hand.
5. Whip the egg whites to soft peaks, then gradually add the remaining sugar and continue whipping until stiff, glossy peaks form.
6. Lighten the batter by folding in approximately one-quarter of the egg whites, then fold in the remaining whites.
7. Pour the batter into the prepared pans and bake at 350°F (180°C) until the cakes are set, approximately 35 to 45 minutes.
8. Cool the cakes 5 minutes before removing from the pans.
9. Cool completely, then cut each cake horizontally into two layers. Spread apricot jam on each layer and restack them, creating two two-layer cakes.
10. Heat the apricot glaze until spreadable. Pour it over the top and sides of each cake.
11. Allow the apricot glaze to cool completely, then pour the Chocolate Glaze or Silky Ganache Deluxe over the top and sides of each cake to create a smooth, glossy coating.

Approximate values per $\frac{1}{10}$-cake serving: **Calories** 450, **Total fat** 21 g, **Saturated fat** 10 g, **Cholesterol** 185 mg, **Sodium** 60 mg, **Total carbohydrates** 56 g, **Protein** 7 g, **Vitamin A** 20%

LONGCHAMP

Chef Jack Shoop, CMC, CMB

Yield: 1 Torte, 10 in. (24 cm)

Ladyfingers (page 479)	as needed	as needed
Classic Genoise (page 440), cut into a 10-in. (24-cm) circle	1 layer	1 layer
Kirsch	3.5 fl. oz.	105 ml
Simple Syrup (page 73), cool	1 qt.	1 lt
Kirsch Mousse (recipe follows)	as needed	as needed
Fresh raspberries	1 pt.	0.5 lt
Italian Meringue (page 413)	as needed	as needed

1. Place a 10-inch (24-centimeter) torte ring that is 1¾ inches (4.5 centimeters) high over a cardboard circle. Line the ring completely with Ladyfingers. Cut the Ladyfingers level with the top of the ring. Place the Classic Genoise inside the ring to form the bottom of the cake.
2. Prepare a Kirsch-flavored syrup by combining the Kirsch and the Simple Syrup. Brush the Classic Genoise and the Ladyfingers with this syrup. Reserve the remaining Kirsch-flavored syrup for another use.
3. Fill the torte with Kirsch Mousse, sprinkling in raspberries as the torte is filled so that the fruit is evenly distributed. The torte should be filled to the top of the ring. Smooth the top of the mousse with an offset spatula.
4. Freeze the torte until set.
5. Spread a thin layer of Italian Meringue over the mousse. Decorate the top of the torte with Italian Meringue piped through a pastry bag fitted with a St. Honoré tip. Pipe the meringue from the center, curving outward to the edge of the torte. Brown the top of the meringue with a propane torch.
6. Remove the torte ring and garnish the torte with fresh raspberries.

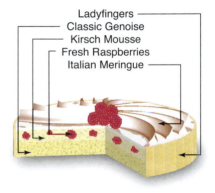

Ladyfingers
Classic Genoise
Kirsch Mousse
Fresh Raspberries
Italian Meringue

Approximate values per 1/12-torte serving: **Calories** 690, **Total fat** 30 g, **Saturated fat** 17 g, **Cholesterol** 267 mg, **Sodium** 171 mg, **Total carbohydrates** 89 g, **Protein** 10 g, **Vitamin A** 25%, **Vitamin C** 35%, **Calcium** 10%

KIRSCH MOUSSE

Yield: 2 qt. (2 lt)

Kirsch	3.5 fl. oz.	105 ml
Sheet gelatin, softened	9 sheets (0.6 oz.)	18 g
Heavy cream	1 qt.	1 lt
Pastry Cream (page 492)	2 lb.	960 g

1. Bring the Kirsch to a simmer over low heat. Remove from the heat, add the softened sheet gelatin and stir until it is completely dissolved.
2. Stir the gelatin mixture into the heavy cream, then whip the cream to soft peaks.
3. Fold the whipped cream into the Pastry Cream and chill until ready to use.

Approximate values per serving: **Calories** 480, **Total fat** 36 g, **Saturated fat** 22 g, **Cholesterol** 245 mg, **Sodium** 96 mg, **Total carbohydrates** 27 g, **Protein** 8 g, **Vitamin A** 29%, **Vitamin C** 41%, **Calcium** 12%

SAFETY ALERT
Propane Torch

Training on how to operate a propane torch is recommended before using it to brown meringue or other dessert preparations. Use extreme caution and follow appropriate safety procedures when using a torch. Keep the gas bottle away from sources of heat. Do not leave the torch unattended. Rest the bottle on a stable surface away from any flammable materials.

CHOCOLATE LAVA CAKES

Yield: 4 Individual Tortes, 2¾ in. × 2½ in. (7 cm × 6 cm) each

Chocolate batter:

Semisweet chocolate (58% cacao), chopped	4 oz.	120 g	228%
Unsalted butter	4 oz.	120 g	228%
Eggs	4 oz. (2½ eggs)	120 g	228%
Granulated sugar	4 oz.	120 g	228%
Vanilla extract	0.15 fl. oz. (1 tsp.)	5 ml	8.5%
Salt	0.06 oz. (¼ tsp.)	1 g	3%
Pastry flour, sifted	1.75 oz.	52 g	100%
Total batter weight:	18 oz.	538 g	1023%

Ganache center:

Heavy cream	1.75 fl. oz.	52 ml
Invert sugar	0.75 oz	22 g
Semisweet chocolate (58% cacao), chopped	2.5 oz.	75 g
Unsalted butter	0.33 oz.	10 g
Total weight:	1 lb. 7 oz.	697 g

Fresh berries	as needed	as needed
Tuile Batter (page 354), baked and cut into strips (optional)	as needed	as needed
Powdered sugar	as needed for garnish	

1. Melt the chocolate with the butter in a bowl over simmering water to 120°F (50°C).
2. Whip the eggs and sugar on medium speed to a thick ribbon, approximately 10 minutes. Add the vanilla and salt.
3. Gently fold in the melted chocolate. Fold in the sifted flour. Refrigerate the soft batter until it firms, at least 1 hour.
4. Prepare the ganache center while the batter chills. Bring the cream and invert sugar to boil in a small saucepan. Pour onto the chopped chocolate and butter, stirring until well combined. (If all the chocolate has not melted, heat briefly in a microwave oven or over a double boiler.)

1. Filling the rings with the batter.

2. Placing the ganache into the batter.

3. Filling the rings with the remaining batter.

5 Cool the ganache until slightly firm, then pipe into 4 rounded mounds on a parchment paper–lined sheet pan. Place in the freezer.

6 Line four 2¾-inch (7-centimeter) torte rings with parchment paper. Place them on a paper-lined sheet pan.

7 Using a pastry bag fitted with a large tip, pipe a 1-inch (2-centimeter) layer of the batter into each ring. Add a frozen ganache mound, then fill each ring with the remaining batter so that the ganache is covered and the rings are three-quarters full.

8 Bake at 400°F (190°C) until the surface no longer trembles and has lost its shine, approximately 16 to 20 minutes.

9 To serve, slide a spatula under each cooked torte and transfer to individual serving plates. Lift off the rings. Dust with powdered sugar and garnish with berries and a tuile cookie, if desired.

Approximate values per serving: **Calories** 780, **Total fat** 28 g, **Saturated fat** 24 g, **Cholesterol** 185 mg, **Sodium** 120 mg, **Total carbohydrates** 140 g, **Protein** 12 g

4 The finished lava cake.

MANGO MASCARPONE TORTE

Yield: 48 Servings, 1 Full-Size Sheet Pan

Mango Gelée (page 607)	2 lb. 9 oz.	1230 g
Vanilla Spongecake (page 478)	2 full sheets	2 full sheets
Granulated sugar	4 oz.	120 g
Mango, fresh or IQF, defrosted and cut into ½-in. (1.2-cm) cubes	3 lb.	1440 g
Unsalted butter	2 oz.	60 g
Vanilla extract	0.3 fl. oz. (2 tsp.)	10 ml
Mascarpone Cream Mousse (page 531)	6 lb. 6 oz.	3060 g
Simple Syrup (page 73)	12 fl. oz.	360 ml
Kirsch or rum	3 fl. oz.	90 ml

❶ Placing the spongecake on top of the mousse.

❶ Place a patterned silicone baking mat on a flat sheet pan fitted with a cake pan extender that measures the same size as the mat, approximately 13½ inches × 21½ inches (35 centimeters × 55 centimeters). Prepare the Mango Gelée and pour it into the pan. Freeze until set, approximately 45 minutes.

❷ Trim each sheet of Vanilla Spongecake to fit the pan. Set aside.

❸ Stir the sugar in a heavy saucepan over medium-high heat until it turns a golden caramel color. Add the mango cubes and cook, stirring until heated through. Add the butter and vanilla and stir to combine. Remove from the heat. Set aside.

❹ Prepare the Mascarpone Cream Mousse. Spread half of the mousse over the gelée in the pan. Place one trimmed sheet of spongecake on top of the mousse. Combine the Simple Syrup and Kirsch. Moisten the spongecake with half of the syrup.

❷ Moistening the cake with syrup.

❺ Spread the mango cubes evenly over the spongecake. Spread the remaining mascarpone mousse in the frame covering the mango cubes. Place the remaining spongecake on top of the mousse and moisten it with the remaining syrup.

❻ Freeze the torte overnight.

❼ Invert the torte onto a clean sheet of parchment paper. Peel off the silicone baking mat. Remove the cake frame, heating it gently with a propane torch if necessary. Trim the edges of the torte, if necessary. Use a hot knife to cut the frozen torte into portions measuring approximately 1¾ inches × 3⅓ inches (4 centimeters × 8.5 centimeters). Allow the portioned torte to thaw in the refrigerator before serving.

Approximate values per 6-oz. (180-g) serving: **Calories** 440, **Total fat** 24 g, Saturated fat 12 g, **Cholesterol** 275 mg, **Sodium** 65 mg, **Total carbohydrates** 48 g, **Protein** 9 g, **Vitamin A** 35%, **Vitamin C** 20%

❸ Peeling off the silicone mat.

❹ Heating the cake frame with a propane torch.

❺ Removing the cake frame.

CARAIBE TORTE

Yield: 4 Tortes, 8 in. × 6 in. (20 cm × 15 cm) each

Chocolate Spongecake (page 442), fully baked	3 half sheets	3 half sheets
Simple Syrup (page 73)	14 fl. oz.	420 ml
Jamaican rum	4 fl. oz.	120 ml
Chocolate Buttercream Filling (page 492)	4 lb.	1920 g
Silky Ganache Deluxe (page 485)	as needed	as needed
Chocolate Meringue Sticks (recipe follows)	as needed for garnish	
White modeling chocolate roses (page 711)	as needed for garnish	

1. Place a rectangular cake frame 16 inches × 12 inches × 2½ inches (41 centimeters × 30 centimeters × 6.5 centimeters) on a flat paper-lined sheet pan.
2. Fit one Chocolate Spongecake layer inside the frame. Flavor the Simple Syrup with the rum and moisten the cake with 6 fluid ounces (180 milliliters) of the rum syrup.
3. Spread half of the Chocolate Buttercream Filling on the cake. Cover the cream with another cake layer, then moisten it with 6 fluid ounces (180 milliliters) of the rum syrup.
4. Spread the remaining Chocolate Buttercream Filling over the cake. Cover with the last cake layer and moisten with the remaining rum syrup.
5. Freeze the torte at least 2 hours.
6. To finish the torte, invert it onto a flat surface and remove the frame and paper. Spread a small layer of room-temperature Silky Ganache Deluxe over the top of the torte. Warm the remaining ganache to 110°F (43°C) and glaze the surface evenly.
7. Once the ganache sets, divide the torte into four equal pieces. Place each piece on a cake board. Garnish the tortes with Chocolate Meringue Sticks and white modeling chocolate roses.

Approximate values per ⅛-torte serving: **Calories** 470, **Total fat** 26 g, **Saturated fat** 15 g, **Cholesterol** 215 mg, **Sodium** 55 mg, **Total carbohydrates** 52 g, **Protein** 7 g, **Vitamin A** 15%

1. Quartering the Caraibe torte.

2. The finished Caraibe torte.

CHOCOLATE MERINGUE STICKS

Yield: Approximately 120 Pieces

Chocolate Meringue (page 411)	1 lb. 8 oz.	720 g

1. Using a small plain tip, pipe the Chocolate Meringue onto a paper-lined sheet pan in strips running the length of the sheet pan.
2. Bake at 225°F (110°C) until crisp, approximately 1 hour.
3. Remove the Chocolate Meringue from the oven and immediately cut the strips into 1½-inch (3.5 centimeter) sticks. Chocolate Meringue Sticks will keep 1 month if stored in a dry place, tightly wrapped in an airtight container.

Chocolate Spongecake
Chocolate Buttercream
Silky Ganache Deluxe
Chocolate Meringue Sticks

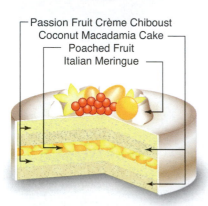

Passion Fruit Crème Chiboust
Coconut Macadamia Cake
Poached Fruit
Italian Meringue

RIO TORTE

Yield: 2 Tortes, 7 in. (17 cm) each

Coconut Macadamia Cake (recipe follows)	4 rounds	4 rounds
Passion Fruit Crème Chiboust (page 516)	1 lb. 10 oz.	780 g
Pineapple and mango cubes, poached	1 lb.	480 g
Italian Meringue (page 413)	1 lb. 7 oz.	690 g
Tropical fruit	as needed	as needed

1. Lightly oil and sugar two 7-inch (17-centimeter) torte rings. Place them on a paper-lined sheet pan. Place one layer of Coconut Macadamia Cake into each ring.
2. Divide half of the Passion Fruit Crème Chiboust evenly between the rings. Scatter the poached pineapple and mango cubes over the cream. Top with the remaining layers of cake.
3. Fill the rings to the top with more crème Chiboust, leveling it to the rim with a long metal spatula. (Because crème Chiboust tends to settle in the ring, reserving some of the cream in the refrigerator and releveling the torte after a few hours is recommended.)
4. Freeze the tortes a minimum of 2 hours.
5. Remove the tortes from the rings and place them on cake boards.
6. Coat the top and sides of each torte with an even layer of Italian Meringue. Decorate the surface of each torte with more Italian Meringue using a pastry bag fitted with a St. Honoré tip. Lightly brown the tortes with a propane torch and decorate with tropical fruit.

Approximate values per ⅛-torte serving: Calories 640, **Total fat** 33 g, **Saturated fat** 18 g, **Cholesterol** 260 mg, **Sodium** 95 mg, **Total carbohydrates** 81 g, **Protein** 10 g, **Vitamin A** 25 %, **Vitamin C** 15 %, **Iron** 15%

COCONUT MACADAMIA CAKE

Yield: 4 Rounds, 7 in. (17 cm) each   **Method:** Egg foam

Egg yolks	8 oz. (13 yolks)	240 g	200%
Granulated sugar	10 oz.	300 g	250%
Heavy cream	10 fl. oz.	300 ml	250%
Macaroon-type coconut	9 oz.	270 g	225%
Vanilla extract	0.5 fl. oz.	15 ml	12%
Cake flour, sifted	4 oz.	120 g	100%
Macadamia nuts, coarsely chopped	6 oz.	180 g	150%
Egg whites	8 oz. (8 whites)	240 g	200%
Total batter weight:	3 lb. 7 oz.	1665 g	1387%

1. In a large bowl, whisk the egg yolks and sugar until well combined. Add the cream, then the coconut, vanilla and flour. Fold in the macadamias.
2. In a separate bowl, whisk the egg whites to medium stiff peaks. Fold one-third of the whipped egg whites into the coconut mixture, then delicately fold in the rest of the egg whites.
3. Divide the cake batter evenly between buttered and floured cake pans. Bake at 375°F (190°C) until the center of the cake bounces back when lightly pressed, approximately 20 minutes. Cool completely before using.

Approximate values per 1-oz. (30-g) serving: **Calories** 130, **Total fat** 90 g, **Saturated fat** 5 g, **Cholesterol** 70 mg, **Sodium** 15 mg, **Total carbohydrates** 10 g, **Protein** 2 g

FRAISIER TORTE

The Fraisier torte is the French pastry chef's answer to strawberry shortcake. Make it when berries are at their peak.

Yield: 4 Tortes, 8 in. × 6 in. (20 cm × 15 cm) each

Pistachio Spongecake (page 478), fully baked	1 full sheet	1 full sheet
Simple Syrup (page 73)	7.5 fl. oz.	225 ml
Raspberry liqueur	2.5 fl. oz.	75 ml
Raspberry purée	2 oz.	60 g
Raspberry Cream Filling (page 517)	2 lb.	960 g
Fresh strawberries, whole	3 lb.	1440 g
French Mousseline Buttercream (page 453)	as needed	as needed
Marzipan	as needed	as needed
Food coloring (optional)	as needed	as needed
Neutral glaze (optional)	as needed	as needed
Fresh berries (optional)	as needed for garnish	
Sugar decorations (optional)	as needed for garnish	

Pistachio Spongecake
Raspberry Cream
Whole Strawberries
Mousseline Buttercream
Marzipan

1. Place a rectangular cake frame measuring 16 inches × 12 inches × 2½ inches (41 centimeters × 30 centimeters × 6.5 centimeters) on a flat paper-lined sheet pan. Do not oil or sugar the frame.

2. Cut the Pistachio Spongecake in two and place one layer, cut side facing up, inside the frame.

3. Combine the Simple Syrup with the raspberry liqueur and raspberry purée. Moisten the spongecake with half of the raspberry syrup.

4. Spread a layer of Raspberry Cream Filling ⅛ inch (3 millimeters) thick evenly over the spongecake.

5. Arrange the strawberries upright on the cream, positioning them close together so that their sides touch. Cover the strawberries evenly with the remaining Raspberry Cream Filling. Top with the remaining spongecake layer, cut side facing toward the cream. Moisten it with the remaining raspberry syrup.

6. In order to obtain a clean cut, chill the assembled cake several hours in the refrigerator.

7. Loosen the cake from the frame by running a knife along the inside edge of the frame. Remove the cake frame. Spread a thin layer of French Mousseline Buttercream on the top surface of the cake. Tint the marzipan a pale color. Roll it out 1/16 inch (1 millimeter) thick and position the marzipan on the top surface of the torte, covering the buttercream.

8. With a serrated knife, trim the sides of the torte evenly to expose the strawberries. Quarter the cake, then transfer it to four cake boards. If desired, coat the marzipan with neutral glaze and decorate with fresh berries and sugar decorations.

Approximate values per ⅛-torte serving: **Calories** 685, **Total fat** 48 g, **Saturated fat** 27 g, **Cholesterol** 298 mg, **Sodium** 37 mg, **Total carbohydrates** 60 g, **Protein** 6 g, **Vitamin A** 35%, **Vitamin C** 45%

EROS TORTE

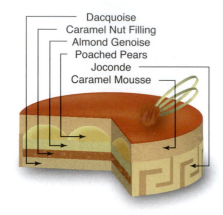

Dacquoise
Caramel Nut Filling
Almond Genoise
Poached Pears
Joconde
Caramel Mousse

Yield: 3 Tortes, 7 in. (17 cm) each

Joconde Spongecake (page 605), baked on a patterned mat	1 half sheet	1 half sheet
Dacquoise (page 424), 7-in. (17-cm) disks	3 disks	3 disks
Caramel Nut Filling or Icing (page 484)	1 lb. 9 oz.	750 g
Almond Genoise (page 477), 7-in. (17-cm) round	1 round	1 round
Simple Syrup (page 73)	4.5 fl. oz.	135 ml
Cointreau or orange liqueur	2.5 fl. oz.	75 ml
Poached Pears in Exotic Syrup (page 579)	15	15
Caramel Mousse (recipe follows)	2 lb. 8 oz.	1200 g
Tart glaze	as needed	as needed
Combed Chocolate Teardrop Ribbons (page 703)	as needed	as needed
Walnut halves	as needed	as needed

1. Oil and sugar three 7-inch (17-centimeter) torte rings and place them on a paper-lined sheet pan. Cut the Joconde Spongecake into three strips measured to fit the rings. Line each ring with a strip of cake, its patterned design facing the ring. Place one Dacquoise disk in the bottom of each ring.
2. Divide the Caramel Nut Filling or Icing evenly among the three rings.
3. Slice the Almond Genoise into three layers. Place one layer in each ring, covering the nut filling. Combine the Simple Syrup and Cointreau and moisten the cake with 2 ounces (60 milliliters) of the syrup.
4. Slice the Poached Pears in Exotic Syrup in half, remove the core and stem and place approximately 10 pear halves in each ring, covering the Almond Genoise layer.
5. Cover the pears with the Caramel Mousse and fill to the rim. Level the top of the tortes by running a long metal spatula over the rim of the ring molds.
6. Freeze the tortes a minimum of 2 hours.
7. Coat the tortes with the tart glaze, then remove the rings. Transfer the tortes onto cake boards. Decorate the tops with Combed Chocolate Teardrop Ribbons and walnut halves.

Approximate values per 1-oz. (30-g) serving: **Calories** 90, **Total fat** 2.5 g, **Saturated fat** 1 g, **Cholesterol** 45 mg, **Sodium** 15 mg, **Total carbohydrates** 16 g, **Protein** 2 g

CARAMEL MOUSSE

Reduce the amount of gelatin by half if the mousse will not need to be sliced, as in a torte or tart.

Yield: Approximately 2 lb. 8 oz. (1200 g)

Glucose or corn syrup	3.5 oz.	105 g
Granulated sugar	6 oz.	180 g
Water	2.5 fl. oz.	75 ml
Unsalted butter	1.5 oz.	45 g
Heavy cream, boiling	6 fl. oz.	180 ml
Vanilla extract	0.5 fl. oz.	15 ml
Cointreau or orange-flavored liqueur	0.5 fl. oz.	15 ml
Egg yolks	3.6 oz. (6 yolks)	108 g
Sheet gelatin, softened	0.5 oz.	15 g
Heavy cream, whipped to soft peaks	18 fl. oz.	540 ml

1 Combine the glucose syrup, 4 ounces (120 grams) of the sugar and the water in a large, deep saucepan. Stir while bringing the mixture to a boil. Wash away the sugar crystals from the sides of the pan. Without stirring any more, cook the mixture to an amber caramel, approximately 350°F (177°C). Do not let the mixture smoke and burn.

2 Carefully add the butter and the boiling cream to the caramel; be aware that the mixture will rise high in the pan. Stir, then bring back to a boil for 2 minutes. Remove from heat and let cool to 86°F (30°C). Add the vanilla and liqueur. Set aside.

3 Place the egg yolks in a bowl and whisk in the remaining sugar. Heat the mixture over a bain marie, whisking constantly until it reaches 160°F (71°C), without scorching the yolks.

4 Transfer to the bowl of a mixer fitted with the whip attachment. Add the softened sheet gelatin to the yolk mixture. Whip until lukewarm, approximately 86°F (30°C), then remove the bowl from the mixer.

5 Fold the yolk mixture into the caramel. Then fold in the whipped cream. Use immediately.

Approximate values per 1-oz. (30-g) serving: **Calories** 110, **Total fat** 8 g, **Saturated fat** 5 g, **Cholesterol** 65 mg, **Sodium** 10 mg, **Total carbohydrates** 7 g, **Protein** 1 g

---

RUBIES TORTE

Yield: 3 Triangular Tortes, 8 in. (20 cm) each

Raspberry Gelée (page 607)	2 lb. 9 oz.	1230 g
Chocolate Almond Flour Cake (page 472)	1 full sheet	1 full sheet
Raspberry Ganache (page 585)	2 lb. 14 oz.	1380 g
Cocoa Gelée (page 608)	as needed	as needed
White and dark chocolate decorations (page 698)	as needed	as needed
Fresh raspberries	as needed	as needed

Flourless Chocolate Cake
Chocolate Decorations
Raspberry Ganache
Raspberry Gelée
Cocoa Gelée

1 Cut four 24-inch- (60-centimeter-) long sheets of aluminum foil. For strength, stack the sheets, then fold up the edges to make a rectangular container measuring 8 inches × 16 inches (20 centimeters × 40 centimeters). Place the foil container on a half-sheet pan.

2 Prepare the Raspberry Gelée and pour it into the foil container. Freeze until the gelée sets.

3 Invert the Chocolate Almond Flour Cake onto a flat surface. Leave the parchment paper attached and cut the cake into three strips measuring approximately 8 inches × 16 inches (20 centimeters × 40 centimeters) each. Transfer one strip of cake, paper side down, to a clean sheet pan.

4 Spread the top of the cake with half of the Raspberry Ganache. Transfer another cake strip, paper side up, onto the ganache. Remove the paper.

5 Spread this layer with half of the remaining ganache. Unwrap the frozen Raspberry Gelée and trim it into a strip measuring 8 inches × 16 inches (20 centimeters × 40 centimeters). Place it onto the ganache-coated cake. Top with the last cake strip, paper side up. Remove the paper and spread the cake layer with the remaining ganache.

6 Freeze until firm, approximately 2 hours.

7 Remove the cake from the freezer and immediately cover it with Cocoa Gelée heated to 120°F (49°C). Cut the cake into three triangular pieces. Place each piece on a cake board and decorate with chocolate decorations and fresh raspberries.

Approximate values per ⅑-torte serving: **Calories** 660, **Total fat** 38 g, **Saturated fat** 20 g, **Cholesterol** 205 mg, **Sodium** 80 mg, **Total carbohydrates** 76 g, **Protein** 13 g, **Vitamin A** 25%, **Vitamin C** 20%, **Iron** 10%

PALOMO TORTE

Yield: 4 Tortes, 7 in. (17 cm) each

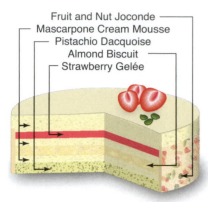

Fruit and Nut Joconde
Mascarpone Cream Mousse
Pistachio Dacquoise
Almond Biscuit
Strawberry Gelée

Strawberry Gelée (page 613)	1 lb. 13 oz.	870 g
Fruit and Nut Joconde (page 605), fully baked	1 half sheet	1 half sheet
Pistachio Dacquoise (page 424), 7-in. (17-cm) disks, fully baked	4 disks	4 disks
Mascarpone Cream Mousse (page 531)	4 lb. 5 oz.	2160 g
Almond Biscuit (page 612)	1 half sheet	1 half sheet
Simple Syrup (page 73)	7.5 fl. oz.	225 ml
Strawberry liqueur	2.5 fl. oz.	75 ml
Strawberry purée	2 oz.	60 g
Neutral glaze	as needed	as needed
White chocolate combed curls (page 701)	as needed	as needed
Strawberries and pistachios	as needed	as needed

1. Prepare the Strawberry Gelée and pour it into four silicone molds or pie tins, slightly smaller than the 7-inch (17-centimeter) torte rings being used. Freeze until needed.

2. Lightly oil and sugar four 7-inch (17-centimeter) torte rings. Place on a paper-lined sheet pan.

3. Cut the Fruit and Nut Joconde into 2-inch- (5-centimeter-) wide strips the length of the sheet pan. Fit the strips tightly into the rings. Place the Pistachio Dacquoise in the bottom of each ring.

4. Spread a small amount of the Mascarpone Cream Mousse in a thin layer on the Pistachio Dacquoise.

5. Cut the Almond Biscuit into four 7-inch (17-centimeter) rounds and place on the Mascarpone Cream Mousse.

6. Combine the Simple Syrup, strawberry liqueur and strawberry purée. Moisten the cake with the strawberry syrup. Cover with a small amount of Mascarpone Cream Mousse.

7. Unmold the frozen Strawberry Gelée by simply pressing it out of the silicone molds, or by briefly placing the pie tins on a heat source, until the disks come free. Place one molded gelée in each ring.

8. Cover with the remaining Mascarpone Cream Mousse and level to the rim of the ring.

9. Freeze until well chilled, approximately 2 hours.

10. Coat the surface of the tortes with neutral glaze. Chill until firm, then remove the rings. Place the tortes on cake boards. Garnish with white chocolate ribbons, fresh strawberries and pistachios.

Approximate values per ⅛-torte serving: **Calories** 580, **Total fat** 35 g, **Saturated fat** 15 g, **Cholesterol** 215 mg, **Sodium** 75 mg, **Total carbohydrates** 54 g, **Protein** 15 g, **Vitamin A** 20%, **Vitamin C** 10%, **Calcium** 10%, **Iron** 10%

BERGAMOT TORTE

Yield: 3 Tortes, 7½ in. (19 cm) each

Patterned Joconde Cake (page 606), fully baked	1 full sheet	1 full sheet
Dacquoise (page 424), 7½-in. (19-cm) disks, fully baked	3 disks	3 disks
Orange Bergamot Curd (page 493)	1 lb. 14 oz.	900 g
Almond Genoise (page 477), 7-in. (17-cm) rounds, fully baked	2 rounds	2 rounds
Granulated sugar	8 oz.	240 g
Orange juice	8 fl. oz.	240 ml
Bergamot essential oil	5–6 drops	5–6 drops
Milk Chocolate Earl Grey Mousse (page 527)	5 lb.	2400 g
Cocoa gelée	as needed	as needed
Edible gold leaf (optional)	as needed for garnish	

edible gold leaf delicate sheets of pure gold used to decorate chocolates and iced cakes; the thin sheets, separated by tissue paper, are sold in packs and are available from cake decorating suppliers. Edible silver leaf, known as *vark*, is also available

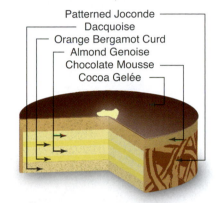

Patterned Joconde
Dacquoise
Orange Bergamot Curd
Almond Genoise
Chocolate Mousse
Cocoa Gelée

1. Lightly oil and sugar three 7½-inch (19-centimeter) torte rings. Place them on a paper-lined sheet pan.

2. Cut the Patterned Joconde Cake into strips ½ inch (1.2 centimeters) narrower than the height of the rings. Fit the strips tightly into the rings with the design facing the ring. Place a layer of Dacquoise in the bottom of each ring.

3. Spread a small amount of Orange Bergamot Curd on the Dacquoise.

4. Slice the Almond Genoise into three layers and place one in each torte ring.

5. Make a syrup from the sugar, orange juice and bergamot oil and moisten the Almond Genoise with half of the syrup. Spread with the remaining Orange Bergamot Curd.

6. Place the remaining Almond Genoise in each ring and moisten well with the syrup.

7. Top each cake with the Milk Chocolate Earl Grey Mousse, filling the rings to the rim and leveling with a flat metal spatula.

8. Freeze until hard, approximately 2 hours.

9. Remove from the freezer and cover the top surface with a thin layer of cocoa gelée.

10. Remove the tortes from the rings, then decorate with edible gold leaf, if desired.

Approximate values per ⅛-torte serving: **Calories** 940, **Total fat** 56 g, **Saturated fat** 29 g, **Cholesterol** 380 mg, **Sodium** 135 mg, **Total carbohydrates** 98 g, **Protein** 16 g, **Vitamin A** 35%, **Vitamin C** 25%, **Calcium** 15%, **Iron** 15%

Hazelnut and Cherry Meringue Cake
Hazelnut Cream Filling
Cherry Gelée
Sliced Almonds

NOBILIS TORTE

Yield: 4 Tortes, 8 in. × 6 in. (20 cm × 15 cm) each

Cherry Gelée (page 613)	4 lb.	1920 g
White chocolate, melted	as needed	as needed
Hazelnut and Cherry Meringue Cake (recipe follows)	2 half sheets	2 half sheets
Hazelnut Cream Filling (page 533)	4 lb. 12 oz.	2280 g
Neutral glaze	as needed	as needed
Sliced almonds	as needed	as needed
Fresh cherries	as needed	as needed

1. Pour the Cherry Gelée into a 16-inch × 12-inch (40-centimeter × 30-centimeter) pan or silicone mold. (Or place a 16-inch × 12-inch × 2-inch [40-centimeter × 30-centimeter × 5-centimeter] cake frame on a sheet pan that has been lined with a silicone baking mat. Pipe a thin strip of white chocolate along the inner bottom edge of the frame to seal the frame to the baking mat. Pour the Cherry Gelée into the frame.) Freeze until set.

2. Position a half-sheet cake frame measuring 16 inches × 12 inches × 2½ inches (40 centimeters × 30 centimeters × 6.5 centimeters) on a paper-lined sheet pan.

3. Fit one layer of Hazelnut and Cherry Meringue Cake inside the frame.

4. Spread half of the Hazelnut Cream Filling evenly over the surface of the cake.

5. Cover with the Cherry Gelée, then spread half of the remaining Hazelnut Cream Filling over the gelée. Top with the second layer of cake. Cover with plastic wrap and freeze at least 2 hours.

6. Invert the cake onto the back side of a flat sheet pan. Remove the cake frame.

7. Using an offset spatula, spread the remaining Hazelnut Cream Filling over the top of the cake. Spread a thin layer of neutral glaze on the surface of the tortes.

8. Refrigerate until set. Cut the cake into four equal pieces. Place on cake boards. Decorate with sliced almonds and fresh cherries.

Approximate values per ⅛-torte serving: **Calories** 680, **Total fat** 40 g, **Saturated fat** 15 g, **Cholesterol** 115 mg, **Sodium** 80 mg, **Total carbohydrates** 69 g, **Protein** 14 g, **Vitamin A** 25%, **Vitamin C** 15%, **Calcium** 10%, **Iron** 10%

HAZELNUT AND CHERRY MERINGUE CAKE

Yield: 3 Half-Sheet Pans

Cake flour, sifted	8 oz.	240 g	100%
Hazelnuts, toasted and coarsely chopped	1 lb. 9 oz.	750 g	312%
Hazelnut flour	9 oz.	270 g	112%
Powdered sugar	14 oz.	420 g	175%
Dried cherries	10 oz.	300 g	125%
Egg whites	2 lb.	960 g	400%
Dried egg whites (optional)	0.5 oz.	15 g	6%
Granulated sugar	1 lb.	480 g	200%
Total batter weight:	7 lb. 2 oz.	3435 g	1430%

1. Stir the cake flour, hazelnuts, hazelnut flour, powdered sugar and dried cherries together in a bowl. Set aside.

2. Whip the liquid egg whites in the bowl of a large mixer fitted with the whip attachment until foaming.

3 Combine the dried egg whites (if using) with the granulated sugar and add the mixture to the whipped egg whites.

4 Whip the egg whites until they hold a firm peak. Fold in the dry ingredients.

5 Spread the mixture using an offset metal spatula over paper-lined sheet pans.

6 Bake at 350°F (180°C) until the cake bounces back when lightly pressed, approximately 40 minutes. Cool completely before using. This cake is a component in Nobilis Torte or it may be filled with whipped cream or any of the buttercream fillings in Chapter 13, Cakes and Icings.

Approximate values per 1-oz. (30-g) serving: **Calories** 100, **Total fat** 5 g, **Saturated fat** 0 g, **Cholesterol** 0 mg, **Sodium** 15 mg, **Total carbohydrates** 13 g, **Protein** 3 g

EMPRESS TORTE

Note: The assembly of this torte is illustrated on page 609.

Yield: 3 Tortes, 7 in. × 2½ in. (17 cm × 6 cm) each

Nougatine Dacquoise (page 424), 7-in. (17-cm) disks, fully baked	3 disks	3 disks
Lime Curd (page 493)	1 lb. 4 oz.	600 g
Almond Genoise (page 477), 7-in. (17-cm) rounds, fully baked	2 rounds	2 rounds
Simple Syrup (page 73)	7 fl. oz.	210 ml
Raspberry purée	8 fl. oz.	240 ml
Raspberry Mousseline (page 528)	3 lb. 8 oz.	1680 g
Neutral glaze	as needed	as needed
Chocolate cutouts (page 698)	as needed	as needed
Raspberries or other fruit	as needed	as needed
Combed chocolate ribbons (page 702)	as needed	as needed
Gerbet Macarons (page 640)	as needed	as needed

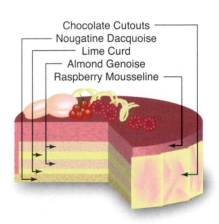

Chocolate Cutouts
Nougatine Dacquoise
Lime Curd
Almond Genoise
Raspberry Mousseline

1 Lightly oil and sugar three 7-inch × 2½-inch (17-centimeter × 6-centimeter) torte rings. Place one Nougatine Dacquoise disk in each ring.

2 Spread a small amount of Lime Curd over each Nougatine Dacquoise layer.

3 Slice the Almond Genoise horizontally in three even layers. Place an Almond Genoise round in each ring.

4 Combine the Simple Syrup and raspberry purée and moisten the cake with half of the raspberry syrup. Cover with the remaining Lime Curd.

5 Place another Almond Genoise layer in the ring and moisten with the remaining raspberry syrup.

6 Fill the rings to the rim with the Raspberry Mousseline and level evenly. Freeze until set, approximately 2 hours.

7 Spread a thin layer of neutral glaze on the surface of the tortes. Let set.

8 Remove the rings and place on cake boards. Carefully heat the sides of the tortes with a propane torch, then overlap chocolate cutouts along the sides of the tortes. Decorate with raspberries or other fruit, chocolate ribbons and Gerbet Macarons.

Approximate values per ⅛-torte serving: **Calories** 600, **Total fat** 29 g, **Saturated fat** 13 g, **Cholesterol** 145 mg, **Sodium** 85 mg, **Total carbohydrates** 77 g, **Protein** 14 g, **Vitamin A** 15%, **Vitamin C** 20%, **Iron** 10%

TIRAMISU TORTE

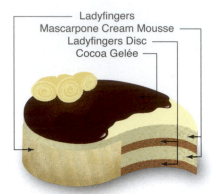

Ladyfingers
Mascarpone Cream Mousse
Ladyfingers Disc
Cocoa Gelée

Yield: 2 Tortes, 7 in. (17 cm) each

Ladyfinger batter (page 479)	2 lb. 14 oz.	1380 g
Simple Syrup (page 73)	9 fl. oz.	270 ml
Coffee or almond liqueur	2 fl. oz.	60 ml
Coffee extract	0.5 fl. oz.	15 ml
Vanilla extract	0.5 fl. oz.	15 ml
Mascarpone Cream Mousse (page 531)	3 lb. 5 oz.	1590 g
Cocoa Gelée (page 608)	as needed	as needed
Cocoa powder (optional)	as needed	as needed
Hollow molded chocolates (page 707)	as needed	as needed
Chocolate fans or decorations (page 697)	as needed	as needed

1. Butter and flour two paper-lined full-sheet pans. Using a plain medium tip, pipe half of the Ladyfinger batter into four disks measuring 7 inches (17.5 centimeters) in diameter.

2. To make the strips of Ladyfingers to line the ring molds, pipe the remaining batter into Ladyfingers 4 inches (10 centimeters) long, placed close together so they join at the sides and form a strip the entire length of the sheet pan. Bake as directed.

3. Lightly oil and sugar two 7-inch (17-centimeter) torte rings. Place them on a paper-lined sheet pan.

4. Cut the strip of Ladyfingers in half lengthwise. Trim the strips of Ladyfingers on each long edge to fit evenly inside the ring molds.

5. Position the Ladyfinger strips inside the rings, cut to size to make a tight fit. Place a Ladyfinger disk on the bottom of each ring.

6. Combine the Simple Syrup, liqueur, coffee extract and vanilla. Moisten the cake with half of this syrup.

7. Divide half of the Mascarpone Cream Mousse between the two molds.

8. Place the second Ladyfinger disk in the rings and moisten with the remaining coffee syrup.

9. Fill with the remaining Mascarpone Cream Mousse, leveling it to the rim.

10. Refrigerate or freeze the tortes 2 hours.

11. Remove from freezer and cover the top surface with a thin layer of Cocoa Gelée heated to 120°F (49°C), or sprinkle lightly with cocoa powder to garnish. Remove the rings, then decorate the tortes with hollow molded chocolates, chocolate fans or other chocolate decorations.

Tiramisu Torte made in a teardrop-shaped mold.

Approximate values per ⅛-torte serving: **Calories** 640, **Total fat** 33 g, **Saturated fat** 18 g, **Cholesterol** 390 mg, **Sodium** 40 mg, **Total carbohydrates** 70 g, **Protein** 17 g, **Vitamin A** 25%

ROLLED FONDANT CALLA LILY CAKE

The pristine surface of a cake covered in rolled fondant lends itself to elegant decoration. This cake is coated with rolled fondant, and the sides are embellished with piped Royal Icing as shown on page 465. It is the elegant calla lily garnish, made from pastillage (page 719) that completes this simple design.

Fondant or Pastillage Calla Lilies (recipe follows)	4 flowers	4 flowers
Filled layer cake coated with fondant, decorated with Royal Icing	1 cake	1 cake
Royal Icing (page 457)	as needed	as needed
Pastillage or fondant curls	2 pieces	2 pieces

1. Position the Fondant or Pastillage Calla Lilies in an attractive grouping on top of the cake. Once the position is decided, remove the flowers and pipe several small mounds of Royal Icing on top of the cake. Position the flowers in the icing.

2. Tuck the pastillage or fondant curls between the flowers.

FONDANT OR PASTILLAGE CALLA LILIES

Yield: 4 Flowers

Rolled fondant or pastillage	10 oz.	300 g
Food coloring, assorted colors	as needed	as needed

1. Photocopy the calla lily template on page 778. Cut out the template to use as a cutting guide.

2. Place 2 ounces (60 grams) of the fondant or pastillage in a small bowl. Add enough deep yellow food coloring to tint the paste a deep yellow color. Divide the tinted paste into four uniform pieces. Roll each piece into a blunt tube measuring approximately 2½ inches (6 centimeters) long. Cover with plastic wrap and set aside.

3. Tint 1 ounce (30 grams) of the rolled fondant or pastillage light green. Cover it with plastic wrap and set aside.

4. To make the calla lily petals, divide the remaining fondant or pastillage into four even pieces. Press out or roll each piece ¼ inch (6 millimeters) thick. Divide the green-tinted paste into 12 small pieces. Roll the small pieces into strips approximately 2 inches (5 centimeters) long. Place three green strips randomly onto the pressed paste. Roll out each piece of pressed paste ½₂ inch (2 millimeters) thick.

5. Place the calla lily template on top of the fondant or pastillage. Using a sharp paring knife, trim each piece into the petal shape, using the outline as a guide. Thin the edges of each petal using the back of a spoon or a marzipan tool.

6. Place a yellow center at the base of the petal and fold, slightly overlapping the base of the flower.

7. Invert a muffin pan onto a sheet pan. Arrange the flowers on the pan, surrounded and cushioned by cotton balls. Allow the flowers to dry at room temperature 48 hours before using.

SAFETY ALERT
Edible Flowers

Real calla lilies, like most flowers in the lily family, are toxic when eaten. Although it is tempting to substitute real calla lilies for sugar ones on a cake, don't. In fact, do not decorate any food item with real lilies. Many flowers and blossoms are toxic, especially those grown from bulbs. Even flowers that would otherwise be edible may contain pesticides that can be harmful if ingested. Use only flowers grown specifically for use as food; purchase edible flowers only from reputable purveyors.

1. Making calla lilies, clockwise from top left: yellow-tinted paste formed into centers; green-tinted paste on petal; rolled-out paste; thinning the edges of a flower petal.

2. Wrapping a petal around a center.

WHITE CHOCOLATE ENGAGEMENT CAKE

This engagement cake takes its inspiration from the purity of white chocolate and the elegance of a cream-colored cake with simple red accent colors. The chocolate decorations are made by sprinkling tempered chocolate with chopped dried cranberries before cutting into small squares.

Filled layer cake iced with French buttercream, 12 in. (30 cm)	1 cake	1 cake
White Modeling Chocolate (page 710)	3 lb. 8 oz.	1680 g
White chocolate decorations (page 698)	as needed	as needed
White Chocolate Heart Centerpiece (procedure follows)	1	1
White chocolate swizzle sticks (page 702)	as needed for garnish	
Organic rose petals, fresh raspberries and red currants	as needed for garnish	

1. Refrigerate the iced cake until it is cold and the buttercream is firm, preferably overnight.
2. Roll out the White Modeling Chocolate 1⁄12 inch (2 millimeters) thick into a circle large enough to drape over and cover the cake on all sides. Do not roll the paste too thin, as this may cause bubbles to form when the finished cake is stored in a refrigerator.
3. Use a rolling pin to transfer the sheet of modeling chocolate to the cake. Drape it over the cake. With the palm of your hand, even out the modeling chocolate and make it smooth. Remove any air bubbles that appear in the surface of the modeling chocolate by pricking them with a toothpick and gently pressing out the air. The hole left behind can be smoothed out with a finger.
4. Using a sharp paring knife or pizza wheel, trim off any extra modeling chocolate along the bottom edge of the cake.
5. Arrange white chocolate decorations along the bottom edge of the cake. Decorate the cake with the White Chocolate Heart Centerpiece, white chocolate swizzle sticks, organic rose petals, fresh raspberries and red currants.

PROCEDURE FOR MAKING A WHITE CHOCOLATE HEART CENTERPIECE

1. Spread tempered white chocolate 1⁄8 inch (3 millimeters) thick onto a sheet of acetate using an offset spatula.
2. Allow the chocolate to set just until the surface loses some of its gloss and feels like leather. Cut out two hearts using heart-shaped cookie cutters. Use a knife to cut out two hollow heart shapes in the center of each heart. Cut out a 2-inch (5-centimeter) circle to be used as the base for the hearts.
3. Once the chocolate has set, remove the cutouts from the acetate.
4. To assemble the centerpiece, cut through the bottom of one of the heart pieces using a heated knife. Slip the heart over the second heart to interlock the two. Use a small amount of melted chocolate to attach the interlocking hearts to the round base.

GREEN FONDANT OR MARZIPAN BOMBE

Like many decorative cake coatings, fondant and marzipan provide a smooth elegant finish and seal in moisture. Fondant, discussed on page 455, tints easily and is versatile. But unlike fondant, marzipan, discussed on page 714, has a delicate almond flavor that enhances the cake it covers. This coated bombe is made from layers of spongecake moistened with simple syrup and filled with chocolate mousse. The bombe is chilled thoroughly, unmolded and then coated with a light layer of buttercream. Before covering with fondant or marzipan, the bombe is again thoroughly chilled overnight in the refrigerator, a wise step to use to ensure a firm foundation when making a specialty cake.

Fondant or marzipan, tinted green	2 lb. 8 oz.	1200 g
Filled torte or bombe made in a 5-qt. (5-lt) mold, iced with buttercream	1 bombe	1 bombe
Nougatine, cut into small squares, decorated with Royal Icing (page 457)	as needed	as needed
Marzipan Flowers (recipe follows)	12	12
Isomalt Lace (page 729)	as needed	as needed
Nougatine curls (page 723)	as needed	as needed
Fresh white currants	as needed	as needed

❶ Applying marzipan strips to the bombe.

❶ Roll out the fondant ⅛ inch (3 millimeters) thick. Cut 9-inch- (27-centimeter-) long strips from the fondant approximately 1½ inches (3 centimeters) wide. Using a sharp knife, cut a wedge approximately 3 inches (7.5 centimeters) from the end of each strip to slightly taper the ends.

❷ Place the iced bombe on a cake board. Arrange the strips of fondant on the bombe with the narrow end at the top. Slightly overlap each strip until the entire surface of the cake is covered.

❸ Trim any excess fondant at the bottom of the bombe using a sharp knife. Position the nougatine squares evenly around the bottom edge of the bombe.

❹ Decorate the top of the bombe with Marzipan Flowers, Isomalt Lace, nougatine curls and white currants.

❷ Close-up of the decorated bombe.

MARZIPAN FLOWERS

Yield: 12 Flowers

Marzipan	6 oz.	180 g
Yellow paste food coloring	as needed	as needed
Simple Syrup (page 73)	as needed	as needed

❶ Roll out 4 ounces (120 grams) of the marzipan ⅛ inch (3 millimeters) thick. Cut it into flower shapes using a small cookie or gum paste cutter.

❷ Using the blunt end of a wooden chopstick or a marzipan tool, press down on the center of each cutout to make a cupped flower shape. Place the shaped marzipan flowers into miniature muffin tins or clean chocolate molds to dry. Set aside.

❸ Tint the remaining marzipan with yellow paste food coloring. Press the tinted marzipan through a sieve and cut the threads into short pieces using a pair of scissors.

❹ Brush a small amount of Simple Syrup in the center of each marzipan flower. Tuck some of the sieved marzipan into the center. Return the finished flowers to the muffin tins or molds to dry.

❸ The finished bombe.

CHAPTER EIGHTEEN

PETITS FOURS AND CONFECTIONS

- understand the uses of the petit four
- prepare an assortment of traditional petits fours and confections
- create petits fours using components from other chapters in this book

PETITS FOURS ARE ANY NUMBER OF SMALL PASTRIES, cookies and miniature desserts that are served after a meal or with afternoon tea. According to British culinary authority Alan Davidson, these pastries may take their name from the small ovens (Fr. *petits fours*) in which these pastries were baked in the 18th century. Long a favorite at receptions and buffets, the petit four is having a renaissance. As pastry chefs work to develop their signature creations, more attention is being paid to the petit four as a way to express the style of the restaurant and its cuisine. They are incorporating small candies or confections into their repertoires. Today, petits fours and confections are often served at the end of a meal or as a dessert on their own when accompanied by ice cream, sorbet, crème brûlée or other creamy products. This chapter discusses petits fours and some of the confections served at the end of the meal. Chocolates and other candies are discussed in more depth in Chapter 20, Chocolate and Sugar Work.

PETITS FOURS—MINIATURE PASTRIES

friandise (free-yon-DEEZ) a small pastry or sweet delicacy often served between or after meals; petit four

Petits fours are any type of pastry small enough to be consumed in one to two bites. They may also be referred to as **friandises**. Made fresh in fine pâtisseries, petits fours offer the host of a large, stand-up gathering the possibility of serving a sweet after a meal. Petits fours also appeal to those seeking dainty, small-scale sweets. Afternoon teas, bridal showers and traditional ladies' luncheons frequently feature petits fours, long a symbol of elegance and refinement.

Meticulously prepared miniature cookies such as cigarettes, langues de chat, mirroirs, French almond macaroons, miniature éclairs and meringues are traditional petits fours. But it is common practice for a pastry chef to make smaller versions of frequently made pastries to create petits fours. For example, when a mousse or cream is prepared for a torte, extra can be made and piped into small tart shells or chocolate cups. This method saves time when the production schedule is well organized.

When preparing petits fours, attention to detail is paramount. Uniformity in size and shape, and consistency of finishing details count a great deal for the eye appeal of petits fours.

Petits fours should:

▶ be no more than one or two small bites. Most should measure no more than 1½ to 2 inches (4 to 5 centimeters) in length.

▶ represent a variety of textures and flavors.

▶ be visually attractive.

▶ complement whatever foods precede or accompany them without duplicating their flavors.

TABLE 18.1	RECOMMENDED PETIT FOUR COMPONENTS		
BASE	**SHAPE**	**FILLING**	**GARNISH**
Baked shortbread or sweet dough	Tartlets, disks, barquettes	Buttercreams, custards, curds, ganache, frozen parfaits, mousses and chiffons	Berries, fruit slices, chocolate ornaments, toasted nuts
Baked meringue or nut meringue	Piped cookies, shells, disks	Crème Chantilly, buttercreams, curds, ganache, frozen parfaits, mousses and chiffons	Chopped pistachios, candied citrus rind, shaved chocolate
Baked éclair paste	Mini éclairs, puffs	Crème Chantilly, curds, frozen parfaits, mousses	Chocolate or fondant glaze, caramel, powdered sugar
Tulipe (tuile batter)	Rolled, cup	Crème Chantilly, white chocolate mousse	Dip in chocolate, then in toasted nuts
Wafer cookies	Piped, then baked	Buttercreams, curds, ganache, jams	Filled and sandwiched together, ends dipped in chocolate
Joconde or other firm spongecake	Filled and layered	Buttercreams, jam, marzipan, ganache	Fondant glaze, decorated with piping gel or chocolate
Poundcake	Sliced and cut out, baked in mini pans	Buttercreams, curds, crème Chantilly, jam	Fondant glaze or chocolate glaze
Chocolate	Molded cups or disks	Mousses, ganache, ice creams, crème Chantilly, hazelnut cream	Berries, fruit slices, candied fruit or nuts, mint leaves

Petit Four Varieties

Petits fours are divided into five broad categories based on preparation method, texture or principal ingredient—fresh, iced, dry, glazed fruit and a broad category called prestige. Confections included in this chapter may also be served along with petits fours as well as the chocolates and truffles discussed in Chapter 20, Chocolate and Sugar Work. These categories assist the bakery and pastry chef in planning the proper assortment of products suitable to the occasion. (See Table 18.1.)

FRESH PETITS FOURS

Fresh petits fours (Fr. *petits fours frais*) are moist miniatures that may contain fruit and fillings such as buttercream, citrus curd, ganache or various mousses. Miniature tartlets or **barquettes** filled with pastry cream and topped with fresh berries, grapes or apricot halves are examples of this type. Nearly all the tarts in this book can be miniaturized and served as petits fours. Diminutive cups made from tempered chocolate, sweet dough (*pâte sucrée*) baked into small shells, miniature rum babas and cream puffs (*pâte à choux*) make excellent containers for cream-filled petits fours. The formulas for Cappuccino Cheesecakes (page 650) and Chocolate Raspberry Mousse Bites (page 651) illustrate the procedure for making fresh petits fours.

barquette a small boat-shaped pastry shell used for miniature cakes or tarts served as canapés or petits fours

PROCEDURE FOR MAKING BARQUETTE SHELLS

❶ Roll out the pastry dough ⅛ inch (3 millimeters) thick.

❷ Press the dough into the barquette shells.

❸ Prick the dough with a fork to allow steam to escape during baking.

❹ Place a second barquette shell on top of the dough to prevent it from rising as it bakes.

ICED PETITS FOURS

Iced petits fours (Fr. *petits fours glacés*) are small cakes, cookies or biscuits iced with fondant or glaze. They are most frequently made from a firm cake such as a joconde that is baked into thin sheets. The thin cake is then layered with jam, ganache or various buttercreams, and often topped with a layer of rolled **marzipan**. Perhaps because of their frequent appearance in holiday mail order catalogs, many in the United States think that this style of cake is the definitive petit four.

marzipan (MAHR-sih-pan) a paste of ground almonds, sugar and glucose syrup used to fill and decorate pastries

Iced petits fours should not exceed 1 inch (2.5 centimeters) in height. Different shapes may be cut as long as they can be consumed in two mouthfuls. A rolling cutter, knife dipped in hot water or petit four cutter ensures uniform pieces. After cutting, the petit four is usually coated with soft fondant; rolling fondant is not used for this purpose. The fondant is heated carefully in a bain marie to 100°F (38°C). Simple syrup or water is added to thin the fondant so that it is just thick enough to coat the petit four. A few drops of pastel food coloring may be added to enhance the coating's appearance. A long **dipping fork**, such as that used when coating chocolates, is inserted into each petit four to hold the layers together when immersing the cakes in the melted fondant. Fondant seals the petits fours, helping them retain moisture but also making them rather sweet. Select a filling that will balance the sweetness. Petits fours filled with jam and coated with fondant will remain moist several days when stored in an airtight container under refrigeration. Tinted royal icing or chocolate is usually piped into delicate flowers or fine scrollwork designs on top of the glazed petit four. Of course these petits fours can also be made without the final glazing process, with just the lightest coating of jam or icing on top, which is perhaps more appropriate for the taste preferences of today's consumer.

dipping fork utensil used to hold chocolate or small pastries for dipping into chocolate or other coating; consists of a narrow handle with two, three or four long, thin prongs, which are easily inserted into small pastries

PROCEDURE FOR PREPARING AN ICED PETIT FOUR

1. Bake a thin, flexible spongecake such as a joconde. Using a serrated or cake knife, trim the edges, then cut the cake into four uniform pieces.
2. Generously moisten one layer of the cake with flavored simple syrup. Spread it with one or more fillings chosen to complement the flavors in the cake, such as raspberry jam, lemon curd or vanilla buttercream.
3. Continue layering the cake, moistened with syrup, and filling, ending with a final layer of cake.
4. Top the cake with a thin sheet of marzipan, if desired.
5. Freeze the cake, then cut it into small uniform squares or shapes.
6. Prepare fondant or glaze. Thin until it is thick enough to coat the cake but the layers of spongecake can be seen through the fondant. Dip the cut pieces of cake into the glaze and place on a cake screen to drain. Alternatively, spoon the coating over the cut cakes placed on an icing screen.
7. Allow the fondant or glaze to dry, then decorate with piped chocolate or royal icing.

PETIT FOUR GLACÉ

MISE EN PLACE
▸ Prepare Joconde Spongecake.
▸ Prepare Simple Syrup.

Yield: 72 Petits Fours, 1¾ in. (4.5 cm) each		**Type:** Iced petit four
Joconde Spongecake (page 605)	1 full sheet	1 full sheet
Simple Syrup (page 73)	4 fl. oz.	120 ml
Raspberry liqueur or purée	2 fl. oz.	60 ml
Raspberry jam	as needed	as needed
Fondant	3 lb.	1440 g
Chocolate decorations	as needed	as needed
Fresh raspberries	1½ pt.	0.75 lt

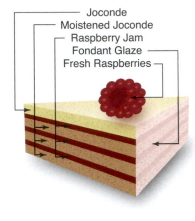

Joconde
Moistened Joconde
Raspberry Jam
Fondant Glaze
Fresh Raspberries

1. Cut the baked Joconde Spongecake crosswise into four equal strips. Place one of the joconde strips on a paper-lined sheet pan. Combine the Simple Syrup and raspberry liqueur and moisten the cake with 1½ fluid ounces (45 milliliters) of this syrup.

2. Spread a thin even layer of raspberry jam on the moistened cake.

3. Cover with another sheet of joconde. Moisten with 1½ fluid ounce (45 milliliters) raspberry syrup and coat with more raspberry jam. Cover with another sheet of joconde and once again repeat the moistening and jam process. Top with the last joconde layer. Freeze until firm.

4. Trim the cake, then cut into small squares or triangles measuring approximately 1¾ inches (4.5 centimeters).

5. Gently heat the fondant to 100°F (38°C) over a bain marie. Remove from the heat and thin the fondant slightly with a small amount of the remaining raspberry syrup. Strain the fondant through a fine sieve to remove any crumbs.

6. Place the cake pieces on an icing screen. Coat with warm fondant, using a large spoon, a squeeze bottle or a pastry bag with a plain small to medium tip. After coating the petits fours, the layers of joconde should still be visible through the fondant.

7. Decorate with chocolate decorations and fresh raspberries.

VARIATION:

Raspberry Petit Four—Omit the fondant and top the cake with neutral glaze before cutting the cake into small triangles.

Approximate values per piece: **Calories** 120, **Total fat** 10 g, **Saturated fat** 0 g, **Cholesterol** 10 mg, **Sodium** 15 mg, **Total carbohydrates** 26 g, **Protein** 1 g

1. Cutting the cake into small rectangles.

2. Pouring fondant over the cakes.

3. Spreading the fondant evenly over the cakes.

DRY PETITS FOURS

Dry petits fours (Fr. *petits fours sec*) are any number of fragile, crunchy dainty cookies. The most common are cookies such as Tulipe Cookies (page 354), Checkerboard Cookies (page 328), nut meringues and small butter cookies or puff pastry products made without a cream filling. These cookies may also be filled with or dipped in chocolate. For example, see Cherry-Almond Florentines (page 648) or Langues de Chat (Cat's Tongue Cookies, page 646). Be aware that when filled, these brittle cookies may become moist and soften in a few hours.

Almond Macaroons

Almond macaroons are a simple yet refined cookie, popular as a petit four. Almond macaroons are made in a number of styles. Those made with almond paste are especially moist and chewy. But French-style almond macaroons (Fr. *macarons*) resemble a meltingly tender baked meringue with a moist interior. These refined cookies require skill to make but are worth the effort.

French-style macaron batter is made by folding finely ground almonds into egg whites beaten with sugar. Proper folding ensures that the macarons will bake with a characteristic smooth surface and a satin sheen. Fold the almond flour into the batter until it becomes shiny and falls from the spatula in thick ribbons. (The French term for this important step is **macaronnage**.) The batter is piped into small rounds on parchment paper or silicone-lined baking mats. For best results, the tip mark left by the piping tip should dissolve within 1 minute. If the batter has been insufficiently folded, the tip mark will remain and the macarons may crack on the surface and be dull after baking. Overmixed batter will be runny. Pipe a test row of the batter to determine whether it has been properly mixed. Macarons are baked until set but not golden brown.

The technique for making macarons is illustrated here with the formula for Gerbet Macarons, which are smooth-topped macarons made with blanched almond flour and usually filled with jam or buttercream.

PROCEDURE FOR PREPARING ALMOND MACARONS

1. To ensure that the egg whites foam smoothly, separate the egg whites 24 hours before using; then refrigerate them until needed. Have all ingredients at room temperature. If the almond flour has been stored in a freezer or refrigerator, warm it briefly in a low oven to remove any moisture.

2. Beat the egg whites and sugar until stiff.

3. Fold in blanched almond flour and powdered sugar until the mixture becomes shiny and falls from a spatula in thick ribbons.

4. Using a small or medium plain tip, pipe the batter onto silicone baking mats or paper-lined sheet pans. Let the piped batter sit 15 minutes to ensure a smooth surface. (If it appears that the macaron batter was underfolded, let the piped batter rest 25 to 30 minutes before baking. If the batter was overfolded and the macarons are spreading, bake at once.)

5. Bake the macarons at 325°F (160°C) until set but not browned, approximately 18 to 22 minutes. Baking at a low temperature ensures that the macarons do not overly darken.

6. Cool the macarons before removing them from the silicone mat or parchment paper. Or pour a few drops of water under the silicone mat or baking paper when the macarons are removed from the oven. The steam created may help release the macarons.

7. Sandwich two macarons together with a small amount of jam, curd or buttercream. Select a filling that complements the color of the macaron batter. Allow the macarons to sit, filled, for several hours before serving so that the filling adheres to the baked shells.

GERBET MACARONS

MISE EN PLACE

▶ Bring almond flour and egg whites to room temperature.

▶ Separate egg whites.

▶ Preheat oven to 325°F (160°C).

Yield: 90 Cookies, approximately 1 in. (2.5 cm) each   **Type:** Dry petit four

Almond flour, room temperature	1 lb. 2 oz.	540 g
Powdered sugar	1 lb. 7 oz.	690 g
Egg whites, room temperature	14 oz. (14 whites)	420 g
Granulated sugar	7 oz.	210 g
Cream of tartar	1 pinch	1 pinch
Dried egg whites	0.3 oz. (2 tsp.)	9 g
Liquid or powdered food coloring (optional)	as needed	as needed
Buttercream, ganache, jam, lemon curd or other filling	as needed	as needed

1. In a food processor fitted with the metal blade, mix the almond flour and powdered sugar until the almond flour is very fine. Set aside.

2. In the bowl of a mixer fitted with the whip attachment, whip the egg whites until foamy. Stir together the granulated sugar, cream of tartar and dried egg whites, then add the mixture to the foamed egg whites in a steady stream.

3. Whip the egg whites on medium speed until the mixture is very stiff. Add the food coloring (if using). Remove the mixture from the machine.

4. Whisk the egg whites using a balloon whisk to restore a uniform smooth appearance to the mixture. Using a spatula, fold in one-quarter of the almond and powdered sugar mixture. Add the remaining dry ingredients and fold the batter until it becomes shiny and falls from the spatula in thick ribbons. If the mixture looks dull, continue to fold until the batter develops a shine.

5. Using a pastry bag fitted with a medium plain tip, pipe the batter onto silicone baking mats or paper-lined sheet pans. Each macaron should measure 1 inch (2.5 centimeters) wide and ¼ inch (6 millimeters) tall. If the mark left by the piping tip does not dissolve within 1 minute, stir the batter a little more, then continue piping.

6. Let the piped batter rest for 15 minutes.

7. Bake at 325°F (160°C) until the macarons can almost be removed from the silicone or parchment paper, approximately 18 to 22 minutes.

8. Allow the cookies to cool, then remove them from the silicone mats or sheet pans.

9. Spread a thin layer of buttercream, ganache, jam, or lemon curd on the bottom (pan side) of one cookie and gently press another cookie onto the filling, top side out.

Approximate values per cookie: **Calories** 30, **Total fat** 1 g, **Saturated fat** 0 g, **Cholesterol** 0 mg, **Sodium** 0 mg, **Total carbohydrates** 4 g, **Protein** 1 g, **Claims**—gluten free

1. Properly whipped egg whites for macarons.

2. Folding the almond flour into the whipped egg whites.

3. Piping the macaron batter before baking.

4. The finished macarons.

GLAZED FRUIT

Glazed fruit coated with caramel or sugar syrup cooked to the hard crack stage (Fr. *petits fours deguisés*) complements any assortment of petits fours. Grapes, strawberries, blackberries, pineapple pieces, citrus segments and many other small pieces of fruit hold up well when coated in crunchy sugar. Often dried fruit such as dates or apricots or conserved fruits such as candied chestnuts (Fr. *marrons glacés*) and kumquats will be stuffed with a nugget of tinted marzipan, then rolled in granulated sugar or coated with melted fondant before serving. The formula for Caramel-Dipped Fruits (page 653) illustrates a glazed fruit petit four. A stunning presentation of glazed fruit on a **showpiece** made from pastillage is shown on page 720.

PETITS FOURS PRESTIGE

Thanks to the invention of silicone molds, the production of petits fours has become easier, faster and therefore more profitable than ever. "New-style" petits fours (Fr. *petits fours prestiges*), made from advanced creams and mousses, have emerged because of the versatility of silicone molds. Cheesecake batter, crème brûlée and other creams and mousses can be poured into these molds, baked and then frozen. Once hardened, the pastries are easily removed and can be placed on prebaked disks made from nougatine, tart dough or chocolate. Garnishing may be simple or elaborate incorporating chocolate decorations and pulled sugar work. Petits fours based on rich buttercream and marzipan have become less popular, but whole new realms of petits fours have been introduced to the discerning guest. Many of the formulas at the end of this chapter, such as Irish Cream Crème Brûlée petits fours (page 652) and Chocolate Raspberry Mousse Bites (page 651), are examples of this prestigious style petit four.

showpiece (Fr. *piece montée*) a decorative sculpture made from chocolate, sugar or other confections; used as a table display and to demonstrate the skills of the pastry chef

CONFECTIONS

Confections are any sort of small sugar-based sweet or candy. These might be hard candies, caramels, chocolate, fruit jellies or fudge as well as many of the small pastries discussed in this chapter. They may be served after a meal along with traditional petits fours or as a special treat. Often restaurants will present a few such sweets when the bill is presented to the customer. This chapter includes a few formulas for simple sweets that work well as petits fours. Caramel and more complex sweets that require advanced candy-making skills are in Chapter 20, Chocolate and Sugar Work.

SERVING AND PRESENTING PETITS FOURS AND CONFECTIONS

Whether served at the conclusion of a formal dinner, presented as the centerpiece of an afternoon tea or passed on butlered trays during a wedding reception, petits fours and confections must be properly selected and presented to maintain eye appeal. In a fine dining restaurant, waiters may present each table with small trays of these small treats as a dessert course or when the check is presented. An attractive assortment of petits fours may be included in a dessert buffet or passed on decorated trays in butler-style service. Often individual petits fours and candies are placed in fluted paper cases. This makes them easy to pick up and leaves the serving tray looking clean and neat.

For presentation platters, the composition of the assortment and the way it is positioned on the tray must be visually pleasing. A classic presentation is to line up parallel rows of the same item so that the guest may select from many types of petits fours without having to reach across the tray. In this arrangement, the waiter monitoring the buffet may easily refill the tray. Footed and tiered trays offer the opportunity to create visual excitement in a limited amount of space. Each level of the tiered tray may contain a different petit four. Intensely flavored and smaller items, such as chocolates or small glazed fruits, may be offered from graduated tiered trays while larger pieces such as miniature tartlets or éclairs are served from flat trays.

Terms to Know

dipping fork	petits fours
French macaron	madeleines
macaronnage	pâte de fruits

1. What are the different types of petits fours and under what circumstances would each type be appropriate?

2. Discuss the techniques you might use to cut iced petits fours to ensure uniform products.

3. What procedures should the pastry chef observe in order to ensure uniformity of product when making petits fours?

4. Using some of the recommended petit four combinations in Table 18.1, plan an assortment of small pastries to be served after a formal banquet. Take into consideration what might be offered as the dessert and explain the reasoning for your selection.

5. Search the Internet for photographs of petits fours used in a buffet display. Analyze the types of petits fours offered and critique the presentation used. **WWW**

Several of the following formulas are combinations of formulas presented in this chapter and other dessert products covered in other chapters. For example, White Chocolate Mousse Bites are made with Shortbread Tart Dough (Pâte Sablée), discussed in Chapter 11, Pies and Tarts. Many of these petits fours use components including nougatine, simple syrup and ganache, discussed elsewhere in this book.

LEMON TARTLETS

Yield: 40 Tartlets, 2 in. (5 cm) each   **Type:** Fresh petit four

Sesame Seed Nougatine (page 724)	1 lb. 12 oz.	840 g
Lemon Curd (page 493)	1 lb. 4 oz.	600 g
Italian Meringue (page 413)	as needed	as needed
Candied orange rind, cut into small rectangles (page 671)	as needed for garnish	

1. Lightly oil 40 small tartlet pans or petit four molds.
2. Roll the Sesame Seed Nougatine very thin. Cut it into circles the size of the tartlet or petit four molds. Line them with the nougatine. Remove the shells from the molds as soon as they hold their shape.
3. Pipe chilled Lemon Curd into the nougatine cups.
4. Pipe a small rosette of Italian Meringue on top of each tartlet. Using a propane torch, lightly brown the surface of the meringue, taking care not to brown the lemon curd or nougatine shell.
5. Garnish each tartlet with a piece of orange rind.

Approximate values per 1-oz. (30-g) serving: **Calories** 180, **Total fat** 10 g, **Saturated fat** 3.5 g, **Cholesterol** 20 mg, **Sodium** 20 mg, **Total carbohydrates** 23 g, **Protein** 3 g

APRICOT PASSION FRUIT GANACHE TARTLETS

Yield: 40 Tartlets, 1½ in. (4 cm) each   **Type:** Fresh petit four

Apricot purée	5 oz.	150 g
Passion fruit purée	2 oz.	60 g
Granulated sugar	3 oz.	90 g
Honey	1 oz.	30 g
Milk chocolate, chopped fine	5 oz.	150 g
Semisweet chocolate, chopped fine	5 oz.	150 g
Unsalted butter, room temperature	2 oz.	60 g
Shortbread Tart Dough shells (page 382), made with almond flour, 1½-in. (4-cm) disks, fully baked	40 disks	40 disks
Dried apricots, sliced thin	3 oz.	90 g
Choclate decorations (page 697)	as needed for garnish	

1. In a nonreactive saucepan heat the apricot and passion fruit purées, sugar and honey to 120°F (49°C).
2. Combine the milk chocolate and semisweet chocolate and melt them to 90°F (32°C). Stir the fruit purée mixture into the melted chocolate until well blended. Stir in the soft butter.
3. Pipe the ganache into the Shortbread Tart Dough shells, filling them to the rim.
4. Refrigerate the tarts until set, then garnish with a slice of dried apricot and chocolate decorations (if using).

Approximate values per tartlet: **Calories** 160, **Total fat** 9 g, **Saturated fat** 5 g, **Cholesterol** 25 mg, **Sodium** 65 mg, **Total carbohydrates** 19 g, **Protein** 2 g

SAN DIEGOS

Yield: 65 Petits Fours, 1½ in. (4 cm) each		Type: Fresh petit four	
Sweet Almond Tart Dough (page 383)	1 lb. 8 oz.	720 g
Hazelnut paste	13 oz.	390 g
Heavy cream	2 fl. oz.	60 ml
Eggs	5 oz. (3 eggs)	150 g
Egg yolks	6.5 oz. (11 yolks)	195 g
Almond paste	1 lb. 5 oz.	630 g
Granulated sugar	5 oz.	150 g
Pistachio compound	2 oz.	60 g
Pistachios, blended to a paste*	3 oz.	90 g
Unsalted butter, melted	9 oz.	270 g
Simple Syrup (page 73)	2 fl. oz.	60 ml
Kirsch	1 fl. oz.	30 ml
Pistachios, finely chopped	10 oz.	300 g
White chocolate decorations (page 699; optional)	as needed for garnish	

1. Roll the Sweet Almond Tart Dough ⅛ inch (3 millimeters) thick. Line the bottom and sides of a paper-lined half-sheet pan with the dough. Prick the dough with a fork.

2. Bake blind at 375°F (190°C) until blond in color, approximately 10 minutes.

3. In the bowl of a mixer fitted with the paddle attachment, blend the hazelnut paste and cream. Beat in one-third of the eggs. Scrape down the bowl and beat in 1½ ounces (45 grams) of the egg yolks.

4. Spread the hazelnut mixture on the baked tart dough. Freeze just until the mixture sets, approximately 15 minutes.

5. In the bowl of a mixer fitted with the paddle attachment, combine the almond paste, sugar and pistachio compound. Add the blended pistachio paste. Add the remaining eggs, one at a time, scraping down the bowl after each is added. Add the remaining egg yolks and the melted butter.

6. Spread the cake batter over the hazelnut mixture. Bake at 350°F (180°C) until the cake bounces back when lightly pressed, approximately 35 to 38 minutes. Let cool.

7. Combine the Simple Syrup and Kirsch. Moisten the cake with the syrup, then cut it into 1½-inch (4-centimeter) squares.

8. Dip the top surface of each petit four in the chopped pistachios. Decorate with a chocolate decoration, if using.

*Pistachio paste is made by blending pistachio nuts in a food processor until a smooth paste is formed.

VARIATION:

Valencias—Replace the pistachio compound with orange compound. Omit the pistachios. Garnish the petits fours with sliced almonds and candied orange rind.

Approximate values per cookie: **Calories** 210, **Total fat** 14 g, **Saturated fat** 4.5 g, **Cholesterol** 65 mg, **Sodium** 35 mg, **Total carbohydrates** 17 g, **Protein** 4 g

Valencias

L'OPÉRA

One of pastry chef Gaston Lenôtre's creations, the Opéra cake should be generously moistened with coffee syrup. This intensifies the flavor and improves the cake's keeping properties.

Yield: 75 Petits Fours, 1 in. × 1½ in. (2.5 cm × 4 cm) each

Type: Iced petit four

Moistened Joconde
Silky Ganache Deluxe
Coffee Buttercream
Chocolate Decorations

Simple Syrup (page 73)	4 fl. oz.	120 ml
Coffee liqueur	1 fl. oz.	30 ml
Coffee extract	1 fl. oz.	30 ml
Vanilla extract	0.3 fl. oz. (2 tsp.)	10 ml
Joconde Spongecake (page 605)	1 full sheet	1 full sheet
Silky Ganache Deluxe (page 485), room temperature	14 oz.	420 g
Traditional French Buttercream (page 483)	1 lb.	480 g
Chocolate decorations (page 700)	as needed for garnish	
Edible gold leaf (optional)	as needed for garnish	

1 Combine the Simple Syrup, coffee liqueur, 1 tablespoon (15 milliliters) of the coffee extract and the vanilla. Set aside.

2 Cut the Joconde Spongecake crosswise into three equal strips. Place one of the joconde strips on a paper-lined sheet pan and moisten with 2 fluid ounces (60 milliliters) of the coffee-vanilla syrup.

3 Evenly spread a thin layer of Silky Ganache Deluxe over the moistened cake. Cover with another sheet of joconde and moisten with 2 fluid ounces (60 milliliters) of the coffee-vanilla syrup.

4 Combine the Traditional French Buttercream with the remaining coffee extract and spread evenly over the cake. Cover with another sheet of joconde and moisten with the remaining syrup.

5 Freeze until hard.

6 Invert the frozen cake onto a sheet pan. Coat the top of the cake with a thin layer of Silky Ganache Deluxe to seal. Heat the remaining ganache to 120°F (49°C), then spread it evenly over the cake with an offset spatula. Let the ganache harden. Trim the edges with a clean, warm knife.

7 Cut the cake into small squares, triangles or rectangles measuring approximately 1 inch × 1½ inches (2.5 centimeters × 4 centimeters). Garnish with chocolate decorations and edible gold leaf, if using.

Approximate values per piece: **Calories** 90, **Total fat** 5 g, **Saturated fat** 3 g, **Cholesterol** 30 mg, **Sodium** 10 mg, **Total carbohydrates** 8 g, **Protein** 1 g

LANGUES DE CHAT
(CAT'S TONGUE COOKIES)

Yield: 65 Sandwich Cookies, 3 in. (7.5 cm) each   **Type:** Dry petit four

Unsalted butter, melted	as needed	as needed
Unsalted butter, softened	8 oz.	240 g
Powdered sugar	13 oz.	390 g
Egg whites	9 oz. (9 whites)	270 g
Vanilla extract	0.15 fl. oz. (1 tsp.)	5 ml
Cake flour	10 oz.	300 g
Pistachios, chopped (optional)	5 oz.	150 g
Semisweet chocolate, melted	as needed	as needed

1. Lightly brush melted butter on a sheet of parchment paper. Allow the butter to solidify. Set aside.
2. Cream the solid unsalted butter and powdered sugar. Gradually add the egg whites, then the vanilla. Fold in the flour using a rubber spatula.
3. In a pastry bag fitted with a plain medium tip, pipe the batter into 3-inch- (7.5-centimeter) long strips. Sprinkle with chopped pistachios (if using).
4. Bake at 400°F (200°C) until light golden, approximately 9 to 10 minutes.
5. Cool the cookies. Spread melted semisweet chocolate on the underside of one cookie, then sandwich it with a second cookie. Dip the ends of each cookie sandwich in additional chocolate.

VARIATION:

Lemon Sandwich Cookies—Omit the melted chocolate. Fill the cookies with Lemon Curd (page 493).

Approximate values per cookie: **Calories** 80, **Total fat** 4 g, **Saturated fat** 2 g, **Cholesterol** 10 mg, **Sodium** 10 mg, **Total carbohydrates** 10 g, **Protein** 1 g

1. Piping batter onto buttered parchment paper.

2. The finished cookies filled with chocolate.

Ladyfingers sprinkled with chopped pistachios.

MADELEINES

Madeleines *are cookies made from spongecake or genoise batter. They are traditionally shaped as small fluted fans using special molds. Madeleines are popular petits fours to serve with tea or coffee, as their somewhat dry, spongy texture is excellent for dipping into a hot beverage. Unlike the classic that launched Marcel Proust on his* Remembrance of Things Past, *this formula incorporates brown butter (beurre noisette) for additional flavor.*

❶ Piping the batter into greased and floured molds.

Yield: 12 Cookies, approximately ¾ oz. (20 g) each

Method: Egg foam

Type: Dry petit four

Unsalted butter	4 oz.	120 g	133%
Eggs	3.2 oz. (2 eggs)	100 g	106%
Granulated sugar	3 oz.	90 g	100%
Lemon zest, grated fine	0.07 oz. (1 tsp.)	2 g	2%
Lemon juice	0.04 fl. oz. (¼ tsp.)	1 ml	1%
Vanilla extract	0.04 fl. oz. (¼ tsp.)	1 ml	1%
Baking powder	0.02 oz. (⅛ tsp.)	0.5 g	0.7%
Cake flour, sifted	3 oz.	90 g	100%
Total batter weight:	10 oz.	404 g	443%

❶ Melt the butter over medium heat; continue cooking until the milk solids turn a golden-brown color. Set aside to cool.

❷ Whisk the eggs and sugar over a bain marie until warm (98°F/37°C). Remove from the heat and whisk in the lemon zest, lemon juice and vanilla.

❸ Sift the baking powder and flour together; stir into the egg mixture. Stir in the melted butter. Cover the bowl and allow the batter to rest 1 hour at room temperature.

❹ Butter and flour the madeleine shells. Spoon or pipe the batter into the shells, filling each three-quarters full.

❺ Bake at 450°F (230°C) until the cookies rise in the center and are very light brown on the bottom and edges, approximately 3 to 4 minutes for 1½-inch (4-centimeter) madeleines and 10 to 12 minutes for 3-inch (7.5-centimeter) madeleines. They should spring back when touched lightly in the center. Remove the madeleines from the oven, invert the pan over a wire cooling rack, and tap lightly to release the cookies from the pan.

Approximate values per cookie: **Calories** 110, **Total fat** 7 g, **Saturated fat** 4 g, **Cholesterol** 45 mg, **Sodium** 10 mg, **Total carbohydrates** 10 g, **Protein** 1 g, **Vitamin A** 6%

❷ The finished cookies.

CHERRY-ALMOND FLORENTINES

Yield: 40 Cookies, 2 in. (5 cm) each   **Type:** Dry petit four

Sweet Tart Dough (page 368), chilled	1 lb. 8 oz.	720 g
Granulated sugar	6 oz.	180 g
Glucose or corn syrup	2 oz.	60 g
Water	3 fl. oz.	90 ml
Unsalted butter, cubed	5 oz.	150 g
Honey	2.5 oz.	75 g
Heavy cream, boiling	3 fl. oz.	90 ml
Vanilla extract	0.15 fl. oz. (1 tsp.)	5 ml
Almonds, sliced, toasted	11 oz.	330 g
Dried cherries	2 oz.	60 g
Semisweet chocolate, tempered	as needed	as needed

SAFETY ALERT
Caramelizing Sugar

Caramelizing sugar can cause serious burns. Use a pair of cotton gloves covered by a pair of rubber gloves such as those used for industrial dishwashing to protect hands from coming into contact with spilled caramel. Take proper precautions to avoid hot sugar coming into direct contact with your skin.

1. Roll the chilled Sweet Tart Dough ⅛ inch (3 millimeters) thick and slightly larger than a half-sheet pan. Line the bottom and sides of the sheet pan with the dough. Prick the dough with a fork.
2. Bake blind at 375°F (190°C) until blond in color, approximately 8 to 11 minutes. Remove from the oven and set aside to cool.
3. Boil the sugar, glucose syrup and water to a golden caramel, approximately 325°F (160°C). Add the butter and honey to the caramel, then add the boiling cream. Bring the mixture to a full boil.
4. Remove from the heat and add the vanilla, almonds and cherries. While still warm, spread the mixture onto the prebaked crust in a thin, even layer.
5. Bake at 375°F (190°C) approximately 20 minutes or until the center has set and is golden brown.
6. Cool completely, trim the edges, then cut into 2-inch (5-centimeter) squares. Excess trimmed from the edges may be ground and used to side mask frosted cakes.
7. Dip one corner of each piece in tempered semisweet chocolate.

Approximate values per cookie: **Calories** 160, **Total fat** 10 g, **Saturated fat** 3.5 g, **Cholesterol** 15 mg, **Sodium** 0 mg, **Total carbohydrates** 15 g, **Protein** 3 g

1. Spreading the cherry-almond mixture over the baked dough.

2. Cutting the cookies.

3. Dipping the finished Cherry-Almond Florentines in chocolate.

CHOCOLATE PECAN CAKES

Yield: 40 Petits Fours, 1¼ in. × 2 in. (3 cm × 5 cm) each

Type: Dry petit four

Unsalted butter, softened	3.5 oz.	105 g	200%
Powdered sugar	3 oz.	90 g	171%
Eggs	3.2 oz. (2 eggs)	96 g	182%
Cake flour	1.75 oz.	50 g	100%
Bittersweet chocolate, melted to 110°F (43°C)	2.5 oz.	75 g	143%
Pecans, coarsely chopped	3 oz.	90 g	171%
Total batter weight:	1 lb.	506 g	967%
Silky Ganache Deluxe (page 485), room temperature	1 lb. 4 oz.	600 g	
Pecan halves	20	20	
Chocolate mesh (page 697)	as needed for garnish		

1. Cream the butter and sugar in the bowl of a mixer fitted with the paddle attachment. Gradually add the eggs. Scrape down the bowl.

2. On low speed add the cake flour. Once it is incorporated, add the melted chocolate and the chopped pecans.

3. Using a bag fitted with a large plain piping tip, pipe the batter into silicone molds or buttered and floured petit four molds.

4. Bake at 375°F (190°C) until the cake bounces back when lightly pressed, approximately 12 minutes. Let cool, then remove the cakes from the molds.

5. Pipe a rosette of Silky Ganache Deluxe onto each cake. Cut the pecan pieces in half. Insert a piece of chocolate mesh and a pecan piece into the ganache.

Approximate values per tartlet: **Calories** 100, **Total fat** 8 g, **Saturated fat** 4 g, **Cholesterol** 20 mg, **Sodium** 0 mg, **Total carbohydrates** 7 g, **Protein** 1 g

CAPPUCCINO CHEESECAKES

Yield: 40 Tartlets, 1½ in. (4 cm) each   **Type:** Fresh petit four

Cream cheese, room temperature	1 lb.	480 g
Granulated sugar	4 oz.	120 g
Eggs	3.2 oz. (2 eggs)	96 g
Sour cream	4 oz.	120 g
Coffee extract	1 fl. oz.	30 ml
Vanilla extract	0.15 fl. oz. (1 tsp.)	5 ml
Sesame Seed Nougatine (page 724), 2-in. (5-cm) disks, fully baked	40 disks	40 disks
Coffee beans	as needed for garnish	
White chocolate decorations (page 699)	as needed for garnish	
Cocoa powder (optional)	as needed for garnish	

① Beat the cream cheese and sugar on low speed in the bowl of a mixer fitted with the paddle attachment. Scrape down the bowl and beat until no lumps remain.

② Add the eggs one at a time, waiting for each egg to be fully incorporated before adding the next. Add the sour cream, then the coffee extract and vanilla.

③ Place a silicone petit four mold on a sheet pan and divide the batter evenly among the molds.

④ Pour water on the sheet pan to create a water bath and bake at 325°F (160°C) until the cheesecakes have set, approximately 25 minutes. Let cool, then freeze until hard.

⑤ Unmold each cheesecake onto a Sesame Seed Nougatine disk. Decorate with a coffee bean and white chocolate decoration, or dust lightly with cocoa powder.

Approximate values per tartlet: **Calories** 120, **Total fat** 7 g, **Saturated fat** 3.5 g, **Cholesterol** 25 mg, **Sodium** 45 mg, **Total carbohydrates** 12 g, **Protein** 2 g

WHITE CHOCOLATE MOUSSE BITES

Yield: 40 Petits Fours, approximately 1½ in. (4 cm) each

Type: Fresh petit four

Heavy cream	5 fl. oz.	150 ml
White chocolate	14 oz.	420 g
Egg yolks	2 oz. (3 yolks)	60 g
Granulated sugar	1 oz.	30 g
Sheet gelatin, softened	0.3 oz.	7 g
Shortbread Tart Dough (page 382), made with almond flour, 1½-in. (4-cm) disks, fully baked	40 disks	40 disks
Rose petals or red seedless grapes	as needed	as needed
White chocolate cutouts (page 698)	as needed for garnish	

1 Whip the cream to soft peaks and set aside.

2 Melt the chocolate to 110°F (43°C) and hold it at that temperature.

3 Place the egg yolks and sugar in a bowl over simmering water. Whip the yolks constantly until they form a thick ribbon and the temperature reaches 158°F (70°C).

4 Remove the yolks from the heat and whip them over an ice bath until they cool to 120°F (49°C). Add the softened sheet gelatin to the yolk mixture, then fold it into the melted chocolate. Fold in the whipped cream using a whisk until just incorporated.

5 Pour the mixture into 1½-inch (4-centimeter) silicone molds. Level the mousse with an offset spatula.

6 Freeze until hard, then unmold each mousse onto a Shortbread Tart Dough disk.

7 Decorate with rose petals or a few small grapes and a white chocolate cutout.

Approximate values per piece: **Calories** 190, **Total fat** 15 g, **Saturated fat** 8 g, **Cholesterol** 70 mg, **Sodium** 50 mg, **Total carbohydrates** 17 g, **Protein** 3 g

---

CHOCOLATE RASPBERRY MOUSSE BITES

Yield: 40 Petits Fours, 1¾ in. (4.5 cm) each   **Type:** Fresh petit four

Heavy cream	10 fl. oz.	300 ml
Granulated sugar	1 oz.	30 g
Raspberry purée, seedless	5 oz.	150 g
Semisweet chocolate, melted to 130°F (54°C)	6 oz.	180 g
Shortbread Tart Dough (page 382), made with hazelnut flour, 1¾-in. (4.5-cm) disks, fully baked	40 disks	40 disks
Fresh blackberries for garnish	as needed for garnish	
Edible flower petals	as needed for garnish	

1 Whip the cream and sugar to soft peaks. Keep chilled.

2 Warm the raspberry purée until it reaches 115°F (46°C). Stir it into the melted chocolate, then immediately fold in the whipped cream.

3 Pour the mixture into 1¾-inch (4.5-centimeter) silicone molds. Level the mousse with an offset spatula. Freeze until hard, then unmold the mousses onto the Shortbread Tart Dough disks.

4 Garnish with fresh blackberries, cut in half, and edible flower petals.

Approximate values per piece: **Calories** 130, **Total fat** 10 g, **Saturated fat** 6 g, **Cholesterol** 40 mg, **Sodium** 35 mg, **Total carbohydrates** 13 g, **Protein** 2 g

IRISH CREAM CRÈME BRÛLÉE

Yield: 40 Petits Fours, 1½ in. (4 cm) each   **Type:** Fresh petit four

Egg yolks	3.3 oz. (5 yolks)	100 g
Brown sugar	3 oz.	90 g
Heavy cream	1 pt.	480 ml
Milk chocolate, chopped fine	3 oz.	90 g
Sheet gelatin, softened	3 sheets (0.2 oz.)	6 g
Irish whiskey	1.5 fl. oz.	45 ml
Coffee extract	0.15 fl. oz. (1 tsp.)	5 ml
Vanilla extract	1 fl. oz.	30 ml
Shortbread Tart Dough (page 382), 1½-in. (4-cm) disks, fully baked	40 disks	40 disks
Chocolate-covered coffee beans	as needed for garnish	
Candied kumquat slices	as needed for garnish	

1. Combine the egg yolks and sugar in a large bowl. Whisk until smooth. Set aside.
2. Heat the cream and milk chocolate until it reaches 150°F (66°C) and whisk it into the yolk mixture.
3. Add the softened sheet gelatin to the cream mixture along with the whiskey, coffee extract and vanilla.
4. Place a silicone petit four mold on a sheet pan and divide the cream mixture evenly among the molds.
5. Pour water onto the sheet pan to create a water bath and bake at 325°F (160°C) until the custards have set, approximately 30 minutes. Let cool, then freeze until hard.
6. Unmold the frozen crème brûlée onto the Shortbread Tart Dough disks. Garnish each with a coffee bean and kumquat slice.

Approximate values per piece: **Calories** 160, **Total fat** 13 g, **Saturated fat** 7 g, **Cholesterol** 80 mg, **Sodium** 45 mg, **Total carbohydrates** 13 g, **Protein** 2 g

CARAMEL-DIPPED FRUITS

Yield: 30 Pieces | **Type:** Glazed fruit

Glucose or corn syrup	1 lb.	480 g
Fondant	12 oz.	360 g
Strawberries, kumquats, seedless grapes, orange segments or fresh figs	30	30

① Place the glucose syrup in a heavy saucepan over medium-high heat. Bring to a boil without stirring.

② Carefully add the fondant to the glucose syrup without stirring. Boil until the mixture reaches a golden caramel.

③ Remove from the heat. Immediately dip the bottom of the pot in a bowl of room-temperature water to stop the cooking process.

④ Using tongs, dip each piece of fruit in the caramel and place on a silicone baking mat or onto a lightly oiled sheet pan to harden.

Note: Decorating Caramel (page 727) used for dipped éclairs may be used to prepare these caramel-dipped fruits; however, caramel made with glucose or corn syrup and fondant is superior at resisting humidity.

Approximate values per piece: **Calories** 90, **Total fat** 0 g, **Saturated fat** 0 g, **Cholesterol** 0 mg, **Sodium** 25 mg, **Total carbohydrates** 23 g, **Protein** 0 g (Values vary depending on fruit selected.)

> ### SAFETY ALERT
> ### Caramelizing Sugar
>
> Caramelizing sugar can cause serious burns. Use a pair of cotton gloves covered by a pair of rubber gloves such as those used for industrial dishwashing to protect hands from coming into contact with spilled caramel. Take proper precautions to avoid hot sugar coming into direct contact with your skin.

Caramel-dipped kumquats.

Caramel-dipped strawberries.

Caramel-dipped grapes.

RASPBERRY PÂTE DE FRUIT

Pâte de fruit is a sugar candy made by gelling fruit purée. When prepared properly, the candy retains the bright color and flavor of the fruit from which is it made. Once the fruit gel sets, it is cut into squares and rolled in granulated sugar. Pâte de fruit can be made from many types of fruit; apricot, cranberry, currant, lemon and orange are popular flavors. These candies are often served as after dinner petits fours.

When preparing the candy mixture, it is important to monitor temperatures carefully and to work quickly. Once the citric acid has been added, the mixture will set very quickly. Once the candy has set, to prevent the sugar from weeping out, making the pâte de fruit sticky, allow the candies to sit out at room temperature loosely covered for at least 48 hours before wrapping them in plastic.

Yield: Approximately 4 lb. (1920 g), 10 dozen candies

Raspberry purée	1 lb. 10 oz.	780 g
Citric acid	0.3 oz.	8 g
Water	0.3 fl. oz.	8 ml
Granulated sugar	2 lb. 3 oz.	1050 g
Apple pectin	0.75 oz.	20 g
Glucose or corn syrup	9 oz.	270 g
Granulated sugar for coating	as needed	as needed

1. Position four candy rulers with their thinnest side down on a silicone baking mat or parchment paper to form an 11-inch (28-centimeter) square.
2. Heat the raspberry purée to 110°F (43°C).
3. Dissolve the citric acid in the water. Set aside.
4. Whisk together 3 ounces (90 grams) of the granulated sugar and the pectin in a small bowl. Add it to the heated purée. Bring the mixture to a boil.
5. Stir in the remaining 2 pounds (960 grams) of sugar and glucose syrup. Bring the mixture back to a boil and cook, stirring constantly with a heat-resistant spatula until the purée reaches 223°F (106°C) on a candy thermometer.
6. Remove from the heat and add the dissolved citric acid. Quickly pour the mixture between the candy rulers. Level with an oiled heat-resistant spatula to a thickness of ⅜ inch (1.3 centimeters) if necessary.
7. Allow the jelled fruit purée to cool and firm, then cut it into 1-inch (2.5-centimeter) squares. Dip each cut piece of candy into granulated sugar.
8. Place the sugar-coated candy squares on parchment paper–lined sheet pans. Cover the sheet trays with parchment paper. Let the trays sit at room temperature for 48 hours to firm before wrapping them.

Approximate values per candy: **Calories** 40, **Total fat** 0 g, **Saturated fat** 0 g, **Cholesterol** 0 mg, **Sodium** 0 mg, **Total carbohydrates** 11 g, **Protein** 0 g, **Claims**—fat free, sodium free, gluten free

MARSHMALLOWS

Yield: 1 Half-Sheet Pan; 4½ Dozen Squares, approximately 2 in. (5 cm) each

Egg whites	5 oz. (5 whites)	150 g
Granulated sugar	1 lb.	480 g
Glucose or corn syrup	4 oz.	120 g
Water	6 fl. oz.	180 ml
Sheet gelatin, softened	10 sheets (0.66 oz.)	20 g
Orange or lemon oil*	10 drops	10 drops
Powdered sugar	as needed	as needed
Cornstarch	as needed	as needed

1. Line a sheet pan with oiled parchment paper or a silicone baking mat. Place the egg whites in the bowl of a mixer fitted with the whip attachment.
2. Bring the sugar, glucose syrup and water to a boil in a heavy saucepan over medium-high heat. Once the mixture begins to boil, start to whip the egg whites on low speed.
3. While the eggs whip, cook the sugar syrup to 265°F (130°C).
4. As soon as the sugar syrup reaches 265°F (130°C), increase the mixer speed to medium-high. Pour the syrup over the whipping egg whites, holding the pan close to the inner wall of the bowl to avoid pouring syrup onto the whip.
5. As soon as all of the syrup has been added to the whipped egg whites, melt the gelatin and pour it into the whipped egg mixture, avoiding the whip attachment.
6. Remove the bowl from the mixer. Gently fold in the orange oil, using a whisk or spatula, without deflating the meringue. Spread the marshmallow in an even layer onto the prepared pan.
7. Let the marshmallow dry, uncovered, 24 hours at room temperature.
8. To portion the marshmallows, sift together equal amounts of powdered sugar and cornstarch. Sprinkle the surface of the marshmallow with half of the mixture. Invert the pan of marshmallow onto a clean sheet of parchment paper. Cut the marshmallow into 2-inch (5-centimeter) squares. Toss the cut pieces of marshmallow in the remaining sugar mixture.

*Orange or lemon compound can be used in place of the oil. Substitute ½ fluid ounce (15 milliliters) of compound for the oil in the formula.

Approximate values per ½-oz. (15-g) serving: **Calories** 35, **Total fat** 0 g, **Saturated fat** 0 g, **Cholesterol** 0 mg, **Sodium** 5 mg, **Total carbohydrates** 8 g, **Protein** 1 g, **Claims**—fat free

1. Adding sugar syrup to the egg whites.

2. Adding gelatin to the whipped egg whites.

3. Spreading the marshmallow into the pan.

CHAPTER NINETEEN

RESTAURANT AND PLATED DESSERTS

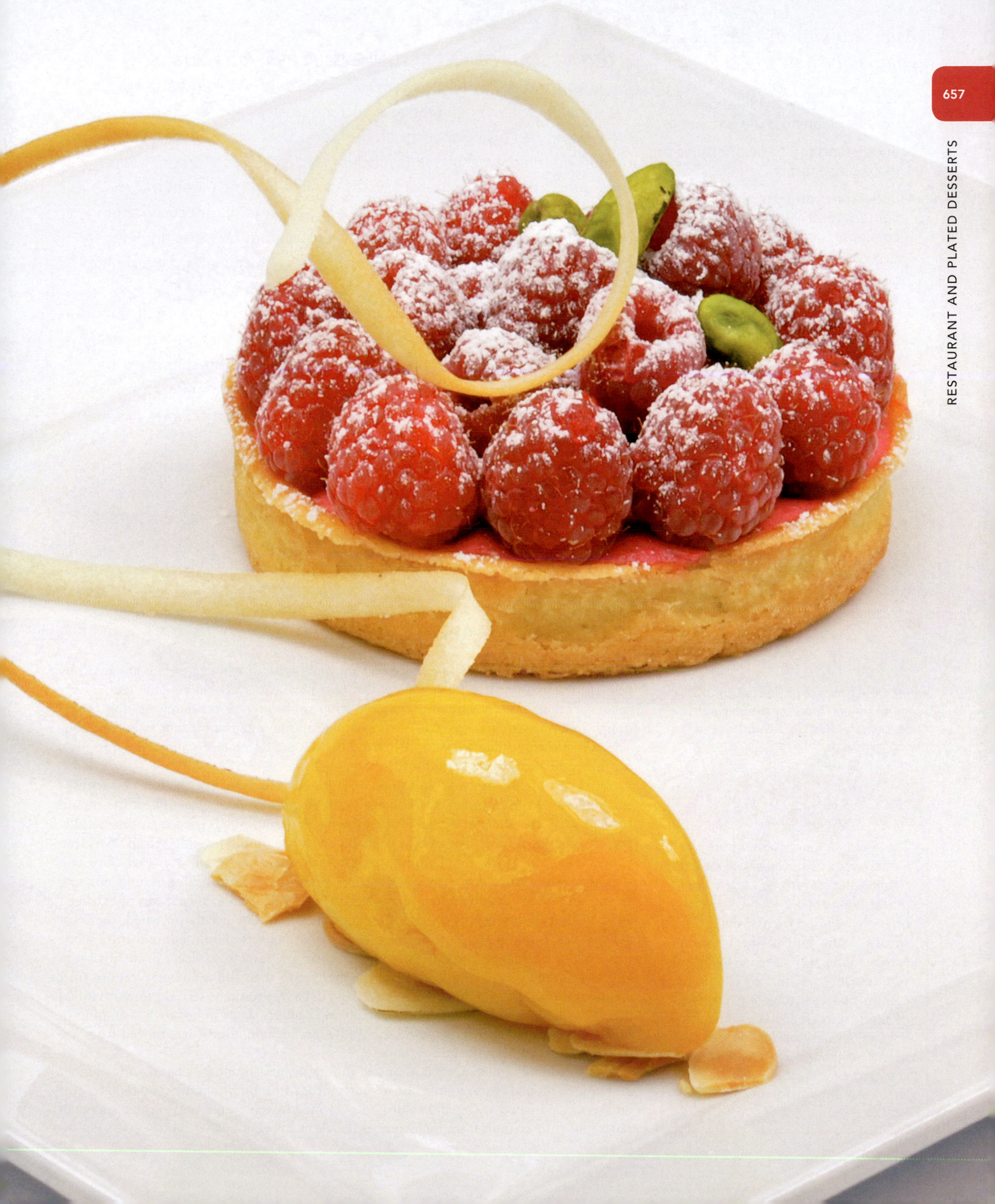

After studying this chapter, you will be able to:

- recognize key considerations that go into planning a dessert menu
- understand the basic principles of plate presentation
- understand and use contemporary flavor pairing concepts
- use a variety of techniques to add visual appeal to plated desserts

A GREAT SOURCE OF EXCITEMENT IN RESTAURANTS today is the interest in presenting desserts with the same care and attention to detail as the main meal. Desserts and the pastry chefs who create them are getting top billing along with the heretofore more prominent chefs de cuisine. Plated desserts may include several sweets on one plate presented in a manner that is visually stunning. A main item may be served hot accompanied by a contrasting cold garnish and something acidic or crunchy as a contrast. Today's restaurant desserts are a far cry from a humble slice of apple crisp and scoop of ice cream, although a well-crafted pie using ripe fruit in season cannot be beat.

Today's restaurant customer, whether in a fine dining establishment or a quick service bakery-café, expects great desserts that are attractively presented. This chapter looks at ways to create and present desserts appropriate for a number of restaurant settings. Elements from topics covered throughout this book are used to create exciting sweets suitable for ending any great meal.

Presentation techniques are divided into two broad categories: those applied to specific desserts and those applied to the plate as a whole. Many of the techniques discussed here are illustrated with desserts that appear elsewhere in this book.

THE RESTAURANT DESSERT

service the process of delivering foods to diners in the proper fashion, appropriately prepared and presented at the correct time

The most attractive desserts are those that are well prepared whose appeal is enhanced by proper presentation. In a retail bakery, this may mean carefully baking and icing a layer cake, spending time on piping decorative icing uniformly or accurately scaling cookie dough to ensure cookies baked to a consistent size. In a restaurant setting, all of the considerations surrounding **service**, delivering the dessert to the customer, come into play, for this is the moment of truth for the pastry chef.

Desserts must be properly portioned both for the economics of the business and for the pleasure of the customer. Iced cakes should be cut into neat slices. The knife should be held so as not to crush the cake when slicing. A clean knife is used each time a cake, pie, cheesecake or other dessert is portioned. The knife should be wiped clean on a clean paper towel after each cut. Dipping the knife in clean hot water after each slice and wiping it will ensure that a cheesecake slices smoothly. Lemon filling should not mar the meringue in a lemon meringue pie because the knife used to slice it was not cleaned after cutting the previous portion. The meringue should be evenly browned, the crust golden and in one piece. Portions of cakes and bar cookies should be uniformly sliced into crisp-edged pieces; each guest should receive the same size piece. Fruit-filled pies and tarts, when sliced, should arrive at the table with their filling intact; pieces of fruit should not tumble onto the serving plate. Cold desserts should be served properly chilled and on cold plates. Ice cream should be cold and hold its shape in its bowl; it should not be runny and melted. A hot soufflé should be served soon after it is removed from the oven and arrive hot at the guest's table.

Any decorative touches, such as sauces and garnishes, should be placed with thought and care. Whipped cream should be carefully piped. Most important, plates should be neat and spotless. Inspect each plate before it leaves the kitchen. Wipe fingerprints, specks of sauce and stray crumbs from their rims with a clean towel.

SWEET ENDINGS

The word *dessert* comes from the French word *deserver*, which means clearing the plates and cutlery from the table. At one time it was a course of fresh fruits and small delicacies served at the end of the meal. In France in the 18th century, the dessert course consisted of elaborate *pieces montées*, towering displays of fruits, nuts, marzipan and other confections designed to impress the guests. Although its meaning has changed over the centuries, dessert is still a moment for the chef and host to shine.

Creating a Basic Dessert Menu

Dessert menus are created to match the type of service, the theme of the operation, the desired price point, the labor available and any other needs expressed by the restaurant's management. A restaurant may offer a quick service menu, prepared by a small staff with limited time for assembling elaborate desserts. In such cases, the dessert menu could be as simple as a selection of cookies. Or, as in a diner, there may be a refrigerated case of assorted layer cakes and cheesecakes prominently displayed. Waiters serve from presliced cakes. In a full-service restaurant where guests spend more time at the table, the clientele demand more varied and complex dessert offerings. Although cheesecake may appear on the menu, it may be paired with a sauce or other complementary garnish.

The theme of the restaurant is reflected in the style of the food and the type of cuisine served. In an establishment offering the authentic cuisine of a specific country, the dessert menu should include items offered in that locale. A guest may expect to see flan on the menu in a Mexican restaurant, for example. In a casual French bistro, profiteroles with chocolate sauce simply presented, as illustrated in the top right photo, would be appropriate. In a fine dining restaurant that caters to well-traveled guests looking for something unusual, the same profiteroles may be presented in a stylish contemporary way, as pictured in the middle photograph to the right. If the theme of the restaurant is American market cuisine, where the chef sources foods locally in season, the pastry chef may be asked to create new menu items only using fruit in season. Rhubarb on the menu at a time other than spring, for example, would be inappropriate.

The selling price of a dessert is based on numerous factors—the cost of the ingredients used to make the dessert as well as the labor involved in its creation. It is the pastry chef's responsibility to design desserts that are appropriate for the operation. Most quick service restaurants offer desserts at modest cost. Take a hot dog stand, for example; with little labor in the kitchen, few would expect baked-to-order soufflés on the menu. Nor would many customers expect to pay for such a luxury in that setting. A dessert that includes several elements on the plate, including a hot garnish added at the last minute, will require more labor to serve than a simple dish of ice cream. Pastry chefs take direction from their superiors and restaurant management, who ultimately decide what is appropriate for the setting.

Classic presentation of ice-cream-filled profiteroles with chocolate sauce.

Modern presentation of profiterole pastries.

Creating New Items for a Dessert Menu

Pastry chefs often turn to their standard repertoire when looking for new ideas for desserts. Rarely is there enough time for new formulas to be developed for each dessert to be served. Instead, restaurant desserts are based on combining various preparations from the pastry kitchen to create specific dishes appropriate for the restaurant. By carefully changing the shape of many basic preparations and combining elements in different ways, as discussed in this book, new desserts can be created. Pastry chefs save time by using one formula to prepare a number of items. With a solid foundation in the core techniques covered in this book, the aspiring pastry chef can prepare a wide variety of baked goods, pastries and desserts.

SHAPING DESSERTS

By varying the shape and size of baking pans specified in a formula, the pastry chef may create a variety of presentations. Cakes and batters may be baked in diverse forms, adjusting the baking time according to the size and type of pan used. A shallow baking sheet or baking sheet with a pan extender will make one large flat cake. From this basic rectangle, many shapes of cake may be cut. The cake can be frosted and cut into individual square portions. The whole sheet cake can be divided into four rectangles, each to be filled and frosted to make four rectangular cakes. (See the cutting diagrams in Appendix IV.) Alternately, before frosting, the sheet cake may be cut into individual rounds using a biscuit cutter, filled, then frosted for individual cakes. (Cake trim is saved and ground to use to mask the sides of a cake.) Cakes as well as muffin batters may be baked in greased muffin tins or loaf pans normally used for breads. Imagine preparing the Orange Chiffon Cake (page 445) in individual muffin tins.

Individual Free-Form Apple Tart

Domed Cheesecake with Pineapple Skewer and Mango Sorbet

Peach and Blueberry Napoleon

Pie and tart doughs are extremely versatile. The same formula for Basic Pie Dough (page 366) or Shortbread Tart Dough (page 382) can be baked in any number of forms beyond the standard round pie pan. A whole apple or peach may be wrapped in pie dough and baked on a baking sheet. The dough can be rolled out and used to make a free-form pie, as shown on page 659. The size of the free-form pie can be small enough so that each serves one person or equivalent to a full-size pie that is then cut into wedges for serving. Pastry chefs often bake miniature pastries, using two or three on a sampler plate to complete one serving. Baked meringues, éclairs, fruit fritters, churros and beignets lend themselves to this type of presentation.

MOLDING CUSTARDS, MOUSSES AND CREAMS

Some preparations, particularly custards, mousses, creams, ice creams and sorbets, can be molded into attractive shapes by using small ramekins, silicone molds, ice cream scoops or ice cube containers. These mixtures are placed into the molds before they set so that, once ready for service, they take the shape of their container. The basic cheesecake mixture on page 498 takes on a new personality when baked in a domed mold as shown here.

CHANGING COMPONENTS

Changing the look of a traditional dessert is as simple as changing the type of crust used in a pie or tart. The classic French Napoleon is made from layers of baked puff pastry, as shown on page 303. Rectangles of shortbread tart dough or sheets of phyllo dough, as shown here, can be baked and assembled to make a customized napoleon-type pastry.

Choux paste and meringue shells can be formed and baked into tart shells. Shortcake is generally made with a type of biscuit that absorbs the juices from the fruit layered on it, as in the Shortcakes formula on page 152. But the pastry chef is not limited; various cakes could be sliced and used to make a type of layered fruit shortcake, including Lemon Tea Bread (page 163), Almond Genoise (page 477) or Coconut Macadamia Cake (page 620).

USING COMPONENTS IN DIFFERENT PREPARATIONS

Proper preparation of a quality dessert requires skill, attention to detail and the proper amount of time to complete the work. Pressed for time in a commercial bakeshop or restaurant kitchen, the pastry chef looks for ways to be efficient while maintaining quality. Using the same formulas in multiple preparations eases the work. Here are several examples of the ways in which two basic preparations—Classic Spongecake (page 442) and Raspberry Mousse (page 530)—can be used to create four different desserts. (The amount of each ingredient, the yield and the baking time will depend on the pans used. These procedures are guidelines only. See the formulas at the end of this chapter for additional ideas.)

RASPBERRY MOUSSE BARS

Classic Spongecake (page 442)
Raspberry Mousse (page 530)

1. Bake the spongecake batter in a half-sheet pan, adjusting the time according to the size of the pan selected.
2. Place the cake in a clean sheet pan fitted with a pan extender. Fill with Raspberry Mousse. Cut into bars for service.

CHOCOLATE RASPBERRY TORTE

Classic Spongecake (page 442)
Simple Syrup (page 73)
Lemon extract
Raspberry Mousse (page 530)
Chocolate Ganache, warm (page 458)
Toasted coconut

1. Bake the spongecake batter in 8-inch (20-centimeter) round pans.
2. Slice the cooled cakes into three layers each. Moisten the sponge with Simple Syrup flavored with lemon extract.
3. Fill alternating layers of the cake with Raspberry Mousse.
4. Coat the cakes with a thin layer of melted Chocolate Ganache. Mask the sides of the cake with toasted coconut.

FRESH RASPBERRY TARTLETS

Shortbread Tart Dough (page 382)
Raspberry Mousse (page 530)
Fresh raspberries
Neutral glaze

1. Make individual tarts with the Shortbread Tart Dough. Bake blind.
2. When cool, fill the shells with Raspberry Mousse and top with fresh raspberries. Coat with neutral glaze.

RASPBERRY CHARLOTTE

Classic Spongecake (page 442)
Apricot jam
Raspberry Mousse (page 530)
Neutral glaze

1. Bake the spongecake batter in a half-sheet pan. Spread the cake with apricot jam and roll tightly as for a jelly roll. Cut the cake into ½-inch- (1.2-centimeter-) thick slices and line the bottom and sides of an 8-inch (20-centimeter) cake pan or mold with the slices of cake.
2. Fill the cake-lined pan with Raspberry Mousse. Let the mousse set until firm. Chill, then unmold. Coat the surface of the Charlotte with neutral glaze.

THE PLATE

While great care is taken creating a dessert, equal care must be taken in presenting it to the customer. **Presentation** is the process of offering the selected foods to diners in a manner that is visually pleasing. When presenting foods, always bear in mind that diners consume first with their eyes and then with their mouths. The colors, textures and shapes on the plate should work together to form a harmonious balance.

Desserts that combine several components and are presented in a manner similar to that of the main meal are called **plated desserts**. The way in which a dessert is placed on a plate is part of the appeal of a plated dessert. The **composition** of the plate should be balanced and harmonious. The main dessert item, the way it is shaped, the items that accompany the dessert and the plate on which it is placed all contribute to the diner's perception of its quality.

Choosing Plates

Restaurant china designed to withstand the rigors of repeated use is available in many shapes, colors and styles. It is often the chef's responsibility to select the china appropriate for the food being served. Frequently, specific plates will be used for specific dishes, such as a tulip sundae glass for an ice cream dish.

SIZE AND SHAPE

Most plates are round, but oval, rectangular, square and triangular plates are now more common. Plates are available in a variety of sizes, from a small 4-inch (10-centimeter) bread plate to a huge 14-inch (35-centimeter) charger or base plate. Plates are typically concave; their depths may vary within a limited range of about 1 inch (2.5 centimeters). Most plates have rims; rim diameters also vary. Soup bowls can be rimmed or rimless. Soup plates are usually larger and shallower than soup bowls and have wide rims. There are also dozens of plates and bowls intended for a specific purpose, such as tall, narrow glasses for ice cream parfaits.

Choose plates large enough to hold the food comfortably without overcrowding or spilling. Oversized, rimmed soup plates are popular for serving ice creams and sorbets or other moist desserts with a sauce. Be careful when using oversized plates, however, as the food may look sparse, creating poor value perception.

Whether the plates are round, oval or less conventionally shaped, be sure to choose one with a size and shape that best highlights the food and supports the composition. For example, in the photograph at left, the rectangular dish with round corners and raised rim accentuates the geometrically simple yet effective composition of the square date bar and spherical scoop of ice cream.

COLORS AND PATTERNS

White and cream are by far the most common colors for restaurant china; almost any food looks good on these neutral colors. Colored and patterned plates can be used quite effectively to accent food, however. The obvious choice is to contrast dark plates with bright- or light-colored foods and light plates with dark-colored foods. The food should always be the focal point of any plate. The colors and shapes in the pattern should blend well and harmonize with the foods served. The zesty parallel lines on the square plate to the left are an artful counterpoint to the textured churros pastries and bowl of dark sauce.

THE COMPOSITION

Plates should be composed to make the dessert appetizing to the customer. Strive for a well-balanced composition, which can be achieved with careful consideration of the shape, size, colors, textures and arrangement of foods on the plate.

composition a completed plate's structure of colors, shapes and arrangements

Chewy Date Bars with Caramel Ice Cream

Churros with Chocolate Sauce

Shapes

For visual interest or pure drama, combine a variety of shapes on the plate when composing a plated dessert. It is exciting to the eye and can make a bold statement. The diamond shape of the Tulipe Cookie perched on top of a triangular wedge of sorbet in the photograph to the right is a bold geometric statement, crisp modern lines that match the snap of the cookie and the bright flavor of the mango sorbet. Adding some height is amusing and can be an effective addition when plating a pastry. Attention should be paid to how the guest will eat the dessert, however. Some creations may be too complicated for the guest to eat comfortably.

Colors

Foods come in a rainbow of colors and to the extent appropriate, foods of different colors should be presented together. Generally, the colors should provide balance and contrast. But no matter how well prepared or planned, some desserts simply have dull and boring colors. If so, try adding another ingredient or garnish for a splash of color.

Textures

Pastry chefs strive to include a variety of textures in their desserts. *Texture* refers to the sensation perceived when eating the product as well as the appearance of the surface of the food. It may be crisp, crumbly, grainy, flaky, smooth or creamy. Many historically popular pastries, such as a well-made éclair, offer a wonderful balance between crisp pastry and creamy filling. The preparations included on a plated dessert should offer a harmonious balance of textures. The trio of chocolate desserts shown to the right offer a similar flavor palate made more interesting by the striking textural contrasts on this sparse, elegant plate. From the right, a fragile wafer cookie contrasts with the cold ice cream, a brittle chocolate box holds a light fluid custard and a gooey cake is coated with a melting chocolate essence.

The pages of this book are filled with formulas for toppings, cookies, and garnishes that can add a pleasing textural contrast to a plated dessert. Among them are the following:

- ▶ Basic Nougatine (page 724)
- ▶ Candied Almonds (page 604)
- ▶ Caramel-Dipped Fruits (page 653)
- ▶ Candied Citrus Peel (page 671)
- ▶ Chocolate Meringue Sticks (page 619)
- ▶ Hazelnut Crisps (page 748)
- ▶ Isomalt Lace (page 729)
- ▶ Marshmallows (page 655)
- ▶ Palmiers (page 302)
- ▶ Peanut Brittle (page 749)
- ▶ Puff Pastry (page 280), dusted with coarse sugar, cut in strips and baked

At the end of this chapter are additional formulas for some useful garnishes.

Flavor

Use judgment in combining elements on the dessert plate so that the flavors of the components will harmonize on the palate. For best results, limit the number of different flavorings in an individual preparation; too many different tastes confuse the palate and muddy flavors. Flavors may be **complementary** or **contrasting**. Complementary flavors are those that are similar to the other flavors in a dish. Chocolate and cocoa are complementary flavors, different variations of the same flavor. Consider layering flavors in a dish by combining similar flavors of different intensities, variations on a theme, such as in the trio of chocolate desserts shown above.

Contrasting flavors are those that are very different, such as sweet and sour, sweet and bitter or fat and acid. Chocolate Mousse, shown to the right, is a perfect example of the contrast between the tartness of the raspberries, the bitter base notes of the chocolate and the sweetness of the mousse made with whipped cream.

Mango Sorbet

A trio of miniature chocolate desserts offers complementary tastes and contrasting textures on one plate.

Chocolate Mousse in a Glass

TABLE 19.1 CLASSIC FLAVOR COMBINATIONS

DOMINANT FLAVOR	FORMS	COMPLEMENTS
Chocolate	Bittersweet or dark	Caramel, coffee, cinnamon, orange
		Fresh berry flavors, particularly those with some acidity: cherry, strawberry, raspberry
		Mint, spearmint or peppermint; basil, rosemary
		Fruit liqueurs or rum
		Dried fruit
		Coconut
	Milk chocolate	Toasted nuts, caramel
	Cocoa	Espresso, vanilla, whiskey
Spices	Allspice	Pears, apples, tree fruit
	Anise or licorice	Almonds and sweet cream
	Cinnamon	Chocolate, apples, pears, caramel
	Ginger	Most fruit and berries, especially apricot, peach, pear and lemon
Herbs	Peppermint	Chocolate, sweet cream
	Spearmint	Chocolate, cherries, strawberries, peaches, melon
Citrus (lemon, lime, mandarin, orange)	Juice	Almonds and almond flavor
		Cream and cream cheese
		Other citrus, honey
		Mint
	Zest	Buttery flavors, pastry, custard, chocolate
		Sweet or tart creamy products, sour cream, cream cheese
Caramel		Most spices, toasted nuts, chocolate
		Sweet or tart creamy products
		Bananas, apples, pears
Nuts	Raw	Fruits and berries
		Sweet or tart creams
		Citrus juice or rind
	Toasted	Buttery pastry, caramel, chocolate, coffee

Blueberry Pie, Vanilla Ice Cream, and fresh blueberries.

Classic flavor combinations are illustrated throughout this book; cinnamon in apple pie and chocolate with mint are two common examples. Table 19.1 lists some other companion flavors. Table 19.2 list examples of plated desserts using some of these flavor combinations. Taste is to a large extent a personal preference. These combinations are time-tested based on the experience of pastry chefs and confectioners. Experimentation will lead to new taste combinations; consider these tables a beginning point.

TEMPERATURE

Closely related to the flavor of food is the temperature at which it is served. Warm foods have a more intense flavor than cold foods. The diner will perceive the aroma of a warm dish before it is tasted. Hot and cold foods served together on a dessert plate please the palate. No wonder that a warm slice of fruit pie with ice cream never goes out of style.

TABLE 19.2 DESSERTS PLATING CONCEPTS USING CLASSIC FLAVOR COMBINATIONS

DOMINANT FLAVOR	COMPLEMENTARY FLAVORS	PLATED DESSERT
Bittersweet chocolate	Cinnamon, rum, coconut	Rum-flavored chocolate mousse garnished with cinnamon Chantilly cream and toasted coconut
Milk chocolate	Toasted hazelnuts, caramel	Milk chocolate hazelnut pie garnished with Chantilly cream, caramel sauce and chocolate shavings
Spices	Allspice, ginger, apples	Warm ginger apple spice cake served with vanilla bean ice cream and custard sauce
Herbs	Spearmint, cherries, melon	Mint, watermelon and cherry salad served with cherry sorbet
Citrus (orange)	Orange, almond, cream, honey	Orange honey mousse garnished with toasted almonds, served with cuccidati cookies
Citrus (lemon)	Cream cheese, lemon rind	Lemon tea bread muffins served with lemon cream cheese spread and lemon curd
Caramel	Chocolate, bananas	Bananas Foster with cocoa nib–spiked chocolate ice cream and chocolate crumble garnish
Nuts	Cream, coffee	Warm walnut fudge brownie, coffee ice cream

Arranging Desserts on the Plate

Having decided on the color, texture and shapes of the foods that will go on the plate, next the pastry chef must decide where to place each individual item to achieve a balanced and unified composition. Mostly this takes judgment and style, but there are a few general guidelines.

GUIDELINES FOR ARRANGING FOODS ON A PLATE

▶ Strike a balance between overcrowding the plate and leaving large gaps of space. Foods should not touch the plate rim nor necessarily be confined in the very center.

▶ Choose a **focal point** for the plate—that is, the point to which the eye is drawn. This is usually the highest point on the plate. Avoid placing foods of equal heights around the edge of the plate, leaving a hole in the center—the eye will naturally be drawn to that gap.

▶ The plate's composition should flow naturally. For example, make the highest point the back of the plate and have the rest of the food become gradually shorter toward the front of the plate. Slicing and fanning fruits or scattering the plate with berries can bring the eye down and help establish flow.

Pears Poached in Red Wine

FIGURE 19.1 ▶ Main elements in a plated dessert might be (from left): molded panna cotta, an individual dome of chocolate mousse, blackberry crisp in a white ramekin, crème brûlée baked in a square mold, cheesecake batter baked in a heart shape, a slice of Empress Torte, and orange chocolate mousse prepared in a domed mold.

FIGURE 19.2 ▶ Textural garnishes for a plated dessert might include (from left): teardrop-shaped meringue cookies, shortbread tart dough squares, brownies, curled nougatine, oatmeal and coconut macaroon cookies, round shortbreads, cuccidati cookies, large sugar cookies.

Composing a Plated Dessert

There is no single thought process that goes into composing a plated dessert. Most chefs follow a few specific steps. It's common to start with the main feature on the plate, whether it is a slice of cake or pie, an individual tart or a molded mousse. Fussing unnecessarily over a plate is not recommended. Something as simple as the Succès pastry (page 426) or an individual fruit tart may need nothing more than a spoonful of fruit coulis to complete its presentation. But when the menu dictates, adding the proper accompaniments transforms it into a pleasing composition. The single poached pear in the photo on page 665, for example, would not be much of a dessert on its own. When combined with complementary components such as sauce, fresh berries, delicate herbs and a crunchy French macaron, it becomes a satisfying whole.

The steps of composing a more complex dessert plate, Orange Milk Chocolate Mousse with Kumquat Sauce, are shown in Figures 19.1 through 19.4. First the dessert is chosen from several different preparations, as shown in Figure 19.1. The size, color and shape of the dessert helps determine what type of plate to use. A modern-style square white plate has been selected for presenting the orange chocolate mousse. Its sloping rim, which suggests a picture frame, accents foods placed within but not touching the edge. For textural contrast, the mousse is placed on a piece of baked chocolate tart dough.

Next, consideration is given to the entire finished plate. With the smooth texture of the main element, a chocolate mousse, more contrasting texture is desired. There are a number of options, as shown in Figure 19.2. What is chosen will affect the design of the plate as well as the flavor experience for the guest eating it. The meringues would add texture, but their whiteness is undesirable on the stark white plate. The brownie, the large oatmeal cookies and the round sugar cookies are too rustic for what will become a more refined presentation. Nougatine is selected because its curved shape adds an interesting visual element. The nougatine itself adds a subtle toasted nut flavor and the desired texture without being overly sweet.

With a basic element positioned on one quadrant of the square plate, there is a great deal of open space remaining. Other elements are added to contribute to the design while layering more complementary flavors on the plate. A chocolate caramel sauce

FIGURE 19.3 ▶ Sauces, fruits and nut garnishes might include (from left): chopped nuts, fresh berries, caramelized peach slices, mango coulis, raspberry sauce, chocolate caramel sauce.

FIGURE 19.4 ▶ Additional plated dessert garnishes might include (from left): fresh organic rose petals, pistachios, dried melon and mango slices, chocolate, thin nougatine, sprigs of fresh herbs.

pooled in the recesses in the molded mousse adds a visual pop to the design. The dark chocolate in the sauce contrasts nicely with the milk chocolate mousse. Either the raspberry sauce or mango coulis pictured in Figure 19.3 could be used, but their flavor would not complement the delicate mousse. Adding a temperature contrast is also appealing. Even though the caramelized peach slices would compliment the plate design and offer the sensation of heat to the plate, a warm kumquat sauce is chosen to echo the citrus note in the chocolate mousse.

The plate now has color, texture and temperature contrasts. And a few additional elements are considered. Orange sorbet is chosen to add another note to the flavor experience—the chill of the frozen garnish and another citrus variation. Some baked streusel crumbled underneath the square of sorbet has a practical application; it keeps the sorbet from sliding on the plate when being served. It also adds another textural element. Then there are a few last touches, shown in Figure 19.4. A slice of dried orange, a fourth citrus element, is chosen and placed in the mousse at a jaunty angle, completing the composition.

PERENNIAL FAVORITES

Year in, year out, certain combinations top the lists of dessert favorites. Pastry chefs and restaurant consultants agree that these dessert flavor profiles are always popular. Build your dessert menu with an offering from each category.

- Fruit desserts from the humble pie to a berry-topped tart appeal to a wide range of consumers. Layer berries or sliced stone fruits in a glass with Chantilly and sorbet and serve with crisp tuile cookies for a contemporary dessert.

- Cheesecake continues to wow customers. It can be a traditional wedge or a lighter version made in an individual mold. Blend in a small amount of locally made farmer's cheese to give it an artisan flavor.

- Lemon desserts such as lemon meringue and Key lime pie, lemon mousse or lemon cake strike the right note. For a refreshing twist, use such exotic citrus as blood oranges or yuzu in a sorbet, curd or sauce.

- Caramel flavors, whether in the form of a hot fudge sundae with hot caramel sauce or a wedge of cake with caramel icing, appear on top restaurant dessert lists. Caramel pairs well with toasted nuts, creams and cheesecakes.

- No dessert menu would be complete without chocolate. Cake, cookies, ice cream, mousses, tarts—there's always room for chocolate.

Slicing strawberry fans to use as a plate garnish.

Organic rose petals coated with sugar.

Forming grapefruit sorbet into a quenelle shape.

Plate Garnishes

Nothing adds more polish to a plated dessert than a bit of plate decorating and garnish. The colors, textures, shapes and arrangements of foods on a plate can be improved or highlighted by decorating a plate with candied fruit, herbs, spices and other garnishes and sauce. If any of these are to be applied after the food is plated, plan to do so quickly so that the dessert is at the proper temperature when it reaches the table.

GARNISHING DESSERTS WITH HERBS AND EDIBLE FLOWERS

Using a sprig of fresh mint, other mild herb, or a fresh flower is one easy way to add color and flow to the design of a dessert plate. Whether the herb is an ingredient in the dish or merely a decoration, it should always complement the dessert and be consistent with the flavorings on the plate. Sprigs of fresh green mint (often with a fresh berry or two or a strawberry cut into a fan) are often the perfect decoration for a dessert plate.

Organic petals of edible flowers such as pansies or roses, pictured here, can be brushed lightly with pasteurized egg white, then dipped in fine granulated sugar to be used as a delicate plate garnish.

FORMING ICE CREAM AND SORBETS FOR GARNISH

Using different-shaped scoops or even two soup spoons helps create attractively molded ice cream or sorbet to garnish plated desserts.

DECORATING PLATES WITH SAUCES

Sauce is an integral part of many deserts. It adds flavor and moisture; it also adds color, texture and flow to the plate. One or more colored sauces can also be used to paint plates. One technique is simply to drizzle or splatter the sauce onto the plate. Alternatively, one or more colored sauces can be applied to a plate using squirt bottles to create abstract patterns or representational designs. Painting the plates with colored sauces also facilitates the visual flow of the design and adds color. This technique is used with cold sauces such as vanilla, caramel, chocolate and fruit-flavored sauces. The sauces must be thick enough to hold the pattern once it is created, and they should be the same viscosity. A thick chocolate sauce can be used to outline a shape on the dessert plate, and then a lighter custard sauce or fruit coulis can be piped inside. The chocolate holds the sauce in place.

PROCEDURE FOR PAINTING A SPIDER WEB DESIGN

❶ Pool one sauce evenly across the entire base of the plate, then apply a contrasting sauce onto the base sauce in a spiral.

❷ Draw a thin-bladed knife or a toothpick through the sauce from the center point toward the edge. Then, leaving a ½-inch (1.2-centimeter) space along the edge, draw a knife blade or toothpick from the edge to the center.

Other patterns can be produced by squirting the sauces onto the plate in different patterns or by pulling a knife tip or toothpick through the sauce in different directions. As shown below, a circle of chocolate and raspberry-sauce dots in a pool of vanilla sauce is pulled to create a border of hearts.

Spoons, spatulas and other simple kitchen tools help when applying sauces, as shown in the following examples.

Painting mango coulis on a plate with a pastry brush.

Applying teardrop shapes of fruit coulis with a soup spoon.

Running a rubber spatula through a line of fruit coulis to create a shadow effect.

DRIED FRUIT SLICES

Dried fruit slices make colorful, elegant or whimsical garnishes for simple or complex presentations. A single slice of dried strawberry can add a spot of color to a dollop of whipped cream. Overlapping slices of dried strawberry used on the fruit trifle shown at right create an airy feeling in the design. Dried fruit slices can also serve a functional purpose on a plated dessert; placing a fruit slice underneath a quenelle of ice cream or sorbet helps keep it from sliding when the plate is served.

Dried fruit slices are prepared by slicing fruit as thin as possible, approximately $\frac{1}{16}$ inch (1 millimeter) thick. Either a mandoline or an electric meat slicer ensures uniform results. The slices are coated in sugar, then dried in the oven at a low temperature. Although parchment paper can be used to line the sheet pans on which the fruit is placed for drying, silicone mats are preferred. With silicone mats, there is little chance of having the fruit stick.

Because the texture and water content of fruit varies, no single method works for all types of fruit. Either powdered sugar, granulated sugar or sugar syrup is needed, depending on the fruit. Three methods and the fruits best suited for each method are outlined here. Follow the method recommended for the type of fruit being used. Although a variety of fruits can be prepared at one time, do not combine a variety of fruit slices on a single sheet pan. Drying slowly at a low temperature ensures that the fruit crisps up before it begins to darken or burn. Dried fruit slices can be kept for several days if stored in airtight containers at room temperature. Humidity will soften the fruit slices. Packets of desiccant used to keep cookies and candy crisp can be placed with the fruit slices to ensure that they retain a crisp texture.

Dried strawberry slices garnish a Reduced-Fat Strawberry Trifle.

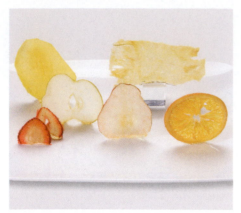

Assorted dried fruit slices (clockwise from left): strawberries, apple, mango, pineapple, orange and pear

METHOD I FOR PREPARING DRIED FRUIT SLICES

Mangoes, pineapple or strawberries	as needed	as needed
Powdered sugar	as needed	as needed

1 Stem, peel and pit the fruit as needed. Slice the fruit as thin as possible, keeping the fruit slices intact.

2 Dip the fruit slices on both sides in powdered sugar, shaking off any excess that clings to the fruit. Place the slices in a single layer on sheet pans lined with parchment paper or silicone baking mats. Fruit slices that overlap will stick together after drying, an effect that may be desirable.

3 Bake at 175°F (80°C) until the slices are uniformly crisp, approximately 90 to 180 minutes. Check the slices every 30 minutes to see that they are not drying out unevenly. If the fruit is browning too quickly, reduce the heat to 150°F (65°C). Rotate the pans occasionally to promote even drying.

METHOD II FOR PREPARING DRIED FRUIT SLICES

Citrus fruit such as lemons, limes, mandarins and oranges, seedless varieties recommended	as needed	as needed
Granulated sugar	as needed	as needed

1 Slice the fruit as thin as possible, keeping the fruit slices intact. Remove the seeds.

2 Dip the fruit slices on both sides in granulated sugar, shaking off any excess that clings to the fruit. Place the slices in a single layer on sheet pans lined with parchment paper or silicone baking mats. Fruit slices that overlap will stick together after drying, an effect that may be desirable.

3 Bake at 175°F (80°C) until the slices are uniformly crisp, approximately 90 to 180 minutes. Check the slices every 30 minutes to see that they are not drying out unevenly. If the fruit is browning too quickly, reduce the heat to 150°F (65°C). Rotate the pans occasionally to promote even drying.

METHOD III FOR PREPARING DRIED FRUIT SLICES

Granulated sugar	4 oz.	120 g
Water	8 fl. oz.	240 ml
Apples, carrots or pears	as needed	as needed

1 Bring the sugar and water to a boil in a small saucepan. Reduce the heat to a very low simmer.

2 Stem and peel the fruit as needed. Slice the fruit as thin as possible, keeping the fruit slices intact. (Carrots may be sliced using a vegetable peeler.) Remove the seeds.

3 Simmer the fruit slices in batches in the sugar syrup until slightly tender, approximately 2 to 3 minutes for the apple or pear slices and 8 to 10 minutes for the carrot slices. Remove the slices from the syrup, draining any excess syrup that clings to the slices. Place them in a single layer on sheet pans lined with parchment paper or silicone baking mats. Fruit slices that overlap will stick together after drying, an effect that may be desirable.

4 Bake at 175°F (80°C) until the slices are uniformly crisp, approximately 90 to 180 minutes. Check the slices every 30 minutes to see that they are not drying out unevenly. If the fruit is browning too quickly, reduce the heat to 150°F (65°C). Rotate the pans occasionally to promote even drying.

CANDIED CITRUS PEEL

Citrus peel is a delicious ingredient in or garnish for many pastries and plated desserts. Oranges, lemons, grapefruits or tangerines may be used. Organic produce is recommended.

Yield: 50–100 Candied Strips

Citrus fruit	5–10 fruits	5–10 fruits
Water	1 qt.	1 lt
Salt	0.1 oz. (½ tsp.)	3 g
Granulated sugar	1 lb.	480 g
Glucose or corn syrup	7 oz.	210 g

1. Wash the fruits. With a sharp knife, cut large, thin pieces of the peel from the citrus fruits. Remove as much of the white pith from the peel as possible.
2. Cut the peel into long, thin strips, approximately ¼ inch (6 millimeters) wide.
3. Bring 1 pint (480 milliliters) of the water and the salt to boil in a saucepan large enough to hold the citrus peel. Add the peel and simmer 2 minutes. Drain.
4. Bring the remaining 1 pint (480 milliliters) of water, the sugar and glucose syrup to a boil. Add the blanched citrus peel and reduce the heat to a low simmer. Cook the peels approximately 15 to 20 minutes, until they are translucent and tender. Store the peels in the syrup in the refrigerator. Or drain the peels on a screen until cool. Sprinkle the drained peels with granulated sugar and store in an airtight container.

Approximate values per piece: **Calories** 35, **Total fat** 0 g, **Saturated fat** 0 g, **Cholesterol** 0 mg, **Sodium** 20 mg, **Total carbohydrates** 9 g, **Protein** 0 g

Drained Orange Peel

Orange Peel Dipped in Sugar

Toasted coconut curls garnishing a rum baba.

TOASTED COCONUT CURLS

These coconut curls can be seen on the Banana Cream Pie (page 374) and on the Rum Babas with Crème Chantilly pictured here.

Yield: 40–50 Curls

Coconut, 5 in. (13 cm), shelled	1 half	1 half

1. Using a vegetable peeler, cut slices from the coconut, keeping some of the brown skin intact. Place the slices of coconut on a parchment-lined sheet pan. Bake at 375°F (190°C) until the slices are crisp and light golden brown, approximately 12 to 15 minutes.

Approximate values per ½-oz. (15-g) serving: **Calories** 45, **Total fat** 5 g, **Saturated fat** 5 g, **Cholesterol** 0 mg, **Sodium** 0 mg, **Total carbohydrates** 5 g, **Protein** 0 g

QUESTIONS FOR DISCUSSION

Terms to Know

presentation	complementary
plated desserts	contrasting
composition	focal point

1. Discuss the factors pastry chefs must consider when creating a dessert menu for a full-service restaurant.

2. Select a basic formula from any of the preceding chapters in this book. Using that one formula, create three different plated dessert presentations.

3. List and describe three different concepts for plating a cut portion of dessert.

4. Select three plates of different sizes, shapes and colors. Plate a portion of a fruit pie or a slice of cake on each plate, with appropriate garnishes, adjusting the plate presentation as needed. Discuss the considerations for each plate.

5. Discuss the impact that the size of kitchen staff has on serving plated desserts. Discuss which components are best suited to including on a dessert plate when kitchen staff is limited.

6. Describe various ways a sauce may be used to decorate a plated dessert.

PROFITEROLES THE MODERN WAY

Yield: 6 Servings

Éclair Paste (page 408)	12 oz.	360 g
Shortbread Tart Dough (page 382), made with hazelnut flour	7 oz.	210 g
Pistachio Ice Cream (page 554) or pastry cream	1 qt.	1 lt
Chocolate Caramel Sauce (page 538)	12 oz.	360 g
Chocolate rings (page 703)	18 rings	18 rings
Edible gold leaf (optional)	as needed for garnish	
Mango Coulis (page 512)	6 oz.	120 g
Fresh blackberries	as needed for garnish	

1. Line two sheet pans with parchment paper. Using a pastry bag with a large plain tip, pipe the Éclair Paste into 30 small circles approximately 1 inch (2.5 centimeters) in diameter. Bake at 350°F (180°C) until golden brown and dried through, approximately 20 to 25 minutes. Let cool.

2. Line up five profiteroles in a row and measure the length and the width of the composition. Roll the Shortbread Tart Dough ⅛ inch (3 millimeters) thick and cut out rectangles of dough that measure the length and width of the cream puff composition.

3. Bake the dough on paper-lined sheet pans at 375°F (190°C) until golden brown, approximately 14 to 16 minutes. Set aside.

4. Using the point of a paring knife, poke a small round opening in the bottom of each profiterole. Fit a pastry bag with a medium plain tip. Fill it with the freshly churned Pistachio Ice Cream or cold pastry cream and quickly pipe the filling into each profiterole. (Wear cotton gloves to prevent the ice cream from melting if necessary.) Freeze the filled profiteroles until ready to serve.

5. For each serving, position five filled profiteroles on a piece of the baked tart dough on a serving plate. Cover with the Chocolate Caramel Sauce. Place three chocolate rings on the composition and decorate with edible gold leaf (if using).

6. Pour Mango Coulis on each plate. Using a rubber spatula, create a design in the sauce. Scatter each plate with fresh blackberries before serving.

Approximate values per serving: **Calories** 920, **Total fat** 60 g, **Saturated fat** 25 g, **Cholesterol** 300 mg, **Sodium** 330 mg, **Total carbohydrates** 89 g, **Protein** 16 g, **Vitamin A** 45%, **Calcium** 20%

WARM CANDIED ORANGE BROWNIE WITH ORANGE MARSHMALLOW AND MANDARIN SORBET

Yield: 24 Servings

Candied Orange Peel (page 671), diced	6 oz.	180 g
Fudge Brownie batter (page 321)	7 lb. 3 oz.	3466 g
Marshmallow (page 655), made with orange oil, cut into 2-in. (5-cm) squares	24 squares	24 squares
Mandarin sorbet (page 557)	2 qt.	2 lt.
Dried orange slices (page 670)	24 slices	24 slices
Chocolate rings (page 703)	24 rings	24 rings

1 Fold the diced Candied Orange Peel into the Fudge Brownie batter. Pan and bake the brownies according to the formula on page 321.

2 Freeze the baked brownies until firm. Remove the brownies from the pan and cut them into 3-inch × 3¼-inch (7.5-centimeter × 8.3-centimeter) bars. Refrigerate the brownies until ready to serve.

3 For each serving, place a brownie square on a microwavable serving plate. Heat until the brownie is warmed through. Place a marshmallow square on top of the brownie and a quenelle of Mandarin Sorbet on top. Decorate with a dried orange slice and a chocolate ring. Serve immediately.

Approximate values per serving: **Calories** 870, **Total fat** 37 g, **Saturated fat** 18 g, **Cholesterol** 130 mg, **Sodium** 65 mg, **Total carbohydrates** 129 g, **Protein** 10 g, **Vitamin C** 25%

LEMON CURD MERINGUE TARTS WITH MANGO COULIS

Yield: 12 Tarts, 2½ in. (7.5 cm) each

Mango purée	1 lb. 4 oz.	600 g
Granulated sugar	5 oz.	150 g
Common (French) Meringue (page 410), 2½-in. (7.5-cm) shells, fully baked	12 shells	12 shells
White chocolate, melted	as needed	as needed
Lemon Curd (page 493)	1 lb. 4 oz.	600 g
Fresh lychees	24	24
Neutral glaze	as needed	as needed
Fresh blackberries	36	36

1 Combine the mango purée and sugar in a blender and process until smooth. Strain if desired. Set aside.

2 Using a pastry brush, gently brush the interior of the meringue shells with white chocolate.

3 Using a pastry bag fitted with a medium plain piping tip, fill the meringue shell to the edge with Lemon Curd.

4 Place two lychees in the center of each tart. Using a pastry brush, glaze the lychees with neutral glaze.

5 Surround the lychees with blackberries. Dot the plate with some of the mango purée.

Approximate values per serving: **Calories** 520, **Total fat** 30 g, **Saturated fat** 18 g, **Cholesterol** 125 mg, **Sodium** 95 mg, **Total carbohydrates** 61 g, **Protein** 5 g, **Vitamin A** 20%, **Vitamin C** 20%

WHITE CHOCOLATE MOUSSE ON RHUBARB WITH STRAWBERRY ICE CREAM

Yield: 6 Servings

Warm Rhubarb in Orange Syrup (recipe follows)	20 oz.	600 g
Dried strawberry slices (page 670)	18	18
Strawberry Ice Cream (page 555)	as needed	as needed
White Chocolate Mousse (page 650) molded, frozen and cut into 5-in. × 1-in. (12.7-cm × 2.5-cm) bars	6	6
Baked Streusel for Crumble (page 389)	as needed	as needed
White chocolate rings (page 703)	as needed	as needed
Fresh raspberries and red and white currants	as needed for garnish	

1. To prepare each serving, place two pieces of Warm Rhubarb in Orange Syrup next to one another on each plate. While the rhubarb cools slightly, position three dried strawberry slices on each plate and top with a quenelle of Strawberry Ice Cream.

2. Position a bar of White Chocolate Mousse on top of the rhubarb stems. Sprinkle with Baked Streusel for Crumble. Decorate with a white chocolate ring and some of the fresh berries. Drizzle some of the sauce from the cooked rhubarb on each plate. Serve immediately.

Approximate values per serving: **Calories** 550, **Total fat** 35 g, **Saturated fat** 22 g, **Cholesterol** 125 mg, **Sodium** 95 mg, **Total carbohydrates** 52 g, **Protein** 5 g, **Vitamin A** 20%, **Vitamin C** 25%, **Calcium** 15%

WARM RHUBARB IN ORANGE SYRUP

Yield: 6 Servings, 20 oz. (600 g)

Granulated sugar	3 oz.	90 g
Rhubarb, cut into 12 5-in. (12.5-cm) pieces	12 oz.	360 g
Orange juice	3 fl. oz.	90 ml
Unsalted butter	1 oz.	30 g
Vanilla extract	0.5 fl. oz.	15 ml
Kirsch or orange liqueur	0.5 fl. oz.	15 ml

1. Stir the sugar in a large sauté pan placed over medium-high heat until it turns a light golden caramel color. Reduce the heat to low and add the rhubarb and orange juice. Heat the rhubarb until it just becomes tender, approximately 1 to 2 minutes. Turn it over and cook for another minute.

2. Swirl in the butter and add the vanilla and Kirsch.

Approximate values per 3-oz. (90-g) serving: **Calories** 120, **Total fat** 4 g, **Saturated fat** 2.5 g, **Cholesterol** 10 mg, **Sodium** 0 mg, **Total carbohydrates** 19 g, **Protein** 1 g, **Vitamin C** 15%

ORANGE MILK CHOCOLATE MOUSSE
WITH KUMQUAT SAUCE

This formula is used in the illustrations for composing a plated dessert on page 666.

Yield: 17 Servings

Orange Milk Chocolate Mousse (page 528)	3 lb. 5 oz.	1590 g
Chocolate Tart Dough (page 384)	24 oz.	720 g
Nougatine curls (page 724)	17 curls	17 curls
Kumquat Sauce (page 537)	10 oz.	300 g
Chocolate Caramel Sauce (page 538)	12 oz.	320 g
Baked Streusel for Crumble (page 389)	as needed	as needed
Orange Sorbet (page 557)	1.5 qt	1.5 lt
Dried orange slices (page 670)	17 slices	17 slices

1. Invert a 13-inch × 11-inch (33-centimeter × 28-centimeter) half-sphere silicone mold with the domes facing up onto a half-sheet pan. Fit the pan with a pan extender the size of the silicone mold.

2. Prepare the Orange Milk Chocolate Mousse. Spread the mousse evenly over the silicone-mold-lined pan. Freeze the mousse until set, at least 12 hours.

3. Invert the pan of mousse onto a clean sheet of parchment paper. Cut the frozen mousse into seventeen uniform bars with two indentations each. Cover and refrigerate the bars.

4. Roll the Chocolate Tart Dough ⅛ inch (3 millimeters) thick. Cut out rectangles of dough the same dimension as the portioned mousse bars. Bake the dough at 375°F (190°C) until crisp, approximately 12 to 14 minutes. Let cool.

5. To plate each serving, place a bar of Orange Milk Chocolate Mousse on top of a tart dough rectangle on a serving plate. Decorate with a nougatine curl. Garnish the plate with some of the Kumquat Sauce. Fill the recesses in the mousse with Chocolate Caramel Sauce.

6. Sprinkle a small area of the plate with the Baked Streusel for Crumble. Use a square scoop to portion some of the Orange Sorbet onto the streusel. Garnish the sorbet with a dried orange slice. Serve immediately.

Approximate values per serving: **Calories** 770, **Total fat** 46 g, **Saturated fat** 23 g, **Cholesterol** 185 mg, **Sodium** 150 mg, **Total carbohydrates** 85 g, **Protein** 10 g, **Vitamin A** 25%, **Iron** 15%

LEMON-LIME MOUSSE WITH BLACK CURRANT SORBET

Yield: 24 Servings

Lemon-Lime Mousse (page 530)	2 lb. 14 oz.	1380 g
Black Currant Sorbet (page 557)	2.5 qt.	2.5 lt
Dacquoise (page 424)	1 half sheet	1 half sheet
Lemon Lace Cookies (recipe follows)	24 cookies	24 cookies
Dried lemon slices (page 670)	24 slices	24 slices
Baked Streusel for Crumble (page 389)	1 lb.	480 g
Black Currant Coulis (page 512)	as needed	as needed

1. Line a half-sheet pan with plastic wrap. Oil and sugar the plastic wrap. Spread the Lemon-Lime Mousse evenly in the pan. Freeze the mousse until firm, at least 2 hours.

2. Invert the frozen mousse onto a clean sheet of parchment paper. Remove the pan and peel off the plastic wrap. Trim the edges and cut the mousse into 2½-inch (6-centimeter) squares. Refrigerate the mousse until ready to plate.

3. Chill a quarter-size sheet pan lined with plastic film in the freezer. Spread the Black Currant Sorbet into an 8-inch (20-centimeter) square on the chilled sheet pan. Freeze until hard.

4. Cut the frozen sorbet into 1-inch × 1½-inch (5-centimeter × 2.5-centimeter) portions. Freeze until ready to plate.

5. Trim the dacquoise into a 16¼-inch × 11-inch (41-centimeter × 27-centimeter) rectangle. Cut the dacquoise lengthwise into four 2¾-inch (7-centimeter) strips. Cut each strip into six pieces.

6. To plate each serving, place a square of mousse on top of a square of dacquoise. Garnish the mousse with a Lemon Lace Cookie and a dried lemon slice. Position on one side of the serving plate.

7. Sprinkle a small amount of Baked Streusel for Crumble on the plate. Place a square of sorbet on top of the streusel. Sauce the plate with Black Currant Coulis.

Approximate values per serving: **Calories** 440, **Total fat** 20 g, **Saturated fat** 11 g, **Cholesterol** 60 mg, **Sodium** 120 mg, **Total carbohydrates** 66 g, **Protein** 4 g, **Vitamin A** 15%

LEMON LACE COOKIES

Yield: 16 Cookies, approximately ⅔ oz. (20 g) each

Method: Wafer cookies

			Rice flour at 100%
Unsalted butter	1.5 oz.	45 g	86%
Lemon juice	2.5 fl. oz.	75 ml	143%
Lemon zest, grated	0.07 oz. (1 tsp.)	2 g	4%
Salt	0.03 oz. (⅛ tsp.)	1 g	2%
Powdered sugar	5 oz.	155 g	285%
Rice flour	1.75 oz.	55 g	100%
Total batter weight:	10.5 oz.	333 g	620%

1. Combine the butter, lemon juice, lemon zest and salt in a bowl. Place the bowl over a bain marie of hot water. Heat just until the butter is melted. Whisk in the powdered sugar and the flour.

2. Stencil or drop the batter onto paper- or silicone-lined sheet pans. Bake at 375°F (190°C) until light golden brown, approximately 6 to 8 minutes.

3. Cool the cookies before removing them from the sheet pans.

Approximate values per ½-oz. (15-g) serving: **Calories** 60, **Total fat** 2 g, **Saturated fat** 1 g, **Cholesterol** 5 mg, **Sodium** 10 mg, **Total carbohydrates** 10 g, **Protein** 0 g

DOMED CHEESECAKE WITH PINEAPPLE SKEWER AND MANGO SORBET

Yield: 2 Servings

Fresh pineapple, peeled	4 oz.	120 g
Lemongrass stalks, cut into 5-in. (13-cm) pieces, or bamboo skewers	2 pieces	2 pieces
Granulated sugar	1 oz.	30 g
Orange juice	2 fl. oz.	60 ml
Unsalted butter	0.3 oz. (2 tsp.)	10 g
Vanilla extract	0.15 fl. oz. (1 tsp.)	5 ml
Coconut liqueur (optional)	0.5 fl. oz.	15 ml
Cheesecake Domes (recipe follows)	2 domes	2 domes
Dried mango slices (page 670)	2 slices	2 slices
Fresh black currants	as needed for garnish	
Baked Streusel for Crumble (page 389)	as needed	as needed
Mango Sorbet (page 547)	as needed	as needed
Fresh blackberries, halved	as needed for garnish	

1. Cut the pineapple into ½-inch- (1.2-centimeter-) thick slices, then cut the slices into 1-inch (2.5-centimeter) squares. Thread three pieces of pineapple onto each piece of lemongrass. Set aside.
2. Stir the sugar in a sauté pan over high heat until it turns a light golden caramel color. Reduce the heat to low, then add the orange juice and the two pineapple skewers to the pan. Heat the pineapple skewers for 2 minutes. Turn them over and cook until the pineapple is warm, approximately 1 to 2 minutes. Swirl in the butter, vanilla and coconut liqueur (if using). Hold the pan in a warm place.
3. To serve, place one Cheesecake Dome on its coconut shortbread round on each serving plate. Decorate each dome with a dried mango slice and black currants.
4. Sprinkle a tablespoon of Baked Streusel for Crumble into a small oval shape on each plate and place a quenelle of Mango Sorbet on top of the streusel.
5. Place one pineapple skewer on each plate. Drizzle each plate with some of the caramel sauce in the pan. Add blackberries sliced in half and serve immediately.

Approximate values per serving: **Calories** 830, **Total fat** 51 g, **Saturated fat** 32 g, **Cholesterol** 220 mg, **Sodium** 350 mg, **Total carbohydrates** 87 g, **Protein** 11 g, **Vitamin A** 60%, **Vitamin C** 60%, **Iron** 15%

CHEESECAKE DOMES

Yield: 20 Pastries

New York Cheesecake batter (page 498)	3 lb.	1440 g
Coconut Shortbread Tart Dough (page 382)	1 lb. 8 oz.	720 g

1. Prepare the New York Cheesecake batter and pour it into 4-ounce (120-gram) domed silicone molds measuring 3⅛ inches (8 centimeters) wide. Bake, let the cheesecakes cool, then refrigerate overnight. (The cheesecakes may be kept frozen.)
2. Roll the Coconut Shortbread Tart Dough ⅛ inch (3 millimeters) thick and cut out 3-inch (7.5-centimeter) rounds from the dough. Bake on paper-lined sheet pans at 375°F (190°C) until golden brown, approximately 14 to 16 minutes. Set aside until cool.
3. Unmold each cheesecake dome onto a baked coconut shortbread round. Refrigerate the domes until ready to serve.

Approximate values per 5-oz. (150-g) serving: **Calories** 550, **Total fat** 43 g, **Saturated fat** 27 g, **Cholesterol** 195 mg, **Sodium** 280 mg, **Total carbohydrates** 36 g, **Protein** 10 g, **Vitamin A** 25%

VANILLA CHEESECAKE WITH SESAME SEED NOUGATINE, COCONUT SAUCE AND SORBET

Yield: 12 Servings

Individual Vanilla Cheesecakes (page 522)	12	12
Sesame Seed Nougatine (page 724), 2-in. (5-cm) disks	24 disks	24 disks
Tuile Batter (page 354), baked into small cups	24 cups	24 cups
Raspberry Sorbet (page 559)	as needed	as needed
Mango Sorbet (page 547)	as needed	as needed
Coconut Sauce (page 539)	as needed	as needed
Fresh cherries	as needed for garnish	
Edible flowers and fresh herbs	as needed for garnsih	

1. Place an Individual Vanilla Cheesecake on a plate. Stand two Sesame Seed Nougatine disks upright next to the cheesecake.
2. Place two Tulipe Cookie cups next to the cheesecake, then fill one with a scoop of Raspberry Sorbet and the other with a scoop of Mango Sorbet.
3. Drizzle Coconut Sauce on the plate. Garnish with fresh cherries, flower petals and herbs.

Approximate values per serving: **Calories** 430, **Total fat** 32 g, **Saturated fat** 19 g, **Cholesterol** 170 mg, **Sodium** 210 mg, **Total carbohydrates** 28 g, **Protein** 8 g, **Vitamin A** 25%

HOT COFFEE SOUFFLÉ WITH CHOCOLATE ICE CREAM SERVED IN TULIPE COOKIE BASKETS

Yield: 10 Servings

Coffee Soufflé (page 525)	10 soufflés	10 soufflés
Tuile Batter (page 354), baked into cups	10 cups	10 cups
Chocolate Ice Cream (page 545)	1 qt.	1 lt
Fresh mint leaves	as needed for garnish	
Chocolate-covered coffee beans	as needed for garnish	

1. Place a baked hot Coffee Soufflé on a plate. Position a Tuile Batter cookie cup next to the soufflé. Quickly place a scoop of Chocolate Ice Cream in the cup. Decorate the ice cream with fresh mint leaves and coffee beans.

Approximate values per serving: **Calories** 230, **Total fat** 11 g, **Saturated fat** 6 g, **Cholesterol** 125 mg, **Sodium** 70 mg, **Total carbohydrates** 29 g, **Protein** 5 g, **Vitamin A** 10%, **Vitamin C** 20%

BRANDIED CHERRY ICE CREAM ON NOUGATINE MOONS

Yield: 6 Servings

Brandied Cherry Ice Cream (page 545)	1.25 qt.	1.25 lt
Chocolate rings (page 703), 2¾ in. (7 cm) in diameter	18 rings	18 rings
Fresh peaches or nectarines	2	2
Granulated sugar	2 oz.	60 g
Orange juice	4 fl. oz.	120 ml
Unsalted butter	0.5 oz.	15 g
Vanilla extract	0.15 fl. oz. (1 tsp.)	5 ml
Orange liqueur or Kirsch (optional)	1 fl. oz.	30 ml
Nougatine Moons (recipe follows)	6 cutouts	6 cutouts
Fresh cherries	as needed for garnish	

1. Prepare the Brandied Cherry Ice Cream and pack it into 2¾-inch (7-centimeter) torte rings. Freeze until the ice cream is solid, preferably overnight.
2. Unmold the ice cream. Cut each cylinder of ice cream into three uniform disks. Return the ice cream to the freezer until firm.
3. Remove the ice cream from the freezer. Slip a chocolate ring over each slice of ice cream. Return the ice cream to the freezer until ready to serve.
4. Peel each peach and cut into 12 slices. Stir the sugar in a sauté pan over high heat until it turns a light golden caramel color. Reduce the heat to low and add the peach slices and orange juice. Heat until the peaches are hot, approximately 3 to 4 minutes. Stir in the butter, vanilla and liqueur (if using). Hold the pan in a warm place.
5. To serve, place a Nougatine Moon on each serving plate. Position three ice cream disks on the nougatine. Garnish the plates with the peaches, the caramel cooking liquid and the fresh cherries. Serve immediately.

Approximate values per serving: **Calories** 750, **Total fat** 41 g, **Saturated fat** 16 g, **Cholesterol** 225 mg, **Sodium** 90 mg, **Total carbohydrates** 89 g, **Protein** 10 g, **Vitamin A** 30%, **Vitamin C** 20%, **Calcium** 15%

NOUGATINE MOONS

Yield: 6 Cutouts

Basic Nougatine (page 724)	14 oz.	420 g

1. Prepare the Basic Nougatine according to the instructions on page 723 through Step 4. Roll out the nougatine approximately ⅛ inch (1 millimeter) thick. Cut out six rounds measuring 5 inches (12.5 centimeters) in diameter. Use the round cutter to remove a section of the nougatine to obtain a half-moon shape. (Save the cut-out pieces for another use.)
2. Store the nougatine cutouts in an airtight container for up to 1 week before using.

Approximate values per 2½-oz. (75-g) serving: **Calories** 280, **Total fat** 12 g, **Saturated fat** 2 g, **Cholesterol** 5 mg, **Sodium** 40 mg, **Total carbohydrates** 45 g, **Protein** 4 g

CHEESECAKE BARS WITH FRESH RED FRUITS

Yield: 12 Servings

New York Cheesecake batter (page 498)	3 lb.	1440 g
Tea-Scented Cherry Cookie dough (page 330)	15 oz.	450 g
Decorating Caramel (page 727), piped into rings	60 rings	60 rings
Decorating Caramel (page 727), warm	as needed	as needed
Mixed berry coulis (page 512)	8 fl. oz.	240 ml
Fresh berries	2 pt.	1 lt
White chocolate cutouts (page 698)	12 cutouts	12 cutouts

1. Prepare the New York Cheesecake batter and pour it into a greased 9-inch- (22-centimeter-) square pan. Bake and cool according to the instructions on page 498. Freeze the cheesecake until very firm.

2. Unmold the cheesecake onto a paper-lined sheet pan.

3. Trim the edges and cut the cheesecake in half. Cut each half into 6 uniform pieces. Refrigerate the cut cheesecake until ready to serve.

4. Roll the Tea-Scented Cherry Cookie dough out into a 9-inch (22-centimeter) square. Divide the dough into 12 uniform pieces the same size as the portioned cheesecake. Bake the dough on a paper-lined sheet pan at 375°F (190°C) until golden brown, approximately 10 to 13 minutes.

5. To plate each serving, dip the caramel rings into warm Decorating Caramel and position them spaced an inch apart along one side of the plate. Pour the coulis under and around the caramel rings. Garnish with the fresh berries.

6. Place a baked cookie rectangle on the plate with a bar of cheesecake on top. Gently break a white chocolate cutout in half. Position it on top of the cheesecake so that a small gap appears. Serve immediately.

Approximate values per serving: **Calories** 650, **Total fat** 39 g, **Saturated fat** 24 g, **Cholesterol** 180 mg, **Sodium** 290 mg, **Total carbohydrates** 66 g, **Protein** 9 g, **Vitamin A** 30%, **Vitamin C** 15%

FLAMBÉED PINEAPPLE IN CRÊPES WITH BLACKBERRY SORBET

Yield: 2 Servings

Unsalted butter	1 oz.	30 g
Fresh pineapple, ½-in. (1.2-centimeter) slices, cored	4 slices	4 slices
Granulated sugar	1 oz.	30 g
Lemon juice	0.15 fl. oz. (1 tsp.)	5 ml
Orange juice	1 fl. oz.	30 ml
Sambuca or Kirsch	0.5 fl. oz.	15 ml
Crêpes (page 416)	2	2
Blackberry Sorbet (page 556)	4 oz.	120 g
Fresh blackberries	as needed for garnish	
Edible flowers, fresh herbs or microgreens	as needed for garnish	

1. Melt the butter over medium-high heat in a sauté pan large enough to hold the pineapple slices. When the butter stops sizzling, add the pineapple slices and cook approximately 1 to 2 minutes on each side, until the slices are lightly browned.
2. While the pineapple cooks, in a medium-sized saucepan cook the sugar, lemon juice and orange juice to a golden caramel. Stop the cooking process by placing the bottom of the pan in a bowl of cold water.
3. Add the pineapple slices to the caramel. Reheat until the syrup is warm and flowing.
4. Add the liqueur and carefully ignite.
5. Heat the crêpes in a 350°F (180°C) oven. Place one on each serving plate. Place the pineapple slices on one half of each warm crêpe.
6. Fold the crêpes to close and decorate each plate with some Blackberry Sorbet and fresh blackberries, edible flowers and herbs. Pour the warm sauce over the crêpes and serve immediately.

Approximate values per serving: **Calories** 330, **Total fat** 12 g, **Saturated fat** 11 g, **Cholesterol** 125 mg, **Sodium** 110 mg, **Total carbohydrates** 56 g, **Protein** 1 g, **Vitamin A** 10%, **Vitamin C** 45%

PALMIERS WITH BAKED NECTARINES, PEACH SORBET AND CHAMPAGNE SABAYON

Yield: 6 Servings

Palmiers (page 302)	12 cookies	12 cookies
Peach Sorbet (page 556)	as needed	as needed
Warm Baked Nectarines, peeled (page 576)	6	6
Champagne Sabayon (page 494)	1 qt.	1 lt
Fresh berries	as needed for garnish	
Fresh herbs or microgreens	as needed for garnish	
Candied orange rind, diced	as needed for garnish	

1 Place a Palmier on the center of a plate. Place a scoop of Peach Sorbet in the center of the Palmier. Stand another Palmier upright behind the scoop of sorbet.

2 Split a Warm Baked Nectarine in half, then cut each piece in two. Arrange the cut slices of nectarine around the sorbet. Surround the dessert with Champagne Sabayon and garnish the plate with berries, herbs and pieces of candied orange rind.

Approximate values per serving: **Calories** 480, **Total fat** 26 g, **Saturated fat** 9 g, **Cholesterol** 120 mg, **Sodium** 65 mg, **Total carbohydrates** 54 g, **Protein** 11 g

WARM PEACHES WITH CHAMPAGNE-ROSE SORBET

Yield: 10 Servings

Warm Baked Peaches (page 576)	10	10
Tuile Batter (page 354), baked into rectangular and triangular shapes	20 cookies	20 cookies
Champagne-Rose Sorbet (page 557)	28 fl. oz.	840 ml
Lace Cookies (recipe follows)	10 cookies	10 cookies
Mango Coulis (page 512)	as needed	as needed
Fresh currants	as needed	as needed

1. Remove the Warm Baked Peaches from the oven. Place one on each serving plate.
2. Place a diamond-shaped Tuile Batter cookie on top of each peach.
3. Unmold a 2-oz. (60-gram) piece of Champagne-Rose Sorbet and center it on the Tulipe Cookie. Insert a triangular Tulipe Cookie into the sorbet.
4. Surround the peach with a curved Lace Cookie, some of the Mango Coulis and fresh currants.

Approximate values per serving: **Calories** 440, **Total fat** 19 g, **Saturated fat** 9 g, **Cholesterol** 40 mg, **Sodium** 25 mg, **Total carbohydrates** 63 g, **Protein** 4 g, **Vitamin A** 10%, **Vitamin C** 15%

LACE COOKIES

Yield: 1 lb. 5 oz. (670 g)   **Method:** Wafer cookie

Unsalted butter, softened	3 oz.	95 g	187%
Granulated sugar	6 oz.	180 g	375%
Almonds, chopped	7 oz.	220 g	437%
Blackberry purée	4 fl. oz.	125 ml	250%
Cake flour	1.6 oz.	50 g	100%
Total batter weight:	1 lb. 5 oz.	670 g	1349%

1. Make a stencil by cutting a 10-inch × ½-inch (25-centimeter × 1.2-centimeter) rectangular hole out of a rigid piece of thin cardboard or plastic. Line a sheet pan with a silicone baking mat. Set aside.
2. Cream the butter in the bowl of a mixer until lump-free. Add the sugar and incorporate well. Add the almonds and the blackberry purée. Mix well, then add the cake flour.
3. Place the stencil on the silicone baking mat. Spread the wafer batter the same thickness as the stencil. Move the stencil and repeat until the sheet tray is covered with stenciled cookie batter.
4. Bake at 400°F (200°C) until the cookies are firm and lightly brown, approximately 6 minutes.
5. As soon as the cookies are removed from the oven, wrap the strips of warm dough around an oiled tube or French-style rolling pin. Once cooled, slide the cookie from the form. Store the cookies tightly sealed in a plastic container.

Approximate values per serving: **Calories** 440, **Total fat** 19 g, **Saturated fat** 9 g, **Cholesterol** 40 mg, **Sodium** 25 mg, **Total carbohydrates** 63 g, **Protein** 4 g, **Vitamin A** 10%, **Vitamin C** 15%

BLACK CURRANT SORBET SERVED ON ICE WITH GERBET MACARONS AND CRÈME BRÛLÉE

Yield: 6 Servings

Crème Brûlée (page 520), unbaked	10 fl. oz.	300 ml
Black Currant Sorbet (page 557)	1 qt.	1 lt
Red Currant Coulis (page 512)	4 oz.	120 g
Ground almonds or almond flour	as needed	as needed
Gerbet Macarons (page 640), 3 in. (7.5 cm) each, tinted pink	12 cookies	12 cookies
Decorating Caramel (page 727), piped into squares	6 squares	6 squares
Fresh red, black and golden currants	as needed for garnish	

1 Fill six square silicone or metal molds measuring approximately 3 inches (7.5 centimeters) each with water. Freeze until ready to serve.

2 Prepare and bake the Crème Brûlée in 2-ounce (60-milliliter) ramekins. Cool completely, then refrigerate until ready to serve.

3 Line a quarter-size sheet pan with plastic wrap. Spread out the Black Currant Sorbet into an even layer in the pan. Freeze until firm, preferably overnight.

4 When the sorbet is sufficiently hard, cut out six 3-inch (7.5-centimeter) squares and six 3-inch (7.5-centimeter) disks of sorbet. Return the sorbet to the freezer until ready to serve. (Save any remaining sorbet for another use.)

5 To plate each serving, caramelize the surface of the Crème Brulée. Place one custard on each serving plate. Spoon some of the Red Currant Coulis over the surface of the custard.

6 Sprinkle some ground almonds on each serving plate. Unmold a square of ice onto the ground almonds.

7 Position one square of the sorbet on top of the ice. Sandwich together two Gerbet Macarons with a disk of sorbet. Place the filled macaron on top of the sorbet. Decorate each plate with a square of caramel decoration and the fresh currants.

Approximate values per serving: **Calories** 500, **Total fat** 160 g, **Saturated fat** 8 g, **Cholesterol** 125 mg, **Sodium** 60 mg, **Total carbohydrates** 83 g, **Protein** 5 g, **Vitamin A** 15%

CHAPTER TWENTY

CHOCOLATE AND SUGAR WORK

After studying this chapter, you will be able to:

- identify a variety of chocolate products
- understand the various procedures for tempering chococlate
- prepare chocolate decorations and candies
- prepare marzipan and nougatine
- make and use pastillage; prepare and use caramel to create spun sugar and caramel decorations
- prepare sugar showpieces

CHOCOLATE WORK, CANDY MAKING AND SUGAR CONFECTIONERY ARE SPECIALTIES within the baking industry. Entire books have been written about these products. The intention of this chapter is to simply provide a solid grounding in the most popular confectionery products. Many students are attracted to the culinary arts for the possibility of artistic expression. Products such as chocolate, marzipan and nougatine afford the pastry chef an opportunity to use delicious food products to sculpt and mold edible treats. With its enticing aroma, silken texture and complex taste, chocolate is a seductive ingredient, appealing to almost everyone. In the right hands chocolate can be transformed into an artistic expression comparable to any piece of sculpture. Although the procedures for handling chocolate may seem complex at first, many are easily mastered. Piping chocolate decorations and making truffles is well within the grasp of most pastry cooks.

This chapter also covers marzipan, nougatine (a type of sugar and nut confection) and simple sugar work used to make edible decorations. These techniques are the basis for more complex sugar work and the crafting of chocolate and sugar showpieces, discussed at the end of this chapter.

CHOCOLATE

Few need to be told of the myriad uses for chocolate in the bakeshop. Chocolate appears in everything from croissants and foamy puddings to cakes, frostings and candies. It flavors foods, enhances texture, holds moisture and helps build emulsions. And it tastes delicious.

Chocolate Production

Cocoa Beans

Chocolate (Fr. *chocolat*) begins as yellow fruit pods dangling from the trunk and main branches of the tropical cacao tree. A native species of the Amazon rainforest, the cacao tree is found in the Caribbean, parts of Africa, Asia and Latin America. Each pod contains approximately 40 almond-sized cocoa beans. After the pods ripen, the beans are scooped out and placed in the sun for several days to dry and ferment. Though time consuming, this process helps develop the aroma and essential oils in the beans. They are then cleaned, dried, cured and roasted to develop flavor and reduce bitterness. Next, the beans are crushed to remove their shells, yielding the prized chocolate **nib**.

Like coffee beans, cocoa beans are blended to the specifications of the chocolate manufacturer to obtain the flavor and aroma desired in their end product, a closely guarded trade secret. Nibs are shipped to manufacturers worldwide where they can be further roasted.

Roasted nibs are crushed into a thick (nonalcoholic) paste known as **chocolate liquor** or **chocolate mass**. Chocolate mass contains about 53 percent fat, known as **cocoa butter**. Chocolate mass is further refined depending on the desired product. If **cocoa powder** is to be produced, virtually all the cocoa butter is removed. Adding more cocoa butter, sugar, milk solids and flavorings to the chocolate mass creates a variety of other products.

Most manufacturers of fine chocolates use the Swiss technique of **conching** to increase smoothness. Conching involves stirring large vats of blended chocolate with a heavy granite roller or paddle to smooth out sugar crystals and mellow the flavor, a process that

conching stirring melted chocolate with large stone or metal rollers to create a smooth texture in the finished chocolate

may last from 12 hours to 3 days. The particle size of unconched chocolate is between 50 and 70 microns in size (one micron is 0.001 millimeter or 0.000039 inch). Fully conched chocolate has a particle size of 18 to 20 microns, resulting in a superior product. Once conched, chocolate is tempered, molded and wrapped for shipment and sale.

Tasting Chocolate

Three primary varieties of cocoa beans are grown commercially: *forastero*, a very hardy, abundant variety that accounts for more than 90 percent of the beans grown; *criollo*, prized for its unique aroma and flavor; and *trinitario*, a flavorful hybrid of the preceding two. Most chocolates are blends of beans, created by their manufacturer to be unique yet consistent. Varietal chocolates, those made from one type of bean grown in one specific area, have become trendy, though expensive, for both chocolate bars and baking chocolates.

Roasting greatly affects the final flavor of chocolate. Generally, German and Spanish manufacturers use a high (or strong) roast; Swiss and American makers use a low (or mild) roast.

Refining is also a matter of national taste. Swiss and German chocolate are the smoothest, followed by English chocolates. American chocolate is noticeably grainier.

Chocolate quality is actually the product of several factors besides flavor. All these factors should be evaluated when selecting chocolates:

▶ Appearance—color should be even and glossy, without any discoloration.
▶ Smell—should be chocolatey with no off-odors or staleness. Complex aromas of vanilla, berries, nuts, toasting, smoke or spice, among others, may be present.
▶ **Break**—should snap cleanly without crumbling.
▶ Texture—should melt quickly and evenly on the tongue.

TYPES OF CHOCOLATE

Unsweetened Chocolate

Unsweetened chocolate is pure hardened chocolate liquor without any added sugar or milk solids. It is frequently used in baking and is sometimes referred to as "baking chocolate." Unsweetened chocolate is approximately 53 percent cocoa butter and 47 percent cocoa solids. Its flavor is pure and chocolatey, but the absence of sugar makes it virtually inedible as is.

Bittersweet and Semisweet Chocolates

Both bittersweet and semisweet chocolates contain at least 35 percent chocolate mass plus additional cocoa butter, sugar, flavorings and sometimes emulsifiers. Generally, semisweet chocolate will be sweeter than bittersweet chocolate, but there are no precise definitions, so flavor and sweetness will vary from brand to brand. Both are excellent eating chocolates and can usually be substituted measure for measure in any formula.

Couverture

Couverture (koo-vehr-TYOOR) refers to high-quality chocolate containing at least 32 percent cocoa butter. Professional chocolatiers generally prefer couverture chocolate, which has a higher **fluidity** than other chocolates when melted. It is available in a range of flavors—bittersweet, semisweet and milk chocolate, for example. Couverture has a glossy appearance and can be used to create a thin, smooth coating on confections and pastries.

Couverture chocolate contains three primary ingredients: cocoa solids, sugar and cocoa butter. (It may also contain a flavoring such as vanilla and lecithin as an emulsifier.) The label on couverture sold in bulk will usually indicate the amount of these primary ingredients. Often it is labeled with a series of numbers, such as 70/30/38. In this example, the couverture has a ratio of

fluidity a physical characteristic of chocolate, its ability to flow when melted; it is determined by the percentage of cocoa butter or fat in the chocolate

Clockwise from lower left: semisweet chips, disks of chocolate liquor, block of bittersweet chocolate, block of milk chocolate, disks of white chocolate, alkalized cocoa powder

FROM CACAO TO CHOCOLATE CHIPS

To understand the history of chocolate, a chef or chocoholic must first understand the fundamental difference between its original use as a beverage and its later transformation into a candy.

The cacao tree (called *theobroma cacao*, meaning "food of the gods") originated in the river valleys of South America and was carried into what is now Mexico by the Mayans before the 7th century A.D. It was cultivated by Mayans, Aztecs and Toltecs not only as a source of food but also as currency. Chocolate was consumed only as a treasured drink. Cacao beans were roasted, crushed to a paste and steeped in water, then thickened with corn flour to create a cold, bitter beverage. Sometimes honey, vanilla or spices, including chiles, were added. The Aztec emperor Montezuma was so enamored with the beverage that he reportedly consumed 50 cups at each meal.

Columbus brought cacao beans to Spain from his fourth voyage to the New World in 1504. (The common term *cocoa* is actually a western European mispronunciation of the proper term *cacao*, caused by confusion with another New World delicacy, the coconut.) But almost 20 years passed before Spanish conquistadors, led by Cortez, understood the beans' value. With Montezuma's encouragement, Cortez and his soldiers slowly acquired a taste for the bitter beverage, spurred on by the intoxicating effects of caffeine.

Cortez's most important contribution to the history of chocolate was to take beans with him when he left Mexico. He planted them on the islands he passed on his return to Spain: Trinidad, Haiti and Fernando Po, from which the giant African cocoa industry grew. Through Cortez's farsighted efforts, Spain controlled all aspects of the cocoa trade until well into the 18th century.

The Spanish began drinking chocolate at home during the 16th century. It was usually mixed with two other expensive imports, sugar and vanilla, and frothed with a carved wooden swizzle stick known as a *molinet*. This thick, cold drink was made from tablets of crushed cocoa beans produced and sold by monks. The Spanish believed that cocoa cured all ills and supplied limitless stamina. In the early 17th century, cocoa beverages, now served hot, crept into France via royal marriages.

Cocoa spread through the rest of Europe by different routes. The Dutch, who had poached on Spanish trade routes for many years, eventually realized the value of the unusual beans they found on Spanish ships. Holland soon became the most important cocoa port outside Spain. From there, a love of cocoa spread to Germany, Scandinavia and Italy. In 1655, England acquired Jamaica and its own cocoa plantations.

Until the Industrial Revolution, cocoa was made by hand using mortar and pestle or stone-grinding disks to crush the cocoa nibs. By the 1700s, cocoa factories had opened throughout Europe. James Baker opened the first cocoa factory in the United States in 1765.

Conrad van Houten, a Dutch chemist, patented "chocolate powder" in 1825. His work marked the beginning of a shift from drinking to eating chocolate. It also paved the way for everything we know as chocolate today. Van Houten developed a screw press that removed most of the cocoa butter from the bean, leaving a brown,

Chocolate Chef, sculpted by Pastry Chef Rubin Foster

flaky powder, essentially the same substance as modern cocoa powder.

Eventually, it was discovered that the extra cocoa butter resulting from the production of cocoa powder could be added to ground beans to make the paste more malleable, smoother and more tolerant of added sugar. The English firm of Fry and Sons introduced the first eating chocolate in 1847. Their recipe was the same then as today: crushed cocoa beans, cocoa butter and sugar.

In 1876, Swiss chocolatier Daniel Peter invented solid milk chocolate using the new condensed milk created by baby food manufacturer Henri Nestlé. Pennsylvania cocoa manufacturer Milton Hershey introduced his milk chocolate bars in 1894, followed by Hershey's Kisses in 1907. Nestlé Foods introduced the chocolate chip, perfect for cookies, in 1939.

70 percent cocoa solids by weight to 30 percent sugar. The last number refers to the percentage of total fat which, in this case, is 38 percent cocoa butter. The high cocoa butter percentage gives couverture its fluidity and deep shine.

Sweet Chocolate

Government standards require that sweet chocolate contain not less than 15 percent chocolate liquor and varying amounts of sugar, milk solids, flavorings and emulsifiers. As the name implies, sweet chocolate is sweeter, and thus less chocolatey, than semisweet chocolate. (Because of brand name confusion, recipes that refer to "German" chocolate mean sweet chocolate.)

Milk Chocolate

The favorite eating chocolate in the United States is milk chocolate. It contains sugar, vanilla, perhaps other flavorings and, of course, milk solids. The milk solids that make the chocolate milder and sweeter than other chocolates also make it less suitable for baking purposes. Do not substitute milk chocolate for dark chocolate in any product that must be baked, as the milk solids tend to burn. If melted slowly and carefully, milk chocolate can be used in glazes, mousses or candies.

Chocolate Chips, Chunks and Pistoles

Chocolate chips are drops of chocolate available in count sizes from 14 to 160 per ounce (the average chips are 800 to 1000 per pound). They are easy additions to cookies, muffins and cakes. Like the larger chocolate chunks, chips are available in many flavors including white chocolate, butterscotch, peanut butter and fruit flavors. Pistoles or callets are small round pieces of chocolate, often of the finest couverture, designed to eliminate the need for chopping chocolate in the bakeshop.

Chocolate Pistoles

Cocoa Powder

The brown powder left after the fat (cocoa butter) is removed from cocoa beans is known as cocoa powder. It does not contain any sweeteners or flavorings and is used primarily in baked goods. Alkalized or Dutch-processed cocoa powder has been treated with an alkaline solution, such as potassium carbonate, to raise the powder's pH from 5.5 to 7 or 8. Alkalized powder is darker and milder than nonalkalized powder and has a reduced tendency to lump. Either can usually be substituted measure for measure in baked goods.

Dutch-Processed Cocoa Powder (left) and American-Style Non-Alkalized Cocoa Powder (right)

Cocoa Butter

Chocolate liquor is approximately 53 percent fat, known as cocoa butter. Cocoa butter has long been prized for its resistance to rancidity and its use as a cosmetic. The complex chemical composition of the fats in cocoa butter gives chocolate its melt-in-the-mouth quality. Fine chocolatiers use chocolate with high percentages of cocoa butter for this reason. But because these fats melt at different temperatures, handling chocolate when making dipped or molded candies requires precise melting techniques. (See pages 692–696.) Pure cocoa butter comes in several forms: solid blocks, small tablets and a powdered or granulated form.

White Chocolate

This ivory-colored substance is not the product of an albino cocoa bean. It is actually a confectionery product that does not contain any chocolate solids or liquor. (Thus it is usually labeled "white confectionery" or "coating" in the United States.) The finest white chocolate couverture contains a minimum of 31 percent cocoa butter, a maximum of 55 percent sugar, 20 percent milk solids, and vanilla or other flavors. Other products replace all or part of the cocoa butter with vegetable oils. These confectionery products will be less expensive than those containing pure cocoa butter, but their flavor and texture will be noticeably inferior. White chocolate melts at a lower temperature than dark chocolate and burns easily. It is excellent for mousses, sauces and candy making but is less often used in baked products.

Gianduja

Gianduja (jan-DOO-yah) is a smooth blend of roasted hazelnut paste and chocolate containing 25 to 38 percent cocoa mass, milk solids and sugar. Used in candy production, mousses and buttercreams, gianduja is a prized confection in Italy.

Imitation Chocolate or Chocolate-Flavored Coating

A less-expensive product substituted in many prepared foods, imitation chocolate is made with hydrogenated vegetable oils instead of cocoa butter, as little as 8 percent defatted cocoa powder and as much as 55 percent sugar, plus emulsifiers, flavorings and perhaps milk solids. The resulting product melts at a higher temperature and requires no tempering.

MELTING CHOCOLATE

Two important rules for melting chocolate:

1. Chocolate must never exceed 120°F (49°C) or there will be a loss of flavor.
2. Water—even a drop in the form of steam—must never touch the chocolate.

When a droplet of water enters melted chocolate, the chocolate becomes lumpy (a process called *seizing*). There must be a minimum of ½ fluid ounce (15 milliliters) of water per ounce (30 grams) of chocolate to keep this from happening. If seizing does occur, the addition of fat such as vegetable shortening, clarified butter, or cocoa butter will somewhat restore the chocolate to a workable condition.

For melting chocolate, unlined copper is the traditional "chocolate pot" because it is so responsive to changes in temperature. Aluminum or heatproof glass also works well. Ideally, chocolate should be heated to 120°F (49°C), the point at which all the different fat fractions in the cocoa butter are melted.

When melting chocolate or cocoa butter, temperatures exceeding 120°F (49°C) adversely affect the flavor. There are many acceptable methods for melting dark chocolate. If the heat source does not exceed 120°F (49°C), it is fine to add the dark chocolate in large pieces and leave it to melt unmonitored. When the heat source is capable of bringing the chocolate over 120°F (49°C), however, the chocolate should be finely chopped or grated to ensure uniformity of melting. The chocolate must be carefully watched and stirred to avoid overheating. If using a double boiler, water in the lower container should not exceed 140°F (60°C) and the upper container should not touch the water. The chocolate should be stirred constantly.

Milk chocolate and white chocolate must always be stirred frequently while melting because they contain milk solids that seed (lump) if left undisturbed.

Remove chocolate from the heat source when it reaches 115°F (46°C), as the temperature may continue to rise, and stir vigorously to prevent overheating and to distribute the cocoa butter evenly.

Always melt chocolate uncovered as moisture could condense on the lid, drop back into the chocolate, and cause seizing.

—from *The Cake Bible*
by Rose Levy Beranbaum

Imitation chocolates have an inferior taste and leave a waxy feel in the mouth, though when quality is no concern they may be used in most cases when chocolate is required. Products containing imitation chocolate should be labeled "chocolate flavored."

STORING CHOCOLATES

All chocolates should be stored at a cool, consistent temperature, away from strong odors and moisture. Neither refrigerating nor freezing is recommended for chocolate storage, however. Dark chocolate, white chocolate and cocoa powder can be kept up to 1 year without loss of flavor. Milk chocolate will not keep as well because it contains milk solids.

BEAN-TO-BAR CHOCOLATE

More and more, *chocolatiers* are interested in the source of their chocolate. Some have become chocolate makers themselves, manufacturing their own chocolate from beans they purchase from growers around the world. The term *bean-to-bar chocolate* is being used to refer to such companies, whether small or industrial scale.

Tempering Chocolate

In order to create chocolate candies with a high gloss and a crisp sharp snap when eaten, chocolate must be tempered. **Tempering** chocolate is a controlled process of melting, cooling and reheating chocolate within set temperature ranges. (See Table 20.1.) High cocoa butter chocolate such as couverture chocolate consists of fat molecules and solid crystals that, when heated above a certain temperature—approximately 90°F (32°C) for dark couverture chocolate and 87°F (30.5°C) for milk and white couverture—unchain and become unstable. Tempering the chocolate rechains these molecules and stabilizes the cocoa butter crystals, making the chocolate homogenous again. Chocolate melted for mousses, creams, ganache and baking requires no tempering. When chocolate is not tempered, it will be crumbly and streaked with gray when dry and will not snap. It takes a long time to set and sticks to candy molds.

Several methods are used to temper chocolate manually—*seeding*, *tabling*, *microwave oven* and *cocoa butter* methods. Each method relies on melting chocolate and heating it to a certain temperature, then cooling and rewarming it. The chocolate must be chopped into small, uniform pieces so that it melts evenly. When melting chocolate, make certain that the chocolate bowl makes no contact with water to avoid overheating. Equally important, steam or water should not enter the chocolate because this would cause it to seize. When

TABLE 20.1	TEMPERATURE RANGES FOR TEMPERING CHOCOLATE		
	MELT	COOL	TEMPER
Dark chocolate couverture	113°F–120°F (45°C–48°C)	78°F (25°C)	86°F–90°F (29°C–32°C)
Milk or white chocolate couverture	104°F–115°F (40°C–46°C)	78°F (25°C)	87°F (30.5°C)

stirring chocolate during tempering, avoid incorporating excess air into the mass, which makes the chocolate thick and unmanageable. Reheating and retempering will restore the chocolate's fluidity.

The ideal room temperature when working with tempered chocolate is between 68°F and 72°F (20°C and 22°C) with low humidity. Always wear gloves when handling chocolate. Gloves are sanitary and keep chocolate from melting as quickly from body heat.

For tempering, use only couverture chocolate or add more cocoa butter; chocolate with a low cocoa butter content, such as chocolate chips made for cookies, will not melt properly. Chocolate manufacturers recommend various temperatures best suited for tempering their blend of chocolate. Follow these temperatures even if they differ from those provided in this book.

Do not heat chocolate over 120°F (49°C) because it may cause the cocoa butter to break down, which makes proper tempering impossible. When one of the tempering techniques has been completed but the temperature of the couverture is above that of the tempered range, it is necessary to repeat the entire process.

SEEDING METHOD

Tempering chocolate using the seeding method requires tempered chocolate as it comes from the manufacturer. Two-thirds of the chocolate is melted either in the microwave or over a bain marie. When the melted portion reaches 118°F (48°C), it is removed from the heat. The remaining chocolate is added and the chocolate is stirred until it melts. This is the seeding process. The crystals in the solid chocolate melt gently without unchaining, thus tempering the entire mass.

PROCEDURE FOR TEMPERING CHOCOLATE BY SEEDING

Place two-thirds of the chopped couverture chocolate or pistoles to be tempered in a dry bowl. Melt the chocolate in a microwave or over barely simmering water. When the chocolate couverture is melted to 118°F (48°C)—or 115°F (46°C) for milk or white chocolate—remove from the heat and seed with the remaining one-third of the chocolate. Stir the mixture using a rubber spatula until the lumps melt. Or use an immersion blender, holding the blade well under the melted chocolate. Check the temperature with an instant-read thermometer. The chocolate must stay below recommended temperatures; dark couverture chocolate needs to be below 90°F (32°C). Milk and white couverture chocolate need to be below 87°F (30.5°C).

TABLING METHOD

The tabling method is the classic method performed by the most experienced chocolatiers but requires practice to master. First the chocolate is melted, then a portion of the chocolate is poured onto a marble slab or cool sanitary surface. The pastry chef stirs the chocolate with a spatula, working it back and forth over the marble, performing the tabling process until it cools. Once the chocolate reaches the desired temperature, the tabled chocolate is heated to 86°F to 90°F (29°C to 32°C) for dark couverture chocolate. Milk and white couverture chocolate are reheated to 87°F (30.5°C). Chocolate tempered successfully by tabling retains its shine and crispness longer than with other methods.

When using this method to temper chocolate, wipe the outside of the bowl before pouring out the chocolate so that no water drips onto the marble. When reheating the chocolate after it has been tabled, its temperature will climb in seconds. If overheated, the chocolate will lose temper, requiring the process to be repeated.

PROCEDURE FOR TEMPERING CHOCOLATE BY TABLING

❶ Place the chopped couverture pieces in a dry stainless steel bowl over a pot of barely simmering water (bain marie). Melt the chocolate to 120°F (49°C) for dark couverture chocolate (115°F [46°C] for milk or white couverture chocolate) while constantly stirring with a rubber spatula. Pour two-thirds of the melted chocolate onto a clean, dry marble slab. Work the chocolate with a bench scraper or palette knife, scraping and turning the mass to cool it.

❷ Work the chocolate until it reaches 78°F (25°C). The chocolate will thicken as it is worked. Scrape the cooled chocolate back into the bowl of melted chocolate. Reheat it over the bain marie until the chocolate reaches 86°F to 90°F (29°C to 32°C) for dark couverture chocolate. Milk and white couverture chocolate are reheated to 87°F (30.5°C). Couverture will climb to this temperature in seconds; do not heat above recommended temperatures or the couverture will lose temper, requiring the process to be repeated.

MICROWAVE OVEN METHOD

Chocolate that has already been tempered may be melted in a microwave oven as long as the chocolate is not heated above temperatures that would unchain the fat molecules. Simply heat the chocolate using the lowest power setting, checking every 10 seconds so as not to exceed the maximum allowed temperatures. The chocolate is then ready for use. This is a simple, quick and hygienic method, but it may require some practice to determine the power range suitable for different microwave ovens. Chocolate tempered using this method may not hold its temper as long as chocolate tempered by other methods.

PROCEDURE FOR TEMPERING CHOCOLATE IN A MICROWAVE OVEN

❶ Place the chopped chocolate in a dry bowl. Place the bowl in the microwave oven. Heat on medium 10 to 12 seconds. Remove the bowl from the microwave and gently stir the chocolate without incorporating any air bubbles into the chocolate. Repeat this process as needed until all pieces are melted.

❷ Check the temperature of the melted chocolate to make certain it stays below 90°F (32°C) to hold its temper. Milk and white couverture chocolate needs to stay below 87°F (30.5°C).

COCOA BUTTER METHOD

Tempering with cocoa butter is a new, hygienic and efficient way to temper chocolate. For this type of tempering, commercially prepared powdered or crystallized cocoa butter is added to the melted couverture at the rate of 1 percent of the weight of the couverture being tempered. (Adding more than 1 percent cocoa butter will not jeopardize the tempering of the chocolate; it will only make the couverture chocolate more fluid.) For example, for 3 pounds (1.5 kilograms) of couverture chocolate, add 0.5 ounce (15 grams) of granulated cocoa butter to the chocolate when tempering. When ground cocoa butter has been stored for 6 months or longer, it becomes resistant to melting properly within the specified temperature ranges. In this case, when adding the cocoa butter, increase the listed temperature by 1°F (0.5°C).

PROCEDURE FOR TEMPERING CHOCOLATE WITH GROUND COCOA BUTTER

❶ Place the chopped couverture pieces in a dry stainless steel bowl over a pot of barely simmering water (bain marie). Melt the chocolate to between 104°F and 115°F (40°C to 46°C). Remove it from the heat. Let it cool to 95°F (35°C) for dark chocolate (93°F [33.5°C] for milk and white chocolate).

❷ Stir in the granulated cocoa butter, stirring until smooth.

❸ Let the chocolate cool to 89°F (31.5°C) for dark chocolate and 86°F (29.5°C) for milk, white and colored chocolate before using. Hold at or below this temperature.

Properly tempered chocolate, lower left, retains its shine. Improperly tempered chocolate, upper right, changes texture, blooms and loses its shine.

transfer sheets flexible sheets of acetate printed with edible designs; used to apply decorative patterns and images onto tempered chocolate

chocolate comb utensil made from hard plastic or rubber with sharp teeth carved into one or more of its sides; used to create patterns in chocolate and icings

HANDLING TEMPERED CHOCOLATE

Incorrectly tempered or improperly stored chocolate may develop a grayish white surface known as **bloom**. Two types of bloom can develop on chocolate. **Fat bloom** occurs when cocoa butter crystals rise and crystallize on the chocolate's surface. Chocolate stored above 70°F (21°C) will develop fat bloom over time. Since fat bloom has no effect on taste, tempering the product will remedy the problem. **Sugar bloom** occurs when moisture collects on the surface of the chocolate and blends with the sugar in the chocolate, leaving a white sugar film. The result is a gritty chocolate that cannot be improved by tempering.

Cool melted chocolate in a room at 65°F (18°C) so that it crystallizes properly. Cookies dipped in chocolate couverture and decorations made of chocolate couverture should cool and harden at this same temperature. Temperatures above 75°F (24°C) may slow the hardening process and cause the chocolate to bloom. Refrigerating the chocolates to harden will make the couverture softer and less crisp. Improperly wrapped chocolate stored under refrigeration causes sugar bloom. Store chocolate work in a cool dry place with low humidity below 70°F (21°C). Chocolate should never be stored under refrigeration. A temperature range of 56°F–60°F (13°C–16°C) is ideal for storing all types of chocolate and chocolate candies.

Chocolate Decorations

Tempered chocolate lends itself to being piped, shaped and formed into tempting decorations to garnish cakes, tarts, petits fours, ice creams and just about anything in the bakeshop. Strips of tempered chocolate may also be used to cover cakes and tortes and to enhance plated desserts.

For most of these items, tempered chocolate is piped or spread with a palette knife over a marble slab or thin sheets of acetate. (Tempered chocolate can also be spread on **transfer sheets**, acetate printed with edible designs. To ensure proper transferring of the printed cocoa butter onto the chocolate, it is important to use tempered couverture chocolate that is at its highest allowable tempered temperature.) Once cooled, the pieces can be stored for use as needed. Plastic **chocolate combs** (see page 702), some designed to create a marbleized effect, bubble wrap and silk screens, are useful tools to create textural effects with chocolate. Chocolate cutouts employ the most basic techniques and are recommended for beginners. Chocolate cigars, curls, shavings and fans require more practice but are simple once mastered. (For chocolate cigars, start using one type of couverture before attempting the two-toned version.) When chocolate sticks to the scraper, let it harden more on the marble before proceeding. If the chocolate flakes into pieces while being scraped off the marble, it has cooled too much. Try rubbing a gloved hand over the chocolate to warm it slightly. There is no waste when making chocolate decorations. Scraps and broken pieces of chocolate may be melted for use in brownies, ganache, icings and other items.

PROCEDURE FOR PIPING CHOCOLATE DECORATIONS

Fill a parchment paper cone with melted chocolate. Snip the tip with a sharp knife. Pipe chocolate filigree patterns onto sheets of acetate or parchment paper.

PROCEDURE FOR PIPING CHOCOLATE MESH

Fill a parchment paper cone with melted chocolate. Snip the tip with a sharp knife. Pipe freestyle patterns to make small or large pieces of chocolate mesh.

PROCEDURE FOR MAKING CHOCOLATE LEAVES

❶ Brush the underside of a clean, dry lemon leaf with tempered couverture. Place the leaf on a wire cooling rack and allow the chocolate to set.

❷ Once the chocolate has set, peel off the lemon leaf.

PROCEDURE FOR MAKING MARBLED CHOCOLATE CUTOUTS

① In a bowl of tempered white couverture chocolate, randomly deposit small amounts of dark tempered couverture. Do not mix together. Pour a row of marbled chocolate onto a sheet of acetate.

② As the white chocolate flows onto the acetate, the dark chocolate forms contrasting ribbons.

③ Spread the marbled chocolate with an offset spatula into a wide band approximately ¹⁄₁₆ inch (1 millimeter) thick. Pushing the chocolate enhances the marbleized effect.

④ Allow the marbled chocolate to set, just until the surface of the chocolate loses some of its gloss, then cut into desired shapes with a paring knife or circular cutter. Allow the chocolate to harden completely, then peel the pieces from the acetate.

PROCEDURE FOR MAKING CHOCOLATE TRANSFER SHEET DECORATIONS

❶ Place a transfer sheet over a sheet of parchment paper on a wooden workbench. (Avoid working on a metal or marble surface, which cools the chocolate rapidly and may hinder proper bonding between the cocoa butter and the chocolate.)

❷ Quickly spread tempered couverture chocolate evenly over the transfer sheet.

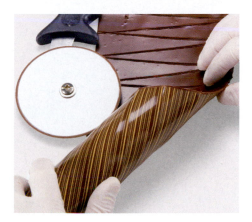

❸ Once the chocolate is no longer glossy and has the firmness of leather, cut it into desired shapes. If curved shapes are desired, immediately roll the sheet by starting from the bottom right corner, rolling toward the top left corner.

❹ For the best sheen, wait at least 4 hours, then peel off the acetate transfer sheets.

Finished chocolate decorations.

PROCEDURE FOR MAKING CHOCOLATE BOXES

1. Cut a clean sponge into 2-inch (5-centimeter) cubes. Cut 4-inch (10-centimeter) squares of plastic wrap. Place a sponge on a square of plastic and gather up the sides, twisting the top to completely enclose the sponge.

2. Dip the plastic-wrapped sponge three quarters of the way into tempered chocolate. Drain the excess chocolate, then place it onto a paper-lined sheet pan or silicone baking mat. Cool and dip again. When hardened, loosen the plastic and remove the sponge. Then peel the plastic off to reveal the chocolate box.

PROCEDURE FOR MAKING CHOCOLATE CIGARETTES

Spread a thin layer of tempered couverture on a clean, dry marble slab. When the couverture has set slightly and the chocolate loses some of its gloss, position a metal dough scraper along one edge of the chocolate. Holding it at a 45-degree angle, push the scraper in a short motion, moving forward approximately 1 inch (2.5 centimeters) to produce uniform curls.

VARIATION:

Two-Toned Chocolate Cigarettes—Spread couverture over an acetate strip. Quickly comb the couverture into stripes. Scrape away excess couverture on the sides of the combed strip. Once the strips have set but have not hardened, cover with a thin layer of contrasting-color tempered couverture.

PROCEDURE FOR MAKING TEMPERED CHOCOLATE SHAVINGS

1. Spread tempered couverture chocolate evenly on a marble slab. Allow to set slightly.

2. Using a metal dough scraper, scrape chocolate forward in a 90-degree angle with a quick motion. If chocolate smears on the scraper, wait a few seconds. If it flakes, it has cooled too much. Rub a gloved hand over the chocolate surface to slightly soften it.

PROCEDURE FOR MAKING UNTEMPERED CHOCOLATE SHAVINGS

1. Select a totally flat sheet pan. Warm the sheet pan to 80°F (27°C) by placing it in a warm oven. Spread nontempered melted couverture chocolate on the back of the sheet pan.

2. Refrigerate the sheet pan until the couverture has hardened.

3. Remove from the refrigerator. Let the chocolate soften slightly. Hold a plastic scraper at a 90-degree angle to the sheet pan and scrape 1-inch (2.5-centimeter) curls from the pan.

4. Transfer the shavings directly onto the cake, tart or pastry. Serve as soon as possible because the untempered chocolate will bloom under refrigeration.

PROCEDURE FOR MAKING CHOCOLATE COMBED CURLS

Place a piece of marble in the freezer for at least 30 minutes. Drop a tablespoon of tempered couverture on the cold marble. Run a chocolate comb over the marble to form parallel lines, leaving a thin chocolate film between them. Holding a dough or pastry scraper at a 90-degree angle, push the scraper forward, using one hand to roll the chocolate into a curled shape. (Note: This garnish appears on the Lactose-Free Chocolate Silk Pie on page 598.)

PROCEDURE FOR MAKING CHOCOLATE FANS

1. Combine 20 ounces (600 grams) tempered couverture with 2 fluid ounces (60 milliliters) peanut oil to make it spread easily and remain pliable when set.
2. Spread the chocolate on a marble slab. Allow it to cool slightly, just until the surface of the chocolate loses some of its gloss.
3. If right-handed, hold a metal scraper in your right hand at a 45-degree angle to the marble in front of the chocolate.
4. Position the middle finger of your left hand on the lower left corner of the scraper, partially touching the chocolate. In a fast motion, scrape forward. The pressure of your left hand will help form the ruffles of chocolate. (Reverse directions if left-handed.)
5. Place fans immediately on cakes to decorate, or store them in an airtight container in a cool dry area below 70°F (21°C).

Scraping lightly cooled chocolate with a flat metal scraper to make chocolate fans.

PROCEDURE FOR MAKING CHOCOLATE STICKS

1. Roll a piece of acetate into a cylinder shape. Secure it with adhesive tape. Cover one end of the cylinder with plastic wrap and secure it with tape.
2. Temper white or dark couverture chocolate. Fill a pastry cone with the tempered chocolate and pipe the chocolate into the cylinder. Set straight in a container.
3. Leave for at least 1 hour before removing tape and film.

PROCEDURE FOR MAKING WHITE CHOCOLATE AND GOLD LEAF SWIZZLE STICKS

1 Freeze a piece of marble until well chilled, at least 30 minutes.

2 Temper white chocolate couverture. Fill a paper pastry cone with the tempered chocolate. Remove the marble from the freezer and pipe the chocolate into parallel lines onto the marble. Quickly dab edible gold leaf onto the chocolate if desired.

3 Place a chocolate stick on top of the white chocolate. Position a knife along one edge of the chocolate. Holding the knife at a 45-degree angle, scrape the chocolate strands from one end and roll them around the chocolate stick. (Note: This garnish appears on the cake on page 630.)

Rolling chocolate stick around piped chocolate.

PROCEDURE FOR MAKING COMBED CHOCOLATE RIBBONS

1 Spread tempered chocolate onto a 5-inch × 2-inch (13-centimeter × 5-centimeter) strip of acetate using an offset spatula. Run a chocolate comb over the acetate to form parallel lines in the band of chocolate.

2 Pipe a thin border of couverture across each end of the combed chocolate to keep the thin strips of chocolate connected once the chocolate hardens.

3 Roll a clean sheet of acetate to make a tube measuring 5 inches (13 centimeters) long with a 2-inch (5-centimeter) opening. Secure with adhesive tape. Carefully slide the chocolate-coated sheet of piped chocolate into the tube, twisting gently as it enters the tube. Place in a cool place until hardened and release by cutting the clear tape.

PROCEDURE FOR MAKING CHOCOLATE TEARDROP RIBBONS

1 Spread tempered chocolate on a 5-inch × 2-inch (13-centimeter × 5-centimeter) strip of acetate. Comb to create lines in the chocolate. Fold the ends of the acetate together with the chocolate inside. Press the ends together and secure with adhesive tape. Place in a cool place until firm.

2 Remove the acetate from the chocolate ribbon, clockwise from upper right. Using a paring knife, separate the strips of chocolate and gently arrange the chocolate loops into a lacy bow.

PROCEDURE FOR MAKING CHOCOLATE RINGS

1 Drop approximately 2 tablespoons tempered chocolate onto a 7-inch × 4-inch (17-centimeter × 10-centimeter) strip of acetate. Run a chocolate comb over the acetate to form parallel lines in the chocolate.

2 Bring the ends of the acetate together to form a tube. Secure with adhesive tape.

3 Place in a curved mold in a cool place until hardened; release by cutting the adhesive tape.

4 Using a paring knife, separate the strips of chocolate into individual rings.

Chocolate Candies

Without a doubt, chocolates are one of the most luxurious items created by the pastry chef. Fillings may be based on buttercream, marzipan, ganache, fondant, liqueur or a combination. Chocolate candies are divided into two categories based on the way they are made: dipped or molded.

Dipped chocolates are made when firm candy centers such as pieces of marzipan, caramel or firm ganache are cut or piped into bite-size pieces and dipped into tempered chocolate. **Molded chocolates** are made when solid plastic or metal molds are coated with chocolate, filled, then sealed with more chocolate. Because the molds hold the chocolate's shape, molded chocolates can be filled with soft creams, mousses, even liqueur syrups.

In general, chocolates made with fresh cream and butter have a shorter shelf life than chocolates made with marzipan, fondant or liqueur. Glucose syrup helps extend the keeping quality of a cream or butter filling; however, not every preparation allows this ingredient.

DIPPED CHOCOLATES

Fillings for dipped chocolates, also known as **centers**, may be fruit jellies, marzipan, firm ganache or nut clusters. Fillings may be poured or spread on silicone baking mats or wax paper. Metal bars called **candy rulers** contain the filling while it sets, then the fillings are cut to size with a knife or a wire cutting device.

STYLES OF CHOCOLATE CANDIES

Chocolate bonbons vary geographically. In Belgium as well as Switzerland, the emphasis is on molded bonbons with well-flavored ganache centers. In France, the bonbons are usually dipped in a thin coating of dark chocolate. Traditionally American chocolate bonbons were characterized by their sweet fillings. Inspired by European chocolate making, new American chocolatiers are working toward a bolder style using exotically flavored centers in a chocolate shell formed by molding or dipping.

centers the firm or soft fillings for chocolate candies

candy rulers steel or aluminum bars of varying lengths and thicknesses used to contain fillings for candies; the metal bars may also be used to roll pastry doughs to a uniform thickness

SPRAYING CHOCOLATE

Pastry chefs find their tools in unlikely places, including the home improvement store. Mason's scrapers and trowels and bubble wrap become decorating tools for spreading icing or creating textured chocolate. One indispensable tool, the heavy-duty paint sprayer, is the secret to applying an elegant chocolate finish on a torte, frozen dessert or chocolate showpiece.

To prepare chocolate for spraying, melt an equal weight of semisweet or bittersweet chocolate and cocoa butter to 120°F (49°C) in a microwave or over a double boiler. The chocolate should be tempered for coating a chocolate showpiece, but tempering is not necessary when spraying tortes or frozen desserts. Pour the chocolate mixture into the clean

and sanitized canister of a new heavy-duty paint sprayer or one sold expressly for spraying chocolate.

Use the same precautions spraying chocolate as for spraying paint. Cover the workbench with parchment paper or silicone mats. Create an enclosed area in which to spray to minimize cleanup. Three sheet pans or three sheets of hard plastic standing upright on a workbench make an open-sided box in which to work. Place the torte or other item to be sprayed on a cake turntable inside the enclosed area created on the workbench. Hold the sprayer a minimum of 18 inches (45 centimeters) away from the torte. Rotate the turntable with one hand while moving the sprayer gently back and forth over the

torte. Spray a thin layer of the chocolate over the entire surface one section at a time. To achieve a matte finish, freeze the torte a minimum of 2 hours and apply the chocolate when the torte is still frozen. Products that are oversprayed become shiny instead of matte. Chocolate is more forgiving than enamel; simply freeze and spray the object again.

Chocolate Spray Gun

Set of Chocolate Dipping Forks

The centers are dipped when sufficiently set. Ideally, the temperature of the centers is near 70°F (21°C) for dipping. Specialized **dipping forks** with two or more long thin prongs may be used to remove the dipped chocolates from the coating. Softer fillings may be piped onto disks of chocolate, marzipan or nougatine before dipping. The dipping fork is inserted into the disk, not the gooey center, making dipping easier. The forks are also used to create patterns on the chocolates after dipping. Ring-shaped dipping spoons help hold round candies like truffles when dipping (see the photograph on page 705).

Chocolates can be garnished using nuts, gold leaf or coffee beans; decorated or streaked with chocolate, candies or violets; imprinted with a dipping fork; and decorated with silk-screened designs.

PROCEDURE FOR DIPPING CHOCOLATES

❶ Place a chilled piped or cut chocolate center on a dipping fork. Dip in tempered couverture.

❷ Wipe away any chocolate that pools under the dipping fork.

❸ Place the dipped chocolate on parchment paper or a silicone mat until firm. (The chocolate may be topped with edible gold leaf or other garnish.)

Chocolate Truffles

Chocolate truffles take their name from the rough, black, highly prized fungus they resemble, but there the similarity ends. Chocolate truffles should have a rich, creamy ganache center with a well-balanced, refined flavor.

To prepare chocolate truffles, a firm ganache is flavored as desired, then piped or allowed to harden. Once firm, the ganache is rolled in cocoa powder, powdered sugar or melted chocolate. The classic French truffle is a small, irregularly shaped ball of bittersweet chocolate dusted with cocoa powder. Americans, however, seem to prefer larger candies, coated with melted chocolate and decorated with nuts or additional chocolate, toasted sliced almonds, chocolate shavings or candied citrus peel. The following formula can be prepared in either style.

DARK CHOCOLATE TRUFFLES

Yield: 150 Medium-Sized Truffles, 4 lb. 4 oz. (2040 g)

Dark chocolate	2 lb.	960 g
Unsalted butter	1 lb.	480 g
Heavy cream	1 pt.	480 ml
Brandy, bourbon or liqueur	4 fl. oz.	120 ml
Cocoa powder (optional)	as needed	as needed
Powdered sugar (optional)	as needed	as needed
Chocolate, tempered (optional)	as needed	as needed

1. Chop the chocolate and butter into small pieces and place in a large metal bowl.
2. Bring the cream to a boil. Immediately pour the hot cream over the chocolate and butter. Stir until the chocolate and butter are completely melted.
3. Stir in the brandy. Pipe the ganache into uniform mounds. Allow the ganache to set slightly, then drop each ball into a pan of sifted cocoa powder or powdered sugar, rolling it around to coat completely. Alternatively, dip the ganache into tempered chocolate. Chocolate-coated truffles may also be coated with chopped toasted nuts.
4. Truffles can be stored in the refrigerator 7 to 10 days. Allow them to soften slightly at room temperature before serving.

Approximate values per truffle: **Calories** 70, **Total fat** 6 g, **Saturated fat** 3.5 g, **Cholesterol** 10 mg, **Sodium** 0 mg, **Total carbohydrates** 4 g, **Protein** 0 g

1. Piping the chocolate truffle mixture into uniform mounds.

2. Chocolate truffles may be dipped into tempered chocolate using a dipping spoon.

3. After dipping in tempered chocolate, truffles may also be coated with chopped toasted nuts.

MOLDING CHOCOLATES

Chocolate lends itself to being molded into small candies or larger, three-dimensional pieces. Chocolates are molded in several stages. A thin layer of chocolate is built up in the mold by filling it with melted chocolate, then pouring out the excess. This is repeated a second time, then the molds are chilled—the **first cooling**. Fillings are poured or piped into the chilled shells, then they are sealed with a thin layer of tempered chocolate. The **second cooling** is the stage when the finished chocolates are chilled before unmolding.

Chocolate molds come in a wide range of designs, sizes and materials. Those made from a polycarbonate material are preferred because they are easy to use and provide superior chocolate sheen. Tin molds rust easily and generally produce less glossy chocolates. Hobbyists usually work with molds made of thin, flexible plastic.

Before using, new or soiled molds are washed in warm water no higher than 120°F (49°C) with a mild unscented detergent. Buffing with cotton balls is usually sufficient to remove any chocolate residue that remains, so molds are not washed after each use. An abrasive is never used to clean chocolate molds, as this would scratch the delicate surface and mar the finished chocolates.

Accurate temperatures and properly prepared molds are needed to ensure success when making molded chocolates. The melted chocolate should be held at the recommended temperatures (see page 693) throughout the molding process. The temperature of the fillings should not exceed 70°F (21°C) to prevent melting the chocolate shells. The molds should also be held at the proper temperatures to ensure successful molding—70°F (21°C) for polycarbonate molds, 78°F (25°C) for metal molds.

When molding chocolates, a large quantity of melted, tempered chocolate is necessary to coat the insides of the shells completely. Not all of the chocolate specified in each formula will be used to make the batch of molded chocolate. Excess can be reserved for use in other bakeshop items or for reuse once it is retempered. The amount of molded candies each batch produces varies according to the size and depth of molds used. Each formula in this book is calculated using the molds in the procedural photographs or those of similar capacity. Overfilled chocolate shells will be impossible to seal neatly. Remove excess filling with a spoon or the suction from a clean squeeze bottle.

PROCEDURE FOR MOLDING CHOCOLATES

❶ Ladle tempered chocolate onto the mold. Spread the chocolate over the surface of the mold with an offset spatula, filling each cavity. Tap the mold on the table a few times to remove any air.

❷ Turn the mold upside down, then tap the sides of the mold with a rubber hammer or a spatula to remove the excess chocolate. The coating should be no thicker than ¹⁄₁₆ inch (1 millimeter).

❸ Invert the mold and scrape the excess couverture from its surface with a metal spatula. Place the mold, chocolate side up, on a paper-lined sheet pan and cool it in a low-humidity refrigerator at 50°F (10°C). Leave the molds in the refrigerator only until the chocolate shells loosen.

④ Remove the molds from the refrigerator. Using a pastry bag fitted with a small plain tip, carefully pipe the filling into the shells to just within ⅟₁₆ inch (1 millimeter) of the rim.

⑤ Cover the filled shells with tempered couverture melted to its highest allowed temperature.

⑥ Scrape excess chocolate from the surface of the mold with an offset spatula.

⑦ After the chocolate has hardened and the shells have shrunk slightly from the sides of their molds, the chocolates are ready for unmolding. Firmly tap a corner of the mold on the table to loosen the chocolates, then invert the mold.

Hollow Chocolate Figure Molding

Three-dimensional chocolate figures are made in two-sided molds with either a closed or an open bottom. In a **closed-bottom mold**, there are two separate molds, one a mirror image of the other. Each mold is filled, then chilled until the chocolate pieces are unmolded. The finished three-dimensional candy is made when two matching pieces are attached together. Closed-bottom chocolate molding is illustrated by the white chocolate dolphins shown on page 708. **Open-bottom molds** are two mirror-image molds hinged or attached together with clips. The molds are coated inside, then closed or clipped together. When the chocolate sets and contracts from the molds, the clips and sides are removed to reveal the completed three-dimensional piece.

As with all tempered chocolate work, a room temperature of 68°F (20°C) with low humidity is recommended. Having the molds at the proper temperature provides consistent results. Chilling molded chocolates in a room or refrigerator at 52°F (11°C) helps the chocolate set and unmold quickly. Colored highlights can be added to molded white chocolate; melt and temper equal parts white chocolate and cocoa butter. Tint the mixture using paste food coloring. Brush, rub or splatter the molds with this tinted mixture before adding the tempered white chocolate couverture.

PROCEDURE FOR CLOSED-BOTTOM CHOCOLATE MOLDING

① Pipe or brush areas of the mold requiring highlighting with a tinted tempered white couverture chocolate mixture.

② Speckle additional details into the mold with the tinted chocolate mixture.

③ Fill the mold with tempered white chocolate couverture. Scrape excess chocolate from the surface of the mold before allowing it to harden.

④ Once the chocolates are unmolded, slightly soften the flat sides of each piece by placing them on a sheet tray that has been warmed in a hot oven.

⑤ Press two matching chocolate pieces together to form the three-dimensional dolphin-shaped candy.

PROCEDURE FOR MOLDING A CHOCOLATE BOWL

❶ With gloved hands, rub the inside of a bowl-shaped mold with a mixture of tinted white chocolate and cocoa butter. Ladle tempered white chocolate couverture into the mold. Tilt the mold to evenly coat it with the chocolate. Scrape excess couverture from the surface of the mold and place in a cool place until the chocolate hardens and shrinks from the sides of the mold.

Hollow Chocolate Spheres

❷ Rap the side of the mold on a table to loosen the chocolate. Unmold the white chocolate bowl once it sets to reveal its patterned surface. (To join two hollow pieces to form a sphere, soften the edge of one bowl on a sheet tray that has been warmed in a hot oven. Press the two pieces together to form the three-dimensional sphere.)

MODELING CHOCOLATE

Modeling chocolate is a type of edible modeling clay used for making cake decorations. Made from melted chocolate, sugar syrup and/or invert sugar such as glucose or corn syrup, modeling chocolate has a smoother texture than marzipan, making it ideal for delicate work. Lifelike chocolate roses are made by tinting white modeling chocolate pink, then sandwiching it between two layers of white modeling chocolate. This creates a delicate mottled material. Modeling chocolate is also used to add small details to chocolate showpieces. Modeling chocolate keeps 6 months when wrapped tightly in plastic and stored in the refrigerator.

PROCEDURE FOR MAKING MODELING CHOCOLATE

❶ Have all ingredients at room temperature.

❷ Melt dark couverture in a microwave or over a bain marie until it reaches 110°F (43°C). For white chocolate, bring it to 90°F (32°C).

❸ Stir together the corn syrup, glucose syrup and fondant if using a combination of sweeteners.

❹ Stir this mixture into the melted chocolate. Add coloring (if using).

❺ Cool the mixture at room temperature several hours.

❻ Knead the mixture thoroughly until well blended. If the cocoa butter separates from the mass, chill the modeling chocolate before kneading.

❼ Let the modeling chocolate rest, wrapped in plastic and stored in the refrigerator overnight, before using to make it easier to handle.

Dark and White Modeling Chocolate

DARK MODELING CHOCOLATE

Yield: 1 lb. 6 oz. (660 g)

Bittersweet chocolate (58% cacao)	1 lb.	480 g
Corn syrup	6 fl. oz.	180 ml

1. Finely chop the chocolate and melt it to 110°F (43°C).
2. Stir in the corn syrup and combine well.
3. Knead the mixture thoroughly until well blended. If the cocoa butter separates from the mass, chill the modeling chocolate before kneading.
4. Wrap the modeling chocolate in plastic wrap and rest at room temperature for a minimum of 2 hours or preferably overnight before using.

Approximate values per ½-oz. (15-g) serving: **Calories** 60, **Total fat** 25 g, **Saturated fat** 1.5 g, **Cholesterol** 0 mg, **Sodium** 0 mg, **Total carbohydrates** 9 g, **Protein** 1 g

WHITE MODELING CHOCOLATE

Making white modeling chocolate requires the addition of cocoa butter to give the finished modeling chocolate a supple texture. When making white modeling chocolate, it is very important to melt the cocoa butter to the recommended temperature. If the temperature is too high, the cocoa butter will not homogenize properly and the paste will separate. If the cocoa butter temperature is too low or the cocoa butter is not added quickly into the other ingredients, part of the cocoa butter will solidify and create lumps in the modeling paste.

When glucose syrup is not available, use the variation, designed for use when only corn syrup is available.

Yield: 4 lb. (1920 g)

Cocoa butter	8 oz.	240 g
Powdered sugar, sifted	1 lb. 8 oz.	720 g
Fondant, firm confectionery style, room temperature*	1 lb.	480 g
Glucose syrup	1 lb.	480 g

1. Melt the cocoa butter over a double boiler until it reaches 90°F (32°C).
2. Place the powdered sugar, fondant and glucose syrup in the bowl of a mixer fitted with the paddle attachment. Add the melted cocoa butter and mix on low speed until well combined, approximately 2 minutes.
3. If the cocoa butter separates from the mixture during mixing, let it cool 15 to 30 minutes and mix again. Wrap the modeling chocolate with plastic wrap and rest at room temperature for a minimum of 2 hours or preferably overnight before using.

*Note: Firm confectionery fondant is used to make candy centers.

VARIATION:

White Modeling Chocolate Made with Corn Syrup—Substitute 12 ounces (360 grams) cream-style fondant in place of the firm fondant and 7 fluid ounces (210 milliliters) corn syrup in place of the glucose syrup in the formula.

Approximate values per ½-oz. (15-g) serving: **Calories** 60, **Total fat** 2 g, **Saturated fat** 1 g, **Cholesterol** 0 mg, **Sodium** 5 mg, **Total carbohydrates** 11 g, **Protein** 0 g

PROCEDURE FOR MAKING MODELING CHOCOLATE ROSES AND LEAVES

❶ Divide the white modeling chocolate into three uniform pieces. Tint one section with pink food coloring, kneading it to distribute the color evenly. Dust a worktable lightly with powdered sugar and roll out each piece of modeling chocolate into an 8-inch × 10-inch (20-centimeter × 25-centimeter) block. Stack the three layers so that the layer of pink modeling chocolate is sandwiched between the two white layers.

❷ Flatten the modeling chocolate with a rolling pin to $\frac{1}{16}$ inch (1 millimeter) thick. Cut 2-inch (5-centimeter) circles out of the dough with a cookie cutter and place them on a sheet of heavy-gauge plastic spaced 2 inches (5 centimeters) apart. Cover the circles with another sheet of heavy-gauge plastic. Thin the upper edges of the disks evenly using a flexible metal spatula to make realistic rose petals.

❸ Roll a scrap of the dough into a 2-inch- (5-centimeter-) tall cone with a narrow tip. Wrap a petal completely around the cone with the upper edge of the petal flush with the top of the cone. Attach another petal around the cone, positioning it at the exact height of the center tip. Fold part of the petal back. Attach the next petal, overlapping the previous petal by approximately $\frac{1}{4}$ inch (6 millimeters). Continue adding petals until the desired size rose is obtained. Cut excess dough from the bottom with scissors.

❹ Flatten additional white modeling chocolate with a rolling pin until it is $\frac{1}{8}$ inch (3 millimeters) thick. Cut the modeling chocolate into leaf shapes using a small paring knife. Use the back of a knife or modeling tools to indent veins in the leaves. Drape the leaves over a dowel or rolling pin to obtain a curved shape and let dry overnight.

❺ Attach the leaves to the finished rose with simple syrup.

Chocolate Showpiece

Chocolate **showpieces** are the ultimate expression of the chocolatiers' art. They are often the centerpiece on a dessert buffet celebrating Valentine's or Mother's Day or a test of one's skill in a competition. Anything one can imagine can be done in chocolate. But planning the design and executing the showpiece require organization.

First the design is planned, keeping in mind both visual and structural balance. Scale is an important consideration; large pieces need to be both structurally sound and movable. When planning the design, make a mock-up in acetate and paper to test the construction. When making a piece in monochromatic colors, ensure that there is a variety of eye-pleasing textures and shapes. Textured plastic for chocolate work can be purchased from baking supply stores, but interesting patterned plastic can also be found at home improvement and art supply stores. White chocolate can be dyed with fat-soluble colors, which often look best when used sparingly. After a chocolate piece is constructed, it is often sprayed with chocolate. (See page 704.) Spraying only part of the piece highlights the contrast between matte and shiny surfaces. Keep in mind that only chocolate pieces completely free of fingerprints can be used without spraying.

MAKING THE CHOCOLATE SHOWPIECE

When making a chocolate showpiece, the work is done in stages, tempering successive batches of chocolate as needed. (Chocolate components firm quickly and need constant attention.) The amount of chocolate required will vary depending on the size of the showpiece. To approximate how much chocolate will be needed, scatter chopped chocolate out onto a worktable in the dimensions of the piece. Then temper that amount of chocolate, adding 15 to 20 percent more as a cushion. Showpieces can be made with chocolate that previously was used for other displays but may have lost its freshness.

The base is usually made first. Once it has set as firm as leather, it is immediately cut and turned over to keep the edges from curling. When assembling a showpiece keep the chocolate at the highest allowable tempered temperature (90°F [32°C] for dark chocolate), to ensure a firm bond between the chocolate pieces. Tempered chocolate piped from small parchment paper cones can be used to bond pieces together. To keep tempered chocolate on hand, set the bowl containing tempered chocolate on top of a heating pad set to low. Or set the bowl containing tempered chocolate in a larger bowl of water that is slightly warmer than the tempered chocolate. Cans of **cold spray**, which dispense compressed air at freezing temperatures, can be used to quickly set the bonded area so the pieces do not have to be held while they set. For proper sheen, it is important to leave chocolate that was molded in plastic or on acetate to set for at least 1 hour before removing the plastic. Four or more hours will produce the highest gloss on the chocolate. Removing the acetate too soon will create disappointing results.

Chocolate flower and pillar showpiece.

This showpiece shown above and in the chapter opening photograph on page 687 is composed of different-sized hollow chocolate pillars. Large abstract flowers decorate the base of the composition. This formula lists the actual weight of the white or dark chocolate used to create the showpiece. These amounts will be helpful in determining how much chocolate will be needed if a smaller or larger piece is desired. For best results, temper more chocolate than needed. Any excess can be remelted and reused.

CHOCOLATE FLOWER AND PILLAR SHOWPIECE

Base, 12 in. × 10 in. (30.5 cm × 25.5 cm)	1 lb. 2 oz.	540 g
Short pillars, 5 in. × 1 in. (13 cm × 2.5 cm)	4 oz.	120 g
Medium pillars, 8 in. × 1 in. (20 cm × 2.5 cm)	6 oz.	180 g
Tall pillars, 10 in. × ¾ in. (25 cm × 2 cm)	6 oz.	180 g
Flower centers (white chocolate)	3 oz.	90 g
Flower petals	3 oz.	90 g
Tempered chocolate for assembly	as needed	as needed

1. For the base: Spread out the tempered chocolate ¼ inch (6 centimeters) thick on a piece of textured plastic approximately 16 inches (40 centimeters) square. Once the chocolate is firm as leather, use a template to cut out the base. To prevent the chocolate base from curling at the edges, immediately flip it over onto a flat surface. Allow the base to cool and firm for at least 1 hour, or up to 4 hours for the highest sheen.

2. For the pillars: While the base cools, make 10 to 14 tubes from plastic acetate in assorted sizes. Fasten the acetate into tubes using tape. Fill a pastry bag with tempered chocolate. One at a time, pipe chocolate into the tubes while holding each one above the bowl of tempered chocolate to catch the excess. When the dripping stops, position the tubes upright on a flat sheet pan.

3 Refrigerate the tubes for 20 minutes. Remove from the refrigerator and let sit at room temperature for at least 1 hour, or up to 4 hours for the highest sheen.

4 For the flower centers: Mold the white chocolate into bowls using the molding technique on page 709, joining the domes together into spheres.

5 For the flower petals: Dip the tip of a paring knife into tempered chocolate and lightly press the knife point onto a strip of acetate. (For the larger flower petals, use a slightly larger chef's knife.) Repeat a few times, and then, before the chocolate begins to set, place the acetate strip inside a curved tuile mold. Or make a mold from a paper tube cut in half horizontally. Let sit at room temperature for at least 1 hour, or up to 4 hours

6 To form the flower: Starting with the smaller petals, dip the base of each one into tempered chocolate. Attach them to the white chocolate spheres in a circular pattern. Surround the first row of petals with the larger ones. Place the flowers on a sheet of parchment or acetate to set.

7 To assemble the showpiece: Apply a small amount of melted chocolate to a solid, decorative board. Remove the plastic from the base and place it on the board. Temper a small amount of chocolate to be used to attach the pieces together.

8 Remove the acetate from the pillars. One at a time, dip the bottom of each pillar into a small amount of tempered chocolate, then position them on the base in an artistic fashion. Freeze the chocolate showpiece for approximately 30 minutes.

9 Prepare an area for spraying chocolate. Melt chocolate for spraying or use chocolate spray in a can.

10 Remove the showpiece from the freezer and spray it from a distance to create a velvet appearance on the piece. Spray the heart of the flowers lightly. Attach the flowers to the base with tempered chocolate.

❶ Tracing the template to make the base.

❷ Filling an acetate tube with chocolate.

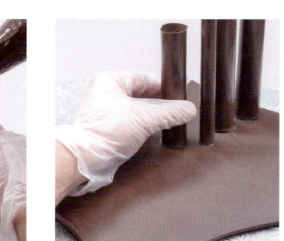

❸ Positioning the chocolate columns on the base.

❹ Forming leaves for the chocolate flowers.

❺ Positioning the chocolate leaves around the white chocolate center to form a blossom.

❻ Spraying the showpiece with chocolate.

❼ Closeup of the finished showpiece.

ALMONDS: FROM THE LAND OF MILK AND HONEY

The first traces of the almond tree are found in parts of China and the Middle East, mainly Iran and the Indus River valley. Almonds are one of the earliest cultivated plants mentioned in ancient texts and the Bible. The Roman Empire introduced the almond into Europe and planted almond orchards in Italy, Sicily, Spain, Portugal, France and North Africa. The first almond tree reached American shores in 1769, when Franciscan monks brought saplings with them from Spain. The climate in San Diego where they settled didn't suit these trees, however, so it was not until the 20th century that the almond took hold in California. Today, California supplies more than 80 percent of the world's almonds. Italy, Spain, Portugal, France, Morocco and Turkey are major foreign producers. Almonds grown in Italy and Spain are prized by confectioners for their excellent aroma and sweet taste.

MARZIPAN

Marzipan is a mixture of almond paste, sugar and glucose or corn syrup that may be colored and used like modeling clay for sculpting small fruits, flowers or other objects. Because of its plasticity, marzipan can also be rolled out and cut into various shapes or used to cover cakes and pastries. It is widely used as an ingredient in chocolate candies and petits fours.

The best-quality marzipan is made from equal parts by weight of fresh almonds and sugar, with liquid sweetener for pliability. With their high fat content (50 percent), almonds need sugar to bring out their delicate flavor. A higher amount of sugar creates a sweeter marzipan that may be more difficult to handle. Quality marzipan is ivory in color, subtle in almond flavor, and short textured but not sticky, and should hold its shape when modeled.

Make the paste in a stainless steel bowl rather than aluminum to prevent discoloration. Wrap marzipan tightly in plastic and then place it in a thick black plastic bag. Proper wrapping keeps the paste from drying out; opaque or black plastic prevents fading from exposure to light. Properly prepared and stored marzipan retains optimum freshness 2 to 3 months.

Marzipan exposed to air will form a crust; therefore, only the amount needed should be removed from the plastic bag. To cover tortes, wedding cakes and pastries, the paste is rolled to approximately ⅛ inch (3 millimeters) thick. Special rolling pins are available to create various patterns on the marzipan sheet. Powdered sugar is used to prevent the marzipan from sticking, as flour will add an undesirable flavor and may cause it to ferment.

MARZIPAN

Yield: 2 lb. 4 oz. (1080 g)

Almond paste	1 lb.	480 g
Glucose or corn syrup	4 oz.	120 g
Powdered sugar, sifted	1 lb.	480 g

1. In the stainless steel bowl of a mixer fitted with the paddle attachment, blend the almond paste and glucose syrup on low speed until well combined.
2. Continuing on low speed, gradually add just enough of the powdered sugar to make a pliable paste that is not oily. Wrap the marzipan tightly in plastic and store in a dry place until ready to use.

Approximate values per ½-oz. (15-g) serving: **Calories** 60, **Total fat** 2 g, **Saturated fat** 0 g, **Cholesterol** 0 mg, **Sodium** 0 mg, **Total carbohydrates** 10 g, **Protein** 1 g

Marzipan Modeling

Marzipan is the perfect medium for making edible decorations. Children's birthday cakes enchant when topped with whimsical animals and balloons. When tinted orange, marzipan can be rolled into Lilliputian carrots used to mark individual portions of carrot cake. When modeling marzipan, color the paste with liquid food coloring before modeling. The marzipan may also be hand-painted or sprayed with edible food coloring after it has been shaped. For either method, water-soluble colors are used. Light brown shades are obtained by adding coffee extract, chocolate tones with cocoa powder. (Sugar syrup may be needed to compensate for the cocoa's drying action.) Marzipan roses may be made according to the instructions on page 711 for modeling chocolate roses.

For marzipan production, uniformity and fine detail is the hallmark of good craftsmanship. **Serial work** refers to modeling identical pieces of molded candies such as marzipan. To create a series of figures of identical weight, calculate the total weight of marzipan to be used. For example, if 10 pears each weighing 1 ounce (30 grams) are needed, scale 10 ounces (300 grams) of marzipan. Tint the paste, if desired, then roll the marzipan into a cylinder measuring 10 inches (25 centimeters) long. Cut the cylinder into 1-inch (2.5-centimeter) segments to obtain 10 pieces of marzipan of identical size and weight. Use this technique to prepare each part of a multipart marzipan figure such as the Happy Pig (page 717) and Hunter the Dog (page 718).

Sugar syrup is used to attach separate pieces of marzipan together to make a complete figure. (Even though egg whites work equally well for assembling, the safety of this practice is questionable.) The basic marzipan figure is based on a pear shape to which other pieces are attached to form details such as leaves for fruits and arms, legs, ears and other features for animal shapes. Additional details are made from melted chocolate, royal icing, dried fruit or other edible decoration.

Proper placement of decorative details makes the difference between an appealing marzipan sculpture and a dull one. When making animal figures, eyes are one of the most important features. The eye indentions should be sufficiently deep to allow for a good amount of royal icing. Eyes should be flush with the face and not bulging too much. Tempered chocolate may be used to add eye details. Placing the pupils of the eyes off to one side, on the left or right or looking up make a lively figure. Place the eyes, ears, nose and mouth relatively close together to create a young and appealing figure.

A light spray with cocoa butter once the figures are finished slows the drying process. It also protects colored marzipan from fading and provides an attractive luster. Cocoa butter may be melted to 90°F (32°C), placed in a pressure sprayer and applied to the figure or brushed on. **Edible food lacquer** may be sparingly used to provide extra shine. Marzipan figures may be made several months ahead and stored in an airtight container in a cool place before serving.

Assortment of marzipan fruit.

edible food lacquer a composition of fats, lecithin and other edible ingredients used to create a shine on marzipan and other confections

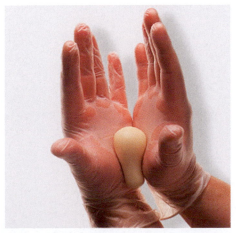
Rolling marzipan into a basic pear shape.

Indenting the marzipan with a sculpting tool to form the eyes for a marzipan figure.

PROCEDURE FOR MAKING MARZIPAN FIGURES

1. Determine the number of finished pieces required.
2. Scale the marzipan. Tint the marzipan if necessary. Then roll and divide the pieces evenly according to the amount needed for each part, if necessary.
3. Shape the different pieces required for the marzipan figure. Attach the pieces together if necessary, using sugar syrup as the glue. Allow the pieces to set approximately 30 minutes.
4. Apply decorative details using marzipan sculpting tools or a small knife.
5. Paint or airbrush colors on the finished pieces. Add decorative details such as royal icing eyes. Spray or brush the finished pieces with cocoa butter or edible food lacquer.

MARZIPAN PEAR

Yield: 1 Pear Figure

Marzipan	0.5 oz.	15 g
Liquid food coloring	as needed	as needed

1. Form the marzipan into a round ball. Roll one end of the ball between your palms to form a pear shape.
2. Airbrush or paint color onto the surface of the marzipan.
3. Attach the pear to a disk of marzipan using sugar syrup.
4. Cut out a leaf shape from tinted marzipan. Attach it to the pear using a marzipan modeling tool or wooden skewer.

Approximate values per ½-oz. (15-g) serving: **Calories** 60, **Total fat** 2 g, **Saturated fat** 0 g, **Cholesterol** 0 mg, **Sodium** 0 mg, **Total carbohydrates** 10 g, **Protein** 1 g

Form the marzipan into a smooth ball (left foreground). Taper the marzipan into a pear shape (center foreground). Indent the tip of the figure with a sculpting tool. Insert a stem and leaf (right) into the marzipan pear. Airbrush or paint the finished pear with food coloring. The finished marzipan pears are shown at the top.

HAPPY PIG

Yield: 1 Pig Figure

Marzipan	5 oz.	150 g
Simple Syrup (page 73)	as needed	as needed
Liquid food coloring	as needed	as needed
Cocoa butter	as needed	as needed
Royal Icing (page 457)	as needed	as needed
Chocolate, melted	as needed	as needed
Chocolate cutouts (page 698)	as needed	as needed

1. For the body, roll 2½ ounces (75 grams) of the marzipan into a ball. Form an oval shape with two blunt ends by rolling the marzipan between gloved palms. Curve the marzipan so that the extensions form the hind legs. Cut a slit into one end of each piece to form the hooves.

2. For the front legs, divide ⅓ ounce (10 grams) of the marzipan into two equal pieces. Roll each piece into tubes ½ inch (1.2 centimeters) long. Indent one end of each rope with a knife or marzipan tool to indicate the hooves. Attach the marzipan to each side of the figure to form the front legs.

3. Roll 1½ ounces (45 grams) marzipan into a pear shape. Flatten the narrow end of the pear shape on the work surface to create a pig snout. Indent two holes for the nose and make a small cut for the mouth. Make indentions for the eyes. Attach the head to the body with a small amount of Simple Syrup.

4. For the ears, divide ⅓ ounce (10 grams) of the marzipan in half. Roll each piece of the marzipan into a small ball, then taper the marzipan into a cone 1 inch (2.5 centimeters) in length. Flatten the cones slightly, then attach them to the head, bending the tips down toward the eyes.

5. For the tail, roll a small amount of marzipan into a thin rope, tapered slightly at the end. Curl and attach it to the body.

6. Airbrush details onto the pig with red food color. Spray the finished figure with cocoa butter. Fill a pastry bag with a small plain tip with Royal Icing. Fill the indentations for the eyes with Royal Icing. Use a toothpick dipped in melted chocolate to add details to the eyes.

7. Place the finished marzipan pig on a chocolate cutout.

Approximate values per ½-oz. (15-g) serving: **Calories** 60, **Total fat** 2 g, **Saturated fat** 0 g, **Cholesterol** 0 mg, **Sodium** 0 mg, **Total carbohydrates** 10 g, **Protein** 1 g

Start with a ball of marzipan. Form the body of the figure and its two legs (upper left). Going counterclockwise: attach two front legs; attach ears onto the head, which has been sculpted with details; two views of the finished pig after it has been airbrushed with color.

HUNTER THE DOG

Yield: 1 Dog Figure

Marzipan	4 oz.	120 g
Simple Syrup (page 73)	as needed	as needed
Cocoa butter	as needed	as needed
Royal Icing (page 457)	as needed	as needed
Chocolate, melted	as needed	as needed

1. For the body, roll 1⅔ ounces (50 grams) of the marzipan into a ball. Taper the ball into a pear shape by rolling the marzipan between gloved hands.
2. Roll ⅓ ounce (10 grams) of the marzipan into a 3-inch- (7.5-centimeter-) long rope. Cut the rope in half, then curve each piece to form the hind legs. Attach each piece of marzipan to the sides of the body with Simple Syrup. Use a modeling tool or toothpick to indent the marzipan to resemble the paws.
3. Roll ⅓ ounce (10 grams) of the marzipan into a 2-inch- (5-centimeter-) long rope. Curve the marzipan rope and place it on the front of the figure to form the front legs.
4. For the tail, roll a small amount of the marzipan into a seamless ball. Taper the marzipan into a pear shape, then attach the narrow end under the figure.
5. For the head, roll 1 ounce (30 grams) of the marzipan into a smooth ball. Taper it into a blunt pear shape. Curve the tapered end slightly to form a turned-up nose. Indent the eyes and mouth with a modeling tool or toothpick. Attach the head to the body of the figure with Simple Syrup.
6. For the ears, divide ⅓ ounce (10 grams) of the marzipan into two equal pieces. Roll into balls. Taper one end to make the pear shape and flatten the tapered end. Attach the marzipan to each side of the head of the figure.
7. Spray the finished figure with cocoa butter. Fill a pastry bag fitted with a small plain tip with Royal Icing. Fill the indentations for the eyes and snout with Royal Icing. Use a toothpick dipped in melted chocolate to add details to the eyes.

Approximate values per ½-oz. (15-g) serving: **Calories** 60, **Total fat** 2 g, **Saturated fat** 0 g, **Cholesterol** 0 mg, **Sodium** 0 mg, **Total carbohydrates** 10 g, **Protein** 1 g

Start with a ball of marzipan (center left); roll into a cone for the body (left). Roll small pieces of marzipan to form the rear and front legs (lower left). Form another piece of marzipan into a pear shape for the head (foreground). Use a modeling tool to indent the cone to make the eyes and nose. Attach the cone to the marzipan body (right). Pipe Royal Icing to add decorative details. Two views of the finished marzipan figure are shown at the top.

PASTILLAGE

Pastillage is a paste made with sugar, cornstarch and gelatin. It can be molded or rolled into sheets, then cut into various shapes. Once dry, pastillage is sturdy and firm like plaster. Although edible, it is rarely consumed. Naturally pure white, it can be painted with cocoa or food coloring. Pastillage is used for showpieces and large decorative items. Decorative work made from pastillage is not temperature or humidity sensitive. Protected from dust, it will keep for a year.

Pastillage is made by blending powdered sugar and starch with water or egg whites or a small amount of corn syrup. Gelatin or gum tragacanth are used as binders and lemon juice, citric acid or cream of tartar as bleaching agents. (When gum tragacanth is used, the finished product is often called *gum paste*.) The addition of more corn syrup and vegetable shortening makes the paste less susceptible to drying out and is recommended when the pastillage is to be used for sculpting flowers. Use stainless steel bowls and nonreactive utensils when making pastillage to keep it from discoloring. A drop of blue liquid food coloring added to the liquid ingredients enhances the whiteness of the paste. The pastillage can be tinted with other colors when mixing. Because pastillage dries out quickly, keep it tightly wrapped in plastic. While working with the paste, keep unused portions covered with plastic wrap and a damp towel until needed.

Ready-to-use pastillage and gum paste products are sold through cake-decorating supply houses. These products are also available in powdered form.

Rolling and Shaping

Although pastillage can be molded into many of the same shapes as for marzipan or modeling chocolate, it is usually rolled flat and then cut into shapes. When rolling pastillage, work on a flat surface that has been lightly dusted with a small amount of a mixture of equal parts cornstarch and powdered sugar. Use a variable-gauge rolling pin to roll the pastillage to an even thickness. Cut the paste as soon as it has been rolled; once exposed to air, pastillage loses malleability and cracks. Once the pieces are cut, transfer them to a flat surface lightly dusted with cornstarch to dry. Pieces of rolled out pastillage can also be pressed into cornstarch-dusted molds or draped over cake pans to shape.

Proper drying prevents pastillage from warping. Let pastillage dry at room temperature, occasionally turning over the large pieces so that they dry evenly on both sides. Small pieces may be turned after 2 hours; larger pieces require more time. Most pastillage pieces will be thoroughly dry after 3 days.

Once it is completely dry, pastillage may be rubbed with fine sandpaper to smooth its surface. Rubbing the dry pastillage in a circular motion with a lightly moistened sponge that has been heated in a microwave oven will add a shine to the material. Brushing the dried pastillage with a **gum arabic** solution will also give the finished work a shiny surface. The gum arabic solution also seals its surface so that the pastillage can be colored after it is assembled and dried. Fresh pastillage, royal icing or tempered white chocolate is used to glue the pieces of pastillage together to make a showpiece.

Although pastillage can be colored during the mixing process, dry pieces can be spray-painted by airbrush before or after assembly.

Pastillage showpiece.

gum arabic a water-soluble gum obtained from several species of the acacia tree

PASTILLAGE

Yield: 2 lb. 9 oz. (1260 g)

Powdered sugar, sifted	2 lb.	960 g
Cornstarch	4 oz.	120 g
Granulated gelatin	0.5 oz.	15 g
Water, warm	4 fl. oz.	120 ml
Glucose or corn syrup	1 oz.	30 g
Lemon juice	0.5 fl. oz.	15 ml
Blue liquid food coloring (optional)	1 drop	1 drop

1 Place the powdered sugar and cornstarch in the stainless steel bowl of a mixer fitted with a stainless steel paddle attachment.

2 Bloom then melt the gelatin in the warm water and stir in the glucose syrup.

3 Make a well in the middle of the dry ingredients in the bowl. Add the liquid mixture and blend the ingredients on low speed. Add the lemon juice and food coloring (if using). Mix until combined.

4 Remove the pastillage from the bowl. Immediately wrap it tightly in plastic.

VARIATION:

Pastillage for Sculpting—Increase the corn syrup to 2 ounces (60 grams) in Step 2. Add 0.5 ounce (15 grams) vegetable shortening with the dry ingredients in Step 3.

GUM ARABIC SOLUTION

Yield: 2 fl. oz. (60 ml)

Boiling water	1 fl. oz.	30 ml
Gum arabic, powdered	1 fl. oz.	30 ml

1 Whisk the ingredients together in a stainless steel bowl until well blended. Use immediately.

Working with Pastillage

The procedure for working with pastillage is illustrated with the Matisse-Inspired Showpiece. When working with pastillage, always keep any unused paste tightly wrapped in plastic to keep it from drying out. Have any templates, molds, knives and other tools in place before starting any pastillage project. Keep a dish of cornstarch nearby for dusting the work surface and utensils. A clean, dry pastry brush is useful for dusting excess cornstarch off the pieces. Identify a cool, dry area in the bakeshop where the pieces can be stored undisturbed to dry.

MATISSE-INSPIRED SHOWPIECE

This showpiece is composed of large leaf shapes balanced on hollow tubes of pastillage placed on a pastillage base. Hand-formed hibiscus flowers decorate the base. This tower makes an impressive display for Caramel-Dipped Fruits (page 653), petits fours or molded and dipped chocolates.

Templates to be used for making the components in this showpiece can be found in Appendix IV, Patterns and Templates. Each component in this showpiece will require several days of drying time. Begin working on all of the pieces simultaneously.

Pastillage showpiece with Caramel Dipped Fruits.

SHOWPIECE TUBE SUPPORTS

Pastillage   2 lb. 8 oz.   1200 g

1. Dust three 1⅓-inch- (3.5-centimeter-) diameter rolling pins with cornstarch.
2. Roll 14 ounces (420 grams) of the pastillage ⅙ inch (4 millimeters) thick on a powdered-sugar-and-cornstarch-dusted work surface. Trim the pastillage into a rectangle measuring approximately 12 inches × 5 inches (30 centimeters × 12.5 centimeters). Place a dusted rolling pin lengthwise on the pastillage. Wrap the pastillage around the rolling pin.
3. Using a knife, trim the excess pastillage. Place the pastillage-wrapped rolling pin seam side down on a parchment-covered sheet pan to dry.
4. Roll 12 ounces (360 grams) of the pastillage as in Step 2, trimming it into a rectangle measuring approximately 10 inches × 5 inches (25 centimeters × 12.5 centimeters). Wrap the pastillage around another cornstarch-dusted rolling pin and transfer to the sheet pan to dry.
5. Roll the remaining pastillage as in Step 2, trimming it into a rectangle measuring approximately 8 inches × 5 inches (20 centimeters × 12.5 centimeters). Wrap the pastillage around another cornstarch-dusted rolling pin and transfer to the sheet pan to dry.
6. Cover the three pastillage-wrapped rolling pins loosely with parchment paper. Let dry at least 2 to 3 days before removing the rolling pins.
7. Gently slide the dry pastillage off the rolling pins. Let it dry at room temperature another 2 days.
8. Using the fine grid of a box grater, sand the bottom and top of the pastillage tubes perfectly level.
9. To add additional detail to the tubes, roll the pastillage into an 18-inch × 4-inch (45-centimeter × 10-centimeter) rectangle. Using a pizza wheel, cut the pastillage lengthwise into ⅕-inch- (5-millimeter-) wide strips. Brush the strips lightly with water and wrap the strips around the pastillage tubes in a spiral design. Lay the tubes seam side down on a parchment-covered sheet pan. Let dry at least 1 day.

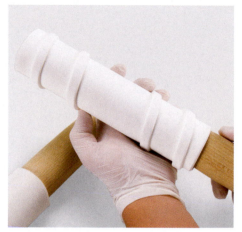

Removing dried pastillage tubes from the rolling pin.

SHOWPIECE BASE

Pastillage   2 lb. 8 oz.   1200 g

1. Roll 1 pound 8 ounces (720 grams) of the pastillage into a circle measuring slightly over 18 inches (45 centimeters) in diameter on a powdered-sugar-and-cornstarch-dusted work surface. Trim the pastillage into a uniform 18-inch- (45-centimeter-) wide circle. Dust off any excess powdered sugar and cornstarch with a clean, dry pastry brush. Transfer it to a flat parchment-covered sheet pan.
2. Knead the pastillage trimmings into the remaining pastillage. Roll it out into a 14-inch (35-centimeter) circle. Transfer it to a flat parchment-covered sheet pan.
3. Allow the circles to dry for 24 hours. Turn the pieces over to keep them from warping. Allow them to dry thoroughly, at least another 24 hours.

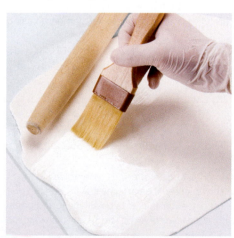

1. Moistening rolled pastillage with water before cutting.

2. Tracing the template with a knife and cutting out a leaf from the pastillage.

SHOWPIECE PHILODENDRON LEAVES

Pastillage	3 lb. 4 oz.	1560 g

1. Photocopy the philodendron leaf template on page 777. Cut out the philodendron leaf outline.
2. Roll out 18 ounces (540 grams) of the pastillage into a rectangle slightly thicker than ⅛ inch (3 millimeters) and the size of the leaf template on a cornstarch-and-powdered-sugar-dusted work surface. Lightly brush the surface of the rolled pastillage with a very thin coating of water.
3. Place the leaf template on the moistened pastillage. Using a blade or sharp knife, cut the pastillage into the leaf shape.
4. Transfer the leaf to a parchment-covered flat sheet pan.
5. Repeat with the remaining pastillage to make a total of three leaves.
6. Let dry 2 to 3 days. The leaves may be turned over after 1 or 2 days of drying; however, a slightly curved shape gives the leaves a natural appearance, which may be desirable.

HIBISCUS-STYLE FLOWERS

Powdered sugar	4 oz.	120 g
Cornstarch	4 oz.	120 g
Pastillage or rolled fondant, per completed flower	1 lb.	480 g
Royal Icing (page 457)	12 oz.	360 g
Stamens* (optional)	as needed	as needed

1. Sift together the powdered sugar and cornstarch. Set aside.
2. Photocopy the hibiscus flower templates on page 778. Cut out both hibiscus flower templates.
3. Lightly dust the work surface with some of the sugar-and-cornstarch mixture. Roll out two-thirds of the pastillage 1/12 inch (2 millimeters) thick. Lightly brush the surface of the rolled pastillage with a very thin coating of water.
4. Place the large flower template on the moistened pastillage. Using a blade or sharp knife, cut the pastillage into four flower shapes.
5. Using a marzipan tool, make ruffled indentions on the edges of the flower petals.
6. Invert a clean muffin tin. Lightly dust it with some of the sugar-and-cornstarch mixture. Fold up the pastillage cutouts into a cupped shape. Place them propped up between the muffin cups. Arrange the flower petals to obtain an attractive shape.
7. Roll out the remaining pastillage and cut out four of the small flower shapes. Using a marzipan tool, make ruffled indentions on the edge of the flower petals. Lightly dust the inside of a clean muffin tin with some of the sugar-and-cornstarch mixture. Fold up the pastillage cutouts into a cupped shape. Place them in the muffin cups. Arrange the flower petals to obtain an attractive shape.
8. Allow the flower shapes to dry thoroughly at room temperature until firm, at least 2 days.
9. To assemble the flowers, pipe a small amount of Royal Icing into the center of each of the larger flower shapes. Place a smaller flower into each large one. Pipe a small dome of Royal Icing in the center of each assembled flower, if desired, and carefully position some flower stamens (if using) in the Royal Icing. Let harden.

*Artificial flower stamens, leaves and decorative elements are sold through cake-decorating wholesalers.

SHOWPIECE ASSEMBLY

Royal Icing (page 457)	10 oz.	300 g

1. Select a work area where the showpiece can remain undisturbed after it is assembled. Spread a thin layer of Royal Icing on the surface to which the showpiece will be attached. A flat serving platter, marble slab or foil-wrapped cake board can be used. Center the large pastillage round on the board. Spread the center of the pastillage round with a thin layer of Royal Icing. Center the smaller pastillage round on top.

2 Before attaching the pastillage tubes, test their position on the board. Take into account the space that the large leaves will take up once they are positioned on top of the upright tubes. Once the tubes are positioned properly, pipe a small ring of Royal Icing on the selected area and place a tube on top. Through the top opening of the tube, pipe approximately 2 tablespoons Royal Icing to make an invisible seal between the tube and the base. Repeat with the other tubes. Allow the showpiece to harden at least 1 day.

3 Pipe a layer of Royal Icing on the top edge of a tube and carefully place the center of a pastillage leaf on top, ensuring that it is stable and balanced. Pipe additional Royal Icing underneath the leaf where it touches the tube.

4 Repeat with the remaining leaves, taking care not to bump into the previous assembled pieces. Position the Hibiscus-Style Flowers around the base.

5 Let the showpiece dry at least 2 days before using to display petits fours, marzipan work or chocolates.

Attaching dry pastillage leaves to pastillage cones.

NOUGATINE

Nougatine is a blend of melted caramelized sugar, sliced toasted almonds and butter. (Closely related is **nougat** candy, the same composition to which egg whites are added.) Nougatine is used as an ingredient in petits fours, chocolates, creams and mousses. When still warm, nougatine is pliable and may be formed into edible dessert containers. Croquembouche is often displayed on an elaborate nougatine showpiece. Unlike other sugar decorations, such as pastillage or gum paste, nougat remains deliciously edible.

Like all nut brittle and sugar candies, nougatine softens easily under humid conditions. Using cocoa butter in the formula helps it resist stickiness. Specialty ingredients can help nougatine stay crisp longer and resist crystallization. Powdered glucose, the dried form of glucose syrup, may be substituted for 10 percent of the sugar in the formula for this purpose. Edible food lacquer can be sprayed on the pieces to help them resist weeping. In all cases, nougatine should be stored in well-sealed containers.

As with other types of sugar work, oiled parchment paper or silicone baking mats are recommended. Oil all tools and work surfaces to be used when making nougatine. A constant warm temperature makes rolling, cutting and shaping nougatine easier; working over a heated surface such as a flat-top stove is recommended. Otherwise, work near a warm oven on a silicone mat or an oiled marble slab. Pieces of nougatine may be assembled into simple or elaborate showpieces. Attach the pieces together using caramel sugar (page 726) or nougatine made without the nuts. Nougatine formulas are versatile and may be made by replacing all or some of the almonds with sliced toasted hazelnuts, walnuts, cocoa nibs, coffee beans or toasted sesame seeds.

nougat a candy made from caramelized sugar, almonds and egg whites known as *turrón* in Spain and *torrone* in Italy

PROCEDURE FOR MAKING NOUGATINE

1 Oil all cooking surfaces, tools, knives, rolling pins and molds with vegetable oil.

2 Melt the sugars, corn syrup, fondant and glucose syrup in a pot, preferably copper, over medium heat.

3 Cook the syrup until caramelized, approximately 320°F–330°F (160°C–166°C). Remove from the heat.

4 Carefully stir in the nuts or other ingredients, then the fat.

5 Pour the mass onto a silicone baking mat, oiled marble or oiled parchment paper. Let cool slightly.

6 Roll the mass to the desired thickness. Cut into desired shapes and form immediately. Should it harden before cutting, reheat nougatine in a warm oven, 275°F (135°C).

7 Store nougatine away from heat and humidity. Excess scraps may be reused or ground for a crunchy topping or an addition to mousses, chocolates or a frozen dessert known as **nougat glacé**.

nougat glacé a still-frozen dessert composed of whipped cream, Italian meringue, chopped nougatine and candied fruits

SAFETY ALERT
Caramelizing Sugar

Caramelizing sugar can cause serious burns. Use a pair of cotton gloves covered by a pair of rubber gloves such as those used for industrial dishwashing to protect hands from coming into contact with spilled caramel. Take proper precautions to avoid hot sugar coming into direct contact with your skin.

❶ Mixing almonds into the cooked glucose syrup and fondant mixture.

❷ Rolling nougatine to the proper thickness.

❸ Cutting and molding the nougatine into shapes.

BASIC NOUGATINE

This formula is recommended for those working in a humid environment.

Yield: 3 lb. 8 oz. (1680 g)

Glucose or corn syrup	14 oz.	420 g
Fondant	1 lb. 3 oz.	570 g
Almonds, sliced, toasted and warm	1 lb. 5 oz.	630 g
Unsalted butter or cocoa butter	2 oz.	60 g

❶ Over medium-high heat, bring the glucose syrup to a boil in a heavy saucepan without stirring.

❷ Add the fondant and let it dissolve without stirring. Cook until the syrup turns a golden amber color, approximately 320°F–330°F (160°C–166°C).

❸ Remove from the heat. Quickly add the almonds, then stir in the butter.

❹ Pour the cooked nougatine out on a silicone baking mat or a lightly oiled marble slab. Wait a few moments before rolling the nougatine to prevent it from sticking to the rolling pin.

❺ Roll the mixture to approximately 1/16 inch (1 millimeter) thick for most uses, slightly thicker for showpieces.

❻ If the nougatine hardens before the required thickness is reached, place it on a silicone mat or lightly oiled sheet pan and reheat in a 275°F (135°C) oven. Nougatine rolled to 1/8-inch (3-millimeter) thickness will take approximately 8 to 10 minutes to soften. Reheat the nougatine anytime during the cutting or shaping process.

❼ When the nougatine is rolled evenly thin, quickly flip the baking mat, nougatine side down, onto a sheet of parchment. (Or lift the nougatine with a spatula and flip onto the paper.) Immediately cut into shapes and press into molds.

❽ Leftover nougatine scraps can be stored in an airtight container. Scraps can be reheated and reworked at a later time. Slightly overlap the pieces on a paper-lined sheet pan and place in a 300°F (150°C) oven. Remove the warm nougatine and roll to form a uniform sheet.

Approximate values per 1-oz. (30-g) serving: **Calories** 100, **Total fat** 40 g, **Saturated fat** 1 g, **Cholesterol** 0 mg, **Sodium** 15 mg, **Total carbohydrates** 15 g, **Protein** 1 g

VARIATIONS:

Hazelnut or Walnut Nougatine—Increase the fondant to 1 pound 6 ounces (660 grams). Substitute 1 pound 5 ounces (630 grams) finely chopped, hot toasted hazelnuts or walnuts for the almonds.

Cocoa Nougatine—Reduce the glucose syrup to 7 ounces (210 grams). Reduce the fondant to 11 ounces (330 grams). Replace the almonds with 8 ounces (240 grams) cocoa nibs and 1/2 ounce (15 grams) cocoa powder. Cook the glucose syrup and fondant until it reaches an amber caramel, then add the cocoa nibs and cocoa powder. Reduce butter to 1 ounce (30 grams) and stir it into the nougatine.

Sesame Seed Nougatine—Reduce the glucose syrup to 7 ounces (210 grams). Reduce the fondant to 11 ounces (330 grams). Substitute 10 ounces (300 grams) hot, toasted sesame seeds for the almonds. Reduce butter to 1 ounce (30 grams).

Coffee Nougatine—Increase the fondant to 1 pound 6 ounces (660 grams). Reduce the almonds to 8 ounces (240 grams). Add 8 ounces (240 grams) finely chopped toasted hazelnuts, 4 ounces (120 grams) hot toasted sesame seeds, and 1 ounce (30 grams) instant coffee to the mixture along with the hot almonds once it caramelizes.

NOUGATINE CUPS

Yield: 12 Cups

Basic Nougatine (page 724)	1 lb. 12 oz.	840 g
Decorating Caramel (page 727)	as needed	as needed

1. Prepare a template for shaping the nougatine. Select a 4-inch- (10-centimeter-) wide martini glass or other cone-shaped object. Invert the glass onto a clean sheet of cardboard, parchment paper or thick plastic. Trace the circumference of the glass onto the material. (The template will produce a cone slightly smaller than the original. To make a cone the exact size of the original, draw the circumference slightly larger than the glass.)

2. Cut a ¼-inch (6-millimeter) pie-shaped wedge out of the circle. Fold the template into a cone shape, trimming it as needed to make an even fit. Lightly oil the template to prevent it from sticking to the nougatine.

3. Prepare the Basic Nougatine. Allow it to cool slightly, then roll it out to a thickness of approximately ⅛ inch (3 millimeters). While the nougatine is still warm, cut the nougatine into six circles, using the template as a guide. Shape the nougatine cutouts into cones and place each one into a cone-shaped glass to cool completely.

4. Roll out the remaining nougatine, rewarming it in a 300°F (149°C) oven as needed. Cut 3-inch (7.5-centimeter) circles out of the nougatine. Attach one circle to the bottom of each nougatine cone using the Decorating Caramel as an adhesive.

5. Use the cups the day they are made or store them in a cool, dry place in an airtight container up to 1 week before using.

Approximate values per 2½-oz. (75-g) serving: **Calories** 280, **Total fat** 12 g, **Saturated fat** 2 g, **Cholesterol** 5 mg, **Sodium** 40 mg, **Total carbohydrates** 45 g, **Protein** 4 g

DECORATIVE SUGAR WORK

Sugar can be used to create a number of doughs, pastes and syrups used for artistic and decorative work. Depending on the temperature to which the sugar is cooked, the sugar will be clear and firm or dark and brittle. As discussed in Chapter 4, Bakeshop Ingredients, sugar cooked to the caramel stage, 338°F (170°C), will darken and add a deep rich flavor to pastries. True caramel is most often used to add a crunchy surface on pastries such as croquembouche and the St. Honoré (see page 420). Sugar that is cooked only to the hard crack stage, 300°F (149°C), will hold its shape without adding the rich flavor.

When making a concentrated cooked sugar syrup or caramel, ensure that the sugar is free of traces of flour or other contaminants that may crystallize the syrup. Sugar cubes may be used in place of granulated sugar for this reason. (Ingredient scoops that travel between food storage containers can introduce contaminants.) When making any cooked sugar syrup, care must be taken to prevent recrystallization of the syrup. Do not stir a sugar solution after it comes to a boil. Using a clean pastry brush dipped in water, brush away any sugar crystals that adhere to the sides of the pan. (The extra water added from the brush evaporates and has no effect on the final product.)

Induction or electric stoves provide steady, reliable heat and are preferred over gas stoves when preparing concentrated sugar syrups such as caramel. The gas flames from an open burner can cook the syrup unevenly, heating the sides of the pan more quickly than the center. The caramel may cook unevenly and may darken before the desired temperature is reached. Once it begins to caramelize, sugar syrup will brown quickly if not removed from the heat. Placing the pan immediately in an ice-water bath helps prevent carryover cooking from burning the sugar syrup.

Pastry chefs presenting their sugar sculpture at an international competition

Caramel syrup, when used to dip pastries such as Merveilleux Pastries (page 422) or cream puffs for croquembouche, may include a high percentage of corn syrup or glucose syrup. These liquid sugars keep the caramel pliable longer, making dipping large numbers of pastries possible.

PROCEDURE FOR PREPARING CARAMEL

1. Combine granulated sugar, corn or glucose syrup (if using), and a small amount of water in a heavy saucepan. Unlined copper may be used.
2. Stir the solution to make sure all sugar crystals dissolve before it reaches a boil. Cover the pan and bring the mixture to a boil. Do not stir the solution after it begins boiling, however.
3. Once the syrup boils, add the interferent if one is specified in the formula. Corn syrup, glucose syrup, cream of tartar or lemon juice may be used.
4. Continue cooking the syrup, brushing down the sides of the pan with cold water to wash off crystals that may be deposited there.
5. Cook the syrup to the desired temperature, using a candy thermometer to gauge the syrup's concentration. Wash off the thermometer probe after placing in the syrup; sugar that clings to it can reseed the syrup.
6. Cook the syrup until it begins to caramelize, approximately 338°F (170°C). Remove the pan from the heat as soon as the desired color is reached but before the caramel begins to burn and smoke. Briefly plunge the bottom of the pan into an ice-water bath to stop the cooking process.

CARAMEL

Yield: 1 ½ pt. (720 ml)

Granulated sugar	1 lb.	480 g
Glucose or corn syrup	8 fl. oz.	240 ml
Water	8 fl. oz.	240 ml

1. Combine the sugar, glucose syrup and water in a heavy saucepan. Stir the mixture, then cover the pan and bring the mixture to a boil.
2. Once the mixture boils, brush the sides of the pan with a pastry brush dipped in clean water to remove any sugar crystals stuck to the pan.
3. Boil the mixture without stirring until it reaches a golden caramel color, approximately 338°F (170°C).
4. Remove the pan from the heat and dip the bottom of the pan in a bowl of cold water for 30 seconds to stop the cooking process.
5. Use to dip éclairs, cream puffs or other items. This caramel may also be used to make caramel cages and for other decorative caramel work.

Approximate values per 1-fl.-oz. (30-ml) serving: **Calories** 40, **Total fat** 0 g, **Saturated fat** 0 g, **Cholesterol** 0 mg, **Sodium** 15 mg, **Total carbohydrates** 10 g, **Protein** 0 g

Decorating Caramel

Decorating caramel is a sugar syrup that is used to make sugar ornaments, spun sugar and other edible decorations. It is cooked just beyond the hard crack stage. By removing the sugar from the heat at a lower temperature than for caramel, the sugar darkens minimally. The danger of carryover cooking burning the syrup is also minimized. At these temperatures, any coloring added to the syrup will be visible in the finished decorations. For the best results when coloring decorating caramel, use food colors that are specifically recommended for use in sugar work. Most paste-type food colors will crystallize the sugar syrup and should not be used. Most liquid and powdered food colors can be used, however. Dissolve powdered food color in alcohol or water before adding to the sugar. Add the food coloring once the syrup has boiled and reaches 265°F–275°F (130°C–135°C). Do not stir. The color will blend in as the syrup bubbles.

Isomalt, a type of invert sugar often used to make **pulled sugar** decorations, discussed on page 732, can be used in place of the granulated sugar in this formula. Because it resists humidity, isomalt is popular for decorative items. When decorating caramel is to be used for dipping fruits, granulated sugar is recommended.

DECORATING CARAMEL

Yield: 14 oz. (420 g)

Water	4 fl. oz.	120 ml
Granulated sugar	10 oz.	300 g
Glucose or corn syrup	4 oz.	120 g
Liquid food coloring (optional)	as needed	as needed

1. Combine the water and sugar in a heavy saucepan. Bring it to a boil. Using a clean pastry brush dipped in water, wash away any sugar crystals that adhere to the sides of the pan.
2. Add the glucose syrup to the boiling liquid. Without stirring, cook the syrup to 275°F (135°C). Add food coloring (if using); pour the food coloring in the center of the pan without stirring. Cook until the syrup reaches 316°F (158°C), or longer if a caramel color is desired.
3. Remove from the heat and dip the bottom of the pan in a bowl filled with cold water; let sit 12 seconds or until the syrup no longer bubbles.
4. Use immediately to make piped sugar decorations, spun sugar or other edible garnishes.

Approximate values per 1-fl.-oz. (30-ml) serving: **Calories** 40, **Total fat** 0 g, **Saturated fat** 0 g, **Cholesterol** 0 mg, **Sodium** 15 mg, **Total carbohydrates** 10 g, **Protein** 0 g

Spun Sugar

Spun sugar is a confection consisting of long, fine, hairlike threads of sugar made by flicking a hot concentrated sugar syrup rapidly across dowels. Mounds or wreaths of these threads are used to decorate ice cream desserts, croquembouche and gâteaux. Making spun sugar is a messy process. The work station used to prepare spun sugar should be covered with paper or heavy plastic to catch sugar that flies around in the process. Some chefs cut the curved ends from a whisk to make a tool for spinning sugar, although a pair of forks may be used instead. Use the formula for Caramel (page 726) or Decorating Caramel (above) to make spun sugar. Remove the pan from the heat and stop the cooking process by immersing the bottom of the pan in cool water for a few seconds. Should the caramel harden, reheat it by placing it over low heat. These fragile threads absorb moisture and soften easily, so they are best used the same day they are made, stored in an airtight container until needed.

SAFETY ALERT
Hot Sugar Syrup

Hot sugar syrup can cause serious burns. Wear a pair of cotton gloves covered by a pair of rubber gloves such as those used for industrial dishwashing to protect hands from coming into contact with spilled caramel. Burns from caramel can be more severe than those from hot oil. Use the utmost care when working with any type of cooked sugar syrup. Take proper precautions to avoid hot sugar coming into direct contact with your skin.

PROCEDURE FOR MAKING SPUN SUGAR

① Lightly oil two 18-inch (45-centimeter) wooden dowels, wooden-handled spoons or wooden rolling pins. Place them 12 inches (30 centimeters) apart on a clean worktable so that they extend off the edge of the table approximately 12 inches (30 centimeters). Line a few sheet pans with paper and place them under the dowels to catch drips.

② Prepare a batch of Caramel (page 726) or Decorating Caramel (page 727).

③ To make the gossamer threads, dip a whisk approximately 3 inches (7.5 centimeters) into the caramel. With a quick flick of the wrist, shake the whisk back and forth over the ends of the dowels. Repeat the process until a mass of threads collects on the dowels.

④ Collect the threads and coil into a nest or other shape. Use to garnish ice cream, cakes or other desserts.

① Gathering spun sugar threads formed on an oiled rolling pin.

② Loosely wrapping the spun sugar into a nest shape.

CARAMEL DECORATIONS

Either type of caramel presented above can be poured from a spoon or piped into decorative shapes to use for garnishing cakes, pastries and plated desserts. Great care must be taken when piping caramel, however, to avoid serious burns. Use precut paper cones. Wear proper gloves to avoid getting burned. Fill the paper cone no more than halfway full, then close the cone carefully. Pipe the caramel onto oiled parchment paper or silicone baking mats so that the cooled sugar releases easily.

Caramel piped into decorative shapes.

Decorative caramel cage.

Decorating caramel can also be piped or drizzled over dome-shaped silicone molds or bowls that have been lightly oiled. Because caramel contracts as it hardens, when working with ceramic or metal shapes, drizzle or pipe the caramel inside the form for best results.

Decorative caramel softens under humid conditions. Store garnishes made from piped sugar tightly sealed in a plastic container. A **drying agent** or **desiccant** such as silica gel may be placed in the storage container, especially under humid conditions or when storing the product for more than a few days. Depending on the humidity, sugar decorations can keep for 4 to 7 days when stored properly.

drying agent any of several products used to remove humidity from the air; particularly useful when storing sugar work, nougatine and other dry cookies, which soften under moist conditions; packets of drying agents are placed in storage containers for such confections; reusable envelopes of silica gel are sold for this purpose

ISOMALT LACE

Isomalt is a type of invert sugar used to make pulled sugar decorations. When baked between sheets of a silicone baking mat, the isomalt melts into an attractive bubble pattern. The sheets can be broken into pieces to decorate cakes such as the one on page 631. It can also be bent and curved while still warm from the oven.

isomalt a type of sugar alcohol used as a sugar substitute and in sugar work. It is a disaccharide, composed of glucose and mannitol that is made from sugar beets

Isomalt	3 oz.	90 g
Food coloring, powdered (optional)	0.3 oz. (⅛ tsp.)	1 g

❶ Line a flat sheet pan with a silicone baking mat. Stir together the isomalt and powdered food coloring (if using). Sprinkle the mixture onto the silicone-mat-lined sheet pan to a thickness of approximately ⅛ inch (3 millimeters). It is not necessary to spread the mixture evenly.

❷ Place a second silicone mat on top of the isomalt. Bake at 375°F (180°C) for approximately 15 minutes. (When baked longer, the isomalt will develop larger holes and a golden color.)

❸ Remove from the oven and let cool. Store in an airtight container with a drying agent.

Approximate values per ½-oz. (15-g) serving: **Calories** 40, **Total fat** 0 g, **Saturated fat** 0 g, **Cholesterol** 0 mg, **Sodium** 0 mg, **Total carbohydrates** 10 g, **Protein** 0 g

SUGAR-BASED CANDIES

Caramel forms the base for a number of delicious confections such as chewy caramel candies and nut brittle. A candy thermometer provides the most accurate temperature reading and should be used when making caramel candies.

CARAMEL CANDIES

This formula makes a soft, chewy caramel candy. Cooking the caramel mixture to the temperature indicated in the formula ensures that the caramel will set properly. If a firmer caramel is desired, cook the mixture 1–2 degrees higher in Steps 2 and 3.

Yield: 1 lb. 10 oz. (780 g), approximately 36 Candies

Heavy cream	1 pt.	480 ml
Granulated sugar	1 lb.	480 g
Glucose or corn syrup	8 oz.	240 g
Vanilla bean, split, seeds scraped	1	1
Unsalted butter	3 oz.	90 g
Semisweet or bittersweet couverture, tempered (optional)	as needed	as needed

1. Position four candy rulers on a silicone baking mat or parchment paper to make an 8-inch (20-centimeter) square.
2. Bring the cream, sugar, glucose syrup and vanilla bean seeds to a boil in a heavy saucepan set over medium-high heat. Cook until the mixture reaches 245°F (118°C) on a candy thermometer.
3. Stir in the butter and continue cooking until the mixture returns to 245°F (118°C).
4. Carefully pour the mixture between the candy rulers, leveling it with an oiled heat-resistant spatula to a thickness of ½ inch (1.2 centimeters).
5. Allow the caramel to cool and firm, then cut it into 1⅓-inch (3.4-centimeter) squares. Wrap each caramel in cellophane, if desired. The candies may also be individually dipped in tempered chocolate couverture, if desired.

Approximate values per candy: **Calories** 100, **Total fat** 6 g, **Saturated fat** 3.5 g, **Cholesterol** 5 mg, **Sodium** 10 mg, **Total carbohydrates** 11 g, **Protein** 1 g

❶ Caramel candy cooling between candy rulers.

❷ Wrapping the cut caramels in cellophane.

PULLED, BLOWN AND POURED SUGAR

One of the most artistic aspects of a pastry chef's range of work is the field of sugar. With pulled and blown sugar, pastry chefs can create towering sculptures and luminous decorations. Success creating decorative sugar garnishes and showpieces requires a firm grasp of the science of sugar crystallization and heat transfer, as well as an artistic eye. This work is technically challenging, and the hot sugar is difficult to handle. These pieces are rarely eaten. Their appeal is in the design, form, color and artistry of the finished piece. Becoming a *décorateur*, the pastry chef skilled in decorative arts, takes repetition, much patience and dedication. But mastering some basic skills is within the reach of a student who is willing to practice.

Ingredients for Pulled, Blown and Poured Sugar

To make pulled and blown sugar, sugar and glucose syrup is cooked into a pliable mass that can be turned into decorative shapes. Many of the basic ingredients for sugar work are quite common; others are available through specialty suppliers. Granulated sugar, the backbone of this specialty, must be free from any impurities, which will hinder the strength of the sugar structure. Superfine or regular granulated sugar or white sugar cubes may be used. **Glucose syrup** is used to slow down the crystallization process when cooking sugar for pulling and blowing. It does, however, raise the final working temperature of the **sugar mass**. Acids also slow down the crystallization process. An acid such as cream of tartar will make the sugar more elastic and easier to work with. But if too much cream of tartar is

Blown and pulled sugar showpiece.

used, the pulled or blown pieces will be unstable and may collapse. Other usable acids are tartaric acid, lemon juice and vinegar. It is extremely difficult to work with sugar in a humid environment. The moisture in the air will make the sugar pieces sticky and difficult to handle. In those conditions, many chefs prefer to work with isomalt as it is not as affected by humidity as recipes made from scratch with sugar, glucose syrup, water and acid.

Pulled and blown sugar pieces are often tinted with appropriate colors. Paste and most liquid food colors are not recommended, as these usually contain acids that can soften the sugar mass and make the finished piece unstable. **Powdered food colors** are preferred. These powders are dissolved in water or alcohol and added to the boiling sugar at the required temperature. Poured sugar pieces can be made opaque with the addition of liquid whitener such as titanium dioxide or calcium carbonate.

Edible food lacquer is used to protect sugar showpieces from humidity. Because most showpieces will not be eaten, they can also be sprayed with shellacs found in hardware stores. Drying agents or desiccants are used to absorb the moisture inside containers of sugar work. Silica gel, sold under many brand names, and other desiccants are sold through specialty suppliers.

Equipment for Pulled, Blown and Poured Sugar

A number of specialized tools are required when making pulled and blown sugar. The most useful pieces of equipment are discussed here.

Latex and insulated gloves help protect the hands from high heat. Some chefs prefer to work without gloves, however, because they feel that the gloves hinder the more delicate aspects of their work. Monitoring the correct temperature of the sugar during cooking and after the mass is formed is essential for sugar work. A **digital thermometer** with a detachable probe is preferred. **Eyedroppers** are used to add the proper amount of cream of tartar or coloring to the sugar mass.

Marble or granite slabs are used to quickly cool down cooked sugar. The sugar mass is usually worked on oiled silicone mats placed on top of a marble slab. **Scissors, cutters** and **knives** that are lightly oiled are used to cut and handle the sugar mass. **Fans** or a blow dryer with a cold setting are used to rapidly cool blown sugar pieces.

An **alcohol burner** is used to partially melt pieces of sugar work and then "glue" the components together. An **infrared heat lamp** is used to soften the sugar mass and to keep it malleable. The lamp fixture is designed to accept an infrared light bulb. The heat from the bulb, usually 250 watts, keeps the sugar mass at the correct temperature. The flexible neck on the lamp allows the chef to move the heat source closer to or further from the sugar mass as needed. For pulled sugar, the mass is kept at approximately 100°F (37°C). For blown sugar, the mass is kept at approximately 175°F (79°C). While sugar sits under the lamp, it must be pulled and folded to distribute the heat evenly before working. To keep drafts from cooling the sugar, the heat lamp may also be positioned over a **heatbox**, which consists of three plastic sides with an open front.

A **sugar pump** and copper **blow pipe** are used to gently inflate sugar for blown pieces.

Sugar Lamp

Sugar Pump and Pipe

Formulas for Pulled and Blown Sugar

Most decorative sugar work is made from a doughlike mixture of cooked sucrose and glucose syrup. First sugar, glucose syrup and water is boiled briskly. Slow boiling may encourage the formation of sugar crystals. When it reaches 285°F (143°C), the soft crack stage, a solution of tartaric acid is added. This helps prevent crystallization and keep the mixture malleable and soft when warm. Then the mixture is cooked to 310°F (155°C), the hard crack stage. To stop the cooking process, the bottom of the pan is plunged into cold water. The mixture is then poured onto an oiled slab and worked into a pliable mass.

Working the sugar mass by pulling and folding is an important step. It aerates the sugar mass, making it pliable, and it gives the mass a satin or pearl-like sheen. (This step is often called *pearling*.) The sugar mixture can be used immediately. It should be cut into pieces of manageable size, which must be kept warm under the heat lamp. Turning them regularly ensures that the sugar stays uniformly warm. Or the extra pieces of sugar can be stored in airtight containers after cooling to be used later, reheating them under a heat lamp or in a microwave oven on low until softened as needed.

BASIC PULLED AND BLOWN SUGAR

Yield: Approximately 2 lb. 8 oz. (1200 g)

Tartaric acid solution:

Cream of tartar	1 oz.	30 g
Water, hot	1 oz.	30 g

Sugar mass:

Granulated sugar	2 lb. 2 oz.	1020 g
Water	14 oz.	420 g
Glucose syrup	7 oz.	210 g
Food coloring (optional)	as needed	as needed

1. Combine the cream of tartar and boiling water. Stir to dissolve. Let cool.
2. Place the sugar and water in a pan over medium-high heat. Whisk the sugar until it dissolves and the mixture starts to boil. Wash the inner sides of the pan with a brush dipped in water to prevent crystallizing of any sugar crystals that stick to the sides of the pan.
3. Boil the mixture for 2 minutes, then add the glucose syrup. Return the mixture to a boil.
4. Cook until the mixture reaches 230°F (110°C). Add the food coloring (if using).
5. Cook until the mixture reaches 285°F (143°C). Add 12 drops of the tartaric acid solution.
6. Remove the mixture from the heat when it reaches 310°F (155°C). Immediately dip the bottom of the pan into cold water to stop the boiling process. Wipe the pan dry.
7. Pour the sugar mixture onto a silicone mat or lightly oiled marble slab. Once the mass has settled and formed a skin on the underside, begin to pull and fold it. Start by pulling from underneath the edges of the sugar mass, using a lightly oiled spatula or gloved fingers. Lifting from the ends, fold the sugar back onto itself. Or use an edge of the silicone baking mat to turn the sugar back onto itself.
8. Move the sugar mass to a cool part of the marble. The mixture will spread out again. Fold over the edges of the sugar mass. Repeat the process until the sugar mass stops spreading.
9. Wearing insulated gloves, pull the sugar mass out between both hands to approximately 20 inches (50 centimeters) in length. Fold the sugar mass over and twist it together. Repeat pulling, twisting and folding the sugar until it develops a satin sheen throughout. Do not overpull as this will cause the mass to overaerate, become opaque and crystallize.
10. Using a sharp, oiled knife, divide the sugar mass into pieces of manageable size. Place a piece of the pulled sugar under a heat lamp to work into pulled or blown sugar. Set the extra pieces aside to be reheated under the heat lamp when needed.

VARIATION:

Poured Sugar—Omit the tartaric acid solution in Step 5. Pour the sugar syrup in Step 7 into the prepared frames or molds.

1. Testing the sugar mass as it begins to cool.

2. Turning the sugar mass over using the silicone mat.

3. Beginning to pull the sugar mass.

4. Pulling the sugar mass until it has a satin sheen.

Working with Pulled, Blown and Poured Sugar

The procedures for working with pulled, blown and poured sugar are illustrated with the Modern Flower Sugar Showpiece. All sugar work starts with the basic pulled sugar formula described earlier. As with all advanced patisserie, practice is essential before success is achieved. Design ideas are easily found in art, design, dance, theater or other books. Opt for simplicity to achieve elegant results. For stability, focus on designs that have a sufficient area touching the base. And selecting appealing colors is important. A monochromatic color scheme is elegant; using too many colors can make the design look cheap and garish.

MODERN FLOWER SUGAR SHOWPIECE

This showpiece combines several relatively simple elements in one design. The base is made from a round disk of poured sugar. Yellow tinted rice is added to the sugar for color and visual texture. A simple twist of pulled sugar forms a column in front of which sits a flower composed of pulled and blown sugar.

PULLED SUGAR FLOWER PETALS

1. Prepare a batch of sugar for pulling. Cut off a piece of sugar of manageable size.
2. Shape the pulled sugar into a ball. Hold it under the heat lamp until it is malleable but not melting. Pull and fold the sugar a few times to ensure a good sheen.
3. Grab an edge of the sugar mass between the thumbs and forefingers of each hand. Pull in an upward and rounded fashion to thin the edge of the sugar mass.
4. For each petal, grab a ⅔-inch (1.5-centimeter) section of the thinned sugar mass between gloved fingers. Pull the mass out to create the petal. Quickly cut the petal from the sugar mass. Set aside to cool.

1. Thinning the edge of the sugar mass.

2. Pulling the sugar to form a petal.

3. The pulled sugar flower petals.

BLOWN SUGAR SPHERE (CORE OF THE FLOWER)

① Pull and fold a warm piece of sugar a few times to ensure a good sheen. Form a 2-inch (5-centimeter) ball and pull it away from the main mass. Cut it off with scissors.

② Indent the ball ½ inch (1.2 centimeters) deep. Elongate the sugar slightly. Set the piece aside under the heat lamp.

③ Quickly heat the copper blow pipe over a gas flame. Wrap a small amount of pulled sugar around the tip of the pipe. Then insert the pipe into the ball of sugar. Press the sugar mass tightly against the pipe, making sure that no air can escape.

④ Holding the air pump in one hand and the piece of pulled sugar in the other, slowly pump in air to form a sphere. (Make certain that the sphere forms at least 1 inch [2.5 centimeters] above the tip of the pipe. This will make it easy to separate from the copper pipe.) If one section of the sphere expands faster than another, rub a gloved hand over it. This will cool down the section, allowing the sugar to expand uniformly.

⑤ Pull a long tail from the top of the sphere.

⑥ Cool the sphere in front of a fan. Once cool and stable, remove the piece from the copper pipe by heating and turning the pipe over the flame of the alcohol burner. Once the sugar is evenly soft, carefully cut off the sphere with scissors. Set aside.

① Forming the sugar mass into a ball around the thumb.

② Heating the copper blow pipe.

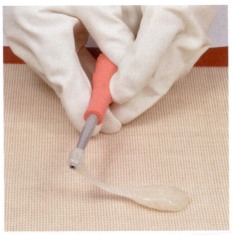

③ Wrapping the sugar around the heated pipe.

④ Blowing the sugar into a sphere.

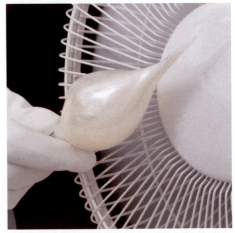

⑤ Cooling the finished sugar sphere in front of a fan.

ASSEMBLING PULLED AND BLOWN SUGAR FLOWER

1. To assemble the flowers, heat the end of each petal over an alcohol burner or dip the end of each petal in cooked pulled sugar syrup.
2. Attach the petals one by one in a circular fashion to the bottom edge of the blown sugar sphere. Overlap the petals slightly, if desired. Set aside.

1. Dipping a flower petal in sugar syrup.

2. Attaching a sugar petal to the center.

3. The finished blown and pulled sugar flower.

POURED SUGAR BASE

Poured or cast sugar is used to make bases and structures for decorative sugar showpieces. It can also be used alone to make eye-catching showpieces. The poured sugar technique is quite simple. The sugar mixture is poured into oiled metal or silicone molds. Place the molds on silicone mats set over marble. This will make it easy to move the sugar to cooler parts of the marble to facilitate cooling.

The cooked sugar syrup can be colored or made opaque by adding titanium dioxide. Opaque cast sugar can be airbrushed once cooled. Lightly oiled aluminum foil can also be used for clear sugar. When wrinkled slightly, the foil will create an interesting texture on the base. If the foil is left on the base, it will reflect light, adding to the visual interest of the piece. Here visual interest is created by sprinkling colored rice into the poured sugar.

Rice, uncooked	as needed	as needed
Yellow liquid food coloring (optional)	as needed	as needed
Pulled and Blown Sugar solution, Poured Sugar variation	1 lb. 8 oz.	720 g

1. Lightly oil the inner walls of two 3-inch (8-centimeter) torte rings and place them on a silicone mat or aluminum foil.
2. Toss the raw rice with a few drops of yellow liquid food coloring (if using).
3. Pour a small amount of the poured sugar syrup in each ring and sprinkle with rice. Pour another amount on top to cover the rice and sprinkle with additional rice. Repeat and finish with the sugar syrup. Allow to cool before removing the rings.

1. Pouring sugar into oiled ring.

2. Sprinkling the sugar with colored rice.

The sugar twist.

PULLED SUGAR TWIST

1. Pull and fold a warm piece of sugar a few times to ensure a good sheen. Pull and twist the sugar into an 8-inch (20-centimeter) section. Cut it off with scissors. Fold and twist the sugar into a decorative shape. Set aside to cool.

MODERN FLOWER SUGAR SHOWPIECE ASSEMBLY

Poured Sugar Base, 3-in. (8-cm) diameter	1	1
Pulled Sugar Twist	1	1
Pulled and Blown Sugar Flower	1	1

1. Place the poured sugar base on a decorative serving tray.
2. Heat the bottom of the Pulled Sugar Twist over an alcohol burner, then attach it to the base. Cool with a fan or blow dryer until set.
3. Attach the sugar flower to the base using pulled sugar syrup or heat it slightly over an alcohol burner.

Placing the flower on the sugar base to complete the showpiece.

CONVENIENCE PRODUCTS

In many food service establishments, space, staffing and time do not permit making chocolates and decorative sugar confections on site. Because chocolate confectionery is such a specialized craft, many high-quality chocolate products are available to fill this need. Prepared chocolate shells come in many forms, from miniature tart shells to unusual molded containers such as tulipe shells, miniature swans, pianos and even tiny ovens designed to be filled with fruit, creams or mousses. Hollow molded chocolate shells used to make truffles and other chocolate candies are also widely available. They come in disposable plastic trays, handy for filling with a signature ganache or other soft center. Chocolate decorations come in various shapes—fans, swirls, circles, triangles and many more, some with designs or logos stenciled on the surface. When purchasing prepared chocolate products, select those made from the highest-quality chocolate, with the highest percentage of cocoa butter and solids and the lowest amount of hydrogenated fat and artificial flavorings. As with all tempered chocolate products, these prepared items require careful storage in a cool dry place.

White or dark chocolate modeling paste made with cocoa powder, cocoa butter and other fats, emulsifiers, milk powder and flavorings is available. Piping chocolate, formulated so it resists blooming, makes decorating cakes with chocolate feasible when tempering chocolate might be difficult. Ganache and truffle fillings are available in tubs. Softening makes them pipeable or spreadable. These are shelf-stable products that may contain hydrogenated fats in place of natural dairy ingredients such as cream or butter. Such products are used to make candy centers and may be customized with the addition of fruit compounds, liqueurs or other flavorings.

Nougatine powder to which water is added is available for making nougatine cups, disks and decorations. Premade nougatine cups and plates on which to serve ice cream or sorbets are also available. Specialty-ingredient catalogs are full of simple and elaborate decorations made from marzipan and sugar. Marzipan plaques on which a greeting may be piped, figures made from colored royal icing and ready-made sculpted marzipan fruit are a few of the many items that may be purchased. Such convenience products allow the pastry chef the freedom to spend more time creating desserts; however, no amount of elaborate decoration will compensate for a poorly executed pastry.

1. What are the basic types of chocolate and their common uses in the pastry kitchen?
2. Why must couverture chocolate be tempered? When is it not necessary to temper chocolate?
3. Discuss the four methods for tempering couverture and discuss the precautions that must be taken when preparing the chocolate.
4. Imagine that you have been asked to prepare a celebration cake for a special event. Describe the type of event and the ways you might use decorative marzipan, nougatine and other items in this chapter to create an appropriate design.
5. Which decorative items from this chapter would not be acceptable to use in making or storing a showpiece that must be entirely edible?

Terms to Know

nib
chocolate liquor
chocolate mass
cocoa butter
break
tempering
seizing
fat and sugar bloom
dipped chocolates
molded chocolates
first cooling
second cooling
closed-bottom mold
open-bottom mold
serial work
pulled sugar
spun sugar
drying agent
sugar mass

ADDITIONAL CHOCOLATE
AND DECORATIVE WORK FORMULAS

MENDIANT (BITTERSWEET CHOCOLATE, NUT AND DRIED FRUIT DISKS)

Yield: 32 Candies   **Method:** Piped

Semisweet or bittersweet couverture, tempered	1 lb.	480 g
Slivered almonds, toasted	32	32
Candied Orange Peel (page 671), cut into uniform pieces	32	32
Pistachios	32	32
Dried cherries	32	32
Walnut quarters	32	32

1. Line two sheet pans with acetate or parchment paper.
2. Pipe out 32 rounds of tempered couverture 1½ inches (4 centimeters) in diameter onto the prepared pans. Working quickly before the chocolate sets, arrange 1 piece of slivered almond, 1 Candied Orange Peel, 1 pistachio, 1 dried cherry and 1 walnut on each mound of chocolate.
3. Allow the chocolate to set before serving or packing.

Approximate values per candy: **Calories** 100, **Total fat** 6 g, **Saturated fat** 0 g, **Cholesterol** 0 mg, **Sodium** 85 mg, **Total carbohydrates** 10 g, **Protein** 1 g

NOBLE (RASPBERRY GANACHE CHOCOLATES)

Yield: 48 Candies, 1 lb. 11 oz. (825 g) Ganache   **Method:** Molded

Raspberry purée	10 oz.	300 g
Glucose or corn syrup	2 oz.	60 g
Semisweet couverture chocolate, chopped fine	10 oz.	300 g
Raspberry liqueur	1.5 fl. oz.	45 ml
Natural raspberry compound (optional)	0.5 oz.	30 g
Trimoline or honey	1 oz.	30 g
Unsalted butter, room temperature	2 oz.	60 g
Red food coloring, fat soluble	as needed	as needed
Cocoa butter, melted	3 oz.	90 g
White chocolate, melted	2 oz.	60 g
Semisweet or bittersweet couverture for coating molds	3 lb.	1440 g

1. Boil the raspberry purée and glucose syrup in a nonreactive saucepan over medium-high heat.
2. Remove from the heat. Add the purée to the chopped couverture chocolate in five increments, stirring between each addition to create an emulsion.
3. Add the raspberry liqueur and raspberry compound (if using), then the trimoline and butter. Let cool to 70°F (21°C).
4. Sift the food coloring, then mix it into half of the melted cocoa butter. Stir in the remaining cocoa butter and the melted white chocolate. Temper. Using a spray gun, spray a thin coating of the colored chocolate into the chocolate molds. Or use a gloved hand to spread a thin layer of the tinted chocolate in each mold.
5. Coat the molds using tempered semisweet or bittersweet couverture. Allow the chocolate-filled molds to sit in the refrigerator until the shells shrink from the sides of the molds.
6. Fill the molds with the cooled ganache to within ⅟₁₆ inch (1 millimeter) from the top. When the filling is sufficiently firm, cover with tempered couverture. Chill, then unmold.

Approximate values per candy: **Calories** 80, **Total fat** 4.5 g, **Saturated fat** 3 g, **Cholesterol** 5 mg, **Sodium** 0 mg, **Total carbohydrates** 11 g, **Protein** 1 g

FAUN (HAZELNUT GANACHE CHOCOLATES)

Yield: 56 Candies, 1 lb. 9 oz. (720 g) Ganache   **Method:** Molded

Gianduja	12 oz.	360 g
Hazelnut paste	13 oz.	390 g
Bittersweet couverture, tempered for coating molds	3 lb.	1440 g

1. Melt the gianduja to 110°F (43°C).
2. Remove from the heat and stir in the hazelnut paste. Let cool to 72°F (22°C).
3. Coat the molds with the tempered couverture and give the chocolate the first cooling.
4. Fill the molds with the ganache to within ¹⁄₁₆ inch (1 millimeter) of the top. When the ganache has set sufficiently, cover it with tempered couverture to seal. Chill the chocolates in a cool area until set, then unmold.

Approximate values per candy: **Calories** 100, **Total fat** 7 g, **Saturated fat** 2.5 g, **Cholesterol** 0 mg, **Sodium** 0 mg, **Total carbohydrates** 10 g, **Protein** 1 g

Assorted molded bonbons, clockwise from left: Baho, Passion, Faun, Noble and Ceylon (bottom).

CEYLON (MILK CHOCOLATE AND CINNAMON GANACHE CHOCOLATES)

Yield: 56 Candies, 1 lb. 9 oz. (765 g) Ganache   **Method:** Molded

Milk chocolate couverture, chopped fine	8 oz.	240 g
Bittersweet couverture, chopped fine	5 oz.	150 g
Heavy cream	9 fl. oz.	270 ml
Ceylon cinnamon sticks, crushed	0.5 oz.	15 g
Glucose or corn syrup	3 oz.	90 ml
Milk chocolate couverture, tempered for coating molds	3 lb.	1440 g

1. Combine the chopped chocolates in a large bowl. Set aside.
2. Bring the cream and cinnamon to a boil. Remove from the heat, cover with plastic film and infuse 20 minutes.
3. Strain the cream and discard the cinnamon. Add the glucose syrup and return to a boil.
4. Add the cream to the chopped chocolate in five increments, stirring after each addition with a rubber spatula to form an emulsion.
5. Let the cinnamon ganache cool to 70°F (21°C).
6. Coat the molds with the tempered couverture and give the chocolate the first cooling.
7. Fill the molds with the ganache to within ¹⁄₁₆ inch (1 millimeter) of the top. When the ganache has set sufficiently, cover it with tempered couverture to seal. Chill the chocolates in a cool area until set, then unmold.

Approximate values per candy: **Calories** 90, **Total fat** 6 g, **Saturated fat** 4 g, **Cholesterol** 10 mg, **Sodium** 10 mg, **Total carbohydrates** 10 g, **Protein** 1 g

PONA (ORANGE CREAM–FILLED CHOCOLATES)

Yield: 48 Candies, 1 lb. 11 oz. (810 g) Filling   **Method:** Molded

Fondant	1 lb. 6 oz.	660 g
Orange marmalade	4 oz.	120 g
Grand Marnier or other orange liqueur	1 fl. oz.	30 ml
Semisweet or bittersweet couverture, tempered for coating molds	3 lb.	1440 g

1. In the bowl of a mixer fitted with the paddle attachment, combine the fondant, marmalade and liqueur.
2. Coat the molds with the tempered couverture and give the chocolate the first cooling.
3. While the chocolate cools, warm the fondant mixture in a bain marie over simmering water to 80°F (25°C). Fill the molds with the fondant mixture to within 1⁄16 inch (1 millimeter) from the top.
4. When the filling has lightly crusted over, after approximately 10 minutes, cover it with tempered couverture. Chill the chocolates in a cool area until set, then unmold.

Approximate values per candy: **Calories** 90, **Total fat** 25 g, **Saturated fat** 1.5 g, **Cholesterol** 0 mg, **Sodium** 5 mg, **Total carbohydrates** 17 g, **Protein** 1 g

CARAVELLE (MARZIPAN, RASPBERRY AND HAZELNUT CHOCOLATES)

Yield: 48 Candies, 1 lb. 12 oz. (480 g) Filling   **Method:** Molded

Marzipan (page 714)	10 oz.	300 g
Fondant	4 oz.	120 g
Raspberry compound	1 oz.	30 g
Raspberry liqueur	1 fl. oz.	30 ml
Semisweet or bittersweet couverture, tempered for coating molds	3 lb.	1440 g
Hazelnuts, toasted	48	48

1. Combine the marzipan, fondant and raspberry compound in the bowl of a mixer fitted with the paddle attachment and mix until the mixture is lump-free.
2. Gradually add the raspberry liqueur.
3. Coat the molds with the tempered couverture and give the chocolate the first cooling.
4. Fill the molds with a small amount of filling and place a toasted hazelnut in each mold.
5. Pipe the remaining filling to within 1⁄16 inch (1 millimeter) from the top. Cover the filling with tempered couverture. Chill the chocolates in a cool area until set, then unmold.

Approximate values per candy: **Calories** 80, **Total fat** 3 g, **Saturated fat** 1.5 g, **Cholesterol** 0 mg, **Sodium** 0 mg, **Total carbohydrates** 12 g, **Protein** 1 g

PASSION (WHITE CHOCOLATE AND PASSION FRUIT GANACHE CHOCOLATES)

Yield: 56 Candies, 1 lb. 11 oz. (795 g) Ganache   **Method:** Molded

Granulated sugar	4 oz.	120 g
Passion fruit purée, warm	8 fl. oz.	240 ml
Heavy cream	2 fl. oz.	60 ml
Vanilla bean, split	½	½
White chocolate, chopped fine	11 oz.	330 g
Unsalted butter	1.5 oz.	45 g
Orange food coloring, fat soluble	as needed	as needed
Cocoa butter, melted	3 oz.	90 g
White chocolate, melted	2 oz.	60 g
Semisweet or bittersweet couverture, tempered for coating molds	3 lb.	1440 g

1. Cook the sugar in a heavy saucepan over medium-high heat, stirring constantly until it forms a golden caramel.
2. Add the passion fruit purée and cream to the caramel. Bring the mixture to a boil, then remove it from the heat.
3. Stir the vanilla bean into the cream with a whisk. Infuse the cream with the vanilla bean 5 minutes, then remove the bean.
4. Add the caramel cream to the chopped white chocolate in five increments, stirring well after each addition. Add the butter, then let the ganache cool to 70°F (21°C).
5. Sift the food coloring, then mix it into half of the melted cocoa butter. Stir in the remaining cocoa butter and melted white chocolate. Temper. Using a spray gun, spray a thin coating of the colored chocolate into the chocolate molds, or use a gloved hand to spread a thin layer of the tinted chocolate in each mold.
6. Coat the molds with the tempered couverture and give the chocolate the first cooling.
7. Fill the molds with the cooled ganache to within ⅟₁₆ inch (1 millimeter) from the top.
8. When the filling has sufficiently firmed, cover it with tempered couverture. Chill the chocolates in a cool area until set, then unmold.

Approximate values per candy: **Calories** 90, **Total fat** 5 g, **Saturated fat** 3 g, **Cholesterol** 5 mg, **Sodium** 5 mg, **Total carbohydrates** 11 g, **Protein** 1 g

SEVILLE (MILK CHOCOLATE, HAZELNUT AND ORANGE GANACHE CHOCOLATES)

Yield: 56 Candies, 1 lb. 13 oz. (870 g) Ganache   **Method:** Molded

Milk chocolate couverture, chopped fine	10 oz.	300 g
Cocoa butter or additional milk chocolate, chopped fine	2 oz.	60 g
Heavy cream	10 fl. oz.	300 ml
Hazelnut paste	3 oz.	90 g
Candied Orange Peel (page 671), chopped fine	3 oz.	90 g
Grand Marnier or orange liqueur	1 fl. oz.	30 ml
Semisweet couverture, tempered for coating molds	3 lb.	1440 g

1. Combine the chopped chocolate and cocoa butter (if using) in a large bowl. Set aside.
2. Boil the cream. Add it to the chocolate mixture in five increments, stirring with a rubber spatula after each addition.
3. Stir in the hazelnut paste, Candied Orange Peel and liqueur.
4. Coat the molds with the tempered couverture and give the chocolate the first cooling.
5. Fill the molds with the ganache to within $\frac{1}{16}$ inch (1 millimeter) from the top.
6. When the filling has sufficiently set, cover it with tempered couverture to seal. Chill the chocolates in a cool area until set, then unmold.

Approximate values per candy: **Calories** 100, **Total fat** 7 g, **Saturated fat** 4 g, **Cholesterol** 10 mg, **Sodium** 5 mg, **Total carbohydrates** 10 g, **Protein** 1 g

BAHO (GINGER, LIME AND CARAMEL CREAM–FILLED CHOCOLATES)

Yield: 56 Candies, 1 lb. 11 oz. (831 g) Filling   **Method:** Molded

Heavy cream	7 fl. oz.	210 ml
Ginger, chopped fine	2 oz.	60 g
Lime zest, grated	0.2 oz. (1 Tbsp.)	6 g
Granulated sugar	10 oz.	300 g
Unsalted butter	4.5 oz.	135 g
Glucose or corn syrup	4 oz.	120 g
Green food coloring, fat soluble	as needed	as needed
Cocoa butter, melted	4 oz.	120 g
White chocolate couverture, tempered for coating molds	3 lb.	1440 g

1. Boil the cream in a nonreactive saucepan. Add the ginger and lime zest and infuse the cream 20 minutes, then strain. Keep the cream warm.
2. Stir the sugar over medium-high heat in a large saucepan using a whisk until a golden caramel is obtained. Remove the caramel from the heat and add the butter.
3. Slowly pour the infused cream into the caramel, whisking constantly. Bring the cream back to a boil and cook, stirring constantly until no lumps of caramel remain.
4. Remove from the heat and add the glucose syrup. Cool the filling to 70°F (21°C) before molding the chocolates.
5. Sift the food coloring and then mix it into the melted cocoa butter. Temper the colored cocoa butter. Using a gloved hand, smear a small amount into the indention of the mold.
6. Coat the molds with the tempered white chocolate couverture and give the chocolates the first cooling.
7. Pipe the filling to within $\frac{1}{16}$ inch (1 millimeter) from the edge.
8. Carefully cover the filling with tempered couverture to seal. Chill the chocolates in a cool area until set, then unmold.

Approximate values per candy: **Calories** 90, **Total fat** 5 g, **Saturated fat** 3.5 g, **Cholesterol** 10 mg, **Sodium** 5 mg, **Total carbohydrates** 11 g, **Protein** 0 g

SAMBA (ANISE GANACHE AND NOUGATINE CHOCOLATES)

Yield: 70 Candies, 1 lb. 13 oz. (892 g) Filling	**Method:** Dipped	
Heavy cream	9 fl. oz.	270 ml
Glucose or corn syrup	1.5 oz.	45 g
Anise seeds, chopped fine	0.25 oz. (4 tsp.)	7.5 g
Semisweet couverture, chopped fine	1 lb. 2 oz.	540 g
Sambuca or anise liqueur	1 fl. oz.	30 ml
Basic Nougatine (page 724), formed into disks 1/16 inch (1 millimeter) thick and 3/4 inch (1.8 centimeters) in diameter	70 disks	70 disks
Bittersweet couverture, tempered for dipping	3 lb.	1440 g

1. Boil the cream and glucose syrup in a nonreactive saucepan. Remove from the heat and add the anise seeds. Cover with plastic film and steep 20 minutes.
2. Strain the mixture and discard the seeds.
3. Melt the chopped couverture until half of the mass is melted.
4. Reheat the infused cream to 180°F (82°C) and pour into the half-melted chocolate. Whisk until thoroughly combined.
5. Let the ganache cool to 80°F (26°C) and add the liqueur.
6. When the mixture starts to set, pipe 1/3-ounce (10-gram) spheres of ganache onto silicone mats or wax paper.
7. Place a nougatine disk flat on the center of each piped sphere.
8. When the chocolates have set, dip in the tempered couverture.

Approximate values per candy: **Calories** 100, **Total fat** 7 g, **Saturated fat** 4 g, **Cholesterol** 5 mg, **Sodium** 5 mg, **Total carbohydrates** 12 g, **Protein** 1 g

VIONI (MILK CHOCOLATE AND VANILLA SQUARES)

Yield: Approximately 128 Candies, 1½ in. × ¾ in. (3.7 cm × 1.8 cm) each

Method: Dipped

Milk chocolate couverture, chopped fine	1 lb. 4 oz.	600 g
Glucose or corn syrup	1 oz.	30 g
Granulated sugar	10 oz.	300 g
Heavy cream	7 fl. oz.	210 ml
Vanilla bean, split	1	1
Unsalted butter, room temperature	2 oz.	60 g
Milk chocolate couverture, tempered for dipping	3 lb.	1440 g

1. Place the chopped couverture in a large bowl. Set aside.
2. In a nonreactive saucepan, bring the glucose syrup to a boil. Add the sugar gradually and stir until it reaches an amber caramel.
3. While the sugar cooks, boil the cream with the vanilla bean and whisk to release the seeds.
4. Deglaze the caramel with the boiling cream. Bring the mixture to a full boil and remove from the heat. Discard the vanilla bean.
5. Add the caramel cream to the chopped couverture in five increments, stirring after each addition with a rubber spatula to form an emulsion. Add the butter.
6. Pour the ganache into a candy frame or between candy rulers spaced to form a 12-inch (30-centimeter) square ½ inch (1.2 centimeters) thick. Let the ganache set.
7. Spread a very thin layer of tempered couverture over the ganache.
8. Cut the ganache into 1½-inch × ¾-inch (3.7-centimeter × 1.8-centimeter) rectangles.
9. Fold 128 small rectangular pieces of transfer sheets lengthwise in half, with the printed cocoa butter on the outside. Set aside.
10. Dip the centers in tempered couverture. Immediately place one folded transfer sheet diagonally on the surface of each dipped chocolate. Let the bonbons crystallize overnight before removing the transfer sheet.

Approximate values per candy: **Calories** 100, **Total fat** 4.5 g, **Saturated fat** 1.5 g, **Cholesterol** 0 mg, **Sodium** 5 mg, **Total carbohydrates** 16 g, **Protein** 1 g

Assorted dipped bonbons, clockwise from left: Rocher, Palets d'Or, Vioni, Mendiant, Irish Cream (bottom).

Ganache poured between candy rulers.

IRISH CREAM (CHOCOLATE GANACHE, COFFEE AND WHISKEY SQUARES)

Yield: Approximately 144 Candies, 1 in. (2.5 cm) each

Method: Dipped

Milk chocolate couverture, chopped fine	1 lb.	480 g
Semisweet couverture, chopped fine	2 oz.	60 g
Heavy cream	8 fl. oz.	240 ml
Coffee extract	0.3 fl. oz.	10 ml
Whiskey	4 fl. oz.	120 ml
Trimoline or honey	0.5 oz.	15 g
Chocolate couverture, tempered	as needed	as needed
Milk chocolate couverture, tempered for dipping	3 lb.	1440 g

1. Combine the chopped couvertures in a large mixing bowl. Set aside.
2. Boil the cream. Add it to the chopped couverture in five increments, stirring with a rubber spatula after each addition to form an emulsion.
3. Stir in the coffee extract, whiskey and trimoline.
4. Pour the chocolate ganache into a candy frame or between candy rulers spaced to form a 12-inch (30-centimeter) square with a thickness of ½ inch (1.2 centimeters). Let the ganache set.
5. Spread a very thin layer of tempered couverture over the ganache. Once the chocolate sets, cut the candy into 1-inch (2.5-centimeter) squares.
6. Coat the individual chocolates with tempered milk chocolate couverture and imprint three lines using a dipping fork.

Approximate values per candy: **Calories** 45, **Total fat** 2.5 g, **Saturated fat** 1.5 g, **Cholesterol** 5 mg, **Sodium** 0 mg, **Total carbohydrates** 4 g, **Protein** 0 g

ROCHERS (CARAMEL, ALMOND AND ORANGE CHOCOLATES)

Yield: 70 Candies   **Method:** Dipped

Slivered almonds	1 lb.	480 g
Granulated sugar	4 oz.	120 g
Water	2 fl. oz.	60 ml
Vanilla bean, split	½	½
White chocolate couverture, chopped fine	11 oz.	330 g
Candied Orange Peel (page 671), fine dice	4 oz.	120 g
Pistachios (optional)	4 oz.	120 g

1. Toast the almonds to light golden brown. Set aside.
2. Boil the sugar and water to 240°F (116°C). Remove from the heat. Scrape the vanilla bean into the syrup. Add the toasted almonds. Stir the mixture until the sugar crystallizes on the almonds.
3. Pour one-third of the crystallized almonds into a sauté pan and stir over medium heat until the sugar coating caramelizes. Spread them on a silicone baking mat or oiled parchment paper. Separate the almonds using an oiled fork. Repeat with the remaining almonds. Let cool.
4. Temper the white chocolate couverture and mix in the caramelized almonds, Candied Orange Peel and pistachios (if using).
5. Using two spoons, shape the mixture into uniform mounds and place the chocolates on a silicone baking mat or paper-lined sheet pan. Let the chocolates harden before storing.

Approximate values per ½-oz. (15-g) candy: **Calories** 70, **Total fat** 4.5 g, **Saturated fat** 1 g, **Cholesterol** 0 mg, **Sodium** 5 mg, **Total carbohydrates** 7 g, **Protein** 2 g

PALETS D'OR (BITTERSWEET AND VANILLA CHOCOLATES)

Yield: Approximately 70 candies, 1 in. (2.5 cm) each

Method: Dipped

Bittersweet couverture, chopped fine	12.5 oz.	375 g
Heavy cream	10 fl. oz.	300 ml
Glucose or corn syrup	2 oz.	60 g
Vanilla bean, split	1	1
Butter, room temperature	2 oz.	60 g
Bittersweet couverture, tempered for dipping	3 lb.	1440 g
Edible gold leaf	as needed	as needed

1. Line several flat sheet pans with sheets of acetate. Set aside the finely chopped bittersweet chocolate in a small bowl.
2. Place the cream in a nonreactive saucepan. Add the glucose syrup and scrape the vanilla seeds into the cream. Bring the mixture to a boil.
3. Remove the cream from the heat and pour it over the chocolate. Stir the mixture with a rubber spatula until it is smooth. Let it cool to 105°F (40°C) and then add the butter.
4. When the mixture starts to set, pipe ⅓-ounce (10-gram) mounds of ganache onto the acetate-lined sheet pans. Immediately cover the piped ganache with another sheet of acetate. Using a flat sheet pan or metal spatula, press the ganache evenly to a thickness of approximately ½ inch (1.2 centimeters). Allow to set for 24 hours.
5. Remove the ganache rounds from the acetate. To prevent the dipping fork from sticking into the ganache, quickly paint a thin layer of bittersweet chocolate onto the top of each ganache round, or use a spray gun to place a thin layer of chocolate on the ganache rounds. Let set for 5 minutes.
6. Dip the chocolates into the tempered couverture and immediately place a small piece of edible gold leaf on each ganache piece. Quickly place a clean piece of acetate on top of the chocolates.
7. Allow the chocolate to set for 24 hours before removing the acetate sheet.

Approximate values per 1-oz. (30-g) serving: **Calories** 150, **Total fat** 110 g, **Saturated fat** 7 g, **Cholesterol** 10 mg, **Sodium** 0 mg, **Total carbohydrates** 13 g, **Protein** 2 g

1. Pressing the piped ganache to an even thickness.

2. Removing the acetate from the bonbons after dipping.

HAZELNUT CRISPS

Yield: 7 oz. (210 g)

Milk chocolate, chopped	1 oz.	30 g
Cocoa butter, chopped fine	1 oz.	30 g
Unsalted butter	0.5 oz.	15 g
Hazelnut paste	3 oz.	90 g
Puffed rice cereal	1.5 oz.	45 g

1. Combine the chocolate and cocoa butter. Melt in the microwave or a bain marie over simmering water to 120°F (49°C).
2. Remove from the heat and add the butter and hazelnut paste in one step. Mix well with a whisk.
3. Fold in the puffed rice cereal.
4. Drop the chocolate-coated cereal by teaspoonfuls onto a silicone mat or paper-lined sheet pan. Or sprinkle the candy while still soft directly onto cakes, tortes or wherever it is to be used.

Approximate values per ½-oz. (15-g) serving: **Calories** 80, **Total fat** 5 g, **Saturated fat** 2.5 g, **Cholesterol** 5 mg, **Sodium** 35 mg, **Total carbohydrates** 7 g, **Protein** 1 g

SUGAR-BASED NOUGATINE

Yield: 3 lb. 13 oz. (1830 g)

Glucose or corn syrup	5 oz.	150 g
Granulated sugar	2 lb.	960 g
Almonds, sliced, toasted and hot	1 lb. 5 oz.	630 g
Unsalted butter or cocoa butter, cut into small pieces	3 oz.	90 g

1. Bring the glucose syrup to a boil in a heavy saucepan over medium-high heat.
2. Stir 4 ounces (120 grams) of the sugar into the glucose syrup. Once the sugar has dissolved, add another 4 ounces (120 grams) of the sugar. Gradually add the remaining sugar when most of the previously added sugar has dissolved. Continue stirring to evenly cook the mixture, approximately 3 to 4 minutes.
3. Reduce the heat. Brush down any sugar crystals that may have stuck to the sides of the pan with a clean brush dipped in clean water. Stir constantly until the mixture caramelizes to a light amber color, approximately 5 to 9 minutes.
4. When the mixture is amber, add the hot toasted almonds at once. Stir rapidly to coat the almonds, then cook 1 more minute. Remove from the heat and stir in the butter.
5. Roll and form the nougatine as needed.

VARIATIONS:

Hazelnut or Walnut Nougatine—Substitute 1 pound 5 ounces (630 grams) finely chopped, hot toasted hazelnuts or walnuts for the almonds.

Coffee Nougatine—Reduce the almonds to 8 ounces (240 grams). Add 8 ounces (240 grams) finely chopped toasted hazelnuts, 4 ounces (120 grams) hot toasted sesame seeds, and 1 ounce (30 grams) instant coffee to the mixture along with the hot almonds once it caramelizes. Reduce the butter to 2 ounces (60 grams).

Approximate values per ½-oz. (15-g) serving: **Calories** 70, **Total fat** 3 g, **Saturated fat** 0.5 g, **Cholesterol** 0 mg, **Sodium** 0 mg, **Total carbohydrates** 9 g, **Protein** 1 g

PEANUT BRITTLE

Yield: 3 lb. (1495 g)

Roasted salted peanuts may be used if a more American-style brittle is desired. Chopping a portion of the nuts will make the brittle flatter and more dense.

Peanuts, raw	1 lb. 4 oz.	600 g
Granulated sugar	1 lb.	480 g
Water	10 fl. oz.	300 ml
Glucose or corn syrup	12 oz.	360 g
Salt	0.2 oz. (1 tsp.)	6 g
Unsalted butter	1 oz.	30 g
Vanilla extract	0.15 fl. oz. (1 tsp.)	5 ml
Baking soda	0.14 oz. (1 tsp.)	4 g

1. Toast the peanuts in a 375°F (190°C) oven until lightly brown and fragrant, approximately 6 to 8 minutes. Set aside.

2. Bring the sugar and water to a boil in a heavy saucepan over medium-high heat. Add the glucose syrup. Wash down the sides of the pan with a clean pastry brush dipped in cold water to remove any sugar crystals that cling to the pan. Boil until the mixture turns a light golden brown caramel color.

3. Remove from the heat. Quickly stir in the salt, butter, vanilla, baking soda and peanuts. Immediately scrape the mixture onto a silicone baking mat or lightly oiled piece of marble. Spread out the mixture with an oiled spatula as thin as possible. Allow the brittle to cool.

4. Break the cooled peanut brittle up into uniform pieces. Store the candy in an airtight container in a cool, dry and dark place, where it will keep up to 3 weeks.

VARIATION:

Hazelnut Brittle—Substitute blanched hazelnuts for the peanuts.

Approximate values per 1 ¼-oz. (35-g) serving: **Calories** 130, **Total fat** 6 g, **Saturated fat** 0 g, **Cholesterol** 0 mg, **Sodium** 85 mg, **Total carbohydrates** 18 g, **Protein** 3 g

Hazelnut Brittle (left) and Peanut Brittle (right)

MEASUREMENT AND CONVERSION CHARTS

MEASUREMENT CONVERSION CHART— FORMULAS FOR EXACT MEASURES

	WHEN YOU KNOW	MULTIPLY BY	TO FIND
Mass (weight)	ounces	28.35	grams
	pounds	0.45	kilograms
	grams	0.035	ounces
	kilograms	2.2	pounds
Volume (capacity)	teaspoons	5.0	milliliters
	tablespoons	15.0	milliliters
	fluid ounces	29.57	milliliters
	cups	0.24	liters
	pints	0.47	liters
	quarts	0.95	liters
	gallons	3.785	liters
	milliliters	0.034	fluid ounces
Temperature	Fahrenheit	$\frac{5}{9}$ (after subtracting 32)	Celsius
	Celsius	$\frac{9}{5}$ (then add 32)	Fahrenheit

ROUNDED MEASURES FOR QUICK REFERENCE

1 oz.		= 30 g
4 oz.		= 120 g
8 oz.		= 240 g
16 oz.	= 1 lb.	= 480 g
32 oz.	= 2 lb.	= 960 g
36 oz.	= 2¼ lb.	= 1000 g (1 kg)
1/4 tsp.	= $\frac{1}{24}$ fl. oz.	= 1 ml
1/2 tsp.	= $\frac{1}{12}$ fl. oz.	= 2.5 ml
1 tsp.	= $\frac{1}{6}$ fl. oz.	= 5 ml
1 Tbsp.	= ½ fl. oz.	= 15 ml
1 c.	= 8 fl. oz.	= 240 ml
2 c. (1 pt.)	= 16 fl. oz.	= 480 ml
4 c. (1 qt.)	= 32 fl. oz.	= 960 ml
4 qt. (1 gal.)	= 128 fl. oz.	= 3.75 lt
32°F	= 0°C	
122°F	= 50°C	
212°F	= 100°C	

CONVERSION GUIDELINES

1 gallon	=	4 quarts
		8 pints
		16 cups (8 fluid ounces each)
		128 fluid ounces
1 fifth bottle	=	approximately 1½ pints or exactly 26.5 fluid ounces
1 measuring cup	=	8 fluid ounces (a coffee cup generally holds 6 fluid ounces)
1 large egg white	=	1 ounce (average)
1 lemon	=	1 to 1¼ fluid ounces of juice
1 orange	=	3 to 3½ fluid ounces of juice

SCOOP SIZES

SCOOP NUMBER	LEVEL MEASURE
6	⅔ cup
8	½ cup
10	⅖ cup
12	⅓ cup
16	¼ cup
20	3⅕ tablespoons
24	2⅔ tablespoons
30	2⅕ tablespoons
40	1⅗ tablespoons

Note: The number of the scoop determines the number of servings in each quart of a mixture; for example, with a No. 16 scoop, one quart of mixture will yield 16 servings.

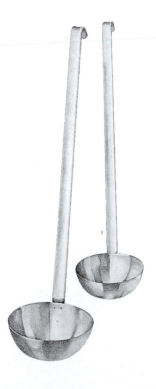

LADLE SIZES

SIZE	PORTION OF A CUP	NUMBER PER QUART	NUMBER PER LITER
1 fl. oz.	⅛	32	34
2 fl. oz.	¼	16	17
2⅔ fl. oz.	⅓	12	13
4 fl. oz.	½	8	8.6
6 fl. oz.	¾	5⅓	5.7

CANNED-GOOD SIZES

SIZE	NO. OF CANS PER CASE	AVERAGE WEIGHT	AVERAGE NO. CUPS PER CAN
No. ½	8	8 oz.	1
No. 1 tall (also known as 303)	2 & 4 doz.	16 oz.	2
No. 2	2 doz.	20 oz.	2½
No. 2½	2 doz.	28 oz.	3½
No. 3	2 doz.	33 oz.	4
No. 3 cylinder	1 doz.	46 oz.	5⅔
No. 5	1 doz.	3 lb. 8 oz.	5½
No. 10	6	6 lb. 10 oz.	13

Various standard cans—(left to right, front row) No. ½ flat, No. ¼; (middle row) No. 300, No. 1 tall, No. ½; (back row) No. 10, No. 3 cyclinder, No. 5.

APPROXIMATE VOLUME AND WEIGHT CONVERSIONS OF KEY BAKESHOP INGREDIENTS

ITEM	APPROXIMATE VOLUME EQUIVALENTS			APPROXIMATE WEIGHT EQUIVALENTS				
	1 OUNCE	¼ OUNCE	1 POUND	1 TSP.		1 TBSP.		1 CUP
				OUNCES	GRAMS	OUNCES	GRAMS	
Butter	2 Tbsp.	1½ tsp.	2 cups	0.17 oz.	5	0.5 oz.	15	8 oz.
Flour, all-purpose	3½ Tbsp.	2⅔ tsp.	3½ cups	0.09 oz.	3	0.3 oz.	9	4.5 oz.
Honey, corn syrup and molasses	4 tsp.	1 tsp.	1⅓ cups	0.25 oz.	7	0.75 oz.	24	12 oz.
Shortening, solid	7 tsp.	1¾ tsp.	2¼ cups	0.15 oz.	4	0.45 oz.	12	7.1 oz.
Sugar, granulated	7 tsp.	1¾ tsp.	2¼ cups	0.15 oz.	4	0.45 oz.	12	7 oz.
Sugar, brown	2 Tbsp.	1½ tsp.	2 cups	0.16 oz.	5	0.5 oz.	15	8 oz.
Sugar, powdered	¼ cup	1 Tbsp.	4 cups	0.08 oz.	2.5	0.25 oz.	8	4 oz.
Baking powder, baking soda and cream of tartar	7 tsp.	1¾ tsp.		0.14 oz.	4	0.4 oz.	12	
Cornstarch	11 tsp.	2¾ tsp.		0.09 oz.	3	0.3 oz.	9	
Dried egg whites	1¾ tsp.	½ tsp.		0.15 oz.	5	0.45 oz.	12	
Gelatin, powdered	10 tsp.	2½ tsp.		0.1 oz.	3	0.3 oz.	9	
Lemon peel	14 tsp.	3½ tsp.		0.07 oz.	2	0.2 oz.	6	
Salt, table	5 tsp.	1¼ tsp.		0.21 oz.	6	0.6 oz.	18	
Salt, kosher	2 Tbsp.	1½ tsp.		0.17 oz.	5	0.5 oz.	15	
Seeds (anise, caraway, dill)	14 tsp.	3½ tsp.		0.07 oz.	2	0.2 oz.	6	
Spices, dry ground	14 tsp.	3½ tsp.		0.07 oz.	2	0.2 oz.	6	
Yeast, active dry	7 tsp.	1¾ tsp.		0.15 oz.	4	0.45 oz.	12	
Yeast, fresh compressed	2 Tbsp.	1½ tsp.		0.17 oz.	5	0.5 oz.	15	
Vanilla extract and other extracts	2 Tbsp.	1½ tsp.		0.15 oz.	5	0.5 oz.	15	

APPENDIX II
FRESH FRUIT AVAILABILITY CHART

The following chart is intended as only a general guide to the best availability of freshly harvested fruit grown in the continental United States. State departments of agriculture can provide charts of local produce availability and information on local farmer's markets and sustainable agriculture programs. The Web sites of environmental groups such as the National Resources Defense Council, American Farmland Trust, and other public and private organizations also provide lists of seasonally available produce organized by state.

PRODUCT	JAN.	FEB.	MAR.	APR.	MAY	JUN.	JUL.	AUG.	SEP.	OCT.	NOV.	DEC.
	WINTER: DEC. 21–MAR. 19		SPRING: MAR. 20–JUN. 20			SUMMER: JUN. 21–SEP. 21			AUTUMN: SEP. 22–DEC. 20			
Apples								x	x	x	x	
Apricots						x	x					
Blueberries					x	x	x	x				
Cantaloupe						x	x	x	x			
Cherries					x	x	x	x				
Chestnuts									x	x	x	x
Citrus	x	x	x	x	x	x			x	x	x	x
Cranberries									x	x	x	x
Dates										x	x	x
Figs						x	x	x	x	x		
Grapes						x	x	x	x	x	x	
Lychees						x	x					
Mangoes					x	x	x	x				
Papayas			x	x	x	x						
Peaches				x		x	x	x				
Pears	x	x	x	x						x	x	x
Pecans											x	x
Persimmons										x	x	x
Pineapples			x	x	x	x	x	x				
Plums						x	x	x	x			
Pomegranates									x	x	x	x
Prickly pears									x	x	x	x
Pumpkins									x	x	x	
Raspberries						x	x	x	x			
Rhubarb		x	x	x	x							
Strawberries		x	x	x	x	x						
Watermelons						x	x	x				

APPENDIX III

VOLUME FORMULAS

When applicable, these formulas were scaled up using the baker's percentage method. Therefore the weight in metric measurements is not the exact equivalent of the weight in ounces and pounds.

CHAPTER 6, QUICK BREADS

SOUR CREAM MUFFINS (PAGE 144)

Yield: 50 Muffins, approximately 4 oz. (120 g) each

All-purpose flour	3 lb. 2 oz.	1500 g
Baking powder	0.7 oz.	21 g
Baking soda	0.7 oz.	21 g
Salt	1 oz.	30 g
Unsalted butter, room temperature	2 lb. 2 oz.	1200 g
Granulated sugar	2 lb. 2 oz.	1200 g
Eggs	1 lb.	495 g
Sour cream	3 lb. 2 oz.	1500 g
Vanilla extract	0.75 fl. oz.	22 ml
Total batter weight:	*12 lb. 7 oz.*	*5989 g*

STREUSEL TOPPING (PAGE 145)

Yield: 9 lb. 9 oz. (4544 g)

All-purpose flour	4 lb.	1920 g
Cinnamon, ground	2.5 oz.	8 g
Salt	0.8 oz.	24 g
Brown sugar	1 lb. 6 oz.	672 g
Granulated sugar	1 lb.	480 g
Whole butter, cold	3 lb.	1440 g
Total weight:	*9 lb. 9 oz.*	*4544 g*

BUTTERMILK PANCAKES (PAGE 147)

Yield: 96 Pancakes, 2 oz. (60 g) each

All-purpose flour	4 lb.	1920 g
Granulated sugar	4 oz.	115 g
Baking powder	1.6 oz.	48 g
Salt	1.3 oz.	38 g
Buttermilk	96 fl. oz.	2880 ml
Unsalted butter, melted	8 oz.	240 g
Eggs, beaten	20 oz.	595 g
Total batter weight:	*12 lb. 2 oz.*	*5836 g*

CREAM SCONES (PAGE 149)

Yield: 90 Scones, approximately 1½ oz. (45 g) each

All-purpose flour	4 lb.	1920 g
Granulated sugar	5.75 oz.	175 g
Baking powder	1.6 oz.	48 g
Baking soda	0.5 oz.	17 g
Salt	0.6 oz.	20 g
Unsalted butter, cold	1 lb.	480 g
Egg yolks	5 oz.	154 g
Half-and-half	44 fl. oz.	1325 ml
Total dough weight:	*8 lb. 9 oz.*	*4137 g*

CHOCOLATE CHERRY SCONES (PAGE 150)

Yield: 50 Scones, approximately 4¼ oz. (130 g) each

Unsalted butter, cold	1 lb. 12 oz.	845 g
Granulated sugar	8 oz.	240 g
Buttermilk	16 fl. oz.	480 ml
Sour cream	2 lb.	960 g
Salt	1.3 oz.	38 g
Vanilla extract	1 fl. oz.	28 ml
All-purpose or pastry flour	4 lb.	1920 g
Baking powder	3.8 oz.	115 g
Sun-dried cherries	2 lb.	960 g
Chocolate chunks	1 lb. 2 oz.	270 g
Total dough weight:	*12 lb. 12 oz.*	*5856 g*

IRISH WHEATEN BREAD (PAGE 152)

Yield: 4 Loaves, 9 in. (24 cm)

Whole-wheat flour, coarse	3 lb.	1440 g
Bread flour	1 lb.	480 g
Sea salt	0.8 oz.	24 g
Baking soda	0.56 oz.	16 g
Unsalted butter, diced	10 oz.	300 g
Low-fat buttermilk	48 fl. oz.	1440 ml
Total dough weight:	*7 lb. 11 oz.*	*3700 g*

MORNING GLORY MUFFINS (PAGE 153)

Yield: 36 Large Muffins, approximately 5 oz. (150 g) each

All-purpose flour	2 lb.	960 g
Granulated sugar	2 lb. 3 oz.	1075 g
Baking soda	1.3 oz.	38 g
Salt	1.2 oz.	35 g
Cinnamon, ground	0.6 oz.	19 g
Carrots, grated	1 lb. 12 oz.	840 g
Raisins	12 oz.	360 g
Pecan pieces	8 oz.	240 g
Coconut, shredded	8 oz.	240 g
Apple, unpeeled, grated	12 oz.	365 g
Eggs	1 lb. 4 oz.	595 g
Corn oil	1 lb. 5 oz.	625 g
Vanilla extract	1.3 fl. oz.	38 ml
Total batter weight:	*11 lb. 4 oz.*	*5406 g*

BRAN MUFFINS WITH RAISINS (PAGE 154)

Yield: 72 Muffins, 3½ oz. (105 g) each

Buttermilk	2 qt.	1920 ml
Wheat bran	20 oz.	600 g
Salt	1.5 oz.	45 g
All-purpose flour	2 lb. 10 oz.	1260 g
Baking powder	1.2 oz.	36 g
Baking soda	1.2 oz.	36 g
Cinnamon, ground	0.8 oz.	24 g
Eggs	13 oz.	390 g
Vegetable oil	12 fl. oz.	360 g
Brown sugar	3 lb.	1440 g
Raisins, conditioned	2 lb.	960 g
Total batter weight:	*14 lb. 11 oz.*	*7031 g*

PUMPKIN MUFFINS (PAGE 154)

Yield: 42 Muffins, approximately 4½ oz. (135 g) each

All-purpose flour	2 lb. 5 oz.	1170 g
Baking soda	0.3 oz.	9 g
Baking powder	0.6 oz.	18 g
Cinnamon, ground	1.4 oz.	34 g
Cloves, ground	0.12 oz.	3 g
Ginger, ground	0.4 oz.	12 g
Cardamom, ground	0.1 oz.	3 g
Eggs	1 lb. 3 oz.	573 g
Granulated sugar	3 lb. 14 oz.	1889 g
Vegetable oil	12 oz.	363 g
Salt	0.75 oz.	23 g
Pumpkin purée	3 lb.	1439 g
Orange juice	18 fl. oz.	538 ml
Total batter weight:	*12 lb. 13 oz.*	*6074 g*

ZUCCHINI BREAD (PAGE 159)

Yield: 6 Loaves, 9 in. × 5 in. (24 cm × 12 cm) each

Eggs	15 oz.	453 g
Corn oil	1 lb. 5 oz.	630 g
Granulated sugar	3 lb. 5 oz.	1612 g
Vanilla extract	0.45 fl. oz.	13 ml
Cinnamon, ground	0.4 oz.	12 g
Salt	0.6 oz.	17 g
Baking soda	0.4 oz.	12 g
Baking powder	0.2 oz.	6 g
All-purpose flour	2 lb. 10 oz.	1260 g
Zucchini, coarsely grated	2 lb.	982 g
Pecans, chopped	11 oz.	352 g
Total batter weight:	*11 lb. 2 oz.*	*5349 g*

JALAPEÑO CHEDDAR CORN MUFFINS (PAGE 160)

Yield: 60 Muffins, approximately 4¼ oz. (130 g) each

Yellow cornmeal	2 lb. 4 oz.	1080 g
Pastry or all-purpose flour	2 lb. 4 oz.	1080 g
Granulated sugar	9 oz.	270 g
Baking powder	1.2 oz.	35 g
Baking soda	0.4 oz.	13 g
Salt	0.7 oz.	19 g
Buttermilk	72 fl. oz.	2160 ml
Eggs	1 lb. 14 oz.	907 g
Grapeseed, olive or vegetable oil	24 fl. oz.	713 ml
Corn kernels	1 lb. 2 oz.	540 g
Grated Cheddar cheese	1 lb. 2 oz.	540 g
Seeded and diced jalapeño peppers	12 oz.	356 g
Total batter weight:	*16 lb.*	*7713 g*

LEMON TEA BREAD (PAGE 163)

Yield: 72 Muffins, approximately 2½ oz. (75 g) each, or 6 Loaves

Unsalted butter, softened	1 lb. 4 oz.	600 g
Granulated sugar	4 lb. 2 oz.	2004 g
Eggs	1 lb. 6 oz.	660 g
Milk	26 fl. oz.	792 ml
All-purpose flour	2 lb. 8 oz.	1200 g
Baking powder	1 oz.	28 g
Salt	0.6 oz.	19 g
Lemon zest, grated	2.4 oz.	72 g
Lemon juice	26 fl. oz.	792 ml
Total batter weight:	*12 lb. 12 oz.*	*6167 g*

GINGERBREAD (PAGE 164)

Yield: 8 Dozen 2-in. (5-cm) Squares; 2 Half-Sheet Pans

Unsalted butter	2 lb.	957 g
Brown sugar	2 lb.	957 g
Molasses	2 lb.	957 g
Eggs	10 oz.	302 g
Vanilla extract	0.6 fl. oz.	17 ml
Salt	1.2 oz.	33 g
Coffee, brewed, warm	24 fl. oz.	722 ml
Pastry or all-purpose flour	3 lb. 8 oz.	1680 g
Baking soda	0.4 oz.	12 g
Baking powder	0.4 oz.	12 g
Ginger, ground	1.5 oz.	50 g
Cinnamon, ground	3 oz.	84 g
Cardamom or cloves, ground	0.14 oz.	4 g
Total batter weight:	*12 lb. 1 oz.*	*5787 g*

SOUR CREAM COFFEECAKE (PAGE 165)

Yield: 4 Tube Cakes, 10 in. (25 cm)

Filling:

All-purpose flour	1.6 oz.	48 g
Cinnamon, ground	0.8 oz.	23 g
Brown sugar	1 lb. 8 oz.	722 g
Pecans, chopped	1 lb.	479 g
Unsalted butter, melted	4 oz.	118 g

Cake:

Unsalted butter	1 lb.	479 g
Granulated sugar	2 lb.	957 g
Eggs	13 oz.	386 g
Sour cream	2 lb.	957 g
Cake flour, sifted	1 lb. 12 oz.	840 g
Salt	0.2 oz.	6 g
Baking powder	0.5 oz.	17 g
Baking soda	0.5 oz.	17 g
Vanilla extract	0.6 fl. oz.	17 ml
Total batter weight:	*10 lb. 9 oz.*	*5066 g*

CHAPTER 7, ARTISAN AND YEAST BREADS

SOFT YEAST DINNER ROLLS (PAGE 190)

Yield: 134 Rolls, approximately 1¼ oz. (38 g) each

Active dry yeast	4 oz.	120 g
Water (temperature controlled)	3 lb.	1439 ml
Bread flour	5 lb. 8 oz.	2640 g
Salt	2 oz.	60 g
Granulated sugar	8 oz.	240 g
Nonfat dry milk powder	4 oz.	120 g
Shortening	4 oz.	120 g
Unsalted butter, softened	4 oz.	120 g
Eggs	6.4 oz.	200 g
Total dough weight:	*10 lb. 8 oz.*	*5059 g*

TRADITIONAL FRENCH BAGUETTES (PAGE 192)

Yield: 16 Loaves, approximately 12 oz. (360 g) each

Old Dough (page 199), room temperature	2 lb. 2 oz.	1022 g
Bread flour	6 lb.	2880 g
Instant yeast	0.7 oz.	23 g
Water (temperature controlled)	61 fl. oz.	1829 ml
Salt	2 oz.	60 g
Total dough weight:	*12 lb. 2 oz.*	*5814 g*

NATURAL SOURDOUGH STARTER (CHEF) (PAGE 194)

Yield: 6 lb. 9 oz. (3145 g)

Spring water, 70°F (21°C)	45 fl. oz.	1350 ml
Organic grapes	15 oz.	445 g
Bread flour	2 lb. 13 oz.	1350 g

SIMPLE SOURDOUGH STARTER (PAGE 198)

Yield: 11 lb. 4 oz. (5415 g)

Active dry yeast	0.45 oz.	15 g
Water, warm	12 fl. oz.	360 ml
Water, room temperature	72 fl. oz.	2160 ml
All-purpose flour	6 lb.	2880 g

POOLISH (PAGE 199)

Yield: 2 lb. 8 oz. (1204 g)

Bread flour, room temperature	1 lb. 4 oz.	600 g
Water, 70°F (21°C)	1 lb. 4 oz.	600 g
Instant yeast	0.14 oz.	4 g

PÂTE FERMENTÉE (OLD DOUGH) (PAGE 199)

Yield: 5 lb. 4 oz. (2535 g)

Bread flour	3 lb. 2 oz.	1500 g
Instant yeast	0.75 oz.	22.5 g
Water, 70°F (21°C)	32.5 fl. oz.	975 ml
Salt	1.25 oz.	37.5 g

WHITE SANDWICH BREAD (PAGE 200)

Yield: 10 Large Loaves

Water (temperature controlled)	60 fl. oz.	1800 ml
Nonfat dry milk powder	6 oz.	180 g
Granulated sugar	4.8 oz.	144 g
Salt	2.4 oz.	72 g
Active dry yeast	2.4 oz.	72 g
Bread flour	7 lb. 8 oz.	3600 g
Unsalted butter, softened	4.8 oz.	144 g
Eggs	16.8 oz.	504 g
Total dough weight:	*13 lb. 9 oz.*	*6516 g*

PULLMAN LOAVES (PAGE 201)

Yield: 6 Loaves, approximately 2 lb. (970 g) each

Dry milk powder	2 oz.	60 g
Bread flour	3 lb. 6 oz.	1620 g
High-gluten flour	3 lb. 6 oz.	1620 g
Water (temperature controlled)	68 fl. oz.	2040 g
Compressed yeast	5 oz.	150 g
Granulated sugar	2.5 oz.	76 g
Salt	2 oz.	60 g
Dough conditioner (optional)	2 oz.	60 g
Unsalted butter, room temperature	5.4 oz.	162 g
Total dough weight:	*12 lb. 2 oz.*	*5848 g*

FRENCH OR ITALIAN BREAD (PAGE 213)

Yield: 8 Loaves, approximately 1 lb. 9 oz. (750 g) each

Water (temperature controlled)	78 fl. oz.	2340 ml
Active dry yeast	2 oz.	57 g
Bread flour	7 lb. 8 oz.	3600 g
Salt	2.4 oz.	72 g
Total dough weight:	*12 lb. 10 oz.*	*6069 g*

MULTIGRAIN SOURDOUGH BREAD (PAGE 214)

Yield: 6 Loaves, 9 in. × 5 in. (22 cm × 13 cm) each

Cracked wheat	13 oz.	396 g
Water, hot	24 fl. oz.	720 ml
Whole butter, melted	6 oz.	180 g
Molasses	4.5 oz.	135 g
Honey	4.5 oz.	135 g
Salt	0.6 oz.	18 g
Nonfat dry milk powder	6 oz.	180 g
Flax seeds	6 oz.	180 g
Sunflower seeds, roasted	6 oz.	180 g
Sourdough starter	4 lb. 2 oz.	1980 g
Active dry yeast	0.4 oz.	12 g
Whole-wheat flour	1 lb. 14 oz.	900 g
Bread flour	1 lb. 14 oz.	900 g
Total dough weight:	*12 lb. 2 oz.*	*5916 g*

NINE-GRAIN BREAD (PAGE 215)

Yield: 6 Loaves, approximately 1 lb. 9 oz. (750 g) each

Nine-grain mix	1 lb.	475 g
Water, room temperature	20 fl. oz.	605 ml
High-gluten flour	3 lb.	1440 g
Vital wheat gluten	2.5 oz.	72 g
Instant yeast	1.5 oz.	43 g
Salt	1.5 oz.	43 g
Water (temperature controlled)	32 fl. oz.	965 ml
Old Dough (page 199), room temperature (optional)	2 lb.	950 g
Total dough weight:	*9 lb. 8 oz.*	*4533 g*

SAN FRANCISCO SOURDOUGH BREAD (PAGE 218)

Yield: 5 Loaves, approximately 2 lb. (960 g) each

Active dry yeast	2.4 oz.	72 g
Water (temperature controlled)	40 fl. oz.	1200 ml
Sourdough starter	1 lb. 14 oz.	890 g
Bread flour	5 lb.	2400 g
Kosher salt	2.4 oz.	72 g
Egg whites, beaten	8 oz.	250 g
Total dough weight:	*10 lb. 2 oz.*	*4884 g*

ENGLISH MUFFINS (PAGE 220)

Yield: 54 Muffins, approximately 3 oz. (90 g) each

Milk	36 fl. oz.	1012 ml
Instant yeast	20.75 oz.	21 g
Pastry flour	3 lb.	1350 g
Bread flour	3 lb.	1350 g
Baking powder (optional)	1.2 oz.	37 g
Granulated sugar	4.5 oz.	126 g
Salt	2 oz.	54 g
Unsalted butter, room temperature	4.8 oz.	150 g
Water (temperature controlled)	36 fl. oz.	1012 ml
Total dough weight:	*11 lb. 4 oz.*	*5112 g*

GRISSINI (DRY ITALIAN-STYLE BREAD STICKS) (PAGE 221)

Yield: 18 Dozen Bread Sticks

Bread flour	8 lb. 12 oz.	4200 g
Instant yeast	2 oz.	60 g
Salt	5.33 oz.	160 g
Water (temperature controlled)	60 fl. oz.	1800 ml
Olive oil	16 fl. oz.	480 ml
Unsalted butter, softened	1 lb.	480 g
Total dough weight:	*13 lb. 15 oz.*	*7180 g*

PIZZA DOUGH (PAGE 226)

Yield: 6 Large Pizzas or 48 Individual Pizzas

Active dry yeast	2.5 oz.	75 g
Water, hot (90°F/32°C)	12 fl. oz.	353 ml
Bread flour	5 lb. 4 oz.	2520 g
Water, cool	36 fl. oz.	1084 ml
Salt	1.2 oz.	35 g
Olive oil	6 fl. oz.	176 ml
Honey	4.2 oz.	126 g
Total dough weight:	*9 lb. 1 oz.*	*4369 g*

PITA BREAD (PAGE 227)

Yield: 72 Individual Pitas

Compressed yeast	11.5 oz.	345 g
Water (temperature controlled)	76 fl. oz.	2290 ml
Bread flour	9 lb.	4320 g
Salt	2.8 oz.	86 g
Vegetable oil	12 fl. oz.	367 ml
Total dough weight:	*15 lb. 6 oz.*	*7408 g*

PRETZELS (PAGE 229)

Yield: 62 Pretzels, approximately 3 oz. (90 g) each

Old Dough (page 199), room temperature	1 lb. 9 oz.	763 g
Bread flour	6 lb.	2880 g
Instant yeast	1.4 oz.	43 g
Water (temperature controlled)	58.5 fl. oz.	1756 ml
Salt	1.4 oz.	43 g
Unsalted butter	4.5 oz.	135 g
Total dough weight:	*11 lb. 9 oz.*	*5620 g*

CHAPTER 8, ENRICHED YEAST BREADS

CHALLAH (PAGE 240)

Yield: 8 Large Loaves

Active dry yeast	2 oz.	60 g
Water, hot (90°F/32°C)	8 fl. oz.	235 ml
Honey	12 fl. oz.	370 ml
Water (temperature controlled)	20 fl. oz.	605 ml
Eggs	1 lb. 11 oz.	806 g
Unsalted butter, melted	15.5 oz.	470 g
Salt	2.2 oz.	67 g
Bread flour	7 lb.	3360 g
Total dough weight:	*12 lb. 6 oz.*	*5973 g*

SWEET BUN DOUGH (PAGE 242)

Yield: 144 Buns, approximately 2 oz. (60 g) each

Compressed yeast	8 oz.	220 g
Water (temperature controlled)	60 fl. oz.	1680 ml
Dry milk powder	8 oz.	220 g
Bread flour	6 lb. 12 oz.	3000 g
Pastry flour	2 lb. 4 oz.	1000 g
Granulated sugar	1 lb. 14 oz.	840 g
Baking powder	2 oz.	56 g
Salt	2 oz.	56 g
Eggs	13 oz.	360 g
Unsalted butter, room temperature	14.4 oz.	400 g
Vegetable shortening or butter	14.4 oz.	400 g
Total dough weight:	*18 lb. 7 oz.*	*8232 g*

CINNAMON SWIRL RAISIN BREAD (PAGE 250)

Yield: 9 Loaves, approximately 1 lb. 14 oz. (840 g) each

Bread flour	5 lb. 1 oz.	2430 g
Potato flour	6 oz.	180 g
Dry milk powder	3.75 oz.	112 g
Water (temperature controlled)	39 fl. oz.	1166 ml
Eggs	12 oz.	365 g
Vanilla extract	0.4 fl. oz.	12 ml
Granulated sugar	13.5 oz.	405 g
Salt	2.3 oz.	68 g
Instant yeast	3 oz.	90 g
Water, warm	6 fl. oz.	180 ml
Unsalted butter, softened	1 lb. 3.5 oz.	583 g
Raisins	4 lb. 2 oz.	1980 g
Cinnamon Sugar (recipe follows)	1 lb. 8 oz.	719 g
Total dough weight:	*17 lb. 8 oz.*	*8290 g*

CINNAMON SUGAR

Yield: 1 lb. 8 oz. (720 g)

Cinnamon, ground	3 oz.	90 g
Granulated sugar	1 lb. 5 oz.	630 g

PAIN DE MIE (SANDWICH BREAD) (PAGE 252)

Yield: 6 Loaves, approximately 1 lb. 14 oz. (900 g) each

Instant yeast	2 oz.	61 g
Water (temperature controlled)	57 fl. oz.	1714 ml
Bread flour	6 lb. 6 oz.	3060 g
Dry milk powder	3 oz.	92 g
Granulated sugar	4 oz.	122 g
Salt	2 oz.	61 g
Unsalted butter, room temperature	12 oz.	367 g
Total dough weight:	*11 lb. 6 oz.*	*5477 g*

MILK BREAD (PAGE 253)

Yield: 21 Loaves, approximately 10 oz. (300 g) each

Milk	59 fl. oz.	1650 ml
Compressed yeast	6.5 oz.	180 g
Bread flour	3 lb. 6 oz.	1500 g
Pastry flour	3 lb. 6 oz.	1500 g
Shortening	13 oz.	360 g
Granulated sugar	10 oz.	300 g
Dough conditioner (optional)	1.5 oz.	45 g
Salt	1.5 oz.	45 g
Eggs	9.75 oz.	270 g
Total dough weight:	*13 lb. 1 oz.*	*5850 g*

HOT CROSS BUNS (PAGE 256)

Yield: 62 Rolls, approximately 3½ oz. (105 g) each

Dough:

Golden raisins, conditioned	1 lb. 4 oz.	600 g
Dark raisins, conditioned	1 lb. 4 oz.	600 g
Candied orange peel	6 oz.	160 g
Bread flour	4 lb. 8 oz.	2000 g
Unsalted butter or shortening	8 oz.	240 g
Granulated sugar	7 oz.	200 g
Dough conditioner (optional)	0.6 oz.	20 g
Dry milk powder	4 oz.	100 g
Compressed yeast	5.5 oz.	160 g
Salt	1.2 oz.	36 g
Eggs	6.4 oz.	200 g
Vanilla extract	0.3 fl. oz.	10 ml
Cardamom, ground	0.14 oz.	4 g
Allspice, ground	0.14 oz.	4 g
Ginger, ground	0.3 oz.	8 g
Cinnamon, ground	0.4 oz.	12 g
Water	38 fl. oz.	1040 ml

Cross dough:

Pastry flour	1 lb.	440 g
Unsalted butter or shortening	3 oz.	80 g
Milk	14 fl. oz.	380 ml
Total dough weight:	*13 lb. 14 oz.*	*6294 g*
Bun Glaze (recipe follows)	11 fl. oz.	330 ml

BUN GLAZE

Yield: 11 fl. oz. (331 ml)

Water	3.5 fl. oz.	105 ml
Granulated sugar	7 oz.	210 g
Ginger, ground	0.04 oz.	1 g
Lemon juice	0.3 fl. oz.	10 ml
Lemon zest, finely grated	0.14 oz.	4 g
Cream of tartar	0.04 oz.	1 g

PECAN STICKY BUNS (PAGE 260)

Yield: 35 Buns, approximately 3 oz. (90 g) each

Dough:

Active dry yeast	3 oz.	90 g
Granulated sugar	6 oz.	180 g
Milk	1.5 fl. oz.	45 ml
Buttermilk	16 fl. oz.	490 ml
Vanilla extract	0.5 fl. oz.	15 ml
Lemon zest, grated	0.6 oz.	18 g
Lemon juice	0.5 fl. oz.	15 ml
Egg yolks	3.6 oz.	108 g
Salt	1.2 oz.	36 g
All-purpose flour	3 lb.	1440 g
Unsalted butter, very soft	1 lb. 8 oz.	720 g
Total dough weight:	*6 lb. 9 oz.*	*3157 g*

Topping:

Honey	9 fl. oz.	270 ml
Brown sugar	9 oz.	270 g
Pecans, chopped	6 oz.	180 g

Filling:

Cinnamon	0.2 oz.	6 g
Pecans, chopped	9 oz.	270 g
Brown sugar	12 oz.	360 g
Unsalted butter, melted	9 oz.	270 g

PARISIAN BRIOCHE (PAGE 263)

Yield: 6 Loaves, approximately 1 lb. 8 oz. (720 g) each

Sponge:

Instant yeast	1 oz.	30 g
Water, warm	8 fl. oz.	240 ml
Bread flour	1 lb.	480 g
Eggs	1 lb.	480 g
Granulated sugar	2 oz.	60 g
Total sponge weight:	*2 lb. 10 oz.*	*1290 g*

Dough:

Instant yeast	0.5 oz.	16 g
Water, warm	2 fl. oz.	60 ml
Sponge	2 lb. 10 oz.	1290 g
High-gluten flour	3 lb. 4 oz.	1560 g
Granulated sugar	8 oz.	240 g
Eggs, lightly beaten	1 lb.	470 g
Salt	1.5 oz.	46 g
Unsalted butter, softened but still pliable	1 lb. 10 oz.	780 g
Total dough weight:	*9 lb. 4 oz.*	*4462 g*

KUGELHOPF (PAGE 264)

Yield: 8 Loaves, approximately 1 lb. 9 oz. (750 g) each

Milk	20 fl. oz.	600 ml
Instant yeast	4 oz.	120 g
Eggs	2 lb.	960 g
Vanilla extract	0.3 fl. oz.	10 ml
Bread flour	4 lb. 4 oz.	2040 g
Granulated sugar	10 oz.	300 g
Salt	1.5 oz.	44 g
Unsalted butter, softened	2 lb. 4 oz.	1080 g
Raisins, conditioned	2 lb.	960 g
Total dough weight:	*12 lb. 10 oz.*	*6114 g*

CHAPTER 9, LAMINATED DOUGHS

PUFF PASTRY (PATE FEUILLETEE) (PAGE 280)

Yield: 9 lb. 8 oz. (4582 g)

Salt	1.5 oz.	45 g
Water, chilled	31 fl. oz.	940 ml
Bread flour, chilled or frozen	1 lb. 14 oz.	900 g
All-purpose flour, chilled or frozen	1 lb. 15.5 oz.	945 g
Unsalted butter, very soft	13.5 oz.	405 g
Unsalted butter, cold	2 lb. 13 oz.	1347 g
Total dough weight:	*9 lb. 8 oz.*	*4582 g*

PARISIAN CROISSANTS (PAGE 287)

Yield: 120 Rolls

Bread flour	4 lb. 8 oz.	2160 g
Salt	2 oz.	60 g
Granulated sugar	12 oz.	360 g
Milk	42 fl. oz.	1250 ml
Active dry yeast	2 oz.	60 g
Unsalted butter, softened	3 lb.	1440 g
Total dough weight:	*11 lb. 2 oz.*	*5330 g*

DANISH PASTRY DOUGH (PAGE 290)

Yield: 108 Pastries

Active dry yeast	1.5 oz.	45 g
Bread flour	1 lb. 14 oz.	900 g
All-purpose flour	1 lb. 14 oz.	900 g
Granulated sugar	12 oz.	360 g
Water (temperature controlled)	12 fl. oz.	360 ml
Milk (temperature controlled)	12 fl. oz.	360 ml
Eggs, room temperature	9.6 oz.	300 g
Salt	0.6 oz.	18 g
Vanilla extract	0.5 fl. oz.	12 ml
Cinnamon, ground	0.12 oz.	3 g
Unsalted butter, melted	4.5 oz.	135 g
Unsalted butter, cold	3 lb.	1440 g
Total dough weight:	*10 lb.*	*4833 g*

CREAM CHEESE FILLING (PAGE 295)

Yield: 6 lb. 13 oz. (3273 g)

Cream cheese	4 lb. 8 oz.	2160 g
Granulated sugar	12 oz.	360 g
Eggs	14.5 oz.	432 g
Vanilla extract	1.5 fl. oz.	45 ml
Lemon zest, grated fine	0.21 oz.	6 g
Pastry flour	9 oz.	270 g

FRANGIPANE (PAGE 295)

Yield: 6 lb. 5 oz. (3030 g)

Almond paste	3 lb.	1440 g
Granulated sugar	6 oz.	180 g
Unsalted butter, softened	1 lb. 5 oz.	630 g
Eggs	1 lb. 4 oz.	600 g
Vanilla extract	1.5 fl. oz.	45 ml
Cake flour	4.5 oz.	135 g

ALMOND PASTE FILLING (PAGE 296)

Yield: 5 lb. 13 oz. (2829 g)

Almond paste, room temperature	3 lb. 12 oz.	1800 g
Unsalted butter, softened	1 lb. 8 oz.	720 g
Salt	0.3 oz.	9 g
Vanilla extract	1 fl. oz.	30 ml
Egg whites	9 oz.	270 g

ALMOND CREAM (PAGE 296)

Yield: 9 lb. 3 oz. (440 g)

Unsalted butter, softened	1 lb. 8 oz.	720 g
Granulated sugar	3 lb.	1440 g
Eggs	1 lb. 8 oz.	750 g
All-purpose flour	15 oz.	450 g
Almonds, ground	2 lb. 4 oz.	1080 g

RICOTTA CHEESE FILLING (PAGE 297)

Yield: 8 lb. 11 oz. (4185 g)

Cream cheese, softened	4 lb. 8 oz.	2160 g
Ricotta	1 lb. 14 oz.	900 g
Granulated sugar	15 oz.	450 g
Eggs	9.6 oz.	300 g
Vanilla extract	0.5 fl. oz.	15 ml
Pastry flour	12 oz.	360 g

THICKENED CHERRIES (PAGE 297)

Yield: 8 lb. 5 oz. (4008 g)

Cherries, IQF	6 lb.	2880 g
Granulated sugar	1 lb. 8 oz.	720 g
Cornstarch	4.5 oz.	135 g
Water	9 fl. oz.	270 ml
Almond extract	0.12 fl. oz.	3 ml

APRICOT FILLING (PAGE 297)

Yield: 6 lb. (2884 g)

Dried apricots	1 lb. 8 oz.	720 g
Orange juice	3 pt.	1440 ml
Granulated sugar	1 lb. 2 oz.	540 g
Salt	0.15 oz.	4.5 g
Unsalted butter	6 oz.	180 g

COCONUT CREAM FILLING (PAGE 298)

Yield: 5 lb. 6 oz. (2605 g)

Unsalted butter, softened	1 lb. 4 oz.	600 g
Granulated sugar	1 lb. 9 oz.	750 g
Salt	1 oz.	30 g
Eggs	1 lb. 4 oz.	600 g
Vanilla extract	0.75 fl. oz.	25 ml
Macaroon coconut	1 lb. 4 oz.	600 g

QUICK PUFF PASTRY (PAGE 299)

Yield: 7 lb. 4 oz. (3576 g)

Unbleached all-purpose flour	2 lb. 5.5 oz.	1140 g
Cake flour	7.5 oz.	228 g
Unsalted butter	3 lb.	1460 g
Salt	0.6 oz.	18 g
Water, very cold	24 fl. oz.	730 ml
Total dough weight:	7 lb. 4 oz.	3576 g

CROISSANTS (PAGE 304)

Yield: 70 Croissants, approximately 2½ oz. (75 g) each

Dough:

Granulated sugar	8 oz.	240 g
Salt	2 oz.	60 g
Dry milk powder	2 oz.	60 g
Eggs	3.2 oz.	100 g
Water, ice cold	36 fl. oz.	1080 ml
Vanilla extract	0.3 fl. oz.	10 ml
Instant yeast	2 oz.	60 g
Bread flour	4 lb.	1920 g
Unsalted butter, softened	3 lb. 12 oz.	1800 g
Total dough weight:	11 lb. 1 oz.	5330 g

Egg wash:

Heavy cream	4 fl. oz.	120 ml
Eggs, lightly beaten	6.4 oz.	192 g

CHAPTER 10, COOKIES AND BROWNIES

CHOCOLATE CHUNK COOKIES (PAGE 313)

Yield: 100 Cookies, approximately 2 oz. (60 g) each

Unsalted butter, softened	2 lb.	960 g
Granulated sugar	1 lb.	480 g
Brown sugar	1 lb. 8 oz.	720 g
Eggs	10 oz.	300 g
Vanilla extract	0.6 fl. oz.	18 ml
Salt	0.8 oz. (2 tsp.)	24 g
Pastry or all-purpose flour	2 lb. 8 oz.	1200 g
Baking soda	0.3 oz.	8 g
Pecans or walnut pieces, chopped	1 lb.	480 g
Chocolate chunks or chips	4 lb.	1920 g
Total dough weight:	12 lb. 11 oz.	6110 g

FUDGE BROWNIES (PAGE 321)

Yield: 8 Dozen Brownies, approximately 2 in. (5 cm) each, 2 Half-Sheet Pans

Unsalted butter, room temperature	2 lb. 4 oz.	1075 g
Unsweetened chocolate	2 lb.	960 g
Eggs	2 lb.	960 g
Granulated sugar	5 lb.	2400 g
Salt	0.4 oz.	11 g
Vanilla extract	2 fl. oz.	60 ml
Coffee extract (optional)	1 fl. oz.	30 ml
Pastry or all-purpose flour	2 lb.	960 g
Pecan pieces	1 lb.	480 g
Total batter weight:	14 lb. 7 oz.	6936 g

OATMEAL COOKIES (PAGE 323)

Yield: 96 Cookies, approximately 2 oz. (60 g) each

All-purpose or pastry flour	1 lb. 15.5 oz.	945 g
Baking soda	0.4 oz.	12 g
Cinnamon, ground	0.6 oz.	18 g
Quick-cooking oats	1 lb. 11 oz.	822 g
Unsalted butter, softened	1 lb. 11 oz.	822 g
Granulated sugar	1 lb. 11 oz.	822 g
Brown sugar	1 lb. 11 oz.	822 g
Eggs	9.5 oz.	284 g
Orange juice concentrate	4.5 fl. oz.	132 ml
Vanilla extract	1.5 fl. oz.	44 ml
Salt	0.6 oz.	18 g
Raisins	2 lb. 4 oz.	1066 g
Total dough weight:	12 lb.	5807 g

CHOCOLATE CHEWIES (PAGE 323)

Yield: 48 Cookies, approximately 3¾ oz. (112 g) each

Powdered sugar	5 lb. 12 oz.	2600 g
Cocoa powder	12 oz.	338 g
Salt	1 oz.	26 g
Vanilla extract	1 fl. oz.	26 ml
Egg whites	1 lb. 8 oz.	676 g
Walnuts or any other nut, chopped coarse	3 lb. 8 oz.	1586 g
Total batter weight:	11 lb. 10 oz.	5252 g

SNICKERDOODLES (CINNAMON BUTTER COOKIES) (PAGE 326)

Yield: 200 Cookies, approximately 1 oz. (30 g) each

Pastry or all-purpose flour	4 lb. 6 oz.	2100 g
Baking powder	0.7 oz.	21 g
Cinnamon, ground	1.4 oz.	42 g
Unsalted butter, softened	2 lb. 8 oz.	1197 g
Granulated sugar	1 lb. 14 oz.	903 g
Brown sugar	2 lb. 8 oz.	1197 g
Eggs	1 lb.	483 g
Vanilla extract	3 fl. oz.	84 ml
Salt	2 oz.	63 g
Total dough weight:	*12 lb. 11 oz.*	*6090 g*

PEANUT BUTTER SANDIES (PAGE 327)

Yield: 18 Dozen, approximately 1⅓ oz. (40 g) each

Pastry or all-purpose flour	6 lb.	2880 g
Baking soda	5.75 oz.	17 g
Baking powder	5.75 oz.	17 g
Unsalted butter, softened	3 lb. 15 oz.	1900 g
Granulated sugar	3 lb. 15 oz.	1900 g
Eggs	13 oz.	403 g
Peanut butter	2 lb. 8 oz.	1210 g
Salt	1.6 oz.	49 g
Peanut halves (optional)	7.5 oz.	230 g
Total dough weight:	*18 lb.*	*8606 g*

TRADITIONAL SHORTBREAD (PAGE 329)

Yield: 21 Dozen Cookies, approximately ½ oz. (15 g) each

Unsalted butter, softened	3 lb.	1436 g
Powdered sugar	1 lb. 8 oz.	718 g
Vanilla extract	1.75 fl. oz.	51 ml
Salt	0.6 oz.	17 g
Pastry or all-purpose flour	3 lb. 9 oz.	1710 g
Total dough weight:	*8 lb. 3 oz.*	*3932 g*

OAT CHOCOLATE CHIP BAR COOKIES (PAGE 334)

Yield: 6 Dozen Bars, approximately 2 in. x 3 in. (5 cm x 7.5 cm) each, 2 Half-Sheet Pans

Pastry or all-purpose flour	1 lb. 8 oz.	720 g
Baking soda	0.25 oz.	8 g
Cinnamon, ground	0.25 oz.	8 g
Unsalted butter, softened	1 lb. 8 oz.	720 g
Brown sugar	1 lb. 8 oz.	720 g
Granulated sugar	12 oz.	360 g
Eggs	10 oz.	302 g
Buttermilk	4 fl. oz.	123 ml
Salt	0.4 oz.	10 g
Vanilla extract	0.65 fl. oz.	19 ml
Quick-cooking oats	1 lb. 12 oz.	835 g
Chocolate chunks	1 lb. 8 oz.	720 g
Walnuts, chopped	12 oz.	360 g
Total batter weight:	*10 lb. 3 oz.*	*4905 g*

CLASSIC PECAN BARS (PAGE 335)

Yield: 16 Dozen Cookies, approximately 2 in. (5 cm) each, 2 Half-Sheet Pans

Sweet Tart Dough (page 368)	5 lb.	2400 g
Filling:		
Brown sugar	1 lb. 14 oz.	900 g
Unsalted butter	1 lb.	480 g
Honey	1 lb. 12 oz.	840 g
Granulated sugar	7 oz.	210 g
Pecans, chopped	4 lb.	1920 g
Heavy cream	8 fl. oz.	240 ml

SUGAR COOKIES (PAGE 339)

Yield: 130 Cookies, approximately 1 oz. (30 g) each

Pastry or all-purpose flour	3 lb.	1440 g
Baking powder	0.4 oz.	13 g
Unsalted butter, softened	2 lb. 4 oz.	1080 g
Granulated sugar	1 lb. 8 oz.	720 g
Powdered sugar	12 oz.	360 g
Salt	0.6 oz.	18 g
Eggs	9.6 oz.	288 g
Vanilla extract	1 fl. oz.	27 ml
Total dough weight:	*8 lb. 3 oz.*	*3946 g*

Decorative Cookie Icing:		
Powdered sugar	5 lb.	2400 g
Lemon juice or water	20 fl. oz.	600 ml
Corn syrup	10 fl. oz.	300 ml
Vanilla extract	0.75 fl. oz.	25 ml

GINGERBREAD COOKIES (PAGE 340)

Yield: 48 Cookies, approximately 2⅓ oz. (70 g) each

Unsalted butter, softened	1 lb.	475 g
Brown sugar	1 lb.	475 g
Molasses, dark	24 fl. oz.	720 ml
Eggs	6.2 oz.	187 g
All-purpose flour	3 lb.	1440 g
Baking soda	0.5 oz.	15 g
Salt	0.4 oz.	11 g
Ginger, ground	0.5 oz.	15 g
Cinnamon, ground	0.3 oz.	8 g
Nutmeg, ground	0.1 oz.	3 g
Cloves, ground	0.1 oz.	3 g
Total dough weight:	*7 lb.*	*3352 g*

SPECULAAS (BELGIAN SPICE COOKIES) (PAGE 341)

Yield: 22 Dozen Cookies, approximately ⅔ oz. (20 g) each

Unsalted butter, softened	2 lb. 4 oz.	1081 g
Brown sugar	3 lb. 10 oz.	1734 g
Eggs	9 oz.	265 g
Milk	4 fl. oz.	122 ml
Salt	0.4 oz.	12 g
Cinnamon, ground	0.5 oz.	14 g
Speculaas Spices (page 341)	1 oz.	28 g
Baking soda	1.3 oz.	40 g
Pastry flour, sifted	4 lb. 8 oz.	2040 g
Total dough weight:	*11 lb. 2 oz.*	*5336 g*

DIJON MUSTARD BLACK PEPPER CRACKERS (PAGE 342)

Yield: 40 Dozen Crackers, approximately ¼ oz. (7 g) each

Dijon mustard	8 oz.	240 g
White wine	8 fl. oz.	240 ml
Pastry or all-purpose flour	2 lb. 8 oz.	1200 g
Quick-cooking oats	1 lb.	480 g
Baking powder	0.5 oz.	16 g
Baking soda	1.1 oz.	33 g
Salt	1.6 oz.	48 g
Granulated sugar	4 oz.	120 g
Black pepper, table grind	4 oz.	120 g
Unsalted butter, cold, diced	1 lb. 8 oz.	720 g
Total dough weight:	*6 lb. 11 oz.*	*3217 g*

PARMESAN SUN-DRIED TOMATO CRACKERS (PAGE 342)

Yield: 30 Dozen Crackers, approximately ¼ oz. (7 g) each

Pastry or all-purpose flour	3 lb.	1440 g
Unsalted butter, cold, diced	1 lb. 8 oz.	720 g
Parmesan cheese, grated	2 lb.	965 g
Sun-dried tomatoes, chopped fine	12 oz.	360 g
Fresh basil, chopped fine	1.2 oz.	36 g
Fresh oregano, chopped fine	0.8 oz.	24 g
Salt	1.2 oz.	36 g
Garlic powder	0.4 oz.	11 g
Balsamic vinegar	8 fl. oz.	245 ml
Total dough weight:	*7 lb. 14 oz.*	*3837 g*

WHOLE-WHEAT CRACKERS (PAGE 343)

Yield: 40 Dozen Crackers, approximately ¼ oz. (7 g) each

Whole-wheat flour, stone ground	2 lb. 8 oz.	1200 g
Quick-cooking oats	1 lb. 8 oz.	720 g
Baking powder	0.5 oz.	16 g
Granulated sugar	2 oz.	60 g
Black pepper	0.8 oz.	24 g
Cayenne pepper, ground	0.5 oz.	17 g
Sesame seeds	4 oz.	120 g
Salt	1.7 oz.	50 g
Unsalted butter, cold, diced	2 lb. 8 oz.	1200 g
Balsamic vinegar	8 fl. oz.	240 ml
Total dough weight:	*7 lb. 9 oz.*	*3647 g*

RUGELACH (PAGE 344)

Yield: 9½ Dozen Cookies, approximately 1½ oz. (45 g) each

Pastry or all-purpose flour	2 lb. 13 oz.	1350 g
Baking soda	0.2 oz.	7 g
Cream cheese, room temperature	1 lb. 11 oz.	8109 g
Granulated sugar	1 lb. 4 oz.	621 g
Lemon zest, grated fine	0.45 oz.	13 g
Unsalted butter, softened	1 lb. 8 oz.	715 g
Salt	0.6 oz.	18 g
Red currant or apricot jam	2 lb. 4 oz.	1080 g
Dried cherries, finely chopped	12 oz.	351 g
Walnuts, chopped coarse	12 oz.	351 g
Total dough weight:	*11 lb. 1 oz.*	*5316 g*

SWEDISH YULE LOGS (PAGE 345)

Yield: 6 Dozen Cookies, approximately 1¾ oz. (45 g) each

Unsalted butter, softened	2 lb. 8 oz.	1195 g
Powdered sugar	7.5 oz.	230 g
Vanilla extract	1 fl. oz.	28 ml
Sherry or vanilla extract	3.75 fl. oz.	115 ml
Cardamom, ground	0.14 oz.	4 g
All-purpose flour	3 lb.	1440 g
Pecans or walnuts, chopped fine	15 oz.	446 g
Total dough weight:	*7 lb. 3 oz.*	*3458 g*

BISCOTTI (PAGE 356)

Yield: 6 Dozen Biscotti, approximately 2 oz. (60 g) each

Cinnamon, ground	0.4 oz.	11 g
Ammonium carbonate or baking powder	0.6 oz.	17 g
Hazelnut flour	1 lb. 4 oz.	595 g
Almond flour	6 oz.	182 g
Pastry or all-purpose flour	2 lb.	960 g
Eggs	16.5 oz.	500 g
Salt	0.4 oz.	12 g
Granulated sugar	2 lb.	960 g
Unsalted butter, melted	1 lb.	480 g
Whole hazelnuts	1 lb. 4 oz.	595 g
Total dough weight:	*8 lb. 15 oz.*	*4301 g*

CHOCOLATE PEANUT BUTTER BROWNIES (PAGE 358)

Yield: 9 Dozen Brownies, 2 in. (5 cm) each, 2 Half-Sheet Pans

Pastry or all-purpose flour	2 lb.	960 g
Baking powder	0.6 oz.	17 g
Eggs	1 lb.	500 g
Granulated sugar	1 lb. 8 oz.	720 g
Brown sugar	1 lb. 8 oz.	720 g
Peanut butter	1 lb. 8 oz.	720 g
Vanilla extract	1 fl. oz.	30 ml
Unsalted butter, melted	6 oz.	182 g
Peanuts, toasted	12 oz.	365 g
Semisweet chocolate chunks	12 oz.	365 g
Chocolate Ganache (page 458)	3 lb.	1440 g
Total batter weight:	*12 lb. 5 oz.*	*6018 g*

CHAPTER 11, PIES AND TARTS

BASIC PIE DOUGH (PAGE 366)

Yield: 15 Pie Shells, 9 in. (22 cm) each

Unsalted butter, chilled	5 lb.	2394 g
Pastry or all-purpose flour	6 lb. 9 oz.	3150 g
Buttermilk or water	20 fl. oz.	600 ml
Salt	2 oz.	60 g
Granulated sugar	2.5 oz.	73 g
Vanilla extract (optional)	2.5 fl. oz.	73 ml
Total dough weight:	*13 lb. 4 oz.*	*6331 g*

SWEET TART DOUGH (PÂTE SUCRÉE) (PAGE 368)

Yield: 15 Shells, 9 in. (22 cm) each

Unsalted butter, softened	2 lb. 8 oz.	1200 g
Powdered sugar	1 lb. 10 oz.	780 g
Eggs	6.5 oz.	201 g
Salt	13 oz.	390 g
Vanilla extract	0.6 fl. oz.	18 ml
All-purpose or pastry flour	7 lb. 4 oz.	3480 g
Total dough weight:	*12 lb. 14 oz.*	*6069 g*

BASIC CRUMB CRUST (PAGE 369)

Yield: 10 Shells, 9 in. (22 cm) each

Graham crackers, crushed	4 lb.	1920 g
Granulated sugar	2 lb.	960 g
Cinnamon, ground	0.6 oz.	17 g
Unsalted butter, melted	1 lb.	480 g
Total dough weight:	*7 lb.*	*3377 g*

BASIC CREAM PIE (PAGE 374)

Yield: 12 Pies, 9 in. (22 cm) each

Granulated sugar	3 lb. 8 oz.	1680 g
Milk	11 pt.	5280 ml
Heavy cream	5 pt.	2400 ml
Egg yolks	1 lb. 3 oz.	576 g
Cornstarch	1 lb. 1 oz.	512 g
Unsalted butter	1 lb.	480 g
Vanilla extract	4 fl. oz.	120 ml
Flaky or sweet tart dough pie shells, baked	12 shells	12 shells

Banana Cream Pie—Layer 3 pounds (1440 grams) sliced bananas (about 12 medium bananas) into the baked shells with the warm cream filling.

Coconut Cream Pie I—Substitute 3 pints (1440 milliliters) coconut milk for 3 pints (1440 milliliters) of the milk.

Coconut Cream Pie II—Stir 2 pounds (960 grams) toasted coconut into the warm cream.

APPLE-CRANBERRY PIE (PAGE 375)

Yield: 6 Pies, 9 in. (22 cm) each

Fresh tart apples such as Granny Smiths, peeled, cored and cut in 1-in. (2.5-cm) cubes	6 lb.	2880 g
Brown sugar	1 lb. 8 oz.	720 g
Granulated sugar	1 lb. 8 oz.	720 g
Orange zest, grated fine	1.2 oz.	36 g
Cinnamon, ground	0.4 oz.	12 g
Salt	0.3 oz.	9 g
Cornstarch	1 oz.	36 g
Orange juice	18 fl. oz.	540 ml
Fresh cranberries, rinsed	6 pt.	3000 ml
Mealy dough pie shells, 9 in. (22 cm), partially baked	6 shells	6 shells
Streusel Topping (page 145)	2 lb. 10 oz.	1260 g

Apple-Rhubarb Pie—Substitute cleaned rhubarb, cut into 1-inch (2.5-centimeter) chunks, for the cranberries. Add 0.06 ounce (1.8 grams) nutmeg.

SHORTBREAD TART DOUGH (PÂTE SABLÉE) (PAGE 382)

Yield: 28 Tart Shells, 8 in. (20 cm) each

Egg yolks, hard-boiled	1 lb. 4 oz.	593 g
Unsalted butter, softened	5 lb. 15 oz.	2870 g
Powdered sugar	2 lb. 11 oz.	1310 g
Vanilla extract	2 fl. oz.	62 ml
Salt	1.2 oz.	37 g
Almond or hazelnut flour	1 lb. 1 oz.	530 g
Pastry or all-purpose flour	6 lb. 8 oz.	3120 g
Total dough weight:	*17 lb. 10 oz.*	*8522 g*

CHOCOLATE TART DOUGH (CHOCOLATE PATE SUCREE) (PAGE 384)

Yield: 16 Tart Shells, 8 in. (20 cm) each

Unsalted butter	3 lb.	1440 g
Granulated sugar	1 lb. 14 oz.	900 g
Salt	0.3 oz.	8 g
Vanilla extract	1.5 fl. oz.	43 ml
Eggs	9 oz.	288 g
Hazelnut or almond flour	9 oz.	288 g
Pastry or all-purpose flour	3 lb.	1440 g
Cocoa powder	15 oz.	446 g
Total dough weight:	*10 lb.*	*4853 g*

PÂTE BRISÉE (PAGE 384)

Yield: 18 Shells, approximately 9 in. (22 cm) each

Unsalted butter, chilled	6 lb.	2872 g
All-purpose or pastry flour	6 lb. 14 oz.	3780 g
Eggs	9.6 oz.	287 g
Salt	2.4 oz.	75 g
Water, ice cold	12 fl. oz.	529 ml
Total dough weight:	*14 lb. 6 oz.*	*7543 g*

CHOCOLATE CREAM PIE (PAGE 386)

Yield: 12 Pies, 9 in. (22 cm) each

Brown sugar	3 lb. 8 oz.	1680 g
Milk	8 qt.	7680 ml
Cocoa powder	4 oz.	120 g
Egg yolks	1 lb. 3 oz.	576 g
Cornstarch	12 oz.	360 g
Bittersweet chocolate (64% cacao), chopped fine	3 lb. 8 oz.	1680 g
Unsalted butter	1 lb.	480 g
Vanilla extract	4 fl. oz.	120 ml
Mealy or sweet tart dough pie shells, 9 in. (22 cm), baked	12 shells	12 shells

FRESH STRAWBERRY PIE (PAGE 387)

Yield: 8 Pies, 9 in. (22 cm) each

Granulated sugar	5 lb. 12 oz.	2760 g
Water	2 pt.	960 ml
Cornstarch	10 oz.	300 g
Water, cold	3 pt.	1440 ml
Salt	0.4 oz.	12 g
Lemon juice	8 fl. oz.	240 ml
Fresh strawberries, rinsed and sliced in half	8 qt.	8 lt
Flaky dough pie shells, 9 in. (22 cm), baked	8 shells	8 shells

PEACH BLACKBERRY MINT CRISP (PAGE 389)

Yield: 24 Servings

Instant tapioca	3 oz.	90 g
Orange juice	12 fl. oz.	360 ml
Peaches, peeled	6 lb.	2880 g
Blackberries, fresh or IQF	2 lb.	960 g
Granulated sugar	1 lb. 8 oz.	720 g
Vanilla extract	0.6 fl. oz.	20 ml
Fresh mint leaves, chopped fine	120	120

BAKED STREUSEL FOR CRUMBLE (PAGE 389)

Yield: 5 lb. 2 oz. (2466 g)

Pastry or all-purpose flour	2 lb.	960 g
Brown sugar	1 lb. 4 oz.	600 g
Unsalted butter, cold, cut in small cubes	1 lb. 12 oz.	840 g
Salt	0.8 oz.	24 g
Cinnamon, ground	0.8 oz.	24 ml
Vanilla extract	0.6 fl. oz.	18 ml

APPLE CRUMB PIE (PAGE 392)

Yield: 6 Pies, 9 in. (22 cm) each

Basic Pie Dough (page 366)	5 lb. 10 oz.	2700 g
Filling:		
Golden Delicious apples, peeled and cored	12 lb.	5760 g
Granny Smith apples, peeled and cored	9 lb.	4320 g
Granulated sugar	3 lb. 6 oz.	1620 g
Lemon juice	3 fl. oz.	90 ml
Vanilla extract	3 fl. oz.	90 ml
Pastry or all-purpose flour	6 oz.	180 g
Cinnamon, ground	1.8 oz.	54 g
Unsalted butter, diced fine	12 oz.	360 g
Streusel Topping (page 145)	2 lb. 10 oz.	1260 g

PECAN PIE (PAGE 392)

Yield: 12 Pies, 9 in. (22 cm) each

Eggs	4 lb.	1920 g
Brown sugar	2 lb. 8 oz.	1200 g
Unsalted butter, barely melted	2 lb.	960 g
Vanilla extract	2 fl. oz.	60 ml
Salt	0.8 oz.	24 g
Maple syrup or dark corn syrup	4 pt.	1920 ml
Glucose or light corn syrup	4 pt.	1920 ml
Pecan halves and pieces	7 lb.	3360 g
Mealy dough pie shells, 9 in. (22 cm), unbaked	12 shells	12 shells

SWEET POTATO PIE (PAGE 393)

Yield: 8 Pies, 9 in. (22 cm) each

Sweet potatoes, peeled and cubed	4 lb.	1920 g
Brown sugar	2 lb. 8 oz.	1200 g
Salt	0.8 oz.	24 g
Cinnamon, ground	0.2 oz.	8 g
Ginger, ground	0.6 oz.	16 g
Allspice, ground	0.6 oz.	16 g
Vanilla extract	1.2 fl. oz.	40 ml
Eggs	1 lb. 11 oz.	800 g
Buttermilk	32 fl. oz.	960 ml
Heavy cream	40 fl. oz.	1200 ml
Mealy dough or sweet tart dough pie shells, 9 in. (22 cm), baked	8 shells	8 shells

LINZER TART (PAGE 401)

Yield: 4 Tarts, 9 in. (22 cm) each

Unsalted butter, softened	2 lb.	963 g
Granulated sugar	2 lb.	963 g
Egg yolks	5.3 oz.	159 g
Orange zest, grated fine	1.6 oz.	48 g
Lemon zest, grated fine	0.8 oz.	24 g
All-purpose flour	2 lb. 12 oz.	1320 g
Hazelnuts, ground fine	1 lb. 8 oz.	713 g
Baking powder	0.5 oz.	16 g
Cinnamon, ground	0.5 oz.	16 g
Cloves, ground	0.13 oz.	4 g
Salt	0.2 oz.	6 g
Total dough weight:	*8 lb. 12 oz.*	*4232 g*
Raspberry preserves	3 lb. 8 oz.	1680 g

CHAPTER 12, PASTRY AND DESSERT COMPONENTS

ÉCLAIR PASTE (PÂTE À CHOUX) (PAGE 408)

Yield: 12 lb. 5 oz.–12 lb. 11 oz. (2958–3054 g) Dough

Milk	2 pt.	480 ml
Water	2 pt.	480 ml
Salt	1.2 oz.	18 g
Unsalted butter	1 lb. 12 oz.	420 g
Bread flour	2 lb. 8 oz.	600 g
Eggs	4 lb.–4 lb. 6 oz.	960–1056 g

COMMON (FRENCH) MERINGUE (PAGE 410)

Yield: 24 Disks, 8 in. (20 cm) each, 4 lb. (2900 g) Meringue

Egg whites	2 lb.	960 g
Granulated sugar	4 lb.	1920 g
Dried egg whites (optional)	1.2 oz.	32 g
Vanilla extract	0.6 fl. oz.	20 ml

ITALIAN MERINGUE (PAGE 413)

Yield: 6 lb. 10 oz. (3120 g)

Granulated sugar	3 lb. 4 oz.	1560 g
Glucose or corn syrup	8 oz.	240 g
Water	12 fl. oz.	360 ml
Egg whites, room temperature	2 lb.	960 g

CRÊPES (PAGE 416)

Yield: 90 Crêpes, 6 in. (15 cm) each

Eggs	1 lb. 14 oz.	895 g
Egg yolks	12 oz.	353 g
Water	36 fl. oz.	1085 ml
Whole milk	54 fl. oz.	1625 ml
Granulated sugar	1 lb. 2 oz.	542 g
Salt	0.6 oz.	18 g
All-purpose flour	2 lb. 10 oz.	1260 g
Unsalted butter, melted	15 oz.	454 g
Total batter weight:	*12 lb. 15 oz.*	*6232 g*

POPOVERS (PAGE 421)

Yield: 60 Popovers

Beef fat or vegetable oil	30 fl. oz.	1080 ml
All-purpose flour	1 lb. 8 oz.	720 g
Salt	0.6 oz.	18 g
Eggs	1 lb. 14 oz.	900 g
Whole milk	48 fl. oz.	1440 ml
Whole butter, melted	9 oz.	270 g
Total batter weight:	*8 lb. 13 oz.*	*4428 g*

CHURROS (FLUTED MEXICAN DOUGHNUT STICKS) (PAGE 422)

Yield: Approximately 90 to 100 Pastries

Cinnamon, ground	1.5 oz.	45 g
Granulated sugar	12 oz.	360 g
Water	48 fl. oz.	1440 g
Salt	0.5 oz.	15 ml
Pastry flour	1 lb. 8 oz.	720 g
Egg whites	9 oz.	270 g
Vanilla extract	0.45 fl. oz.	15 ml
Total batter weight:	*5 lb. 15 oz.*	*2865 g*

CHAPTER 13, CAKES AND ICINGS

CLASSIC GENOISE (PAGE 440)

Yield: 6 Full-Sheet Pans or 12 Rounds, 8 in. (20 cm) each

Eggs	6 lb.	2884 g
Granulated sugar	3 lb.	1442 g
Unsalted butter, melted (optional)	9 oz.	275 g
Vanilla extract	1.7 fl. oz.	48 ml
Cake flour	3 lb. 6 oz.	1620 g
Total batter weight:	*13 lb.*	*6269 g*

CLASSIC SPONGECAKE (PAGE 442)

Yield: 12 Rounds, 9 in. (22 cm) each

Eggs	4 lb. 13 oz.	2331 g
Granulated sugar	2 lb. 12 oz.	1348 g
Vanilla extract	1.5 fl. oz.	50 ml
All-purpose flour, sifted	2 lb. 10 oz.	1260 g
Total batter weight:	*10 lb. 4 oz.*	*4989 g*

ANGEL FOOD CAKE (PAGE 444)

Yield: 4 Tube Cakes, 10 in. (25 cm) each

Granulated sugar	3 lb.	1440 g
Cake flour, sifted	14 oz.	418 g
Salt	0.2 oz.	6 g
Egg whites	3 lb.	1440 g
Cream of tartar	1.2 oz.	36 g
Vanilla extract	2 fl. oz.	60 ml
Total batter weight:	*7 lb. 1 oz.*	*3400 g*

Chocolate Angel Food Cake—Combine 4 ounces (115 grams) cocoa powder with 7.5 fluid ounces (230 milliliters) warm water and 1.2 fluid ounces (36 milliliters) vanilla extract in a bowl. Set aside. Whisk a very large spoonful of the whipped egg whites into the cocoa mixture, folding it into the remaining egg whites at the end of Step 2.

ORANGE CHIFFON CAKE (PAGE 445)

Yield: 4 Tube Cakes, 10 in. (25 cm) each

Cake flour, sifted	2 lb.	960 g
Granulated sugar	3 lb.	1440 g
Baking powder	1.6 oz.	48 g
Salt	0.8 oz.	24 g
Vegetable oil	1 pt.	480 ml
Egg yolks	1 lb.	480 g
Water, cool	8 fl. oz.	240 ml
Orange juice	1 pt.	480 ml
Orange zest, grated fine	0.8 oz.	24 g
Vanilla extract	2 fl. oz.	58 ml
Egg whites	2 lb.	960 g
Total batter weight:	*10 lb. 13 oz.*	*5194 g*

Glaze:

Powdered sugar, sifted	12 oz.	360 g
Orange juice	4 fl. oz.	120 ml
Orange zest, grated fine	0.5 oz.	120 g

SIMPLE BUTTERCREAM (PAGE 451)

Yield: 12 lb. 9 oz. (6040 g)

Lightly salted butter, softened	4 lb.	1920 g
Pasteurized egg (optional)	8 oz.	240 g
Powdered sugar, sifted	8 lb.	3840 g
Vanilla extract	1.2 fl. oz.	40 ml

Light Chocolate Buttercream—Dissolve 4 ounces (120 grams) sifted cocoa powder in 8 fluid ounces (240 milliliters) cool water. Add to the buttercream along with the vanilla.

Lemon Buttercream—Decrease the vanilla extract to 0.6 fluid ounce (20 milliliters). Add 0.6 fluid ounce (20 milliliters) lemon extract and 0.8 ounce (24 grams) finely grated lemon zest.

ITALIAN BUTTERCREAM (PAGE 452)

Yield: 10 lb. 10 oz. (4800 g)

Egg whites	1 lb. 12 oz.	800 g
Granulated sugar	3 lb. 6 oz.	1500 g
Lightly salted butter, softened but not melted	5 lb. 8 oz.	2500 g

FRENCH MOUSSELINE BUTTERCREAM (PAGE 453)

Yield: 4 qt. (4 lt)

Granulated sugar	3 lb. 4 oz.	1560 g
Water	1 pt.	480 ml
Egg yolks	1 lb. 3 oz.	576 g
Lightly salted butter, softened but not melted	6 lb.	2880 g
Italian Meringue (page 413)	2 lb.	960 g
Vanilla, coffee, lemon or other flavoring extract	4 fl. oz.	120 ml

BASIC FUDGE ICING (PAGE 454)

Yield: Approximately 8 lb. (3840 g)

Powdered sugar, sifted	6 lb.	2880 g
Unsalted butter	9 oz.	270 g
Shortening	6 oz.	180 g
Corn syrup or glucose	6 oz.	180 g
Water	12 fl. oz.	360 ml
Salt	0.1 oz.	3 g
Vanilla extract	0.5 fl. oz.	15 ml

COCOA FUDGE ICING (PAGE 455)

Yield: 9 lb. 2 oz. (4380 g)

Unsalted butter, room temperature	2 lb. 4 oz.	1080 g
Cocoa powder, unsweetened	2 lb. 4 oz.	1080 g
Glucose or corn syrup	1 lb. 8 oz.	720 g
Water	24 fl. oz.	720 ml
Vanilla extract	1.5 fl. oz.	45 ml
Salt	0.6 oz.	15 g
Powdered sugar, sifted	1 lb. 8 oz.	720 g

CHOCOLATE GLAZE (PAGE 456)

Yield: 3 lb. 4 oz. (1560 g)

Unsweetened chocolate	1 lb.	480 g
Semisweet chocolate	1 lb.	480 g
Unsalted butter	1 lb.	480 g
Light corn syrup	4 oz.	120 g

ROYAL ICING (PAGE 457)

Yield: 2 lb. 10 oz. (1266 g)

Powdered sugar	2 lb. 4 oz.	1080 g
Egg whites, pasteurized, room temperature	6 oz.	180 g
Lemon juice	0.25 fl. oz.	6 ml

CHOCOLATE GANACHE (PAGE 458)

Yield: 8 lb. 4 oz. (3960 g)

Bittersweet chocolate (58–68% cocoa)	4 lb.	1920 g
Heavy cream	4 pt.	1920 ml
Almond or coffee liqueur	4 fl. oz.	120 ml

COCONUT PECAN ICING (PAGE 473)

Yield: 11 lb. 5 oz. (5430 g)

Evaporated milk	48 fl. oz.	1440 ml
Granulated sugar	3 lb.	1440 g
Egg yolks	12 oz.	360 g
Unsalted butter	1 lb. 8 oz.	720 g
Vanilla extract	1 fl. oz.	30 ml
Coconut, flaked	1 lb. 8 oz.	720 g
Pecans, chopped	1 lb. 8 oz.	720 g

DEVIL'S FOOD CAKE (PAGE 474)

Yield: 4 Layer Cakes, 9 in. (22 cm) each

Pastry flour	2 lb. 2 oz.	1020 g
Cocoa powder	1 lb.	480 g
Baking powder	0.6 oz.	16 g
Baking soda	0.6 oz.	16 g
Unsalted butter, melted	1 lb. 4 oz.	600 g
Eggs	1 lb. 3 oz.	571 g
Buttermilk	32 fl. oz.	960 ml
Vanilla extract	1 fl. oz.	30 ml
Granulated sugar	3 lb. 12 oz.	1795 g
Salt	0.4 oz.	12 g
Brewed coffee, hot	32 fl. oz.	959 ml
Total batter weight:	*13 lb. 7 oz.*	*6459 g*

ALMOND GENOISE (PAGE 477)

Yield: 8 Rounds, 7 in. (17 cm) each

Almond paste	12 oz.	355 g
Granulated sugar	1 lb. 8 oz.	720 g
Egg yolks	2.5 oz.	77 g
Eggs	3 lb. 4 oz.	1555 g
Vanilla extract	2 fl. oz.	58 ml
Cake flour, sifted	2 lb.	960 g
Unsalted butter, melted	10 oz.	297 g
Total batter weight:	*8 lb. 6 oz.*	*4022 g*

VANILLA SPONGECAKE (PAGE 478)

Yield: 2 Full-Sheet Pans, 18 in. × 24 in. (45 cm × 60 cm)

Eggs	1 lb. 7 oz.	690 g
Egg yolks	8.5 oz.	250 g
Granulated sugar	1 lb. 4 oz.	597 g
Vanilla extract	3 fl. oz.	89 ml
Cake flour, sifted	11 oz.	330 g
Egg whites	14 oz.	419 g
Powdered sugar, sifted	4 oz.	119 g
Total batter weight:	*5 lb. 3 oz.*	*2494 g*

Chocolate Spongecake—Reduce the cake flour to 8 ounces (240 grams) and sift it with 3 ounces (90 grams) cocoa powder.

LADYFINGERS (PAGE 479)

Yield: 425 Cookies, approximately 4 in. (10 cm) each

Bread flour	1 lb. 8 oz.	720 g
Cornstarch	1 lb. 3 oz.	576 g
Egg yolks	2 lb. 1 oz.	1008 g
Vanilla extract	0.75 fl. oz.	21 ml
Egg whites	3 lb. 9 oz.	1728 g
Granulated sugar	2 lb. 4 oz.	1080 g
Total batter weight:	*10 lb. 10 oz.*	*5133 g*

CREAM CHEESE ICING (PAGE 482)

Yield: 14 lb. 5 oz. (6885 g)

Cream cheese, softened	9 lb.	4320 g
Powdered sugar	3 lb. 12 oz.	1800 g
Unsalted butter, softened	1 lb. 8 oz.	720 g
Vanilla extract	1.5 fl. oz.	45 ml

TRADITIONAL FRENCH BUTTERCREAM (PAGE 483)

Yield: 11 lb. 4 oz. (5400 g)

Granulated sugar	3 lb. 9 oz.	1710 g
Corn syrup or glucose	9 oz.	270 g
Water	18 fl. oz.	540 ml
Eggs	15 oz.	450 g
Egg yolks	1 lb. 2 oz.	540 g
Unsalted butter, room temperature	4 lb. 14 oz.	2340 g
Vanilla extract	3 fl. oz.	90 ml

SILKY GANACHE DELUXE (PAGE 485)

Yield: 12 lb. 8 oz. (6000 g)

Heavy cream	64 fl. oz.	1920 ml
Granulated sugar	1 lb. 4 oz.	600 g
Corn syrup or glucose	1 lb. 4 oz.	600 g
Semisweet or bittersweet chocolate (58–68% cocoa)	4 lb. 12 oz.	2280 g
Unsalted butter	1 lb. 4 oz.	600 g

ORANGE MILK CHOCOLATE GANACHE (PAGE 485)

Yield: 8 lb. 8 oz. (4080 g)

Heavy cream	32 fl. oz.	960 ml
Milk	24 fl. oz.	720 ml
Glucose or corn syrup	8 oz.	240 g
Unsalted butter	8 oz.	240 g
Milk chocolate	3 lb. 8 oz.	1680 g
Bittersweet chocolate	8 oz.	240 g
Orange oil (not extract)	8–12 drops	8–12 drops

CHAPTER 14, CUSTARDS, CREAMS AND SAUCES

VANILLA CUSTARD SAUCE (CRÈME ANGLAISE) (PAGE 490)

Yield: 7.5 qt. (7200 ml)

Half-and-half	6 qt.	6 lt
Vanilla beans, split	6	6
Egg yolks	3 lb.	1440 g
Granulated sugar	3 lb. 12 oz.	1800 g

PASTRY CREAM (CRÈME PÂTISSIÈRE) (PAGE 492)

Yield: 9 lb. (4320 g)

Milk	3 qt.	3 lt
Vanilla beans, split	3	3
Granulated sugar	1 lb. 6.5 oz.	675 g
Egg yolks	1 lb. 2 oz.	540 g
Cornstarch	7.5 oz.	225 g
Unsalted butter	6 oz.	180 g

LEMON OR LIME CURD (PAGE 493)

Yield: 7 lb. 14 oz. (3720 g)

Lemon juice	24 fl. oz.	720 ml
Granulated sugar	2 lb. 7 oz.	1170 g
Lemon zest, grated fine	1 oz.	30 g
Eggs	1 lb. 8 oz.	720 g
Unsalted butter, room temperature	2 lb. 4 oz.	1080 g

BAKED CRÈME BRÛLÉE (PAGE 497)

Yield: 40 Servings, approximately 4 oz. (120 g) each

Milk	32 fl. oz.	960 ml
Heavy cream	96 fl. oz.	2880 ml
Vanilla beans, split	2	2
Granulated sugar	1 lb. 12 oz.	840 g
Egg yolks	1 lb. 8 oz.	720 g

NEW YORK CHEESECAKE (PAGE 498)

Yield: 8 Cakes, 8 in. (20 cm) each

Crust:		
Graham crackers, crushed	4 lb.	1920 g
Unsalted butter, melted	1 lb. 8 oz.	720 g
Batter:		
Cream cheese, room temperature	13 lb. 8 oz.	6480 g
Granulated sugar	3 lb. 8 oz.	1680 g
Eggs	3 lb. 3 oz.	1536 g
Cake flour or cornstarch	8 oz.	240 g
Vanilla extract	2 fl. oz.	60 ml
Lemon zest, grated fine	0.4 oz.	12 g
Heavy cream	56 fl. oz.	1680 ml
Total batter weight:	*24 lb. 4 oz.*	*11,688 g*

BAVARIAN CREAM (PAGE 503)

Yield: 8 qt. (8 lt)

Milk	56 fl. oz.	1680 ml
Heavy cream	56 fl. oz.	1680 ml
Granulated sugar	1 lb. 8 oz.	720 g
Vanilla beans, split	4	4
Egg yolks	1 lb. 3 oz.	576 g
Sheet gelatin, softened	32 sheets (2 oz.)	60 g
Heavy cream, whipped to soft peaks	4 qt.	3840 ml

LIME CHIFFON (PAGE 505)

Yield: 64 Servings

Granulated gelatin	2 oz.	60 g
Water	40 fl. oz.	1200 ml
Granulated sugar	3 lb. 8 oz.	1680 g
Fresh lime juice	24 fl. oz.	720 ml
Lime zest, grated fine	1.5 oz.	48 g
Egg yolks, pasteurized	1 lb. 3 oz.	576 g
Egg whites, pasteurized	2 lb.	960 g

CLASSIC CHOCOLATE MOUSSE (PAGE 506)

Yield: 2½–3 gal. (6–8 lt)

Bittersweet chocolate (60–64% cocoa)	3 lb. 12 oz.	1800 g
Unsalted butter	2 lb. 4 oz.	1080 g
Egg yolks, pasteurized	1 lb. 1 oz.	504 g
Egg whites, pasteurized	2 lb. 12 oz.	1320 g
Granulated sugar	10 oz.	300 g
Heavy cream	1 qt.	960 ml

FRUIT COULIS (PAGE 512)

Yield: 7 lb. 8 oz. (3600 g)

Fruit purée, strained	6 lb.	2880 g
Granulated sugar	15 oz.	450 g
Glucose or corn syrup	6 oz.	180 g
Lemon juice	3 fl. oz.	90 ml

CARAMEL SAUCE (PAGE 512)

Yield: 12 qt. (12 lt)

Granulated sugar	13 lb. 8 oz.	6 kg
Water	3 pt.	1440 ml
Lemon juice	6 fl. oz.	180 ml
Heavy cream, room temperature	6 qt.	6 lt
Unsalted butter, cut into pieces	15 oz.	450 g

DARK CHOCOLATE SYRUP (PAGE 513)

Yield: 6 qt. (6 lt)

Cocoa powder	1 lb. 8 oz.	720 g
Water	9 pt.	4320 ml
Granulated sugar	6 lb.	2880 g
Unsalted butter	2 lb. 4 oz.	108 g
Heavy cream	12 fl. oz.	360 ml

RASPBERRY CREAM FILLING (PAGE 517)

Yield: 10 lb. (4880 g)

Traditional French Buttercream (page 483)	4 lb. 6 oz.	2100 g
Pastry Cream (page 492)	3 lb. 12 oz.	1800 g
Raspberry purée	1 lb. 9 oz.	750 g
Raspberry compound	5 oz.	150 g

ORANGE MILK CHOCOLATE MOUSSE (PAGE 528)

Yield: 13 lb. 8 oz. (6478 g)

Egg yolks, pasteurized	1 lb.	480 g
Water	1 pt.	480 ml
Granulated sugar	1 lb.	480 g
Sheet gelatin, softened	24 sheets (1.5 oz.)	45 g
Cointreau or Grand Marnier	3 fl. oz.	88 ml
Milk chocolate	4 lb.	1920 g
Orange essential oil	1 fl. oz.	30 ml
Heavy cream, whipped to soft peaks	7 pt.	3360 ml

WHITE CHOCOLATE MOUSSE (PAGE 529)

Yield: 12 lb. (6 kg)

White chocolate, chopped fine	5 lb. 1 oz.	2430 g
Heavy cream	36 fl. oz.	1080 ml
Egg yolks, pasteurized	7.2 oz.	216 g
Granulated sugar	6 oz.	180 g
Heavy cream, whipped to soft peaks	114 fl. oz.	3420 ml

LEMON-LIME MOUSSE (PAGE 530)

Yield: 11 lb. 11 oz. (5608 g)

Lemon juice	1 pt.	480 ml
Lime juice	1 pt.	480 ml
Sheet gelatin, softened	16 sheets (1 oz.)	30 g
Grand Marnier	4 fl. oz.	120 ml
Egg whites, pasteurized	1 lb.	480 g
Granulated sugar	1 lb. 12 oz.	840 g
Water	12 fl. oz.	360 ml
Heavy cream, whipped to soft peaks	3 qts. 8 fl. oz.	3120 ml

HONEY MOUSSE (PAGE 532)

Yield: 4 lb. (2190 g)

Egg whites, pasteurized	8 oz.	240 g
Granulated sugar	4 oz.	120 g
Honey	12 oz.	360 g
Water	6 fl. oz.	180 ml
Sheet gelatin, softened	16 sheets (1 oz.)	30 g
Vanilla extract	2 fl. oz.	60 ml
Grand Marnier	2 fl. oz.	60 ml
Candied citrus rind, diced (optional)	6 oz.	180 g
Heavy cream, whipped to soft peaks	2 pt.	960 ml

RASPBERRY SAUCE (PAGE 533)

Yield: Approximately 4 qt. (4 lt)

Raspberries, fresh or IQF	8 lb.	4 kg
Granulated sugar	3 lb. 6 oz.	1680 g
Lemon juice	4 fl. oz.	120 ml

BUTTERSCOTCH SAUCE (PAGE 535)

Yield: 8 qt. (8 lt)

Granulated sugar	6 lb.	2880 g
Light corn syrup	9 lb.	4320 g
Unsalted butter	1 lb.	480 g
Heavy cream	40 fl. oz.	1200 ml
Scotch whisky	16 fl. oz.	480 ml

CHAPTER 15, ICE CREAM AND FROZEN DESSERTS

FRENCH ICE CREAM BASE (PAGE 554)

Yield: 6 qt. (6 lt)

Whole milk	80 fl. oz.	3200 ml
Heavy cream	56 fl. oz.	1680 ml
Egg yolks	1 lb.	480 g
Granulated sugar	1 lb. 12 oz.	840 g
Glucose or corn syrup	4 oz.	120 g
Ice cream stabilizer (optional)	1.2 oz.	40 g

CHOCOLATE ICE CREAM (PAGE 555)

Yield: 6 qt. (6 lt)

Egg yolks	1 lb. 2 oz.	540 g
Granulated sugar	1 lb. 14 oz.	900 g
Cocoa powder	9 oz.	270 g
Milk	6 pt.	2880 ml
Heavy cream	18 fl. oz.	540 ml
Semisweet chocolate, chopped	1 lb. 8 oz.	720 g

STRAWBERRY ICE CREAM (PAGE 555)

Yield: 6 qt. (6 lt)

Water	48 fl. oz.	1440 ml
Granulated sugar	30 oz.	900 g
Pectin-based ice cream stabilizer (optional)	0.4 oz.	12 g
Glucose or corn syrup	3 lb.	1440 g
Strawberry purée	6 lb.	2880 ml
Heavy cream	36 fl. oz.	1080 ml

LEMON SORBET (PAGE 558)

Yield: 6 qt. (6 lt)

Lemon juice	4 pt.	2000 ml
Water	4 pt.	2000 ml
Granulated sugar	4 lb.	2000 g

GRAPEFRUIT SORBET (PAGE 559)

Yield: 6 qt. (6 lt)

Fresh grapefruit juice	4 qt.	4 lt
Granulated sugar	2 lb.	960 g

CHAPTER 17, TORTES AND SPECIALTY CAKES

COCOA GELÉE (PAGE 608)

Yield: 10 lb. (4800 g)

Water	32 fl. oz.	960 ml
Granulated sugar	4 lb.	1920 g
Heavy cream	42 fl. oz.	1260 ml
Cocoa powder, sifted	1 lb. 4 oz.	600 g
Sheet gelatin, softened	32 sheets (2 oz.)	60 g
Vanilla extract	2.5 fl. oz.	80 ml

SACHER TORTE (PAGE 614)

Yield: 8 Cakes, 9 in. (22 cm) each

All-purpose flour	2 lb. 8 oz.	1200 g
Cocoa powder, alkalized	12 oz.	360 g
Unsalted butter, softened	3 lb. 2 oz.	1500 g
Granulated sugar	4 lb. 8 oz.	2160 g
Egg yolks	2 lb. 2 oz.	1020 g
Hazelnuts, toasted and ground	12 oz.	360 g
Egg whites	3 lb. 8 oz.	1680 g
Total batter weight:	*17 lb. 4 oz.*	*8280 g*
Apricot jam	4 lb. 8 oz.	2160 g

Photocopy and enlarge these templates if desired before using.

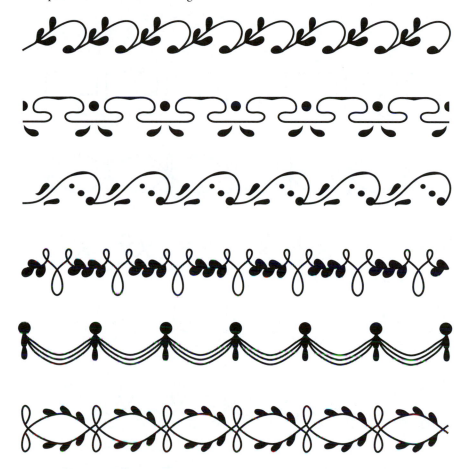

Piping Scroll Designs

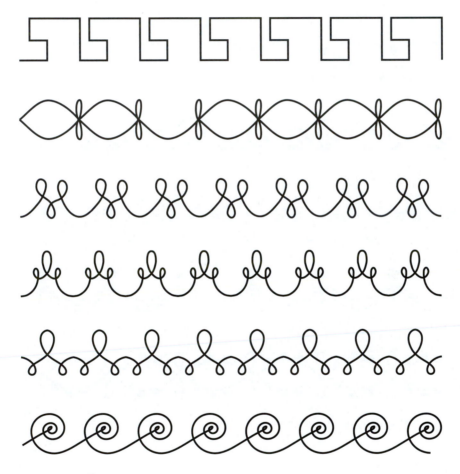

Piping Scroll Designs

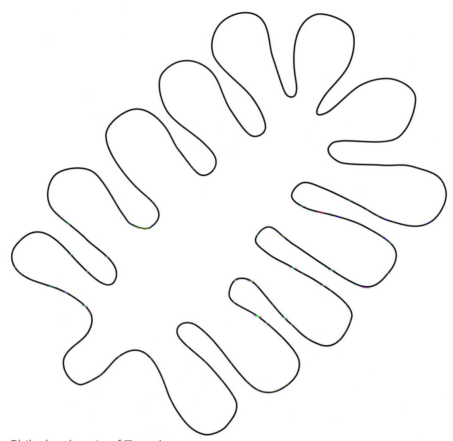

Philodendron Leaf Template

Hibiscus Flowers and Calla Lily Templates

CAKE CUTTING DIAGRAMS

Cutting Half Sheet Cakes and Bars (12 × 18 inches/30 × 45 centimeters)

The number of cuts will be doubled for a full-size sheet pan (24 × 18 inches/61 × 45 centimeters)

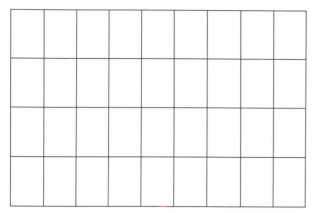

4 × 9 = 36 Rectangular Pieces, 3 × 2 in. (7 × 5 cm) each

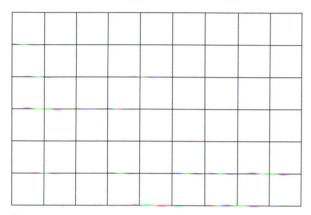

6 × 9 = 54 Square Pieces, 2 × 2 in. (5 × 5 cm) each

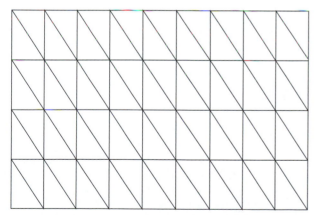

72 Triangular Pieces, 3 × 2 in. (7 × 5 cm) each

1 Cut the cake into 36 pieces (4 × 9), 3 × 2 in. (7 × 5 cm) each.

2 Then cut each rectangle into half diagonally, creating 72 triangles.

Cutting a Pie or Cake into Uniform Portions

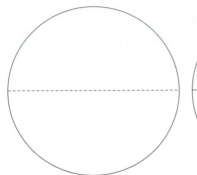 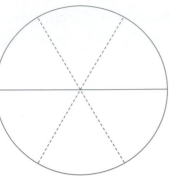 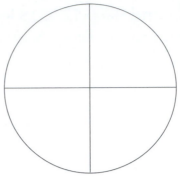 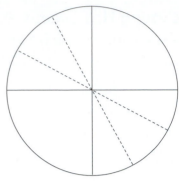

❶ Cut the pie or cake in half.

❷ In order to produce 6 portions, cut across the pie or cake diagonally, so that each half is cut into thirds.

❸ When the total number of portions is divisible by four, begin by cutting the pie or cake into even quarters.

❹ Then cut each quarter into the number of slices necessary to produce the number of portions desired. In the example here, the total yield will be 12 portions.

Cutting a Pie or Cake into 10 Portions

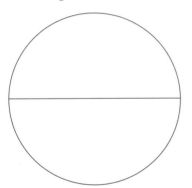 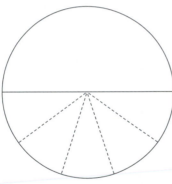 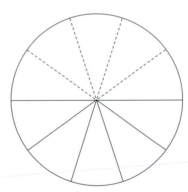

❶ Cut the pie or cake in half.

❷ Cut one half of the pie or cake into 5 uniform slices.

❸ Cut the remaining half of the pie or cake into 5 uniform slices.

Cutting Large Round Cake Layers

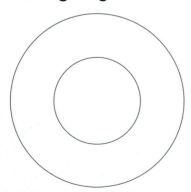 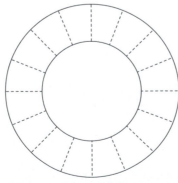 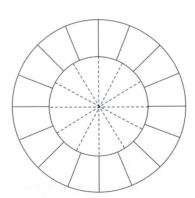

❶ Cut a circle halfway from the edge of the cake.

❷ Cut portions in the outer ring of the cake.

❸ After the outer ring of portions have been removed, then cut portions from the inner ring of the cake.

GLOSSARY

absorption—the ability of flour to absorb moisture when mixed into a dough; varies according to protein content and growing and storage conditions of the flour

acid—foods such as citrus juice, vinegar and wine that have a sour or sharp flavor (most foods are slightly acidic); acids have a pH of less than 7

acidulation—the browning of cut fruit caused by the reaction of an enzyme (polyphenoloxidase) with the phenolic compounds present in these fruits; this browning is often mistakenly attributed to exposure to oxygen

additives—substances added to many foods to prevent spoilage or to improve appearance, texture, flavor or nutritional value; may be synthetic materials copied from nature (for example, sugar substitutes) or naturally occurring substances (for example, lecithin); some food additives may cause allergic reactions in sensitive people

aerate—(1) to whip air into a mixture to lighten it, such as beating egg whites to a foam; (2) to incorporate air into a mixture through sifting and mixing

agave—a type of succulent plant native to the Southwest and the Americas; a syrup made from its thick pointed leaves is used as a natural sweetener

aging—the period during which freshly milled flour is allowed to rest so that it will whiten and produce less sticky doughs; the aging of flour can be chemically accelerated

allergens—substances that may cause allergic reactions in some people

amaranth—tiny oval seeds of a type of annual herb plant native to South America; used as a cooked grain and flour

aroma—the sensations, as interpreted by the brain, of what we detect when a substance comes in contact with sense receptors in the nose

artisan—a person who works in a skilled craft or trade; one who works with his or her hands; applied to bread bakers and confectioners who prepare foods using traditional methods

baba—a small, light yeast cake soaked in rum syrup; traditionally baked in an individual cylindrical mold, giving the finished product a mushroom shape

bacteria—single-celled microorganisms, some of which can cause diseases, including food-borne diseases

bain marie—(ban mah-ree) (1) a hot-water bath used to gently cook food or keep cooked food hot; (2) a metal container for holding food in a hot-water bath

bake blind—to bake a pie shell or tart shell unfilled using baking weights or beans to support the crust as it bakes

bake-off—the procedure of cooking a prepared dough or other pastry item that has been produced elsewhere and is merely finished on site

baker's peel—a flat-handled paddle used to slide food, particularly bread and pizza, into a deck oven

baker's percentage—a system for measuring ingredients in a formula by expressing them as a percentage of the total flour weight

baking—a dry-heat cooking method in which foods are surrounded by hot, dry air in a closed environment; similar to roasting, the term *baking* is usually applied to breads, pastries, vegetables and fish

baking powder—a mixture of sodium bicarbonate and one or more acids, generally cream of tartar and/or sodium aluminum sulfate, used to leaven baked goods; it releases carbon dioxide gas if moisture is present in a formula; single-acting baking powder releases carbon dioxide gas in the presence of moisture only; double-acting baking powder releases some carbon dioxide gas upon contact with moisture, and then more gas is released when heat is applied

baking soda—sodium bicarbonate, an alkaline compound that releases carbon dioxide gas when combined with an acid and moisture; used to leaven baked goods

baking weights—small ceramic or metal disks used to keep pie crust from bubbling up during baking; used when baking an unfilled pie or tart shell; also known as *pie weights*

banneton—(BAN-eh-tohn) a traditional woven basket, often lined with canvas, in which yeast bread is placed to rise before baking

barquette—a small boat-shaped pastry shell used for miniature cakes or tarts served as canapés or petits fours

base—a substance that neutralizes an acid in a liquid solution; ingredients such as sodium bicarbonate (baking soda) that have an alkaline or bitter flavor; bases have a pH higher than 7

batter—(1) a semiliquid mixture containing flour or other starch used to make cakes and breads; the gluten development is minimized and the liquid forms the continuous medium in which other ingredients are dispersed; generally contains more fat, sugar and liquids than a dough; (2) a semiliquid mixture of liquid and starch used to coat foods for deep-frying

Baumé scale—(boh-may) *see* **hydrometer**

Bavarian cream—a sweet dessert mixture made by thickening custard sauce with gelatin and then folding in whipped cream; the final product is poured into a mold and chilled until firm

bean flour—cooked beans, including chickpeas, soybeans and white beans, that are dried, then ground into a fine powder; used in place of gluten-forming wheat flours

beating—a mixing method in which foods are vigorously agitated to incorporate air or develop gluten; a spoon or electric mixer fitted with a paddle is used

beignets—squares or strips of éclair paste that are deep-fried and dusted with powdered sugar; squares or strips of éclair paste or yeast dough similar to doughnuts

bench rest—allowing bread dough, usually covered, to ferment in bulk on a worktable

biga—Italian term for a dry yeast dough starter that requires a long fermentation

biscuit—(1) a small, flaky quick bread leavened with baking soda or baking powder for a light, tender texture; the dough is rolled out and cut into circles or dropped from a spoon; (2) any dry, flat cake, usually leavened with baking powder and/or baking soda; (3) (bee-SQUEE) a type of dry sponge cake used to make multilayered tortes

biscuit method—a mixing method used to make biscuits, scones and flaky doughs; it involves cutting cold fat into the flour and other dry ingredients before any liquid is added

blanching—very briefly and partially cooking a food in boiling water or hot fat; used to assist preparation (for example, to loosen peels from fruits or vegetables), as part of a combination cooking method, to remove undesirable flavors or to prepare a food for freezing

blending—a mixing method in which two or more ingredients are combined just until they are evenly distributed

bloom—(1) a white, powdery layer that sometimes appears on chocolate; (2) to soften granulated gelatin in a liquid before melting and using

boiling—a moist-heat cooking method that uses convection to transfer heat from a hot (approximately 212°F/100°C) liquid to the food submerged in it

bombe—(bahm) two or more flavors of ice cream, or ice cream and sherbet, shaped in a spherical mold; each flavor is a separate layer that forms the shell for the next flavor

bombe mixture—(Fr. *pâte à bombe*) egg yolks cooked with sugar syrup and whipped, used as a base for still-frozen desserts and cakes

bouchées—(boo-SHAY) small puff pastry shells that can be filled and served as bite-size hors d'oeuvre or petits fours

boulanger (boo-lawn-JHAY) French for "baker"

bran—the tough outer layer of a cereal grain and the part highest in fiber

bread flour—blended flour made from hard winter wheat with a protein content between 12 and 15 percent

brioche—(bree-OHSH) a rich yeast bread containing large amounts of eggs and butter

broiling—a dry-heat cooking method in which foods are cooked by heat radiating from an overhead source

brotform—(BROT-form) a traditional basket made from coiled willow in which yeast bread is placed to rise before baking; the basket leaves circular marks in the dough; heavy plastic versions are available for commercial food service use

buckwheat flour—dark, nutty-tasting flour milled from the seeds of the buckwheat plant and used to make bread, cereals and baked goods

bulk fermentation—the rise given to the entire mass of yeast dough before the dough is shaped

bun—any of a variety of small, round yeast rolls; may be sweet or savory

buttercream—a light, smooth, fluffy frosting of sugar, fat and flavorings; egg yolks or whipped egg whites are sometimes added; the three principal kinds are simple, Italian and French

cake—in American usage, refers to a broad range of pastries, including layer cakes, coffeecakes and gâteaux; can refer to almost anything that is baked, tender, sweet and sometimes frosted

cake comb—a utensil made from hard plastic, metal or rubber with sharp teeth cut into one or more of its sides; used to create patterns in icings and chocolate

cake flour—a finely milled soft wheat flour with a protein content of less than 8 percent; used to produce tender products

calorie—a unit of energy measured by the amount of heat required to raise 1000 grams of water 1 degree Celsius; it is also written as *kilocalorie* or *kcal* and is used as a measure of food energy

candy rulers—steel or aluminum bars of varying lengths and thicknesses used to contain fillings for candies; the metal bars may also be used as guidelines for rolling pastry dough to a uniform thickness

cannoli—an Italian pastry made from a dough shell curled into a tube, deep-fried and filled with sweetened ricotta cheese

caramelization—the process of cooking sugars; the browning of sugar enhances the flavor and appearance of foods

carbohydrates—a group of compounds composed of oxygen, hydrogen and carbon, the human body's primary source of energy

(4 calories per gram); carbohydrates are classified as simple (including certain sugars) and complex (including starches and fiber)

carryover cooking/baking—the cooking that occurs after a food is removed from a heat source; it is accomplished by the residual heat remaining in the food

charlotte—a dessert made in a mold lined with ladyfingers and filled with a custard cream stabilized with gelatin

cheesecloth—a light, fine mesh gauze used to strain liquids and make sachets

china cap—a cone-shaped strainer made of perforated metal

cholesterol—a fatty substance found in foods derived from animal products and in the human body; in excess, it has been linked to heart disease

chop—to cut an item into small pieces where uniformity of size and shape is neither feasible nor necessary

choux pastry—(shoo) *see* **éclair paste**

churros—a Mexican and Spanish pastry in which sticks of éclair paste flavored with cinnamon are deep-fried and rolled in sugar while still hot

citric acid—an acid found in citrus fruit juice, used to enhance flavor in foods and to prevent crystallization of sugar syrups; available in liquid or powdered form

citrus—fruits characterized by a thick rind, most of which is a bitter white pith (albedo) with a thin exterior layer of colored skin (zest); their flesh is segmented and juicy and varies from bitter to tart to sweet

clarified butter—purified butterfat; the butter is melted and the water and milk solids are removed

club roll—a small oval-shaped roll made of crusty French bread

coagulation—the irreversible transformation of proteins from a liquid or semiliquid state to a drier, solid state; usually accomplished through the application of heat

cocoa butter—the fat found in cocoa beans and used in fine chocolates

coconut cream—(1) a coconut-flavored liquid made like coconut milk but with less water; it is creamier and thicker than coconut milk; (2) the thick fatty portion that separates and rises to the top of canned or frozen coconut milk. Do not substitute cream of coconut for true coconut cream.

coconut milk—a coconut-flavored liquid made by pouring boiling water over shredded coconut; may be sweetened or unsweetened. Do not substitute cream of coconut for coconut milk.

coconut water—the thin, slightly opaque liquid contained within a fresh coconut

composition—a completed plate's structure of colors, shapes and arrangements

compound butter—(Fr. *beurre composé*) fresh butter blended with spices, herbs and or seasonings; used to flavor sauces or as flavorful spreads; these blends may be savory or sweet

concentrate—also known as a *fruit paste* or *compound*; a reduced fruit purée, without a gel structure, used as a flavoring

conching—stirring melted chocolate with large stone or metal rollers to create a smooth texture in the finished chocolate

conditioning—soaking dried fruit in liquid before use so that the fruit remains tender after baking

conduction—the transfer of heat from one item to another through direct contact

confectionery—transforming sugar into sweets; also refers to the trade of candy making

convection—the transfer of heat caused by the natural movement of molecules in a fluid (whether air, water or fat) from a warmer area to a cooler one; mechanical convection is the movement of molecules caused by stirring

conversion factor—(C.F.) the number used to increase or decrease ingredient quantities to change the yield of a formula

cookery—the art, practice or work of cooking

cookie press—also known as a *cookie gun*; a hollow tube fitted with a plunger and an interchangeable decorative tip or plate; soft cookie dough is pressed through the tip to create shapes or patterns

cookies—small, sweet, flat pastries; usually classified by preparation or make-up techniques as drop, icebox, bar, cutout, pressed and wafer

cooking—(1) the transfer of energy from a heat source to a food; this energy alters the food's molecular structure, changing its texture, flavor, aroma and appearance; (2) the preparation of food for consumption

cooking medium—the air, fat, water or steam in which a food is cooked

coring—the process of removing the seeds or pit from a fruit or fruit-vegetable

coupe—(koop) an ice cream sundae, especially one served with a fruit topping

cream filling—a pie filling made of flavored pastry cream thickened with cornstarch

cream of coconut—a canned commercial product consisting of thick, sweetened coconut-flavored liquid; used for baking and in beverages

creaming—a mixing method in which softened fat and sugar are vigorously combined to incorporate air

creams—also known as *crèmes*; include light, fluffy or creamy-textured dessert foods made with whipped cream or whipped egg whites, such as Bavarian creams, chiffons, mousses and crème Chantilly

crème anglaise—(khrem ahn-GLEHZ) also known as *crème à l'anglaise*; see **vanilla custard sauce**

crème brûlée—(krehm broo-LAY) French for "burnt cream"; used to describe a rich dessert custard topped with a crust of caramelized sugar

crème caramel—(khrem kair-ah-MEHL) like crème renversée (rehn-vehr-SAY) and flan, a custard baked over a layer of caramelized sugar and inverted for service

crème Chantilly—(khrem shan-TEE) heavy cream whipped to soft peaks and flavored with sugar and vanilla; used to garnish pastries or desserts or folded into cooled custard or pastry cream for fillings

crème Chiboust—(khrem chee-BOOS) a vanilla pastry cream lightened by folding in Italian meringue; traditionally used in gâteau St. Honoré

crème pâtissière—(khrem pah-tees-SYEHR) *see* **pastry cream**

crêpe—(krayp) a thin, delicate unleavened griddlecake made with a very thin egg batter

cooked in a very hot sauté pan; used in sweet and savory preparations

crêpes flambées—(krayp flahm-BAY) a dessert preparation consisting of thin pancakes filled with fruit, jam or other fillings served flaming; produced by igniting brandy, rum or other liquor so that the alcohol burns off and the flavor of the liquor is retained

croissant—(krwah-SAHN) a crescent-shaped roll made from a rich, laminated yeast dough

croquembouche—(krow-kem-BOOSH) a pyramid of small choux puffs, each filled with pastry cream; a French tradition for Christmas and weddings, it is held together with caramelized sugar and decorated with spun sugar or marzipan flowers

croûte, en—(awn KROOT) describes a food encased in a bread or pastry crust

cruller—a Dutch pastry in which a loop or strip of twisted éclair paste is deep-fried

crumb—the interior of bread or cake; may be elastic, aerated, fine or coarse grained

crumb coat—a thin layer of icing applied to a cake to seal loose surface crumbs before a final decorative layer of icing is applied

cuisine—the ingredients, seasonings, cooking procedures and styles attributable to a particular group of people; the group can be defined by geography, history, ethnicity, politics, culture or religion

curd—(1) the solid portion of milk when it separates, which becomes cheese; (2) a stirred custard made from eggs, sugar, butter and fruit juice, usually citrus

curdling—the separation of milk or egg mixtures into solid and liquid components; caused by overcooking, high heat or the presence of acids

custard—any liquid thickened by the coagulation of egg proteins; its consistency depends on the ratio of eggs to liquid and the type of liquid used; custards can be baked in the oven or cooked in a bain marie or on the stove top

cutting—(1) reducing a food to smaller pieces; (2) a mixing method in which solid fat is incorporated into dry ingredients until only lumps of the desired size remain

deck oven—an oven with stationary, individually heated shelves; products can be baked on each deck's floor (hearth) either in or out of pans

deep-frying—a dry-heat cooking method that uses convection to transfer heat to a food submerged in hot fat; foods to be deep-fried are usually first coated in batter or breading

density—the relationship between the mass and volume of a substance ($D = m/v$); as more and more solids are dissolved in a liquid, the liquid becomes heavier or denser; sugar density is measured on the Baumé scale using a saccharometer

détrempe—(day-trup-eh) a paste made with flour and water during the first stage of preparing pastry doughs, especially rolled-in doughs

develop—to mix dough to the point when the protein bond in the flour forms gluten and the dough becomes smooth and elastic

dipping fork—a utensil used to hold chocolate or small pastries for dipping into chocolate or other coating; consists of a narrow handle with two, three or four long, thin prongs, which are easily inserted into small foods

docker—a hand tool designed to pierce holes in the surface of bread, cracker, pastry and pizza dough before baking to release air bubbles so the product bakes evenly

docking—pricking small holes in an unbaked dough or crust to allow steam to escape and to prevent the dough from rising when baked

dough—a mixture of flour and other ingredients used in baking; has a low moisture content, with gluten forming the continuous medium into which other ingredients are embedded; it is often stiff enough to cut into shapes

dough conditioner—enzymes, emulsifiers and yeast foods added to bread dough to improve gluten development or to soften the dough for faster mixing and shorter fermentation times; available as a powdered blend

dough hook—a mixer attachment used when kneading bread dough or other heavy mixtures

dry-heat cooking methods—cooking methods, principally broiling, grilling, roasting and baking, sautéing, pan-frying and deep-frying, that use air or fat to transfer heat through conduction and convection; dry-heat

cooking methods allow surface sugars to caramelize

drying agent—products such as silica gel used to remove humidity from the air for storing sugar work, nougatine and dry cookies, which would soften under moist conditions

dulce de leche—(DUL-say de LAY-chay) a thick, caramel-like syrup made by slowly heating sweetened milk; used as a sauce or spread, especially in Latin American, Spanish and South American cooking

dumpling—any of a variety of small starchy products made from doughs or batters that are simmered or steamed; can be plain or filled

durum wheat—a species of very hard wheat with a particularly high amount of protein; it is used to make couscous or milled into semolina, which is used for making pasta

dusting—lightly coating the surface of an unbaked dough product with a powdery substance such as flour or cornmeal, usually to prevent sticking or to give the product a decorative finish

éclairs—(ay-clayrz) baked fingers of éclair paste filled with pastry cream; the top is then coated with chocolate glaze or fondant

éclair paste—also known as *pâte à choux* or *choux pastry*; a soft dough that produces hollow baked products with crisp exteriors; used for making éclairs, cream puffs and savory products

edible food lacquer—a composition of fats, lecithin and other edible ingredients used to create a shine on marzipan and other confections

egg wash—a mixture of beaten eggs (whole eggs, yolks or whites) and a liquid, usually milk or water, used to coat doughs before baking to add sheen

emulsification—the process by which generally unmixable liquids, such as oil and water, are forced into a uniform distribution

emulsifier—a substance, natural or chemical, added to a mixture to assist in the binding of unmixable liquids; lecithin found in egg yolks or mono- and diglycerides are commonly used emulsifiers

emulsify—the process of combining a fat and a liquid into a homogeneous mixture, accomplished by proper blending of ingredients

emulsion—(1) a uniform mixture of two unmixable liquids; (2) flavoring oils such as orange and lemon, mixed into water with the aid of emulsifiers

endosperm—the largest part of a cereal grain and a source of protein and carbohydrates (starch); the part used primarily in milled products

entremet—(AHN-truh-may) (1) a contemporary dessert torte made with layers of spongecake, mousse and other fillings; (2) in traditional menu usage the term refers to desserts

essential oils—pure oils extracted from the skins, peels and other parts of plants; used to give their aroma and taste to flavoring agents in foods, cosmetics and other products

evaporation—the process by which heated water molecules move faster and faster until the water turns to a gas (steam) and vaporizes; evaporation is responsible for the drying of foods during cooking

extracts—concentrated mixtures of ethyl alcohol and flavoring oils such as vanilla, almond and lemon

fats—(1) a group of compounds composed of oxygen, hydrogen and carbon atoms that supply the body with energy (9 calories per gram); fats are classified as saturated, monounsaturated or polyunsaturated; (2) the general term for butter, lard, shortening, oil and margarine used as cooking media or ingredients

fermentation—the process by which yeast converts sugar into alcohol and carbon dioxide; it also refers to the time that yeast dough is left to rise, that is, the time it takes for carbon dioxide gas cells to form and become trapped in the gluten network

feuilletage—(fuh-yuh-TAHZH) French for "flaky"; used to describe puff pastry or the process for making puff pastry

feuilletées—(fuh-yuh-TAY) square, rectangular or diamond-shaped puff pastry boxes; may be filled with a sweet or savory mixture

fiber—also known as *dietary fiber*; the indigestible carbohydrates found in grains, fruits and vegetables; fiber aids digestion

flambé—(flahm-BAY) to ignite brandy, rum or other liquor so that the alcohol burns off and the flavor of the liquor is retained

flan—a firm custard baked over a layer of caramelized sugar and inverted for service

flat icing—an opaque white sugar glaze used to decorate Danish pastry and coffeecakes

flavor—an identifiable or distinctive quality of a food, drink or other substance perceived with the combined senses of taste, touch and smell

flavoring—an item that adds a new taste to a food and alters its natural flavors; flavorings include herbs, spices, vinegars and condiments; the terms *seasoning* and *flavoring* are often used interchangeably

flax—a grain plant also known as *linseed*, rich in omega-3 fatty acids; flax hulls and seeds are crushed into a meal or flour to release beneficial compounds

flour—a powdery substance of varying degrees of fineness made by milling grains such as wheat, corn or rye

fluidity—a physical characteristic of chocolate, its ability to flow when melted; it is determined by the percentage of cocoa butter or fat in the chocolate

foam icing—a coating for cakes made from meringue cooked with a hot sugar syrup; also known as *Italian meringue*

folding—a mixing method in which light, airy ingredients are incorporated into heavier ingredients by gently moving them from the bottom of the bowl up over the top in a circular motion, usually with a rubber spatula

fondant—(FAHN-dant) a sweet, thick opaque sugar paste commonly used for glazing pastries such as napoleons or making candies

food allergy—a reaction by the immune system to foods; symptoms include digestive problems, hives, swollen airways or the life-threatening reaction known as *anaphylaxis*

food intolerance—an abnormal physical response to food that is not immune-mediated

formula—a recipe; the term is most often used in the bakeshop

frangipane—(fran-juh-pahn) a sweet almond and egg filling cooked inside pastry

French buttercream—a cake icing or filling made with egg yolks into which a hot sugar syrup is beaten before butter and flavorings are added; also known as *mousseline buttercream*

friable—easily crumbled; said of a baked good with a low moisture and high fat content such as a butter cookie

friandise—(free-ohn-DEEZE) a small pastry or sweet delicacy often served between or after meals; a petit four

friction factor—the temperature increase a mixer generates in bread dough as it is being kneaded

fritters—deep-fried sweet or savory cakes often made from chopped fruits or vegetables coated in batter

frosting—also known as *icing*; a sweet decorative coating used as a filling between the layers or as a coating over the top and sides of a cake

fruit—the edible organ that develops from the ovary of a flowering plant and contains one or more seeds (pips or pits)

frying—a dry-heat cooking method in which foods are cooked in hot fat; includes sautéing, stir-frying, pan-frying and deep-frying

fudge—a cooked mixture of sugar, corn syrup, butter or cream and flavorings made into a soft candy or thick icing

ganache—(ga-nosh) a rich blend of chocolate and heavy cream and, optionally, flavorings, used as a pastry or candy filling or frosting

garnish—(1) food used as an attractive decoration; (2) a subsidiary food used to add flavor or character to the main ingredient in a dish

gâteau—(gah-toe) (1) in American usage, refers to any cake-type dessert; (2) in French usage, refers to various pastry items made with puff pastry, éclair paste, short dough or sweet dough

gelatin—a natural product derived from collagen, an animal protein, used to thicken liquids when chilled; available in two forms: granulated gelatin and sheet (also called *leaf*) gelatin

gelatinization—the process by which starch granules are cooked; they absorb moisture when placed in a liquid and heated; as the moisture is absorbed, the product swells, softens and clarifies slightly

gelato—(jah-laht-to) an Italian-style ice cream that is denser than American-style ice cream

genoise—(zhen-waahz) (1) a form of whipped-egg cake that uses whole eggs whipped with sugar; (2) a French spongecake

germ—the smallest portion of a cereal grain and the only part that contains fat

glaçage—(glah-sahge) browning or glazing a food, usually under a salamander or broiler

glaze—(1) any shiny coating applied to food or created by browning; (2) a thin, flavored coating poured or dripped onto a cake or pastry

glucose—(1) an important energy source for the body; also known as *blood sugar*; (2) a thick, sweet syrup made from cornstarch, composed primarily of dextrose; light corn syrup can usually be substituted for it in baked goods or candy making; also sold in a powdered form

gluten—an elastic network of proteins created when wheat flour is moistened and manipulated; it gives structure and strength to baked goods and is responsible for their volume, texture and appearance; the proteins necessary for gluten formation are glutenin and gliaden

gold leaf—delicate sheets of gold used to decorate chocolate and iced cakes; the thin sheets, separated by tissue paper, are sold in packs available from cake decorating suppliers; edible silver leaf, known as *vark*, is also available

gougère—(goo-ZHAIR) éclair paste flavored with cheese or herbs, baked and served as a savory hors d'oeuvre

gourmet foods—foods of the highest quality, perfectly prepared and beautifully presented

grains—(1) grasses that bear edible seeds, including corn, rice and wheat; (2) the fruit (that is, the seed or kernel) of such grasses

grind—to pulverize or reduce food to small particles using a mechanical grinder or food processor

grinding—a milling process in which grains are reduced to a powder; the powder can be of differing degrees of fineness or coarseness

gum arabic—a water-soluble gum obtained from several species of the acacia tree

gum paste—a smooth dough of sugar and gelatin that can be colored and used to make decorations, especially for pastries

Hazard Analysis Critical Control Points (HACCP)—a rigorous system of self-inspection used to manage and maintain sanitary conditions in all types of food service operations; it focuses on the flow of food through the food service facility to identify any point or step in preparation (known as a *critical control point*) where some action must be taken to prevent or minimize a risk or hazard

hearth—the heated bottom surface of a baking oven on which foods are directly baked

herb—any of a large group of aromatic plants whose leaves, stems or flowers are used as a flavoring; used either dried or fresh

high-ratio cake—a form of creamed-fat cake that uses emulsified shortening and has a two-stage mixing method

homogenization—the process by which milkfat is prevented from separating out of milk products

hotel pan—a rectangular, stainless steel pan with a lip allowing it to rest in a storage shelf or steam table; available in several standard sizes

hull—also known as the *husk*; the outer covering of a fruit, seed or grain

humectant—a substance such as corn syrup, glucose syrup or honey that absorbs moisture, making baked goods soft and tender

hybrid—the result of crossbreeding genetically different species; often a unique product

hydrogenated fat—unsaturated, liquid fats that are chemically altered to remain solid at room temperature, such as solid shortening or margarine

hydrogenation—the process used to harden oils; hydrogen atoms are added to unsaturated fat molecules, making them partially or completely saturated and thus solid at room temperature

hydrometer—a device used to measure specific gravity; it shows degrees of concentration on the Baumé scale; also known as a *saccharometer*

hygroscopic—describes a food that readily absorbs moisture from the air

infuse—to flavor a liquid by steeping it with ingredients such as tea, coffee, herbs or spices

instant-read thermometer—a thermometer used to measure the internal temperature of foods; the stem is inserted in the food, producing an instant temperature readout

interferent—a substance such as glucose syrup or lemon juice that helps stop sugar from recrystallizing when dissolved in a solution

IQF (individually quick-frozen)—describes the technique of rapidly freezing each individual item of food such as slices of fruit, berries or pieces of fish before packaging; IQF foods are not packaged with syrup or sauce

isomalt—a type of sugar alcohol used as a sugar substitute and in sugar work. It is a disaccharide, composed of glucose and mannitol that is made from sugar beets

Italian buttercream—a cake icing or filling made from meringue cooked with hot sugar syrup into which butter and flavorings are beaten

jam—a fruit gel made from fruit pulp and sugar

jelly—a fruit gel made from fruit juice and sugar

juice—the liquid extracted from any fruit or vegetable

Kaiser roll—a large round yeast roll with a crisp crust and a curved pattern stamped on the top; used primarily for sandwiches

kneading—a mixing method in which dough is worked to develop gluten

kuchen—(KOO-ken) a German-style cake, often yeasted

kugelhopf—(KOO-guhl-hopf) a light, buttery yeast cake studded with nuts and raisins and baked in a special fluted mold; a specialty of Germany, the Alsace region of France and other central European countries

lactose—a disaccharide that occurs naturally in mammalian milk; milk sugar

lamination—incorporating fat such as butter into a pastry dough, making a laminated dough with hundreds of crisp layers, as for puff pastry and croissants

leavener—an ingredient or process that produces or incorporates gases in a baked product in order to increase volume, provide structure and give texture

lecithin—a natural emulsifier found in egg yolks and soybeans

levain—the French term for "leavening"; it refers to a dough made from a sourdough

culture that forms the basis for French-style sourdough bread

liqueur—a strong, sweet, syrupy alcoholic beverage made by mixing or redistilling neutral spirits with fruits, flowers, herbs, spices or other flavorings; also known as a *cordial*

liquor—an alcoholic beverage made by distilling grains, vegetables or other foods; includes rum, whiskey and vodka

macerate—to soak foods in a flavorful liquid, usually alcoholic, to soften them

Maillard reaction—the process whereby sugar breaks down and darkens in the presence of protein and heat; nonenzymatic browning

make-up—the cutting, shaping and forming of dough products before baking

malting—soaking, sprouting and drying barley or other grains to develop enzymes; malted grains may be added to wheat flour to improve its baking qualities

mandoline—a stainless steel, hand-operated slicing device with adjustable blades

marmalade—a citrus jelly that contains unpeeled slices of citrus fruit

marquise—(mahr-KEE) a frozen mousselike dessert, usually chocolate

marzipan—(MAHR-sih-pan) a paste of ground almonds, sugar and glucose syrup used to fill and decorate pastries

master baker—a professional title given exclusively to highly skilled and experienced bakers who have demonstrated their professional knowledge in written and practical exams

meal—the coarsely ground seeds of any edible grain such as corn or oats

melting—the process by which certain foods, especially those high in fat, gradually soften and then liquefy when heated

menu—a list of foods and beverages available for purchase

meringue—(muh-reng) a foam made of beaten egg whites and sugar

metric system—a measurement system based on decimal units in which the gram, liter and meter are the basic units of weight, volume and length, respectively

microorganisms—single-celled organisms as well as tiny plants and animals that can be seen only through a microscope

microwave cooking—a heating method that uses radiation generated by a special oven to penetrate the food; it agitates water molecules, creating friction and heat; this energy then spreads throughout the food by conduction (and by convection in liquids)

millet—a high-protein cereal grain cooked and eaten like rice; ground and used in combination with wheat flour in baking

milling—the process by which grain is ground into flour or meal

mise en place—(meez on plahs) French for "putting in place"; refers to the preparation and assembly of all necessary ingredients and equipment before cooking begins

mix—(1) to combine ingredients in such a way that they are evenly dispersed throughout the mixture; (2) a blend of dry ingredients to which liquid, eggs and other ingredients are added in order to make a batter or dough

moist-heat cooking methods—cooking methods, principally simmering, poaching, boiling and steaming, that use water or steam to transfer heat through convection; moist-heat cooking methods are used to emphasize the natural flavors of foods

molder—a mechanical device that shapes divided bread dough into forms before proofing and baking

molding—the process of shaping foods, particularly custards, tortes and mousses, into attractive, hard-edged shapes by using metal rings, circular cutters or other forms

molds—(1) algaelike fungi that form long filaments or strands; for the most part, molds affect only food appearance and flavor; (2) containers used for shaping foods

molecular gastronomy—a culinary movement that investigates the use of chemistry, physics and scientific principles in restaurant cooking

mortar and pestle—a hard bowl (the mortar) in which foods such as spices are ground or pounded into a powder with a club-shaped tool (the pestle)

mousse—(moose) a soft, creamy food, either sweet or savory, lightened by adding whipped cream, beaten egg whites or both

mousseline—(moose-uh-leen) a cream, sauce or buttercream lightened by folding in whipped cream

mouth feel—the sensation, other than flavor, that a food or beverage has in the mouth; a function of the item's body, texture and, to a lesser extent, temperature

muffin method—a mixing method used to make quick-bread batters; it involves combining liquid fat with other liquid ingredients before adding them to the dry ingredients

Napoleon—a many-layered pastry made from baked sheets of puff pastry filled with pastry cream or whipped cream

neapolitan—a three-layered loaf or cake of ice cream; each layer is a different flavor and a different color, a typical combination being chocolate, vanilla and strawberry

nectar—the diluted, sweetened juice of peaches, apricots, guavas, black currants or other fruits, the juice of which would be too thick or too tart to drink straight

noisette—French for "hazelnut"

no-time dough—yeast dough formulated with additional yeast and dough conditioners to accelerate fermentation to 15 to 30 minutes

nougat—a candy made from caramelized sugar, almonds and egg whites; known as *turrón* in Spain and *torrone* in Italy

nougat glacé—a frozen dessert composed of crumbled nougatine folded into Italian meringue and whipped cream

nougatine—a confection made from toasted nuts and caramelized sugar used as a decoration, as an ingredient or in showpieces

nut—(1) the edible single-seed kernel of a fruit surrounded by a hard shell; (2) generally, any seed or fruit with an edible kernel in a hard shell

nutrients—the chemical substances found in food that nourish the body by promoting growth, facilitating body functions and providing energy; the six categories of nutrients are proteins, carbohydrates, fats, water, minerals and vitamins

oil—a type of fat that remains liquid at room temperature

oven spring—the rapid rise of yeast goods when first placed in a hot oven; results from the temporary increase in yeast activity and the expansion of trapped gases

overrun—a measure of the air churned into an ice cream; expressed as a percentage, which reflects the increase in volume of the ice cream greater than the amount of the base used to produce the product

palate—(1) the complex of smell, taste and touch receptors that contribute to a person's ability to recognize and appreciate flavors; (2) the range of an individual's recognition and appreciation of flavors

pan-frying—a dry-heat cooking method in which food is cooked in a moderate amount of hot fat

panettone—(pan-eh-TONE-nay) a sweet Italian yeast bread filled with raisins, candied fruits, anise seeds and nuts; traditionally baked in a rounded cylindrical mold and served as a breakfast bread or dessert during the Christmas holidays

papain—an enzyme found in papayas that breaks down proteins; used as the primary ingredient in many commercial meat tenderizers

parbaked—describes bread that has been baked until the gluten structure is set and yeast activity has stopped but without browning; a frequent procedure for preparing bread that will be frozen for resale

parboiling—partially cooking a food in boiling or simmering liquid; similar to blanching, but the cooking time is longer

parchment (paper)—heat-resistant paper used throughout the bakeshop for tasks such as lining baking pans, making pastry cones for piping and covering foods during shallow poaching

parfait—ice cream served in a long, slender glass with alternating layers of topping or sauce; also the name of the mousselike preparation that forms the basis for some still-frozen desserts

Paris-Brest—(pa-REE breast) rings of baked éclair paste cut in half horizontally and filled with light pastry cream and/or whipped cream; the top is dusted with powdered sugar or drizzled with chocolate glaze

Parisienne; Parisian—(1) the smaller scoop on a two-scoop melon ball cutter; (2) small spheres of fruits or vegetables cut with a tiny melon ball cutter

pasteurization—the process of heating something to a prescribed temperature for a specific period in order to destroy pathogenic bacteria

pastillage—(pahst-tee-azh) a paste made of sugar, cornstarch and gelatin; it may be cut or molded into decorative shapes

pastry—may refer to a group of doughs made primarily with flour, water and fat; pastry can also refer to foods made with these doughs or to a large variety of fancy baked goods

pastry bag—a cone-shaped cloth, plastic or parchment bag used to control the application of icings, fillings and batters

pastry cream—also known as *crème pâtissière*; a stirred custard made with egg yolks, sugar and milk and thickened with starch; used for pastry and pie fillings

pâte—(paht) French for "dough"

pâte à bombe—*see* **bombe mixture**

pâte à choux—(paht ah shoo) *see* **éclair paste**

pâte brisée—(paht bree-zay) a dough that produces a very flaky baked product containing little or no sugar; flaky dough is used for prebaked pie shells or crusts; mealy dough is a less flaky product used for custard, cream or fruit pie crusts

pâte feuilletée—(paht fuh-yuh-tay) also known as *puff pastry*; a rolled-in dough used for pastries, cookies and savory products; it produces a rich and buttery but not sweet baked product with hundreds of light, flaky layers

pâte sucrée—(paht soo-kray) a dough containing sugar that produces a very rich, crisp (not flaky) baked product; also known as *sweet dough*, it is used for tart shells

pathogen—any organism that causes disease; usually refers to bacteria

pâtissier—(pah-tees-ee-yay) a pastry chef; the person responsible for all baked items, including breads, pastries and desserts

pearl sugar—large-grain sugar formed into opaque pellets for decorating cookies and breads

pectin—a gelatin-like carbohydrate obtained from certain fruits; used to thicken jams and jellies

pH—a measurement of the acid or alkali content of a solution, expressed on a scale of 0 to 14.0. A pH of 7.0 is considered neutral or balanced. The lower the pH value, the more acidic the substance. The higher the pH value, the more alkaline the substance

plasticity—a physical characteristic of fat; its capability of being shaped or molded

poaching—a moist-heat cooking method that uses convection to transfer heat from a hot (approximately 160°F–180°F [71°C–82°C]) liquid to the food submerged in it; used for whole fruits such as apricots, peaches and pears

pomes—members of the Rosaceae family; tree fruits with a thin skin and firm flesh surrounding a central core containing many small seeds (called *pips* or *carpels*); include apples, pears and quince

poolish—French term for a yeast dough sponge fermented for a long period at cool temperatures

pot de crème—(poh duh KHREM) (1) a rich French egg and cream custard; (2) a ceramic or porcelain cup in which custard is baked and served

potentially hazardous foods—foods on which pathogenic bacteria can thrive

preserve—(1) a fruit gel that contains large pieces or whole fruits; (2) to extend the shelf life of a food by subjecting it to a process such as irradiation, canning, vacuum-packing, drying or freezing and/or by adding preservatives

profiterole—(pro-feet-uh-roll) a small round pastry made from éclair paste filled with a savory filling and served as an hors d'oeuvre or filled with ice cream, topped with sauce and served as a dessert

proof box—a heat- and humidity-controlled cabinet in which yeast-leavened dough is placed to rise immediately before baking

proofing—the rise given to shaped yeast products just prior to baking

proteins—a group of compounds composed of oxygen, hydrogen, carbon and nitrogen atoms necessary for manufacturing, maintaining and repairing body tissues and as an alternative source of energy (4 calories per gram); protein chains are constructed of various combinations of amino acids

pudding—a thick, spoonable dessert custard, usually made with eggs, milk, sugar and flavorings and thickened with flour or another starch

puff pastry—*see* **pâte feuilletée**

Pullman—a long rectangular loaf of bread for slicing; also, the lidded pan in which this bread is baked

pumpernickel—(1) coarsely ground rye flour; (2) bread made with this flour

punch—to fold dough after it has fermented and risen in order to relax the gluten, reactivate the yeast and allow gases to escape

purée—(pur-ray) (1) to process food to achieve a smooth pulp; (2) food that is processed by mashing, straining or fine chopping to achieve a smooth pulp

quiche—(keesh) a savory tart filled with custard and other ingredients such as cheese, ham and vegetables

quick bread—a bread, including loaves and muffins, leavened by chemical leaveners or steam rather than yeast

quinoa—(keen-wa) tiny, spherical seeds of a plant native to South America, cooked like grain or ground and used as flour

rack oven—an oven in which multiple trays of baked goods are loaded onto racks rolled directly into the oven

ramekin—a small, ovenproof dish, usually ceramic

rancidity—a chemical change in fats caused by exposure to air, light or heat that results in objectionable flavors and odors

recipe—a set of written instructions for producing a specific food or beverage; also known as a *formula*

reduction—a liquid cooked until a portion of it evaporates, reducing the volume of the liquid; used to concentrate flavor and thicken liquids

retardation—chilling a yeasted dough under refrigeration to slow yeast activity and to extend fermentation or proofing time

ripe—(1) describes fully grown and developed fruit; the fruit's flavor, texture and appearance are at their peak and the fruit is ready to eat; (2) describes an unpleasant odor indicating that a food, especially meat, poultry, fish or shellfish, may be past its prime

rognures—(roh-nure) French for "trimmings" or "scraps"; generally refers to scraps of uncooked dough

rolled fondant—a cooked mixture of sugar, glucose syrup and water with the consistency of a dough; draped over cakes to create a perfectly smooth, plasterlike surface

rolled-in dough—a dough in which a fat is incorporated in many layers by using a rolling and folding procedure; it is used for flaky baked goods such as croissants, puff pastry and Danish pastry; also called *laminated dough*

roll-in—(1) a shorthand expression for the butter or other fat used in layering laminated dough; also referred to as *lock-in fat*; (2) the procedure of incorporating fat such as butter into a pastry dough to create hundreds of crisp layers

roulade—(roo-lahd) a filled and rolled spongecake

rounding—the process of shaping dough into smooth, round balls; used to stretch the outside layer of gluten into a smooth coating

royal icing—also known as *decorator's icing*; an uncooked mixture of confectioner's sugar and egg whites that becomes hard and brittle when dry; used for making intricate cake decorations

sabayon—(zah-by-on) also known as *zabaglione*; a foamy, stirred custard sauce made by whisking eggs, sugar and wine over low heat

sanding sugar—granulated sugar with a large, coarse crystal structure that prevents it from dissolving easily; used for decorating cookies and pastries

saturated fats—fats found mainly in animal products and tropical oils; usually solid at room temperature; the body has more difficulty breaking down saturated fats than either monounsaturated or polyunsaturated fats

sauce—generally, a thickened liquid used to flavor and enhance other foods

sautéing—(saw-tay-ing) a dry-heat cooking method that uses conduction to transfer heat from a hot pan to food with the aid of a small amount of hot fat; cooking is usually done quickly over high temperatures

savarin—(sa-va-RAHN) a rich, yeasted cake prepared from baba dough baked into a small round ring, the center of which may be filled with whipped cream and candied fruit

savory—(1) describes spiced or seasoned, as opposed to sweet, foods; (2) (savoury) a highly seasoned last course of a traditional English dinner

scald—to heat a liquid, usually milk, to just below the boiling point

scale up (down)—to increase (decrease) a recipe or formula mathematically

scaling—measuring ingredients or portions on a scale

score—to cut shallow gashes across the surface of a food before cooking

season—(1) traditionally, to enhance flavor by adding salt; (2) more commonly, to enhance flavor by adding salt and/or pepper as well as herbs and spices; (3) to prepare a pot, pan or other cooking surface to prevent sticking

seasoning—an item added to enhance the natural flavors of a food without dramatically changing its taste; salt is the most common seasoning, although all herbs and spices are often referred to as seasonings

semifreddi—(seh-mee-frayd-dee) also known as *still-frozen desserts*; items made with frozen mousse, custard or cream into which large amounts of whipped cream or meringue are folded in order to incorporate air; layers of spongecake and/or fruits may be added for flavor and texture; includes frozen soufflés, marquise, mousses and neapolitans

service—the process of delivering foods to diners in the proper fashion, appropriately prepared and presented at the correct time

sheeter—a machine for rolling out dough between rollers set over a canvas surface

sherbet—a frozen mixture of fruit juice or fruit purée that contains milk and/or eggs for creaminess

shocking—also called *refreshing*; the technique of quickly chilling blanched or parcooked foods in ice water; prevents further cooking and sets colors

shortening—(1) a white, flavorless, solid fat formulated for baking or deep-frying; (2) any fat used in baking to tenderize the product by shortening gluten strands

showpiece—(Fr. *piece montée*) a decorative sculpture made from chocolate, sugar or other confections; used as a table display and to demonstrate the skills of the pastry chef

side masking—the technique of coating only the sides of a cake with garnish

sifting—passing one or more dry ingredients through a wire mesh to remove lumps, combine and aerate

simmering—(1) a moist-heat cooking method that uses convection to transfer heat from a hot (approximately 185°F–205°F [85°C–96°C]) liquid to the food submerged in it; (2) maintaining the temperature of a liquid just below the boiling point

simple syrup—a mixture of sugar dissolved in water; used in icings, mousses, frozen desserts and confectionery

smoke point—the temperature at which a fat begins to break down and smoke

solid pack—describes canned fruits or vegetables with little or no water added

sorbet—(sore-bay) a frozen mixture of fruit juice or fruit purée; similar to sherbet but without milk products

sorghum—(1) grain harvested from a plant that resembles corn, used primarily for animal feed and food processing applications; also called *milo*; when ground, sorghum may be blended with other flours to make gluten-free preparations; (2) a dark, thick, sweet syrup similar to molasses

soufflé—(soo-flay) either a sweet or savory fluffy dish made with a custard base lightened with whipped egg whites and then baked; the whipped egg whites cause the dish to puff when baked

sourdough—a fermented mixture of flour and water added to dough for leavening and flavoring

specific gravity—the weight of an ingredient or a mixture in relation to the weight of water

spice—any of a group of strongly flavored or aromatic portions of plants (other than leaves) used as flavorings, condiments or aromatics; usually used in dried form, either whole or ground

sponge—a thick flour-and-water batter, which may or may not contain commercial yeast; used to improve the flavor and texture of yeast breads

sponge method—a yeast dough mixing method in which flour, water and sometimes yeast are premixed and allowed to ferment; after the sponge has fermented, the remainder of the formula ingredients are incorporated

spread—the flattening of cookie dough when it heats and bakes, controlled by the formula, ingredients (especially sugar and fat) and temperature

springform pan—a baking pan with a separate bottom and side wall held together with a clamp that is released to free the baked product

spun sugar—a decoration made by flicking caramelized sugar rapidly over a dowel to create long, fine, hairlike threads

staling—*see* **starch retrogradation**

standardized recipe—a recipe producing a known quality and quantity of food for a specific operation

starch—complex carbohydrates from plants that are edible and either digestible or indigestible (fiber); often used as thickening agents

starch retrogradation—the process whereby starch molecules in a batter or dough lose moisture after baking; the result is baked goods that are dry or stale

steaming—a moist-heat cooking method in which heat is transferred from steam to the food being cooked by direct contact; the food to be steamed is placed in a basket or rack above a boiling liquid in a covered pan

steep—to soak food in a hot liquid in order to either extract its flavor or impurities or soften its texture

St. Honoré—the patron saint of the pastry chef; also the name for a light, crisp pastry composed of puff pastry topped with cream puffs filled with custard and coated with hard caramel; also the name for a piping tip that produces a wedge-shaped design, which is often used to pipe in the filling

stirring—a mixing method in which ingredients are gently mixed by hand until evenly blended, usually with a spoon, whisk or rubber spatula

stollen—(STOH-lunn) a sweet German yeast bread filled with dried fruit and marzipan, shaped like a folded oval coated with powdered sugar

stone fruits—members of the genus *Prunus*, also known as *drupes*; tree or shrub fruits with a thin skin, soft flesh and one woody stone or pit; include apricots, cherries, nectarines, peaches and plums

straight dough method—a mixing method for yeast breads in which all ingredients are simply combined and mixed; also known as the *direct method*

strain—to pour foods through a sieve, mesh strainer or cheesecloth to separate or remove the liquid component

streudel—(stroo-DUL) a layered pastry filled with cooked fruit, nuts and the like

streusel—(stroo-zel) a crumbly mixture of fat, flour, sugar and sometimes nuts and spices; used to top baked goods

sucrose—the chemical name for refined or table sugar; it is refined from the raw sugars found in the large tropical grass called sugarcane and the root of the sugar beet; a disaccharide composed of one molecule each of glucose and fructose

sugar—a carbohydrate that provides the body with energy and gives a sweet taste to foods

sugar beet—(*Beta vulgaris*) a plant with a high concentration of sucrose in its root; a major source of refined sugar

sugarcane—(*Saccharum officinarum*) a tropical grass native to Southeast Asia; the primary source of sugar

sugar syrups—either simple syrups (thin mixtures of sugar and water) or cooked syrups (melted sugar cooked until it reaches a specific temperature)

sundae—a great and gooey concoction of ice cream, sauces (hot fudge, marshmallow and caramel, for example), toppings (nuts, candies and fresh fruit) and whipped cream

supreme—an intact segment of citrus fruit with all membrane removed

syrup pack—describes canned fruits with a light, medium or heavy syrup added

tart—(1) a sweet or savory filling in a baked crust made in a shallow, straight-sided pan without a top crust; (2) a flavor that is sharp, acidic or sour

tartlet—a small, single-serving tart

taste—the sensations, as interpreted by the brain, of what we detect when food, drink or other substances come into contact with our taste buds

temperature danger zone—the broad range of temperatures between 41°F and 135°F (5°C and 57°C) at which bacteria multiply rapidly

tempering—(1) heating gently and gradually; refers to the process of slowly adding a hot liquid to eggs or other foods to raise their temperature without causing them to curdle; (2) a process for melting chocolate during which the temperature of the cocoa butter is carefully stabilized; this keeps the chocolate smooth and glossy

thickening agents—ingredients used to thicken liquids; include starches (flour, cornstarch and arrowroot) and gelatin

torte—in Central and Eastern European usage, refers to a rich cake in which all or part of the flour is replaced with finely chopped nuts or bread crumbs; also refers to any multilayered sweet cake

transfer sheets—flexible sheets of acetate printed with edible designs; used to apply decorative patterns and images onto tempered chocolate

trimoline—invert sugar syrup used commercially to prevent crystallization in candies and fondant fillings

truffles—(1) rich chocolate candies made with ganache; (2) an edible fungus considered a delicacy

tube pan—a deep round baking pan with a hollow tube in the center

tunneling—the holes that may form in baked goods as the result of overmixing

turns—the number of times that laminated dough is rolled and folded

umami—often called the "fifth taste"; refers to the rich, full taste perceived in the presence of the natural amino acid glutamate and its commercially produced counterpart known as *monosodium glutamate (MSG)*; cheeses, meats, rich stocks, soy sauce, shellfish, fatty fish, mushrooms, tomatoes and wine are all high in glutamate

unsaturated fats—fats that are normally liquid (oils) at room temperature; they may be monounsaturated (from plants such as olives and avocados) or polyunsaturated (from grains and seeds such as corn, soybeans and safflower as well as from fish)

vacherin—(VACH-ran) a baked meringue disk or cake layered with ice cream

vanilla custard sauce—also known as *crème anglaise*; a stirred custard made with egg yolks, sugar and milk or half-and-half and flavored with vanilla; served with or used in dessert preparations

vanillin—(1) whitish crystals of vanilla flavor that often develop on vanilla beans during storage; (2) synthetic vanilla flavoring

vegetarianism—eating a plant-based diet; ovo vegetarians eat eggs; lacto vegetarians eat some dairy; ovo-lacto vegetarians eat eggs and dairy; vegans consume no animal products of any kind

vent—(1) to allow the circulation or escape of a liquid or gas; (2) to cool a pot of hot liquid by setting the pot on blocks in a cold-water bath and allowing cold water to circulate around it

Viennese table—a lavish dessert buffet offered at receptions and catered events featuring an assortment of sliced tortes, elegant pastries, mousses, fruits and confections

Viennoiserie—(vienneh-wah-zer-ee) term applied to the category of enriched pastry doughs that includes brioche, croissants, Danish pastries and other laminated dough products

vinegar—a thin, sour liquid used as a preservative, cooking ingredient and cleaning solution

vol-au-vents—(vul-oh-vanz) deep, individual portion-sized puff pastry shells; often filled with a savory mixture and served as an appetizer or a main course

volume—the space occupied by a substance; volume measurements are commonly expressed as liters, teaspoons, tablespoons, cups, pints and gallons

wash—a glaze applied to dough before baking; a commonly used wash is made with whole egg and water

water bath—*see* **bain marie**

water pack—describes canned fruit with water or fruit juice added

weight—the mass or heaviness of a substance; weight measurements are commonly expressed as grams, ounces and pounds

whipping—a mixing method in which foods are vigorously beaten to incorporate air; a whisk or electric mixer fitted with a whip is used

whole butter—butter that is not clarified, whipped or reduced in fat content; it may be salted or unsalted

windowpane test—a procedure to check that yeast dough has been properly kneaded; a piece of the kneaded dough is pulled apart to see if it stretches without breaking

wine—an alcoholic beverage made from the fermented juice of grapes; may be sparkling (effervescent) or still (noneffervescent) or fortified with additional alcohol

work station—a work area in the kitchen dedicated to a particular task, such as broiling or salad making; work stations using the same or similar equipment for related tasks are grouped together into work sections

xanthan gum—a stabilizer produced by fermenting the sugars in corn; used to thicken, stabilize and emulsify prepared sauces, dairy products, ice creams and baked goods

yeasts—microscopic fungi whose metabolic processes are responsible for fermentation; they are used for leavening bread and in cheese, beer and wine making

yield—the total amount of a product produced by a formula expressed in total weight, volume or number of units of the product

zabaglione—*see* **sabayon**

zest—the thin, colored outer portion of the rind of citrus fruit; contains the oil that provides flavor and aroma

BIBLIOGRAPHY
AND RECOMMENDED READING

GENERAL INTEREST

Davidson, Alan. *The Oxford Companion to Food.* Oxford, England: Oxford University Press, 1999.

Dornenburg, Andrew, and Karen Page. *Culinary Artistry.* New York: Wiley, 1996.

Escoffier, Auguste. *The Escoffier Cook Book and Guide to the Fine Art of Cookery for Connoisseurs, Chefs, Epicures.* (Trans. of *Le Guide culinaire.*) New York: Crown, 1969.

Labensky, Steven, Gaye G. Ingram, and Sarah R. Labensky. *Prentice Hall Essentials Dictionary of Culinary Arts.* Upper Saddle River, N.J.: Prentice Hall, 2008.

Larousse Gastronomique. English ed. New York: Potter, 2001.

Molt, Mary. *Food for Fifty.* 13th ed. Upper Saddle River, N.J.: Prentice Hall, 2011.

Pépin, Jacques. *The Art of Cooking.* New York: Knopf, 1987.

———. *La Technique.* New York: Pocket Books, 1987.

Point, Fernand. *Fernand Point: Ma Gastronomie.* English ed. Wilton, Conn.: Lyceum Books, 1974.

Willan, Anne. *La Varenne Pratique.* New York: Crown, 1989.

CULINARY HISTORY

Coe, Sophie D., and Michael D. Coe. *The True History of Chocolate.* New York: Thames & Hudson, 1996.

Cooper, Ann. *A Woman's Place Is in the Kitchen: The Evolution of Women Chefs.* Stamford, Conn.: Thomson, 1997.

Dupaigne, Bernard. *The History of Bread.* New York: Abrams, 1999.

Freedman, Paul, ed. *Food: The History of Taste (California Studies in Food and Culture).* Berkeley: University of California Press, 2007.

Kaplan, Steven Laurence. *Good Bread Is Back: A Contemporary History of French Bread, The Way It Is Made, and the People Who Make It.* Durham, N.C.: Duke University Press, 2006.

Lovegren, Sylvia. *Fashionable Food: Seven Decades of Food Fads.* New York: Macmillan General Reference, 1995.

Mintz, Sidney W. *Sweetness and Power: The Place of Sugar in Modern History.* New York: Viking Press, 1995.

Montanari, Massimo. *Food Is Culture (Arts and Traditions of the Table: Perspectives on Culinary History).* Trans. by Albert Sonnenfeld. New York: Columbia University Press, 2006.

Norman, Barbara. *Tales of the Table: A History of Western Cuisine.* Englewood Cliffs, N.J.: Prentice Hall, 1972.

Quinzio, Jeri. *Of Sugar and Snow: A History of Ice Cream Making.* Berkeley: University of California Press, 2010.

Revel, Jean-François. *Culture and Cuisine.* (Trans. of *Un Festin en paroles.*) New York: Da Capo Press, 1982.

Toussaint-Samat, Maguelonne. *A History of Food.* Trans. by Anthea Bell. Cambridge, Mass.: Blackwell, 1992.

Wheaton, Barbara Ketcham. *Savoring the Past: The French Kitchen and Table from 1300 to 1789.* Reprint ed. New York: Touchstone Books, 1996.

Willan, Anne. *Great Cooks and Their Recipes: From Taillevent to Escoffier.* Boston: Little, Brown, 1992.

TOOLS

Bridge, Fred, and Jean F. Tibbetts. *The Well-Tooled Kitchen.* New York: Morrow, 1991.

Williams, Chuck, ed. *Williams-Sonoma Kitchen Companion.* New York: Time-Life Books, 2000.

Wolf, Burton, ed. *The New Cooks' Catalogue.* New York: Knopf, 2000.

GENERAL INGREDIENTS

Aftel, Mandy, and Daniel Patterson. *Aroma: The Magic of Essential Oils in Food and Fragrance.* New York: Artisan, 2004.

Davidson, Alan. *Fruit: A Connoisseur's Guide and Cookbook.* New York: Simon & Schuster, 1991.

Dowell, Philip, and Adrian Bailey. *Cook's Ingredients.* New York: Morrow, 1980.

Jenkins, Steven. *Steven Jenkins' Cheese Primer.* New York: Workman, 1996.

McCalman, Max, and David Gibbons. *Mastering Cheese.* New York: Clarkson Potter, 2009.

Morris, Sallie, and Lesley Mackley. *The Spice Ingredients Cookbook.* New York: Lorenz Books, 1997.

Norman, Jill. *The Complete Book of Spices.* New York: Viking Studio Books, 1991.

Ortiz, Elisabeth Lambert. *The Encyclopedia of Herbs, Spices and Flavorings.* New York: Dorling Kindersley, 1992.

Page, Karen, and Andrew Dornenburg. *The Flavor Bible: The Essential Guide to Culinary Creativity, Based on the Wisdom of America's Most Imaginative Chefs.* New York: Little, Brown, 2008.

Payne, Rolce Redard, and Dorrit Speyer Senior. *Cooking with Fruit.* New York: Crescent Books, 1995.

Schapira, Joel, and Karl Schapira. *The Book of Coffee and Tea.* New York: St. Martin's Press, 1975.

Schneider, Elizabeth. *Uncommon Fruits and Vegetables: A Commonsense Guide.* New York: Morrow, 1998.

Ward, Susie Claire Clifton, and Jenny Stacey. *The Gourmet Atlas.* New York: Macmillan, 1997.

FOOD SCIENCE

Figoni, Paula. *How Baking Works.* 3rd ed. Hoboken, N.J.: Wiley, 2011.

McGee, Harold. *On Food and Cooking: The Science and Lore of the Kitchen.* 2nd ed. New York: Scribner, 2004.

McWilliams, Margaret. *Foods: Experimental Perspectives.* 7th ed. Upper Saddle River, N.J.: Prentice Hall, 2012.

National Restaurant Association Educational Foundation. *ServSafe Coursebook.* 5th ed. Upper Saddle River, N.J.: Prentice Hall, 2011.

Parsons, Russ. *How to Read a French Fry.* Boston: Houghton Mifflin, 2001.

Pyler, E. J., and L. A. Gorton. *Baking Science and Technology Vol. 2: Formulation and Production.* 4th ed. Kansas City, Mo.: Sosland, 2009.

This, Hervé. *Molecular Gastronomy: Exploring the Science of Flavor.* Trans. by Malcolm DeBevoise. New York: Columbia University Press, 2005.

QUICK BREADS, YEAST BREADS AND LAMINATED DOUGHS

Albright, Barbara, and Leslie Weiner. *Mostly Muffins.* New York: St. Martin's Press, 1984.

Alston, Elizabeth. *Biscuits and Scones.* New York: Potter, 1988.

Amendola, Joseph. *The Bakers' Manual.* 3rd ed. New York: Wiley, 2002.

Assire, Jérome. *The Book of Bread.* New York: Flammarion, 1996.

Bellouet, Gérard-Joë, and Jean-Michel Perruchon. *Apprenez l'Art des Petits Fours Sucreés et Saleés.* Paris: Bellouet Conseil, 2002.

Bertinet, Richard. *Dough: Simple Contemporary Breads.* London: Kyle Books, 2005.

Calvel, Raymond, et al. *The Taste of Bread.* Gaithersburg, Md.: Aspen, 2001.

Clayton, Bernard. *Bernard Clayton's New Complete Book of Breads.* Revised ed. New York: Fireside Books, 1995.

David, Elizabeth. *English Bread and Yeast Cookery.* Notes by Karen Hess. New York: Viking Press, 1980.

Glezer, Maggie. *A Blessing of Bread: The Many Rich Traditions of Jewish Bread Making around the World.* New York: Artisan, 2004.

Hamelman, Jeffrey. *Bread: A Baker's Book of Techniques and Recipes.* New York: Wiley, 2004.

Hanneman, L. J. *Bakery: Bread and Fermented Goods.* London: Heinemann, 1980.

Leader, Daniel, and Judith Blahnik. *Bread Alone.* New York: Morrow, 1993.

Ortiz, Joe. *The Village Baker: Classic Regional Breads from Europe and America.* Berkeley, Calif.: Ten Speed Press, 1993.

Pyler, E. J. *Handbook of Basic Technical Baking Terminology.* Kansas City, Mo.: Sosland, 1994.

Reinhart, Peter. *Bread Baker's Apprentice.* Berkeley, Calif.: Ten Speed Press, 2002.

———. *Crust and Crumb.* Berkeley, Calif.: Ten Speed Press, 1998.

Schunemann, Claus. *Baking, the Art and Science: A Practical Handbook for the Baking Industry.* Calgary, Canada: Baker Tech, 1988.

Suas, Michel. *Advanced Bread and Pastry.* Clifton Park, N.Y.: Delmar Cengage, 2009.

CUSTARDS, CREAMS AND SAUCES

Clarke, Chris. *The Science of Ice Cream.* London: Royal Society of Chemistry, 2005.

Larousse, David Paul. *The Sauce Bible: Guide to the Saucier's Craft.* New York: Wiley, 1993.

Migoya, Francisco J., and The Culinary Institute of America. *Frozen Desserts.* Hoboken, N.J.: Wiley, 2008.

Peterson, James. *Sauces: Classical and Contemporary Sauce Making.* 2nd ed. New York: Van Nostrand Reinhold, 1998.

DESSERTS AND PASTRIES

Bertrand, Philippe, and Philippe Marand. *L'Éveil des Sens. Toute la Sensualité du Goût: Pâtisseries et Desserts Cuisinés pur beurre de Cacao.* London: Kirra Editions, 2003.

Braker, Flo. *The Simple Art of Perfect Baking.* Shelburne, Vt.: Chapters, 1992.

Daley, Regan. *In the Sweet Kitchen: The Definitive Baker's Companion.* New York: Artisan, 2001.

Ducasse, Alain, and Frédéric Robert. *Le Grand Livre de Cuisine d'Alain Ducasse: Desserts et Pâtisserie.* Paris: Hachette Littérature, 2002.

Fletcher, Helen S. *The New Pastry Cook.* New York: Morrow, 1986.

French Culinary Institute. *The Fundamental Techniques of Classic Pastry Arts.* New York: Stewart, Tabori & Chang, 2009.

Friberg, Bo. *The Professional Pastry Chef.* 4th ed. New York: Wiley, 2002.

Healy, Bruce, and Paul Bugat. *Mastering the Art of French Pastry.* Woodbury, N.Y.: Barron's, 1984.

Heatter, Maida. *Maida Heatter's Book of Great Desserts.* Kansas City, Kans.: Andrews McMeel, 1999.

Hyman, Philip, and Mary Hyman, trans. *The Best of Gaston Lenôtre's Desserts.* Woodbury, N.Y.: Barron's, 1983.

———. *Lenôtre's Ice Creams and Candies.* Woodbury, N.Y.: Barron's, 1979.

Lewis, Matt, and Renato Poliafito. *Baked: New Frontiers in Baking.* New York: Stewart, Tabori & Chang, 2008.

Luchetti, Emily. *A Passion for Desserts.* San Francisco: Chronicle Books, 2003.

Madison, Deborah. *Seasonal Fruit Desserts: From Orchard, Farm, and Market.* New York: Clarkson Potter, 2010.

Maglieri, Nick. *Nick Maglieri's Perfect Pastry.* New York: Macmillan, 1989.

———. *The Modern Baker.* New York: Dorling Kindersley, 2008.

Patent, Greg. *Baking in America.* Boston: Houghton Mifflin, 2002.

Perruchon, Jean-Michel. *Entremets Petits Gateaux Fusion.* France: Bellouet Conseil Editions, 2009.

Peters, Colette. *Cakes to Dream On.* New York: Wiley, 2004.

Prueitt, Elisabeth M., and Chad Robertson. *Tartine.* San Francisco: Chronicle Books, 2006.

Purdy, Susan G. *A Piece of Cake.* Reprint. New York: Macmillan, 1993.

Schreiber, Cory, and Julie Richardson. *Rustic Fruit Desserts: Crumbles, Buckles, Cobblers, Pandowdies, and More.* Berkeley, Calif.: Ten Speed Press, 2009.

Silverton, Nancy. *Desserts by Nancy Silverton.* New York: Harper & Row, 1986.

Sur la Table and Cindy Mushet. *The Art and Soul of Baking.* Kansas City, Mo.: Andrews McMeel, 2008.

Yockelson, Lisa. *Baking by Flavor.* New York: Wiley, 2002.

HEALTHFUL BAKING AND NUTRITION

Baskette, Michael, and James Painter. *The Art of Nutritional Cooking.* 3rd ed. Upper Saddle River, N.J.: Prentice Hall, 2009.

Boyce, Kim. *Good to the Grain: Baking with Whole-Grain Flours.* New York: Stewart, Tabori & Chang, 2010.

Egan, Maureen, and Susan Davis Allen. *Healthful Quantity Baking.* New York: Wiley, 1992.

Freyberg, Nicholas, and Willis A. Gortner. *The Food Additives Book.* New York: Bantam Books, 1982.

King Arthur Flour Whole Grain Baking: Delicious Recipes Using Nutritious Whole Grains. King Arthur Flour Cookbooks. Woodstock, Vt.: Countryman Press, 2006.

CHOCOLATE, SUGAR AND DECORATIVE WORK

Bau, Frédéric. *Au Coeur des Saveurs.* Barcelona, Spain: Montagud Editores, 1998.

Boyle, Tish, and Timothy Moriarty. *Grand Finales: A Neoclassic View of Plated Desserts.* New York: Wiley, 2000.

Garrett, Toba. *Wedding Cake Art and Design: A Professional Approach.* Hoboken, N.J.: Wiley, 2010.

Gordon, Clay. *Discover Chocolate: The Ultimate Guide to Buying, Tasting, and Enjoying Fine Chocolate.* New York: Gotham Books, 2007.

Greweling, Peter. *Chocolates and Confections. Formula, Theory and Technique for the Artisan Confectioner.* Hoboken, N.J.: Wiley, 2007.

Minifie, Bernard W. *Chocolate, Cocoa, and Confectionery: Science and Technology.* 3rd ed. Gaithersburg, Md.: Aspen, 1989.

Morató, Ramon. *Chocolate.* Stuttgart, Germany: Matthaes Vertag, 2010.

Prescilla, Maricel. *The New Taste of Chocolate.* Berkeley, Calif.: Ten Speed Press, 2001.

Recchiuti, Michael, and Fran Gage. *Chocolate Obsession: Confections and Treats to Create and Savor.* New York: Stewart, Tabori & Chang, 2005.

Teubner, Christian, ed. *The Chocolate Bible.* New York: Penguin Studio, 1997.

Wybauw, Jean Pierre. *Chocolate Decorations.* Tielt, Belgium: Uitgeverij Lannoo Nv., 2007.

BOOKS BY CONTRIBUTING CHEFS

Beranbaum, Rose Levy. *The Bread Bible.* New York: Norton, 2003.

———. *Rose's Heavenly Cakes.* Hoboken, N.J.: Wiley, 2009.

Brennan, Pip, Jimmy Brennan, and Ted Brennan. *Breakfast at Brennan's and Dinner, Too.* New Orleans, La.: Brennan's, 1994.

Gand, Gale, and Julia Moskin. *Gale Gand's Just a Bite.* New York: Clarkson Potter, 2001.

Gand, Gale, and Lisa Weiss. *Chocolate and Vanilla.* New York: Clarkson Potter, 2006.

Guerithault, Vincent. *Vincent's Cookbook.* Berkeley, Calif.: Ten Speed Press, 1994.

Malgieri, Nick. *Bake! Essential Techniques for Perfect Baking.* London: Kyle Books, 2010.

Medrich, Alice. *Chewy Gooey Crispy Crunchy Melt-in-Your-Mouth Cookies.* New York: Artisan, 2010.

———. *Chocolat.* New York: Warner Books, 1990.

Milliken, Mary Sue, and Susan Feniger. *City Cuisine.* New York: Morrow, 1989.

RECIPE INDEX

Page numbers in **boldface** indicate location of the main recipe; main recipes on page followed by **V** have variations. Page numbers in *italics* indicate a variation of a main recipe.

SUBJECT INDEX

PHOTO CREDITS